M000294431

Alignment Guide for

Anderson and Ray

KRUGMAN'S

Economics

for the AP® Course

Third Edition

Find a complete correlation guide to College Board's current curriculum framework for AP® Macroeconomics and AP® Microeconomics at

www.highschool.bfwpub.com/krugmanAP3e

KRUGMAN'S
Economics
for the AP® Course

Third Edition

David Anderson
Centre College

Margaret Ray
University of Mary Washington

bedford, freeman & worth
high school publishers

BOSTON | NEW YORK

Krugman's Economics for the AP® Course
Third Edition

Senior Vice President, Content Strategy: Charles Linsmeier
Senior Program Director, High School: Ann Heath
Development Editor: Andrew Sylvester
Editorial Assistant: Carla Duval
Senior Marketing Manager: Janie Pierce-Bratcher
Marketing Assistant: Kelly Noll
Media Editor: Kim Morté
Media Producer: Jodi Isman
Director, Content Management Enhancement: Tracey Kuehn
Senior Managing Editor: Lisa Kinne
Senior Content Project Manager: Won McIntosh
Senior Workflow Project Manager: Paul Rohloff
Senior Photo Editor: Cecilia Varas
Photo Researcher: Richard Fox, Lumina Datamatics, Inc.
Director of Design, Content Management: Diana Blume
Design Services Manager: Natasha Wolfe
Cover Designer: John Callahan
Interior Designer: Tamara Newnam
Illustration Coordinator: Janice Donnola
Illustrations: Network Graphics
Composition: Lumina Datamatics, Inc.
Printing and Binding: Transcontinental Printing
Cover credit: Michael Ventura/Alamy

Library of Congress Control Number: 2018962415
ISBN-10: 1-319-11327-3
ISBN-13: 978-1-319-11327-8
© 2019, 2015, 2011 by Worth Publishers
All rights reserved.
Printed in Canada
3 4 5 6 7 8   25 24 23 22 21 20

Worth Publishers
Bedford, Freeman & Worth, High School Publishers
One New York Plaza, Suite 4600
New York, NY 10004-1562
highschool.bfwpub.com/catalog

To beginning students everywhere,
which we all were at one time.

About the Authors

David Anderson is the Paul G. Blazer Professor of Economics at Centre College. He received his BA in economics from the University of Michigan and his MA and PhD in economics from Duke University. Anderson has been involved in the AP® Economics program for more than two decades. For five years he led the grading of one or both of the AP® Economics exams, and he speaks regularly at AP® conferences and workshops. He has authored dozens of scholarly articles and 15 books, including *Explorations in Economics, Survey of Economics, Cracking the AP® Economics Exam, Economics by Example, Favorite Ways to Learn Economics,* and *Environmental Economics and Natural Resource Management.* His research is primarily on economic education, environmental economics, law and economics, and labor economics. Anderson loves teaching introductory economics and has won awards for excellence and innovation in the classroom. His favorite hobby is running, and he competes in marathons and triathlons. He lives in Danville, Kentucky, with his wife and two children.

Margaret Ray is professor of economics and director of the Center for Economic Education at the University of Mary Washington, where she specializes in teaching introductory economics. She received her BS in economics from Oklahoma State University and her PhD in economics from the University of Tennessee. In 2012 she received her MEd in curriculum and instruction and became certified to teach K–12 social studies. She has taught AP® Economics at several high schools in Virginia and has received the Council on Economic Education's Excellence in Teaching Economics award. She has been involved in the AP® Economics program since 1992, serving as a reader and question leader, writing test items, overseeing the AP® course audit, writing College Board "Special Focus" articles, and editing the Council on Economic Education's AP® Macroeconomics resource. She has been a College Board® Endorsed Consultant for economics since 2001, and she conducts several professional development workshops and institutes each year. Her favorite hobby is showing hunter-jumper horses adopted from racehorse rescue organizations. She lives on a farm in Spotsylvania, Virginia, with her two daughters.

Ligaya Franklin

Paul Krugman, recipient of the 2008 Nobel Memorial Prize in Economic Sciences, is a faculty member of the Graduate Center of the City University of New York, associated with the Luxembourg Income Study, which tracks and analyzes income inequality around the world. Previously he taught at Princeton University for 14 years. He received his BA from Yale and his PhD from MIT. Before Princeton, he taught at Yale, Stanford, and MIT. He also spent a year on the staff of the Council of Economic Advisers (1982–1983). His research has included pathbreaking work on international trade, economic geography, and currency crises. In 1991, Krugman received the American Economic Association's John Bates Clark medal. In addition to his teaching and academic research, Krugman writes extensively for nontechnical audiences. He is a regular op-ed columnist for *The New York Times*.

Robin Wells was a lecturer and researcher in economics at Princeton University. She received her BA from the University of Chicago and her PhD from the University of California at Berkeley; she then did postdoctoral work at MIT. She has taught at the University of Michigan, the University of Southampton (United Kingdom), Stanford, and MIT.

Key Contributors and Advisors

We would like to thank the following individuals, and other anonymous contributors, for helping us to improve the quality and usability of the third edition. We are grateful for their thoughtful reviews, accuracy checks, and contributions to developing stronger AP® style questions and answers. We are also grateful for their contributions to the supporting resources.

Laura Adams, The Money Girl

Patricia Brazill, Irondequoit High School, New York (retired)

Jim Chasey, Homewood-Flossmoor High School, Illinois (retired)

Eric Dodge, Hanover College, Indiana

Thomas Dunn, Florida Atlantic University, Florida

David Frank, Bartram Trail High School, Florida

Mike Fullington, Port Charlotte High School, Florida

Roland Lewin, Santa Barbara City College, California

Jessica Marshall, The University of Mary Washington, Virginia

Julie Meek, West Plano High School, Texas

Sally Meek, West Plano High School, Texas

Ravi Radhakrishnan, Centre College, Kentucky

Jennifer Raphaels, Ridge High School, New Jersey

Martha Rush, Mounds View High School, Minnesota

Sandra Wright, Adlai E. Stevenson High School, Illinois

Brief Contents

Contents

Contents   **xi**

SECTION 10 ▶ BEHIND THE SUPPLY CURVE: PROFIT, PRODUCTION, AND COSTS 509

SECTION 11 ▶ MARKET STRUCTURES: PERFECT COMPETITION AND MONOPOLY 565

SECTION 14   MARKET FAILURE AND THE ROLE OF GOVERNMENT   711

Incentives Matter, for Better or Worse

AP® PRACTICE EXAMS

ENRICHMENT MODULES

To the Student

How to Get the Most from This Program

The AP® Economics course represents a wonderful opportunity for high school students to be challenged by the rigor of a college-level course while learning life-relevant concepts from the discipline of economics. We understand the unique challenges of teaching and learning AP® Economics and have designed this book and its support program to be the most effective possible resources to help you succeed.

Intent on promoting the efficiency and effectiveness of AP® Economics courses, we started with the best available college-level introduction to economics—Krugman and Wells' *Economics*. To this solid foundation we brought our years of experience in reading thousands and thousands of student AP® Macroeconomics and Microeconomics exams and in conducting workshops and trainings for high school economics teachers. The result is an easy-to-read and use program that adheres closely to the AP® curriculum framework and works to prepare you for the AP® exam from day one while mastering the fundamental ideas of economics.

Take a look at the pages that follow for an introduction to the features that will help you realize success in the course and on the AP® economics exams.

To learn about the digital and other resources that support this textbook, visit:
www.highschool.bfwpub.com/krugmanAP3e

READ THE TEXT and use the features to help grasp the big ideas.

Knowing how to use your text effectively will help you learn the concepts and realize success on the AP® exam. By putting all of the pieces together as you work through the text, you will complete the entire puzzle by the end of the course.

SECTION 2

Supply and Demand

Module 5 Supply and Demand: Introduction and Demand

Module 6 Supply and Demand: Supply

Module 7 Supply and Demand: Equilibrium

Module 8 Supply and Demand: Price Controls (Ceilings and Floors)

Module 9 Supply and Demand: Quantity Controls

economics by example *The Coffee Market's Hot; Why Are Bean Prices Not?*

Blue Jean Blues

These days you may be used to paying $50, $100, or more for a pair of blue jeans, but consumers in 2012 may have been shocked by a dramatic increase in the price of jeans compared to the previous year. Or maybe not: fashions change, and maybe they thought they were paying the price for being fashionable. But consumers in 2012 weren't paying for some new innovation in fashion—they were paying for cotton. Jeans are made of denim, a particular weave of cotton. In 2011, when jeans manufacturers were buying supplies for the coming year, the price of cotton climbed to more than triple its level just two years earlier. In March 2011, the price of a pound of cotton hit an all-time high, the highest cotton price since record keeping began in 1870.

Why were cotton prices so high? On one side, demand for clothing of all kinds was surging. On the supply side, severe weather events hit world cotton production. Most notably, Pakistan, the world's fourth-largest cotton producer, was hit by devastating floods that put one-fifth of the country underwater and virtually destroyed its cotton crop. But by 2012 the supply of cotton rebounded and the price of cotton fell by 62% (a change that would be reflected in clothing prices in 2013). After some smaller ups and downs in the intervening five years, the price of cotton in 2018 remained at approximately 59% of its 2011 high.

The rise in cotton prices in 2011 was not all bad news for everyone connected with the cotton trade. In the United States, cotton producers had not been hit by bad weather and were benefiting from the higher prices. American farmers responded to high cotton prices by sharply increasing the acreage they devoted to the crop. None of these measures were enough, however, to produce immediate price relief.

Wait a minute: how, exactly, does flooding in Pakistan translate into higher jeans prices or more polyester instead of cotton, in your T-shirts? It's a matter of supply and demand—but what does that mean? Many people use "supply and demand" as a catchphrase to mean "the laws of the marketplace at work." To economists, however,

> Each section is divided into **short Modules** to help you tackle concepts in manageable chunks.

> Read the **Opening Story.** Each section opens with a compelling story that often extends through the Modules. These opening stories, drawn from news headlines and world events, are designed to pique your interest and build your intuition as you prepare to learn about the economics concepts that follow.

MOD 5

Supply and Demand: Introduction and Demand

In this Module, you will learn to:
• Explain what a competitive market is and how it is described by the supply and demand model
• Draw a demand curve and interpret its meaning
• Discuss the difference between movements along the demand curve and changes in demand
• List and describe the factors that shift the demand curve

Introduction and Demand

Levis may be a popular brand of jeans, but they account for only a tiny fraction of all cotton transactions.

A **competitive market** is a market in which there are many buyers and sellers of the same good or service, none of whom can influence the price at which the good or service is sold.

The **supply and demand model** is a model of how a competitive market works.

Cotton sellers and cotton buyers constitute a *market*—a group of producers and consumers who exchange a good or service for payment. In this section, we'll focus on a particular type of market known as a *competitive market*. Roughly, a **competitive market** is one in which there are many buyers and sellers of the same good or service. More precisely, the key feature of a competitive market is that no individual's actions have a noticeable effect on the price at which the good or service is sold. It's important to understand, however, that this is not an accurate description of every market. For example, it's not an accurate description of the market for cola beverages. That's because in the market for cola beverages, Coca-Cola and Pepsi account for such a large proportion of total sales that they are able to influence the price at which cola beverages are bought and sold. But it is an accurate description of the market for cotton. The global marketplace for cotton is so huge that even a jeans retailer as large as Levi Strauss & Co. accounts for only a tiny fraction of transactions, making it unable to influence the price at which cotton is bought and sold.

It's a little hard to explain why competitive markets are different from other markets until we've seen how a competitive market works. For now, let's just say that it's easier to model competitive markets than other markets.

When a market is competitive, its behavior is well described by the **supply and demand model**. Because many markets *are* competitive, the supply and demand model is a very useful one indeed.

There are six key elements in the supply and demand model:

• The *demand curve*
• The set of factors that cause the demand curve to shift
• The *supply curve*
• The set of factors that cause the supply curve to shift
• The *market equilibrium*, which includes the *equilibrium price* and *equilibrium quantity*
• The way the market equilibrium changes when the supply curve or demand curve shifts

To explain the supply and demand model, we will examine each of these elements in turn. In this Module we begin with the demand curve and then discuss the factors that cause the demand curve to shift.

The Demand Curve

How many pounds of cotton, packaged in the form of blue jeans, do consumers around the world want to buy in a given year? You might at first think that we can answer this question by multiplying the number of pairs of blue jeans purchased

AP® EXAM TIP

For success on the AP® exam you must be able to draw, label, and interpret supply and demand graphs. These graphs are also the foundation of other graphs you will learn in the course.

50   Section 2   Supply and Demand

> Scan the **Learning Objectives** for an overview of the critical concepts you will be tackling in the Module. Focus on mastering these skills.

> Watch for the yellow **Key Term** boxes, which highlight the vocabulary you must master to realize success on the AP® exam. The terms are repeated in the Section Review and in the Glossary/Glosario at the end of the book.

> Pay attention to the **AP® Exam Tip** boxes. They provide helpful advice on what to read closely and what common pitfalls to avoid so you can ace the AP® exam.

STUDY THE GRAPHS and figures. To succeed on the AP® exam, you must be able to draw and interpret graphs correctly.

Figures and **graphs** hold volumes of information. Study them carefully, read the captions, and pay attention to any related AP® Exam Tips. Mastering the creation and interpretation of economic models is important to realizing success on the AP® exam. Color is used consistently throughout the book to distinguish between demand (blue) and supply (red) curves.

Market equilibrium occurs at point *E*, where the supply curve and the demand curve intersect. In equilibrium, the quantity demanded is equal to the quantity supplied. In this market, the equilibrium price is $1 per pound and the equilibrium quantity is 10 billion pounds per year.

MODULE 5 REVIEW

Adventures in AP® Economics

Watch the video: *Demand*

Check Your Understanding

1. Explain whether each of the following events represents (i) a *change in* demand (a *shift* of the demand curve) or (ii) a *movement along* the demand curve (a *change in the quantity demanded*).
   a. A store owner finds that customers are willing to p[ay] more for umbrellas on rainy days.
   b. When XYZ Mobile, a cellular plan provider, offered reduced rates on data charges, its volume data usa[ge]

   c. People buy more long-stem roses the week of Valentine's Day, even though the prices are higher

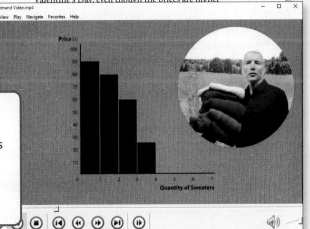

Watch the **Adventures in AP® Economics Videos.** Created by author David Anderson, each short video reviews a key graph or concept presented in the section. Watch the videos as many times as needed to make sure that you understand the material. Each video is highlighted at the end of the relevant Module, and all associated videos are listed at the end of the section.

section 2 economics by example

The Coffee Market's Hot; Why Are Bean Prices Not?
Insights into Supply and Demand

Under fifteenth-century Turkish law, a wife could divorce her husband if he failed to provide her with a daily quota of coffee. Coffee is no longer grounds for divorce, but it is the world's most popular beverage after water and a common element of cozy getaways

can have cinnamon in your latte thanks to the wor[ld] supply and demand.

Because they explain so much, let's explore the concepts of supply and demand.

Read the **economics by example** case at the end of each section for a deep dive into the concepts. Each article offers colorful examples and real-life applications of core principles, providing valuable insight into the many ways that your life is immersed in economics.

MODULE 8 REVIEW

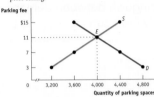

Check Your Understanding

1. On game days, homeowners near Middletown University's stadium used to rent parking spaces in their driveways to fans at a going rate of $11. A new town ordinance now sets a maximum parking fee of $7. Use the accompanying supply and demand diagram to show how each of the following can result from the price ceiling.

Parking fee

Quantity of parking spaces

a. Some homeowners now think it's not worth the hassle to rent out spaces.
b. Some fans who used to carpool to the game now drive alone.
c. Some fans can't find parking and leave without seeing the game.
Explain how each of the following adverse effects arises from the price ceiling.
d. Some fans now arrive several hours early to find parking.
e. Friends of homeowners near the stadium regularly attend games, even if they aren't big fans. But some serious fans have given up because of the parking situation.
f. Some homeowners rent spaces for more than $7 but pretend that the buyers are nonpaying friends or family.

2. True or false? Explain your answer. A price ceiling below the equilibrium price in an otherwise efficient market
a. increases quantity supplied.
b. makes some people who want to consume the good worse off.
c. makes all producers worse off.

Answer the **Check Your Understanding** questions at the end of each Module to make sure you grasp the content. If you struggle to answer these questions, go back and reread the Module.

Feeling confident? Test yourself by answering each of the seven AP®-style Module-ending **multiple-choice questions**. These practice questions help you become comfortable with the types of questions you'll see in the multiple-choice section of the AP® exam. Many of the questions ask you to analyze data or interpret tables and graphs.

TACKLE THE AP® TEST: Multiple-Choice Questions

1. A price ceiling
   a. is an example of a price control.
   b. is intended to decrease price below the equilibrium.
   c. was established in New York City after World War II.
   d. benefits some consumers.
   e. is all of the above.

2. An effective minimum wage law
   a. is an example of a price ceiling.
   b. benefits all workers.
   c. reduces the quantity of labor supplied.
   d. reduces the quantity of labor demanded.
   e. is all of the above.

3. To be effective, a price ceiling must be set
   a. above the equilibrium price.
   b. below the equilibrium price.
   c. equal to the equilibrium price.
   d. by the federal government.
   e. on the market for housing.

4. Refer to the graph provided. A price floor set at $5 will result in

5. Effective price ceilings are inefficient because they
   a. create shortages.
   b. lead to wasted resources.
   c. decrease quality.
   d. create black markets.
   e. do all of the above.

Use the graph provided to answer questions 6 and 7.

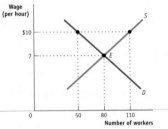

Wage (per hour)

Number of workers

TACKLE THE AP® TEST: Free-Response Questions

1. Refer to the graph provided to answer the following questions.

Wage (per hour)

Number of workers

a. What are the equilibrium wage and quantity of workers in this market?
b. For it to have an effect, where would the government have to set a minimum wage?
c. If the government set a minimum wage at $8,
   i. how many workers would supply their labor?
   ii. how many workers would be hired?
   iii. how many workers would want to work that did *not* want to work for the equilibrium wage?
   iv. how many previously employed workers would no longer have a job?

Rubric for FRQ 1 (6 points)

1 point: equilibrium wage = $6, quantity of labor = 1,800

1 point: The minimum wage will have an effect if it is set anywhere above $6.

1 point: 2,600 workers would supply their labor

1 point: 1,000 workers would be hired

1 point: 800 (the number of workers who would want to work for $8 but did not supply labor for $6)

1 point: 800 (at the equilibrium wage of $6, 1,800 workers were hired; at a wage of $8, 1,000 workers would be hired. 1,800 − 1,000 = 800)

2. Draw a correctly labeled graph of a housing market in equilibrium. On your graph, illustrate an effective legal limit (ceiling) on rent. Identify the quantity of housing demanded, the quantity of housing supplied, and the size of the resulting surplus or shortage.
(6 points)

Two "mini **AP®-style free-response questions**" are also provided at the end of each Module. The FRQs on the AP® exam are much more complex, but these practice FRQs prepare you to read questions carefully, analyze graphs and data, and answer the questions that are asked. A sample grading rubric is given for the first FRQ to show you how answers are scored and to help you learn to write thoughtful and complete answers. The second problem asks you to practice answering an FRQ on your own.

SECTION 2 Review

▶ SECTION 2 Review Video

Adventures in AP® Economics Videos
Mod 5: Demand
Mod 6: Supply
Mod 7: Market Equilibrium

Module 5

1. The **supply and demand model** illustrates how a **competitive market**, one with many buyers and sellers of the same product, works.

2. The **demand schedule** shows the **quantity demanded** at each price and is represented graphically by a **demand curve**. The **law of demand** says that demand curves slope downward, meaning that as price decreases, the quantity demanded increases.

3. A **movement along the demand curve** occurs when the price changes and causes a change in the quantity demanded. When economists talk of **changes in demand**, they mean shifts of the demand curve—a

change in the quantity demanded at any given price. An increase in demand causes a rightward shift of the demand curve. A decrease in demand causes a leftward shift.

4. There are five main factors that shift the demand curve:
   - a change in tastes
   - a change in the prices of related goods, such as **substitutes** or **complements**
   - a change in income: when income rises, the demand for **normal goods** increases and the demand for **inferior goods** decreases
   - a change in expectations

Module 6

5. The **supply schedule** shows the **quantity supplied** at each price and is represented graphically by a **supply curve**. According to the **law of supply**, supply curves slope upward, meaning that as price increases, the quantity demanded increases.

6. A **movement along the supply curve** occurs when the price changes and causes a change in the quantity supplied. When economists talk of **changes in supply**, they mean shifts of the supply curve—a change in

the quantity supplied at any given price. An increase in supply causes a rightward shift of the supply curve. A decrease in supply causes a leftward shift.

7. There are five main factors that shift the supply curve:
   - a change in **input** prices
   - a change in the prices of related goods and services
   - a change in expectations
   - a change in the number of producers
   - a change in technology

Module 7

8. An economic situation is in **equilibrium** when no individual would be better off doing something different. The supply and demand model is based on the principle that the price in a market moves to its

demand has the oppo_
reduces the equilibri_
librium quantity; a de_
effect.

> Start your review of each section by watching the **Section Review Video**, which reviews the key models and concepts in the section. Then **watch** or rewatch any of the **Adventures in AP® Economics Videos** that address content you find difficult.

> Read the **Section Review** and study the **Key Terms** at the end of each section. Understanding the language of economics is critical to being successful on the AP® exam.

Key Terms

Competitive market, p. 50
Supply and demand model, p. 50
Demand schedule, p. 51
Quantity demanded, p. 52
Demand curve, p. 52
Law of demand, p. 52
Change in demand, p. 52
Movement along the demand curve, p. 53
Substitutes, p. 56
Complements, p. 56
Normal good, p. 56
Inferior good, p. 56
Individual demand curve, p. 57
Quantity supplied, p. 60

Supply schedule, p. 60
Supply curve, p. 60
Law of supply, p. 60
Change in supply, p. 60
Movement along the supply curve, p. 62
Input, p. 63
Individual supply curve, p. 65
Equilibrium, p. 68
Equilibrium price, p. 68
Equilibrium quantity, p. 68
Surplus, p. 70
Shortage, p. 71
Price controls, p. 77
Price ceiling, p. 77
Price floor, p. 77

Inefficient allocation to consumers, p. 80
Wasted resources, p. 80
Inefficiently low quality, p. 80
Black market, p. 81
Minimum wage, p. 82
Inefficient allocation of sales among sellers, p. 83
Inefficiently high quality, p. 84
Quantity control or quota, p. 88
License, p. 88
Demand price, p. 89
Supply price, p. 89
Wedge, p. 91
Quota rent, p. 91
Deadweight loss, p. 91

AP® Exam Practice Questions

Multiple-Choice Questions

1. Which of the following changes will most likely result in an increase in the demand for hamburgers in your hometown?
   a. The price of hot dogs decreases.
   b. The price of drinks sold at hamburger restaurants increases.
   c. Income in your town decreases and hamburgers are a normal good.
   d. The local newspaper publishes a story on health problems caused by red meat.
   e. The number of vegetarians in your town decreases and the population size remains the same.

Refer to the following table and information to answer Questions 21–24.

Only fishing boats licensed by the U.S. government are allowed to catch swordfish in the waters off the North Atlantic coast. The following table shows hypothetical demand and supply schedules for swordfish caught in the United States each year.

Price of swordfish (per pound)	Quantity of swordfish (millions of pounds per year)	
	Quantity demanded	Quantity supplied
$20	6	15
18	7	13
16	8	11
14	9	9
12	10	7

21. If the government establishes a quota of 7 million pounds in the market, what will the demand price of swordfish be (per pound)?
   a. $20   d. $14
   b. $18   e. $12
   c. $16

22. If the government establishes a quota of 7 million pounds in the market, what will the supply price of swordfish be (per pound)?
   a. $20   d. $14
   _. $10   _. $12

Free-Response Questions

1. Pablo Picasso painted only 1,000 paintings during his "Blue Period."
   a. Draw a correctly labeled graph of the market for Picasso "Blue Period" paintings showing each of the following:
      i. the supply and demand curves for paintings
      ii. the equilibrium price and quantity of paintings
   b. List the five principal factors that will lead to a change in the price of paintings in this market.
   c. Show the effect on price in your market for paintings if wealthy art collectors decide that it is essential to acquire Picasso "Blue Period" paintings for their collections. **(5 points)**

2. The market for less-skilled labor in a large city is perfectly competitive.
   a. Draw a correctly labeled graph of the market for less skilled labor showing each of the following:
      i. the supply of labor and the demand for labor
      ii. the equilibrium wage and quantity of labor (measured as the number of workers)
   b. On your graph from part a, illustrate the effect of an advance in technology that makes workers more productive. Identify the new equilibrium price and quantity as _ and Q_

> Test yourself at the end of each section by tackling the **AP® Exam Practice Questions**, which include 25 multiple-choice questions and an additional set of FRQs. These questions draw from concepts covered across multiple Modules and give you the chance to prove that you've mastered the economics content *and* the types of questions you'll see on the AP® exam!

MOD 45

Putting It All Together

In this Module, you will learn to:
- Use macroeconomic models to conduct policy analysis
- Improve your approach to free-response macroeconomics questions

Having completed our study of basic macroeconomic models, we can use them to analyze scenarios and evaluate policy recommendations. In this Module we develop a step-by-step approach to macroeconomic analysis. You can adapt this approach to problems involving any macroeconomic model, including models of aggregate demand and supply, production possibilities, money markets, and the Phillips curve. By the end of this module you will be able to combine mastery of the principles of macroeconomics with problem solving skills to analyze a new scenario on your own.

A Structure for

In our study of macroeconomics many different forms. No matter problems have the following com

1. *A starting point.* To analyze any
2. *A pivotal event.* This might be

> **Module 45: Putting It All Together,** the final Module in macroeconomics, teaches you how to use what you have learned to answer comprehensive, "real-world" questions about the macroeconomy, like the type you will see in the long FRQ on the AP® exam.

AP® Macroeconomics Exam
Practice Test

Multiple-Choice Questions

Refer to the figure below to answer Question 1.

1. A movement from point *B* to point *A* illustrates which of the following?
   a. a choice to produce only capital goods
   b. an advance in technology
   c. a decrease in available resources used to produce consumer goods
   d. an increase in the price of capital goods

3. According to the concept of comparative advantage, which of the following is true when countries specialize and trade?
   a. Each country obtains an absolute advantage.
   b. Total world output increases.
   c. The production possibilities curve for both countries shifts outward.
   d. Prices fall in both countries.
   e. Deadweight loss is created.

Refer to the figure below to answer Question 4.

> Test your knowledge and readiness for the AP® exam by taking the end-of-book **AP®-style Practice Exam for Macro- or Microeconomics.** Each includes 60 multiple-choice questions and three FRQs per exam, just like the official tests. Time yourself to simulate the actual exams.

EM

Enrichment Modules

Module A Financial Markets and Crise
Module B Behavioral Economics
Module C The Economics of Informati
Module D Indifference Curves and Co

> Learning about economics doesn't stop after you take the exam in May. Continue your study of economics with **Enrichment Modules** and the **Financial Literacy Handbook** to help round out the course and to prepare you for further economics study in college and beyond.

FLH

Financial Literacy Handbook

By Laura Adams ("The Money Girl")

Part 1 Take It to the Bank
Part 2 Get Interested in Money Math
Part 3 Learn to Earn

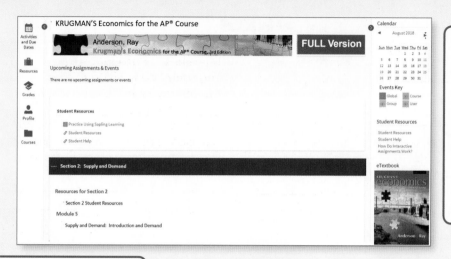

Created and supported by educators, the **new Online Homework and e-book program** includes all of the resources you need in one convenient place. The interactive, mobile-ready e-book allows you to read and reference the text when you are working online or to download it to read when an internet connection is not available.

Hundreds of **online homework questions** allow you to do your homework efficiently. The program offers hints and guidance for every answer choice to help you learn even when the answer you select is wrong.

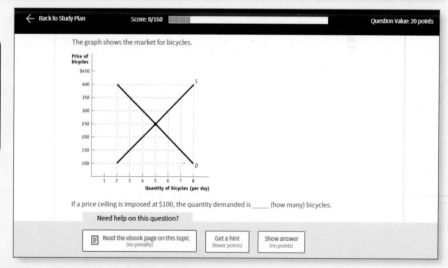

LearningCurve adaptive quizzing offers individualized question sets and feedback. Test yourself and get extra practice on areas of confusion without stressing about grades.

Use the **Strive for a 5 Guide** companions to the macro and/or micro portion of this text. Each Guide was written to work hand-in-glove with the text and includes a study guide followed by tips and advice on taking the exam and two more full AP® practice exams per guide.

Basic Economic Concepts

Indiapicture/Alamy

Common Ground

The annual meeting of the American Economic Association draws thousands of economists, young and old, famous and obscure. There are booksellers, business meetings, and quite a few job interviews. But mainly the economists gather to talk and listen. During the busiest times, 60 or more presentations may be taking place simultaneously, on questions that range from the future of the stock market to who does the cooking in two-earner families.

What do these people have in common? An expert on the stock market probably knows very little about the economics of housework, and vice versa. Yet an economist who wanders into the wrong seminar and ends up listening to presentations on some unfamiliar topic is nonetheless likely to hear much that is familiar. The reason is that all economic analysis is based on a set of common principles that apply to many different issues.

Some of these principles involve *individual choice*—for economics is, at its core, about the choices that individuals make. Do you choose to work during the summer or take a back-packing trip? Do you text with friends or meet them at a movie? These decisions involve *making a choice* from among a limited number of alternatives—limited because no one can have everything that he or she wants. Every question in economics at its most basic level involves individuals making choices.

To understand how an economy works, you need to understand more than how individuals make choices. None of us lives like Robinson Crusoe, alone on an island. We must make decisions in an environment that is shaped by the decisions of others. Indeed, in our global economy even the simplest decisions you make—say, what to have for breakfast—are shaped by the decisions of thousands of other people, from the banana grower in Costa Rica who decided to grow the fruit you eat to the farmer in Iowa who provided the corn in your cornflakes. Because each of us depends on so many others—and they, in turn, depend on us—our choices interact. So, although all economics at

a basic level is about individual choice, in order to understand behavior within an economy we must also understand economic *interaction*—how my choices affect your choices, and vice versa.

Microeconomics helps us understand many important economic interactions by looking at individual choice and the markets for individual goods—for example, the market for cereal. *Macroeconomics* is our window for viewing economy-wide interactions in order to understand how they lead to the ups and downs we see in the economy as a whole.

In this section we discuss the study of economics and the difference between microeconomics and macroeconomics. We also introduce the major topics within macroeconomics and the use of models to study the economy. Finally, we present the *production possibilities curve* model and use it to understand basic economic activity, including trade between two economies. Because the study of economics relies on graphical models, an appendix on the use of graphs follows the end of this section.

The Study of Economics

In this Module, you will learn to:
- Explain how scarcity and choice are central to the study of economics
- Discuss the importance of opportunity cost in decision making
- Distinguish between microeconomic concepts and macroeconomic concepts
- Explain the difference between positive economics and normative economics
- Identify areas of agreement and disagreement among economists

Individual Choice: The Core of Economics

Economics is the study of scarcity and choice.

Individual choice is decisions by individuals about what to do, which necessarily involve decisions about what not to do.

Economics is the study of scarcity and choice. Every economic issue involves, at its most basic level, **individual choice**—decisions by individuals about what to do and what *not* to do. In fact, you might say that it isn't economics if it isn't about choice.

When you shop online there are thousands of different products available, and it is extremely unlikely that you—or anyone else—could afford to buy everything you might want to have. Besides, there's only so much space in your room. Given the limitations on your budget and your living space, you must choose which products to buy and which to pass up.

Casimiro/Alamy

The fact that those products are available in the first place involves choice—the online stores chose to put them there, and the manufacturers of the products chose to produce them. An **economy** is a system that coordinates choices about production with choices about consumption and distributes goods and services to the people who want them. The United States has a **market economy**, in which production and consumption are the result of decentralized decisions by many firms and individuals. There is no central authority telling people what to produce or where to ship it. Each individual producer makes what he or she thinks will be most profitable, and each consumer buys what he or she chooses.

An alternative to a market economy is a **command economy**, in which industry is publicly owned and there *is* a central authority making production and consumption decisions. Command economies have been tried, most notably in the Soviet Union between 1917 and 1991 and in North Korea today, but they don't work very well. Producers in the Soviet Union routinely found themselves unable to produce because they did not have crucial raw materials, or they succeeded in producing but then found that nobody wanted what the central authority had them produce. Consumers were often unable to find necessary items—command economies are famous for long lines at shops.

At the root of the problem with command economies is a lack of **incentives**, which are rewards or punishments that motivate particular choices. In market economies, producers are free to charge higher prices when there is a shortage of something, and to keep the resulting profits. High prices and profits provide incentives for producers to make more of the most-needed goods and services and to eliminate shortages.

In fact, economists tend to be skeptical of any attempt to change people's behavior that doesn't change their incentives. For example, a plan that calls on manufacturers to reduce pollution voluntarily probably won't be effective; a plan that gives them a financial incentive to do so is more likely to succeed.

Property rights, which establish ownership and grant individuals the right to trade goods and services with each other, create many of the incentives in market economies. With the right to own property comes the incentive to produce things of value, either to keep, or to trade for mutual gain. And ownership creates an incentive to put resources to their best possible use. Property rights to a lake, for example, give

An **economy** is a system for coordinating a society's productive and consumptive activities.

In a **market economy**, the decisions of individual producers and consumers largely determine what, how, and for whom to produce, with little government involvement in the decisions.

In a **command economy**, industry is publicly owned and a central authority makes production and consumption decisions.

Incentives are rewards or punishments that motivate particular choices.

Property rights establish ownership and grant individuals the right to trade goods and services with each other.

the owners an incentive not to pollute that lake if its use for recreation, serenity, or sale has great value.

In any economy, the decisions of what to do with the next ton of pollution, the next hour of free time, and the next dollar of spending money are *marginal decisions*. They involve trade-offs at the margin: comparing the costs and benefits of doing a little bit more of an activity versus a little bit less. The gain from doing something one more time is called the *marginal benefit*. The cost of doing something one more time is the *marginal cost*. If the marginal benefit of making another car, reading another page, or buying another latte exceeds the marginal cost, the activity should continue. But if the cost of one more exceeds the benefit of one more—that is, if the marginal cost exceeds the marginal benefit—the activity should stop. The study of such decisions, known as **marginal analysis**, plays a central role in economics because the formula of doing things until the marginal benefit no longer exceeds the marginal cost is the key to deciding "how much" to do of any activity.

All economic activities involve individual choice. Let's take a closer look at what this means for the study of economics.

Resources Are Scarce

You can't always get what you want. Almost everyone would like to have a beautiful home in a great location, help with the housecleaning, a luxury car, and frequent vacations at fancy resorts. But even in a rich country like the United States, not many families can afford all of that. So each family must make choices—whether to go to Disney World this year or buy a better car, whether to make do with a small backyard or accept a longer commute in order to live where land is cheaper.

Limited income isn't the only thing that keeps people from having everything they want. Time is also in limited supply: there are only 24 hours in a day. And because the time we have is limited, choosing to spend time on one activity also means choosing not to spend time on a different activity—spending time studying for an exam means forgoing a night at the movies. Indeed, many people feel so limited by the number of hours in the day that they are willing to trade money for time. For example, convenience stores usually charge higher prices than larger supermarkets. But they fulfill a valuable role by catering to customers who would rather pay more than spend the time traveling farther to a supermarket where they might also have to wait in longer lines.

Why do individuals have to make choices? The ultimate reason is that *resources are scarce*. A **resource** is anything that can be used to produce something else. The economy's resources, sometimes called *factors of production*, can be classified into four categories: **land** (including timber, water, minerals, and all other resources that come from nature), **labor** (the effort of workers), **capital** (machinery, buildings, tools, and all other manufactured goods used to make other goods and services), and **entrepreneurship** (risk taking, innovation, and the organization of resources for production). A resource is **scarce** when there is not enough of it available to satisfy the various ways a society wants to use it. For example, there are limited supplies of oil and coal, which currently provide most of the energy used to produce and deliver everything we buy. And in a growing world economy with a rapidly increasing human population, even clean air and water have become scarce resources.

Just as individuals must make choices, the scarcity of resources means that society as a whole must make choices. One way for a society to make choices is simply to allow them to emerge as the result of many individual choices. For example, there are only so many hours in a week, and Americans must decide how to spend their time. How many hours will they spend going to supermarkets to get lower prices rather than saving time by shopping at convenience stores? The answer is the sum of individual decisions: society's choice about where to shop is simply the sum of the choices made by the millions of individuals in the economy.

For various reasons, there are some decisions that are best not left to individual choice. For example, the authors of this book live in areas that until recently

Marginal analysis is the study of the costs and benefits of doing a little bit more of an activity versus a little bit less.

AP® EXAM TIP

Students of microeconomics should pay close attention to *marginal analysis*, as it is often tested on the AP® exam. Any time you see "marginal," think "additional."

A **resource** is anything that can be used to produce something else.

Land refers to all resources that come from nature, such as minerals, timber, and petroleum.

Labor is the effort of workers.

Capital refers to manufactured goods used to make other goods and services.

Entrepreneurship describes the efforts of entrepreneurs in organizing resources for production, taking risks to create new enterprises, and innovating to develop new products and production processes.

A **scarce** resource is not available in sufficient quantities to satisfy all the various ways a society wants to use it.

AP® EXAM TIP

Be careful when you see key terms you think you already know, because economists have special meanings for many words. For example, economists use the term *land* in reference to all sorts of natural resources and raw materials such as silicon, cotton, and even water.

were mainly farmland but are now being rapidly built up. Most local residents feel that their communities would be more pleasant places to live if some land were left undeveloped. But the benefit an individual landowner receives from his or her undeveloped land is often small relative to the financial incentive to sell the land to a developer. So a trend has emerged in many communities across the United States of local governments purchasing undeveloped land and preserving it as open space with broad appeal to residents and visitors. Decisions about how to use scarce resources are often best left to individuals but sometimes should be made at a higher, community-wide, level.

Opportunity Cost: The Real Cost of Something Is What You Must Give Up to Get It

Suppose it is your last year of high school and you must decide which college to attend. You have narrowed your choices to a small liberal arts college near home or a large state university several hours away. If you decide to attend the local liberal arts college, what is the cost of that decision? Of course, you will have to pay for tuition, books, and housing no matter which college you choose. Added to the cost of choosing the local college is the forgone opportunity to attend the large state university, your next best alternative. Economists call the value of the next best alternative that you must give up when you make a particular choice an **opportunity cost**.

The real cost of an item is its **opportunity cost**: the value of the next best alternative that you must give up in order to get the item.

Opportunity costs are crucial to individual choice because, in the end, all costs are opportunity costs. That's because with every choice, an alternative is forgone—money or time spent on one thing can't be spent on another. If you spend $15 on a pizza, you forgo the opportunity to spend that $15 on a hamburger. If you spend Saturday afternoon at the swimming pool, you can't spend Saturday afternoon doing homework. And if you attend one school, you can't attend another.

The pool and school examples show that economists are concerned with more than just costs paid in dollars and cents. The forgone opportunity to do homework has no direct monetary cost, but it is an opportunity cost nonetheless. And if the local college and the state university have the same tuition and fees, the cost of choosing one school over the other has nothing to do with payments and everything to do with forgone opportunities.

Now suppose tuition and fees at the state university are $5,000 less than at the local college. In that case, what you give up to attend the local college is the ability to attend the state university *plus* the enjoyment you could have gained from spending $5,000 on other things. So the opportunity cost of a choice includes all the costs—whether or not they are monetary costs—of making that choice.

The choice to go to college *at all* provides an important final example of opportunity costs. High school graduates can either go to college or seek immediate employment. Even with a full scholarship that would make college "free" in terms of monetary costs, going to college would still be an expensive proposition because most young people, if they were not in college, would have a job. By going to college, students forgo the income they could have earned if they had gone straight to work instead. Therefore, the opportunity cost of attending college is the value of all necessary monetary payments for tuition and fees *plus* the forgone income from the best available job that could take the place of going to college.

For most people the value of a college degree far exceeds the value of alternative earnings, with notable exceptions. The opportunity cost of going to college is high for people who could earn a lot during what would otherwise be their college years. Basketball star Thon Maker bypassed college because the opportunity cost would have included his $11.6 million contract with the Milwaukee Bucks. Facebook co-founder Mark Zuckerberg, Microsoft co-founder Bill Gates, and singer Taylor Swift are among the high achievers who decided that the opportunity cost of completing college was prohibitive.

Thon Maker understood the concept of opportunity cost.

Microeconomics Versus Macroeconomics

We have presented economics as the study of choices and described how, at its most basic level, economics is about individual choice. The branch of economics concerned with how individuals make decisions and how those decisions interact is called **microeconomics**. Microeconomics focuses on choices made by individuals, households, or firms—the smaller parts that make up the economy as a whole.

    Macroeconomics focuses on the bigger picture—the overall ups and downs of the economy. When you study macroeconomics, you learn how economists explain these fluctuations and how governments can use economic policy to minimize the damage they cause. Macroeconomics focuses on **economic aggregates**—economic measures such as the unemployment rate, the inflation rate, and gross domestic product—that summarize data across many different markets.

    Table 1.1 lists some typical questions that involve economics. A microeconomic version of the question appears on the left, paired with a similar macroeconomic question on the right. By comparing the questions, you can begin to get a sense of the difference between microeconomics and macroeconomics.

Microeconomics is the study of how individuals, households, and firms make decisions and how those decisions interact.

Macroeconomics is concerned with the overall ups and downs of the economy.

Economic aggregates are economic measures that summarize data across many different markets.

Table 1.1	Microeconomic Versus Macroeconomic Questions
Microeconomic Questions	**Macroeconomic Questions**
Should I go to college or get a job after high school?	How many people are employed in the economy as a whole this year?
What determines the salary that Citibank offers to a new college graduate?	What determines the overall salary levels paid to workers in a given year?
What determines the cost to a high school of offering a new course?	What determines the overall level of prices in the economy as a whole?
What government policies should be adopted to make it easier for low-income students to attend college?	What government policies should be adopted to promote employment and growth in the economy as a whole?
What determines the number of iPhones exported to France?	What determines the overall trade in goods, services, and financial assets between the United States and the rest of the world?

    As these questions illustrate, microeconomics focuses on how individuals and firms make decisions, and the consequences of those decisions. For example, a school will use microeconomics to determine how much it would cost to offer a new course, which includes the instructor's salary, the cost of class materials, and so on. By weighing the costs and benefits, the school can then decide whether or not to offer the course. Macroeconomics, in contrast, examines the *overall* behavior of the economy—how the actions of all of the individuals and firms in the economy interact to produce a particular economy-wide level of economic performance. For example, macroeconomics is concerned with the general level of prices in the economy and how high or low they are relative to prices last year, rather than with the price of a particular good or service.

Positive Versus Normative Economics

Economic analysis draws on a set of basic economic principles. But how are these principles applied? That depends on the purpose of the analysis. Economic analysis that is used to answer questions about the way the economy works, questions that have definite right and wrong answers, is known as **positive economics**. In contrast, economic analysis that involves saying how the economy *should* work is known as **normative economics**.

Positive economics is the branch of economic analysis that describes the way the economy actually works.

Normative economics makes prescriptions about the way the economy should work.

Imagine you are an economic adviser to the governor of your state and the governor is considering an increase in the toll charged along the state turnpike. Below are three questions the governor might ask you.

1. How much revenue will the tolls yield next year without an increase?

2. How much higher would that revenue be if the toll were raised from $1.00 to $1.50?

3. Should the toll be raised, bearing in mind that a toll increase would lower the volume of traffic and air pollution in the area but impose a financial hardship on frequent commuters?

There is a big difference between the first two questions and the third one. The first two are questions about facts. Your forecast of next year's toll revenue without any increase will be proved right or wrong when the numbers actually come in. Your estimate of the impact of a change in the toll is a little harder to check—the increase in revenue depends on other factors besides the toll, and it may be hard to disentangle the causes of any change in revenue. Still, in principle there is only one right answer.

But the question of whether or not tolls should be raised may not have a "right" answer—two people who agree on the effects of a higher toll could still disagree about whether raising the toll is a good idea. For example, someone who lives near the turnpike but doesn't commute on it will care a lot about noise and air pollution but not so much about commuting costs. A regular commuter who doesn't live near the turnpike will have the opposite priorities.

This example highlights a key distinction between the two roles of economic analysis and presents another way to think about the distinction between positive and normative analysis: positive economics is about description and normative economics is about prescription. Positive economics occupies most of the time and effort of economists.

Looking back at the three questions the governor might ask, it is worth noting a subtle but important difference between questions 1 and 2. Question 1 asks for a simple prediction about next year's revenue—a forecast. Question 2 is a "what if" question, asking how revenue would change if the toll were to increase. Economists are often called upon to answer both types of questions. Economic *models*, which provide simplified representations of reality using, for example, graphs or equations, are especially useful for answering "what if" questions.

The answers to such questions often serve as a guide to policy, but they are still predictions, not prescriptions. That is, they tell you what will happen if a policy is changed, but they don't tell you whether or not that result is good. Suppose that your economic model tells you that the governor's proposed increase in highway tolls will raise property values in communities near the road but will tax or inconvenience people who currently use the turnpike to get to work. Does that information make this proposed toll increase a good idea or a bad one? It depends on whom you ask. As we've just seen, someone who is very concerned with the communities near the road will support the increase, but someone who is very concerned with the welfare of drivers will feel differently. That's a value judgment—it's not a question of positive economic analysis.

Still, economists often do engage in normative economics and give policy advice. How can they do this when there may be no "right" answer? One answer is that economists are also citizens, and we all have our opinions. But economic analysis can often be used to show that some policies are clearly better than others, regardless of individual opinions.

Suppose that policies A and B achieve the same goal, but policy A makes everyone better off than policy B—or at least makes some people better off without making other people worse off. Then A is clearly more beneficial than B. That's not a value judgment: we're talking about how best to achieve a goal, not about the goal itself.

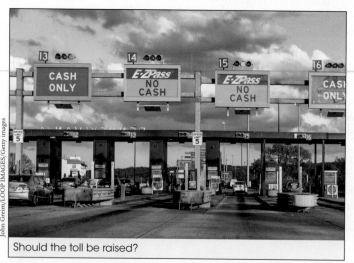

Should the toll be raised?

For example, two different policies have been used to help low-income families obtain housing: rent control, which limits the rents landlords are allowed to charge, and rent subsidies, which provide families with additional money with which to pay rent. Almost all economists agree that subsidies are the preferable policy. (In Module 75 we'll see why this is so.) And so the great majority of economists, whatever their personal politics, favor subsidies over rent control.

When policies can be clearly ranked in this way, then economists generally agree. But it is no secret that economists sometimes disagree.

When and Why Economists Disagree

Economists have a reputation for disagreeing with each other. Where does this reputation come from? One important answer is that media coverage tends to exaggerate the real differences in views among economists. If nearly all economists agree on an issue—for example, the proposition that rent controls lead to housing shortages—reporters and editors are likely to conclude that there is no story worth covering, and so the professional consensus tends to go unreported. But when there is some issue on which prominent economists take opposing sides, such as whether cutting taxes right now would help the economy, that does make a good news story. So you hear much more about the areas of disagreement among economists than you do about the many areas of agreement.

It is also worth remembering that economics, unavoidably, is often tied up in politics. On a number of issues, powerful interest groups know what opinions they want to hear. Therefore, they have an incentive to find and promote economists who profess those opinions, which gives these economists a prominence and visibility out of proportion to their support among their colleagues.

Although the appearance of disagreement among economists exceeds the reality, it remains true that economists often *do* disagree about important things. For example, some highly respected economists argue vehemently that the U.S. government should replace the income tax with a *value-added tax* (a national sales tax, which is the main source of government revenue in many European countries). Other equally respected economists disagree. What are the sources of this difference of opinion?

One important source of differences is in values: as in any diverse group of individuals, reasonable people can differ. In comparison to an income tax, a value-added tax typically falls more heavily on people with low incomes. So an economist who values a society with more social and income equality will likely oppose a value-added tax. An economist with different values will be less likely to oppose it.

A second important source of differences arises from the way economists conduct economic analysis. Economists base their conclusions on models formed by making simplifying assumptions about reality. Two economists can legitimately disagree about which simplifications are appropriate—and therefore arrive at different conclusions.

Suppose that the U.S. government were considering a value-added tax. One economist may rely on a simplification of reality that focuses on the administrative costs of tax systems—that is, the costs of monitoring compliance, processing tax forms, collecting the tax, and so on. This economist might then point to the well-known high costs of administering a value-added tax and argue against the change. Another economist may think that the right way to approach the question is to ignore the administrative costs and focus on how the proposed law would change individual savings behavior. The second economist might point to studies suggesting that value-added taxes promote higher consumer saving, a desirable result. Because the economists have made different simplifying assumptions, they arrive at different conclusions. And so the two economists may find themselves on different sides of the issue.

Most disputes like this are eventually resolved by the accumulation of evidence that shows which of the various simplifying assumptions made by economists does a better job of fitting the facts. However, in economics, as in any science, it can take a long time before research settles important disputes—decades, in some cases. And since the economy is always changing in ways that make old approaches invalid or raise new policy questions, there are always new issues on which economists disagree. The policy maker must then decide which economist to believe.

MODULE 1 REVIEW

Check Your Understanding

1. Provide an example of a resource from each of the four categories of resources.

2. What type of resource is each of the following?
   a. time spent making pizzas at a restaurant
   b. a bulldozer
   c. a river

3. You make $45,000 per year at your current job with Whiz Kids Consultants. You are considering a job offer from Brainiacs, Inc., which would pay you $50,000 per year. Is each of the following elements an opportunity cost of accepting the new job at Brainiacs, Inc.? Answer yes or no, and explain your answer.
   a. the increased time spent commuting to your new job
   b. the $45,000 salary from your old job
   c. the more spacious office at your new job

4. Identify each of the following statements as positive or normative, and explain your answer.
   a. Society should take measures to prevent people from engaging in dangerous personal behavior.
   b. People who engage in dangerous personal behavior impose higher costs on society through higher medical costs.

TACKLE THE AP® TEST: Multiple-Choice Questions

1. Which of the following is an example of capital?
   a. a cheeseburger dinner
   b. a construction worker
   c. petroleum
   d. a factory
   e. an acre of farmland

2. Which of the following is not an example of resource scarcity?
   a. There is a finite amount of petroleum in the world.
   b. Farming communities are experiencing droughts.
   c. There are not enough physicians to satisfy all desires for health care in the United States.
   d. Cassette tapes are no longer being produced.
   e. Teachers would like to have more instructional technology in their classrooms.

3. Suppose that you prefer reading a book you already own to watching videos and that you prefer watching videos to listening to music. If these are your only three choices, what is the opportunity cost of reading?
   a. watching videos and listening to music
   b. watching videos
   c. listening to music
   d. sleeping
   e. the price of the book

4. Which of the following statements is normative?
   a. The price of gasoline is rising.
   b. The price of gasoline is too high.
   c. Gas prices are expected to fall in the near future.
   d. Cars can run on gasoline, electricity, or diesel fuel.
   e. When the price of gasoline rises, drivers buy less gasoline.

5. Which of the following questions is studied in microeconomics?
   a. Should I go to college or get a job after I graduate?
   b. What government policies should be adopted to promote employment in the economy?
   c. How many people are employed in the economy this year?
   d. Has the overall level of prices in the economy increased or decreased this year?
   e. What determines the overall salary levels paid to workers in a given year?

6. Which of the following exist(s) in a command economy but not in a market economy?
   a. property rights for individuals
   b. land, labor, capital, and entrepreneurship
   c. plenty of incentives to motivate firms to produce what consumers need
   d. an absence of long lines of customers at shops
   e. a central authority making production and consumption decisions

7. All opportunity costs are
   a. nonmonetary.
   b. forgone monetary payments.
   c. losses of time.
   d. values of alternatives that must be given up.
   e. related to educational opportunities.

TACKLE THE AP® TEST: Free-Response Questions

1. Define the term *resources*, and list the four categories of resources. What characteristic of resources results in the need to make choices?

> **Rubric for FRQ 1 (6 points)**
>
> **1 point:** Resources are anything that can be used to produce something else.
>
> **1 point each:** The four categories of the economy's resources are land, labor, capital, and entrepreneurship.
>
> **1 point:** The characteristic that results in the need to make choices is scarcity.

2. In what type of economic analysis do questions have a "right" or "wrong" answer? In what type of economic analysis do questions not necessarily have a "right" answer? On what type of economic analysis do economists tend to disagree most frequently? Why might economists disagree? Explain. **(5 points)**

Introduction to Macroeconomics

> **In this Module, you will learn to:**
> - Explain what a business cycle is and why policy makers seek to diminish the severity of business cycles
> - Describe how employment and unemployment are measured
> - Define aggregate output and explain how it changes over the business cycle
> - Define inflation and deflation and explain why price stability is preferred
> - Explain how economic growth determines a country's standard of living
> - Summarize the crucial role of models—simplified representations of reality—in economics

Today many people enjoy walking, biking, and horseback riding through New York's beautiful Central Park. But in 1932 there were many people living there in squalor. At that time, Central Park contained one of many "Hoovervilles"—the shantytowns that had sprung up across America as a result of a catastrophic economic slump that had started in 1929. Millions of people were out of work and unable to feed, clothe, and house themselves and their families. Beginning in 1933, the U.S. economy would stage a partial recovery. But joblessness stayed high throughout the 1930s—a period that came to be known as the Great Depression.

Why the name "Hooverville"? These shantytowns were named after President Herbert Hoover, who had been elected in 1928. When the Depression struck, people blamed the president: neither he nor his economic advisers seemed to understand what had happened or to know what to do to improve the situation. At that time, the field of macroeconomics—the study of the overall ups and downs of the economy—was still in its infancy. It was only after the economy was plunged into catastrophe that economists began to closely examine how the economy works and to develop policies that might prevent such disasters in the future. To this day, the effort to understand economic slumps and find ways to prevent them is at the core of macroeconomics.

American Stock Archive/Getty Images

In this module we will begin to explore the key features of macroeconomic analysis. We will look at some of the field's major concerns, including business cycles, employment, aggregate output, price stability, and economic growth.

The Business Cycle

The alternation between economic downturns and upturns in the macroeconomy is known as the **business cycle**. The economy experiences occasional economic downturns known as **recessions**, periods in which output and employment are falling. These are followed by economic upturns—periods in which output and employment are rising—known as **expansions** or *recoveries*. A **depression** is a very deep and prolonged downturn; fortunately, the United States hasn't had one since the Great Depression of the 1930s.

When does a downturn officially become a recession? Economists in many countries mark the beginning of a recession after two consecutive quarters (a quarter is three months) of falling output in the economy. In the United States, the National Bureau of Economic Research (NBER), a private, nonprofit research group, marks the beginning and end of recessions. Rather than following rigid guidelines for this determination, the NBER considers a variety of economic indicators with an emphasis on employment and production levels.

According to the NBER, there have been 11 recessions in the United States since World War II. During that period the average recession lasted 11 months, and the average expansion lasted 58 months. The average length of a business cycle, from the beginning of one recession to the beginning of the next recession, has been 5 years and 8 months. The shortest business cycle was 18 months and the longest was 10 years and 8 months. The *Great Recession*, which you'll read more about in later modules, started in December 2007 and ended in June 2009. **Figure 2.1** shows the history of the U.S. unemployment rate since 1989 and the timing of business cycles. Recessions are indicated in the figure by shaded areas.

The business cycle is an enduring feature of the economy. But even though ups and downs seem to be inevitable, most people believe that macroeconomic analysis has guided policies that help smooth out the business cycle and stabilize the economy. What happens during a business cycle, and how can macroeconomic policies address the downturns? Let's look at three issues: employment and unemployment, aggregate output, and inflation and deflation.

The **business cycle** is the alternation between economic downturns, known as *recessions*, and economic upturns, known as *expansions*.

Recessions are periods of economic downturns when output and employment are falling.

Expansions, or recoveries, are periods of economic upturns when output and employment are rising.

A **depression** is a very deep and prolonged downturn.

Figure 2.1   The U.S. Unemployment Rate and the Timing of Business Cycles, 1989–2018

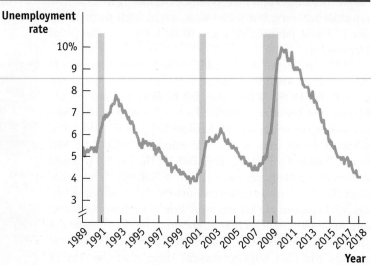

The unemployment rate, a measure of joblessness, rises sharply during recessions (indicated by shaded areas) and usually falls during expansions.
Data Source: Bureau of Labor Statistics.

Employment, Unemployment, and the Business Cycle

Although not as severe as a depression, a recession is clearly an undesirable event. Like a depression, a recession leads to joblessness, reduced production, reduced incomes, and lower living standards. To understand how job loss relates to the adverse effects of recessions, we need to understand something about how the labor force is structured. **Employment** is the total number of people who are currently working for pay, and **unemployment** is the total number of people who are actively looking for work but aren't currently employed. A country's **labor force** is the sum of employment and unemployment.

The **unemployment rate**—the percentage of the labor force that is unemployed—is usually a good indicator of what conditions are like in the job market. A high unemployment rate signals a poor job market in which jobs are hard to find; a low unemployment rate indicates a good job market in which jobs are relatively easy to find. In general, during recessions the unemployment rate is rising, and during expansions it is falling. Look again at Figure 2.1, which shows the unemployment rate from 1989 through early 2018. The graph shows significant changes in the unemployment rate. Note that even in the most prosperous times there is some unemployment. A booming economy, like that of the late 1990s, can push the unemployment rate down to 4% or even lower. But a severe recession, like the one that began in 2007, can push the unemployment rate into double digits.

Employment is the number of people who are currently working for pay in the economy.

Unemployment is the number of people who are actively looking for work but aren't currently employed.

The **labor force** is equal to the sum of employment and unemployment.

The **unemployment rate** is the percentage of the labor force that is unemployed.

Aggregate Output and the Business Cycle

Rising unemployment is the most painful consequence of a recession, and falling unemployment is the most urgently desired feature of an expansion. But the business cycle isn't just about jobs—it's also about **output**: the quantity of goods and services produced. During the business cycle the economy's level of output and its unemployment rate move in opposite directions. At lower levels of output, fewer workers are needed, and the unemployment rate is relatively high. Growth in output requires the efforts of more workers, which lowers the unemployment rate. To measure the rise and fall of an economy's output, we look at **aggregate output**—the economy's total production of goods and services for a given time period, usually a year. Aggregate output normally falls during recessions and rises during expansions.

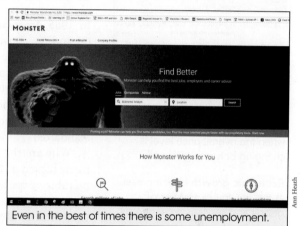

Even in the best of times there is some unemployment.

Ann Heath

Output is the quantity of goods and services produced.

Aggregate output is the economy's total production of goods and services for a given time period.

Inflation, Deflation, and Price Stability

In 1970 the average worker in the United States was paid $3.40 an hour. By February 2018 the average hourly earnings for such a worker had risen to $26.75. Three cheers for economic progress!

But wait—American workers were paid much more in 2018, but they also faced a much higher cost of living. In 1970 a new car cost only about $3,500; by 2018 the average new car cost more than $36,000. The price of a loaf of white bread went from about $0.20 to $1.27. And the price of a pound of tomatoes rose from just $0.19 to $2.03. If we compare the percentage increase in earnings between 1970 and 2018 with the increase in the overall price level (the price level for all goods and services), we see that the average worker's paycheck goes only slightly farther today than it did in 1970. In other words, the increase in the cost of living wiped out many of the wage gains of the typical worker from 1970 to 2018. What caused this situation?

Between 1970 and 2018, the economy experienced substantial **inflation**, a rise in the overall price level. The opposite of inflation is **deflation**, a fall in the overall price level. A change in the prices of a few goods changes the opportunity cost of

A rising overall price level is **inflation**.

A falling overall price level is **deflation**.

Economic growth has made the luxuries of the 1950s commonplace today.

purchasing those goods but does not constitute inflation or deflation. These terms are reserved for more general changes in the prices of goods and services throughout the economy.

Both inflation and deflation can pose problems for the economy. Inflation discourages people from holding on to cash, because if the price level is rising, cash loses value. That is, if the price level rises, a dollar will buy less than it would before. As we will see later in our more detailed discussion of inflation, in periods of rapidly rising prices, people stop holding cash altogether and instead trade goods for goods.

Deflation can cause the opposite problem. That is, if the overall price level falls, a dollar will buy more than it would before. In this situation it can be more attractive for people with cash to hold on to it rather than to invest in new factories and other productive assets. This can deepen a recession.

In later modules we will look at other costs of inflation and deflation. For now, note that economists have a general goal of **price stability**—meaning that the overall price level is changing only slowly if at all—because it avoids uncertainty about prices and helps to keep the economy stable.

> The economy has **price stability** when the overall price level is changing only slowly if at all.
>
> **Economic growth** is an increase in the maximum amount of goods and services an economy can produce.

Economic Growth

In 1955 Americans were delighted with the nation's prosperity. The economy was expanding, consumer goods that had been rationed during World War II were available for everyone to buy, and most Americans believed, rightly, that they were better off than citizens of any other nation, past or present. Yet by today's standards Americans were quite poor in 1955. For example, in 1955 only 33% of American homes contained washing machines, and hardly anyone had air conditioning. If we turn the clock back to 1905, we find that life for most Americans was startlingly primitive by today's standards.

Why are the vast majority of Americans today able to afford conveniences that many lacked in 1955? The answer is **economic growth**, an increase in the maximum possible output of an economy. Unlike the short-term increases in aggregate output that occur as an economy recovers from a downturn in the business cycle, economic growth is an increase in productive capacity that permits a sustained rise in aggregate output over time. **Figure 2.2** shows annual figures for U.S. real gross domestic

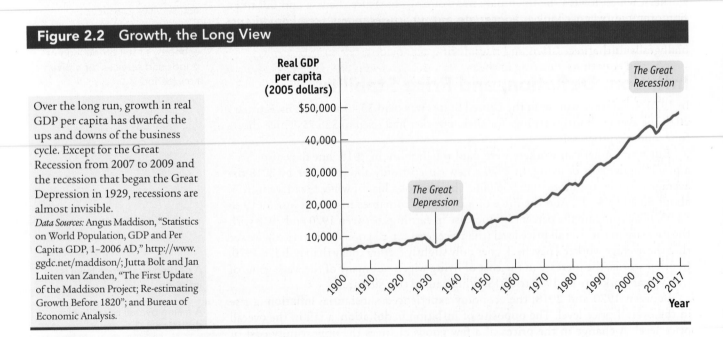

Figure 2.2   Growth, the Long View

Over the long run, growth in real GDP per capita has dwarfed the ups and downs of the business cycle. Except for the Great Recession from 2007 to 2009 and the recession that began the Great Depression in 1929, recessions are almost invisible.
Data Sources: Angus Maddison, "Statistics on World Population, GDP and Per Capita GDP, 1–2006 AD," http://www.ggdc.net/maddison/; Jutta Bolt and Jan Luiten van Zanden, "The First Update of the Maddison Project; Re-estimating Growth Before 1820"; and Bureau of Economic Analysis.

product (GDP) per capita—the value of final goods and services produced in the United States per person—from 1900 to 2017. As a result of this economic growth, the U.S. economy's aggregate output per person was more than eight times as large in 2017 as it was in 1900.

Economic growth is fundamental to a nation's prosperity. A sustained rise in output per person allows for higher wages and a rising standard of living. The need for economic growth is urgent in poorer, less developed countries, where a lack of basic necessities makes growth a central concern of economic policy. As you will see when studying macroeconomics, the goal of economic growth can be in conflict with the goal of hastening recovery from an economic downturn. What is good for economic growth can be bad for short-run stabilization of the business cycle, and vice versa.

We have seen that macroeconomics is concerned with the long-run trends in aggregate output as well as the short-run ups and downs of the business cycle. Now that we have a general understanding of the important topics studied in macroeconomics, we are almost ready to apply economic principles to real economic issues. To do this requires one more step—an understanding of how economists use *models*.

> **AP® EXAM TIP**
>
> For the AP® Exam you should know that some increases in output do not represent economic growth. Economic growth is an increase in the economy's potential output. Temporary fluctuations in economic conditions often alter real GDP (output) when there has been no change in the economy's potential output.

The Use of Models in Economics

In 1901, one year after their first glider flights at Kitty Hawk, the Wright brothers built something else that would change the world—a wind tunnel. This was an apparatus that let them experiment with many different designs for wings and control surfaces. These experiments gave them knowledge that would make heavier-than-air flight possible. Needless to say, testing an airplane design in a wind tunnel is cheaper and safer than building a full-scale version and hoping it will fly. More generally, models play a crucial role in almost all scientific research—economics included.

A **model** is any simplified version of reality that is used to better understand a real-life situation. But how do we create a simplified representation of an economic situation? One possibility—an economist's equivalent of a wind tunnel—is to find or create a real but simplified economy. For example, economists interested in the economic role of money have studied the system of exchange that developed in World War II prison camps, in which cigarettes became a universally accepted form of payment, even among prisoners who didn't smoke.

Another possibility is to simulate the workings of the economy on a computer. For example, when changes in tax law are proposed, government officials use *tax models*—large mathematical computer programs—to assess how the proposed changes would affect different groups of people. Models can also be depicted by graphs and equations. Starting in the next module you will see how graphical models illustrate the relationships between variables and reveal the effects of changes in the economy.

Models are important because their simplicity allows economists to focus on the influence of only one change at a time. That is, they allow us to hold everything else constant and to study how one change affects the overall economic outcome. So when building economic models, it is important to make the **other things equal assumption**, which means that all other relevant factors remain unchanged. Sometimes the Latin phrase *ceteris paribus*, which means "other things equal," is used.

But it isn't always possible to find or create a small-scale version of the whole economy, and a computer program is only as good as the data it uses. (Programmers have a saying: garbage in, garbage out.) For many purposes, the most effective form of economic modeling is the construction of "thought experiments": simplified, hypothetical versions of real-life situations. And as you will see throughout this book, economists' models are very often in the form of a graph. In the next Module we will look at the *production possibilities curve*, a model that helps economists think about the choices to be made in every economy.

A **model** is a simplified representation used to better understand a real-life situation.

The **other things equal assumption** means that all other relevant factors remain unchanged. This is also known as the *ceteris paribus* assumption.

MODULE 2 REVIEW

Check Your Understanding

1. Describe two types of models used by economists.

2. Describe who gets hurt in a recession and how they are hurt.

TACKLE THE AP® TEST: Multiple-Choice Questions

1. During the recession phase of a business cycle, which of the following is likely to increase?
- **a.** the unemployment rate
- **b.** the price level
- **c.** economic growth rate
- **d.** the labor force
- **e.** wages

2. The labor force is made up of everyone who is
- **a.** employed.
- **b.** old enough to work.
- **c.** actively seeking work.
- **d.** employed or unemployed.
- **e.** employed or capable of working.

3. Which of the following provides a long-term increase in the productive capacity of an economy?
- **a.** an expansion
- **b.** a recovery
- **c.** a recession
- **d.** a depression
- **e.** economic growth

4. Which of the following is the most likely result of inflation?
- **a.** falling employment
- **b.** a dollar will buy more than it did before
- **c.** people are discouraged from holding cash
- **d.** price stability
- **e.** low aggregate output per capita

5. The other things equal assumption allows economists to
- **a.** avoid making assumptions about reality.
- **b.** focus on the effects of only one change at a time.
- **c.** avoid making the *ceteris paribus* assumption.
- **d.** allow nothing to change in their model.
- **e.** reflect all aspects of the real world in their model.

6. In the United States, a recession officially begins after
- **a.** the NBER makes a judgment call that it has.
- **b.** the business cycle stops rising.
- **c.** two consecutive quarters of falling aggregate output.
- **d.** six weeks or rising unemployment.
- **e.** a depression has worsened for two consecutive months.

7. Which of the following could not be considered an economic model?
- **a.** a graph
- **b.** an equation
- **c.** a computer simulation
- **d.** the economy itself
- **e.** a real but simplified economy

TACKLE THE AP® TEST: Free-Response Questions

1. Define *expansion* and *economic growth* and explain the difference between these two concepts.

2. Define *inflation* and explain why an increase in the price of donuts does not indicate that inflation has occurred. **(2 points)**

Rubric for FRQ 1 (3 points)

1 point: An expansion is the period of recovery after an economic downturn.

1 point: Economic growth is an increase in the productive capacity of the economy.

1 point: An expansion can occur regardless of any increase in the economy's long-term potential for production, and it only lasts until the next downturn, while economic growth increases the economy's ability to produce more goods and services over the long term.

The Production Possibilities Curve Model

In this Module, you will learn to:
- Explain the importance of trade-offs in economic analysis
- Describe what the production possibilities curve model tells us about efficiency, opportunity cost, and economic growth
- Explain why increases in the availability of resources and improvements in technology are the two sources of economic growth

A good economic model can be a tremendous aid to understanding. In this Module, we look at the *production possibilities curve*, a model that helps economists think about the *trade-offs* every economy faces. The production possibilities curve helps us understand three important aspects of the real economy: efficiency, opportunity cost, and economic growth.

Trade-offs: The Production Possibilities Curve

Some historians say that the true story of Alexander Selkirk inspired Daniel Defoe's 1719 novel about shipwrecked hero Robinson Crusoe. In 1704, Selkirk was a crew member on a ship that he correctly feared was not seaworthy. Before the ship met its fate at the bottom of the sea, Selkirk quarreled with the captain about the need for repairs, and then abandoned the ship during a stop at a deserted island near Chile. As in the story of Robinson Crusoe, Selkirk was alone and had limited resources: the natural resources of the island, a few items he brought from the ship, and, of course, his own time and effort. With only these resources, he had to make a life for four and a half years. In effect, he became a one-man economy.

One of the important principles of economics we introduced in Module 1 was that resources are scarce. As a result, any economy—whether it contains one person or millions of people—faces trade-offs. You make a **trade-off** when you give up something in order to have something else. For example, if a castaway on a tropical island devotes more resources to catching fish, he benefits by catching more fish, but he cannot use those same resources to gather coconuts, so the trade-off is that he has fewer coconuts.

To think about the trade-offs necessary in any economy, economists often use the **production possibilities curve** model. The idea behind this model is to improve our understanding of trade-offs by considering a simplified economy that produces only two goods. This simplification enables us to show the trade-offs graphically.

Figure 3.1 shows a hypothetical production possibilities curve for Alex, a castaway alone on an island, who must make a trade-off between fish production and coconut production. The curve shows the maximum quantity of fish Alex can catch during a week *given* the quantity of coconuts he gathers, and vice versa. That is, it answers questions of the form, "What is the maximum quantity of fish Alex can catch if he also gathers 9 (or 15, or 30) coconuts?"

There is a crucial distinction between points *inside* or *on* the production possibilities curve (the shaded area) and points *outside* the production possibilities curve. If a production point lies inside or on the curve—like point C, at which Alex catches 20 fish and gathers 9 coconuts—it is feasible. After all, the curve tells us

You make a **trade-off** when you give up something in order to have something else.

The **production possibilities curve** illustrates the trade-offs facing an economy that produces only two goods. It shows the maximum quantity of one good that can be produced for each possible quantity of the other good produced.

Figure 3.1 The Production Possibilities Curve

The production possibilities curve illustrates the trade-offs facing an economy that produces two goods. It shows the maximum quantity of one good that can be produced, given the quantity of the other good produced. Here, the maximum quantity of coconuts that Alex can gather depends on the quantity of fish he catches, and vice versa. His feasible production is shown by the area *inside* or *on* the curve. Production at point *D* is not feasible. Production at point *C* is feasible but not efficient and indicates underutilized resources. Points *A* and *B* are feasible and *productively efficient*.

AP® EXAM TIP

Be prepared to draw a correctly labeled production possibilities curve and use it to identify opportunity cost, efficient points, inefficient points, and unattainable points. Unemployment results in production at a point below the production possibilities curve—that is, feasible but inefficient.

that if Alex catches 20 fish, he could also gather a maximum of 15 coconuts, so he could certainly gather 9 coconuts. However, a production point that lies outside the curve—such as point *D*, which would have Alex catching 40 fish and gathering 30 coconuts—isn't feasible.

In Figure 3.1 the production possibilities curve intersects the horizontal axis at 40 fish. This means that if Alex devoted all his resources to catching fish, he would catch 40 fish per week but would have no resources left over to gather coconuts. The production possibilities curve intersects the vertical axis at 30 coconuts. This means that if Alex devoted all his resources to gathering coconuts, he could gather 30 coconuts per week but would have no resources left over to catch fish. Thus, if Alex wants 30 coconuts, the trade-off is that he can't have any fish.

The curve also shows less extreme trade-offs. For example, if Alex decides to catch 20 fish, he would be able to gather at most 15 coconuts; this production choice is illustrated by point *A*. If Alex decides to catch 28 fish, he could gather at most 9 coconuts, as shown by point *B*.

Thinking in terms of a production possibilities curve simplifies the complexities of reality. The real-world economy produces millions of different goods. Even a castaway on an island would produce more than two different items (for example, he would need clothing and housing as well as food). But in this model we imagine an economy that produces only two goods, because in a model with many goods, it would be much harder to study trade-offs, efficiency, and economic growth.

Efficiency

An economy is **efficient** if there is no way to make anyone better off without making at least one person worse off.

The production possibilities curve is useful for illustrating the general economic concept of efficiency. An economy is **efficient** if there are no missed opportunities—meaning that there is no way to make some people better off without making other people worse off. For example, suppose a course you are taking meets in a classroom that is too small for the number of students—some may be forced to sit on the floor or stand—despite the fact that a larger classroom nearby is empty during the same period. Economists would say that this is an *inefficient* use of resources because there is a way to make some people better off without making anyone worse off—after all, the larger classroom is empty. The school is not using its resources efficiently. When an economy is using all of its resources efficiently, the only way one person can be made better off is by rearranging the use of resources in such a way that the change makes someone else worse off. So in our classroom example, if all larger classrooms were already fully occupied, we could say that the school was run in an efficient way; your classmates could be made better off only by making people in the larger classroom worse off—by moving them to the room that is too small.

Returning to our castaway example, as long as Alex produces a combination of coconuts and fish that is on the production possibilities curve, his production is efficient. At point *A*, the 15 coconuts he gathers are the maximum quantity he can get *given* that he has chosen to catch 20 fish; at point *B*, the 9 coconuts he gathers are the maximum he can get *given* his choice to catch 28 fish; and so on. If an economy is producing at a point on its production possibilities curve, we say that the economy has achieved **productive efficiency**.

Now suppose that for some reason Alex was at point *C*, producing 20 fish and 9 coconuts. Then this one-person economy would definitely not be productively efficient and would therefore be inefficient: it is missing the opportunity to produce more of both goods.

Another example of inefficiency in production occurs when people in an economy are involuntarily unemployed: they want to work but are unable to find jobs. When that happens, the economy is not productively efficient because it could produce more output if those people were employed. The production possibilities curve shows the amount that can *possibly* be produced if all resources are fully employed. In other words, changes in unemployment move the economy closer to, or further away from, the production possibilities curve (*PPC*). But the curve itself is determined by what would be possible if there were no unemployment in the economy. Greater unemployment is represented by points farther below the *PPC*—the economy is not reaching its possibilities if it is not using all of its resources. Lower unemployment is represented by points closer to the *PPC*—as unemployment decreases, the economy moves closer to reaching its possibilities.

Although the production possibilities curve helps clarify what it means for an economy to achieve productive efficiency, it's important to understand that productive efficiency is only *part* of what's required for the economy as a whole to be efficient. Efficiency also requires that the economy allocate its resources so that consumers are as well off as possible. If an economy does this, we say that it has achieved **allocative efficiency**. To see why allocative efficiency is as important as productive efficiency, notice that points *A* and *B* in Figure 3.1 both represent situations in which the economy is productively efficient, because in each case it can't produce more of one good without producing less of the other. But these two situations may not be equally desirable. Suppose that Alex prefers point *B* to point *A*—that is, he would rather consume 28 fish and 9 coconuts than 20 fish and 15 coconuts. Then point *A* is inefficient from the point of view of the economy as a whole: it's possible to make Alex better off without making anyone else worse off. (Of course, in this castaway economy there isn't anyone else; Alex is all alone.)

This example shows that efficiency for the economy as a whole requires *both* productive and allocative efficiency. To be efficient, an economy must produce as much of each good as it can, given the production of other goods, and it must also produce the mix of goods that people most want to consume.

A crowded classroom reflects inefficiency if switching to a larger classroom would make some students better off without making anyone worse off.

An economy achieves **productive efficiency** if it produces at a point on its production possibilities curve.

An economy achieves **allocative efficiency** if it produces at the point along its production possibilities curve that makes consumers as well off as possible.

Opportunity Cost

The production possibilities curve is also useful as a reminder that the true cost of any good is not only its price, but also everything else in addition to money that must be given up in order to get that good—the *opportunity cost*. If, for example, Alex decides to go from point *A* to point *B*, he will produce 8 more fish but 6 fewer coconuts. So the opportunity cost of those 8 fish is the 6 coconuts not gathered. Since 8 extra fish have an opportunity cost of 6 coconuts, 1 fish has an opportunity cost of $6/8 = 3/4$ of a coconut.

Is the opportunity cost of an extra fish in terms of coconuts always the same, no matter how many fish Alex catches? In the example illustrated by Figure 3.1, the answer is yes. If Alex increases his catch from 28 to 40 fish, an increase of 12, the number of coconuts he gathers falls from 9 to zero. So his opportunity cost per additional fish is $9/12 = 3/4$ of a coconut, the same as it was when his catch went from 20 fish to 28.

AP® EXAM TIP

Opportunity Cost = Opportunity Lost (the financial or nonfinancial cost of a choice not taken)

However, the fact that in this example the opportunity cost of an additional fish in terms of coconuts is always the same is a result of an assumption we've made, an assumption that's reflected in the way Figure 3.1 is drawn. Specifically, whenever we assume that the opportunity cost of an additional unit of a good doesn't change regardless of the output mix, the production possibilities curve is a straight line.

Moreover, as you might have already guessed, the slope of a straight-line production possibilities curve is equal to the opportunity cost—specifically, the opportunity cost for the good measured on the horizontal axis in terms of the good measured on the vertical axis. In Figure 3.1, the production possibilities curve has a *constant slope* of $-\frac{3}{4}$, implying that Alex faces a *constant opportunity cost* per fish equal to $\frac{3}{4}$ of a coconut. (A review of how to calculate the slope of a straight line is found in the Section 1 Appendix.) This is the simplest case, but the production possibilities curve model can also be used to examine situations in which opportunity costs change as the mix of output changes.

Figure 3.2 illustrates a different assumption, a case in which Alex faces *increasing opportunity cost*. Here, the more fish he catches, the more coconuts he has to give up to catch an additional fish, and vice versa. For example, to go from producing zero fish to producing 20 fish, he has to give up 5 coconuts. That is, the opportunity cost of those 20 fish is 5 coconuts. But to increase his fish production from 20 to 40—that is, to produce an additional 20 fish—he must give up 25 more coconuts, a much higher opportunity cost. As you can see in Figure 3.2, when opportunity costs are increasing rather than constant, the production possibilities curve is a concave-shaped (bowed out) curve rather than a straight line.

> **AP® EXAM TIP**
>
> The AP® Exam may test your understanding that the use of specialized resources makes the production possibilities curve *concave to the origin*, meaning that it is bowed out as shown in Figure 3.2.

Figure 3.2   Increasing Opportunity Cost

The concave (bowed-out) shape of the production possibilities curve reflects increasing opportunity cost. In this example, to produce the first 20 fish, Alex must give up 5 coconuts. But to produce an additional 20 fish, he must give up 25 more coconuts. The opportunity cost of fish increases because as Alex catches more fish, he must make increasing use of resources specialized for coconut production.

Although it's often useful to work with the simple assumption that the production possibilities curve is a straight line, in reality, opportunity costs are typically increasing. When only a small amount of a good is produced, the opportunity cost of producing that good is relatively low because the economy needs to use only those resources that are especially well suited for its production. For instance, if an economy grows only a small amount of corn, that corn can be grown in places where the soil and climate are perfect for growing corn but less suitable for growing anything else, such as wheat. So growing that corn involves giving up only a small amount of wheat production. Once the economy grows a lot of corn, however, land that is well suited for wheat but isn't so great for corn must be used to produce corn anyway. As a result, increases in corn production involve sacrificing more and more wheat per unit of corn. In other words, as more of a good is produced, its opportunity cost typically rises because resources specialized for the production of that good are used up and resources specialized for the production of the other good must be used instead.

In some cases, there is no specialization of resources, meaning that all resources are equally suitable for the production of each good. That might be the case when the two goods are leather belts and leather hats, pizzas and calzones, or cappuccinos and lattes. When there is no specialization of resources, the opportunity cost of each unit remains the same as more of a good is made. For example, assuming that two leather belts could be made with the labor, leather, and other resources needed to make one leather hat, the opportunity cost of each leather hat is two belts. When no resources are specialized for the production of either good, the production possibilities curve is a straight, downward-sloping line like the one in Figure 3.1.

Economic Growth

Finally, the production possibilities curve helps us understand what it means to talk about *economic growth*. We introduced the concept of economic growth in Module 2, saying that it allows *a sustained rise in aggregate output and an increase in our standard of living*. But are we really justified in saying that the economy has grown over time? After all, although the U.S. economy produces more of many things than it did a century ago, it produces less of other things—for example, horse-drawn carriages. In other words, production of many goods is actually down. So how can we say for sure that the economy as a whole has grown?

The answer, illustrated in **Figure 3.3**, is that economic growth means an *expansion of the economy's production possibilities*: the economy *can* produce more of everything. For example, if Alex's production is initially at point *A* (20 fish and 25 coconuts), economic growth means that he could move to point *E* (25 fish and 30 coconuts). Point *E* lies outside the original curve, so in the production possibilities curve model, growth is shown as an outward shift of the curve. Unless the *PPC* shifts outward, the points beyond the *PPC* are unattainable. Those points beyond a given *PPC* are beyond the economy's production possibilities.

Figure 3.3 Economic Growth

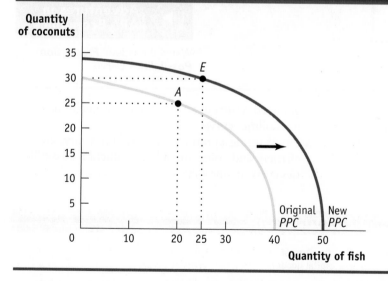

Economic growth results in an *outward shift* of the production possibilities curve because production possibilities are expanded. The economy can now produce more of everything. For example, if production is initially at point *A* (20 fish and 25 coconuts), it could move to point *E* (25 fish and 30 coconuts). The opposite, a leftward shift due to decreases in factors of production or productivity, would represent economic contraction.

What can cause the production possibilities curve to shift outward? There are two general sources of economic growth. One is an increase in the availability of resources (sometimes called factors of production) used to produce goods and services: labor, land, capital, and entrepreneurship. To see how adding to an economy's resources leads to economic growth, suppose that fish become more abundant in the waters around Alex's island. He can then catch more fish in the course of a day spent fishing. We can't say how many more fish Alex will catch; that depends on how much time he decides to spend fishing now that there are more fish in his part of the sea. But because the increased fish population makes his fishing more productive, he can catch more fish without reducing the number of

Technology is the technical means for producing goods and services.

coconuts he gathers, or he can gather more coconuts without reducing his fish catch. So his production possibilities curve shifts outward.

The other source of economic growth is progress in **technology**, the technical means for the production of goods and services. Suppose Alex figures out a better way either to catch fish or to gather coconuts—say, by inventing a fishing net or a wagon for transporting coconuts. Either invention would shift his production possibilities curve outward. However, the shift would not be a simple outward expansion of every point along the *PPC*. Technology specific to the production of only one good has no effect if all resources are devoted to the other good: a fishing net will be of no use if Alex produces nothing but coconuts. So the point on the *PPC* that represents the number of coconuts that can be produced if there is no fishing will not change. In real-world economies, innovations in the techniques we use to produce goods and services have been a crucial force behind economic growth.

Remember, economic growth means an increase in what the economy *can* produce. What the economy actually produces depends on the choices people make. After his production possibilities expand, Alex might not choose to produce both more fish and more coconuts; he might choose to increase production of only one good, or he might even choose to produce less of one good. For example, if he gets better at catching fish, he might decide to go on an all-fish diet and skip the coconuts, just as the introduction of motor vehicles led most people to give up horse-drawn carriages. But even if, for some reason, he chooses to produce either fewer coconuts or fewer fish than before, we would still say that his economy has grown, because he *could* have produced more of everything. If an economy's production possibilities curve shifts inward, the economy has become smaller. This could happen if the economy loses resources or technology (for example, if it experiences war or a natural-disaster).

The production possibilities curve is a very simplified model of an economy, yet it teaches us important lessons about real-life economies. It gives us our first clear sense of what constitutes economic efficiency, it illustrates the concept of opportunity cost, and it shows what economic growth is all about.

MODULE 3 REVIEW

Adventures in AP® Economics

Watch the video: *Production Possibilities Curve*

Check Your Understanding

1. True or false? Explain your answer.
   a. An increase in the amount of resources available to Alex for use in producing coconuts and fish does not change his production possibilities curve.
   b. A technological change that allows Alex to catch more fish relative to any amount of coconuts gathered results in a change in his production possibilities curve.
   c. Points inside a production possibilities curve are efficient and points outside a production possibilities curve are inefficient.

TACKLE THE AP® TEST: Multiple-Choice Questions

Refer to the graph to answer questions 1–5.

1. Which point(s) on the graph represent productive efficiency?
   a. *B* and *C*
   b. *A* and *D*
   c. *A, B, C,* and *D*
   d. *A, B, C, D,* and *E*
   e. *A, B, C, D, E,* and *F*

2. For this economy, an increase in the quantity of capital goods produced without a corresponding decrease in the quantity of consumer goods produced
   a. cannot happen because there is always an opportunity cost.
   b. is represented by a movement from point *E* to point *A*.
   c. is represented by a movement from point *C* to point *B*.
   d. is represented by a movement from point *E* to point *B*.
   e. is only possible with an increase in resources or technology.

3. An increase in unemployment could be represented by a movement from point
   a. *D* to point *C*.
   b. *B* to point *A*.
   c. *C* to point *F*.
   d. *B* to point *E*.
   e. *E* to point *B*.

4. Which of the following might allow this economy to move from point *B* to point *F*?
   a. more workers
   b. discovery of new resources
   c. building new factories
   d. technological advances
   e. all of the above

5. This production possibilities curve shows the trade-off between consumer goods and capital goods. Since capital goods are a resource, an increase in the production of capital goods today will increase the economy's production possibilities in the future. Therefore, all other things equal (*ceteris paribus*), producing at which point today will result in the largest outward shift of the *PPC* in the future?
   a. *A*
   b. *B*
   c. *C*
   d. *D*
   e. *E*

6. The production possibilities curve will certainly be straight if
   a. making more of one good means that less of the other good can be made.
   b. the opportunity cost of making each good increases as more is made.
   c. no resources are specialized for the production of either good.
   d. the opportunity cost of making the first unit of each good is the same.
   e. the economy experiences decreasing opportunity costs for the production of both goods.

7. Allocative efficiency is achieved
   a. at every point along a production possibilities curve.
   b. at every point above a production possibilities curve.
   c. at every point below a production possibilities curve.
   d. at the point on a production possibilities curve that minimizes the use of resources.
   e. at the point along a production possibilities curve that makes consumers as well off as possible.

TACKLE THE AP® TEST: Free-Response Questions

1. Refer to the graph. Assume that the country is producing at point *C*.
   a. Does this country's production possibilities curve exhibit increasing opportunity costs? Explain.
   b. Suppose point *C* is initially the allocatively efficient point for this country, but then the country goes to war. Before any of the country's resources are lost in the fighting, which point is the most likely to be allocatively efficient for the country when it is at war? Explain.

   c. If the economy entered into a recession, the country would move from point *C* to which point? Explain.

Quantity of military goods ("guns")

Quantity of social goods ("butter")

2. Assume that an economy can choose between producing food and producing shelter at a constant opportunity cost. Draw a correctly labeled production possibilities curve for the economy. On your graph:
   a. Use the letter *E* to label one of the points that is productively efficient.
   b. Use the letter *U* to label one of the points at which there might be unemployment.
   c. Use the letter *I* to label one of the points that is not feasible. **(5 points)**

Rubric for FRQ 1 (6 points)

1 point: Yes

1 point: The *PPC* is concave (bowed outward), so with each additional unit of butter produced, the opportunity cost in terms of gun production (indicated by the slope of the line) increases. Likewise, as more guns are produced, the opportunity cost in terms of butter increases.

1 point: B

1 point: The country would choose an efficient point with more (but not all) military goods with which to fight the war. Point *A* would be an unlikely choice because at that point there is no production of any social goods, some of which are needed to maintain a minimal standard of living.

1 point: E

1 point: A recession, which causes unemployment, is represented by a point below the *PPC*.

Comparative Advantage and Trade

> **In this Module, you will learn to:**
> - Explain how trade leads to gains for an individual or an economy
> - Explain the difference between absolute advantage and comparative advantage
> - Describe how comparative advantage leads to gains from trade in the global marketplace

Gains from Trade

AP® EXAM TIP

Take note! The content in this Module frequently shows up in both the free-response and the multiple-choice sections of the AP® exam.

In a market economy, individuals engage in **trade**: they provide goods and services to others and receive goods and services in return.

There are **gains from trade**: people can get more of what they want through trade than they could if they tried to be self-sufficient. This increase in output is due to **specialization**: each person specializes in the task that he or she is good at performing.

A family could try to take care of all its own needs—growing its own food, sewing its own clothing, providing itself with entertainment, and writing its own economics textbooks. But trying to live that way would be very hard. The key to a much better standard of living for everyone is **trade**, meaning that people divide tasks among themselves and each person provides a good or service that other people want in return for different goods and services that he or she wants.

The reason we have an economy, rather than many self-sufficient individuals, is that there are **gains from trade**: by dividing tasks and trading, two people (or 7 billion people) can each get more of what they want than they could get by being self-sufficient. Gains from trade that arise from this division of tasks is known as **specialization**, which allows each person to engage in a task that he or she is particularly good at performing.

The advantages of specialization, and the resulting gains from trade, were the starting point for Adam Smith's 1776 book *The Wealth of Nations*, which many regard as the beginning of economics as a discipline. Smith's book begins with a description of an eighteenth-century pin factory where, rather than each of the 10 workers making a pin from start to finish, each worker specialized in one of the many steps in pin-making:

> One man draws out the wire, another straights it, a third cuts it, a fourth points it, a fifth grinds it at the top for receiving the head; to make the head requires two or three distinct operations; to put it on, is a particular business, to whiten the pins is another; it is even a trade by itself to put them into the paper; and the important business of making a pin is, in this manner, divided into about eighteen distinct operations. . . . Those ten persons, therefore, could make among them upwards of forty-eight thousand pins in a day. But if they had all wrought separately and independently, and without any of them having been educated to this particular business, they certainly could not each of them have made twenty, perhaps not one pin a day. . . .

The same principle applies when we look at how people divide tasks among themselves and trade in an economy. The economy as a whole can produce more when each person *specializes* in a task and *trades* with others.

The benefits of specialization are the reason a person typically focuses on the production of only one type of good or service. It takes many years of study and experience to become a doctor; it also takes many years of study and experience to become a commercial airline pilot. Many doctors might have the potential to become excellent pilots, and vice versa, but it is very unlikely that anyone who decided to pursue both careers would be as good a pilot or as good a doctor as someone who specialized in only one of those professions. So it is to everyone's advantage when individuals specialize in their career choices.

Markets are what allow a doctor and a pilot to specialize in their respective fields. Because markets for

Mike Fuentes/Bloomberg via Getty Images

The concept of specialization allows for the mass production of most of the devices and appliances that we use today.

commercial flights and for doctors' services exist, a doctor is assured that she can find a flight and a pilot is assured that he can find a doctor. As long as individuals know that they can find the goods and services that they want in the market, they are willing to forgo self-sufficiency and specialize instead.

Comparative Advantage and Gains from Trade

The production possibilities curve model is particularly useful for illustrating gains from trade—trade based on *comparative advantage*. Let's stick with Alex being stranded on his island, but now let's suppose that a second castaway, Kirk, is washed ashore. Can Alex and Kirk benefit from trading with each other?

It's obvious that there will be potential gains from trade if the two castaways do different things particularly well. For example, if Alex is a skilled fisherman and Kirk is very good at climbing trees, clearly it makes sense for Alex to catch fish and Kirk to gather coconuts—and for the two men to trade the products of their efforts.

But one of the most important insights in all of economics is that there are gains from trade even if one of the trading parties isn't especially good at anything. Suppose, for example, that Kirk is less well suited to primitive life than Alex; he's not nearly as good at catching fish, and compared to Alex, even his coconut-gathering leaves something to be desired. Nonetheless, what we'll see is that both Alex and Kirk can live better by trading with each other than either could alone.

For the purposes of this example, let's go back to the simple case of straight-line production possibilities curves. Alex's production possibilities are represented by the production possibilities curve in panel (a) of **Figure 4.1**, which is the same as the production possibilities curve in Figure 3.1. According to this *PPC*, Alex could catch 40 fish, but only if he gathered no coconuts, and he could gather 30 coconuts, but only if he caught no fish. Recall that this means that the slope of his production possibilities curve is $-\frac{3}{4}$: his opportunity cost of 1 fish is $\frac{3}{4}$ of a coconut.

Panel (b) of Figure 4.1 shows Kirk's production possibilities. Like Alex's, Kirk's production possibilities curve is a straight line, implying a constant opportunity cost of fish in terms of coconuts. His production possibilities curve has a constant slope of -2. Kirk is less productive all around: at most he can produce 10 fish or 20 coconuts. But he

Roderick Chen/Getty Images

Figure 4.1 Production Possibilities for Two Castaways

(a) Alex's Production Possibilities

Quantity of coconuts

For each fish Alex loses 3/4 of a coconut

30

1
$-\frac{3}{4}$

Alex's PPC

0   40

Quantity of fish

(b) Kirk's Production Possibilities

Quantity of coconuts

For each fish Kirk loses 2 coconuts

20 1
-2

Kirk's PPC

0   10

Quantity of fish

Here, each of the two castaways has a constant opportunity cost of fish, and therefore a straight-line production possibilities curve. In

Alex's case, each fish has an opportunity cost of ¾ of a coconut. In Kirk's case, each fish has an opportunity cost of 2 coconuts.

is particularly bad at fishing: whereas Alex sacrifices ¾ of a coconut per fish caught, for Kirk the opportunity cost of a fish is 2 whole coconuts. **Table 4.1** summarizes the two castaways' opportunity costs of fish and coconuts.

Table 4.1	Alex's and Kirk's Opportunity Costs of Fish and Coconuts	
	Alex's Opportunity Cost	**Kirk's Opportunity Cost**
One fish	¾ coconut	2 coconuts
One coconut	4/3 fish	½ fish

Now, Alex and Kirk could go their separate ways, each living on his own side of the island, catching his own fish and gathering his own coconuts. Let's suppose that they start out that way and make the consumption choices shown in **Figure 4.2**: in the absence of trade, Alex consumes 28 fish and 9 coconuts per week, while Kirk consumes 6 fish and 8 coconuts.

Figure 4.2   Comparative Advantage and Gains from Trade

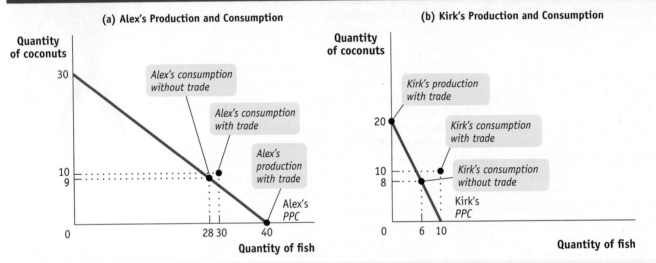

By specializing and trading, the two castaways can produce and consume more of both goods. Alex specializes in catching fish, his comparative advantage, and Kirk—who has an *absolute* disadvantage in both goods but a *comparative* advantage in coconuts—specializes in gathering coconuts. The result is that each castaway can consume more of both goods than either could without trade.

But is this the best they can do? No, it isn't. Given that the two castaways have different opportunity costs, they can strike a deal that makes both of them better off. **Table 4.2** shows how such a deal works: Alex specializes in the production of fish, catching 40 per week, and gives 10 to Kirk. Meanwhile, Kirk specializes in the production of coconuts, gathering 20 per week, and gives 10 to Alex. The result is shown by the points above the PPCs in Figure 4.2. Alex now consumes more of both goods than before: instead of 28 fish and 9 coconuts, he consumes 30 fish and 10 coconuts. Kirk also consumes more, going from 6 fish and 8 coconuts to 10 fish and 10 coconuts. As Table 4.2 also shows, both Alex and Kirk experience gains from trade: Alex's consumption of fish increases by two, and his consumption of coconuts increases by one. Kirk's consumption of fish increases by four, and his consumption of coconuts increases by two.

So both castaways are better off when they each specialize in what they are good at and trade with each other. It's a good idea for Alex to catch the fish for both of them, because his opportunity cost of a fish is only ¾ of a coconut not gathered versus 2 coconuts for Kirk. Correspondingly, it's a good idea for Kirk to gather coconuts for both of them.

Or we could describe the situation in a different way. Because Alex is so good at catching fish, his opportunity cost of gathering coconuts is high: 4/3 of a fish not caught for every coconut gathered. Because Kirk is a pretty bad fisherman, his opportunity cost of gathering coconuts is much less, only ½ of a fish per coconut.

Table 4.2	How the Castaways Gain from Trade				
		Without Trade		**With Trade**		Gains from Trade
		Production	Consumption	Production	Consumption	
Alex	Fish	28	28	40	30	+2
	Coconuts	9	9	0	10	+1
Kirk	Fish	6	6	0	10	+4
	Coconuts	8	8	20	10	+2

An individual has a **comparative advantage** in producing something if the opportunity cost of that production is lower for that individual than for other people. In other words, Kirk has a comparative advantage over Alex in producing a particular good or service if Kirk's opportunity cost of producing that good or service is lower than Alex's. In this case, Kirk has a comparative advantage in gathering coconuts, and Alex has a comparative advantage in catching fish.

Notice that Alex is actually better than Kirk at producing both goods: Alex can catch more fish in a week, and he can also gather more coconuts. This means that Alex has an **absolute advantage** in both activities: he can produce more output with a given amount of input (in this case, his time) than Kirk can. It might seem as though Alex has nothing to gain from trading with less competent Kirk. But we've just seen that Alex can indeed benefit from a deal with Kirk, because *comparative*, not *absolute*, advantage is the basis for mutual gain. It doesn't matter that it takes Kirk more time to gather a coconut; what matters is that for him the opportunity cost of that coconut in terms of fish is lower. So, despite his absolute disadvantage in both activities, Kirk has a comparative advantage in coconut gathering. Meanwhile Alex, who can use his time better by catching fish, has a comparative disadvantage in coconut gathering.

Mutually Beneficial Terms of Trade

The **terms of trade** indicate the rate at which one good can be exchanged for another. In our story, Alex and Kirk traded 10 coconuts for 10 fish, so each coconut traded for 1 fish. Why not some other terms of trade, such as ¾ fish per coconut? Indeed, there are many terms of trade that would make both Alex and Kirk better off than if they didn't trade. But there are also terms that Alex or Kirk would certainly reject. For example, Alex would not trade 2 fish per coconut, because he only gives up ⅓ fish per coconut without trade.

To find the range of mutually beneficial terms of trade for a coconut, look at each person's opportunity cost of producing a coconut. *Any price per coconut between the opportunity cost of the coconut producer and the opportunity cost of the coconut buyer will make both sides better off than in the absence of trade.* We know that Kirk will produce coconuts because he has a comparative advantage in gathering coconuts. Kirk's opportunity cost is ½ fish per coconut. Alex, the buyer of coconuts, has an opportunity cost of ⅓ fish per coconut. So any terms of trade between ½ fish per coconut and ⅓ fish per coconut would benefit both Alex and Kirk.

To understand why, consider the opportunity costs summarized in Table 4.1. When Kirk doesn't trade with Alex, Kirk can gain ½ fish by giving up a coconut, because his opportunity cost of each coconut is ½ fish. Kirk will clearly reject any deal with Alex that provides him with less than ½ fish per coconut—he's better off not trading at all and getting ½ fish per coconut. But Kirk benefits from trade if he receives more than ½ fish per coconut. So the terms of 1 fish per coconut, as in our story, are acceptable to Kirk.

When Alex doesn't trade with Kirk, Alex gives up ⅓ fish to get a coconut—his opportunity cost of a coconut is ⅓ fish. Alex will reject any deal that requires him to pay more than ⅓ fish per coconut. But Alex benefits from trade if he pays less than ⅓ fish per coconut. The terms of 1 fish per coconut are thus acceptable to Alex as well. Both islanders would also be made better off by terms of ¾ fish per coconut or ⁵⁄₄ fish per coconut or any other price between ½ fish and ⅓ fish per coconut. The islanders' negotiation skills determine where the terms of trade fall within that range.

An individual has a **comparative advantage** in producing a good or service if the opportunity cost of producing the good or service is lower for that individual than for other people.

An individual has an **absolute advantage** in producing a good or service if he or she can make more of it with a given amount of time and resources. Having an absolute advantage is not the same thing as having a comparative advantage.

The **terms of trade** indicate the rate at which one good can be exchanged for another.

AP® EXAM TIP

The mutually beneficial terms of trade for a good fall between the producer's opportunity cost for the good and the buyer's opportunity cost for the good.

AP® EXAM TIP

The producer with the *absolute advantage* can produce the largest quantity of the good. However, it is the producer with the *comparative advantage*, and not necessarily the one with the absolute advantage, who should specialize in the production of that good to achieve mutual gains from trade.

So remember, Alex and Kirk will engage in trade only if the "price" of the good each person obtains from trade is less than his own opportunity cost of producing the good. The same is true for international trade. Whenever two parties trade voluntarily, the terms of trade for each good are found between the opportunity cost of the producer and the opportunity cost of the buyer.

The story of Alex and Kirk clearly simplifies reality. Yet it teaches us some very important lessons that also apply to the real economy. First, the story illustrates the gains from trade. By agreeing to specialize and trade, Alex and Kirk can each consume more of both goods than if each tried to be self-sufficient. Second, the story demonstrates a key point that is often overlooked in real-world arguments: as long as potential trading partners have different opportunity costs, *each has a comparative advantage in something and each has a comparative disadvantage in something else, so each can benefit from trade.*

The idea of comparative advantage applies to many activities in the economy. Perhaps its most important application is in trade—not between individuals, but between countries. So let's look briefly at how the model of comparative advantage helps us understand both the causes and the effects of international trade.

Comparative Advantage and International Trade

Look at the label on a manufactured good sold in the United States, and there's a good chance you will find that it was produced in some other country—in China, Japan, or even Canada. On the other hand, many U.S. industries sell a large portion of their output overseas. This is particularly true for the agriculture, high technology, and entertainment industries.

Should we celebrate this international exchange of goods and services, or should it cause us concern? Politicians and the public often question the desirability of international trade, arguing that the nation should produce goods for itself rather than buy them from foreigners. Industries around the world demand protection from foreign competition: Japanese farmers want to keep out American rice, and American steelworkers want to keep out European steel. These demands are often supported by public opinion.

Economists, however, have a very positive view of international trade. Why? Because they view it in terms of comparative advantage. **Figure 4.3** shows how international

Figure 4.3 Comparative Advantage and International Trade

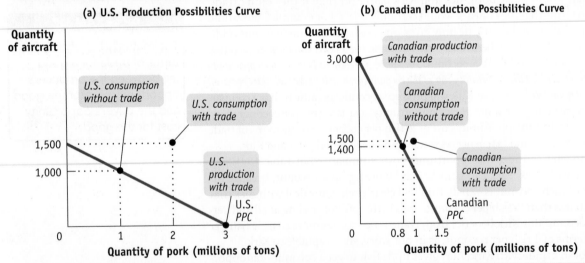

In this hypothetical example, Canada and the United States produce only two goods: pork and aircraft. Aircraft are measured on the vertical axis and pork on the horizontal axis. Panel (a) shows the U.S. production possibilities curve. It is relatively flat, implying that the United States has a comparative advantage in pork production. Panel (b) shows the Canadian production possibilities curve. It is relatively steep, implying that Canada has a comparative advantage in aircraft production. Just like two individuals, both countries gain from specialization and trade.

trade can be interpreted in terms of comparative advantage. Although the example is hypothetical, it is based on an actual pattern of international trade: American exports of pork to Canada and Canadian exports of aircraft to the United States. Panels (a) and (b) illustrate hypothetical production possibilities curves for the United States and Canada, with pork measured on the horizontal axis and aircraft measured on the vertical axis. The U.S. production possibilities curve is flatter than the Canadian production possibilities curve, implying that producing one more ton of pork costs fewer aircraft in the United States than it does in Canada. This means that the United States has a comparative advantage in pork and Canada has a comparative advantage in aircraft.

Although the consumption points in Figure 4.3 are hypothetical, they illustrate a general principle: as in the example of Alex and Kirk, the United States and Canada can both achieve mutual gains from trade. If the United States concentrates on producing pork and sells some of its output to Canada, while Canada concentrates on aircraft and sells some of its output to the United States, both countries can consume more than if they insisted on being self-sufficient. For example, the United States could trade 1 million tons of pork for 1,500 aircraft from Canada. This would allow both countries to consume at a point outside of their production possibilities curves.

Moreover, these mutual gains don't depend on each country's being better at producing one kind of good. Even if, say, one country has remarkably productive workers who give it an absolute advantage in both industries, there are still mutual gains from trade.

MODULE 4 REVIEW

Adventures in AP® Economics

Watch the video:
Comparative Advantage and Absolute Advantage

Check Your Understanding

1. In Italy, an automobile can be produced by 8 workers in one day and a washing machine by 3 workers in one day. In the United States, an automobile can be produced by 6 workers in one day, and a washing machine by 2 workers in one day.
   a. Which country has an absolute advantage in the production of automobiles? in washing machines?
   b. Which country has a comparative advantage in the production of washing machines? in automobiles?
   c. What type of specialization results in the greatest gains from trade between the two countries?

2. Refer to the story of Alex and Kirk illustrated by Figure 4.1 in the text. Explain why Alex and Kirk are willing to engage in a trade of 1 fish for 1½ coconuts.

TACKLE THE AP® TEST: Multiple-Choice Questions

Refer to the graph below to answer questions 1–6 below.

1. Use the graph to determine which country has an absolute advantage in producing each good.

Absolute advantage in wheat production	Absolute advantage in textile production
a. Country A	Country B
b. Country A	Country A
c. Country B	Country A
d. Country B	Country B
e. Country A	Neither country

2. For Country A, the opportunity cost of a bushel of wheat is
   a. ½ unit of textiles.
   b. ⅔ unit of textiles.
   c. 1⅓ units of textiles.
   d. 1½ units of textiles.
   e. 2 units of textiles.

3. Use the graph to determine which country has a comparative advantage in producing each good.

	Comparative advantage in wheat production	Comparative advantage in textile production
a.	Country A	Country B
b.	Country A	Country A
c.	Country B	Country A
d.	Country B	Country B
e.	Country A	Neither country

4. If the two countries specialize and trade, which of the choices below describes the countries' imports?

	Import wheat	Import textiles
a.	Country A	Country A
b.	Country A	Country B
c.	Country B	Country B
d.	Country B	Country A
e.	Neither country	Country B

5. What is the highest price Country B is willing to pay to buy wheat from Country A?
   a. ½ unit of textiles
   b. ⅔ unit of textiles
   c. 1 unit of textiles
   d. 1½ units of textiles
   e. 2 units of textiles

6. What are the mutually beneficial terms of trade, measured in units of wheat from Country A per unit of textiles from Country B?
   a. between 1 and 2
   b. between ⅔ and 2
   c. between ½ and 1½
   d. between ⅔ and 1½
   e. between ½ and 2

7. There are opportunities for mutually beneficial trade between two countries whenever
   a. one can produce more of everything than the other.
   b. the production possibilities curves of the two countries are identical.
   c. each country has a comparative advantage in making something.
   d. the countries are similar in size.
   e. no country has an absolute advantage in producing both goods.

TACKLE THE AP® TEST: Free-Response Questions

1. Refer to the graph below to answer the following questions.

a. What is the opportunity cost of a bushel of corn in each country?
b. Which country has an absolute advantage in computer production? Explain.
c. Which country has a comparative advantage in corn production? Explain.
d. If each country specializes, what good will Country B import? Explain.
e. What is the minimum price Country A will accept to export corn to Country B? Explain.

Rubric for FRQ 1 (9 points)
1 point: Country A, ¼ computer; Country B, 1¼ computers
1 point: Country B
1 point: Because Country B can produce more computers than Country A (500 versus 200)
1 point: Country A

1 point: Because Country A can produce corn at a lower opportunity cost (¼ computer versus 1¼ computers)
1 point: Corn
1 point: Country B has a comparative advantage in the production of computers, so it will produce computers and import corn (Country A has a comparative advantage in corn production, so it will specialize in corn and import computers from Country B).
1 point: ¼ computer
1 point: Country A's opportunity cost of producing corn is ¼ computer, so that is the lowest price it will accept to sell corn to Country B.

2. Refer to the table below to answer the following questions. These two countries are producing textiles and wheat using equal amounts of resources. The table indicates the maximum weekly output for workers who produce wheat or textiles.

	Weekly output per worker	
	Country A	Country B
Bushels of wheat	15	10
Units of textiles	60	60

a. What is the opportunity cost of producing a bushel of wheat for each country?
b. Which country has the absolute advantage in wheat production?
c. Which country has the comparative advantage in textile production? Explain. **(5 points)**

▶ SECTION 1 Review Video

Adventures in AP® Economics Videos

Mod 3: Production Possibilities Curves
Mod 4: Comparative Advantage & Absolute Advantage
Appendix: Graphing Tips & Tricks

Module 1

1. Everyone has to make choices about what to do and what *not* to do. **Individual choice** is the basis of **economics**—if it doesn't involve choice, it isn't economics. The **economy** is a system that coordinates choices about production and consumption. In a **market economy**, these choices are made by many firms and individuals. In a **command economy**, these choices are made by a central authority. **Incentives** are rewards or punishments that motivate particular choices and can be lacking in a command economy where producers cannot set their own prices or keep their own profits. **Property rights** create incentives in market economies by establishing ownership and granting individuals the right to trade goods and services for mutual gain. In any economy, decisions are informed by **marginal analysis**—the study of the costs and benefits of doing something a little bit more or a little bit less.

2. The reason choices must be made is that **resources**—anything that can be used to produce something else—are **scarce**. The four categories of resources are **land**, **labor**, **capital**, and **entrepreneurship**. Individuals are limited in their choices by money and time; economies are limited by their supplies of resources.

3. Because you must choose among limited alternatives, the true cost of anything is what you must give up to get it—all costs are **opportunity costs**.

4. Economists use economic models for **positive economics**, which describes how the economy works, and for **normative economics**, which prescribes how the economy *should* work. Positive economics often involves making forecasts. Economics can determine correct answers for positive questions, but typically not for normative questions, which involve value judgments. Exceptions occur when policies designed to achieve a certain prescription can be clearly ranked in terms of preference.

5. There are two main reasons economists disagree. One, they may disagree about which simplifications to make in a model. Two, economists may disagree—like everyone else—about values.

6. **Microeconomics** is the branch of economics that studies how people make decisions and how those decisions interact. **Macroeconomics** is concerned with the overall ups and downs of the economy and focuses on **economic aggregates** such as the unemployment rate and gross domestic product, that summarize data across many different markets.

Module 2

7. Economies experience ups and downs in economic activity. This pattern is called the **business cycle**. The downturns are known as **recessions**; the upturns are known as **expansions**. A **depression** is a long, deep downturn.

8. Workers are counted in **unemployment** figures only if they are actively seeking work but aren't currently employed. The sum of **employment** and unemployment is the **labor force**. The **unemployment rate** is the percentage of the labor force that is unemployed.

9. As the unemployment rate rises, the **output** for the economy as a whole—the **aggregate output**—generally falls.

10. A short-term increase in aggregate output made possible by a decrease in unemployment does not constitute **economic growth**, which is an increase in the maximum amount of output an economy can produce.

11. Rises and falls in the overall price level constitute **inflation** and **deflation**. Economists prefer that prices change only slowly if at all, because such **price stability** helps keep the economy stable.

12. Almost all economics is based on **models**, "thought experiments" or simplified versions of reality, many of which use analytical tools such as mathematics and graphs. An important assumption in economic models is the **other things equal (ceteris paribus) assumption**, which allows analysis of the effect of change in one factor by holding all other relevant factors unchanged.

Module 3

13. One important economic model is the **production possibilities curve**, which illustrates the **trade-offs** facing an economy that produces only two goods. The production possibilities curve illustrates three elements: opportunity cost (showing how much less of one good must be produced if more of the other good is produced), **efficiency** (an economy achieves **productive efficiency** if it produces on the production possibilities curve and **allocative efficiency** if it produces the mix of goods and services that people want to consume), and economic growth (an outward shift of the production possibilities curve).

14. There are two basic sources of growth in the production possibilities curve model: an increase in resources and improved **technology**.

Module 4

15. There are **gains from trade**: by engaging in the **trade** of goods and services with one another, the members of an economy can all be made better off. Underlying gains from trade are the advantages of **specialization**, of having individuals specialize in the tasks they are comparatively good at.

16. The existence of **comparative advantages** explains the source of gains from trade between individuals and countries. Having a comparative advantage means that you can make a good or service at a lower opportunity cost than everyone else. This is often confused with an **absolute advantage**, which is an ability to produce more of a particular good or service than anyone else. This confusion leads some to erroneously conclude that there are no gains from trade between people or countries.

17. As long as a comparative advantage exists between two parties, there are opportunities for mutually beneficial trade. The **terms of trade** indicate the rate at which one good can be exchanged for another. The range of mutually beneficial terms of trade for a good are found between the producer's opportunity cost of making the good and the buyer's opportunity cost of making the same good.

Key Terms

Economics, p. 2
Individual choice, p. 2
Economy, p. 2
Market economy, p. 2
Command economy, p. 2
Incentives, p. 2
Property rights, p. 2
Marginal analysis, p. 3
Resource, p. 3
Land, p. 3
Labor, p. 3
Capital, p. 3
Entrepreneurship, p. 3
Scarce, p. 3
Opportunity cost, p. 4
Microeconomics, p. 5
Macroeconomics, p. 5

Economic aggregates, p. 5
Positive economics, p. 5
Normative economics, p. 5
Business cycle, p. 10
Recessions, p. 10
Expansions, p. 10
Depression, p. 10
Employment, p. 11
Unemployment, p. 11
Labor force, p. 11
Unemployment rate, p. 11
Output, p. 11
Aggregate output, p. 11
Inflation, p. 11
Deflation, p. 11
Price stability, p. 12
Economic growth, p. 12

Model, p. 13
Other things equal (*ceteris paribus*) assumption, p. 13
Trade-off, p. 15
Production possibilities curve, p. 15
Efficient, p. 16
Productive efficiency, p. 17
Allocative efficiency, p. 17
Technology, p. 20
Trade, p. 22
Gains from trade, p. 22
Specialization, p. 22
Comparative advantage, p. 25
Absolute advantage, p. 25
Terms of trade, p. 25

AP® Exam Practice Questions

Multiple-Choice Questions

1. In a market economy, most choices about production and consumption are made by which of the following?
   a. politicians
   b. many individuals and firms
   c. the government
   d. managers
   e. economists

2. Which of the following pairs indicates a category of resources and an example of that resource?

Category	Example
a. money	investment
b. capital	money
c. capital	minerals
d. land	factory
e. land	timber

3. You can either go to a movie or study for an exam. Which of the following is an opportunity cost of studying for the exam?
   a. a higher grade on the exam
   b. the price of a movie ticket
   c. the cost of paper, pens, books, and other study materials
   d. the enjoyment from seeing the movie
   e. the sense of achievement from learning

4. Which of the following situations is explained by increasing opportunity costs?
   a. More people go to college when the job market is good.
   b. More people do their own home repairs when hourly wages fall.
   c. There are more parks in crowded cities than in suburban areas.

d. Convenience stores cater to busy people.

e. People with higher wages are more likely to mow their own lawns.

5. Which of the following is a normative statement?

   a. The unemployment rate is expected to rise.

   b. Individuals purchase more of a good when the price rises.

   c. The government should increase the minimum wage.

   d. An increase in the tax rate on wage earnings reduces the incentive to work.

   e. Public education generates greater benefits than costs.

6. Falling output in an economy is consistent with which of the following?

   a. a recession

   b. an expansion

   c. a recovery

   d. falling unemployment

   e. long-term economic growth

7. Which of the following is a goal for the economy?

   a. declining labor force

   b. inflation

   c. deflation

   d. rising aggregate output

   e. rising unemployment rate

Refer to the following table and information for Questions 8–11.

Suppose that Atlantis is a small, isolated island in the South Atlantic. The inhabitants grow potatoes and catch fish. The following table shows the maximum annual output combinations of potatoes and fish that can be produced.

Maximum annual output options	Quantity of potatoes (pounds)	Quantity of fish (pounds)
A	1,000	0
B	800	300
C	600	500
D	400	600
E	200	650
F	0	675

8. Atlantis can produce which of the following combinations of output?

   Pounds of potatoes   *Pounds of fish*

   a. 1,000   675

   b. 600   600

   c. 400   600

   d. 300   800

   e. 200   675

9. If Atlantis is efficient in production, what is the opportunity cost of increasing the annual output of potatoes from 600 to 800 pounds?

   a. 200 pounds of fish

   b. 300 pounds of fish

   c. 500 pounds of fish

   d. 675 pounds of fish

   e. 800 pounds of fish

10. As Atlantis produces more potatoes, what is true about the opportunity cost of producing potatoes?

    a. It stays the same.

    b. It continually increases.

    c. It continually decreases.

    d. It increases and then decreases.

    e. It decreases and then increases.

11. Which of the following combinations of output is efficient?

    Pounds of potatoes   *Pounds of fish*

    a. 1,000   0

    b. 600   600

    c. 400   500

    d. 300   400

    e. 0   0

Refer to the following information for Questions 12–13.

In the ancient country of Roma, only two goods—spaghetti and meatballs—are produced. There are two tribes in Roma, the Tivoli and the Frivoli. By themselves, in a given month, the Tivoli can produce 30 pounds of spaghetti and no meatballs, 50 pounds of meatballs and no spaghetti, or any combination in between. In the same month, the Frivoli can produce 40 pounds of spaghetti and no meatballs, 30 pounds of meatballs and no spaghetti, or any combination in between.

12. Which tribe has a comparative advantage in meatball and spaghetti production?

    Meatballs   *Spaghetti*

    a. Tivoli   Tivoli

    b. Frivoli   Frivoli

    c. Tivoli   Frivoli

    d. Frivoli   Tivoli

    e. Neither   both

13. In AD 100, the Frivoli discovered a new technique for making meatballs and doubled the quantity of meatballs they could produce each month. After the discovery of this new technique in Frivoli only, which tribe had an absolute advantage in meatball production, and which had a comparative advantage in meatball production?

    Absolute advantage   *Comparative advantage*

    a. Tivoli   Tivoli

    b. Frivoli   Frivoli

    c. Tivoli   Frivoli

    d. Frivoli   Tivoli

    e. Frivoli   both

14. Which of the following is a basic source of economic growth in the production possibilities model?

    a. specialization

    b. efficiency

    c. opportunity cost

    d. trade-offs

    e. improved technology

15. Comparative advantage explains which of the following?

    a. a country's ability to produce more of a particular good or service

    b. when production is considered efficient

    c. why the production possibilities curve is bowed outward

    d. the source of gains from trade

    e. why the production possibilities curve shifts outward

16. If there is no specialization of resources in the production of milk and cream, the production possibilities curve for an economy that produces these two goods is
 a. bowed out and downward-sloping.
 b. straight and downward-sloping.
 c. bowed in and downward-sloping.
 d. horizontal.
 e. vertical.

17. Suppose that in a day Nigel can make three placemats or one gallon of maple syrup, and Pauline can make two placemats or two gallons of maple syrup. Which of the following terms of trade would be mutually beneficial for Nigel and Pauline?
 a. Nigel trades one placemat for ½ gallon of maple syrup from Pauline.
 b. Pauline trades one placemat for ½ gallon of maple syrup from Nigel.
 c. Nigel trades one placemat for two gallons of maple syrup from Pauline.
 d. Pauline trades one placemat for two gallons of maple syrup from Nigel.
 e. Nigel trades one placemat for ¼ gallon of maple syrup from Pauline.

18. If Country A has an absolute advantage in making butter and is considering trade with Country B, we know that
 a. Country A also has a comparative advantage in making butter.
 b. Country B has a comparative advantage in making butter.
 c. Country A can make more butter than Country B can with a given amount of input.
 d. if the two countries trade, Country A should specialize in making butter.
 e. if the two countries trade, Country B should specialize in making butter.

19. Economic growth is defined as an increase in
 a. the output of an economy.
 b. the employment level in an economy.
 c. the spending level in an economy.
 d. the quality of life in an economy.
 e. the maximum possible output of an economy.

20. The study of the costs and benefits of doing a little bit more of an activity instead of a little bit less is called
 a. economics.　　　　**d.** marginal analysis.
 b. microeconomics.　　**e.** market analysis.
 c. macroeconomics.

21. The fundamental problem with command economies is a lack of
 a. central authority.　　**d.** land.
 b. workers.　　　　　　**e.** opportunity cost.
 c. incentives.

22. The labor force is made up entirely by
 a. employed workers.
 b. unemployed workers.
 c. employed workers and retired workers.
 d. employed workers and unemployed workers.
 e. college students and employed workers.

23. Consumers in the country of Isolandia prefer to eat a balanced mix of cereal and fruit, and the country does not engage in international trade. If Isolandia produces at a point on its production possibilities curve at which only cereal is made, then the country achieves
 a. productive efficiency but not allocative efficiency.
 b. allocative efficiency but not productive efficiency.
 c. neither productive efficiency nor allocative efficiency.
 d. economic growth and allocative efficiency.
 e. economic growth and productive efficiency.

24. The country of Sneedleham makes needles and ham at a constant opportunity cost. If Sneedleham acquires more resources but the opportunity cost of producing each good remains the same, how will the country's production possibilities curve change?
 a. It will shift inward and become steeper.
 b. It will shift outward and become steeper.
 c. It will change from being linear to being bowed outward.
 d. It will shift inward with no change in slope.
 e. It will shift outward with no change in slope.

25. Which of the following is true about the *ceteris paribus* assumption?
 a. It makes the use of more complicated but more rewarding models.
 b. It means "maximize profit at all costs."
 c. It simplifies the study of how a single change affects an economy.
 d. It means "the customer is always right."
 e. It means "people behave rationally."

Free-Response Questions

1. The Hatfield family lives on the east side of the Hatatoochie River, and the McCoy family lives on the west side. Each family's diet consists of fried chicken and corn-on-the-cob, and each is self-sufficient, raising its own chickens and growing its own corn.

 Assume the Hatfield family has a comparative advantage in the production of corn.
 a. Draw a correctly labeled graph showing a hypothetical production possibilities curve for the McCoy family.
 b. Which family has the comparative advantage in the production of chickens? Explain.
 c. Assuming that each family is producing efficiently, how can the two families increase their consumption of both chicken and corn? **(5 points)**

2. Suppose the country of Lunchland produces only peanut butter and jelly using resources that are not equally useful for producing both goods.
   a. Draw a correctly labeled production possibilities curve graph for Lunchland and label the following:
      i. point *A*, indicating an inefficient use of resources.
      ii. point *B*, indicating quantities of peanut butter and jelly that are currently not possible.
   b. Identify two things that could happen to enable Lunchland to produce or consume the quantities identified in part a (ii). **(5 points)**

3. Fields Farm and Romano Farm have identical resources and produce oranges and/or peaches at a constant opportunity cost. The table below shows the maximum quantity of oranges and peaches each farm could produce if it devoted all of its resources to that fruit.

   a. On a correctly labeled graph and using the numbers in the table, draw the production possibilities curve for Romano Farm.
   b. What is Fields Farm's opportunity cost of producing one bushel of peaches?
   c. Suppose each farm agrees to specialize in one good and trade for the other good.
      i. Which farm should specialize in peaches? Explain.
      ii. If the farms specialize as indicated in part c (i), would the terms of trade of four oranges in exchange for one peach be acceptable to both farms? Explain.
   d. Now suppose Romano Farm obtains new technology used only for the production of peaches. Show the effect of this change on the graph drawn for part a. **(5 points)**

| | Output (bushels per day) | |
	Oranges	Peaches
Fields Farm	80	40
Romano Farm	60	20

SECTION 1 APPENDIX

Graphs in Economics

In this Appendix, you will learn to:
- Recognize the importance of graphs in studying economics
- Describe the basic components of a graph
- Explain how graphs illustrate the relationship between variables
- Explain how to calculate the slope of a curve and discuss what the slope value means
- Describe how to calculate areas represented on graphs
- Explain how to interpret numerical graphs

Getting the Picture

Whether you're reading about economics in the *Wall Street Journal* or in your economics textbook, you will see many graphs. Visual presentations can make it much easier to understand verbal descriptions, numerical information, or ideas. In economics, graphs are the type of visual presentation used to facilitate understanding. To fully understand the ideas and information being discussed, you need to know how to interpret these visual aids. This Module explains how graphs are constructed and interpreted and how they are used in economics.

Graphs, Variables, and Economic Models

One reason to attend college is that a bachelor's degree provides access to higher-paying jobs. Additional degrees, such as MBAs or law degrees, increase earnings even more. If you were to read an article about the relationship between educational attainment and income, you would probably see a graph showing the income levels for workers with different levels of education. This graph would depict the idea that, in general, having more education increases a person's income. This graph, like most graphs in economics, would depict the relationship between two economic variables. A **variable** is a measure that can take on more than one value, such as the number of years of education a person has, the price of a can of soda, or a household's income.

*A **variable** is a measure that can take on more than one value.*

As you learned in this Section, economic analysis relies heavily on *models*, simplified representations of real situations. Most economic models describe the relationship between two variables, simplified by holding constant other variables that may affect the relationship. For example, an economic model might describe the relationship between the price of a can of soda and the number of cans of soda that consumers will buy, assuming that everything else that affects consumers' purchases of soda stays constant. This type of model can be depicted mathematically, but illustrating the relationship in a graph makes it easier to understand. Next, we show how graphs that depict economic models are constructed and interpreted.

How Graphs Work

Most graphs in economics are built in a two-dimensional space defined by two perpendicular lines that show the values of two or more variables. These graphs help people visualize the relationship between the variables. A first step in understanding the use of such graphs is to see how the values of variables are indicated by the points on the graphs.

Two-Variable Graphs

Figure A.1 shows a typical two-variable graph. It illustrates the data in the accompanying table on outside temperature and the number of sodas a typical vendor can expect to sell at a baseball stadium during one game. The first column shows the values of outside temperature (the first variable) and the second column shows the values of

---

Figure A.1   Plotting Points on a Two-Variable Graph

x-variable: Outside temperature	y-variable: Number of sodas sold	Point
0°F	10	A
10	0	B
40	30	C
60	50	D
80	70	E

The data from the table are plotted where outside temperature (the independent variable) is measured along the horizontal axis and number of sodas sold (the dependent variable) is measured along the vertical axis. Each of the five combinations of temperature and sodas sold is represented by a point: *A, B, C,* *D,* or *E.* Each point in the graph is identified by a pair of values. For example, point *C* corresponds to the pair (40, 30)—an outside temperature of 40°F (the value of the *x*-variable) and 30 sodas sold (the value of the *y*-variable).

---

the number of sodas sold (the second variable). Five combinations or pairs of the two variables are shown, denoted by points A through E in the third column.

Now let's turn to graphing the data in this table. In any two-variable graph, one variable is called the x-variable and the other is called the y-variable. Here we have made outside temperature the x-variable and number of sodas sold the y-variable. The solid horizontal line in the graph is called the **horizontal axis** or **x-axis**, and values of the x-variable—outside temperature—are measured along it. Similarly, the solid vertical line in the graph is called the **vertical axis** or **y-axis**, and values of the y-variable—number of sodas sold—are measured along it. At the **origin**, the point where the two axes meet, each variable is equal to zero. As you move rightward from the origin along the x-axis, values of the x-variable are positive and increasing. As you move up from the origin along the y-axis, values of the y-variable are positive and increasing.

> The solid horizontal line that goes through the origin on a graph is called the **horizontal axis** or **x-axis**.
>
> The solid vertical line that goes through the origin on a graph is called the **vertical axis** or **y-axis**.
>
> The two axes meet at the **origin**.

You can plot each of the five points A through E on this graph by using a pair of numbers—the values that the x-variable and the y-variable take on for a given point. In Figure A.1, at point C, the x-variable takes on the value 40 and the y-variable takes on the value 30. You plot point C by drawing a line straight up from 40 on the x-axis and a horizontal line across from 30 on the y-axis. We write point C as (40, 30). We write the origin as (0, 0).

Looking at point A and point B in Figure A.1, you can see that when one of the variables for a point has a value of zero, it will lie on one of the axes. If the value of the x-variable is zero, the point will lie on the vertical axis, like point A. If the value of the y-variable is zero, the point will lie on the horizontal axis, like point B. (The location of point B was chosen to illustrate this fact and not because soda sales will really decrease when the temperature rises.)

Most graphs that depict relationships between two economic variables represent a **causal relationship**, a relationship in which the value of one variable directly influences or determines the value of the other variable. In a causal relationship, the determining variable is called the **independent variable**; the variable it determines is called the **dependent variable**. In our example of soda sales, the outside temperature is the independent variable. It directly influences the number of sodas that are sold, which is the dependent variable in this case.

> A **causal relationship** is one in which the value of one variable directly influences or determines the value of the other variable.
>
> In a causal relationship, the determining variable is called the **independent variable** and the determined variable is called the **dependent variable**.

By convention, we put the independent variable on the horizontal axis and the dependent variable on the vertical axis. Figure A.1 is constructed consistent with this convention: the independent variable (outside temperature) is on the horizontal axis and the dependent variable (number of sodas sold) is on the vertical axis. An important exception to this convention is in graphs showing the economic relationship between the price and quantity of a product: although price is generally the independent variable that determines quantity, price is always measured on the vertical axis.

Curves on a Graph

Panel (a) of **Figure A.2** contains some of the same information as Figure A.1, with a line drawn through the points B, C, D, and E. Such a line on a graph is called a **curve**, regardless of whether it is a straight line or a curved line. If the curve that shows the relationship between two variables is a straight line, or linear, the variables have a **linear relationship**. When the curve is not a straight line, it is nonlinear, and the variables have a **nonlinear relationship**.

A point on a curve indicates the value of the y-variable for a specific value of the x-variable. For example, point D indicates that at a temperature of 60°F, a vendor can expect to sell 50 sodas. The shape and orientation of a curve reveal the general nature of the relationship between the two variables. The upward tilt of the curve in panel (a) of Figure A.2 suggests that vendors can expect to sell more sodas at higher outside temperatures.

When variables are related in this way—that is, when an increase in one variable is associated with an increase in the other variable—the variables are said to have a **positive relationship**. This relationship is illustrated by a curve that slopes upward from left to right. Because the relationship between outside temperature and number of sodas sold is also linear, as illustrated by the curve in panel (a) of Figure A.2, it is a positive linear relationship.

> A line on a graph is called a **curve**, regardless of whether it is a straight line or a curved line.
>
> If a curve that shows the relationship between two variables is a straight line, or linear, the variables have a **linear relationship**.
>
> When a curve is not a straight line, it is nonlinear, and the variables have a **nonlinear relationship**.
>
> When an increase in one variable is associated with an increase in the other variable, the variables are said to have a **positive relationship**.

Figure A.2 Drawing Curves

(a) Positive Linear Relationship

(b) Negative Linear Relationship

The curve in panel (a) illustrates the relationship between the two variables, outside temperature and number of sodas sold. The two variables have a positive linear relationship: positive because the curve has an upward tilt, and linear because it is a straight line. The curve implies that an increase in the *independent* variable (outside temperature) leads to an increase in the dependent variable (number of sodas sold). The curve in panel (b) is also a straight line, but it tilts downward. The two variables here,

outside temperature and number of hot drinks sold, have a negative linear relationship: an increase in the *independent* variable (outside temperature) leads to a decrease in the dependent variable (number of hot drinks sold). The curve in panel (a) has a horizontal intercept at point *B*, where it hits the horizontal axis. The curve in panel (b) has a vertical intercept at point *J*, where it hits the vertical axis, and a horizontal intercept at point *M*, where it hits the horizontal axis.

When an increase in one variable is associated with a decrease in the other variable, the two variables are said to have a **negative relationship**.

When an increase in one variable is associated with a decrease in the other variable, the two variables are said to have a **negative relationship**. Two variables that have such a relationship are the outside temperature and the number of hot drinks a vendor can expect to sell at a baseball stadium. This relationship is illustrated by a curve that slopes downward from left to right, like the curve in panel (b) of Figure A.2. Because this curve is also linear, the relationship it depicts is a negative linear relationship.

We've been looking at positive and negative relationships between variables that also have causal relationships. In some other cases the relationships shown on graphs can be misleading in terms of causality. For example, a graph displaying the size of a city's police force on the horizontal axis and the city's crime rate on the vertical axis might show a positive relationship, but this does not indicate that having more police causes the crime rate to rise. Instead, it may be that cities with higher crime rates employ more police, meaning that a higher crime rate is the cause for a larger police force. Another explanation could be that having more police leads to an increase in the number of existing crimes that are detected. Or perhaps big cities with large police forces have higher crime rates for reasons quite unrelated to policing. The important point is that a positive or negative relationship between two variables does not provide sufficient information to conclude that one variable causes the other to change.

The **horizontal intercept** indicates the value of the *x*-variable when the value of the *y*-variable is zero.

The **vertical intercept** indicates the value of the *y*-variable when the value of the *x*-variable is zero.

Return for a moment to the curve in panel (a) of Figure A.2, and you can see that it hits the horizontal axis at point *B*. This point, known as the **horizontal intercept**, shows the value of the *x*-variable when the value of the *y*-variable is zero: for example, when it is 10°F, no sodas are sold. In panel (b) of Figure A.2, the curve hits the vertical axis at point *J*. This point, called the **vertical intercept**, indicates the value of the *y*-variable when the value of the *x*-variable is zero: 70 hot drinks are sold when the temperature is 0°F.

A Key Concept: The Slope of a Curve

The **slope** of a curve is a measure of how steep it is; the slope indicates how sensitive the y-variable is to a change in the x-variable. In our example of outside temperature and the number of cans of soda a vendor can expect to sell, the slope of the curve would indicate how many more cans of soda the vendor could expect to sell with each 1° increase in temperature. Interpreted this way, the slope gives meaningful information. Even without numbers for x and y, it is possible to arrive at important conclusions about the relationship between the two variables by examining the slope of a curve at various points.

> The **slope** of a curve is a measure of how steep it is; the slope indicates how sensitive the y-variable is to a change in the x-variable.

The Slope of a Linear Curve

The slope, or steepness, of a linear curve is measured by dividing the "rise" between two points on the curve by the "run" between those same two points. The rise is the change in the value of the y-variable, and the run is the change in the value of the x-variable. Here is the formula:

$$\frac{\text{Change in } y}{\text{Change in } x} = \frac{\Delta y}{\Delta x} = \text{slope}$$

In the formula, the symbol Δ (the Greek uppercase delta) stands for "change in." When a variable increases, the change in that variable is positive; when a variable decreases, the change in that variable is negative.

The slope of a curve is positive when the rise (the change in the y-variable) has the same sign as the run (the change in the x-variable). That's because when two numbers have the same sign, the ratio of those two numbers is positive. The curve in panel (a) of Figure A.2 has a positive slope: along the curve, both the y-variable and the x-variable increase. The slope of a curve is negative when the rise and the run have different signs. That's because when two numbers have different signs, the ratio of those two numbers is negative. The curve in panel (b) of Figure A.2 has a negative slope: along the curve, an increase in the x-variable is associated with a decrease in the y-variable.

Figure A.3 illustrates how to calculate the slope of a linear curve. Let's focus first on panel (a). From point A to point B the value of the y-variable changes from 25 to 20 and the value of the x-variable changes from 10 to 20. So the slope of the line between these two points is

$$\frac{\text{Change in } y}{\text{Change in } x} = \frac{\Delta y}{\Delta x} = \frac{-5}{10} = -\frac{1}{2} = -0.5$$

Because a straight line is equally steep at all points, the slope of a straight line is the same at all points. In other words, a straight line has a constant slope. You can check this by calculating the slope of the linear curve between points A and B and between points C and D in panel (b) of Figure A.3.

$$\frac{\Delta y}{\Delta x} = \frac{10}{2} = 5$$

$$\frac{\Delta y}{\Delta x} = \frac{20}{4} = 5$$

Horizontal and Vertical Curves and Their Slopes

When a curve is horizontal, the value of y along that curve never changes—it is constant. Everywhere along the curve, the change in y is zero. Now, zero divided by any number is zero. So regardless of the value of the change in x, the slope of a horizontal curve is always zero.

Figure A.3 Calculating the Slope

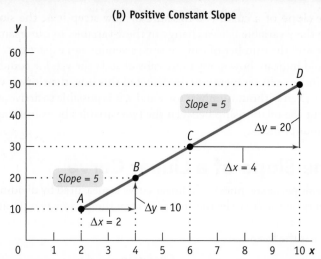

Panels (a) and (b) show two linear curves. Between points A and B on the curve in panel (a), the change in y (the rise) is -5 and the change in x (the run) is 10. So the slope from A to B is $\frac{\Delta y}{\Delta x} = \frac{-5}{10} = -\frac{1}{2} = -0.5$, where the negative sign indicates that the curve is downward-sloping. In panel (b), the curve has a slope from A to B of $\frac{\Delta y}{\Delta x} = \frac{10}{2} = 5$. The slope from C to D is

$\frac{\Delta y}{\Delta x} = \frac{20}{4} = 5$. The slope is positive, indicating that the curve is upward-sloping. Furthermore, the slope between A and B is the same as the slope between C and D, making this a linear curve. The slope of a linear curve is constant: it is the same regardless of where it is calculated along the curve.

If a curve is vertical, the value of x along the curve never changes—it is constant. Everywhere along the curve, the change in x is zero. This means that the slope of a vertical line is a ratio with zero in the denominator. A ratio with zero in the denominator is an infinitely large number that is considered "undefined." So the slope of a vertical line is typically described as infinite or undefined.

A vertical or a horizontal curve has a special implication: it means that the x-variable and the y-variable are unrelated. Two variables are unrelated when a change in one variable (the independent variable) has no effect on the other variable (the dependent variable). If, as is usual, the y-variable is the dependent variable, the curve showing the relationship between the dependent variable and the unrelated independent variable is horizontal. For instance, suppose you eat lasagna once a week regardless of the number of hours you spend studying that week. Then the curve on a graph that shows lasagna meals per week on the vertical axis and study hours per week on the horizontal axis would be horizontal at the height of one. If the x-variable is the dependent variable and the independent variable is unrelated to the dependent variable, the curve is vertical.

The Slope of a Nonlinear Curve

A **nonlinear curve** is one along which the slope changes.

A **nonlinear curve** is one along which the slope changes. Panels (a), (b), (c), and (d) of **Figure A.4** show various nonlinear curves. Panels (a) and (b) show nonlinear curves whose slopes change as you follow the line's progression, but the slopes always remain positive. Although both curves tilt upward, the curve in panel (a) gets steeper as the line moves from left to right in contrast to the curve in panel (b), which gets flatter. A curve that is upward-sloping and gets steeper, as in panel (a), is said to have a *positive and increasing* slope. A curve that is upward-sloping but gets flatter, as in panel (b), is said to have a *positive and decreasing* slope.

When we calculate the slope along these nonlinear curves, we obtain different values for the slope at different points. How the slope changes along the curve determines the curve's shape. For example, in panel (a) of Figure A.4, the slope of the curve is a

Figure A.4 Nonlinear Curves

(a) Positive and Increasing Slope

(b) Positive and Decreasing Slope

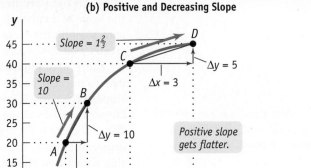

(c) Negative and Increasing Slope

(d) Negative and Decreasing Slope

In panel (a) the slope of the curve from A to B is $\frac{\Delta y}{\Delta x} = \frac{10}{4} = 2.5$, and from C to D it is $\frac{\Delta y}{\Delta x} = \frac{15}{1} = 15$. The slope is positive and increasing; it gets steeper as it moves to the right. In panel (b) the slope of the curve from A to B is $\frac{\Delta y}{\Delta x} = \frac{10}{1} = 10$, and from C to D, it is $\frac{\Delta y}{\Delta x} = \frac{5}{3} = 1\frac{2}{3}$. The slope is positive and decreasing; it gets flatter as it moves to the right. In panel (c) the slope from A to B

is $\frac{\Delta y}{\Delta x} = \frac{-10}{3} = -3\frac{1}{3}$, and from C to D it is $\frac{\Delta y}{\Delta x} = \frac{-15}{1} = -15$.
The slope is negative and increasing; it gets steeper as it moves to the right. And in panel (d) the slope from A to B is $\frac{\Delta y}{\Delta x} = \frac{-20}{1} = -20$, and from C to D it is $\frac{\Delta y}{\Delta x} = \frac{-5}{3} = -1\frac{2}{3}$. The slope is negative and decreasing; it gets flatter as it moves to the right. The slope in each case has been calculated by using the *arc method*—that is, by drawing a straight line connecting two points along a curve. The average slope between those two points is equal to the slope of the straight line between those two points.

positive number that steadily increases as the line moves from left to right, whereas in panel (b), the slope is a positive number that steadily decreases.

The slopes of the curves in panels (c) and (d) are negative numbers. For simplicity, economists often prefer to express a negative number as its **absolute value**, which is the value of the negative number without the minus sign. In general, we denote the absolute value of a number by two parallel bars around the number; for example, the absolute value of -4 is written as $|-4| = 4$. In panel (c), the absolute value of the slope steadily increases as the line moves from left to right. The curve therefore has a *negative and increasing* slope. And in panel (d), the absolute value of the slope of the curve steadily decreases along the curve. This curve therefore has a *negative and decreasing* slope.

The **absolute value** of a number is the value of that number without a minus sign, whether or not the number was negative to begin with.

Maximum and Minimum Points

The slope of a nonlinear curve can change from positive to negative or vice versa. When the slope of a curve changes from positive to negative, it creates what is called a *maximum point* on the curve. When the slope of a curve changes from negative to positive, it creates a *minimum point*.

Panel (a) of **Figure A.5** illustrates a curve along which the slope changes from positive to negative as the line moves from left to right. When x is between 0 and 50, the slope of the curve is positive. When x equals 50, the curve attains its highest point—the largest value of y along the curve. This point is called the **maximum point** of the curve. When x exceeds 50, the slope becomes negative as the curve turns downward. Many important curves in economics are hill-shaped like this one. An example is the curve that shows how the profit of a firm changes as it produces more output—firms maximize profit by reaching the top of the hill.

In contrast, the curve shown in panel (b) of Figure A.5 is U-shaped: it has a slope that changes from negative to positive. When x equals 50, the curve reaches its lowest point—the smallest value of y along the curve. This point is called the **minimum point** of the curve. Various important curves in economics, such as the curve that represents how a firm's cost per unit changes as output increases, are U-shaped like this one.

> The point along a curve with the largest value of y is called the **maximum point** of the curve.

> The point along a curve with the smallest value of y is called the **minimum point** of the curve.

Figure A.5 Maximum and Minimum Points

Panel (a) shows a curve with a maximum point, the point at which the slope changes from positive to negative. Panel (b) shows a curve with a minimum point, the point at which the slope changes from negative to positive.

Calculating the Area Below or Above a Curve

Sometimes it is useful to be able to measure the size of the area below or above a curve. To keep things simple, we'll only calculate the area below or above a linear curve.

How large is the shaded area below the linear curve in panel (a) of **Figure A.6**? First, note that this area has the shape of a right triangle. A right triangle is a triangle in which two adjacent sides form a 90° angle. We will refer to one of these sides as the *height* of the triangle and the other side as the *base* of the triangle. For our purposes, it doesn't matter which of these two sides we refer to as the base and which as the height. Calculating the area of a right triangle is straightforward: *multiply the height of the triangle by the base of*

Figure A.6 Calculating the Area Below and Above a Linear Curve

(a) Area Below a Linear Curve

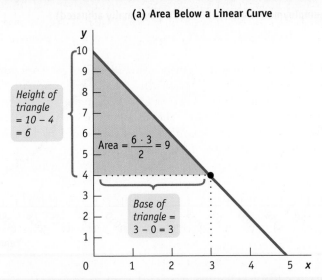

Height of triangle = 10 − 4 = 6

Area = $\frac{6 \cdot 3}{2}$ = 9

Base of triangle = 3 − 0 = 3

(b) Area Above a Linear Curve

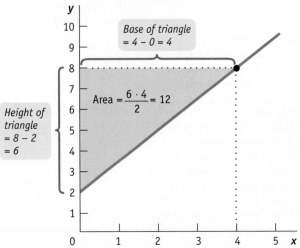

Base of triangle = 4 − 0 = 4

Area = $\frac{6 \cdot 4}{2}$ = 12

Height of triangle = 8 − 2 = 6

The area below or above a linear curve forms a right triangle. The area of a right triangle is calculated by multiplying the height of the triangle by the base of the triangle and dividing the result by 2. In panel (a) the area of the shaded triangle is 9. In panel (b) the area of the shaded triangle is 12.

the triangle and divide the result by 2. The height of the triangle in panel (a) of Figure A.6 is 10 − 4 = 6 and the base of the triangle is 3 − 0 = 3, so the area of that triangle is

$$\frac{6 \times 3}{2} = 9$$

How about the shaded area above the linear curve in panel (b) of Figure A.6? We can use the same formula to calculate the area of this right triangle. The height of the triangle is 8 − 2 = 6 and the base of the triangle is 4 − 0 = 4, so the area of that triangle is

$$\frac{6 \times 4}{2} = 12$$

Graphs That Depict Numerical Information

Graphs can also be used as a convenient way to summarize and display data without assuming some underlying causal relationship. Graphs that simply display numerical information are called *numerical graphs*. Here we will consider four types of numerical graphs: *time-series graphs, scatter diagrams, pie charts,* and *bar graphs*. These are widely used to display real empirical data about different economic variables, because they often help economists and policy makers identify patterns or trends in the economy.

Types of Numerical Graphs

You have probably seen graphs in newspapers that show what has happened over time to economic variables such as the unemployment rate or stock prices. A **time-series graph** has successive dates on the horizontal axis and the values of a variable that occurred on those dates on the vertical axis. For example, **Figure A.7** shows the unemployment rate in the United States from 1989 to 2018. A line connecting the points that correspond to the unemployment rate for each month during those years gives a clear idea of the overall trend in unemployment during that period.

A **time-series graph** has successive dates on the horizontal axis and the values of a variable that occurred on those dates on the vertical axis.

Figure A.7   Time-Series Graph

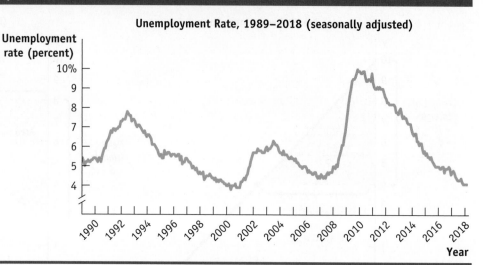

Unemployment Rate, 1989–2018 (seasonally adjusted)

Time-series graphs show successive dates on the *x*-axis and values for a variable on the *y*-axis. This time-series graph shows the seasonally adjusted unemployment rate in the United States from 1989 to 2018. The two short diagonal lines toward the bottom of the *y*-axis are a *truncation sign* indicating that a piece of the axis was cut out to save space.
Data Source: Bureau of Labor Statistics.

Figure A.8 is an example of a different kind of numerical graph. It represents information from a sample of 184 countries on average life expectancy and gross domestic product (GDP) per capita—a rough measure of a country's standard of living. Each point in the graph indicates an average resident's life expectancy and the log of GDP per capita for a given country. (Economists have found that the log of GDP rather than the simple level of GDP is more closely tied to average life expectancy.) The points lying in the upper right of the graph, which show combinations of high life expectancy and high log of GDP per capita, represent economically advanced countries such as the United States. Points lying in the bottom left of the graph, which show combinations of low life expectancy and low log of GDP per capita, represent economically less advanced countries such as Afghanistan and Sierra Leone. The pattern of points indicates that there is a positive relationship between life expectancy and log of GDP per capita: on the whole, people live longer in countries with a higher standard of living. This type of graph is called a **scatter diagram**, a diagram in which each point corresponds to an actual observation of the *x*-variable and the *y*-variable. In scatter diagrams, a curve is typically fitted to the scatter of points; that is, a curve is drawn that approximates as closely as possible the general relationship between the variables. As you can see, the

Each point on a **scatter diagram** corresponds to an actual observation of the *x*-variable and the *y*-variable.

Figure A.8   Scatter Diagram

In a scatter diagram, each point represents the corresponding values of the *x*- and *y*-variables for a given observation. Here, each point indicates the observed average life expectancy and the log of GDP per capita of a given country for a sample of 184 countries. The upward-sloping fitted line here is the best approximation of the general relationship between the two variables.
Data Source: World Bank (2015).

Standard of Living and Average Life Expectancy

fitted curve in Figure A.8 is upward-sloping, indicating the underlying positive relationship between the two variables. Scatter diagrams are often used to show how a general relationship can be inferred from a set of data.

A **pie chart** shows the share of a total amount that is accounted for by various components, usually expressed in percentages. For example, **Figure A.9** is a pie chart that depicts the various sources of revenue for the U.S. government budget in 2017, expressed in percentages of the total revenue amount, $3,316 billion. As you can see, payroll tax receipts (the revenues collected to fund Social Security, Medicare, and unemployment insurance) accounted for 35% of total government revenue, and individual income tax receipts accounted for 48%.

A **pie chart** shows the share of a total amount that is accounted for by various components, usually expressed in percentages.

Figure A.9   Pie Chart

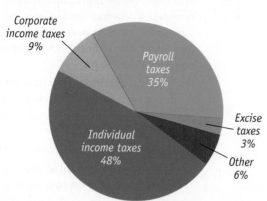

Receipts by Source for U.S. Government Budget 2017 (total: $3,316 billion)

Corporate income taxes 9%
Payroll taxes 35%
Individual income taxes 48%
Excise taxes 3%
Other 6%

A pie chart shows the percentages of a total amount that can be attributed to various components. This pie chart shows the percentages of total federal revenues received from each source.
Data Source: Office of Management and Budget.

A **bar graph** uses bars of various heights or lengths to indicate values of a variable. In the bar graph in **Figure A.10**, the bars show the 2016 unemployment rates for workers with various levels of education. Exact values of the variable that is being measured may be written at the end of the bar, as in this figure. For instance, the unemployment rate for workers with a high school diploma but no college education was 5.2%. Even without the precise values, comparing the heights or lengths of the bars can give useful insight into the relative magnitudes of the different values of the variable.

A **bar graph** uses bars of various heights or lengths to indicate values of a variable.

Figure A.10   Bar Graph

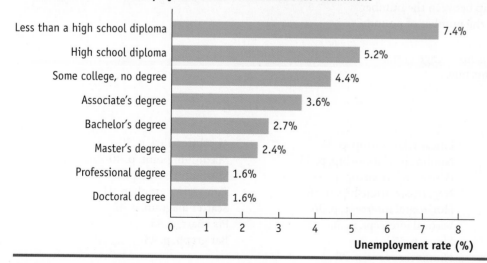

Unemployment Rates and Educational Attainment

Less than a high school diploma	7.4%
High school diploma	5.2%
Some college, no degree	4.4%
Associate's degree	3.6%
Bachelor's degree	2.7%
Master's degree	2.4%
Professional degree	1.6%
Doctoral degree	1.6%

Unemployment rate (%)

A bar graph measures a variable by using bars of various heights or lengths. This bar graph shows the unemployment rate for workers with various education levels.
Data Source: Bureau of Labor Statistics.

SECTION
1
Appendix Review

Adventures in
AP® Economics

Watch the video:
Graphing Tricks & Tips

Check Your Understanding

1. Study the four accompanying diagrams. Consider the following statements and indicate which diagram matches each statement. For each statement, tell which variable would appear on the horizontal axis and which on the vertical. In each of these statements, is the slope positive, negative, zero, or undefined?

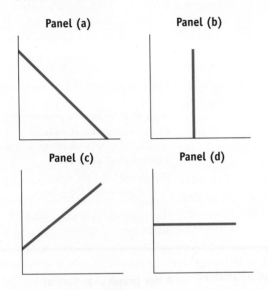

Panel (a)   Panel (b)

Panel (c)   Panel (d)

a. If the price of movies increases, fewer consumers go to see movies.

b. Workers with more experience typically have higher incomes than less experienced workers.

c. Regardless of the temperature outside, Americans consume the same number of hot dogs per day.

d. Consumers buy more frozen yogurt when the price of ice cream goes up.

e. Research finds no relationship between the number of diet books purchased and the number of pounds lost by the average dieter.

f. Regardless of its price, there is no change in the quantity of salt that Americans buy.

2. During the Reagan administration, economist Arthur Laffer argued in favor of lowering income tax rates in order to increase tax revenues. Like most economists, he believed that at tax rates above a certain level, tax revenue would fall (because high taxes would discourage some people from working) and that people would refuse to work at all if they received no income after paying taxes. This relationship between tax rates and tax revenue is graphically summarized in what is widely known as the Laffer curve. Plot the Laffer curve relationship, assuming that it has the shape of a nonlinear curve. The following questions will help you construct the graph.

a. Which is the independent variable? Which is the dependent variable? On which axis do you therefore measure the income tax rate? On which axis do you measure income tax revenue?

b. What would tax revenue be at a 0% income tax rate?

c. The maximum possible income tax rate is 100%. What would tax revenue be at a 100% income tax rate?

d. Estimates now show that the maximum point on the Laffer curve is (approximately) at a tax rate of 80%. For tax rates less than 80%, how would you describe the relationship between the tax rate and tax revenue, and how is this relationship reflected in the slope? For tax rates higher than 80%, how would you describe the relationship between the tax rate and tax revenue, and how is this relationship reflected in the slope?

Key Terms

Variable, p. 34
Horizontal axis/x-axis, p. 35
Vertical axis/y-axis, p. 35
Origin, p. 35
Causal relationship, p. 35
Independent variable, p. 35
Dependent variable, p. 35
Curve, p. 35

Linear relationship, p. 35
Nonlinear relationship, p. 35
Positive relationship, p. 35
Negative relationship, p. 36
Horizontal intercept, p. 36
Vertical intercept, p. 36
Slope, p. 37
Nonlinear curve, p. 38

Absolute value, p. 39
Maximum point, p. 40
Minimum point, p. 40
Time-series graph, p. 41
Scatter diagram, p. 42
Pie chart, p. 43
Bar graph, p. 43

What's to Love About Economics?
Virtues of the Economic Way of Thinking

Economics is the most popular major at many of America's best colleges. People with training in economics are recruited not only by financial institutions, but also by governments, corporations, international organizations, consulting firms, public utilities, research institutes, and intelligence agencies. What makes economics so interesting and relevant that great students want to dive into it and myriad employers angle for workers with economic wisdom? Get ready to wade into some of the many reasons.

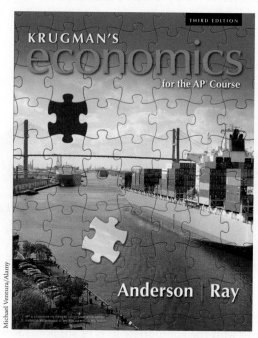

Michael Ventura/Alamy

Economics is Everywhere

Economics doesn't simply appear in books or lurk in bank vaults. Economics is above you in airplanes, below you in coal mines, behind the fabric content of your clothing, and underpinning the politics of your nation. Economics is the study of limited resources and unlimited wants. The broad scope of this discipline results from the limits on virtually every human want. Beyond money, there are limited supplies of time, information, clean water and air, potential spouses, employers, employees, NCAA Final

Four basketball tickets, and everything you would buy if you won the lottery. Economics is behind your choice to go to school, the cinnamon in your latte, your adherence to laws (or lack thereof), and the public policies of your government. Economics is also the lens through which people who seek happiness should look before making decisions.

Suppose you love hot dogs. You know that eating hot dogs causes weight gain, but the first few bites create a lot of pleasure and not a lot of weight. As your hunger is satisfied, the benefit of each additional bite decreases and its cost (in terms of indigestion and excessive caloric intake) increases. You should eat more *until the additional benefit of another bite equals the additional cost*. With the additional benefit falling and the additional cost rising, the next bite, and every subsequent bite, would do more harm than good.

Economists call the additional benefit from 1 more of something the *marginal benefit* and the additional cost of 1 more of something the *marginal cost*. Thus, you should eat until the marginal cost equals the marginal benefit. If it's the best hot dog you've ever tasted, the marginal benefit is higher, and you'll take more bites. Sometimes even indigestion is well justified. In 2017, high marginal benefits led Joey Chestnut to eat 72 hot dogs in 10 minutes—he won $10,000 and fame at the Nathan's Hot Dog Eating Contest.

The study of where marginal benefit meets marginal cost leads to the efficient outcomes that economists cherish. How many hours should you spend in the library? How many laps should you swim in the pool? How much time should you spend in the shower? The answer is always the same: Just do it until the marginal benefit equals the marginal cost and you couldn't do any better.

Dennis Van Tine/Photoshot/AGE Fotostock

Economic Tools Can Address Weighty Issues

It's no secret that economic theory helps business people make decisions about prices, production levels, and manufacturing methods that maximize profits. The economic way of thinking also applies to the most difficult dilemmas facing society. Economic theory can address troubling problems with poverty, crime, pollution, education, health care, the legal system, child care, transportation systems, water shortages, population growth, biodiversity loss, sustainable development, and energy, to name a few.

Consider the issue of how to punish people who break the law. Suppose that each song illegally downloaded from the internet costs society $1 in lost wages for sound studio employees, advertisers, musicians, music retailers, and others in the music industry. Again, efficiency dictates that each activity should continue until the additional (or marginal) benefit equals the additional (or marginal) cost. For simplicity, assume that the marginal cost to society of illegally downloading a song remains constant at $1 and that the value of the time spent downloading is negligible. If the benefit to the recipient from illegally downloading another song exceeds the cost to society, the download creates a net gain for society and it is efficient (although still illegal) to carry it out.

How can we bring about the efficient level of illegal downloading? One way would be to successfully enforce a penalty of $1 for each illegal download. If music lovers had to pay a $1 fine per download, they would only download songs that were worth at least $1 to them. Inefficient downloads—those worth less than the $1 cost to society—would not occur. The trouble is that it would be very expensive to detect and take legal action against every illegal download.

Economic theory can help with that problem, too. Suppose the levels of policing were such that only half of all illegal downloads resulted in a fine. With a 50% chance of having to pay $2, the expected fine per song illegally downloaded would be ½ × $2, or $1. Music lovers who made decisions on the basis of the expected fine would still download only when their benefit from a song exceeded the cost to society.

The expected fine would also be $1 if there were a 1-in-10 chance of paying $10, a 1-in-100 chance of paying $100, or a 1-in-1,000 chance of paying $1,000. For music lovers who don't have a particular preference for, or aversion to, risk taking, any of these combinations would provide the proper incentive to limit illegal downloads to the efficient number. With this in mind, law enforcement costs can be reduced without altering the incentives to obey the law by raising fines and lowering enforcement levels.

Economic Findings Can Be Specific and Compelling

What special powers do people trained in economics have that allow them to make strong arguments and precise recommendations? They may not be superheroes, but they brandish quantitative tools, detailed methods of reasoning, the high-road goal of maximizing social welfare, and the use of assumptions to leap tall complexities in a single bound. Let's look at each of these powers in turn.

Quantitative Tools

Economists delve deeply into quantitative methods that yield precise answers to important questions. Because economics is about the realities facing each of us on a daily basis, the meatiest topics within economics are concrete and visible and can be discussed without advanced math, as is the case in this book. If this exposition whets your appetite for the rigorous side of economics, you will encounter more mathematical models in advanced textbooks. As you read on about economic findings, you may well become persuaded that the evidence gained by applying quantitative tools provides benefits that far exceed any associated costs.

For example, citizens and legislators in many states are grappling with the appropriate level of support for rooftop solar-power systems. One question is whether households that create more electricity than they need should receive credit for energy they feed into the electrical grid for other households to use. There is concern that, because they pay lower utility bills, households with solar panels might not pay their fair share of the costs of operating the local power utility. On the other hand, by contributing to the local energy supply, those households may help their communities avoid costly upgrades to their power plants. Thanks to quantitative tools, economists can advance this debate from "Gee, we like clean energy, but we want everyone to pay their fair share for the power grid, so we're confused" to "The rooftop solar-power systems in this area will provide an estimated net benefit of $36 million to households with no solar power over the systems' lifetimes" (paraphrased from a 2014 study by Energy and Environmental Economics, Inc., commissioned by the state of Nevada). Sure, estimates may differ, depending on the research method and the underlying assumptions, but it is useful to obtain objective estimates of the costs and benefits of such decisions as an alternative to acting purely on the basis of gut feelings and stabs in the dark. The quantitative tools of economics make these estimates possible.

Economic Reasoning

The crux of economic reasoning, as you've already read, is that any activity should be continued until the additional benefits from doing so equal the additional costs. Consideration of these costs and benefits can yield estimates of just how loud a sound system should be, how long one should sunbathe on the beach, how low a thermostat should be set, and how far one should go in school. The availability of specific answers to common puzzles is one reason why some people get excited about economics.

For instance, using information on the costs and benefits of going to school for each year, students can pinpoint the best plans for their formal educations. The Bureau of Labor Statistics reports the median earnings of adults working full time in the United States, broken down by levels of educational attainment. In 2017, workers who had finished high school earned $9,516 more than workers with no diploma. Workers with bachelor's degrees earned $23,712 more than high school graduates, and those with advanced degrees earned $16,484 on top of that. The financial benefits of education are augmented by any nonfinancial benefits a particular person would receive from the higher-paying jobs to which education provides access, such as more job security, lighter physical burdens, and cleaner working conditions. For comparison, the direct costs of going to school for another year are readily available—typically about $25,000 for each year of college. These costs can be combined with the cost of forgoing work to attend school and with the nonfinancial burdens of school to determine the appropriate educational goals for a particular student.

Clear and Defensible Objectives

Economic analysis can be applied in myriad contexts to pursue objectives ranging from profit maximization to everlasting bliss. When economists consider public policy, the default goal is the greatest possible net gain to society. This goal is achieved by addressing questions of what, how, and for whom to produce, with an eye on *efficiency*. Think of efficiency as maximizing the size of the "pie" that represents social well-being, profit, personal happiness, or any other particular objective. Efficient outcomes exhaust all opportunities for net gains.

Once the net gains from government policies are maximized, society must grapple with the *equity* consideration of how to divide the pie among potential recipients. For example, public lands could be opened to loggers, sold to developers, maintained as parks for tourists, or donated to the homeless. It would be efficient to use the land for the purpose that provides the greatest overall net benefits, but the most efficient outcome often conflicts with equity considerations. The greatest net benefits might come from a park, but interests in equity point toward helping the homeless. Economists study taxes, subsidies, and entitlement programs that can distribute the gains from efficiency in a more equitable manner. For example, if a particular tract of public land would be more valuable to park visitors than to the homeless, the best solution might be to create a park on the land, impose a tax on visitors, and use the tax revenues to pay for homeless shelters elsewhere.

Simplifying Assumptions

Sometimes less is more. Just as it's easier to follow a map that isn't muddled with markings for every tree, telephone wire, and parking space, researchers find simplifications useful when studying cause and effect. Consider the common assumption of *ceteris paribus*—the Latin phrase meaning that influences other than the one being studied remain unchanged. Suppose Tour de France winner Chris Froome is biking down a mountain at 40 miles per hour and gets a flat tire. How will his speed be affected? Admittedly, many elements might come into play. If the tire blew out as Chris flew over a guardrail and went into a free fall, his speed would increase. Wet roads, a collision, or fatigue would all reduce his speed and reinforce the influence of the flat tire. Some people might throw up their hands and say it's impossible to determine for sure what would happen to Chris's speed when his tire went flat.

An economist is more likely to say, "*Ceteris paribus*, the bike will slow down." The economist is assuming that, except for the blowout, all elements of the situation—the weather, the biker's upright position, and so on—will remain the same. The *ceteris paribus* assumption allows the economist to address the issue in question without being hampered by complexities. Economists use the *ceteris paribus* assumption when studying, for example, the effect of consumer demand on prices or the effect of labor unions on employee benefits. In reality, demand changes often coincide with changes in production costs that also affect prices, and unionization is one of many determinants of employee benefits; however, it is useful to isolate influences and assess them one at a time. In the end, economists can combine their data on individual influences to determine the result of several simultaneous changes, whereas skeptics who don't like to make assumptions are getting nowhere fast.

Another noteworthy and controversial assumption is that individuals behave rationally. Associated with the rationality assumption are expectations that people prefer more of a good thing, have goals, learn, and are consistent enough in their behaviors to exhibit *transitive preferences*. Suppose you prefer jazz to reggae music and you prefer reggae to classical music. Given a choice between jazz and classical, which type of music would you select? If the answer is jazz, you are exhibiting the rationality of transitive preferences because

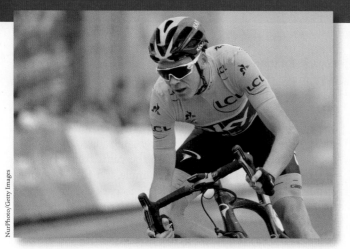
NurPhoto/Getty Images

Conclusion

Thanks for giving economics a try. With these readings and this class under your belt, you will become more adept at making wise decisions, allocating resources, and maximizing the satisfaction of yourself and society. Regardless of whether you choose to devote your professional life to the social science of economics, it's a good bet that the benefits you receive from this class will exceed the costs.

Critical Thinking Questions

your response is consistent with your preference ordering of jazz first, then reggae, and then classical music. An answer of classical music would violate that rationality. More generally, economists assume that individuals will make the appropriate decisions to maximize their happiness and that firms will likewise act to maximize their profits.

Is it rational to assume that people behave rationally? Economists think so for several reasons. Without transitive preferences it would be painfully difficult to make common decisions. If you liked cola better than water, juice better than cola, and (in violation of transitivity) water better than juice, you would cycle through these choices endlessly and spend far too much time in the beverage aisle of the grocery store. Firms with managers who behave irrationally are unlikely to last long, and the same could be said of people. Anyone who eats nails and sleeps in swimming pools is unlikely to survive to pass his or her irrational genes on to the next generation. Do business managers study the graphs and equations that indicate profit-maximizing prices and quantities? Sometimes they do, and other times they may use less formal analyses to derive similar conclusions. Likewise, Nobel laureate Milton Friedman noted that although expert pool players don't really measure all the angles and distances between billiard balls on a pool table or make complex mathematical calculations to find the speed and trajectory with which to strike the balls, they often take their shots as if they did.

Of course, all of us have those mornings when we start to brush our hair with a toothbrush and pour orange juice into our cereal. Economic theory can endure a few missteps by individuals or even a few people who never get things right. Economic theory yields useful conclusions as long as, on average, people's decisions are more rational than random, and that's true for most of us even on a bad day.

1. Do law enforcement agencies really seek an efficient amount of lawbreaking rather than no lawbreaking? Consider some illegal activities that might sometimes create more good than harm. How do the penalties for these crimes compare with the penalties for more serious crimes that are less likely ever to be efficient? How much should people be fined for doing something that society really wants to prohibit from ever happening?

2. Is it common for marginal costs to increase and marginal benefits to decrease? What is the marginal benefit from the first, second, and third practices for the swim team in a day? What is the marginal cost of the first, second, and third swim practices? (It is important to remember that costs and benefits are not strictly financial.) How successful are you at carrying out activities until the marginal cost equals the marginal benefit?

3. How would economists go about analyzing the likely influence of a forecast of heavy snow on the quantity of tickets sold for the *Nutcracker* ballet? What other changes could influence ticket sales? What assumptions should be made? Why?

4. Is it rational for some people to end their formal education with high school degrees, some to finish with college degrees, and some to obtain graduate degrees? Beyond the ability to pay tuition, what are some other reasons why different people stay in school for different lengths of time? How might the nonmonetary cost of college differ among individuals? How might the benefits of attending college differ among individuals?

Supply and Demand

> **economics by example** *The Coffee Market's Hot; Why Are Bean Prices Not?*

Blue Jean Blues

These days you may be used to paying $50, $100, or more for a pair of blue jeans, but consumers in 2012 may have been shocked by a dramatic increase in the price of jeans compared to the previous year. Or maybe not: fashions change, and maybe they thought they were paying the price for being fashionable. But consumers in 2012 weren't paying for some new innovation in fashion—they were paying for cotton. Jeans are made of denim, a particular weave of cotton. In 2011, when jeans manufacturers were buying supplies for the coming year, the price of cotton climbed to more than triple its level just two years earlier. In March 2011, the price of a pound of cotton hit an all-time high, the highest cotton price since record keeping began in 1870.

Why were cotton prices so high? On one side, demand for clothing of all

kinds was surging. On the supply side, severe weather events hit world cotton production. Most notably, Pakistan, the world's fourth-largest cotton producer, was hit by devastating floods that put one-fifth of the country underwater and virtually destroyed its cotton crop. But by 2012 the supply of cotton rebounded and the price of cotton fell by 62% (a change that would be reflected in clothing prices in 2013). After some smaller ups and downs in the intervening five years, the price of cotton in 2018 remained at approximately 59% of its 2011 high.

The rise in cotton prices in 2011 was not all bad news for everyone connected with the cotton trade. In the United States, cotton producers had not been hit by bad weather and were benefiting from the higher prices. American farmers responded to high cotton prices by sharply increasing

the acreage they devoted to the crop. None of these measures were enough, however, to produce immediate price relief.

Wait a minute: how, exactly, does flooding in Pakistan translate into higher jeans prices or more polyester instead of cotton, in your T-shirts? It's a matter of supply and demand—but what does that mean? Many people use "supply and demand" as a catchphrase to mean "the laws of the marketplace at work." To economists, however, the concept of supply and demand has a precise meaning: it is a *model* of market behavior that is extremely useful for understanding many—but not all—markets.

In this section, we lay out the pieces that make up the *supply and demand model*, put them together, and show how this model can be used to understand how most markets behave.

Supply and Demand: Introduction and Demand

> **In this Module, you will learn to:**
> - Explain what a competitive market is and how it is described by the supply and demand model
> - Draw a demand curve and interpret its meaning
> - Discuss the difference between movements along the demand curve and changes in demand
> - List and describe the factors that shift the demand curve

Introduction and Demand

Cotton sellers and cotton buyers constitute a *market*—a group of producers and consumers who exchange a good or service for payment. In this section, we'll focus on a particular type of market known as a *competitive market*. Roughly, a **competitive market** is one in which there are many buyers and sellers of the same good or service. More precisely, the key feature of a competitive market is that no individual's actions have a noticeable effect on the price at which the good or service is sold. It's important to understand, however, that this is not an accurate description of every market. For example, it's not an accurate description of the market for cola beverages. That's because in the market for cola beverages, Coca-Cola and Pepsi account for such a large proportion of total sales that they are able to influence the price at which cola beverages are bought and sold. But it *is* an accurate description of the market for cotton. The global marketplace for cotton is so huge that even a jeans retailer as large as Levi Strauss & Co. accounts for only a tiny fraction of transactions, making it unable to influence the price at which cotton is bought and sold.

It's a little hard to explain why competitive markets are different from other markets until we've seen how a competitive market works. For now, let's just say that it's easier to model competitive markets than other markets.

When a market is competitive, its behavior is well described by the **supply and demand model**. Because many markets *are* competitive, the supply and demand model is a very useful one indeed.

There are six key elements in the supply and demand model:

- The *demand curve*
- The set of factors that cause the demand curve to shift
- The *supply curve*
- The set of factors that cause the supply curve to shift
- The *market equilibrium*, which includes the *equilibrium price* and *equilibrium quantity*
- The way the market equilibrium changes when the supply curve or demand curve shifts

To explain the supply and demand model, we will examine each of these elements in turn. In this Module we begin with the demand curve and then discuss the factors that cause the demand curve to shift.

The Demand Curve

How many pounds of cotton, packaged in the form of blue jeans, do consumers around the world want to buy in a given year? You might at first think that we can answer this question by multiplying the number of pairs of blue jeans purchased

A competitive market is a market in which there are many buyers and sellers of the same good or service, none of whom can influence the price at which the good or service is sold.

The **supply and demand model** is a model of how a competitive market works.

Levis may be a popular brand of jeans, but they account for only a tiny fraction of all cotton transactions.

Nor Gal/Shutterstock.com

AP® EXAM TIP

For success on the AP® exam you must be able to draw, label, and interpret supply and demand graphs. These graphs are also the foundation of other graphs you will learn in the course.

around the world each day by the amount of cotton it takes to make a pair of jeans, and then multiplying by 365. But that's not enough to answer the question because how many pairs of jeans—in other words, how many pounds of cotton—consumers want to buy depends on the price of cotton. When the price of cotton rises, as it did in 2011, some people will respond to the higher price of cotton clothing by buying fewer cotton garments or, perhaps, by switching completely to garments made from other materials, such as synthetics or linen. In general, the quantity of cotton clothing, or of any good or service that people want to buy (taking "want" to mean they are willing and able to buy it), depends on the price. The higher the price, the less of the good or service people want to purchase; alternatively, the lower the price, the more they want to purchase.

So the answer to the question "How many pounds of cotton do consumers want to buy?" depends on the price of a pound of cotton. If you don't yet know what the price will be, you can start by making a table of how many pounds of cotton people would want to buy at a number of different prices. Such a table is known as a *demand schedule*. This, in turn, can be used to draw a *demand curve*, which is one of the key elements of the supply and demand model.

The Demand Schedule and the Demand Curve

A **demand schedule** is a table that shows how much of a good or service consumers will want to buy at different prices. On the right side of **Figure 5.1**, we show a hypothetical demand schedule for cotton. It's hypothetical in that it doesn't use actual data on the world demand for cotton. The demand schedule assumes that all cotton is of equal quality.

According to the table, if cotton costs $1 a pound, consumers around the world will want to purchase 10 billion pounds of cotton over the course of a year. If the price is

A **demand schedule** shows how much of a good or service consumers will be willing and able to buy at different prices.

Figure 5.1 The Demand Schedule and the Demand Curve

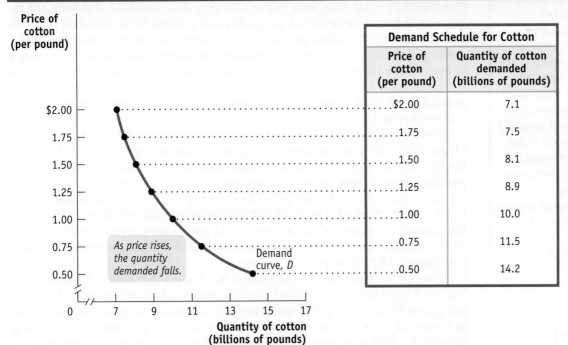

Demand Schedule for Cotton	
Price of cotton (per pound)	Quantity of cotton demanded (billions of pounds)
$2.00	7.1
1.75	7.5
1.50	8.1
1.25	8.9
1.00	10.0
0.75	11.5
0.50	14.2

The demand schedule for cotton yields the corresponding demand curve, which shows how much of a good or service consumers want to buy at any given price. The demand curve and the demand schedule reflect the law of demand: As price rises, the quantity demanded falls. Similarly, a decrease in price raises the quantity demanded. As a result, the demand curve is downward-sloping.

$1.25 a pound, they will want to buy only 8.9 billion pounds; if the price is only $0.75 a pound, they will want to buy 11.5 billion pounds; and so on. So the higher the price, the fewer pounds of cotton consumers will want to purchase. In other words, as the price rises, the **quantity demanded** of cotton—the actual amount consumers are willing and able to buy at a specific price—falls.

The graph in Figure 5.1 is a visual representation of the information in the table. The vertical axis shows the price of a pound of cotton and the horizontal axis shows the quantity of cotton in pounds. Each point on the graph corresponds to one of the entries in the table. The curve that connects these points is a **demand curve**, a graphical representation of the demand schedule, which is another way of showing the relationship between the quantity demanded and the price.

Note that the demand curve shown in Figure 5.1 slopes downward. This reflects the general proposition that a higher price reduces the quantity demanded. For example, jeans-makers know they will sell fewer pairs of jeans when the price of jeans is higher, reflecting a $2 price per pound of cotton, compared to the number they will sell when the price of jeans is lower, reflecting a price of only $1 per pound of cotton. When the price of jeans is relatively high, some people buy pants less often, and some people buy pants made of wool, linen, or synthetics instead of cotton. In the real world, demand curves almost always slope downward. It is so likely that, all other things being equal, a higher price for a good will lead people to demand a smaller quantity of it, that economists are willing to call it a "law"—the **law of demand**.

Shifts of the Demand Curve

Even though cotton prices were higher in 2013 than they had been in 2012, total world consumption of cotton was higher in 2013. How can we reconcile this fact with the law of demand, which says that a higher price reduces the quantity demanded, all other things being equal?

The answer lies in the crucial phrase *all other things being equal*. In this case, all other things weren't equal: there were changes between 2012 and 2013 that increased the quantity of cotton demanded at any given price. For one thing, the world's population increased by 77 million, and therefore the number of potential wearers of cotton clothing increased. In addition, higher incomes in countries like China allowed people to buy more clothing than before. These changes led to an increase in the quantity of cotton demanded at any given price. **Figure 5.2** illustrates this phenomenon using the demand schedule and demand curve for cotton. (As before, the numbers in Figure 5.2 are hypothetical.)

The table in Figure 5.2 shows two demand schedules. The first is a demand schedule for 2012, the same one shown in Figure 5.1. The second is a demand schedule for 2013. It differs from the 2012 demand schedule due to factors such as a larger population and higher incomes, factors that led to an increase in the quantity of cotton demanded at any given price. So at each price, the 2013 schedule shows a larger quantity demanded than the 2012 schedule. For example, the quantity of cotton consumers wanted to buy at a price of $1 per pound increased from 10 billion to 12 billion pounds per year, the quantity demanded at $1.25 per pound went from 8.9 billion to 10.7 billion pounds, and so on.

What is clear from this example is that the changes that occurred between 2012 and 2013 generated a *new* demand schedule, one in which the quantity demanded was greater at any given price than in the original demand schedule. The two curves in Figure 5.2 show the same information graphically. As you can see, the demand schedule for 2013 corresponds to a new demand curve, D_2, that is to the right of the demand curve for 2012, D_1. This **change in demand** shows the increase in the quantity demanded at any given price, represented by the shift in position of the original demand curve, D_1, to its new location at D_2.

The **quantity demanded** is the actual amount of a good or service consumers are willing and able to buy at some specific price. It is shown as a single point in a demand schedule or along a demand curve.

A **demand curve** is a graphical representation of the demand schedule. It shows the relationship between quantity demanded and price.

The **law of demand** says that a higher price for a good or service, all other things being equal, leads people to demand a smaller quantity of that good or service.

A **change in demand** is a shift of the demand curve, which changes the quantity demanded at any given price.

Figure 5.2 An Increase in Demand

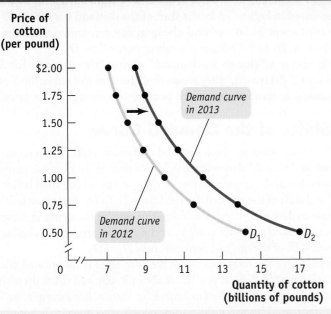

Demand Schedules for Cotton		
Price of cotton (per pound)	Quantity of cotton demanded (billions of pounds)	
	in 2012	in 2013
$2.00	7.1	8.5
1.75	7.5	9.0
1.50	8.1	9.7
1.25	8.9	10.7
1.00	10.0	12.0
0.75	11.5	13.8
0.50	14.2	17.0

Increases in population and income, among other changes, generate an increase in demand—a rise in the quantity demanded at any given price. This is represented by the two demand schedules—one showing demand in 2012, before the rise in population and income, and the other showing demand in 2013, after the rise in population and income—and their corresponding demand curves. The increase in demand shifts the demand curve to the right.

It's crucial to make the distinction between such changes in demand and **movements along the demand curve**, changes in the quantity demanded of a good that result from a change in that good's price. **Figure 5.3** illustrates the difference.

The movement from point A to point B is a movement along the demand curve: the quantity demanded rises due to a fall in price as you move down D_1. Here, a fall in the price of cotton from $1.50 to $1 per pound generates a rise in the quantity demanded

A **movement along the demand curve** is a change in the quantity demanded of a good that is the result of a change in that good's price.

Figure 5.3 A Movement Along the Demand Curve Versus a Shift of the Demand Curve

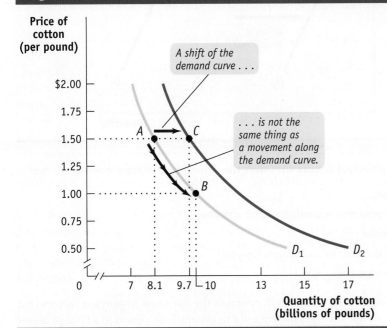

The rise in the quantity demanded when going from point A to point B reflects a movement along the demand curve: it is the result of a fall in the price of the good. The rise in the quantity demanded when going from point A to point C reflects a change in demand: this shift to the right is the result of a rise in the quantity demanded at any given price.

from 8.1 billion to 10 billion pounds per year. But the quantity demanded can also rise when the price is unchanged if there is an *increase in demand*—a rightward shift of the demand curve. This is illustrated in Figure 5.3 by the shift of the demand curve from D_1 to D_2. Holding the price constant at $1.50 a pound, the quantity demanded rises from 8.1 billion pounds at point A on D_1 to 9.7 billion pounds at point C on D_2.

When economists talk about a "change in demand," saying "the demand for X increased" or "the demand for Y decreased," they mean that the demand curve for X or Y shifted—*not* that the quantity demanded rose or fell because of a change in the price.

Understanding Shifts of the Demand Curve

Figure 5.4 illustrates the two basic ways in which demand curves can shift. When economists talk about an "increase in demand," they mean a *rightward* shift of the demand curve: at any given price, consumers demand a larger quantity of the good or service than before. This is shown by the rightward shift of the original demand curve D_1 to D_2. And when economists talk about a "decrease in demand," they mean a *leftward* shift of the demand curve: at any given price, consumers demand a smaller quantity of the good or service than before. This is shown by the leftward shift of the original demand curve D_1 to D_3.

What caused the demand curve for cotton to shift? We have already mentioned two reasons: changes in population and income. If you think about it, you can come up with other things that would be likely to shift the demand curve for cotton. For example, suppose that the price of polyester rises. This will induce some people who previously bought polyester clothing to buy cotton clothing instead, increasing the demand for cotton.

Figure 5.4   Shifts of the Demand Curve

Any event that increases demand shifts the demand curve to the right, reflecting a rise in the quantity demanded at any given price. Any event that decreases demand shifts the demand curve to the left, reflecting a fall in the quantity demanded at any given price.

There are five principal factors that shift the demand curve for a good or service:

- Changes in tastes
- Changes in the prices of related goods or services
- Changes in income
- Changes in the number of consumers (buyers)
- Changes in expectations

Although this is not an exhaustive list, it contains the five most important factors that can shift demand curves. Changes in demand can generally be viewed as a change in one of these factors. So when we say that the quantity of a good or service demanded falls as its price rises, all other things being equal, we are in fact stating that the factors that shift demand are remaining unchanged.

Table 5.1 gives an overview of the ways that these five factors can shift demand. Next, we explore in detail how these factors shift the demand curve.

Table 5.1	**Factors That Shift Demand**		
When this happens . . .	**. . . demand increases**	**But when this happens . . .**	**. . . demand decreases**

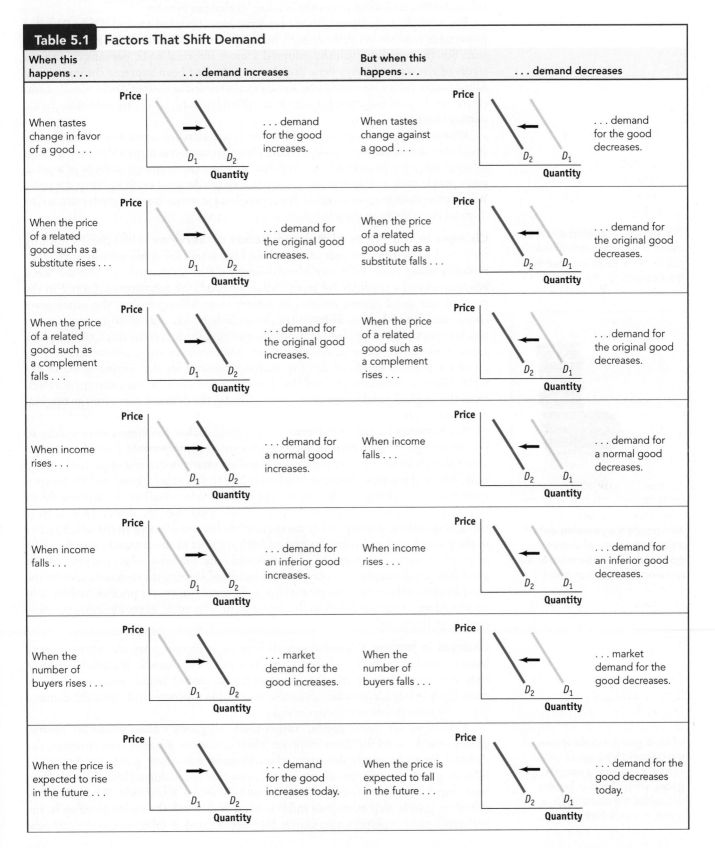

When tastes change in favor of a good . . .	. . . demand for the good increases.	When tastes change against a good . . .	. . . demand for the good decreases.
When the price of a related good such as a substitute rises . . .	. . . demand for the original good increases.	When the price of a related good such as a substitute falls . . .	. . . demand for the original good decreases.
When the price of a related good such as a complement falls . . .	. . . demand for the original good increases.	When the price of a related good such as a complement rises . . .	. . . demand for the original good decreases.
When income rises . . .	. . . demand for a normal good increases.	When income falls . . .	. . . demand for a normal good decreases.
When income falls . . .	. . . demand for an inferior good increases.	When income rises . . .	. . . demand for an inferior good decreases.
When the number of buyers rises . . .	. . . market demand for the good increases.	When the number of buyers falls . . .	. . . market demand for the good decreases.
When the price is expected to rise in the future . . .	. . . demand for the good increases today.	When the price is expected to fall in the future . . .	. . . demand for the good decreases today.

Changes in Tastes Why do people want what they want? Fortunately, we don't need to answer that question—we just need to acknowledge that people have certain preferences, or tastes, that determine what they choose to consume and that these tastes can change. Economists usually lump together changes in demand due to fads, beliefs, cultural shifts, and so on under the heading of changes in *tastes*.

For example, once upon a time men wore hats. Up until around World War II, a respectable man wasn't fully dressed unless he wore a dignified hat along with his suit. But the returning soldiers adopted a more informal style, perhaps due to the rigors of the war. And President Eisenhower, who had been supreme commander of Allied Forces before becoming president, often went hatless. After World War II, it was clear that the demand curve for hats had shifted leftward, reflecting a decrease in the demand for hats.

Economists have little to say about the forces that influence consumers' tastes. (Marketers and advertisers, however, have plenty to say about them!) However, a *change* in tastes has a predictable impact on demand. When tastes change in favor of a good, more people want to buy it at any given price, so the demand curve shifts to the right. When tastes change against a good, fewer people want to buy it at any given price, so the demand curve shifts to the left.

Changes in the Prices of Related Goods or Services While there's nothing quite like a comfortable pair of all-cotton blue jeans, for some purposes khakis—typically made from polyester blends—aren't a bad alternative. Khakis are what economists call a *substitute* for jeans. A pair of goods are **substitutes** if a rise in the price of one good (jeans) makes consumers more willing to buy the other good (polyester-blend khakis). Substitutes are usually goods that in some way serve a similar function: coffee and tea, muffins and doughnuts, train rides and airplane rides. A rise in the price of the alternative good induces some consumers to purchase the original good *instead* of it, shifting demand for the original good to the right. Likewise, when the price of the alternative good falls, some consumers switch from the original good to the alternative, shifting the demand curve for the original good to the left.

But sometimes a fall in the price of one good makes consumers *more* willing to buy another good. Such pairs of goods are known as **complements**. Complements are goods that in some sense are consumed together: smartphones and apps, cookies and milk, cars and gasoline. Because consumers like to consume a good and its complement together, a change in the price of one of the goods will affect the demand for its complement. In particular, when the price of one good rises, the demand for its complement decreases, shifting the demand curve for the complement to the left. So a rise in the price of cookies is likely to cause a leftward shift in the demand curve for milk, as people consume fewer snacks of cookies and milk. Likewise, when the price of one good falls, the demand for its complement increases, shifting the demand curve for the complement to the right. This means that if, for some reason, the price of cookies falls, we should see a rightward shift in the demand curve for milk, as people consume more cookies *and* more milk.

Changes in Income When individuals have more income, they are normally more likely to purchase a good or service at any given price. For example, if a family's income rises, it is more likely to take that summer trip to Disney World—and therefore also more likely to buy plane tickets. So a rise in consumer incomes will cause the demand curves for most goods to shift to the right.

Why do we say "most goods," rather than "all goods"? Most goods are **normal goods**—the demand for them increases when consumer incomes rise. However, the demand for some goods decreases when incomes rise—these goods are known as **inferior goods**. Usually an inferior good is one that is considered less desirable than more expensive alternatives—such as a bus ride versus a taxi ride. When they can afford to, people stop buying an inferior good and switch their consumption to the preferred, more expensive alternative. So when a good is inferior, a rise in income

Two goods are **substitutes** if a rise in the price of one of the goods leads to an increase in the demand for the other good.

Two goods are **complements** if a rise in the price of one of the goods leads to a decrease in the demand for the other good.

When a rise in income increases the demand for a good—the normal case—it is a **normal good**. When a rise in income decreases the demand for a good, it is an **inferior good**.

shifts the demand curve to the left. And, not surprisingly, a fall in income shifts the demand curve to the right.

Consider the difference between so-called casual-dining restaurants such as Applebee's and Olive Garden and fast-food chains such as McDonald's and KFC. When their incomes rise, Americans tend to eat out more at casual-dining restaurants. However, some of this increased dining out comes at the expense of fast-food venues—to some extent, people visit McDonald's less once they can afford to move upscale. So casual dining is a normal good, while fast food appears to be an inferior good.

Changes in the Number of Consumers (Buyers) As we've already noted, one of the reasons for rising cotton demand between 2012 and 2013 was a growing world population. Because of population growth, overall demand for cotton would have risen even if the demand of each individual wearer of cotton clothing had remained unchanged. How the number of consumers affects the market demand curve is described in detail in the next section.

Changes in Expectations When consumers have some choice about when to make a purchase, current demand for a good or service is often affected by expectations about its future price. For example, savvy shoppers often wait for seasonal sales—say, buying next year's holiday gifts during the post-holiday markdowns. In this case, expectations of a future drop in price lead to a decrease in demand today. Alternatively, expectations of a future rise in price are likely to cause an increase in demand today. For example, if you heard that the price of jeans would increase next year, you might go out and buy an extra pair now.

Changes in expectations about future income can also lead to changes in demand. If you learned today that you would inherit a large sum of money sometime in the future, you might borrow some money today and increase your demand for certain goods. On the other hand, if you learned that you would earn less in the future than you thought, you might reduce your demand for some goods and save more money today.

Individual Versus Market Demand Curves

In talking about demand we have discussed both an individual's demand for blue jeans and the market demand for blue jeans. Now let's distinguish between an **individual demand curve**, which shows the relationship between quantity demanded and price for an individual consumer, and a market demand curve, which shows the combined demand by all consumers. For example, suppose that Darla is a consumer of cotton blue jeans; also suppose that all blue jeans are the same, so they sell for the same price. Panel (a) of **Figure 5.5** shows how many pairs of jeans she will buy per year at any given price per pair. Then D_{Darla} is Darla's individual demand curve.

The *market demand curve* shows how the combined quantity demanded by all consumers depends on the market price of that good. (Most of the time, when economists refer to the demand curve, they mean the market demand curve.) The market demand curve is the *horizontal sum* of the individual demand curves of all consumers in that market. To see what we mean by the term *horizontal sum*, assume for a moment that there are only two consumers of blue jeans, Darla and Dino. Dino's individual demand curve, D_{Dino}, is shown in panel (b). Panel (c) shows the market demand curve. At any given price, the quantity demanded by the market is the sum of the quantities demanded by Darla and Dino. For example, at a price of $30 per pair, Darla demands three pairs of jeans per year and Dino demands two pairs per year. So the quantity demanded by the market is five pairs per year.

Clearly, the quantity demanded by the market at any given price is larger with Dino present than it would be if Darla were the only consumer. The quantity demanded at any given price would be even larger if we added a third consumer, then a fourth, and so on. So an increase in the number of consumers leads to an increase in demand.

An **individual demand curve** illustrates the relationship between quantity demanded and price for an individual consumer.

Figure 5.5 Individual Demand Curves and the Market Demand Curve

(a) Darla's Individual Demand Curve

Price of blue jeans (per pair)

$30

0   3

D_{Darla}

Quantity of blue jeans (pairs)

(b) Dino's Individual Demand Curve

Price of blue jeans (per pair)

$30

0   2

D_{Dino}

Quantity of blue jeans (pairs)

(c) Market Demand Curve

Price of blue jeans (per pair)

$30

0   5

D_{Market}

Quantity of blue jeans (pairs)

Darla and Dino are the only two consumers of blue jeans in the market. Panel (a) shows Darla's individual demand curve: the number of pairs of jeans she will buy per year at any given price. Panel (b) shows Dino's individual demand curve. Given that Darla and Dino are the only two consumers, the *market demand curve*, which shows the quantity of blue jeans demanded by all consumers at any given price, is shown in panel (c). The market demand curve is the *horizontal sum* of the individual demand curves of all consumers. In this case, at any given price, the quantity demanded by the market is the sum of the quantities demanded by Darla and Dino.

MODULE 5 REVIEW

Adventures in AP® Economics

Watch the video: **Demand**

Check Your Understanding

1. Explain whether each of the following events represents (i) a *change in* demand (a *shift* of the demand curve) or (ii) a *movement along* the demand curve (a *change in the quantity demanded*).
   a. A store owner finds that customers are willing to pay more for umbrellas on rainy days.
   b. When XYZ Mobile, a cellular plan provider, offered reduced rates on data charges, its volume data usage by users increased sharply.
   c. People buy more long-stem roses the week of Valentine's Day, even though the prices are higher than at other times during the year.
   d. A sharp rise in the price of gasoline leads many commuters to join carpools in order to reduce their gasoline purchases.

TACKLE THE AP® TEST: Multiple-Choice Questions

1. Which of the following is true in a competitive market?
   a. there are many buyers and sellers
   b. each firm sells a different variety of the product
   c. buyers can influence the market price
   d. sellers can influence the market price
   e. all of the above

2. The law of demand states that the relationship between price and the quantity demanded is
   a. positive.
   b. negative.
   c. direct.
   d. unclear.
   e. weak.

3. Which of the following would increase demand for a normal good? A decrease in
   a. price.
   b. income.
   c. the price of a substitute.
   d. consumer taste for a good.
   e. the price of a complement.

4. A decrease in the price of butter would most likely decrease the demand for
   a. margarine.   **d.** milk.
   b. bagels.   **e.** syrup.
   c. jelly.

5. If an increase in income leads to a decrease in demand, the good is
   a. a complement.   **d.** abnormal.
   b. a substitute.   **e.** normal.
   c. inferior.

6. Which of the following will occur if consumers expect the price of a good to fall in the coming months?
   a. The quantity demanded will rise today.
   b. The quantity demanded will remain the same today.
   c. Demand will increase today.
   d. Demand will decrease today.
   e. No change will occur today.

7. Which of the following will increase the demand for disposable diapers?
   a. a new "baby boom"
   b. concern over the environmental effect of landfills
   c. a decrease in the price of cloth diapers
   d. a move toward earlier potty training of children
   e. a decrease in the price of disposable diapers

TACKLE THE AP® TEST: Free-Response Questions

1. Create a table with two hypothetical prices for a good and two corresponding quantities demanded. Choose the prices and quantities so that they illustrate the law of demand. Using your data, draw a correctly labeled graph showing the demand curve for the good. Using the same graph, illustrate an increase in demand for the good.

2. Draw a correctly labeled graph showing the demand for apples. On your graph, illustrate what happens to the demand for apples if a new report from the Surgeon General finds that an apple a day really *does* keep the doctor away. **(3 points)**

Rubric for FRQ 1 (6 points)

Price	Quantity
$4	10
2	14

1 point: Table with data labeled "Price" (or "*P*") and "Quantity" (or "*Q*")

1 point: Values in the table show a negative relationship between *P* and *Q*

1 point: Graph with "Price" on the vertical axis and "Quantity" on the horizontal axis

1 point: Negatively-sloped curve labeled "Demand" or "*D*"

1 point: Demand curve correctly plots the data from the table

1 point: A second demand curve (with a label such as D_2) shown to the right of the original demand curve

---

Supply and Demand: Supply

MOD 6

> **In this Module, you will learn to:**
> • Draw a supply curve and interpret its meaning
> • Discuss the difference between movements along the supply curve and changes in supply
> • List and describe the factors that shift the supply curve

The Supply Curve

Some parts of the world are especially well suited to growing cotton, and the United States is one of those. But even in the United States, some land is better suited

to growing cotton than other land. Whether American farmers restrict their cotton-growing to only the most ideal locations or expand it to less suitable land depends on the price they expect to get for their cotton. Moreover, there are many other areas in the world where cotton could be grown—such as Pakistan, Brazil, Turkey, and China. Whether farmers there actually grow cotton depends, again, on the price.

So just as the quantity of cotton that consumers want to buy depends on the price they have to pay, the quantity that producers are willing to produce and sell—the **quantity supplied**—depends on the price they are offered.

The Supply Schedule and the Supply Curve

The **quantity supplied** is the actual amount of a good or service people are willing to sell at some specific price.

A **supply schedule** shows how much of a good or service producers would supply at different prices.

A **supply curve** shows the relationship between the quantity supplied and the price.

The **law of supply** says that, other things being equal, the price and quantity supplied of a good are positively related.

A **change in supply** is a shift of the supply curve, which changes the quantity supplied at any given price.

The table in **Figure 6.1** shows how the quantity of cotton made available varies with the price—that is, it shows a hypothetical **supply schedule** for cotton.

A supply schedule works the same way as the demand schedule shown in Figure 5.1: in this case, the table shows the number of pounds of cotton farmers are willing to sell at different prices. At a price of $0.50 per pound, farmers are willing to sell only 8 billion pounds of cotton per year. At $0.75 per pound, they're willing to sell 9.1 billion pounds. At $1, they're willing to sell 10 billion pounds, and so on.

In the same way that a demand schedule can be represented graphically by a demand curve, a supply schedule can be represented by a **supply curve**, as shown in Figure 6.1. Each point on the curve represents an entry from the table.

Suppose that the price of cotton rises from $1 to $1.25; we can see that the quantity of cotton farmers are willing to sell rises from 10 billion to 10.7 billion pounds. This is the normal situation for a supply curve: a higher price leads to a higher quantity supplied. Some economists refer to this positive relationship as the **law of supply**. So just as demand curves normally slope downward, supply curves normally slope upward: the higher the price being offered, the more of any good or service producers will be willing to sell.

Shifts of the Supply Curve

For many decades following World War II, cotton remained relatively cheap. One reason is that the amount of land cultivated for cotton expanded. However, the major factor accounting for cotton's relative cheapness was advances in production technology, with output per acre more than quadrupling during this same period. **Figure 6.2** illustrates these events in terms of the supply schedule and the supply curve for cotton.

The table in Figure 6.2 shows two supply schedules. The schedule before improved cotton-growing technology was adopted is the same one as in Figure 6.1. The second schedule shows the supply of cotton *after* the improved technology was adopted. Just as a change in demand schedules leads to a shift of the demand curve, a change in supply schedules leads to a shift of the supply curve—a **change in supply**. This is shown in Figure 6.2 by the shift of the supply curve before the adoption of new cotton-growing

AP® EXAM TIP

A change in demand does not affect supply (either the supply schedule or the supply curve). However, if a change in demand causes a change in price, it will affect the quantity supplied by causing a movement along the supply curve.

Figure 6.1 The Supply Schedule and the Supply Curve

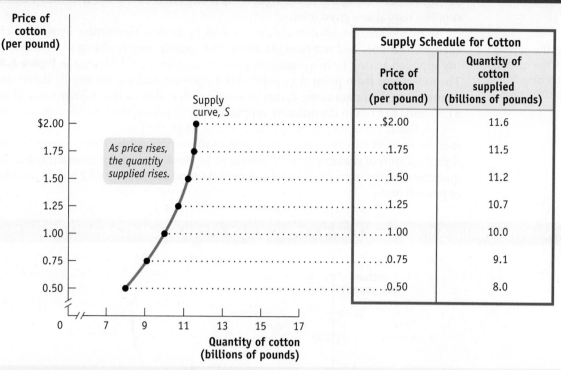

Supply Schedule for Cotton	
Price of cotton (per pound)	Quantity of cotton supplied (billions of pounds)
$2.00	11.6
1.75	11.5
1.50	11.2
1.25	10.7
1.00	10.0
0.75	9.1
0.50	8.0

The supply schedule for cotton is plotted to yield the corresponding supply curve, which shows how much of a good producers are willing to sell at any given price. The supply curve and the supply schedule reflect the fact that supply curves are usually upward-sloping: the quantity supplied rises when the price rises.

Figure 6.2 An Increase in Supply

Supply Schedules for Cotton		
Price of cotton (per pound)	Quantity of cotton supplied (billions of pounds)	
	Before new technology	After new technology
$2.00	11.6	13.9
1.75	11.5	13.8
1.50	11.2	13.4
1.25	10.7	12.8
1.00	10.0	12.0
0.75	9.1	10.9
0.50	8.0	9.6

The adoption of improved cotton-growing technology generated an increase in supply—a rise in the quantity supplied at any given price. This event is represented by the two supply schedules—one showing supply before the new technology was adopted, the other showing supply after the new technology was adopted—and their corresponding supply curves. The increase in supply shifts the supply curve to the right.

technology, S_1, to its new position after the adoption of new cotton-growing technology, S_2. Notice that S_2 lies to the right of S_1, a reflection of the fact that the quantity supplied rises at any given price.

As in the analysis of demand, it's crucial to draw a distinction between such changes in supply and **movements along the supply curve**—changes in the quantity supplied arising from a change in price. We can see this difference in **Figure 6.3**. The movement from point A to point B is a movement along the supply curve: the quantity supplied rises along S_1 due to a rise in price. Here, a rise in price from $1 to $1.50 leads to a rise in the quantity supplied from 10 billion to 11.2 billion pounds of cotton. But the quantity supplied can also rise when the price is unchanged if there is an increase in supply—a rightward shift of the supply curve. This is shown by the rightward shift of the supply curve from S_1 to S_2. Holding the price constant at $1, the quantity supplied rises from 10 billion pounds at point A on S_1 to 12 billion pounds at point C on S_2.

A **movement along the supply curve** is a change in the quantity supplied of a good arising from a change in the good's price.

Figure 6.3   A Movement Along the Supply Curve Versus a Shift of the Supply Curve

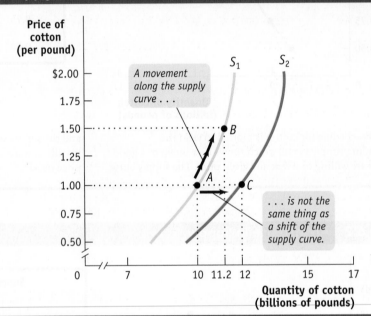

The increase in quantity supplied when going from point A to point B reflects a movement along the supply curve: it is the result of a rise in the price of the good. The increase in quantity supplied when going from point A to point C reflects a shift of the supply curve: it is the result of an increase in the quantity supplied at any given price.

Understanding Shifts of the Supply Curve

Figure 6.4 illustrates the two basic ways in which supply curves can shift. When economists talk about an "increase in supply," they mean a *rightward* shift of the supply curve: at any given price, producers supply a larger quantity of the good than before. This is shown in Figure 6.4 by the rightward shift of the original supply curve S_1 to S_2. And when economists talk about a "decrease in supply," they mean a *leftward* shift of the supply curve: at any given price, producers supply a smaller quantity of the good than before. This is represented by the leftward shift of S_1 to S_3.

Shifts of the supply curve for a good or service are typically the result of a change in one of five factors (though, as in the case of demand, there are other possible causes):

- input prices
- the prices of related goods or services
- producer expectations
- the number of producers
- technology

Figure 6.4　Shifts of the Supply Curve

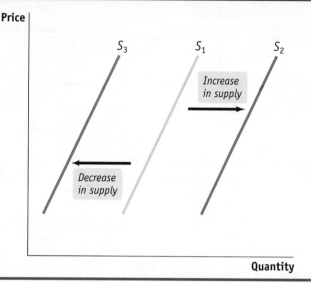

Any event that increases supply shifts the supply curve to the right, reflecting a rise in the quantity supplied at any given price. Any event that decreases supply shifts the supply curve to the left, reflecting a fall in the quantity supplied at any given price.

Table 6.1 (on the next page) provides an overview of the factors that shift supply.

Changes in Input Prices　To produce output, you need *inputs*. An **input** is any good or service that is used to produce another good or service. For example, to make vanilla ice cream, you need vanilla beans, cream, sugar, and so on. Inputs, like outputs, have prices. And an increase in the price of an input makes the production of the final good more costly for those who produce and sell it. So producers are less willing to supply the final good at any given price, and the supply curve shifts to the left. For example, fuel is a major cost for airlines. When oil prices surged in 2007–2008, airlines began cutting back on their flight schedules and some went out of business. Similarly, a fall in the price of an input makes the production of the final good less costly for sellers. They are more willing to supply the good at any given price, and the supply curve shifts to the right.

Changes in the Prices of Related Goods or Services　A single producer often produces a mix of goods rather than a single product. For example, an oil refinery produces gasoline from crude oil, but it also produces heating oil and other products from the same raw material. When a producer sells several products, the quantity of any one good it is willing to supply at any given price depends on the prices of its other co-produced goods.

This effect can run in either direction. An oil refiner will supply less gasoline at any given price when the price of heating oil rises, shifting the supply curve for gasoline to the left. But it will supply more gasoline at any given price when the price of heating oil falls, shifting the supply curve for gasoline to the right. This means that gasoline and other co-produced oil products are *substitutes in production* for refiners.

In contrast, due to the nature of the production process, other goods can be *complements in production*. For example, producers of crude oil—oil-well drillers—often find that oil wells also produce natural gas as a by-product of oil extraction. The higher the price at which a driller can sell its natural gas, the more oil wells it will drill and the more oil it will supply at any given price for oil. As a result, natural gas is a complement in production for crude oil.

Changes in Producer Expectations　Just as changes in consumer expectations can shift the demand curve, they can also shift the supply curve. When suppliers have some choice about when they put their good up for sale, changes in the expected future price of the good can lead a supplier to supply less or more of the good today.

An **input** is a good or service that is used to produce another good or service.

AP® EXAM TIP

A change in supply is shown by a shift of the curve, indicating a change in the quantity supplied at every price. Remember, "left is less and right is more." But looks can be deceiving. When supply decreases, the supply curve shifts to the left—which is up, not down. When supply increases, the supply curve shifts to the right—which is down, not up. To avoid confusion, always think "right" and "left" (not "up" and "down") when shifting supply and demand curves.

Table 6.1 Factors That Shift Supply

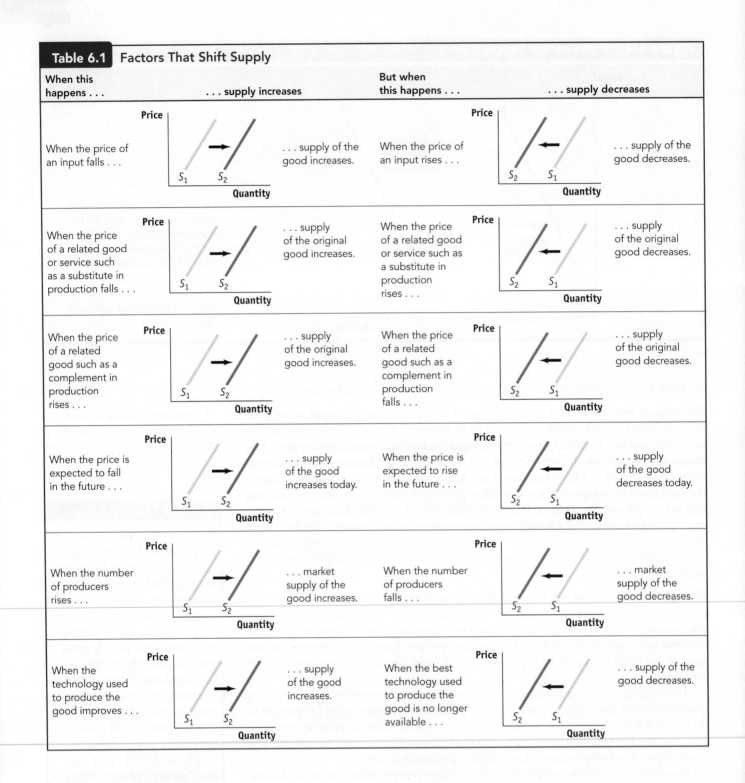

When this happens . . .	. . . supply increases	But when this happens . . .	. . . supply decreases
When the price of an input falls . . .	. . . supply of the good increases.	When the price of an input rises . . .	. . . supply of the good decreases.
When the price of a related good or service such as a substitute in production falls . . .	. . . supply of the original good increases.	When the price of a related good or service such as a substitute in production rises . . .	. . . supply of the original good decreases.
When the price of a related good such as a complement in production rises . . .	. . . supply of the original good increases.	When the price of a related good such as a complement in production falls . . .	. . . supply of the original good decreases.
When the price is expected to fall in the future . . .	. . . supply of the good increases today.	When the price is expected to rise in the future . . .	. . . supply of the good decreases today.
When the number of producers rises . . .	. . . market supply of the good increases.	When the number of producers falls . . .	. . . market supply of the good decreases.
When the technology used to produce the good improves . . .	. . . supply of the good increases.	When the best technology used to produce the good is no longer available . . .	. . . supply of the good decreases.

For example, gasoline and other oil products are often stored for significant periods of time at oil refineries before being sold to consumers. In fact, storage is normally part of producers' business strategy. Knowing that the demand for gasoline peaks in the summer, oil refiners normally reserve some of their gasoline produced during the spring for sale in the summer. Similarly, knowing that the demand for heating oil peaks in the winter, they normally reserve some of their heating oil produced during the fall for sale in the winter. In each case, producers make a decision of when to sell a given product based on a comparison of the current price versus the expected future price. This example illustrates how changes in expectations can alter supply: an increase in the anticipated future price of a good or service reduces supply today, a leftward shift of the supply curve. Similarly, a fall in the anticipated future price increases supply today, a rightward shift of the supply curve.

Changes in the Number of Producers Just as a change in the number of consumers affects the demand curve, a change in the number of producers affects the supply curve. A market with many producers will supply a larger quantity of a good than a market with a single producer, all other things equal.

Changes in Technology When economists talk about "technology," they mean all the methods people can use to turn inputs into useful goods and services. In that sense, the whole complex sequence of activities that turn cotton from Pakistan into the pair of jeans hanging in your closet is technology.

Improvements in technology enable producers to spend less on inputs yet still produce the same output. When a better technology becomes available, reducing the cost of production, supply increases, and the supply curve shifts to the right. As we have already mentioned, improved technology enabled farmers to more than quadruple cotton output per acre planted over the past several decades. Improved technology is the main reason that, until recently, cotton remained relatively cheap even as worldwide demand grew.

> ### AP® EXAM TIP
>
> The mnemonic *I-RENT* can help you remember the factors that shift supply. Supply is shifted by changes in . . . **I**nput (resource) prices, prices of **R**elated goods and services, producer **E**xpectations, the **N**umber of producers, and **T**echnology.

Individual Versus Market Supply Curves

Now that we have introduced the market supply curve, let's examine how it is related to a producer's **individual supply curve**. Look at panel (a) in **Figure 6.5**. The individual supply curve shows the relationship between quantity supplied and price for an individual producer. For example, suppose that Mr. Silva is a Brazilian cotton farmer and that panel (a) of Figure 6.5 shows how many pounds of cotton he will supply per year at any given price. Then S_{Silva} is his individual supply curve.

An **individual supply curve** illustrates the relationship between quantity supplied and price for an individual producer.

Figure 6.5 Individual Supply Curves and the Market Supply Curve

Panel (a) shows the individual supply curve for Mr. Silva, S_{Silva}, the quantity of cotton he will sell at any given price. Panel (b) shows the individual supply curve for Mr. Liu, S_{Liu}. The market supply curve, which shows the quantity of cotton supplied by all producers at any given price, is shown in panel (c). The market supply curve is the horizontal sum of the individual supply curves of all producers.

The *market supply curve* shows how the combined total quantity supplied by all individual producers in the market depends on the market price of that good. Just as the market demand curve is the horizontal sum of the individual demand curves of all consumers, the market supply curve is the horizontal sum of the individual supply curves of all producers. Assume for a moment that there are only two producers of cotton, Mr. Silva and Mr. Liu, a Chinese cotton farmer. Mr. Liu's individual supply curve is shown in panel (b). Panel (c) shows the market supply curve. At any given price, the quantity supplied to the market is the sum of the quantities supplied by Mr. Silva and Mr. Liu. For example, at a price of $2 per pound, Mr. Silva supplies 3,000 pounds of cotton per year and Mr. Liu supplies 2,000 pounds per year, making the quantity supplied to the market 5,000 pounds.

Clearly, the quantity supplied to the market at any given price is larger with Mr. Liu present than it would be if Mr. Silva were the only supplier. The quantity supplied at a given price would be even larger if we added a third producer, then a fourth, and so on. So an increase in the number of producers leads to an increase in supply and a rightward shift of the supply curve.

MODULE 6 REVIEW

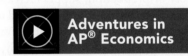

Watch the video: **Supply**

Check Your Understanding

1. Explain whether each of the following events represents (i) a change in supply or (ii) a *movement along* the supply curve.
   a. During a real estate boom that causes house prices to rise, more homeowners put their houses up for sale.
   b. Many strawberry farmers open temporary roadside stands during harvest season, even though prices are usually low at that time.
   c. Immediately after the school year begins, fewer young people are available to work. Fast-food chains must raise wages, which represent the price of labor, to attract workers.
   d. Many construction workers temporarily move to areas that have suffered hurricane damage, lured by higher wages.

   e. Since new technologies have made it possible to build larger cruise ships (which are cheaper to run per passenger), Caribbean cruise lines have offered more cabins, at lower prices, than before.

2. After each of the following events, will the supply curve for the good that is mentioned shift to the left, shift to the right, or remain unchanged?
   a. The coffee berry borer beetle destroys large quantities of coffee berries.
   b. Consumers demand more bike helmets than ever.
   c. The number of tea producers increases.
   d. The price of leather, an input in wallet production, increases.

TACKLE THE AP® TEST: Multiple-Choice Questions

1. The law of supply states that the relationship between price and quantity supplied is
   a. positive.
   b. negative.
   c. indirect.
   d. unclear.
   e. weak.

2. Because the market supply curve is the sum of individual producers' supply curves, an increase in the number of producers will cause which of the following?
   a. the supply curve to shift to the left
   b. the supply curve to shift to the right

   c. a movement to the right along the supply curve
   d. a movement to the left along the supply curve
   e. the supply to decrease

3. Which of the following will decrease the supply of rice?
   a. There is a technological advance that affects the production of *all* goods.
   b. The price of rice falls.
   c. The price of corn (which consumers regard as a substitute for rice) decreases.
   d. The wages of workers producing rice increase.
   e. The demand for rice decreases.

4. An increase in the demand for steak, which increases the price of steak, will lead to an increase in which of the following?
  a. the supply of steak
  b. the supply of hamburger (a substitute in production)
  c. the supply of chicken (a substitute in consumption)
  d. the supply of leather (a complement in production)
  e. the demand for leather

5. A technological advance in textbook production will lead to which of the following?
  a. a decrease in textbook supply
  b. an increase in textbook demand
  c. an increase in textbook supply
  d. a movement along the supply curve for textbooks
  e. an increase in textbook prices

6. Expectations among hiking-boot makers that boot prices will rise significantly in the future will lead to which of the following now?
  a. an increase in boot supply
  b. no change in boot supply
  c. a decrease in boot supply
  d. a movement to the left along the boot supply curve
  e. a movement to the right along the boot supply curve

7. Starch from the stalks of potato plants is used to make packing peanuts, a complement in production. A decrease in potato demand that lowers potato prices will cause which of the following in the packing-peanut market?
  a. an increase in supply and no change in demand
  b. an increase in supply and a decrease in demand
  c. a decrease in both demand and supply
  d. a decrease in supply and no change in demand
  e. a decrease in supply and an increase in demand

TACKLE THE AP® TEST: Free-Response Questions

1. Tesla Motors makes sports cars powered by lithium batteries.
  a. Draw a correctly labeled graph showing a hypothetical supply curve for Tesla sports cars.
  b. On the same graph, show the effect of a major new discovery of lithium that lowers the price of lithium.
  c. Suppose Tesla Motors expects to be able to sell its cars for a higher price next month. Explain the effect that will have on the supply of Tesla cars this month.

Rubric for FRQ 1 (4 points)

Quantity of cars

1 point: Graph with "Price" or "*P*" on the vertical axis and "Quantity" or "*Q*" on the horizontal axis

1 point: A positively sloped curve labeled "Supply" or "*S*"

1 point: A second supply curve shown to the right of the original supply curve with a label such as S_2, indicating that it is the new supply curve

1 point: Correct explanation that the expectation of higher prices next month would lead to a decrease in the supply of Tesla cars this month because the company will want to sell more of its cars when the price is higher

---

2. Suppose AP® economics students at your school offer tutoring services to students in regular economics courses.
  a. Draw a correctly labeled graph showing the supply curve for tutoring services measured in hours. Label the supply curve "S_1."
  b. Suppose the wage paid for babysitting, an alternative activity for AP® economics students, increases. Show the effect of this wage increase on the graph you drew for part a. Label the new supply curve "S_2."
  c. Suppose instead that the number of AP® economics students increases. Show the effect of this increase in AP® economics students on the same graph you drew for parts a and b. Label the new supply curve "S_3."
  (3 points)

Supply and Demand: Equilibrium

> **In this Module, you will learn to:**
> - Explain how supply and demand curves determine a market's equilibrium price and equilibrium quantity
> - Describe how changes in price move the market back to equilibrium in the case of a shortage or surplus
> - Explain how equilibrium price and quantity are affected when there is a change in either supply or demand
> - Explain how equilibrium price and quantity are affected when there is a simultaneous change in both supply and demand

Supply, Demand, and Equilibrium

We have now covered the first four key elements in the supply and demand model: the demand curve, the supply curve, and the set of factors that shift each curve. The next step is to put these elements together to show how they can be used to predict the price at which the good is bought and sold, as well as the quantity transacted.

Orlando Sentinel/Getty Images

In competitive markets the interaction of supply and demand tends to move toward what economists call *equilibrium*. Imagine a busy afternoon at your local supermarket; there are long lines at the checkout counters. Then one of the previously closed registers opens. The first thing that happens is a rush to the newly opened register. But soon enough things settle down and shoppers have rearranged themselves so that the line at the newly opened register is about as long as all the others. This situation— all the checkout lines are now the same length, and none of the shoppers can be better off by doing something different—is what economists call **equilibrium**.

The concept of equilibrium helps us understand the price at which a good or service is bought and sold as well as the quantity transacted of the good or service. A competitive market is in equilibrium when the price has moved to a level at which the quantity of a good demanded equals the quantity of that good supplied. At that price, no individual seller could make herself better off by offering to sell either more or less of the good, and no individual buyer could make himself better off by offering to buy more or less of the good. Recall the shoppers at the supermarket who cannot make themselves better off (cannot save time) by changing lines. Similarly, at the market equilibrium, the price has moved to a level that exactly matches the quantity demanded by consumers to the quantity supplied by sellers.

The price that matches the quantity supplied and the quantity demanded is the **equilibrium price**; the quantity bought and sold at that price is the **equilibrium quantity**. The equilibrium price is also known as the market-clearing price: it is the price that "clears the market" by ensuring that every buyer willing to pay that price finds a seller willing to sell at that price, and vice versa. So how do we find the equilibrium price and quantity?

An economic situation is in **equilibrium** when no individual would be better off doing something different.

A competitive market is in equilibrium when the price has moved to a level at which the quantity demanded of a good equals the quantity supplied of that good. The price at which this takes place is the **equilibrium price**, also referred to as the market-clearing price. The quantity of the good bought and sold at that price is the **equilibrium quantity**.

Finding the Equilibrium Price and Quantity

The easiest way to determine the equilibrium price and quantity in a market is by putting the supply curve and the demand curve on the same diagram. Since the supply curve shows the quantity supplied at any given price and the demand curve shows the quantity demanded at any given price, the price at which the two curves cross is the equilibrium price: the price at which quantity supplied equals quantity demanded.

Figure 7.1 combines the demand curve from Figure 5.1 and the supply curve from Figure 6.1. They *intersect* at point *E*, which is the equilibrium of this market; $1 is the equilibrium price and 10 billion pounds is the equilibrium quantity.

Let's confirm that point *E* fits our definition of equilibrium. At a price of $1 per pound, cotton farmers are willing to sell 10 billion pounds a year and cotton consumers want to buy 10 billion pounds a year. So at the price of $1 a pound, the quantity of cotton supplied equals the quantity demanded. Notice that at any other price the market would not clear: every willing buyer would not be able to find a willing seller, or vice versa. More specifically, if the price were more than $1, the quantity supplied would exceed the quantity demanded; if the price were less than $1, the quantity demanded would exceed the quantity supplied.

The model of supply and demand, then, predicts that given the demand and supply curves shown in Figure 7.1, 10 billion pounds of cotton would change hands at a price of $1 per pound. But how can we be sure that the market will arrive at the equilibrium price? We begin by answering three simple questions:

1. Why do all sales and purchases in a market take place at the same price?
2. Why does the market price fall if it is above the equilibrium price?
3. Why does the market price rise if it is below the equilibrium price?

Figure 7.1 Market Equilibrium

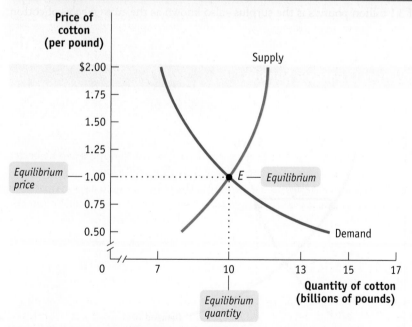

Market equilibrium occurs at point *E*, where the supply curve and the demand curve intersect. In equilibrium, the quantity demanded is equal to the quantity supplied. In this market, the equilibrium price is $1 per pound and the equilibrium quantity is 10 billion pounds per year.

Why Do All Sales and Purchases in a Market Take Place at the Same Price?

There are some markets where the same good can sell for many different prices, depending on who is selling or who is buying. For example, have you ever bought a souvenir in a "tourist trap" and then seen the same item on sale somewhere else (perhaps even in the shop next door) for a lower price? Because tourists don't know which shops offer the best deals and don't have time for comparison shopping, sellers in tourist areas can charge different prices for the same good.

But in any market in which the buyers and sellers have both been around for some time, sales and purchases tend to converge at a generally uniform price, so we can safely talk about *the* market price. It's easy to see why. Suppose a seller offered a potential buyer a price noticeably above what the buyer knew other people were paying. The buyer would clearly be better off shopping elsewhere—unless the seller were prepared to offer a better deal. Conversely, a seller would not be willing to sell for significantly less than the amount he knew most buyers were paying; he would be better off waiting to get a more reasonable customer. So in any well-established, ongoing market, all sellers receive and all buyers pay approximately the same price. This is what we call the *market price*.

Why Does the Market Price Fall If It Is Above the Equilibrium Price?

Suppose the supply and demand curves are as shown in Figure 7.1 but the market price is above the equilibrium level of $1—say, $1.50. This situation is illustrated in **Figure 7.2**. Why can't the price stay there?

As the figure shows, at a price of $1.50 there would be more pounds of cotton available than consumers wanted to buy: 11.2 billion pounds versus 8.1 billion pounds. The difference of 3.1 billion pounds is the **surplus**—also known as the *excess supply*—of cotton at $1.50.

There is a **surplus** of a good or service when the quantity supplied exceeds the quantity demanded. Surpluses occur when the price is above its equilibrium level.

Figure 7.2 Price Above Its Equilibrium Level Creates a Surplus

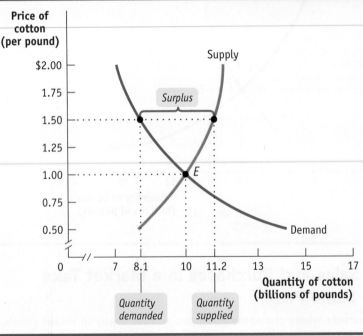

The market price of $1.50 is above the equilibrium price of $1. This creates a surplus: at a price of $1.50, producers would like to sell 11.2 billion pounds but consumers want to buy only 8.1 billion pounds, so there is a surplus of 3.1 billion pounds. This surplus will push the price down until it reaches the equilibrium price of $1.

This surplus means that some cotton farmers are frustrated: at the current price, they cannot find consumers who want to buy their cotton. The surplus offers an incentive for those frustrated would-be sellers to offer a lower price in order to poach business from other producers and entice more consumers to buy. The result of this price cutting will be to push the prevailing price down until it reaches the equilibrium price. So the price of a good will fall whenever there is a surplus—that is, whenever the market price is above its equilibrium level.

Why Does the Market Price Rise If It Is Below the Equilibrium Price?

Now suppose the price is below its equilibrium level—say, at $0.75 per pound, as shown in **Figure 7.3**. In this case, the quantity demanded, 11.5 billion pounds, exceeds the quantity supplied, 9.1 billion pounds, implying that there are would-be buyers who cannot find cotton: there is a **shortage**, also known as an *excess demand*, of 2.4 billion pounds.

When there is a shortage, there are frustrated would-be buyers—people who want to purchase cotton but cannot find willing sellers at the current price. In this situation, either buyers will offer more than the prevailing price or sellers will realize that they can charge higher prices. Either way, the result is to drive up the prevailing price. This bidding up of prices happens whenever there are shortages—and there will be shortages whenever the price is below its equilibrium level. So the market price will always rise if it is below the equilibrium level.

There is a **shortage** of a good or service when the quantity demanded exceeds the quantity supplied. Shortages occur when the price is below its equilibrium level.

Figure 7.3   Price Below Its Equilibrium Level Creates a Shortage

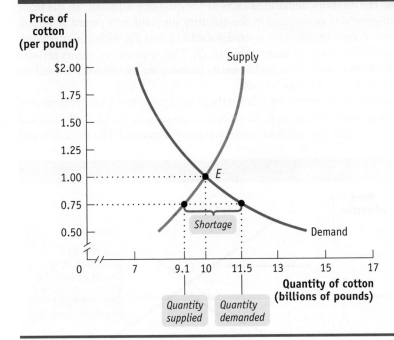

The market price of $0.75 is below the equilibrium price of $1. This creates a shortage: consumers want to buy 11.5 billion pounds, but only 9.1 billion pounds are for sale, so there is a shortage of 2.4 billion pounds. This shortage will push the price up until it reaches the equilibrium price of $1.

Using Equilibrium to Describe Markets

We have now seen that a market tends to have a single price, the equilibrium price. If the market price is above the equilibrium level, the ensuing surplus leads buyers and sellers to take actions that lower the price. And if the market price is below the equilibrium level, the ensuing shortage leads buyers and sellers to take actions that raise the price. So the market price always *moves toward* the equilibrium price, the price at which there is neither surplus nor shortage.

Changes in Supply and Demand

The 2010 floods in Pakistan came as a surprise, but the subsequent increase in the price of cotton was no surprise at all. Suddenly there was a decrease in supply: the quantity of cotton available at any given price fell. Predictably, a decrease in supply raises the equilibrium price.

The flooding in Pakistan is an example of an event that shifted the supply curve for a good without having much effect on the demand curve. There are many such events. There are also events that shift the demand curve without shifting the supply curve. For example, a medical report that chocolate is good for you increases the demand for chocolate but does not affect the supply. Events generally shift either the supply curve or the demand curve, but not both; it is therefore useful to ask what happens in each case.

What Happens When the Demand Curve Shifts

Cotton and polyester are substitutes: if the price of polyester rises, the demand for cotton will increase, and if the price of polyester falls, the demand for cotton will decrease. But how does the price of polyester affect the *market equilibrium* for cotton?

Figure 7.4 shows the effect of a rise in the price of polyester on the market for cotton. The rise in the price of polyester increases the demand for cotton. Point E_1 shows the equilibrium corresponding to the original demand curve, with P_1 the equilibrium price and Q_1 the equilibrium quantity bought and sold.

An increase in demand is indicated by a *rightward* shift of the demand curve from D_1 to D_2. At the original market price P_1, this market is no longer in equilibrium: a shortage occurs because the quantity demanded exceeds the quantity supplied. So the price of cotton rises and generates an increase in the quantity supplied, an upward *movement along the supply curve*. A new equilibrium is established at point E_2, with a higher equilibrium price, P_2, and higher equilibrium quantity, Q_2. This sequence of events reflects a general principle: *When demand for a good or service increases, the equilibrium price and the equilibrium quantity of the good or service both rise.*

What would happen in the reverse case, a fall in the price of polyester? A fall in the price of polyester reduces the demand for cotton, shifting the demand curve to the *left*. At the original price, a surplus occurs as quantity supplied exceeds quantity demanded. The price falls and

Figure 7.4 Equilibrium and Shifts of the Demand Curve

The original equilibrium in the market for cotton is at E_1, at the intersection of the supply curve and the original demand curve, D_1. A rise in the price of polyester, a substitute, shifts the demand curve rightward to D_2. A shortage exists at the original price, P_1, causing both the price and quantity supplied to rise, a movement along the supply curve. A new equilibrium is reached at E_2, with a higher equilibrium price, P_2, and a higher equilibrium quantity, Q_2. When demand for a good or service increases, the equilibrium price and the equilibrium quantity of the good or service both rise.

leads to a decrease in the quantity supplied, resulting in a lower equilibrium price and a lower equilibrium quantity. This illustrates another general principle: *When demand for a good or service decreases, the equilibrium price and the equilibrium quantity of the good or service both fall.*

To summarize how a market responds to a change in demand: *An increase in demand leads to a rise in both the equilibrium price and the equilibrium quantity. A decrease in demand leads to a fall in both the equilibrium price and the equilibrium quantity.* That is, a change in demand causes equilibrium price and quantity to move in the same direction.

What Happens When the Supply Curve Shifts

In the real world, it is a bit easier to predict changes in supply than changes in demand. Physical factors that affect supply, such as weather or the availability of inputs, are easier to get a handle on than the fickle tastes that affect demand. Still, with supply as with demand, what we can best predict are the *effects* of shifts of the supply curve.

As we mentioned earlier, devastating floods in Pakistan sharply reduced the supply of cotton in 2010. **Figure 7.5** shows how this shift affected the market equilibrium. The original equilibrium is at E_1, the point of intersection of the original supply curve, S_1, and the demand curve, with an equilibrium price P_1 and equilibrium quantity Q_1. As a result of the bad weather, supply decreases and S_1 shifts *leftward* to S_2. At the original price P_1, a shortage of cotton now exists and the market is no longer in equilibrium. The shortage causes a rise in price and a fall in quantity demanded, an upward movement along the demand curve. The new equilibrium is at E_2, with an equilibrium price P_2 and an equilibrium quantity Q_2. In the new equilibrium, E_2, the price is higher and the equilibrium quantity lower than before. This can be stated as a general principle: *When supply of a good or service decreases, the equilibrium price of the good or service rises and the equilibrium quantity of the good or service falls.*

What happens to the market when supply increases? An increase in supply leads to a *rightward* shift of the supply curve. At the original price, a surplus now exists; as a result, the equilibrium price falls and the quantity demanded rises. This describes what happened to the market for cotton as new technology increased cotton yields. We can formulate a general principle: *When supply of a good or service increases, the equilibrium price of the good or service falls and the equilibrium quantity of the good or service rises.*

To summarize how a market responds to a change in supply: *An increase in supply leads to a fall in the equilibrium price and a rise in the equilibrium quantity. A decrease in supply leads to a rise in the equilibrium price and a fall in the equilibrium quantity.* That is, a change in supply causes equilibrium price and quantity to move in opposite directions.

AP® EXAM TIP

The graph never lies! To determine what happens to price and quantity when supply or demand shifts, draw the graph of a market in equilibrium and then shift the appropriate curve to show the new equilibrium price and quantity. Compare the old equilibrium price and quantity to the new equilibrium one to find your answer! Draw quick graphs to help you answer multiple choice questions about changes in equilibrium quantity and price.

Figure 7.5 Equilibrium and Shifts of the Supply Curve

The original equilibrium in the market for cotton is at E_1. Bad weather in cotton-growing areas causes a fall in the supply of cotton and shifts the supply curve leftward from S_1 to S_2. A new equilibrium is established at E_2, with a higher equilibrium price, P_2, and a lower equilibrium quantity, Q_2.

Simultaneous Shifts of Supply and Demand Curves

Finally, it sometimes happens that simultaneous events shift *both* the demand and supply curves at the same time. This is not unusual; in real life, supply curves and demand curves for many goods and services shift quite often because the economic environment continually changes. **Figure 7.6** illustrates two examples of simultaneous shifts of the supply and demand curves. In both panels there is an increase in demand—that is, a rightward shift of the demand curve, from D_1 to D_2—for example, representing an increase in the demand for cotton due to changing tastes. Notice that the rightward shift in panel (a) is larger than the one in panel (b): we can suppose that panel (a) represents a year in which many more people than usual choose to buy jeans and cotton T-shirts and panel (b) represents a normal year. Both panels also show a decrease in supply—that is, a leftward shift of the supply curve from S_1 to S_2. Also notice that the leftward shift in panel (b) is relatively larger than the one in panel (a): we can suppose that panel (b) represents the effect of particularly bad weather in Pakistan and panel (a) represents the effect of a much less severe weather event.

In both cases, the equilibrium price rises from P_1 to P_2 as the equilibrium moves from E_1 to E_2. But what happens to the equilibrium quantity, the quantity of cotton bought and sold? In panel (a) the increase in demand is large relative to the decrease in supply, and the equilibrium quantity rises as a result. In panel (b), the decrease in supply is large relative to the increase in demand, and the equilibrium quantity falls as a result. That is, when demand increases and supply decreases, the actual quantity bought and sold can go either way, depending on *how much* the demand and supply curves have shifted.

In general, when supply and demand shift in opposite directions, we can't predict what the ultimate effect will be on the quantity bought and sold. What we can say is that a curve that shifts a disproportionately greater distance than the other curve will have a disproportionately greater effect on the quantity bought and sold (as we saw in

Figure 7.6 Simultaneous Shifts of the Demand and Supply Curves

In panel (a) there is a simultaneous rightward shift of the demand curve and leftward shift of the supply curve. Here the increase in demand is relatively larger than the decrease in supply, so the equilibrium price and equilibrium quantity both rise. In panel (b) there is also a simultaneous rightward shift of the demand curve and leftward shift of the supply curve. Here the decrease in supply is relatively larger than the increase in demand, so the equilibrium price rises and the equilibrium quantity falls.

panel (b)). That said, we can make the following prediction about the outcome when the supply and demand curves shift in opposite directions:

- When demand increases and supply decreases, the equilibrium price rises but the change in the equilibrium quantity is ambiguous.
- When demand decreases and supply increases, the equilibrium price falls but the change in the equilibrium quantity is ambiguous.

But suppose that the demand and supply curves shift in the same direction. Before 2010, this was the case in the global market for cotton, where both supply and demand had increased over the past decade. Can we safely make any predictions about the changes in price and quantity? In this situation, the change in quantity bought and sold can be predicted, but the change in price is ambiguous. The two possible outcomes when the supply and demand curves shift in the same direction (which you should check for yourself) are as follows:

- When both demand and supply increase, the equilibrium quantity rises but the change in the equilibrium price is ambiguous.
- When both demand and supply decrease, the equilibrium quantity falls but the change in the equilibrium price is ambiguous.

> **AP® EXAM TIP**
>
> One way to avoid missing the impact of a simultaneous shift is to treat each shift individually and identify the impact on equilibrium. Then identify the common results and the results that are in opposition. If the equilibrium prices for each individual shift are moving in opposite directions, you know that result is ambiguous.

MODULE 7 REVIEW

Adventures in AP® Economics

Watch the video:
Market Equilibrium

Check Your Understanding

1. In the following three situations, the market is initially in equilibrium. After each event described below, does a surplus or shortage exist at the original equilibrium price? What will happen to the equilibrium price as a result?
   a. In 2018 there was a bumper crop of wine grapes.
   b. After a hurricane, Florida hoteliers often find that many people cancel their upcoming vacations, leaving them with empty hotel rooms.
   c. After a heavy snowfall, many people want to buy second-hand snowblowers at the local tool shop.

2. For each of the following examples, explain how the indicated change affects supply or demand for the good in question and how the shift you describe affects the equilibrium price and quantity.
   a. As the price of gasoline fell in the United States during the 1990s, more people bought large cars.

   b. Technological innovation in the use of recycled paper has lowered the cost of paper production.
   c. When a movie-streaming service lowers its price, local movie theaters have more unfilled seats.

3. Periodically, a computer-chip maker such as Intel introduces a new chip that is faster than the previous one. In response, demand for computers using the earlier chip decreases as customers put off purchases in anticipation of machines containing the new chip. Simultaneously, computer makers increase their production of computers containing the earlier chip in order to clear out their stocks of those chips. Draw two diagrams of the market for computers containing the earlier chip: (a) one in which the equilibrium quantity falls in response to these events and (b) one in which the equilibrium quantity rises. What happens to the equilibrium price in each diagram?

TACKLE THE AP® TEST: Multiple-Choice Questions

1. Which of the following is true about equilibrium?
   a. It is a concept used only in economics.
   b. Economists use it only in the supply and demand model.
   c. It occurs where supply equals demand.
   d. It can occur when there is either a shortage or a surplus.
   e. It is a point at which there is no tendency for change.

2. Price will tend to fall when
   a. there is a shortage.
   b. quantity demanded is greater than quantity supplied.
   c. quantity supplied is less than quantity demanded.

   d. price is above equilibrium.
   e. price is below equilibrium.

3. Which of the following describes what will happen in the market for tomatoes if a salmonella outbreak is attributed to tainted tomatoes?
   a. Supply will decrease and price will increase.
   b. Supply will decrease and price will decrease.
   c. Demand will decrease and price will increase.
   d. Demand will decrease and price will decrease.
   e. Supply and demand will both decrease.

4. Which of the following will lead to an increase in the equilibrium price of product X? A(n)
   a. increase in consumer incomes if product X is an inferior good.
   b. increase in the price of machinery used to produce product X.
   c. technological advance in the production of good X.
   d. decrease in the price of good Y (a substitute for good X).
   e. expectation by consumers that the price of good X is going to fall.

5. The equilibrium price will rise, but the equilibrium quantity may increase, decrease, or stay the same if
   a. demand increases and supply decreases.
   b. demand increases and supply increases.
   c. demand decreases and supply increases.
   d. demand decreases and supply decreases.
   e. demand increases and supply does not change.

6. An increase in the number of buyers and a technological advance will cause
   a. demand to increase and supply to increase.
   b. demand to increase and supply to decrease.
   c. demand to decrease and supply to increase.
   d. demand to decrease and supply to decrease.
   e. no change in demand and an increase in supply.

7. Which of the following is certainly true if demand and supply increase at the same time?
   a. The equilibrium price will increase.
   b. The equilibrium price will decrease.
   c. The equilibrium quantity will increase.
   d. The equilibrium quantity will decrease.
   e. The equilibrium quantity may increase, decrease, or stay the same.

TACKLE THE AP® TEST: Free-Response Questions

1. Draw a correctly labeled graph showing the market for tomatoes in equilibrium. Label the equilibrium price "P_E" and the equilibrium quantity "Q_E." On your graph, draw a horizontal line indicating a price, labeled "P_C", that would lead to a shortage of tomatoes. Label the size of the shortage on your graph.

Rubric for FRQ 1 (6 points)

1 point: Graph with the vertical axis labeled "Price" or "P" and the horizontal axis labeled "Quantity" or "Q"

1 point: Downward-sloping demand curve labeled "Demand" or "D"

1 point: Upward-sloping supply curve labeled "Supply" or "S"

1 point: Equilibrium price "P_E" labeled on the vertical axis and quantity "Q_E" labeled on the horizontal axis at the intersection of the supply and demand curves

1 point: Price line at a price "P_C" below the equilibrium price

1 point: Correct indication of the shortage, which is the horizontal distance between the quantity demanded and the quantity supplied at the height of P_C

2. Draw a correctly labeled graph showing the market for cups of coffee in equilibrium. On your graph, show the effect of a decrease in the price of coffee beans on the equilibrium price and the equilibrium quantity in the market for cups of coffee. **(5 points)**

Supply and Demand: Price Controls (Ceilings and Floors)

In this Module, you will learn to:
- Explain the workings of price controls, one way government intervenes in markets
- Describe how price controls can create problems and make a market inefficient
- Explain why economists are often deeply skeptical of attempts to intervene in markets
- Identify who benefits and who loses from price controls

Why Governments Control Prices

In Module 7, you learned that a market moves to equilibrium—that is, the market price moves to the level at which the quantity supplied equals the quantity demanded. But this equilibrium price does not necessarily please either buyers or sellers.

After all, buyers would always like to pay less if they could, and sometimes they can make a strong moral or political case that they should pay lower prices. For example, what if the equilibrium between supply and demand for apartments in a major city leads to rental rates that an average working person can't afford? In that case, a government might well be under pressure to impose limits on the rents landlords can charge.

Sellers, however, would always like to get more money for what they sell, and sometimes they can make a strong moral or political case that they should receive higher prices. For example, consider the labor market: the price for an hour of a worker's time is called the *wage rate*. What if the equilibrium in the market for less skilled workers leads to wage rates that yield an income below the poverty level? In that case, a government might well be pressured to require employers to pay a rate no lower than some specified minimum wage.

In other words, there is often a strong political demand for governments to intervene in markets. And powerful interests can make a compelling case that a market intervention favoring them is "fair." When a government intervenes to regulate prices, we say that it imposes **price controls**. These controls typically take the form of either an upper limit, a **price ceiling**, or a lower limit, a **price floor**.

Unfortunately, it's not easy to tell a market what to do. As we will now see, when a government tries to legislate prices—whether it legislates them *down* by imposing a price ceiling or *up* by imposing a price floor—there are certain predictable and unpleasant side effects.

We make an important assumption in this Module: the markets in question are efficient before price controls are imposed. Markets can sometimes be inefficient, as is the case, for example, in a market dominated by a *monopolist*, a single seller who has the power to influence the market price. When markets are inefficient, price controls potentially move the market closer to efficiency without necessarily causing problems. In practice, however, price controls often *are* imposed on markets that are efficient—like the New York City apartment market. And so the analysis in this Module applies to many important real-world situations.

Price controls are legal restrictions on how high or low a market price may go. They can take two forms: a **price ceiling**, a maximum price sellers are allowed to charge for a good or service, or a **price floor**, a minimum price buyers are required to pay for a good or service.

S. Greg Panosian/Getty Images

Price Ceilings

Aside from rent control, there are not many price ceilings in the United States today. But at times they have been widespread. Price ceilings are typically imposed during crises—wars, harvest failures, natural disasters—because these events often lead to sudden price increases that hurt many people but produce big gains for a lucky few.

The U.S. government imposed ceilings on many prices during World War II: the war sharply increased demand for raw materials, such as aluminum and steel, and price controls prevented those with access to these raw materials from earning huge profits. Price controls on oil were imposed in 1973, when an embargo by Arab oil-exporting countries seemed likely to generate huge profits for U.S. oil companies. Price controls were imposed on California's wholesale electricity market in 2001, when a shortage created big profits for a few power-generating companies but led to higher electricity bills for consumers.

Believe it or not, rent control in New York is a legacy of World War II: it was imposed because wartime production created an economic boom, which increased demand for apartments at a time when the labor and raw materials that might have been used to build them were being used to win the war instead. Although most price controls were removed soon after the war ended, New York's rent limits were retained and gradually extended to buildings not previously covered, leading to some very strange situations.

You can rent a one-bedroom apartment in Manhattan on fairly short notice—if you are able and willing to pay several thousand dollars a month or live in a less-than-desirable area. Yet some people pay only a small fraction of this amount for comparable apartments, and others pay only slightly more for bigger apartments in better locations.

Aside from producing great deals for some renters, however, what are the broader consequences of New York's rent control system? To answer this question, we turn to the supply and demand model.

How Price Ceilings Cause Inefficiencies

To see what can go wrong when a government imposes a price ceiling on an efficient market, consider **Figure 8.1**, which shows a simplified model of the market for apartments in New York. For the sake of simplicity, we imagine that all apartments are exactly the same and so would rent for the same price in an unregulated market. The table in the figure shows the demand and supply schedules; the demand and supply curves are shown on the left. We show the quantity of apartments on the horizontal axis and the monthly rent per apartment on the vertical axis. You can see that in an unregulated

Figure 8.1 The Market for Apartments in the Absence of Government Controls

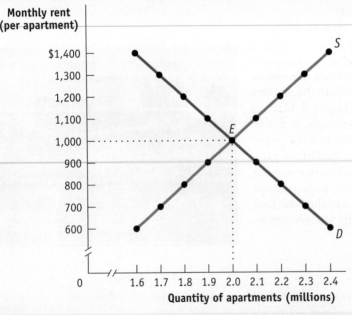

Monthly rent (per apartment)	Quantity of apartments (millions)	
	Quantity demanded	Quantity supplied
$1,400	1.6	2.4
1,300	1.7	2.3
1,200	1.8	2.2
1,100	1.9	2.1
1,000	2.0	2.0
900	2.1	1.9
800	2.2	1.8
700	2.3	1.7
600	2.4	1.6

Without government intervention, the market for apartments reaches equilibrium at point *E* with a market rent of $1,000 per month and 2 million apartments rented.

market the equilibrium would be at point *E*: 2 million apartments would be rented for $1,000 each per month.

Shortages Now suppose that the government imposes a price ceiling, limiting rents to a price below the equilibrium price—say, no more than $800. **Figure 8.2** shows the effect of the price ceiling, represented by the line at $800. At the enforced rental rate of $800, landlords have less incentive to offer apartments, so they won't be willing to supply as many as they would at the equilibrium rate of $1,000. They will choose point *A* on the supply curve, offering only 1.8 million apartments for rent, 200,000 fewer than in the unregulated market. At the same time, more people will want to rent apartments at a price of $800 than at the equilibrium price of $1,000; as shown at point *B* on the demand curve, at a monthly rent of $800 the quantity of apartments demanded rises to 2.2 million, 200,000 more than in the unregulated market and 400,000 more than are actually available at the price of $800. So there is now a persistent shortage of rental housing: at that price, there are 400,000 more people who want to rent than are able to find apartments.

Do price ceilings always cause shortages? No. If a price ceiling is set above the equilibrium price, it won't have any effect. Suppose that the equilibrium rental rate on apartments is $1,000 per month and the city government sets a ceiling of $1,200. Who cares? In this case, the price ceiling won't be binding—it won't actually constrain market behavior—and it will have no effect.

Inefficient Allocation to Consumers Rent control doesn't just lead to a shortage in available apartments. It can also lead to misallocation of the apartments that are available: people who urgently need a place to live may not be able to find an apartment, while some apartments may be occupied by people with much less urgent needs.

In the case shown in Figure 8.2, 2.2 million people would like to rent an apartment at $800 per month, but only 1.8 million apartments are available. Of those 2.2 million who are seeking an apartment, some want an apartment badly and are willing to pay a high price to get one. Others have a less urgent need and are only willing to pay a low price, perhaps because they have alternative housing. An efficient allocation of apartments would reflect these differences: people who really want an apartment will get one and people who aren't all that eager to find an apartment won't. In an inefficient distribution of apartments, the opposite will happen: some people who are not especially

Figure 8.2 The Effects of a Price Ceiling

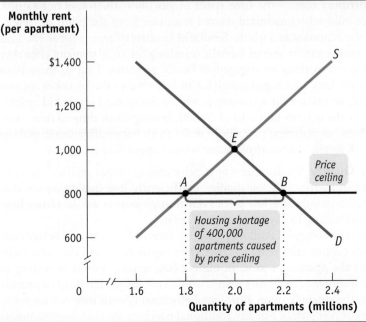

The black horizontal line represents the government-imposed price ceiling on rents of $800 per month. This price ceiling reduces the quantity of apartments supplied to 1.8 million, point *A*, and increases the quantity demanded to 2.2 million, point *B*. This creates a persistent shortage of 400,000 units: 400,000 of the people who want apartments at the legal rent of $800 cannot get them.

Price ceilings often lead to inefficiency in the form of **inefficient allocation to consumers**: people who want the good badly and are willing to pay a high price don't get it, and those who care relatively little about the good and are only willing to pay a relatively low price do get it.

eager to find an apartment will get one and others who are very eager to find an apartment won't. Because people usually get apartments through luck or personal connections under rent control, rent control generally results in an **inefficient allocation to consumers** of the few apartments available.

To see the inefficiency involved, consider the plight of the Lees, a family with young children who have no alternative housing and would be willing to pay up to $1,500 for an apartment—but are unable to find one. Also consider George, a retiree who lives most of the year in Florida but still has a lease on the New York apartment he moved into 40 years ago. George pays $800 per month for this apartment, but if the rent were even slightly more—say, $850—he would give it up and stay with his children when he is in New York.

This allocation of apartments—George has one and the Lees do not—is a missed opportunity: there is a way to make the Lees and George both better off at no additional cost. The Lees would be happy to pay George, say, $1,200 a month to sublease his apartment, which he would happily accept since the apartment is worth no more than $849 a month to him. George would prefer the money he gets from the Lees to keeping his apartment; the Lees would prefer to have the apartment rather than the money. So both would be made better off by this transaction—and nobody else would be made worse off.

Generally, if people who really want apartments could sublease them from people who are less eager to live there, both those who gain apartments and those who trade their occupancy for money would be better off. However, subleasing is illegal under rent control because it would occur at prices above the price ceiling. The fact that subletting is illegal doesn't mean it never happens. In fact, chasing down illegal subletting is a major business for New York private investigators. A report in the *New York Times* described how private investigators use hidden cameras and other tricks to prove that the legal tenants in rent-controlled apartments actually live in the suburbs, or even in other states, and have subleased their apartments at two or three times the controlled rent. Subleasing is a kind of black market activity, which we will discuss shortly. For now, just notice that the aggressive pursuit of illegal subletting surely discourages the practice, so there isn't enough subletting to eliminate the inefficient allocation of apartments.

Price ceilings typically lead to inefficiency in the form of **wasted resources**: people expend money, effort, and time to cope with the shortages caused by the price ceiling.

Wasted Resources Another reason a price ceiling causes inefficiency is that it leads to **wasted resources**: people expend money, effort, and time to cope with the shortages caused by the price ceiling. Back in 1979, U.S. price controls on gasoline led to shortages that forced millions of Americans to spend hours each week waiting in lines at gas stations. The opportunity cost of the time spent in gas lines—the wages not earned, the leisure time not enjoyed—constituted wasted resources from the point of view of consumers and of the economy as a whole. Similarly, because of rent control, the Lees will spend all their spare time for several months searching for an apartment, time they would rather have spent working or engaged in family activities. That is, there is an opportunity cost to the Lees' prolonged search for an apartment—the leisure or income they had to forgo. If the market for apartments worked freely, the Lees would quickly find an apartment at the equilibrium rent of $1,000, leaving them time to earn more or to enjoy themselves—an outcome that would make them better off without making anyone else worse off. Again, rent control creates missed opportunities.

Inefficiently Low Quality Yet another way a price ceiling causes inefficiency is by causing goods to be of inefficiently low quality. **Inefficiently low quality** means that sellers offer low-quality goods at a low price even though buyers would rather have higher quality and are willing to pay a higher price for it.

Price ceilings often lead to inefficiency in that the goods being offered are of **inefficiently low quality**: sellers offer low quality goods at a low price even though buyers would prefer a higher quality at a higher price.

Again, consider rent control. Landlords have no incentive to provide better conditions because they cannot raise rents to cover their repair costs and they can easily find tenants to rent the apartment as is. In many cases, tenants would be willing to pay much more for improved conditions than it would cost for the landlord to provide them—for example, the upgrade of an antiquated electrical system that cannot safely run air conditioners or computers. But any additional payment for such improvements would be legally considered a rent increase, which is prohibited. Indeed, rent-controlled apartments are notoriously badly maintained, rarely painted, subject to frequent electrical and plumbing problems, and sometimes even hazardous to inhabit. As one former manager of Manhattan buildings explained, "At unregulated apartments we'd do most things that the tenants requested. But on the rent-regulated units, we did absolutely only what the law required. . . . We had a perverse incentive to make those tenants unhappy. With regulated apartments, the ultimate objective is to get people out of the building [because rents can be raised for new tenants]."

This whole situation is a missed opportunity—some tenants would be happy to pay for better conditions, and landlords would be happy to provide them for payment. But such an exchange would occur only if the market were allowed to operate freely.

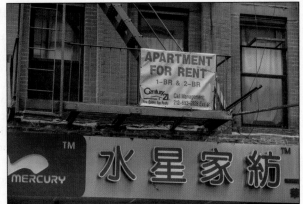

Signs advertising apartments to rent or sublet are common in New York City.

Black Markets And that leads us to a last aspect of price ceilings: the incentive they provide for illegal activities, specifically the emergence of **black markets**. We have already described one kind of black market activity— illegal subletting by tenants. But it does not stop there. Clearly, there is a temptation for a landlord to say to a potential tenant, "Look, you can have this place if you slip me an extra few hundred in cash each month"—and for the tenant to agree, if he or she is one of those people who would be willing to pay much more than the maximum legal rent.

What's wrong with black markets? In general, it's a bad thing if people break *any* law because it encourages disrespect for the law in general. Worse yet, in this case illegal activity worsens the position of those who try to be honest. If the Lees are scrupulous about upholding the rent control law but other people—who may need an apartment less than the Lees—are willing to bribe landlords, the Lees may *never* find an apartment.

A **black market** is a market in which goods or services are bought and sold illegally—either because it is illegal to sell them at all or because the prices charged are legally prohibited by a price ceiling.

So Why Are There Price Ceilings?

We have seen three common results of price ceilings:

- a persistent shortage of the good;
- inefficiency arising from this persistent shortage in the form of inefficiently low quantity, inefficient allocation of the good to consumers, resources wasted in searching for the good, and the inefficiently low quality of the good offered for sale; and
- the emergence of illegal, black market activity.

Given these unpleasant consequences, why do governments still sometimes impose price ceilings? Why does rent control, in particular, persist in New York City?

One answer is that although price ceilings may have adverse effects, they do benefit some people. In practice, New York's rent control rules—which are more complex than our simple model—hurt most residents but give a small minority of renters much cheaper housing than they would get in an unregulated market. And those who benefit from the controls may be better organized and more vocal than those who are harmed by them.

Also, when price ceilings have been in effect for a long time, buyers may not have a realistic idea of what would happen without them. In our previous example, the rental rate in an unregulated market (Figure 8.1) would be only 25% higher than in the regulated market (Figure 8.2): $1,000 instead of $800. But how would renters know that? Indeed, they might have heard about black market transactions at much higher prices— the Lees or some other family paying George $1,200 or more—and would not realize that these black market prices are much higher than the price that would prevail in a fully unregulated market.

A last answer is that government officials often do not understand supply and demand analysis! It is a great mistake to suppose that economic policies in the real world are always sensible or well informed.

> ### AP® EXAM TIP
>
> When it comes to price controls, the ceiling is down low and the floor is up high. That is, to have any effect, a price ceiling must be below the equilibrium price, and a price floor must be above the equilibrium price.

Price Floors

Sometimes governments intervene to push market prices up instead of down. *Price floors* have been widely legislated for agricultural products, such as wheat and milk, as a way to support the incomes of farmers. Historically, there were also price floors on services such as trucking and air travel, although these were phased out by the U.S. government in the 1970s. If you have ever worked in a fast-food restaurant, you are likely to have encountered a price floor: governments in many countries, including the United States, maintain a lower limit on the hourly wage rate paid for a worker's labor—that is, a floor on the price of labor—called the **minimum wage**.

Just like price ceilings, price floors are intended to help some people but generate predictable and undesirable side effects. **Figure 8.3** shows hypothetical supply and demand curves for butter. Left to itself, the market would move to equilibrium at point *E*, with 10 million pounds of butter bought and sold at a price of $1 per pound.

The **minimum wage** is a legal floor on the hourly wage rate paid for a worker's labor.

Figure 8.3 The Market for Butter in the Absence of Government Controls

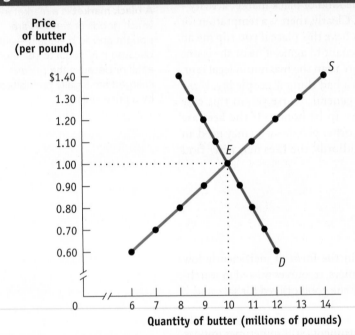

Price of butter (per pound)	Quantity of butter (millions of pounds)	
	Quantity demanded	Quantity supplied
$1.40	8.0	14.0
1.30	8.5	13.0
1.20	9.0	12.0
1.10	9.5	11.0
1.00	10.0	10.0
0.90	10.5	9.0
0.80	11.0	8.0
0.70	11.5	7.0
0.60	12.0	6.0

Without government intervention, the market for butter reaches equilibrium at a price of $1 per pound with 10 million pounds of butter bought and sold.

Now suppose that the government, in order to help dairy farmers, imposes a price floor on butter of $1.20 per pound. Its effects are shown in **Figure 8.4**, where the line at $1.20 represents the price floor. At a price of $1.20 per pound, producers would want to supply 12 million pounds (point *B* on the supply curve) but consumers would want to buy only 9 million pounds (point *A* on the demand curve). So the price floor leads to a persistent surplus of 3 million pounds of butter.

Does a price floor always lead to an unwanted surplus? No. Just as in the case of a price ceiling, the floor may not be binding—that is, it may be irrelevant. If the equilibrium price of butter is $1 per pound but the floor is set at only $0.80, the floor has no effect.

But suppose that a price floor *is* binding: what happens to the unwanted surplus? The answer depends on government policy. In the case of agricultural price floors, governments buy up unwanted surplus. For example, the U.S. government has at times found itself warehousing thousands of tons of butter, cheese, and other farm products.

Figure 8.4 The Effects of a Price Floor

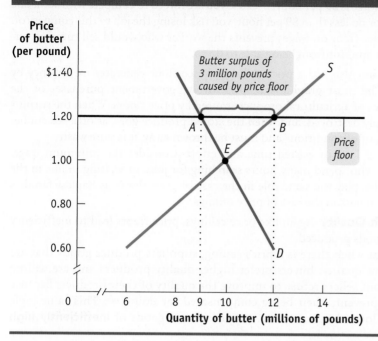

The dark horizontal line represents the government-imposed price floor of $1.20 per pound of butter. The quantity of butter demanded falls to 9 million pounds, and the quantity supplied rises to 12 million pounds, generating a persistent surplus of 3 million pounds of butter.

(The European Commission, which administers price floors for a number of European countries, once found itself the owner of a so-called butter mountain, equal in weight to the entire population of Austria.) The government then has to find a way to dispose of these unwanted goods.

Some countries pay exporters to sell products at a loss overseas; this is standard procedure for the European Union. The United States gives surplus food away to schools, which use the products in school lunches. In some cases, governments have actually destroyed the surplus production. To avoid the problem of dealing with the unwanted surplus, the U.S. government typically pays farmers not to produce the products at all.

When the government is not prepared to purchase the unwanted surplus, a price floor means that would-be sellers cannot find buyers. This is what happens when there is a price floor on the wage rate paid for an hour of labor, the *minimum wage*: when the minimum wage is above the equilibrium wage rate, some people who are willing to work—that is, sell labor—cannot find employers who want to hire them—that is, buy labor. The result is *unemployment*—a surplus of workers in the market.

How a Price Floor Causes Inefficiency

The persistent surplus that results from a price floor creates missed opportunities—inefficiencies—that resemble those created by the shortage that results from a price ceiling.

Inefficiently Low Quantity Because a price floor raises the price of a good to consumers, it reduces the quantity of that good demanded; because sellers can't sell more units of a good than buyers are willing to buy, a price floor reduces the quantity of a good bought and sold below the market equilibrium quantity. Notice that this is the *same* effect as a price ceiling. You might be tempted to think that a price floor and a price ceiling have opposite effects, but both have the effect of reducing the quantity of a good bought and sold.

Inefficient Allocation of Sales Among Sellers Like a price ceiling, a price floor can lead to *inefficient allocation*—but in this case **inefficient allocation of sales among sellers** rather than inefficient allocation to consumers.

Price floors lead to **inefficient allocation of sales among sellers**: those who would be willing to sell the good at the lowest price are not always those who manage to sell it.

Suppose you would be willing to sell your English tutoring services for $5 per hour, but the minimum wage is $9 per hour. Because you are forced to compete with someone who would tutor for no less than $9 per hour, you risk losing the job to this competitor. In this case, the price floor on wages prevents the worker who would sell tutoring services for the lowest amount from being able to do so.

Wasted Resources Also like a price ceiling, a price floor generates inefficiency by *wasting resources*. The most graphic examples involve government purchases of the unwanted surpluses of agricultural products caused by price floors. When the surplus production is simply destroyed, and when the stored produce goes, as officials euphemistically put it, "out of condition" and must be thrown away, it is pure waste.

Price floors also lead to wasted time and effort. Consider the minimum wage. Would-be workers who spend many hours searching for jobs, or waiting in line in the hope of getting jobs, play the same role in the case of price floors as hapless families searching for apartments in the case of price ceilings.

Inefficiently High Quality Again like price ceilings, price floors lead to inefficiency in the quality of goods produced.

We've seen that when there is a price ceiling, suppliers produce goods that are of inefficiently low quality: buyers prefer higher-quality products and are willing to pay for them, but sellers refuse to improve the quality of their products because the price ceiling prevents their being compensated for doing so. This same logic applies to price floors, but in reverse: suppliers offer goods of **inefficiently high quality**.

Price floors often lead to inefficiency in that goods of **inefficiently high quality** are offered: sellers offer high-quality goods at a high price, even though buyers would prefer a lower quality at a lower price.

How can this be? Isn't high quality a good thing? Yes, but only if it is worth the cost. Suppose that suppliers spend a lot of money to make goods of very high quality but that this level of quality isn't worth much to consumers, who would rather receive the money spent on that quality in the form of a lower price. This represents a missed opportunity: suppliers and buyers could make a mutually beneficial deal in which buyers got goods of lower quality for a much lower price.

A good example of the inefficiency of high quality comes from the days when transatlantic airfares were set artificially high by international treaty. Forbidden to compete for customers by offering lower ticket prices, airlines instead offered expensive services, like lavish in-flight meals that went largely uneaten. At one point the regulators tried to restrict this practice by defining maximum service standards—for example, that snack service should consist of no more than a sandwich. One airline then introduced what it called a "Scandinavian Sandwich," a towering affair that forced regulators to convene another conference to define *sandwich*. All of this was wasteful, especially considering that what passengers really wanted was less food and lower airfares.

Since the deregulation of U.S. airlines in the 1970s, passengers have experienced a large decrease in ticket prices accompanied by a decrease in the quality of in-flight service—smaller seats, lower-quality food, and so on. Everyone complains about the service—but thanks to lower fares, the number of people flying on U.S. carriers has grown several hundred percent since airline deregulation.

Illegal Activity Finally, like price ceilings, price floors provide incentives for illegal activity. For example, in countries where the minimum wage is far above the equilibrium wage rate, workers desperate for jobs sometimes agree to work off the books for employers who conceal their employment from the government—or bribe the government inspectors. This practice, known in Europe as "black labor," is especially common in southern European countries such as Italy and Spain.

Matej Kastelic/Alamy

So Why Are There Price Floors?

To sum up, a price floor creates various negative side effects:

- a persistent surplus of the good;
- inefficiency arising from the persistent surplus in the form of inefficiently low quantity, inefficient allocation of sales among sellers, wasted resources, and an inefficiently high level of quality offered by suppliers; and
- the temptation to engage in illegal activity, particularly bribery and corruption of government officials.

So why do governments impose price floors when they have so many negative side effects? The reasons are similar to those for imposing price ceilings. Government officials often disregard warnings about the consequences of price floors either because they believe that the relevant market is poorly described by the supply and demand model or, more often, because they do not understand the model. Above all, just as price ceilings are often imposed because they benefit some influential buyers of a good, price floors are often imposed because they benefit some influential sellers.

MODULE 8 REVIEW

Check Your Understanding

1. On game days, homeowners near Middletown University's stadium used to rent parking spaces in their driveways to fans at a going rate of $11. A new town ordinance now sets a maximum parking fee of $7. Use the accompanying supply and demand diagram to show how each of the following can result from the price ceiling.

Parking fee (y-axis): $15, 11, 7, 3
Quantity of parking spaces (x-axis): 0, 3,200, 3,600, 4,000, 4,400, 4,800

a. Some homeowners now think it's not worth the hassle to rent out spaces.
b. Some fans who used to carpool to the game now drive alone.

c. Some fans can't find parking and leave without seeing the game.

Explain how each of the following adverse effects arises from the price ceiling.

d. Some fans now arrive several hours early to find parking.
e. Friends of homeowners near the stadium regularly attend games, even if they aren't big fans. But some serious fans have given up because of the parking situation.
f. Some homeowners rent spaces for more than $7 but pretend that the buyers are nonpaying friends or family.

2. True or false? Explain your answer. A price ceiling below the equilibrium price in an otherwise efficient market
   a. increases quantity supplied.
   b. makes some people who want to consume the good worse off.
   c. makes all producers worse off.

3. The state legislature mandates a price floor for gasoline of P_F per gallon. Assess the following statements and illustrate your answer using the figure provided.

a. Proponents of the law claim it will increase the income of gas station owners. Opponents claim it will hurt gas station owners because they will lose customers.

b. Proponents claim consumers will be better off because gas stations will provide better service. Opponents claim consumers will be generally worse off because they prefer to buy gas at cheaper prices.

c. Proponents claim that they are helping gas station owners without hurting anyone else. Opponents claim that consumers are hurt and will end up doing things like buying gas in a nearby state or on the black market.

TACKLE THE AP® TEST: Multiple-Choice Questions

1. A price ceiling
   a. is an example of a price control.
   b. is intended to decrease price below the equilibrium.
   c. was established in New York City after World War II.
   d. benefits some consumers.
   e. is all of the above.

2. An effective minimum wage law
   a. is an example of a price ceiling.
   b. benefits all workers.
   c. reduces the quantity of labor supplied.
   d. reduces the quantity of labor demanded.
   e. is all of the above.

3. To be effective, a price ceiling must be set
   a. above the equilibrium price.
   b. below the equilibrium price.
   c. equal to the equilibrium price.
   d. by the federal government.
   e. on the market for housing.

4. Refer to the graph provided. A price floor set at $5 will result in

   a. a shortage of 100 units.
   b. a surplus of 100 units.
   c. a shortage of 200 units.
   d. a surplus of 200 units.
   e. a surplus of 50 units.

5. Effective price ceilings are inefficient because they
   a. create shortages.
   b. lead to wasted resources.
   c. decrease quality.
   d. create black markets.
   e. do all of the above.

Use the graph provided to answer questions 6 and 7.

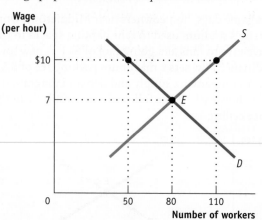

6. If the government establishes a minimum wage at $10, how many workers will benefit from the higher wage?
   a. 30   **d.** 80
   b. 50   **e.** 110
   c. 60

7. With a minimum wage of $10, how many workers are unemployed (would like to work, but are unable to find a job)?
   a. 30   **d.** 80
   b. 50   **e.** 110
   c. 60

TACKLE THE AP® TEST: Free-Response Questions

1. Refer to the graph provided to answer the following questions.

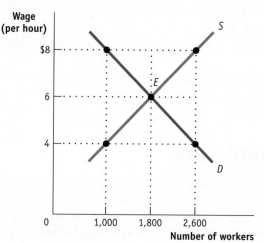

a. What are the equilibrium wage and quantity of workers in this market?

b. For it to have an effect, where would the government have to set a minimum wage?

c. If the government set a minimum wage at $8,

   i. how many workers would supply their labor?

   ii. how many workers would be hired?

   iii. how many workers would want to work that did *not* want to work for the equilibrium wage?

   iv. how many previously employed workers would no longer have a job?

Rubric for FRQ 1 (6 points)

1 point: equilibrium wage = $6, quantity of labor = 1,800

1 point: The minimum wage will have an effect if it is set anywhere above $6.

1 point: 2,600 workers would supply their labor

1 point: 1,000 workers would be hired

1 point: 800 (the number of workers who would want to work for $8 but did not supply labor for $6)

1 point: 800 (at the equilibrium wage of $6, 1,800 workers were hired; at a wage of $8, 1,000 workers would be hired. 1,800 − 1,000 = 800)

---

2. Draw a correctly labeled graph of a housing market in equilibrium. On your graph, illustrate an effective legal limit (ceiling) on rent. Identify the quantity of housing demanded, the quantity of housing supplied, and the size of the resulting surplus or shortage. **(6 points)**

Supply and Demand: Quantity Controls

> **In this Module, you will learn to:**
> - Explain the workings of quantity controls, another way government intervenes in markets
> - Describe how quantity controls create problems and can make a market inefficient
> - Explain who benefits and who loses from quantity controls

Controlling Quantities

In the 1930s, New York City instituted a system of licensing for taxicabs: only taxis with a "medallion" were allowed to pick up passengers. Because this system was intended to ensure quality, medallion owners were supposed to maintain certain standards, including safety and cleanliness. A total of 11,787 medallions were issued when this program began, with taxi owners paying $10 for each medallion.

In 1995, there were still only 11,787 licensed taxicabs in New York, even though the city had meanwhile become the financial capital of the world, a place where hundreds of thousands of people in a hurry tried to hail a cab every day. (An additional 400 medallions were issued in 1995; after several rounds of sales of additional medallions, in 2017 there were approximately 13,587 medallions.) The result of this restriction on the number of taxis was that a New York City taxi medallion became very valuable: if you wanted to operate a taxi in New York, you had to lease a medallion from someone else or buy one for a going price of several hundred thousand dollars. Prices for taxi medallions topped $1 million at their height, but as we discuss below, innovations in ride sharing in recent years has significantly impacted their value—an unintended consequence of quantity control.

A **quantity control**, or **quota**, is an upper limit on the quantity of some good that can be bought or sold.

A **license** gives its owner the right to supply a good or service.

A taxi medallion system is a form of **quantity control**, or **quota**, by which the government regulates the quantity of a good that can be bought and sold rather than regulating the price. Typically, the government limits quantity in a market by issuing **licenses**; only people with a license can legally supply the good. A taxi medallion is just such a license. The government of New York City limits the number of taxi rides that can be sold by limiting the number of taxis to only those who hold medallions. There are many other cases of quantity controls, ranging from limits on how much foreign currency (for instance, British pounds or Mexican pesos) people are allowed to buy to the quantity of clams New Jersey fishing boats are allowed to catch. Section 8 discusses quotas on goods imported from other countries.

Some attempts to control quantities are undertaken for good economic reasons, some for bad ones. In many cases, as we will see, quantity controls introduced to address a temporary problem become politically hard to remove later because the beneficiaries don't want them abolished, even after the original reason for their existence is long gone. But whatever the reasons for such controls, they have certain predictable—and usually undesirable—economic consequences.

The Anatomy of Quantity Controls

To understand why a New York taxi medallion has value, we consider a simplified version of the market for taxi rides, shown in **Figure 9.1**. Just as we assumed in the analysis of rent control that all apartments were the same, we now suppose that all taxi rides are the same—ignoring the real-world complication that some taxi rides are longer, and therefore more expensive, than others. The table in the figure shows supply and demand schedules. The equilibrium—indicated by point *E*

Figure 9.1 The Market for Taxi Rides in the Absence of Government Controls

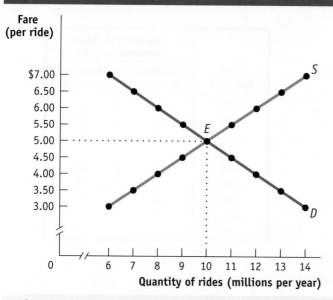

Fare (per ride)	Quantity of rides (millions per year)	
	Quantity demanded	Quantity supplied
$7.00	6	14
6.50	7	13
6.00	8	12
5.50	9	11
5.00	10	10
4.50	11	9
4.00	12	8
3.50	13	7
3.00	14	6

Without government intervention, the market reaches equilibrium with 10 million rides taken per year at a fare of $5 per ride.

in the figure and by the shaded entries in the table—is a fare of $5 per ride, with 10 million rides taken per year. (You'll see in a minute why we present the equilibrium this way.)

The New York medallion system limits the number of taxis, but each taxi driver can offer as many rides as he or she can manage. (Now you know why New York taxi drivers are so aggressive!) To simplify our analysis, however, we will assume that a medallion system limits the number of taxi rides that can legally be given to 8 million per year.

Until now, we have derived the demand curve by answering questions of the form: "How many taxi rides will passengers want to take if the price is $5 per ride?" But it is possible to reverse the question and ask instead: "At what price will consumers want to buy 10 million rides per year?" The price at which consumers want to buy a given quantity—in this case, 10 million rides at $5 per ride—is the **demand price** of that quantity. You can see from the demand schedule in Figure 9.1 that the demand price of 6 million rides is $7 per ride, the demand price of 7 million rides is $6.50 per ride, and so on.

Similarly, the supply curve represents the answer to questions of the form: "How many taxi rides would taxi drivers supply at a price of $5 each?" But we can also reverse this question to ask: "At what price will producers be willing to supply 10 million rides per year?" The price at which producers will supply a given quantity—in this case, 10 million rides at $5 per ride—is the **supply price** of that quantity. We can see from the supply schedule in Figure 9.1 that the supply price of 6 million rides is $3 per ride, the supply price of 7 million rides is $3.50 per ride, and so on.

Now we are ready to analyze a quota. We have assumed that the city government limits the quantity of taxi rides to 8 million per year. Medallions, each of which carries the right to provide a certain number of taxi rides per year, are made available to selected people in such a way that a total of 8 million rides will be provided. Medallion holders may then either drive their own taxis or rent their medallions to others for a fee.

Figure 9.2 shows the resulting market for taxi rides, with the black vertical line at 8 million rides per year representing the quota. Because the quantity of rides is limited to 8 million, consumers must be at point A on the demand curve, corresponding to the shaded entry in the demand schedule: the demand price of 8 million rides is

Ann Heath

The **demand price** of a given quantity is the price at which consumers will demand that quantity.

The **supply price** of a given quantity is the price at which producers will supply that quantity.

Figure 9.2　Effect of a Quota on the Market for Taxi Rides

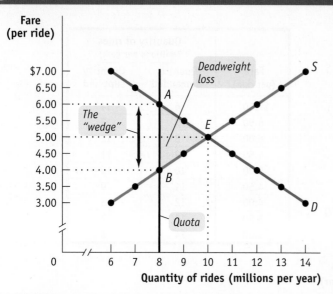

Fare (per ride)	Quantity of rides (millions per year)	
	Quantity demanded	Quantity supplied
$7.00	6	14
6.50	7	13
6.00	8	12
5.50	9	11
5.00	10	10
4.50	11	9
4.00	12	8
3.50	13	7
3.00	14	6

The table shows the demand price and the supply price corresponding to each quantity: the price at which that quantity would be demanded and supplied, respectively. The city government imposes a quota of 8 million rides by selling enough medallions for only 8 million rides, represented by the black vertical line. The price paid by consumers rises to $6 per ride, the demand price of 8 million rides, shown by point A.

The supply price of 8 million rides is only $4 per ride, shown by point B. The difference between these two prices is the quota rent per ride, the earnings that accrue to the owner of a medallion. The quota rent drives a wedge between the demand price and the supply price. Because the quota discourages mutually beneficial transactions, it creates a *deadweight loss* equal to the shaded triangle.

AP® EXAM TIP

You won't have to draw the quota graph on the AP® exam, but you will have to understand the implications of quotas on quantity and deadweight loss. Drawing a quick graph will lead you to relevant answers. Start with a market in equilibrium. Add a vertical line to the left of the equilibrium quantity to illustrate a quota (note: a quota to the right of equilibrium quantity will have no effect). Where the quota line crosses the demand and supply curves gives you the demand and supply prices. The deadweight loss is the triangle to the right of the "wedge" between these prices, below the demand curve, and above the supply curve.

$6 per ride. Meanwhile, taxi drivers must be at point B on the supply curve, corresponding to the shaded entry in the supply schedule: the supply price of 8 million rides is $4 per ride.

But how can the price received by taxi drivers be $4 when the price paid by taxi riders is $6? The answer is that in addition to the market in taxi rides, there is also a market in medallions. Medallion-holders may not always want to drive their taxis: they may be ill or on vacation. Those who do not want to drive their own taxis will sell the right to use the medallion to someone else. So we need to consider two sets of transactions here, and so two prices: (1) the transactions in taxi rides and the price at which these will occur and (2) the transactions in medallions and the price at which these will occur. It turns out that since we are looking at two markets, the $4 and $6 prices will both be right.

To see how all of this works, consider two imaginary New York taxi drivers, Sunil and Harriet. Sunil has a medallion but can't use it because he's recovering from a severely sprained wrist. So he's looking to rent his medallion out to someone else. Harriet doesn't have a medallion but would like to rent one. Furthermore, at any point in time there are many other people like Harriet who would like to rent a medallion. Suppose Sunil agrees to rent his medallion to Harriet. To make things simple, assume that any driver can give only one ride per day and that Sunil is renting his medallion to Harriet for one day. What rental price will they agree on?

To answer this question, we need to look at the transactions from the viewpoints of both drivers. Once she has the medallion, Harriet knows she can make $6 per day—the demand price of a ride under the quota. And she is willing to rent the medallion only if she makes at least $4 per day—the supply price of a ride under the quota. So Sunil cannot demand a rent of more than $2—the difference between $6 and $4. And if Harriet offered Sunil less than $2—say, $1.50—there would be other eager drivers willing to offer him more, up to $2. So, in order to get the medallion, Harriet must offer Sunil at least $2. Since the rent can be no more than $2 and no less than $2, it must be exactly $2.

It is no coincidence that $2 is exactly the difference between $6, the demand price of 8 million rides, and $4, the supply price of 8 million rides. In every case in which the supply of a good is legally restricted, there is a **wedge** between the demand price of the quantity transacted and the supply price of the quantity transacted. This wedge, illustrated by the double-headed arrow in Figure 9.2, has a special name: the **quota rent**. It is the earnings that accrue to the medallion holder from ownership of a valuable commodity, the medallion. In the case of Sunil and Harriet, the quota rent of $2 goes to Sunil because he owns the medallion, and the remaining $4 from the total fare of $6 goes to Harriet.

So Figure 9.2 also illustrates the quota rent in the market for New York taxi rides. The quota limits the quantity of rides to 8 million per year, a quantity at which the demand price of $6 exceeds the supply price of $4. The wedge between these two prices, $2, is the quota rent that results from the restrictions placed on the quantity of taxi rides in this market.

But wait a second. What if Sunil doesn't rent out his medallion? What if he uses it himself? Doesn't this mean that he gets a price of $6? No, not really. Even if Sunil doesn't rent out his medallion, he could have rented it out, which means that the medallion has an *opportunity cost* of $2: if Sunil decides to use his own medallion and drive his own taxi rather than renting his medallion to Harriet, the $2 represents his opportunity cost of not renting out his medallion. That is, the $2 quota rent is now the rental income he forgoes by driving his own taxi. In effect, Sunil is in two businesses—the taxi-driving business and the medallion-renting business. He makes $4 per ride from driving his taxi and $2 per ride from renting out his medallion. It doesn't make any difference that in this particular case he has rented his medallion to himself! So regardless of whether the medallion owner uses the medallion himself or herself, or rents it to others, it is a valuable asset. And this is represented in the going price for a New York City taxi medallion. Notice, by the way, that quotas—like price ceilings and price floors—don't always have a real effect. If the quota were set at 12 million rides—that is, above the equilibrium quantity in an unregulated market—it would have no effect because it would not be binding.

The Costs of Quantity Controls

Like price controls, quantity controls can have some predictable and undesirable side effects. The first is the by-now-familiar problem of inefficiency due to missed opportunities: quantity controls prevent mutually beneficial transactions from occurring, transactions that would benefit both buyers and sellers. Looking back at Figure 9.2, you can see that starting at the quota of 8 million rides, New Yorkers would be willing to pay at least $5.50 per ride for an additional 1 million rides and that taxi drivers would be willing to provide those rides as long as they got at least $4.50 per ride. These are rides that would have taken place if there had been no quota. The same is true for the next 1 million rides: New Yorkers would be willing to pay at least $5 per ride when the quantity of rides is increased from 9 to 10 million, and taxi drivers would be willing to provide those rides as long as they got at least $5 per ride. Again, these rides would have occurred without the quota. Only when the market has reached the unregulated market equilibrium quantity of 10 million rides are there no "missed-opportunity rides"—the quota of 8 million rides has caused 2 million "missed-opportunity rides." A buyer would be willing to buy the good at a price that the seller would be willing to accept, but such a transaction does not occur because it is forbidden by the quota. Economists have a special term for the lost gains from missed opportunities such as these: **deadweight loss**. Generally, when the demand price exceeds the supply price, there is a deadweight loss. Figure 9.2 illustrates the deadweight loss with a shaded triangle between the demand and supply curves. This triangle represents the missed gains from taxi rides

A quantity control, or quota, drives a **wedge** between the demand price and the supply price of a good; that is, the price paid by buyers ends up being higher than that received by sellers. The difference between the demand and supply price at the quota amount is the **quota rent,** the earnings that accrue to the license-holder from ownership of the right to sell the good. It is equal to the market price of the license when the licenses are traded.

Deadweight loss is the value of forgone mutually beneficial transactions.

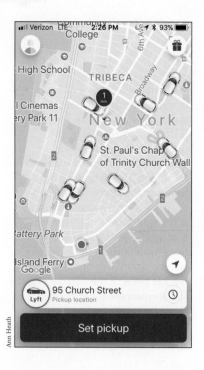
Ann Heath

prevented by the quota, a loss that is experienced by both disappointed would-be riders and frustrated would-be drivers.

Because there are transactions that people would like to make but are not allowed to, quantity controls generate an incentive to get around or even break the law. Taxi regulation applies only to those drivers who are hailed by passengers on the street. A car service that makes prearranged pickups does not need a medallion. This distinction gives an advantage to ride-sharing services, such as Uber and Lyft, that compete with taxis to provide rides. Ride-sharing services allow registered individuals to provide ride services using their own vehicles. Between 2006 and 2016, New York City taxi trips fell by more than 100,000 per month as the number of cars connected with Uber grew to over 46,000, and taxi fares fell by almost 4%. Taxis are still subject to regulations that don't apply to the new ride-sharing services, while the increased competition has reduced taxi fares. As a result, many medallion owners are finding it increasingly difficult to make a profit, and the value of taxi medallions has fallen from a high of $1.3 million just a few years ago to under $250,000 in 2017.

In the previous Module, we saw price controls result in black market activity. Here we see quantity controls lead to innovation in the market for taxi rides that diminishes the value of taxi medallions. The examples in these Modules illustrate that it is difficult for government to control market forces—and attempts to implement price and quantity controls lead to predictable—and often undesirable—consequences.

MODULE 9 REVIEW

Check Your Understanding

1. Suppose that the supply and demand for taxi rides is given by Figure 9.1 and a quota is set at 6 million rides. Replicate the graph from Figure 9.1, and identify each of the following on your graph:
   a. the price of a ride
   b. the quota rent
   c. the deadweight loss resulting from the quota.
   Suppose the quota on taxi rides is increased to 9 million.
   d. What happens to the quota rent and the deadweight loss?

2. Again replicate the graph from Figure 9.1. Suppose that the quota is 8 million rides and that demand decreases due to a decline in tourism. Show on your graph the smallest parallel leftward shift in demand that would result in the quota no longer having an effect on the market.

TACKLE THE AP® TEST: Multiple-Choice Questions

1. Which of the following gives its owner the right to supply a good or service?
   a. a quota
   b. a license
   c. a supply price
   d. a wedge
   e. paying the quota rent

2. Which of the following leads to efficiency in a market?
   a. a price ceiling
   b. a price floor
   c. a quantity control
   d. a quota
   e. none of the above

Refer to the graph provided for Questions 3–5.

3. If the government established a quota of 1,000 in this market, the demand price would be
   a. less than $4.
   b. $4.
   c. $6.
   d. $8.
   e. more than $8.

4. If the government established a quota of 1,000 in this market, the supply price would be
   a. less than $4.   d. $8.
   b. $4.   e. more than $8.
   c. $6.

5. If the government established a quota of 1,000 in this market, the quota rent would be
   a. $2.   d. $8.
   b. $4.   e. more than $8.
   c. $6.

6. Binding quotas lead to which of the following?
   a. inefficiency due to missed opportunities
   b. incentives to evade or break the law
   c. a shortage in the market
   d. deadweight loss
   e. all of the above

7. Which of the following would decrease the effect a quota has on the quantity sold in a market?
   a. decrease in demand
   b. increase in supply
   c. increase in demand
   d. price ceiling above the equilibrium price
   e. none of the above

TACKLE THE AP® TEST: Free-Response Questions

1. Draw a correctly labeled graph illustrating hypothetical supply and demand curves for the U.S. automobile market. Label the equilibrium price and quantity. Suppose the government institutes a quota to limit automobile production. Draw a vertical line labeled "$Q_{ineffective}$" to show the level of a quota that would have no effect on the market. Draw a vertical line labeled "$Q_{effective}$" to show the level of a quota that would have an effect on the market. Shade in and label the deadweight loss resulting from the effective quota.

Rubric for the FRQ (5 points)

1 point: Correctly labeled supply and demand diagram (vertical axis labeled "Price" or "P," horizontal axis labeled "Quantity" or "Q," upward-sloping supply curve with label, downward-sloping demand curve with label)

1 point: Equilibrium at the intersection of supply and demand with the equilibrium price labeled on the vertical axis and the equilibrium quantity labeled on the horizontal axis

1 point: Vertical line to the right of equilibrium quantity labeled $Q_{ineffective}$

1 point: Vertical line to the left of equilibrium quantity labeled $Q_{effective}$

1 point: The triangle to the right of the effective quota line and to the left of supply and demand curves shaded in and labeled as the deadweight loss

2. Draw a correctly labeled graph of the market for taxicab rides. On the graph, draw and label a vertical line showing the level of an effective quota. Label the demand price, the supply price, and the quota rent. **(6 points)**

Module 5

1. The **supply and demand model** illustrates how a **competitive market**, one with many buyers and sellers of the same product, works.

2. The **demand schedule** shows the **quantity demanded** at each price and is represented graphically by a **demand curve**. The **law of demand** says that demand curves slope downward, meaning that as price decreases, the quantity demanded increases.

3. A **movement along the demand curve** occurs when the price changes and causes a change in the quantity demanded. When economists talk of **changes in demand**, they mean shifts of the demand curve—a

change in the quantity demanded at any given price. An increase in demand causes a rightward shift of the demand curve. A decrease in demand causes a leftward shift.

4. There are five main factors that shift the demand curve:
   - a change in tastes
   - a change in the prices of related goods, such as **substitutes** or **complements**
   - a change in income: when income rises, the demand for **normal goods** increases and the demand for **inferior goods** decreases
   - a change in expectations

Module 6

5. The **supply schedule** shows the **quantity supplied** at each price and is represented graphically by a **supply curve**. According to the **law of supply**, supply curves slope upward, meaning that as price increases, the quantity demanded increases.

6. A **movement along the supply curve** occurs when the price changes and causes a change in the quantity supplied. When economists talk of **changes in supply**, they mean shifts of the supply curve—a change in

the quantity supplied at any given price. An increase in supply causes a rightward shift of the supply curve. A decrease in supply causes a leftward shift.

7. There are five main factors that shift the supply curve:
   - a change in **input** prices
   - a change in the prices of related goods and services
   - a change in expectations
   - a change in the number of producers
   - a change in technology

Module 7

8. An economic situation is in **equilibrium** when no individual would be better off doing something different. The supply and demand model is based on the principle that the price in a market moves to its **equilibrium price**, or market-clearing price, the price at which the quantity demanded is equal to the quantity supplied. This quantity is the **equilibrium quantity**. When the price is above its market-clearing level, there is a **surplus** that pushes the price down. When the price is below its market-clearing level, there is a **shortage** that pushes the price up.

9. An increase in demand increases both the equilibrium price and the equilibrium quantity; a decrease in

demand has the opposite effect. An increase in supply reduces the equilibrium price and increases the equilibrium quantity; a decrease in supply has the opposite effect.

10. Shifts of the demand curve and the supply curve can happen simultaneously. When they shift in opposite directions, the change in price is predictable but the change in quantity is not. When they shift in the same direction, the change in quantity is predictable but the change in price is not. In general, the curve that shifts the greater distance has a greater effect on the changes in price and quantity.

Module 8

11. Even when a market is efficient, governments often intervene to pursue greater fairness or to please a powerful interest group. Interventions can take the form of **price controls** or quantity controls (quotas), both of which generate predictable and undesirable side effects, consisting of various forms of inefficiency and illegal activity.

12. A **price ceiling**, a maximum market price below the equilibrium price, benefits successful buyers but creates persistent shortages. Because the price is maintained below the equilibrium price, the quantity demanded is increased and the quantity supplied is decreased compared to the equilibrium quantity. This leads to predictable problems, including **inefficient allocation**

to consumers, **wasted resources**, and **inefficiently low quality**. It also encourages illegal activity as people turn to **black markets** to get the good. Because of these problems, price ceilings have generally lost favor as an economic policy tool. But some governments continue to impose them either because they don't understand the effects or because the price ceilings benefit some influential group.

13. A **price floor**, a minimum market price above the equilibrium price, benefits successful sellers but creates a

persistent surplus: because the price is maintained above the equilibrium price, the quantity demanded is decreased and the quantity supplied is increased compared to the equilibrium quantity. This leads to predictable problems: inefficiencies in the form of **inefficient allocation of sales among sellers**, wasted resources, and **inefficiently high quality**. It also encourages illegal activity and black markets. The most well-known kind of price floor is the **minimum wage**, but price floors are also commonly applied to agricultural products.

Module 9

14. **Quantity controls**, or **quotas**, limit the quantity of a good that can be bought or sold. The government issues **licenses** to individuals, the right to sell a given quantity of the good. The owner of a license earns a **quota rent**, earnings that accrue from ownership of the right to sell the good. It is equal to the difference between the **demand price** at the quota amount, what consumers are willing to pay for that amount, and the **supply price** at the quota

amount, what suppliers are willing to accept for that amount. Economists say that a quota drives a **wedge** between the demand price and the supply price; this wedge is equal to the **quota rent**. By limiting mutually beneficial transactions, quantity controls generate inefficiency. Like price controls, quantity controls lead to **deadweight loss** and encourage innovation or illegal activity.

Key Terms

AP® Exam Practice Questions

Multiple-Choice Questions

1. Which of the following changes will most likely result in an increase in the demand for hamburgers in your hometown?

   a. The price of hot dogs decreases.

   b. The price of drinks sold at hamburger restaurants increases.

   c. Income in your town decreases and hamburgers are a normal good.

   d. The local newspaper publishes a story on health problems caused by red meat.

   e. The number of vegetarians in your town decreases and the population size remains the same.

2. Which of the following changes will most likely result in a decrease in the supply of guitars?
   a. The popularity of guitar music increases.
   b. Consumer incomes decrease.
   c. A new firm enters the guitar industry.
   d. The guitar-making process is reengineered to be more efficient.
   e. The wages of guitar makers increase.

3. Which of the following will most likely result in a decrease in the quantity of lemons demanded?
   a. an increase in the price of lemons
   b. an increase in the price of limes
   c. an increase in the price of lemonade
   d. an increase in the number of lemonade stands
   e. a decrease in consumer income

4. Which of the following will occur if consumer incomes increase?
   a. The demand for inferior goods will increase.
   b. The demand for normal goods will increase.
   c. The demand for all goods will increase.
   d. The demand for normal goods will decrease.
   e. The demand for all goods will decrease.

5. If two goods are complements, an increase in the price of one good will cause which of the following?
   a. a decrease in the demand for the other
   b. a decrease in the quantity demanded of the other
   c. an increase in the demand for the other
   d. an increase in the quantity demanded of the other
   e. no change in the demand for the other

6. An increase in the wages of workers producing a good will most likely lead to which of the following?
   a. a decrease in the quantity of the good supplied
   b. a decrease in the supply of the good
   c. an increase in the quantity of the good supplied
   d. an increase in the supply of the good
   e. no change in the supply of the good

7. Which of the following is true at the equilibrium price in a market?
   a. Consumers who purchase the good may be better off buying something else instead.
   b. The market has not yet cleared.
   c. There is a tendency for the price to decrease over time.

d. There may be either a surplus or a shortage of the good.
e. The quantity demanded of the good equals the quantity supplied.

8. A survey indicated that chocolate is America's favorite ice cream flavor. Which of the following will lead to a decrease in the price of chocolate ice cream?
   a. A drought in the Midwest causes farmers to reduce the number of dairy cows they raise.
   b. A new report from the American Medical Association concludes that chocolate has significant health benefits.
   c. The price of vanilla ice cream increases.
   d. New freezer technology lowers the cost of producing ice cream.
   e. The price of ice cream toppings decreases.

9. Which of the following events will increase both the price and the quantity of pizza?
   a. The price of mozzarella cheese increases.
   b. New health hazards of eating pizza are widely publicized.
   c. The price of pizza ovens rises.
   d. Consumers expect the price of pizza to fall next week.
   e. Consumer income falls and pizza is an inferior good.

Use the following situation and diagram to answer Questions 10–15.

For the last 70 years, the U.S. government has used price supports to provide income assistance to U.S. farmers. At times, the government has used price floors, which it maintains by buying up the surplus farm products. At other times, it has used target prices, giving the farmer an amount equal to the difference between the market price and the target price for each unit sold.

10. What are the equilibrium price and quantity in the market for corn?

Price	Quantity
a. $1	800
b. $1	1,200
c. $3	1,000
d. $5	800
e. $5	1,200

11. If the government sets a price floor of $5 per bushel, how many bushels of corn are produced?

a. 0

b. 400

c. 800

d. 1,000

e. 1,200

12. If the government sets a price floor of $5 per bushel, how many bushels of corn are purchased by consumers?

a. 0

b. 400

c. 800

d. 1,000

e. 1,200

13. How many bushels of corn are purchased by the government if it maintains a price floor of $5 by buying all surplus corn?

a. 0

b. 400

c. 800

d. 1,000

e. 1,200

14. How much does a price floor of $5 cost the government if it maintains the price floor by buying any surplus corn?

a. $0

b. $2,000

c. $4,000

d. $5,000

e. $6,000

15. How much revenue do corn farmers receive if there is a price floor at $5?

a. $0

b. $1,200

c. $3,000

d. $4,000

e. $6,000

Use the following diagram to answer Questions 16–20.

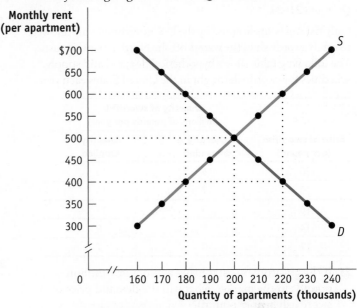

16. Where must an effective price ceiling in this market be set?

a. at $500

b. above $400

c. above $500

d. below $600

e. below $500

17. If the government sets a price ceiling at $400, how many apartments will be demanded by consumers?

a. 0

b. 40,000

c. 180,000

d. 200,000

e. 220,000

18. How many apartments will be offered for rent if the government sets a price ceiling at $400?

a. 0

b. 40,000

c. 180,000

d. 200,000

e. 220,000

19. A price ceiling set at $400 will result in which of the following in the market for apartments?

a. a surplus of 40,000 apartments

b. a surplus of 220,000 apartments

c. no surplus or shortage

d. a shortage of 40,000 apartments

e. a shortage of 220,000 apartments

20. A price ceiling set at $600 will result in which of the following in the market for apartments?

a. a surplus of 40,000 apartments

b. a surplus of 220,000 apartments

c. no surplus or shortage

d. a shortage of 40,000 apartments

e. a shortage of 220,000 apartments

Refer to the following table and information to answer Questions 21–24.

Only fishing boats licensed by the U.S. government are allowed to catch swordfish in the waters off the North Atlantic coast. The following table shows hypothetical demand and supply schedules for swordfish caught in the United States each year.

Price of swordfish (per pound)	Quantity of swordfish (millions of pounds per year)	
	Quantity demanded	Quantity supplied
$20	6	15
18	7	13
16	8	11
14	9	9
12	10	7

21. If the government establishes a quota of 7 million pounds in the market, what will the demand price of swordfish be (per pound)?

  a. $20   **d.** $14

  b. $18   **e.** $12

  c. $16

22. If the government establishes a quota of 7 million pounds in the market, what will the supply price of swordfish be (per pound)?

  a. $20   **d.** $14

  b. $18   **e.** $12

  c. $16

23. What is the quota rent per pound of swordfish received by licensed fishing boats when the government sets a quota of 7 million pounds?

  a. $0   **d.** $18

  b. $6   **e.** $30

  c. $12

24. If there is a quota of 7 million pounds and swordfish fishing licenses are traded in a market, how much will the price of a fishing license be per pound?

  a. $0   **d.** $18

  b. $6   **e.** $30

  c. $12

25. When transactions do not occur due to price or quantity controls, what is the term for the lost gains?

  a. wasted resources

  b. inefficient quality

  c. price wedge

  d. black market losses

  e. deadweight loss

Free-Response Questions

1. Pablo Picasso painted only 1,000 paintings during his "Blue Period."

  a. Draw a correctly labeled graph of the market for Picasso "Blue Period" paintings showing each of the following:

    i. the supply and demand curves for paintings

    ii. the equilibrium price and quantity of paintings

  b. List the five principal factors that will lead to a change in the price of paintings in this market.

  c. Show the effect on price in your market for paintings if wealthy art collectors decide that it is essential to acquire Picasso "Blue Period" paintings for their collections. **(5 points)**

2. The market for less-skilled labor in a large city is perfectly competitive.

  a. Draw a correctly labeled graph of the market for less skilled labor showing each of the following:

    i. the supply of labor and the demand for labor

    ii. the equilibrium wage and quantity of labor (measured as the number of workers)

  b. On your graph from part a, illustrate the effect of an advance in technology that makes workers more productive. Identify the new equilibrium price and quantity as P_{new} and Q_{new}.

  c. Assume that after the advance in technology, the government decides to impose a minimum wage. On your graph, draw a line indicating an effective minimum wage. **(8 points)**

3. Assume the market for sandals is perfectly competitive.

  a. Draw a correctly labeled graph of the market for sandals showing each of the following:

    i. the supply of sandals and the demand for sandals

    ii. the equilibrium price and quantity in the market for sandals, labeled P_1 and Q_1

  b. On your graph from part a, illustrate the effect on the equilibrium price and quantity of sandals if consumer income increases and sandals are a normal good. Label the new equilibrium price and quantity P_2 and Q_2.

  c. If the wages of workers producing sandals decrease at the same time consumer income increases, will the equilibrium quantity of sandals increase, decrease, or remain the same compared to Q_1 and P_1? Explain. **(8 points)**

The Coffee Market's Hot; Why Are Bean Prices Not?

Insights into Supply and Demand

Under fifteenth-century Turkish law, a wife could divorce her husband if he failed to provide her with a daily quota of coffee. Coffee is no longer grounds for divorce, but it is the world's most popular beverage after water and a common element of cozy getaways and productive workdays. Diamonds are another element that cements marriages, but although the price of diamonds drives people to steal, coffee beans have become a steal, costing only a few dollars a pound in the retail market. The paradoxical fall of coffee prices as popularity rises can be explained with the allied concepts of supply and demand.

can have cinnamon in your latte thanks to the workings of supply and demand.

Because they explain so much, let's explore the concepts of supply and demand.

Supply

The supply curve exhibits the relationship between the price and the quantity supplied. According to the *"law" of supply*, as the price increases, the quantity suppliers would be willing to supply increases, and as the price decreases, the willingly supplied quantity decreases. This suggests, for example, that the Reno Philharmonic Orchestra would be willing to put on more performances per week if it could command an $80 ticket price than if it could command a $60 ticket price. This positive relationship between price and quantity is illustrated by the upward slope of the supply curve in the accompanying diagram.

Supply, Demand, and the Great Explorers

The story of supply and demand began long ago. Let's pick it up with the great explorers of the fifteenth and sixteenth centuries. In 1492, Christopher Columbus sailed the ocean blue in search of a westward route to Asia and its gold. In 1519, Ferdinand Magellan proved that the Earth is round on an expedition to the Spice Islands, where cinnamon, nutmeg, and cloves were abundant. The royalty of Spain paid generously for these trips because gold was precious and, at that time in Europe, some spices were worth more than their weight in gold. Why were these products so expensive? Because the combination of high demand and limited supply leads to high prices. Thanks to the incentives that high prices provide, new trade routes were established, supply increased, and spices became affordable. In other words, Europeans came to America and you

It is likely that the law of supply describes your own behavior as well. Think about how many hours of burger flipping, lawn mowing, or babysitting you would supply per week at various prices. If you would supply more

Charido/Alamy

hours for $50 per hour than for $5 per hour, your supply curve has an upward slope. Let's examine why that's probably the case, using the economic concept of opportunity cost.

The *opportunity cost* of a particular action is the value of the next-best alternative action. Part of the opportunity cost of going to college is the money you could have earned working at McDonald's instead. The opportunity cost of an hour of babysitting is the value you would have received from your next-best use of that hour. Your first hour of babysitting would substitute for the least valuable alternative activity that day—perhaps perusing YouTube. Additional hours of babysitting must be carved out of more and more valuable alternatives, such as spending time with friends, sleeping, and (as a last resort!) studying economics. Losses of activities like these constitute the opportunity cost of each hour of babysitting. You are rational to babysit until the opportunity cost of one more hour of babysitting would be the loss of an activity that you value more highly than the hourly wage for babysitting. Your babysitting will obey the law of supply because an increase in the wage (that is, an increase in the price of babysitting) justifies the loss of additional alternative activities and makes you willing to supply a larger quantity of babysitting hours.

In some cases opportunity costs rise because, to make more and more of a good, producers must use inputs that are less and less specialized for making that good. For instance, farmers begin producing soybeans on the land best suited for that crop. As more soybeans are grown, farmers must use land that is less suitable for soybeans, which means lower yields or larger expenditures on fertilizers and irrigation. Similarly, as more silver is mined, mines must be dug deeper and in areas with lower concentrations of silver. The rising opportunity cost of gradually shifting to ill-suited inputs causes the marginal cost—the cost of making one more unit—to increase.

Even when output is increased by adding identical units of a particular input, *diminishing returns* can cause an increase in the marginal cost of production. Diminishing returns set in when successive units of one input added to a fixed quantity of another input contribute less and less to the level of output. The classic example is adding seeds to a flowerpot: if you keep adding seeds, the additional returns in terms of flowers will eventually decrease, and, at some point, there will be so many seeds in the pot that another seed will find no soil. Similarly, as more fishers are added to a fishing boat, or more tractors are added to a farm, they will eventually experience redundancy and congestion. When another unit of input contributes less to output than the preceding unit, the marginal cost rises. And with the cost of making each additional unit rising, firms require higher prices in exchange for larger quantities, and the supply curve is upward-sloping.

Junos/Getty Images

A change in the marginal cost of producing each unit shifts the supply curve. When the marginal cost falls, the supply increases, and the supply curve shifts downward and to the right (as from the light red supply curve to the dark red supply curve in the figure). For example, an improvement in fishing-net technology could lower the cost of catching fish and increase the supply. An *increase* in the marginal cost shifts the supply curve upward and to the left.

You can find the market supply curve by adding up the quantities supplied by all the individual firms at each price. Suppose the fish market consists of two firms: Fred's Fish and Fay's Fish. If, for a price of $1 each, Fay would supply 10 fish and Fred would supply 6 fish, then the market supply is 16 fish (10 from Fay plus 6 from Fred) at $1. The market supply at any other price is determined in the same way—by adding up the quantities supplied by all firms at that price.

Note that a change in the *price* of fish does not change the marginal cost of catching fish, so it does not shift the supply curve. Rather, it causes a movement to a new point along the existing supply curve, as from the point labeled "Initial equilibrium" to point A in the figure. To distinguish between these two types of changes, we call a movement along a stationary supply curve a *change in the quantity supplied,* and a shift in the supply curve itself a *change in supply.*

Demand

The demand curve shows the relationship between the price and the quantity demanded. The demand for a good depends on the benefits it conveys. Whether it is fish, clothing, coffee, or almost anything else, the *marginal benefit*—the benefit gained from one more—generally decreases as quantity increases because needs become satisfied and desires become satiated. The first beverage you drink in a week keeps you alive, whereas the 50th provides no such benefit. The height of the market demand curve at each quantity indicates the most that anyone would be willing to pay for that unit of the good. With benefits decreasing as individuals receive more and more of a good, the height of the market demand curve decreases, giving it a negative slope, as shown in the figure. The downward-sloping nature of the demand curve embodies the *"law" of demand*: as the price of a good decreases, the quantity demanded increases. This makes sense because lower prices justify the purchase of additional, less-valuable units.

Consider your demand for canned tuna fish. Your first can in a week provides the important benefits of protein, minerals, omega-3 fatty acids (to reduce the risk of heart disease), and a welcome break from peanut butter and jelly. Perhaps you'd pay up to $5 for the benefits of a first can of tuna. (You are unlikely to need to pay $5 for a can of tuna, but the demand curve describes the most you would pay if you had to, not what you must or do pay.) If so, your demand curve has a height of $5 at the quantity of

1. A second can of tuna provides a little more variety and more of the same nutrients. Getting those benefits for the second time in a week isn't as essential as getting them the first time, but perhaps a second can is worth $1 to you. In that case, your demand curve has a height of $1 at a quantity of 2. A third can is even less important and may have you craving a break from tuna fish. Let's say you would pay up to 30 cents for a third can, and you wouldn't pay anything for any more tuna. Your demand curve thus has the height of 30 cents at a quantity of 3 and a height of 0 at every higher quantity.

It is rational for you to buy cans of tuna fish until the benefit you receive from 1 more can is no longer worth at least as much as the price you must pay for it. If the price were $6, you wouldn't buy any tuna fish because even the first can is only worth $5 to you. If the price were $4, you would buy 1 can because it's rational to pay $4 for something that's worth $5. At a price of $1 or less, you would buy the second can, which is worth $1 to you, and if the price were 30 cents or less, you would buy 3 cans but no more.

The market demand curve is found by adding up the quantities demanded by all individuals in the market at each price. Suppose you and I are the only consumers in the tuna fish market. If, at a price of $1, I would buy 3 cans of tuna fish and you would buy 2, then the market demand is 5 at a price of $1. The demand at any other price can be determined in the same way—by adding up the quantities demanded by all consumers.

Because the demand curve reflects consumers' willingness to pay for each additional unit of a good or service, the curve will shift upward and to the right, as from the light blue demand curve to the dark blue demand curve in the figure, when the willingness to pay increases. This could result from

- a change in income
- a successful advertising campaign
- expectations of an upcoming increase in prices

- an increase in the price of substitutes, such as peanut butter and jelly
- a decrease in the price of complementary goods, such as bread
- an increase in the number of tuna fish consumers

The opposite of these changes would cause the demand curve to shift downward and to the left.

The effect of a change in income depends on the type of good in question. A *normal good* is one that consumers buy more of when their incomes increase; an *inferior good* is one that consumers buy less of when their incomes increase. Whether a good is normal or inferior depends on individual preferences. For some people, tuna fish might be a normal good. A higher income might lead other people to buy more steak and less tuna fish, so for them, steak would be normal and tuna fish would be inferior. Other examples of goods that are inferior for some people include secondhand clothing, rides on public buses, store-brand soda, and Spam. An increase in income shifts the demand curves for normal goods upward and to the right, and shifts the demand curves for inferior goods downward and to the left. Again, the opposite is also true.

The Marriage of Supply and Demand

The supply and demand curves reside on the same graph, with the price per unit measured on the vertical axis and the quantity of a particular good measured on the horizontal axis. The curves meet at the *equilibrium point*, which is so named because it represents a balance between the quantity demanded and the quantity supplied. The price directly to the left of the equilibrium point is the *equilibrium price*, and the quantity directly below the equilibrium point is the *equilibrium quantity*. If the price is initially set above the equilibrium price, the quantity supplied will exceed the quantity demanded, and the resulting surplus will lead suppliers to lower their price. If the price begins below the equilibrium price, the quantity demanded will exceed the quantity supplied, and the resulting shortage will motivate an increase in the price. Thus, we expect the price to reach the equilibrium level and stay there until a shift occurs in either the supply curve or the demand curve. We can find the effect of any shift by drawing the new curve and comparing the new and old equilibrium points.

Now we are equipped to explain the happenings in the spice and coffee markets of the past and present. In the sixteenth century, the supply of cinnamon in Europe was very small. We represent a relatively small supply with the light red "smaller supply" curve on the left side of the graph. Suppose the light blue "smaller demand" curve represents demand. To discover the influence of supply fluctuations on price, compare the price level (height) at the initial equilibrium of the light-colored supply and demand curves and at equilibrium point C at the intersection of the dark blue "larger supply" curve and the light blue demand curve. With limited supply, the price is higher, which helps to explain the high equilibrium price fetched by cinnamon and other spices imported by Europeans 500 years ago. The supply of spices to Europe and America increased dramatically after Columbus, Magellan, and other explorers established faster and safer trade routes to Asia. As more and more ships brought spices to Western shores, the supply curve shifted from left to right and the equilibrium price fell.

The Coffee Crisis

To examine recent activity in the coffee market, we must consider the effect on prices of changes in demand. Starting again at the initial equilibrium of the light-colored demand and supply curves in the figure, an increase in the popularity of coffee shifts the demand curve to the right. This demand shift indicates that people are willing to buy more coffee at any given price. What happens to the equilibrium price when demand increases? It rises to the level of equilibrium point *A*, and the higher price entices an increase in the quantity of coffee supplied. Note that the change in demand has not affected the cost of producing coffee, which depends on input costs rather than demand, so the supply curve does not shift. Point *A* is on the same supply curve that we started with, but the price has risen because the demand curve shifted outward.

U.S. consumers demand roughly $2.4 trillion worth of imported goods annually. The United States is the largest importer of coffee, which, after oil, is the most traded commodity in the world. More than 500 billion cups of coffee are consumed worldwide each year. But as increasing demand led Starbucks, Inc., to open tens of thousands of retail outlets around the world, the price of coffee beans declined. Let's examine the paradox of coffee prices in the context of supply and demand.

Teerawut Masawat/Alamy

The price of coffee rose fairly steadily in the 2000s and reached $2.89 per pound in the world market in 2011. This price provided healthy profits for coffee growers and led to a rapid expansion in the allocation of land to coffee farming in countries such as Vietnam and Brazil. The fruits of these plantings became available three years later. Although coffee demand was robust during that period, supply increased by *even more than* demand. The dark-colored curves in the figure represent the larger demand and the much larger supply of coffee in the mid-to-late 2010s. An increase in demand lifts prices, but an increase in supply lowers them, and the downward effect on prices was dominant in this case. Despite the large demand, prices were depressed by the overarching supply glut. Prices as low as $1.00 per pound sunk the incomes of some 25 million farmers in 50 countries. Over time, some farmers have been able to respond to the low prices by switching to other crops. The resulting decrease in supply, and its upward influence on prices, mark the beginning of the end of the latest coffee crisis.

Conclusion

Supply is determined by the marginal cost of production, which generally increases with quantity. Demand is determined by marginal benefit, which tends to fall as quantity increases. The price-setting duo of supply and demand, along with the predominant influence of a large supply of coffee beans, explain why coffee prices are low despite the long lines at Starbucks. Similar paradoxes abound. Why are essentials, such as food and water, inexpensive, whereas nonessential jewels and professional ball players command lofty prices? The answer lies in the abundant supply of food and water and the limited availability of jewels and great ball players. Sometimes it is the demand side that is neglected. Struggles to combat high oil prices have focused on the supply side—seeking new sources and tapping into petroleum reserves. A decrease in the demand for oil would also lower prices, although that may be unlikely given consumers' appetite for gasoline consumption. Whether trying to explain, predict, or influence prices, keep in mind that supply and demand work together to determine price and that both can be influenced by policy.

Critical Thinking Questions

1. Although the supply of Jeeps expanded in the late 2010s, people were paying higher prices than ever for those vehicles. Explain how an increase in price can accompany an increase in supply.

2. As your income increases, what do you think will happen to your demand curve for Folgers Coffee? What will happen to your demand curve for Starbucks coffee? Are these goods, therefore, normal or inferior for you?

3. To help coffee farmers, some organizations sell "fair trade" coffee for a price that is higher than the price of most other coffee. Why do you suppose they are able to sell some coffee at the higher price? What would happen to the quantity of coffee supplied and demanded if a law prevented the price of coffee from falling below the fair-trade price?

SECTION 3

Economic Indicators and the Business Cycle

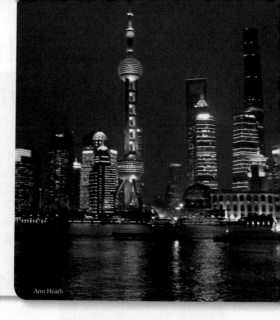

Ann Heath

economics by example *How Can GDP Be Up When We're Feeling Down?*

The New #2

"China Passes Japan as Second-Largest Economy." That was the headline in the *New York Times* on August 15, 2010. Today, the United States and China are still the two largest economies in the world and China's economy has grown to more than double the size of Japan's economy.

But wait a minute—what does it mean to say that the United States and China are the two largest economies in the world or that China's economy is larger than Japan's? After all, these economies are producing very different mixes of goods. China's greatest strength is in relatively low-tech production. Japan, by contrast, is very much a

high-tech nation and dominates world output of goods like electronic sensors for automobiles. How can you compare the sizes of two economies when they aren't producing the same things? The answer is that comparisons of national economies are based on the *value* of their production. When news reports declared that China's economy had overtaken Japan's, they meant that China's *gross domestic product*, or *GDP*—a measure of the overall value of goods and services produced—had surpassed Japan's GDP.

GDP is one of the most important measures used to track the macroeconomy—that is, to quantify movements in

the overall level of output and prices. Measures such as GDP, unemployment rates, and *price indexes* play a central role in the formulation of economic policy because policy makers need to know what's going on and anecdotes are no substitute for hard data. These measures are also important for business decisions—to such an extent that corporations and other players are willing to pay consulting firms for early estimates of what official economic measurements will find.

In this section we explain three of the most useful macroeconomic measures: gross domestic product, unemployment, and inflation.

The Circular Flow and Gross Domestic Product

> **In this Module, you will learn to:**
> - Explain how economists use aggregate measures to track the performance of the economy
> - Draw and interpret the circular-flow diagram of the economy
> - Define and calculate gross domestic product (GDP)

The National Accounts

Almost all countries calculate a set of numbers known as the *national income and product accounts*. The **national income and product accounts**, often referred to simply as the **national accounts**, keep track of the spending of consumers, sales of producers, business investment spending, government purchases, and a variety of other flows of money among different sectors of the economy. In the United States, these numbers are calculated by the Bureau of Economic Analysis, a division of the U.S. government's Department of Commerce. Let's see how they work.

The Circular-Flow Diagram

To understand the principles behind the national accounts, it helps to look at a graphic called the *circular-flow diagram*. This diagram is a simplified representation of the macroeconomy. It shows the flows of money, goods and services, and factors of production through the economy and allows us to visualize the key concepts behind the national accounts. The underlying principle is that the flow of money into each market or sector is equal to the flow of money coming out of that market or sector.

The Simple Circular-Flow Diagram

The U.S. economy is a vastly complex entity, with more than a hundred million workers employed by millions of companies, producing millions of different goods and services. Yet you can learn some very important things about the economy by considering a simple diagram, shown in **Figure 10.1**. This simple model of the macroeconomy represents the transactions that take place in the economy by two kinds of flows: physical things such as goods, services, labor, or raw materials flow in one direction, and payments for these things flow in the opposite direction. In this figure, the physical flows are shown in yellow and the money flows are shown in green.

The simplest circular-flow diagram illustrates an economy that contains only two groups: households and firms. A **household** consists of either an individual or a group of people who share their income. A **firm** is an organization that produces goods and services for sale—and that employs members of households. As you can see in Figure 10.1, households are shown on the top and firms are shown on the bottom.

There are two kinds of markets in the simple economy illustrated in Figure 10.1. To the right are **product markets** in which households buy the products (goods and services) they want from firms. Household payments for goods and services is called **consumer spending**. Consumer spending produces a flow of goods and services to the households and a return flow of money to the firms.

National income and product accounts, or **national accounts,** keep track of the flows of money among different sectors of the economy.

A **household** is a person or group of people who share income.

A **firm** is an organization that produces goods and services for sale.

Product markets are where goods and services are bought and sold.

Consumer spending is household spending on goods and services.

Figure 10.1 The Circular-Flow Diagram

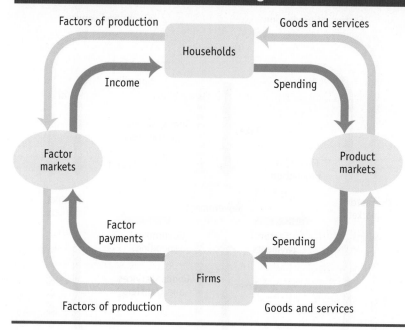

This diagram represents the flows of money, factors of production, and goods and services in the economy. In the markets for goods and services, households purchase goods and services from firms, generating a flow of money to the firms and a flow of goods and services to the households. The money flows back to households as firms purchase factors of production from the households in factor markets.

To the left are **factor markets** in which firms buy the factors of production (also known as resources) they need to produce goods and services from households. Households ultimately own, and receive income from, all of the factors of production: labor, land, capital, and entrepreneurship. While the best-known factor market is the *labor market* and most households derive the bulk of their income from wages earned by selling their labor, households receive income in the form of rent, interest, and profit as well as wages.

This simple circular-flow diagram omits a number of real-world complications. However, the diagram is a useful aid to thinking about the economy—and we can use it as the starting point for developing a more realistic (and therefore more complicated) circular-flow model.

The Expanded Circular-Flow Diagram

Figure 10.2 is an expanded circular-flow diagram that shows how the government is involved in flows between the households and firms in the economy.

In Figure 10.2, the flows between households and firms remain, but flows to and from the government are added. The government injects funds into the circular flow through government spending, and funds leak out of the circular flow through taxing. **Government spending** is the total of purchases made by federal, state, and local governments, including everything from national military spending on ammunition to your local public school's spending on chalk, erasers, and teacher salaries. The government uses tax payments received from households and firms to finance much of its spending. **Taxes** are payments that firms and households are required to make to the government, and **tax revenue** refers to the funds the government receives from taxes.

Firms must pay taxes on the consumer and government spending they receive through the product markets. The funds remaining after taxes are then allocated to pay wages, rent, interest, and profit to households through the factor markets. Households must also pay taxes to the government. After paying taxes, households allocate their remaining income—*disposable income*—to consumer spending. **Disposable income** is the total amount of household income available to spend on consumption.

Factor markets are where resources, especially capital and labor, are bought and sold.

Government spending is total expenditures on goods and services by federal, state, and local governments.

Taxes are required payments to the government. **Tax revenue** is the total amount the government receives from taxes.

Disposable income, equal to income plus government transfers minus taxes, is the total amount of household income available to spend on consumption.

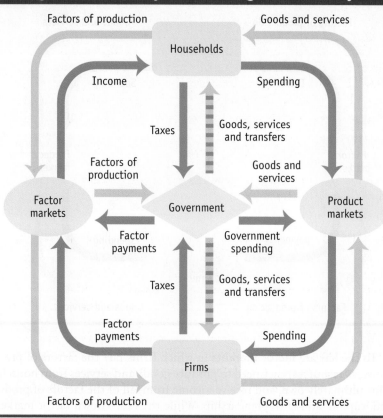

A circular flow of funds connects the three sectors of the economy—households, firms, and government. Taxes flow to the government from both firms and households. *Government spending* on goods and services flows to the product market. Goods and services flow from the product market to the government and then on from the government to both households and firms.

Government transfers are payments that the government makes to individuals without expecting a good or service in return.

Private savings, equal to disposable income minus consumer spending, is a household's disposable income that is not spent on consumption.

Financial markets channel private savings into investment spending and government borrowing.

Government borrowing is the amount of funds borrowed by the government in the financial markets.

Investment spending is spending on new productive physical capital, such as machinery and structures, and on changes in inventories.

In addition to collecting taxes from households and firms, the government makes payments and transfers goods and services to households and firms. **Government transfers** are payments that the government makes to households or firms without expecting a good or service in return. So in addition to receiving income from selling factors of production, some households receive income in the form of government transfers. Unemployment insurance payments are one example of a government transfer. Finally, the government uses part of its spending to provide goods and services to households and firms.

Adding Financial Markets to the Circular Flow

The circular-flow diagram can be made even more realistic, and more complicated, by adding the financial markets. Because a circular-flow diagram becomes very complicated when we include financial markets, let's simply use the idea of flows between markets and sectors we learned from Figures 10.1 and 10.2 to discuss how financial markets are involved in the financial flows in the economy.

Some households do not spend all of their disposable income on goods and services. But that unspent income does not disappear from the circular flow. Household income that is not spent on consumption becomes the household's savings. Since household savings is not spent, it leaks out of the circular flow. This **private savings** is frequently held by financial institutions (such as banks) that inject it back into the circular flow in the form of loans. **Financial markets** channel private savings into **government borrowing** and **investment spending**. The government borrows funds to pay for government spending not covered by tax revenue and firms borrow funds to finance investment spending. The financial sector of the economy is discussed in detail in Section 5.

Investment spending includes firms' spending on new productive capital. For example, an automobile company that is building a new factory will buy investment goods—machinery like stamping presses and welding robots. Firms also accumulate an *inventory* of finished cars in preparation for shipment to dealers. **Inventories** are goods and raw materials that firms hold to facilitate their operations. The national accounts include inventories as part of investment spending. Increases in inventories of finished goods are counted as investment spending because, like machinery, they influence the ability of a firm to make future sales. Spending on additional inventory is a form of investment spending by a firm. Conversely, decreasing inventories reduces investment spending because it leads to lower future sales.

It's also important to understand that investment spending includes spending on the construction of any structure, including a new house. Why include the construction of homes as investment spending? Because, like a factory, a new house produces a future stream of output—housing services for its occupants.

Adding the Rest of the World to the Circular Flow

The rest of the world participates in the U.S. economy in three ways. First, some of the goods and services produced in the United States are sold to residents of other countries. For example, more than half of America's annual wheat and cotton crops are sold abroad. Goods and services sold to other countries are known as **exports**. Payments for exports lead to an injection of funds from the rest of the world into the United States' circular flow. Second, some of the goods and services purchased by residents of the United States are produced abroad. For example, many consumer goods are made in China. Goods and services purchased from other countries are known as **imports**. Import purchases lead to a leakage of funds out of the United States' circular flow. Third, foreigners can participate in U.S. financial markets. Foreign lending—lending by foreigners to borrowers in the United States—generates a flow of funds into the United States from the rest of the world. Conversely, foreign borrowing—borrowing by foreigners from U.S. lenders—leads to a flow of funds out of the United States to the rest of the world. The international sector of the economy is discussed in detail in Section 8.

The underlying principle of this expanded circular flow is still that the inflow of money into each market or sector must equal the outflow of money coming from that market or sector. And we can use the monetary flows within the circular-flow model to measure the size of an economy. Calculating the dollar value of all the final goods and services produced in an economy, shown in the circular flow, gives us the economy's gross domestic product, one of the most important measures used to track the macroeconomy.

Inventories are stocks of goods and raw materials held to facilitate business operations.

Exports are goods and services sold to other countries.

Imports are goods and services purchased from other countries.

Gross domestic product, or **GDP**, is the total value of all final goods and services produced in the economy during a given year.

The **expenditure approach** to calculating GDP adds up **aggregate spending** on domestically produced final goods and services in the economy—the sum of consumer spending, investment spending, government purchases of goods and services, and exports minus imports.

The **income approach** to calculating GDP adds up the total factor income earned by households from firms in the economy, including rent, wages, interest, and profit.

Gross Domestic Product

Gross domestic product, or **GDP**, is the total value of all *final goods and services* produced in an economy during a given period, usually a year. In 2017, the GDP of the United States was $19,485 billion, or about $59,825 per person. The calculation of a country's GDP can be explained using our circular-flow model.

There are three approaches to the calculation of GDP. The **expenditure approach** adds up **aggregate spending** on domestically produced final goods and services in the economy—shown in the top half of Figure 10.2. The **income approach** adds up the total factor income earned by households from firms in the economy, including rent, wages, interest, and profit—shown in the bottom half of Figure 10.2. Recall from the discussion on circular flow that inflows must equal outflows, so these approaches

The United States is a net importer of goods and services, such as these toys made on a production line in China.

The **value-added approach** to calculating GDP surveys firms and adds up their contributions to the value of final goods and services.

will yield the same result. The **value-added approach**, the third and most complex approach to calculating GDP, surveys firms and adds up their individual contributions to the value of each final good and service.

Government statisticians use all three approaches to calculate GDP. To illustrate how they work, we will consider a hypothetical economy, shown in **Figure 10.3**. This economy consists of three firms—American Motors, Inc., which produces one car per year; American Steel, Inc., which produces the steel that goes into the car; and American Ore, Inc., which mines the iron ore that goes into the steel. GDP in this economy is $21,500, the value of the one car per year the economy produces. Let's look at how the three different methods of calculating GDP yield the same result.

Figure 10.3   Calculating GPD

Aggregate spending on domestically produced final goods and services = $21,500

	American Ore, Inc.	American Steel, Inc.	American Motors, Inc.	Total factor income
Value of sales	$4,200 (ore)	$9,000 (steel)	$21,500 (car)	
Intermediate goods	0	4,200 (iron ore)	9,000 (steel)	
Wages	2,000	3,700	10,000	$15,700
Interest payments	1,000	600	1,000	2,600
Rent	200	300	500	1,000
Profit	1,000	200	1,000	2,200
Total expenditure by firm	4,200	9,000	21,500	
Value added per firm = Value of sales – cost of intermediate goods	4,200	4,800	12,500	

Total payments to factors = $21,500

Sum of value added = $21,500

In this hypothetical economy consisting of three firms, GDP can be calculated in three different ways: measuring GDP as the value of production of final goods and services by summing each firm's value added, measuring GDP as aggregate spending on domestically produced final goods and services, and measuring GDP as factor income earned by households from firms in the economy.

The Expenditure Approach

The most common way to calculate GDP is by adding up aggregate spending on domestically produced final goods and services. That is, GDP can be measured by the flow of funds into firms, but it is important that this measurement be carried out in a way that avoids double-counting. A consumer's purchase of a new car from a dealer is one example of a sale of **final goods and services**: goods and services sold to the final, or end, user. But an automobile manufacturer's purchase of steel from a steel foundry or glass from a glassmaker is an example of a sale of **intermediate goods and services**: goods and services that are inputs into the production of final goods and services. In the case of intermediate goods and services, the purchaser—another firm—is *not* the final user.

In terms of our steel and auto example, we don't want to count both consumer spending on a car (represented in Figure 10.3 by the sales price of the car) and the auto producer's spending on steel (represented in Figure 10.3 by the price of a car's worth of steel). If we counted both, we would be counting the steel embodied in the car twice. We solve this problem by counting only the value of sales to *final*

Final goods and services are goods and services sold to the final, or end, user.

Intermediate goods and services are goods and services bought from one firm by another firm to be used as inputs into the production of final goods and services.

buyers, such as consumers, firms that purchase investment goods, the government, or foreign buyers. In other words, in order to avoid the double-counting of spending, we omit sales of intermediate goods and services from one business to another when estimating GDP using spending data. You can see from Figure 10.3 that aggregate spending on final goods and services—the finished car—is $21,500.

As we've already pointed out, the national accounts *do* include investment spending by firms as a part of final spending. That is, an auto company's purchase of steel to make a car isn't considered a part of final spending, but the company's purchase of new machinery for its factory *is* considered a part of final spending. What's the difference? Steel is an input that is used up in production; machinery will last for a number of years. Since purchases of capital goods that will last for a considerable time aren't closely tied to current production, the national accounts consider such purchases a form of final sales.

Steel is an intermediate good because it is sold to other product manufacturers, such as automakers or refrigerator makers, and rarely to the final consumer.

There are four groups that purchase goods and services in an economy: households, firms, the government, and foreigners. The expenditure approach to calculating GDP adds up the spending by these four sources of aggregate spending. The largest category of spending is consumer spending by households, which we will denote with the symbol C. The three other components of spending are investment spending by firms, which we will denote by I; government purchases of goods and services, which we will denote by G; and spending by foreigners on domestically produced goods and services—that is, exports—which we will denote by X.

In reality, not all of this final spending goes toward domestically produced goods and services. Some of the consumption, investment, and government spending is for goods and services produced in other countries—imports. We must take account of spending on imports, which we will denote by M. Income spent on imports is income not spent on domestic goods and services—it is income that has "leaked" across national borders. So to calculate domestic production using spending data, we must subtract spending on imports. Putting this all together gives us the following equation, which breaks GDP down by the four sources of aggregate spending:

(10-1) $\quad GDP = C + I + G + (X - M)$

Note that the value of $(X - M)$—the difference between the value of exports and the value of imports—is known as **net exports**. We'll be seeing a lot of Equation 10-1 in later Modules!

The Income Approach

Another way to calculate GDP is to add up all the income earned by factors of production in the economy—the wages earned by labor; the interest earned by those who lend their savings to firms and the government; the rent earned by those who lease their land or structures to firms; and the profits (money not paid to wages, interest, or rent) earned by the owners of the firms' physical capital. This income approach is a valid measure because the money firms earn by selling goods and services must go somewhere.

Figure 10.3 shows how this calculation works for our simplified economy. The shaded column at the far right shows the total wages, interest, and rent paid by all these firms, as well as their total profit. Adding up all of these yields a total factor income of $21,500—again, equal to GDP.

We won't emphasize the income approach as much as the expenditure approach to calculating GDP. It's important to keep in mind, however, that all the money spent on domestically produced goods and services generates factor income to households—that is, there really is a circular flow.

AP® EXAM TIP

Exports represent the flow of goods and services out of the economy into another country, with payment for the exports flowing back in. Imports represent the flow of goods and services into the economy from another country, with payment for the imports flowing back out. Because of this constant exchange of goods and services and payments, we focus on net flow in or out.

Net exports are the difference between the value of exports and the value of imports $(X - M)$.

AP® EXAM TIP

Remember that imports are subtracted when using the expenditure approach. If exports exceed imports, then net exports will be positive, indicating a net outflow of goods and services and a net inflow of payments. If imports exceed exports, then net exports will be negative, indicating a net inflow of goods and services and a net outflow of payments.

The Value-Added Approach

The final way to calculate GDP is to add up the contribution of each firm along the way to the total value of the final good or service. For example, in Figure 10.3, the total value of the sale of all goods, intermediate and final, is $34,700: $21,500 from the sale of the car, plus $9,000 from the sale of the steel, plus $4,200 from the sale of the iron ore. Yet we know that GDP—the total value of all final goods and services in a given year—is only $21,500. Another way to avoid double-counting is to count only the **value added** by each producer in the calculation of GDP: the difference between the value of its sales and the value of the inputs it purchases from other businesses. That is, at each stage of the production process we subtract the cost of inputs—the intermediate goods—at that stage. In this case, the value added by the auto producer is the dollar value of the cars it manufactures *minus* the cost of the steel it buys, or $12,500. The value added by the steel producer is the dollar value of the steel it produces *minus* the cost of the ore it buys, or $4,800. Only the ore producer, who we have assumed doesn't buy any inputs, has value added equal to its total sales, $4,200. The sum of the value added by all three producers is $12,500 + $4,800 + $4,200 = $21,500, equal to GDP.

Calculating GDP

Now that we know how GDP is calculated in principle, let's see what it looks like in practice.

Figure 10.4 shows the breakdown of GDP according to the four components of aggregate spending.

Figure 10.4   U.S. GDP in 2018 (Q2) and its Components

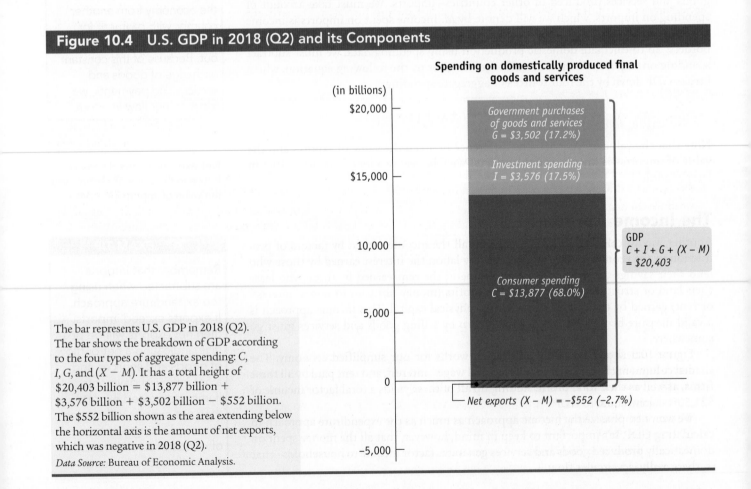

The bar represents U.S. GDP in 2018 (Q2). The bar shows the breakdown of GDP according to the four types of aggregate spending: *C*, *I*, *G*, and (*X − M*). It has a total height of $20,403 billion = $13,877 billion + $3,576 billion + $3,502 billion − $552 billion. The $552 billion shown as the area extending below the horizontal axis is the amount of net exports, which was negative in 2018 (Q2).

Data Source: Bureau of Economic Analysis.

The bar in Figure 10.4 corresponds to the expenditure approach to calculating GDP, showing the breakdown by the four types of aggregate spending. Within the bar, consumer spending (C), which was 68% of GDP, dominates. Investment spending (I) constituted 17.5% of GDP; government purchases of goods and services (G) constituted 17.2% of GDP. But some of that spending was on foreign-produced goods and services. In 2018 (Q2), the value of net exports, the difference between the value of exports and the value of imports ($X - M$ in Equation 10-1), was negative—the United States was a net importer of foreign goods and services. The 2018 (Q2) value of $X - M$ was −$552 billion, or −2.7% of GDP. Thus, a portion of the bar extends below the horizontal axis to represent the negative value for net exports.

GDP: What's In and What's Out?

Let's pause here and emphasize some things that are and are not included in GDP. GDP is the total value of all final goods and services produced in an economy during a given year. GDP *includes* investment by firms in new capital goods, new construction of structures, and inventories.

Intermediate goods, used goods, financial assets (like stocks and bonds), and goods and services produced in other countries are not included in GDP. Recall that including intermediate goods in GDP leads to double-counting, so only final goods are included. Used goods are not included in GDP for a similar reason. Used goods were already counted in the year that they were produced and to include them again would be to double-count them. Financial assets such as stocks and bonds are not included in GDP because they don't represent either the production or the sale of final goods and services. A bond represents a promise to repay with interest, and a stock represents ownership of a firm. And obviously foreign-produced goods and services are not included in calculations of gross *domestic* product because they were not produced domestically.

> ### AP® EXAM TIP
>
> Understand what is and is not included as part of investment spending (I). Investment spending is spending on capital, the construction of structures (residential as well as commercial), and changes to inventories. Spending on inputs is not considered part of investment spending. Inputs, such as steel, are used up in production, but capital, like a metal stamp machine, is not.

> ### AP® EXAM TIP
>
> Know what is and is not included in GDP. *Included*: domestically produced final goods and services, capital goods, new construction of structures, and changes to inventories. *Not included*: intermediate goods and services, inputs, used goods, financial assets such as stocks and bonds, and foreign-produced goods and services.

Adventures in AP® Economics

Watch the video: *The Circular Flow*

MODULE 10 REVIEW

Check Your Understanding

1. Explain why the three methods of calculating GDP produce the same estimate of GDP.

2. Identify each of the sectors to which firms make sales. What are the various ways in which households are linked with other sectors of the economy?

3. Consider Figure 10.3. Explain why it would be incorrect to calculate total value added as $30,500, the sum of the sales price of a car and a car's worth of steel.

TACKLE THE AP® TEST: Multiple-Choice Questions

1. The circular-flow diagram is a simple model of the macroeconomy in which
   a. the flow of money into each market or sector exceeds the flow of money coming out of that market or sector.
   b. the value of stocks equals the value of bonds.
   c. households own the factors of production.
   d. there is only one household and one firm.
   e. goods and services are sold in factor markets.

2. Which of the following leaks out of the circular flow in the expanded circular-flow model?
   a. investment spending
   b. government borrowing
   c. private savings
   d. the value of exports
   e. government spending

3. Which of the following is injected into the circular flow in the expanded circular-flow model?
   a. the value of imports
   b. government transfer payments
   c. taxes
   d. private savings
   e. factor payments

4. GDP is equal to
   a. the total value of all final goods and services produced in an economy during a given period.
   b. $C + I + G + M$.
   c. the total value of intermediate goods plus final goods.
   d. the total income received by producers of final goods and services.
   e. the total of all goods and services sold during a year.

5. Which of the following is included in GDP?
   a. changes to inventories
   b. intermediate goods
   c. used goods
   d. financial assets (stocks and bonds)
   e. foreign-produced goods

6. Which of the following is *not* included in GDP?
   a. capital goods such as machinery
   b. imports
   c. the value of domestically produced services
   d. government purchases of goods and services
   e. the construction of structures

7. Which of the following components makes up the largest percentage of GDP measured by aggregate spending?
   a. consumer spending
   b. investment spending
   c. government purchases of goods and services
   d. exports
   e. imports

TACKLE THE AP® TEST: Free-Response Questions

1. Will each of the following transactions be included in GDP for the United States? Explain why or why not.
   a. Coca-Cola builds a new bottling plant in the United States.
   b. Delta sells one of its existing airplanes to Korean Air.
   c. Ms. Moneybags buys an existing share of Disney stock.
   d. A California winery produces a bottle of Chardonnay and sells it to a customer in Montreal, Canada.
   e. An American buys a bottle of French perfume in Tulsa, Oklahoma.
   f. A book publisher produces too many copies of a new book; the books don't sell this year, so the publisher adds the surplus books to its inventories.

2. Draw a correctly labeled circular-flow diagram showing the flows of funds between the markets for goods and services and the factor markets. Add the government to your diagram, and show how money leaks out of the economy to the government and how money is injected back into the economy by the government. **(5 points)**

> **Rubric for FRQ 1 (6 points)**
>
> **1 point:** Yes. New structures built in the United States are included in U.S. GDP.
>
> **1 point:** No. The airplane is used, and sales of used goods are not included in GDP.
>
> **1 point:** No. This is a transfer of ownership—not new production.
>
> **1 point:** Yes. This is an export.
>
> **1 point:** No. This is an import—it was not produced in the United States.
>
> **1 point:** Yes. Additions to inventories are considered investments.

Interpreting Real Gross Domestic Product

In this Module, you will learn to:
- Differentiate between real GDP and nominal GDP
- Explain why real GDP is the appropriate measure of economic activity

Creating the National Accounts

The national accounts owe their creation to the Great Depression. As the economy plunged, government officials found their ability to respond crippled by the lack of adequate information. They could only guess at what was happening to the economy as a whole. In response to this perceived lack of information, the Department of Commerce commissioned Simon Kuznets, a young Russian-born economist, to develop a set of national income accounts. (Kuznets later won the Nobel Prize in economics for his work.) The first version of these accounts was presented to Congress in 1937. Kuznets's initial estimates fell short of the full modern set of accounts because they focused on income rather than production.

The push to complete the national accounts came during World War II, when policy makers were in even more need of comprehensive measures of the economy's performance. The federal government began issuing estimates of gross domestic product and gross national product in 1942. In January 2000, in its publication *Survey of Current Business*, the Department of Commerce ran an article titled "GDP: One of the Great Inventions of the 20th Century." This may seem a bit over the top, but national income accounting, invented in the United States, has since become a tool of economic analysis and policy making around the world.

National accounts were an important tool for policy makers to measure economic performance during World War II.

What GDP Tells Us

Why was it so important to create the national accounts? What exactly does the value of GDP tell us?

The most important use of GDP is as a measure of the size of the economy, providing us a scale against which to compare the economic performance of other years or other countries. For example, in 2017, U.S. GDP was $19,485 billion. By comparison, Japan's GDP that year was $4,781.2 billion, and the combined GDP of the countries that make up the European Union was $17,277.6 billion. This comparison tells us that Japan, although it has the world's third-largest national economy, has a significantly smaller economy than the United States. And when taken in aggregate, Europe's economy is almost as large as the U.S. economy.

Still, one must be careful when using GDP numbers, especially when making comparisons over time. That's because part of the increase in the value of GDP over time represents increases in the *prices* of goods and services rather than an increase in output. For example, U.S. GDP was $8,578 billion in 1997 and had more than doubled to $19,458 billion by 2017. But U.S. production didn't actually double over that period; part of the increase was due to an increase in the price of goods and services. To measure actual changes in aggregate output, we need to use a modified version of GDP that is adjusted for price changes, known as *real GDP*. We'll see how real GDP is calculated next.

Real GDP: A Measure of Aggregate Output

At the beginning of this section we described how China passed Japan as the world's second-largest economy in 2010. At the time, Japan's economy was weakening: during the second quarter of 2010, output declined by an annual rate of 6.3%. Oddly, however, GDP was up. In fact, Japan's GDP measured in yen, its national currency, rose by an annual rate of 4.8% during the quarter. How was that possible? The answer is that Japan was experiencing inflation at the time. As a result, the yen value of Japan's GDP rose although output actually fell.

The moral of this story is that the commonly cited GDP number is an interesting and useful statistic, one that provides a good way to compare the size of different economies, but it's not a good measure of the economy's growth over time. GDP can grow because the economy grows, but it can also grow simply because of inflation. Even if an economy's output doesn't change, GDP will go up if the prices of the goods and services the economy produces increase. Likewise, GDP can fall either because the economy is producing less or because prices have fallen.

To measure the economy's growth with accuracy, we need a measure of **aggregate output**: the total quantity of final goods and services the economy produces. As we noted above, the measure that is used for this purpose is known as *real GDP*. By tracking real GDP over time, we avoid the problem of changes in prices distorting the value of changes in production over time. Let's look first at how real GDP is calculated and then at what it means.

Calculating Real GDP

To understand how real GDP is calculated, imagine an economy in which only two goods, apples and oranges, are produced and in which both goods are sold only to final consumers. The outputs and prices of the two fruits for two consecutive years are shown in **Table 11.1**.

Table 11.1	Calculating GDP and Real GDP in a Simple Economy	
	Year 1	Year 2
Quantity of apples (billions)	2,000	2,200
Price of an apple	$0.25	$0.30
Quantity of oranges (billions)	1,000	1,200
Price of an orange	$0.50	$0.70
GDP (billions of dollars)	$1,000	$1,500
Real GDP (billions of year 1 dollars)	$1,000	$1,150

The first thing we can say about these data is that the value of sales increased from year 1 to year 2. In the first year, the total value of sales was (2,000 billion × $0.25) + (1,000 billion × $0.50) = $1,000 billion; in the second, it was (2,200 billion × $0.30) + (1,200 billion × $0.70) = $1,500 billion, which is 50% larger. But it is also clear from the table that this increase in the dollar value of GDP overstates the real growth in the economy. Although the quantities of both apples and oranges increased, the prices of both apples and oranges also rose. So part of the 50% increase in the dollar value of GDP simply reflects higher prices, not increased production.

To estimate the true increase in aggregate output produced, we have to ask the following question: How much would GDP have gone up if prices had *not* changed? To answer this question, we need to find the value of output in year 2 expressed in year 1 prices. In year 1, the price of apples was $0.25 each and the price of oranges $0.50 each. So year 2 output *at year 1 prices* is (2,200 billion × $0.25) + (1,200 billion × $0.50) = $1,150 billion. Since output in year 1 at year 1 prices was $1,000 billion, GDP measured in year 1 prices rose 15%—from $1,000 billion to $1,150 billion.

AP® EXAM TIP

Aggregate output is the total quantity of final goods and services produced within an economy.

Now we can define **real GDP**: it is the total value of all final goods and services produced in the economy during a year, calculated as if prices had stayed constant at the level of some given base year in order to remove the effects of price changes. A real GDP number always comes with information about what the base year is. A GDP number that has not been adjusted for changes in prices is calculated using the prices in the year in which the output is produced. Economists call this measure **nominal GDP**, or GDP at current prices. Our first calculation above used nominal GDP to measure the change in output from year 1 to year 2, which is why we overstated the true growth in output: we claimed it to be 50%, when in fact it was only 15%. By comparing output in the two years using a common set of prices—the year 1 prices in this example—we are able to focus solely on changes in the quantity of output by eliminating the influence of changes in prices.

Table 11.2 shows a real-life version of our apples and oranges example. The second column shows nominal GDP in 2000, 2009, and 2017. The third column shows real GDP for each year in 2009 dollars (that is, using the value of the dollar in the year 2009). For 2009, the nominal GDP and the real GDP are the same. But real GDP in 2000 expressed in 2009 dollars was higher than nominal GDP in 2000, reflecting the fact that prices were in general higher in 2009 than in 2000. Real GDP in 2017 expressed in 2009 dollars, however, was less than nominal GDP in 2017 because prices in 2009 were lower than in 2017.

Real GDP is the total value of all final goods and services produced in the economy during a given year, calculated using the prices of a selected base year in order to remove the effects of price changes.

Nominal GDP is the total value of all final goods and services produced in the economy during a given year, calculated with the prices current in the year in which the output is produced.

Table 11.2	Nominal Versus Real GDP in 2000, 2009, and 2017	
	Nominal GDP (billions of current dollars)	Real GDP (billions of 2009 dollars)
2000	$10,285	$12,560
2009	14,419	14,419
2017	19,386	17,092

Data Source: Bureau of Economic Analysis.

Paul Maguire/Alamy

You might have noticed that there is an alternative way to calculate real GDP using the data in Table 11.1. Why not measure it using the prices of year 2 rather than year 1 as the base-year prices? This procedure seems equally valid. According to that calculation, real GDP in year 1 at year 2 prices is (2,000 billion × $0.30) + (1,000 billion × $0.70) = $1,300 billion; real GDP in year 2 at year 2 prices is $1,500 billion, the same as nominal GDP in year 2. So using year 2 prices as the base year, the growth rate of real GDP is equal to ($1,500 billion − $1,300 billion)/$1,300 billion = 0.154, or 15.4%. This is slightly higher than the figure we got from the previous calculation, in which year 1 prices were the base-year prices. In that calculation, we found that real GDP increased by 15.0%. Neither answer, 15.4% versus 15.0%, is more "correct" than the other. In reality, the government economists who put together the U.S. national accounts have adopted a method to measure the change in real GDP known as chain-linking, which uses the average between the GDP growth rate calculated using an early base year and the GDP growth rate calculated using a late base year. As a result, U.S. statistics on real GDP are always expressed in *chained dollars*, which splits the difference between using early and late base years.

Real GDP per Capita

GDP is a measure of a country's aggregate output. Other things equal, a country with a larger population will have higher GDP simply because there are more people working. If we want to compare GDP across countries but we want to eliminate the effect of differences in population size, we use the measure **GDP per capita**—GDP divided by the size of the population, equivalent to the average GDP per person. Correspondingly, real GDP per capita is the average real GDP per person.

GDP per capita is GDP divided by the size of the population; it is equivalent to the average GDP per person.

What Real GDP Doesn't Measure

Real GDP per capita can be a useful measure in some circumstances, such as in a comparison of labor productivity between two countries. However, despite the fact that it is a rough measure of the average real output per person, real GDP per capita has well-known limitations as a measure of a country's living standards. Every once in a while, economists are accused of believing that growth in real GDP per capita is the only thing that matters—that is, thinking that increasing real GDP per capita is a goal in itself. In fact, economists rarely make that mistake. Let's take a moment to be clear about why a country's real GDP per capita is not a sufficient measure of human welfare in that country and why growth in real GDP per capita is not an appropriate policy goal in itself.

Real GDP does not include many of the things that contribute to happiness, such as leisure time, volunteerism, housework, and natural beauty. And real GDP increases with expenditures on some things that make people unhappy, including disease, divorce, crime, and natural disasters.

Real GDP per capita is a measure of an economy's average aggregate output per person—an indication of the economy's potential for certain achievements. Having studied the income approach to calculating GDP, you know that the value of output corresponds to the value of income. A country with a relatively high GDP per capita can afford relatively high expenditures on health, education, and other goods and services that contribute to a high quality of life. But how output is actually used is another matter. To put it differently, your income might be higher this year than last year, but whether you use that higher income to actually improve your quality of life is up to you. There is not a one-to-one match between real GDP and the quality of life. The real GDP per capita measure does not indicate how income is distributed. It doesn't include some sources of well-being, and it does include some things that are detriments to well-being.

MODULE 11 REVIEW

Check Your Understanding

1. Assume there are only two goods in the economy, french fries and onion rings. In year 1, 1,000,000 servings of french fries were sold for $0.40 each and 800,000 servings of onion rings were sold for $0.60 each. From year 1 to year 2, the price of french fries rose to $0.50 and the servings sold fell to 900,000; the price of onion rings fell to $0.51 and the servings sold rose to 840,000.
   a. Calculate nominal GDP in year 1 and year 2. Calculate real GDP in year 2 using year 1 prices.
   b. Why would an assessment of growth using nominal GDP be misguided?

2. Indicate the effect of each of the following on real GDP:
   a. Chevrolet increases its production of Corvettes.
   b. Consumer expenditures increase as a result of inflation.
   c. $50 billion is spent on hurricane cleanup.
   d. Citizens spend 10,000 hours as neighborhood watch volunteers.

TACKLE THE AP® TEST: Multiple-Choice Questions

1. Which of the following is true of real GDP?
   a. It is adjusted for changes in prices.
   b. It is always equal to nominal GDP.
   c. It decreases whenever aggregate output increases.
   d. It is equal to nominal GDP minus the inflation rate.
   e. All of the above are true.

2. The best measure for comparing a country's aggregate output over time is
   a. nominal GDP.
   b. real GDP.
   c. nominal GDP per capita.
   d. real GDP per capita.
   e. average GDP per capita.

3. Use the information provided in the table below for an economy that produces only apples and oranges. Assume year 1 is the base year.

	Year 1	Year 2
Quantity of apples	3,000	4,000
Price of an apple	$0.20	$0.30
Quantity of oranges	2,000	3,000
Price of an orange	$0.40	$0.50

What was the value of real GDP in each year?

	Year 1	Year 2
a.	$1,400	$2,700
b.	$1,900	$2,700
c.	$1,400	$2,000
d.	$1,900	$2,000
e.	$1,400	$1,900

4. Real GDP per capita is an imperfect measure of the quality of life in part because it
   a. includes the value of leisure time.
   b. excludes expenditures on education.
   c. includes expenditures on natural disasters.
   d. excludes expenditures on entertainment.
   e. includes the value of housework.

5. Refer to the data in the table below.

	Nominal GDP in billions of dollars
United States	$19,458.0
Japan	4,781.2
European Union	17,277.6

Which of the following can be determined with the information in the table?
   a. Residents of Japan were worse off than residents of the United States or the European Union.
   b. The European Union had a higher nominal GDP per capita than the United States.
   c. The United States had a larger economy than the European Union.
   d. Residents of the European Union were better off than residents of Japan or the United States.
   e. Japan experienced larger increases in prices than the United States or Japan.

6. Which of the following would cause real GDP to exceed nominal GDP?
   a. a large increase in aggregate output
   b. a large decease in aggregate output
   c. a significant decrease in prices
   d. an increase in population
   e. using the value-added approach to calculate GDP

7. Which of the following would lead to an increase in real GDP per capita all other things equal?
   a. a decrease in population
   b. an increase in population
   c. an increase in prices
   d. a decrease in aggregate output
   e. the use of chain-linking

TACKLE THE AP® TEST: Free-Response Questions

1. The economy of Britannica produces three goods: computers, T-shirts, and sunglasses. The accompanying table shows the prices and output of the three goods for year 1 and year 2.

Year	Computers Price	Computers Quantity	T-shirts Price	T-shirts Quantity	Sunglasses Price	Sunglasses Quantity
Year 1	$900	10	$10	100	$15	2
Year 2	1,050	12	14	110	17	3

   a. Calculate the nominal GDP in Britannica for year 1.

   b. Calculate the real GDP in Britannica for year 1 using year 1 as the base year.
   c. Calculate the real GDP in Britannica for year 2 using year 1 as the base year.

Rubric for FRQ 1 (3 points)

1 point: ($900 × 10) + ($10 × 100) + ($15 × 2) = $9,000 + $1,000 + $30 = $10,030

1 point: Real GDP equals nominal GDP in the base year, so this answer is the same as in part a.

1 point: ($900 × 12) + ($10 × 110) + ($15 × 3) = $10,800 + $1,100 + $45 = $11,945

2. The country of Hungry produces only pizzas and the country of Thirsty produces only smoothies. Use the information in the table to answer the following questions:

  a. Calculate the number of pizzas made in Hungry and the number of smoothies made in Thirsty in each year.

  b. Calculate the real GDP in each country in year 2 using year 1 prices.

  c. In which country did real GDP increase the most between year 1 and year 2?

  d. In which country did real GDP per capita decrease the most between year 1 and year 2? Show your work.

(6 points)

	Nominal GDP	Price	Population
Hungry			
Year 1	$10,000	$10	5
Year 2	20,000	10	16
Thirsty			
Year 1	$10,000	$10	5
Year 2	30,000	20	10

The Meaning and Calculation of Unemployment

> **In this Module, you will learn to:**
> - Explain how unemployment is measured
> - Calculate the unemployment rate
> - Summarize the significance of the unemployment rate for the economy
> - Explain the relationship between the unemployment rate and economic growth

The Unemployment Rate

A Gallup poll in March 2016 found that 26% of Americans mentioned "economic issues" as the nation's most important problem, with "unemployment/jobs" cited most frequently as the source of economic concerns. **Figure 12.1** shows the U.S.

Figure 12.1 The U.S. Unemployment Rate, 1948–2017

The unemployment rate has fluctuated widely over time. It always rises during recessions, which are shown by the shaded bars. It usually, but not always, falls during periods of economic expansion.

Data Source: Bureau of Labor Statistics; National Bureau of Economic Research.

unemployment rate from 1948 through 2017. As you can see, the unemployment rate has fluctuated widely over the past 70 years. What does the unemployment rate mean, and why is it a major concern for U.S. citizens? To make sense of the attention paid to employment and unemployment, we need to first understand how they are defined and measured.

Defining and Measuring Unemployment

It's easy to define employment: you are **employed** if and only if you have a job.

Unemployment, however, is a more subtle concept. Just because a person isn't working doesn't mean that we consider that person *unemployed*. For example, in April 2017 there were 42 million retired workers in the United States receiving Social Security checks. Most of them were probably happy that they were no longer working, so we wouldn't consider someone who has settled into a comfortable retirement to be unemployed. There were also 10 million disabled U.S. workers receiving benefits because they were unable to work. Again, although they weren't working, we wouldn't normally consider them to be unemployed.

The U.S. Census Bureau, the federal agency that collects data on unemployment, considers the unemployed to be those individuals who are "jobless, looking for jobs, and available for work." Retired people don't count because they aren't looking for jobs; those who are unable to work don't count because they aren't available for work. More specifically, an individual is considered unemployed if he or she doesn't currently have a job and has been actively seeking a job during the past four weeks. So the **unemployed** are people who are actively looking for work but aren't currently employed.

A country's **labor force** is the sum of the employed and the unemployed—that is, the people who are currently working and the people who are currently looking for work. The **labor force participation rate**, defined as the share of the working-age population that is in the labor force, is calculated as follows:

(12-1) $\text{Labor force participation rate} = \dfrac{\text{Labor force}}{\text{Population age 16 and older}} \times 100$

The **unemployment rate**, defined as the percentage of the total number of people in the labor force who are unemployed, is calculated as follows:

(12-2) $\text{Unemployment rate} = \dfrac{\text{Number of unemployed workers}}{\text{Labor force}} \times 100$

To estimate the numbers that go into calculating the unemployment rate, the U.S. Census Bureau carries out a monthly survey called the Current Population Survey, which involves interviewing a random sample of 60,000 American families. People are asked whether they are currently employed. If they are not employed, they are asked whether they have been looking for a job during the past four weeks. The results are then scaled up, using estimates of the total population, to estimate the total number of employed and unemployed Americans.

The Significance of the Unemployment Rate

In general, the unemployment rate is a good indicator of how easy or difficult it is to find a job given the current state of the economy. When the unemployment rate is low, for example when it was 4.4% in 2017, nearly everyone who wants a job can find one—available workers are so scarce that employers joke that if the worker is breathing, he or she will be hired! By contrast, in the midst of a recession it is much harder to find a job. For example, in 2009, the unemployment rate in 17 states rose to over 10% (close to 15% in Michigan), with many highly qualified workers having lost their jobs and having

Education & Exploration 1/Alamy

Employed people are currently holding a job in the economy, either full time or part time.

Unemployed people are actively looking for work but aren't currently employed.

The **labor force** is equal to the sum of the employed and the unemployed.

The **labor force participation rate** is the percentage of the population aged 16 or older that is in the labor force.

The **unemployment rate** is the percentage of the total number of people in the labor force who are unemployed.

AP® EXAM TIP

You will need to calculate the size of the labor force, the labor force participation rate, and the unemployment rate. Remember: an unemployed person must be willing and able to work and be actively seeking employment. The labor force is made up of both employed and unemployed people. The labor force participation rate is the percent of the *population* in the labor force, and the unemployment rate is the percent of the *labor force* that is unemployed.

a hard time finding new ones. Although the unemployment rate is a good indicator of current labor market conditions, it is not a perfect measure.

Issues with the Unemployment Rate as a Measure of the True Level of Unemployment

Frequently, some of the people who would like to work but aren't working still don't get counted as unemployed. In particular, an individual who has given up looking for a job for the time being because there are no jobs available isn't counted as unemployed because he or she has not been searching for a job during the previous four weeks. Individuals who want to work but aren't currently searching because they see little prospect of finding a job given the state of the job market are known as **discouraged workers**. Because it does not count discouraged workers, the measured unemployment rate may understate the percentage of people who want to work but are unable to find jobs.

Discouraged workers are part of a larger group known as **marginally attached workers**. These are people who say they would like to have a job and have looked for work in the recent past but are not currently looking for work. The difference between discouraged workers and other marginally attached workers is that the other marginally attached workers ended their job search for a reason other than a belief that no job was available for them. For example, they may have gone back to school or become disabled. Marginally attached workers are also not included when calculating the unemployment rate.

Finally, another category of workers who are frustrated in their ability to find work but aren't counted as unemployed are the **underemployed**: workers who are currently employed but would like to work more hours or are overqualified for their jobs. For example, some part-time workers would like to work full time, and some college graduates work as fast-food clerks. Again, they aren't counted in the unemployment rate.

The Bureau of Labor Statistics is the federal agency that calculates the official unemployment rate. It also calculates broader "measures of labor underutilization" that include the three categories of frustrated workers. **Figure 12.2** shows what happens to the measured unemployment rate once marginally attached workers (including discouraged workers) and the underemployed are counted. The broadest measure of unemployment and underemployment, known as *U6*, is the sum of these three measures plus the unemployed; it is substantially higher than the rate usually quoted by the news media. But U6 and the unemployment rate move very much in parallel, so changes in the unemployment rate remain a good guide to what's happening in the overall labor market.

On the other hand, the unemployment rate may indicate a larger issue with unemployment than actually exists in the economy. When searching for work, it's normal for people to take at least a few weeks to find a suitable job. Yet a worker who is quite confident of finding a job, but has not yet accepted a position, is counted as unemployed. As a consequence, the unemployment rate never falls to zero, even in boom times when jobs are plentiful. In addition, people may indicate that they are willing and able to work and are seeking employment when they are not. For example, often people must indicate that they have looked for work in order to receive unemployment benefits. If someone indicates that they have looked for work to qualify for benefits, when in reality they are not seeking a job, the unemployment rate will be overstated.

Finally, it's important to realize that the unemployment rate varies greatly among demographic groups. Other things equal, jobs are generally easier to find for more experienced workers and for workers during their "prime" working years, from ages 25 to 54. For younger workers, as well as workers nearing retirement age, jobs are typically

Discouraged workers are non-working people who are capable of working but have given up looking for a job due to the state of the job market.

Marginally attached workers would like to be employed and have looked for a job in the recent past but are not currently looking for work.

The **underemployed** are workers who would like to work more hours or who are overqualified for their jobs.

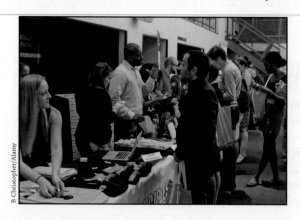

Figure 12.2 Alternative Measures of Unemployment, 1994–2017

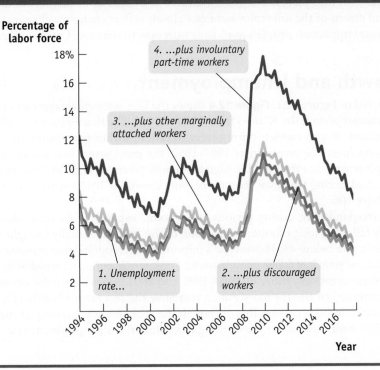

The unemployment number usually quoted in the news media counts someone as unemployed only if he or she has been looking for work during the past four weeks. Broader measures also count discouraged workers, other marginally attached workers, and the underemployed. These broader measures show a higher unemployment rate—but they move closely in parallel with the more narrow rate.

Data Source: Bureau of Labor Statistics.

harder to find. **Figure 12.3** shows unemployment rates for different groups in the second quarter of 2018, when the U.S. unemployment rate dipped below 4%. As you can see, the unemployment rate for African-American workers was much higher than the national average; the unemployment rate for White teenagers (ages 16–19) was almost three times the national average; and the unemployment rate for Black or African-American teenagers, at 23.1%, was over five times the national average. (Bear in mind that a teenager isn't considered unemployed, even if he or she isn't working, unless that teenager is looking for work but can't find it.) So even at a time when the overall unemployment rate was relatively low, jobs were hard to find for some groups.

Figure 12.3 Unemployment Rates of Different Groups, 2018 (Q2)

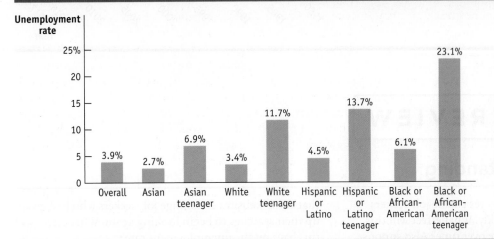

Unemployment rates vary greatly among different demographic groups. For example, although the overall unemployment rate in the second quarter of 2018 was 3.9%, the unemployment rate among Asian teenagers was 6.9%. As a result, even during periods of low overall unemployment, unemployment remains a serious problem for some groups.

Data Source: Bureau of Labor Statistics.

Although the unemployment rate is not an exact measure of the percentage of people unable to find jobs, it is a good indicator of overall labor market conditions. The ups and downs of the unemployment rate closely reflect economic changes that have a significant impact on people's lives. Let's turn now to the causes of these fluctuations.

Growth and Unemployment

Compared to Figure 12.1, **Figure 12.4** shows the U.S. unemployment rate over a somewhat shorter period, the 37 years from 1980 to 2017. The shaded bars represent periods of recession. As you can see, during every recession, without exception, the unemployment rate rose. The recession of 1981–1982, the most severe one shown, pushed the unemployment rate into double digits: unemployment peaked in November 1982 at 10.8%. And during the most recent recession shown, in 2010 the unemployment rate rose above 10%.

Correspondingly, during periods of economic expansion the unemployment rate usually falls. The long economic expansion of the 1990s eventually brought the unemployment rate below 4%. However, it's important to recognize that *economic expansions aren't always periods of falling unemployment*. Look at the periods immediately following two recent recessions, those of 1990–1991 and 2001. In each case the unemployment rate continued to rise for more than a year after the recession was officially over. The explanation in both cases is that, although the economy was growing as measured by real GDP, it was not growing fast enough to reduce the unemployment rate.

Figure 12.4   Unemployment and Recessions, 1980–2017

This figure shows a close-up of the unemployment rate from 1980 through the end of 2017, with the shaded bars indicating recessions. It's clear that unemployment always rises during recessions and *usually* falls during expansions. But in both the early 1990s and the early 2000s, unemployment continued to rise for some time after the recession was officially declared over.

Data Source: Bureau of Labor Statistics; National Bureau of Economic Research.

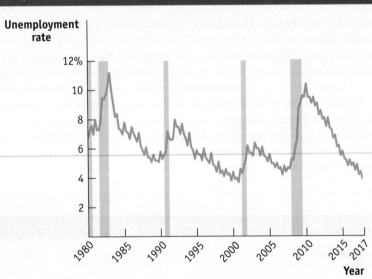

MODULE 12 REVIEW

Check Your Understanding

1. Suppose that employment websites enable job-seekers to find suitable jobs more quickly. What effect will this have on the unemployment rate over time? Also suppose that these websites encourage job-seekers who had given up their searches to begin looking again. What effect will this have on the unemployment rate?

2. In which of the following cases would the worker be counted as unemployed? Explain.
   a. Rosa, an older worker, has been laid off and gave up looking for work months ago.
   b. Anthony, a schoolteacher, has chosen not to work during his three-month summer break.
   c. Grace, an investment banker, has been laid off and is currently searching for another position.
   d. Sergio, a classically trained musician, can only find work playing for local parties.
   e. Natasha, a graduate student, went back to school because jobs were scarce.

3. Which of these statements is consistent with the observed relationship between growth in real GDP and changes in the unemployment rate? Explain.
   a. A rise in the unemployment rate accompanies a fall in real GDP.
   b. An exceptionally strong business recovery is associated with a greater percentage of the labor force being employed.
   c. Negative real GDP growth is associated with a fall in the unemployment rate.

TACKLE THE AP® TEST: Multiple-Choice Questions

1. To be considered unemployed, a person must
   a. collect unemployment insurance.
   b. work more than 30 hours per week.
   c. have been laid off from a job that was held for one year or longer.
   d. not be working but want to have a job.
   e. not be working but be available for and actively seeking a job.

Use the information for a hypothetical economy presented in the following table to answer Questions 2–4.

Population age 16 and older = 200,000
Labor force = 100,000
Number of people working part time = 20,000
Number of people working full time = 70,000

2. What is the labor force participation rate?
   a. 70%   **d.** 10%
   b. 50%   **e.** 5%
   c. 20%

3. How many people are unemployed?
   a. 10,000
   b. 20,000
   c. 30,000
   d. 100,000
   e. 110,000

4. What is the unemployment rate?
   a. 70%   **d.** 10%
   b. 50%   **e.** 5%
   c. 20%

5. The unemployment problem in an economy may be understated by the unemployment rate due to
   a. people lying about seeking a job.
   b. discouraged workers.
   c. job candidates with one offer but waiting for more.
   d. overemployed workers.
   e. none of the above.

6. The unemployment problem in an economy may be overstated by the unemployment rate due to
   a. people taking their time to transition between available jobs.
   b. discouragement.
   c. marginally attached workers.
   d. underemployment.
   e. people saying they did not look for work when they actually did.

7. If real GDP is falling, which of the following is true?
   a. The economy is in an expansion.
   b. Unemployment is rising.
   c. The number of discouraged workers is decreasing.
   d. Underemployment is falling.
   e. None of the above are true.

TACKLE THE AP® TEST: Free-Response Questions

1. Use the data provided in the following table to calculate each of the following. Show how you calculate each.
   a. the size of the labor force
   b. the labor force participation rate
   c. the unemployment rate

Population age 16 and older = 12 million
Employment = 5 million
Unemployment = 1 million

2. What is the labor market classification of each of the following individuals? Be as specific as possible, and explain your answer.
   a. Julie has a graduate degree in mechanical engineering. She works full time mowing lawns.
   b. Jeff was laid off from his previous job. He would very much like to work at any job, but, after looking for work for a year, he has stopped looking for work.
   c. Ian is working 25 hours per week at a bookstore and has no desire to work full time.
   d. Raj has decided to take a year off from work to stay home with his daughter. **(4 points)**

MOD 13

The Causes and Categories of Unemployment

> **In this Module, you will learn to:**
> - Identify the factors that determine the natural rate of unemployment
> - Explain the three different types of unemployment and their causes

Unemployment in the Economy

Fast economic growth tends to reduce the unemployment rate. So how low can the unemployment rate go? You might be tempted to say zero, but that isn't feasible. Over the past half century, the national unemployment rate has never dropped below 2.9%, showing that there is unemployment even when the economy is doing well and many businesses are having a hard time finding workers. To understand why an economy always has unemployment, we need to examine the nature of labor markets and how they can lead to substantial measured unemployment. We also need to recognize that there are three distinct types of unemployment: frictional, structural, and cyclical. Our starting point is the observation that, even in the best of times, jobs are constantly being created and destroyed.

Job Creation and Job Destruction

Even during good times, most Americans know someone who has lost his or her job. The U.S. unemployment rate in June 2017 was only 4.4%, relatively low by historical standards, yet in that month there were 5.3 million "job separations"— terminations of employment that occurred because a worker was either fired or quit voluntarily.

There are many reasons for such job loss. One is structural change in the economy: industries rise and fall as new technologies emerge and consumers' tastes change. For example, employment in high-tech industries such as telecommunications surged in the late 1990s but slumped severely after 2000. However, structural change also brings the creation of new jobs: the number of jobs in the U.S. health care sector has surged as new medical technologies have emerged and the aging of the population has increased the demand for medical care. The U.S. health care sector is predicted to continue to add more jobs than any other sector in the coming years. Poor management performance or bad luck at individual companies also leads to job loss for their employees.

This constant churning of the workforce is an inevitable feature of the modern economy. And this churning, in turn, is one source of *frictional unemployment*—one main reason that there is a considerable amount of unemployment even when jobs are abundant.

The U.S. health care sector is predicted to be a source of job creation in the future.

Frictional Unemployment

Workers who lose their jobs involuntarily due to job destruction often choose not to take the first new jobs offered. For example, suppose a skilled programmer, laid off because her software company's product line was unsuccessful, sees a job listing for low-paying clerical work. She might respond to the post and get the job—but that would be foolish. Instead, she should take the time to look for a job that takes advantage of her skills and pays accordingly. In addition, individual workers are constantly leaving jobs voluntarily, typically for personal reasons—family moves, dissatisfaction, and better job prospects elsewhere.

Economists say that workers who spend time looking for employment are engaged in job search. If all workers and all jobs were alike, job search wouldn't be necessary; if information about jobs and workers were perfect, job search would be very quick. In practice, however, it's normal for a worker who leaves or loses a job, or a young worker seeking a first job, to spend at least a few weeks searching.

Frictional unemployment is unemployment due to the time workers spend in job search. A certain amount of frictional unemployment is inevitable, for two reasons. One is the constant process of job creation and job destruction. The other is the fact that new workers are always entering the labor market. For example, in August 2017, out of 3.5 million workers counted as unemployed, 0.73 million were new entrants to the workforce and another 2.2 million were "re-entrants"—people who had come back after being out of the workforce for a time.

A limited amount of frictional unemployment is relatively harmless and may even be a good thing. The economy is more productive if workers take the time to find jobs that are well matched to their skills, and workers who are unemployed for a brief period while searching for the right job don't experience great hardship. In fact, when there is a low unemployment rate, periods of unemployment tend to be quite short, suggesting that much of the unemployment is frictional. **Figure 13.1** shows the composition

> ### AP® EXAM TIP
>
> Be prepared to identify the type of unemployment—frictional, structural, or cyclical—given a specific scenario in both the multiple-choice and free-response questions on the AP® exam.

Frictional unemployment is unemployment due to the time workers spend in job search.

Figure 13.1   Distribution of the Unemployed by Duration of Unemployment, 2010 and 2017

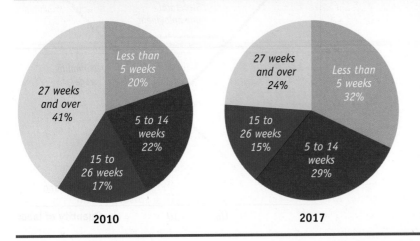

2010

2017

In years when the unemployment rate is low, most unemployed workers are unemployed for only a short period. In 2017, a year of low unemployment, 32% of the unemployed had been unemployed for less than 5 weeks and 61% for less than 15 weeks. The short duration of unemployment for most workers suggests that most unemployment in 2017 was frictional. In early 2010, by contrast, only 20% of the unemployed had been unemployed for less than 5 weeks, but 41% had been unemployed for 27 or more weeks, indicating that during periods of high unemployment, a smaller share of unemployment is frictional.

Data Source: Bureau of Labor Statistics.

of unemployment in 2017, when the unemployment rate was only 4.4%: 32.5% of the unemployed had been unemployed for less than 5 weeks and only 38.8% had been unemployed for 15 or more weeks. Just 24.2% were considered to be "long-term unemployed"—unemployed for 27 or more weeks. The picture looked very different in 2010, after unemployment had been high for an extended period of time.

In periods of higher unemployment, workers tend to be jobless for longer periods of time, suggesting that a smaller share of unemployment is frictional. By early 2010, when unemployment had been high for several months, for instance, the fraction of unemployed workers considered "long-term unemployed" had jumped to 41%.

Public policy designed to help workers who lose their jobs can lead to frictional unemployment as an unintended side effect. Most economically advanced countries provide benefits to laid-off workers as a way to tide them over until they find a new job. In the United States, these benefits typically replace only a small fraction of a worker's income and expire after 26 weeks, in most cases. In other countries, particularly some in Europe, benefits are more generous and last longer. The drawback to this generosity is that it reduces the incentive to quickly find a new job. By keeping more people searching for longer, the benefits increase frictional unemployment.

Structural Unemployment

Frictional unemployment exists even when the number of people seeking jobs is equal to the number of jobs being offered—that is, the existence of frictional unemployment doesn't mean that there is a surplus of labor. Sometimes, however, there is a *persistent surplus* of job-seekers in a particular labor market. For example, there may be more workers with a particular skill than there are jobs available using that skill, or there may be more workers in a particular geographic region than there are jobs available in that region. **Structural unemployment** is unemployment that results from a mismatch between job seekers and the types of jobs available in the economy. This mismatch can be due to workers lacking the skills required for the available jobs. It can also occur when there are more people seeking jobs in a labor market than there are jobs available at the current wage rate.

The supply and demand model tells us that the price of a good, service, or factor of production tends to move toward an equilibrium level that matches the quantity supplied with the quantity demanded. This is equally true, in general, of labor markets. **Figure 13.2** shows a typical market for labor. The labor demand curve indicates that

Structural unemployment is unemployment that results when workers lack the skills required for the available jobs, or there are more people seeking jobs in a labor market than there are jobs available at the current wage rate.

Figure 13.2 The Effect of Minimum Wage on the Labor Market

When the government sets a minimum wage, W_F, that exceeds the market equilibrium wage rate, W_E, the number of workers, Q_S, who would like to work at that minimum wage is greater than the number of workers, Q_D, demanded at that wage rate. This surplus of labor is considered structural unemployment.

when the price of labor—the wage rate—increases, employers demand less labor. The labor supply curve indicates that when the price of labor increases, more workers are willing to supply labor at the prevailing wage rate. These two forces coincide to lead to an equilibrium wage rate for any given type of labor in a particular location. That equilibrium wage rate is shown as W_E.

Even at the equilibrium wage rate, W_E, there will still be some frictional unemployment. That's because there will always be some workers engaged in job search even when the number of jobs available is equal to the number of workers seeking jobs. But there wouldn't be any structural unemployment caused by a surplus of labor, as there is when the wage rate is persistently above W_E. Factors that can lead to a wage rate in excess of W_E include minimum wages, labor unions, and *efficiency wages*.

Minimum Wages

As explained in Module 8, a minimum wage is a government-mandated floor on the price of labor. In the United States in 2018, the national minimum wage was $7.25 an hour. For many American workers, the minimum wage is irrelevant; the market equilibrium wage for these workers is well above this price floor. But for less skilled workers, the minimum wage may be binding—it affects the wages that people are actually paid and can lead to structural unemployment. In countries that have higher minimum wages, the range of workers for whom the minimum wage is binding is larger.

Figure 13.2 shows the effect of a binding minimum wage. In this market, there is a legal floor on wages, W_F, which is above the equilibrium wage rate, W_E. This leads to a persistent surplus in the labor market: the quantity of labor supplied, Q_S, is larger than the quantity demanded, Q_D. In other words, more people want to work than can find jobs at the minimum wage, leading to structural unemployment.

Given that minimum wages—that is, binding minimum wages—generally lead to structural unemployment, you might wonder why governments impose them. The rationale is to help ensure that people who work can earn enough income to afford at least a minimally comfortable lifestyle. However, this may come at a cost, because it may eliminate employment opportunities for some workers who would have willingly worked for lower wages. As illustrated in Figure 13.2, not only are there more sellers of labor than there are buyers, but there are also fewer people working at a minimum wage (Q_D) than there would have been with no minimum wage at all (Q_E).

Although economists broadly agree that a high minimum wage has the employment-reducing effects shown in Figure 13.2, there is some question about whether this is a good description of how the minimum wage actually works in the United States. The minimum wage in the United States is quite low compared with that in other wealthy countries. For three decades, from the 1970s to the mid-2000s, the U.S. minimum wage was so low that it was not binding for the vast majority of workers— employers paid most workers more than the minimum wage. In addition, some researchers have produced evidence that increases in the minimum wage actually lead to higher employment when, as was the case in the United States at one time, the minimum wage is low compared to average wages. They argue that firms that employ low-skilled workers sometimes restrict their hiring in order to keep wages low and that, as a result, the minimum wage can sometimes be increased without any loss of jobs. Most economists, however, agree that a sufficiently high minimum wage *does* lead to structural unemployment.

Labor Unions

The actions of *labor unions* can have effects similar to those of minimum wages, leading to structural unemployment. By bargaining collectively for all of a firm's workers, unions can often win higher wages from employers than workers would have obtained by bargaining individually. This process, known as *collective bargaining*, is intended to tip the scales of bargaining power more toward workers and away from employers. Labor unions exercise bargaining power by threatening firms with a *labor strike*, a collective

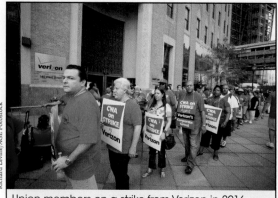
Union members on a strike from Verizon in 2016.

refusal to work. The threat of a strike can have very serious consequences for firms that have difficulty replacing striking workers. In such cases, workers acting collectively can exercise more power than they could if they acted individually.

When workers have greater bargaining power, they tend to demand and receive higher wages. Unions also bargain over benefits, such as health care and pensions, which we can think of as additional wages. Indeed, economists who study the effects of unions on wages find that unionized workers earn higher wages and more generous benefits than non-union workers with similar skills. The result of these increased wages can be the same as the result of a minimum wage: labor unions push the wage that workers receive above the equilibrium wage. Consequently, there are more people willing to work at the wage being paid than there are jobs available. Like a binding minimum wage, this leads to structural unemployment.

Efficiency Wages

Efficiency wages are wages that employers set above the equilibrium wage rate as an incentive for better employee performance.

Actions by firms may also contribute to structural unemployment. Firms may choose to pay **efficiency wages**—wages that employers set above the equilibrium wage rate as an incentive for their workers to deliver better performance.

Employers may feel the need for such incentives for several reasons. For example, employers often have difficulty directly observing how hard an employee works. They can, however, elicit more work effort by paying above-market wages: employees receiving these higher wages are more likely to work harder to ensure that they aren't fired, which would cause them to lose their higher wages.

When many firms pay efficiency wages, the result is a pool of workers who want jobs but can't find them. So the use of efficiency wages by firms leads to structural unemployment.

Cyclical Unemployment and the Natural Rate of Unemployment

The **natural rate of unemployment** is the unemployment rate that arises from the effects of frictional plus structural unemployment.

Cyclical unemployment is the deviation of the actual rate of unemployment from the natural rate.

Because some frictional unemployment is inevitable and because many economies also suffer from structural unemployment, a certain amount of unemployment is normal, or "natural." Actual unemployment fluctuates around this normal level. The **natural rate of unemployment** is the rate of unemployment that arises from the effects of frictional plus structural unemployment. It is the normal, or *minimum feasible*, unemployment rate around which the actual unemployment rate fluctuates.

There is no specific value for the natural rate of unemployment, but **Figure 13.3** provides estimates of the natural rates of unemployment in the relatively wealthy countries that belong to the Organization for Economic Cooperation and Development (OECD). **Cyclical unemployment** is the deviation of the actual rate of unemployment from the natural rate; that is, it is the difference between the actual and natural rates of unemployment. As the name suggests, cyclical unemployment is the share of unemployment that arises from the business cycle. Jobs lost due to a recession will return after the economy moves into expansion. We'll see later that public policy cannot keep the unemployment rate persistently below the natural rate without leading to accelerating inflation.

We can summarize the relationships between the various types of unemployment as follows:

(13-1) Natural unemployment =
        Frictional unemployment + Structural unemployment

(13-2) Actual unemployment =
        Natural unemployment + Cyclical unemployment

Figure 13.3 Natural Rate of Unemployment in OECD Countries

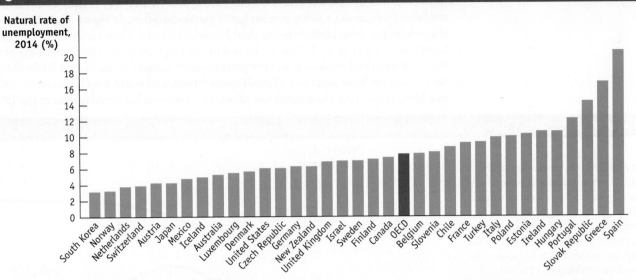

Among members of the OECD, estimates of the natural rates of unemployment in 2014 ranged from 3.2% in South Korea to 20.7% in Spain. The blue bar shows the average across all the OECD countries, 7.8%. The U.S. natural rate of unemployment, 6.1%, is low relative to both the average rate and the rates in the major European economies of the United Kingdom, Germany,

Italy, France, and Spain. As mentioned earlier, the rates in Europe may be elevated by frictional unemployment caused by generous unemployment benefits. In addition, high minimum wages in Europe can discourage employers from offering jobs and lead to higher rates of structural unemployment.

Data Source: OECD.

Perhaps because of its name, people often imagine that the natural rate of unemployment is a constant that doesn't change over time and can't be affected by policy. Neither proposition is true. Let's take a moment to stress two facts: the natural rate of unemployment changes over time, and it can be affected by economic policies.

Changes in the Natural Rate of Unemployment

Private-sector economists and government agencies need estimates of the natural rate of unemployment both to make forecasts and to conduct policy analyses. Almost all these estimates show that the U.S. natural rate rises and falls over time. For example, the Federal Reserve Bank of St. Louis believes that the U.S. natural rate of unemployment was 5.28% in 1950, rose to 6.27% by the end of the 1970s, and then fell to a low of 4.92% in 2009. Between 2009 and 2011, the estimated natural rate of unemployment increased to 5.15% but fell back to 4.74% in 2018. European countries have experienced even larger swings in their natural rates of unemployment.

What causes the natural rate of unemployment to change? The most important factors are changes in the characteristics of the labor force, changes in labor market institutions, and changes in government policies. Let's look briefly at each factor.

Changes in Labor Force Characteristics

In 2017 the overall rate of unemployment in the United States was 4.4%. Young workers, however, had much higher unemployment rates: 14% for teenagers and 7.4% for workers aged 20 to 24. Workers aged 25 to 54 had an unemployment rate of only 3.7%.

In general, unemployment rates tend to be lower for experienced workers than for inexperienced workers. Because experienced workers tend to stay in a given job longer than do inexperienced ones, they have lower frictional unemployment. Also, because older workers are more likely than young workers to be family breadwinners, they have a stronger incentive to find and keep jobs.

> **AP® EXAM TIP**
>
> The natural rate of unemployment is never zero because frictional employment always exists. Think of the natural rate as the lowest feasible level of unemployment that can be reached—a level that will be identified in the models of the macroeconomy presented later in the course. Numerical estimates of the natural rate differ based on when, where, and why they are estimated, but the concept of the natural unemployment rate is always the same.

One reason the natural rate of unemployment rose during the 1970s was a large rise in the number of new workers—children of the post–World War II baby boom entered the labor force, as did a rising percentage of married women. As **Figure 13.4** shows, both the percentage of the labor force less than 25 years old and the percentage of women in the labor force surged in the 1970s. By the end of the 1990s, however, the share of women in the labor force had leveled off and the percentage of workers under 25 had fallen sharply. As a result, the labor force as a whole is more experienced today than it was in the 1970s, one likely reason that the natural rate of unemployment is lower today than in the 1970s.

Figure 13.4 The Changing Makeup of the U.S. Labor Force, 1948–2016

In the 1970s the percentage of the labor force consisting of women rose rapidly, as did the percentage under age 25. These changes reflected the entry of large numbers of women into the paid labor force for the first time and the fact that baby boomers were reaching working age. The natural rate of unemployment may have risen because many of these workers were relatively inexperienced. Today, the labor force is much more experienced, which is one possible reason the natural rate has fallen since the 1970s.
Data Source: Bureau of Labor Statistics.

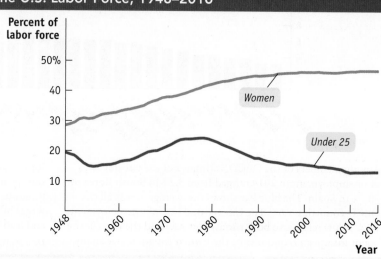

Changes in Labor Market Institutions

As we pointed out earlier, unions that negotiate wages above the equilibrium level can be a source of structural unemployment. Some economists believe that strong labor unions are one of the reasons for the high natural rate of unemployment in Europe. In the United States, a sharp fall in union membership after 1980 may have been one reason the natural rate of unemployment fell between the 1970s and the 1990s.

Other institutional changes may also have been at work. For example, some labor economists believe that temporary employment agencies reduce frictional unemployment by matching workers to jobs. Furthermore, internet websites have reduced frictional unemployment by making information about job openings and job-seekers more widely available, thereby helping workers avoid a prolonged job search.

Technological change, coupled with labor market institutions, can also affect the natural rate of unemployment. Technological change leads to an increase in the demand for skilled workers who are familiar with the relevant technology and a reduction in the demand for unskilled workers. Economic theory predicts that wages should increase for skilled workers and decrease for unskilled workers. But if wages for unskilled workers cannot go down—say, due to a binding minimum wage—increased structural unemployment, and therefore a higher natural rate of unemployment, will result.

Online job search engines have reduced frictional unemployment by helping to match employers with job-seekers.

Changes in Government Policies

A high minimum wage can cause structural unemployment. Generous unemployment benefits can increase frictional unemployment. So government policies intended to help workers can have the undesirable side effect of raising the natural rate of unemployment.

Some government policies, however, may reduce the natural rate. Two examples are job training and employment subsidies. Job-training programs are supposed to provide unemployed workers with skills that widen the range of jobs they can perform. Employment subsidies are payments either to workers or to employers that provide a financial incentive to accept or offer jobs.

MODULE 13 REVIEW

Check Your Understanding

1. Explain the following statements.
   a. Frictional unemployment always exists.
   b. Frictional unemployment accounts for a larger share of total unemployment when the unemployment rate is low.

2. Why does collective bargaining have the same general effect on unemployment as a minimum wage? Illustrate your answer with a diagram.

3. Suppose the United States dramatically increases benefits for unemployed workers. Explain what will happen to the natural rate of unemployment.

TACKLE THE AP® TEST: Multiple-Choice Questions

1. A person who moves to a new state and takes two months to find a new job can be categorized as experiencing which type of unemployment?
   a. frictional   d. natural
   b. structural   e. full
   c. cyclical

2. What type of unemployment is created by a recession?
   a. frictional   d. natural
   b. structural   e. full
   c. cyclical

3. A person who is unemployed because of a mismatch between the quantity of labor supplied and the quantity of labor demanded is experiencing what type of unemployment?
   a. frictional   d. natural
   b. structural   e. full
   c. cyclical

4. Which of the following is true of the natural rate of unemployment?
   a. It includes frictional unemployment.
   b. It includes cyclical unemployment.
   c. It includes all types of unemployment.
   d. It is equal to 0%.
   e. All of the above are true.

5. Which of the following can affect the natural rate of unemployment in an economy over time?
   a. labor force characteristics such as age and work experience
   b. the existence of labor unions
   c. advances in technologies that help workers find jobs
   d. government job-training programs
   e. all of the above

6. Which of the following can lead to structural unemployment?
   a. minimum wage laws
   b. labor unions
   c. efficiency wages
   d. technological change
   e. all of the above

7. Actual unemployment is equal to natural unemployment
   a. minus structural unemployment.
   b. plus cyclical unemployment.
   c. plus frictional unemployment.
   d. minus cyclical unemployment.
   e. minus frictional unemployment.

TACKLE THE AP® TEST: Free-Response Questions

1. a. The natural rate of unemployment is made up of which types of unemployment?
   b. Explain how cyclical unemployment relates to the natural rate of unemployment.
   c. List three factors that can lead to a change in the natural rate of unemployment.

Rubric for FRQ 1 (6 points)

1 point: The natural rate of unemployment is made up of frictional unemployment . . .

1 point: . . . plus structural unemployment.

1 point: Cyclical unemployment is the deviation of the actual rate of unemployment from the natural rate. *Or,* cyclical unemployment is the difference between the actual and natural rates of unemployment.

1 point: Changes in labor force characteristics

1 point: Changes in labor market institutions such as unions

1 point: Changes in government policies

2. In each of the following situations, what type of unemployment is Melanie facing? Explain.

   a. After completing a complex graphic design project, Melanie is laid off. Her prospects for a new job requiring similar skills are good, and she has signed up with a programmer placement service. She has passed up offers for low-paying jobs.

   b. Melanie loses her programming job because the development of new packaged software programs means employers no longer need to hire as many programmers.

   c. Due to the current slump in investment spending, Melanie has been laid off from her programming job. Her employer promises to rehire her when business picks up. **(6 points)**

MOD 14

Inflation: An Overview

> **In this Module, you will learn to:**
> - Calculate the rate of inflation
> - Specify the economic costs of inflation
> - Identify who is helped and who is hurt by inflation
> - Explain why policy makers try to maintain a stable rate of inflation
> - Differentiate between real and nominal values of income, wages, and interest rates
> - Discuss the problems of deflation and disinflation

Inflation and Deflation

Inflation in the United States has fluctuated between 0.12% and 3.14% since 2010 and is expected to remain in that range up to 2022 and beyond. During the same period, inflation in the European Union has remained below 3%. In general, inflation in major Western economies has remained fairly low in recent decades, for reasons we will investigate in later Modules. But other economies have had to deal with much higher rates of inflation in recent years. **Table 14.1** lists all countries in the world with an inflation

Table 14.1	Countries with an Inflation Rate over 10% in 2017
Country	**Inflation Rate (%)**
Egypt	10.2
Argentina	10.6
Sierra Leone	11.3
Azerbaijan	12.4
Haiti	13.4
Ukraine	13.9
Kazakhstan	14.6
Nigeria	15.7
Ghana	17.5
Zambia	17.9
Mozambique	19.2
Malawi	21.7
Democratic Republic of the Congo	22.4
Venezuela	254.9

Data adapted from World Economic Forum, 2018.

rate above 10% in 2017. Notice that many of these countries are in sub-Saharan Africa or the former Soviet Union. But the country with the highest inflation rate by far in 2017 is a South American country, Venezuela.

In 2017, Venezuela experienced inflation of 255% with predictions that it could rise even higher in the years to come. Venezuela has been experiencing *hyperinflation*, very high and accelerating rates of inflation. Observers describe the path of Venezuela's economy, as illustrated by its inflation rate, as a "death spiral." But Venezuela's hyperinflation is still not as bad as the worst hyperinflation experienced by Hungary in 1945, Yugoslavia in 1992, and Zimbabwe in 2008, where inflation rates doubled *daily*.

Why is high inflation a problem in an economy? Why are policy makers so concerned about hyperinflation that they get anxious when they see the inflation rate moving upward even slightly? The answer is that inflation imposes costs on the economy—but not in the way most people think.

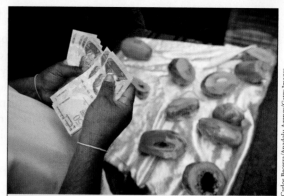

Due to hyperinflation, a kilogram of papaya (a little more than 2 pounds) can cost Venezuelans the equivalent of over $60 (USD).

The Level of Prices Doesn't Matter . . .

The most common misconception about inflation is that an increase in the price level makes everyone poorer—after all, a given amount of money buys less. But inflation does *not* make everyone poorer. To see why, it's helpful to imagine what would happen if a country replaced its currency with a new currency.

An example of this kind of currency conversion happened in 2002, when France, like a number of other European countries, replaced its national currency, the franc, with the euro. People turned in their franc coins and notes, and received euro coins and notes in exchange, at a rate of 6.55957 francs per euro. At the same time, all contracts were restated in euros at the same rate of exchange. For example, if a French citizen had a home mortgage debt of 500,000 francs, this became a debt of 500,000/6.55957 = 76,224.51 euros. If a worker's contract specified that he or she should be paid 100 francs per hour, it became a contract specifying a wage of 100/6.55957 = 15.2449 euros per hour, and so on. Since the eurozone was originally formed, eight additional countries have joined and replaced their national currencies with the euro. The most recent addition to the eurozone was Lithuania, which adopted the euro as its national currency in 2015.

You could imagine doing the same thing in the United States, replacing the dollar with a "new dollar" at a rate of exchange of, say, 7 to 1. If you owed $140,000 on your home, that would become a debt of 20,000 new dollars. If you had a wage rate of $14 an hour, it would become 2 new dollars an hour, and so on. This would bring the overall U.S. price level back to about what it was when John F. Kennedy was president.

So would everyone be richer as a result because prices would be only one-seventh as high? Of course not. Prices would be lower, but so would wages and incomes. If you cut a worker's wage to one-seventh of its previous value, but also cut all prices to one-seventh of their previous level, the worker's **real wage**—the wage rate divided by the price level to adjust for the effects of inflation or deflation—doesn't change. In fact, bringing the overall price level back to what it was during the Kennedy administration would have no effect on overall purchasing power, because doing so would reduce income exactly as much as it reduced prices. Conversely, the rise in prices that has actually taken place since the early 1960s hasn't made America poorer, because it has also raised incomes by the same amount: **real income**—income divided by the price level to adjust for the effects of inflation or deflation—hasn't been affected by the rise in overall prices.

The moral of this story is that the *level* of prices doesn't matter: the United States would be no richer than it is now if the overall level of prices was still as low as it was in 1961; conversely, the rise in prices over the past 45 years hasn't made us poorer.

The **real wage** is the wage rate divided by the price level to adjust for the effects of inflation or deflation.

Real income is income divided by the price level to adjust for the effects of inflation or deflation.

. . . But the Rate of Change of Prices Does

The **inflation rate** is the percentage increase in the overall level of prices per year.

The conclusion that the level of prices doesn't matter might seem to imply that the inflation rate doesn't matter either. But that's not true.

To see why, it's crucial to distinguish between the *level of prices* and the *inflation rate*. In the next Module, we will discuss precisely how the level of prices in the economy is measured using price indexes such as the consumer price index. For now, let's look at the **inflation rate**, the percentage increase in the overall level of prices per year. The inflation rate is calculated as follows:

$$\text{Inflation rate} = \frac{\text{Price level in year 2} - \text{Price level in year 1}}{\text{Price level in year 1}} \times 100$$

Figure 14.1 highlights the difference between the price level and the inflation rate in the United States since 1969, with the price level measured along the left vertical axis and the inflation rate measured along the right vertical axis. In the 2000s, the overall level of prices in the United States was much higher than it was in 1969—but that, as we've learned, didn't matter. The inflation rate in the 2000s, however, was much lower than in the 1970s—and that almost certainly made the economy richer than it would have been if high inflation had continued.

Economists believe that high rates of inflation impose significant economic costs. The most important of these costs are *shoe-leather costs*, *menu costs*, and *unit-of-account costs*. We'll discuss each in turn.

Figure 14.1 The Price Level Versus the Inflation Rate, 1969–2017

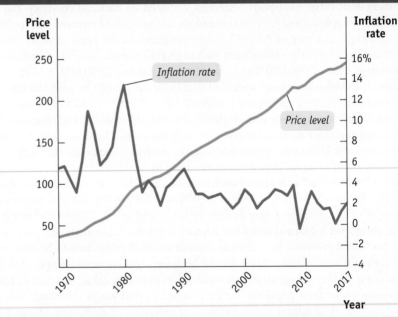

Over the past 48 years, the price level has continuously gone up. But the *inflation rate*—the rate at which consumer prices are rising—has had both ups and downs.
Data Source: Bureau of Labor Statistics.

Shoe-Leather Costs

People hold money—cash in their wallets and bank deposits from which they can withdraw funds—for convenience in making transactions. A high inflation rate, however, discourages people from holding money, because the purchasing power of the cash in their wallets and the funds in their bank accounts steadily erodes as the overall level of prices rises. This leads people to search for ways to reduce the amount of money they hold, often at considerable economic cost.

During the most famous of all inflations, the German *hyperinflation* of 1921–1923, merchants employed runners to take their cash to the bank many times a day to convert it into something that would hold its value, such as a stable foreign currency. In an effort to avoid having the purchasing power of their money eroded, people used up valuable resources—the time and labor of the runners—that could have been used productively elsewhere. During the German hyperinflation, so many banking transactions were taking place that the number of employees at German banks nearly quadrupled—from around 100,000 in 1913 to 375,000 in 1923. More recently, Brazil experienced hyperinflation during the early 1990s; during that episode, the Brazilian banking sector grew so large that it accounted for 15% of GDP, more than twice the size of the financial sector in the United States measured as a share of GDP. The large increase in the Brazilian banking sector that was needed to cope with the consequences of inflation represented a loss of real resources to its society.

Increased costs of transactions caused by inflation are known as **shoe-leather costs**, an allusion to the wear and tear caused by the extra running around that takes place when people are trying to avoid holding money. Shoe-leather costs are substantial in economies with very high inflation rates, as anyone who has lived in such an economy—say, one suffering inflation of 100% or more per year—can attest. Most estimates suggest, however, that the shoe-leather costs of inflation at the rates seen in the United States—which in peacetime has never had inflation above 15%—are quite small.

Menu Costs

In a modern economy, most of the things we buy have a listed price. There's a price listed under each item on a supermarket shelf, a price printed on advertisements, and a price listed for each dish on a restaurant's menu. Changing a listed price has a real cost, called a **menu cost**. For example, to change a price in a supermarket may require a clerk to change the price listed under the item on the shelf and an office worker to change the price associated with the item's UPC code in the store's computer. In the face of inflation, of course, firms are forced to change prices more often than they would if the price level was more or less stable. This means higher costs for the economy as a whole.

In times of very high inflation rates, menu costs can be substantial. During the Brazilian inflation of the early 1990s, for instance, supermarket workers reportedly spent half of their time replacing old price stickers with new ones. When the inflation rate is high, merchants may decide to stop listing prices in terms of the local currency and use either an artificial unit—in effect, measuring prices relative to one another—or a more stable currency, such as the U.S. dollar. This is exactly what the Israeli real estate market began doing in the mid-1980s: prices were quoted in U.S. dollars, even though payment was made in Israeli shekels. And this is also what happened in Zimbabwe when, in May 2008, official estimates of the inflation rate reached 1,694,000%.

Menu costs are also present in low-inflation economies, but they are not severe. In low-inflation economies, businesses might update their prices only sporadically—not daily or even more frequently, as is the case in high-inflation or hyperinflation economies. And technological advances have made menu costs less and less important, since prices can be changed electronically and fewer merchants attach price stickers to merchandise. But it still takes some type of effort to determine and implement any price change.

Unit-of-Account Costs

In the Middle Ages, contracts were often specified "in kind": for example, a tenant might be obliged to provide his landlord with a certain number of cattle each year (the phrase *in kind* actually comes from an ancient word for *cattle*). This may have made sense at the time, but it would be an awkward way to conduct modern business. Instead, we state contracts in monetary terms: a renter owes a certain number of dollars per month, a company that issues a bond promises to pay the bondholder the dollar value of the bond when it comes due, and so on. We also tend to make our economic calculations in dollars: a family planning its budget, or a small business owner trying to figure out how well the business is doing, makes estimates of the amount of money coming in and going out.

During the German hyperinflation of the early 1920s, people burned worthless paper money in their stoves.

Shoe-leather costs are the increased costs of transactions caused by inflation.

Menu costs are the real costs of changing listed prices.

This role of the dollar as a basis for contracts and calculation is called the *unit-of-account* role of money. It's an important aspect of the modern economy. Yet it's a role that can be degraded by inflation, which causes the purchasing power of a dollar to change over time—a dollar next year is worth less than a dollar this year. The effect, many economists argue, is to reduce the quality of economic decisions: the economy as a whole makes less efficient use of its resources because of the uncertainty caused by changes in the unit of account, the dollar. The **unit-of-account costs** of inflation are the costs arising from the way inflation makes money a less reliable unit of measurement.

Unit-of-account costs arise from the way inflation makes money a less reliable unit of measurement.

Unit-of-account costs may be particularly important in the tax system, because inflation can distort the measures of income on which taxes are collected. Here's an example: assume that the inflation rate is 10%, so that the overall level of prices rises 10% each year. Suppose that a business buys an asset, such as a piece of land, for $100,000 and then resells it a year later at a price of $110,000. In a fundamental sense, the business didn't make a profit on the deal: in real terms, it got no more for the land than it paid for it, because the $110,000 would purchase no more goods than the $100,000 would have a year earlier. But U.S. tax law would say that the business made a capital gain of $10,000, and it would have to pay taxes on that phantom gain.

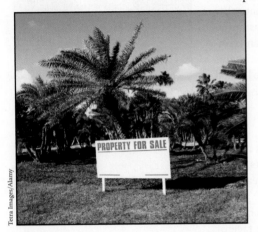

During the 1970s, when the United States had a relatively high inflation rate, the distorting effects of inflation on the tax system were a serious problem. Some businesses were discouraged from productive investment spending because they found themselves paying taxes on phantom gains. Meanwhile, some unproductive investments became attractive because they led to phantom losses that reduced tax bills. When the inflation rate fell in the 1980s—and tax rates were reduced—these problems became much less important.

Winners and Losers from Inflation

As we've just learned, a high inflation rate imposes overall costs on the economy. In addition, inflation can produce winners and losers within the economy. The main reason inflation sometimes helps some people while hurting others is that economic transactions, such as loans, often involve contracts that extend over a period of time and these contracts are normally specified in nominal—that is, in dollar—terms. In the case of a loan, the borrower receives a certain amount of funds at the beginning, and the loan contract specifies how much he or she must repay at some future date. But what that dollar repayment is worth in real terms—that is, in terms of purchasing power—depends greatly on the rate of inflation over the intervening years of the loan.

The *interest rate* on a loan is the percentage of the loan amount that the borrower must pay to the lender, typically on an annual basis, in addition to the repayment of the loan amount itself. Economists summarize the effect of inflation on borrowers and lenders by distinguishing between *nominal* interest rates and *real* interest rates. The **nominal interest rate** is the interest rate that is actually paid for a loan, unadjusted for the effects of inflation. For example, the interest rates advertised on student loans and every interest rate you see listed by a bank is a nominal rate. The **real interest rate** is the nominal interest rate adjusted for inflation. This adjustment is achieved by simply subtracting the inflation rate from the nominal interest rate. For example, if a loan carries a nominal interest rate of 8%, but the inflation rate is 5%, the real interest rate is 8% − 5% = 3%.

The **nominal interest rate** is the interest rate actually paid for a loan.

The **real interest rate** is the nominal interest rate minus the rate of inflation.

When a borrower and a lender enter into a loan contract, the contract normally specifies a nominal interest rate. But each party has an expectation about the future rate of inflation and therefore an expectation about the real interest rate on the loan. If the actual inflation rate is *higher* than expected, borrowers gain at the expense of lenders: borrowers will repay their loans with funds that have a lower real value than had been expected—since the funds can purchase fewer goods and services than expected due to the surprisingly high inflation rate. Conversely, if the inflation rate is *lower* than expected, lenders will gain at the expense of borrowers: borrowers must repay their loans with funds that have a higher real value than had been expected.

Historically, the fact that inflation creates winners and losers has sometimes been a major source of political controversy. In 1896 William Jennings Bryan electrified the Democratic presidential convention with a speech in which he declared, "You shall not crucify mankind on a cross of gold." What he was actually demanding was an inflationary policy. At the time, the U.S. dollar had a fixed value in terms of gold. Bryan wanted the U.S. government to abandon the gold standard and print more money, which would have raised the level of prices and, he believed, helped the nation's farmers who were deeply in debt.

Home mortgages (loans for the purchase of homes) are the most important source of gains and losses from inflation. Americans who took out mortgages in the early 1970s quickly found their real payments reduced by higher-than-expected inflation: by 1983, the purchasing power of a dollar was only 45% of what it had been in 1973. Those who took out mortgages in the early 1990s were not so lucky, because the inflation rate fell to lower-than-expected levels in the following years: in 2003 the purchasing power of a dollar was 78% of what it had been in 1993.

Because gains for some and losses for others result from inflation that is either higher or lower than expected, yet another problem arises: uncertainty about the future inflation rate discourages people from entering into any form of long-term contract. This is an additional cost of high inflation, because high rates of inflation are usually unpredictable, too. In countries with high and uncertain inflation, long-term loans are rare. This, in turn, makes it difficult for people to commit to long-term investments.

One last point: unexpected deflation—a surprise fall in the price level—creates winners and losers, too. Between 1929 and 1933, as the U.S. economy plunged into the Great Depression, the price level fell by 35%. This meant that debtors, including many farmers and homeowners, saw a sharp rise in the real value of their debts, which led to widespread bankruptcy and helped create a banking crisis, as lenders found their customers unable to pay back their loans.

Inflation Is Easy; Disinflation Is Hard

There is not much evidence that a rise in the inflation rate from, say, 2% to 5% would do a great deal of harm to the economy. Still, policy makers generally move forcefully to bring inflation back down when it creeps above 2% or 3%. Why? Because experience shows that bringing the inflation rate down—a process called **disinflation**—is very difficult and costly once a higher rate of inflation has become well established in the economy.

Figure 14.2 shows the inflation rate and the unemployment rate in the United States over a crucial decade, from 1978 to 1988. The decade began with an alarming rise in the inflation rate, but by the end of the period inflation averaged only about 4%. This was considered a major economic achievement—but it came at a high cost. Much of the fall in inflation probably resulted from the very severe recession of 1981–1982, which drove the unemployment rate to 10.8%—its highest level since the Great Depression.

Many economists believe that this period of high unemployment was necessary, because they believe that the only way to reduce inflation that has become deeply embedded in the economy is through policies that temporarily depress the economy. The best way to avoid having to put the economy through a wringer to reduce inflation, however, is to avoid having a serious inflation problem in the first place. So, policy makers respond forcefully to signs that inflation may be accelerating as a form of preventive medicine for the economy.

Disinflation is the process of bringing the inflation rate down.

Figure 14.2 The Cost of Disinflation

The U.S. inflation rate peaked in 1980 and then fell sharply. Progress against inflation, however, was accompanied by a temporary but very large increase in the unemployment rate, demonstrating the high cost of disinflation.

Data Source: Bureau of Labor Statistics.

MODULE 14 REVIEW

Adventures in AP® Economics

Check Your Understanding

Watch the video: *Real and Nominal Values*

1. The widespread use of technology has revolutionized the banking industry, making it much easier for customers to access and manage their money. Does this mean that the shoe-leather costs of inflation are higher or lower than they used to be? Explain.

2. Most people in the United States have grown accustomed to a modest inflation rate of around 2–3%. Who would gain and who would lose if inflation came to a complete stop for several years? Explain.

TACKLE THE AP® TEST: Multiple-Choice Questions

1. Which of the following is true regarding the price level in an economy?
   a. An increase in the price level is called inflation.
   b. The price level only increases over time.
   c. A decrease in the price level is called disinflation.
   d. The price level decreases during a recession.
   e. All of the above are true.

2. If your nominal wage doubles at the same time as prices double, your real wage will
   a. increase.
   b. decrease
   c. not change.
   d. double.
   e. be impossible to determine.

3. If inflation causes people to frequently convert their dollars into other assets, the economy experiences what type of cost?
   a. price level   d. unit-of-account
   b. shoe-leather   e. none of the above
   c. menu

4. Because dollars are used as the basis for contracts, inflation leads to which type of cost?
   a. price level   d. unit-of-account
   b. shoe-leather   e. none of the above
   c. menu

5. Changing the listed price when inflation leads to a price increase is an example of which type of cost?
   a. price level   d. unit-of-account
   b. shoe-leather   e. none of the above
   c. menu

6. The real interest rate is the nominal interest rate
   a. plus the rate of inflation.
   b. minus the rate of inflation.
   c. multiplied by the rate of inflation.
   d. divided by the rate of inflation.
   e. charged by banks during inflationary periods.

7. If your real wage decreases while your nominal wage stays the same, the economy must have experienced
   a. inflation.
   b. deflation.
   c. disinflation.
   d. zero inflation.
   e. unemployment.

TACKLE THE AP® TEST: Free-Response Questions

1. In the following examples: (i) indicate whether inflation imposes a net cost on the economy; (ii) explain your answer; and (iii) identify the type of net cost involved if there is one.
   a. When inflation is expected to be high, workers get paid more frequently and make more trips to the bank.
   b. Lanwei is reimbursed by her company for her work-related travel expenses. Sometimes, however, the company takes a long time to reimburse her. So when inflation is high, she is less willing to travel for her job.
   c. Hector Homeowner has a mortgage loan that he took out five years ago with a fixed 6% nominal interest rate. Over the years, the inflation rate has crept up unexpectedly to its present level of 7%.
   d. In response to unexpectedly high inflation, the manager of Cozy Cottages of Cape Cod must reprint and resend expensive color brochures correcting the price of rentals this season.

Rubric for FRQ 1 (11 points)

1 point: There is a net cost to the economy.

1 point: There is an increase in the cost of financial transactions imposed by inflation.

1 point: This type of cost is called a shoe-leather cost.

1 point: There is a net cost to the economy.

1 point: Lanwei's forgone output is a cost to the economy.

1 point: This type of cost is called a unit-of-account cost.

1 point: There is no net cost to the economy.

1 point: Hector gains and the bank loses because the money Hector pays back is worth less than expected.

1 point: There is a net cost to the economy.

1 point: Cozy Cottages must reprint and resend expensive brochures when inflation causes rental prices to rise.

1 point: This type of cost is called a menu cost.

2. You borrow $1,000 for one year at 5% interest to buy a couch. Although you did not anticipate any inflation, there is unexpected inflation of 5% over the life of your loan.
   a. What was the real interest rate on your loan?
   b. Explain how you gained from the inflation.
   c. Who lost as a result of the situation described? Explain. **(4 points)**

MOD 15

The Measurement and Calculation of Inflation

In this Module, you will learn to:
- Explain what a price index is and how it is calculated
- Calculate the inflation rate using the values of a price index
- Describe the importance of the consumer price index and other price indexes

Price Indexes and the Aggregate Price Level

The **aggregate price level** is a measure of the overall level of prices in the economy.

In the summer of 2008, Americans were facing sticker shock at the gas pump: the price of a gallon of regular gasoline had risen from about $3 in late 2007 to more than $4 in most places. Many other prices were also up. Some prices, though, were heading down: the prices of some foods, like eggs, were coming down from a run-up earlier in the year, and virtually anything involving electronics was also getting cheaper. Yet practically everyone felt that the overall cost of living seemed to be rising. But how fast?

Clearly there was a need for a single number that would summarize what was happening to consumer prices. Just as macroeconomists find it useful to have a single number to represent the overall level of output, they also find it useful to have a single number to represent the overall level of prices: the **aggregate price level**. Yet a huge variety of goods and services are produced and consumed in the economy. How can we summarize the prices of all these goods and services with a single number? The answer lies in the concept of a *price index*—a concept best introduced with an example.

Market Baskets and Price Indexes

Suppose that a frost in Florida destroys most of the citrus harvest. As a result, the price of oranges rises from $0.20 each to $0.40 each, the price of grapefruit rises from $0.60 to $1.00, and the price of lemons rises from $0.25 to $0.45. How much has the price of citrus fruit increased?

One way to answer that question is to state three numbers—the changes in prices for oranges, grapefruit, and lemons. But this is a very cumbersome method. Rather than having to recite three numbers in an effort to track changes in the prices of citrus fruit, we would prefer to have some kind of overall measure of the *average* price change.

A **market basket** is a hypothetical set of consumer purchases of goods and services.

To measure average price changes for consumer goods and services, economists track changes in the cost of a typical consumer's *consumption bundle*—a typical group of goods and services purchased. A hypothetical consumption bundle, used to measure changes in the overall price level, is known as a **market basket**. For our market basket in this example we will suppose that, before the frost, a typical consumer bought 200 oranges, 50 grapefruit, and 100 lemons over the course of a year.

Table 15.1 shows the pre-frost and post-frost costs of this market basket. Before the frost, it cost $95; after the frost, the same basket of goods cost $175. Since $175/$95 = 1.842, the post-frost basket costs 1.842 times the cost of the pre-frost basket, a cost increase of 84.2%. In this example, the average price of citrus fruit has increased 84.2% since the base year as a result of the frost, where the base year is the initial year used in the measurement of the price change.

Table 15.1	Calculating the Cost of a Market Basket	
	Pre-frost	**Post-frost**
Price of orange	$0.20	$0.40
Price of grapefruit	0.60	1.00
Price of lemon	0.25	0.45
Cost of market basket (200 oranges, 50 grapefruit, 100 lemons)	(200 × $0.20) + (50 × $0.60) + (100 × $0.25) = $95.00	(200 × $0.40) + (50 × $1.00) + (100 × $0.45) = $175.00

AP® EXAM TIP

The term *market basket* refers to a group of goods and services that represents what consumers buy. On the AP® exam, market baskets usually consist of three or four goods, a simplification of the market basket used to compute the Consumer Price Index, or CPI, the most commonly used price index.

Economists use the same method to measure changes in the overall price level: they track changes in the cost of buying a given market basket. The changes are calculated relative to a **base year**, the year chosen as the one to use for comparison. Using a market basket and a base year, we obtain what is known as a **price index**, a measure of the overall price level compared to the prices in the base year. A price index is calculated for a specific year using a specified base year. A price index can be calculated using the following formula:

(15-1) $\text{Price index in a given year} = \dfrac{\text{Cost of market basket in a given year}}{\text{Cost of market basket in base year}} \times 100$

In our example, the citrus fruit market basket cost $95 in the base year, the year before the frost. So by applying Equation 15-1, we define the price index for citrus fruit as (cost of market basket in the current year/$95) × 100, yielding an index of 100 for the period before the frost and 184.2 after the frost. You should note that applying Equation 15-1 to calculate the price index for the base year always results in a price index of (cost of market basket in base year/cost of market basket in base year) × 100 = 100.

The price index makes it clear that the average price of citrus has risen 84.2% as a consequence of the frost. Because of its simplicity and intuitive appeal, the method we've just described is used to calculate a variety of price indexes to track average price changes among a variety of different groups of goods and services. Examples include the *consumer price index* and the *producer price index*, which we'll discuss shortly. Price indexes are also the basis for measuring inflation. The price level mentioned in the inflation rate formula in Module 14 is simply a price index value, and the inflation rate is determined as the annual percentage change in an official price index. The inflation rate from year 1 to year 2 is thus calculated using the following formula, with year 1 and year 2 being consecutive years.

(15-2) $\text{Inflation rate} = \dfrac{\text{Price index in year 2} - \text{Price index in year 1}}{\text{Price index in year 1}} \times 100$

Typically, a news report that cites "the inflation rate" is referring to the annual percentage change in the consumer price index.

The **base year** is the year arbitrarily chosen for comparison when calculating a price index. The price level compares the price of the market basket of goods in a given year to its price in the base year.

A **price index** measures the cost of purchasing a given market basket in a given year. The index value is always equal to 100 in the selected base year.

AP® EXAM TIP

Any year can be chosen as the base year. If the price of a market basket is higher in a given year than in the base year, the price index will be greater than 100; if it is lower, the price index will be lower than 100. Remember: the price index in the base year is always equal to 100 because prices in the base year are always 100% of what they are in the base year!

The Consumer Price Index

The most widely used measure of the overall price level in the United States is the **consumer price index** (often referred to simply as the **CPI**), which is intended to show how the cost of all purchases by a typical urban family has changed over time. It is calculated by surveying market prices for a market basket that is constructed to represent the consumption of a typical family of four living in a typical American city. Rather than having a single base year, the CPI currently has a base period of 1982–1984.

The **consumer price index,** or **CPI**, measures the cost of the market basket of a typical urban American family.

The market basket used to calculate the CPI is far more complex than the three-fruit market basket we described above. In fact, to calculate the CPI, the Bureau of Labor Statistics sends its employees out to survey supermarkets, gas stations, hardware stores, hospitals, and so on—some 23,000 retail outlets in 87 cities. Every month it tabulates about 80,000 prices, on everything from romaine lettuce to a medical checkup. **Figure 15.1** shows the weight of major categories in the consumer price index as of December 2016. **Figure 15.2** shows how the CPI has changed since measurement began in 1913. Since 1940, the CPI has risen steadily, although its annual percentage increases in recent years have been much smaller than those of the 1970s and early 1980s. A logarithmic scale is used so that equal percentage changes in the CPI appear the same.

AP® EXAM TIP

The CPI is the most commonly used price index on the AP® exam. Make sure you learn how to calculate a price index value for a given year. Also make sure you can calculate the inflation rate using price index values.

Figure 15.1   The Makeup of the Consumer Price Index in 2016

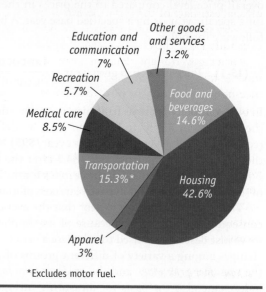

This chart shows the percentage shares of major types of spending in the CPI as of December 2016.
Data Source: Bureau of Labor Statistics.

*Excludes motor fuel.

Figure 15.2   The CPI, 1913–2017

Since 1940, the CPI has risen steadily. But the annual percentage increases in recent years have been much smaller than those of the 1970s and early 1980s. (The vertical axis is measured on a logarithmic scale so that equal percentage changes in the CPI appear the same.)
Data Source: Bureau of Labor Statistics.

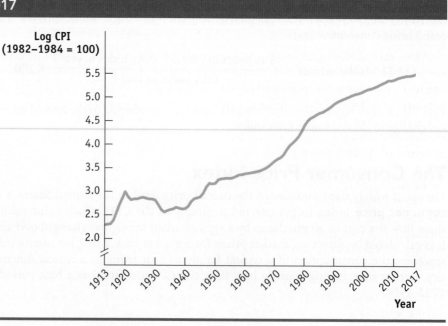

Indexing to the CPI

The CPI has a direct and immediate impact on millions of Americans. The reason is that many payments are tied, or "indexed," to the CPI—the amount paid for goods and services rises or falls when the CPI rises or falls.

The practice of indexing payments to consumer prices goes back to the founding of the United States. In 1780, the Massachusetts State Legislature recognized that the pay of its soldiers needed to be increased because of inflation occurring during the Revolutionary War. The legislature adopted a formula that made a soldier's pay proportional to the cost of a market basket consisting of 5 bushels of corn, 68 pounds of beef, 10 pounds of sheep's wool, and 16 pounds of sole leather.

Today, 61 million people receive checks from Social Security, a national program that accounts for almost a quarter of current total federal spending. The amount of an individual's check is determined by a formula that reflects his or her previous payments into the system, as well as other factors. In addition, all Social Security payments are adjusted each year to offset any increase in consumer prices over the previous year. The CPI is used to calculate the official estimate of the inflation rate used to adjust these payments annually. So every percentage point added to the official estimate of the rate of inflation adds 1% to the checks received by tens of millions of individuals.

A small change in the CPI has large consequences for those who depend on Social Security payments.

Other government payments are also indexed to the CPI. In addition, income tax brackets—the bands of income levels that determine a taxpayer's income tax rate—are indexed to the CPI. In the private sector, many private contracts, including some wage settlements, contain cost-of-living allowances (called COLAs) that adjust payments in proportion to changes in the CPI.

Because the CPI plays such an important and direct role in people's lives, it is a politically sensitive number. The Bureau of Labor Statistics, which calculates the CPI, takes great care in collecting and interpreting price and consumption data. It uses a complex method in which households are surveyed to determine what they buy and where they shop, and a carefully selected sample of stores are surveyed to get representative prices. However, there is still controversy about whether the CPI accurately measures inflation.

How Accurate Is the CPI?

Some economists believe that the consumer price index systematically overstates the actual rate of inflation. Why? Suppose the price of everything in the market basket used to calculate the CPI increased by 10% over the past year. The typical consumer might not need to spend 10% more this year to be as well off as last year, for three reasons.

First, each item remains in the studied market basket for four years. Yet consumers frequently alter the mix of goods and services they buy, reducing purchases of products that have become relatively more expensive and increasing purchases of products that have become relatively cheaper. For example, suppose that the price of hamburgers suddenly doubled. Americans currently eat a lot of hamburgers, but in the face of such a price rise many of them would switch to chicken sandwiches, pizza, or other substitutes whose prices hadn't increased as much. As a result, a price index based on a market basket with a lot of hamburgers in it would overstate the true rise in the cost of living. This is called **substitution bias**.

The second reason arises from product improvements. It's likely that over the years your favorite toothpaste, laundry detergent, and snack foods have both increased in price and come out in "new and improved" versions. If what you're getting is really better than before, you aren't paying more for the same product. Rather, you're paying more and getting more. The Bureau of Labor Statistics does its best to make adjustments for changes in product quality, but it is hard to measure the extent to which consumers are getting more as opposed to simply paying more.

Substitution bias occurs in the CPI because, over time, items with prices that have risen most receive too much weight (because households substitute away from them), while items with prices that have risen least are given too little weight (because households shift their spending toward them).

The third reason that inflation rate estimates may be misleading is innovation. Every new year brings new items, such as new electronic gadgets, new smartphone apps, new health care solutions, and new clothing options. By widening the range of consumer choice, innovation makes a given amount of money worth more. That is, innovation creates benefits similar to those of a fall in consumer prices. For all of these reasons, changes in the CPI may overstate changes in the cost of maintaining a particular standard of living. However, with more frequent updates of the market basket, among other tweaks in its methods, the Bureau of Labor Statistics has improved the accuracy of the CPI in recent years. And, despite some remaining controversy, the CPI remains the basis for most estimates of inflation.

The United States is not the only country that calculates a consumer price index. In fact, nearly every country calculates one. As you might expect, the market baskets that make up these indexes differ quite a lot from country to country. In poor countries, where people must spend a high proportion of their income just to feed themselves, food makes up a large share of the price index. Among high-income countries, differences in consumption patterns lead to differences in the price indexes: the Japanese price index puts a larger weight on raw fish and a smaller weight on beef than ours does, and the French price index puts a larger weight on wine.

Other Price Measures

The **producer price index,** or **PPI,** measures the prices of goods and services purchased by producers.

There are two other price measures that are also widely used to track economy-wide price changes. One is the **producer price index** (or **PPI,** which used to be known as the *wholesale price index*). As its name suggests, the producer price index measures the cost of a typical basket of goods and services—containing raw commodities such as steel, electricity, coal, and so on—purchased by producers. Because commodity producers are relatively quick to raise prices when they perceive a change in overall demand for their goods, the PPI often responds to inflationary or deflationary pressures more quickly than the CPI. As a result, the PPI is often regarded as an "early warning signal" of changes in the inflation rate.

The **GDP deflator** for a given year is 100 times the ratio of nominal GDP to real GDP in that year.

The other widely used price measure is the *GDP deflator;* it isn't exactly a price index, although it serves the same purpose. Recall how we distinguished between nominal GDP (GDP in current prices) and real GDP (GDP calculated using the prices of a base year). The **GDP deflator** for a given year is 100 times the ratio of nominal GDP to real GDP in that year. Since the Bureau of Economic Analysis— the source of the GDP deflator—calculates real GDP using a base year of 2009, the nominal GDP and the real GDP for 2009 are the same. This makes the GDP deflator for 2009 equal to 100. For this reason, later in this book you will see measures of the aggregate price level with the designation "GDP Deflator, 2009 = 100." And in many cases you will see real GDP measured in 2009 dollars. Inflation raises nominal GDP but not real GDP, causing the GDP deflator to rise. If nominal GDP doubles but real GDP does not change, the GDP deflator indicates that the aggregate price level has doubled.

Perhaps the most important point about the different inflation rates generated by these three measures of prices is that they usually move closely together (although the producer price index tends to fluctuate more than either of the other two measures). **Figure 15.3** shows the annual percentage changes in the three indexes since 1930. By all three measures, the U.S. economy experienced deflation during the early years of the Great Depression, inflation during World War II, accelerating inflation during the 1970s, and a return to relative price stability in the 1990s. Notice, by the way, the dramatic ups and downs in producer prices. This reflects large swings in energy and food prices, which play a much bigger role in the PPI than they do in either the CPI or the GDP deflator.

Figure 15.3 The CPI, the PPI, and the GDP Deflator

The figure shows that the three different measures of inflation usually move closely together. Each reveals a drastic acceleration of inflation during the 1970s and a return to relative price stability in the 1990s.

Data Source: Bureau of Labor Statistics; Bureau of Economic Analysis.

MODULE 15 REVIEW

Check Your Understanding

1. Consider Table 15.1 but suppose that the market basket is composed of 100 oranges, 50 grapefruit, and 200 lemons. How does this change the pre-frost and post-frost consumer price indexes? Explain. Generalize your answer to explain how the construction of the market basket affects the CPI.

2. For each of the following events, explain how the use of a 10-year-old market basket would bias measurements of price changes over the past decade.

   a. A typical family owns more cars than it would have a decade ago. Over that time, the average price of a car has increased more than the average prices of other goods.

   b. Virtually no households had tablet PCs a decade ago. Now many households have them, and their prices have been falling.

3. If the consumer price index increased from 214.537 in year 1 to 218.056 in year 2, what was the inflation rate between year 1 and year 2?

TACKLE THE AP® TEST: Multiple-Choice Questions

1. If the cost of a market basket of goods increases from $100 in year 1 to $108 in year 2, what does the consumer price index in year 2 equal if year 1 is the base year?
   a. 8
   b. 10
   c. 100
   d. 108
   e. 110

2. If the consumer price index increases from 80 to 120 from one year to the next, the inflation rate over that time period was
   a. 20%.
   b. 40%.
   c. 50%.
   d. 80%.
   e. 120%.

3. Which of the following is true of the CPI?
   a. It is the most common measure of the price level.
   b. It measures the price of a typical market basket of goods.
   c. It is used to index social security payments.
   d. It is calculated for a particular base year or period.
   e. All of the above are true.

4. The value of a price index in the base year is
   a. 0.
   b. 100.
   c. 200.
   d. the same as the inflation rate.
   e. equal to the average cost of a market basket of goods.

5. If your wage doubles at the same time as the consumer price index goes from 100 to 300, your real wage
   a. doubles.
   b. falls.
   c. increases.
   d. stays the same.
   e. cannot be determined.

6. A market basket is
   a. made up of all goods and services purchased by a family.
   b. a hypothetical consumption bundle.
   c. a set of goods and services typically purchased by producers.
   d. an arbitrary set of goods and services purchased by an individual.
   e. a fixed set of goods and services identified in 1982.

7. Use Table 15.1 to answer the following question. What is the value of the price index in the pre-frost and post-frost year if the post-frost year is the base year?

	Pre-frost	Post-frost
Price of orange	$0.20	$0.40
Price of grapefruit	0.60	1.00
Price of lemon	0.25	0.45
Cost of market basket (200 oranges, 50 grapefruit, 100 lemons)	(200 × $0.20) + (50 × $0.60) + (100 × $0.25) = $95.00	(200 × $0.40) + (50 × $1.00) + (100 × $0.45) = $175.00

	Pre-frost	Post-frost
a.	54	100
b.	100	54
c.	184	100
d.	100	184
e.	54	184

TACKLE THE AP® TEST: Free-Response Questions

1. Suppose the year 2010 is the base year for a price index. Between 2010 and 2030 prices double and at the same time your nominal income increases from $40,000 to $80,000.
   a. What is the value of the price index in 2010?
   b. What is the value of the price index in 2030?
   c. What is the percentage increase in your nominal income between 2010 and 2030?
   d. What has happened to your real income between 2010 and 2030? Explain.

2. The accompanying table contains the values of the CPI for year 1 and year 2.
   a. What does the CPI measure?
   b. Calculate the inflation rate from year 1 to year 2.

Year	CPI
1	229.6
2	233.0

(2 points)

Rubric for FRQ 1 (5 points)

1 point: 100

1 point: 200

1 point: 100%

1 point: It stayed the same.

1 point: Real income is a measure of the purchasing power of my income, and because my income and the price level both doubled, the purchasing power of my income has not been affected: $40,000/100 = $80,000/200.

SECTION

3

Review

SECTION 3 Review Video

Adventures in AP® Economics Videos
Mod 10: The Circular Flow
Mod 14: Real and Nominal Values

Module 10

1. Economists keep track of the flows of money between sectors with the **national income and product accounts**, or **national accounts**. **Households** earn income via the **factor markets** from wages, interest on bonds, profit accruing to owners of stocks, and rent on land. In addition, they receive **government transfers**. **Disposable income**, total household income minus taxes plus government transfers, is allocated to **consumer spending** (*C*) in the **product markets** and **private savings**. Via the **financial markets**, private savings and foreign lending are channeled to **investment spending** (*I*), government borrowing, and foreign borrowing. Government purchases of goods and services (*G*) are paid for by **tax revenues** and **government borrowing**. **Exports** (*X*) generate an inflow of funds into the country from the rest of the world, but **imports** (*M*) lead to an outflow of funds to the rest of the world.

Foreigners can also buy stocks and bonds in the U.S. financial markets.

2. **Gross domestic product**, or **GDP**, measures the value of all **final goods and services** produced in the economy. It does not include the value of **intermediate goods and services**, but it does include inventories and **net exports** ($X - M$). There are three approaches to calculating GDP: the **value-added approach** of adding up the **value added** by all producers; the **expenditure approach** of adding up all spending on domestically produced final goods and services, leading to the equation $GDP = C + I + G + X - M$, also known as **aggregate spending**; and the **income approach** of adding up all the income paid by domestic **firms** to factors of production. These three methods are equivalent because in the economy as a whole, total income paid by domestic firms to factors of production must equal total spending on domestically produced final goods and services.

Module 11

3. **Real GDP** is the value of the final goods and services produced, calculated using the prices of a selected base year. Except in the base year, real GDP is not the same as **nominal GDP**, the value of **aggregate output** calculated using current prices. Analysis of the growth rate of aggregate output must use real GDP because doing so eliminates any change in the value of aggregate output due solely to price changes. Real **GDP per capita** is a

measure of average aggregate output per person but is not in itself an appropriate policy goal. U.S. statistics on real GDP are always expressed in "chained dollars," which means they are calculated with the chain-linking method of averaging the GDP growth rate found using an early base year and the GDP growth rate found using a late base year.

Module 12

4. **Employed** people currently hold a part-time or full-time job; **unemployed** people do not hold a job but are actively looking for work. Their sum is equal to the **labor force**; the **labor force participation rate** is the percentage of the population age 16 or older that is in the labor force.

5. The **unemployment rate**, the percentage of the labor force that is unemployed and actively looking for work, can overstate or understate the true level of unemployment. It can overstate because it counts as unemployed those who are continuing to search for a job despite having been offered one. It can understate because it

ignores frustrated workers, such as **discouraged workers, marginally attached workers**, and the **underemployed**. In addition, the unemployment rate varies greatly among different groups in the population; it is typically higher for younger workers and for workers near retirement age than for workers in their prime working years.

6. The unemployment rate is affected by the business cycle. The unemployment rate generally falls when the growth rate of real GDP is above average and generally rises when the growth rate of real GDP is below average.

Module 13

7. Job creation and destruction, as well as voluntary job separations, lead to **frictional unemployment**. **Structural unemployment** results when workers lack the skills required for the available jobs. In addition, a variety of factors, such as minimum wages, unions, and **efficiency wages**, result in a situation in which there is a surplus of labor at the market wage rate, creating structural unemployment. As a result, the **natural rate of unemployment**, the sum of frictional and structural unemployment, is well above zero, even when jobs are plentiful.

8. The actual unemployment rate is equal to the natural rate of unemployment, the share of unemployment that is independent of the business cycle, plus **cyclical unemployment**, the share of unemployment that depends on fluctuations in the business cycle.

9. The natural rate of unemployment changes over time, largely in response to changes in labor force characteristics, labor market institutions, and government policies.

Module 14

10. Inflation does not, as many assume, make everyone poorer by raising the level of prices. That's because if wages and incomes are adjusted to take into account a rising price level, **real wages** and **real income** remain unchanged. However, a high **inflation rate** imposes overall costs on the economy: **shoe-leather costs, menu costs**, and **unit-of-account costs**.

11. Inflation can produce winners and losers within the economy, because long-term contracts are generally written in dollar terms. Loans typically specify a **nominal interest rate**, which differs from the **real interest rate** due to inflation. A higher-than-expected inflation rate is good for borrowers and bad for lenders. A lower-than-expected inflation rate is good for lenders and bad for borrowers.

12. **Disinflation**, the process of bringing the inflation rate down, usually comes at the cost of a higher unemployment rate. So policy makers try to prevent inflation from becoming excessive in the first place.

Module 15

13. To measure the **aggregate price level**, economists calculate the cost of purchasing a **market basket**. A **price index** is the ratio of the current cost of that market basket to the cost in a selected **base year**, multiplied by 100.

14. The inflation rate is calculated as the annual percentage change in a price index, typically based on the **consumer price index**, or **CPI**, the most common measure of the aggregate price level. The CPI is frequently used for indexing payments, but CPI may overstate the rise in price levels because of factors like **substitution bias**, product improvements, and innovation. A similar index for goods and services purchased by firms is the **producer price index**, or **PPI**. Finally, economists also use the **GDP deflator**, which measures the price level by calculating the ratio of nominal to real GDP times 100.

Key Terms

AP® Exam Practice Questions

Multiple-Choice Questions

Refer to the following diagram for Questions 1–3.

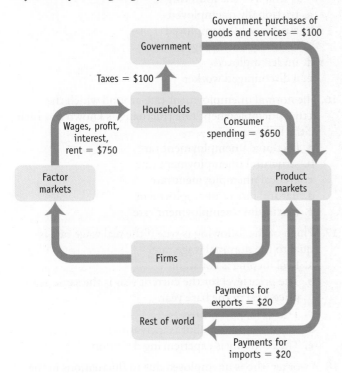

1. What is the value of GDP?
- **a.** $550
- **b.** $650
- **c.** $750
- **d.** $770
- **e.** $790

2. What is the value of disposable income?
- **a.** $750
- **b.** $650
- **c.** $550
- **d.** $530
- **e.** $510

3. The $750 of wages, profit, interest, and rent shown by the arrow pointing into the factor markets box illustrates the calculation of GDP using which approach?
- **a.** value-added
- **b.** aggregate spending
- **c.** expenditure
- **d.** income
- **e.** resource

Refer to the following table for Questions 4–6.

Category	Components of GDP (billions of dollars)
Consumer spending	
Durable goods	$1,000
Nondurable goods	2,000
Services	7,000
Private Investment Spending	
Fixed investment spending	1,700
Nonresidential	1,400
Structures	500
Equipment and software	900
Residential	300
Change in private inventories	−100
Net exports	
Exports	1,500
Imports	2,000
Government purchases of goods and services and investment spending	
Federal	1,400
State and local	1,600

4. What is the value of GDP?
- **a.** $10,000
- **b.** $11,600
- **c.** $14,100
- **d.** $15,100
- **e.** $18,100

5. What is the value of net exports?
- **a.** $3,500
- **b.** $2,000
- **c.** $1,500
- **d.** $500
- **e.** −$500

6. Which of the following refers to a loan in the form of an IOU that pays interest?
- **a.** stock
- **b.** bond
- **c.** disposable income
- **d.** government transfer
- **e.** investment

7. Investment spending includes spending on which of the following?
   a. stocks
   b. physical capital
   c. inputs
   d. services
   e. reductions in inventories

8. Which of the following is included in the calculation of GDP?
   a. intermediate goods and services
   b. used goods
   c. stocks and bonds
   d. foreign-produced goods and services
   e. domestically produced capital goods

9. Which of the following is true for the current year if real GDP is greater than nominal GDP?
   a. The price level has decreased since the base year.
   b. The consumer price index has increased since the base year.
   c. The economy is experiencing inflation.
   d. There has been economic growth.
   e. Net exports are positive.

10. A country's labor force is equal to which of the following?
    a. the number of people aged 16 and above
    b. the number of people employed plus the number retired
    c. the number of people employed plus the number unemployed
    d. the number of people working for pay
    e. the number of people employed for pay plus the number who have given up looking for work

11. The number of people who are considered unemployed is equal to the number of people who are not working and
    a. are receiving unemployment compensation.
    b. have given up seeking work.
    c. plan to look for work in the future.
    d. have looked for work in the recent past.
    e. are actively seeking work.

12. The unemployment rate is the number of people unemployed divided by the number
    a. employed.
    b. employed plus the number discouraged.
    c. in the labor force.
    d. in the population aged 16 and above.
    e. in the population.

13. The number of people counted as unemployed includes which of the following types of workers?
    a. discouraged workers
    b. aspiring workers seeking their first job
    c. underemployed workers

d. retired workers
e. part-time workers

14. A worker who is not working while engaged in a job search after moving to a new city is considered to be which of the following?
    a. frictionally unemployed
    b. structurally unemployed
    c. cyclically unemployed
    d. underemployed
    e. a discouraged worker

15. A worker who is not working because his or her skills are no longer demanded in the labor market is considered to be which of the following?
    a. frictionally unemployed
    b. structurally unemployed
    c. cyclically unemployed
    d. underemployed
    e. a discouraged worker

16. The normal unemployment rate around which the actual unemployment rate fluctuates is known as which of the following?
    a. frictional unemployment rate
    b. structural unemployment rate
    c. cyclical unemployment rate
    d. natural rate of unemployment
    e. maximum unemployment rate

17. Which of the following is true if the real wage rate is equal to the nominal wage rate?
    a. Real income is constant.
    b. The price level for the current year is the same as the price level in the base year.
    c. The CPI is increasing.
    d. The demand for labor is increasing.
    e. The economy is experiencing deflation.

18. A worker who is unemployed due to fluctuations in the business cycle is considered to be which of the following?
    a. frictionally unemployed
    b. structurally unemployed
    c. cyclically unemployed
    d. underemployed
    e. a discouraged worker

19. When inflation makes money a less reliable unit of measurement, the economy is experiencing which of the following costs of inflation?
    a. unit-of-account   d. measurement
    b. shoe-leather   e. monetary
    c. menu

20. Bringing down the inflation rate is known as
    a. negative inflation.   d. disinflation.
    b. deflation.   e. contraction.
    c. bubble popping.

21. The real interest rate is equal to the nominal interest rate
    a. minus the inflation rate.
    b. plus the inflation rate.
    c. divided by the inflation rate.
    d. times the inflation rate.
    e. plus the real interest rate divided by the inflation rate.

22. Who loses from unanticipated inflation?
    a. borrowers
    b. the government
    c. investors
    d. mortgage owners
    e. people on fixed incomes

23. Assume a country has a population of 1,000. If 400 people are employed and 100 people are unemployed, what is the country's unemployment rate?
    a. 50%   d. 20%
    b. 40%   e. 10%
    c. 25%

24. Which of the following changes will result in an increase in the natural rate of unemployment?
    a. More teenagers focus on their studies and do not look for jobs until after college.
    b. The government increases the time during which an unemployed worker can receive benefits.
    c. Greater access to the internet makes it easier for job-seekers to find a job.
    d. Union membership declines.
    e. Opportunities for job training improve.

25. If the consumer price index rises from 120 to 132, what is the inflation rate?
    a. 8%   d. 20%
    b. 10%   e. 32%
    c. 12%

Free-Response Questions

1. Draw a correctly labeled simple circular-flow diagram.
   a. On your diagram, illustrate each of the following:
      i. Households and firms
      ii. The factor and product markets
   b. Add the government to your diagram to illustrate how taxes, government spending, and goods and services enter and exit the circular flow. **(7 points)**

2. Assume the country of Technologia invests in an online application that efficiently matches job-seekers with employers and significantly reduces the time required for job searches.
   a. Which type of unemployment will Technologia's investment affect?
   b. Will unemployment increase or decrease?
   c. Given the change in unemployment from part b, what will happen to the natural rate of unemployment in Technologia? Explain.
   d. Given your answer to part b, what will happen to real GDP in Technologia? Explain. **(6 points)**

3. Use the price level information in the table below to answer the following questions. Assume year 2 is the base year.

Price level	
Year 1	$400
Year 2	$800
Year 3	$1,000
Year 4	$800

   a. Calculate the price index for year 1 and 2. Show your work.
   b. Calculate the inflation rate between year 1 and year 2. Show your work.
   c. The economy experienced deflation between which two years? Explain.
   d. The economy experienced disinflation between which two years? Explain. **(5 points)**

How Can GDP Be Up When We're Feeling Down?

The Divergence of Gross Domestic Product and Measures of Well-being

Gross domestic product (GDP) is the market value of all final goods and services produced in a country within a given period. Some policy makers target GDP growth as if it embodied everything that is good, but as a measure of well-being, GDP is flawed. GDP figures can mislead because some goods and services are purchased in response to problems, such as pollution and terrorism, and many of the true joys of life, such as time spent with friends and family, are left out of GDP. So it is not surprising to economists when surveys such as the Harris Poll of Happiness indicate that, even as GDP rises, the proportion of Americans who report being very happy remains at about one-third.

Ammentorp Photography/Alamy

Consider a typical worker, a blissful retiree, and an unemployed worker who got divorced and had heart bypass surgery in the same year. The typical employed worker contributes about $132,000 worth of output to GDP each year. The litigation costs for a contested divorce with custody issues run about $75,000, as do the health care costs for heart bypass surgery. Although the retiree may be the happiest member of this bunch, she added nothing to GDP, whereas the victim of bad luck is responsible for the largest contribution. A country beset with bad luck—wars, hurricanes, disease, crime—runs up a large GDP, too. This chapter explains the methods of calculating gross domestic product, the weakness of GDP as a measure of contentment, and alternative measures that give more accurate indications of both burdens and bliss.

Measuring GDP

GDP may not be the root of happiness, but it is a valuable measure of output, with implications for employment and economic growth. In 1991, GDP replaced gross national product (GNP) as the primary measure of production used by U.S. economists. The difference is that GDP measures the value of goods and services produced by anyone on U.S. soil, whereas GNP measures the value of U.S. citizens' production anywhere in the world. Thus, Serena Williams's winnings at Wimbledon were part of U.S. *GNP* because she is a U.S. citizen, and part of British *GDP* because she earned them on British soil. Government agencies and private corporations use GDP figures widely to get a read on the direction of the economy. For example, the Central Intelligence Agency (CIA) uses GDP per capita (GDP divided by the number of citizens) as a benchmark for the standard of living in nations around the world, and the board of governors of the Federal Reserve System and the president's Council of Economic Advisers use GDP as a gauge of the economy's performance and a basis for policy decisions.

GDP is calculated by the Bureau of Economic Analysis (BEA), an agency of the U.S. Department of Commerce. There are three primary ways of compiling the GDP figure.

First, the *expenditure approach* adds up the following to obtain the total expenditure on goods and services:

- consumption spending by households
- investment spending by businesses
- government spending
- net exports (exports minus imports)

In order to avoid double counting, only spending on "final" goods and services is included. This means that expenditures on raw materials such as iron ore, and on intermediate goods such as car engines, are not counted until such inputs become part of a completed product (such as a car), and spending on goods purchased to be resold isn't counted until the goods are sold to the ultimate consumer.

The investment component of GDP includes business spending on machinery and other capital goods, new construction of both businesses and homes, and goods that are produced and held as net additions to inventories. The purchase of stocks and bonds and the deposit of money into banks do not represent production and are not counted as investment. By adding up all these expenditures, the BEA can determine the value of final goods and services produced within a particular year.

Second, the *value-added approach*, similar to the expenditure approach, examines output values, but the method of avoiding double-counting is different. Rather than considering only final goods and services, the value-added approach examines raw and intermediate goods and services as well, and it counts only the incremental change in value from one step in the production process to the next. If $1 worth of cotton becomes $5 worth of fabric which becomes a $30 dress, the value-added approach is to add together the $1 value of the cotton, the $4 increase in value when the cotton becomes fabric, and the $25 increase in value when the fabric becomes a dress, to get the same $30 figure that the expenditure approach takes from the final sale of the dress: $30 = $1 + ($5 − $1) + ($30 − $5).

Zoonar GmbH/Alamy

Third, the *income approach* is based on the logic that workers receive the market value of goods and services as income. *National income* is the sum of:

- employee compensation
- interest payments (such as on bank deposits and bonds)
- rental income received by landlords
- corporate profits
- proprietors' (that is, businesses owners') income

To find GDP, national income must be adjusted by adding items that are part of the value of production but not part of income, and by removing items that count toward income but not toward production. Specifically, this entails:

1. subtracting government subsidies, which are part of income but don't constitute payment for a good
2. adding the value of new capital purchased to replace old *capital*, called *capital consumption*, or *depreciation*, because those purchases are made with depreciation reserves that don't count toward income
3. adding *net foreign factor income*, which is the difference between what foreign investors earn on assets in the United States and what U.S. investors earn from their assets elsewhere

In theory, all three of these approaches lead to the same estimate of GDP. In practice, they are similar. In 2017, the BEA estimated GDP to be $19,500 trillion and national income to be $16,677 trillion. After making the adjustments as previously explained to estimate GDP using national income, the difference between the two GDP estimates was a "statistical discrepancy" of $34 billion, or less than 1 percent. As they say, that's not bad for government work.

Out with the Bads and In with the Goods

Policy makers and the media often herald GDP growth as a uniformly splendid event. In fact, increases in GDP may or may not be desirable. GDP increases when money is spent to deal with social failures, such as (1) excessive pollution and crime; (2) burdens placed on future generations by farming techniques that cause soil erosion and by manufacturing that depletes nonrenewable resources; and (3) when paid activities replace unpaid activities, like when the work of nannies replaces unpaid parenting, subscriptions to digital services replace interpersonal contact, and fast-food replaces home-cooked meals. A better measure of progress would exclude expenditures that signal bad situations and include the value of beneficial nonmarket activities. This section identifies the categories of expenditure that should and should not be parts of an accurate indicator of social well-being.

The Bads

Defensive goods and services are those necessitated by problems that make society worse off, as with corruption; natural disasters; disease; and such perils of economic growth as pollution, congestion, and work-related stress. For instance, in a typical year, about $700 billion of the U.S. GDP is spent on police, prisons, security systems, and other purchases to help deal with the problem of crime. If the crime rate worsens, this component of GDP will increase, but society will be worse off. As another example, billions of dollars are spent each year to treat chronic back pain, which is often caused by injury, depression, or the stress and strain of fast-paced jobs. Back pain has become a leading reason to visit a doctor, but the need to spend more on this or any other burgeoning malady does not reflect a better life. The same is true for expenditures on counterterrorism, drug treatment, oil spills, malignancies, psychologists, and funerals. Increased expenditures on defensive goods and services indicate that the quality of life has diminished, and these expenditures should be subtracted from GDP to obtain a more accurate measure of social well-being.

As step 2 of the adjustment from national income to GDP in the previous section indicates, capital consumption (depreciation) is part of GDP. This erosion in the value of capital during the production process is not an indication of better living. Suppose that $5,000 worth of silk-screening equipment must be replaced because of wear and tear after the production of $100,000 worth of Hard Rock Cafe T-shirts. GDP would increase by $105,000 because it includes capital consumption, whereas the net gain for society would be $100,000 worth of new products because $5,000 worth of new capital would be required to replace the worn-out machinery. The U.S. government publishes net national product (NNP) figures that adjust GDP to account for the depreciation of traditional (human-made) capital. NNP does not account for losses of forests, oil reserves, and other natural capital associated with increases in GDP. A true measure of social well-being would reflect the losses of all types of capital.

The Goods

Nonmarket production provides benefits to society in the absence of explicit prices and purchases. Work performed for the benefit of the worker and the worker's family—child care, gardening, housework, do-it-yourself home improvements—is not included in GDP, although the same duties *are* counted in GDP when performed by a paid professional. Production in the *underground economy*, or *cash economy*, is not reported to the government and is not part of GDP, despite available estimates that its value approaches $2 trillion per year in the United States. And the volunteer work performed at churches, charities, nursing homes, schools, and elsewhere goes uncounted in GDP. It is important to include these goods and services, to the extent possible, in a true measure of social well-being.

Improvements in GDP and national income don't necessarily correspond with improvements in income distribution, nor do they guarantee that most people are earning higher incomes. It may be that a small percentage of people are earning more, whereas most people's incomes are stagnating or even declining. If a gauge of income distribution is desired within a measure of social well-being, the *Gini coefficient* could serve that purpose. The Gini coefficient ranges from 0 to 1, increasing as income inequality worsens. A coefficient of 0 means that everyone receives the same income, and a coefficient of 1 means that the richest person receives all the income. As a few examples, the Gini coefficient is 0.31 in Canada, 0.39 in the United States, and 0.46 in Mexico.

Finally, as elated as people might be about weekends, days off, and the prospect of early retirement, the quality and quantity of leisure time don't find their way into GDP calculations. GDP would be higher if everyone worked incessantly, but then people would have no time in which to enjoy the bumper crop of output. An ideal measure of social well-being would reflect the opportunities for leisure time.

Alternative Measures

Economists have proposed several indicators of well-being and progress as alternatives to GDP. Examples include:

- the Gallup-Sharecare Well-Being Index
- the Genuine Progress Indicator (GPI)
- the Human Development Index
- the Index of Sustainable Economic Welfare (ISEW)
- the OECD Better Life Index

All of these measures include a financial component related to GDP but incorporate other determinants of well-being, such as health, the environment, education, community, and the depletion of natural resources. For instance, the Genuine Progress Indicator is based on 26 economic, social, and environmental factors, and the Human Development Index is based on five measures of income, education, and health.

Patti McConville/Alamy

Visit www.oecdbetterlifeindex.org for an opportunity to design your own welfare index by placing more weight on the things you deem particularly important.

Most of the alternative indexes have diverged from GDP in recent decades. For example, the Genuine Progress Indicator suggests that GDP is out of line with the true value of progress by trillions of dollars, and GPI per capita has stagnated since 1977, even as GDP per capita has increased. GDP calculations are relevant to employment and productivity, but a measure of social well-being would serve as a better guide for decisions that aim to improve our quality of life. Politicians have a tendency to focus on rising GDP values, and they have largely ignored arguments by economists, such as Nobel laureate James Tobin, about the need to consider alternative indexes. Lobbying efforts by economists, and groups such as Redefining Progress, continue, and 20 U.S. states have joined dozens of nations in calculating their GPI or other "beyond GDP" measures.

Conclusion

> Gross national product does not allow for the health of our children, the quality of their education, or the joy of their play. It does not include the beauty of our poetry or the strength of our marriages; the intelligence of our public debate or the integrity of our public officials. It measures neither our wit nor our courage; neither our wisdom nor our learning; neither our compassion nor our devotion to our country; it measures everything, in short, except that which makes life worthwhile.
>
> —Robert F. Kennedy, 1968

Gross domestic product and national income are valid and useful measures of output and economic activity. However, despite their central roles as gauges for success, they do not accurately reflect well-being. Consider the $86,511 median income in Shenandoah, a section of East Baton Rouge parish in Louisiana. This figure eclipses the $59,039 median income for the United States as a whole and indicates a high volume of output in nearby chemical, plastics, oil, and gas industries. In fact, Louisiana workers are rated among the most productive workers in the nation. Even so, the high levels of output and median income in Shenandoah may not fully explain the overall quality of life there. The parish experiences relatively high rates of crime, cancer, and income inequality, all of which may influence the well-being of residents in ways that cannot be captured in median income and output figures. In any location, GDP rises with smoke-blackened skies, broken homes that force both parents to work full time, disease, and disaster, so wise policy makers will consult alternative measures of progress.

Critical Thinking Questions

1. The CIA uses GDP as an indicator of economic activity in countries around the world. How would you explain to a noneconomist CIA director what GDP can and cannot tell the CIA about those countries?

2. Prostitution, gambling, and some types of drug use are legal in some countries and illegal in others. What implication does this have for international GDP comparisons? What other issues might cloud such comparisons?

3. Suppose that in 2017, a track star earned $15,000 as a waitress, and won a gold medal at the World Track Championships. In 2018, she had a leg injury that kept her from running, but she earned $100,000 coaching and endorsing a shoe company. In 2019, she spent $125,000 to fight cancer. In which year did this person add the most to GDP? In which year did she experience the most joy? In which year did her personal welfare reach its lowest point? What does this indicate about the relationships among income, GDP, and happiness?

4. Categorize each of the following items as being *in* or *out* of U.S. GDP in the relevant year:
   a. the prize money U.S. track star Emma Coburn won in Europe
   b. the used toboggan you bought on eBay
   c. the Whopper you bought for lunch
   d. the massage you bought your dad for Father's Day
   e. the Monet painting you bought your mother for Mother's Day
   f. the coffee beans that Starbucks roasted in December but didn't sell until the following year

5. How could leisure time be included in a measure of social well-being? Can you think of measurable values that coincide with leisure?

National Income and Price Determination

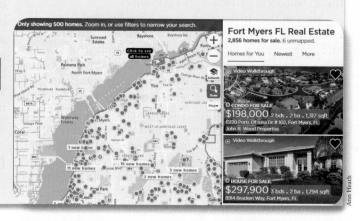

economics by example
How Much Debt Is Too Much?

From Boom to Bust

Ft. Myers, Florida, was a boomtown back in 2005. Jobs were plentiful: the unemployment rate was less than 3%. The shopping malls were humming, and new stores were opening everywhere.

But then the boom went bust. Jobs became scarce, and by 2010, the unemployment rate was above 13%. Stores had few customers, and many were closing. One new business was flourishing, however. Marc Joseph, a real estate agent, began offering "foreclosure tours": visits to homes that had been seized by banks after the owners were unable to make mortgage payments.

What happened? Ft. Myers was one of many cities that boomed because of a surge in home construction, fueled in part by speculators who bought houses not to live in, but because they believed they could resell those houses at much higher prices. Home construction gave jobs to construction workers, electricians, real estate agents, and others. These workers, in turn, spent money locally, creating jobs for sales workers, waiters, gardeners, and more. These workers also spent money locally, creating further expansion, and so on.

The boom turned into a bust when home construction came to a virtual halt. It turned out that speculation had been feeding on itself: people were buying houses as investments, then selling them to other people who were also buying houses as investments. The prices had risen to levels far beyond what people who actually wanted to live in houses were willing to pay.

The abrupt collapse of the housing market pulled the local economy down, as the process that had created the earlier boom operated in reverse. But just as economic booms are followed by economic busts, economic busts are followed by economic booms. Since hitting their low in 2011, housing prices in Ft. Meyers have increased by 78%. The Case-Shiller Home Price Index shows significant increases in housing prices in many cities from 2012 to 2017. For example, in 2017, housing prices in Boston had increased to 11% higher than during the peak of the previous housing bubble. In Seattle, they had increased to 43% more than during the previous bubble, in Dallas 42%, and in the San Francisco Bay area 10%.

The boom and bust in Ft. Myers illustrates, on a small scale, the way booms and busts often happen for the economy as a whole. The business cycle is often driven by ups or downs in investment spending—either residential investment spending (spending on home construction) or nonresidential investment spending (such as spending on construction of office buildings, factories, and shopping malls). Changes in investment spending, in turn, indirectly lead to changes in consumer spending, which magnify—or *multiply*—the effect of the investment spending changes on the economy as a whole.

In this section we'll study how this process works on a grand scale. As a first step, we introduce *multiplier* analysis and show how it helps us understand the business cycle. We then explore how *aggregate supply* and *aggregate demand* determine the levels of prices and real output in an economy. Finally, we use the aggregate demand–aggregate supply model to visualize the state of the economy and examine the effects of economic policy.

Income and Expenditure

In this Module, you will learn to:

- Understand the relationship between disposable income and consumer spending and how expected future income and aggregate wealth affect consumer spending
- Identify the determinants of investment spending
- Explain why investment spending is considered a leading indicator of the future state of the economy
- Describe the multiplier process by which initial changes in spending lead to further changes in spending

Consumer Spending

Should you splurge on a restaurant meal or save money by eating at home? Should you buy a new car and, if so, how expensive a model? Should you redo that bathroom or live with it for another year? In the real world, households are constantly confronted with such choices—not just about the consumption mix but also about how much to spend in total. These choices, in turn, have a powerful effect on the economy: consumer spending normally accounts for two-thirds of total spending on final goods and services. But what determines how much consumers spend?

Current Disposable Income and Consumer Spending

The most important factor affecting a family's consumer spending is its current disposable income—income after taxes are paid and government transfers are received. It's obvious from daily life that people with high disposable incomes on average drive more expensive cars, live in more expensive houses, and spend more on meals, clothing, and entertainment than people with lower disposable incomes. And the relationship between current disposable income and spending is clear in the data.

The Bureau of Labor Statistics (BLS) collects annual data on family income and spending. Since the income figures include transfers from the government, what the BLS calls a household's after-tax income is equivalent to its current disposable income. Recall from Module 10 that disposable income is the total amount of household income available to spend on consumption.

A **consumption function** uses an equation or a graph to show how a household's consumer spending varies with the household's current disposable income.

Figure 16.1 shows the graph of a consumption function. Household consumer spending is measured on the vertical axis, and household disposable income is measured on the horizontal axis. The vertical intercept is the amount the household would spend if its current disposable income were zero. The intercept is greater than zero because a household with no disposable income must still consume goods and services and can buy some things by borrowing or using its savings.

As a household's income rises above zero, its consumption can increase. A household can choose to spend all of each additional dollar of income it receives, or it can choose to spend none of it. The actual increase in consumer spending when disposable income rises by $1 is called the **marginal propensity to consume**, or **MPC**. When

A **consumption function** shows how a household's consumer spending varies with the household's current disposable income.

The **marginal propensity to consume**, or **MPC**, is the increase in consumer spending when disposable income rises by $1.

Figure 16.1   The Consumption Function

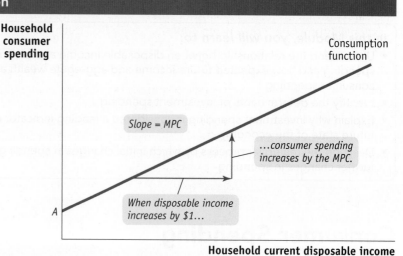

The consumption function relates a household's current disposable income to its consumer spending. The vertical intercept, *A*, is the amount the household would spend if its current disposable income were zero. The slope of the consumption function is the marginal propensity to consume, or *MPC*: the amount the household spends out of each additional $1 of current disposable income.

consumer spending changes because of a rise or fall in disposable income, the *MPC* is the change in consumer spending divided by the change in disposable income:

$$\text{(16-1)} \quad MPC = \frac{\Delta \text{ Consumer spending}}{\Delta \text{ Disposable income}}$$

where the symbol Δ (delta) means "change in." For example, if a household's spending goes up by $6 when disposable income goes up by $10, *MPC* is $6/$10 = 0.6.

Because consumers normally spend only a portion of an additional dollar of disposable income, *MPC* is a number between 0 and 1. The additional disposable income that consumers don't spend is saved. The **marginal propensity to save**, or *MPS*, is the fraction of an additional $1 of disposable income that is saved. Because consumers must either spend or save an additional dollar, the *MPC* plus the *MPS* will equal 1; therefore the *MPC* = 1 − *MPS* and the *MPS* = 1 − *MPC*.

The **marginal propensity to save**, or *MPS*, is the increase in household savings when disposable income rises by $1.

A household's total consumption spending at any level of disposable income equals the value of the intercept plus some fraction of disposable income, determined by the *MPC*. Recall that the slope of any line is "rise over run." Looking at the consumption function in Figure 16.1, you can see that the rise is the change in consumer spending and the run is equal to the change in disposable income. Because $MPC = \dfrac{\Delta \text{ Counsumer spending}}{\Delta \text{ Disposable income}}$, for each $1 "run" in disposable income, consumer spending "rises" by the amount of the *MPC*, so the slope of the consumption function is the *MPC*.

An individual household's consumption function shows a microeconomic relationship between the household's current disposable income and its spending on goods and services. Macroeconomists study the aggregate consumption function, which shows the relationship between current disposable income and consumer spending for the economy as a whole. We can represent this relationship with the following equation:

$$\text{(16-2)} \quad C = A + MPC \times Y_D$$

Here, *C* is aggregate consumer spending, Y_D is aggregate current disposable income, and *A* is the amount of consumer spending when disposable income is zero. Using data from 2012, the *MPC* in the United States was estimated to be $0.52. This figure implies that the marginal propensity to save (*MPS*) was $1 − $0.52 = $0.48.

Shifts of the Aggregate Consumption Function

The aggregate consumption function shows the relationship between current disposable income and consumer spending for the economy as a whole, other things equal. When things other than current disposable income cause households to consume more or less at every level of income, the aggregate consumption function will shift. There are two principal causes of shifts of the aggregate consumption function: changes in expected future disposable income and changes in aggregate wealth.

Changes in Expected Future Disposable Income

Milton Friedman argued that consumer spending depends primarily on the income people expect to have over the long term rather than on their current income. This argument is known as the *permanent income hypothesis*. Suppose you land a really good, well-paying job upon graduating from college—but the job, and the paychecks, won't start for several months. So your disposable income hasn't risen yet. Even so, it's likely that you will start spending more on final goods and services right away—maybe buying nicer work clothes than you originally planned—because you know that higher income is coming.

Conversely, suppose you have a good job but learn that the company is planning to downsize your division, raising the possibility that you may lose your job and have to take a lower-paying one somewhere else. Even though your disposable income hasn't gone down yet, you might well cut back on spending even while still employed, to save for a rainy day.

Both of these examples show how expectations about future disposable income can either increase or decrease consumer spending at all levels of disposable income.

Changes in Aggregate Wealth

Imagine two individuals, Maria and Mark, both of whom expect to earn $30,000 this year. Suppose, however, that they have different histories. Maria has been working steadily for the past 10 years, owns her own home, and has $200,000 in the bank. Mark is the same age as Maria, but he has been in and out of work, hasn't managed to buy a house, and has very little in savings. In this case, Maria has something that Mark doesn't have: wealth. Even though they have the same disposable income, other things equal, you'd expect Maria to spend more on consumption than Mark. That is, *wealth* has an effect on consumer spending.

The effect of wealth on spending is emphasized by an influential economic model of how consumers make choices about spending versus saving called the *life-cycle hypothesis*. According to this hypothesis, consumers plan their spending over their lifetime, not just in response to their current disposable income. As a result, people try to *smooth* their consumption over their lifetimes—they save some of their current disposable income during their years of peak earnings (typically occurring during a worker's 40s and 50s) and live off the wealth they accumulated while working during their retirement. We won't go into the details of this hypothesis but will simply point out that it implies an important role for wealth in determining consumer spending. For example, a middle-aged couple who have accumulated a lot of wealth—who have paid off the mortgage on their house and already own plenty of stocks and bonds—will, other things equal, spend more on goods and services than a couple who have the same current disposable income but still need to save for their retirement.

Because wealth affects household consumer spending, changes in wealth across the economy can shift the aggregate consumption function. A rise in aggregate wealth—say, because of a booming stock market—increases aggregate consumption at all levels of disposable income in the same way as does an expected increase in future disposable income. A decline in aggregate wealth—say, because of a fall in housing prices as occurred in 2008—reduces aggregate consumption at all levels of disposable income.

Rubberball/Mike Kemp/Getty Images

Investment Spending

Although consumer spending is much greater than investment spending, booms and busts in investment spending tend to drive the business cycle. In fact, most recessions originate as a fall in investment spending. **Figure 16.2** illustrates this point; it shows the annual percentage change of investment spending and consumer spending in the

Figure 16.2 Fluctuations in Investment Spending and Consumer Spending

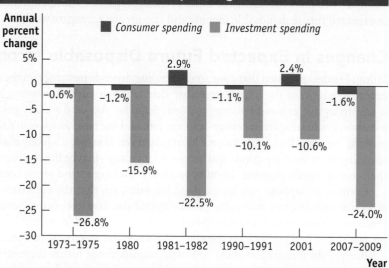

The bars illustrate the annual percentage change in investment spending and consumer spending during six recent recessions. As the heights of the bars show, swings in investment spending were much larger in percentage terms than those in consumer spending. The pattern has led economists to believe that recessions typically originate as a slump in investment spending.

United States, both measured in 2005 dollars, during six recessions from 1973 to 2009. As you can see, swings in investment spending are much more dramatic than those in consumer spending. In addition, economists believe that declines in consumer spending are usually the result of slumps in investment spending that trigger the spending multiplier process. Soon we'll examine in more detail how investment spending affects consumer spending.

Before we do that, however, let's analyze the factors that determine investment spending, which are somewhat different from those that determine consumer spending. **Planned investment spending** is the investment spending that firms *intend* to undertake during a given period. For reasons explained shortly, the level of investment spending that businesses *actually* carry out is sometimes not the same level as was planned. Planned investment spending depends on three principal factors: the interest rate, the expected future level of real GDP, and the current level of production capacity. First, we'll analyze the effect of the interest rate.

Planned investment spending is the investment spending that businesses intend to undertake during a given period.

The Interest Rate and Investment Spending

Interest rates have their clearest effect on one particular form of investment spending: spending on residential construction—that is, on the construction of homes. The reason is straightforward: home-builders only build houses they think they can sell, and houses are more affordable—and therefore more likely to sell—when the interest rate is low. Consider a potential home-buying family that needs to borrow $150,000 to buy a house. At an interest rate of 7.5%, a 30-year home mortgage will mean payments of $1,048 per month. At an interest rate of 5.5%, those payments would be only $851 per month, making houses significantly more affordable.

Interest rates also affect other forms of investment spending. Firms with investment spending projects will go ahead with a project only if they expect a rate of return higher than the cost of the funds they would have to borrow to finance that project. If the interest rate rises, fewer projects will pass that test, and, as a result, investment spending will be lower.

You might think that a firm faces a different trade-off if it can fund its investment project with its past profits rather than through borrowing. Past profits used to finance investment spending are called *retained earnings*. But even if a firm pays for investment spending out of retained earnings, the trade-off it must make in deciding whether or not to fund a project

Interest rates have a direct impact on whether or not construction companies decide to invest in the construction of new homes.

Dmitry Kalinovsky/Shutterstock

remains the same because it must take into account the opportunity cost of its funds. For example, instead of purchasing new equipment, the firm could lend out the funds and earn interest. The forgone interest earned is the opportunity cost of using retained earnings to fund an investment project. So the trade-off the firm faces when comparing a project's rate of return to the market interest rate has not changed because it uses retained earnings rather than borrowed funds. Either way, a rise in the market interest rate makes any given investment project less profitable. Conversely, a fall in the interest rate makes some investment projects that were unprofitable before profitable at the new lower interest rate. As a result, some projects that had been unfunded before will be funded now.

So planned investment spending—spending on investment projects that firms voluntarily decide whether or not to undertake—is negatively related to the interest rate. Other things equal, a higher interest rate leads to a lower level of planned investment spending.

Expected Future Real GDP, Production Capacity, and Investment Spending

Suppose a firm has enough capacity to continue to produce the amount of goods it is currently selling but doesn't expect its sales to grow in the future. Then it will engage in investment spending only to replace existing equipment and structures that wear out or are rendered obsolete by new technologies. But if, instead, the firm expects its sales to grow rapidly in the future, it will find its existing production capacity insufficient for its future production needs. So the firm will undertake investment spending to meet those needs. This implies that, other things equal, firms will undertake more investment spending when they expect their sales to grow.

Now suppose that the firm currently has considerably more capacity than necessary to meet current production needs. Even if it expects sales to grow, it won't have to undertake investment spending for a while—not until the growth in sales catches up with its excess capacity. This illustrates the fact that, other things equal, the current level of productive capacity has a negative effect on investment spending: other things equal, the higher the current capacity, the lower the investment spending.

If we put together the effects on investment spending of (1) growth in expected future sales and (2) the size of current production capacity, we can see one situation in which firms will most likely undertake high levels of investment spending: when they expect sales to grow rapidly. In that case, even excess production capacity will soon be used up, leading firms to resume investment spending.

What is an indicator of high expected growth in future sales? It's a high expected future growth rate of real GDP. A higher expected future growth rate of real GDP results in a higher level of planned investment spending, but a lower expected future growth rate of real GDP leads to lower planned investment spending.

Inventories and Unplanned Investment Spending

Most firms maintain inventories, stocks of goods held to satisfy future sales. Firms hold inventories so they can quickly satisfy buyers—a consumer can purchase an item off the shelf rather than waiting for it to be manufactured. In addition, businesses often hold inventories of their inputs to be sure they have a steady supply of necessary materials and spare parts. At the beginning of 2018, the overall value of inventories in the U.S. economy was estimated at over $1.9 trillion, roughly 10% of GDP.

As we explained in Module 10, a firm that increases its inventories is engaging in a form of investment spending. Suppose, for example, that the U.S. auto industry produces 800,000 cars per month but sells only 700,000. The remaining 100,000 cars are added to the inventory at auto company warehouses or car dealerships, ready to be sold in the future.

Inventory investment is the value of the change in total inventories held in the economy during a given period. Unlike other forms of investment spending, inventory investment can actually be negative. If, for example, the auto industry reduces its inventory over the course of a month, we say that it has engaged in negative inventory investment.

Inventory investment is the value of the change in inventories held in the economy during a given period. Inventory investment is unplanned when a difference between actual sales and expected sales leads to the change in inventories. Actual inventory investment is the sum of planned and unplanned inventory investment.

To understand inventory investment, think about a manager stocking the canned goods section of a supermarket. The manager tries to keep the store fully stocked so that shoppers can almost always find what they're looking for. But the manager does not want the shelves too heavily stocked because shelf space is limited and products can spoil. Similar considerations apply to many firms and typically lead them to manage their inventories carefully. However, sales fluctuate. And because firms cannot always accurately predict sales, they often find themselves holding larger or smaller inventories than they had intended. When a firm's inventories are higher than intended due to an unforeseen decrease in sales, the result is unplanned inventory investment. An unexpected increase in sales depletes inventories and causes the value of unplanned inventory investment to be negative.

In any given period, actual investment spending is equal to planned investment spending plus unplanned inventory investment. If we let $I_{Unplanned}$ represent unplanned inventory investment, $I_{Planned}$ represent planned investment spending, and I represent actual investment spending, then the relationship among all three can be represented as

$$(16\text{-}3) \quad I = I_{Unplanned} + I_{Planned}$$

To see how unplanned inventory investment can occur, let's continue to focus on the auto industry and make the following assumptions. First, let's assume that a firm must determine each month's production volume in advance, before it knows the volume of actual sales. Second, let's assume that it anticipates selling 800,000 cars next month and that it plans neither to add to nor subtract from existing inventories. In that case, it will produce 800,000 cars to match anticipated sales.

Now imagine that next month's actual sales are less than expected, only 700,000 cars. As a result, the value of 100,000 cars will be added to investment spending as unplanned inventory investment.

The auto industry will, of course, eventually adjust to this slowdown in sales and the resulting unplanned inventory investment. It is likely that the firm will cut next month's production volume in order to reduce inventories. In fact, economists who study macroeconomic variables in an attempt to determine the future path of the economy pay careful attention to changes in inventory levels. Rising inventories typically indicate positive unplanned inventory investment and a slowing economy, as sales are less than had been forecast. Falling inventories typically indicate negative unplanned inventory investment and a growing economy, as sales are greater than forecast. In the next section, we will see how production adjustments in response to fluctuations in sales and inventories ensure that the value of final goods and services actually produced is equal to desired purchases of those final goods and services.

The Spending Multiplier: An Informal Introduction

The story of the boom and bust in Ft. Myers that opens this Section involves a chain reaction in which an initial rise or fall in spending leads to changes in income, which lead to further changes in spending, and so on. Let's examine that chain reaction more closely, this time thinking through the effects of changes in spending on the economy as a whole.

To simplify our analysis, we will make the following four assumptions that we will reconsider in later modules:

1. We assume that producers are willing to supply additional output at a fixed price. That is, an additional $1 billion in spending will not drive up the overall level of prices. As a result, changes in overall spending translate into changes in aggregate output, as measured by real GDP. This assumption isn't too unrealistic in the short run, but later in this section we'll learn that it needs to be changed when we think about the long-run effects of changes in demand.

2. We assume the interest rate remains constant.

3. We assume that there is no government spending and no taxes.

4. We assume that exports and imports are zero.

Given these simplifying assumptions, consider what happens if there is a change in investment spending. Specifically, imagine that for some reason home-builders decide to spend an extra $100 billion on home construction over the next year.

The direct effect of this increase in investment spending will be to increase income and the value of aggregate output by the same amount. That happens because each dollar spent on home construction translates into a dollar's worth of income for construction workers, suppliers of building materials, electricians, and so on. If the process stopped there, the increase of $100 billion in residential investment spending would raise overall income by exactly $100 billion.

But the process doesn't stop there. Many businesses, such as those that support home improvement and interior design, benefit during housing booms. The increase in aggregate output leads to an increase in disposable income that flows to households in the form of profits and wages. The increase in households' disposable income leads to a rise in consumer spending, which, in turn, induces firms to increase output yet again. This generates another rise in disposable income, which leads to another round of consumer spending increases, and so on. In other words, the initial increase in investment spending results in multiple rounds of increases in aggregate output.

How large is the total effect on aggregate output if we sum the effect from all these rounds of spending increases? With the assumption of no taxes and no international trade, each $1 increase in spending raises both real GDP and disposable income by $1. So the $100 billion increase in investment spending initially raises real GDP by $100 billion. The corresponding $100 billion increase in disposable income leads to a second-round increase in consumer spending, which raises real GDP by a further $MPC \times \$100$ billion. This is followed by a third-round increase in consumer spending of $MPC \times MPC \times \$100$ billion, and so on. After an infinite number of rounds, the total effect on real GDP is

Many businesses, such as those that support home improvement and interior design, benefit during housing booms.

Increase in investment spending	$= \$100$ billion
+ Second-round increase in consumer spending	$= MPC \times \$100$ billion
+ Third-round increase in consumer spending	$= MPC^2 \times \$100$ billion
+ Fourth-round increase in consumer spending	$= MPC^3 \times \$100$ billion

$$\text{Total increase in real GDP} = (1 + MPC + MPC^2 + MPC^3 + \cdots) \times \$100 \text{ billion}$$

The $100 billion increase in investment spending sets off a chain reaction in the economy, and the net result is a change in real GDP that is a multiple of the size of that initial change in spending.

How large is this multiple? Clearly, the size of the MPC is integral to determining how much spending is passed on each round. To determine the exact amount of the multiple, we can use the mathematical fact that an infinite series of the form $1 + x + x^2 + x^3 + \cdots$, where x is between 0 and 1, is equal to $1/(1 - x)$. The total effect of a $100 billion increase in investment spending, I, taking into account all the subsequent increases in consumer spending (and assuming no taxes and no international trade), is given by the following equation:

$$(16\text{-}4) \quad \begin{array}{c}\text{Total increase}\\ \text{in real GDP from}\\ \$100 \text{ billion rise in } I\end{array} = \frac{1}{(1 - MPC)} \times \$100 \text{ billion}$$

Let's consider a numerical example in which $MPC = 0.6$; in other words, each \$1 in additional disposable income causes a \$0.60 rise in consumer spending. A \$100 billion increase in investment spending raises real GDP by \$100 billion in the first round. The second-round increase in consumer spending raises real GDP by an additional $0.6 \times \$100$ billion, or \$60 billion. The third-round increase in consumer spending raises real GDP by $0.6 \times \$60$ billion, or \$36 billion. This process continues until the amount of spending in another round would be virtually zero. In the end, real GDP rises by \$250 billion as a consequence of the initial \$100 billion rise in investment spending:

$$\frac{1}{(1 - 0.6)} \times \$100 \text{ billion} = 2.5 \times \$100 \text{ billion} = \$250 \text{ billion}$$

Notice that even though there can be a nearly endless number of rounds of expansion of real GDP, the total rise in real GDP is limited to \$250 billion. The reason is that at each stage some of the rise in disposable income "leaks out" because it is saved, leaving less to be spent in the next round. How much of each additional dollar of disposable income is saved depends on MPS, the marginal propensity to save.

We've described the effects of a change in investment spending, but the same analysis can be applied to any other change in spending. The important thing is to distinguish between the initial change in aggregate spending, before real GDP rises, and the additional change in aggregate spending caused by the change in real GDP as the chain reaction unfolds. For example, suppose that a boom in housing prices makes consumers feel richer and that, as a result, they are willing to spend more at any given level of disposable income. This will lead to an initial rise in consumer spending, before real GDP rises. But it will also lead to subsequent rounds of higher consumer spending as real GDP and disposable income rise.

An **autonomous change in aggregate spending** is an initial rise or fall in aggregate spending that is the cause, not the result, of a series of income and spending changes.

The **spending multiplier** is the ratio of the total change in real GDP caused by an autonomous change in aggregate spending to the size of that autonomous change. It indicates the total rise in real GDP that results from each \$1 of an initial rise in spending.

An initial rise or fall in aggregate spending at a given level of real GDP is called an **autonomous change in aggregate spending**. It is autonomous—which means "self-governing"—because it is the cause, not the result, of the chain reaction just described. Formally, the **spending multiplier** is the ratio of the total change in real GDP caused by an autonomous change in aggregate spending to the size of that autonomous change. If we let ΔAAS stand for the autonomous change in aggregate spending and ΔY stand for the total change in real GDP, then the spending multiplier is equal to $\Delta Y / \Delta AAS$. We've already seen how to find the value of the spending multiplier. Assuming no taxes and no trade, the total change in real GDP caused by an autonomous change in aggregate spending is

$$(16\text{-}5) \quad \Delta Y = \frac{1}{(1 - MPC)} \times \Delta AAS$$

So the spending multiplier is

$$(16\text{-}6) \quad \frac{\Delta Y}{\Delta AAS} = \frac{1}{(1 - MPC)}$$

Notice that the size of the spending multiplier depends on MPC. If the marginal propensity to consume is high, so is the spending multiplier. This is true because the size of MPC determines how large each round of expansion is compared with the previous round. To put it another way, the higher MPC is, the less disposable income "leaks out" into savings at each round of expansion.

In later Modules we'll use the concept of the spending multiplier to analyze the effects of fiscal and monetary policies. We'll also see that the spending multiplier changes when we introduce various complications, including taxes and foreign trade.

MODULE 16 REVIEW

Check Your Understanding

1. Explain why a decline in investment spending caused by a change in business expectations leads to a fall in consumer spending.

2. What is the spending multiplier if the marginal propensity to consume is 0.5? What is it if *MPC* is 0.8?

3. Suppose a crisis in the capital markets makes consumers unable to borrow and unable to save money. What implication does this have for the effects of expected future disposable income on consumer spending?

4. For each event, explain whether the initial effect is a change in planned investment spending or a change in unplanned inventory investment, and indicate the direction of the change.
   a. an unexpected increase in consumer spending
   b. a sharp rise in the interest rate
   c. a sharp increase in the economy's growth rate of real GDP
   d. an unanticipated fall in sales

TACKLE THE AP® TEST: Multiple-Choice Questions

1. Changes in which of the following leads to a shift of the aggregate consumption function?
   a. an increase in expected future disposable income
   b. an increase in the *MPC*
   c. a decrease in the *MPC*
   d. an increase in current disposable income
   e. a decrease in current disposable income

2. The slope of a household's consumption function is equal to
   a. the real interest rate.
   b. the inflation rate.
   c. the marginal propensity to consume.
   d. the rate of increase in household current disposable income.
   e. the tax rate.

3. Given the aggregate consumption function $C = \$1.6$ trillion $+ 0.5Y_D$, if aggregate current disposable income is $2.0 trillion, aggregate consumption spending will equal
   a. $3.6 trillion.
   b. $2.6 trillion.
   c. $2.0 trillion.
   d. $1.6 trillion.
   e. $0.6 trillion.

4. The level of planned investment spending is negatively related to
   a. the rate of return on investment.
   b. the level of consumer spending.
   c. the level of actual investment spending.
   d. the interest rate.
   e. all of the above.

5. Actual investment spending in any period is equal to
   a. planned investment spending + unplanned inventory investment.
   b. planned investment spending − unplanned inventory investment.
   c. planned investment spending + inventory decreases.
   d. unplanned inventory investment + inventory increases.
   e. unplanned inventory investment − inventory increases.

6. If the *MPS* is equal to 0.1, what is the value of the spending multiplier?
   a. 0.1
   b. 0.9
   c. 1.11
   d. 9
   e. 10

7. An autonomous increase in aggregate spending of $100 million would lead to a total increase in real GDP of how much if the *MPC* is equal to 0.8?
   a. $80 million
   b. $100 million
   c. $125 million
   d. $500 million
   e. $800 million

1. Use the aggregate consumption function provided to answer the following questions:

$$C = \$1.5 \text{ trillion} + 0.8Y_D$$

   a. What is the value of the marginal propensity to consume?
   b. What is the level of aggregate consumer spending if disposable income is equal to zero?
   c. Suppose aggregate current disposable income is $4.0 trillion. Calculate the amount of aggregate consumer spending.
   d. What is the value of the spending multiplier? Show your work.
   e. By how much would real GDP increase if there were an autonomous increase in aggregate spending equal to $5 billion? Show your work.

Rubric for FRQ 1 (5 points)
1 point: 0.8
1 point: $1.5 trillion
1 point: $4.7 trillion
1 point: $1/(1 − 0.8) = 5$
1 point: $5 billion(5) = $25 billion

2. List the three most important factors affecting planned investment spending. Explain how each is related to actual investment spending. **(6 points)**

MOD 17

Aggregate Demand: Introduction and Determinants

In this Module, you will learn to:
- Use the aggregate demand curve to illustrate the relationship between the aggregate price level and the quantity of aggregate output demanded in the economy
- Explain how the real wealth effect, the interest rate effect, and the exchange rate effect give the aggregate demand curve a negative slope
- Identify the factors that can shift the aggregate demand curve

Aggregate Demand

The **aggregate demand curve** shows the relationship between the aggregate price level and the quantity of aggregate output demanded by households, businesses, the government, and the rest of the world.

The Great Depression, the great majority of economists agree, was the result of a massive negative demand shock. What does that mean? When economists talk about a fall in the demand for a particular good or service, they're referring to a leftward shift of the demand curve. Similarly, when economists talk about a negative demand shock to the economy as a whole, they're referring to a leftward shift of the **aggregate demand curve**, a curve that shows the relationship between the aggregate price level and the quantity of aggregate output demanded by households, firms, the government, and the rest of the world.

Figure 17.1 shows what the aggregate demand curve may have looked like in 1933, at the end of the 1929–1933 recession. The horizontal axis shows the total quantity of domestic goods and services demanded, measured in 2005 dollars. Real GDP is used to

Figure 17.1 The Aggregate Demand Curve

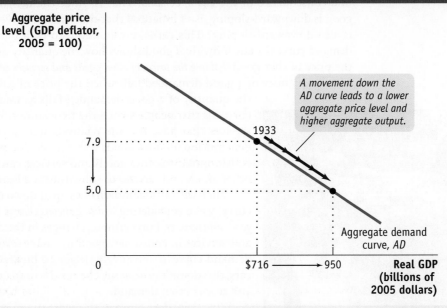

The aggregate demand curve shows the relationship between the aggregate price level and the quantity of aggregate output demanded. Corresponding to the actual 1933 data, here the total quantity of goods and services demanded at an aggregate price level of 7.9 is $716 billion in 2005 dollars. According to our hypothetical curve, however, if the aggregate price level had been only 5.0, the quantity of aggregate output demanded would have risen to $950 billion.

measure aggregate output, and we will use the two terms interchangeably. The vertical axis shows the aggregate price level, measured by the GDP deflator. With these variables on the axes, we can draw a curve, AD, that shows how much aggregate output would have been demanded at any given aggregate price level. Since AD is meant to illustrate aggregate demand in 1933, one point on the curve corresponds to actual data for 1933, when the aggregate price level was 7.9 and the total quantity of domestic final goods and services purchased was $716 billion in 2005 dollars.

As drawn in Figure 17.1, the aggregate demand curve is downward-sloping, indicating a negative relationship between the aggregate price level and the quantity of aggregate output demanded. A higher aggregate price level, other things equal, reduces the quantity of aggregate output demanded; a lower aggregate price level, other things equal, increases the quantity of aggregate output demanded. According to Figure 17.1, if the price level in 1933 had been 5.0 instead of 7.9, the total quantity of domestic final goods and services demanded would have been $950 billion in 2005 dollars instead of $716 billion.

The first key question about the aggregate demand curve involves its negative slope.

Why Is the Aggregate Demand Curve Downward-Sloping?

In Figure 17.1, the curve AD slopes downward. Why? Recall the basic equation of national income accounting:

(17-1) $GDP = C + I + G + (X - M)$

where C is consumer spending, I is investment spending, G is government purchases of goods and services, X is exports to other countries, and M is imports. If we measure these variables in constant dollars—that is, in prices of a base year—then $C + I + G + (X - M)$ represents the quantity of domestically produced final goods and services demanded during a given period. G is decided by the government, but the other variables are private-sector decisions. To understand why the aggregate demand curve slopes downward, we need to understand why a rise in the aggregate price level reduces C, I, and $(X - M)$.

You might think that the downward slope of the aggregate demand curve is a natural consequence of the *law of demand*. That is, since the demand curve for any one good is downward-sloping, isn't it natural that the demand curve for aggregate output is also downward-sloping? This turns out, however, to be a misleading parallel. The demand curve for any individual good shows how the quantity demanded depends on the price of that good, *holding the prices of other goods and services constant*. The main reason the quantity of a good demanded falls when the price of that good rises—that is,

the quantity of a good demanded falls as we move up the demand curve—is that people switch their consumption to other goods and services that have become relatively less expensive. But aggregate demand includes *all* goods and services, so the idea of switching consumption to other goods and services can't apply—there are no other goods and services to substitute at a lower relative price!

When we consider movements up or down the aggregate demand curve, we're considering *a simultaneous change in the prices of all final goods and services*. Furthermore, changes in the composition of goods and services in consumer spending aren't relevant to the aggregate demand curve: if consumers decide to buy fewer clothes but more cars, this doesn't necessarily change the total quantity of final goods and services they demand.

Why, then, does a rise in the aggregate price level lead to a fall in the quantity of all domestically produced final goods and services demanded? There are three reasons: the *real wealth effect*, the *interest rate effect*, and the *exchange rate effect* of a change in the aggregate price level.

When the aggregate price level falls, the purchasing power of consumers' assets rises, leading shoppers to place more items in their carts.

The Real Wealth Effect

An increase in the aggregate price level, other things equal, reduces the purchasing power of many assets. Consider, for example, someone who has $5,000 in a bank account. If the aggregate price level were to rise by 25%, that $5,000 would buy only as much as $4,000 would have bought previously. With the loss in purchasing power, the owner of that bank account would probably scale back his or her consumption plans. Millions of other people would respond the same way, leading to a fall in spending on final goods and services, because a rise in the aggregate price level reduces the purchasing power of everyone's bank account.

Correspondingly, a fall in the aggregate price level increases the purchasing power of consumers' assets and leads to more consumer demand. The **real wealth effect** of a change in the aggregate price level is the change in consumer spending caused by the altered purchasing power of consumers' assets. Because of the real wealth effect, consumer spending, C, falls when the aggregate price level rises, leading to a downward-sloping aggregate demand curve.

The **real wealth effect** of a change in the aggregate price level is the change in consumer spending caused by the altered purchasing power of consumers' assets.

The Interest Rate Effect

Economists use the term *money* in its narrowest sense to refer to cash and bank deposits on which people can withdraw funds. People and firms hold money because it reduces the cost and inconvenience of making transactions. An increase in the aggregate price level, other things equal, reduces the purchasing power of a given amount of money holdings. To purchase the same basket of goods and services as before, people and firms now need to hold more money. So, in response to an increase in the aggregate price level, the public tries to increase its money holdings, either by borrowing more or by selling assets such as bonds. This reduces the funds available for lending to other borrowers and drives interest rates up. A rise in the interest rate reduces investment spending because it makes the cost of borrowing higher. It also reduces consumer spending because households save more of their disposable income. So a rise in the aggregate price level depresses investment spending, I, and consumer spending, C, through its effect on the purchasing power of money holdings, an effect known as the **interest rate effect** of a change in the aggregate price level. This also leads to a downward-sloping aggregate demand curve.

The **interest rate effect** of a change in the aggregate price level is the change in investment and consumer spending caused by altered interest rates that result from changes in the demand for money.

The Exchange Rate Effect

Net exports $(X - M)$ are the fourth component of the basic equation of national income accounting. A change in the aggregate price level will also have an effect on net exports for two reasons that can help to explain why the aggregate demand curve slopes downward. First, there is the direct effect on net exports. As the domestic aggregate price level changes, a country's goods and services become more or less expensive relative to those goods and services in other countries. For example, as the domestic aggregate price level increases relative to the aggregate price level in another country, exports become more expensive for foreign buyers and imports become less expensive. This increase in the price level results in a decrease in net exports and real GDP, so the AD curve has a negative slope.

Second, there is an indirect effect on net exports through the foreign exchange market where currencies are exchanged. As the domestic aggregate price level changes, it causes a change in domestic interest rates, which affects financial investment flows between countries. For example, as the domestic aggregate price level and interest rates decrease relative to other countries, domestic financial investors invest more in other countries, where the return on their investment is higher. The resulting increase in the flow of domestic currency to other countries causes a decrease in the value of that currency in the foreign exchange market (known as the exchange rate—discussed in detail in Section 8). The decrease in the value of the domestic currency increases net exports because domestic goods and services become relatively cheaper for foreign buyers with now higher-valued currency. This is called the **exchange rate effect** of a change in the aggregate price level. The decrease in the price level results in an increase in real GDP, so the AD curve has a negative slope.

The **exchange rate effect** of a change in the aggregate price level is the change in net exports caused by a change in the value of the domestic currency, which leads to change in the relative price of domestic and foreign goods and services.

Shifts of the Aggregate Demand Curve

When we introduced the analysis of supply and demand in the market for an individual good, we stressed the importance of the distinction between *movements along* the demand curve and *shifts of* the demand curve. The same distinction applies to the aggregate demand curve. Figure 17.1 shows a *movement along* the aggregate demand curve, a change in the aggregate quantity of goods and services demanded as the aggregate price level changes. But there can also be *shifts of* the aggregate demand curve, changes in the quantity of goods and services demanded at any given price level, as shown in **Figure 17.2**. When we talk about an increase in aggregate demand, we mean a shift

---

Figure 17.2 Shifts of the Aggregate Demand Curve

(a) Rightward Shift

(b) Leftward Shift

Panel (a) shows the effect of events that increase the quantity of aggregate output demanded at any given aggregate price level, such as a rise in consumer optimism about future income or a rise in government spending. Such changes shift the aggregate demand curve to the right, from AD_1 to AD_2.

Panel (b) shows the effect of events that decrease the quantity of aggregate output demanded at any given aggregate price level, such as a fall in wealth caused by a stock market decline. This shifts the aggregate demand curve leftward from AD_1 to AD_2.

of the aggregate demand curve to the right, as shown in panel (a) by the shift from AD_1 to AD_2. A rightward shift occurs when the quantity of aggregate output demanded increases at any given aggregate price level. A decrease in aggregate demand means that the *AD* curve shifts to the left, as in panel (b). A leftward shift implies that the quantity of aggregate output demanded falls at any given aggregate price level.

A number of factors can shift the aggregate demand curve. Among the most important factors are changes in expectations, changes in wealth, and the size of the existing stock of physical capital. In addition, both fiscal and monetary policy can shift the aggregate demand curve. All five factors set the spending multiplier process in motion. By causing an initial rise or fall in real GDP, they change disposable income, which leads to additional changes in aggregate spending, which lead to further changes in real GDP, and so on. For an overview of factors that shift the aggregate demand curve, see **Table 17.1**.

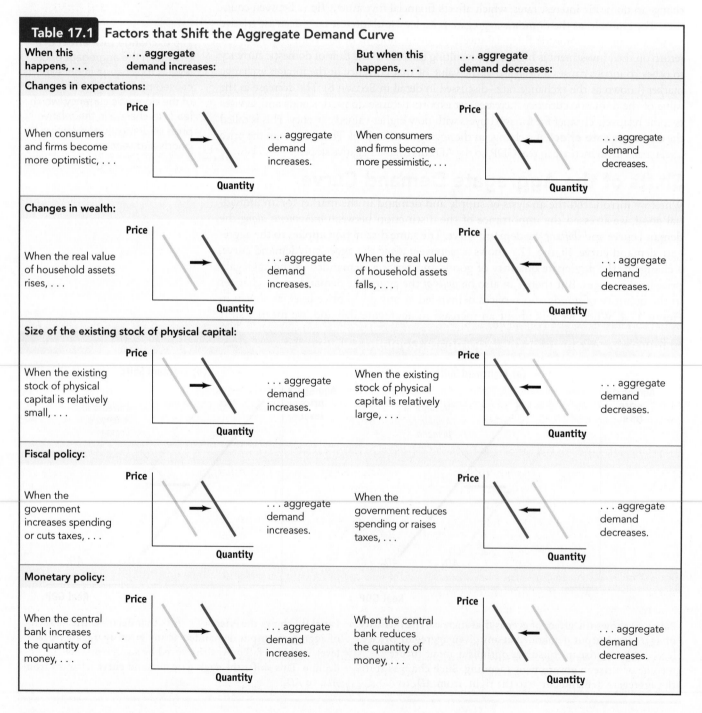

Table 17.1 Factors that Shift the Aggregate Demand Curve

When this happens, . . .	. . . aggregate demand increases:		But when this happens, . . .	. . . aggregate demand decreases:	
Changes in expectations:					
When consumers and firms become more optimistic, . . .	*(graph: Price vs. Quantity, rightward shift)*	. . . aggregate demand increases.	When consumers and firms become more pessimistic, . . .	*(graph: Price vs. Quantity, leftward shift)*	. . . aggregate demand decreases.
Changes in wealth:					
When the real value of household assets rises, . . .	*(graph: Price vs. Quantity, rightward shift)*	. . . aggregate demand increases.	When the real value of household assets falls, . . .	*(graph: Price vs. Quantity, leftward shift)*	. . . aggregate demand decreases.
Size of the existing stock of physical capital:					
When the existing stock of physical capital is relatively small, . . .	*(graph: Price vs. Quantity, rightward shift)*	. . . aggregate demand increases.	When the existing stock of physical capital is relatively large, . . .	*(graph: Price vs. Quantity, leftward shift)*	. . . aggregate demand decreases.
Fiscal policy:					
When the government increases spending or cuts taxes, . . .	*(graph: Price vs. Quantity, rightward shift)*	. . . aggregate demand increases.	When the government reduces spending or raises taxes, . . .	*(graph: Price vs. Quantity, leftward shift)*	. . . aggregate demand decreases.
Monetary policy:					
When the central bank increases the quantity of money, . . .	*(graph: Price vs. Quantity, rightward shift)*	. . . aggregate demand increases.	When the central bank reduces the quantity of money, . . .	*(graph: Price vs. Quantity, leftward shift)*	. . . aggregate demand decreases.

Changes in Expectations

Both consumer spending and planned investment spending depend in part on people's expectations about the future. Consumers base their spending not only on the income they have now but also on the income they expect to have in the future. Firms base their planned investment spending not only on current conditions but also on the sales they expect to make in the future. As a result, changes in expectations can push consumer spending and planned investment spending up or down. If consumers and firms become more optimistic, aggregate spending rises; if they become more pessimistic, aggregate spending falls. In fact, short-run economic forecasters pay careful attention to surveys of consumer and business sentiment. In particular, forecasters watch the Consumer Confidence Index, a monthly measure calculated by the Conference Board, and the Michigan Consumer Sentiment Index, a similar measure calculated by the University of Michigan.

The loss of wealth resulting from the stock market crash of 1929 was a significant factor leading to the Great Depression.

Changes in Wealth

Consumer spending depends in part on the value of household assets. When the real value of these assets rises, the purchasing power they embody also rises, leading to an increase in aggregate spending. For example, in the 1990s, there was a significant rise in the stock market that increased aggregate demand. And when the real value of household assets falls—for example, because of a stock market crash—the purchasing power they embody is reduced and aggregate demand also falls. The stock market crash of 1929 was a significant factor leading to the Great Depression. Similarly, a sharp decline in real estate values was a major factor depressing consumer spending in 2008.

Size of the Existing Stock of Physical Capital

Firms engage in planned investment spending to add to their stock of physical capital. Their incentive to spend depends in part on how much physical capital they already have: the more they have, the less they will feel a need to add more, other things equal. The same applies to other types of investment spending—for example, if a large number of houses have been built in recent years, this will depress the demand for new houses and, as a result, will also tend to reduce residential investment spending. In fact, that's part of the reason for the deep slump in residential investment spending that began in 2006. The housing boom of the previous few years had created an oversupply of houses: by spring 2008, the inventory of unsold houses on the market was equal to more than 11 months of sales, and prices had fallen more than 20% from their peak. This gave the construction industry little incentive to build even more homes.

Government Policies and Aggregate Demand

One of the key insights of macroeconomics is that the government can have a powerful influence on aggregate demand and that, in some circumstances, this influence can be used to improve economic performance.

The two main ways the government can influence the aggregate demand curve are through *fiscal policy* and *monetary policy*. We'll briefly discuss their influence on aggregate demand, leaving a full-length discussion for later.

Fiscal Policy Fiscal policy is the use of either government spending—government purchases of final goods and services and government transfers—or tax policy to stabilize the economy. In practice, governments often respond to recessions by increasing spending, cutting taxes, or both. They often respond to inflation by reducing spending or increasing taxes.

The effect of government purchases of final goods and services, G, on the aggregate demand curve is *direct* because government purchases are themselves a component of aggregate demand. So an increase in government purchases shifts the aggregate demand curve to the right and a decrease shifts it to the left. History's most dramatic example

Fiscal policy is the use of government purchases of goods and services, government transfers, or tax policy to stabilize the economy.

of how increased government purchases affect aggregate demand was the effect of wartime government spending during World War II. Because of the war, purchases by the U.S. federal government surged 400%. This increase in purchases is usually credited with ending the Great Depression. In the 1990s, Japan used large public works projects—such as government-financed construction of roads, bridges, and dams—in an effort to increase aggregate demand in the face of a slumping economy.

In contrast, changes in either tax rates or government transfers influence the economy *indirectly* through their effect on disposable income. A lower tax rate means that consumers get to keep more of what they earn, increasing their disposable income. An increase in government transfers also increases consumers' disposable income. In either case, this increases consumer spending and shifts the aggregate demand curve to the right. A higher tax rate or a reduction in transfers reduces the amount of disposable income received by consumers. This reduces consumer spending and shifts the aggregate demand curve to the left.

Monetary Policy In the next section, we will study the Federal Reserve System and monetary policy in detail. At this point, we just need to note that the Federal Reserve controls **monetary policy**—the use of changes in the quantity of money or the interest rate to stabilize the economy. We've just discussed how a rise in the aggregate price level, by reducing the purchasing power of money holdings, causes a rise in the interest rate. That, in turn, reduces both investment spending and consumer spending.

But what happens if the quantity of money in the hands of households and firms changes? In modern economies, the quantity of money in circulation is largely determined by the decisions of a *central bank* created by the government. As we'll learn in more detail later, the Federal Reserve, the U.S. central bank, is a special institution that is neither exactly part of the government nor exactly a private institution. When the central bank increases the quantity of money in circulation, households and firms have more money, which they are willing to lend out. The effect is to drive the interest rate down at any given aggregate price level, leading to higher investment spending and higher consumer spending. That is, increasing the quantity of money shifts the aggregate demand curve to the right. Reducing the quantity of money has the opposite effect: households and firms have less money holdings than before, leading them to borrow more and lend less. This raises the interest rate, reduces investment spending and consumer spending, and shifts the aggregate demand curve to the left.

Monetary policy is the central bank's use of changes in the quantity of money or the interest rate to stabilize the economy.

MODULE 17 REVIEW

Check Your Understanding

1. Determine the effect on aggregate demand of each of the following events. Explain whether it represents a movement along the aggregate demand curve (up or down) or a shift of the curve (leftward or rightward).
   a. a rise in the interest rate caused by a change in monetary policy
   b. a fall in the real value of money in the economy due to a higher aggregate price level
   c. news of a worse-than-expected job market next year
   d. a fall in tax rates
   e. a rise in the real value of assets in the economy due to a lower aggregate price level
   f. a rise in the real value of assets in the economy due to a surge in real estate values

TACKLE THE AP® TEST: Multiple-Choice Questions

1. Which of the following does NOT explain the slope of the aggregate demand curve?
   a. the real wealth effect of a change in the aggregate price level
   b. the interest rate effect of a change in the aggregate price level
   c. the product-substitution effect of a change in the aggregate price level
   d. the exchange rate effect of a change in the aggregate price level
   e. a change in interest-sensitive consumer spending resulting from a change in interest rates

2. Which of the following will shift the aggregate demand curve to the right?
   a. a decrease in wealth
   b. pessimistic consumer expectations
   c. a decrease in the existing stock of capital
   d. contractionary fiscal policy
   e. a decrease in the quantity of money

3. The Consumer Confidence Index is used to measure which of the following?
   a. the level of consumer spending
   b. the rate of return on investments
   c. consumer expectations
   d. planned investment spending
   e. the level of current disposable income

4. Decreases in the stock market decrease aggregate demand by decreasing which of the following?
   a. consumer wealth
   b. the price level
   c. the stock of existing physical capital
   d. interest rates
   e. tax revenues

5. Which of the following government policies will shift the aggregate demand curve to the left?
   a. a decrease in the quantity of money
   b. an increase in government purchases of goods and services
   c. a decrease in taxes
   d. a decrease in interest rates
   e. an increase in government transfers

6. A change in consumer spending that results from a change in consumers' purchasing power is known as the _____ effect of a change in the aggregate price level.
   a. interest rate   d. price
   b. exchange rate   e. income
   c. real wealth

7. A change in real GDP that results when the domestic price level increases relative to a foreign price level is the _____ effect of a change in the price level.
   a. foreign   d. price
   b. exchange rate   e. income
   c. real wealth

TACKLE THE AP® TEST: Free-Response Questions

1. a. Draw a correctly labeled graph showing aggregate demand.
   b. On your graph from part a, illustrate an increase in aggregate demand.
   c. List the four factors that shift aggregate demand.
   d. Describe a change in each determinant of aggregate demand that would lead to the shift you illustrated in part b.

Rubric for FRQ 1 (12 points)

1 point: Vertical axis labeled "Aggregate price level" (or "Price level")

1 point: Horizontal axis labeled "Real GDP"

1 point: Downward-sloping curve labeled "AD" (or "AD_1")

1 point: AD curve shifted to the right

1 point: Expectations

1 point: Wealth

1 point: Size of existing stock of physical capital

1 point: Government policies

1 point: Consumers/Producers more confident

1 point: Increase in wealth

1 point: Lower existing stock of physical capital

1 point: An increase in government spending or in the money supply

2. Identify the three effects that cause the aggregate demand curve to have a downward slope. Explain each. **(6 points)**

Aggregate Supply: Introduction and Determinants

> **In this Module, you will learn to:**
> - Use the aggregate supply curve to illustrate the relationship between the aggregate price level and the quantity of aggregate output supplied in the economy
> - Identify the factors that can shift the aggregate supply curve
> - Explain why the aggregate supply curve is different in the short run from in the long run

Aggregate Supply

The **aggregate supply curve** shows the relationship between the aggregate price level and the quantity of aggregate output supplied in the economy.

Between 1929 and 1933, there was a sharp fall in aggregate demand—a reduction in the quantity of goods and services demanded at any given price level. One consequence of the economy-wide decline in demand was a fall in the prices of most goods and services. By 1933, the GDP deflator (one of the price indexes) was 26% below its 1929 level, and other indexes were down by similar amounts. A second consequence was a decline in the output of most goods and services: by 1933, real GDP was 27% below its 1929 level. A third consequence, closely tied to the fall in real GDP, was a surge in the unemployment rate from 3% to 25%.

The association between the plunge in real GDP and the plunge in prices wasn't an accident. Between 1929 and 1933, the U.S. economy was moving down its **aggregate supply curve**, which shows the relationship between the economy's aggregate price level (the overall price level of final goods and services in the economy) and the total quantity of final goods and services, or aggregate output, producers are willing to supply. (As you will recall, we use real GDP to measure aggregate output, and we'll often use the two terms interchangeably.) More specifically, between 1929 and 1933, the U.S. economy moved down its *short-run aggregate supply curve*.

The Short-Run Aggregate Supply Curve

The period from 1929 to 1933 demonstrated that there is a positive relationship in the short run between the aggregate price level and the quantity of aggregate output supplied. That is, a rise in the aggregate price level is associated with a rise in the quantity of aggregate output supplied, other things equal; a fall in the aggregate price level is associated with a fall in the quantity of aggregate output supplied, other things equal. To understand why this positive relationship exists, consider the most basic question facing a producer: is producing a unit of output profitable or not? Let's define profit per unit:

(18-1) Profit per unit of output =
Price per unit of output − Production cost per unit of output

Thus, the answer to the question depends on whether the price the producer receives for a unit of output is greater or less than the cost of producing that unit of output. At any given point in time, many of the costs producers face are fixed per unit of output and can't be changed for an extended period of time. Typically, the largest source of inflexible production cost is the wages paid to workers. *Wages* here refers to all forms of worker compensation, including employer-paid health care and retirement benefits in addition to earnings.

Wages are typically an inflexible production cost because the dollar amount of any given wage paid, called the **nominal wage**, is often determined by contracts that were signed in the past. And even when there are no formal contracts, there are often informal agreements between management and workers, making companies reluctant to change wages in response to economic conditions. For example, companies usually will not reduce wages during poor economic times—unless the downturn has been particularly long and severe—for fear of generating worker resentment. Correspondingly, companies typically won't raise wages during better economic times—until they are at risk of losing workers to competitors—because they don't want to encourage workers to routinely demand higher wages. As a result of both formal and informal agreements, then, the economy is characterized by **sticky wages**: nominal wages that are slow to fall even in the face of high unemployment and slow to rise even in the face of labor shortages. It's important to note, however, that nominal wages cannot be sticky forever: ultimately, formal contracts and informal agreements will be renegotiated to take into account changed economic circumstances. How long it takes for nominal wages to become flexible is an integral component of what distinguishes the short run from the long run.

The positive relationship between the aggregate price level and the quantity of aggregate output producers are willing to supply during the time period when many production costs, particularly nominal wages, can be taken as fixed is illustrated by the **short-run aggregate supply curve**. The positive relationship between the aggregate price level and aggregate output in the short run gives the short-run aggregate supply curve its upward slope. **Figure 18.1** shows a hypothetical short-run aggregate supply curve, *SRAS,* that matches actual U.S. data for 1929 and 1933. On the horizontal axis is aggregate output (or, equivalently, real GDP)—the total quantity of final goods and services supplied in the economy—measured in 2005 dollars. On the vertical axis is the aggregate price level as measured by the GDP deflator, with the value for the year 2005 equal to 100. In 1929, the aggregate price level was 10.6 and real GDP was $977 billion. In 1933, the aggregate price level was 7.9 and real GDP was only $716 billion. The movement down the *SRAS* curve corresponds to the deflation and fall in aggregate output experienced over those years.

The **nominal wage** is the dollar amount of the wage paid.

Sticky wages are nominal wages that are slow to fall even in the face of high unemployment and slow to rise even in the face of labor shortages.

AP® EXAM TIP

The upward slope of the short-run aggregate supply curve is explained by sticky wages. Sticky wages means that nominal wages are slow to rise and fall in response to unemployment levels because of set wage contracts and agreements. In the long run these agreements expire and wages become flexible.

The **short-run aggregate supply curve** shows the positive relationship between the aggregate price level and the quantity of aggregate output supplied that exists in the short run, the time period when many production costs can be taken as fixed.

Figure 18.1 The Short-Run Aggregate Supply Curve

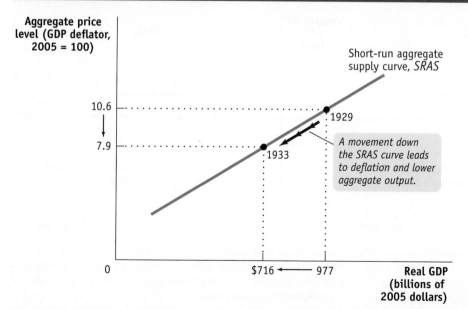

The short-run aggregate supply curve shows the relationship between the aggregate price level and the quantity of aggregate output supplied in the short run, the period in which many production costs such as nominal wages are fixed. Here we show numbers corresponding to the Great Depression, from 1929 and 1933: when deflation occurred and the aggregate price level fell from 10.6 (in 1929) to 7.9 (in 1933), firms responded by reducing the quantity of aggregate output supplied from $977 billion to $716 billion measured in 2005 dollars.

Shifts of the Short-Run Aggregate Supply Curve

Figure 18.1 shows a *movement along* the short-run aggregate supply curve, as the aggregate price level and aggregate output fell from 1929 to 1933. But there can also be *shifts of* the short-run aggregate supply curve, as shown in **Figure 18.2**. Panel (a) of Figure 18.2 shows a *decrease in short-run aggregate supply*—a leftward shift of the short-run aggregate supply curve. Aggregate supply decreases when producers reduce the quantity of aggregate output they are willing to supply at any given aggregate price level. Panel (b) shows an *increase in short-run aggregate supply*—a rightward shift of the short-run aggregate supply curve. Aggregate supply increases when producers increase the quantity of aggregate output they are willing to supply at any given aggregate price level.

To understand why the short-run aggregate supply curve can shift, it's important to recall that producers make output decisions based on their profit per unit of output. The short-run aggregate supply curve illustrates the relationship between the aggregate price level and aggregate output: because some production costs are fixed in the short run, a change in the aggregate price level leads to a change in producers' profit per unit of output and, in turn, leads to a change in aggregate output. But other factors besides the aggregate price level can affect profit per unit and, in turn, aggregate output. Changes in these other factors, which we will read about next, will shift the short-run aggregate supply curve.

To develop some intuition, suppose something happens that raises production costs—say, an increase in the price of oil. At any given price of output, a producer now earns a smaller profit per unit of output. As a result, producers reduce the quantity supplied at any given aggregate price level, and the short-run aggregate supply curve shifts to the left. If, by contrast, something happens that lowers production costs—say, a fall in the nominal wage—a producer now earns a higher profit per unit of output at any given price of output. This leads producers to increase the quantity of aggregate output supplied at any given aggregate price level, and the short-run aggregate supply curve shifts to the right.

Now we'll look more closely at the link between important factors that affect producers' profit per unit and shifts in the short-run aggregate supply curve.

Figure 18.2 Shifts of the Short-Run Aggregate Supply Curve

Panel (a) shows a decrease in short-run aggregate supply: the short-run aggregate supply curve shifts leftward from $SRAS_1$ to $SRAS_2$, and the quantity of aggregate output supplied at any given aggregate price level falls. Panel (b) shows an increase in short-run aggregate supply: the short-run aggregate supply curve shifts rightward from $SRAS_1$ to $SRAS_2$, and the quantity of aggregate output supplied at any given aggregate price level rises.

Changes in Commodity Prices

A surge in the price of oil caused problems for the U.S. economy in the 1970s and in early 2008. Oil is a *commodity*, a standardized input bought and sold in bulk quantities. An increase in the price of a commodity—in this case, oil—raised production costs across the economy and reduced the quantity of aggregate output supplied at any given aggregate price level, shifting the short-run aggregate supply curve to the left. Conversely, a decline in commodity prices reduces production costs, leading to an increase in the quantity supplied at any given aggregate price level and a rightward shift of the short-run aggregate supply curve.

Why isn't the influence of commodity prices already captured by the short-run aggregate supply curve? Because commodities—unlike, say, soft drinks—are not a final good, their prices are not included in the calculation of the aggregate price level. Furthermore, commodities represent a significant cost of production to most suppliers, just like nominal wages do. So changes in commodity prices have large impacts on production costs. And in contrast to non-commodities, the prices of commodities can sometimes change drastically due to industry-specific shocks to supply—such as wars in the Middle East or rising Chinese demand that leaves less oil for the United States.

Signs of the times: high oil prices caused high gasoline prices in 2008.

Changes in Nominal Wages

As we explained, at any given point in time, nominal wages are fixed because they are set by contracts or informal agreements made in the past, but these wages can change once enough time has passed for terms to be renegotiated. Suppose, for example, that there is an economy-wide rise in the cost of health care insurance premiums paid by employers as part of employees' wages. From the employers' perspective, this is equivalent to a rise in nominal wages because it is an increase in employer-paid compensation. So this rise in nominal wages increases production costs and shifts the short-run aggregate supply curve to the left. Conversely, suppose there is an economy-wide fall in the cost of such premiums. This is equivalent to a fall in nominal wages from the point of view of employers; it reduces production costs and shifts the short-run aggregate supply curve to the right.

An important historical fact is that during the 1970s, the surge in the price of oil had the indirect effect of also raising nominal wages. This "knock-on" effect occurred because many wage contracts included *cost-of-living allowances* that automatically raised the nominal wage when consumer prices increased. Through this channel, the surge in the price of oil—which led to an increase in overall consumer prices—ultimately caused a rise in nominal wages. So the economy, in the end, experienced two leftward shifts of the aggregate supply curve: the first generated by the initial surge in the price of oil and the second generated by the induced increase in nominal wages. The negative effect on the economy of rising oil prices was greatly magnified through the cost-of-living allowances in wage contracts. Today, cost-of-living allowances in wage contracts are rare.

Changes in Productivity

An increase in productivity means that a worker can produce more units of output with the same quantity of inputs. For example, the introduction of bar-code scanners in retail stores greatly increased the ability of a single worker to stock, inventory, and resupply store shelves. As a result, the cost to a store of "producing" a dollar of sales fell and profit rose. And, correspondingly, the quantity supplied increased. (Think of Walmart or Costco and the increase in the number of their stores as an increase in aggregate supply.) So a rise in productivity, whatever the source, increases producers' profits and shifts the short-run aggregate supply curve to the right. Conversely, a fall in productivity—say, due to new regulations that require workers to spend more time filling out forms—reduces the number of units of output a worker can produce with the same quantity of inputs. Consequently, the cost per unit of output rises, profit falls, and quantity supplied falls. This shifts the short-run aggregate supply curve to the left.

Almost every good purchased today has a UPC bar code on it, which allows stores to scan and track merchandise with great speed.

Changes in Expectations about Inflation

If inflation is expected to be higher than previously thought, workers will seek higher nominal wages to keep pace with the higher prices. Suppose you saw prices rising more rapidly than in the recent past. You might expect a particularly high inflation rate over the coming year. To prevent the expected inflation from eroding your real wages, you and other workers would pressure employers to raise nominal wages. As we've discussed, nominal wages are temporarily inflexible due to wage contracts, but when contracts are renewed and nominal wages rise, the short-run aggregate supply curve shifts to the left. Likewise, if inflation is expected to be lower than previously thought, workers will accept lower nominal wages and the short-run aggregate supply curve will shift to the right.

For a summary of the factors that shift the short-run aggregate supply curve, see **Table 18.1**.

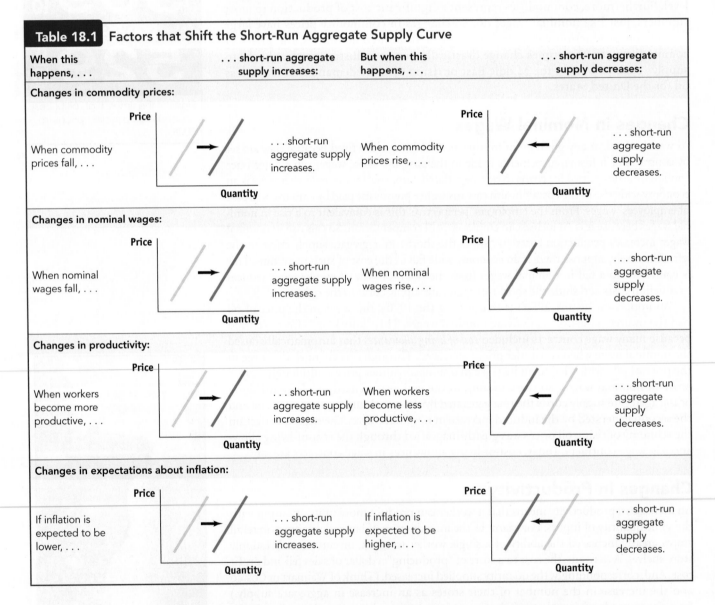

| Table 18.1 | Factors that Shift the Short-Run Aggregate Supply Curve |

When this happens, . . .	. . . short-run aggregate supply increases:	But when this happens, . . .	. . . short-run aggregate supply decreases:
Changes in commodity prices:			
When commodity prices fall, . . .	. . . short-run aggregate supply increases.	When commodity prices rise, . . .	. . . short-run aggregate supply decreases.
Changes in nominal wages:			
When nominal wages fall, . . .	. . . short-run aggregate supply increases.	When nominal wages rise, . . .	. . . short-run aggregate supply decreases.
Changes in productivity:			
When workers become more productive, . . .	. . . short-run aggregate supply increases.	When workers become less productive, . . .	. . . short-run aggregate supply decreases.
Changes in expectations about inflation:			
If inflation is expected to be lower, . . .	. . . short-run aggregate supply increases.	If inflation is expected to be higher, . . .	. . . short-run aggregate supply decreases.

The Long-Run Aggregate Supply Curve

We've just seen that in the short run, a fall in the aggregate price level leads to a decline in the quantity of aggregate output supplied. This is partially the result of nominal wages that are sticky in the short run. But as we mentioned earlier, contracts and informal agreements are renegotiated in the long run. So in the long run, nominal wages—like the aggregate price level—are flexible, not sticky. Wage flexibility greatly alters the long-run relationship between the aggregate price level and aggregate supply. In fact, in the long run the aggregate price level has *no* effect on the quantity of aggregate output supplied.

To see why, let's conduct a thought experiment. Imagine that you could wave a magic wand—or maybe a magic bar-code scanner—and cut *all prices* in the economy in half at the same time. By "all prices" we mean the prices of all inputs, including nominal wages, as well as the prices of final goods and services. What would happen to aggregate output, given that the aggregate price level has been halved and all input prices, including nominal wages, have been halved?

The answer is: nothing. Consider Equation 18-1 again: each producer would receive a lower price for its product, but costs would fall by the same proportion. As a result, every unit of output that was profitable to produce before the change in prices would still be profitable to produce after the change in prices. So a halving of *all* prices in the economy has no effect on the economy's aggregate output. In other words, changes in the aggregate price level now have no effect on the quantity of aggregate output supplied.

In reality, of course, no one can change all prices by the same proportion at the same time. But let's consider the *long run*, the period of time over which all prices are fully flexible. In the long run, inflation or deflation has the same effect as someone changing all prices by the same proportion. As a result, changes in the aggregate price level do not change the quantity of aggregate output supplied in the long run. That's because changes in the aggregate price level, in the long run, will be accompanied by equal proportional changes in *all* input prices, including nominal wages.

The **long-run aggregate supply curve**, illustrated in **Figure 18.3** by the curve *LRAS*, shows the relationship between the aggregate price level and the quantity of aggregate output supplied that would exist if all prices, including nominal wages, were fully flexible. The long-run aggregate supply curve is vertical because changes in the aggregate price level have *no* effect on aggregate output in the long run. At an aggregate price level of 15.0, for example, the quantity of aggregate output supplied is $800 billion in 2005 dollars. If the aggregate price level falls by 50% to 7.5, the quantity of aggregate output supplied is unchanged in the long run at $800 billion in 2005 dollars.

It's important to understand not only that the *LRAS* curve is vertical but also that its position along the horizontal axis marks an important benchmark for output. The horizontal intercept in Figure 18.3, where *LRAS* touches the horizontal axis ($800 billion in 2005 dollars), is the economy's **potential output**, Y_P: the level of real GDP the economy

> The **long-run aggregate supply curve** shows the relationship between the aggregate price level and the quantity of aggregate output supplied that would exist if all prices, including nominal wages, were fully flexible.

> **Potential output** is the level of real GDP the economy would produce if all prices, including nominal wages, were fully flexible.

Figure 18.3 The Long-Run Aggregate Supply Curve

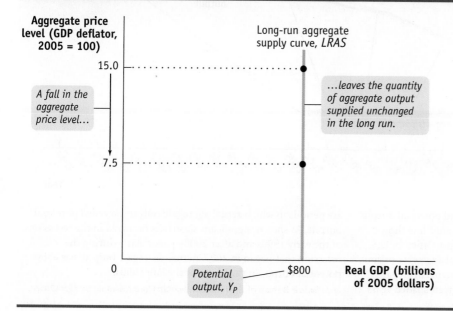

Aggregate price level (GDP deflator, 2005 = 100)

Long-run aggregate supply curve, *LRAS*

15.0

A fall in the aggregate price level...

...leaves the quantity of aggregate output supplied unchanged in the long run.

7.5

0

Potential output, Y_P

$800

Real GDP (billions of 2005 dollars)

> The long-run aggregate supply curve shows the quantity of aggregate output supplied when all prices, including nominal wages, are flexible. It is vertical at potential output, Y_p, because in the long run a change in the aggregate price level has no effect on the quantity of aggregate output supplied.

The **full-employment level of output** is the level of real GDP the economy can produce if all resources are fully employed.

would produce if all prices, including nominal wages, were fully flexible. Another way to describe Y_p is the **full-employment output level**, the GDP that the economy can attain with full employment of all of its resources. The full-employment output level is consistent with the natural rate of unemployment from Module 13.

In reality, the actual level of real GDP is almost always either above or below potential output. We'll see why later, when we discuss the *AD–AS* model. Still, an economy's potential output is an important number because it defines the trend around which actual aggregate output fluctuates from year to year.

In the United States, the Congressional Budget Office (CBO) estimates annual potential output for the purpose of federal budget analysis. In **Figure 18.4**, the CBO's estimates of U.S. potential output from 1989 to 2017 are represented by the orange line and the actual values of U.S. real GDP over the same period are represented by the blue line. Years shaded purple on the horizontal axis correspond to periods in which actual aggregate output fell short of potential output, while years shaded green correspond to periods in which actual aggregate output exceeded potential output.

As you can see, U.S. potential output has risen steadily over time—implying a series of rightward shifts of the *LRAS* curve. What has caused these rightward shifts? The answer lies in the factors related to long-run growth:

- increases in the quantity of resources, including land, labor, capital, and entrepreneurship
- increases in the quality of resources, such as a better-educated workforce
- technological progress

Over the long run, as the size of the labor force and the productivity of labor both rise, the level of real GDP that the economy is capable of producing also rises. Indeed, one

Figure 18.4 Actual and Potential Output from 1989 to 2017

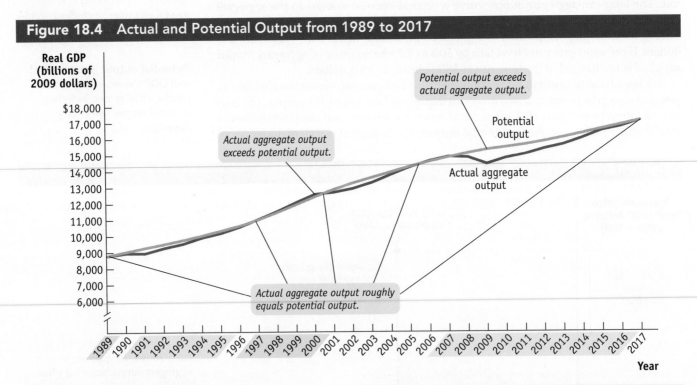

This figure shows the performance of actual and potential output in the United States from 1989 to 2017. The orange line shows estimates, produced by the Congressional Budget Office, of U.S. potential output, and the blue line shows actual aggregate output. The purple-shaded years are periods in which actual aggregate output fell below potential output, while the green-shaded years are periods in which actual aggregate output exceeded potential output. As shown, significant shortfalls occurred in the recessions of the early 1990s and after 2000—particularly during the recession that began in 2007. Actual aggregate output was above potential output in the boom of the late 1990s.

Data Source: Bureau of Economic Research; Congressional Budget Office.

way to think about economic growth is that it is the growth in the economy's potential output. We generally think of the long-run aggregate supply curve as shifting to the right over time as an economy experiences long-run growth.

From the Short Run to the Long Run

As you can see in Figure 18.4, the economy normally produces more or less than potential output: actual aggregate output was below potential output in the early 1990s, above potential output in the late 1990s, and below potential output for most of the 2000s. So the economy is normally operating at a point on its short-run aggregate supply curve—but not at a point on its long-run aggregate supply curve. Why, then, is the long-run curve relevant? Does the economy ever move from the short run to the long run? And if so, how?

The first step to answering these questions is to understand that the economy is always in one of only two states with respect to the short-run and long-run aggregate supply curves. It can be on both curves simultaneously by being at a point where the curves cross (as in those few years in Figure 18.4 in which actual aggregate output and potential output roughly coincided). Or it can be on the short-run aggregate supply curve but not the long-run aggregate supply curve (as in those years in which actual aggregate output and potential output *did not* coincide). But that is not the end of the story. If the economy is on the short-run but not the long-run aggregate supply curve, the short-run aggregate supply curve will shift over time until the economy is at a point where both curves cross—a point where actual aggregate output is equal to potential output.

Figure 18.5 illustrates how this process works. In both panels *LRAS* is the long-run aggregate supply curve, $SRAS_1$ is the initial short-run aggregate supply curve, and the aggregate price level is at P_1. In panel (a) the economy starts at the initial production point, A_1, which corresponds to a quantity of aggregate output supplied, Y_1, that is higher than potential output, Y_P. Producing an aggregate output level (such as Y_1) that is higher than potential output (Y_P) is possible only because nominal wages have not yet

Figure 18.5 From the Short Run to the Long Run

In panel (a), the initial short-run aggregate supply curve is $SRAS_1$. At the aggregate price level, P_1, the quantity of aggregate output supplied, Y_1, exceeds potential output, Y_P. Eventually, low unemployment will cause nominal wages to rise, leading to a leftward shift of the short-run aggregate supply curve from $SRAS_1$ to $SRAS_2$. In panel (b), the reverse happens: at the aggregate price level, P_1, the quantity of aggregate output supplied is less than potential output. High unemployment eventually leads to a fall in nominal wages over time and a rightward shift of the short-run aggregate supply curve.

fully adjusted upward. Until this upward adjustment in nominal wages occurs, producers are earning high profits and producing a high level of output. But a level of aggregate output higher than potential output means a low level of unemployment. Because jobs are abundant and workers are scarce, nominal wages will rise over time, gradually shifting the short-run aggregate supply curve leftward. Eventually, it will be in a new position, such as $SRAS_2$. (Later, we'll show where the short-run aggregate supply curve ends up. As we'll see, that depends on the aggregate demand curve as well.)

In panel (b), the initial production point, A_1, corresponds to an aggregate output level, Y_1, that is lower than potential output, Y_P. Producing an aggregate output level (such as Y_1) that is lower than potential output (Y_P) is possible only because nominal wages have not yet fully adjusted downward. Until this downward adjustment occurs, producers are earning low (or negative) profits and producing a low level of output. An aggregate output level lower than potential output means high unemployment. Because workers are abundant and jobs are scarce, nominal wages will fall over time, shifting the short-run aggregate supply curve gradually to the right. Eventually, it will be in a new position, such as $SRAS_2$.

We'll see in the next module that these shifts of the short-run aggregate supply curve will return the economy to potential output in the long run.

MODULE 18 REVIEW

Check Your Understanding

1. Determine the effect on short-run aggregate supply of each of the following events. Explain whether it represents a movement along the *SRAS* curve or a shift of the *SRAS* curve.
   a. A rise in the consumer price index (CPI) leads producers to increase output.
   b. A fall in the price of oil leads producers to increase output.
   c. A rise in legally mandated retirement benefits paid to workers leads producers to reduce output.

2. Suppose the economy is initially at potential output and the quantity of aggregate output supplied increases. What information would you need to determine whether this was due to a movement along the *SRAS* curve or a shift of the LRAS curve?

TACKLE THE AP® TEST: Multiple-Choice Questions

1. Which of the following will shift the short-run aggregate supply curve? A change in
   a. profit per unit at any given price level.
   b. commodity prices.
   c. nominal wages.
   d. productivity.
   e. all of the above

2. Because changes in the aggregate price level have no effect on aggregate output in the long run, the long-run aggregate supply curve is
   a. vertical.
   b. horizontal.
   c. fixed.
   d. negatively sloped.
   e. positively sloped.

3. The horizontal intercept of the long-run aggregate supply curve is
   a. at the origin.
   b. negative.
   c. at potential output.
   d. equal to the vertical intercept.
   e. always the same as the horizontal intercept of the short-run aggregate supply curve.

4. A decrease in which of the following will cause the short-run aggregate supply curve to shift to the left?
   a. commodity prices
   b. the cost of health care insurance premiums paid by employers
   c. nominal wages
   d. productivity
   e. the use of cost-of-living allowances in labor contracts

5. That employers are reluctant to decrease nominal wages during economic downturns and raise nominal wages during economic expansions is one reason nominal wages are described as
   a. long-run.
   b. unyielding.
   c. flexible.
   d. real.
   e. sticky.

6. The short-run aggregate supply curve is upward-sloping due to
   a. the real wealth effect.
   b. the interest rate effect.
   c. sticky wages.
   d. flexible prices.
   e. the substitution effect.

7. The full-employment level of output corresponds to which of the following?
   a. potential output
   b. the horizontal intercept of the long-run aggregate demand curve
   c. short-run equilibrium
   d. the level of real GDP when wages are sticky
   e. all of the above

TACKLE THE AP® TEST: Free-Response Questions

1. a. Draw a correctly labeled graph illustrating a long-run aggregate supply curve.
   b. On your graph from part a, label potential output.
   c. On your graph from part a, illustrate an increase in long-run aggregate supply.
   d. What could have caused the change you illustrated in part c? List three possible causes.

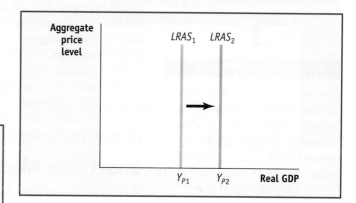

Rubric for FRQ 1 (8 points)

1 point: Vertical axis labeled "Aggregate price level" (or "Price level")

1 point: Horizontal axis labeled "Real GDP"

1 point: Vertical curve labeled "LRAS" (or "$LRAS_1$")

1 point: Potential output labeled Y_p (or Y_{p1}) on the horizontal axis at the intercept of the long-run aggregate supply curve

1 point: Long-run aggregate supply curve shifted to the right

1 point: An increase in the quantity of resources (land, labor, capital, or entrepreneurship)

1 point: An increase in the quality of resources

1 point: Technological progress

2. a. Draw a correctly labeled short-run aggregate supply curve.
   b. On your graph from part a, illustrate a decrease in short-run aggregate supply.
   c. List three types of changes, including the factor that changes and the direction of the change, that could lead to a decrease in short-run aggregate supply. **(6 points)**

Equilibrium in the Aggregate Demand–Aggregate Supply Model

> **In this Module, you will learn to:**
> - Explain the difference between short-run and long-run macroeconomic equilibrium
> - Describe the causes and effects of demand shocks and supply shocks
> - Determine if an economy is experiencing a recessionary gap or an inflationary gap and explain how to calculate the size of an output gap

The *AD–AS* Model

In the **AD–AS model,** the aggregate supply curve and the aggregate demand curve are used together to analyze economic fluctuations.

The **short-run equilibrium aggregate price level** is the aggregate price level in the short-run macroeconomic equilibrium.

Short-run equilibrium aggregate output is the quantity of aggregate output produced in the short-run macroeconomic equilibrium.

From 1929 to 1933, the U.S. economy moved down the short-run aggregate supply curve as the aggregate price level fell. In contrast, from 1979 to 1980, the U.S. economy moved up the aggregate demand curve as the aggregate price level rose. In each case, the cause of the movement along the curve was a shift of the other curve. In 1929–1933, it was a leftward shift of the aggregate demand curve—a major fall in consumer spending during the Great Depression. In 1979–1980, it was a leftward shift of the short-run aggregate supply curve—a dramatic fall in short-run aggregate supply caused by the oil *price shock*.

To understand the behavior of the economy, we must put the aggregate supply curve and the aggregate demand curve together. The **AD–AS model** is the basic model we use to understand economic fluctuations—changes in real GDP, employment, and the aggregate price level.

Short-Run Macroeconomic Equilibrium

We'll begin our analysis by focusing on the short run. **Figure 19.1** shows the aggregate demand curve and the short-run aggregate supply curve in the same diagram. The point at which the *AD* and *SRAS* curves intersect, E_{SR}, is the short-run macroeconomic equilibrium: the point at which the quantity of aggregate output supplied is equal to the quantity demanded by domestic households, businesses, the government, and the rest of the world. The aggregate price level at E_{SR}, P_E, is the **short-run equilibrium aggregate price level**. The level of aggregate output at E_{SR}, Y_E, is the **short-run equilibrium aggregate output**.

We have seen that a shortage of any individual good causes its market price to rise and a surplus of the good causes its market price to fall. These forces ensure that the market reaches equilibrium. A similar logic applies to short-run macroeconomic equilibrium. If the aggregate price level is above its equilibrium level, the quantity of aggregate output supplied exceeds the quantity of aggregate output demanded. This leads to a fall in the aggregate price level and pushes it toward its equilibrium level. If the aggregate price level is below its equilibrium level, the quantity of aggregate output supplied is less than the quantity of aggregate output demanded. This leads to a rise in the aggregate price level, again pushing it toward its equilibrium level. In the discussion that follows, we'll assume that the economy is always in short-run macroeconomic equilibrium.

We'll also make another important simplification based on the observation that, in reality, there is a long-term upward trend in both aggregate output and the aggregate price level. We'll assume that a fall in either variable really means a fall compared to the long-run trend. For example, if the aggregate price level normally rises 4% per year, a year in which the aggregate price level rises only 3% would count, for our purposes, as a 1% decline. In fact, since the Great Depression there have been very few years in which the aggregate price level of any major nation actually declined—Japan's period of deflation from 1995 to 2005 is one

Figure 19.1 The AD–AS Model

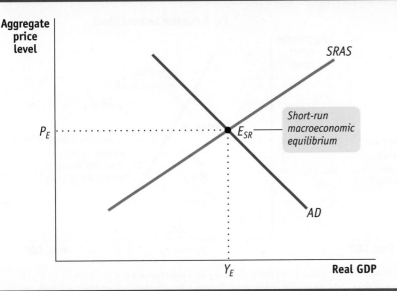

The *AD–AS* model combines the aggregate demand curve and the short-run aggregate supply curve. Their point of intersection, E_{SR}, is the point of short-run macroeconomic equilibrium where the quantity of aggregate output demanded is equal to the quantity of aggregate output supplied. P_E is the short-run equilibrium aggregate price level, and Y_E is the short-run equilibrium level of aggregate output.

of the few exceptions (which we will explain later). However, there have been many cases in which the aggregate price level fell relative to the long-run trend.

The short-run equilibrium aggregate output and the short-run equilibrium aggregate price level can change because of shifts of either the *AD* curve or the *SRAS* curve. Let's look at each case in turn.

Shifts of Aggregate Demand: Short-Run Effects

An event that shifts the aggregate demand curve, such as a change in expectations or wealth, the effect of the size of the existing stock of physical capital, or the use of fiscal or monetary policy, is known as a **demand shock**. The Great Depression was caused by a negative demand shock, the collapse of wealth and loss of business and consumer confidence that followed the stock market crash of 1929 and the banking crises of 1930–1931. The Great Depression was ended by a positive demand shock— the huge increase in government purchases during World War II. In 2008, the U.S. economy experienced another significant negative demand shock as the housing market turned from boom to bust, leading consumers and firms to scale back their spending. The associated financial crisis and economic recovery that followed the 2008 negative demand shock are discussed in Enrichment Module A.

Figure 19.2 shows the short-run effects of negative and positive demand shocks. A negative demand shock shifts the aggregate demand curve, *AD*, to the left, from AD_1 to AD_2, as shown in panel (a). The economy moves down along the *SRAS* curve from E_1 to E_2, leading to lower short-run equilibrium aggregate output and a lower short-run equilibrium aggregate price level. A positive demand shock shifts the aggregate demand curve, *AD*, to the right, as shown in panel (b). Here, the economy moves up along the *SRAS* curve, from E_1 to E_2. This leads to higher short-run equilibrium aggregate output and a higher short-run equilibrium aggregate price level. Demand shocks cause aggregate output and the aggregate price level to move in the same direction.

AP® EXAM TIP

When asked on the exam to graph the effect of a change, make sure you understand whether the question is asking you to graph the short run or the long run. If short run or long run is not specified, graph the short run.

An event that shifts the aggregate demand curve is a **demand shock**.

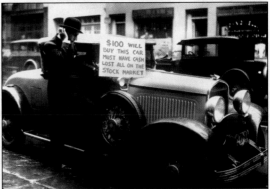

The Great Depression was caused by a negative demand shock and was ended by a positive demand shock.

Shifts of the *SRAS* Curve

An event that shifts the short-run aggregate supply curve, such as a change in commodity prices, nominal wages, or productivity, is known as a **supply shock**. A *negative* supply

An event that shifts the short-run aggregate supply curve is a **supply shock**.

Figure 19.2 Demand Shocks

(a) A Negative Demand Shock

A negative demand shock...

SRAS

...leads to a lower aggregate price level and lower aggregate output.

P_1
$\downarrow$
P_2

E_1

E_2

AD_1

AD_2

$Y_2 \longleftarrow Y_1$

Aggregate price level

Real GDP

(b) A Positive Demand Shock

A positive demand shock...

SRAS

...leads to a higher aggregate price level and higher aggregate output.

P_2
$\uparrow$
P_1

E_2

E_1

AD_2

AD_1

$Y_1 \longrightarrow Y_2$

Aggregate price level

Real GDP

A demand shock shifts the aggregate demand curve, moving the aggregate price level and aggregate output in the same direction. In panel (a), a negative demand shock shifts the aggregate demand curve leftward from AD_1 to AD_2, reducing the aggregate price level from P_1 to P_2 and aggregate output from Y_1 to Y_2. In panel (b), a positive demand shock shifts the aggregate demand curve rightward, increasing the aggregate price level from P_1 to P_2 and aggregate output from Y_1 to Y_2.

shock raises production costs and reduces the quantity producers are willing to supply at any given aggregate price level, leading to a leftward shift of the short-run aggregate supply curve. The U.S. economy experienced severe negative supply shocks following disruptions to world oil supplies in 1973 and 1979. In contrast, a *positive* supply shock reduces production costs and increases the quantity supplied at any given aggregate price level, leading to a rightward shift of the short-run aggregate supply curve. The United States experienced a positive supply shock between 1995 and 2000, when the increasing use of the internet and other information technologies caused productivity growth to surge.

The effects of a negative supply shock are shown in panel (a) of **Figure 19.3**. The initial equilibrium is at E_1, with aggregate price level P_1 and aggregate output Y_1. The disruption in the oil supply causes the short-run aggregate supply curve to shift to the left, from $SRAS_1$ to $SRAS_2$. As a consequence, aggregate output falls and the aggregate price level rises, an upward movement along the AD curve. At the new equilibrium, E_2, the short-run equilibrium aggregate price level, P_2, is higher, and the short-run equilibrium aggregate output level, Y_2, is lower than before.

Stagflation is the combination of inflation and stagnating (or falling) aggregate output.

The combination of inflation and falling aggregate output shown in panel (a) has a special name: **stagflation**, for "stagnation plus inflation." When an economy experiences stagflation, it's very unpleasant: falling aggregate output leads to rising unemployment, and people feel that their purchasing power is squeezed by rising prices. Stagflation in the 1970s led to a mood of national pessimism. As we'll see shortly, it also poses a dilemma for policy makers.

A positive supply shock, shown in panel (b), has exactly the opposite effects. A rightward shift of the $SRAS$ curve, from $SRAS_1$ to $SRAS_2$ results in a rise in aggregate output and a fall in the aggregate price level, a downward movement along the AD curve. The favorable supply shocks of the late 1990s led to a combination of full employment and declining inflation. That is, the aggregate price level fell compared with the long-run trend. For a few years, this combination produced a great wave of national optimism.

The distinctive feature of supply shocks, both negative and positive, is that, unlike demand shocks, they cause the aggregate price level and aggregate output to move in *opposite* directions.

Figure 19.3 Supply Shocks

(a) A Negative Supply Shock

(b) A Positive Supply Shock

A supply shock shifts the short-run aggregate supply curve, moving the aggregate price level and aggregate output in opposite directions. Panel (a) shows a negative supply shock, which shifts the short-run aggregate supply curve leftward and causes

stagflation—lower aggregate output and a higher aggregate price level. Panel (b) shows a positive supply shock, which shifts the short-run aggregate supply curve rightward, generating higher aggregate output and a lower aggregate price level.

There's another important contrast between supply shocks and demand shocks. As we've seen, monetary policy and fiscal policy enable the government to shift the *AD* curve, meaning that governments are in a position to create the kinds of shocks shown in Figure 19.2. It's much harder for governments to shift the *AS* curve. Are there good policy reasons to shift the *AD* curve? We'll turn to that question soon. First, however, let's look at the difference between short-run macroeconomic equilibrium and long-run macroeconomic equilibrium.

Long-Run Macroeconomic Equilibrium

Figure 19.4 combines the aggregate demand curve with both the short-run and long-run aggregate supply curves. The aggregate demand curve, *AD*, crosses the short-run

Figure 19.4 Long-Run Macroeconomic Equilibrium

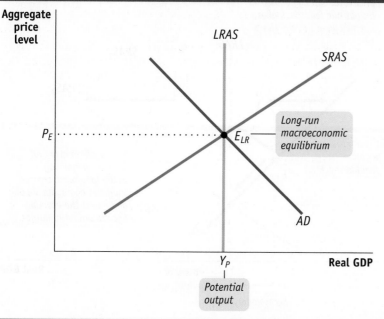

Here the point of short-run macroeconomic equilibrium also lies on the long-run aggregate supply curve, *LRAS*. As a result, short-run equilibrium aggregate output is equal to potential output, Y_P. The economy is in long-run macroeconomic equilibrium at E_{LR}.

aggregate supply curve, $SRAS$, at E_{LR}. Here we assume that enough time has elapsed that the economy is also on the long-run aggregate supply curve, $LRAS$. As a result, E_{LR} is at the intersection of all three curves—$SRAS$, $LRAS$, and AD. So short-run equilibrium aggregate output is equal to potential output, Y_P. Such a situation, in which the point of short-run macroeconomic equilibrium is on the long-run aggregate supply curve, is known as *long-run macroeconomic equilibrium*.

To see the significance of long-run macroeconomic equilibrium, let's consider what happens if a demand shock moves the economy away from long-run macroeconomic equilibrium. In **Figure 19.5**, we assume that the initial aggregate demand curve is AD_1 and the initial short-run aggregate supply curve is $SRAS_1$. So the initial macroeconomic equilibrium is at E_1, which lies on the long-run aggregate supply curve, $LRAS$. The economy, then, starts from a point of short-run and long-run macroeconomic equilibrium, and short-run equilibrium aggregate output equals potential output at Y_1.

Now suppose that for some reason—such as a sudden worsening of business and consumer expectations—aggregate demand falls and the aggregate demand curve shifts leftward to AD_2. This results in a lower equilibrium aggregate price level at P_2 and a lower equilibrium aggregate output level at Y_2 as the economy settles in the short run at E_2. The short-run effect of such a fall in aggregate demand is what the U.S. economy experienced in 1929–1933: a falling aggregate price level and falling aggregate output.

Aggregate output in this new short-run equilibrium, E_2, is below potential output. When this happens, the economy faces a **recessionary gap**. A recessionary gap inflicts a great deal of pain because it corresponds to high unemployment.

But this isn't the end of the story. In the face of high unemployment, nominal wages eventually fall, as do any other sticky prices, ultimately leading producers to increase output. As a result, a recessionary gap causes the short-run aggregate supply curve to gradually shift to the right. This process continues until $SRAS_1$ reaches its new position at $SRAS_2$, bringing the economy to equilibrium at E_3, where AD_2, $SRAS_2$, and $LRAS$ all intersect. At E_3, the economy is back in long-run macroeconomic equilibrium; it is back

There is a **recessionary gap** when aggregate output is below potential output.

Figure 19.5   Short-Run Versus Long-Run Effects of a Negative Demand Shock

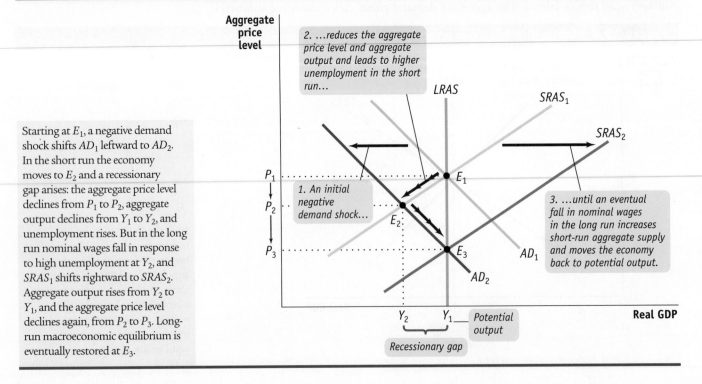

Starting at E_1, a negative demand shock shifts AD_1 leftward to AD_2. In the short run the economy moves to E_2 and a recessionary gap arises: the aggregate price level declines from P_1 to P_2, aggregate output declines from Y_1 to Y_2, and unemployment rises. But in the long run nominal wages fall in response to high unemployment at Y_2, and $SRAS_1$ shifts rightward to $SRAS_2$. Aggregate output rises from Y_2 to Y_1, and the aggregate price level declines again, from P_2 to P_3. Long-run macroeconomic equilibrium is eventually restored at E_3.

at potential output Y_1 but at a lower aggregate price level, P_3, reflecting a long-run fall in the aggregate price level.

What if, instead of a decrease in aggregate demand, there was an increase? The results are shown in **Figure 19.6**, where we again assume that the initial aggregate demand curve is AD_1 and the initial short-run aggregate supply curve is $SRAS_1$. The initial macroeconomic equilibrium, at E_1, lies on the long-run aggregate supply curve, $LRAS$. Initially, then, the economy is in long-run macroeconomic equilibrium.

Now suppose that aggregate demand rises, and the AD curve shifts rightward to AD_2. This results in a higher aggregate price level, at P_2, and a higher aggregate output level, at Y_2, as the economy settles in the short run at E_2. Aggregate output in this new short-run equilibrium is above potential output, and unemployment is low in order to produce this higher level of aggregate output. When this happens, the economy experiences an **inflationary gap**. As in the case of a recessionary gap, this isn't the end of the story. In the face of low unemployment, nominal wages will rise, as will other sticky prices. An inflationary gap causes the short-run aggregate supply curve to shift gradually to the left as producers reduce output in the face of rising nominal wages. This process continues until $SRAS_1$ reaches its new position at $SRAS_2$, where AD_2, $SRAS_2$, and $LRAS$ all intersect. At E_3, the economy is back in long-run macroeconomic equilibrium. It is back at potential output, but at a higher price level, P_3, reflecting a long-run rise in the aggregate price level.

To summarize the analysis of how the economy responds to recessionary and inflationary gaps, we can focus on the **output gap**, the difference between actual aggregate output and potential output. In the long run, the output gap tends toward zero.

If there is a recessionary gap, so that the output gap is negative, nominal wages eventually fall, moving the economy back to potential output and bringing the output gap back to zero. If there is an inflationary gap, so that the output gap is positive, nominal wages eventually rise, also moving the economy back to potential output and again bringing the output gap back to zero. So supply or demand shocks affect aggregate output in the short run but not in the long run.

> ### AP® EXAM TIP
>
> Know how to draw each of the three possible states of the economy: long-run equilibrium, a recessionary gap, and an inflationary gap. In long-run equilibrium, AD and $SRAS$ intersect on the $LRAS$ curve at potential output. In a recessionary gap, the intersection of AD and $SRAS$ showing short-run equilibrium should be to the left of $LRAS$ and potential output, and in an inflationary gap, this intersection should be to the right.

There is an **inflationary gap** when aggregate output is above potential output.

The **output gap** is the difference between actual aggregate output and potential output.

Figure 19.6 Short-Run Versus Long-Run Effects of a Positive Demand Shock

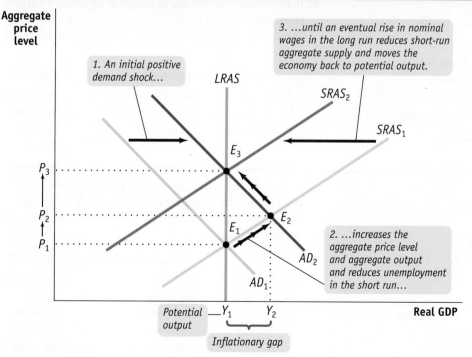

Starting at E_1, a positive demand shock shifts AD_1 rightward to AD_2, and the economy moves to E_2 in the short run. This results in an inflationary gap as aggregate output rises from Y_1 to Y_2, the aggregate price level rises from P_1 to P_2, and unemployment falls to a low level. In the long run, $SRAS_1$ shifts leftward to $SRAS_2$ as nominal wages rise in response to low unemployment at Y_2. Aggregate output falls back to Y_1, the aggregate price level rises again to P_3, and the economy returns to long-run macroeconomic equilibrium at E_3.

MODULE 19 REVIEW

Adventures in
AP® Economics

Watch the video:
*Aggregate Demand and
Aggregate Supply*

Check Your Understanding

1. Describe the short-run effects of each of the following shocks on the aggregate price level and on aggregate output:
   a. The government sharply increases the minimum wage, raising the wages of many workers.
   b. Solar energy firms launch a major program of investment spending.
   c. Congress raises taxes and cuts spending.
   d. Severe weather destroys crops around the world.

2. Suppose a rise in productivity increases potential output and creates a recessionary gap. With no policy action, explain the process by which the economy moves from this recessionary gap to a long-run equilibrium.

TACKLE THE AP® TEST: Multiple-Choice Questions

1. Which of the following causes a negative supply shock?
   a. a technological advance
   b. increasing productivity
   c. an increase in oil prices
   d. a decrease in government spending
   e. a decrease in consumption

2. Which of the following causes a positive demand shock?
   a. an increase in wealth
   b. pessimistic consumer expectations
   c. a decrease in government spending
   d. an increase in taxes
   e. a relatively high existing stock of capital

3. During stagflation, what happens to the aggregate price level and real GDP?

	Aggregate price level	Real GDP
a.	decreases	increases
b.	decreases	decreases
c.	increases	increases
d.	increases	decreases
e.	stays the same	stays the same

   Refer to the graph for Questions 4 and 5.

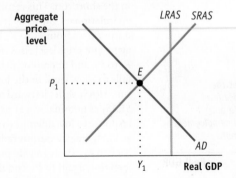

4. Which of the following statements is true if this economy is operating at P_1 and Y_1?
   a. The level of aggregate output equals potential output.
   b. The economy is in short-run macroeconomic equilibrium.
   c. The economy is in long-run macroeconomic equilibrium.
   d. There is an inflationary gap.
   e. Wages will rise and *SRAS* will shift to the right.

5. The economy depicted in the graph is experiencing a(n)
   a. contractionary gap.   d. demand gap.
   b. recessionary gap.   e. supply gap.
   c. inflationary gap.

6. If an economy is initially in long-run equilibrium and then experiences a positive demand shock, what will happen to wages, the aggregate price level, and real GDP in the long run?

	Wages	Aggregate price level	Real GDP
a.	increase	increase	no change
b.	increase	increase	increase
c.	increase	no change	increase
d.	decrease	increase	decrease
e.	decrease	decrease	decrease

7. If an economy is initially in long-run equilibrium and then experiences a negative demand shock, what will happen to wages, the aggregate price level, and real GDP in the long run?

	Wages	Aggregate price level	Real GDP
a.	decrease	decrease	no change
b.	increase	increase	increase
c.	increase	no change	increase
d.	decrease	increase	decrease
e.	decrease	decrease	decrease

TACKLE THE AP® TEST: Free-Response Questions

1. Refer to the following graph, with the economy operating at P_1 and Y_1.
   a. Is the economy in short-run macroeconomic equilibrium? Explain.
   b. Is the economy in long-run macroeconomic equilibrium? Explain.
   c. What type of gap exists in this economy?
   d. What will happen to the size of the output gap in the long run?

2. Draw a correctly labeled aggregate demand and aggregate supply graph illustrating an economy in long-run macroeconomic equilibrium. **(5 points)**

Economic Policy and the Aggregate Demand–Aggregate Supply Model

MOD 20

In this Module, you will learn to:
- Discuss how the *AD–AS* model is used to formulate macroeconomic policy
- Explain the rationale for stabilization policy
- Describe the importance of fiscal policy as a tool for managing economic fluctuations
- Identify the policies that constitute expansionary fiscal policy and those that constitute contractionary fiscal policy

Macroeconomic Policy

We've just seen that the economy will eventually trend back to potential output. Most macroeconomists believe, however, that the adjustment process typically takes a decade or more. In particular, if aggregate output is below potential output, the economy can suffer an extended period of depressed aggregate output and high unemployment before it returns to normal.

"In the long run, we are all dead."
—John Maynard Keynes
(1883–1946)

Stabilization policy is the use of government policy to reduce the severity of recessions and rein in excessively strong expansions.

This belief in the economy's tendency toward self-correction is the background to one of the most famous quotations in economics: John Maynard Keynes's declaration, "In the long run we are all dead." Economists usually interpret Keynes as having recommended that governments not wait for the economy to correct itself. Instead, it is argued by many economists, but not all, that the government should use fiscal policy to push the economy back to potential output in the aftermath of a shift of the aggregate demand curve. This is the rationale for active **stabilization policy**, which is the use of government policy to reduce the severity of recessions and rein in excessively strong expansions.

Can stabilization policy improve the economy's performance? As we saw in Figure 18.4, the answer certainly appears to be yes. Under active stabilization policy, the U.S. economy returned to potential output in 1996 after an approximately five-year recessionary gap. Likewise, in 2001, it also returned to potential output after an approximately four-year inflationary gap. These periods are much shorter than the decade or more that economists believe it would take for the economy to return to potential output in the absence of active stabilization policy. However, as we'll see shortly, the ability to improve the economy's performance is not always guaranteed. It depends on the kinds of shocks the economy faces.

Policy in the Face of Demand Shocks

Imagine that the economy experiences a negative demand shock, like the one shown by the shift from AD_1 to AD_2 in Figure 19.5. Monetary and fiscal policy shift the aggregate demand curve. If policy makers react quickly to the fall in aggregate demand, they can use monetary or fiscal policy to shift the aggregate demand curve back to the right. And if policy were able to perfectly anticipate shifts of the aggregate demand curve and counteract them, it could short-circuit the whole process shown in Figure 19.5. Instead of going through a period of low aggregate output and falling prices, the government could manage the economy so that it would stay at E_1.

Why might a policy that short-circuits the adjustment shown in Figure 19.5 and maintains the economy at its original equilibrium be desirable? For two reasons: First, the temporary fall in aggregate output that would happen without policy intervention is a bad thing, particularly because such a decline is associated with high unemployment. Second, as discussed in Module 14, *price stability* is generally regarded as a desirable goal. So preventing deflation—a fall in the aggregate price level—is a good thing.

Does this mean that policy makers should always act to offset declines in aggregate demand? Not necessarily. As we'll see, some policy measures to increase aggregate demand, especially those that increase budget deficits, may have long-term costs in terms of lower long-run growth. Furthermore, in the real world policy makers aren't perfectly informed, and the effects of their policies aren't perfectly predictable. This creates the danger that stabilization policy will do more harm than good; that is, attempts to stabilize the economy may end up creating more instability. Despite these qualifications, most economists believe that a good case can be made for using macroeconomic policy to offset major negative shocks to the *AD* curve.

Should policy makers also try to offset positive shocks to aggregate demand? It may not seem obvious that they should. After all, even though inflation may be a bad thing, isn't more output and lower unemployment a good thing? Again, not necessarily. Most economists now believe that any short-run gains from an inflationary gap must be paid back later. So policy makers today usually try to offset positive as well as negative demand shocks. For reasons we'll explain later, attempts to eliminate recessionary gaps and inflationary gaps usually rely on monetary rather than fiscal policy. For now, let's explore how macroeconomic policy can respond to supply shocks.

Responding to Supply Shocks

In panel (a) of Figure 19.3, we showed the effects of a negative supply shock: in the short run such a shock leads to lower aggregate output but a higher aggregate price level. As we've noted, policy makers can respond to a negative *demand* shock by using monetary and fiscal policy to return aggregate demand to its original level. But what can or should they do about a negative *supply* shock?

In contrast to the case of a demand shock, there are no easy remedies for a supply shock. That is, there are no government policies that can easily counteract the changes in production costs that shift the short-run aggregate supply curve. So the policy response to a negative supply shock cannot aim to simply push the curve that shifted back to its original position.

In addition, if you consider using monetary or fiscal policy to shift the aggregate demand curve in response to a supply shock, the right response isn't obvious. Two bad things are happening simultaneously: a fall in aggregate output, leading to a rise in unemployment, *and* a rise in the aggregate price level. Any policy that shifts the aggregate demand curve alleviates one problem only by making the other problem worse. If the government acts to increase aggregate demand and limit the rise in unemployment, it reduces the decline in output but causes even more inflation. If it acts to reduce aggregate demand, it curbs inflation but causes a further rise in unemployment.

Is Stabilization Policy Stabilizing?

We've described the theoretical rationale for stabilization policy as a way of responding to demand shocks. But does stabilization policy actually stabilize the economy? One way we might try to answer this question is to look at the long-term historical record, as shown in **Figure 20.1**.

Before World War II, the U.S. government didn't really have a stabilization policy, largely because macroeconomics as we know it didn't exist, and there was no consensus about what to do. Since World War II, and especially since 1960, active stabilization policy has become standard practice.

So here's the question: Has the economy actually become more stable since the government began trying to stabilize it? The answer is a qualified yes. It's qualified because data from the pre–World War II era are less reliable than more modern data. But there still seems to be a clear reduction in the size of economic fluctuations.

Figure 20.1 shows the number of unemployed as a percentage of the nonfarm labor force since 1890. (We focus on nonfarm workers sometimes because farmers, though they often suffer economic hardship, are rarely reported as unemployed.) Even ignoring the huge spike in unemployment during the Great Depression, unemployment seems to have varied a lot more before World War II than after. It's also worth noticing that

Figure 20.1 Stabilization Policy 1890–2017

The data show the number of unemployed as a percentage of the nonfarm labor force from 1890 to 2017. The unemployment rate fluctuated significantly before World War II compared to the years after, suggesting that the government's stabilization policies were effective.

the peaks in postwar unemployment in 1975 and 1982 corresponded to major supply shocks—the kind of shock for which stabilization policy has no good answer.

It's possible that the greater stability of the economy reflects good luck rather than policy. But on the face of it, the evidence suggests that stabilization policy is indeed stabilizing.

Fiscal Policy: The Basics

Let's begin with the obvious: modern governments spend a great deal of money and collect a lot in taxes. **Figure 20.2** shows government spending and tax revenue as percentages of GDP for a selection of high-income countries in 2015. As you can see, the French government sector is relatively large, accounting for more than half of the French economy. The government of the United States plays a smaller role in the economy than do the governments of Canada or most European countries. But that role is still sizable. As a result, changes in the federal budget—changes in government spending or in taxation—can have large effects on the U.S. economy.

To analyze these effects, we begin by showing how taxes and government spending affect the economy's flow of income. Then we can see how changes in spending and tax policy affect aggregate demand.

Figure 20.2 Government Spending and Tax Revenue for Some High-Income Countries in 2015

Government spending and tax revenue are represented as a percentage of GDP. France has a particularly large government sector, representing nearly 6% of its GDP. The U.S. government sector, although sizable, is smaller than the government sectors of Canada and most European countries.

Data Source: OECD; Official Development Assistance.

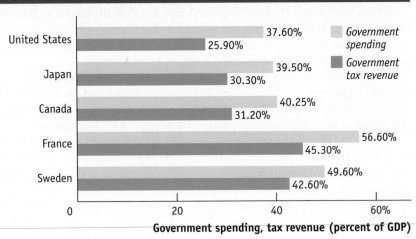

Taxes and Government Spending

In the circular-flow diagram discussed in Module 10, we showed the circular flow of income and spending in the economy as a whole. One of the sectors represented in that figure was the government. Funds flow *into* the government in the form of taxes and government borrowing; funds flow *out* in the form of government purchases of goods and services and government transfers to households.

What kinds of taxes do Americans pay, and where does the money go? **Figure 20.3** shows the composition of U.S. tax revenue in 2016. Taxes, of course, are required payments to the government. In the United States, taxes are collected at the national level by the federal government; at the state level by each state government; and at local levels by counties, cities, and towns. At the federal level, the main taxes are income taxes on both personal income and corporate profits as well as *social insurance* taxes, which we'll explain shortly. At the state and local levels, the picture is more complex: these governments rely on a mix of sales taxes, property taxes, income taxes, and fees of various kinds. Overall, taxes on personal income and corporate profits accounted for 49% of total government revenue in 2016; social insurance taxes accounted for 23.7%; and a variety of other taxes, collected mainly at the state and local levels, accounted for the rest.

Figure 20.3 Sources of Tax Revenue by All Levels of Government in the United States, 2016

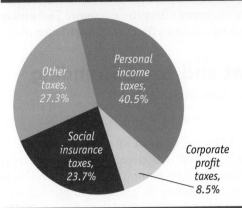

Personal income taxes, taxes on corporate profits, and social insurance taxes account for most government tax revenue. The rest is a mix of property taxes, sales taxes, and other sources of revenue.

Data Source: OECD.

Figure 20.4 shows the composition of total U.S. government spending in 2016, which takes two forms. One form is purchases of goods and services. This includes everything from ammunition for the military to the salaries of public schoolteachers (who are treated in the national accounts as providers of a service—education). The big items here are national defense and education. The large category labeled "Other goods and services" consists mainly of state and local spending on a variety of services, from police and firefighters to highway construction and maintenance.

The other form of government spending is government transfers, which are payments by the government to households for which no good or service is provided in return. In the modern United States, as well as in Canada and Europe, government transfers represent a very large proportion of the budget. Most U.S. government spending on transfer payments is accounted for by three big programs:

Government transfers on their way: Social Security checks are run through a printer at the U.S. Treasury printing facility in Philadelphia, Pennsylvania.

William Thomas Cain/Getty Images

- Social Security, which provides guaranteed income to older Americans, disabled Americans, and the surviving spouses and dependent children of deceased beneficiaries
- Medicare, which covers much of the cost of health care for Americans over age 65
- Medicaid, which covers much of the cost of health care for Americans with low incomes

The term **social insurance** is used to describe government programs that are intended to protect families against economic hardship. These include Social Security,

Social insurance programs are government programs intended to protect families against economic hardship.

Figure 20.4 Government Spending in the United States, 2016

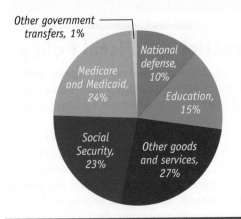

The two types of government spending are purchases of goods and services and government transfers. The big items in government purchases are national defense and education. The big items in government transfers are Social Security and the Medicare and Medicaid health care programs.

Data Source: Bureau of Economic Analysis.

Medicare, and Medicaid, as well as smaller programs such as unemployment insurance and food stamps. In the United States, social insurance programs are largely paid for with special, dedicated taxes on wages—the social insurance taxes we mentioned earlier.

But how do tax policy and government spending affect the economy? The answer is that taxation and government spending have a strong effect on aggregate spending.

The Government Budget and Total Spending

Let's recall the basic equation of national income accounting:

$$(20\text{-}1) \quad GDP = C + I + G + (X - M)$$

The left-hand side of this equation is GDP, the value of all final goods and services produced in the economy. The right-hand side is aggregate spending, the total spending on final goods and services produced in the economy. Aggregate spending is the sum of consumer spending (C), investment spending (I), government purchases of goods and services (G), and the value of exports (X) minus the value of imports (M). It includes all the sources of aggregate demand.

The government directly controls one of the variables on the right-hand side of Equation 20-1: government purchases of goods and services (G). But that's not the only effect fiscal policy has on aggregate spending in the economy. Through changes in taxes and transfers, it also influences consumer spending (C) and, in some cases, investment spending (I).

To see why the budget affects consumer spending, recall that *disposable income*, the total income households have available to spend, is equal to the total income they receive from wages, dividends, interest, and rent, *minus* taxes, *plus* government transfers. So either an increase in taxes or a decrease in government transfers *reduces* disposable income. And a fall in disposable income, other things equal, leads to a fall in consumer spending. Conversely, either a decrease in taxes or an increase in government transfers *increases* disposable income. And a rise in disposable income, other things equal, leads to a rise in consumer spending.

The government's ability to affect investment spending is a more complex story, which we won't discuss in detail. The important point is that the government taxes profits, and changes in the rules that determine how much a business owes can increase or decrease the incentive to spend on investment goods.

Because the government itself is one source of spending in the economy, and because taxes and transfers can affect spending by consumers and firms, the government can use changes in taxes or government spending to *shift the aggregate demand curve*, and there can be good reasons for doing so. In early 2008, for example, there was bipartisan agreement that the U.S. government should act to prevent a fall in aggregate demand—that is, to move the aggregate demand curve to the right of where it would otherwise be. The resulting Economic Stimulus Act of 2008 was a classic example of fiscal policy: the use of taxes, government transfers, or government purchases of goods and services to stabilize the economy by shifting the aggregate demand curve.

Expansionary and Contractionary Fiscal Policy

Why would the government want to shift the aggregate demand curve? Because it wants to close either a recessionary gap, created when aggregate output falls below potential output, or an inflationary gap, created when aggregate output exceeds potential output.

Figure 20.5 shows the case of an economy facing a recessionary gap. *SRAS* is the short-run aggregate supply curve, *LRAS* is the long-run aggregate supply curve, and AD_1 is the initial aggregate demand curve. At the initial short-run macroeconomic equilibrium, E_1, aggregate output is Y_1, below potential output, Y_P. What the government would like to do is increase aggregate demand, shifting the aggregate demand curve rightward to AD_2. This would increase aggregate output, making it equal to

Figure 20.5 Expansionary Fiscal Policy Can Close a Recessionary Gap

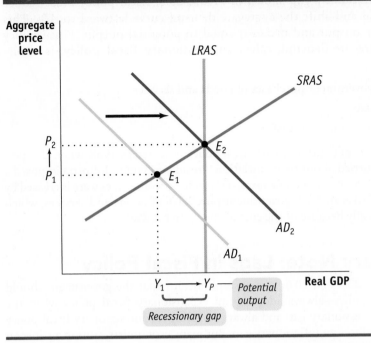

At E_1 the economy is in short-run macroeconomic equilibrium and there is a recessionary gap of $Y_P - Y_1$. Expansionary fiscal policy shifts the aggregate demand curve rightward from AD_1 to AD_2, moving the economy to long-run macroeconomic equilibrium.

potential output. Fiscal policy that increases aggregate demand, called **expansionary fiscal policy**, normally takes one of three forms:

Expansionary fiscal policy increases aggregate demand.

- an increase in government purchases of goods and services
- a cut in taxes
- an increase in government transfers

Figure 20.6 shows the opposite case—an economy facing an inflationary gap. At the initial equilibrium, E_1, aggregate output is Y_1, above potential output, Y_P.

Figure 20.6 Contractionary Fiscal Policy Can Close an Inflationary Gap

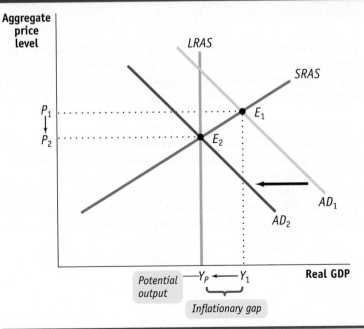

At E_1 the economy is in short-run macroeconomic equilibrium and there is an inflationary gap of $Y_1 - Y_P$. Contractionary fiscal policy shifts the aggregate demand curve leftward from AD_1 to AD_2, moving the economy to long-run macroeconomic equilibrium.

Module 20 Economic Policy and the Aggregate Demand–Aggregate Supply Model **197**

Policy makers often try to head off inflation by eliminating inflationary gaps. To eliminate the inflationary gap shown in Figure 20.6, fiscal policy must reduce aggregate demand and shift the aggregate demand curve leftward to AD_2. This reduces aggregate output and makes it equal to potential output. Fiscal policy that reduces aggregate demand, called **contractionary fiscal policy**, is implemented by

Contractionary fiscal policy reduces aggregate demand.

- a reduction in government purchases of goods and services
- an increase in taxes
- a reduction in government transfers

A classic example of contractionary fiscal policy occurred in 1968, when U.S. policy makers grew worried about rising inflation. President Lyndon Johnson imposed a temporary 10% surcharge on income taxes—everyone's income taxes were increased by 10%. He also tried to scale back government purchases of goods and services, which had risen dramatically because of the cost of the Vietnam War.

A Cautionary Note: Lags in Fiscal Policy

Looking at Figures 20.5 and 20.6, it may seem obvious that the government should actively use fiscal policy—always adopting an expansionary fiscal policy when the economy faces a recessionary gap and always adopting a contractionary fiscal policy when the economy faces an inflationary gap. But many economists caution against an extremely active stabilization policy, arguing that a government that tries too hard to stabilize the economy through fiscal policy, or a central bank that does the same with monetary policy, can end up making the economy less stable.

We'll leave discussion of the warnings associated with monetary policy to later Modules. In the case of fiscal policy, one key reason for caution is that there are important *time lags* in its use. To understand the nature of these lags, think about what has to happen before the government increases spending to fight a recessionary gap. First, the government has to realize that the recessionary gap exists: economic data take time to collect and analyze, and recessions are often recognized only months after they have begun. Second, the government has to develop a spending plan, which can itself take months, particularly if politicians take time debating how the money should be spent and passing legislation. Finally, it takes time to spend money. For example, a road construction project begins with activities such as surveying that don't involve spending large sums. It may be quite some time before the big spending begins.

Because of these lags, an attempt to increase spending to fight a recessionary gap may take so long to get going that the economy has already recovered on its own. In fact, the recessionary gap may have turned into an inflationary gap by the time the fiscal policy takes effect. In that case, the fiscal policy will make things worse instead of better.

This doesn't mean that fiscal policy should never be actively used. In early 2008, for example, there was good reason to believe that the U.S. economy had begun a lengthy slowdown caused by turmoil in the financial markets, so as discussed in Enrichment Module A, a fiscal stimulus that was designed to arrive within a few months would almost surely push aggregate demand in the right direction. But the problem of lags makes the actual use of both fiscal and monetary policy harder than you might think from a simple analysis like the one we have just given.

MODULE 20 REVIEW

Adventures in
AP® Economics

Watch the video:
Fiscal Policy

Check Your Understanding

1. In each of the following cases, determine whether the policy is an expansionary or contractionary fiscal policy:
   a. Several military bases around the country, which together employ tens of thousands of people, are closed.
   b. The number of weeks an unemployed person is eligible for unemployment benefits is increased.
   c. The federal tax on gasoline is increased.

2. Explain why federal disaster relief, which quickly disburses funds to victims of natural disasters such as hurricanes, floods, and large-scale crop failures, will stabilize the economy more effectively after a disaster than relief that must be legislated.

3. Suppose someone says, "Using monetary or fiscal policy to pump up the economy is counterproductive—you get a brief high, but then you have the pain of inflation."
   a. Explain what this means in terms of the *AD–AS* model.
   b. Is this a valid argument against stabilization policy? Why or why not?

TACKLE THE AP® TEST: Multiple-Choice Questions

1. Which of the following contributes to the lag in implementing fiscal policy?
   a. It takes time for Congress and the president to pass spending and tax changes.
   b. Current economic data takes time to collect and analyze.
   c. It takes time for policy makers to realize an output gap exists.
   d. It takes time for changes in spending and tax policy to take effect.
   e. All of the above contribute.

2. Which of the following is a government transfer program?
   a. Social Security
   b. Medicare/Medicaid
   c. unemployment insurance
   d. food stamps
   e. all of the above

3. Which of the following is an example of expansionary fiscal policy?
   a. increasing taxes
   b. increasing government spending
   c. decreasing government transfers
   d. decreasing interest rates
   e. increasing the money supply

4. Which of the following is a fiscal policy that is appropriate to combat inflation?
   a. decreasing taxes
   b. decreasing government spending
   c. increasing government transfers
   d. decreasing interest rates
   e. expansionary fiscal policy

5. A cut in income taxes is an example of
   a. an expansionary fiscal policy.
   b. a contractionary fiscal policy.
   c. an expansionary monetary policy.
   d. a contractionary monetary policy.
   e. none of the above.

6. Which of the following is an example of a fiscal policy appropriate to combat unemployment?
   a. increasing taxes
   b. increasing government spending
   c. decreasing government transfers
   d. increasing interest rates
   e. contractionary fiscal policy

7. Which of the following is an example of a fiscal policy appropriate to combat a recession?
   a. increasing taxes
   b. decreasing government spending
   c. expansionary fiscal policy
   d. increasing interest rates
   e. decreasing the money supply

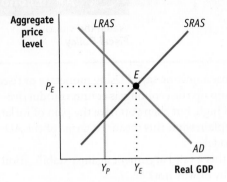

1. Refer to the graph above.
   a. What type of gap exists in this economy?
   b. What type of fiscal policy is appropriate in this situation?
   c. List the three variables the government can change to implement fiscal policy.
   d. How would the government change each of the three variables to implement the policy you listed in part b?

2. a. Draw a correctly labeled graph showing an economy experiencing a recessionary gap.
   b. What type of fiscal policy is appropriate in this situation?
   c. Give an example of what the government could do to implement the type of policy you listed in part b. **(6 points)**

Fiscal Policy and Multiplier Effects

In this Module, you will learn to:
- Explain why fiscal policy has a multiplier effect
- Calculate the tax multiplier
- Describe how automatic stabilizers influence the multiplier effect

The Spending Multiplier and Estimates of the Influence of Government Policy

An expansionary fiscal policy, like the American Recovery and Reinvestment Act of 2009, pushes the aggregate demand curve to the right. A contractionary fiscal policy, like Lyndon Johnson's tax surcharge, pushes the aggregate demand curve to the left. For policy makers, however, knowing the direction of the shift isn't enough: they need estimates of *how much* the aggregate demand curve will be shifted by a given policy. To get these estimates, they use the concept of the multiplier.

Multiplier Effects of Changes in Government Purchases

Suppose that a government decides to spend $50 billion to build bridges and roads. The government's purchases of goods and services will directly increase total spending on final goods and services by $50 billion. But there will also be an indirect effect because the government's purchases will start a chain reaction throughout the economy. The firms producing the goods and services purchased by the government will earn revenues that flow to households in the form of wages, profit, interest, and rent. This increase in disposable income will lead to a rise in consumer spending. The rise in consumer spending, in turn, will induce firms to increase output, leading to a further rise in disposable income, which will lead to another round of consumer spending increases, and so on.

In Module 16 we learned about the *spending multiplier*: the factor by which we multiply the amount of an autonomous change in aggregate spending to find the resulting change in real GDP. An increase in government purchases of goods and services is an example of an autonomous increase in aggregate spending. Any increase in government purchases of goods and services will lead to a series of additional purchases, resulting in an even larger final increase in real GDP. The initial change in spending multiplied by the spending multiplier gives us the final change in real GDP.

Let's consider a simple case that does not involve taxes or international trade. In this case, any change in GDP accrues entirely to households. Assume that the aggregate price level is fixed, so that any increase in nominal GDP is also a rise in real GDP, and that the interest rate is fixed. In that case, the spending multiplier is $1/(1 - MPC)$. Recall that MPC is the *marginal propensity to consume*, the fraction of an additional \$1 in disposable income that is spent. For example, if the marginal propensity to consume is 0.5, the spending multiplier is $1/(1 - 0.5) = 1/0.5 = 2$. Given a spending multiplier of 2, a \$50 billion increase in government purchases of goods and services would increase real GDP by \$100 billion. Of that \$100 billion, \$50 billion is the initial effect from the increase in G, and the remaining \$50 billion is the subsequent effect of more production leading to more income which leads to more consumer spending, which leads to more production, and so on.

When the government hires Boeing to build military aircraft, Boeing employees spend their earnings on things like cars, and the automakers spend their earnings on things like education, and so on, creating a multiplier effect.

What happens if government purchases of goods and services are reduced instead? The math is exactly the same, except that there's a minus sign in front: if government purchases of goods and services fall by \$50 billion and the marginal propensity to consume is 0.5, real GDP falls by \$100 billion. This is the result of less production leading to less income, which leads to less consumption, which leads to less production, and so on.

Multiplier Effects of Changes in Government Transfers and Taxes

Expansionary or contractionary fiscal policy need not take the form of changes in government purchases of goods and services. Governments can also change transfer payments or taxes. In general, however, a change in government transfers or taxes shifts the aggregate demand curve by *less* than an equal-sized change in government purchases, resulting in a smaller effect on real GDP.

To see why, imagine that instead of spending \$50 billion on building bridges, the government simply hands out \$50 billion in the form of government transfers. In this case, there is no direct effect on aggregate demand as there was with government purchases of goods and services. Real GDP and income grow only because households spend some of that \$50 billion—and they probably won't spend it all. In fact, they will spend additional income according to the MPC. If the MPC is 0.5, households will spend only 50 cents of every additional dollar they receive in transfers.

Table 21.1 shows a hypothetical comparison of two expansionary fiscal policies assuming an MPC equal to 0.5 and a multiplier equal to 2: one in which the government directly purchases \$50 billion in goods and services and one in which the government makes transfer payments instead, sending out \$50 billion in checks to consumers.

Table 21.1	Hypothetical Effects of a Fiscal Policy with a Multiplier of 2	
Effect on real GDP	**$50 billion rise in government purchases of goods and services**	**$50 billion rise in government transfer payments**
First round	$50 billion	$25 billion
Second round	$25 billion	$12.5 billion
Third round	$12.5 billion	$6.25 billion
.	.	.
.	.	.
.	.	.
Eventual effect	$100 billion	$50 billion

In each case, there is a first-round effect on real GDP, either from purchases by the government or from purchases by the consumers who received the checks. This first round is followed by a series of additional rounds as rising real GDP raises income (all of which is disposable under our assumption of no taxes), which in turn raises consumption.

However, the first-round effect of the transfer program is smaller; because we have assumed that the *MPC* is 0.5, only $25 billion of the $50 billion is spent, with the other $25 billion saved. As a result, all the further rounds are smaller, too. In the end, the transfer payment increases real GDP by only $50 billion. In comparison, a $50 billion increase in government purchases produces a $100 billion increase in real GDP.

A tax cut has an effect similar to the effect of a transfer. It increases disposable income, leading to a series of increases in consumer spending. But the overall effect is smaller than that of an equal-sized increase in government purchases of goods and services: the autonomous increase in aggregate spending is smaller because households save part of the amount of the tax cut. They save a fraction of the tax cut equal to their *MPS* (which equals $1 - MPC$). So, for each $1 decrease in taxes, spending increases only by the portion of the dollar that is not saved: the *MPC*. A tax increase has the opposite effect. For each $1 of additional taxes collected, savings decrease by the *MPS* and spending decreases by the *MPC*.

The **tax multiplier** is the factor by which a change in tax collections changes real GDP.

The **tax multiplier** is the factor by which we multiply a change in tax collections to find the total change in real GDP. Recall that the spending multiplier is $1/(1 - MPC)$. The tax multiplier has "*MPC*" in place of "1" in the numerator to reflect the initial spending decrease of *MPC* for each $1 of taxes collected. And the tax multiplier is negative because spending decreases when taxes increase, and spending increases when taxes decrease. This makes the tax multiplier

$$-MPC/(1 - MPC)$$

For example, if the *MPC* is 0.80, then the tax multiplier is $-0.80/(1 - 0.80) = -4$. So a $10 billion increase in taxes would cause a change in spending of $-4 \times \$10$ billion $= -\$40$ billion.

The multiplier for a change in transfers is the same as the tax multiplier, except the multiplier is positive, because when transfers increase, spending increases, and when transfers decrease, spending decreases. In our example above, the *MPC* was 0.5, so the multiplier was $0.5/(1 - 0.5) = 1$. This explains why the $50 billion increase in transfers led to a $50 billion total increase in real GDP. If the *MPC* had been 0.75, the multiplier would have been $0.75/(1 - 0.75) = 3$, and the $50 billion increase in transfers would have led to a $3 \times \$50$ billion $= \$150$ billion total increase in real GDP.

When a government collects taxes to cover its expenditures, it keeps the budget balanced. This activates both the spending multiplier and the tax multiplier. The spending multiplier applies to the government spending, and the tax multiplier applies to the equivalent taxes. We can use the example above to see what happens when government spending and taxes increase by the same amount. The increase in spending of $50 billion multiplies by 2 (the spending multiplier is 2 when *MPC* is 0.5), causing a total increase in real GDP of $100 billion. An equivalent increase in taxes of $50 billion would be multiplied by −1 (this is the tax multiplier when MPC is 0.5), causing a total decrease in real GDP of −$50 billion. The net effect on real GDP is an increase of $100 billion − $50 billion = $50 billion. Notice that this figure is the same as the original change in both government spending and taxes!

We find the **balanced budget multiplier** by adding the spending and tax multipliers together: $[1/(1 - MPC)] + [(-MPC)/(1 - MPC)] = (1 - MPC)/(1 - MPC) = 1$. The balanced budget multiplier shows that the factor by which we multiply a simultaneous change in both spending and taxes to find the resulting total change in real GDP is always equal to 1, as confirmed by our example above. So each $1 of government spending funded with new tax collections increases aggregate spending by $1.

While a balanced budget simplifies the multiplier story, the existence of taxes that depend on real GDP complicate it. In the real world, governments rarely impose **lump-sum taxes**, for which the amount owed is independent of the taxpayer's income. Instead, the great majority of tax revenue is raised with taxes that depend positively on the level of real GDP. As we'll discuss shortly, these taxes make the spending and tax multipliers smaller.

In practice, economists often argue that it also matters *who* among the population gets tax cuts or increases in government transfers. For example, compare the effects of an increase in unemployment benefits with the effects of a cut in taxes on profits distributed to shareholders as dividends. Consumer surveys suggest that the average unemployed worker will spend a higher share of any increase in his or her disposable income than would the average recipient of dividend income. That is, people who are unemployed tend to have a higher *MPC* than people who own a lot of stocks, because the latter tend to be wealthier and tend to save more of any increase in disposable income. If that's true, a dollar spent on unemployment benefits increases aggregate demand more than a dollar's worth of dividend tax cuts. Such arguments played an important role in debates about the final provisions of the 2008 stimulus package.

How Taxes Affect the Multiplier

Government taxes capture some part of the increase in real GDP that occurs in each round of the multiplier process, since most government taxes depend positively on real GDP. As a result, disposable income increases by considerably less than $1 for each $1 spent once we include taxes in the model.

The increase in government tax revenue when real GDP rises isn't the result of a deliberate decision or action by the government. It's a consequence of the way the tax laws are written, which causes most sources of government revenue to increase *automatically* when real GDP goes up. For example, income tax receipts increase when real GDP rises because the amount each individual owes in taxes depends positively on his or her income, and households' taxable income rises when real GDP rises. Sales tax receipts increase when real GDP rises because people with more income spend more on goods and services. And corporate profit tax receipts increase when real GDP rises because profits increase when the economy expands.

The effect of these automatic increases in tax revenue is to reduce the size of the spending and tax multipliers. Remember, the multipliers are the result of a chain reaction in which higher real GDP leads to higher disposable income, which leads to higher consumer spending, which leads to further increases in real GDP. The fact that the government siphons off some of any increase in real GDP means that at each stage of this process, the increase in consumer spending is smaller than it would be if taxes weren't part of the picture. As a result, these multipliers become smaller.

Many macroeconomists believe it's a good thing that taxes reduce the multipliers in real life. Most, though not all, recessions are the result of negative demand shocks. The same mechanism that causes tax revenue to increase when the economy expands causes it to decrease when the economy contracts. Since tax receipts decrease when real GDP

The **balanced budget multiplier** is the factor by which a change in both spending and taxes changes real GDP.

Lump-sum taxes are taxes that don't depend on the taxpayer's income.

An historical example of discretionary fiscal policy was the Works Progress Administration (WPA), a relief measure established during the Great Depression that put the unemployed to work building bridges, roads, buildings, and parks.

falls, the effects of these negative demand shocks are smaller than they would be if there were no taxes. In other words, the decrease in tax revenue reduces the adverse effect of the initial fall in aggregate demand. The automatic decrease in government tax revenue generated by a fall in real GDP—caused by a decrease in the amount of taxes households pay—acts like an automatic expansionary fiscal policy implemented in the face of a recession. Similarly, when the economy expands, the government finds itself automatically pursuing a contractionary fiscal policy—a tax increase. Government spending and taxation rules that cause fiscal policy to be automatically expansionary when the economy contracts and automatically contractionary when the economy expands, without requiring any deliberate action by policy makers, are called **automatic stabilizers**.

Automatic stabilizers are government spending and taxation rules that cause fiscal policy to be automatically expansionary when the economy contracts and automatically contractionary when the economy expands.

The rules that govern tax collection aren't the only automatic stabilizers, although they are the most important ones. Some types of government transfers also play a stabilizing role. For example, more people receive unemployment insurance when the economy is depressed than when it is booming. The same is true of Medicaid and food stamps. So transfer payments tend to rise when the economy is contracting and fall when the economy is expanding. Like changes in tax revenue, these automatic changes in transfers tend to reduce the size of the multipliers because the total change in disposable income that results from a given rise or fall in real GDP is smaller.

As in the case of government tax revenue, many macroeconomists believe that it's a good thing that government transfers reduce the spending and tax multipliers. Expansionary and contractionary fiscal policies that are the result of automatic stabilizers are widely considered helpful to macroeconomic stabilization, because they blunt the extremes of the business cycle. But what about fiscal policy that *isn't* the result of automatic stabilizers? **Discretionary fiscal policy** is fiscal policy that is the direct result of deliberate actions by policy makers rather than automatic adjustment. For example, during a recession, the government may pass legislation that cuts taxes and increases government spending in order to stimulate the economy. In general, mainly due to problems with time lags as discussed in Module 20, economists tend to support the use of discretionary fiscal policy only in special circumstances, such as during an especially severe recession.

Discretionary fiscal policy is fiscal policy that is the result of deliberate actions by policy makers rather than rules.

MODULE 21 REVIEW

Check Your Understanding

1. Explain why a $500 million increase in government purchases of goods and services will generate a larger rise in real GDP than a $500 million increase in government transfers.

2. Explain why the tax multiplier is smaller than the spending multiplier for a decrease in government purchases.

3. The country of Boldovia has no unemployment insurance benefits and a tax system that uses only lump-sum taxes. The neighboring country of Moldovia has generous unemployment benefits and a tax system in which residents must pay a percentage of their income. Which country will experience greater variation in real GDP in response to demand shocks, positive and negative? Explain.

TACKLE THE AP® TEST: Multiple-Choice Questions

1. The marginal propensity to consume
   a. has a negative relationship to the spending multiplier.
   b. is always equal to 1.
   c. represents the proportion of a consumer's income that is spent.
   d. is equal to 1/*MPS*.
   e. is the increase in consumption when disposable income increases by $1.

2. The maximum effect on real GDP of a $100 million increase in government purchases of goods and services will be
   a. an increase of $100 million.
   b. an increase of more than $100 million.
   c. an increase of less than $100 million.
   d. an increase of either more than or less than $100 million, depending on the *MPC*.
   e. a decrease of $100 million.

3. The presence of income taxes has what effect on the spending multiplier? They
  a. increase it.   **d.** negate it.
  b. decrease it.   **e.** have no effect on it.
  c. destabilize it.

4. A lump-sum tax is
  a. higher as income increases.
  b. lower as income increases.
  c. independent of income.
  d. the most common form of tax.
  e. a type of business tax.

5. Which of the following is NOT an automatic stabilizer?
  a. income taxes
  b. unemployment insurance
  c. Medicaid
  d. food stamps
  e. monetary policy

6. The maximum effect on real GDP of a $100 million increase in taxes will be
  a. an increase of $100 million.
  b. a decrease of more than $100 million.
  c. a decrease of less than $100 million.
  d. an increase of more than $100 million.
  e. an increase of either more than or less than $100 million, depending on the *MPC*.

7. If the *MPC* is 0.75 and government spending and taxes are both increased by $10 million, which of the following is true?
  a. The spending multiplier is 5.
  b. The tax multiplier is equal to −4.
  c. The budget deficit will increase.
  d. Real GDP will decrease by $10 million.
  e. The balanced budget multiplier is equal to 1.

TACKLE THE AP® TEST: Free-Response Questions

1. Assume the *MPC* in an economy is 0.8 and the government increases government purchases of goods and services by $60 million. Also assume the absence of taxes, international trade, and changes in the aggregate price level.
  a. What is the value of the spending multiplier?
  b. By how much will real GDP change as a result of the increase in government purchases?
  c. What would happen to the size of the effect on real GDP if the *MPC* fell? Explain.
  d. If we relax the assumption of no taxes, automatic changes in tax revenue as income changes will have what effect on the size of the spending multiplier?
  e. Suppose the government collects $60 million in taxes to balance its $60 million in expenditures. By how much would real GDP change as a result of this increase in both government spending and taxes?

> **Rubric for FRQ 1 (6 points)**
> **1 point:** Spending multiplier = $1/(1 − MPC) = 1/(1 − 0.8)$
>   = $1/0.2 = 5$
> **1 point:** $60 million × 5 = $300 million
> **1 point:** It would decrease.

> **1 point:** The spending multiplier is $1/(1 − MPC)$. A fall in *MPC* increases the denominator, $(1 − MPC)$, and therefore decreases the spending multiplier.
> **1 point:** Decrease it
> **1 point:** $60 million × 1 = $60 million

2. A change in government purchases of goods and services results in a change in real GDP equal to $200 million. Assume the absence of taxes, international trade, and changes in the aggregate price level.
  a. Suppose that the *MPC* is equal to 0.75. What was the size of the change in government purchases of goods and services that resulted in the increase in real GDP of $200 million?
  b. Now suppose that the change in government purchases of goods and services was $20 million. What value of the spending multiplier would result in an increase in real GDP of $200 million?
  c. Given the value of the spending multiplier you calculated in part b, what marginal propensity to save would have led to that value of the spending multiplier? **(3 points)**

Module 16

1. The **consumption function** shows how an individual household's consumer spending is determined by its current disposable income. The aggregate consumption function shows the relationship for the entire economy. The aggregate consumption function shifts in response to changes in expected future disposable income and changes in aggregate wealth.

2. **Planned investment spending** depends negatively on the interest rate and on existing production capacity; it depends positively on expected future real GDP.

3. Firms hold inventories of goods so that they can satisfy consumer demand quickly. **Inventory investment** is positive when firms add to their inventories, negative when they reduce them. Often, however, changes in inventories are not a deliberate decision but the result of mistakes in forecasts about sales. The result is

unplanned inventory investment, which can be either positive or negative. **Actual investment spending** is the sum of planned investment spending and unplanned inventory investment.

4. An **autonomous change in aggregate spending** leads to a chain reaction in which the total change in real GDP is equal to the spending multiplier times the initial change in aggregate spending. The size of the **spending multiplier**, $1/(1 - MPC)$, depends on the **marginal propensity to consume, MPC**, the fraction of an additional dollar of disposable income spent on consumption. The larger the MPC, the larger the multiplier and the larger the change in real GDP for any given autonomous change in aggregate spending. The fraction of an additional dollar of disposable income that is saved is called the **marginal propensity to save, MPS**.

Module 17

5. The **aggregate demand curve** shows the relationship between the aggregate price level and the quantity of aggregate output demanded.

6. The aggregate demand curve is downward-sloping for three reasons. The first is the **real wealth effect** of a change in the aggregate price level—a higher aggregate price level reduces the purchasing power of households' wealth and reduces consumer spending. The second is the **interest rate effect** of a change in the aggregate price level—a higher aggregate price level reduces the purchasing power of households' and firms' money holdings, leading to a rise in interest rates and a fall in investment spending and consumer spending. The third is the **exchange rate effect** of a change in the aggregate price level—an increase in the aggregate price level

increases the relative price of exports and decreases the relative price of imports, which decreases net exports.

7. The aggregate demand curve shifts because of changes in expectations, changes in wealth not due to changes in the aggregate price level, and the effect of the size of the existing stock of physical capital. Policy makers can also influence aggregate demand. **Fiscal policy** is the use of taxes, government transfers, or government purchases of goods and services to shift the aggregate demand curve. **Monetary policy** is the Fed's use of changes in the quantity of money or the interest rate to stabilize the economy, which involves shifting the aggregate demand curve.

Module 18

8. The **aggregate supply curve** shows the relationship between the aggregate price level and the quantity of aggregate output supplied.

9. The **short-run aggregate supply curve** is upward-sloping because **nominal wages** are **sticky** in the short run: a higher aggregate price level leads to higher profit per unit of output and increased aggregate output in the short run.

10. Changes in commodity prices, nominal wages, and productivity lead to changes in producers' profits and shift the short-run aggregate supply curve.

11. In the long run, all prices, including nominal wages, are flexible and the economy produces at its **potential output**. Another way to describe potential output is as the **full-employment output level**—the GDP that the economy can attain with full employment of all of its resources. If actual aggregate output exceeds potential output, nominal wages will eventually rise in response to low unemployment and aggregate output will fall. If potential output exceeds actual aggregate output, nominal wages will eventually fall in response to high unemployment and aggregate output will rise. So the **long-run aggregate supply curve** is vertical at potential output.

Module 19

12. In the **AD–AS** model, the intersection of the short-run aggregate supply curve and the aggregate demand curve is the point of **short-run equilibrium aggregate price level** and the level of **short-run equilibrium aggregate output**.

13. Economic fluctuations occur because of a shift of the aggregate demand curve (a *demand shock*) or the short-run aggregate supply curve (a *supply shock*). A **demand shock** causes the aggregate price level and aggregate output to move in the same direction as the economy moves along the short-run aggregate supply curve. A **supply shock** causes them to move in opposite directions as the economy moves along the aggregate demand curve. A particularly nasty occurrence is **stagflation**—inflation and falling aggregate output—which is caused by a negative supply shock.

14. Demand shocks have only short-run effects on aggregate output because the economy is self-correcting in the long run. In a **recessionary gap**, an eventual fall in nominal wages moves the economy to long-run macroeconomic equilibrium, in which aggregate output is equal to potential output. In an **inflationary gap**, an eventual rise in nominal wages moves the economy to long-run macroeconomic equilibrium. We can use the **output gap**, the percentage difference between actual aggregate output and potential output, to summarize how the economy responds to recessionary and inflationary gaps. Because the economy tends to be self-correcting in the long run, the output gap always tends toward zero.

Module 20

15. The high cost—in terms of unemployment—of a recessionary gap and the future adverse consequences of an inflationary gap lead many economists to advocate active **stabilization policy**: using fiscal or monetary policy to offset demand shocks. There can be drawbacks, however, because such policies may contribute to a long-term rise in the budget deficit, leading to lower long-run growth. Also, poorly timed policies can increase economic instability.

16. Negative supply shocks pose a policy dilemma: a policy that counteracts the fall in aggregate output by increasing aggregate demand will lead to higher inflation, but a policy that counteracts inflation by reducing aggregate demand will deepen the output slump.

17. The government plays a large role in the economy, collecting a large share of GDP in taxes and spending a large share both to purchase goods and services and to make transfer payments, largely for **social insurance**. Fiscal policy is the government's tool for stabilizing the economy, although many economists caution that a very active fiscal policy may in fact make the economy less stable due to time lags in policy formulation and implementation.

18. Government purchases of goods and services directly affect aggregate demand, and changes in taxes and government transfers affect aggregate demand indirectly by changing households' disposable income. **Expansionary fiscal policy** shifts the aggregate demand curve rightward; **contractionary fiscal policy** shifts the aggregate demand curve leftward.

Module 21

19. Fiscal policy has a multiplier effect on the economy, the size of which depends upon the fiscal policy. Except in the case of lump-sum taxes, taxes reduce the size of the spending and tax multipliers. Expansionary fiscal policy leads to an increase in real GDP, while contractionary fiscal policy leads to a decrease in real GDP. Because part of any change in taxes or transfers is absorbed by savings in the first round of spending, changes in government purchases of goods and services have a more powerful effect on the economy than equal-size changes in taxes or transfers.

20. The **tax multiplier** indicates the total change in aggregate spending that results from each $1 increase in tax collections. It is smaller than the spending multiplier because some of the tax collections would have been saved, not spent. Smaller still, with a value of 1, is the **balanced budget multiplier**, which indicates the total increase in aggregate spending that results from each $1 increase in both government spending and taxes.

21. Rules governing taxes—with the exception of **lump-sum taxes**—and some transfers act as **automatic stabilizers**, reducing the size of the spending multiplier and automatically reducing the size of fluctuations in the business cycle. In contrast, **discretionary fiscal policy** arises from deliberate actions by policy makers rather than from the business cycle.

Key Terms

Consumption function, p. 157
Marginal propensity to consume (MPC), p. 157
Marginal propensity to save (MPS), p. 158
Planned investment spending, p. 160
Inventory investment, p. 161
Autonomous change in aggregate spending, p. 164
Spending multiplier, p. 164
Aggregate demand curve, p. 166
Real wealth effect, p. 168
Interest rate effect, p. 168
Exchange rate effect, p. 169
Fiscal policy, p. 171
Monetary policy, p. 172

Aggregate supply curve, p. 174
Nominal wage, p. 175
Sticky wages, p. 175
Short-run aggregate supply curve, p. 175
Long-run aggregate supply curve, p. 179
Potential output, p. 179
Full-employment output level, p. 180
AD–AS model, p. 184
Short-run equilibrium aggregate price level, p. 184
Short-run equilibrium aggregate output, p. 184
Demand shock, p. 185

Supply shock, p. 185
Stagflation, p. 186
Recessionary gap, p. 188
Inflationary gap, p. 189
Output gap, p. 189
Stabilization policy, p. 192
Social insurance, p. 195
Expansionary fiscal policy, p. 197
Contractionary fiscal policy, p. 198
Tax multiplier, p. 202
Balanced budget multiplier, p. 203
Lump-sum taxes, p. 203
Automatic stabilizers, p. 204
Discretionary fiscal policy, p. 204

AP® Exam Practice Questions

Multiple-Choice Questions

1. Which of the following will occur if the federal government reduces defense spending?
   a. Aggregate demand will increase.
   b. Aggregate demand will decrease.
   c. There will be no change in aggregate demand or supply.
   d. Aggregate supply will increase.
   e. Aggregate supply will decrease.

2. Which of the following will occur if an increase in interest rates leads to a decrease in investment spending?
   a. Aggregate demand will increase.
   b. Aggregate demand will decrease.
   c. There will be no change in aggregate demand or supply.
   d. Aggregate supply will increase.
   e. Aggregate supply will decrease.

3. Which of the following will occur as a result of an increase in the aggregate price level?
   a. Aggregate demand will increase.
   b. Aggregate demand will decrease.
   c. There will be no change in aggregate demand or supply.
   d. Aggregate supply will increase.
   e. Aggregate supply will decrease.

4. Which of the following will occur if the price of steel decreases as a result of the discovery of new deposits of iron ore used to make steel?
   a. Aggregate demand will increase.
   b. Aggregate demand will decrease.
   c. There will be no change in aggregate demand or supply.
   d. Aggregate supply will increase.
   e. Aggregate supply will decrease.

5. Sticky nominal wages in the short run cause the short-run aggregate supply curve to
   a. shift to the right.   d. slope downward.
   b. shift to the left.   e. be vertical.
   c. slope upward.

6. As a result of the real wealth effect, a higher aggregate price level will reduce which of the following?
   a. households' purchasing power
   b. interest rates
   c. investment spending
   d. nominal wages
   e. aggregate demand

7. The interest rate effect of a decrease in the aggregate price level will increase which of the following?
   a. the purchasing power of money holdings
   b. investment spending
   c. interest rates
   d. aggregate supply
   e. aggregate demand

8. Which of the following types of shocks poses a policy dilemma due to the inability to use stabilization policy to address inflation and unemployment at the same time?
   a. negative supply shock
   b. positive supply shock
   c. negative demand shock
   d. positive demand shock
   e. negative budget shock

9. A higher aggregate price level leads to higher profit per unit of output and increased output in the short run because of which of the following?
   a. the real wealth effect
   b. the interest rate effect
   c. sticky nominal wages
   d. productivity gains
   e. stabilization policy

10. If potential output is equal to actual aggregate output, which of the following is true?
    a. The economy is experiencing inflation.
    b. The economy is experiencing cyclical unemployment.
    c. Nominal wages are sticky.
    d. The economy is in long-run equilibrium.
    e. The aggregate price level is rising.

11. Which of the following is true about the long-run aggregate supply curve?
    a. It is horizontal.
    b. It is the result of nominal wages being fully flexible.
    c. It is the result of sticky prices.
    d. It is upward-sloping.
    e. It intersects the horizontal axis at the actual level of real GDP.

12. Short-run equilibrium aggregate output is the quantity of aggregate output produced when
    a. the aggregate demand curve and the short-run aggregate supply curve are identical.
    b. the quantity of aggregate output supplied is equal to the quantity demanded.
    c. the economy reaches its potential output.
    d. the short-run aggregate supply curve is vertical.
    e. all prices, including nominal wages, are fully flexible.

13. The collapse of wealth and business and consumer confidence that caused the Great Depression is an example of which type of shock?
    a. negative supply shock
    b. positive supply shock
    c. negative demand shock
    d. positive demand shock
    e. negative recessionary shock

14. Which of the following is an example of a positive demand shock?
    a. a large increase in defense spending
    b. the stock market crash of 1929
    c. the discovery of a large, previously unknown oil field
    d. a reduction in the aggregate price level
    e. an increase in nominal wages

15. A positive supply shock will lead to which of the following?
    a. stagflation
    b. an increase in the aggregate price level
    c. a recession
    d. a rightward shift of the short-run aggregate supply curve
    e. an increase in aggregate output along with inflation

16. Which of the following is an example of a negative supply shock?
    a. Production costs decrease.
    b. Information technologies lead to productivity growth.
    c. The stock market collapses.
    d. The government runs a budget deficit.
    e. World oil supplies are disrupted.

17. Which of the following is true when the economy is experiencing a recessionary gap?
    a. Potential output is below aggregate output.
    b. Aggregate demand is below aggregate supply.
    c. There is high unemployment.
    d. The aggregate price level is rising.
    e. The economy has self-corrected.

18. When the economy is experiencing an inflationary gap, the output gap is
    a. positive.
    b. negative.
    c. zero.
    d. decreasing.
    e. increasing.

19. Which of the following leads to self-correction when the economy is experiencing a recessionary gap?
    a. Nominal wages and prices rise.
    b. The short-run aggregate supply curve decreases.
    c. The long-run aggregate supply curve decreases.
    d. The short-run aggregate supply curve shifts to the right.
    e. Unemployment leads to an increase in aggregate demand.

20. Which type of policy can be used to address a decrease in aggregate output to below potential output?
    a. expansionary
    b. contractionary
    c. indiscretionary
    d. recessionary
    e. inflationary

21. If the marginal propensity to consume is equal to 0.80, the spending multiplier is
   a. 0.80.
   b. 1.25.
   c. 4.00.
   d. −4.00.
   e. 5.00.

22. If the marginal propensity to consume is 0.75, an initial increase in aggregate spending of $1,000 will lead to a total change in real GDP equal to
   a. $750.
   b. $1,000.
   c. $1,333.
   d. $4,000.
   e. $7,500.

23. If the marginal propensity to consume is 0.9, every $10 billion increase in taxes will cause a change in spending equal to
   a. $100 billion.
   b. $90 billion.
   c. $9 billion.
   d. −$10 billion.
   e. −$90 billion.

24. Compared to an increase in taxes, an equal-sized increase in government spending will have what effect on real GDP?
   a. a larger, negative effect
   b. a smaller, negative effect
   c. a larger, positive effect
   d. a smaller, positive effect
   e. an equal, offsetting effect

25. Which of the following is an example of an automatic stabilizer?
   a. the Works Progress Administration established during the Great Depression
   b. lump-sum taxes
   c. a balanced budget requirement for the government
   d. sales taxes
   e. economic stimulus checks from the government

Free-Response Questions

1. Consider an economy operating at full employment.
   a. Draw a correctly labeled aggregate supply and aggregate demand graph for the economy. On your graph, show each of the following:
      i. equilibrium price level, labeled P_1
      ii. equilibrium output level, labeled Y_1

   b. Assume the government increases transfer payments to families with dependent children.
      i. Show the effect of the increase in transfer payments on your graph.
      ii. Label the new short-run equilibrium price level P_2 and the new short-run equilibrium output level Y_2.
   c. Refer to the new short-run equilibrium shown on your graph in response to part b.
      i. The new short-run equilibrium illustrates what type of output gap?
      ii. What type of fiscal policy would be appropriate for an economy facing a persistent gap of the type you identified in part i? **(7 points)**

2. Assume the *MPS* for an economy is 0.1.
   a. What is the value of the spending multiplier? Show your work.
   b. What is the value of the tax multiplier? Show your work.
   c. What is the maximum increase in real GDP as a result of an increase in government spending of $200 million? Show your work.
   d. If government spending and taxes are both increased by $200 million, what is the net effect on real GDP? Explain. **(5 points)**

3. The real GDP in Macroland is currently $100 million below potential output.
   a. What type of gap is Macroland experiencing? What type of policy would be used to close this gap?
   b. If the *MPC* in Macroland is 0.8, what is the value of the spending multiplier? Show your work.
   c. To return Macroland to long-run equilibrium, by how much should the government change taxes? Show your work.
   d. Would the change in government spending needed to close the gap be greater than, less than, or equal to the change in taxes? Explain. **(7 points)**

How Much Debt Is Too Much?

Expenditure Smoothing, Ricardian Equivalence, Expansionary Fiscal Policy, and Investments in the Future

The Debt and the Deficit

Attractive as it may sound to live within our means—spending no more than we earn—strict adherence to that policy would prevent many worthwhile exceptions. Income tends to arrive in fits and starts for individuals, businesses, and governments alike. Work opportunities fluctuate, and sales and tax revenues rise and fall with the seasons, the economy, and consumer sentiment. For example, department stores and jewelry stores make about 15% and 25% of their sales, respectively, in the month of December, whereas expenditures on inventory must be made months in advance. To establish a household, start a business, or defend a democracy, money is needed up front, but the returns can be a long time coming. The inevitable mismatch in timing between expenditures and revenues necessitates borrowing, deficits, and debt. Here we explore theories relevant to the decisions of whether and when to borrow.

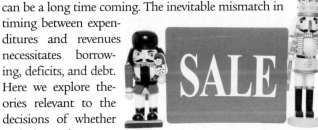
chris brignell/Alamy

A *deficit* is the amount by which expenditures exceed revenues in one period—usually a year. If revenues exceed expenditures, there is a *surplus*. Over time, *debt* accumulates as the sum of past deficits minus past surpluses. Individuals, businesses, and nations can carry sizable debt loads without much trouble if their assets and incomes are sufficient. And debtors are abundant—the average U.S. household's personal debt is about $95,000. Major corporations such as the Ford Motor Company routinely amass billions of dollars of debt. And the U.S. national debt—the total debt owed by the federal government—exceeds the U.S. gross domestic product.

The U.S. national debt was $0.9 trillion in 1980, $3.2 trillion in 1990, $5.7 trillion in 2000, $13.6 trillion in 2010, and more than $20.5 trillion in 2018. Government debt is used to finance expenditures in excess of tax collections. About three-quarters of the U.S. national debt is held by the public. This includes individuals, corporations, state and local governments within the United States, foreign governments, and other entities outside the U.S. government. Anyone can help finance the debt by purchasing U.S. savings bonds, state and local government series securities, or Treasury bills, notes (T-notes), bonds, or Treasury inflation-protected securities (TIPS).

Debt and Decision Making

Nobel laureate Milton Friedman's *permanent income hypothesis* suggests that it makes sense for individuals to smooth expenditures and spend a relatively constant portion of their lifetime income each year. Many of those who invest in higher education spend roughly the first third of their lives going to school and earning very little, the second third earning sizable incomes, and the last third earning very little again. Rather than living in poverty during the early and late stages of life, many people borrow enough during the early years to live comfortably, pay back their debts and become net creditors (lenders) during the lucrative years, and then live on their accumulated surpluses during retirement. For example, a professional who earns an average of $100,000 a year for 30 years of work has lifetime earnings of $3 million. If she expects to live 90 years, the permanent income hypothesis suggests that this individual would spend $3 million/90 = $33,333 (adjusted for inflation) each year of her life. Reduced needs for spending during youth, and uncertainty about future income and longevity, are among the reasons why expenditure levels aren't truly even throughout one's life, but a glance at the student parking lot at any elite college confirms that those who plan to earn a lot begin spending their lifetime earnings before the flow of revenues actually begins.

The concept of expenditure smoothing makes sense for other entities as well. Rather than missing out on opportunities to grow when they need to grow, prudent corporations and governments accumulate debt if doing so creates

Enigma/Alamy

benefits that exceed the burdens of borrowing. The trick is to stop borrowing before that trend is reversed.

Whether to finance tax cuts, wars, education spending, or hurricane relief, there are several valid rationales for a government to accumulate debt. One of the fathers of classical economics, David Ricardo, claimed that it makes no difference whether government expenditures are financed with debt or taxes because citizens treat government spending as a liability either way. The idea, called *Ricardian equivalence*, is that when the government borrows money, taxpayers know they must repay the loan eventually, and they increase their savings by enough to repay the borrowed funds plus interest at the appropriate time. If the government borrows $300 billion to finance new roads and bridges, according to this theory, each American would place his or her $1,000 share of this debt into an account where it would accumulate interest at about the same rate as the government's loan. Then, whenever the government collects taxes to repay the $300 billion plus interest, the citizens will have the appropriate amount ready to send in.

Because U.S. citizens hold about half of the publicly held debt themselves, the process is often more direct: rather than depositing more money into savings, many citizens invest in the very bonds used to finance the debt. If you purchase a $1,000 Treasury bond, your investment goes directly to finance government expenditures. When the government raises taxes to repurchase the bond, the payment you receive for the bond will be enough to cover the taxes used to retire it. Whether you held the debt directly in the form of a government bond or deposited funds into an account that would cover the tax repayment, Ricardian equivalence would mean that the debt burden could be carried and repaid without undue trauma for those who must pick up the check.

To the extent that it holds, Ricardian equivalence also has the simplifying result that tax-financed expenditures and debt-financed expenditures have the same effect on the economy. With expansionary fiscal policy, the government may try to increase demand by spending money on, say, a national highway system, as President Franklin D. Roosevelt did, or a hydroelectric dam, as President Herbert Hoover did during the Great Depression. In today's dollars, the Hoover Dam cost about $1 billion. If the government paid $1 billion to build a new dam by raising taxes by $1 billion, consumers would have that much less to spend and save. If, instead, the dam was paid for by selling $1 billion worth of Treasury bonds, Ricardian equivalence suggests that taxpayers would collectively save $1 billion for a future tax day. Either way, the fiscal policy would have the same effect.

Despite the logic of the theory, tax cuts and swelling deficits have not stimulated high savings rates in modern times. One explanation is that taxpayers would save enough to repay the debt if they expected the burden to fall squarely on them, but instead, they anticipate that another generation will foot the bill, and they do not care quite as much about the next generation as they do about themselves.

Debt can be justified even when it is more consequential than under Ricardian equivalence. For instance, the generations that completed the transcontinental railroad in 1869 and the transcontinental highway in 1935 created liabilities that passed through generations, but those who ultimately repaid the debts probably valued the ability to travel and transport goods across the country more highly than the amount of debt they shouldered. The same may be true for expenditures on new medicines, environmental protection, education, peace, political stability, technology, and research in any number of areas pertinent to future generations.

The Downside of Debt

The interest payments on the U.S. national debt amount to more than $450 billion per year. Without the debt, those interest payments could instead be spent on favored programs or returned to the citizens. The National Priorities Project reports that out of each dollar of tax revenues, roughly,

29 cents goes to health

23 cents goes to military spending

13 cents goes to pay interest on the national debt

8 cents goes to unemployment and labor

6 cents goes to veterans' benefits

5 cents goes to food and agriculture

4 cents goes to government

3 cents goes to transportation

3 cents goes to education

2 cents goes to housing and community

2 cents goes to energy and the environment

1 cent goes to international affairs

1 cent goes to science

That means that if we didn't have a debt to pay interest on, we could spend 5 times as much on education, 7 times as much on energy and the environment, or 14 times as much on science without raising taxes. When drawing the line between too much national debt and not enough, opportunity costs such as these should be weighed against the benefits of debt, as discussed in the previous section.

With Americans holding more than half of the publicly held debt, we can be consoled that a majority of the interest payments go to Americans. Of course, it would be nice if we could make these payments in exchange for needed goods and services instead of needed debt

Andy Dean Photography/Shutterstock

financing. There is also the problem that, even if the payments remain within the country, taxation to pay interest on the debt redistributes money from taxpayers to relatively wealthy creditors.

Ricardian equivalence would take the bite out of the debt burden, but the question is, Do you have $64,000 set aside to repay your individual share of the national debt? If not, debt repayment may cause a jolt to your way of life. The economy as a whole may also reel from the repayment of what is now $6 trillion owed to foreign purchasers of the U.S. debt. In 2017, for example, China and Japan owned $1.2 trillion and $1.1 trillion worth of U.S. debt, respectively.

Major tax cuts, like many other debt-financed policy measures, are often defended as a form of expansionary fiscal policy. Even if Ricardian equivalence is off base, the intended boost in demand from this debt creation is also threatened by increases in interest rates that dampen investment expenditures. In a process called *crowding out*, government borrowing competes with private borrowing to drive the interest rate up and investment expenditures down. Supply and demand in the market for money determine the interest rate paid to borrow money, just as supply and demand in the market for espressos determine the price paid for espressos. When the government increases its demand for money, the price of money—the interest rate—increases. This makes it more expensive for private borrowers to obtain money for investments in businesses, homes, factory expansions, technology upgrades, and so on. With *full crowding out*, each dollar of debt-financed government spending raises the interest rate enough to eliminate, or "crowd out," $1 of private spending. In reality, we usually experience only *partial crowding out*, meaning that each dollar of debt-financed government spending raises the interest rate enough to crowd out less than $1 of private expenditure.

Government debt also has a detrimental effect on the domestic savings rate and the exchange rate between the U.S. dollar and foreign currencies. Former Federal Reserve chair Alan Greenspan said, "Reducing the federal budget deficit (or preferably moving it to surplus) appears to be the most effective action that could be taken to augment domestic savings." To finance government debt, dollars that could otherwise be saved must be spent on government securities—those Treasury bills, T-notes, and the like mentioned earlier. Almost $4 trillion worth of the U.S. government debt has been purchased by private individuals, mutual funds, pension funds, and other domestic savings programs.

The foreign-owned debt poses a threat to currency exchange rates. If foreign investors for some reason lost confidence in their purchases of U.S. debt, they would sell their securities and exchange the dollars they received for their home currencies. The subsequent increase in the supply of dollars and increase in the demand for other currencies would lower the value of the U.S. dollar relative to other currencies. This would increase the cost of goods imported into the United States, while making U.S. exports less expensive for buyers in other countries.

In response to the assortment of problems with a large debt, there have been many valiant efforts to harness government expenditures. President Ronald Reagan introduced the Balanced Budget and Emergency Deficit Control Act of 1985 this way: "This legislation will impose the discipline we now lack by locking us into a spending reduction plan. It will establish a maximum allowable deficit ceiling beginning with our current 1986 deficit of $180 billion, and then it will reduce that deficit in equal steps to a balanced budget in calendar year 1990." The Budget Enforcement Act of 1990, extended in 1993 and 1997, replaced the previous system of deficit limits with stricter enforcement mechanisms meant to cap many types of government spending. The legislation was there, but, regrettably, the hoped-for discipline was not. Rather than balancing the budget, Congress raised the limits and enacted emergency spending bills. More recently, the ceiling on national debt rose gradually from $14.3 trillion in 2010 to at least $20.5 trillion in 2018.

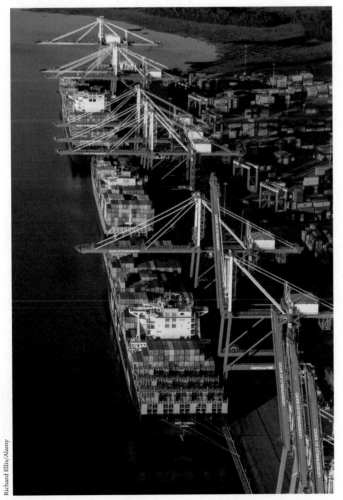

Richard Ellis/Alamy

Conclusion

It is a mistake to pass up the opportunity to borrow seed money for tomorrow's gardens. Debt creation can be an appropriate way for individuals, businesses, and governments to accommodate differences in timing between revenues and worthwhile expenditures. The line between too much debt and not enough comes when another dollar of debt-financed purchases does not justify the burden imposed on those who must repay the debt. Expenditures on research and development, health, education, infrastructure, conservation, and diplomacy are often among those that adequately serve current and future generations. Government debt can also be used for the purpose of expansionary fiscal policy, although the effects of crowding out and Ricardian equivalence weaken the intended influence on the economy.

The considerable assets and credibility of the U.S. government allow it to carry a sizable debt for extended periods with impunity not available to smaller entities. However, the validity of limited debt financing can invite overindulgence at every level. By all reasonable standards, the $20-plus trillion U.S. national debt warrants concern, making debt repayment a priority for many economists and policy makers.

Critical Thinking Questions

1. Do you see evidence to support the permanent income hypothesis? That is, do you see people borrowing money when they are young to smooth their expenditures over time? Do people with the potential to earn higher incomes in the future borrow more money now?

2. Suppose the government borrows money to fund the projects listed below. From the standpoint of the people who will repay the debt created by these projects, how do you think the benefits will compare to the costs?
   a. research to cure Alzheimer's disease
   b. hurricane recovery assistance
   c. NASA's Mars Exploration Program

3. If the United States eliminated its national debt, how would you recommend that the country reallocate the $450 billion per year that would be saved on interest payments?

4. Does your behavior correspond with Ricardian equivalence? How much do you have in savings for the purpose of paying your share of the national debt? If you don't have enough to pay your share, explain your reasoning. What would happen to your standard of living if you had to repay your share of the government debt within five years?

5. How do you explain the reelection of so many lawmakers who do not balance the budget?

SECTION 5

The Financial Sector

economics by example *How Should We Wield the Tool of Monetary Policy?*

Funny Money

On October 2, 2004, FBI and Secret Service agents seized a shipping container that had just arrived in Newark, New Jersey, on a ship from China. Inside the container, under cardboard boxes containing plastic toys, they found what they were looking for: more than $300,000 in counterfeit $100 bills. Two months later, another shipment with $3 million in counterfeit bills was intercepted. Government and law enforcement officials began alleging publicly that these bills—which were high-quality fakes, very hard to tell from the real thing—were being produced by the government of North Korea.

Even before the 2004 seizure, the U.S. government was working to enhance the security of its currency. The design of the one-dollar bill has not been updated since it debuted in 1963, but other denominations have been redesigned to make counterfeiting more difficult; the $20 bill in 2003, the $50 bill in 2004, the $10 bill in 2006 and the $5 bill in 2008. In 2013, the United States again redesigned the $100 bill, adding two new,

advanced anti-counterfeiting features: a color-changing image of a bell and a woven 3D ribbon that scrolls when the bill is tilted. While the new design is believed to have been successful in deterring most counterfeiters, a 2016 report indicated that North Korea was probably still active in counterfeiting, though their improved counterfeit bills were not being detected.

The funny thing about the efforts, on the part of both the counterfeiters and law enforcement, is that elaborately decorated pieces of paper have little or no intrinsic value. Indeed, a $100 bill printed with blue or orange ink literally wouldn't be worth the paper it was printed on. But if the ink on that decorated piece of paper is just the right shade of green, people will think that it's *money* and will accept it as payment for very real goods and services. Why? Because they believe, correctly, that they can do the same thing: exchange that piece of green paper for real goods and services.

In fact, here's a riddle: if a fake $100 bill from North Korea enters the United

States, and nobody ever realizes it's fake, who gets hurt? Accepting a fake $100 bill isn't like buying a car that turns out to be a lemon or a meal that turns out to be inedible; as long as the bill's counterfeit nature remains undiscovered, it will pass from hand to hand just like a real $100 bill. The answer to the riddle is that the real victims of North Korean counterfeiting are U.S. taxpayers because counterfeit dollars reduce the revenues available to pay for the operations of the U.S. government. Accordingly, the Secret Service diligently monitors the integrity of U.S. currency, promptly investigating any reports of counterfeit dollars.

The efforts of the Secret Service attest to the fact that money isn't like ordinary goods and services. In this section we'll look at the role money plays, the workings of a modern monetary system, and the institutions that sustain and regulate it. We'll then see how models of the money and loanable funds markets help us understand *monetary policy* as carried out by central banks.

MOD 22

Saving, Investment, and the Financial System

> **In this Module, you will learn to:**
> - Describe the relationship between savings and investment spending
> - Explain how financial intermediaries help investors achieve diversification
> - Identify the purposes of the four principal types of financial assets: stocks, bonds, loans, and bank deposits

Matching Up Savings and Investment Spending

Two instrumental sources of economic growth are increases in the skills and knowledge of the workforce, known as *human capital*, and increases in capital—goods used to make other goods—which can also be called *physical capital* to distinguish it from human capital. In many countries, human capital is largely provided by the government through public education. (In countries with a large private education sector, like the United States, private post-secondary education is also an important source of human capital.) But physical capital, with the exception of infrastructure such as roads and bridges, is mainly created through private investment spending—that is, spending by firms rather than by the government.

Who pays for private investment spending? In some cases it's the people or corporations who actually do the spending—for example, a family that owns a business might use its own savings to buy new equipment or a new building, or a corporation might reinvest some of its own profits to build a new factory. In the modern economy, however, individuals and firms who create physical capital often do it with other people's money—money that they borrow or raise by selling stock. If they borrow money to create physical capital, they are charged an *interest rate*. The **interest rate** is the price, calculated as a percentage of the amount borrowed, charged by lenders to borrowers for the use of their savings for one year.

To understand how investment spending is financed, we need to look first at how savings and investment spending are related to each other for the economy as a whole.

Google's private investment spending is used to create physical capital, such as their corporate facilities.

The **interest rate** is the price, calculated as a percentage of the amount borrowed, charged by lenders to borrowers for the use of their savings for one year.

According to the **savings–investment spending identity,** savings and investment spending are always equal for the economy as a whole.

The Savings–Investment Spending Identity

The most basic point to understand about savings and investment spending is that they are always equal. This is not a theory; it's a fact of accounting called the **savings–investment spending identity**.

To see why the savings–investment spending identity must be true, first imagine a highly simplified economy in which there is no government and no interaction with other countries. The overall income of this simplified economy, by definition, would be equal to total spending in the economy. Why? Because the only way people could earn income would be by selling something to someone else, and every dollar spent in the economy would create income for somebody. So, in this simplified economy,

$$\text{(22-1)} \quad \text{Total income} = \text{Total spending}$$

So, what can people do with income? They can either spend it on consumption or save it. Then it must be true that

$$\text{(22-2)} \quad \text{Total income} = \text{Consumer spending} + \text{Savings}$$

Meanwhile, spending consists of either consumer spending or investment spending:

(22-3) Total spending = Consumer spending + Investment spending

Putting these together, we get:

(22-4) Consumer spending + Savings = Consumer spending + Investment spending

Subtract consumer spending from both sides, and we get:

(22-5) Savings = Investment spending

As we said, it's a basic accounting fact that savings equals investment spending for the economy as a whole.

So far, however, we've looked only at a simplified economy in which there is no government and no economic interaction with the rest of the world. Bringing these realistic complications back into the story changes things in two ways.

First, households are not the only parties that can save in an economy. In any given year, the government can save, too, if it collects more tax revenue than it spends. When this occurs, the difference is called a **budget surplus** and is equivalent to savings by the government. If, alternatively, government spending exceeds tax revenue, there is a **budget deficit**—a negative budget surplus. In this case, we often say that the government is "dissaving": by spending more than its tax revenues, the government is engaged in the opposite of saving. We'll define the term **budget balance** to refer to both cases, with the understanding that the budget balance can be positive (a budget surplus) or negative (a budget deficit). **National savings** is equal to the sum of private savings and the budget balance, whereas private savings is disposable income (income after taxes) minus consumption.

Second, the fact that any one country is part of a wider world economy means that savings need not be spent on physical capital located in the same country in which the savings are generated. That's because the savings of people who live in any one country can be used to finance investment spending that takes place in other countries. So any given country can receive *inflows* of funds—foreign savings that finance investment spending in the country. Any given country can also generate *outflows* of funds—domestic savings that finance investment spending in another country.

The net effect of international inflows and outflows of funds on the total savings available for investment spending in any given country is known as the **capital inflow** into that country, equal to the total inflow of foreign funds minus the total outflow of domestic funds to other countries. Like the budget balance, a capital inflow can be negative—that is, more capital can flow out of a country than flows into it. In recent years, the United States has experienced a consistent net inflow of capital from foreigners, who view our economy as an attractive place to put their savings. In January 2018, for example, net capital inflows into the United States were $120 billion.

It's important to note that, from a national perspective, a dollar generated by national savings and a dollar generated by capital inflow are not equivalent. Yes, they can both finance the same dollar's worth of investment spending, but any dollar borrowed from a saver must eventually be repaid with interest. A dollar that comes from national savings is repaid with interest to someone domestically—either a private party or the government. But a dollar that comes as capital inflow must be repaid with interest to a foreigner. So a dollar of investment spending financed by a capital inflow comes at a higher *national* cost—the interest that must eventually be paid to a foreigner—than a dollar of investment spending financed by national savings.

The application of the savings–investment spending identity to an economy that is open to inflows or outflows of capital means that investment spending is equal to savings, where savings is equal to national savings *plus* capital inflow. That is, in an economy with a positive capital inflow, some investment spending is funded by the savings of foreigners. And, in an economy with a negative capital inflow (a net outflow), some portion of national savings funds investment spending in other

The **budget surplus** is the difference between tax revenue and government spending when tax revenue exceeds government spending.

The **budget deficit** is the difference between tax revenue and government spending when government spending exceeds tax revenue.

The **budget balance** is the difference between tax revenue and government spending.

National savings, the sum of private savings and the budget balance, is the total amount of savings generated within the economy.

Capital inflow is equal to the total inflow of foreign funds minus the total outflow of domestic funds to other countries.

The corner of Wall and Broad Streets is at the center of New York City's financial district.

countries. In the United States in 2017, investment spending totaled $2,916 billion. Private savings were $1,388 billion, offset by a budget deficit of $485 billion and supplemented by capital inflows. Notice that these numbers don't quite add up; because data collection isn't perfect, there will always be a "statistical discrepancy." But we know that this is an error in the data, not in the theory, because the savings–investment spending identity must hold in reality.

The Financial System

Financial markets are where households invest their current savings and their accumulated savings, or **wealth**, by purchasing *financial assets*.

A **financial asset** is a paper claim that entitles the buyer to future income from the seller. For example, when a saver lends funds to a company, the loan is a financial asset sold by the company and purchased by the saver. The loan entitles the saver to future income from the company. A household can also invest its current savings or wealth by purchasing a **physical asset**, a claim on a tangible object, such as a preexisting house or a preexisting piece of equipment. This claim gives the owner the right to dispose of the object as he or she wishes (for example, rent it or sell it).

If you were to go to your local bank and get a loan—say, to buy a new car—you and the bank would be creating a financial asset: your loan. A *loan* is one important kind of financial asset in the real world, one that is owned by the lender—in this case, your local bank. In creating that loan, you and the bank would also be creating a **liability**, a requirement to pay money in the future. So, although your loan is a financial asset from the bank's point of view, it is a liability from your point of view: a requirement that you repay the loan, including any interest. In addition to loans, there are three other important kinds of financial assets: stocks, bonds, and *bank deposits*. Because a financial asset is a claim to future income that someone has to pay, it is also someone else's liability. Shortly, we'll explain in detail who bears the liability for each type of financial asset.

These four types of financial assets—loans, stocks, bonds, and bank deposits—exist because the economy has developed a set of specialized markets, such as the stock market and the bond market, and specialized institutions, such as banks, that facilitate the flow of funds from lenders to borrowers. A well-functioning financial system is a critical ingredient in achieving long-run growth because it encourages greater savings and investment spending. It also ensures that savings and investment spending are undertaken efficiently. To understand how this occurs, we first need to know what tasks the financial system needs to accomplish. Then we can see how the job gets done.

Three Tasks of a Financial System

There are three important problems facing borrowers and lenders: *transaction costs*, *financial risk*, and the desire for *liquidity*. The three tasks of a financial system are to reduce these problems in a cost-effective way. Doing so enhances the efficiency of financial markets: it makes it more likely that lenders and borrowers will make mutually beneficial trades—trades that make society as a whole richer.

Reducing Transaction Costs

Transaction costs are the expenses of actually putting together and executing a deal. For example, arranging a loan requires spending time and money negotiating the terms of the deal, verifying the borrower's ability to pay, drawing up and executing legal documents, and so on. Suppose a large business decides that it wants to raise $1 billion for investment spending. No individual would be willing to lend that much. And negotiating individual

A household's **wealth** is the value of its accumulated savings.

A **financial asset** is a paper claim that entitles the buyer to future income from the seller.

A **physical asset** is a claim on a tangible object that gives the owner the right to dispose of the object as he or she wishes.

A **liability** is a requirement to pay money in the future.

Transaction costs are the expenses of negotiating and executing a deal.

loans from thousands of different people, each willing to lend a modest amount, would impose very large total costs because each individual transaction would incur a cost. Total costs would be so large that the entire deal would probably be unprofitable for the business.

Fortunately, that's not necessary: when large businesses want to borrow money, they either get a loan from a bank or sell bonds in the bond market. Obtaining a loan from a bank avoids large transaction costs because it involves only a single borrower and a single lender. We'll explain more about how bonds work in the next section. For now, it is enough to know that the principal reason there is a bond market is that it allows companies to borrow large sums of money without incurring large transaction costs.

Reducing Risk

A second problem that real-world borrowers and lenders face is **financial risk**, uncertainty about future outcomes that involve financial losses or gains. Financial risk (which from now on we'll simply call "risk") is a problem because the future is uncertain; it holds the potential for losses as well as gains.

Most people are risk-averse, although to differing degrees. A well-functioning financial system helps people reduce their exposure to risk. Suppose the owner of a business expects to make a greater profit if she buys additional capital equipment but isn't completely sure of this result. She could pay for the equipment by using her savings or selling her house. But if the profit is significantly less than expected, she will have lost her savings, or her house, or both. That is, she would be exposing herself to a lot of risk due to uncertainty about how well or poorly the business performs. So, being risk-averse, this business owner wants to share the risk of purchasing new capital equipment with someone, even if that requires sharing some of the profit if all goes well. How can she do this? By selling shares of her company to other people and using the money she receives from selling shares, rather than money from the sale of her other assets, to finance the equipment purchase. By selling shares in her company, she reduces her personal losses if the profit is less than expected: she won't have lost her other assets. But if things go well, the shareholders earn a share of the profit as a return on their investment.

By selling a share of her business, the owner has been able to invest in several things in a way that lowers her total risk. She has maintained her investment in her bank account, a financial asset; in ownership of her house, a physical asset; and in ownership of the unsold portion of her business, also a physical asset. By engaging in diversification—investing in several assets with unrelated, or independent, risks—our business owner has lowered her total risk of loss. The desire of individuals to reduce their total risk by engaging in diversification is why we have stocks and a stock market.

Providing Liquidity

The third and final task of the financial system is to provide investors with *liquidity*, which—like risk—becomes relevant because the future is uncertain. Suppose that you want to start a new business at some point. Even if you have no concerns about the risk of the business failing, you probably won't want to invest all of your savings into the business. This is because you might suddenly find yourself in need of cash—say, to pay for a medical emergency. Money invested in a business is not easily converted into cash in the event that it is needed for other purposes. For this reason, savvy investors like you are reluctant to lock up too much money in businesses among other large purchases.

An asset is **liquid** if, as with money deposited in a bank, it can be quickly converted into cash without much loss of value. An asset is **illiquid** if, as with a business, car, or home, it cannot. The reluctance to invest heavily in illiquid assets would deter business growth and many major purchases if financial systems offered no remedy. As we'll see, however, the initial sale of stocks and bonds can resolve some liquidity problems by raising money for new and expanding projects. And, by taking deposits and lending them out, banks allow individuals to own liquid assets (their deposits) while financing investments in illiquid assets such as businesses and homes.

Financial risk is uncertainty about future outcomes that involve financial losses and gains.

An asset is **liquid** if it can be quickly converted into cash without much loss of value.

An asset is **illiquid** if it cannot be quickly converted into cash without much loss of value.

To help lenders and borrowers make mutually beneficial deals, then, the economy needs ways to reduce transaction costs, to reduce and manage risk through diversification, and to provide liquidity. How does it achieve these tasks? With a variety of financial assets.

Types of Financial Assets

In the modern economy there are four main types of financial assets: loans, bonds, stocks, and bank deposits. In addition, financial innovation has allowed the creation of a wide range of *loan-backed securities*, assets created by pooling individual loans and selling shares in that pool. Each type of asset serves a somewhat different purpose. We'll explain loans, bonds, and stocks first. Then we'll turn to bank deposits when we explain the role banks play as financial intermediaries.

Loans

A **loan** is a lending agreement between an individual lender and an individual borrower.

A **loan** is a lending agreement between an individual lender and an individual borrower. Most people encounter loans in the form of bank loans to finance the purchase of a car or a house. And small businesses usually use bank loans to buy new equipment.

The good aspect of loans is that a given loan is usually tailored to the needs of the borrower. Before a small business can get a loan, it usually has to discuss its business plans, its profits, and so on with the lender. This process results in a loan that meets the borrower's needs and ability to repay.

The bad aspect of loans is that making a loan to an individual person or a business typically involves a lot of transaction costs, such as the cost of negotiating the terms of the loan, investigating the borrower's credit history and ability to repay, and so on. To minimize these costs, large borrowers such as major corporations and governments often take a more streamlined approach: they sell (or issue) bonds.

Bonds

A *bond* is an IOU issued by the borrower. Normally, the seller of the bond promises to pay a fixed sum of interest each year and to repay the principal—the value stated on the face of the bond—to the owner of the bond on a particular date. So a bond is a financial asset from its owner's point of view and a liability from its issuer's point of view. A bond issuer sells a number of bonds with a given interest rate and maturity date to whoever is willing to buy them, a process that avoids costly negotiation of the terms of a loan with many individual lenders.

Bond purchasers can acquire information free of charge on the quality of the bond issuer, such as the bond issuer's credit history, from *bond-rating agencies*, rather than having to incur the expense of investigating it themselves. A particular concern for investors is the possibility of default, the risk that the bond issuer might fail to make payments as specified by the bond contract. Once a bond's risk of default has been rated, it can be sold on the bond market as a more or less standardized product—a product with clearly defined terms and quality. In general, bonds with a higher default risk must pay a higher interest rate to attract investors.

Another important advantage of bonds is that they are easy to resell. This provides liquidity to bond purchasers. Indeed, a bond will often pass through many hands before it finally comes due. Loans, in contrast, are much more difficult to resell because, unlike bonds, they are not standardized: they differ in size, quality, terms, and so on. This makes them a lot less liquid than bonds.

Stocks

A *stock* is a share in the ownership of a company. A share of stock is a financial asset from its owner's point of view and a liability from the company's point of view. Not all companies sell shares of their stock; "privately held" companies are owned by an individual or a few partners, who gets to keep all of the company's profit. Most large companies, however, do sell stock. For example, as this book goes to press, Microsoft has almost 7.7 billion shares outstanding; if you buy one of those shares, you are entitled to less than one-eight billionth of the company's profit, as well as 1 of 7.7 billion votes on company decisions.

Why does Microsoft, historically a very profitable company, allow you to buy a share in its ownership? Why don't Bill Gates and Paul Allen, the two founders of Microsoft, keep complete ownership for themselves and just sell bonds for their investment spending needs? The reason, as we have just learned, is risk: few individuals are risk-tolerant enough to face the risk involved in being the sole owner of a large company.

Reducing the risk that business owners face, however, is not the only way in which the existence of stocks improves society's welfare: it also improves the welfare of investors who buy stocks (that is, shareowners, or shareholders). Shareowners are able to enjoy the higher returns over time that stocks generally offer in comparison to bonds. Over the past century, the average annual return on U.S. stocks has been about 7% after adjusting for inflation; for U.S. bonds the average annual return during the same time period has been only about 2%. But as investment companies warn you, "Past performance is no guarantee of future performance." And there is a downside: owning the stock of a given company is riskier than owning a bond issued by the same company. Why? Loosely speaking, a bond is a promise while a stock is a hope: by law, a company must pay what it owes its lenders (bondholders) before it distributes any profit to its shareholders. And if the company should fail (that is, be unable to pay its interest obligations and declare bankruptcy), its physical and financial assets go to its bondholders—its lenders—while its shareholders typically receive nothing. So, although a stock generally provides a higher return to an investor than a bond, it also carries higher risk.

The financial system has devised ways to help investors as well as business owners simultaneously manage risk and enjoy somewhat higher returns. It does that through the services of institutions known as *financial intermediaries*.

Financial Intermediaries

A **financial intermediary** is an institution that transforms funds gathered from many individuals into financial assets. The most important types of financial intermediaries are *mutual funds, pension funds, life insurance companies,* and *banks.* About three-quarters of the financial assets owned by Americans are held through these intermediaries rather than directly.

A **financial intermediary** is an institution that transforms the funds it gathers from many individuals into financial assets.

Mutual Funds

As we've explained, owning shares of a company entails risk in return for a higher potential reward. But it should come as no surprise that stock investors can lower their total risk by engaging in diversification. By owning a *diversified portfolio* of stocks—a group of stocks in which risks are unrelated to, or offset, one another—rather than concentrating investment in the shares of a single company or a group of related companies, investors can reduce their risk. In addition, financial advisers, aware that most people are risk-averse, almost always advise their clients to diversify not only their stock portfolio but also their entire wealth by holding other assets in addition to stocks—assets such as bonds, real estate, and cash. (And, for good measure, to have plenty of insurance in case of accidental losses!)

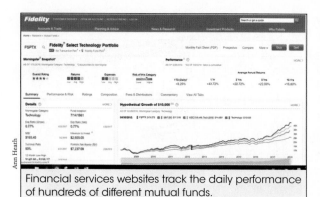

Financial services websites track the daily performance of hundreds of different mutual funds.

However, for individuals who don't have a large amount of money to invest—say $1 million or more—building a diversified stock portfolio can incur high transaction costs (particularly fees paid to stockbrokers) because they are buying a few shares of a lot of companies. Fortunately for such investors, mutual funds help solve the problem of achieving diversification without high transaction costs. A mutual fund is a financial intermediary that creates a stock portfolio by buying and holding shares in companies and then selling *shares of the stock portfolio* to individual investors. By buying these shares, investors with a relatively small amount of money to invest can indirectly hold a diversified portfolio, achieving a better return for any given level of risk than they could otherwise achieve.

Pension Funds and Life Insurance Companies

In addition to mutual funds, many Americans have holdings in pension funds, non-profit institutions that collect the savings of their members and invest those funds in a wide variety of assets, providing their members with income when they retire. Although pension funds are subject to some special rules and receive special treatment for tax purposes, they function much like mutual funds. They invest in a diverse array of financial assets, allowing their members to achieve more cost-effective diversification and conduct more market research than they would be able to individually.

Americans also have substantial holdings in the policies of life insurance companies, which guarantee a payment to the policyholder's beneficiaries (typically, the family) when the policyholder dies. By enabling policyholders to cushion their beneficiaries from financial hardship arising from their death, life insurance companies also improve welfare by reducing risk.

Banks

Recall the problem of liquidity: other things equal, people want assets that can be readily converted into cash. Bonds and stocks are much more liquid than physical assets or loans, yet the transaction costs of selling bonds or stocks to meet a sudden expense can be large. Furthermore, for many small and moderate-sized companies, the cost of issuing bonds and stocks is too large, given the modest amount of money they seek to raise. A *bank* is an institution that helps resolve the conflict between lenders' needs for liquidity and the financing needs of borrowers who don't want to use the stock or bond markets.

A bank works by first accepting funds from *depositors*: when you put your money in a bank, you are essentially becoming a lender by lending the bank your money. In return, you receive credit for a **bank deposit**—a claim on the bank, which is obliged to give you your cash if and when you demand it. So a bank deposit is a financial asset owned by the depositor and a liability of the bank that holds it.

A bank, however, keeps only a fraction of its customers' deposits in the form of ready cash. Most of its deposits are lent out to businesses, buyers of new homes, and other borrowers. These loans come with a long-term commitment by the bank to the borrower: as long as the borrower makes his or her payments on time, the loan cannot be recalled by the bank and converted into cash. So a bank enables those who wish to borrow for long lengths of time to use the funds of those who wish to lend but simultaneously want to maintain the ability to get their cash back on demand. More formally, a **bank** is a financial intermediary that provides liquid financial assets in the form of deposits to lenders and uses their funds to finance borrowers' investment spending on illiquid assets.

In essence, a bank is engaging in a kind of mismatch: lending for long periods of time but also subject to the condition that its depositors could demand their funds back at any time. How can it manage that?

A **bank deposit** is a claim on a bank that obliges the bank to give the depositor his or her cash when demanded.

A **bank** is a financial intermediary that provides liquid assets in the form of bank deposits to lenders and uses those funds to finance borrowers' investment spending on illiquid assets.

The bank counts on the fact that, on average, only a small fraction of its depositors will want their cash at the same time. On any given day, some people will make withdrawals and others will make new deposits; these will roughly cancel each other out. So the bank needs to keep only a limited amount of cash on hand to satisfy its depositors. In addition, if a bank becomes financially incapable of paying its depositors, individual bank deposits are currently guaranteed to depositors up to $250,000 by the Federal Deposit Insurance Corporation, or FDIC, a federal agency. This reduces the risk to a depositor of holding a bank deposit, in turn reducing the incentive to withdraw funds if concerns about the financial state of the bank should arise. So, under normal conditions, banks need to hold only a fraction of their depositors' cash.

By reconciling the needs of savers for liquid assets with the needs of borrowers for long-term financing, banks play a key economic role.

MODULE 22 REVIEW

Check Your Understanding

1. Rank the following assets from the lowest level to the highest level of (i) transaction costs, (ii) risk, and (iii) liquidity. Ties are acceptable for items that have indistinguishable rankings.
   a. a bank deposit with a guaranteed interest rate
   b. a share of a highly diversified mutual fund, which can be quickly sold
   c. a share of the family business, which can be sold only if you find a buyer and all other family members agree to the sale

2. What relationship would you expect to find between the level of development of a country's financial system and the country's level of economic development? Explain in terms of the country's levels of savings and investment spending.

TACKLE THE AP® TEST: Multiple-Choice Questions

1. Which of the following is a task of the financial system?
   a. decreasing transaction costs
   b. increasing risk
   c. creating illiquidity
   d. increasing inefficiency
   e. creating capital outflow

2. Which of the following is NOT a type of financial asset?
   a. bonds
   b. stocks
   c. bank deposits
   d. loans
   e. houses

3. The federal government is said to be "dissaving" when
   a. there is a budget deficit.
   b. there is a budget surplus.
   c. there is no budget surplus or deficit.
   d. savings does not equal investment spending.
   e. national savings equals private savings.

4. A nonprofit institution collects the savings of its members and invests those funds in a wide variety of assets in order to provide its members with income after retirement. This describes a
   a. mutual fund.
   b. bank.
   c. savings and loan institution.
   d. pension fund.
   e. life insurance company.

5. A financial intermediary that provides liquid financial assets in the form of deposits to lenders and uses their funds to finance borrowers' investment spending on illiquid assets is called a
   a. mutual fund.
   b. bank.
   c. corporation.
   d. pension fund.
   e. life insurance company.

6. It is a basic accounting fact that the level of investment for the economy as a whole must equal the level of
   a. capital inflows.
   b. capital outflows.
   c. wealth.
   d. financial assets.
   e. savings.

7. Bonds are
   a. IOUs issued by a borrower.
   b. a financial asset for the bond owner.
   c. a liability for the bond issuer.
   d. easy to resell.
   e. all of the above

1. Identify and describe the three tasks of a well-functioning financial system.

Rubric for FRQ 1 (6 points)

1 point: Decrease transaction costs

1 point: A well-functioning financial system facilitates investment spending by allowing companies to borrow large sums of money without incurring large transaction costs.

1 point: Decrease risk

1 point: A well-functioning financial system helps people reduce their exposure to risk, so that they are more willing to engage in investment spending in the face of uncertainty in the economy.

1 point: Provide liquidity

1 point: A well-functioning financial system allows the fast, low-cost conversion of assets into cash.

2. List and describe the four most important types of financial intermediaries. **(4 points)**

MOD 23

The Definition and Measurement of Money

> **In this Module, you will learn to:**
> - Identify the functions of money
> - Explain the various roles money plays and the many forms it takes in the economy
> - Describe how the amount of money in the economy is measured

The Meaning of Money

In everyday conversation, people often use the word *money* to mean "wealth." If you ask, "How much money does Elon Musk have?" the answer will be something like, "Oh, $20 billion or so, but who's counting?" That is, the number will include the value of the stocks, bonds, real estate, and other assets he owns.

But the economist's definition of money doesn't include all forms of wealth. The dollar bills in your wallet are money; other forms of wealth—such as cars, houses, and stocks—aren't money. Let's examine what, according to economists, distinguishes money from other forms of wealth.

What Is Money?

Money is any asset that can easily be used to purchase goods and services.

Money is defined in terms of what it does: **money** is any asset that can easily be used to purchase goods and services. For ease of use, money must be widely accepted by sellers. It is also desirable for money to be durable, portable, uniform, in limited supply, and divisible into smaller units, as with dollars and cents. In Module 22 we defined an asset as *liquid* if it can easily be converted into cash. Money consists of cash itself, which is liquid by definition, as well as other assets that are highly liquid.

You can see the distinction between money and other assets by asking yourself how you pay for groceries. The person at the cash register will accept dollar bills in return for milk and frozen pizza—but he or she won't accept stock certificates or a collection of vintage baseball cards. If you want to convert stock certificates or vintage baseball cards into groceries, you have to sell them—trade them for money—and then use the money to buy groceries.

Of course, many stores allow you to pay for goods with a debit card or check linked to your bank account. Does that mean that your bank account is money, even if you haven't converted it into cash? Yes. Currency in circulation—actual cash in the hands of the public—is considered money. So are checkable bank deposits—bank accounts on which people can write checks or debit funds.

Are currency and checkable bank deposits the only assets that are considered money? It depends. As we'll see later, there are two widely used definitions of the **money supply**, the total value of financial assets in the economy that are considered money. The narrower definition considers only the most liquid assets to be money: currency in circulation, traveler's checks, and checkable bank deposits. The broader definition includes these three categories plus other assets that are "almost" checkable, such as savings account deposits that can be transferred into a checking account online with a few clicks. Both definitions of the money supply, however, make a distinction between those assets that can easily be used to purchase goods and services, and those that can't.

> The **money supply** is the total value of financial assets in the economy that are considered money.

Money plays a crucial role in generating *gains from trade* because it makes indirect exchange possible. Think of what happens when a cardiac surgeon buys a new refrigerator. The surgeon has valuable services to offer—namely, performing heart operations. The owner of the store has valuable goods to offer: refrigerators and other appliances. It would be extremely difficult for both parties if, instead of using money, they had to directly barter the goods and services they sell. In a barter system, a cardiac surgeon and an appliance store owner could trade only if the store owner happened to want a heart operation *and* the surgeon happened to want a new refrigerator. This is known as the problem of finding a "double coincidence of wants": in a barter system, two parties can trade only when each wants what the other has to offer. Money solves this problem: individuals can trade what they have to offer for money and trade money for what they want.

Because the ability to make transactions with money rather than relying on bartering makes it easier to achieve gains from trade, the existence of money increases welfare, even though money does not directly produce anything. As Adam Smith put it, money "may very properly be compared to a highway, which, while it circulates and carries to market all the grass and corn of the country, produces itself not a single pile of either."

Let's take a closer look at the roles money plays in the economy.

Roles of Money

Money plays three main roles in any modern economy: it is a *medium of exchange*, a *store of value*, and a *unit of account*.

> A **medium of exchange** is an asset that individuals acquire for the purpose of trading for goods and services rather than for their own consumption.

Medium of Exchange

Our cardiac surgeon/appliance store owner example illustrates the role of money as a **medium of exchange**—an asset that individuals use to trade for goods and services rather than for consumption. People can't eat dollar bills; rather, they use dollar bills to trade for food among other goods and services.

In normal times, the official money of a given country—the dollar in the United States, the peso in Mexico, and so on—is also the medium of exchange in virtually all transactions in that country. During troubled economic times, however, other goods or assets often play that role instead. For example, during economic turmoil people often turn to other countries' moneys as the medium of exchange: U.S. dollars have played this role in troubled Latin American countries, as have euros in troubled Eastern European countries. In a famous example, cigarettes functioned as the medium of exchange in World War II prisoner-of-war camps, for smokers and nonsmokers alike, because they could be easily traded for other items. During the extreme German inflation of 1923, goods such as eggs and lumps of coal briefly became mediums of exchange.

Gambling at the Stalag 383 prisoner of war camp during World War II was carried out using cigarettes as currency.

Store of Value

A **store of value** is a means of holding purchasing power over time.

In order to act as a medium of exchange, money must also be a **store of value**—a means of holding purchasing power over time. To see why this is necessary, imagine trying to operate an economy in which ice cream cones were the medium of exchange. Such an economy would quickly suffer from, well, monetary meltdown: your medium of exchange would often turn into a sticky puddle before you could use it to buy something else. Of course, money is by no means the only store of value. Any asset that holds its purchasing power over time is a store of value. Examples include farmland and classic cars. So the store-of-value role is a necessary but not a distinctive feature of money.

Unit of Account

A **unit of account** is a measure used to set prices and make economic calculations.

Finally, money normally serves as the **unit of account**—the commonly accepted measure individuals use to set prices and make economic calculations. To understand the importance of this role, consider a historical fact: during the Middle Ages, peasants typically were required to provide landowners with goods and labor rather than money in exchange for a place to live. For example, a peasant might be required to work on the landowner's land one day a week and also hand over one-fifth of his harvest. Today, rents, like other prices, are almost always specified in money terms. That makes things much clearer: imagine how hard it would be to decide which apartment to rent if modern landowners followed medieval practice. Suppose, for example, that Mr. Smith says he'll let you have a place if you clean his house twice a week and bring him a pound of steak every day, whereas Ms. Jones wants you to clean her house just once a week but wants four pounds of chicken every day. Who's offering the better deal? It's hard to say. If, on the other hand, Mr. Smith wants $600 a month and Ms. Jones wants $700, the comparison is easy. In other words, without a commonly accepted measure, the terms of a transaction are harder to determine, making it more difficult to make transactions and achieve gains from trade.

Types of Money

In some form or another, money has been in use for thousands of years. For most of that period, people used **commodity money**: the medium of exchange was a good, normally gold or silver, that had intrinsic value in other uses. These alternative uses gave commodity money value independent of its role as a medium of exchange. For example, the cigarettes that served as money in World War II POW camps were valuable because many prisoners smoked. Gold was valuable because it was used for jewelry and ornamentation, aside from the fact that it was minted into coins.

Commodity money is a good used as a medium of exchange that has intrinsic value in other uses.

By 1776, the year in which the United States declared its independence and Adam Smith published *The Wealth of Nations*, there was widespread use of paper money in addition to gold and silver coins. Unlike modern dollar bills, however, this paper money consisted of notes issued by private banks, which promised to exchange their notes for gold or silver coins on demand. So the paper currency that initially replaced commodity money was **commodity-backed money**, a medium of exchange with no intrinsic value whose ultimate value was guaranteed by a promise that it could always be converted into valuable goods on demand.

Commodity-backed money is a medium of exchange with no intrinsic value whose ultimate value is guaranteed by a promise that it can be converted into valuable goods.

The big advantage of commodity-backed money over simple commodity money, like gold and silver coins, was that it tied up fewer valuable resources. Although a note-issuing bank still had to keep some gold and silver on hand, it had to keep only enough to satisfy demand for redemption of its notes. And it could rely on the fact that only a fraction of its paper notes would be redeemed on a normal day. So the bank needed to keep only a portion of the total value of its notes in circulation in the form of gold and silver in its vaults. It could lend out the remaining gold and silver to those who wished to use it. This allowed society to use the remaining gold and silver for other purposes, all with no loss in the ability to achieve gains from trade.

When issued, this commodity-backed one-dollar silver certificate could have been converted into silver.

In a famous passage in *The Wealth of Nations*, Adam Smith described paper money as a "waggon-way through the air." Smith was making an analogy between money and an imaginary highway that did not absorb the valuable land beneath it. An actual highway provides a useful service but at a cost: land that could be used to grow crops is instead paved over. If the highway could be built through the air, it wouldn't destroy useful land. As Smith understood, when banks replaced gold and silver money with paper notes, they accomplished a similar feat: they reduced the amount of real resources used by society to provide the functions of money.

At this point you may ask, why make any use at all of gold and silver in the monetary system, even to back paper money? In fact, today's monetary system goes even further than the system Smith admired, having eliminated any role for gold and silver. A U.S. dollar bill isn't commodity money, and it isn't even commodity-backed. Rather, its value arises entirely from the fact that it is generally accepted as a means of payment, a role that is ultimately decreed by the U.S. government. Money whose value derives entirely from its official status as a means of exchange is known as **fiat money** because it exists by government *fiat*, a historical term for a policy declared by a ruler.

Fiat money has two major advantages over commodity-backed money. First, it is even more of a "waggon-way through the air"—it doesn't tie up any real resources, except for the paper it's printed on. Second, the money supply can be managed based on the needs of the economy, instead of being determined by the amount of gold and silver prospectors happen to discover.

On the other hand, fiat money poses some risks. One such risk is counterfeiting. Counterfeiters usurp a privilege of the U.S. government, which has the sole legal right to print dollar bills. And the benefit that counterfeiters get by exchanging fake bills for real goods and services comes at the expense of the U.S. federal government, which covers a small but nontrivial part of its own expenses by issuing new currency to meet a growing demand for money.

The larger risk is that government officials who have the authority to print money will be tempted to abuse the privilege by printing so much money that they create inflation.

Fiat money is a medium of exchange whose value derives entirely from its official status as a means of payment.

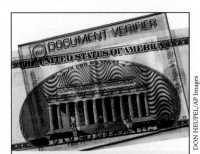

The image of a valid U.S. five-dollar bill shows a pattern in the background of the Lincoln Memorial image as seen through a Document Security Systems, Inc. document verifier.

DON HEUPEL/AP Images

Measuring the Money Supply

The Federal Reserve (an institution we'll talk more about shortly) calculates the size of two **monetary aggregates**, overall measures of the money supply, which differ in how strictly money is defined. The two aggregates are known, rather cryptically, as M1 and M2. (There used to be a third aggregate named—you guessed it—M3, but in 2006 the Federal Reserve concluded that measuring it was no longer useful.) M1, the narrowest definition, contains only currency in circulation (also known as cash), traveler's checks, and checkable bank deposits. M2 starts with M1 and adds several other kinds of assets, often referred to as *near-moneys*—financial assets that aren't directly usable as a medium of exchange but can be readily converted into cash or checkable bank deposits. Examples include savings accounts and time deposits such as small-denomination certificates of deposit (CDs), which aren't checkable but can be withdrawn at any time before their maturity date by paying a penalty. Other types of assets in M2 include money market funds, which are mutual funds that invest only in liquid assets and bear a close resemblance to bank deposits. These near-moneys pay interest while cash (currency in circulation) does not; in addition, they typically pay higher interest rates than any offered on checkable bank deposits. Because currency and checkable deposits are directly usable as a medium of exchange, however, M1 is the most liquid measure of money.

In September 2017, M1 was valued at $3,527 billion, with approximately 43% accounted for by currency in circulation, approximately 57% accounted for by checkable bank deposits, and less than 1% accounted for by traveler's checks. In turn, M1 made up more than 25% of M2, valued at $13.86 trillion in 2017.

A **monetary aggregate** is an overall measure of the money supply.

> ### AP® EXAM TIP
>
> On the AP® exam, references to the money supply usually refer to the M1 measure.

MODULE 23 REVIEW

Check Your Understanding

1. Suppose you hold a gift certificate, good for certain products at participating stores. Is this gift certificate money? Why or why not?

2. Although most bank accounts pay some interest, depositors can get a higher interest rate by buying a certificate of deposit, or CD. The difference between a CD and a checking account is that the depositor pays a penalty for withdrawing the money before the CD comes due—a period of months or even years. Small CDs are counted in M2, but not in M1. Explain why they are not part of M1.

3. Explain why a system of commodity-backed money uses resources more efficiently than a system of commodity money.

TACKLE THE AP® TEST: Multiple-Choice Questions

1. When you use money to purchase lunch, money is serving which role?
   a. medium of exchange
   b. store of value
   c. unit of account
   d. measure of usefulness
   e. all of the above

2. When you decide you want "$10 worth" of a product, money is serving which role?
   a. medium of exchange
   b. store of value
   c. unit of account
   d. measure of usefulness
   e. all of the above

3. In the United States, the dollar is
   a. backed by silver.
   b. backed by gold and silver.
   c. commodity-backed money.
   d. commodity money.
   e. fiat money.

4. Which of the following is the most liquid monetary aggregate?
   a. M1
   b. M2
   c. M3
   d. near-moneys
   e. dollar bills

5. Which of the following is the best example of using money as a store of value?
   a. A customer pays in advance for $10 worth of gasoline at a gas station.
   b. A babysitter puts her earnings in a dresser drawer while she saves to buy a bicycle.
   c. Travelers buy meals on board an airline flight.
   d. Foreign visitors to the United States convert their currency to dollars at the airport.
   e. You use $1 bills to purchase soda from a vending machine.

6. Using salt as money is an example of
   a. fiat money.
   b. commodity money.
   c. commodity-backed money.
   d. a monetary aggregate.
   e. near-money.

7. In the United States, the money supply is
   a. made up of only currency in circulation.
   b. made up of only illiquid assets.
   c. considered commodity-backed.
   d. commonly defined as either M1 or M2.
   e. always defined to include "near moneys."

TACKLE THE AP® TEST: Free-Response Questions

1. a. What does it mean for an asset to be liquid?
   b. Which of the assets listed below is the most liquid? Explain.
      A Federal Reserve note (dollar bill)
      A savings account deposit
      A house
   c. Which of the assets listed in part b is the least liquid? Explain.
   d. In which monetary aggregate(s) calculated by the Federal Reserve are checkable deposits included?

2. a. The U.S. dollar derives its value from what? In other words, what "backs" U.S. currency?

   b. What is the term used to describe the type of money used in the United States today?

   c. In addition to the type of money described in part b, what two other types of money have been used in the past? Define each. **(5 points)**

The Time Value of Money

In this Module, you will learn to:
- Explain why a dollar today is worth more than a dollar a year from now
- Use the concept of present value to make better decisions about costs and benefits that come in the future

The Concept of Present Value

Individuals often face financial decisions that will have consequences long into the future. For example, when you decide to attend college, you are committing yourself to years of study, which you expect will pay off for the rest of your life. So the decision to attend college is a decision to embark on a long-term project.

The basic rule in deciding whether or not to undertake a project is that you should compare the benefits of that project with its costs, implicit as well as explicit. But making these comparisons can sometimes be difficult because the benefits and costs of a project may not arrive at the same time. Sometimes the costs of a project come at an earlier date than the benefits. For example, going to college involves large immediate costs: tuition, income forgone because you are in school, and so on. The benefits, such as a higher salary in your future career, come later, often much later. In other cases, the benefits of a project come at an earlier date than the costs. If you take out a loan to pay for a vacation cruise, the satisfaction of the vacation will come immediately, but the burden of making payments will come later.

How, specifically, is time an issue in economic decision making?

Borrowing, Lending, and Interest

In general, having a dollar today is worth more than having a dollar a year from now. To see why, let's consider two examples.

First, suppose that you get a new job that comes with a $1,000 bonus, which will be paid at the end of the first year. But you would like to spend the extra money now—say, on new clothes for work. Can you do that? The answer is yes—you can borrow money today and use the bonus to repay the debt a year from now. But if that is your plan, you cannot borrow the full $1,000 today. You must borrow *less* than that because a year from now you will have to repay the amount borrowed *plus interest*.

Now consider a different scenario. Suppose that you are paid a bonus of $1,000 today, and you decide that you don't want to spend the money until a year from now. What do you do with it? You put it in the bank; in effect, you are lending the $1,000 to the bank, which in turn lends it out to its customers who wish to borrow. At the end of a year, you will get *more* than $1,000 back—you will receive the $1,000 plus the interest earned.

All of this means that having $1,000 today is worth more than having $1,000 a year from now. As any borrower or lender knows, this is what allows a lender to charge a borrower interest on a loan: borrowers are willing to pay interest in order to have money today rather than waiting until they acquire that money later on. Most interest rates are stated as the percentage of the borrowed amount that must be paid to the lender for each year of the loan. Whether money is actually borrowed for 1 month or 10 years, and regardless of the amount, the same principle applies: money in your pocket today is worth more than money in your pocket tomorrow. To keep things simple in the discussions that follow, we'll restrict ourselves to examples of loans of $1.

Because the value of money depends on when it is paid or received, you can't evaluate a project by simply adding up the costs and benefits when those costs and benefits arrive at different times. You must take time into account when evaluating the project because $1 that is paid to you today is worth more than $1 that is paid to you a year from now. Similarly, $1 that you must pay today is more burdensome than $1 that you must pay next year. Fortunately, there is a simple way to adjust for these complications so that we can correctly compare the value of dollars received and paid out at different times.

In the next section, we'll see how the interest rate can be used to convert future benefits and costs into what economists call *present values*. By using present values when evaluating a project, you can evaluate a project *as if* all relevant costs and benefits were occurring today rather than at different times. This allows people to "factor out" the complications created by time. We'll start by defining the concept of present value.

Defining Present Value

The key to the concept of present value is to understand that you can use the interest rate to compare the value of a dollar realized (paid or received) today with the value of a dollar realized later. Why the interest rate? Because the interest rate correctly measures the cost to you of delaying the receipt of a dollar of benefit and, correspondingly, the benefit to you of delaying the payment of a dollar of cost. Let's illustrate this with some examples.

Suppose that you are evaluating whether or not to take a job in which your employer promises to pay you a bonus at the end of the first year. What is the value to you today of $1 of bonus money to be paid one year in the future? Or, to put the question somewhat differently, what amount would you be willing to accept today as a substitute for receiving $1 one year from now?

To answer this question, begin by observing that you need *less* than $1 today in order to be assured of having $1 one year from now. Why? Because any money that you have today can be lent out at interest—say, by depositing it in a bank account so that the bank can then lend it out to its borrowers. The accumulation of interest turns any amount you have today into a greater sum, called the **future value** of today's amount, at the end of the loan period.

Let's work this out mathematically. We'll use the symbol r to represent the interest rate, expressed in decimal terms—that is, if the interest rate is 10%, then $r = 0.10$. If you lend out $X for one year, at the end of that year you will receive your $X back, plus the interest on your $X, which is $X \times r$. Thus, at the end of the year you will receive:

(24-1)   Future value of $X in one year $= \$X + \$X \times r = \$X \times (1 + r)$

The **future value** of some current amount of money is the amount to which it will grow as interest accumulates over a specified period of time.

Jorg Greuel/Getty Images

The next step is to find out how much you would have to lend out today to have $1 a year from now. To do that, we just need to set the future value in Equation 24-1 equal to $1 and solve for $X. That is, we solve the following equation for $X:

$$(24\text{-}2) \quad \$X \times (1 + r) = \$1$$

When we rearrange Equation 24-2 to solve for $X, we find the amount you need to lend out today in order to receive $1 one year from now. Economists have a special name for $X—it's called the **present value** of $1:

$$(24\text{-}3) \quad \text{Present value of \$1 realized in one year} = \$X = \$1/(1 + r)$$

This means that you would be willing to accept $X today in place of each $1 to be paid to you one year in the future. The reason is that, if you were to lend out $X today, you would be assured of receiving $1 one year from now.

To find the value of $X we simply need to plug the actual value of r (a value determined by the financial markets) into Equation 24-3. Let's assume that the interest rate is 10%, which means that $r = 0.10$. In that case:

$$\$X = \$1/(1 + 0.10) = \$1/1.10 = \$0.91$$

So you would be willing to accept $0.91 today in exchange for every $1 to be paid to you one year in the future. That is, the present value of $1 realized in one year is $0.91. Note that the present value of any given amount will change as the interest rate changes.

To see that this technique works for evaluating future costs as well as evaluating future benefits, consider the following example. Suppose you enter into an agreement that obliges you to pay $1 one year from now—say, to pay off a car loan from your parents when you graduate in a year. How much money would you need today to ensure that you have $1 in a year? The answer is $X, the present value of $1, which in our example is $0.91. The reason $0.91 is the right answer is that if you lend it out for one year at an interest rate of 10%, you will receive $1 in return at the end. So if, for example, you must pay back $5,000 one year from now, then you need to deposit $5,000 × 0.91 = $4,550 into a bank account today earning an interest rate of 10% in order to have $5,000 one year from now. (There is a slight discrepancy due to rounding.) In other words, today you need to have the present value of $5,000, which equals $4,550, in order to be assured of paying off your debt in a year.

These examples show us that the present value concept provides a way to calculate the value today of $1 that is realized in a year—regardless of whether that $1 is realized as a benefit (the bonus) or a cost (the car loan payback). To evaluate a project today that has benefits, costs, or both to be realized in a year, we just use the relevant interest rate to convert those future dollars into their present values. In that way we have "factored out" the complication that time creates for decision making.

The **present value** of $1 realized one year from now is $1/(1 + r)$: the amount of money you must lend out today in order to have $1 in one year. It is the value to you today of $1 realized one year from now.

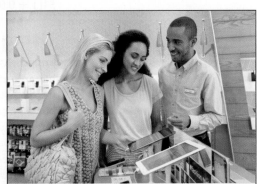

Having it someday in the future isn't the same as having it now.

Present Value in the Long Run

In the next section, we will use the present value concept to evaluate a project. But before we do that, it is worthwhile to note that the present value method can be used for projects in which the $1 is realized more than a year later—say, two, three, or even more years. Suppose you are considering a project that will pay you $1 *two* years from today. What is the value to you today of $1 received two years into the future? We can find the answer with extensions of the formulas we've already seen.

Let's call $V the amount of money you need to lend today at an interest rate of r in order to have $1 in two years. So if you lend $V today, in one year you will receive:

$$(24\text{-}4) \quad \text{Future value of \$V in one year} = \$V \times (1 + r)$$

And if you re-lend that sum for another year, at the end of the second year you will receive:

(24-5)   Future value of $V in two years $= \$V \times (1 + r) \times (1 + r) = \$V \times (1 + r)^2$

For example, if $r = 0.10$, then $\$V \times (1.10)^2 = \$V \times 1.21$.

Now we are ready to find the present value of $1 realized in two years. First we set the future value in Equation 24-5 equal to $1:

(24-6)   Condition satisfied when $1 is received two years
from now as a result of lending $V today: $\$V \times (1 + r)^2 = \$1$

Rearranging Equation 24-6, we can solve for $V:

(24-7) $\$V = \$1/(1 + r)^2$

Given $r = 0.10$ and using Equation 24-7, we arrive at:

$$\$V = \$1/(1.10)^2 = \$1/1.21 = \$0.83$$

So, when the interest rate is 10%, $1 realized two years from today is worth $0.83 today because by lending out $0.83 today you can be assured of having $1 in two years. And that means that the present value of $1 realized two years into the future is $0.83.

Equation 24-7 points the way toward a general expression for present value, where $1 is paid after N years:

(24-8)   Present value of $1 received in N years $= \$1/(1 + r)^N$

Likewise, each $1 lent today for N years has a future value of:

(24-9)   Future value of today's $1 in N years $= \$1(1 + r)^N$

For example, $1 lent for five years at an interest rate of 6% has a future value of $\$1(1 + 0.06)^5 = \$1.34$.

Using Present Value

Suppose you have three choices for a project to undertake. Project A costs nothing and has an immediate payoff to you of $100. Project B requires that you pay $10 today in order to receive $115 a year from now. Project C gives you an immediate payoff of $119 but requires that you pay $20 a year from now. Let's assume that the annual interest rate is 10%—that is, $r = 0.10$.

The problem in evaluating these three projects is that their costs and benefits are realized at different times. That is, of course, where the concept of present value becomes extremely helpful: by using present value to convert any dollars realized in the future into today's value, you factor out the issue of time. Appropriate comparisons can be made using the **net present value** of a project—the present value of current and future benefits minus the present value of current and future costs. The best project to undertake is the one with the highest net present value.

The **net present value** of a project is the present value of current and future benefits minus the present value of current and future costs.

Table 24.1 shows how to calculate net present value for each of the three projects. The second and third columns show how many dollars are realized and when they are realized; costs are indicated by a minus sign. The fourth column shows the equations used to convert the flows of dollars into their present value, and the fifth column shows the actual amounts of the total net present value for each of the three projects.

For instance, to calculate the net present value of project B, we need to calculate the present value of $115 received in one year. The present value of $1 received in one year would be $\$1/(1 + r)$. So the present value of $115 is equal to $115 \times \$1/(1 + r)$; that is, $\$115/(1 + r)$. The net present value of project B is the present value of today's and future benefits minus the present value of today's and future costs: $-\$10 + \$115/(1 + r)$.

Table 24.1 The Net Present Value of Three Hypothetical Projects

Project	Dollars realized today	Dollars realized one year from today	Present value formula	Net present value given $r = 0.10$
A	$100	—	$100	$100.00
B	−$10	$115	$-\$10 + \$115/(1 + r)$	$94.55
C	$119	−$20	$\$119 - \$20/(1 + r)$	$100.82

From the fifth column, we can immediately see which is the preferred project—it is project C. That's because it has the highest net present value, $100.82, which is higher than the net present value of project A ($100) and much higher than the net present value of project B ($94.55).

This example shows how important the concept of present value is. If we had failed to use the present value calculations and instead simply added up the dollars generated by each of the three projects, we could easily have been misled into believing that project B was the best project and project C was the worst when the reverse is actually the case.

Determining the value of a bond is another example of the need to consider present value. Recall from Module 22 that a bond is an IOU issued by its seller with a promise to pay back the value of the bond plus interest on the maturity date. The price paid by the buyer is the principle value of the bond. The interest is the bond seller's payment for the benefit of having access to funds today. Because interest rates are determined in the market, they can change between the time a bond is purchased and its repayment. Higher interest rates increase the opportunity cost of holding money. When the market interest rate increases, bond sellers must pay that higher interest rate on new bonds they sell. Because newly issued bonds pay a higher interest rate, older bonds that pay a lower interest rate are now less valuable. A buyer looking to resell an older bond must lower the price to reflect the fact that the older bond pays an interest rate that is now below the market interest rate paid on newly issued bonds. Put simply, an increase in the interest rate decreases the present value of a bond (and, conversely, a decrease in the interest rate increases the present value of a bond). Therefore, the interest rate and the price of bonds are inversely related.

A final example of present value at work is seen with lottery jackpots. On March 30, 2012, Mega Millions set the record (surpassed in 2016) for the largest jackpot ever in North America, with a payout of $656 million. Well, sort of. That $656 million was available only if you chose to take your winnings in the form of an *annuity*, consisting of an annual payment for the next 26 years. If you wanted cash up front, the jackpot was only $471 million and change.

Why was Mega Millions so stingy about quick payoffs? It was all a matter of present value. If the winner had been willing to take the annuity, the lottery would have invested the jackpot money, buying U.S. government bonds (in effect lending the money to the federal government). The money would have been invested in such a way that the investments would pay just enough to cover the annuity. This worked, of course, because at the interest rates prevailing at the time, the present value of a $656 million annuity spread over 26 years was just about $471 million. To put it another way, the opportunity cost to the lottery of that annuity in present value terms was $471 million.

So why didn't they just call it a $471 million jackpot? Well, $656 million sounds more impressive! But receiving $656 million over 26 years is essentially the same as receiving $471 million today.

David Gould/Getty Images

MODULE 24 REVIEW

Check Your Understanding

1. Consider the three hypothetical projects shown in Table 24.1. This time, however, suppose that the interest rate is only 2%.
   a. Calculate the net present values of the three projects. Which one is now preferred?

   b. Explain why the preferred choice is different with a 2% interest rate than with a 10% interest rate.

TACKLE THE AP® TEST: Multiple-Choice Questions

1. The interest rate on a loan measures which of the following?
   a. the amount the borrower must pay back
   b. the cost of using a dollar tomorrow rather than today
   c. the benefit of using a dollar today
   d. the price of borrowing money calculated as a percentage of the amount borrowed
   e. all of the above

2. If the interest rate is zero, then the present value of a dollar received at the end of the year is
   a. more than $1.
   b. equal to $1.
   c. less than $1.
   d. zero.
   e. infinite.

3. If the interest rate is 10%, the present value of $1 paid to you one year from now is
   a. $0.
   b. $0.89.
   c. $0.91.
   d. $1.
   e. more than $1.

4. If the interest rate is 5%, the future value of $100 lent today is
   a. $90.
   b. $95.
   c. $100.
   d. $105.
   e. $110.

5. What is the present value of $100 realized two years from now if the interest rate is 10%?
   a. $80
   b. $83
   c. $90
   d. $100
   e. $110

6. If you are choosing between multiple projects with costs and benefits that accrue over multiple years, you should select the project with the highest
   a. present value.
   b. future value.
   c. net present value.
   d. interest rate.
   e. project cost.

7. Which of the following is true as the interest rate increases?
   a. the price of bonds decreases
   b. future value decreases
   c. net present value increases
   d. the cost of borrowing decreases
   e. the opportunity cost of spending decreases

TACKLE THE AP® TEST: Free-Response Questions

1. a. Calculate the net present value of each of the three hypothetical projects described below. Assume the interest rate is 5%.
   Project A: You receive an immediate payoff of $1,000.
   Project B: You pay $100 today in order to receive $1,200 a year from now.
   Project C: You receive $1,200 today but must pay $200 one year from now.
   b. Which of the three projects would you choose to undertake based on your net present value calculations? Explain.

> **Rubric for FRQ 1 (5 points)**
>
> **1 point:** Project A net present value: $1,000
>
> **1 point:** Project B net present value: $-$100 + ($1,200/1.05) = $1,042.86
>
> **1 point:** Project C net present value: $1,200 − ($200/1.05) = $1,009.52
>
> **1 point:** Choose project B.
>
> **1 point:** It has the highest net present value.

2. a. What is the future value of a three-year loan of $1,000 at 5% interest? Show your work.
   b. What is the present value of $1,000 received in three years if the interest rate is 5%? Show your work. **(4 points)**

Banking and Money Creation

In this Module, you will learn to:
- Describe the role of banks in the economy
- Identify the reasons for and types of banking regulation
- Explain how banks create money

The Monetary Role of Banks

Over 40% of M1, the narrowest definition of the money supply, consists of currency in circulation—those bills and coins held by the public. It's obvious where U.S. currency comes from: it's printed or minted by the U.S. Treasury. But the rest of M1 consists of bank deposits, and deposits account for a significant portion of M2, the broader definition of the money supply. By either measure, then, bank deposits are an important part of the money supply. And this fact brings us to our next topic: the monetary role of banks.

What Banks Do

A bank is a *financial intermediary* that uses bank deposits, which you will recall are liquid assets, to finance borrowers' investments in illiquid assets such as businesses and homes. Banks can lend depositors' money to investors and thereby create liquidity because it isn't necessary for a bank to keep all of its deposits on hand. Except in the case of a *bank run*—which we'll discuss shortly—all of a bank's depositors won't want to withdraw their funds at the same time.

However, banks can't lend out *all* the funds placed in their hands by depositors because they have to satisfy any depositor who wants to withdraw his or her funds. In order to meet these demands, a bank must keep substantial quantities of liquid assets on hand. In the modern U.S. banking system, these assets take the form of either currency in the bank's vault or deposits held in the bank's own account at the Federal Reserve. As we'll see shortly, the latter can be converted into currency more or less instantly. Currency in bank vaults and bank deposits held by central banks are called **bank reserves**. Because bank reserves are in bank vaults and at the Federal Reserve, not held by the public, they are not part of currency in circulation.

To understand the role of banks in determining the money supply, we start by introducing a simple tool for analyzing a bank's financial position: a T-account. A business's T-account summarizes its financial position by showing, in a single table, the business's assets and liabilities, with assets on the left and liabilities on the right. **Figure 25.1** shows the T-account for a hypothetical business that *isn't* a bank—Samantha's Smoothies. According to Figure 25.1, Samantha's Smoothies owns a building worth $30,000 and has $15,000 worth of smoothie-making equipment. These are assets, so they're on

Bank reserves are the currency that banks hold in their vaults plus their deposits at the Federal Reserve.

Figure 25.1   A T-Account for Samantha's Smoothies

Assets		Liabilities and Owner's Equity	
Building	$30,000	Loan from bank	$20,000
Smoothie-making machines	$15,000	Owner's equity	$25,000

A T-account summarizes a business's financial position. Its assets, in this case consisting of a building and some smoothie-making machinery, are on the left side. Its liabilities—the money it owes to a local bank—are on the right side, along with the owner's equity.

the left side of the table. To finance its opening, the business borrowed $20,000 from a local bank. That's a liability, so the loan is on the right side of the table. *Owner's equity* of $25,000 balances the two sides of the T-account. Owner's equity is equal to the amount of assets minus the amount of liabilities and represents the owner's financial investment in the business. By looking at the T-account, you can immediately see what Samantha's Smoothies owns and what it owes. This type of table is called a T-account because the lines in the table make a T-shape.

Samantha's Smoothies is an ordinary, nonbank business. Now let's look at the T-account for a hypothetical bank, First Street Bank, which is the repository of $1 million in bank deposits.

Figure 25.2 shows First Street's financial position. The loans First Street has made are on the left side because they are assets: they represent funds that those who have borrowed from the bank are expected to repay. The bank's only other assets, in this simplified example, are its reserves, which, as we've learned, can take the form of either cash in the bank's vault or deposits at the Federal Reserve. On the right side we show the bank's liabilities, which in this example consist entirely of deposits made by customers at First Street. These are liabilities because they represent funds that must ultimately be repaid to depositors. Notice, by the way, that in this example First Street's assets are larger than its liabilities by the amount of the bank's capital. That's the way it's supposed to be! In fact, banks are required by law to maintain assets larger than their liabilities by a specific percentage.

Figure 25.2   Assets and Liabilities of First Street Bank

First Street Bank's assets consist of $1,000,000 in loans and $100,000 in reserves. Its liabilities consist of $1,000,000 in deposits—money owed to people who have placed funds in First Street's hands; this amount is combined with the bank's capital of $100,000.

Assets		Liabilities and Bank's Capital	
Loans	$1,000,000	Deposits	$1,000,000
Reserves	$100,000	Bank's capital	$100,000

In this example, First Street Bank holds reserves equal to 10% of its customers' bank deposits. The fraction of bank deposits that a bank holds as reserves is its **reserve ratio**.

In the modern American system, the Federal Reserve—which, among other things, regulates banks operating in the United States—sets a **required reserve ratio**, which is the smallest fraction of bank deposits that a bank must hold. To understand why banks are regulated, let's consider a problem banks can face: *bank runs*.

The Problem of Bank Runs

A bank can lend out most of the funds deposited in its care because in normal times only a small fraction of its depositors want to withdraw their funds on any given day. But what would happen if, for some reason, all or at least a large fraction of its depositors *did* try to withdraw their funds during a short period of time, such as a couple of days?

The answer is that the bank wouldn't be able to raise enough cash to meet those demands. The reason is that banks convert most of their depositors' funds into loans made to borrowers; that's how banks earn revenue—by charging interest on loans. Bank loans, however, are illiquid: they can't easily be converted into cash on short notice. To see why, imagine that First Street Bank has lent $100,000 to Drive-a-Peach Used Cars, a local dealership. To raise cash to meet demands for withdrawals, First Street can sell its Drive-a-Peach loan to someone else—another bank or an individual investor. But if First Street tries to sell the loan quickly, potential buyers will be wary: they will suspect that First Street wants to sell the loan because there is significant risk that the loan might not be repaid. As a result, First Street Bank can sell the loan quickly only by offering it for sale at a deep discount—say, a discount of 50%, or $50,000.

The upshot is that, if a significant number of First Street's depositors suddenly decided to withdraw their funds, the bank's efforts to raise the necessary cash quickly would force it to sell off its assets very cheaply. Inevitably, this would lead to a *bank failure*: the bank would be unable to pay off its depositors in full.

What might lead First Street's depositors to rush to pull their money out? A plausible answer is a spreading rumor that the bank is in financial trouble. Even if depositors aren't sure the rumor is true, they are likely to play it safe and get their money out while they still can. And it gets worse: a depositor who simply thinks that *other* depositors are going to panic and try to get their money out will realize that this could "break the bank." So he or she joins the rush. In other words, fear about a bank's financial condition can be a self-fulfilling prophecy: depositors who believe that other depositors will rush to the exit will rush to the exit themselves.

A **bank run** is a phenomenon in which many of a bank's depositors try to withdraw their funds due to fears of a bank failure. Moreover, bank runs aren't bad only for the bank in question and its depositors. Historically, they have often proved contagious, with a run on one bank leading to a loss of faith in other banks, causing additional bank runs. A wave of bank runs that swept across the United States at the start of the Great Depression eventually led 40% of banks to fail by the end of 1932. In response to that experience and similar experiences in other countries, the United States and most other modern governments have established a system of bank regulations that protects depositors and prevents most bank runs.

> A **bank run** is a phenomenon in which many of a bank's depositors try to withdraw their funds due to fears of a bank failure.

Bank Regulation

Should you worry about losing money in the United States due to a bank run? No. After the banking crises of the 1930s, the United States and most other countries put into place a system designed to protect depositors and the economy as a whole against bank runs. This system has three main features: *deposit insurance*, *capital requirements*, and *reserve requirements*. In addition, banks have access to the *discount window*, a source of loans from the Federal Reserve when they're needed.

Deposit Insurance

Almost all banks in the United States advertise themselves as a "member of the FDIC"—the Federal Deposit Insurance Corporation. Recall from Module 22 that the FDIC provides deposit insurance, a guarantee that depositors will be paid even if the bank can't come up with the funds, up to a maximum amount per account. As this book was going to press, the FDIC guaranteed the first $250,000 of each account.

It's important to realize that deposit insurance doesn't just protect depositors if a bank actually fails. The insurance also eliminates the main reason for bank runs: since depositors know their funds are safe even if a bank fails, they have no incentive to rush to pull them out because of a rumor that the bank is in trouble.

Capital Requirements

Deposit insurance, although it protects the banking system against bank runs, creates a well-known incentive problem. Because depositors are protected from loss, they have no incentive to monitor their bank's financial health, allowing risky behavior by the bank to go undetected. At the same time, the owners of banks have an incentive to engage in overly risky investment behavior, such as making questionable loans at high interest rates. That's because if all goes well, the owners profit; and if things go badly, the government covers the losses through federal deposit insurance.

To reduce the incentive for excessive risk-taking, regulators require that the owners of banks hold substantially more assets than the value of bank deposits. That way, the bank will have assets larger than its deposits even if some of its loans go bad, and losses will accrue against the bank owners' assets, rather than against the government. The excess of a bank's assets over its bank deposits and other liabilities is called the *bank's capital*. For example, First Street Bank has capital of $100,000, equal to 9% of the total value of its assets. In practice, a bank is required to have capital equal to at least 7% of the value of its assets.

Reserve Requirements

Reserve requirements are rules set by the Federal Reserve that determine the required reserve ratio for banks.

Another regulation used to reduce the risk of bank runs is **reserve requirements**, rules set by the Federal Reserve that establish the required reserve ratio for banks. For example, in the United States, the required reserve ratio for checkable bank deposits is currently between zero and 10%, depending on the amount deposited at the bank.

The Discount Window

One final protection against bank runs is the fact that the Federal Reserve stands ready to lend money to banks through a channel known as the discount window. The ability to borrow money means a bank can avoid being forced to sell its assets at fire-sale prices in order to satisfy the demands of a sudden rush of depositors demanding cash. Instead, it can turn to the Federal Reserve and borrow the funds it needs to pay off depositors.

Determining the Money Supply

Without banks, there would be no checkable deposits, and so the quantity of currency in circulation would equal the money supply. In that case, the money supply would be determined solely by whoever controls government minting and printing presses. But banks do exist, and through their creation of checkable bank deposits, they affect the money supply in two ways. First, banks remove some currency from circulation: dollar bills that are sitting in bank vaults, as opposed to sitting in people's wallets, aren't part of the money supply. Second, and much more importantly, banks create money by accepting deposits and making loans—that is, they make the money supply larger than just the value of currency in circulation. Our next topic is how banks create money and what determines the amount of money they create.

AP® EXAM TIP

When we say that banks create money, we mean that they increase the amount recorded in depositors' accounts; they don't print more currency—only the Treasury does that. The AP® exam will ask about the money creation process—make sure you distinguish between creating and printing money.

How Banks Create Money

To see how banks create money, let's examine what happens when someone decides to deposit currency in a bank. Consider the example of Silas, a miser who keeps a shoebox full of cash under his bed. Suppose Silas realizes that it would be safer, as well as more convenient, to deposit that cash in the bank and to use his debit card when shopping. Assume that he deposits $1,000 into a checkable account at First Street Bank. What effect will Silas's actions have on the money supply?

Panel (a) of **Figure 25.3** shows the initial effect of his deposit. First Street Bank credits Silas with $1,000 in his account, so the economy's checkable bank deposits rise by $1,000. Meanwhile, Silas's cash goes into the vault, raising First Street's reserves by $1,000 as well.

This initial transaction has no effect on the money supply. Currency in circulation, part of the money supply, falls by $1,000; checkable bank deposits, also part of the money supply, rise by the same amount.

But this is not the end of the story because First Street Bank can now lend out part of Silas's deposit. Assume that it holds 10% of Silas's deposit—$100—in reserves and lends the rest out in cash to Silas's neighbor, Mary. The effect of this second stage is shown in panel (b) of Figure 25.3. First Street's deposits remain unchanged, and so does the value of its assets. But the composition of its assets changes: by making the loan, it reduces its reserves by $900, so that they are only $100 larger than they were before Silas

Jonathan Kitchen/Getty Images

Figure 25.3 Effect on the Money Supply of Turning Cash into a Checkable Deposit at First Street Bank

(a) Initial Effect Before Bank Makes a New Loan

Assets		Liabilities	
Loans	No change	Checkable deposits	+$1,000
Reserves	+$1,000		

(b) Effect When Bank Makes a New Loan

Assets		Liabilities	
Loans	+$900	No change	
Reserves	−$900		

When Silas deposits $1,000 (which had been stashed under his bed) into a checkable bank account, there is initially no effect on the money supply: currency in circulation falls by $1,000, but checkable bank deposits rise by $1,000. The corresponding entries on the bank's T-account, depicted in panel (a), show deposits initially rising by $1,000 and the bank's reserves initially rising by $1,000. In the second stage, depicted in panel (b), the bank holds 10% of Silas's deposit ($100) as reserves and lends out the rest ($900) to Mary. As a result, its reserves fall by $900 and its loans increase by $900. Its liabilities, including Silas's $1,000 deposit, are unchanged. The money supply, the sum of checkable bank deposits and currency in circulation, has now increased by $900—the $900 now held by Mary.

made his deposit. In the place of the $900 reduction in reserves, the bank has acquired an IOU, its $900 cash loan to Mary. So by putting $900 of Silas's cash back into circulation by lending it to Mary, First Street Bank has, in fact, increased the money supply. That is, the sum of currency in circulation and checkable bank deposits has risen by $900 compared to what it had been when Silas's cash was still under his bed. Although Silas is still the owner of $1,000, now in the form of a checkable deposit, Mary has the use of $900 in cash from her loan.

This may not be the end of the story either. Suppose that Mary uses her cash to buy a laptop from Acme Computers. What does Anne Acme, the store's owner, do with the cash? If she holds on to it, the money supply doesn't increase any further. But suppose she deposits the $900 into a checkable bank deposit—say, at Second Street Bank. Second Street Bank, in turn, will keep only part of that deposit in reserves, lending out the rest, creating still more money.

Assume that Second Street Bank, like First Street Bank, keeps 10% of any bank deposit in reserves and lends out the rest. Then it will keep $90 in reserves and lend out $810 of Anne's deposit to another borrower, further increasing the money supply.

Table 25.1 shows the process of money creation we have described so far. At first the money supply consists only of Silas's $1,000. After he deposits the cash into a checkable bank deposit and the bank makes a loan, the money supply rises to $1,900. After the second deposit and the second loan, the money supply rises to $2,710. And the process will, of course, continue from there. (Although we have considered the case in which Silas places his cash in a checkable bank deposit, the results would be the same if he put it into any type of near-money.) This process will also work in reverse. When loans are repaid, money is destroyed.

Table 25.1 How Banks Create Money

	Currency in circulation	Checkable bank deposits	Money supply
First stage: Silas keeps his cash under his bed.	$1,000	$0	$1,000
Second stage: Silas deposits cash in First Street Bank, which lends out $900 to Mary, who then pays it to Anne Acme.	900	1,000	1,900
Third stage: Anne Acme deposits $900 in Second Street Bank, which lends out $810 to another borrower.	810	1,900	2,710

This process of money creation and destruction may sound familiar. Recall the *spending multiplier process* that we described in Module 16: an initial increase in spending leads to a rise in real GDP, which leads to a further rise in spending, which leads to a further rise in real GDP, and so on. What we have here is another kind of multiplier—the *money multiplier*. Next, we'll learn what determines the size of this multiplier.

Reserves, Bank Deposits, and the Money Multiplier

In tracing out the effect of Silas's deposit in Table 25.1, we assumed that the funds a bank lends out always end up being deposited either in the same bank or in another bank—so funds disbursed as loans come back to the banking system, even if not to the lending bank itself. In reality, some of these loaned funds may be held by borrowers in their wallets and not deposited in a bank, meaning that some of the loaned amount "leaks" out of the banking system. Such leaks reduce the size of the money multiplier, just as leaks of real income into savings reduce the size of the real GDP multiplier. (Bear in mind, however, that the "leak" here comes from the fact that borrowers keep some of their funds in currency, rather than the fact that consumers save some of their income.) But let's set that complication aside for a moment and consider how the money supply is determined in a "checkable-deposits-only" monetary system, in which funds are always deposited in bank accounts and none are held in wallets as currency. That is, in our checkable-deposits-only monetary system, any and all funds borrowed from a bank are immediately deposited into a checkable bank account. We'll assume that banks are required to satisfy a minimum reserve ratio of 10% and that every bank lends out all of its **excess reserves**, reserves over and above the amount needed to satisfy the minimum reserve ratio.

Now suppose that for some reason a bank suddenly finds itself with $1,000 in excess reserves. What happens? The answer is that the bank will lend out that $1,000, which will end up as a checkable bank deposit somewhere in the banking system, launching a money multiplier process very similar to the process shown in Table 25.1. In the first stage, the bank lends out its excess reserves of $1,000, which becomes a checkable bank deposit somewhere. The bank that receives the $1,000 deposit keeps 10%, or $100, as reserves and lends out the remaining 90%, or $900, which again becomes a checkable bank deposit somewhere. The bank receiving this $900 deposit again keeps 10%, which is $90, as reserves and lends out the remaining $810. The bank receiving this $810 keeps $81 in reserves and lends out the remaining $729, and so on. As a result of this process, the total increase in checkable bank deposits is equal to a sum that looks like:

$$\$1,000 + \$900 + \$810 + \$729 + \ldots$$

We'll use the symbol *rr* for the reserve ratio. More generally, the total increase in checkable bank deposits that is generated when a bank lends out $1,000 in excess reserves is:

(25-1) $\$1,000 + \$1,000 \times (1 - rr) + \$1,000 \times (1 - rr)^2 + \$1,000 \times (1 - rr)^3 + \ldots$

As we saw in Module 16, an infinite series of this form can be simplified to $\$1,000/rr$. We will formally define the money multiplier in the next section, but we can now see its usefulness: it is the factor by which we multiply an initial increase in excess reserves to find the total resulting increase in checkable bank deposits:

$$\textbf{(25-2)} \quad \text{Money multiplier} = \frac{1}{rr}$$

Given a reserve ratio of 10%, or 0.1, a $1,000 increase in excess reserves will increase the total value of checkable bank deposits by $\$1,000 \times 1/rr = \$1,000/0.1 = \$10,000$. In fact, in a checkable deposits-only monetary system, the total value of checkable bank deposits will be equal to the value of bank reserves divided by the reserve ratio.

Excess reserves are a bank's reserves over and above its required reserves.

Or to put it a different way, if the reserve ratio is 10%, each $1 of reserves held by a bank supports $1/rr = \$1/0.1 = \$10$ of checkable bank deposits.

The Money Multiplier in Reality

In reality, the determination of the money supply is more complicated than our simple model suggests because it depends not only on the ratio of reserves to bank deposits but also on the fraction of the money supply that individuals choose to hold in the form of currency. In fact, we already saw this in our example of Silas depositing the cash instead of holding it under his bed: when he chose to hold a checkable bank deposit instead of currency, he set in motion an increase in the money supply.

To define the money multiplier in practice, we need to understand that central banks control the **monetary base**, the sum of currency in circulation and the reserves held by banks. A central bank does not determine how that sum is allocated between bank reserves and currency in circulation. Consider Silas and his deposit one more time: by taking the cash from under his bed and depositing it in a bank, he reduced the quantity of currency in circulation but increased bank reserves by an equal amount. So while the allocation of the monetary base changes—the amount in reserves grows and the amount in circulation shrinks—the total of these two, the monetary base, remains unchanged.

The monetary base is different from the money supply in two ways. First, bank reserves, which are part of the monetary base, aren't considered part of the money supply. A $1 bill in someone's wallet is considered part of the money supply because it's available for an individual to spend, but a $1 bill held as bank reserves in a bank vault or deposited at a central bank isn't considered part of the money supply because it's not available for spending. Second, checkable bank deposits, which are part of the money supply because they are available for spending, aren't part of the monetary base.

Figure 25.4 shows the two concepts schematically. The circle on the left represents the monetary base, consisting of bank reserves plus currency in circulation. The circle on the right represents the money supply, consisting mainly of currency in circulation plus checkable or near-checkable bank deposits. As the figure indicates, currency in circulation is part of both the monetary base and the money supply. But bank reserves aren't part of the money supply, and checkable or near-checkable bank deposits aren't part of the monetary base. Normally, most of the monetary base actually consists of currency in circulation, which also makes up about half of the money supply.

Now we can formally define the **money multiplier**: it's the ratio of the money supply to the monetary base. Most importantly, this tells us the total number of dollars created in the banking system by each $1 addition to the monetary base. We have seen that in a simple situation in which banks hold no excess reserves and all cash is deposited in banks, the money multiplier is $1/rr$. So if the reserve requirement is 0.1 (the minimum required ratio for most checkable deposits in the United States), the money multiplier

The **monetary base** is the sum of currency in circulation and bank reserves.

Currency held as bank reserves isn't part of the money supply, but it is part of the monetary base.

The **money multiplier** is the ratio of the money supply to the monetary base. It indicates the total number of dollars created in the banking system by each $1 addition to the monetary base.

Figure 25.4 The Monetary Base and the Money Supply

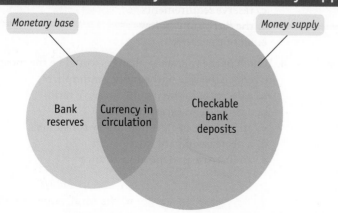

Monetary base

Money supply

Bank reserves

Currency in circulation

Checkable bank deposits

The monetary base is equal to bank reserves plus currency in circulation. It is different from the money supply, which consists mainly of checkable or near-checkable bank deposits plus currency in circulation. Each dollar of bank reserves backs several dollars of bank deposits, making the money supply larger than the monetary base.

is $1/0.1 = 10$; if the Federal Reserve adds $100 to the monetary base, the money supply will increase by $10 \times \$100 = \$1,000$. Normally, the actual money multiplier in the United States, using M1 as our measure of money, is about 1.9. That's a lot smaller than 10. Normally, the reason the actual money multiplier is so small arises from the fact that people hold significant amounts of cash, and a dollar of currency in circulation, unlike a dollar in reserves, doesn't support multiple dollars of the money supply. In fact, currency in circulation normally accounts for more than 90% of the monetary base.

MODULE 25 REVIEW

Adventures in AP® Economics

Watch the video: **The Money Multiplier**

Check Your Understanding

1. Suppose you are a depositor at First Street Bank. You hear a rumor that the bank has suffered serious losses on its loans. Every depositor knows that the rumor isn't true, but each thinks that most other depositors believe the rumor. Why, in the absence of deposit insurance, could this lead to a bank run? How does deposit insurance change the situation?

2. A con artist has a great idea: he'll open a bank without investing any capital and lend all the deposits at high interest rates to real estate developers. If the real estate market booms, the loans will be repaid and he'll make high profits. If the real estate market goes bust, the loans won't be repaid and the bank will fail—but he will not lose any of his own wealth. How would modern bank regulation frustrate his scheme?

3. Assume that total reserves are equal to $200 and total checkable bank deposits are equal to $1,000. Also assume that the public does not hold any currency and banks hold no excess reserves. Now suppose that the required reserve ratio falls from 20% to 10%. Trace out how this leads to an expansion in bank deposits.

4. Take the example of Silas depositing his $1,000 in cash into First Street Bank and assume that the required reserve ratio is 10%. But now assume that each recipient of a bank loan keeps half the loan in cash and deposits the rest. Trace out the resulting expansion in the money supply through at least three rounds of deposits.

TACKLE THE AP® TEST: Multiple-Choice Questions

1. Bank reserves include which of the following?
   a. currency in circulation
   b. bank deposits held in accounts at the Federal Reserve
   c. customer deposits in bank checking accounts
   d. the monetary base
   e. all of the above

2. The fraction of bank deposits *actually* held as reserves is the
   a. reserve ratio.
   b. required reserve ratio.
   c. excess reserve ratio.
   d. reserve requirement.
   e. monetary base.

3. Bank regulation includes which of the following?
   a. deposit insurance
   b. capital requirements
   c. reserve requirements
   d. the discount window
   e. all of the above

4. Which of the following changes would be the most likely to reduce the size of the money multiplier?
   a. a decrease in the required reserve ratio
   b. a decrease in excess reserves
   c. an increase in cash holding by consumers
   d. a decrease in bank runs
   e. an increase in deposit insurance

5. The monetary base equals
  a. currency in circulation.
  b. bank reserves.
  c. currency in circulation − bank reserves.
  d. currency in circulation + bank reserves.
  e. currency in circulation/bank reserves.

6. If a bank has $100,000 in deposits and holds $5,000 in required reserves, what is the value of the money multiplier?
  a. 0.05   d. 20
  b. 0.5   e. 50
  c. 5

7. If the reserve ratio is 10% and excess reserves increase by $1,000, what is the maximum possible increase in checkable deposits throughout the banking system?
  a. $0
  b. $100
  c. $1,000
  d. $10,000
  e. $100,000

TACKLE THE AP® TEST: Free-Response Questions

1. How will each of the following affect the money supply through the money multiplier process? Explain.
  a. People hold more cash.
  b. Banks hold more excess reserves.
  c. The Fed increases the required reserve ratio.

Rubric for FRQ 1 (6 points)

1 point: a: It will decrease.

1 point: Money held as cash does not support multiple dollars in the money supply.

1 point: b: It will decrease.

1 point: Excess reserves are not loaned out and therefore do not expand the money supply.

1 point: c: It will decrease.

1 point: Banks will have to hold more as reserves and therefore loan out less.

2. Suppose the required reserve ratio is 5%.
  a. If a bank has deposits of $100,000 and holds $10,000 as reserves, how much of the $10,000 is excess reserves? Explain.
  b. If a bank holds no excess reserves and it receives a new deposit of $1,000, how much of that $1,000 can the bank lend out and how much is the bank required to add to its reserves? Explain.
  c. By how much can an increase in excess reserves of $2,000 change the money supply in a checkable deposits-only system? Explain. **(4 points)**

The Federal Reserve System: The U.S. Central Bank

In this Module, you will learn to:
• Discuss what events led to the creation of a U.S. central bank
• Describe the structure of the Federal Reserve System
• Explain how the Federal Reserve has responded to major financial crises

The Federal Reserve System

Who's in charge of ensuring that banks maintain enough reserves? Who decides how large the monetary base will be? The answer, in the United States, is an institution known as the Federal Reserve (or, informally, as "the Fed"). The Federal Reserve is a **central bank**—an institution that oversees and regulates a country's banking system

A **central bank** is an institution that oversees and regulates the banking system and controls the monetary base.

The Eccles Building in Washington, D.C., houses the main offices of the Federal Reserve.

AP® Exam Tip

The Federal Reserve is responsible for conducting monetary policy for the United States. Other nations have central banks with different names.

and controls its monetary base. Other central banks include the Bank of England, the Bank of Japan, and the European Central Bank, or ECB.

An Overview of the Twenty-first Century American Banking System

Under normal circumstances, banking is a rather staid and unexciting business. Fortunately, bankers and their customers like it that way. However, there have been repeated episodes in which "sheer panic" would be the best description of banking conditions—the panic induced by a bank run and the specter of the collapse of a bank or multiple banks, leaving depositors penniless, bank shareholders wiped out, and borrowers unable to get credit. In the previous section, we introduced some of the regulations that help maintain stability in the banking system. In this section, we'll give an overview of the behavior and regulation of the American banking system over the last century.

The creation of the Federal Reserve System in 1913 was largely a response to lessons learned in the Panic of 1907. In 2008, the United States found itself in the midst of a financial crisis that in many ways mirrored the Panic of 1907, which occurred almost exactly 100 years earlier.

Crisis in American Banking at the Turn of the Twentieth Century

The creation of the Federal Reserve System in 1913 marked the beginning of the modern era of American banking. From 1864 until 1913, American banking was dominated by a federally regulated system of national banks. They alone were allowed to issue currency, and the currency notes they issued were printed by the federal government with uniform size and design. How much currency a national bank could issue depended on its capital. Although this system was an improvement on the earlier period in which banks issued their own notes with no uniformity and virtually no regulation, the national banking regime still suffered numerous bank failures and major financial crises—at least one and often two per decade.

The main problem afflicting the system was that the money supply was not sufficiently responsive: it was difficult to shift currency around the country to respond quickly to local economic changes. In particular, there was often a tug-of-war between New York City banks and rural banks for adequate amounts of currency. Rumors that a bank had insufficient currency to satisfy demands for withdrawals would quickly lead to a bank run. A bank run would then spark a contagion, setting off runs at other nearby banks, sowing widespread panic and devastation in the local economy. In response, bankers in some locations pooled their resources to create local clearinghouses that would jointly guarantee a member's liabilities in the event of a panic, and some state governments began offering deposit insurance on their banks' deposits.

However, the cause of the Panic of 1907 was different from those of previous crises; in fact, its cause was eerily similar to the roots of the 2008 crisis. Ground zero of the 1907 panic was New York City, but the consequences devastated the entire country, leading to a deep four-year recession. The crisis originated in institutions in New York known as trusts, bank-like institutions that accepted deposits but that were originally intended to manage only inheritances and estates for wealthy clients. Because these trusts were supposed to engage only in low-risk activities, they were less regulated, had lower reserve requirements, and had lower cash reserves than national banks. However, as the American economy boomed during the first decade of the twentieth century, trusts began speculating in real estate and the stock market, areas of speculation forbidden to national banks.

In both the Panic of 1907, which led to an epidemic of bank runs like the one pictured here, and the financial crisis of 2008, large losses from risky speculation destabilized the banking system.

Being less regulated than national banks, trusts were able to pay their depositors higher returns. Yet trusts took a free ride on national banks' reputation for soundness, with depositors considering them equally safe. As a result, trusts grew rapidly: by 1907, the total assets of trusts in New York City were as large as those of national banks. Meanwhile, the trusts declined to join the New York Clearinghouse, a consortium of New York City national banks that guaranteed one another's soundness; joining the clearinghouse would have required the trusts to hold higher cash reserves, reducing their profits.

The Panic of 1907 began with the failure of the Knickerbocker Trust, a large New York City trust that failed when it suffered massive losses in unsuccessful stock market speculation. Quickly, other New York trusts came under pressure, and frightened depositors began queuing in long lines to withdraw their funds. The New York Clearinghouse declined to step in and lend to the trusts, and even healthy trusts came under serious assault. Within two days, a dozen major trusts had gone under. Credit markets froze, and the stock market fell dramatically as stock traders were unable to get credit to finance their trades and business confidence evaporated.

Fortunately, one of New York City's wealthiest men, the banker J. P. Morgan, quickly stepped in to stop the panic. Understanding that the crisis was spreading and would soon engulf healthy institutions, trusts and banks alike, he worked with other bankers, wealthy men such as John D. Rockefeller, and the U.S. Secretary of the Treasury to shore up the reserves of banks and trusts so they could withstand the onslaught of withdrawals. Once people were assured that they could withdraw their money, the panic ceased. Although the panic itself lasted little more than a week, it and the stock market collapse decimated the economy. A four-year recession ensued, with production falling 11% and unemployment rising from 3% to 8%.

Responding to Banking Crises: The Creation of the Federal Reserve

Concerns over the frequency of banking crises and the unprecedented role of J. P. Morgan in saving the financial system prompted the federal government to initiate banking reform. In 1913 the national banking system was eliminated and the Federal Reserve System was created as a way to compel all deposit-taking institutions to hold adequate reserves and to open their accounts to inspection by regulators. The Panic of 1907 convinced many that the time for centralized control of bank reserves had come. The Federal Reserve was given the sole right to issue currency in order to make the money supply sufficiently responsive to satisfy economic conditions around the country.

The Structure of the Fed

The legal status of the Fed is unusual: it is not exactly part of the U.S. government, but it is not really a private institution either. Strictly speaking, the Federal Reserve System consists of two parts: the Board of Governors and the 12 regional Federal Reserve Banks.

The Board of Governors, which oversees the entire system from its offices in Washington, D.C., is constituted like a government agency: its seven members are appointed by the president and must be approved by the Senate. However, they are appointed for 14-year terms, to insulate them from political pressure in their conduct of monetary policy. Although the chair is appointed more frequently—every four years—it is traditional for the chair to be reappointed and serve a much longer term. For example, William McChesney Martin was chair of the Fed from 1951 until 1970. Alan Greenspan, appointed in 1987, served as the Fed's chair until 2006.

The 12 Federal Reserve Banks each serve a region of the country, known as a *Federal Reserve district*, providing various banking and supervisory services. One of their jobs, for example, is to audit the books of private-sector banks to ensure their financial health. Each regional bank is run by a board of directors chosen from the local banking and business community. The Federal Reserve Bank of New York plays a special role: it carries out *open market operations*, usually the main tool of monetary policy. **Figure 26.1** shows the 12 Federal Reserve districts and the city in which each regional Federal Reserve Bank is located.

Figure 26.1 The Federal Reserve System

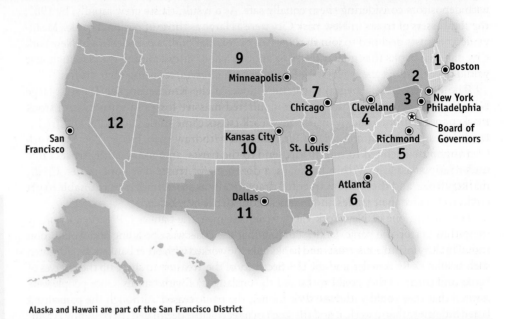

The Federal Reserve System consists of the Board of Governors in Washington, D.C., plus 12 regional Federal Reserve Banks. This map shows each of the 12 Federal Reserve districts.

Data Source: Board of Governors of the Federal Reserve System.

Alaska and Hawaii are part of the San Francisco District

Decisions about monetary policy are made by the Federal Open Market Committee, which consists of the Board of Governors plus five of the regional bank presidents. The president of the Federal Reserve Bank of New York is always on the committee, and the other four seats rotate among the 11 other regional bank presidents. The chair of the Board of Governors normally also serves as the chair of the Federal Open Market Committee.

The effect of this complex structure is to create an institution that is ultimately accountable to the voting public because the Board of Governors is chosen by the president and confirmed by the Senate, all of whom are themselves elected officials. But the long terms served by board members, as well as the indirectness of their appointment process, largely insulate them from short-term political pressures.

The Effectiveness of the Federal Reserve System

Although the Federal Reserve System standardized and centralized the holding of bank reserves, it did not eliminate the potential for bank runs because banks' reserves were still less than the total value of their deposits. The potential for more bank runs became a reality during the Great Depression. Plunging commodity prices hit American farmers particularly hard, precipitating a series of bank runs in 1930, 1931, and 1933, each of which started at midwestern banks and then spread throughout the country. After the failure of a particularly large bank in 1930, federal officials realized that the economy-wide effects compelled them to take a less hands-off approach and to intervene more vigorously. In 1932, the Reconstruction Finance Corporation (RFC) was established and given the authority to make loans to banks in order to stabilize the banking sector. In addition, the Glass-Steagall Act of 1933, which increased the ability of banks to borrow from the Federal Reserve System, was passed. A loan to a leading Chicago bank from the Federal Reserve appears to have stopped a major banking crisis in 1932. However, the beast had not yet been tamed. Banks became fearful of borrowing from the RFC because doing so signaled weakness to the public.

In the midst of the catastrophic bank run of 1933, the new U.S. president, Franklin D. Roosevelt, was inaugurated. He immediately declared a "bank holiday," closing all banks until regulators could get a handle on the problem. In March 1933, emergency measures were adopted that gave the RFC extraordinary powers to stabilize and restructure the banking industry by providing capital to banks either by loans or by outright purchases of bank shares. With the new regulations, regulators closed nonviable banks and recapitalized viable ones by allowing the RFC to buy preferred shares in banks (shares that gave the U.S. government more rights than regular shareholders) and by greatly expanding banks' ability to borrow from the Federal Reserve. By 1933, the RFC had invested over $17 billion (2013 dollars) in bank capital—one-third of the total capital of all banks in the United States at that time—and purchased shares in almost one-half of all banks. The RFC loaned more than $34 billion (2013 dollars) to banks during this period.

Economic historians uniformly agree that the banking crises of the early 1930s greatly exacerbated the severity of the Great Depression, rendering monetary policy ineffective as the banking sector broke down and currency, withdrawn from banks and stashed under beds, reduced the money supply.

Like Franklin D. Roosevelt, President Obama, shown here meeting with economic advisers, was faced with a major financial crisis upon taking office.

Although the powerful actions of the RFC stabilized the banking industry, new legislation was needed to prevent future banking crises. The Glass-Steagall Act of 1933 separated banks into two categories, **commercial banks**, depository banks that accepted deposits and were covered by deposit insurance, and **investment banks**, which engaged in creating and trading financial assets such as stocks and corporate bonds but were not covered by deposit insurance because their activities were considered more risky. Regulation Q, which was part of the Glass-Steagall Act, prevented commercial banks from paying interest on checking accounts, in the belief that this would promote unhealthy competition between banks. In addition, investment banks were much more lightly regulated than commercial banks. The most important measure for the prevention of bank runs, however, was the adoption of federal deposit insurance (with an original limit of $2,500 per deposit).

A **commercial bank** accepts deposits and is covered by deposit insurance.

An **investment bank** trades in financial assets and is not covered by deposit insurance.

These measures were clearly successful, and the United States enjoyed a long period of financial and banking stability. As memories of the bad old days dimmed, Depression-era bank regulations were lifted. Regulation Q was eliminated in 1980 and by 1999, the Glass-Steagall Act had been so weakened that commercial banks could deal in stocks and bonds among other financial assets.

The Savings and Loan Crisis of the 1980s

Along with banks, the banking industry also included savings and loans (also called S&Ls or thrifts), institutions established to accept savings and turn them into long-term mortgages for home-buyers. S&Ls were covered by federal deposit insurance and were tightly regulated for safety. However, trouble hit in the 1970s, as high inflation led savers to withdraw their funds from low-interest-paying S&L accounts and put them into higher-paying money market accounts. In addition, the high inflation rate severely eroded the value of the S&Ls' assets, the long-term mortgages they held on their books.

In order to improve S&Ls' competitive position versus banks, Congress eased regulations to allow S&Ls to undertake much more risky investments in addition to long-term home mortgages. However, the new freedom did not bring with it increased oversight, leaving S&Ls with less oversight than banks.

Not surprisingly, during the real estate boom of the 1970s and 1980s, S&Ls engaged in overly risky real estate lending. Also, corruption occurred as some S&L executives used their institutions as private piggy banks. By the early 1980s, a large number of S&Ls had failed. Because accounts were covered by federal deposit insurance, the liabilities of a failed S&L were now liabilities of the federal government. From 1986 through 1995, the federal government closed over 1,000 failed S&Ls, costing U.S. taxpayers over $124 billion.

In a classic case of shutting the barn door after the horse has escaped, in 1989 Congress put in place comprehensive oversight of S&L activities. It also empowered Fannie Mae and Freddie Mac to take over much of the home mortgage lending previously done by S&Ls. Fannie Mae and Freddie Mac are quasi-governmental agencies created during the Great Depression to make homeownership more affordable for low- and moderate-income households. There is evidence that the S&L crisis helped cause a steep slowdown in the finance and real estate industries, leading to the recession of the early 1990s.

Back to the Future: The Financial Crisis of 2008

The financial crisis of 2008 shared features of previous crises. Like the Panic of 1907 and the S&L crisis, it involved institutions that were not as strictly regulated as deposit-taking banks, as well as excessive speculation. And like the crises of the early 1930s, it involved a U.S. government that was reluctant to take aggressive action until the scale of the devastation became clear. Enrichment Module A: Financial Markets and Crises provides a detailed account of the financial crisis of 2008. To summarize the situation briefly, historically low interest rates helped cause a boom in housing between 2003 and 2006. With home prices rising steadily, loans to home-buyers with questionable finances seemed deceptively safe, and the number of such loans exploded. But then housing prices started falling in 2006, leaving many borrowers with homes that were worth less than the mortgage loans used to buy them. The resulting losses for lenders caused a collapse of trust in the financial system. Lending institutions were reluctant to make loans, and firms had difficulty obtaining enough money to continue their operations.

Beginning in mid-2007, the Federal Reserve took ambitious steps to make more cash available in the economy. It provided liquidity to the troubled financial system through discount window lending, and bought large quantities of other assets, mainly long-term government debt and the debt of Fannie Mae and Freddie Mac. The Fed and the Treasury Department also rescued several firms whose collapse could have been catastrophic for the economy, including the investment bank Bear Stearns and the insurance company AIG.

By the fall of 2010, the financial system was relatively stable, and major institutions had repaid much of the money the federal government had injected during the crisis. It was generally expected that taxpayers would end up losing little if any money. Like earlier crises, the crisis of 2008 led to changes in banking regulation, most notably the Dodd-Frank financial regulatory reform bill enacted in 2010. And similar to what happened in the aftermath of previous financial crises, economic recovery has spurred discussion of deregulation. As of this writing in 2018, the Fed is considering easing regulations imposed after the 2007–2009 financial crisis as a way to improve banking industry profitability, efficiency, and competitiveness.

The Dodd-Frank Act, passed in 2010, was one of the many regulations passed in the aftermath of the 2007–2009 financial crisis.

Brooks Kraft/Getty Images

MODULE 26 REVIEW

Check Your Understanding

1. What are the similarities between the Panic of 1907, the S&L crisis, and the crisis of 2008?

2. Why did the creation of the Federal Reserve fail to prevent the bank runs of the Great Depression? What measures stopped the bank runs?

TACKLE THE AP® TEST: Multiple-Choice Questions

1. Which of the following contributed to the creation of the Federal Reserve System?
   a. the bank panic of 1907
   b. the Great Depression
   c. the savings and loan crisis of the 1980s
   d. the financial crisis of 2008
   e. the aftermath of World War II

2. Which of the following institutions controls the monetary base?
   a. the central bank
   b. the Treasury
   c. Congress
   d. commercial banks
   e. investment banks

3. Which of the following is NOT a role of the Federal Reserve System?
   a. controlling bank reserves
   b. printing currency (Federal Reserve notes)
   c. carrying out monetary policy
   d. supervising and regulating banks
   e. holding reserves for commercial banks

4. Who oversees the Federal Reserve System?
   a. Congress
   b. the president of the United States
   c. the Federal Open Market Committee
   d. the Board of Governors of the Federal Reserve System
   e. the Reconstruction Finance Corporation

5. Which of the following contributed to the financial crisis of 2008?
   a. excessive speculation
   b. inadequate regulation
   c. delays in aggressive action by the government
   d. low interest rates leading to a housing boom
   e. all of the above

6. The Federal Open Market Committee is made up of which of the following?
   a. members of the Board of Governors
   b. five voting Federal Reserve Bank presidents
   c. the president of the Federal Reserve Bank of New York
   d. eleven Federal Reserve Bank presidents on a rotating basis
   e. all of the above

7. Which of the following is true regarding central banks?
   a. They only exist in the United States and Europe.
   b. They oversee and regulate the banking system.
   c. They are structured to be part public and part private.
   d. They include multiple regional reserve banks.
   e. All of the above are true.

TACKLE THE AP® TEST: Free-Response Questions

1. a. What group determines monetary policy?
   b. How many members serve in this group?
   c. Who always serves in this group?
   d. Who sometimes serves in this group? Explain.

   Rubric for FRQ 1 (5 points)

   1 point: The Federal Open Market Committee (FOMC)

   1 point: 12

   1 point: Members of the Board of Governors and the New York Federal Reserve Bank president

   1 point: 4 of the other 11 Federal Reserve Bank presidents

   1 point: The 11 other Federal Reserve Bank presidents rotate their service on the FOMC.

   ---

2. a. What does the Board of Governors of the Federal Reserve System do?
   b. How many members serve on the group?
   c. Who appoints members?
   d. How long do members serve?
   e. Why do they serve a term of this length?
   f. How long does the chair serve?
   (6 points)

Central Banks and Monetary Policy

> **In this Module, you will learn to:**
> - Describe the functions of the Federal Reserve System and other central banks
> - Explain the primary tools a central bank uses to influence the economy

The Federal Reserve System

In the previous Module, you learned that the Federal Reserve System serves as the central bank of the United States. The Fed is only one of a number of central banks around the world, and it is much younger than Sweden's Sveriges Riksbank (founded in 1668) and Britain's Bank of England (founded in 1694). But in general, other central banks operate in much the same way as the Fed so we will start with a discussion of the U.S. Federal Reserve System.

The Fed has two parts: the Board of Governors, which is part of the U.S. government, and the 12 regional Federal Reserve Banks, which are privately owned. But what are the functions of the Federal Reserve System, and how does it serve them?

The Functions of the Federal Reserve System

Today, the Federal Reserve's functions fall into four basic categories: providing financial services to depository institutions, supervising and regulating banks and other financial institutions, maintaining the stability of the financial system, and conducting monetary policy. Let's look at each in turn.

Provide Financial Services

The 12 regional Federal Reserve Banks provide financial services to depository institutions such as banks and other large institutions, including the U.S. government. The Federal Reserve is sometimes referred to as the "banker's bank" because it holds reserves, clears checks, provides cash, and transfers funds for commercial banks—all services that banks provide for their customers. The Federal Reserve also acts as the banker and fiscal agent for the federal government. The U.S. Treasury has its checking account with the Federal Reserve, so when the federal government writes a check, it is written on an account at the Fed.

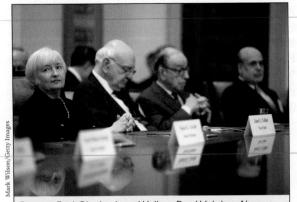

Former Fed Chairs Janet Yellen, Paul Volcker, Alan Greenspan, and Ben Bernanke.

Supervise and Regulate Banking Institutions

The Federal Reserve System is charged with ensuring the safety and soundness of the nation's banking and financial system. Each regional Federal Reserve Bank examines and regulates commercial banks in its district. The Board of Governors also engages in regulation and supervision of financial institutions.

Maintain the Stability of the Financial System

As we have seen, one of the major reasons the Federal Reserve System was created was to provide the nation with a safe and stable monetary and financial system. The Fed is charged with maintaining the integrity of the financial system. As part of this function, Federal Reserve banks provide liquidity to financial institutions to ensure their safety and soundness.

Conduct Monetary Policy

One of the Federal Reserve's most important functions is the conduct of monetary policy. As we will see, the Federal Reserve uses the tools of monetary policy to prevent or address extreme macroeconomic fluctuations in the U.S. economy.

What the Fed Does

How does the Fed perform its functions? The Federal Reserve has three main policy tools at its disposal: *reserve requirements*, the *discount rate*, and, perhaps most importantly, *open market operations*. These tools play a part in how the Fed performs each of its functions as outlined below.

The Reserve Requirement

In our discussion of bank runs, we noted that the Fed sets a minimum required reserve ratio, currently between zero and 10% for checkable bank deposits. Banks that fail to maintain at least the required reserve ratio on average over a two-week period face penalties.

What does a bank do if it has insufficient reserves to meet the Fed's reserve requirement? Normally, it borrows additional reserves from other banks via the federal funds market, a financial market that allows banks that fall short of the reserve requirement to borrow reserves (usually just overnight) from banks that are holding excess reserves. The interest rate in this market is determined by supply and demand, but the supply and demand for bank reserves are both strongly affected by Federal Reserve actions. Later we will see how the **federal funds rate**, the interest rate at which funds are borrowed and lent among banks in the federal funds market, plays a key role in modern monetary policy.

In order to alter the money supply, the Fed can change reserve requirements. If the Fed reduces the required reserve ratio, banks will lend a larger percentage of their deposits, leading to more loans and an increase in the money supply via the money multiplier. Alternatively, if the Fed increases the required reserve ratio, banks are forced to reduce their lending, leading to a fall in the money supply via the money multiplier. Under current practice, however, the Fed doesn't use changes in reserve requirements to actively manage the money supply. The last significant change in reserve requirements was in 1992.

> The **federal funds rate** is the interest rate that banks charge other banks for loans, as determined in the federal funds market.

The Discount Rate

Banks in need of reserves can also borrow from the Fed. The interest rate the Fed charges on those loans is called the **discount rate** because the transactions take place through a lending facility known as the *discount window* (even though the discount window no longer refers to a literal window through which the Fed makes loans to banks). Discount rates are set by each individual reserve bank and must be approved by the Board of Governors. Typically, they are set just above the federal funds rate and move with other short-term interest rates.

The Fed can alter the money supply by changing the discount rate. For example, beginning in the fall of 2007, the Fed reduced the spread between the federal funds rate and the discount rate as part of its response to the ongoing financial crisis. As a result, by the spring of 2008 the discount rate was only 0.25 percentage points above the federal funds rate.

If the Fed reduces the spread between the discount rate and the federal funds rate, the cost to banks of being short of reserves falls. Banks respond by increasing their lending, and the money supply increases via the money multiplier. If the Fed increases the spread between the discount rate and the federal funds rate, bank lending falls—and so will the money supply via the money multiplier.

The Fed normally doesn't use the discount rate to actively manage the money supply. As we mentioned earlier, however, there was a temporary surge in lending through the discount window in 2007 in response to the financial crisis. Today, normal monetary policy is conducted almost exclusively using the Fed's third policy tool: open market operations.

> The **discount rate** is the interest rate the Fed charges on loans to banks.

AP® EXAM TIP

The interest rate targeted by the Federal Reserve when it conducts monetary policy is the federal funds rate. The discount rate is the rate the Federal Reserve charges banks when they borrow from the Fed. Be careful not to confuse these two interest rates on the AP® exam!

Open Market Operations

Like the banks it oversees, the Federal Reserve has assets and liabilities. The Fed's assets consist of its holdings of debt issued by the U.S. government, mainly short-term U.S. government bonds with a maturity of less than one year, known as U.S. Treasury bills. Remember, the Fed and the U.S. government are not one entity; U.S. Treasury bills held by the Fed are a liability of the government but an asset of the Fed. The Fed's liabilities consist of currency in circulation and bank reserves. **Figure 27.1** summarizes the normal assets and liabilities of the Fed in the form of a T-account.

Figure 27.1 The Federal Reserve's Assets and Liabilities

The Federal Reserve holds its assets mostly in short-term government bonds called U.S. Treasury bills. Its liabilities are the monetary base—currency in circulation plus bank reserves.

Assets	Liabilities
Government debt (Treasury bills)	Monetary base (Currency in circulation + bank reserves)

An **open market operation** is a purchase or sale of government debt (bond) by the Fed.

In an **open market operation**, the Federal Reserve buys or sells U.S. Treasury bills, normally through a transaction with *commercial banks*—banks that mainly make business loans, as opposed to home loans. The Fed never buys U.S. Treasury bills directly from the federal government. There's a good reason for this: when a central bank buys government debt directly from the government, it is lending directly to the government—in effect, the central bank is issuing money to finance the government's budget deficit. As we'll see later in the book, this has historically been a formula for disastrous levels of inflation.

The two panels of **Figure 27.2** show the changes in the financial position of both the Fed and commercial banks that result from open market operations. When the Fed buys U.S. Treasury bills from a commercial bank, it pays by crediting the

Figure 27.2 Open Market Operations by the Federal Reserve

(a) An Open Market Purchase of $100 Million

	Assets		Liabilities	
Federal Reserve	Treasury bills	+$100 million	Monetary base	+$100 million

	Assets		Liabilities
Commercial banks	Treasury bills	−$100 million	No change
	Reserves	+$100 million	

(b) An Open Market Sale of $100 Million

	Assets		Liabilities	
Federal Reserve	Treasury bills	−$100 million	Monetary base	−$100 million

	Assets		Liabilities
Commercial banks	Treasury bills	+$100 million	No change
	Reserves	−$100 million	

In panel (a), the Federal Reserve increases the monetary base by purchasing U.S. Treasury bills from private commercial banks in an open market operation. Here, a $100 million purchase of U.S. Treasury bills by the Federal Reserve is paid for by a $100 million increase in the monetary base. This will ultimately lead to an increase in the money supply via the money multiplier as banks lend out some of these new reserves. In panel (b), the Federal

Reserve reduces the monetary base by selling U.S. Treasury bills to private commercial banks in an open market operation. Here, a $100 million sale of U.S. Treasury bills leads to a $100 million reduction in commercial bank reserves, resulting in a $100 million decrease in the monetary base. This will ultimately lead to a fall in the money supply via the money multiplier as banks reduce their loans in response to a fall in their reserves.

bank's reserve account by an amount equal to the value of the Treasury bills. This is illustrated in panel (a): the Fed buys $100 million of U.S. Treasury bills from commercial banks, which increases the monetary base by $100 million because it increases bank reserves by $100 million. When the Fed sells U.S. Treasury bills to commercial banks, it debits the banks' accounts, reducing their reserves. This is shown in panel (b), where the Fed sells $100 million of U.S. Treasury bills. Here, bank reserves and the monetary base decrease.

You might wonder where the Fed gets the funds to purchase U.S. Treasury bills from banks. The answer is that it simply creates them with the stroke of the pen—or, these days, the click of the button—that credits the banks' accounts with extra reserves. The Fed issues currency to pay for Treasury bills only when banks want the additional reserves in the form of currency. Remember, the modern dollar is fiat money, which isn't backed by anything. So the Fed can add to the monetary base at its own discretion.

The change in bank reserves caused by an open market operation doesn't directly affect the money supply (recall from Module 25 that bank reserves are not part of the money supply). Instead, it starts the money multiplier in motion. After the $100 million increase in reserves shown in panel (a), commercial banks would lend out their additional reserves, immediately increasing the money supply by $100 million. Some of those loans would be deposited back into the banking system, increasing reserves again and permitting a further round of loans, and so on, leading to a rise in the money supply. An open market sale has the reverse effect: bank reserves fall, requiring banks to reduce their loans, leading to a fall in the money supply.

Economists often say, loosely, that the Fed controls the money supply—checkable deposits plus currency in circulation. In fact, it controls only the monetary base—bank reserves plus currency in circulation. But by increasing or decreasing the monetary base, the Fed can exert a powerful influence on both the money supply and interest rates. This influence is the basis of monetary policy, discussed in detail in Modules 28 and 29.

The European Central Bank

Central banks in other countries operate in much the same way as the Fed. That's especially true of the only other central bank that rivals the Fed in terms of importance to the world economy: the European Central Bank.

The European Central Bank in Frankfurt, Germany.

The European Central Bank, known as the ECB, was created in January 1999 when 11 European nations abandoned their national currencies, adopted the euro as their common currency, and placed their joint monetary policy in the ECB's hands. (Eight more countries have joined since 1999.) The ECB instantly became an extremely important institution: although no single European nation has an economy anywhere near as large as that of the United States, the combined economies of the eurozone, the group of countries that have adopted the euro as their currency, are roughly as big as the U.S. economy. As a result, the ECB and the Fed are the two giants of the monetary world.

Like the Fed, the ECB has a special status: it's not a private institution, but it's not exactly a government agency either. In fact, it can't be a government agency because there is no pan-European government! Luckily for puzzled Americans, there are strong analogies between European central banking and the Federal Reserve System.

First of all, the ECB, which is located in Frankfurt, Germany, isn't really the counterpart of the whole Federal Reserve System: it's the equivalent of the Board of Governors in Washington. The European counterparts of the regional Federal Reserve Banks are Europe's national central banks: the Bank of France, the Bank of Italy, and so on. Until 1999, each of these national banks was its country's equivalent to the Fed. For example, the Bank of France controlled the French monetary base.

Today these national banks, like regional Feds, provide various financial services to local banks and businesses and conduct open market operations, but the making of monetary policy has moved upstream to the ECB. Still, the various European national central banks aren't small institutions: in total, they employ more than 50,000 people; in 2018, the ECB employed about 2,500.

Each country in the eurozone chooses who runs its own national central bank. The ECB's Executive Board is the counterpart of the Fed's Board of Governors; its members are chosen by unanimous consent of the eurozone national governments. The counterpart of the Federal Open Market Committee is the ECB's Governing Council. Just as the Fed's Open Market Committee consists of the Board of Governors plus a rotating group of regional Fed presidents, the ECB's Governing Council consists of the Executive Board plus the heads of the national central banks.

Like the Fed, the ECB is ultimately answerable to voters. Given the fragmentation of political forces across national boundaries, however, it appears to be even more insulated than the Fed from short-term political pressures.

MODULE 27 REVIEW

Adventures in AP® Economics

Watch the video: *Monetary Policy and the Federal Reserve System*

Check Your Understanding

1. Assume that any money lent by a bank is deposited back into the banking system as a checkable deposit and that the reserve ratio is 10%. Trace out the effects of a $100 million open market purchase of U.S. Treasury bills by the Fed on the value of checkable bank deposits. What is the size of the money multiplier?

TACKLE THE AP® TEST: Multiple-Choice Questions

1. Which of the following is a function of a central bank?
   a. conduct monetary policy
   b. conduct fiscal policy
   c. regulate foreign central banks
   d. print currency
   e. collect taxes

2. Which of the following financial services does the Federal Reserve provide for commercial banks?
   a. clearing checks
   b. holding reserves
   c. making loans
   d. providing cash
   e. all of the above

3. When the Fed makes a loan to a commercial bank, it charges
   a. no interest.
   b. the prime rate.
   c. the federal funds rate.
   d. the discount rate.
   e. the market interest rate.

4. If the Fed purchases U.S. Treasury bills from a commercial bank, what happens to bank reserves and the money supply?

	Bank reserves	Money supply
a.	increase	decrease
b.	increase	increase
c.	decrease	decrease
d.	decrease	increase
e.	increase	no change

5. When banks make loans to each other, they charge the
   a. prime rate.
   b. discount rate.
   c. federal funds rate.
   d. CD rate.
   e. mortgage rate.

6. Which of the following is true of the Federal Reserve system?
   a. It has the same structure as other central banks.
   b. It is made up of four regional reserve banks.
   c. Key decision makers are appointed by the president and approved by the Senate.
   d. It is completely independent of the government.
   e. It is responsible for printing currency and minting coins.

7. Which of the following occurs when a central bank sells government bonds?
   a. Bank reserves are increased.
   b. The monetary base is increased.
   c. The money supply decreases.
   d. Lending by banks increases.
   e. The discount rate increases.

TACKLE THE AP® TEST: Free-Response Questions

1. Assume an economy is experiencing a recession.
   a. What are the three major tools a central bank can use to address the recession?
   b. What would the central bank do with each tool to increase the money supply? Explain for each.

Rubric for FRQ 1 (9 points)

1 point: The discount rate

1 point: The reserve requirement

1 point: Open market operations

1 point: Decrease the discount rate

1 point: A lower discount rate makes it cheaper to borrow from the central bank so the money supply increases.

1 point: Decrease the reserve requirement

1 point: A lower reserve requirement allows banks to loan more, increasing the money supply.

1 point: Buy bonds

1 point: When the central bank buys bonds, banks' excess reserves increase. When lent out, these excess reserves increase the money supply with the assistance of the money multiplier.

2. What are the four basic functions of the Federal Reserve system and what part of the system is responsible for each? **(8 points)**

The Money Market

In this Module, you will learn to:
- Illustrate the relationship between the demand for money and the interest rate with a graph
- Explain why the liquidity preference model determines the interest rate in the short run

The Demand for Money

Remember that M1, the most commonly used definition of the money supply, consists of currency in circulation (cash), plus checkable bank deposits, plus traveler's checks. M2, a broader definition of the money supply, consists of M1 plus deposits that can easily be transferred into checkable deposits. You also learned why people hold money—to make it easier to purchase goods and services. Now we'll go deeper, examining what determines *how much* money individuals and firms want to hold at any given time.

The Opportunity Cost of Holding Money

Most economic decisions involve trade-offs at the margin. That is, individuals decide how much of a good to consume by determining whether the benefit they'd gain from consuming a bit more of that good is worth the cost. The same decision process is used when deciding how much money to hold.

Individuals and firms find it useful to hold some of their assets in the form of money because of the convenience money provides: money can be used to make purchases directly, while other assets can't. But there is a price to be paid—an opportunity cost— for that convenience: money held in your wallet earns no interest.

As an example of how convenience makes it worth incurring some opportunity costs, consider the fact that even today—with the prevalence of credit cards, debit cards, and ATMs—people continue to keep cash in their wallets rather than leave

Cash in your pocket might not earn you any interest, but it is still the most convenient option in some situations, such as when you leave a tip at a restaurant.

the funds in an interest-bearing account. They do this because they don't want to have to go to an ATM to withdraw money every time they want to make a small purchase. In other words, the convenience of keeping some cash in your wallet is more valuable than the interest you would earn by keeping that money in the bank.

Even holding money in a checking account involves a trade-off between convenience and interest payments. That's because you can earn a higher interest rate by putting your money in assets other than a checking account. For example, many banks offer certificates of deposit, or CDs, which pay a higher interest rate than ordinary bank accounts. But CDs also carry a penalty if you withdraw the funds before a certain amount of time—say, six months—has elapsed. An individual who keeps funds in a checking account is forgoing the higher interest rate those funds would have earned if placed in a CD in return for the convenience of having cash readily available when needed.

Since 2007, interest rates have fallen to historical lows, which has decreased the opportunity cost of holding money. **Table 28.1** illustrates the opportunity cost of holding money in a specific month. The first row shows the interest rate on one-year certificates of deposit—that is, the interest rate individuals could get if they were willing to tie their funds up for one year. In November 2017, one-year CDs yielded 1.65%. The second row shows the interest rate on interest-bearing bank accounts (specifically, those included in M1). Funds in these accounts were more accessible than those in CDs, but the price of that convenience was a much lower interest rate, only 0.65%. Finally, the last row shows the interest rate on currency—cash in your wallet—which, of course, was zero.

Table 28.1	Selected Interest Rates, November 2017
One-year CDs	1.65%
Interest-bearing demand deposits	0.65
Currency	0

Source: Bankrate.com.

Table 28.1 shows the opportunity cost of holding money at one point in time, but the opportunity cost of holding money changes when the overall level of interest rates changes. Specifically, when the overall level of interest rates falls, the opportunity cost of holding money falls, too.

Short-Term and Long-Term Interest Rates

Short-term interest rates are the interest rates on financial assets that mature within a year.

Because there are many alternatives to holding money in your wallet, each with its own interest payment, there are many different interest rates in the economy. But all **short-term interest rates**—rates on financial assets that come due, or mature, within a year—tend to move together, with rare exceptions. The reason short-term interest rates tend to move together is that CDs and other short-term assets (like one-month and three-month U.S. Treasury bills) are in effect competing for the same business. Any short-term asset that offers a lower-than-average interest rate will be sold by investors, who will move their wealth into a higher-yielding short-term asset. The selling of the asset, in turn, forces its interest rate up because investors must be rewarded with a higher rate in order to induce them to buy it. Conversely, investors will move their wealth into any short-term financial asset that offers an above-average interest rate. The purchase of the asset drives its interest rate down when sellers find they can lower the rate of return on the asset and still find willing buyers. So interest rates on short-term financial assets tend to be roughly the same because no asset will consistently offer a higher-than-average or a lower-than-average interest rate.

Long-term interest rates are interest rates on financial assets that mature a number of years in the future.

At any given moment, **long-term interest rates**—interest rates on financial assets that mature, or come due, a number of years in the future—may be different from short-term interest rates. The difference between short-term and long-term interest rates is sometimes important as a practical matter. Let's look at why.

Consider the case of Millie, who has already decided to place $1,000 in CDs for the next two years. However, she hasn't decided whether to put the money in a two-year CD at a 5% rate of interest, or in a one-year CD, at a 4% rate of interest, and then another one-year CD at a new rate of interest the following year.

You might think that the two-year CD is a clearly better deal—but it may not be. Suppose that Millie expects the rate of interest on one-year CDs to rise sharply next year. If she puts her funds in a one-year CD this year, she will be able to reinvest the money at a much higher rate next year. And this could give her a two-year rate of return that is higher than if she put her funds into the two-year CD. For example, if the rate of interest on one-year CDs rises from 4% this year to 8% next year, putting her funds in two successive one-year CDs will give her an annual rate of return over the next two years of about 6%, better than the 5% rate on two-year CDs.

The same considerations apply to investors deciding between short-term and long-term bonds. If they expect short-term interest rates to rise, investors may buy short-term bonds even if long-term bonds offer a higher interest rate. If they expect short-term interest rates to fall, investors may buy long-term bonds even if short-term bonds offer a higher interest rate.

In practice, long-term interest rates reflect the average expectation in the market about what's going to happen to short-term rates in the future. When long-term rates are higher than short-term rates, the market is signaling that it expects short-term rates to rise in the future. Moreover, short-term rates, rather than long-term rates, affect money demand because the decision to hold money involves trading off the convenience of holding cash versus the payoff from holding assets that mature in the short term—a year or less.

For our current purposes, however, it's useful to ignore the distinction between short-term and long-term rates and assume that there is only one interest rate.

AP® EXAM TIP

In addition to the Federal Funds Rate and the Discount Rate, the AP® exam generally focuses on the role of interest rates in the economy by considering a single, representative short-run interest rate, r or i (though we know there are many different interest rates).

The Money Demand Curve

Because the overall level of interest rates affects the opportunity cost of holding money, the quantity of money individuals and firms want to hold, other things equal, is negatively related to the interest rate. In **Figure 28.1**, the horizontal axis shows the quantity of money demanded and the vertical axis shows the nominal interest rate, r, which you can think of as a representative short-term interest rate such as the rate on one-month CDs. Why do we place the nominal interest rate and not the real interest rate on the vertical axis? Because the opportunity cost of holding money includes both the real return that could be earned on a bank deposit and the erosion in purchasing power caused by inflation. The nominal interest rate includes both the forgone real return and the expected loss due to inflation. Hence, r in Figure 28.1 and all subsequent figures is the nominal interest rate.

Figure 28.1   The Money Demand Curve

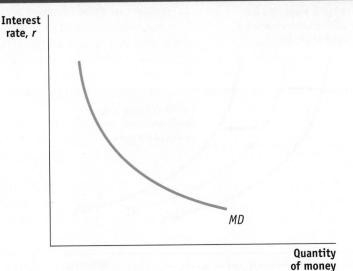

The money demand curve *(MD)* illustrates the relationship between the interest rate and the quantity of money demanded. It slopes downward: a higher interest rate leads to a higher opportunity cost of holding money and reduces the quantity of money demanded.

The **money demand curve (MD)** shows the relationship between the quantity of money demanded and the interest rate.

The relationship between the interest rate and the quantity of money demanded by the public is illustrated by the **money demand curve, MD,** in Figure 28.1. The money demand curve slopes downward because, other things equal, a higher interest rate increases the opportunity cost of holding money, leading the public to reduce the quantity of money it demands. For example, if the interest rate is very low—say, 0.15%, a common rate for one-month CDs in 2017—the interest forgone by holding money is relatively small. As a result, individuals and firms will tend to hold relatively large amounts of money to avoid the cost and nuisance of converting other assets into money when making purchases. By contrast, if the interest rate is relatively high—say, 15%, a level it reached in the United States in the early 1980s—the opportunity cost of holding money is high. People will respond by keeping only small amounts in cash and deposits, converting assets into money only when needed.

You might ask why we draw the money demand curve with the interest rate—as opposed to rates of return on other assets, such as stocks or real estate—on the vertical axis. The answer is that, for most people, the relevant question is whether to hold money or put the funds in the form of other assets that can be turned fairly quickly and easily into money. Stocks don't fit that definition because there are significant broker's fees when you sell stock (which is why stock market investors are advised not to buy and sell too often); selling real estate involves even larger fees and can take a long time as well. So the relevant comparison is between money and assets that are "close to" money—fairly liquid assets like CDs. And, as we've already seen, the interest rates on all these assets normally move closely together.

Shifts of the Money Demand Curve

Like the demand curve for an ordinary good, the money demand curve can be shifted by a number of factors. As **Figure 28.2** shows, an increase in the demand for money corresponds to a rightward shift of the *MD* curve, raising the quantity of money demanded at any given interest rate; a fall in the demand for money corresponds to a leftward shift of the *MD* curve, reducing the quantity of money demanded at any given interest

---

Figure 28.2   Increases and Decreases in the Demand for Money

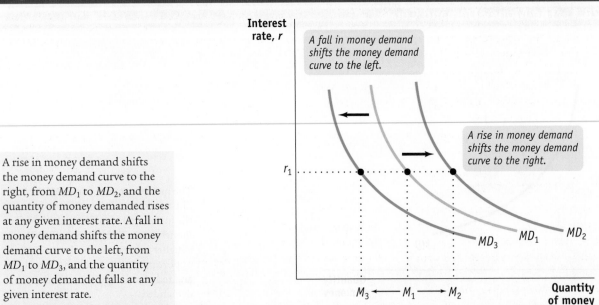

A rise in money demand shifts the money demand curve to the right, from MD_1 to MD_2, and the quantity of money demanded rises at any given interest rate. A fall in money demand shifts the money demand curve to the left, from MD_1 to MD_3, and the quantity of money demanded falls at any given interest rate.

A fall in money demand shifts the money demand curve to the left.

A rise in money demand shifts the money demand curve to the right.

rate. The most important factors causing the money demand curve to shift are changes in the aggregate price level, changes in real GDP, changes in banking technology, and changes in banking institutions.

Changes in the Aggregate Price Level

Americans keep a lot more cash in their wallets and funds in their checking accounts today than they did in the past. One reason is that they have to if they want to be able to buy anything: almost everything costs more now than it did decades ago, when you could get a burger, fries, and a drink at McDonald's for 45 cents and a gallon of gasoline for 29 cents. So higher prices increase the demand for money (a rightward shift of the *MD* curve), and lower prices decrease the demand for money (a leftward shift of the *MD* curve).

We can actually be more specific than this: other things equal, the demand for money is *proportional* to the price level. That is, if the aggregate price level rises by 20%, the quantity of money demanded at any given interest rate, such as r_1 in Figure 28.2, also rises by 20%—the movement from M_1 to M_2. Why? Because if the price of everything rises by 20%, it takes 20% more money to buy the same basket of goods and services. And if the aggregate price level falls by 20%, at any given interest rate the quantity of money demanded falls by 20%—shown by the movement from M_1 to M_3 at the interest rate r_1. As we'll see later, the fact that money demand is proportional to the price level has important implications for the long-run effects of monetary policy.

Changes in Real GDP

Households and firms hold money as a way to facilitate purchases of goods and services. The larger the quantity of goods and services they buy, the larger the quantity of money they will want to hold at any given interest rate. So an increase in real GDP—the total quantity of goods and services produced and sold in the economy—shifts the money demand curve rightward. A fall in real GDP shifts the money demand curve leftward.

Changes in Technology

There was a time, not so long ago, when withdrawing cash from a bank account required a visit during the bank's hours of operation. Since most people did their banking during lunch hour, they often found themselves standing in line. As a result, people limited the number of times they needed to withdraw funds by keeping substantial amounts of cash on hand. Not surprisingly, this tendency diminished greatly with the advent of ATMs and debit cards in the 1970s. More recent examples of technology that has reduced the need for cash include online payment services like PayPal and mobile wallet services that allow payments to be made using smartphones. Changes in technology such as these decrease the demand for money and shift the money demand curve to the left.

These events illustrate how changes in technology can affect the demand for money. In general, advances in information technology have tended to reduce the demand for money by making it easier for the public to make purchases without holding significant amounts of cash.

Changes in Institutions

Changes in institutions can increase or decrease the demand for money. For example, until Regulation Q was eliminated in 1980, U.S. banks weren't allowed to offer interest on checking accounts. So the interest you would forgo by holding funds in a checking account instead of an interest-bearing asset made the opportunity cost of holding funds in checking accounts very high. When banking regulations changed, allowing banks to pay interest on checking account funds, the demand for money rose and shifted the money demand curve to the right.

Recent technologies have made it easy for people to use their smartphones to make purchases, further decreasing the demand for money.

AP® EXAM TIP

Changes in the aggregate price level, real GDP, technology, and banking institutions shift the money demand curve. On the AP® exam you may be given scenarios in which you must determine the direction of a shift in this curve based on a change in one of these factors.

The Supply of Money

As we discussed in detail in Modules 26 and 27, the supply of money in the economy is set by the central bank to achieve its target interest rate. In the United States, the Federal Reserve's Open Market Committee issues a press release announcing any changes in its target interest rate. Below is an excerpt from the beginning of the press release issued by the Fed in June 2017:

> *Consistent with its statutory mandate, the Committee seeks to foster maximum employment and price stability. The Committee continues to expect that, with gradual adjustments in the stance of monetary policy, economic activity will expand at a moderate pace, and labor market conditions will strengthen somewhat further. Inflation on a 12-month basis is expected to remain somewhat below 2 percent in the near term but to stabilize around the Committee's 2 percent objective over the medium term. Near-term risks to the economic outlook appear roughly balanced, but the Committee is monitoring inflation developments closely.*
>
> *In view of realized and expected labor market conditions and inflation, the Committee decided to raise the target range for the federal funds rate to 1 to 1-1/4 percent. The stance of monetary policy remains accommodative, thereby supporting some further strengthening in labor market conditions and a sustained return to 2 percent inflation.*

Remember that the federal funds rate is the rate at which banks lend reserves to each other to meet the required reserve ratio. As the statement implies, at each of its eight-times-a-year meetings, the Federal Open Market Committee sets a target value for the federal funds rate. It's then up to Fed officials to achieve that target. This is done by the Open Market Desk at the Federal Reserve Bank of New York, which buys and sells short-term U.S. government debt, known as Treasury bills, to achieve that target.

As we've already seen, other short-term interest rates, such as the rates on CDs, move with the federal funds rate. So when the Fed raised its target for the federal funds rate in June 2017, many other short-term interest rates also increased.

How does the Fed go about achieving a *target federal funds rate*? And more to the point, how is a central bank able to affect interest rates at all?

The Equilibrium Interest Rate

Recall that, for simplicity, we've assumed that there is only one interest rate paid on nonmonetary financial assets, both in the short run and in the long run. To understand how the interest rate is determined, consider **Figure 28.3**, which illustrates the *liquidity preference model* of the interest rate; this model says that the interest rate is determined by the supply and demand for money in the market for money. Figure 28.3 combines the money demand curve, *MD*, with the **money supply curve**, *MS*, which shows the relationship between the quantity of money supplied by the Federal Reserve and the interest rate.

The **money supply curve** shows the relationship between the quantity of money supplied and the interest rate.

A central bank can increase or decrease the money supply: it usually does this through *open market operations*. In the United States, the Fed buys or sells Treasury bills, but it can also lend via the *discount window* or change *reserve requirements*. Let's assume for simplicity that the Fed, using one or more of these methods, simply chooses the level of the money supply that it believes will achieve its interest rate target. Then the money supply curve is a vertical line, *MS* in Figure 28.3, with a horizontal intercept corresponding to the money supply chosen by the Fed, $\overline{M}$. The money market equilibrium is at *E*, where *MS* and *MD* cross. At *E*, the quantity of money demanded equals the money supply, $\overline{M}$, leading to an equilibrium interest rate of r_E.

To understand why r_E is the equilibrium interest rate, consider what happens if the money market is at a point like *L*, where the interest rate, r_L, is below r_E. At r_L the public wants to hold the quantity of money M_L, an amount larger than the actual money

Figure 28.3   Equilibrium in the Money Market

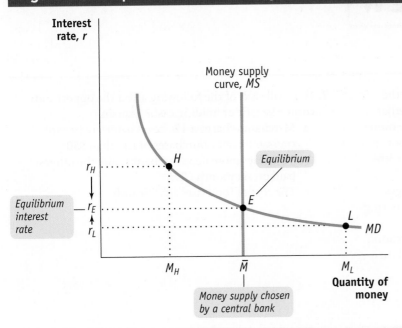

The money supply curve, MS, is vertical at the money supply chosen by the central bank, $\overline{M}$. The money market is in equilibrium at the interest rate r_E: the quantity of money demanded by the public is equal to $\overline{M}$, the quantity of money supplied. At a point such as L, the interest rate, r_L, is below r_E and the corresponding quantity of money demanded, M_L, exceeds the money supply, $\overline{M}$. In an attempt to shift their wealth out of nonmoney interest-bearing financial assets and raise their money holdings, investors drive the interest rate up to r_E. At a point such as H, the interest rate r_H is above r_E and the corresponding quantity of money demanded, M_H, is less than the money supply, $\overline{M}$. In an attempt to shift out of money holdings into nonmoney interest-bearing financial assets, investors drive the interest rate down to r_E.

supply, $\overline{M}$. This means that at point L, the public wants to shift some of its wealth out of interest-bearing assets such as high-denomination CDs (which are nonmoney assets) into money. This has two implications. One is that the quantity of money demanded is *more* than the quantity of money supplied. The other is that the quantity of interest-bearing nonmoney assets demanded is *less* than the quantity supplied. So those trying to sell nonmoney assets will find that they have to offer a higher interest rate to attract buyers. As a result, the interest rate will be driven up from r_L until the public wants to hold the quantity of money that is actually available, $\overline{M}$. That is, the interest rate will rise until it is equal to r_E.

Now consider what happens if the money market is at a point such as H in Figure 28.3, where the interest rate r_H is above r_E. In that case the quantity of money demanded, M_H, is less than the quantity of money supplied, $\overline{M}$. Correspondingly, the quantity of interest-bearing nonmoney assets demanded is greater than the quantity supplied. Those trying to sell interest-bearing nonmoney assets will find that they can offer a lower interest rate and still find willing buyers. This leads to a fall in the interest rate from r_H. It falls until the public wants to hold the quantity of money that is actually available, $\overline{M}$. Again, the interest rate will end up at r_E.

AP® EXAM TIP

The AP® exam requires you to be able to draw a correctly labeled money market graph. The nominal interest rate is measured along the vertical axis and the quantity of money is measured along the horizontal axis. And perhaps most crucially, the money supply curve is vertical!

Two Models of the Interest Rate

Here we have developed the liquidity preference model of the interest rate. In this model, the equilibrium interest rate is the rate at which the quantity of money demanded equals the quantity of money supplied in the money market. This model is different from, but consistent with, another model known as the *loanable funds model* of the interest rate, which is developed in the next module. In the loanable funds model, we will see that the interest rate matches the quantity of loanable funds supplied by savers with the quantity of loanable funds demanded for investment spending.

Check Your Understanding

1. Explain how each of the following would affect the quantity of money demanded, and indicate whether each change would cause a movement along the money demand curve or a shift of the money demand curve.
   a. The short-term interest rate rises from 5% to 30%.
   b. All prices fall by 10%.
   c. New wireless technology automatically charges supermarket purchases to credit cards, eliminating the need to stop at the cash register.
   d. In order to avoid paying taxes, a vast underground economy develops in which workers are paid their wages in cash rather than with checks.

2. How will each of the following affect the opportunity cost or benefit of holding cash? Explain.
   a. Merchants charge a 1% fee on debit/credit card transactions for purchases of less than $50.
   b. To attract more deposits, banks raise the interest paid on six-month CDs.
   c. The cost of food rises significantly.

TACKLE THE AP® TEST: Multiple-Choice Questions

1. A change in which of the following will cause movement along the money demand curve?
   a. the aggregate price level
   b. technology
   c. real GDP
   d. banking institutions
   e. the interest rate

2. Which of the following will decrease the demand for money, shifting the demand curve to the left?
   a. an increase in the interest rate
   b. inflation
   c. an increase in real GDP
   d. an increase in the availability of ATMs
   e. the elimination of Regulation Q

3. What will happen to the money supply and the equilibrium interest rate if the Federal Reserve sells Treasury securities?

	Money supply	Equilibrium interest rate
a.	increase	increase
b.	decrease	increase
c.	increase	decrease
d.	decrease	decrease
e.	decrease	no change

4. Which of the following is true regarding short-term and long-term interest rates?
   a. Short-term interest rates are always above long-term interest rates.
   b. Short-term interest rates are always below long-term interest rates.
   c. Short-term interest rates are always equal to long-term interest rates.
   d. Short-term interest rates are more important for determining the demand for money.
   e. Long-term interest rates are more important for determining the demand for money.

5. The quantity of money demanded rises (that is, there is a movement along the money demand curve) when
   a. the aggregate price level increases.
   b. the aggregate price level falls.
   c. real GDP increases.
   d. new technology makes banking easier.
   e. short-term interest rates fall.

6. Which of the following will lead to an increase in the interest rate?
   a. an increase in real GDP
   b. a decrease in the aggregate price level
   c. an increase in the money supply
   d. open market bond purchases
   e. a decrease in the federal funds rate

7. Which of the following is true of the money demand curve?
   a. It is set by the central bank.
   b. It is vertical.
   c. It is horizontal.
   d. It illustrates the opportunity cost of holding money.
   e. It shows a positive relationship between the interest rate and the quantity of money held as cash.

TACKLE THE AP® TEST: Free-Response Questions

1. Draw three correctly labeled graphs of the money market to illustrate the effect of each of the following three changes.
   a. The aggregate price level increases.
   b. Real GDP falls.
   c. There is a dramatic increase in online banking.

Rubric for FRQ 1 (6 points)

1 point: The vertical axis is labeled "Interest rate" or "r" and the horizontal axis is labeled "Quantity of money."

1 point: The money supply curve is vertical and labeled.

1 point: The money demand curve is negatively sloped and labeled.

1 point: a: The money demand curve shifts right.

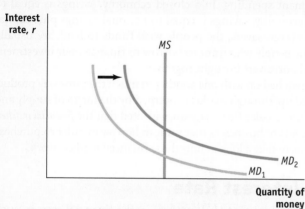

1 point: b: The money demand curve shifts left.

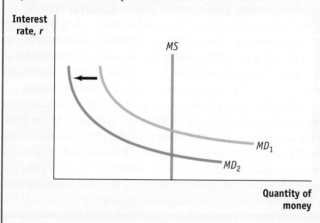

1 point: c: The money demand curve shifts left.

2. Draw a correctly labeled graph showing equilibrium in the money market. Label the equilibrium interest rate r_E and label an interest rate below the equilibrium interest rate r_L. Explain what occurs in the market when the interest rate is at r_L and what steps will lead the market to eventually return to equilibrium. **(7 points)**

The Market for Loanable Funds

> **In this Module, you will learn to:**
> • Describe how the loanable funds market matches savers and investors
> • Identify the determinants of supply and demand in the loanable funds market
> • Explain how the two models of interest rates can be reconciled

The Market for Loanable Funds

Recall from the circular-flow model in Module 10 that, for the economy as a whole, savings always equals investment spending. In a closed economy, savings is equal to national savings. In an open economy, savings is equal to national savings plus capital inflow. At any given time, however, savers, the people with funds to lend, are usually not the same as borrowers, the people who want to borrow to finance their investment spending. How are savers and borrowers brought together?

Savers and borrowers are matched up with one another in much the same way producers and consumers are matched up: through markets governed by the forces of supply and demand. In our discussion of the circular-flow diagram, we noted that the *financial markets* channel the savings of households to businesses that want to borrow in order to purchase capital equipment. It's now time to take a look at how those financial markets work.

The Equilibrium Interest Rate

There are a large number of different financial markets in the financial system, such as the bond market and the stock market. However, economists often work with a simplified model in which they assume that there is just one market that brings together those who want to lend money (savers) and those who want to borrow money (firms with investment spending projects). This hypothetical market is known as the **loanable funds market**. The price that is determined in the loanable funds market is the interest rate, denoted by r. It is the return a lender receives for allowing borrowers the use of a dollar for one year, calculated as a percentage of the amount borrowed.

Recall that in the money market, the *nominal* interest rate is of central importance and always serves as the "price" measured on the vertical axis. Investors and savers in the loanable funds market care about the *real* interest rate, which tells them the price paid for the use of money aside from the amount paid to keep up with inflation. However, in the real world neither borrowers nor lenders know what the future inflation rate will be when they make a deal, so actual loan contracts specify a nominal interest rate rather than a real interest rate. For this reason, and because it facilitates comparisons between the money market and the loanable funds market, the figures in this section are drawn with the vertical axis measuring the *nominal interest rate for a given expected future inflation rate*. As long as the expected inflation rate is unchanged, changes in the nominal interest rate also lead to changes in the real interest rate. We take up the influence of inflation later in this module.

We should also note at this point that, in reality, there are many different kinds of nominal interest rates because there are many different kinds of loans—short-term loans, long-term loans, loans made to corporate borrowers, loans made to governments, and so on. In the interest of simplicity, we'll ignore those differences and assume that there is only one type of loan. **Figure 29.1** illustrates the hypothetical demand for loanable funds. On the horizontal axis we show the quantity of loanable funds demanded. On the vertical axis we show the interest rate, which is the "price" of borrowing. To see why the demand curve for loanable funds, D_{LF}, slopes downward, imagine that there are many businesses, each of which has one potential investment project. How does a given business

Financial markets are where savers and borrowers can match up.

The **loanable funds market** is a hypothetical market that brings together those who want to lend money and those who want to borrow money.

AP® EXAM TIP

When expectations about the future inflation rate remain unchanged, the real interest rate and the nominal interest rate rise and fall together; either rate can appear on the vertical axis of the loanable funds graph. We use the nominal interest rate here for comparability with the money market graph. If a question asks you to draw conclusions about the real interest rate on the basis of the loanable funds graph, simply label the vertical axis "real interest rate."

Figure 29.1 The Demand for Loanable Funds

The demand curve for loanable funds (D_{LF}) slopes downward: the lower the interest rate, the greater the quantity of loanable funds demanded. Here, reducing the interest rate from 12% to 4% increases the quantity of loanable funds demanded from $150 billion to $450 billion.

decide whether or not to borrow money to finance its project? The decision depends on the interest rate the business faces and the **rate of return** on its project—the profit earned on the project expressed as a percentage of its cost. This can be expressed in a formula as:

The **rate of return** on a project is the profit earned on the project expressed as a percentage of its cost.

$$\textbf{(29-1)} \quad \text{Rate of return} = \frac{\text{Revenue from project} - \text{Cost of project}}{\text{Cost of project}} \times 100$$

For example, a project that costs $300,000 and produces revenue of $315,000 provides a rate of return of $[(\$315,000 - \$300,000)/\$300,000] \times 100 = 5\%$.

A business will want a loan when the rate of return on its project is greater than or equal to the interest rate. So, for example, at an interest rate of 12%, only businesses with projects that yield a rate of return greater than or equal to 12% will want a loan. A business will not pay 12% interest to fund a project with a 5% rate of return. The demand curve in Figure 29.1 shows that if the interest rate is 12%, businesses will want to borrow $150 billion (point A); if the interest rate is only 4%, businesses will want to borrow a larger amount, $450 billion (point B). That's a consequence of our assumption that the demand curve slopes downward: the lower the interest rate, the larger the total quantity of loanable funds demanded. Why do we make that assumption? Because, in reality, the number of potential investment projects that yield at least 4% is always greater than the number that yield at least 12%.

Figure 29.2 shows the hypothetical supply of loanable funds. Again, the interest rate plays the same role that the price plays in ordinary supply and demand analysis. Savers incur an opportunity cost when they lend to a business; the funds could instead be spent on consumption—say, a nice vacation. Whether a given individual becomes a lender by making funds available to borrowers depends on the interest rate received in return. By saving your money today and earning interest on it, you are rewarded with higher consumption in the future when your loan is repaid with interest. So it is a good assumption that more people are willing to forgo current consumption and make a loan when the interest rate is higher. As a result, our hypothetical supply curve of loanable funds slopes upward. In Figure 29.2, lenders will supply $150 billion to the loanable funds market at an interest rate of 4% (point X); if the interest rate rises to 12%, the quantity of loanable funds supplied will rise to $450 billion (point Y).

Figure 29.2　The Supply of Loanable Funds

The supply curve for loanable funds (S_{LF}) slopes upward: the higher the interest rate, the greater the quantity of loanable funds supplied. Here, increasing the interest rate from 4% to 12% increases the quantity of loanable funds supplied from $150 billion to $450 billion.

The equilibrium interest rate is the interest rate at which the quantity of loanable funds supplied equals the quantity of loanable funds demanded. As you can see in **Figure 29.3**, the equilibrium interest rate, r_E, and the total quantity of lending, Q_E, are determined by the intersection of the supply and demand curves, at point E. Here, the equilibrium interest rate is 8%, at which $300 billion is lent and borrowed. Investment spending projects with a rate of return of 8% or more are funded; projects with a rate of return of less than 8% are not. Correspondingly, only lenders who are willing to accept an interest rate of 8% or less will have their offers to lend funds accepted.

Figure 29.3 shows how the market for loanable funds matches up desired savings with desired investment spending: in equilibrium, the quantity of funds that savers want to lend is equal to the quantity of funds that firms want to borrow. The figure also shows that this

Figure 29.3　Equilibrium in the Loanable Funds Market

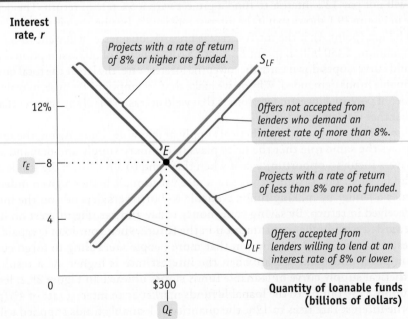

At the equilibrium interest rate, the quantity of loanable funds supplied equals the quantity of loanable funds demanded. Here, the equilibrium interest rate is 8%, with $300 billion of funds lent and borrowed. Investment spending projects with a rate of return of 8% or higher receive funding; those with a lower rate of return do not. Lenders who demand an interest rate of 8% or lower have their offers of loans accepted; those who demand a higher interest rate do not.

matchup is efficient in two senses. First, the right investments get made: the investment spending projects that are actually financed have higher rates of return than those that do not get financed. Second, the right people do the saving: the potential savers who actually lend funds are willing to lend for lower interest rates than those who do not. The insight that the loanable funds market leads to an efficient use of savings, although drawn from a highly simplified model, has important implications for real life. As we'll see shortly, it is the reason that a well-functioning financial system increases an economy's long-run economic growth rate.

Before we get to that, however, let's look at how the market for loanable funds responds to shifts of demand and supply.

Shifts in the Demand for Loanable Funds

The equilibrium interest rate changes when there are shifts of the demand curve for loanable funds, the supply curve for loanable funds, or both. Let's start by looking at the causes and effects of changes in demand.

The factors that can cause the demand curve for loanable funds to shift include the following:

- *Changes in perceived business opportunities.* A change in beliefs about the rate of return on investment spending can increase or reduce the amount of desired spending at any given interest rate. For example, in 2017, the U.S. Small Business Optimism Index reached its highest level since the survey began in 1973, with a record level of small business owners indicating they planned to increase expenditures for capital and inventories. Increases in investment by small businesses shift the demand for loanable funds to the right. A decrease in business optimism, such as the United States experienced between 2006 and 2009 as a result of the financial crisis, shifts the demand for loanable funds to the left.

Increased optimism among small business owners will cause the demand curve for loanable funds to shift.

Another way to affect perceived business opportunities is through a government **investment tax credit**, which firms can deduct from their taxes. For example, an investment tax credit for renewable energy provides an incentive for firms to invest in solar, wind, or other forms of renewable energy. The investment tax credit would increase the rate of return on these investments, thereby increasing the demand for loanable funds and shifting the demand curve for loanable funds to the right.

- *Changes in the government's borrowing.* Governments that run budget deficits are major sources of the demand for loanable funds. As a result, changes in the budget deficit can shift the demand curve for loanable funds. For example, between 2000 and 2003, as the U.S. federal government went from a budget surplus to a budget deficit, net federal borrowing went from *minus* $189 billion—that is, in 2000 the federal government was actually providing loanable funds to the market because it was paying off some of its debt—to *plus* $377.6 billion because in 2003 the government had to borrow large sums to pay its bills. In 2009, net federal borrowing again increased as the budget deficit rose to an historical high of $1,412.7 billion. Changes in the federal budget position have the effect, other things equal, of shifting the demand curve for loanable funds. Increases in government borrowing shift the demand for loanable funds to the right and decreases shift it to the left.

An **investment tax credit** is an amount that firms are allowed by law to deduct from their taxes based on their investment spending.

Figure 29.4 shows the effects of an increase in the demand for loanable funds. S is the supply of loanable funds, and D_{LF1} is the initial demand curve. The initial equilibrium interest rate is r_1. An increase in the demand for loanable funds means that the quantity of funds demanded rises at any given interest rate, so the demand curve shifts rightward to D_{LF2} As a result, the equilibrium interest rate rises to r_2.

The fact that, other things equal, an increase in the demand for loanable funds leads to a rise in the interest rate has one especially important implication: beyond concern about repayment, there are other reasons to be wary of government budget deficits. As we've already seen, an increase in the government's deficit shifts the demand curve for loanable funds to

Figure 29.4 An Increase in the Demand for Loanable Funds

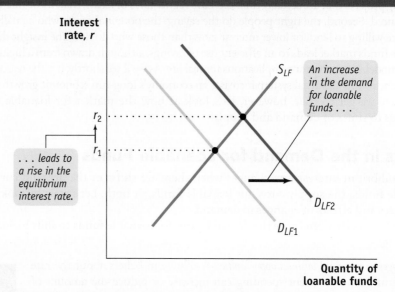

If the quantity of funds demanded by borrowers rises at any given interest rate, the demand for loanable funds shifts rightward from D_{LF1} to D_{LF2}. As a result, the equilibrium interest rate rises from r_1 to r_2.

Crowding out occurs when a government deficit drives up the interest rate and leads to reduced investment spending.

the right, which leads to a higher interest rate. If the interest rate rises, businesses will cut back on their investment spending. So a rise in the government budget deficit tends to reduce overall investment spending. Economists call the negative effect of government budget deficits on investment spending **crowding out**. The threat of crowding out is a key source of concern about persistent budget deficits, which we discuss further in the next Module.

Shifts in the Supply of Loanable Funds

Like the demand for loanable funds, the supply of loanable funds can shift. Among the factors that can cause the supply of loanable funds to shift are the following:

Capital inflows can lead to an increase in investment spending in areas like residential property.

- *Changes in private saving behavior.* A number of factors can cause the level of private savings to change at any given rate of interest. For example, between 2000 and 2006 rising home prices in the United States made many homeowners feel richer, making them willing to spend more and save less. This had the effect of shifting the supply of loanable funds to the left. The drop in home prices between 2006 and 2009 had the opposite effect, shifting the supply of loanable funds to the right.

- *Changes in capital inflows.* Capital flows into a country can change as investors' perceptions of that country change. For example, from 2009 to 2016, Brazil experienced large capital inflows because international investors believed that years of economic reforms made it a safe place to put their funds. The United States has received large capital inflows between 2009 and 2017, with much of the money coming from China.

Figure 29.5 shows the effects of an increase in the supply of loanable funds. D_{LF} is the demand for loanable funds, and S_{LF1} is the initial supply curve. The initial equilibrium interest rate is r_1. An increase in the supply of loanable funds means that the quantity of funds supplied rises at any given interest rate, so the supply curve shifts rightward to S_{LF2}. As a result, the equilibrium interest rate falls to r_2.

Inflation and Interest Rates

Anything that shifts either the supply of loanable funds curve or the demand for loanable funds curve changes the interest rate. Historically, major changes in interest rates have been driven by many factors, including changes in government policy and

Figure 29.5 An Increase in the Supply of Loanable Funds

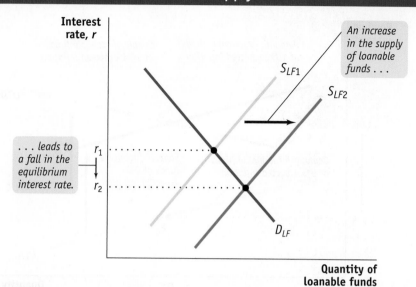

An increase in the supply of loanable funds . . .

S_{LF1}

S_{LF2}

. . . leads to a fall in the equilibrium interest rate.

r_1

r_2

D_{LF}

Interest rate, r

Quantity of loanable funds

If the quantity of funds supplied by lenders rises at any given interest rate, the supply of loanable funds shifts rightward from S_{LF1} to S_{LF2}. As a result, the equilibrium interest rate falls from r_1 to r_2.

technological innovations that created new investment opportunities. However, arguably the most important factor affecting interest rates over time—the reason, for example, why interest rates today are much lower than they were in the late 1970s and early 1980s—is changing expectations about future inflation, which shift both the supply of and the demand for loanable funds.

To understand the effect of expected inflation on interest rates, recall our discussion in Module 14 of the way inflation creates winners and losers—for example, the way that high U.S. inflation in the 1970s and 1980s reduced the real value of homeowners' mortgages, which was good for the homeowners but bad for the banks. We know that economists capture the effect of inflation on borrowers and lenders by distinguishing between the *nominal interest rate* and the *real interest rate*, where the distinction is as follows:

Real interest rate = Nominal interest rate − Inflation rate

The true cost of borrowing is the real interest rate, not the nominal interest rate. To see why, suppose a firm borrows $10,000 for one year at a 10% nominal interest rate. At the end of the year, it must repay $11,000—the amount borrowed plus the interest. But suppose that over the course of the year the average level of prices increases by 10%, so that the real interest rate is zero. Then the $11,000 repayment has the same purchasing power as the original $10,000 loan. In effect, the borrower has received a zero-interest loan.

Similarly, the true payoff to lending is the real interest rate, not the nominal rate. The bank that makes the one-year $10,000 loan at a 10% nominal interest rate receives an $11,000 repayment at the end of the year. But the 10% increase in the average level of prices means that the purchasing power of the money the bank gets back is no more than that of the money it lent out. In effect, the bank has made a zero-interest loan.

The expectations of borrowers and lenders about future inflation rates are normally based on recent experience. In the late 1970s, after a decade of high inflation, borrowers and lenders expected future inflation to be high. By the late 1990s, after a decade of fairly low inflation, borrowers and lenders expected future inflation to be low. And these changing expectations about future inflation had a strong effect on the nominal interest rate, largely explaining why interest rates were much lower in the early years of the twenty-first century than they were in the early 1980s.

Let's look at how changes in the expected future rate of inflation are reflected in the loanable funds model. In **Figure 29.6**, the curves S_{LF0} and D_{LF0} show the supply of and demand for loanable funds given that the expected future rate of inflation is 0%. In that case, equilibrium is at E_0 and the equilibrium nominal interest rate is 4%. Because expected

AP® EXAM TIP

Even though the real interest rate is equal to the nominal interest rate minus the inflation rate, simply knowing two of the values will not necessarily tell you the effect on the third. For example, an increase in the nominal interest rate and a decrease in the inflation rate will both lead to an increase in the real interest rate. But if both the nominal interest rate and the inflation rate increase at the same time, it is impossible to tell what will happen to the real interest rate unless you know which rate changed by more.

Figure 29.6   The Fisher Effect

D_{LF0} and S_{LF0} are the demand and supply curves for loanable funds when the expected future inflation rate is 0%. At an expected inflation rate of 0%, the equilibrium nominal interest rate is 4%. An increase in expected future inflation pushes both the demand and supply curves upward by 1 percentage point for every percentage point increase in expected future inflation. D_{LF10} and S_{LF10} are the demand and supply curves for loanable funds when the expected future inflation rate is 10%. The 10 percentage point increase in expected future inflation raises the equilibrium nominal interest rate to 14%. The expected real interest rate remains at 4%, and the equilibrium quantity of loanable funds also remains unchanged.

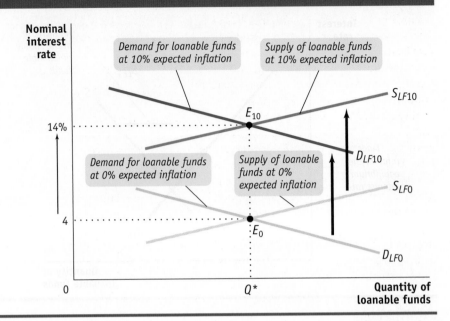

future inflation is 0%, the equilibrium expected real interest rate over the life of the loan, the real interest rate expected by borrowers and lenders when the loan is contracted, is also 4%.

Now suppose that the expected future inflation rate rises to 10%. The demand curve for funds shifts upward to D_{LF10}: borrowers are now willing to borrow as much at a nominal interest rate of 14% as they were previously willing to borrow at 4%. That's because with a 10% inflation rate, a borrower who pays a 14% nominal interest rate pays a 4% real interest rate. Similarly, the supply curve of funds shifts upward to S_{LF10}: lenders require a nominal interest rate of 14% to persuade them to lend as much as they would previously have lent at 4%. That's because with a 10% inflation rate, a lender who receives a 14% nominal interest rate receives a 4% real interest rate. The new equilibrium is at E_{10}: the result of an increase in the expected future inflation rate from 0% to 10% is that the equilibrium nominal interest rate rises from 4% to 14%.

This situation can be summarized as a general principle, named the *Fisher effect* after the American economist Irving Fisher, who proposed it in 1930: an increase in expected inflation drives up the nominal interest rate by the same number of percentage points, leaving the expected real interest rate unchanged. The central point is that both lenders and borrowers base their decisions on the expected real interest rate. As a result, a change in the expected rate of inflation does not affect the equilibrium quantity of loanable funds or the expected real interest rate; all it affects is the equilibrium nominal interest rate.

Reconciling the Two Interest Rate Models

In Module 28 we developed what is known as the liquidity preference model of the interest rate. In that model, the equilibrium interest rate is the rate at which the quantity of money demanded equals the quantity of money supplied in the money market. In the loanable funds model, we see that the interest rate matches the quantity of loanable funds supplied by savers with the quantity of loanable funds demanded for investment spending. How do the two models compare?

The Interest Rate in the Short Run

As we explained using the liquidity preference model, a fall in the interest rate leads to a rise in investment spending, I, which then leads to a rise in both real GDP and consumer spending, C. The rise in real GDP doesn't lead only to a rise in consumer spending, however. It also leads to a rise in savings: at each stage of the multiplier process, part of the increase in disposable income is saved. How much do savings rise? According to the *savings–investment spending identity*, total savings in the economy is always equal to investment spending. This tells us that when a fall in the interest rate leads to higher investment spending, the resulting increase in real GDP generates exactly enough additional savings to match the rise in investment spending. To put it another way, after a fall in the interest rate, the quantity of savings supplied rises exactly enough to match the quantity of savings demanded.

Figure 29.7 shows how our two models of the interest rate are reconciled in the short run by the links among changes in the interest rate, changes in real GDP, and changes in savings. Panel (a) represents the liquidity preference model of the interest rate. MS_1 and MD_1 are the initial supply and demand curves for money. According to the liquidity preference model, the equilibrium interest rate in the economy is the rate at which the quantity of money supplied is equal to the quantity of money demanded in the money market. Panel (b) represents the loanable funds model of the interest rate. S_{LF1} is the initial supply curve and D_{LF} is the demand curve for loanable funds. According to the loanable funds model, the equilibrium interest rate in the economy is the rate at which the quantity of loanable funds supplied is equal to the quantity of loanable funds demanded in the market for loanable funds.

Figure 29.7   The Short-Run Determination of the Interest Rate

Panel (a) shows the liquidity preference model of the interest rate: the equilibrium interest rate matches the money supply to the quantity of money demanded. In the short run, the interest rate is determined in the money market, where an increase in the money supply, from $\overline{M}_1$ to $\overline{M}_2$, pushes the equilibrium interest rate down, from r_1 to r_2. Panel (b) shows the loanable funds model of the interest rate. The fall in the interest rate in the money market leads, through the multiplier effect, to an increase in real GDP and savings; a rightward shift of the supply curve of loanable funds, from S_{LF1} to S_{LF2}; and a fall in the interest rate, from r_1 to r_2. As a result, the new equilibrium interest rate in the loanable funds market matches the new equilibrium interest rate in the money market at r_2.

In Figure 29.7, both the money market and the market for loanable funds are initially in equilibrium at E_1 with the same interest rate, r_1. You might think that this would happen only by accident, but in fact it will always be true. To see why, let's look at what happens when the central bank increases the money supply from $\overline{M}_1$ to $\overline{M}_2$. This pushes the money supply curve rightward to MS_2, causing the equilibrium interest rate in the market for money to fall to r_2, and the economy moves to a short-run equilibrium at E_2. What happens in panel (b), in the market for loanable funds? In the short run, the fall in the interest rate due to the increase in the money supply leads to a rise in real GDP, which generates a rise in savings through the multiplier process. This rise in savings shifts the supply curve for loanable funds rightward, from S_{LF1} to S_{LF2}, moving the equilibrium in the loanable funds market from E_1 to E_2 and also reducing the equilibrium interest rate in the loanable funds market. And we know that savings rise by exactly enough to match the rise in investment spending. This tells us that the equilibrium rate in the loanable funds market falls to r_2, the same as the new equilibrium interest rate in the money market.

In the short run, then, the supply and demand for money determines the interest rate, and the loanable funds market follows the lead of the money market. When a change in the supply of money leads to a change in the interest rate, the resulting change in real GDP causes the supply of loanable funds to change as well. As a result, the equilibrium interest rate in the loanable funds market is the same as the equilibrium interest rate in the money market.

Notice our use of the phrase "in the short run." Changes in aggregate demand affect aggregate output only in the short run. In the long run, aggregate output is equal to potential output. So our story about how a fall in the interest rate leads to a rise in aggregate output, which leads to a rise in savings, applies only in the short run. In the long run, as we'll see next, the determination of the interest rate is quite different because the roles of the two markets are reversed. In the long run, the loanable funds market determines the equilibrium interest rate, and it is the market for money that follows the lead of the loanable funds market.

The Interest Rate in the Long Run

In the short run an increase in the money supply leads to a fall in the interest rate, and a decrease in the money supply leads to a rise in the interest rate. In the long run, however, changes in the money supply don't affect the interest rate.

Figure 29.8 shows why. As in Figure 29.7, panel (a) shows the liquidity preference model of the interest rate and panel (b) shows the supply and demand for loanable funds. We assume that in both panels the economy is initially at E_1, in long-run macroeconomic equilibrium at potential output with the money supply equal to $\overline{M}_1$. The demand curve for loanable funds is D_{LF}, and the initial supply curve for loanable funds is S_{LF1}. The initial equilibrium interest rate in both markets is r_1.

Figure 29.8   The Long-Run Determination of the Interest Rate

Panel (a) shows the liquidity preference model long-run adjustment to an increase in the money supply from $\overline{M}_1$ to $\overline{M}_2$; panel (b) shows the corresponding long-run adjustment in the loanable funds market. As we discussed in Figure 29.7, the increase in the money supply reduces the interest rate from r_1 to r_2, increases real GDP, and increases savings in the short run. This is shown in panel (a) and panel (b) as the movement from E_1 to E_2. In the long run, however, the increase in the money supply raises wages and other nominal prices; this shifts the money demand curve in panel (a) from MD_1 to MD_2, leading to an increase in the interest rate from r_1 to r_2 as the economy moves from E_2 to E_3. The rise in the interest rate causes a fall in real GDP and a fall in savings, shifting the loanable funds supply curve back to S_{LF1} from S_{LF2} and moving the loanable funds market from E_2 back to E_1. In the long run, the equilibrium interest rate is the rate that matches the supply and demand for loanable funds when real GDP equals potential output.

Now suppose the money supply rises from $\overline{M}_1$ to $\overline{M}_2$. As we saw in Figure 29.7, this initially reduces the interest rate to r_2. However, in the long run the aggregate price level will rise by the same proportion as the increase in the money supply (due to the *neutrality of money*, a topic presented in detail in the next section). A rise in the aggregate price level increases money demand by the same proportion. So in the long run the money demand curve shifts right to MD_2, and the equilibrium interest rate rises back to its original level, r_1.

Panel (b) of Figure 29.8 shows what happens in the market for loanable funds. We saw earlier that an increase in the money supply leads to a short-run rise in real GDP and that this rise shifts the supply of loanable funds rightward from S_{LF1} to S_{LF2}. In the long run, however, real GDP falls back to its original level as wages and other nominal prices rise. As a result, the supply of loanable funds, S_{LF}, which initially shifted from S_{LF1} to S_{LF2}, shifts back to S_{LF1}.

In the long run, then, changes in the money supply do not affect the interest rate. So what determines the interest rate in the long run—that is, what determines r_1 in Figure 29.8? The answer is the supply and demand for loanable funds. More specifically, in the long run the equilibrium interest rate is the rate that matches the supply of loanable funds with the demand for loanable funds when real GDP equals potential output.

MODULE 29 REVIEW

Check Your Understanding

1. Use a diagram of the loanable funds market to illustrate the effect of the following events on the equilibrium interest rate and quantity of loanable funds.
   a. An economy is opened to international movements of capital, and a capital inflow occurs.
   b. Retired people generally save less than working people at any interest rate. The proportion of retired people in the population goes up.

2. Explain what is wrong with the following statement: "Savings and investment spending may not be equal in

the economy as a whole in equilibrium because when the interest rate rises, households will want to save more money than businesses will want to invest."

3. Suppose that expected inflation rises from 3% to 6%.
   a. How will the real interest rate be affected by this change?
   b. How will the nominal interest rate be affected by this change?
   c. What will happen to the equilibrium quantity of loanable funds?

TACKLE THE AP® TEST: Multiple-Choice Questions

1. A business will decide whether or not to borrow money to finance a project based on a comparison of the interest rate with the _____ from its project.
   a. expected revenue
   b. profit
   c. rate of return
   d. cost generated
   e. demand generated

2. The real interest rate equals the
   a. nominal interest rate plus the inflation rate.
   b. nominal interest rate minus the inflation rate.

   c. nominal interest rate divided by the inflation rate.
   d. nominal interest rate times the inflation rate.
   e. federal funds rate.

3. Which of the following will increase the demand for loanable funds?
   a. a federal government budget surplus
   b. an increase in perceived business opportunities
   c. a decrease in the interest rate
   d. positive capital inflows
   e. a decrease in private saving rates

4. Which of the following will increase the supply of loanable funds?
   a. an increase in perceived business opportunities
   b. decreased government borrowing
   c. an increase in private saving rates
   d. an increase in the expected inflation rate
   e. a decrease in capital inflows

5. Both lenders and borrowers base their decisions on
   a. expected real interest rates.
   b. expected nominal interest rates.
   c. real interest rates.
   d. nominal interest rates.
   e. nominal interest rates minus real interest rates.

6. The graph of the loanable funds market is different than that of the money market in which of the following ways?
   a. The demand curve slopes downward.
   b. The demand curve slopes upward.
   c. The supply curve slopes downward.
   d. The supply curve slopes upward.
   e. Price is on the vertical axis.

7. If the real interest rate decreases at the same time the inflation rate decreases, what must be true of the nominal interest rate?
   a. The nominal interest rate fell sharply.
   b. The nominal interest rate increased by more than the inflation rate decreased.
   c. The nominal interest rate increased by less than the inflation rate decreased.
   d. The nominal interest rate was unchanged.
   e. The change in the nominal interest rate cannot be determined.

TACKLE THE AP® TEST: Free-Response Questions

1. Draw a correctly labeled graph showing equilibrium in the loanable funds market.

   Rubric for FRQ 1 (6 points)

   1 point: Vertical axis labeled "Interest rate" or "r"

   1 point: Horizontal axis labeled "Quantity of loanable funds"

   1 point: Downward-sloping demand curve for loanable funds (labeled)

   1 point: Upward-sloping supply curve for loanable funds (labeled)

   1 point: Equilibrium quantity of loanable funds shown on horizontal axis below where curves intersect

   1 point: Equilibrium interest rate shown on vertical axis across from where curves intersect

   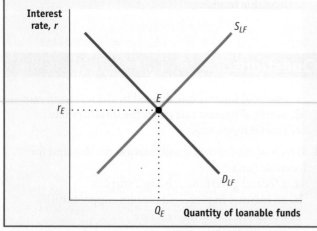

2. Does each of the following affect either the supply or the demand for loanable funds, and if so, does the affected curve increase (shift to the right) or decrease (shift to the left)?
   a. There is an increase in capital inflows into the economy.
   b. Businesses are pessimistic about future business conditions.
   c. The government increases borrowing.
   d. The private saving rate decreases. **(4 points)**

SECTION 5 Review

SECTION 5 Review

SECTION 5 Review Video

Adventures in AP® Economics Videos
Mod 25: The Money Multiplier
Mod 27: Monetary Policy and the Federal Reserve System

Module 22

1. Investment in physical capital is necessary for long-run economic growth. So in order for an economy to grow, it must channel savings into investment spending. The price charged per year by lenders to investors and other borrowers for the use of their savings is the **interest rate**, which is calculated as a percentage of the amount borrowed.

2. According to the **savings–investment spending identity**, savings and investment spending are always equal for the economy as a whole. The government is a source of savings when it runs a positive **budget balance**, also known as a **budget surplus**; it is a source of dissavings when it runs a negative budget balance, also known as a **budget deficit**. In a closed economy, savings is equal to **national savings**, the sum of private savings plus the budget balance. In an open economy, savings is equal to national savings plus **capital inflow** of foreign savings. When a capital outflow, or negative capital inflow, occurs, some portion of national savings is funding investment spending in other countries.

3. Households invest their current savings or **wealth**— their accumulated savings—by purchasing assets. Assets come in the form of either a **financial asset**, a paper claim that entitles the buyer to future income from the seller, or a **physical asset**, a claim on a tangible object that gives the owner the right to dispose of it as desired.

Module 23

7. **Money** is any asset that can easily be used to purchase goods and services. Currency in circulation and checkable bank deposits are both considered part of the **money supply**. Money plays three roles: it is a **medium of exchange** used for transactions, a **store of value** that holds purchasing power over time, and a **unit of account** in which prices are stated.

8. Over time, **commodity money**, which consists of goods possessing value aside from their role as money, such as gold and silver coins, was replaced by

Module 24

10. The accumulation of interest causes any amount of money loaned today to grow into a larger amount, called the **future value**, over the loan period.

11. In order to evaluate a project in which costs or benefits are realized in the future, you must first transform them into their **present values** using the interest rate, r.

A financial asset is also a **liability** from the point of view of its seller. There are four main types of financial assets: loans, bonds, stocks, and **bank deposits**. Each of them serves a different purpose in addressing the three fundamental tasks of a financial system: reducing **transaction costs**—the cost of making a deal; reducing **financial risk**—uncertainty about future outcomes that involves financial gains and losses; and providing **liquid** assets— assets that can be quickly converted into cash without much loss of value (in contrast to **illiquid** assets, which are not easily converted).

4. Although many small and moderate-size borrowers use bank **loans** to fund investment spending, larger companies typically issue bonds. Business owners reduce their risk by selling stock.

5. **Financial intermediaries** are critical components of the financial system. Mutual funds and pension funds allow small investors to diversify and life insurance companies allow families to reduce risk.

6. A **bank** allows individuals to hold liquid bank deposits that are then used to finance investments in illiquid assets. Banks can perform this mismatch because on average only a small fraction of depositors withdraw their savings at any one time. Banks are a key ingredient in long-run economic growth.

commodity-backed money, such as paper currency backed by gold. Today the dollar is pure **fiat money**, whose value derives solely from its official role.

9. The Federal Reserve calculates two measures of the money supply. M1 is the narrowest **monetary aggregate**; it contains only currency in circulation, traveler's checks, and checkable bank deposits. M2 includes a wider range of assets called near-moneys, mainly other forms of bank deposits, that can easily be converted into checkable bank deposits.

The present value of $1 realized one year from now is $1/(1 + r)$, the amount of money you must lend out today to have $1 one year from now. Once this transformation is done, you should choose the project with the highest **net present value**.

Module 25

12. Banks allow depositors immediate access to their funds, but they also lend out most of the funds deposited in their care. To meet demands for cash, they maintain **bank reserves** composed of both currency held in vaults and deposits at a central bank. The **reserve ratio** is the ratio of bank reserves to bank deposits. A T-account summarizes a bank's financial position, with loans and reserves counted as assets, and deposits counted as liabilities.

13. Banks have sometimes been subject to **bank runs**, most notably in the early 1930s. The modern banking system has four safeguards to prevent bank runs: deposit insurance, capital requirements for bank owners (to reduce the incentive to make overly risky loans with depositors' funds), legally mandated **reserve requirements**, and Federal Reserve lending through its discount window.

14. When currency is deposited in a bank, it starts a multiplier process in which banks lend out **excess reserves**, leading to an increase in the money supply—so banks create money. If the entire money supply consisted of checkable bank deposits, the money supply would be equal to the value of reserves divided by the reserve ratio. In reality, much of the **monetary base** consists of currency in circulation, and the **money multiplier** is the ratio of the money supply to the monetary base.

Module 26

15. The Federal Reserve or "the Fed" is the **central bank** of the United States. In response to the Panic of 1907, the Fed was created to centralize holding of reserves, inspect banks' books, and make the money supply sufficiently responsive to varying economic conditions.

16. The Great Depression sparked widespread bank runs in the early 1930s, which greatly worsened and lengthened the depth of the Depression. Federal deposit insurance was created, and the government recapitalized banks by lending to them and by buying shares of banks. By 1933, banks had been separated into two categories: **commercial** (covered by deposit insurance) and **investment** (not covered). Public acceptance of deposit insurance finally stopped the bank runs of the Great Depression.

17. The savings and loan (thrift) crisis of the 1980s arose because insufficiently regulated S&Ls engaged in overly risky speculation and incurred huge losses. Depositors in failed S&Ls were compensated with taxpayer funds because they were covered by deposit insurance. However, the crisis caused steep losses in the financial and real estate sectors, resulting in a recession in the early 1990s.

18. As housing prices rose between 2003 and 2006, lenders made large quantities of questionable mortgage loans. When housing prices tumbled, massive losses by banks and nonbank financial institutions led to widespread collapse in the financial system. To prevent another Great Depression, the Fed and the U.S. Treasury expanded lending to bank and nonbank institutions, provided capital through the purchase of bank shares, and purchased private debt. Because much of the crisis originated in nontraditional bank institutions, the crisis of 2008 raised the question of whether a wider safety net and broader regulation were needed in the financial sector.

Module 27

19. The central bank regulates banks and sets reserve requirements. To meet those requirements, banks in the United States borrow and lend reserves in the federal funds market at the **federal funds rate**. U.S. banks can also borrow from the Fed at the **discount rate**.

20. **Open market operations** by the central bank are the principal tool of monetary policy. In the United States, the Fed can increase or reduce the monetary base by buying U.S. Treasury bills from banks or selling U.S. Treasury bills to banks.

Module 28

21. The **money demand curve** arises from a trade-off between the opportunity cost of holding money and the liquidity that money provides. The opportunity cost of holding money depends on **short-term interest rates**, not **long-term interest rates**. Changes in the aggregate price level, real GDP, technology, and institutions shift the money demand curve.

22. According to the liquidity preference model of the interest rate, the interest rate is determined in the money market by the money demand curve and the **money supply curve**. The central bank can change the interest rate in the short run by shifting the money supply curve.

23. In the United States, the Fed uses open market operations to achieve a target federal funds rate, which other short-term interest rates generally follow. In the EU, the European Central Bank (ECB) conducts monetary policy.

Module 29

24. The hypothetical **loanable funds market** shows how loans from savers are allocated among borrowers with investment spending projects. In equilibrium, only those projects with a **rate of return** greater than or equal to the equilibrium interest rate will be funded. By showing how gains from trade between lenders and borrowers are maximized, the loanable funds market shows why a well-functioning financial system leads to greater long-run economic growth. Government budget deficits can raise the interest rate and can lead to **crowding out** of investment spending. Changes in perceived business opportunities, including incentives such as **investment tax credits**, and in government borrowing shift the demand curve for loanable funds; changes in private savings and capital inflows shift the supply curve.

25. Because neither borrowers nor lenders can know the future inflation rate, loans specify a nominal interest rate rather than a real interest rate. For a given expected future inflation rate, shifts of the demand and supply curves of loanable funds result in changes in the underlying real interest rate, leading to changes in the nominal interest rate. According to the Fisher effect, an increase in expected future inflation raises the nominal interest rate by the same number of percentage points, so that the expected real interest rate remains unchanged.

Key Terms

Interest rate, p. 216
Savings–investment spending identity, p. 216
Budget surplus, p. 217
Budget deficit, p. 217
Budget balance, p. 217
National savings, p. 217
Capital inflow, p. 217
Wealth, p. 218
Financial asset, p. 218
Physical asset, p. 218
Liability, p. 218
Transaction costs, p. 218
Financial risk, p. 219
Liquid, p. 219
Illiquid, p. 219
Loan, p. 220
Financial intermediary, p. 221

Bank deposit, p. 222
Bank, p. 222
Money, p. 224
Money supply, p. 225
Medium of exchange, p. 225
Store of value, p. 226
Unit of account, p. 226
Commodity money, p. 226
Commodity-backed money, p. 226
Fiat money, p. 227
Monetary aggregate, p. 227
Future value, p. 230
Present value, p. 231
Net present value, p. 232
Bank reserves, p. 235
Reserve ratio, p. 236
Required reserve ratio, p. 236
Bank run, p. 237

Reserve requirements, p. 238
Excess reserves, p. 240
Monetary base, p. 241
Money multiplier, p. 241
Central bank, p. 243
Commercial bank, p. 247
Investment bank, p. 247
Federal funds rate, p. 251
Discount rate, p. 251
Open market operation, p. 252
Short-term interest rates, p. 256
Long-term interest rates, p. 256
Money demand curve, p. 258
Money supply curve, p. 260
Loanable funds market, p. 264
Rate of return, p. 265
Investment tax credit, p. 267
Crowding out, p. 268

AP® Exam Practice Questions

Multiple-Choice Questions

1. The interest rate is
   a. the opportunity cost of lending money.
   b. the price borrowers pay for the use of lenders' savings.
   c. a percentage of the amount saved by borrowers.
   d. the rate charged by banks to hold savings for one year.
   e. the amount earned by using profits to build a new factory.

2. Which of the following identities is true in a simplified economy with no government and no interaction with other countries?
   a. consumer spending = investment spending
   b. total income = consumer spending − investment spending
   c. total spending = investment spending + savings
   d. investment spending = total spending − savings
   e. savings = investment spending

3. A budget surplus exists when the government does which of the following?
   a. saves
   b. collects less tax revenue than it spends
   c. has a negative budget balance
   d. increases the national debt
   e. uses expansionary fiscal policy

4. Which of the following is a task of an economy's financial system?
   a. maximizing risk
   b. increasing transaction costs
   c. decreasing diversification
   d. eliminating liquidity
   e. enhancing the efficiency of financial markets

5. A financial intermediary that resells shares of a stock portfolio is a
   a. mutual fund.
   b. pension fund.
   c. loan-backed security.
   d. bond broker.
   e. depository institution.

6. Which of the following assets is most liquid?
   a. stock
   b. bond
   c. loan
   d. mutual fund
   e. cash

7. When money acts as a means of holding purchasing power over time, it is serving which function?
   a. medium of exchange
   b. source of liquidity
   c. store of value
   d. unit of account
   e. source of wealth

8. Which of the following is an example of using money as a unit of account?
   a. buying a new T-shirt
   b. purchasing $10 worth of candy
   c. keeping the dollar you receive each year for your birthday for 10 years
   d. putting money into your savings account
   e. paying for lunch with your debit card

9. Which of the following is a desirable characteristic of money?
   a. fixed supply
   b. large denominations
   c. made of precious metal
   d. widely accepted
   e. backed by commodities

10. Fiat money derives its value from which of the following?
   a. its official status
   b. the good being used as a medium of exchange

c. a promise it can be converted into something valuable
   d. gold or silver
   e. exchange rates

11. The M1 money supply includes which of the following?
   a. near-moneys
   b. checkable deposits
   c. savings accounts
   d. time deposits
   e. mutual funds

12. The present value of $1 you receive one year from now is equal to
   a. $1(1 + r)$.
   b. $1/(1 - r)$.
   c. $1/(1 + r)$.
   d. $1(1 + r^2)$.
   e. $1(1 + r)^2$.

13. If the interest rate is 2%, the amount received one year from now as a result of lending $1,000 today is
   a. $980.
   b. $1,000.
   c. $1,020.
   d. $1,200.
   e. $2,000.

14. The liquid assets banks keep in their vaults are known as bank
   a. deposits.
   b. savings.
   c. reserves.
   d. money.
   e. returns.

15. The required reserve ratio is
   a. the most cash that banks are allowed to hold in their vault.
   b. set by the central bank.
   c. responsible for most bank runs.
   d. equal to 5% of bank deposits.
   e. the fraction of bank loans held as reserves.

16. If rr is the reserve requirement, the money multiplier is equal to
   a. rr.
   b. $1 - rr$.
   c. $1/rr$.
   d. rr^2.
   e. $1/rr^2$.

17. Which of the following is part of the money supply but not part of the monetary base?
   a. checkable bank deposits
   b. bank reserves
   c. currency in circulation
   d. deposits at the central bank
   e. savings accounts

18. The Federal Reserve is a(n)
   a. single central bank located in New York.
   b. government agency overseen by the Secretary of the Treasury.
   c. system of 10 regional banks.
   d. institution that oversees the banking system.
   e. depository institution that lends to large corporations.

19. The Federal Reserve is charged with doing all of the following EXCEPT
    a. providing financial services to commercial banks.
    b. supervising and regulating banks.
    c. maintaining the stability of the financial system.
    d. conducting monetary policy.
    e. insuring bank deposits.

20. Which of the following will increase the demand for money?
    a. a fall in the aggregate price level
    b. an increase in real GDP
    c. technological advances
    d. open market operations by the central bank
    e. a decrease in the interest rate

21. The money supply curve is
    a. upward sloping.
    b. vertical.
    c. horizontal.
    d. downward sloping.
    e. U-shaped.

22. When banking regulations were changed so that banks could pay interest on checking accounts, what was the effect on interest rates and the equilibrium quantity of money?

	Interest rate	Quantity of money
a.	increase	decrease
b.	decrease	increase
c.	increase	increase
d.	decrease	decrease
e.	increase	no change

23. Which of the following will shift the supply curve for loanable funds to the right?
    a. an increase in the rate of return on investment spending
    b. an increase in the government budget deficit
    c. a decrease in the national saving rate
    d. an increase in expected inflation
    e. capital inflows from abroad

24. Crowding out is illustrated by which of the following changes in the loanable funds market?
    a. a decreasing equilibrium interest rate
    b. an increase in the demand for loanable funds
    c. a decrease in the demand for loanable funds
    d. an increase in the supply of loanable funds
    e. a decrease in the supply of loanable funds

25. The supply curve for loanable funds is
    a. upward sloping.
    b. vertical.
    c. horizontal.
    d. downward sloping.
    e. U-shaped.

Free-Response Questions

1. a. Draw a correctly labeled graph of the market for loanable funds. On your graph, indicate each of the following:
        i. the equilibrium interest rate, labeled r_1
        ii. the equilibrium quantity of loanable funds, labeled Q_1
    b. Use your graph from (a) to show how an increase in government spending affects the loanable funds market. On the graph, indicate each of the following:
        i. the new equilibrium interest rate, labeled r_2
        ii. the new equilibrium quantity of loanable funds, labeled Q_2
    c. Explain how the new interest rate (r_2) affects the level of real GDP. **(5 points)**

2. a. Draw a correctly labeled graph of the money market. On your graph, indicate each of the following:
        i. the equilibrium interest rate, labeled r_1
        ii. the equilibrium quantity of money, labeled Q_1
    b. Use your graph from (a) to show how an increase in the aggregate price level affects the money market. On the graph, indicate each of the following:
        i. the new equilibrium interest rate, labeled r_2
        ii. the new equilibrium quantity of loanable funds, labeled Q_2
    c. Explain how the new interest rate (r_2) affects the level of real GDP. **(6 points)**

3. Suppose the required reserve ratio is 10% and a bank has deposits of $100 million and holds reserves of $12 million.
    a. Calculate the bank's required reserves. Show your work.
    b. Calculate the bank's excess reserves. Show your work.
    c. If the bank receives a new deposit of $1,000:
        i. How much must the bank hold as reserves? Show your work.
        ii. How much can the bank lend out? Explain.
    d. Assume the bank's excess reserves are increased by $500.
        i. What is the value of the money multiplier? Show your work.
        ii. By how much could the additional excess reserves increase the money supply? Show your work.
        (6 points)

How Should We Wield the Tool of Monetary Policy?

Money, the Fed, and Schools of Economic Thought

Money gets a bad rap. The proverb that money is the root of all evil is at least as old as the Bible. The coins and bills that constitute money for most people are called *fiat currency* because they would have little use if not for the government decree, or "fiat," that makes them valuable. They are adopted merely as a convenience. Without dollars, there would be no less greed, but every type of commerce for every reason would be carried out with less convenience. When fiat currency is unavailable, buyers and sellers resort to cumbersome bartering and the use of *commodity money*, such as precious metals, shells, beads, salt, or anything else that has value as a commodity. Inmates can't hold fiat currency in prison, but

the number of cigarettes it takes to buy a tattoo is well known in the prison yard. Some summer camps don't allow campers to hold fiat currency, but no small amount of commerce goes on between campers for commodity money, such as candy bars.

A more tenable concern over money might be that the central bank, the Federal Reserve or "Fed" in the United States, has made too little (or too much) of it available in the economy at a particular time. There is considerable disagreement about the real and lasting effects of fine-tuning the money supply. Here we provide an overview of money, the Federal Reserve System, and the battlefield of economic theory on which the Fed strategizes about monetary policy.

Show Me the Money

Money serves three primary functions:

- It is *a medium of exchange*. Rather than carting products around to trade for other products, which can be difficult if you're in the refrigerator business or if the person who has what you want doesn't want what you have, people use money, which is easy to carry around and is accepted by all.

- It is *a store of value*. You can hold cash in your pocket or bury it in a pickle jar for use in the future, whereas storing value in output, such as economics lectures or tomatoes, simply doesn't work.

- It is *a unit of account*. Dollars, yen, baht, and other units of currency provide standard ways of measuring expenditures.

Beyond cash and standard bank deposits, the money supply has several other components that deserve mention. A *money market mutual fund* is made up of short-term, low-risk financial securities, such as Treasury bills. *Retail money market funds* are those offered primarily to individuals. *Time deposits*, such as certificates of deposit, are deposits that can't be withdrawn for a specified period without a financial penalty.

The money supply is measured in terms of *M1* and *M2*: M1 includes cash, checking account deposits, and traveler's checks; M2 is M1 plus savings accounts, time deposits, and retail money market mutual funds.

The Federal Reserve System

The *Federal Reserve System* has the mission of formulating monetary policy to achieve price stability and economic growth. The Fed oversees a *fractional reserve banking system* in which only a fraction of bank deposits is actually retained by the banks and the rest is loaned out. Banks earn profits on the difference between the interest rates they pay depositors and the higher interest rates that loan recipients pay the banks. The board of governors of the Fed determines the *reserve requirement*, which is the minimum fraction of deposits that a bank must retain either in the vault or in a reserve account at the Fed. When a bank falls short of the required level of reserves, it can borrow in the *federal funds market* from banks that have excess reserves. The interest rate that banks pay each other in this market is called the *federal funds rate*.

The Fed has three primary tools for influencing the money supply. The main line of attack is *open market operations* conducted by specialists at the Federal Reserve's Open Market Desk in New York to manipulate the reserves held by banks. To increase the reserves, the folks at the Open Market Desk purchase government securities, such as Treasury bonds, through securities dealers in the market that is open to banks, businesses, and individuals. The Fed's payments for these securities end up as reserves in the sellers' accounts at commercial banks. To decrease the money supply, the Fed sells part of its multi-trillion dollar portfolio of Treasury securities on the open market. Payments for these securities diminish commercial banks' reserve accounts.

Changes in bank reserves set the wheels of monetary policy in motion. With fewer reserves, banks have less money to lend out, so the amount of money in circulation decreases. As our knowledge of supply and demand would predict, a decrease in the supply of reserves also causes the price of borrowing reserves—the federal funds rate—to increase. This makes it more expensive for banks to borrow from each other and triggers subsequent increases in interest rates paid by bank customers. The result is less borrowing and spending in the economy. The opposite is also true: when security purchases by the Fed increase the level of reserves, the federal funds rate and other interest rates drop, and more money flows into the economy. These monetary policy transactions are orchestrated by the Federal Open Market Committee, which consists of the seven members of the Fed's board of governors and five of the presidents of the 12 Federal Reserve System banks.

The Fed's control of the reserve requirement constitutes a rarely used but powerful second tool with which to influence the money supply. To understand that tool we must first examine the process of *money creation*. Suppose a Fed purchase of $1,000 worth of bonds gives a bank $1,000 worth of reserves, all of which is lent out to Tina. If Tina deposits the money into her checking account and the reserve requirement is 10%, $100 out of Tina's $1,000 deposit must be held by her bank as *required reserves*. The other $900 is *excess reserve* and can be lent out, say, to Finn. If Finn deposits his $900 (or buys things from people who deposit the money), 10% of that $900—$90—must be held as required reserves and $810 can be lent out. If each loan is subsequently deposited and every bank lends out its excess reserves, the $1,000 deposit ultimately creates $9,000 worth of new loans (the $900 plus the $810 and so on). No more loans can be made at that point because the

Fed's entire $1,000 injection of new money must be held as required reserves. Why? Because when deposited, the $9,000 in new loans along with Tina's $1,000 initial deposit amount to $10,000 in total deposits, 10% of which is $1,000.

The *money multiplier* indicates the total amount of deposits that can develop out of each $1 of new deposits, and equals 1 divided by the reserve requirement. With a reserve requirement of 10%, or 0.10, the multiplier is $1/0.10 = 10$, which explains why the $1,000 deposit ultimately became $10 \times \$1,000$, or $10,000 in deposits. Because the Fed controls the reserve requirement, it controls the amount of money created in this process. If it changed the reserve requirement to 20%, the money multiplier would become $1/0.20 = 5$, and a $1,000 deposit could develop into $5 \times \$1,000 = \$5,000$ in deposits. The money multiplier is diminished when money leaks out of the cycle of loans and deposits, as when people hold significant amounts of money as cash, banks hold excess reserves, or expenditures are made on imports.

As a third tactic for controlling the money supply, the boards of directors of the 12 regional Federal Reserve banks, in consultation with the Board of Governors of the Fed, control the interest rate paid by banks and other depository institutions when they borrow money from their regional Federal Reserve bank. This rate is called the *discount rate*, and the lending facility within each Federal Reserve bank is called the *discount window*. When the discount rate is raised, less money is borrowed, and so there is less money in the economy. Although the availability of funds from other sources limits the direct influence of discount rate changes, a change in this rate is considered an important signal of the intent of Fed policy.

The Fed also uses the informal power of *moral suasion*—pressure or persuasion without force—to convey its policy interests and intentions through public statements, published studies, educational programs, and conferences.

The Monetary Policy Debate

Adherents to various schools of economic thought have differing views on monetary policy. The monetarists, championed by Nobel laureate Milton Friedman and following in the footsteps of the classical economists before them, focus on policy implications in the long run, after the economy has had time to adjust to changes. Monetarist and classical economists believe money is *neutral*, meaning that the level of output is independent of the money supply in the long run. If this is true, Fed policies to alter the money supply affect the inflation rate but not the long-term growth rate of output.

Monetarists question the Fed's ability to fine-tune the economy and achieve short-run stability with monetary policy. They acknowledge that variations in the money supply can have short-run effects on demand and output, but are skeptical of the Fed's ability to master the complex dynamics of the economy and yield the desired result. Monetarists worry that, even if the Fed accurately assesses a downturn in the economy and carries out a flawless monetary expansion, the economy may correct itself before the additional money gets into consumers' hands, and the additional spending at that point might only cause inflation. Monetarists prefer a more passive "monetary rule" of letting the money supply grow steadily at the rate of output growth rather than making adjustments in response to short-run demand problems.

Like monetarists, the earlier classical economists believed that the economy could heal itself in a reasonable amount of time. When that didn't happen during the Great Depression of 1929–1939, British economist John Maynard Keynes became convinced that the economy sometimes needs a nudge. His favored solution was changes in taxes and government spending, which economists call *fiscal policy*. Keynes reasoned that, after a change in total or "aggregate" demand, rigidity in wages and prices prevents the economy from adjusting swiftly back to long-run equilibrium. He explained that wages can be sticky (inflexible) because of multiyear wage contracts, and that prices can be sticky due to the hassle of making price adjustments in catalogs, price lists, and menus.

Keynes saw the possible transmission of monetary growth to output growth this way: (1) an increase in the money supply could decrease the price of borrowing money—the interest rate; (2) a lower interest rate could encourage investment, which is a component of aggregate demand; (3) with higher aggregate demand, the price, GDP, and employment levels could all increase. However, Keynes pointed out that this chain of events might be broken at several points. For example, if the demand for money is relatively flat, an increase in the money supply will not cause the interest rate to fall. And if the demand for investment isn't responsive to the interest rate, investment won't increase even if there is a substantial decrease in the interest rate.

Based on differing takes on these possibilities, some Keynesians argue that monetary policy is powerless, and others are more optimistic about its benefits, the consensus being that fiscal policy is the preferred fix.

Keynes said that inflation could be countered with higher taxes or less government spending, either of which would lower aggregate demand. Unemployment, conversely, could be remedied by lower taxes or higher spending to boost aggregate demand. The proposed trade-off between unemployment and inflation is known as the *Phillips relationship*, named after New Zealand economist William Phillips. But in the 1970s, the United States experienced *stagflation*: high rates of inflation accompanied high levels of unemployment. Just as the Great Depression made people question classical economic policies, stagflation created concern over Keynesian policies. How could aggregate demand be used to moderate the economy if the Phillips relationship did not hold and unemployment and inflation were both a problem at the same time? An increase in aggregate demand might cure the unemployment problem, but the corresponding inflation would go through the roof.

Skepticism about Keynesian policy in the 1970s left an opening for alternative schools of thought. Nobel laureate Robert Lucas wrote that *rational expectations* would undermine monetary or fiscal policy. His theory was that individuals and firms would anticipate policy responses to upturns and downturns in the economy. For instance, at the onset of a recession, people would anticipate the government response of increasing aggregate demand and the subsequent price increases. They would respond with price and wage increases that increased the cost of production, decreased the quantity demanded, and negated the influence of the expansionary policy.

In the late 1970s and early 1980s, Fed policy more closely resembled the monetarists' suggestion of steady monetary growth without countercyclical responses. During that period, the alarming inflation rate came down, but the economy remained sluggish. In the 1980s, there was much fanfare for *supply-side economics*, which emphasized shifting aggregate supply with tax cuts rather than attempting to move aggregate demand. The results were mixed, with inflation under control but a burgeoning government debt and a looming recession that began in 1990.

Although Keynes himself did not favor adjustments in the money supply to moderate the economy, the Keynesian approach of activist policy making was gradually coupled with the classical belief that the money supply does matter. The outcome was the *neoclassical–Keynesian synthesis*—a hybrid of the previous schools of thought that embraces activist fiscal and monetary policy. Throughout the 1990s and beyond, both types of policy were used in efforts to moderate the economy, with modest success.

Today, as they say, everything old is new again, including a neo-Keynesian school of economics. The new Keynesians have several arguments for the existence of sticky wages and prices that prevent the economy from self-adjusting to full employment:

- **Menu costs:** The expense of printing new menus, catalogs, signs, and price lists makes people reluctant to change prices frequently.

- **Efficiency wages:** Some firms pay amounts in excess of the market wage, called efficiency wages, in order to hire, retain, and encourage the best workers.

Xinhua/Alamy

- **Staggered pricing:** If firms have staggered pricing schedules and can't all change their prices at the same time, there is a disincentive to raise prices by very much because the first firms to charge more risk losing customers to firms that keep their prices steady.

Neo-Keynesians also argue that sticky wages and prices debunk the rational expectations hypothesis because stickiness means that prices can't easily be adjusted to a level that negates the influence of policy changes.

With each of these schools of thought having gone through the wringer of bad times and policy ineffectiveness, none is as strong as it once was. When the Great Recession hit in 2007, there was plenty of activist policy on both the monetary and fiscal sides. Between 2008 and 2014, the Fed injected about $3.5 trillion into the economy in three rounds of "quantitative easing," achieved by purchasing Treasury securities and mortgage-backed securities. In 2009, the federal government attempted to stimulate the economy by investing more than $800 billion in such things as infrastructure, education, health care, tax credits, and direct financial assistance to low-income households. Today, economists are still tinkering with the theories discussed here, trying to find the best possible bases for stabilization policy.

Conclusion

Whether the money supply should be manipulated for the sake of employment and growth depends on a larger set of puzzles: How rigid are prices and the level of output? How responsive are interest rates to changes in the money supply, and how responsive are investments to changes in interest rates? Can the economy heal itself? And can the central bank or the government act quickly and accurately enough to rescue an economy in trouble?

Monetarists believe that in the long run, the money supply affects inflation rates but not long-term growth. They advocate steady growth in the money supply that is proportional to output growth. Like classical economists, monetarists generally believe that the economy can take care of itself.

Keynesians favor policy responses to undesired swings in the economy. Keynes suggested expansionary fiscal policy to bolster sagging aggregate demand, saying that the transmission mechanism between the money supply and aggregate demand may be impeded. Neoclassical economists, neo-Keynesians, supply-siders, and believers in rational expectations bring their own important points to the table, and assure continued progress in critical areas of macroeconomic policy.

Critical Thinking Questions

1. Which of the economic theories discussed in this chapter do you think is closest to the truth? Explain your answer with reference to real-world economic phenomena.

2. Explain how the money-creation process works and discuss reasons why the amount of money created might be less than the largest amount possible.

3. On a graph that measured M1 and M2 on the vertical axis and time on the horizontal axis, would the two lines ever cross? Why or why not?

4. In a period of low inflation and high unemployment, how might the policy recommendations differ among these schools of thought: monetarists, Keynesian, and neoclassical–Keynesian synthesis?

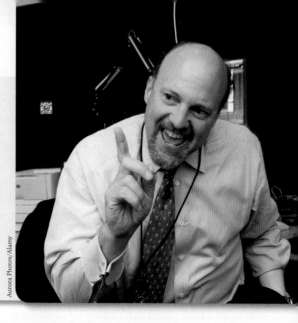

Long-Run Consequences of Stabilization Policies

economics by example *Will Technology Put Everyone Out of Work?*

The Fed as First Responder

Jim Cramer's *Mad Money* is a popular show on CNBC, a cable TV network that specializes in business and financial news. In October 2017, Cramer said the United States was experiencing a "bull market"—one in which investment prices rise faster than their historical average. Cramer noted, "It's a bifurcated bull, but a bull all the same." But it was a different story a decade earlier, on August 3, 2007, when Cramer was so alarmed about negatives he felt were invisible to the Federal Reserve that he screamed about Fed leaders:

"Bernanke is being an academic! It is no time to be an academic. . . . **He has no idea how bad it is out there. He has no idea! He has no idea!** . . . and Bill Poole? Has no idea what it's like out there! . . . They're nuts! **They know nothing!** . . . The Fed is asleep! Bill Poole is a shame! He's shameful!!"

Who were Bernanke and Bill Poole? In the previous section, we described the role of the Federal Reserve System, the U.S. central bank. At the time of Cramer's tirade, Ben Bernanke, a former Princeton professor of economics, was the chair of the Fed's Board of Governors, and William Poole, a former Brown professor of economics, was the president of the Federal Reserve Bank of St. Louis. Both men, because of their positions, were members of the Federal Open Market Committee, which meets eight times a year to set monetary policy. In 2007, Cramer was crying out for the Fed to change monetary policy in order to address what he perceived to be a growing financial crisis.

Why was Cramer screaming at the Federal Reserve rather than, say, the U.S. Treasury—or, for that matter, the president? The answer is that the Fed's control of monetary policy makes it the first line of response to macroeconomic difficulties—very much including the financial crisis that had Cramer so upset. Indeed, within a few weeks, the Fed swung into action with a dramatic reversal of its previous policies.

In Section 4, we developed the aggregate demand and supply model and introduced the use of fiscal policy to stabilize the economy. In Section 5, we introduced money, banking, and the Federal Reserve System, and began to look at how monetary policy is used to stabilize the economy. In this section, we use the models introduced in Sections 4 and 5 to further develop our understanding of stabilization policies (both fiscal and monetary), including their long-run effects on the economy. In addition, we introduce the Phillips curve—a short-run trade-off between unexpected inflation and unemployment—and investigate the role of expectations in the economy. We end the section with a brief summary of the history of macroeconomic thought and how the modern consensus view of stabilization policy has developed.

Long-Run Implications of Fiscal Policy: Deficits and the Public Debt

In this Module, you will learn to:
- Explain the cyclically adjusted budget balance
- Identify problems posed by a large public debt
- Discuss why implicit liabilities of the government can be a cause for concern

In Module 20 we discussed how discretionary fiscal policy can be used to stabilize the economy in the short run. During a recession, an expansionary fiscal policy—raising government spending, lowering taxes, or both—can be used to shift the aggregate demand curve to the right. And when there are inflationary pressures in the economy, a contractionary fiscal policy—lowering government spending, raising taxes, or both—can be used to shift the aggregate demand curve to the left. But how do these policies affect the economy over a longer period of time? In this Module we will look at some of the long-term effects of fiscal policy, including budget balance, debt, and liabilities.

The Budget Balance

Headlines about the government's budget tend to focus on just one point: whether the government is running a budget surplus or a budget deficit and, in either case, how big. People usually think of surpluses as good: when the federal government ran a record surplus in 2000, many people regarded it as a cause for celebration. Conversely, people usually think of deficits as bad: when the Congressional Budget Office projected a $534 billion federal deficit in 2016, many people regarded it as a cause for concern.

The digital National Debt Clock, located in midtown Manhattan, displays the current gross national debt of the United States. As of March 23, 2018 it exceeded 20 trillion dollars.

How do surpluses and deficits fit into the analysis of fiscal policy? Are deficits ever a good thing and surpluses ever a bad thing? To answer those questions, let's look at the causes and consequences of surpluses and deficits.

The Budget Balance as a Measure of Fiscal Policy

What do we mean by surpluses and deficits? The budget balance, which we defined in Module 22, is the difference between the government's tax revenue and its spending, both on goods and services and on government transfers, in a given year. That is, the budget balance—savings by government—is defined by Equation 30-1:

$$\text{(30-1)} \quad \text{Budget balance} = T - G - TR$$

where T is the value of tax revenues, G is government purchases of goods and services, and TR is the value of government transfers. A budget surplus is a positive budget balance, and a budget deficit is a negative budget balance.

Other things equal, expansionary fiscal policies—increased government purchases of goods and services, higher government transfers, or lower taxes—reduce the budget balance for that year. That is, expansionary fiscal policies make a budget surplus smaller or a budget deficit bigger. Conversely, contractionary fiscal policies—reduced government purchases of goods and services, lower government transfers, or higher taxes—increase the budget balance for that year, making a budget surplus bigger or a budget deficit smaller.

> **AP® EXAM TIP**
>
> Fiscal policy affects the budget balance. When spending exceeds taxes, there is a budget deficit, and when taxes exceed spending, there is a budget surplus. You need to be able to identify changes in the budget balance and analyze their long-run affects on the economy.

You might think this means that changes in the budget balance can be used to measure fiscal policy. In fact, economists often do just that: they use changes in the budget balance as a quick way to assess whether current fiscal policy is expansionary or contractionary. But they always keep in mind two reasons this quick approach is sometimes misleading:

- Two different changes in fiscal policy that have equal-sized effects on the budget balance may have quite unequal effects on the economy. As we have already seen, changes in government purchases of goods and services have a larger effect on real GDP than equal-sized changes in taxes and government transfers.

- Often, changes in the budget balance are themselves the result, not the cause, of fluctuations in the economy.

To understand the second point, we need to examine the effects of the business cycle on the budget.

The Business Cycle and the Cyclically Adjusted Budget Balance

Historically, there has been a strong relationship between the federal government's budget balance and the business cycle. The budget tends to move into deficit when the economy experiences a recession, but deficits tend to get smaller or even turn into surpluses when the economy is expanding. **Figure 30.1** shows the federal budget deficit as a percentage of GDP from 1970 to 2017. Shaded areas indicate recessions; unshaded areas indicate expansions. As you can see, the federal budget deficit increased around the time of each recession and usually declined during expansions. In fact, in the late stages of the long expansion from 1991 to 2000, the deficit actually became negative— the budget deficit became a budget surplus.

Figure 30.1 The U.S. Federal Budget Deficit and the Business Cycle

The budget deficit as a percentage of GDP tends to rise during recessions (indicated by shaded areas) and fall during expansions.

Data Source: Bureau of Economic Analysis; National Bureau of Economic Research.

The relationship between the business cycle and the budget balance is even more clear if we compare the budget deficit as a percentage of GDP with the unemployment rate, as we do in **Figure 30.2**. The budget deficit almost always rises when the unemployment rate rises and falls when the unemployment rate falls.

Is this relationship between the business cycle and the budget balance evidence that policy makers engage in discretionary fiscal policy? Not necessarily. It is largely automatic stabilizers that drive the relationship shown in Figure 30.2. As we learned in the

Figure 30.2 The U.S. Federal Budget Deficit and the Unemployment Rate

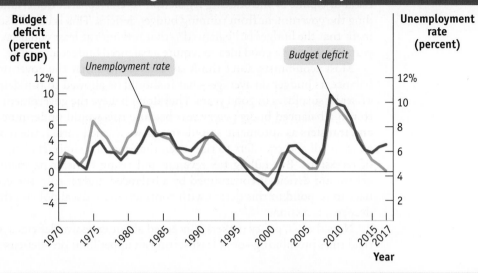

There is a close relationship between the budget balance and the business cycle: a recession moves the budget balance toward deficit, but an expansion moves it toward surplus. Here the budget deficit as a percentage of GDP moves closely in tandem with the unemployment rate.

Data Source: Bureau of Economic Analysis; Bureau of Labor Statistics.

discussion of automatic stabilizers in Module 21, government tax revenue tends to rise and some government transfers, such as unemployment insurance payments, tend to fall when the economy expands. Conversely, government tax revenue tends to fall and some government transfers tend to rise when the economy contracts. So the budget tends to move toward surplus during expansions and toward deficit during recessions even without any deliberate action on the part of policy makers.

In assessing budget policy, it's often useful to separate movements in the budget balance due to the business cycle from movements due to discretionary fiscal policy changes. The former are affected by automatic stabilizers and the latter by deliberate changes in government purchases, government transfers, or taxes. It's important to realize that business-cycle effects on the budget balance are temporary: both recessionary gaps (in which real GDP is below potential output) and inflationary gaps (in which real GDP is above potential output) tend to be eliminated in the long run. Removing their effects on the budget balance sheds light on whether the government's taxing and spending policies are sustainable in the long run. In other words, do the government's tax policies yield enough revenue to fund its spending in the long run? As we'll learn shortly, this is a fundamentally more important question than whether the government runs a budget surplus or deficit in the current year.

To separate the effect of the business cycle from the effects of other factors, many governments produce an estimate of what the budget balance would be if there was neither a recessionary nor an inflationary gap. The **cyclically adjusted budget balance** is an estimate of what the budget balance would be if real GDP were exactly equal to potential output. It takes into account the extra tax revenue the government would collect and the transfers it would save if a recessionary gap were eliminated—or the revenue the government would lose and the extra transfers it would make if an inflationary gap were eliminated.

The **cyclically adjusted budget balance** is an estimate of what the budget balance would be if real GDP were exactly equal to potential output.

Should the Budget Be Balanced?

Persistent budget deficits can cause problems for both the government and the economy. Yet politicians are always tempted to run deficits because this allows them to cater to voters by cutting taxes without cutting spending or by increasing spending without increasing taxes. As a result, there are occasional attempts by policy makers to force fiscal discipline by introducing legislation—even a constitutional amendment—forbidding the government from running budget deficits. This is usually stated as a requirement that the budget be "balanced"—that revenues at least equal spending each fiscal year. Would it be a good idea to require a balanced budget annually?

Most economists don't think so. They believe that the government should only balance its budget on average—that it should be allowed to run deficits in bad years, offset by surpluses in good years. They don't believe the government should be forced to run a balanced budget *every year* because this would undermine the role of taxes and transfers as automatic stabilizers. As we learned earlier, the tendency of tax revenue to fall and transfers to rise when the economy contracts helps to limit the size of recessions. But falling tax revenue and rising transfer payments push the budget toward deficit. If constrained by a balanced-budget rule, the government would have to respond to this deficit with contractionary fiscal policies that would tend to deepen a recession.

Nonetheless, policy makers concerned about excessive deficits sometimes feel that rigid rules prohibiting—or at least setting an upper limit on—deficits are necessary.

Long-Run Implications of Fiscal Policy

During the 1990s, the Japanese government engaged in massive deficit spending in an effort to increase aggregate demand. That policy was partly successful: although Japan's economy was sluggish during the 1990s, it avoided a severe slump comparable to what happened to many countries in the 1930s. Yet the fact that Japan was running large budget deficits year after year made many observers uneasy, as Japan's **government debt**—the accumulation of past budget deficits, minus past budget surpluses—climbed to alarming levels. Now that we understand how budget deficits and surpluses arise, let's take a closer look at their long-run effects on the economy.

Deficits, Surpluses, and Debt

Government debt is the accumulation of past budget deficits, minus past budget surpluses.

When a family spends more than it earns over the course of a year, it has to raise the extra funds either by selling assets or by borrowing. And if a family borrows year after year, it will eventually end up with a lot of debt.

The same is true for governments. With a few exceptions, governments don't raise large sums by selling assets such as national parkland. Instead, when a government spends more than the tax revenue it receives—when it runs a budget deficit—it almost always borrows the extra funds. And governments that run persistent budget deficits end up with substantial debts.

To interpret the numbers that follow, you need to know a slightly peculiar feature of federal government accounting. For historical reasons, the U.S. government does not keep the books by calendar years. Instead, budget totals are kept by fiscal years, which currently run from October 1 to September 30 and are labeled by the calendar year in which they end. For example, fiscal 2013 began on October 1, 2012, and ended on September 30, 2013.

At the end of fiscal 2016, the total debt of the U.S. federal government was $19.9 trillion, or about 106% of gross domestic product. However, part of that debt represented special accounting rules specifying that the federal government as a whole owes funds to certain government programs, especially Social Security. We'll explain those rules shortly. For now, however, let's focus on public debt: government debt held by individuals and institutions outside the government. At the end of fiscal 2016, the federal government's public debt was "only" $14.2 trillion, or about 77% of GDP.

U.S. federal government public debt at the end of fiscal 2016 was larger than it was at the end of fiscal 2015 because the federal government ran a budget deficit during fiscal 2015. A government that runs persistent budget deficits will experience a rising level of debt. Why is this a problem?

Problems Posed by Rising Government Debt

There are two reasons to be concerned when a government runs persistent budget deficits. We described one reason in the previous module: when the economy is at potential output and the government borrows funds in the financial markets, it is competing with firms that plan to borrow funds for investment spending. As a result, the government's borrowing may lead to a *crowding out* of private investment and reduction in economic growth. Let's see why.

Government borrowing increases the demand for loanable funds (D_{LF}), which increases the real interest rate (r). A higher real interest rate decreases investment spending (I) and interest-sensitive consumption (interest-sensitive C; consumption financed by borrowing, such as spending on houses and cars), which leads to a decrease in aggregate demand (AD) and, therefore, in real GDP. This chain of events can be illustrated as

$$\uparrow \text{government borrowing} \rightarrow \uparrow D_{LF} \rightarrow \uparrow r \rightarrow \downarrow I/\text{investment-sensitive } C \rightarrow \downarrow AD \rightarrow \downarrow \text{real GDP}$$

In the long run, the decrease in investment can lead to lower rate of capital accumulation and therefore lower economic growth.

The second reason: today's deficits, by increasing the government's debt, place financial pressure on future budgets. The impact of current deficits on future budgets is straightforward. Like individuals, governments must pay their bills, including interest payments on their accumulated debt. When a government is deeply in debt, those interest payments can be substantial. In fiscal 2016, the U.S. federal government paid 1.3% of GDP—$240.1 billion—in interest on its debt. And although this is a relatively large fraction of GDP, other countries pay even greater fractions of their GDP to service their debt. For example, in 2016, Greece paid interest of about 3.2% of GDP.

Other things equal, a government paying large sums in interest must raise more revenue from taxes or spend less than it would otherwise be able to afford—or it must borrow even more to cover the gap. And a government that borrows to pay interest on its outstanding debt pushes itself even deeper into debt. This process can eventually push a government to the point at which lenders question its ability to repay. Like consumers who have maxed out their credit cards, the government will find that lenders are unwilling to lend any more funds. The result can be that the government defaults on its debt—it stops paying what it owes. Default is often followed by deep financial and economic turmoil.

The idea of a government defaulting sounds far-fetched, but it is not impossible. In the 1990s, Argentina, a relatively high-income developing country, was widely praised for its economic policies—and it was able to borrow large sums from foreign lenders. By 2001, however, Argentina's interest payments were spiraling out of control, and the country stopped paying the sums that were due. In the end, Argentina reached a settlement with most of its lenders under which it paid less than a third of the amount originally due. Similarly, the government of Greece faced default in 2012, and bond holders agreed to trade their bonds for new ones worth less than half as much. In the same year, concerns about economic frailty forced the governments of Ireland, Portugal, Italy, and Spain to pay high interest rates on their debt to compensate for the risk of default.

Default creates havoc in a country's financial markets and badly shakes public confidence in both the government and the economy. For example, Argentina's debt default was accompanied by a crisis in the country's banking system and a very severe recession. And even if a highly indebted government avoids default, a heavy debt burden typically forces it to slash spending or raise taxes, politically unpopular measures that can also damage the economy.

Public sector workers in Athens protest layoffs related to austerity measures in the wake of Greece's economic crisis.

One question some people ask is: can't a government that has trouble borrowing just print money to pay its bills? Yes, it can, but this leads to another problem: inflation. In fact, budget problems are the main cause of very severe inflation, as we'll see later. The point for now is that governments do not want to find themselves in a position where the choice is between defaulting on their debts and inflating those debts away.

Concerns about the long-run effects of deficits need not rule out the use of fiscal policy to stimulate the economy when it is depressed. However, these concerns do mean that governments should try to offset budget deficits in bad years with budget surpluses in good years. In other words, governments should run a budget that is approximately balanced over time. How often do they actually do so?

Deficits and Debt in Practice

Figure 30.3 shows how the U.S. federal government's budget deficit and its debt have evolved since 1940. Panel (a) shows the federal deficit as a percentage of GDP. As you can see, the federal government ran huge deficits during World War II. It briefly ran surpluses after the war, but it has normally run deficits ever since, especially after 1980. This seems inconsistent with the advice that governments should offset deficits in bad times with surpluses in good times.

The **debt–GDP ratio** is the government's debt as a percentage of GDP.

However, panel (b) of Figure 30.3 shows that these deficits have not led to runaway debt. To assess the ability of governments to pay their debt, we often use the **debt–GDP ratio**, the government's debt as a percentage of GDP. We use this measure, rather than simply looking at the size of the debt, because GDP, which measures the size of the economy as a whole, is a good indicator of the potential taxes the government can collect. If the government's debt grows more slowly than GDP, the burden of paying that debt is actually falling compared with the government's potential tax revenue.

Figure 30.3 U.S. Federal Deficits and Debt

Panel (a) shows the U.S. federal budget deficit as a percentage of GDP since 1940. The U.S. government ran huge deficits during World War II and has usually run smaller deficits ever since. Panel (b) shows the U.S. debt–GDP ratio. Comparing panels (a) and (b), you can see that in many years the debt–GDP ratio has declined in spite of government deficits. This seeming paradox reflects the fact that the debt–GDP ratio can fall, even when debt is rising, as long as GDP grows faster than debt.

Data Source: Office of Management and Budget.

As you can see from Figure 30.3, the government paid for World War II by borrowing on a huge scale. By the war's end, the public debt was more than 100% of GDP, and many people worried about how it could ever be paid off.

The truth is that it never was paid off. In 1946, the public debt was $242 billion; that number dipped slightly in the next few years, as the United States ran postwar budget surpluses, but the government budget went back into deficit in 1950 with the start of the Korean War. By 1962, the public debt was back up to $248 billion.

But by that time nobody was worried about the fiscal health of the U.S. government because the debt–GDP ratio had fallen by more than half. The reason? Vigorous economic growth, plus mild inflation, had led to a rapid rise in GDP. The experience was a clear lesson in the peculiar fact that modern governments can run deficits forever, as long as they aren't too large.

What we see from panel (b) is that, although the federal debt has grown in almost every year, the debt–GDP ratio fell for 30 years after the end of World War II. This shows that the debt–GDP ratio can fall, even when debt is rising, as long as GDP grows faster than debt. Growth and inflation sometimes allow a government that runs persistent budget deficits to have a declining debt–GDP ratio nevertheless.

Implicit Liabilities

Looking at Figure 30.3, you might be tempted to conclude that, until the 2008 economic crisis struck, the U.S. federal budget was in fairly decent shape: the return to budget deficits after 2001 caused the debt–GDP ratio to rise a bit, but that ratio was still low compared with both historical experience and some other wealthy countries. However, experts on long-run budget issues view the situation of the United States (and other countries with high public debt, such as Japan and Greece) with alarm. The reason is the problem of *implicit liabilities*. Implicit liabilities are spending promises made by governments that are effectively a debt despite the fact that they are not included in the usual debt statistics.

The largest implicit liabilities of the U.S. government arise from two transfer programs that principally benefit older Americans: Social Security and Medicare. The third-largest implicit liability, Medicaid, benefits low-income families. In each of these cases, the government has promised to provide transfer payments to future as well as current beneficiaries. So these programs represent a future debt that must be honored, even though the debt does not currently show up in the usual statistics. Together, these three programs currently account for almost 40% of federal spending.

The implicit liabilities created by these transfer programs worry fiscal experts. **Figure 30.4** shows why. It shows actual spending on Social Security and on Medicare and Medicaid as percentages of GDP from 1980 to 2017, with Congressional Budget Office projections of spending through 2047. According to these projections, spending on Social Security will rise substantially over the next few decades and spending on the two health care programs will soar. Why?

In the case of Social Security, the answer is demography. Social Security is a "pay-as-you-go" system: current workers pay payroll taxes that fund the benefits of current retirees. So the ratio of the number of retirees drawing benefits to the number of workers paying into Social Security has a major impact on the system's finances. There was a

Figure 30.4 Future Demands on the Federal Budget

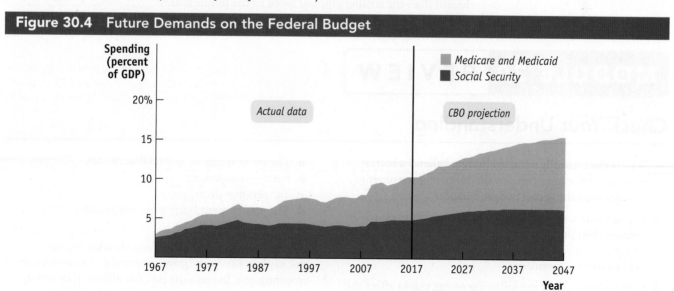

This figure shows actual and projected spending on social insurance programs as a share of GDP. Partly as a result of an aging population, but mainly because of rising health care costs, these programs are expected to become much more expensive over time, posing problems for the federal budget.

Data Source: Congressional Budget Office.

huge surge in the U.S. birth rate between 1946 and 1964, the years of the baby boom. Many baby boomers are currently of working age—which means they are paying taxes, not collecting benefits. But more and more are starting their retirements, and as more and more of them do so, they will stop earning income that is taxed and start collecting benefits. As a result, the ratio of retirees receiving benefits to workers paying into the Social Security system will rise. In 2013, there were 35 retirees for every 100 workers paying into the system. By 2030, according to the Social Security Administration, that number will rise to 46; by 2050, it will rise to 48; and by 2080 that number will be 51 retirees for every 100 workers. This increase will raise benefit payments relative to the size of the economy.

The aging of the baby boomers, by itself, poses a problem, but the projected rise in Medicare and Medicaid spending is a much more serious concern. The main story behind projections of higher Medicare and Medicaid spending is the long-run tendency of health care spending to rise faster than overall spending, both for government-funded and for private-funded health care.

To some extent, the implicit liabilities of the U.S. government are already reflected in debt statistics. We mentioned earlier that the government had a total debt of $19.9 trillion at the end of fiscal 2016, but that only $14.2 trillion of that total was owed to the public. The main explanation for that discrepancy is that both Social Security and part of Medicare (the hospital insurance program) are supported by *dedicated taxes*: their expenses are paid out of special taxes on wages. At times, these dedicated taxes yield more revenue than is needed to pay current benefits. In particular, since the mid-1980s the Social Security system has been taking in more revenue than it currently needs in order to prepare for the retirement of the baby boomers. This surplus in the Social Security system has been used to accumulate a *Social Security trust fund*, which was $2.84 trillion at the end of fiscal 2017.

The money in the trust fund is held in the form of U.S. government bonds, which are included in the $19.9 trillion in total debt. You could say that there's something funny about counting bonds in the Social Security trust fund as part of government debt. After all, these bonds are owed by one part of the government (the government outside the Social Security system) to another part of the government (the Social Security system itself). But the debt corresponds to a real, if implicit, liability: promises by the government to pay future retirement benefits. So, many economists argue that the gross debt of $19.9 trillion, the sum of public debt and government debt held by Social Security and other trust funds, is a more accurate indication of the government's fiscal health than the smaller amount owed to the public alone.

MODULE 30 REVIEW

Check Your Understanding

1. Why is the cyclically adjusted budget balance a better measure of the long-run sustainability of government policies than the actual budget balance?

2. Explain why states required by their constitutions to balance their budgets are likely to experience more severe economic fluctuations than states that are not held to that requirement.

3. Explain how each of the following events would affect the public debt or implicit liabilities of the U.S. government, other things equal. Would the public debt or implicit liabilities be larger or smaller if they occurred?

   a. The growth rate of real GDP increases.
   b. Retirees live longer.
   c. Tax revenue decreases.
   d. The government borrows to pay interest on its current public debt.

4. Use a graph of the loanable funds market to show and explain how large government deficits can lead to crowding out. Explain the possible effects of crowding out on short-run aggregate output and long-run economic growth.

TACKLE THE AP® TEST: Multiple-Choice Questions

1. If government spending exceeds tax revenues, which of the following is necessarily true? There is a
   a. positive budget balance.
   b. budget deficit.
   c. recession.
   d. government debt.
   e. contractionary fiscal policy.

2. Which of the following fiscal policies is expansionary?

	Taxes	Government spending
a.	increase by $100 million	increases by $100 million
b.	decrease by $100 million	decreases by $100 million
c.	increase by $100 million	decreases by $100 million
d.	decrease by $100 million	increases by $100 million
e.	both (a) and (d)	

3. The cyclically adjusted budget deficit is an estimate of what the budget balance would be if real GDP were
   a. greater than potential output.
   b. equal to nominal GDP.
   c. equal to potential output.
   d. falling.
   e. calculated during a recession.

4. During a recession in the United States, what happens automatically to tax revenues and government spending?

	Tax revenues	Government spending
a.	increase	increases
b.	decrease	decreases
c.	increase	decreases
d.	decrease	increases
e.	decrease	does not change

5. Which of the following is a reason to be concerned about persistent budget deficits?
   a. crowding out
   b. government default
   c. the opportunity cost of future interest payments
   d. higher interest rates leading to decreased long-run growth
   e. all of the above

6. In the United States, implicit liabilities
   a. are included in U.S. debt statistics.
   b. represent future government revenue.
   c. account for almost 90% of federal spending.
   d. are future debt of the government.
   e. are considered the same as a tax liability.

7. Which of the following is used to assess a government's ability to pay its debt?
   a. debt–GDP ratio
   b. interest owed on the debt
   c. interest owed on the debt as a percent of GDP
   d. total debt per capita
   e. total tax revenue

TACKLE THE AP® TEST: Free-Response Questions

1. Consider the information provided below for the hypothetical country of Zeta.

   Tax revenues = $2,000

   Government purchases of goods and services = $1,500

   Government transfers = $1,000

   Real GDP = $20,000

   Potential output = $18,000

   a. Is the budget balance in Zeta positive or negative? What is the amount of the budget balance?
   b. Zeta is currently in what phase of the business cycle? Explain.
   c. Is Zeta implementing the appropriate fiscal policy given the current state of the economy? Explain.
   d. How does Zeta's cyclically adjusted budget deficit compare with its actual budget deficit? Explain.

   > **Rubric for FRQ 1 (8 points)**
   > **1 point:** Negative
   > **1 point:** −$500
   > **1 point:** Expansion
   > **1 point:** Real GDP > potential output
   > **1 point:** No
   > **1 point:** Zeta is running a budget deficit during an expansion.
   > **1 point:** It is larger.
   > **1 point:** If real GDP equaled potential output, then tax revenues would be lower and government transfers would be higher.

2. In Module 29 you learned about the market for loanable funds, which is intimately related to our current topic of budget deficits. Use a correctly labeled graph of the market for loanable funds to illustrate the effect of a persistent budget deficit. Identify and explain the effect persistent budget deficits can have on private investment. **(6 points)**

Monetary Policy and the Interest Rate

In this Module, you will learn to:
- Describe how a central bank implements monetary policy by moving the interest rate to affect aggregate output
- Explain why monetary policy is the main tool for stabilizing the economy

Central banks have some more creative ways than this to stabilize the economy.

In Modules 28 and 29 we developed models of the money market and the loanable funds market. We also saw how these two markets are consistent and related. In the short run, the interest rate is determined in the money market and the loanable funds market adjusts in response to changes in the money market. However, in the long run, the interest rate is determined by matching the supply and demand of loanable funds that arise when real GDP equals potential output. Now we are ready to use these models to explain how a central bank can use monetary policy to stabilize the economy in the short run.

Monetary Policy and the Interest Rate

Let's examine how a central bank can use changes in the money supply to change the interest rate. **Figure 31.1** shows what happens when a central bank increases the money supply from $\overline{M}_1$ to $\overline{M}_2$. The economy is originally in equilibrium at E_1, with the equilibrium interest rate r_1 and the money supply $\overline{M}_1$. When the central bank increases the money supply to $\overline{M}_2$, the money supply curve shifts to the right, from MS_1 to MS_2, and the equilibrium interest rate falls to r_2. Why? Because r_2 is the only interest rate at which the public is willing to hold the quantity of money actually supplied, $\overline{M}_2$. So an increase in the money supply drives the interest rate down. Similarly, a reduction in the money supply drives the interest rate up. By adjusting the money supply up or down, the central bank can set the interest rate.

In the United States, at each meeting the Federal Open Market Committee of the Federal Reserve decides on the interest rate to prevail for the next six weeks, until its

Figure 31.1 The Effect of an Increase in the Money Supply on the Interest Rate

A central bank can lower the interest rate by increasing the money supply. Here, the equilibrium interest rate falls from r_1 to r_2 in response to an increase in the money supply from $\overline{M}_1$ to $\overline{M}_2$.

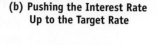

Figure 31.2 Setting the Federal Funds Rate

The Federal Reserve sets a target for the federal funds rate and uses open-market operations to achieve that target. In both panels the target rate is r_T. In panel (a) the initial equilibrium interest rate, r_1, is above the target rate. The Fed increases the money supply by making an open-market purchase of Treasury bills, pushing the money supply curve

rightward, from MS_1 to MS_2, and driving the interest rate down to r_T. In panel (b) the initial equilibrium interest rate, r_1, is below the target rate. The Fed reduces the money supply by making an open-market sale of Treasury bills, pushing the money supply curve leftward, from MS_1 to MS_2, and driving the interest rate up to r_T.

next meeting. The Fed sets a **target federal funds rate**, a desired level for the federal funds rate. This target is then enforced by the Open Market Desk of the Federal Reserve Bank of New York, which adjusts the money supply through *open-market operations*—the purchase or sale of Treasury bills—until the actual federal funds rate equals the target rate. The other tools of monetary policy, lending through the discount window and changes in reserve requirements, aren't used on a regular basis.

Figure 31.2 shows how interest rate targeting by the Federal Reserve works. In both panels, r_T is the target federal funds rate. In panel (a), the initial money supply curve is MS_1 with money supply $\overline{M}_1$, and the equilibrium interest rate, r_1, is above the target rate. To lower the interest rate to r_T, the Fed makes an open-market purchase of Treasury bills, which leads to an increase in the money supply via the money multiplier. This is illustrated in panel (a) by the rightward shift lead to a crowding out of private investment and reduction in economic growth. Let's see why of the money supply curve from MS_1 to MS_2 and an increase in the money supply to $\overline{M}_2$. This drives the equilibrium interest rate *down* to the target rate, r_T.

Panel (b) shows the opposite case. Again, the initial money supply curve is MS_1 with money supply $\overline{M}_1$. But this time the equilibrium interest rate, r_1, is below the target federal funds rate, r_T. In this case, the Fed will make an open-market sale of Treasury bills, leading to a fall in the money supply to $\overline{M}_2$ via the money multiplier. The money supply curve shifts leftward from MS_1 to MS_2, driving the equilibrium interest rate *up* to the target federal funds rate, r_T.

The Fed sets a **target federal funds rate** and uses open-market operations to achieve that target.

AP® EXAM TIP

The interest rate that the Fed targets is the federal funds rate—the interest rate that commercial banks charge each other for overnight loans. The Fed affects the federal funds rate by changing the supply of money. Be careful not to confuse the federal funds rate with the discount rate, which is the rate Federal Reserve banks charge commercial banks for overnight loans.

Monetary Policy and Aggregate Demand

Previous Modules explored how fiscal policy can be used to stabilize the economy by influencing aggregate demand. Now we will see how monetary policy—changes in the money supply or the interest rate, or both—can play the same role.

Expansionary and Contractionary Monetary Policy

Previously we said that monetary policy shifts the aggregate demand curve. We can now explain how that works: through the effect of monetary policy on the interest rate.

Figure 31.3 illustrates the process. Suppose that the central bank wants to reduce interest rates, so it expands the money supply. As we've seen, this leads to a lower interest rate. A lower interest rate, in turn, will lead to more investment spending, which will lead to higher real GDP, which will lead to higher consumer spending, and so on through the multiplier process. So the total quantity of goods and services demanded at any given aggregate price level rises when the quantity of money increases, and the *AD* curve shifts to the right. Monetary policy that shifts the *AD* curve to the right, as illustrated in the top portion of Figure 31.3, is known as **expansionary monetary policy**.

Expansionary monetary policy is monetary policy that increases aggregate demand.

Figure 31.3 Expansionary and Contractionary Monetary Policy

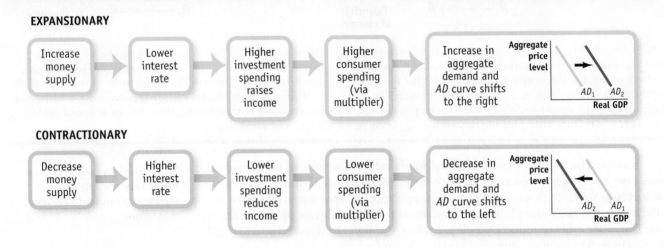

The top portion shows what happens when the central bank adopts an expansionary monetary policy and increases the money supply. Interest rates fall, leading to higher investment spending, which raises income, which, in turn, raises consumer spending and shifts the *AD* curve to the right. The bottom portion shows what happens when the central bank adopts a contractionary monetary policy and reduces the money supply. Interest rates rise, leading to lower investment spending and a reduction in income. This lowers consumer spending and shifts the *AD* curve to the left.

Contractionary monetary policy is monetary policy that reduces aggregate demand.

Suppose, alternatively, that the central bank contracts the money supply. This leads to a higher interest rate. The higher interest rate leads to lower investment spending, which leads to lower real GDP, which leads to lower consumer spending, and so on. So the total quantity of goods and services demanded falls when the money supply is reduced, and the *AD* curve shifts to the left. Monetary policy that shifts the *AD* curve to the left, as illustrated in the lower portion of Figure 31.3, is called **contractionary monetary policy**.

Monetary Policy in Practice

We have learned that policy makers try to fight recessions. They also try to ensure *price stability*: low (though usually not zero) inflation. Actual monetary policy reflects a combination of these goals.

In general, the Federal Reserve and other central banks tend to engage in expansionary monetary policy when actual real GDP is below potential output. Panel (a) of **Figure 31.4** shows the U.S. output gap, which we defined as the percentage difference

Figure 31.4 Tracking Monetary Policy Using the Output Gap, Inflation, and the Taylor Rule

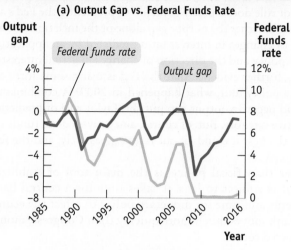

(a) Output Gap vs. Federal Funds Rate

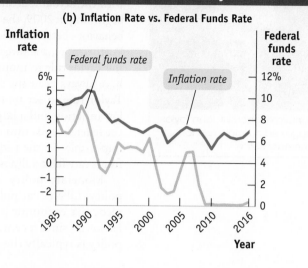

(b) Inflation Rate vs. Federal Funds Rate

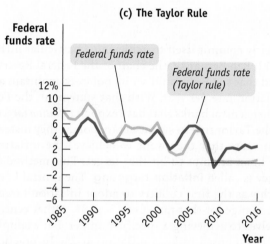

(c) The Taylor Rule

Panel (a) shows that the federal funds rate tends to rise when there is a large positive output gap. Panel (b) shows that the federal funds rate tends to be high when inflation is high and low when inflation is low. Panel (c) shows the Taylor rule in action. The blue-green line shows the actual federal funds rate from 1985 to 2016. The red line shows the interest rate the Fed *should* have set according to the Taylor rule. The fit isn't perfect—in fact, for a period after 2009 the Taylor rule suggests a negative interest rate, an impossibility—but the Taylor rule does a better job of tracking U.S. monetary policy than either the output gap or the inflation rate alone.

Data Sources: Bureau of Economic Analysis, Board of Governors, Congressional Budget Office.

---

between actual real GDP and potential output, versus the federal funds rate since 1985. (Recall that the output gap is positive when actual real GDP exceeds potential output.) As you can see, the Fed has tended to raise interest rates when the output gap is rising—that is, when the economy is developing an inflationary gap—and to cut rates when the output gap is falling.

One reason the Fed was willing to keep interest rates low in the late 1990s was that inflation was low. Panel (b) of Figure 31.4 compares the inflation rate, measured as the rate of change in consumer prices excluding food and energy, with the federal funds rate. You can see how low inflation during the mid-1990s and early 2000s helped encourage loose monetary policy both in the late 1990s and in 2002–2003.

In 1993, Stanford economist John Taylor suggested that monetary policy should follow a simple rule that takes into account concerns about both the business cycle and inflation. The **Taylor rule for monetary policy** is a rule for setting the federal funds rate that takes into account both the inflation rate and the output gap. He also suggested that actual monetary policy often looks as if the Federal Reserve was, in fact, more or less following the proposed rule. The rule Taylor originally suggested was as follows:

$$\text{Federal funds rate} = 1 + (1.5 \times \text{inflation rate}) + (0.5 \times \text{output gap})$$

AP® EXAM TIP

On the AP® exam, if you are asked what policy the central bank could use to correct a particular problem in the economy, identify the correct open-market operation (buying bonds or selling bonds) and be prepared to explain how it would affect interest rates, investment, aggregate demand, and real GDP/the price level.

The **Taylor rule for monetary policy** is a rule for setting the federal funds rate that takes into account both the inflation rate and the output gap.

Stanford economist John Taylor suggested a simple rule for monetary policy.

Panel (c) of Figure 31.4 compares the federal funds rate specified by the Taylor rule with the actual federal funds rate from 1985 to 2016. With the exception of a period beginning in 2009, the Taylor rule does a pretty good job of predicting the Fed's actual behavior—better than looking at either the output gap alone or the inflation rate alone. Furthermore, the direction of changes in interest rates predicted by an application of the Taylor rule to monetary policy and the direction of changes in actual interest rates have always been the same—further evidence that the Fed is using some form of the Taylor rule to set monetary policy. But, what happened in 2009? A combination of low inflation and a large and negative output gap put the Taylor rule of prediction of the federal funds into negative territory. But, of course, a negative federal funds rate is impossible. So the Fed did the best it could—it cut rates aggressively, and the federal funds rate fell to almost zero.

Monetary policy, rather than fiscal policy, is the main tool of stabilization policy. Like fiscal policy, it is subject to lags: it takes time for a central bank to recognize economic problems and time for monetary policy to affect the economy. However, since a central bank moves much more quickly than Congress, monetary policy is typically the preferred tool.

Inflation Targeting

Until 2012, the Fed did not explicitly commit itself to achieving a particular inflation rate. However, in January 2012, Ben Bernanke, the chair of the Federal Reserve

In 2012, Fed Chair Ben Bernanke announced that the Fed would now have an explicit inflation target.

at the time, announced that the Fed would set its policy to maintain an approximately 2% inflation rate per year. With that statement, the Fed joined a number of other central banks that have explicit *inflation targets*. So rather than using the Taylor rule to set monetary policy, they instead announce the inflation rate that they want to achieve—the inflation target—and set policy in an attempt to hit that target. This method of setting monetary policy is called **inflation targeting**. The central bank of New Zealand, which was the first country to adopt inflation targeting in 1988, specified a range for that target of 1% to 3%. Other central banks commit themselves to achieving a specific number. For example, the Bank of England is supposed to keep inflation at 2%. In practice, there doesn't seem to be much difference between these versions: central banks with a target range for inflation seem to aim for the middle of that range, and central banks with a fixed target tend to give themselves considerable wiggle room.

Inflation targeting occurs when the central bank sets an explicit target for the inflation rate and sets monetary policy in order to hit that target.

One major difference between inflation targeting and the Taylor rule is that inflation targeting is forward-looking rather than backward-looking. That is, the Taylor rule adjusts monetary policy in response to *past* inflation, but inflation targeting is based on a forecast of *future* inflation.

Advocates of inflation targeting argue that it has two key advantages, *transparency* and *accountability*. First, economic uncertainty is reduced because the public knows the objective of an inflation-targeting central bank. Second, the central bank's success can be judged by seeing how closely actual inflation rates have matched the inflation target, making central bankers accountable.

Critics of inflation targeting argue that it's too restrictive because there are times when other concerns—like the stability of the financial system—should take priority over achieving any particular inflation rate. Indeed, in late 2007 and early 2008 the Fed cut interest rates much more than either the Taylor rule or inflation targeting would have dictated because it feared that turmoil in the financial markets would lead to a major recession (which it did).

MODULE 31 REVIEW

Check Your Understanding

1. Assume that there is an increase in the demand for money at every interest rate. Using a diagram, show what effect this will have on the equilibrium interest rate for a given money supply.

2. Now assume that the Fed is following a policy of targeting the federal funds rate. What will the Fed do in the situation described in Question 1 to keep the federal funds rate unchanged? Illustrate with a diagram.

3. Suppose the economy is currently suffering from a recessionary gap and the central bank uses an expansionary monetary policy to close that gap. Describe the short-run effect of this policy on the following.
   a. the money supply curve
   b. the equilibrium interest rate
   c. investment spending
   d. consumer spending
   e. aggregate output

TACKLE THE AP® TEST: Multiple-Choice Questions

1. At each meeting of the Federal Open Market Committee, the Federal Reserve sets a target for which of the following?
   a. prime interest rate
   b. federal funds rate
   c. discount rate
   d. market interest rate
   e. mortgage interest rate

2. Which of the following actions can the central bank take to decrease the equilibrium interest rate?
   a. increase the money supply
   b. increase money demand
   c. decrease the money supply
   d. decrease money demand
   e. both (a) and (d)

3. Contractionary monetary policy attempts to _____ aggregate demand by _____ interest rates.
   a. decrease   increasing
   b. increase   decreasing
   c. decrease   decreasing
   d. increase   increasing
   e. increase   maintaining

4. Which of the following is a goal of monetary policy?
   a. zero inflation
   b. deflation
   c. price stability
   d. increased potential output
   e. decreased actual real GDP

5. When implementing monetary policy, the central bank attempts to achieve
   a. an explicit target real GDP growth rate.
   b. zero inflation.
   c. a low rate of deflation.
   d. an explicit target inflation rate.
   e. 4–5% inflation.

6. The Taylor rule for monetary policy sets the federal funds rate based on
   a. the output gap only.
   b. the inflation rate only.
   c. both the output gap and the inflation rate.
   d. neither the output gap nor the inflation rate.
   e. all economic data and conditions.

7. Which of the following correctly describes how a decrease in the money supply will ultimately affect real GDP?
   a. $\downarrow MS \to \uparrow i \to \downarrow I \to \uparrow C \to \downarrow AD \to \downarrow$ real GDP
   b. $\downarrow MS \to \uparrow i \to \downarrow I \to \downarrow C \to \downarrow AD \to \downarrow$ real GDP
   c. $\downarrow MS \to \uparrow i \to \uparrow I \to \uparrow C \to \downarrow AD \to \downarrow$ real GDP
   d. $\downarrow MS \to \downarrow i \to \downarrow I \to \downarrow C \to \uparrow AD \to \downarrow$ real GDP
   e. $\downarrow MS \to \downarrow i \to \downarrow I \to \downarrow C \to \downarrow AD \to \downarrow$ real GDP

TACKLE THE AP® TEST: Free-Response Questions

1. a. Give the equation for the Taylor rule.
   b. How well does the Taylor rule fit the Fed's actual behavior? Explain.
   c. Suppose the inflation rate is 1% and the output gap is 3%. What federal funds rate does the Taylor rule predict?
   d. Suppose the inflation rate increases by 2 percentage points. If the Fed follows the Taylor rule, what specific change in the target federal funds rate will the Fed seek? Identify the general type of policy the Fed uses to achieve that sort of change.

2. **a.** What can the central bank do with each of its three primary tools to implement expansionary monetary policy during a recession?
   b. Use a correctly labeled graph of the money market to explain how the central bank's use of expansionary monetary policy affects interest rates in the short run.
   c. Explain how the interest rate change you graphed in part b affects aggregate supply and demand in the short run.
   d. Use a correctly labeled aggregate demand and supply graph to show how expansionary monetary policy affects aggregate output in the short run. **(11 points)**

MOD 32

Money, Output, and Prices in the Long Run

> **In this Module, you will learn to:**
> - Identify the effects of an inappropriate monetary policy
> - Explain the concept of monetary neutrality and its relationship to the long-term economic effects of monetary policy

In the previous Module we discussed how expansionary and contractionary monetary policy can be used to stabilize the economy. The Federal Reserve can use its monetary policy tools to change the money supply and cause the equilibrium interest rate in the money market to increase or decrease. But what if a central bank pursues a monetary policy that is not appropriate? That is, what if a central bank pursues expansionary policy during an expansion or contractionary policy during a recession? In this Module we consider how a counterproductive action by a central bank can actually destabilize the economy in the short run. We also introduce the long-run effects of monetary policy. As we learned in the last section, the money market (where monetary policy has its effect on the money supply) determines the interest rate only in the short run. In the long run, the interest rate is determined in the market for loanable funds. Here we look at long-run adjustments and consider the long-run effects of monetary policy.

Money, Output, and Prices

Because of its expansionary and contractionary effects, monetary policy is generally the policy tool of choice to help stabilize the economy. However, not all actions by central banks are productive. In particular, as we'll see later, central banks sometimes print money not to fight a recessionary gap but to help the government pay its bills, an action that typically destabilizes the economy.

What happens when a change in the money supply pushes the economy away from, rather than toward, long-run equilibrium? The economy is self-correcting in the long run: a demand shock has only a temporary effect on aggregate output. If the demand shock is the result of a change in the money supply, we can make a stronger statement: in the long run, changes in the quantity of money affect the aggregate price level, but they do not change real aggregate output or the interest rate. To see why, let's look at what happens if the central bank permanently increases the money supply.

Short-Run and Long-Run Effects of an Increase in the Money Supply

To analyze the long-run effects of monetary policy, it's helpful to think of the central bank as choosing a target for the money supply rather than for the interest rate. In assessing the effects of an increase in the money supply, we return to the analysis of the long-run effects of an increase in aggregate demand.

Figure 32.1 shows the short-run and long-run effects of an increase in the money supply when the economy begins at potential output Y_1. The initial short-run aggregate

Figure 32.1   The Short-Run and Long-Run Effects of an Increase in the Money Supply

An increase in the money supply reduces the interest rate and increases aggregate demand . . .

. . . but the eventual rise in nominal wages leads to a fall in short-run aggregate supply and aggregate output falls back to potential output.

An increase in the money supply generates a positive short-run effect (seen in the shift from E_1 to E_2), but no long-run effect, on real GDP (see the shift back to E_3).

supply curve is $SRAS_1$, the long-run aggregate supply curve is $LRAS$, and the initial aggregate demand curve is AD_1. The economy's initial equilibrium is at E_1, a point of both short-run and long-run macroeconomic equilibrium because it is on both the short-run and the long-run aggregate supply curves. Real GDP is at potential output Y_1.

Now suppose there is an increase in the money supply. Other things equal, an increase in the money supply reduces the interest rate, which increases investment spending, which leads to a further rise in consumer spending, and so on. So an increase in the money supply increases the demand for goods and services, shifting the AD curve rightward to AD_2. In the short run, the economy moves to a new short-run macroeconomic equilibrium at E_2. The price level rises from P_1 to P_2, and real GDP rises from Y_1 to Y_2. That is, both the aggregate price level and aggregate output increase in the short run.

But the aggregate output level, Y_2, is above potential output. Production at a level above potential output leads to low unemployment, which brings about a rise in nominal wages over time, causing the short-run aggregate supply curve to shift leftward. This process stops only when the $SRAS$ curve ends up at $SRAS_2$ and the economy ends up at point E_3, a point of both short-run and long-run macroeconomic equilibrium. The long-run effect of an increase in the money supply, then, is that the aggregate price level has increased from P_1 to P_3, but aggregate output is back at potential output Y_1. In the long run, a monetary expansion raises the aggregate price level but has no effect on real GDP.

If the money supply decreases, the story we have just told plays out in reverse. Other things equal, a decrease in the money supply raises the interest rate, which decreases investment spending, which leads to a further decrease in consumer spending, and so on. So a decrease in the money supply decreases the demand for goods and services at any given aggregate price level, shifting the aggregate demand curve to the left. In the short run, the economy moves to a new short-run macroeconomic equilibrium at a level of real GDP below potential output and a lower aggregate price level. That is, both the aggregate price level and aggregate output decrease in the short run. But what happens over time? When the aggregate output level is below potential output, nominal wages fall. When this happens, the short-run aggregate supply curve shifts rightward. This process stops only when the *SRAS* curve ends up at a point of both short-run and long-run macroeconomic equilibrium. The long-run effect of a decrease in the money supply, then, is that the aggregate price level decreases, but aggregate output is back at potential output. In the long run, a monetary contraction decreases the aggregate price level but has no effect on real GDP.

Monetary Neutrality

How much does a change in the money supply change the aggregate price level in the long run? The answer is that a change in the money supply leads to a proportional change in the aggregate price level in the long run. For example, if the money supply falls 25%, the aggregate price level falls 25% in the long run; if the money supply rises 50%, the aggregate price level rises 50% in the long run.

How do we know this? Consider the following thought experiment: suppose all prices in the economy—prices of final goods and services and also factor prices, such as nominal wage rates—double. And suppose the money supply doubles at the same time. What difference does this make to the economy in real terms? None. All real variables in the economy—such as real GDP and the real value of the money supply (the amount of goods and services it can buy)—are unchanged. So there is no reason for anyone to behave any differently.

We can state this argument in reverse: if the economy starts out in long-run macroeconomic equilibrium and the money supply changes, restoring long-run macroeconomic equilibrium requires restoring all real values to their original values. This includes restoring the real value of the money supply to its original level. So if the money supply falls 25%, the aggregate price level must fall 25%; if the money supply rises 50%, the price level must rise 50%; and so on.

This analysis demonstrates the concept known as **monetary neutrality**, in which changes in the money supply have no real effects on the economy. In the long run, the only effect of an increase in the money supply is to raise the aggregate price level by an equal percentage. Economists argue that *money is neutral in the long run.*

According to the concept of **monetary neutrality**, changes in the money supply have no real effects on the economy.

Changes in the Money Supply and the Interest Rate in the Long Run

In the short run, an increase in the money supply leads to a fall in the interest rate, and a decrease in the money supply leads to a rise in the interest rate. Module 29 explained that in the long run it's a different story: changes in the money supply don't affect the interest rate at all. Here we'll review that story and discuss the reasons behind it in greater detail.

Figure 32.2 shows the money supply curve and the money demand curve before and after the Fed increases the money supply. We assume that the economy is initially at E_1, in long-run macroeconomic equilibrium at potential output, and with money supply $\overline{M}_1$.

Figure 32.2 The Long-Run Determination of the Interest Rate

In the short run, an increase in the money supply from $\overline{M}_1$ to $\overline{M}_2$ pushes the interest rate down from r_1 to r_2 and the economy moves to E_2, a short-run equilibrium. In the long run, however, the aggregate price level rises in proportion to the increase in the money supply, leading to an increase in money demand at any given interest rate in proportion to the increase in the aggregate price level, as shown by the shift from MD_1 to MD_2. The result is that the quantity of money demanded at any given interest rate rises by the same amount as the quantity of money supplied. The economy moves to long-run equilibrium at E_3 and the interest rate returns to r_1.

The initial equilibrium interest rate, determined by the intersection of the money demand curve MD_1 and the money supply curve MS_1, is r_1.

Now suppose that the money supply increases from $\overline{M}_1$ to $\overline{M}_2$. In the short run, the economy moves from E_1 to E_2 and the interest rate falls from r_1 to r_2. Over time, however, the aggregate price level rises, and this raises money demand, shifting the money demand curve rightward from MD_1 to MD_2. The economy moves to a new long-run equilibrium at E_3, and the interest rate rises to its original level of r_1.

How do we know that the long-run equilibrium interest rate is the original interest rate, r_1? Because the eventual increase in money demand is proportional to the increase in money supply, thus counteracting the initial downward effect on interest rates. Let's follow the chain of events to see why. With monetary neutrality, an increase in the money supply is matched by a proportional increase in the price level in the long run. If the money supply rises by, say, 50%, the price level will also rise by 50%. Changes in the price level, in turn, cause proportional changes in the demand for money. So a 50% increase in the money supply raises the aggregate price level by 50%, which increases the quantity of money demanded at any given interest rate by 50%. Thus, at the initial interest rate of r_1, the quantity of money demanded rises exactly as much as the money supply, and r_1 is again the equilibrium interest rate. In the long run, then, changes in the money supply do not affect the interest rate.

However, this is a good time to recall the dictum of John Maynard Keynes: "In the long run we are all dead." In the long run, changes in the money supply don't have any effect on real GDP, interest rates, or anything else except the price level. But it would be foolish to conclude from this that the Fed is irrelevant. Monetary policy does have powerful real effects on the economy in the short run, often making the difference between recession and expansion. And that matters a lot for society's welfare.

MODULE 32 REVIEW

Check Your Understanding

1. Suppose the economy begins in long-run macroeconomic equilibrium. What is the long-run effect on the aggregate price level of a 5% increase in the money supply? Explain.

2. Suppose the economy begins in long-run macroeconomic equilibrium. What is the long-run effect on the interest rate of a 5% increase in the money supply? Explain.

1. In the long run, changes in the quantity of money affect which of the following?
   a. real aggregate output
   b. real interest rates
   c. the aggregate price level
   d. real wages
   e. all of the above

2. An increase in the money supply will lead to which of the following in the short run?
   a. higher interest rates
   b. decreased investment spending
   c. decreased consumer spending
   d. increased aggregate demand
   e. lower real GDP

3. A 10% decrease in the money supply will change the aggregate price level in the long run by
   a. zero.   d. 20%.
   b. less than 10%.   e. more than 20%.
   c. 10%.

4. Monetary neutrality means that, in the long run, changes in the money supply
   a. cannot happen.
   b. have no effect on the economy.
   c. have no real effect on the economy.
   d. increase real GDP.
   e. change real interest rates.

5. Percentage increases in the money supply and average annual increases in the price level for a country provide evidence that
   a. the changes in the two variables are exactly equal.
   b. the money supply and aggregate price level are unrelated.
   c. money neutrality holds only in wealthy countries.
   d. monetary policy is ineffective.
   e. money is neutral in the long run.

6. In the long run, real GDP will tend to
   a. move above potential output.
   b. equal potential output.
   c. move below potential output.
   d. move either above or below potential output.
   e. decrease.

7. Which of the following is the long-run response of the money demand curve to an increase in money supply?
   a. It shifts to the right.
   b. It decreases.
   c. It becomes vertical.
   d. There is a movement to the right along the curve.
   e. It does not change.

1. Assume the central bank increases the quantity of money by 25%, even though the economy is initially in both short-run and long-run macroeconomic equilibrium. Describe the effects, in the short run and in the long run (giving numbers where possible), on the following:
   a. aggregate output
   b. the aggregate price level
   c. the real value of the money supply (its purchasing power for goods and services)
   d. the interest rate

> **Rubric for FRQ 1 (8 points)**
>
> **1 point:** Aggregate output rises in the short run.
>
> **1 point:** Aggregate output falls back to potential output in the long run.
>
> **1 point:** The aggregate price level rises in the short run (by less than 25%).
>
> **1 point:** The aggregate price level rises by 25% in the long run.

> **1 point:** The real value of the money supply increases in the short run.
>
> **1 point:** The real value of the money supply does not change (relative to its original value) in the long run.
>
> **1 point:** The interest rate falls in the short run.
>
> **1 point:** The interest rate rises back to its original level in the long run.

2. a. Draw a correctly labeled graph of aggregate demand and aggregate supply showing an economy in long-run macroeconomic equilibrium.
   b. On your graph, show what happens in the short run if the central bank increases the money supply to pay off a government deficit. Explain.
   c. On your graph, show what will happen in the long run. Explain. **(6 points)**

Types of Inflation, Disinflation, and Deflation

In this Module, you will learn to:
- Use the classical model of the price level
- Explain why efforts to collect an inflation tax by printing money can lead to high rates of inflation and even hyperinflation
- Define the types of inflation: cost-push and demand-pull

We have seen that monetary policy affects economic welfare in the short run. Let's take a closer look at two phenomena that are the focus of monetary policy: inflation and deflation.

Money and Inflation

In 2016, Venezuela had the highest rate of inflation in the world, estimated at 254%. Although the United States has not experienced inflation levels that high, in the late 1970s and early 1980s, consumer prices were rising at an annual rate as high as 13%—for comparison, the inflation rate was around 2% in 2018. The policies that the Federal Reserve instituted to reduce high inflation in the 1970s led to the deepest recession the United States had experienced since the Great Depression. As we'll see later, moderate levels of inflation such as those experienced in the United States—even the double-digit inflation of the late 1970s—can have complex causes. Very high inflation is associated with rapid increases in the money supply, but the causes of moderate inflation, the type experienced in the United States, are quite different.

A peaceful protest by Venezuelan activists protesting against inflation, shortages, and the recession in Caracas, Venezuela, in summer 2015.

To understand what causes inflation, we need to revisit the effect of changes in the money supply on the overall price level. Then we'll turn to the reasons why governments sometimes increase the money supply very rapidly.

The Classical Model of Money and Prices

We learned that in the short run an increase in the money supply increases real GDP by lowering the interest rate and stimulating investment spending and consumer spending. However, in the long run, as nominal wages and other sticky prices rise, real GDP falls back to its original level. So in the long run, an increase in the money supply does not change real GDP. Instead, other things equal, it leads to an equal percentage rise in the overall price level; that is, the prices of all goods and services in the economy, including nominal wages and the prices of intermediate goods, rise by the same percentage as the money supply. And when the overall price level rises, the aggregate price level—the prices of all final goods and services—rises as well. As a result, in the long run, a change in the *nominal* money supply, M, leads to a change in the aggregate price level, P, that leaves the *real* quantity of money, M/P, at its original level. As a result, there is no long-run effect on aggregate demand or real GDP. For example, when Turkey dropped six zeros from its currency, the Turkish lira, in January 2005, Turkish real GDP did not change. The only thing that changed was the number of zeros in prices: instead of something costing 2,000,000 lira, it cost 2 lira.

The Turkish currency is the *lira*. When Turkey made 1,000,000 "old" lira equivalent to 1 "new" lira, real GDP was unaffected because of the neutrality of money.

To repeat, this is what happens in the long run. When analyzing large changes in the aggregate price level, however, macroeconomists often find it useful to ignore the distinction between the short run and the long run. Instead, they work with a simplified model in which the effect of a change in the money supply on the aggregate price level takes place instantaneously rather than over a long period of time. You might be concerned about this assumption given the emphasis we've placed on the difference between the short run and the long run. However, for reasons we'll explain shortly, this is a reasonable assumption to make in the case of high inflation.

The simplified model in which the real quantity of money, M/P, is always at its long-run equilibrium level is known as the *classical model of the price level* because it was commonly used by "classical" economists prior to the influence of John Maynard Keynes. To understand the classical model and why it is useful in the context of high inflation, let's revisit the AD–AS model and what it says about the effects of an increase in the money supply. (Unless otherwise noted, we will always be referring to changes in the *nominal* supply of money.)

Figure 33.1 reviews the effects of an increase in the money supply according to the AD–AS model. The economy starts at E_1, a point of short-run and long-run macroeconomic equilibrium. It lies at the intersection of the aggregate demand curve, AD_1, and the short-run aggregate supply curve, $SRAS_1$. It also lies on the long-run aggregate supply curve, $LRAS$. At E_1, the equilibrium aggregate price level is P_1.

Figure 33.1 The Classical Model of the Price Level

Starting at E_1, an increase in the money supply shifts the aggregate demand curve rightward, as shown by the movement from AD_1 to AD_2. There is a new short-run macroeconomic equilibrium at E_2 and a higher price level at P_2. In the long run, nominal wages adjust upward and push the $SRAS$ curve leftward to $SRAS_2$. The total percent increase in the price level from P_1 to P_3 is equal to the percent increase in the money supply.

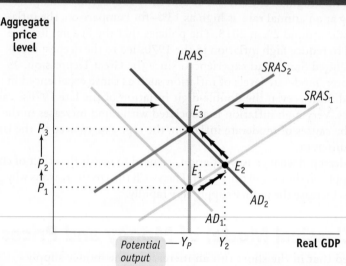

Now suppose there is an increase in the money supply. This is an expansionary monetary policy, which shifts the aggregate demand curve to the right, to AD_2, and moves the economy to a new short-run macroeconomic equilibrium at E_2. Over time, however, nominal wages adjust upward in response to low unemployment and the rise in the aggregate price level, and the $SRAS$ curve shifts to the left, to $SRAS_2$. The new long-run macroeconomic equilibrium is at E_3, and real GDP returns to its initial level. The long-run increase in the aggregate price level from P_1 to P_3 is proportional to the increase in the money supply. As a result, in the long run, changes in the money supply have no effect on the real quantity of money, M/P, or on real GDP. In the long run, money—as we learned—is *neutral*.

The classical model of the price level ignores the short-run movement from E_1 to E_2, assuming instead that the economy moves directly from one long-run equilibrium to another long-run equilibrium. In other words, it assumes that the economy moves directly from E_1 to E_3 and that real GDP never changes in response to a change in the money supply. In effect, in the classical model the effects of money supply changes are analyzed as if the short-run as well as the long-run aggregate supply curves were vertical.

In reality, this is a poor assumption during periods of low inflation. With a low inflation rate, it may take a while for workers and firms to react to a monetary expansion by raising wages and prices. In this scenario, some nominal wages and the prices of some goods are sticky in the short run. As a result, under low inflation there is an upward-sloping *SRAS* curve, and changes in the money supply can indeed change real GDP in the short run.

But what about periods of high inflation? In the face of high inflation, economists have observed that the short-run stickiness of nominal wages and prices tends to vanish. Workers and businesses, sensitized to inflation, are quick to raise their wages and prices in response to changes in the money supply. This implies that under high inflation there is a quicker adjustment of wages and prices of intermediate goods than occurs in the case of low inflation. So the short-run aggregate supply curve shifts leftward more quickly and there is a more rapid return to long-run equilibrium under high inflation. As a result, the classical model of the price level is much more likely to be a good approximation of reality for economies experiencing persistently high inflation.

The consequence of this rapid adjustment of all prices in the economy is that in countries with persistently high inflation, changes in the money supply are quickly translated into changes in the inflation rate. What leads a country to increase its money supply so much that the result is an inflation rate in the hundreds, thousands, or even millions of percent?

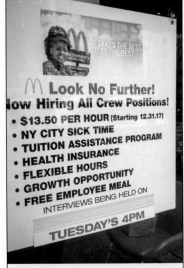

With low inflation, wages can be sticky as it takes time for workers and employers to react to expansionary monetary policy.

The Inflation Tax

Modern economies use fiat money—pieces of paper that have no intrinsic value but are accepted as a medium of exchange. In the United States and most other wealthy countries, the decision about how many pieces of paper—dollars—to issue is placed in the hands of a central bank that is somewhat independent of the political process. However, this independence can always be taken away if politicians decide to seize control of monetary policy.

So what is to prevent a government from paying for some of its expenses not by raising taxes or borrowing but simply by printing money? Nothing. In fact, governments, including the U.S. government, do it all the time. How can the U.S. government do this, given that the Federal Reserve, not the U.S. Treasury, issues money? The answer is that the Treasury and the Federal Reserve work in concert. The Treasury issues debt to finance the government's purchases of goods and services, and the Fed *monetizes* the debt by creating money and buying the debt back from the public through open-market purchases of Treasury bills. In effect, the U.S. government can and does raise revenue by printing money.

For example, in February 2010, the U.S. monetary base—bank reserves plus currency in circulation—was $559 billion larger than it had been a year earlier. This occurred because, over the course of that year, the Federal Reserve had issued $559 billion in money or its electronic equivalent and put it into circulation mainly through open-market operations. To put it another way, the Fed created money out of thin air and used it to buy valuable government securities from the private sector. It's true that the U.S. government pays interest on debt owned by the Federal Reserve—but the Fed, by law, hands the interest payments it receives on government debt back to the Treasury, keeping only enough to fund its own operations. In effect, then, the Federal Reserve's actions enabled the government to pay off $559 billion in outstanding government debt by printing money.

An alternative way to look at this is to say that the right to print money is itself a source of revenue. Economists refer to the revenue generated by the government's right to print money as *seigniorage*, an archaic term that goes back to the Middle Ages. It refers to the right to stamp gold and silver into coins, and charge a fee for doing so, that medieval lords—seigneurs, in France—reserved for themselves.

Seigniorage accounts for only a tiny fraction (less than 1%) of the U.S. government's budget. Furthermore, concerns about seigniorage don't have any influence on the

Old school seigniorage.

Federal Reserve's decisions about how much money to print; the Fed is worried about inflation and unemployment, not revenue. But this hasn't always been true, even in the United States: during the Civil War, both sides relied on seigniorage to help cover budget deficits. And there have been many occasions in history when governments turned to their printing presses as a crucial source of revenue. According to the usual scenario, a government finds itself running a large budget deficit—and lacks either the competence or the political will to eliminate this deficit by raising taxes or cutting spending. Furthermore, the government can't borrow to cover the gap because potential lenders won't extend loans, given the fear that the government's weakness will continue and leave it unable to repay its debts.

In such a situation, a government ends up printing money to cover the budget deficit. But by printing money to pay its bills, a government increases the quantity of money in circulation. And as we've just seen, increases in the money supply translate into equally large increases in the aggregate price level. So printing money to cover a budget deficit leads to inflation.

Who ends up paying for the goods and services the government purchases with newly printed money? The people who currently hold money pay because inflation erodes the purchasing power of their money holdings. In other words, a government imposes an **inflation tax**, a reduction in the value of the money held by the public, by printing money to cover its budget deficit and creating inflation.

It's helpful to think about what this tax represents. If the inflation rate is 5%, then a year from now $1 will buy goods and services worth only about $0.95 today. So a 5% inflation rate in effect imposes a tax rate of 5% on the value of all money held by the public.

But why would any government push the inflation tax to rates of hundreds or thousands of percent? We turn next to the process by which high inflation turns into explosive hyperinflation.

The Logic of Hyperinflation

Inflation imposes a tax on individuals who hold money. And, like most taxes, it will lead people to change their behavior. In particular, when inflation is high, people have a strong incentive to either spend money quickly or acquire interest-bearing assets. The goal is to avoid holding money and thereby reduce the burden of the inflation tax. During the German hyperinflation after World War I, people began using eggs or lumps of coal as a medium of exchange. They did this because lumps of coal maintained their real value over time but money did not. Indeed, during the peak of German hyperinflation, people often burned paper money, which was less valuable than wood.

We are now prepared to understand how countries can get themselves into situations of extreme inflation. Suppose the government prints enough money to pay for a given quantity of goods and services each month. The increase in the money supply causes the inflation rate to rise, which means the government must print more money each month to buy the same quantity of goods and services. If the desire to reduce money holdings causes people to spend money faster than the government prints money, prices increase faster than the money supply. As a result, the government must accelerate the rate of growth of the money supply, which leads to an even higher rate of inflation. As this process becomes self-reinforcing, it can easily spiral out of control.

Here's an analogy: imagine a city government that tries to raise a lot of money with a special fee on taxi rides. The fee will raise the cost of taxi rides, and this will cause people to turn to substitutes, such as walking or taking the bus. As taxi use declines, the government finds that its tax revenue declines and it must impose a higher fee to raise the same amount of revenue as before. You can imagine the ensuing vicious circle: the government imposes fees on taxi rides, which leads to less taxi use, which causes the government to raise the fee on taxi rides, which leads to even less taxi use, and so on.

An **inflation tax** is a reduction in the value of money held by the public caused by inflation.

In the 1920s, hyperinflation made German currency worth so little that children made kites from banknotes.

Substitute the real money supply for taxi rides and the inflation rate for the increase in the fee on taxi rides, and you have the story of hyperinflation. A race develops between the government printing presses and the public: the presses churn out money at a faster and faster rate to try to compensate for the fact that the public is reducing its real money holdings. At some point the inflation rate explodes into hyperinflation, and people are unwilling to hold any money at all (and resort to trading in eggs and lumps of coal). The government is then forced to abandon its use of the inflation tax and shut down the printing presses.

Moderate Inflation and Disinflation

The governments of wealthy, politically stable countries such as the United States and Britain don't find themselves forced to print money to pay their bills. Yet over the past 40 years, both countries, along with a number of other nations, have experienced uncomfortable episodes of inflation. In the United States, the inflation rate peaked at 13% in 1980. In Britain, the inflation rate reached 26% in 1975. Why did policy makers allow this to happen?

Using the aggregate demand and supply model, we can see that there are two possible changes that can lead to an increase in the aggregate price level: a decrease in aggregate supply or an increase in aggregate demand. Inflation that is caused by a significant increase in the price of an input with economy-wide importance is called **cost-push inflation**. For example, it is argued that the oil crisis in the 1970s led to an increase in energy prices in the United States, causing a leftward shift of the aggregate supply curve, increasing the aggregate price level. However, aside from crude oil, it is difficult to think of examples of inputs with economy-wide importance that experience significant price increases.

Inflation that is caused by an increase in aggregate demand is known as **demand-pull inflation**. When a rightward shift of the aggregate demand curve leads to an increase in the aggregate price level, the economy experiences demand-pull inflation. This is sometimes described by the phrase "too much money chasing too few goods," which means that the aggregate demand for goods and services is outpacing the aggregate supply and driving up the prices of goods. For example, large increases in government spending during World War II led to large increases in income and consumer spending after the war ended. Because production during the war had shifted from consumer goods to military goods to support the war effort, the supply of consumer goods was limited. Demand-pull inflation resulted from the combination of high consumer demand ("too much money") and low supply of consumer goods ("too few goods").

In the short run, policies that produce a booming economy also tend to lead to higher inflation, and policies that reduce inflation tend to depress the economy. This creates both temptations and dilemmas for governments.

Imagine yourself as a politician facing reelection in a year and suppose that inflation is fairly low at the moment. You might well be tempted to pursue expansionary policies that will push the unemployment rate down, as a way to please voters, even if your economic advisers warn that this will eventually lead to higher inflation. You might also be tempted to find different economic advisers, who will tell you not to worry: in politics, as in ordinary life, wishful thinking often prevails over realistic analysis.

Conversely, imagine yourself as a politician in an economy suffering from inflation. Your economic advisers will probably tell you that the only way to bring inflation down is to push the economy into a recession, which will lead to temporarily higher unemployment. Are you willing to pay that price? Maybe not.

This political asymmetry—inflationary policies often produce short-term political gains, but policies to bring inflation down carry short-term political costs—explains how countries with no need to impose an inflation tax sometimes end up with serious

Cost-push inflation is inflation that is caused by a significant increase in the price of an input with economy-wide importance.

Demand-pull inflation is inflation that is caused by an increase in aggregate demand.

AP® EXAM TIP

Inflation and deflation are shown as changes in price level on the vertical axis of the aggregate supply and demand graph. Inflation caused by a rightward shift of the aggregate demand curve is known as demand-pull inflation. Inflation caused by a leftward shift of the aggregate supply curve is known as cost-push inflation (because the leftward shift is caused by an increase in production costs). Make sure you can graph and explain cost-push inflation and demand-pull inflation!

inflation problems. For example, that 26% rate of inflation in Britain was largely the result of the British government's decision in 1971 to pursue highly expansionary monetary and fiscal policies. Politicians disregarded warnings that these policies would be inflationary and were extremely reluctant to reverse course even when it became clear that the warnings had been correct.

But why do expansionary policies lead to inflation? We will answer that question in Module 34.

MODULE 33 REVIEW

Check Your Understanding

1. Explain why a large increase in the money supply causes a larger short-run increase in real GDP in an economy that previously had low inflation than in an economy that previously had high inflation. What does this say about situations in which the classical model of the price level applies?

2. Suppose that all wages and prices in an economy are indexed to inflation, meaning that they increase at the same rate as the price level. Can there still be an inflation tax?

TACKLE THE AP® TEST: Multiple-Choice Questions

1. The real quantity of money is
   a. equal to M/P.
   b. equal to real GDP in the short run.
   c. higher in the long run if the Fed buys bonds.
   d. higher when the economy experiences inflation.
   e. all of the above.

2. In the classical model of the price level
   a. only the short-run aggregate supply curve is vertical.
   b. both the short-run and long-run aggregate supply curves are vertical.
   c. only the long-run aggregate supply curve is vertical.
   d. both the short-run aggregate demand and supply curves are vertical.
   e. both the long-run aggregate demand and supply curves are vertical.

3. The classical model of the price level is most applicable in
   a. the United States.
   b. periods of high inflation.
   c. periods of low inflation.
   d. recessions.
   e. depressions.

4. An inflation tax is
   a. imposed by governments to offset price increases.
   b. paid directly as a percentage of the sale price on purchases.
   c. the result of a decrease in the value of money held by the public.

   d. generally levied by states rather than the federal government.
   e. higher during periods of low inflation.

5. Revenue generated by the government's right to print money is known as
   a. seigniorage.
   b. an inflation tax.
   c. hyperinflation.
   d. fiat money.
   e. monetary funds.

6. An increase in the price level resulting from an increase in energy prices is an example of
   a. demand-pull inflation.
   b. re-inflation.
   c. cost-push inflation.
   d. input inflation.
   e. hyperinflation.

7. Demand-pull inflation is caused by which of the following?
   a. an increase in wages
   b. "too little money chasing too few goods"
   c. contractionary monetary policy
   d. an increase in aggregate demand
   e. a decrease in aggregate supply

TACKLE THE AP® TEST: Free-Response Questions

1. Use a correctly labeled aggregate demand and aggregate supply graph to illustrate cost-push inflation. Give an example of what might cause cost-push inflation in the economy.

Rubric for FRQ 1 (9 points)

1 point: Graph labeled "Aggregate price level" or "PL" on the vertical axis and "Real GDP" on the horizontal axis

1 point: AD downward-sloping and labeled

1 point: SRAS upward-sloping and labeled

1 point: LRAS vertical and labeled

1 point: Potential output labeled at horizontal intercept of LRAS

1 point: Long-run macroeconomic equilibrium aggregate price level labeled on vertical axis at intersection of SRAS, LRAS, and AD

1 point: Leftward shift of the SRAS curve

1 point: Higher equilibrium aggregate price level at new intersection of SRAS and AD

1 point: This could be caused by anything that would shift the short-run aggregate supply curve to the left, such as an increase in the price of energy, labor, or another input with economy-wide importance.

2. Draw a correctly labeled aggregate demand and aggregate supply graph showing an economy in long-run macroeconomic equilibrium. On your graph, show the effect of an increase in the money supply, according to the classical model of the price level. **(4 points)**

Inflation and Unemployment: The Phillips Curve

In this Module, you will learn to:
- Identify an output gap in the economy and its corresponding level of unemployment
- Use the Phillips curve to show the nature of the short-run trade-off between inflation and unemployment
- Explain why there is no long-run trade-off between inflation and unemployment
- Discuss why expansionary policies are limited due to the effects of expected inflation
- Explain why even moderate levels of inflation can be hard to end
- Identify the problems with deflation that lead policy makers to prefer a low but positive inflation rate

The Output Gap and the Unemployment Rate

Why do expansionary policies lead to inflation? To answer that question, we need to look first at the relationship between output and unemployment. In Module 18 we

There is a balance between potential output and the unemployment rate.

introduced the concept of *potential output*, the level of real GDP that the economy would produce once all prices had fully adjusted. Potential output typically grows steadily over time, reflecting long-run growth. However, as we learned from the aggregate demand–aggregate supply model, actual aggregate output fluctuates around potential output in the short run: a recessionary gap arises when actual aggregate output falls short of potential output; an inflationary gap arises when actual aggregate output exceeds potential output. Recall that the percentage difference between the actual level of real GDP and potential output is called the *output gap*. A positive or negative output gap occurs when an economy is producing more or less than what would be "expected" because all prices have not yet adjusted. And, as we've learned, wages are the prices in the labor market.

Meanwhile, we learned in Module 13 that the unemployment rate is composed of cyclical unemployment and natural unemployment, the portion of the unemployment rate unaffected by the business cycle. So there is a relationship between the unemployment rate and the output gap. This relationship is defined by two rules:

- When actual aggregate output is equal to potential output, the actual unemployment rate is equal to the natural rate of unemployment.

- When the output gap is positive (an inflationary gap), the unemployment rate is *below* the natural rate. When the output gap is negative (a recessionary gap), the unemployment rate is *above* the natural rate.

In other words, fluctuations of aggregate output around the long-run trend of potential output correspond to fluctuations of the unemployment rate around the natural rate.

This makes sense. When the economy is producing less than potential output—when the output gap is negative—it is not making full use of its productive resources. Among the resources that are not fully used is labor, the economy's most important resource. So we would expect a negative output gap to be associated with unusually high unemployment. Conversely, when the economy is producing more than potential output, it is temporarily using resources at higher-than-normal rates. With this positive output gap, we would expect to see lower-than-normal unemployment.

The Short-Run Phillips Curve

Our next step in understanding the decisions facing governments is to show that there is a short-run trade-off between unemployment and inflation—lower unemployment tends to lead to higher inflation, and vice versa. This key concept is shown by the *Phillips curve*.

The origins of the Phillips curve lie in a famous 1958 paper by the New Zealand–born economist Alban W. H. Phillips. Looking at historical data for Britain, he found that when the unemployment rate was high, the wage rate tended to fall, and when the unemployment rate was low, the wage rate tended to rise. Using data from Britain, the United States, and elsewhere, other economists soon found a similar apparent relationship between the unemployment rate and the rate of inflation—that is, the rate of change in the aggregate price level. For example, **Figure 34.1** shows the U.S. unemployment rate and the rate of consumer price inflation over each subsequent year from 1955 to 1968, with each dot representing one year's data.

Looking at evidence like Figure 34.1, many economists concluded that there is a negative short-run relationship between the unemployment rate and the inflation rate, represented by the **short-run Phillips curve**, or *SRPC*. (We'll explain the

The **short-run Phillips curve (SRPC)** represents the negative short-run relationship between the unemployment rate and the inflation rate.

difference between the short-run and the long-run Phillips curve soon.) **Figure 34.2** shows a hypothetical short-run Phillips curve.

Figure 34.1   Unemployment and Inflation, 1955–1968

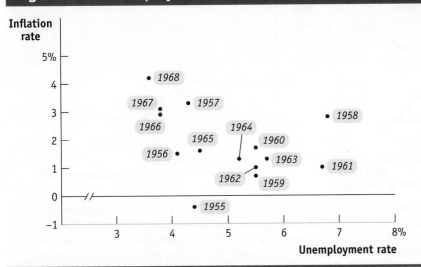

Each dot shows the average U.S. unemployment rate for one year and the percentage increase in the consumer price index over the subsequent year. Data like this lay behind the initial concept of the Phillips curve.

Data Source: Bureau of Labor Statistics.

Figure 34.2   The Short-Run Phillips Curve

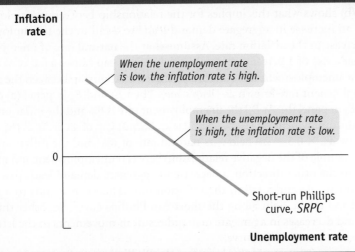

The short-run Phillips curve, *SRPC*, slopes downward because the relationship between the unemployment rate and the inflation rate is negative.

We can better understand the shape of the Phillips curve by examining its ties to the *AD–AS* model. Panel (a) of **Figure 34.3** shows how changes in the aggregate price level and the output gap depend on changes in aggregate demand. Assume that in year 1 the aggregate demand curve is AD_1, the long-run aggregate supply curve is *LRAS*, and the short-run aggregate supply curve is *SRAS*. The initial macroeconomic equilibrium is at E_1, where the price level is 100 and real GDP is $10 trillion. Notice that at E_1 real GDP is equal to potential output, so the output gap is zero.

Now consider what happens if aggregate demand shifts rightward to AD_2 and the economy moves to E_2. At E_2, Real GDP is $10.4 trillion, $0.4 trillion more than potential output—forming a 4% output gap. Meanwhile, at E_2 the aggregate price level has risen to 102—a 2% increase. So panel (a) indicates that in this example a zero output gap is associated with zero inflation and a 4% output gap is associated with 2% inflation.

Figure 34.3   The AD–AS Model and the Short-Run Phillips Curve

(a) An Increase in Aggregate Demand . . .

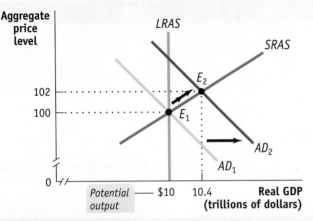

(b) . . . Leads to Both Inflation and a Fall in the Unemployment Rate.

Shifts in aggregate demand lead to movements along the Phillips curve. In panel (a), the economy is initially in equilibrium at E_1. If the aggregate demand curve remains at AD_1, there is an output gap of zero and 0% inflation. If the aggregate demand curve shifts out to AD_2, the positive output gap reduces unemployment to 4%, and inflation rises to 2%. Assuming that the natural rate of unemployment is 6%, the implications for unemployment and inflation are shown in panel (b): with aggregate demand at AD_1, 6% unemployment and 0% inflation will result; if aggregate demand increases to AD_2, 4% unemployment and 2% inflation will result.

Panel (b) shows what this implies for the relationship between unemployment and inflation: an increase in aggregate demand leads to a fall in the unemployment rate and an increase in the inflation rate. Assume that the natural rate of unemployment is 6% and that a rise of 1 percentage point in the output gap causes a fall of ½ percentage point in the unemployment rate (this is a predicted relationship between the output gap and unemployment rate known as *Okun's law*). Then E_1 and E_2 in panel (a) correspond to E_1 and E_2 in panel (b). At E_1, the unemployment rate is 6% and the inflation rate is 0%. At E_2, the unemployment rate is 4%—because an output gap of 4% reduces the unemployment rate by 4% × 0.5 = 2% below its natural rate of 6%—and the inflation rate is 2%. This is an example of the negative relationship between unemployment and inflation.

Going in the other direction, a decrease in aggregate demand leads to a rise in the unemployment rate and a fall in the inflation rate. This corresponds to a movement downward and to the right along the short-run Phillips curve. So, other things equal, increases and decreases in aggregate demand result in movements to the left and right along the short-run Phillips curve.

Changes in aggregate supply also affect the Phillips curve. Previously, we discussed the effect of *supply shocks*, such as sudden changes in the price of oil, that shift the short-run aggregate supply curve. Such shocks also shift the short-run Phillips curve. In general, a negative supply shock shifts *SRPC* up, as the inflation rate increases for every level of the unemployment rate, and a positive supply shock shifts it down as the inflation rate falls for every level of the unemployment rate. Both outcomes are shown in **Figure 34.4.**

But supply shocks are not the only factors that can shift the Phillips curve. In the early 1960s, Americans had little experience with inflation, as inflation rates had been low for decades. But by the late 1960s, after inflation had been steadily increasing for a number of years, Americans had come to expect future inflation. In 1968 two economists—Milton Friedman and Edmund Phelps—independently set forth a crucial hypothesis: that expectations about future inflation directly affect the present inflation rate. Today most economists accept that the *expected inflation rate*—the rate of inflation that employers and workers expect in the near future—is the most important factor, other than the unemployment rate, affecting inflation.

Figure 34.4 The Short-Run Phillips Curve and Supply Shocks

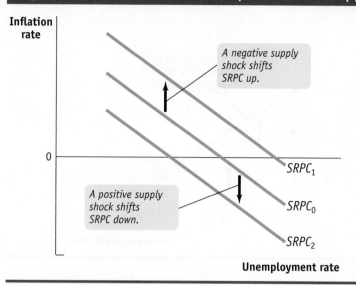

A negative supply shock shifts the *SRPC* up, and a positive supply shock shifts the *SRPC* down.

Inflation Expectations and the Short-Run Phillips Curve

The expected rate of inflation is the rate that employers and workers expect in the near future. One of the crucial discoveries of modern macroeconomics is that changes in the expected rate of inflation affect the short-run trade-off between unemployment and inflation and shift the short-run Phillips curve.

Why do changes in expected inflation affect the short-run Phillips curve? Put yourself in the position of a worker or employer about to sign a contract setting the worker's wages over the next year. For a number of reasons, the wage rate they agree to will be higher if everyone expects high inflation (including rising wages) than if everyone expects prices to be stable. The worker will want a wage rate that takes into account future declines in the purchasing power of earnings. He or she will also want a wage rate that won't fall behind the wages of other workers. And the employer will be more willing to agree to a wage increase now if hiring workers later will be even more expensive. Also, rising prices will make paying a higher wage rate more affordable for the employer because the employer's output will sell for more.

For these reasons, an increase in expected inflation shifts the short-run Phillips curve upward: the actual rate of inflation at any given unemployment rate is higher when the expected inflation rate is higher. In fact, macroeconomists believe that the relationship between changes in expected inflation and changes in actual inflation is one-to-one. That is, when the expected inflation rate increases, the actual inflation rate at any given unemployment rate will increase by the same amount. When the expected inflation rate falls, the actual inflation rate at any given level of unemployment will fall by the same amount.

Figure 34.5 shows how the expected rate of inflation affects the short-run Phillips curve. First, suppose that the expected rate of inflation is 0%. $SRPC_0$ is the short-run Phillips curve when the public expects 0% inflation. According to $SRPC_0$, the actual inflation rate will be 0% if the unemployment rate is 6%; it will be 2% if the unemployment rate is 4%.

Alternatively, suppose the expected rate of inflation is 2%. In that case, employers and workers will build this expectation into wages and prices: at any given unemployment rate, the actual inflation rate will be 2 percentage points higher than it would be if people expected 0% inflation. $SRPC_2$, which shows the Phillips curve when the expected inflation rate is 2%, is $SRPC_0$ shifted upward by 2 percentage

AP® EXAM TIP

Be prepared to explain how a change in expected inflation will affect the macroeconomy. Inflationary expectations shift the *SRAS* curve as well as the *SRPC*. An increase in expected inflation shifts the *SRAS* curve to the left and the *SRPC* to the right. A decrease in expected inflation shifts the *SRAS* curve to the right and the *SRPC* to the left.

Figure 34.5 Expected Inflation and the Short-Run Phillips Curve

An increase in expected inflation shifts the short-run Phillips curve up. $SRPC_0$ is the initial short-run Phillips curve with an expected inflation rate of 0%; $SRPC_2$ is the short-run Phillips curve with an expected inflation rate of 2%. Each additional percentage point of expected inflation raises the actual inflation rate at any given unemployment rate by 1 percentage point.

points at every level of unemployment. According to $SRPC_2$, the actual inflation rate will be 2% if the unemployment rate is 6%; it will be 4% if the unemployment rate is 4%.

What determines the expected rate of inflation? In general, people base their expectations about inflation on experience. If the inflation rate has hovered around 0% in the last few years, people will expect it to be around 0% in the near future. But if the inflation rate has averaged around 5% lately, people will expect inflation to be around 5% in the near future.

Since expected inflation is an important part of the modern discussion about the short-run Phillips curve, you might wonder why it was not in the original formulation of the Phillips curve. The answer lies in history. Think back to what we said about the early 1960s: at that time, people were accustomed to low inflation rates and reasonably expected that future inflation rates would also be low. It was only after 1965 that persistent inflation became a fact of life. So only then did it become clear that expected inflation would play an important role in price-setting.

Inflation and Unemployment in the Long Run

The short-run Phillips curve says that at any given point in time there is a trade-off between unemployment and inflation. According to this view, policy makers have a choice: they can choose to accept the price of high inflation in order to achieve low unemployment, or they can reject high inflation and pay the price of high unemployment. In fact, during the 1960s many economists believed that this trade-off represented a real choice.

However, this view was greatly altered by the later recognition that expected inflation affects the short-run Phillips curve. In the short run, expectations often diverge from reality. In the long run, however, any consistent rate of inflation will be reflected in expectations. If inflation is consistently high, as it was in the 1970s, people will come to expect more of the same; if inflation is consistently low, as it has been in recent years, low inflation will become part of expectations. So what does the trade-off between inflation and unemployment look like in the long run, when actual inflation is incorporated into expectations? Most macroeconomists believe that, in fact, there is no long-run trade-off. That is, it is not possible to achieve lower unemployment in the long run by accepting higher inflation. To see why, we need to introduce another concept: the *long-run Phillips curve.*

The Long-Run Phillips Curve

Figure 34.6 reproduces the two short-run Phillips curves from Figure 34.5, $SRPC_0$ and $SRPC_2$. It also adds an additional short-run Phillips curve, $SRPC_4$, representing a 4% expected rate of inflation. In a moment, we'll explain the significance of the vertical long-run Phillips curve, $LRPC$.

Figure 34.6 The NAIRU and the Long-Run Phillips Curve

$SRPC_0$ is the short-run Phillips curve when the expected inflation rate is 0%. At a 4% unemployment rate, the economy is at point A with an actual inflation rate of 2%. The higher inflation rate will be incorporated into expectations, and the $SRPC$ will shift upward to $SRPC_2$. If policy makers act to keep the unemployment rate at 4%, the actual inflation rate will rise to 4% (point B). Inflationary expectations will be revised upward again, and $SRPC$ will shift to $SRPC_4$. At a 4% unemployment rate the actual inflation rate will rise to 6% (point C). Here, an unemployment rate of 6% is the NAIRU, or nonaccelerating inflation rate of unemployment. As long as unemployment is at the NAIRU, the actual inflation rate will match expectations and remain constant. The long-run Phillips curve, $LRPC$, passes through E_0, E_2, and E_4, and is vertical showing no long-run trade-off between unemployment and inflation.

Suppose that the economy has had a 0% inflation rate in the past. In that case, the current short-run Phillips curve will be $SRPC_0$, reflecting a 0% expected inflation rate. If the unemployment rate is 6%, the actual inflation rate will be 0%.

Also suppose that policy makers decide to trade off lower unemployment for a higher rate of inflation. They use monetary policy, fiscal policy, or both to drive the unemployment rate down to 4%. This puts the economy at point A on $SRPC_0$, leading to an actual inflation rate of 2%.

Over time, the public will come to expect a 2% inflation rate. *This increase in inflationary expectations will shift the short-run Phillips curve upward* to $SRPC_2$. Now, when the unemployment rate is 6%, the actual inflation rate will be 2%. Given this new short-run Phillips curve, policies adopted to keep the unemployment rate at 4% will lead to a 4% actual inflation rate—point B on $SRPC_2$—rather than point A with a 2% actual inflation rate.

Eventually, the 4% actual inflation rate gets built into expectations about the future inflation rate, and the short-run Phillips curve shifts upward yet again to $SRPC_4$. To keep the unemployment rate at 4% would now require accepting a 6% actual inflation rate, point C on $SRPC_4$, and so on. In short, a persistent attempt to trade off lower unemployment for higher inflation leads to *accelerating* inflation over time.

To avoid accelerating inflation over time, the unemployment rate must be high enough that the actual rate of inflation matches the expected rate of inflation. This is the situation at E_0 on $SRPC_0$: when the expected inflation rate is 0% and the unemployment rate is 6%, the actual inflation rate is 0%. It is also the situation at E_2 on $SRPC_2$: when the expected inflation rate is 2% and the unemployment rate is 6%, the actual inflation rate is 2%. And it is the situation at E_4 on $SRPC_4$: when the expected inflation rate is 4% and the unemployment rate is 6%, the actual inflation rate is 4%. As we'll learn shortly, this relationship between accelerating inflation and the unemployment rate is known as the *natural rate hypothesis*.

The nonaccelerating inflation rate of unemployment, or NAIRU, is the unemployment rate at which inflation does not change over time.

The unemployment rate at which inflation does not change over time—6% in Figure 34.6—is known as the **nonaccelerating inflation rate of unemployment**, or **NAIRU** for short. Keeping the unemployment rate below the NAIRU leads to ever-accelerating inflation and cannot be maintained. Most macroeconomists believe that there is a NAIRU and that there is no long-run trade-off between unemployment and inflation.

We can now explain the significance of the vertical line in Figure 34.6. It is the **long-run Phillips curve** (**LRPC**), which shows the relationship between unemployment and inflation in the long run, after expectations of inflation have had time to adjust to experience. It is vertical because any unemployment rate below the NAIRU leads to ever-accelerating inflation. In other words, the long-run Phillips curve shows that there are limits to expansionary policies because an unemployment rate below the NAIRU cannot be maintained in the long run. Moreover, there is a corresponding point we have not yet emphasized: any unemployment rate above the NAIRU leads to decelerating inflation.

The **nonaccelerating inflation rate of unemployment**, or **NAIRU**, is the unemployment rate at which inflation does not change over time.

The **long-run Phillips curve** (**LRPC**) shows the relationship between unemployment and inflation after expectations of inflation have had time to adjust to experience.

The Natural Rate of Unemployment, Revisited

Recall the concept of the natural rate of unemployment, the portion of the unemployment rate unaffected by the swings of the business cycle. Now we have introduced the concept of the NAIRU. How do these two concepts relate to each other?

The answer is that the NAIRU is another name for the natural rate. The level of unemployment the economy "needs" in order to avoid accelerating inflation is equal to the natural rate of unemployment.

In fact, economists estimate the natural rate of unemployment by looking for evidence about the NAIRU from the behavior of the inflation rate and the unemployment rate over the course of the business cycle. For example, in the late 1980s, and again in the late 1990s, European inflation began to accelerate as European unemployment rates, which had been above 9%, began to fall, approaching 8%. Through this unpleasant experience, the major European countries learned, to their dismay, that their natural rates of unemployment were 9% or more.

In Figure 30.4 we cited Congressional Budget Office estimates of the U.S. natural rate of unemployment. The CBO has a model that predicts changes in the inflation rate based on the deviation of the actual unemployment rate from the natural rate. Given data on actual unemployment and inflation, this model can be used to deduce estimates of the natural rate—and that's where the CBO numbers come from.

The Costs of Disinflation

Through experience, policy makers have found that bringing inflation down is a much harder task than increasing it. The reason is that once the public has come to expect continuing inflation, bringing inflation down is painful.

A persistent attempt to keep unemployment below the natural rate leads to accelerating inflation that becomes incorporated into expectations. To reduce inflationary expectations, policy makers need to run the process in reverse, adopting contractionary policies that keep the unemployment rate above the natural rate for an extended period of time. The process of bringing down inflation that has become embedded in expectations is known as *disinflation*.

Disinflation can be very expensive. The U.S. retreat from high inflation at the beginning of the 1980s appears to have cost the equivalent of about 18% of a year's real GDP, the equivalent of roughly $2.6 trillion today. The justification for paying these costs is that they lead to a permanent gain. Although the economy does not recover the short-term production losses caused by disinflation, it no longer suffers from the costs associated with persistently high inflation.

Some economists argue that the costs of disinflation can be reduced if policy makers explicitly state their determination to reduce inflation. A clearly announced, credible policy of disinflation, they contend, can reduce expectations of future inflation and so shift the short-run Phillips curve downward. Some economists believe that the clear determination of the Federal Reserve to combat the inflation of the 1970s was credible enough that the costs of disinflation, huge though they were, were lower than they might otherwise have been.

Deflation

Before World War II, *deflation*—a falling aggregate price level—was almost as common as inflation. In fact, the U.S. consumer price index on the eve of World War II was 30% lower than it had been in 1920. After World War II, inflation became the norm in all countries. But in the 1990s, deflation reappeared in Japan and proved difficult to reverse. Concerns about potential deflation played a crucial role in U.S. monetary policy in the early 2000s and again in late 2008. In fact, in late 2008, the United States experienced a brief period of deflation.

Why is deflation a problem? And why is it hard to end?

Deflation can be a good thing for lenders but a bad thing for borrowers.

Debt Deflation

Deflation, like inflation, produces both winners and losers—but in the opposite direction. Due to the falling price level, a dollar in the future has a higher real value than a dollar today. So lenders, who are owed money, gain under deflation because the real value of borrowers' payments increases. Borrowers lose because the real burden of their debt rises.

In a famous analysis at the beginning of the Great Depression, economist Irving Fisher claimed that the effects of deflation on borrowers and lenders can worsen an economic slump. In effect, deflation takes real resources away from borrowers and redistributes them to lenders. Fisher argued that borrowers, who lose from deflation, are typically short of cash and will be forced to cut their spending sharply when their debt burden rises. However, lenders are less likely to increase spending sharply when the values of the loans they own rise. The overall effect, said Fisher, is that deflation reduces aggregate demand, deepening an economic slump, which, in a vicious circle, may lead to further deflation. The effect of deflation in reducing aggregate demand, known as *debt deflation*, probably played a significant role in the Great Depression.

Effects of Expected Deflation

Like expected inflation, expected deflation affects the nominal interest rate. Consider Figure 29.6 from Section 5 (repeated here as **Figure 34.7**), which demonstrates how expected inflation affects the equilibrium interest rate. As shown, the equilibrium nominal interest rate is 4% if the expected inflation rate is 0%. Clearly, if the expected inflation rate is −3%—meaning that the public expects deflation at 3% per year—the equilibrium nominal interest rate will be 4% − 3% = 1%.

But what would happen if the expected rate of inflation were −5%? Would the nominal interest rate fall to −1%, meaning that lenders are paying borrowers 1% on their debt? No. Nobody would lend money at a negative nominal rate of interest because they could do better by simply holding cash. This illustrates what economists call the **zero bound** on the nominal interest rate: it cannot go below zero.

This zero bound can limit the effectiveness of monetary policy. Suppose the economy is depressed, with output below potential output and the unemployment rate above the natural rate. Normally, the central bank can respond by cutting interest rates so as to increase aggregate demand. If the nominal interest rate is already zero, however, the central bank cannot push it down any further. Banks refuse to lend and consumers and firms refuse to spend because, with a negative inflation rate and a 0% nominal interest rate, holding cash yields a positive real rate of return. Any further increases in the monetary base will either be held in bank vaults or held as cash by individuals and firms, without being spent.

A situation in which conventional monetary policy to fight a slump—cutting interest rates—can't be used because nominal interest rates are up against the zero bound is known as *liquidity trap*. A liquidity trap can occur whenever there is a sharp reduction in demand for loanable funds—which is exactly what happened during the Great Depression.

There is a **zero bound** on the nominal interest rate: it cannot go below zero.

Figure 34.7 The Fisher Effect

D_{LF0} and S_{LF0} are the demand and supply curves for loanable funds when the expected future inflation rate is 0%. At an expected inflation rate of 0%, the equilibrium nominal interest rate is 4%. An increase in expected future inflation pushes both the demand and supply curves upward by 1 percentage point for every percentage point increase in expected future inflation. D_{LF10} and S_{LF10} are the demand and supply curves for loanable funds when the expected future inflation rate is 10%. The 10 percentage point increase in expected future inflation raises the equilibrium nominal interest rate to 14%. The expected real interest rate remains at 4%, and the equilibrium quantity of loanable funds also remains unchanged.

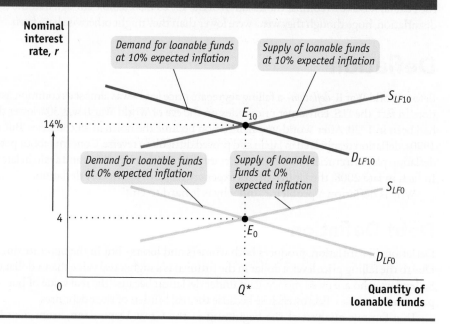

From 2008 until 2015, the Federal Reserve also found itself up against the zero bound. In the aftermath of the bursting of the housing bubble and the ensuing financial crisis, the interest on short-term U.S. government debt fell to virtually zero.

MODULE 34 REVIEW

Adventures in AP® Economics

Watch the video: *The Phillips Curve*

Check Your Understanding

1. Explain why a decrease in aggregate demand causes a movement along the short-run Phillips curve.

2. Why is there no long-run trade-off between unemployment and inflation?

3. Why is disinflation so costly for an economy? Are there ways to reduce these costs?

4. Why won't anyone lend money at a negative nominal rate of interest? How can this pose problems for monetary policy?

TACKLE THE AP® TEST: Multiple-Choice Questions

1. The long-run Phillips curve is
   a. equivalent to the short-run Phillips curve.
   b. the short-run Phillips curve plus expected inflation.
   c. negatively sloped.
   d. horizontal.
   e. none of the above.

2. The short-run Phillips curve shows a _____ relationship between _____.
   a. negative; the aggregate price level and aggregate output
   b. positive; the aggregate price level and aggregate output
   c. negative; unemployment and inflation
   d. positive; unemployment and aggregate output
   e. positive; unemployment and the aggregate price level

3. An increase in expected inflation will shift
   a. the short-run Phillips curve downward.
   b. the short-run Phillips curve upward.
   c. the long-run Phillips curve upward.
   d. the long-run Phillips curve downward.
   e. neither the short-run nor the long-run Phillips curve.

4. Bringing down inflation that has become embedded in expectations is called
   a. deflation.
   b. negative inflation.
   c. anti-inflation.
   d. unexpected inflation.
   e. disinflation.

5. Debt deflation is
   a. the effect of deflation in decreasing aggregate demand.
   b. an idea proposed by Irving Fisher.
   c. a contributing factor in causing the Great Depression.
   d. due to differences in how borrowers/lenders respond to inflation losses/gains.
   e. all of the above

6. The nonaccelerating inflation rate of unemployment, or NAIRU,
   a. is the same as the natural rate of unemployment.
   b. is the unemployment rate associated with the long-run Phillips curve.
   c. is the unemployment rate at which inflation does not change.
   d. shows there is no long-run trade-off between inflation and unemployment.
   e. all of the above

7. Which of the following will cause the short-run Phillips curve to shift to the right?
   a. a positive supply shock
   b. a negative demand shock
   c. an increase in inflation expectations
   d. a decrease in oil prices
   e. all of the above

TACKLE THE AP® TEST: Free-Response Questions

1. a. Draw a correctly labeled graph showing a short-run Phillips curve with an expected inflation rate of 0% and the corresponding long-run Phillips curve.
   b. On your graph, label the nonaccelerating inflation rate of unemployment.
   c. On your graph, show what happens in the long run if the government decides to decrease the unemployment rate below the nonaccelerating inflation rate of unemployment. Explain.

> **1 point:** New SRPC is labeled, for example as "$SRPC_1$" and shown above the original $SRPC_0$
>
> **1 point:** When the unemployment rate moves below the NAIRU, it creates inflation and moves the economy to a point such as A. This leads to positive inflationary expectations, which shift the SRPC up as shown by $SRPC_1$.

2. Consider the accompanying figure.

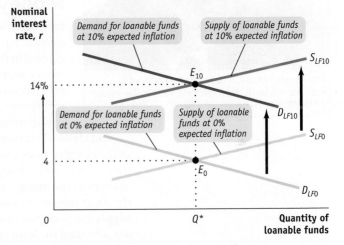

Rubric for FRQ 1 (8 points)

1 point: Vertical axis labeled "Inflation rate"

1 point: Horizontal axis labeled "Unemployment rate"

1 point: Downward-sloping curve labeled "$SRPC_0$"

1 point: Vertical curve labeled "$LRPC$"

1 point: $SRPC_0$ crosses horizontal axis where it crosses $LRPC$

1 point: NAIRU is labeled where $SRPC_0$ crosses $LRPC$ and horizontal axis

a. What is the nominal interest rate if expected inflation is 0%?
b. What would the nominal interest rate be if the expected inflation rate were −2%? Explain.
c. What would the nominal interest rate be if the expected inflation rate were −6%? Explain.
d. What would a negative nominal interest rate mean for lenders? How much lending would take place at a negative nominal interest rate? Explain.
e. What effect does a nominal interest rate of zero have on monetary policy? What is this situation called?
(6 points)

MOD 35

History and Alternative Views of Macroeconomics

Classical Macroeconomics

Norwegian economist Ragnar Frisch, who coined the term *macroeconomics* in the midst of the Great Depression.

The term *macroeconomics* appears to have been coined in 1933 by the Norwegian economist Ragnar Frisch. The timing, during the worst year of the Great Depression, was no accident. Still, there were economists analyzing what we now consider macroeconomic issues—the behavior of the aggregate price level and aggregate output—before then.

Money and the Price Level

Previously, we described the *classical model of the price level*. According to the classical model, prices are flexible, making the aggregate supply curve vertical even in the short run. In this model, other things equal, an increase in the money supply leads to a proportional rise in the aggregate price level, with no effect on aggregate output. As a result, increases in the money supply lead to inflation, and that's all. Before the 1930s, the classical model of the price level dominated economic thinking about the effects of monetary policy.

Did classical economists really believe that changes in the money supply affected only aggregate prices, without any effect on aggregate output? Probably not. Historians of economic thought argue that before 1930 most economists were aware that changes in the money supply affected aggregate output as well as aggregate prices in the short run—or, to use modern terms, they were aware that the short-run aggregate supply curve sloped upward. But they regarded such short-run effects as unimportant, stressing the long run instead. It was this attitude that led John Maynard Keynes to scoff at the focus on the long run, in which, as he said, "we are all dead."

The Business Cycle

Of course, classical economists were also aware that the economy did not grow smoothly. The American economist Wesley Mitchell pioneered the quantitative study of business cycles. In 1920, he founded the National Bureau of Economic Research (NBER), an independent, nonprofit organization that to this day has the official role of declaring the beginnings of recessions and expansions. Thanks to Mitchell's work, the *measurement* of business cycles was well advanced by 1930. But there was no widely accepted *theory* of business cycles.

In the absence of any clear theory, views about how policy makers should respond to a recession were conflicting. Some economists favored expansionary monetary and fiscal policies to fight a recession. Others believed that such policies would worsen the slump or merely postpone the inevitable. For example, in 1934 Harvard's Joseph

Schumpeter, now famous for his early recognition of the importance of technological change, warned that any attempt to alleviate the Great Depression with expansionary monetary policy "would, in the end, lead to a collapse worse than the one it was called in to remedy." When the Great Depression hit, the policy-making process was paralyzed by this lack of consensus. In many cases, economists now believe, policy makers took steps in the wrong direction.

Necessity, however, was the mother of invention. As we'll explain next, the Great Depression provided a strong incentive for economists to develop theories that could serve as a guide to policy—and economists responded.

The Great Depression and the Keynesian Revolution

The Great Depression demonstrated, once and for all, that economists cannot safely ignore the short run. Not only was the economic pain severe, it threatened to destabilize societies and political systems. In particular, the economic plunge helped Adolf Hitler rise to power in Germany.

The whole world wanted to know how this economic disaster could be happening and what should be done about it. But because there was no widely accepted theory of the business cycle, economists gave conflicting and, we now believe, often harmful advice. Some believed that only a huge change in the economic system—such as having the government take over much of private industry and replace markets with a command economy—could end the slump. Others argued that slumps were natural—even beneficial—and that nothing should be done.

Some economists, however, argued that the slump both could have and should have been cured without giving up on the basic idea of a market economy. In 1930, the British economist John Maynard Keynes compared the problems of the U.S. and British economies to those of a car with a defective alternator. Getting the economy running, he argued, would require only a modest repair, not a complete overhaul.

Nice metaphor. But what was the nature of the trouble?

The work of John Maynard Keynes (right), seen here with U.S. Treasury Secretary Henry Morgenthau, Jr., legitimized the use of monetary and fiscal policy to smooth out the business cycle.

Keynes's Theory

In 1936, Keynes presented his analysis of the Great Depression—his explanation of what was wrong with the economy's alternator—in a book titled *The General Theory of Employment, Interest, and Money*. In 1946, the great American economist Paul Samuelson wrote that "it is a badly written book, poorly organized. . . . Flashes of insight and intuition intersperse tedious algebra. . . . We find its analysis to be obvious and at the same time new. In short, it is a work of genius." *The General Theory* isn't easy reading, but it stands with Adam Smith's *The Wealth of Nations* as one of the most influential books on economics ever written.

As Samuelson's description suggests, Keynes's book is a vast stew of ideas. Keynesian economics mainly reflected two innovations. First, Keynes emphasized the short-run effects of shifts in aggregate demand on aggregate output, rather than the long-run determination of the aggregate price level. As Keynes's famous remark about being dead in the long run suggests, until his book appeared, most economists had treated short-run macroeconomics as a minor issue. Keynes focused the attention of economists on situations in which the short-run aggregate supply curve slopes upward and shifts in the aggregate demand curve affect aggregate output and employment as well as aggregate prices.

Figure 35.1 illustrates the difference between Keynesian and classical macroeconomics. Both panels of the figure show the short-run aggregate supply curve, *SRAS*; in both it is assumed that for some reason the aggregate demand curve shifts leftward from AD_1 to AD_2—let's say in response to a fall in stock market prices that leads households to reduce consumer spending.

Figure 35.1 Classical Versus Keynesian Macroeconomics

(a) The Classical View

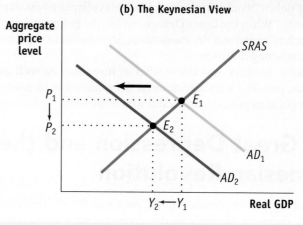

(b) The Keynesian View

One important difference between classical and Keynesian economics involves the short-run aggregate supply curve. Panel (a) shows the classical view: the *SRAS* curve is vertical, so shifts in aggregate demand affect the aggregate price level but not aggregate output. Panel (b) shows the Keynesian view: in the short run the *SRAS* curve slopes upward, so shifts in aggregate demand affect aggregate output as well as aggregate prices.

Panel (a) shows the classical view: the short-run aggregate supply curve is vertical. The decline in aggregate demand leads to a fall in the aggregate price level, from P_1 to P_2, but no change in aggregate output. Panel (b) shows the Keynesian view: the short-run aggregate supply curve slopes upward, so the decline in aggregate demand leads to both a fall in the aggregate price level, from P_1 to P_2, and a fall in aggregate output, from Y_1 to Y_2. As we've already explained, many classical macroeconomists would have agreed that panel (b) was an accurate story in the short run—but they regarded the short run as unimportant. Keynes disagreed. (Just to be clear, there isn't any diagram that looks like panel (b) of Figure 35.1 in Keynes's *The General Theory*. But Keynes's discussion of aggregate supply, translated into modern terminology, clearly implies an upward-sloping *SRAS* curve.)

Second, classical economists emphasized the role of changes in the money supply in shifting the aggregate demand curve, paying little attention to other factors. Keynes, however, argued that other factors, especially changes in "animal spirits"—these days usually referred to with the bland term *business confidence*—are mainly responsible for business cycles. Before Keynes, economists often argued that a decline in business confidence would have no effect on either the aggregate price level or aggregate output, as long as the money supply stayed constant. Keynes offered a very different picture.

Keynes's ideas have penetrated deeply into the public consciousness, to the extent that many people who have never heard of Keynes, or have heard of him but think they disagree with his theory, use Keynesian ideas all the time. For example, suppose that a business commentator says something like this: "Because of a decline in business confidence, investment spending slumped, causing a recession." Whether the commentator knows it or not, that statement is pure Keynesian economics.

Policy to Fight Recessions

The main practical consequence of Keynes's work was that it legitimized *macroeconomic policy activism*—the use of monetary and fiscal policy to smooth out the business cycle.

Macroeconomic policy activism wasn't something completely new. Before Keynes, many economists had argued for using monetary expansion to fight economic downturns—though others were fiercely opposed. Some economists had even argued that temporary budget deficits were a good thing in times of recession—though others disagreed strongly. In practice, during the 1930s many governments followed policies that we would now call Keynesian. In the United States, the administration of Franklin Roosevelt engaged in modest deficit spending in an effort to create jobs. But these efforts were half-hearted. Roosevelt's advisers were deeply divided over the appropriate policies to adopt.

It would make a good story if Keynes's ideas had led to a change in economic policy that brought the Great Depression to an end. Unfortunately, that's not what happened. In fact, in 1937 Roosevelt gave in to advice from non-Keynesian economists who urged him to balance the budget and raise interest rates, even though the economy was still depressed. The result was a renewed slump. Still, the way the Depression ended did a lot to convince economists that Keynes was right.

The basic message from Keynes's work was that economic recovery requires fiscal expansion—deficit spending to create jobs. And that is what eventually happened, but as a result of a very large and expensive war, World War II.

Figure 35.2 shows the U.S. unemployment rate and the federal budget deficit as a share of GDP from 1930 to 1947. As you can see, deficit spending during the 1930s was on a modest scale. In 1940, as the risk of war grew larger, the United States began a large military buildup, and the budget moved deep into deficit. After the attack on Pearl Harbor on December 7, 1941, the country began deficit spending on an unprecedented scale: in fiscal 1943, which began in July 1942, the deficit was 30% of GDP. Today that would be a deficit of $4.3 trillion.

FDR's decision to take the advice of his non-Keynesian advisers and adopt policies to balance the budget and raise interest rates led to a renewed slump.

Figure 35.2 Budget Deficit and Unemployment Rate, 1930–1947

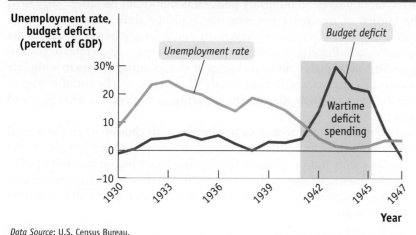

Data Source: U.S. Census Bureau.

Modest deficit spending in the 1930s caused the unemployment rate to decrease from 25% to 15%, whereas large increases in deficit spending during World War II brought the unemployment rate to a low of 1.2% in 1944.

Source: U.S. Census Bureau.

And the economy recovered. Of course, World War II wasn't intended as a Keynesian fiscal policy, but it demonstrated that expansionary fiscal policy can, in fact, create jobs in the short run.

Today, by contrast, there is broad consensus about the useful role monetary and fiscal policy can play in fighting recessions. It would be wrong, however, to suggest that Keynes's ideas have been fully accepted by all modern macroeconomists. In the decades that followed the publication of *The General Theory*, Keynesian economics faced a series of challenges, some of which succeeded in modifying the macroeconomic consensus in important ways.

Challenges to Keynesian Economics

Keynes's ideas fundamentally changed the way economists think about business cycles. However, they did not go unquestioned. In the decades that followed the publication of *The General Theory*, Keynesian economics faced a series of challenges. As a result, the consensus of macroeconomists retreated somewhat from the strong version of Keynesianism that prevailed in the 1950s. In particular, economists became much more aware of the limits to macroeconomic policy activism.

The Revival of Monetary Policy

Keynes's *The General Theory* suggested that monetary policy wouldn't be very effective in depression conditions. Many modern macroeconomists agree: in the previous module, we introduced the concept of a *liquidity trap*, a situation in which monetary policy is ineffective because the interest rate is down against the zero bound. In the 1930s, when Keynes wrote, interest rates, in fact, were very close to 0%.

But even when the era of near-0% interest rates came to an end after World War II, many economists continued to emphasize fiscal policy and downplay the usefulness of monetary policy. Eventually, however, macroeconomists reassessed the importance of monetary policy. A key milestone in this reassessment was the 1963 publication of *A Monetary History of the United States, 1867–1960* by Milton Friedman and Anna Schwartz. Friedman and Schwartz showed that business cycles had historically been associated with fluctuations in the money supply. In particular, the money supply fell sharply during the onset of the Great Depression. Friedman and Schwartz persuaded many, though not all, economists that the Great Depression could have been avoided if the Federal Reserve had acted to prevent that monetary contraction. They persuaded most economists that monetary policy should play a key role in economic management.

The revival of interest in monetary policy was significant because it suggested that the burden of managing the economy could be shifted away from fiscal policy—meaning that economic management could largely be taken out of the hands of politicians. Fiscal policy, which must involve changing tax rates or government spending, necessitates political choices. If the government tries to stimulate the economy by cutting taxes, it must decide whose taxes will be cut. If it tries to stimulate the economy with government spending, it must decide what to spend the money on.

Economists and co-authors Milton Friedman and Anna Schwartz.

Monetary policy, by contrast, does not involve such choices: when the central bank cuts interest rates to fight a recession, it cuts everyone's interest rate at the same time. So a shift from relying on fiscal policy to relying on monetary policy makes macroeconomics a more technical, less political issue. In fact, monetary policy in most major economies is set by an independent central bank that is insulated from the political process.

Monetarism

Monetarism asserts that GDP will grow steadily if the money supply grows steadily.

After the publication of *A Monetary History*, Milton Friedman led a movement, called *monetarism*, that sought to eliminate macroeconomic policy activism while maintaining the importance of monetary policy. **Monetarism** asserted that GDP will grow steadily if the money supply grows steadily. The monetarist policy prescription was to have the central bank target a constant rate of growth of the money supply, such as 3% per year, and maintain that target regardless of any fluctuations in the economy.

Like Keynes, Friedman asserted that the short run is important and that short-run changes in aggregate demand affect aggregate output as well as aggregate prices. Friedman also argued that policy should have been much more expansionary during the Great Depression. However, monetarists argued that most of the efforts of policy makers to smooth out the business cycle actually made things worse. We have already discussed concerns over the usefulness of *discretionary fiscal policy*—changes in taxes or government spending, or both—in response to the state of the economy. As we explained, government perceptions about the economy often lag behind reality, and there are further lags in changing fiscal policy and in its effects on the economy. As a result, discretionary fiscal policies intended to fight a recession often end up feeding a boom, and vice versa. According to monetarists, *discretionary monetary policy*, changes in the interest rate or the money supply by the central bank in order to stabilize the economy, faces the same problem of lags as fiscal policy, but to a lesser extent.

Friedman also argued that if the central bank followed his advice and refused to change the money supply in response to fluctuations in the economy, fiscal policy would be much less effective than Keynesians believed. Earlier we analyzed the phenomenon of *crowding out*, in which government deficits drive up interest rates and lead to reduced investment spending. Friedman and others pointed out that if the money supply is held fixed while the government pursues an expansionary fiscal policy, crowding out will limit the effect of the fiscal expansion on aggregate demand.

Figure 35.3 illustrates this argument. Panel (a) shows aggregate output and the aggregate price level. AD_1 is the initial aggregate demand curve and *SRAS* is the short-run aggregate supply curve. At the initial equilibrium, E_1, the level of aggregate output is Y_1 and the aggregate price level is P_1. Panel (b) shows the money market. *MS* is the money supply curve and MD_1 is the initial money demand curve, so the initial interest rate is r_1.

Figure 35.3 Fiscal Policy with a Fixed Money Supply

(a) The increase in aggregate demand from an expansionary fiscal policy is limited when the money supply is fixed . . .

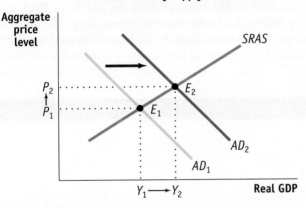

(b) . . . because the increase in money demand drives up the interest rate, crowding out some investment spending.

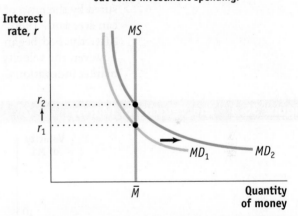

In panel (a) an expansionary fiscal policy shifts the *AD* curve rightward, driving up both the aggregate price level and aggregate output. However, this leads to an increase in the demand for money. If the money supply is held fixed, as in panel (b), the increase in money demand drives up the interest rate, reducing investment spending and offsetting part of the fiscal expansion.

Now suppose the government increases purchases of goods and services. We know that this will shift the *AD* curve rightward, as illustrated by the shift from AD_1 to AD_2; that aggregate output will rise, from Y_1 to Y_2, and that the aggregate price level will rise, from P_1 to P_2. Both the rise in aggregate output and the rise in the aggregate price level, however, will increase the demand for money, shifting the money demand curve rightward from MD_1 to MD_2. This drives up the equilibrium interest rate to r_2. Friedman's point was that this rise in the interest rate reduces investment spending, partially offsetting the initial rise in government spending. As a result, the rightward shift of the *AD* curve is smaller than multiplier analysis indicates. And Friedman argued that with a constant money supply, the multiplier is so small that there's not much point in using fiscal policy.

The Quantity Theory of Money emphasizes the positive relationship between the price level and the money supply. It relies on the velocity equation ($M \times V = P \times Y$).

The velocity of money is the ratio of nominal GDP to the money supply. It is a measure of the number of times the average dollar bill is spent per year.

But Friedman didn't favor activist monetary policy either. He argued that the problem of time lags that limit the ability of discretionary fiscal policy to stabilize the economy also apply to discretionary monetary policy. Friedman's solution was to put monetary policy on "autopilot." The central bank, he argued, should follow a *monetary policy rule*, a formula that determines its actions and leaves it relatively little discretion. During the 1960s and 1970s, most monetarists favored a monetary policy rule of slow, steady growth in the money supply. Underlying this view was the **Quantity Theory of Money**, which relies on the concept of the **velocity of money**, the ratio of nominal GDP to the money supply. Velocity is a measure of the number of times the average dollar bill in the economy turns over per year between buyers and sellers (e.g., I tip the Starbucks barista a dollar, she uses it to buy lunch, and so on). This concept gives rise to the *velocity equation*:

$$(35\text{-}1) \quad M \times V = P \times Y$$

where M is the money supply, V is velocity, P is the aggregate price level, and Y is real GDP.

Monetarists believed, with considerable historical justification, that the velocity of money was stable in the short run and changed only slowly in the long run. As a result, they claimed, steady growth in the money supply by the central bank would ensure steady growth in spending, and therefore in GDP.

Monetarism strongly influenced actual monetary policy in the late 1970s and early 1980s. It quickly became clear, however, that steady growth in the money supply didn't ensure steady growth in the economy: the velocity of money wasn't stable enough for such a simple policy rule to work. **Figure 35.4** shows how events eventually undermined the monetarists' view. The figure shows the velocity of money, as measured by the ratio of nominal GDP to M1, from 1960 to the middle of 2017. As you can see, until 1980, velocity followed a fairly smooth, seemingly predictable trend. After the Fed began to adopt monetarist ideas in the late 1970s and early 1980s, however, the velocity of money began moving erratically—probably due to financial market innovations.

Figure 35.4 The Velocity of Money

From 1960 to 1980, the velocity of money was stable, leading monetarists to believe that steady growth in the money supply would lead to a stable economy. After 1980, however, velocity began moving erratically, undermining the case for traditional monetarism.

Data Sources: Bureau of Economic Analysis; Federal Reserve Bank of St. Louis.

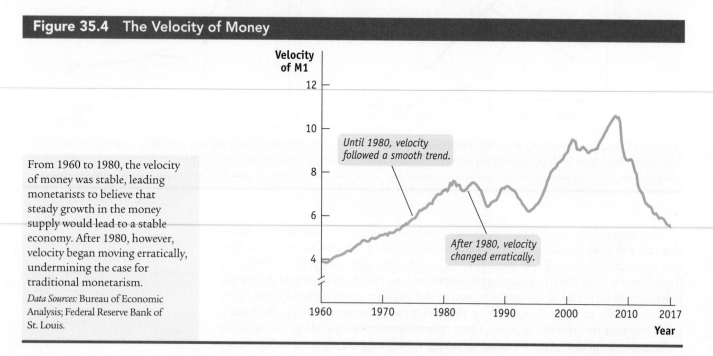

As we'll see later, the concern that originally motivated the monetarists—that too much discretionary monetary policy can actually destabilize the economy—has become widely accepted.

Inflation and the Natural Rate of Unemployment

At the same time that monetarists were challenging Keynesian views about how macroeconomic policy should be conducted, a somewhat broader group of economists was emphasizing the limits to what activist macroeconomic policy could achieve.

In the 1940s and 1950s, many Keynesian economists believed that expansionary fiscal policy could be used to achieve full employment on a permanent basis. In the 1960s, however, many economists realized that expansionary policies could cause problems with inflation, but they still believed policy makers could choose to trade off low unemployment for higher inflation even in the long run.

In 1968, however, Edmund Phelps and Milton Friedman, working independently, proposed the concept of the natural rate of unemployment. In Module 34 we saw that the natural rate of unemployment is also the nonaccelerating inflation rate of unemployment, or NAIRU. According to the *natural rate hypothesis*, because inflation is eventually embedded in expectations, to avoid accelerating inflation over time, the unemployment rate must be high enough that the actual inflation rate equals the expected rate of inflation. Attempts to keep the unemployment rate below the natural rate will lead to an ever-rising inflation rate.

The natural rate hypothesis limits the role of activist macroeconomic policy compared to earlier theories. Because the government can't keep unemployment below the natural rate, its task is not to keep unemployment low but to keep it *stable*—to prevent large fluctuations in unemployment in either direction.

The Friedman–Phelps hypothesis made a strong prediction: that the apparent trade-off between unemployment and inflation would not survive an extended period of rising prices. Once inflation was embedded in the public's expectations, inflation would continue even in the face of high unemployment. Sure enough, that's exactly what happened in the 1970s. This accurate prediction was one of the triumphs of macroeconomic analysis, and it convinced the great majority of economists that the natural rate hypothesis was correct. In contrast to traditional monetarism, which declined in influence as more evidence accumulated, the natural rate hypothesis has become almost universally accepted among macroeconomists, with a few qualifications.

Signs like these at a W.T. Grant store in San Jose, California, in 1972 tried to lure customers with their promise of lower prices.

The Political Business Cycle

One final challenge to Keynesian economics focused not on the validity of the economic analysis but on its political consequences. A number of economists and political scientists pointed out that activist macroeconomic policy lends itself to political manipulation.

Statistical evidence suggests that election results tend to be determined by the state of the economy in the months just before the election. In the United States, if the economy is growing rapidly and the unemployment rate is falling in the six months or so before Election Day, the incumbent party tends to be reelected even if the economy performed poorly in the preceding three years.

This creates an obvious temptation to abuse activist macroeconomic policy: pump up the economy in an election year, and pay the price in higher inflation and/or higher unemployment later. The result can be unnecessary instability in the economy, a political business cycle caused by the use of macroeconomic policy to serve political ends.

One way to avoid a political business cycle is to place monetary policy in the hands of an independent central bank, insulated from political pressure. The political business cycle is also a reason to limit the use of discretionary fiscal policy to extreme circumstances.

Rational Expectations, Real Business Cycles, and New Classical Macroeconomics

As we have seen, one key difference between classical economics and Keynesian economics is that classical economists believed that the short-run aggregate supply curve is vertical, but Keynes emphasized the idea that the aggregate supply curve slopes upward in the short run. As a result, Keynes argued that *demand shocks*—shifts in the aggregate demand curve—can cause fluctuations in aggregate output.

The challenges to Keynesian economics that arose in the 1950s and 1960s—the renewed emphasis on monetary policy and the natural rate hypothesis—didn't question the view that an increase in aggregate demand leads to a rise in aggregate output in the short run nor that a decrease in aggregate demand leads to a fall in aggregate output in the short run. In the 1970s and 1980s, however, some economists developed an approach to the business cycle known as *new classical macroeconomics*, which returned to the classical view that shifts in the aggregate demand curve affect only the aggregate price level, not aggregate output. The new approach evolved in two steps. First, some economists challenged traditional arguments about the slope of the short-run aggregate supply curve based on the concept of *rational expectations*. Second, some economists suggested that changes in productivity caused economic fluctuations, a view known as *real business cycle theory*.

Rational Expectations

In the 1970s, a concept known as rational expectations had a powerful impact on macroeconomics. *Rational expectations*, a theory originally introduced by John Muth in 1961, is the view that individuals and firms make decisions optimally, using all available information.

For example, workers and employers bargaining over long-term wage contracts need to estimate the inflation rate they expect over the life of that contract. Rational expectations says that in making estimates of future inflation, they won't just look at past rates of inflation; they will also take into account available information about monetary and fiscal policy. Suppose that prices didn't rise last year, but that the monetary and fiscal policies announced by policy makers made it clear to economic analysts that there would be substantial inflation over the next few years. According to rational expectations, long-term wage contracts will be adjusted today to reflect this future inflation, even though prices didn't rise in the past.

Rational expectations can make a major difference to the effects of government policy. According to the original version of the natural rate hypothesis, a government attempt to trade off higher inflation for lower unemployment would work in the short run but would eventually fail because higher inflation would get built into expectations. According to rational expectations, we should remove the word *eventually*: if it's clear that the government intends to trade off higher inflation for lower unemployment, the public will understand this, and expected inflation will immediately rise.

Many macroeconomists don't believe the rational expectations hypothesis accurately describes how the economy behaves. *New Keynesian economics*, a set of ideas that became influential in the 1990s, argues that market imperfections interact to make many prices in the economy temporarily sticky. For example, one new Keynesian argument points out that monopolists don't have to be too careful about setting prices exactly "right": if they set a price a bit too high, they'll lose some sales but make more profit on each sale; if they set the price too low, they'll reduce the profit per sale but sell more. As a result, even small costs to changing prices can lead to substantial price stickiness and make the economy as a whole behave in a Keynesian fashion.

Over time, new Keynesian ideas combined with actual experience have reduced the practical influence of the rational expectations concept. Nonetheless, the idea of rational expectations served as a useful caution for macroeconomists who had become excessively optimistic about their ability to manage the economy.

Real Business Cycles

In the 1980s, a number of economists argued that slowdowns in productivity growth, which they attributed to pauses in technological progress, are the main cause of recessions. *Real business cycle theory* claims that fluctuations in the rate of growth of total factor productivity cause the business cycle. *Total factor productivity*, discussed in more detail in Section 7, refers to the amount of output that can be produced with a given level of inputs. When inputs become more productive, they can produce more output. Total factor productivity grows over time, but that growth isn't smooth. Believing that the aggregate supply curve is vertical, real business cycle theorists attribute the source of business cycles to shifts of the aggregate supply curve: a recession occurs when a slowdown in productivity growth shifts the aggregate supply curve leftward, and a recovery occurs when a pickup in productivity growth shifts the aggregate supply curve rightward. In the early days of real business cycle theory, the theory's proponents denied that changes in aggregate demand had any effect on aggregate output.

The current status of real business cycle theory, however, is somewhat similar to that of rational expectations. The theory is widely recognized as having made valuable contributions to our understanding of the economy, and it serves as a useful caution against too much emphasis on aggregate demand. But many of the real business cycle theorists themselves now acknowledge that their models need an upward-sloping aggregate supply curve to fit the economic data—and that this gives aggregate demand a potential role in determining aggregate output. And as we have seen, policy makers strongly believe that aggregate demand policy has an important role to play in fighting recessions.

MODULE 35 REVIEW

Check Your Understanding

1. The figure below shows the behavior of M1 before, during, and after the 2001 recession. What would a classical economist have said about the Fed's policy?

2. What would the figure in Question 1 have looked like if the Fed had been following a monetarist policy since 1996?

3. Now look at Figure 35.4, which shows the path of the velocity of money. What problems do you think the United States would have had if the Fed had followed a monetarist policy since 1996?

4. In addition to praising aggressive monetary policy, an Economic Report of the President says that "tax cuts can boost economic activity by raising after-tax income and enhancing incentives to work, save, and invest." Which part of the report is a Keynesian statement and which part is not? Explain your answer.

5. Let's say that the United States experiences a recession and in response the Fed decides to implement an aggressive monetary policy. After the recession ends, most observers conclude that the aggressive monetary expansion should be given credit for ending the recession.
   a. What would rational expectations theorists say about this conclusion?
   b. What would real business cycle theorists say?

1. Which of the following is true about Keynesian economics?
   a. It was created in response to World War I.
   b. It focuses on changes in the aggregate supply curve over time.
   c. It proposes that the short-run aggregate supply curve is vertical.
   d. It focuses on short-run changes in aggregate demand.
   e. It hinges on the idea that in the short run we're all dead.

2. Which of the following is a central point of monetarism?
   a. Business cycles are associated with fluctuations in money demand.
   b. Activist monetary policy is the best way to address business cycles.
   c. Discretionary monetary policy is effective while discretionary fiscal policy is not.
   d. The Fed should follow a monetary policy rule.
   e. All of the above are central points.

3. The natural rate hypothesis says that the unemployment rate should be
   a. below the NAIRU.
   b. high enough that the actual rate of inflation equals the expected rate.
   c. as close to zero as possible.
   d. 5%.
   e. left wherever the economy sets it.

4. The main difference between the classical model of the price level and Keynesian economics is that
   a. the classical model assumes a vertical short-run aggregate supply curve.
   b. Keynesian economics assumes a vertical short-run aggregate supply curve.
   c. the classical model assumes an upward-sloping long-run aggregate supply curve.
   d. Keynesian economics assumes a vertical long-run aggregate supply curve.
   e. the classical model assumes that aggregate demand cannot change in the long run.

5. That fluctuations in total factor productivity growth cause the business cycle is the main tenet of which theory?
   a. Keynesian
   b. classical
   c. rational expectations
   d. real business cycle
   e. natural rate

6. In the velocity equation, $M \times V = P \times Y$, nominal GDP is represented by
   a. Y d. $M \times Y$
   b. $P \times Y$ e. $(P \times Y)/M$
   c. M

7. Which of the following led to recovery from the Great Depression?
   a. spending on World War II
   b. expansionary fiscal policy by politicians persuaded by Keynesian economics
   c. the Fed taking action to decrease interest rates
   d. the use of new classical macroeconomics
   e. discovery of the natural rate hypothesis

1. a. According to monetarism, business cycles are associated with fluctuations in what?
   b. Does monetarism advocate discretionary fiscal policy? Discretionary monetary policy?
   c. What monetary policy does monetarism suggest?
   d. What is the velocity equation? Indicate what each letter in the equation stands for.
   e. Use the velocity equation to explain the major conclusion of monetarism.

> **1 point:** M is the money supply.
> **1 point:** V is the velocity of money.
> **1 point:** P is the aggregate price level.
> **1 point:** Y is real GDP.
> **1 point:** Since V is stable, a steady growth of M will lead to a steady growth in GDP.

Rubric for FRQ 1 (10 points)

1 point: The money supply
1 point: No
1 point: No
1 point: A monetary policy rule
1 point: $M \times V = P \times Y$

2. For each of the following economic theories, identify its fundamental conclusion.
   a. the classical model of the price level
   b. Keynesian economics
   c. monetarism
   d. the natural rate hypothesis
   e. rational expectations
   f. real business cycle theory **(6 points)**

Consensus and Conflict in Modern Macroeconomics

> *In this Module, you will learn to:*
> - List and describe the elements of the modern macroeconomic consensus
> - Explain the main remaining disputes

The Modern Consensus

The 1970s and the first half of the 1980s were a stormy period for the U.S. economy (and for other major economies, too). There was a severe recession in 1974–1975, then two back-to-back recessions in 1979–1982 that sent the unemployment rate to almost 11%. At the same time, the inflation rate soared into double digits—and then plunged. As we have seen, these events left a strong mark on macroeconomic thought.

After about 1985, however, the economy settled down. The recession of 1990–1991 was much milder than the 1974–1975 recession or the double-dip slump from 1979 to 1982, and the inflation rate generally stayed below 4%. The period of relative calm in the economy from 1985 to 2007 came to be known as the *Great Moderation*. To a large extent, the calmness of the economy was marked by a similar calm in macroeconomic policy discussion. In fact, it seemed that a broad consensus had emerged about several key macroeconomic issues.

Unfortunately, the Great Moderation was followed by the *Great Recession*, the severe and persistent slump that followed the 2008 financial crisis. We'll talk shortly about the policy disputes caused by the Great Recession. First, however, let's examine the apparent consensus that emerged during the Great Moderation. It combines a belief in monetary policy as the main tool of stabilization, with skepticism toward the use of fiscal policy, and an acknowledgement of the policy constraints imposed by the natural rate of unemployment and the political business cycle.

Unfortunately, the relative calm of the Great Moderation was followed by the Great Recession.

Five Key Questions About Macroeconomic Policy

To understand the modern consensus, where it came from, and what still remains in dispute, we'll look at how macroeconomists have changed their answers to five key questions about macroeconomic policy. The five questions, and the answers given by macroeconomists over the past 90 years, are summarized in **Table 36.1**. (In the table, new classical economics is subsumed under classical economics, and new Keynesian economics is subsumed under the modern consensus.) Notice that classical macroeconomics said no to each question; basically, classical macroeconomists didn't think macroeconomic policy could accomplish very much. But let's go through the questions one by one.

Is Expansionary Monetary Policy Helpful in Fighting Recessions?

As we've seen, classical macroeconomists generally believed that expansionary monetary policy was ineffective or even harmful in fighting recessions. In the early years of Keynesian economics, macroeconomists weren't against monetary expansion during recessions, but they tended to doubt its effectiveness. Milton Friedman and his followers convinced economists that monetary policy was effective after all.

AP® EXAM TIP

The AP® exam tests your understanding of economic models and concepts, not your knowledge of the history and current state of the economy or various economic schools of thought. However, knowledge of the history and development of the models and concepts we use today (the modern macroeconomic consensus) will help you better understand the assumptions, application, and shortcomings of the models that will be tested.

Table 36.1 Five Key Questions About Macroeconomic Policy

	Classical macroeconomics	Keynesian macroeconomics	Monetarism	Modern consensus
Is expansionary monetary policy helpful in fighting recessions?	No	Not very	Yes	Yes, except in special circumstances
Is expansionary fiscal policy effective in fighting recessions?	No	Yes	No	Yes
Can monetary and/or fiscal policy reduce unemployment in the long run?	No	Yes	No	No
Should fiscal policy be used in a discretionary way?	No	Yes	No	No, except in special circumstances
Should monetary policy be used in a discretionary way?	No	Yes	No	Still in dispute

Nearly all macroeconomists now agree that monetary policy can be used to shift the aggregate demand curve and to reduce economic instability. The classical view that changes in the money supply affect only aggregate prices, not aggregate output, has few supporters today. The view once held by some Keynesian economists—that changes in the money supply have little effect—has equally few supporters. Now, it is generally agreed that monetary policy is ineffective only in the case of a liquidity trap.

Is Expansionary Fiscal Policy Effective in Fighting Recessions?

Classical macroeconomists were, if anything, even more opposed to fiscal expansion than to monetary expansion. Keynesian economists, on the other hand, gave fiscal policy a central role in fighting recessions. Monetarists argued that fiscal policy was ineffective as long as the money supply was held constant. But that strong view has become relatively rare.

Most macroeconomists now agree that fiscal policy, like monetary policy, can shift the aggregate demand curve. Most macroeconomists also agree that the government should not seek to balance the budget regardless of the state of the economy: they agree that the role of the budget as an automatic stabilizer helps keep the economy on an even keel.

Can Monetary and/or Fiscal Policy Reduce Unemployment in the Long Run?

Classical macroeconomists didn't believe the government could do anything about unemployment. Some Keynesian economists moved to the opposite extreme, arguing that expansionary policies could be used to achieve a permanently low unemployment rate, perhaps at the cost of some inflation. Monetarists believed that unemployment could not be kept below the natural rate.

Almost all macroeconomists now accept the natural rate hypothesis and agree on the limitations of monetary and fiscal policy. They believe that effective monetary and fiscal policy can limit the size of fluctuations of the actual unemployment rate around the natural rate but can't keep unemployment below the natural rate.

Should Fiscal Policy Be Used in a Discretionary Way?

As we've already seen, views about the effectiveness of fiscal policy have gone back and forth, from rejection by classical macroeconomists, to a positive view by Keynesian economists, to a negative view once again by monetarists. Today, most macroeconomists believe that tax cuts and spending increases are at least somewhat effective in increasing aggregate demand. However, *discretionary fiscal policy* is subject to the various types of lags discussed in Module 20. All too often, policies intended to fight a slump affect aggregate demand after the economy has turned around, and end up intensifying a boom.

As a result, the macroeconomic consensus gives monetary policy the lead role in economic stabilization. Discretionary fiscal policy plays the leading role only in special circumstances when monetary policy is ineffective and fiscal policy is likely to take effect before the economy has recovered. For example, many macroeconomists favored the use of discretionary fiscal policy in 2008–2010, when interest rates were near the zero bound and the economy was likely to remain depressed for an extended period.

Should Monetary Policy Be Used in a Discretionary Way?

Classical macroeconomists didn't think that monetary policy should be used to fight recessions; Keynesian economists didn't oppose discretionary monetary policy, but they were skeptical about its effectiveness. Monetarists argued that discretionary monetary policy was doing more harm than good. Where are we today? This remains an area of dispute.

Today there is a broad consensus among macroeconomists on these points:

- Monetary policy should play the main role in stabilization policy.
- The central bank should be independent, insulated from political pressures, in order to avoid a political business cycle.
- Discretionary fiscal policy should be used sparingly, both because of policy lags and because of the risks of a political business cycle.

However, the Great Moderation was upended by events that posed very difficult questions—questions that rage on to this day. We'll now examine what happened and why the ongoing debate is so fierce.

Crisis and Aftermath

The Great Recession shattered any sense among macroeconomists that they had entered a permanent era of agreement over key policy questions. Given the nature of the slump, however, this should have come as no surprise. Why? Because the severity of the slump arguably made the policies that seemed to work during the Great Moderation inadequate.

During the Great Moderation, there had been broad agreement that the job of stabilizing the economy was best carried out by having the Federal Reserve and its counterparts abroad raise or lower interest rates as the economic situation warranted. But what should be done if the economy is deeply depressed, while the interest rates the Fed normally controls are already close to zero and can go no lower (that is, when the economy is in a liquidity trap)? Some economists called for aggressive discretionary fiscal policy and/or unconventional monetary policies that might achieve results despite the zero lower bound. Others strongly opposed these measures, arguing either that they would be ineffective or that they would produce undesirable side effects. In 2008, the Fed took a series of unconventional monetary policy actions in response to the deepening recession and financial crisis.

In 2008, the Fed took a series of unconventional monetary policy actions in response to the deepening recession and financial crisis.

The Debate over Fiscal Policy

In 2009, a number of governments, including that of the United States, responded with expansionary fiscal policy, or "stimulus," generally taking the form of a mix of temporary spending measures and temporary tax cuts. From the start, however, these efforts were highly controversial.

"I'll pause for a moment so you can let this information sink in."

Supporters of fiscal stimulus offered three main arguments for breaking with the normal presumption against discretionary fiscal policy:

1. They argued that discretionary fiscal expansion was needed because the usual tool for stabilizing the economy, monetary policy, could no longer be used now that interest rates were near zero.

2. They argued that one normal concern about expansionary fiscal policy—that deficit spending would drive up interest rates, crowding out private investment spending—was unlikely to be a problem in a depressed economy. Again, this was because interest rates were close to zero and likely to stay there as long as the economy was depressed.

3. Finally, they argued that another concern about discretionary fiscal policy—that it might take a long time to get going—was less of a concern than usual given the likelihood that the economy would be depressed for an extended period.

These arguments generally won the day in early 2009. However, opponents of fiscal stimulus raised two main objections:

1. They argued that households and firms would see any rise in government spending as a sign that tax burdens were likely to rise in the future, leading to a fall in private spending that would undo any positive effect. This is known as the *Ricardian equivalence* argument.

2. They also warned that spending programs might undermine investors' faith in the government's ability to repay its debts, leading to an increase in long-term interest rates despite increases in the money supply.

In fact, by 2010 a number of economists were arguing that the best way to boost the economy was actually to cut government spending, which they argued would increase private-sector confidence and lead to a rise in output and employment. This notion is referred to as the doctrine of "expansionary austerity," and it was especially popular in Britain and Europe, where it was supported by officials at the European Central Bank.

Critics of fiscal stimulus pointed out that the U.S. stimulus had failed to deliver a convincing fall in unemployment; stimulus advocates, however, had warned from the start that this was likely to happen because the stimulus was too small compared with the depth of the slump. Meanwhile, austerity programs in Britain and elsewhere had also failed to deliver an economic turnaround and, in fact, had seemed to deepen the slump. Supporters of these programs, however, argued that they were nonetheless necessary to head off a potential collapse of confidence.

One thing that was clear, however, was that those who had predicted a sharp rise in U.S. interest rates due to budget deficits, leading to conventional crowding out, had been wrong: by the summer of 2012 and again in the summer of 2016, U.S. long-term rates hit record lows, and rates have remained low into 2018 despite continuing large deficits.

MODULE 36 REVIEW

Check Your Understanding

1. What debates has the modern consensus resolved?

2. What debates has the modern consensus not resolved?

TACKLE THE AP® TEST: Multiple-Choice Questions

1. Which of the following is an example of an opinion on which economists have reached a broad consensus?
   a. Monetary policy is not helpful in fighting recessions.
   b. Fiscal policy is not helpful in fighting recessions.
   c. Fiscal and monetary policy can reduce unemployment in the long run.
   d. Discretionary fiscal policy should only be used to fight recessions under special circumstances.
   e. Discretionary monetary policy should always be used to fight recessions.

2. The use of discretionary monetary policy was made more difficult during the Great Recession because
   a. interest rates were near zero.
   b. the Federal Reserve was unwilling to take action to prevent unemployment.
   c. it would require deficit spending that would increase the national debt.
   d. the economic downturn was not expected to last very long.
   e. crowding out would negate any effects on the economy.

3. Which of the following was one of the main arguments against using fiscal stimulus during the Great Recession?
   a. Monetary policy could no longer be used because interest rates were so low.
   b. The crowding out of private investment was no longer a problem in the depressed economy.
   c. Implementation lags were less of a concern than usual because the economy was likely to be depressed for an extended period.
   d. Consumers would see an increase in government spending as a signal that the tax burden would decrease in the future, and therefore they would spend more.
   e. Spending programs might undermine investors' faith in the government's ability to repay its debts, leading to an increase in long-term interest rates.

4. Which of the following is a major source of disagreement among macroeconomists?
   a. The Fed conducted the appropriate amount of quantitative easing during the Great Recession.
   b. The central bank should be independent, insulated from political pressures.
   c. Discretionary fiscal policy should be used sparingly.
   d. Monetary policy should play the main role in stabilization policy.
   e. Budget deficits caused high rates of inflation shortly after the Great Recession.

5. Which of the following best describes the 23 years prior to the Great Recession?
   a. a period of growing disagreement among macroeconomists
   b. a period of high inflation
   c. a period of consensus building among economists
   d. a period of consistently high unemployment
   e. the Great Depression

6. Crowding out is less likely to be a result of expansionary fiscal policy when
   a. federal government debt is already large.
   b. the economy is experiencing inflation.
   c. business confidence and returns on investment are low.
   d. the economy is expanding.
   e. interest rates are low.

7. The Ricardian equivalence argument asserts that when households and firms see government spending increase, it creates the expectation that
   a. private spending will also increase.
   b. taxes will increase in the future.
   c. interest rates will soon fall.
   d. tax rates will decrease as a result.
   e. the federal deficit will decrease.

TACKLE THE AP® TEST: Free-Response Questions

1. What is the consensus view of macroeconomists on each of the following?
   a. monetary policy and aggregate demand
   b. when monetary policy is ineffective
   c. fiscal policy and aggregate demand
   d. a balanced budget mandate
   e. the effectiveness of discretionary fiscal policy

Rubric for FRQ 1 (5 points)
1 point: Monetary policy can shift aggregate demand in the short run.
1 point: Monetary policy is ineffective when in a liquidity trap.
1 point: Fiscal policy can shift aggregate demand.

1 point: This is not a good idea. Fluctuations in the budget act as an automatic stabilizer for the economy.
1 point: It is usually counterproductive (for example, due to lags in implementation).

2. a. What type of policy is used to address a recession: expansionary or contractionary?
   b. What change in government spending would address recession: an increase or a decrease?
   c. Should the Federal Reserve buy or sell bonds to address a recession? Explain.
   d. Is expansionary fiscal policy effective in fighting recessions? Explain. **(4 points)**

Module 30

1. Some of the fluctuations in the budget balance are due to the effects of the business cycle. In order to separate the effects of the business cycle from the effects of discretionary fiscal policy, governments estimate the **cyclically adjusted budget balance**, an estimate of the budget balance if the economy were at potential output.

2. U.S. government budget accounting is calculated on the basis of fiscal years that run from October 1 to September 30. Annual budget deficits, minus budget surpluses, accumulate into **government debt**. Persistent budget deficits have long-run consequences because they lead to an increase in public debt—government debt held by the individuals and institutions outside the government. This can be a problem for two reasons. Public debt may cause *crowding out* of investment spending, which may lead to a decrease in long-run economic growth. And in extreme cases, rising debt may lead to government default, resulting in economic and financial turmoil.

3. A widely used measure of fiscal health is the **debt–GDP ratio**. This number can remain stable or fall even in the face of moderate budget deficits if GDP rises over time. However, a stable debt–GDP ratio may give a misleading impression that all is well because modern governments often have large implicit liabilities. The largest implicit liabilities of the U.S. government come from Social Security, Medicare, and Medicaid, the costs of which are increasing due to the aging of the population and rising medical costs.

Module 31

4. The central bank can use monetary policy to change the interest rate. In the United States, this involves the Fed setting a **target federal funds rate**. **Expansionary monetary policy** reduces the interest rate by increasing the money supply. This increases investment spending and consumer spending, which in turn increases aggregate demand and real GDP in the short run. **Contractionary monetary policy** raises the interest rate by reducing the money supply. This reduces investment spending and consumer spending, which in turn reduces aggregate demand and real GDP in the short run.

5. The Federal Reserve and other central banks try to stabilize their economies, limiting fluctuations of actual output to around potential output, while also keeping inflation low but positive. Under the **Taylor rule for monetary policy**, the target interest rate rises when there is inflation, or a positive output gap, or both; the target interest rate falls when inflation is low or negative, or when the output gap is negative, or both. Some central banks engage in **inflation targeting**, which is a forward-looking policy rule, whereas the Taylor rule is a backward-looking policy rule. In practice, the Fed appears to operate on a loosely defined version of the Taylor rule. In 2012, the Fed adopted an explicit inflation target as well. Because monetary policy is subject to fewer implementation lags than fiscal policy, monetary policy is the preferred policy tool for stabilizing the economy.

Module 32

6. In the long run, changes in the money supply affect the aggregate price level but not real GDP or the interest rate. Data show that the concept of **monetary neutrality** holds: changes in the money supply have no real effect on the economy in the long run.

Module 33

7. In analyzing high inflation, economists use the classical model of the price level, which says that changes in the money supply lead to proportional changes in the aggregate price level even in the short run.

8. Governments sometimes print money in order to finance budget deficits. When they do, they impose an **inflation tax**, generating tax revenue equal to the inflation rate times the money supply, on those who hold money. Revenue from the real inflation tax, the inflation rate times the real money supply, is the real value of resources captured by the government. In order to avoid paying the inflation tax, people reduce their real money holdings and force the government to increase inflation to capture the same amount of real inflation tax revenue. In some cases, this leads to a vicious circle of a shrinking real money supply and a rising rate of inflation, leading to hyperinflation and a fiscal crisis.

9. Countries that don't need to print money to cover government deficits can still stumble into moderate inflation. When an increase in the price of a key input such as oil decreases aggregate supply, the result is **cost-push**

inflation. Inflation caused by an increase in aggregate demand is called **demand-pull inflation**.

Module 34

11. At a given point in time, there is a downward-sloping relationship between unemployment and inflation known as the **short-run Phillips curve**. This curve is shifted by changes in the expected rate of inflation. The **long-run Phillips curve**, which shows the relationship between unemployment and inflation once expectations have had time to adjust, is vertical. It defines the **nonaccelerating inflation rate of unemployment**, or **NAIRU**, which is equal to the natural rate of unemployment.

12. Once inflation has become embedded in expectations, getting inflation back down can be difficult because disinflation can be very costly, requiring the sacrifice of

10. A positive output gap is associated with lower-than-normal unemployment; a negative output gap is associated with higher-than-normal unemployment.

large amounts of aggregate output and imposing high levels of unemployment. However, policy makers in the United States and other wealthy countries were willing to pay that price of bringing down the high inflation of the 1970s.

13. Deflation poses several problems. It can lead to debt deflation, in which a rising real burden of outstanding debt intensifies an economic downturn. Also, interest rates are more likely to run up against the **zero bound** in an economy experiencing deflation. When this happens, the economy enters a liquidity trap, rendering conventional monetary policy ineffective.

Module 35

14. Classical macroeconomics asserted that monetary policy affected only the aggregate price level, not aggregate output, and that the short run was unimportant. By the 1930s, measurement of business cycles was a well-established subject, but there was no widely accepted theory of business cycles.

15. Keynesian economics attributed the business cycle to shifts of the aggregate demand curve, often the result of changes in business confidence. Keynesian economics also offered a rationale for macroeconomic policy activism.

16. In the decades that followed Keynes's work, economists came to agree that monetary policy as well as fiscal policy is effective under certain conditions. **Monetarism** is a doctrine that called for a monetary policy rule as opposed to discretionary monetary policy. On the basis of the **Quantity Theory of Money** and a belief that the **velocity of money** was stable, monetarists argued that GDP would grow steadily if the money supply grew steadily. This idea was influential for a time but was eventually rejected by many macroeconomists.

17. The natural rate hypothesis became almost universally accepted, limiting the role of macroeconomic policy to stabilizing the economy rather than seeking a permanently low unemployment rate. Fears of a political business cycle concocted to advance the careers of the politicians in power led to a consensus that monetary policy should be insulated from politics.

18. The rational expectations hypothesis suggests that even in the short run there might not be a trade-off between inflation and unemployment because expected inflation would change immediately in the face of expected changes in policy. Real business cycle theory claims that changes in the rate of growth of total factor productivity are the main cause of business cycles. Both of these versions of new classical macroeconomics received wide attention and respect, but policy makers and many economists haven't accepted the conclusion that monetary and fiscal policy are ineffective in changing aggregate output.

19. New Keynesian economics argues that market imperfections can lead to price stickiness, so that changes in aggregate demand have effects on aggregate output after all.

Module 36

20. The modern consensus is that monetary and fiscal policy are both effective in the short run but that neither can reduce the unemployment rate in the long run. Discretionary fiscal policy is considered generally unadvisable, except in special circumstances.

21. There are continuing debates about the appropriate role of monetary policy. Some economists advocate the explicit use of an inflation target, but others oppose it. There's also a debate about what kind of unconventional monetary policy, if any, should be adopted to address a liquidity trap.

Key Terms

Cyclically adjusted budget balance, p. 287
Government debt, p. 288
Debt–GDP ratio, p. 290
Target federal funds rate, p. 295
Expansionary monetary policy, p. 296
Contractionary monetary policy, p. 296

Taylor rule for monetary policy, p. 297
Inflation targeting, p. 298
Monetary neutrality, p. 302
Inflation tax, p. 308
Cost-push inflation, p. 309
Demand-pull inflation, p. 309
Short-run Phillips curve, p. 312

Nonaccelerating inflation rate of unemployment (NAIRU), p. 318
Long-run Phillips curve, p. 318
Zero bound, p. 319
Monetarism, p. 326
Quantity Theory of Money, p. 328
Velocity of money, p. 328

AP® Exam Practice Questions

Multiple-Choice Questions

1. The budget balance is equal to
   a. total spending by the government.
   b. taxes minus transfer payments.
   c. taxes minus government spending and transfer payments.
   d. the sum of deficits and surpluses over time.
   e. total tax revenues collected.

2. The cyclically adjusted budget deficit adjusts the actual budget deficit for the effect of
   a. discretionary fiscal policy.
   b. discretionary monetary policy.
   c. inflation.
   d. transfer payments.
   e. the business cycle.

3. The public debt increases when
   a. the government collects more in taxes than it spends.
   b. the government runs a budget deficit.
   c. taxes exceed transfer payments.
   d. the budget balance is positive.
   e. individuals borrow for goods like houses and cars.

4. Which of the following is a potential problem with persistent increases in government debt?
   a. Government borrowing may crowd out private investment.
   b. Government debt is caused by budget deficits, which are always bad for the economy.
   c. It will always lead the government to default.
   d. It creates inflation because the government has to print money to pay it off.
   e. It causes automatic stabilizers to raise taxes in the future.

5. The Federal Open Market Committee sets a target for which of the following?
   a. the income tax rate
   b. the federal funds rate
   c. the money supply
   d. the prime interest rate
   e. the unemployment rate

6. Which of the following will occur if the Federal Reserve buys Treasury bills?
   a. The money supply will increase.
   b. The money supply curve will shift to the left.
   c. The money demand curve will shift to the right.
   d. Interest rates will rise.
   e. Aggregate demand will decrease.

7. Which of the following actions would the Federal Reserve use to address inflation?
   a. make an open-market sale of Treasury bills
   b. increase the money supply
   c. lower the discount rate
   d. decrease money demand
   e. raise taxes

8. The Taylor rule sets the target federal funds rate based on which of the following?
   a. the inflation rate only
   b. the unemployment rate only
   c. the output gap only
   d. both the inflation rate and the unemployment rate
   e. both the output gap and the inflation rate

9. An increase in the money supply will generate which of the following?
   a. a negative short-run effect on real GDP
   b. an increase in real GDP in the long run
   c. a decrease in real GDP in the long run
   d. a decrease in the aggregate price level in the long run
   e. an increase in the aggregate price level in the short run and the long run

10. According to the concept of monetary neutrality, changes in the money supply will affect which of the following in the long run?
    a. only real values
    b. the aggregate price level
    c. employment
    d. aggregate output
    e. aggregate demand

11. An inflation tax is the result of
    a. the federal government running a budget surplus.
    b. the Federal Reserve raising the federal funds rate.
    c. an increase in the demand for money.
    d. printing money to cover a budget deficit.
    e. contractionary fiscal policy.

12. An increase in the aggregate price level caused by a significant increase in the price of an input with economy-wide importance is called
    a. demand-pull inflation.
    b. seigniorage inflation.
    c. supply-push inflation.
    d. cost-push inflation.
    e. input-pull inflation.

13. Which of the following is true when the output gap is negative?
    a. Aggregate output is above potential output.
    b. The unemployment rate is below the natural rate.
    c. The economy is experiencing inflation.
    d. Potential output is above aggregate output.
    e. The natural rate of unemployment is decreasing.

14. The short-run Phillips curve shows the relationship between the inflation rate and the
    a. GDP growth rate.
    b. unemployment rate.
    c. employment rate.
    d. real interest rate.
    e. nominal interest rate.

15. An increase in expected inflation has what effect on the short-run Phillips curve?
    a. a movement up and to the left along the curve
    b. a movement down and to the right along the curve
    c. an upward shift of the curve
    d. a downward shift of the curve
    e. an increase in the slope of the curve

16. The long-run Phillips curve is
    a. horizontal.
    b. vertical.
    c. upward-sloping.
    d. downward-sloping.
    e. U-shaped.

17. The long-run Phillips curve illustrates which of the following?
    a. a positive relationship between unemployment and inflation
    b. a negative relationship between unemployment and inflation
    c. that unemployment will always return to the NAIRU
    d. that unemployment will adjust so that the economy experiences 2% inflation
    e. that output will adjust so that there is no unemployment or inflation in the long run

18. The process of bringing down the rate of inflation that has become embedded in expectations is known as
    a. disinflation.
    b. deflation.
    c. negative inflation.
    d. debt deflation.
    e. monetary policy.

19. A liquidity trap occurs when conventional monetary policy is ineffective because
    a. the short-run Phillips curve is negatively sloped.
    b. the public will not buy or sell Treasury bills.
    c. the unemployment rate cannot go below 5%.
    d. the nominal interest rate cannot be negative.
    e. the real interest rate cannot be negative.

20. According to the Quantity Theory of Money,
    a. the money supply times velocity is equal to nominal GDP.
    b. velocity varies significantly with the business cycle.
    c. changes in the money supply have no long-run effect on the economy.
    d. activist monetary policy is necessary to promote economic growth.
    e. monetary policy rules promote business-cycle fluctuations.

21. Which of the following best describes the difference between the classical and Keynesian views of the slope of the short-run aggregate supply curve?

	Classical	Keynesian
a.	vertical	positive
b.	vertical	horizontal
c.	horizontal	positive
d.	horizontal	negative
e.	horizontal	vertical

22. Which of the following measures the number of times the average dollar bill is spent per year?
    a. the NAIRU
    b. the inflation tax
    c. the unit of account
    d. the velocity of money
    e. $(M + P)/Y$

23. Which of the following equations represents the Quantity Theory of Money?
    a. $M \times V$ = nominal GDP
    b. $M \times V$ = real GDP
    c. $M \times V$ = full employment GDP
    d. $M \times P = V \times Y$
    e. $Y/M = V$

24. The natural rate hypothesis states that the actual inflation rate must equal the expected inflation rate to avoid
    a. high unemployment.
    b. deflation.
    c. recession.
    d. expanding the deficit.
    e. accelerating inflation.

25. Which of the following is accepted as part of the modern macroeconomic consensus?
    a. Monetary policy cannot be used to fight recessions.
    b. Expansionary fiscal policy effectively fights recessions.
    c. Monetary policy can be used to decrease unemployment in the long run.
    d. Discretionary fiscal policy should be used regularly to prevent business cycles.
    e. Discretionary monetary policy should be used regularly to prevent business cycles.

Free-Response Questions

1. Draw a correctly labeled graph showing a short-run Phillips curve.
    a. On your graph, show a long-run Phillips curve and label
       i. the NAIRU
       ii. the equilibrium inflation rate
    b. On your graph, show the effect of an increase in the expected inflation rate. **(6 points)**

2. Draw a correctly labeled graph of the market for loanable funds.
    a. On your graph, show each of the following:
       i. the equilibrium interest rate, labeled r_1
       ii. the equilibrium quantity of loanable funds, labeled Q_1
    b. Assume the government uses deficit spending to finance a decrease in taxes.
       i. On your graph from (a), illustrate the effect of the increased government deficit in the market for loanable funds. Label the new equilibrium interest rate and quantity of loanable funds r_2 and Q_2.
       ii. Explain why the increase in the government deficit had the effect you illustrated on your graph. **(6 points)**

3. Draw a correctly labeled aggregate demand and aggregate supply graph illustrating an economy that is experiencing a recession.
    a. On your graph, label the equilibrium price level, PL_1, and the equilibrium level of real GDP, Y_1.
    b. According to the macroeconomic consensus, what discretionary policy is most likely to help fight the recession?
    c. Use your graph from (a) to illustrate and explain how the discretionary policy you indicated in part (b) could effectively eliminate the recession. **(8 points)**

Will Technology Put Everyone Out of Work?

Unemployment, Creative Destruction, and Quality of Life

Robots are making our cars these days. They're stamping metal, screwing in bolts, welding, and painting. Robots also make furniture, hamburgers, and Oreo cookies. ATMs do the work of bank tellers. Travelocity.com and Orbitz.com take the place of travel agents. Grocery stores now have self-checkout lines, and self-service kiosks are cropping up like weeds. Some McDonald's restaurants even have kiosks in their play areas so that customers don't need to visit the friendly human at the counter. With Netflix streaming movies, who needs a sales-clerk at a DVD store? Airlines now allow travelers to bypass the check-in desk and obtain their boarding passes from a machine—if they haven't printed them beforehand via the internet or sent them to their cell phone. And if you ask an internet search engine to find stories about "technology killing jobs," that technology will lead you to an abundance of claims that it is. As the government and the Federal Reserve craft stabilization policies to address unemployment, should they treat technology as a threat? Let's consider the sources of unemployment and the counterpoints to the argument that robots will soon eat our lunch.

ppicturelibrary/Alamy

There's No Discounting the Value of a Good Job

It's easy to imagine tropical islands as heaven on earth, but even places with sun and sand can have sobering problems. If you've studied Haiti, the Philippines, Jamaica, or St. Lucia, you've learned about poverty and populations with many needs. In contrast, residents of Aruba and Hawaii generally enjoy high standards of health and education, low crime rates, and comfortable living conditions. Part of the formula for island bliss that Aruba and Hawaii have, and Haiti and the other islands lack, is an abundance of jobs.

Hawaii has the triple bonus of thriving tourism, several active military installations, and flourishing agriculture, among other fruitful industries. Aruba has ample jobs from tourism, retail trade, and oil refining. Good jobs are central to human satisfaction on the mainland as well. When people don't live in their favorite place in the world, it is often because their employment opportunities are elsewhere. Given the importance of jobs, it is understandable that emotions run high when it appears that technology will displace workers.

Technology has the potential to affect three broad categories of unemployment. If a worker with employable skills loses her job due to technology, she is *frictionally unemployed* while she looks for a new job. Frictional unemployment exists because there are "frictions" in the labor market that prevent an instantaneous, flawless pairing of workers and employers even when the workers have useful skills. After losing or leaving a job, completing education, or finishing a seasonal job, it takes time for workers to discover, acquire, and begin new work. This makes frictional unemployment necessary and ever-present in our economy.

Suppose widespread fear of technology-related job loss caused many households to lower their spending and save money for difficult times ahead. The resulting decrease in aggregate demand would slow the economy and cause layoffs. Workers who lose their jobs due to such a downturn in the economy's cycle of peaks and troughs experience *cyclical unemployment*. The large-scale layoffs during the Great Recession of 2007–2009 were another example of cyclical unemployment. The job losses included 107,357 layoffs at General Motors, 73,056 layoffs at Citigroup, and 47,540 layoffs at Hewlett-Packard. Many cyclically unemployed workers regain employment when the economy recovers and begins to climb toward a new peak.

Through most of the twentieth century, elevators were directed by human operators who flipped levers to send the elevator cars up and down. With button controls of elevators came the loss of jobs for people who had developed the skill of safe and accurate elevator maneuvering. This is an example of *structural unemployment*, which occurs when a worker lacks the skills necessary for available jobs. Technology and innovation have a long history of creating structural unemployment. The invention of the light bulb put many candle makers out of work. The automobile was a bane to people in the horse and buggy industries. Automatic telephone exchanges have eliminated the jobs of half a million switchboard operators since the 1970s. Until the personal computer became practical in the 1980s, résumés were professionally typeset, and writers without a lot of time, patience, and correction tape would hire typists to convert their handwritten notes into typed letters, reports, and book manuscripts.

Even with all these job losses, the unemployment rate has always recovered. The average unemployment rate since World War II has been about 6%. In 2000, the rate dipped below 4%; in 2009, the rate reached 10%; but by 2017, the rate was back to 4%. The next section explains why the U.S. workforce's successful adaptation to change is likely to continue.

Technology: Friend or Foe?

> Over the long sweep of American generations and waves of economic change, we simply have not experienced a net drain of jobs to advancing technology.
>
> —Alan Greenspan, former chair of the Federal Reserve

Necessity may be the mother of invention, but unemployment need not be its offspring. Former Federal Reserve chair Alan Greenspan's words suggest that technology creates at least as many jobs as it eliminates. The fear that technological advances will cause widespread unemployment can be countered in a number of ways. To begin with, mature industries do little for job creation; innovation is the real engine for growth in that area. Technology is the source of new industries that employ large numbers of people. In the United States in 2017, the computer systems design industry employed 2,014,750 workers, the computer and electronics manufacturing industry employed 1,037,260 workers, and the telecommunications industry employed 781,400 workers. Among older industries, beverage and tobacco product manufacturing employed 256,460, textile mills employed 111,870, and apparel manufacturing employed 123,000. Despite its extensive use of robots, the transportation equipment manufacturing industry employed 1,622,020 workers, making it one of the largest employers in the manufacturing sector.

Technology can increase the productivity of workers, and thus the usefulness of those workers to employers and customers. An eye doctor who uses surgical lasers accomplishes more than colleagues who don't. The same applies to a drug enforcement officer with night-vision glasses, a librarian with a barcode scanner, and a secretary with a computer. Some types of technology will increase the demand for the workers who use them. For instance, robot-assisted surgery is less invasive and more precise than traditional surgery, which increases the demand for doctors who perform that type of surgery.

In other cases, the increased productivity of some workers will lead to the layoff of other workers. A chiropractor with a robotic massage table can treat more patients in a day because she can adjust one patient's spine while another patient is receiving a massage. Likewise, a pizza chef with an automatic mixer can make more pizzas singlehandedly. The demand for labor depends on both the price of the good being made and the additional output gained from hiring another worker. If pizza prices remained constant, an increase in worker productivity would increase the demand for pizza chefs, because by making more pizzas, each chef would be worth more to the pizzerias. However, the increased productivity of chefs would increase the market supply of pizzas and lower the equilibrium price. If the price falls by a lot and the marginal product of labor rises by a little, each chef's contribution to revenue will decrease, and fewer chefs will be hired. If the price falls less than in proportion to the increase in marginal product, more chefs will be hired. In the case of pizza, despite technology-boosted increases in supply, high demand has kept the price of pizza up, so pizza chefs have no reason for concern.

When workers do lose their jobs due to technology, that is not the end of the story. New jobs are simultaneously created in other new industries—those engines of job growth—that make the robots and mixers and such. And then there are the industries that technology creates. For example, two centuries ago the tourism industry was virtually nonexistent in North America, and people who traveled long distances were called explorers. In 1804, it took explorers Meriwether Lewis and William Clark 18 months to travel from St. Louis to the Pacific Ocean. Thanks to modern transportation technology that can whisk people from St. Louis to the Pacific in less than five hours, tourism is now among the largest industries in the United States and the world. The usual trade-offs exist—the arrival of the airplane and the family car resulted

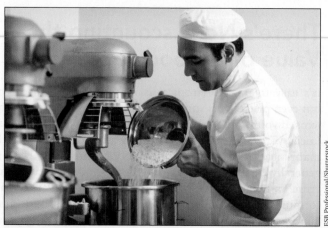

in lost jobs in the passenger rail industry—yet far more jobs were created in the airline and automobile industries than were ever lost on the railroads. Sometimes the trade-offs have minimal impact: the industries that produce spacecraft and launchers, satellites, air conditioners, computer software, and semiconductors have displaced few, if any, workers.

Technology has enabled some industries to exist by placing within the financial reach of the masses products that otherwise would be prohibitively expensive. A handmade watch would cost a pretty penny, and a handmade car would cost a fortune. Both items are now made with the extensive use of robots. Even handmade paper costs about $2 per sheet. One can only imagine how much a textbook would cost if hand-printed.

Technological improvements also bolster the demand for products. Flat-screen technology made it possible to fit televisions in more places. High-tech special effects attract more people to the movies. GPS speed and distance tracking gives runners a new reason to buy a watch. And even the self-service kiosks at McDonald's may reduce the lines and attract more customers.

It's also important to remember that robots and other machines don't keep any of the revenues they generate; all of the money spent on technology goes to people. When technology creates efficiency and reduces costs, all the benefits are passed on to humans in the form of lower prices and higher profits. In contrast, a dismissive stance toward technology—a prohibition of the robots that pour chocolate into molds, seal packages, and turn screws—would be detrimental to society. Such a stance would yield a large number of undesirable, low-paying jobs. There would be far less output to go around, and prices would be painfully high.

The structural unemployment problem is one of too few skills, not of too many workers. Given the shortage of skilled workers in the United States, each year the H-1B non-immigration visa program welcomes more than 65,000 guest workers from other countries for up to six years to do work that no available American citizens are qualified to perform. These individuals include teachers, occupational therapists, engineers, speech pathologists, lawyers, pharmacists, registered nurses, financial consultants, and accountants. Several related immigration programs fill similar needs.

Technology and innovation revitalize the economy and minimize cyclical unemployment. The challenge is to help the structurally unemployed gain new skills and share in the benefits. For this, the U.S. Department of Labor has embraced programs such as the High Growth Job Training Initiative, which identifies needed skill sets and helps community colleges convey those skills to unemployed workers. Unemployment insurance provides a safety net of roughly two-thirds of a worker's weekly income, up to a state-determined maximum, for at least 26 weeks. More generally, a focus on education and training would address these problems, whereas an antitechnology focus would be counterproductive in terms of overall employment and the quality of life.

Technology, Jobs, and the Quality of Life

Industrial mutation . . . incessantly revolutionizes the economic structure from within, incessantly destroying the old one, incessantly creating a new one. This process of creative destruction is the essential fact about capitalism.

—Joseph Schumpeter

Innovation and what Schumpeter calls "creative destruction" are critical to the American way of life. With high-tech machinery and fertilizers, food is produced at a rate that, contrary to the expectations of doomsayers such as Thomas Malthus, has kept pace with population growth. Medical advances have doubled the life expectancy of humans since the Middle Ages. Computers inform us, entertain us, and race through computations so that we need not. The destruction that accompanies creation becomes evident when such new products and processes make some skills obsolete. In 1800, 80% of the U.S. workforce was engaged in agriculture. In 1900, the figure was 38%. Now it is about 2%. Without technological advances such as the mechanical cotton pickers that made hand-picking skills obsolete by around 1950, there would be more jobs in the fields. By accepting innovation, however, we have relegated many of the dirty, difficult, and dangerous jobs to machines and created a host of new industries with high-paying jobs.

The number of jobs has grown at least as fast as the workforce so far, but what if robots ran the whole manufacturing show, including the new industries? We already see expansion in the service sector, which creates jobs and increases our standard of living by putting humans at the service of other humans. Technical efficiency in manufacturing could free up money and workers to expand the benefits received from service industries, such as health care, education, entertainment, environmental cleanup, and tourism. Just as the Schwan's Company employs 14,000 people and simplifies customers' lives by delivering prepared food to their doors, consumers could increase their use of cleaning services, personal trainers, musicians, artists, marriage counselors, massage therapists, beauty consultants, and innumerable other service workers.

Steve Skjold/Alamy

Robots can also grant us more leisure time. Technology has helped to increase the productivity per labor hour at an average rate of 2.5% per year since the 1970s, meaning higher incomes with less work. After a long history of workweeks in excess of 50 hours, the Fair Labor Standards Act of 1938 shortened the workweek to 40 hours in 1940, with mandated overtime pay of 1.5 times the standard wage rate for hourly workers who exceed 40 hours. With continued advancements in technology, we may enjoy income growth along with workweeks of 35 hours or less, as is common in France and Germany already.

A steady flow of innovation since *Homo sapiens* first appeared has done much for our standard of living without a net loss of jobs. What's next? The pattern is likely to continue. The high-tech horizon offers more new industries, such as commercial space travel, alternative energy sources, such as ocean thermal energy conversion, and nanotechnology—a form of molecular engineering that might allow circuits and devices to be built up from single atoms and molecules. Technology can free us from mundane tasks and allow humans to enjoy a more positive work experience. As improvements occur, the challenge for society is to assist the hardest-hit workers with appropriate retraining, to reassure everyone that the sky is not falling, and to make good use of the advances that ensue.

Conclusion

The importance of jobs translates into strong emotions when potential threats to employment are identified. That same importance should compel us to examine real and imagined reasons for job loss carefully. Structural employment as a result of changes in technology is a real, short-term phenomenon in some industries, as it has been for centuries. But by encouraging technological innovation, we enrich the economy with new industries and jobs, improve the productivity of workers, advance the quality of life, and promote growth in real wages—none of which are earned by robots. In adapting to technological change, policy makers should focus on helping those with limited job skills train for the many jobs that remain unfilled. As robots save us money and time by screwing in bolts and cleaning out test tubes, perhaps more attention can be granted to the solvable social, environmental, and health problems to which society could devote a nearly endless amount of work effort.

Critical Thinking Questions

1. Americans eat almost 10 billion donuts each year. How sensitive do you think the demand for donuts is to their price (that is, how price elastic is the demand for donuts)? How much higher do you think the price of donuts would be in the absence of mechanical wheat harvesters, dough mixers, and fryers? What can you conclude about the relationship between technology and employment in the donut industry on the basis of your thoughts about demand elasticity and price?

2. Suppose technology gradually replaced every job, and robots did everything from managing stores and designing bridges to finding cancer cures and creating artwork.
   a. Out of all the jobs that exist, which ones do you think would be the last handed over to robots? Explain your answer.
   b. Once robots were doing it all, what would happen to our standard of living? Would humans become penniless? Why or why not?

3. Describe one type of technology not mentioned in the chapter that
   a. caused an increase in the demand for workers in existing industries.
   b. caused a decrease in the demand for workers in existing industries.
   c. created a new industry with a large number of employees.

Consequences of Public Policy for Economic Growth

economics by example *Why Are Some Countries Rich and Others Poor?*

Grown in China

China is growing—and so are the Chinese. Over the past century the average height of Chinese adults has increased by 10 centimeters (almost 4 inches!) The countries with the largest average height are still in Europe, and the average Chinese citizen is still a lot shorter than the average European or American. But at the current rates of growth, the difference will be largely gone in the next couple of generations.

There's no mystery about why the Chinese have grown taller—they grew richer. Genetics certainly play a role in determining an individual's height, but a report in *Scientific American* notes that environmental factors, such as nutrition, can account for 20% to 40% of height differences. In the early twentieth century, China was a much poorer country and many families couldn't afford to give their children adequate

nutrition. As a result, their children grew up to be shorter adults than they would have been on a healthier diet. However, average income in China has been increasing steadily since the 1980s, and the development of the Chinese economy has led to increased access to food. Today, young adults in China are much taller on average than before the 1980s.

Although it continues to be a relatively poor country, China has made great economic strides over the past 60 years. Its recent history is probably the world's most dramatic example of economic growth—a sustained increase in the productive capacity of an economy. Yet despite its impressive performance, China is playing catch-up with the United States. It's still relatively poor because many other nations began their own processes of economic growth earlier—in the case of the United States

and European countries, more than a century ago.

Unlike a short-run increase in real GDP caused by an increase in aggregate demand or short-run aggregate supply, we'll see that economic growth pushes the production possibilities curve outward and shifts the long-run aggregate supply curve to the right. Because economic growth is a long-run concept, we often refer to it as *long-run economic growth* for clarity. Many economists have argued that long-run economic growth—why it happens and how to achieve it—is the single most important issue in macroeconomics. In this section, we present some facts about long-run growth, look at the factors that economists believe determine its pace, examine how government policies can help or hinder growth, and address questions about the environmental sustainability of growth.

Long-Run Economic Growth

Comparing Economies Across Time and Space

Before we analyze the sources of long-run economic growth, it's useful to have a sense of just how much the U.S. economy has grown over time and how large the gaps are between wealthy countries like the United States and countries that have yet to achieve a comparable standard of living. So let's take a look at the numbers.

Real GDP per Capita

The key statistic used to track economic growth is *real GDP per capita*—real GDP divided by the population size. Economists focus on GDP because, as we have learned, GDP measures the total value of an economy's production of final goods and services as well as the income earned in that economy in a given year. We use *real* GDP because we want to separate changes in the quantity of goods and services from the effects of a rising price level. We focus on real GDP *per capita* because we want to isolate the effect of changes in the population. For example, other things equal, an increase in the population lowers the standard of living for the average person—there are now more people to share a given amount of real GDP. An increase in real GDP that only matches an increase in population leaves the real GDP per capita unchanged.

Although we learned in Section 6 that growth in real GDP per capita should not be a policy goal in and of itself, it does serve as a very useful summary measure of a country's economic progress over time. **Figure 37.1** shows real GDP per capita for the United States, India, and China, measured in 2005 dollars, from 1910 to 2016. (We'll talk more about India and China in a moment.) The vertical axis is drawn so that equal percentage changes in real GDP per capita across countries are the same size in the graph.

To give a sense of how much the U.S. economy grew during the last century, **Table 37.1** shows real GDP per capita at 20-year intervals, expressed as a percentage of the 1910, 2010, and 2016 levels. In 1930, the U.S. economy already produced 125% as much per person as it did in 1910. In 2016, it produced 698% as much per person as it did in 1910. Alternatively, in 1910, the U.S. economy produced only 14% as much per person as it did in 2016.

The income of the typical family normally grows more or less in proportion to per capita income. For example, a 1% increase in real GDP per capita corresponds, roughly, to a 1% increase in the income of the median or typical family—a family at the center of the income distribution. In 2016, the median American household had an income of about $59,039. Since Table 37.1 tells us that real GDP per capita in 1910 was only 14% of its 2016 level, a typical family in 1910 probably had purchasing power only 14% as large as the purchasing power of a typical family in 2016.

DNY59/Getty Images

For many decades Americans dreamed of owning a single-family home in a well-manicured neighborhood.

Figure 37.1 Economic Growth in the United States, India, and China over the Past Century

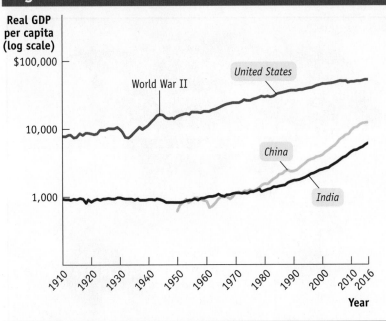

Real GDP per capita from 1910 to 2016, measured in 2005 dollars, is shown for the United States, India, and China (*note:* data for China prior to 1950 is unavailable). Equal percentage changes in real GDP per capita are drawn the same size. India and China currently have a much higher growth rate than the United States. However, China has only recently attained the standard of living achieved in the United States in 1910, while India is still poorer than the United States was in 1910.

Data Source: University of Groningen, Groningen Growth and Development Centre, Maddison Project Database: https://www.rug.nl/ggdc/historicaldevelopment/maddison/.

That would be equivalent to an annual income of around $8,265 in today's dollars, representing a standard of living that we would now consider severe poverty. If the average American family today were forced to live as an average family from 1910, they would feel quite deprived.

Yet many people in the world have a standard of living equal to or lower than that of the United States a century ago. That's the message about China and India in Figure 37.1: despite dramatic economic growth in China over the last four decades and the less dramatic acceleration of economic growth in India, China has only recently attained the standard of living that the United States enjoyed in 1910, while India is still poorer than the United States was in 1910. And much of the world today is poorer than China and India.

You can get a sense of how poor much of the world remains by looking at **Figure 37.2**, a map of the world in which countries are classified according to their 2018 levels of GDP per capita, in U.S. dollars. As you can see, large parts of the world have very low incomes. Generally speaking, the countries of Europe and North America, as well as a few in the Pacific, have high incomes. The median global GDP per capita is under $12,000. In fact, today many of the world's people live in countries with a lower standard of living than the United States had a century ago.

Table 37.1 U.S. Real GDP per Capita

Year	Percentage of 1910 real GDP per capita	Percentage of 2010 real GDP per capita	Percentage of 2016 real GDP per capita
1910	100%	15%	14%
1930	125	19	17
1950	200	30	28
1970	315	48	45
1990	487	75	69
2010	649	100	92
2016	698	107	100

Data Source: University of Groningen, Groningen Growth and Development Centre, Maddison Project Database: https://www.rug.nl/ggdc/historicaldevelopment/maddison/

Figure 37.2 Per Capita Incomes Around the World, 2018

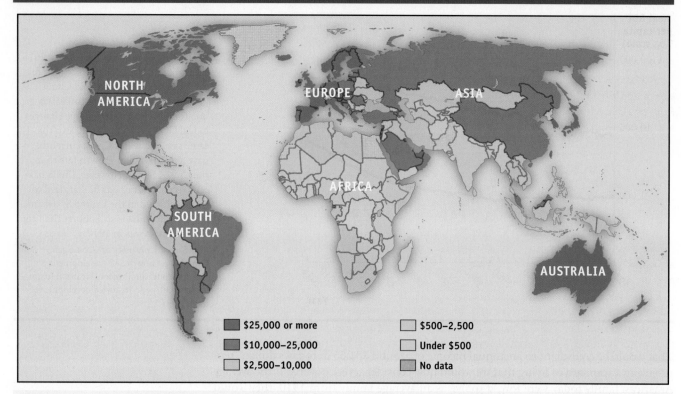

Legend:
- $25,000 or more
- $10,000–25,000
- $2,500–10,000
- $500–2,500
- Under $500
- No data

Although the countries of Europe and North America—along with a few in East Asia—have high per capita incomes, much of the world is still very poor. Today, more than 50% of the world's population lives in countries with a lower standard of living than the United States had a century ago.

Data Source: International Monetary Fund.

When Did Long-Run Growth Begin?

In 2018, the United States was much richer than it was in 1953; in 1953, it was much richer than it had been in 1903. But how did 1853 compare with 1803? Or 1753? How far back does long-run economic growth go?

The answer is that long-run growth is a relatively modern phenomenon. The U.S. economy was already growing steadily by the mid-nineteenth century—think railroads. But if you go back to the period before 1800, you find a world economy that grew extremely slowly by today's standards. Furthermore, the population grew almost as fast as the economy, so there was very little increase in output per person. According to the economic historian Angus Maddison, from the year 1000 to 1800, real aggregate output around the world grew less than 0.2% per year, with population rising at about the same rate. Economic stagnation meant unchanging living standards. For example, information on prices and wages from sources such as monastery records shows that workers in England weren't significantly better off in the early eighteenth century than they had been five centuries earlier. And it's a good bet that they weren't much better off than Egyptian peasants in the age of the pharaohs. However, long-run economic growth has increased significantly since 1800. In the last 50 years or so, real GDP per capita worldwide has grown at a rate of about 2% per year. Let's examine the implications of high and low growth rates.

Prior to the advent of the railroad, growth moved at the pace of a horse-drawn wagon.

Growth Rates

How did the United States manage to produce nearly seven times more per person in 2016 than in 1910? A little bit at a time. Long-run economic growth is normally a gradual process in which real GDP per capita grows at most a few percent per year. From 1910 to 2010, real GDP per capita in the United States increased by an average of 2.1% each year.

To have a sense of the relationship between the annual growth rate of real GDP per capita and the long-run change in real GDP per capita, it's helpful to keep in mind the **Rule of 70**, a mathematical formula that tells us how long it takes real GDP per capita, or any other variable that grows gradually over time, to double. The approximate answer is:

$$(37\text{-}1) \quad \text{Number of years for variable to double} = \frac{70}{\text{Annual growth rate of variable}}$$

The **Rule of 70** tells us that the time it takes a variable that grows gradually over time to double is approximately 70 divided by that variable's annual growth rate.

(Note that the Rule of 70 can only be applied to a positive growth rate.)

So if real GDP per capita grows at 1% per year, it will take 70 years to double. If it grows at 2% per year, it will take only 35 years to double. Applying the Rule of 70 to the 2.1% average growth rate in the United States implies that it should have taken 33.3 years for real GDP per capita to double; it would have taken 100 years—three periods of 33.3 years each—for U.S. real GDP per capita to double three times. That is, the Rule of 70 implies that over the course of 100 years, U.S. real GDP per capita should have increased by a factor of 2 × 2 × 2 = 8. And this turns out to be a pretty good approximation of reality. Over the century from 1910 to 2010 real GDP per capita rose just about eightfold.

Figure 37.3 shows the average annual rate of growth of real GDP per capita for selected countries from 1980 to 2016. Some countries were notable success stories: we've already mentioned China, which has made spectacular progress. India, although not matching China's performance, has also achieved impressive growth.

Some countries, though, have had very disappointing growth. This includes many of the countries in Africa and South America, where growth rates below 1% are common. A few countries, such as Zimbabwe, have actually slid backward.

What explains these differences in growth rates? To answer that question, we need to examine the sources of long-run growth.

Figure 37.3 Comparing Recent Growth Rates

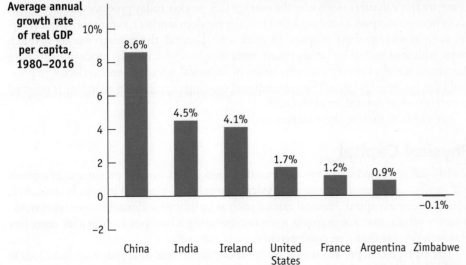

Here the average annual rate of growth of real GDP per capita from 1980 to 2016 is shown for selected countries. China and, to a lesser extent, India and Ireland have achieved impressive growth. The United States, Argentina, and France have had moderate growth. Still others, such as Zimbabwe, had negative growth.
Data Source: World Bank.

The Sources of Long-Run Growth

Long-run economic growth depends almost entirely on one ingredient: rising *productivity*. However, a number of factors affect the growth of productivity. Let's look first at why productivity is the key ingredient. After that, we'll examine what affects it.

The Crucial Importance of Productivity

Sustained growth in real GDP per capita occurs only when the amount of output produced by the average worker increases steadily. The term **labor productivity** (or **productivity**, for short) is used to refer either to output per worker or, in some cases, to output per hour. The number of hours worked by an average worker differs to some extent across countries, although this isn't an important factor in the difference between living standards in, say, India and the United States. In this book we'll focus on output per worker. For the economy as a whole, productivity—output per worker—is simply real GDP divided by the number of people working.

You might wonder why we say that higher productivity is the only source of long-run growth in real GDP per capita. Can't an economy also increase its real GDP per capita by putting more of the population to work? The answer is, yes, but there is more to it than that. For short periods of time, an economy can experience a burst of growth in output per capita by putting a higher percentage of the population to work. That happened in the United States during World War II, when millions of women who previously worked only in the home entered the paid workforce. The percentage of adult civilians employed outside the home rose from 50% in 1941 to 58% in 1944, and you can see the resulting bump in real GDP per capita during those years in Figure 37.1.

Over the longer run, however, the rate of employment growth is never very different from the rate of population growth. Over the course of the twentieth century, for example, the population of the United States rose at an average rate of 1.3% per year and employment rose 1.5% per year. Real GDP per capita rose 1.9% per year; of that, 1.7%—that is, almost 90% of the total increase—was the result of rising productivity. In general, overall real GDP can grow because of population growth, but any large increase in real GDP *per capita* must be the result of increased output *per worker*. That is, it must be due to higher productivity.

We have just seen that increased productivity is the key to long-run economic growth. But what leads to higher productivity?

Explaining Growth in Productivity

There are three main reasons why the average U.S. worker today produces far more than his or her counterpart a century ago. First, the modern worker has far more *physical capital*, such as tools and office space, to work with. Second, the modern worker is much better educated and so possesses much more *human capital*. Finally, modern firms have the advantage of a century's accumulation of technical advancements reflecting a great deal of *technological progress*. The accumulated existing capital in an economy is referred to as its stock of capital, or *capital stock*.

Let's look at each of these factors in turn.

Physical Capital

Module 22 explained that capital—manufactured goods used to produce other goods and services—is often described as **physical capital** to distinguish it from human capital and financial capital. Physical capital such as buildings and machinery makes workers more productive. For example, a worker operating a backhoe can dig a lot more feet of trench per day than one equipped with only a shovel.

The average U.S. private-sector worker today makes use of approximately $130,000 worth of physical capital—far more than a U.S. worker had 100 years ago and far more than the average worker in most other countries has today.

Human Capital

It's not enough for a worker to have good equipment—he or she must also know what to do with it. **Human capital** refers to the improvement in labor created by the education and knowledge embodied in the workforce.

The human capital of the United States has increased dramatically over the past century. A century ago, although most Americans were able to read and write, very few had an extensive education. In 1910, only 13.5% of Americans over 25 had graduated from high school and only 3% had four-year college degrees. By 2015 those percentages were 88% and 33%, respectively. It would be impossible to run today's economy with a population as poorly educated as that of a century ago.

Analyses based on *growth accounting*, described later in this section, suggest that education—and its effect on productivity—is an even more important determinant of growth than increases in physical capital.

The combination of better education and high-tech tools has allowed the average U.S. worker today to produce far more than workers in the past.

Technology

Probably the most important driver of productivity growth is progress in **technology**, which is broadly defined as the technical means for the production of goods and services. We'll see shortly how economists measure the impact of technology on growth.

Workers today are able to produce more than those in the past, even with the same amount of physical and human capital, because technology has advanced over time. It's important to realize that economically important technological progress need not be flashy or rely on cutting-edge science. Historians have noted that past economic growth has been driven not only by major inventions, such as the railroad or the semiconductor chip, but also by thousands of modest innovations. The flat-bottomed paper bag, patented in 1870, made packing groceries and many other goods much easier. The Post-it note, introduced in 1981, has had surprisingly large benefits for office productivity. Experts attribute much of the productivity surge that took place in the United States late in the twentieth century to new technology adopted by retail companies, such as computerized inventories and bar codes, rather than to high-technology companies.

Human capital is the improvement in labor created by the education and knowledge of members of the workforce.

Technology is the technical means for the production of goods and services.

MODULE 37 REVIEW

Check Your Understanding

1. Why do economists focus on real GDP per capita as a measure of economic progress rather than on some other measure, such as nominal GDP per capita or real GDP?

2. Apply the Rule of 70 to the data in Figure 37.3 to determine how long it will take each of the countries listed there to double its real GDP per capita. Will India's real GDP per capita exceed that of the United States in the future if growth rates remain the same? Why or why not?

3. Although China and India currently have growth rates much higher than the U.S. growth rate, the typical Chinese or Indian household is far poorer than the typical American household. Explain why.

TACKLE THE AP® TEST: Multiple-Choice Questions

1. Which of the following is true about income levels for countries around the world compared to the United States?
   a. More than 50% of the world's population lives in countries with a lower income than the United States.
   b. Countries in Asia have a lower average income than the rest of the countries in the world.
   c. Countries with the lowest average income level are found in Africa and South America.
   d. China recently attained the same average income level as the United States.
   e. All of Europe has an average income level equal to or above the United States.

2. Which of the following is the key statistic used to track economic growth?
   a. GDP
   b. real GDP
   c. real GDP per capita
   d. median real GDP
   e. median real GDP per capita

3. According to the Rule of 70, if a country's real GDP per capita grows at a rate of 2% per year, it will take how many years for real GDP per capita to double?
   a. 3.5
   b. 20
   c. 35
   d. 70
   e. It will never double at that rate.

4. If a country's real GDP per capita doubles in 10 years, what is its average annual rate of growth of real GDP per capita?
   a. 3.5%
   b. 7%
   c. 10%
   d. 70%
   e. 700%

5. Long-run economic growth depends almost entirely on
   a. technological change.
   b. rising productivity.
   c. increased labor force participation.
   d. rising real GDP per capita.
   e. population growth.

6. Long-run economic growth could be caused by an increase in
   a. capital stock.
   b. investment.
   c. consumption.
   d. aggregate demand.
   e. short-run aggregate supply.

7. Which of the following leads to an increase in human capital?
   a. education
   b. job training
   c. work experience
   d. increased knowledge
   e. all of the above

TACKLE THE AP® TEST: Free-Response Questions

1. Refer to the figure below to answer each of the questions that follow.

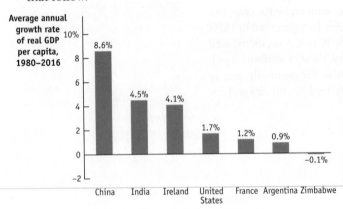

Average annual growth rate of real GDP per capita, 1980–2016

China 8.6%
India 4.5%
Ireland 4.1%
United States 1.7%
France 1.2%
Argentina 0.9%
Zimbabwe −0.1%

a. If growth continued at the rates shown in the figure, which of the seven countries would have had a lower real GDP per capita in 2017 than in the previous year? Explain.

b. If growth continued at the rates shown in the figure, which of the seven countries would have had the largest increase in real GDP per capita in 2017? Explain.

c. If growth continues at the rates shown in the figure, real GDP per capita for which of the seven countries will at least double over the next 10 years? Explain.

> **Rubric for FRQ 1 (6 points)**
>
> **1 point:** Zimbabwe
>
> **1 point:** It has a negative average annual growth rate of real GDP per capita.
>
> **1 point:** It cannot be determined.
>
> **1 point:** The figure provides data for growth rates, but not for the level of real GDP per capita. Higher growth rates do not indicate higher levels.
>
> **1 point:** China
>
> **1 point:** A country has to have an average annual growth rate of 7% or higher for real GDP to at least double in 10 years. China has a growth rate of 8.9%.

2. Increases in real GDP per capita result primarily from changes in what variable? (*Hint:* This is a general source of long-run growth and not a particular input such as capital.) Define that variable. Increases in what other variable could also lead to increased real GDP per capita? Why is this other factor less significant? **(4 points)**

Productivity and Growth

In this Module, you will learn to:
- Illustrate changes in productivity using an aggregate production function
- Discuss how growth has varied among several important regions of the world and explain why the convergence hypothesis applies to economically advanced countries

Economic Growth and the Aggregate Production Function

We know that productivity is higher, other things equal, when workers are equipped with more physical capital, more human capital, better technology, or any combination of the three. Economists use an **aggregate production function** to show how productivity depends on the quantities of physical and human capital per worker as well as the state of technology. In general, all three factors tend to rise over time, as workers are equipped with more machinery, receive more education, and benefit from technological advances. The aggregate production function allows economists to represent the effects of these three factors on overall productivity.

The Law of Diminishing Returns

In analyzing historical economic growth, economists have discovered a crucial fact about the estimated aggregate production function: it exhibits **diminishing returns to physical capital**. That is, when the amount of human capital per worker and the state of technology are held fixed, each successive increase in the amount of physical capital per worker leads to a smaller increase in productivity. **Table 38.1** gives a hypothetical example of how the level of physical capital per worker might affect the level of real GDP per worker, holding human capital per worker and the state of technology fixed. In this example, we measure the quantity of physical capital in terms of the dollars' worth of investment.

The **aggregate production function** is a hypothetical function that shows how productivity (output per worker) depends on the quantities of physical capital per worker and human capital per worker as well as the state of technology.

An aggregate production function exhibits **diminishing returns to physical capital** when, holding the amount of human capital per worker and the state of technology fixed, each successive increase in the amount of physical capital per worker leads to a smaller increase in productivity.

Table 38.1	A Hypothetical Example: How Physical Capital per Worker Affects Productivity, Holding Human Capital and Technology Fixed
Physical capital investment per worker	**Real GDP per worker**
$0	$0
15,000	30,000
30,000	45,000
45,000	55,000

AP® EXAM TIP

The concept of diminishing returns is applied throughout economics. The general idea is that the more you do anything, the harder it is to keep doing it. Because the activity gets harder to do, the returns from doing it diminish. For example, the longer your study session, the less you learn in each additional hour. This same idea applies to investing in physical capital—each added unit will increase productivity by less and less. Diminishing returns explains the shape of the aggregate production function.

As you can see from the table, there is a big payoff from the first $15,000 invested in physical capital: real GDP per worker rises by $30,000. The second $15,000 worth of physical capital also raises productivity, but by not as much: real GDP per worker goes up by only $15,000. The third $15,000 worth of physical capital raises real GDP per worker by only $10,000.

To see why the relationship between physical capital per worker and productivity exhibits diminishing returns, think about how having farm equipment affects the productivity of farm workers. A little bit of equipment makes a big difference: a worker equipped with a tractor can do much more than a worker without one. And, other things equal, a worker using more expensive equipment will be more productive: a worker

Christopher May/Alamy

with a $30,000 tractor will normally be able to cultivate more farmland in a given amount of time than a worker with a $15,000 tractor because the more expensive machine will be more powerful, perform more tasks, or both.

But will a worker with a $30,000 tractor, holding human capital and technology constant, be twice as productive as a worker with a $15,000 tractor? Probably not: there's a huge difference between not having a tractor at all and having even an inexpensive tractor; there's much less difference between having an inexpensive tractor and having a better tractor. A worker with a $150,000 tractor won't be 10 times as productive: a tractor can be improved only so much. Because the same is true of other kinds of equipment, the aggregate production function shows diminishing returns to physical capital.

Figure 38.1 is a graphical representation of the aggregate production function with diminishing returns to physical capital. As the *productivity curve* illustrates, more physical capital per worker leads to more output per worker. But each $30,000 increment in physical capital per worker adds less to productivity. By comparing points *A*, *B*, and *C*, you can also see that, as physical capital per worker rises, output per worker also rises—but at a diminishing rate. Going from point *A* to point *B*, representing a $30,000 increase in physical capital per worker, leads to an increase of $20,000 in real GDP per worker. Going from point *B* to point *C*, a second $30,000 increase in physical capital per worker, leads to an increase of only $10,000 in real GDP per worker.

Figure 38.1   Physical Capital and Productivity

Other things equal, a greater quantity of physical capital per worker leads to higher real GDP per worker but is subject to diminishing returns: each successive addition to physical capital per worker produces a smaller increase in productivity. Starting at point *A*, with $20,000 in physical capital per worker, a $30,000 increase in physical capital per worker leads to an increase of $20,000 in real GDP per worker. At point *B*, with $50,000 in physical capital per worker, a $30,000 increase in physical capital per worker leads to an increase of only $10,000 in real GDP per worker.

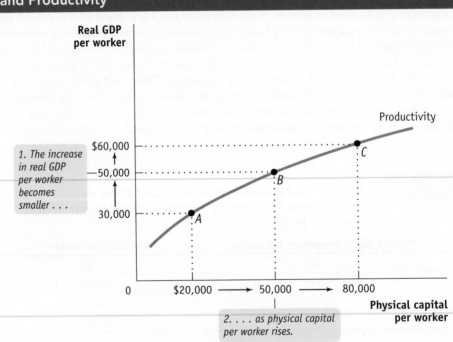

It's important to realize that diminishing returns to physical capital is an "other things equal" phenomenon: additional amounts of physical capital are less productive *when the amount of human capital per worker and the technology are held fixed*. Diminishing returns may disappear if we increase the amount of human capital per worker, or improve the technology, or both when the amount of physical capital per worker is increased. For example, a worker with a $30,000 tractor who has also been trained in the most advanced cultivation techniques may in fact be more than twice as productive as a worker with only a $15,000 tractor and no additional human capital. But diminishing returns to any one input—regardless of whether it is physical capital, human capital, or labor—is a pervasive characteristic of production. Typical estimates suggest that, in practice, a 1% increase in the quantity of physical capital per worker increases output per worker by only one-third of 1%, or 0.33%.

Growth Accounting and Total Factor Productivity

In practice, all the factors contributing to higher productivity rise during the course of economic growth: both physical capital and human capital per worker increase, and technology advances as well. But how does a technological advance affect the aggregate production function?

To see how a change in technology is shown using an aggregate production function, assume that there is no increase in human capital per worker so that we can focus on changes in physical capital and in technology. In **Figure 38.2**, the lower curve shows the same hypothetical relationship between physical capital per worker and output per worker shown in Figure 38.1. Let's assume that this was the relationship given the technology available in 1950. The upper curve also shows a relationship between physical capital per worker and productivity, but this time given the technology available in 2020. (We've chosen a 70-year stretch to allow us to use the Rule of 70.) The 2020 curve is shifted up compared to the 1950 curve because technologies developed over the previous 70 years make it possible to produce more output for a given amount of physical capital per worker than was possible with the technology available in 1950. (Note that the two curves are measured in constant dollars.)

Figure 38.2   Technological Progress and Productivity Growth

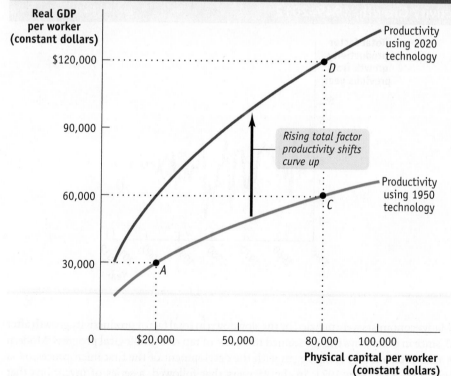

Technological progress shifts the productivity curve upward. Here we hold human capital per worker fixed. We assume that the lower curve (the same curve as in Figure 38.1) reflects technology in 1950 and the upper curve reflects technology in 2020. Holding technology and human capital fixed, quadrupling physical capital per worker from $20,000 to $80,000 leads to a doubling of real GDP per worker, from $30,000 to $60,000. This is shown by the movement from point A to point C, reflecting an approximately 1% per year rise in real GDP per worker. In reality, technological progress shifted the productivity curve upward and the actual rise in real GDP per worker is shown by the movement from point A to point D. Real GDP per worker grew 2% per year, leading to a quadrupling during the period. The extra 1% in growth of real GDP per worker is due to higher total factor productivity.

Let's assume that between 1950 and 2020 the amount of physical capital per worker rose from $20,000 to $80,000. If this increase in physical capital per worker had taken place without any technological progress, the economy would have moved from A to C: output per worker would have risen, but only from $30,000 to $60,000, or 1% per year (using the Rule of 70 tells us that a 1% growth rate over 70 years doubles output).

In fact, however, the economy moved from *A* to *D*: output rose from $30,000 to $120,000, or 2% per year. There was an increase in both physical capital per worker and technological progress, which shifted the aggregate production function.

In this case, 50% of the annual 2% increase in productivity—that is, 1% in annual productivity growth—is due to higher *total factor productivity*, the amount of output that can be produced with a given amount of factor inputs. So when total factor productivity increases, the economy can produce more output with the same quantity of physical capital, human capital, and labor.

Most estimates find that increases in total factor productivity are central to a country's economic growth. Economists believe that observed increases in total factor productivity in fact measure the economic effects of technological progress. All of this implies that technological change is crucial to economic growth. The Bureau of Labor Statistics estimates the growth rate of both labor productivity and total factor productivity for nonfarm business in the United States. According to the Bureau's estimates, over the period from 1948 to 2010, American labor productivity rose 2.3% per year. Only 49% of that rise is explained by increases in physical and human capital per worker; the rest is explained by rising total factor productivity—that is, by technological progress.

However, from the early 1970s through the mid-1990s, the United States went through a slump in total factor productivity growth. **Figure 38.3** shows Bureau of Labor Statistics estimates of annual total factor productivity growth since 1949. As you can see, there was a large fall in the productivity growth rate beginning in the early 1970s. Because higher total factor productivity plays such a key role in long-run growth, the economy's overall growth was also disappointing, leading to a widespread sense that economic progress had ground to a halt.

Figure 38.3   Total Factor Productivity Growth, 1949–2012

Notice that the scale on the vertical axis starts at –6% so that zero total productivity growth is shown above the horizontal axis. A decline in total factor productivity occurs when the growth rate is below zero (negative), and an increase in total factor productivity occurs when the growth rate is above zero (positive).

Data Source: Congressional Budget Office.

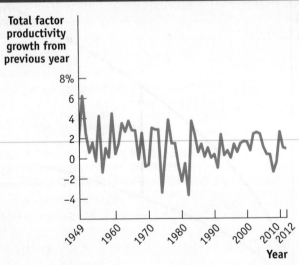

Many economists were puzzled by the slowdown in total factor productivity growth after 1973, since in other ways the era seemed to be one of rapid technological progress. Modern information technology really began with the development of the first microprocessor—a computer on a chip—in 1971. In the 25 years that followed, a series of inventions that seemed revolutionary became standard equipment in the business world: fax machines, desktop computers, cell phones, and e-mail. Yet the rate of growth of productivity remained stagnant. In a famous remark, MIT economics professor and Nobel laureate Robert Solow, a pioneer in the analysis of economic growth, declared that the information technology revolution could be seen everywhere except in the economic statistics.

Why didn't information technology produce large rewards? Economist Paul A. David pointed out that another miracle technology—electric power—had spread through the economy, again with surprisingly little impact on productivity growth at first. The reason, he suggested, was that a new technology doesn't yield its full potential if you use it in old ways.

For example, a traditional factory around 1900 was a multistory building with machinery tightly crowded together and designed to be powered by a steam engine in the basement. This design had limitations: it was very difficult to move people and materials around. Yet owners who electrified their factories initially maintained the multistory, tightly packed layout. Only with the switch to spread-out, one-story factories that took advantage of the flexibility of electric power—most famously Henry Ford's auto assembly line—did productivity take off. Similarly, total factor productivity finally took off in the mid-1990s once people adjusted their ways of doing business to take advantage of new technologies—by, for example, replacing letters with faxes and e-mail—just as David predicted they would.

What About Natural Resources?

In our discussion so far, we haven't mentioned natural resources, which certainly have an effect on productivity. Other things equal, countries that are abundant in valuable natural resources, such as highly fertile land or rich mineral deposits, have higher real GDP per capita than less fortunate countries. The most obvious modern example is the Middle East, where enormous oil deposits have made a few sparsely populated countries very rich. For instance, Kuwait's real GDP per capita increased from $4,429 to $29,040 between 1965 and 2017 based on its oil resources.

The discovery of oil deposits can have a significant effect on real GDP, but in most cases natural resources have a less dramatic effect on productivity compared to human or physical capital.

But other things are often not equal. In the modern world, natural resources are a much less important determinant of productivity than human or physical capital for the great majority of countries. For example, some nations with very high real GDP per capita, such as Singapore, have very few natural resources. Some resource-rich nations, such as Nigeria (which has sizable oil deposits), are very poor.

Historically, natural resources played a much more prominent role in determining productivity. In the nineteenth century, the countries with the highest real GDP per capita were those abundant in rich farmland and mineral deposits: the United States, Canada, Argentina, and Australia. As a consequence, natural resources figured prominently in the development of economic thought. In a famous book published in 1798, *An Essay on the Principle of Population*, the English economist Thomas Malthus made the fixed quantity of land in the world the basis of a pessimistic prediction about future productivity. As population grew, he pointed out, the amount of land per worker would decline. And, other things equal, this would cause productivity to fall. In fact, his view was that improvements in technology or increases in physical capital would lead only to temporary improvements in productivity because they would always be offset by the pressure of rising population and more workers on the supply of land. In the long run, he concluded, the great majority of people were condemned to living on the edge of starvation. Only then would death rates be high enough and birth rates low enough to prevent rapid population growth from outstripping productivity growth.

It hasn't turned out that way, although many historians believe that Malthus's prediction of falling or stagnant productivity was valid for much of human history. Population pressure probably did prevent large productivity increases until the eighteenth century. But in the time since Malthus wrote his book, any negative effects on productivity from population growth have been far outweighed by other, positive factors—advances in technology, increases in human and physical capital, and the opening up of enormous amounts of cultivatable land in the New World.

It remains true, however, that we live on a finite planet, with limited supplies of resources such as oil and limited ability to absorb environmental damage. We address the concerns these limitations pose for economic growth later in this section.

Success, Disappointment, and Failure

Rates of long-run economic growth differ markedly around the world. Let's look at three regions that have had quite different experiences with economic growth over the last few decades.

Figure 38.4 shows trends since 1960 in real GDP per capita in 2005 dollars for three countries: Argentina, Nigeria, and South Korea. We have chosen these countries because each is a particularly striking example of what has happened in its region. South Korea's amazing rise is part of a larger success story in East Asia. Argentina's slow progress, interrupted by repeated setbacks, is more or less typical of the disappointment that has characterized Latin America. And Nigeria's unhappy story—real GDP per capita is considerably lower than South Korea's real GDP per capita, despite the two countries having similar values in the 1960s. This is unfortunately, an experience shared by many African countries.

Figure 38.4   Success and Disappointment

Real GDP per capita from 1960 to 2016, measured in 2005 dollars, is shown for Argentina, South Korea, and Nigeria, using a logarithmic scale. South Korea and some other East Asian countries have been highly successful at achieving economic growth. Argentina, like much of Latin America, has had several setbacks, slowing its growth. Nigeria's standard of living in 2012 remained below that of South Korea and Argentina. Nigeria's experience is consistent with many other African countries, where real GDP per capita continues to lag behind countries in East Asia and Latin America.

Data Source: World Bank.

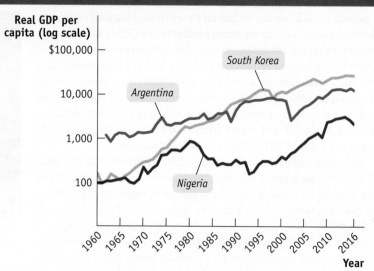

East Asia's Miracle

In 1960, South Korea was a very poor country. In fact, in 1960 its real GDP per capita was lower than that of India today. But, as you can see from Figure 38.4, beginning in the early 1960s, South Korea began an extremely rapid economic ascent: real GDP per capita grew about 7% per year for more than 30 years. Today South Korea, though still somewhat poorer than Europe and the United States, looks very much like an economically advanced country.

South Korea's economic growth is unprecedented in history: it took the country only 35 years to achieve growth that required centuries elsewhere. South Korea was part of a phenomenon referred to as the East Asian economic miracle. High growth rates first appeared in South Korea, Taiwan, Hong Kong, and Singapore but then spread across East Asia and Southeast Asia, most notably to China. Since 1975, Asia's real GDP per capita has increased by 6% per year, three times America's historical rate of growth.

How have the Asian countries achieved such high growth rates? The answer is that all of the sources of productivity growth have been firing on all cylinders. Very high savings rates, the percentage of GDP that is saved nationally in any given year, have allowed the countries to significantly increase the amount of physical capital per worker. Very good basic education has permitted a rapid improvement in human capital. And these countries have experienced substantial technological progress.

Countries in East Asia, such as South Korea, have enjoyed unprecedented growth since the 1970s, thanks largely to the adoption of modern technology and the accumulation of human capital.

Why hadn't any economy in the past achieved this kind of growth? Most economic analysts think that East Asia's growth spurt was possible because by the time East Asian economies began to move into the modern world, they could benefit from adopting the technological advances that had been generated in technologically advanced countries such as the United States. In 1900, the United States could not have moved quickly to a modern level of productivity because much of the technology that powers the modern economy, from jet planes to computers, hadn't been invented yet. In 1970, South Korea probably still had lower labor productivity than the United States had in 1900, but it could rapidly upgrade its productivity by adopting technology that had been developed in the United States, Europe, and Japan over the previous century. This was aided by a huge investment in human capital through widespread schooling.

The East Asian experience demonstrates that economic growth can be especially fast in countries that are playing catch-up to other countries with higher GDP per capita. On this basis, many economists have suggested a general principle known as the *convergence hypothesis*. It says that differences in real GDP per capita among countries tend to narrow over time because countries that start with lower real GDP per capita tend to have higher growth rates. We'll look at the evidence for the convergence hypothesis later in this section.

Even before we get to that evidence, however, we can say right away that starting with a relatively low level of real GDP per capita is no guarantee of rapid growth, as the examples of Latin America and Africa both demonstrate.

Latin America's Disappointment

In 1900, Latin America was not regarded as an economically backward region. Natural resources, including both minerals and cultivable land, were abundant. Some countries, notably Argentina, attracted millions of immigrants from Europe in search of a better life. Measures of real GDP per capita in Argentina, Uruguay, and southern Brazil were comparable to those in economically advanced countries.

Since about 1920, however, growth in Latin America has been disappointing. As Figure 38.4 shows in the case of Argentina, it has remained disappointing to this day. The fact that South Korea is now much richer than Argentina would have seemed inconceivable a few generations ago.

Why has Latin America stagnated? Comparisons with East Asian success stories suggest several factors. The rates of savings and investment spending in Latin America have been much lower than in East Asia, partly as a result of irresponsible government policy that has eroded savings through high inflation, bank failures, and other disruptions. Education—especially broad basic education—has been underemphasized: even Latin American nations rich in natural resources often failed to channel that wealth into their educational systems. And political instability, leading to irresponsible economic policies, has taken a toll.

In the 1980s, many economists came to believe that Latin America was suffering from excessive government intervention in markets. They recommended opening the economies to imports, selling off government-owned companies, and, in general, freeing up individual initiative. The hope was that this would produce an East Asian–type economic surge. So far, however, only one Latin American nation, Chile, has achieved rapid growth. It now seems that pulling off an economic miracle is harder than it looks.

Relatively low rates of savings, investment spending, and education, along with political instability, have hampered economic growth in Latin America.

David R. Frazier Photolibrary, Inc./Alamy

Africa's Troubles

Sub-Saharan Africa is home to over one billion people, more than three times the population of the United States. On average, they are very poor, nowhere close to U.S. living standards 100 or even 200 years ago. And economic progress has been both slow and uneven, as the example of Nigeria, the most populous nation in the region, suggests. In fact, real GDP per capita in sub-Saharan Africa actually fell 13% from 1980 to 1994, although it has recovered since then. The consequence of this poor growth performance has been intense and continuing poverty.

This is a very disheartening picture. What explains it?

Perhaps first and foremost is the problem of political instability. In the years since 1975, large parts of Africa have experienced savage civil wars (often with outside powers backing rival sides) that have killed millions of people and made productive investment spending impossible. The threat of war and general anarchy has also inhibited other important preconditions for growth, such as education and provision of necessary infrastructure.

Property rights are also a problem. The lack of legal safeguards means that property owners are often subject to extortion because of government corruption, making them averse to owning property or improving it. This is especially damaging in a country that is very poor.

While many economists see political instability and government corruption as the leading causes of underdevelopment in Africa, some—most notably Jeffrey Sachs of Columbia University and the United Nations—believe the opposite. They argue that Africa is politically unstable because Africa is poor. And Africa's poverty, they go on to claim, stems from its extremely unfavorable geographic conditions—much of the continent is landlocked, hot, infested with tropical diseases, and cursed with poor soil.

Sachs, along with economists from the World Health Organization, has highlighted the importance of health problems in Africa. In poor countries, worker productivity is often severely hampered by malnutrition and disease. In particular, tropical diseases such as malaria can be controlled only with an effective public health infrastructure, something that is lacking in much of Africa. Economists continue to study regions of Africa to determine whether modest amounts of aid given directly to residents for the purposes of increasing crop yields, reducing malaria, and increasing school attendance can produce self-sustaining gains in living standards.

Although the example of African countries represents a warning that long-run economic growth cannot be taken for granted, there are some signs of hope. Mauritius has developed a successful textile industry. Several African countries that are dependent on exporting commodities such as coffee and oil have benefited from the higher prices of those commodities. And Africa's economic performance since the mid-1990s has been generally much better than it was in preceding decades.

MODULE 38 REVIEW

Check Your Understanding

1. Describe the shift in, or movement along, the aggregate production function caused by each of the following:
   a. The amounts of physical and human capital per worker are unchanged, but there is significant technological progress.
   b. The amount of physical capital per worker grows, but the level of human capital per worker and technology are unchanged.

2. Multinomics, Inc., is a large company with many offices around the country. It has just adopted a new computer system that will affect virtually every function performed within the company. Why might a period of time pass before employees' productivity is improved by the new computer system? Why might there be a temporary decrease in employees' productivity?

TACKLE THE AP® TEST: Multiple-Choice Questions

1. Which of the following is a source of productivity growth?
   a. increased physical capital
   b. increased human capital
   c. increased worker education and training
   d. technological progress
   e. all of the above

2. Which of the following is an example of physical capital?
   a. machinery
   b. health care
   c. education
   d. money
   e. all of the above

3. The following statement describes which area of the world? "This area has experienced growth rates unprecedented in history and now looks economically advanced."
   a. North America
   b. Latin America
   c. Europe
   d. East Asia
   e. Africa

4. Which of the following is cited as an important factor preventing long-run economic growth in Africa?
   a. political instability
   b. lack of property rights
   c. unfavorable geographic conditions
   d. poor health
   e. all of the above

5. The "convergence hypothesis"
   a. states that differences in real GDP per capita among countries widen over time.
   b. states that low levels of real GDP per capita are associated with higher growth rates.
   c. states that low levels of real GDP per capita are associated with lower growth rates.
   d. contradicts the Rule of 70.
   e. has been proven by evidence from all parts of the world.

6. The aggregate production function shows the relationship between real GDP and
   a. physical capital.
   b. technology.
   c. human capital.
   d. the price level.
   e. unemployment.

7. Diminishing returns to physical capital explains why the aggregate production function shows real GDP
   a. increasing at a decreasing rate.
   b. increasing at an increasing rate.
   c. decreasing at a decreasing rate.
   d. decreasing at an increasing rate.
   e. diminishing at a constant rate.

TACKLE THE AP® TEST: Free-Response Questions

1. a. Draw a correctly labeled graph of a productivity curve that illustrates diminishing returns to physical capital.
   b. Explain what it is about your productivity curve that indicates that there are diminishing returns to physical capital.
   c. On your graph, illustrate the effect of technological progress.
   d. How is the level of human capital per worker addressed on your graph?

1 point: Equal increases in physical capital per worker lead to smaller increases in real GDP per worker.

1 point: Upward shift of production function is labeled to indicate technological progress.

1 point: Human capital per worker is held constant.

Rubric for FRQ 1 (7 points)

1 point: Vertical axis is labeled "Real GDP per worker."

1 point: Horizontal axis is labeled "Physical capital per worker."

1 point: Upward-sloping curve is labeled "Aggregate production function" or "Productivity."

1 point: Curve increases at a decreasing rate (the slope is positive and decreasing).

2. Croatia is a small country in Eastern Europe.
   a. Suppose that in Croatia each successive increase in the amount of physical capital per worker leads to the same increase in productivity. Use a correctly labeled graph to show what Croatia's productivity curve would look like.
   b. Suppose instead that each successive increase in the amount of physical capital per worker leads to a larger increase in productivity. Use a correctly labeled graph to show what Croatia's productivity curve would look like.
   c. Between 1991 and 1995, Croatia fought a war for independence from Yugoslavia. This war destroyed a significant portion of the physical capital in Croatia. Supposing all other things remained unchanged, explain how the effect of this change would be illustrated on your graph from part a.
   d. After the war, Croatia invested in education that increased each worker's ability to make productive use of any given amount of capital. Explain how this affected Croatia's productivity curve. **(5 points)**

MOD 39

Growth Policy: Why Economic Growth Rates Differ

> **In this Module, you will learn to:**
> - Discuss the factors that explain why long-run growth rates differ so much among countries
> - Explain the challenges to growth posed by the scarcity of natural resources, environmental degradation, and efforts to make growth sustainable

Why Growth Rates Differ

In 1820, according to estimates by the economic historian Angus Maddison, Mexico had somewhat higher real GDP per capita than Japan. Today, Japan has higher real GDP per capita than most European nations and Mexico is a poor country, though by no means among the poorest. The difference? Over the long run, real GDP per capita grew at 1.9% per year in Japan but at only 1.2% per year in Mexico.

As this example illustrates, even small differences in growth rates have large consequences over the long run. So why do growth rates differ across countries and across periods of time?

Explaining Differences in Growth Rates

As one might expect, economies with rapid growth tend to be economies that add physical capital, increase their human capital, or experience rapid technological progress. Striking economic success stories, like Japan in the 1950s and 1960s or China today, tend to be countries that do all three: rapidly add to their physical capital, upgrade their educational level, and make fast technological progress.

Adding to Physical Capital

One reason for differences in growth rates among countries is that some countries are increasing their stock of physical capital much more rapidly than others, through high rates of investment spending. In the 1960s, Japan was the fastest-growing major economy; it also spent a much higher share of its GDP on investment goods than other major economies. Today, China is the fastest-growing major economy, and it similarly spends a very large share of its GDP on investment goods. In 2016, investment spending was 44% of China's GDP, compared with only 16% in the United States.

Where does the money for high investment spending come from? We have already analyzed how financial markets channel savings into investment spending. The key point is that investment spending must be paid for either out of savings from domestic households or by an inflow of foreign capital—that is, savings from foreign households. Foreign capital has played an important role in the long-run economic growth of some countries, including the United States, which relied heavily on foreign funds during its early industrialization. For the most part, however, countries that invest a large share of their GDP are able to do so because they have high domestic savings. One reason for differences in growth rates, then, is that countries have different rates of savings and investment spending.

AP® EXAM TIP

Understand the difference between long-run economic growth and short-run fluctuations. Economic growth is caused by increased levels of investment in physical capital, human capital, and technology. Refer to investment *in capital stock* when discussing long-run growth to make it clear that you understand the specific type of investment that causes it.

Adding to Human Capital

Just as countries differ substantially in the rate at which they add to their physical capital, there have been large differences in the rates at which countries add to their human capital through education.

A case in point is the comparison between Argentina and China. In both countries, the average educational level has risen steadily over time, but it has risen much faster in China. **Figure 39.1** shows the average years of education of adults in China, which we have highlighted as a spectacular example of long-run growth, and in Argentina, a country whose growth has been disappointing. Seventy years ago, the population of Argentina was much more educated than that of China, where much of the population was illiterate. Today, the average educational level in China is still slightly below that in Argentina—but that's mainly because there are still many elderly adults who never received basic education. In terms of high school and college education, China has outstripped once-rich Argentina.

Over the past several decades, China has made significant investments in human capital in the form of education, embodied in these recent graduates from Beijing's Tsinghua University.

Figure 39.1   China's Students Are Catching Up

In both China and Argentina, the average educational level—measured by the number of years the average adult aged 25 or older has spent in school—has risen over time. Although China still lags behind Argentina, it is catching up—and China's success at adding human capital is one key to its spectacular long-run growth.

Data Source: Robert Barro and Jong-Wha Lee, "A New Data Set of Educational Attainment in the World, 1950–2010," NBER Working Paper No. 15902 (April 2010).

Technological Progress

The advance of technology is a key force behind economic growth. But what drives advances in technology?

Scientific advances make new technologies possible. To take the most spectacular example in today's world, the semiconductor chip—which is the basis for all modern information technology—could not have been developed without the theory of quantum mechanics in physics.

But science alone is not enough: scientific knowledge must be translated into useful products and processes. And that often requires devoting a lot of resources to research and development, or R&D, spending to create new technologies and prepare them for practical use.

Thomas Edison is best known as the inventor of the light bulb and the phonograph. But his biggest invention may surprise you: he invented research and development. Before Edison's time, of course, there had been many inventors. Some of them worked in teams. But in 1875 Edison created something new: his Menlo Park, New Jersey, laboratory. It employed 25 men full time to generate new products and processes for business. In other words, he did not set out to pursue a particular idea and then cash in. He created an organization whose purpose was to create new ideas year after year.

Thomas Alva Edison in his laboratory in New Jersey in 1901.

Edison's Menlo Park lab is now a museum. "To name a few of the products that were developed in Menlo Park," says the museum's website, "we can list the following: the carbon button mouthpiece for the telephone, the phonograph, the incandescent light bulb and the electrical distribution system, the electric train, ore separation, the Edison effect bulb, early experiments in wireless, the grasshopper telegraph, and improvements in telegraphic transmission."

You could say that before Edison's lab, technology just sort of happened: people came up with ideas, but businesses didn't plan to make continuous technological progress. Now R&D operations, often much bigger than Edison's original team, are standard practice throughout the business world.

The R&D conducted by Edison was paid for by the private sector, which still is common today. The United States became the world's leading economy in large part because American businesses were among the first to make systematic research and development a part of their operations. However, some R&D is conducted by governments.

Developing new technology is one thing; applying it is another. There have often been notable differences in the pace at which different countries take advantage of new technologies. America's surge in productivity growth after 1995, as firms learned to make use of information technology, was initially not matched in Europe.

The Role of Government in Promoting Economic Growth

Governments can play an important role in promoting—or blocking—all three sources of long-term economic growth: physical capital, human capital, and technological progress.

Governments and Physical Capital

Governments play an important direct role in building **infrastructure**: roads, power lines, ports, information networks, and other parts of an economy's physical capital that provide a foundation for economic activity. Although some infrastructure is provided by private companies, much of it is either provided by the government or requires a great deal of government regulation and support. Ireland, whose economy really took off in the 1990s, is often cited as an example of the importance of government-provided infrastructure: the government invested in an excellent telecommunications infrastructure in the 1980s, and this helped make Ireland a favored location for high-technology companies.

Poor infrastructure—for example, a power grid that often fails, cutting off electricity to homes and businesses—is a major obstacle to economic growth in some countries. To provide good infrastructure, an economy must be able to afford it, but it must also have the political discipline to maintain it and provide for the future.

Perhaps the most crucial infrastructure is something we rarely think about: basic public health measures in the form of a clean water supply and disease control. As we'll see in the next section, poor health infrastructure is a major obstacle to economic growth in poor countries, especially those in Africa.

Governments also play an important indirect role in making high rates of private investment spending possible. Both the amount of savings and the ability of an economy to direct savings into productive investment spending depend on the economy's institutions, notably its financial system. In particular, a well-functioning banking system is very important for economic growth because, in most countries, it is the principal way in which savings are channeled into business investment spending. If a country's citizens trust their banks, they will place their savings in bank deposits, which the banks will

Poor health infrastructure can be a major obstacle to economic growth in countries like Zambia.

Roads, power lines, ports, information networks, and other underpinnings for economic activity are known as **infrastructure**.

then lend to their business customers. But if people don't trust their banks, they will hoard gold or foreign currency, keeping their savings in safe deposit boxes or under their mattresses, where it cannot be turned into productive investment spending. A well-functioning financial system requires appropriate government regulation that assures depositors that their funds are protected.

Governments and Human Capital

An economy's physical capital is created mainly through investment spending by individuals and private companies. Much of an economy's human capital, by contrast, is the result of government spending on education. In wealthy countries, the government pays for the great bulk of primary and secondary education, although individuals pay a significant share of the costs of higher education.

As a result, differences in the rate at which countries add to their human capital largely reflect government policy. For example, East Asia now has a more educated population than Latin America. This isn't because East Asia is richer than Latin America and so can afford to spend more on education. Until very recently, East Asia, on average, was poorer than Latin America. Instead, it reflects the fact that Asian governments made broad education of the population a higher priority.

Governments and Technology

Technological progress is largely the result of private initiative. But important R&D is done by government agencies. For example, Brazil's agricultural boom was made possible by government researchers who discovered that adding crucial nutrients to the soil would allow crops to be grown on previously unusable land. Government researchers also developed new varieties of soybeans and breeds of cattle that flourish in Brazil's tropical climate.

Political Stability, Property Rights, and Excessive Government Intervention

There's not much point in investing in a business if rioting mobs are likely to destroy it. And why save your money if someone with political connections can steal it? Political stability and protection of property rights are crucial ingredients in long-run economic growth.

Long-run economic growth in successful economies, such as that of the United States, has been possible because there are good laws, institutions that enforce those laws, and a stable political system that maintains those institutions. The law must say that your property is really yours so that someone else can't take it away. The courts and the police must be honest so that they can't be bribed to ignore the law. And the political system must be stable so that the law doesn't change capriciously.

Americans take these preconditions for granted, but they are by no means guaranteed. Aside from the disruption caused by war or revolution, many countries find that their economic growth suffers due to corruption among the government officials who should be enforcing the law. And even when governments aren't corrupt, excessive government intervention can be a brake on economic growth. If large parts of the economy are supported by government subsidies, protected from imports, or otherwise insulated from competition, productivity tends to suffer because of a lack of incentives. As we saw in Module 38, excessive government intervention is one often-cited explanation for slow growth in Latin America.

Is World Growth Sustainable?

In the previous Module, we described the views of Thomas Malthus, the nineteenth-century economist who warned that the pressure of population growth would tend to limit the standard of living. Malthus was right—about the past: for nearly 6,000 years, from the origins of civilization until his own time, limited land supplies effectively prevented any large rise in real incomes per capita. Since then, however, technological progress and rapid accumulation of physical and human capital have allowed the world to defy Malthusian pessimism.

But will this always be the case? Some skeptics have expressed doubt about whether long-run economic growth is sustainable—whether it can continue in the face of the limited supply of natural resources and the impact of growth on the environment.

Natural Resources and Growth, Revisited

In 1972, a group of scientists and leaders called the Club of Rome made a big splash with a book titled *The Limits to Growth*, which argued that long-run economic growth wasn't sustainable due to limited supplies of nonrenewable resources such as oil and natural gas. These "neo-Malthusian" concerns at first seemed to be validated by a sharp rise in resource prices in the 1970s, then came to seem foolish when resource prices fell sharply in the 1980s. After 2005, however, resource prices rose sharply again, leading to renewed concern about resource limitations to growth. **Figure 39.2** shows the real price of oil—the price of oil adjusted for inflation in the rest of the economy. The rise and fall of concerns about resource-based limits to growth have more or less followed the rise and fall of oil prices shown in this figure.

Figure 39.2 The Real Price of Oil, 1949–2016

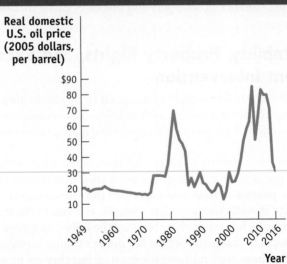

The real price of natural resources, such as oil, rose dramatically in the 1970s and then fell just as dramatically in the 1980s. Since 2005, however, the real prices of natural resources have increased.

Data Sources: Energy Information Administration, Bureau of Labor Statistics.

Differing views about the impact of limited natural resources on long-run economic growth turn on the answers to three questions:

• How large are the supplies of key natural resources?

• How effective will technology be at providing alternatives to natural resources?

• Can long-run economic growth continue in the face of resource scarcity?

It's mainly up to geologists to answer the first question. Unfortunately, there's wide disagreement among the experts, especially about the prospects for future oil production. Some analysts believe that there is so much untapped oil in the ground that world oil production can continue to rise for several decades. Others—including a number of oil company executives—believe that the growing difficulty of finding new oil fields will cause oil production to plateau—that is, stop growing and eventually begin a gradual decline—in the fairly near future. Some analysts believe that we have already reached that plateau.

The answer to the second question, whether there are alternatives to certain natural resources, will come from engineers. There's no question that there are many alternatives to the natural resources currently being depleted, and some of these alternatives are already being exploited. For example, "unconventional" oil extracted from Canadian tar sands is already making a significant contribution to world oil supplies, and electricity generated by wind turbines is rapidly becoming big business around the world.

The third question, whether economies can continue to grow in the face of resource scarcity, is mainly a question for economists. And most, though not all, economists are optimistic: they believe that modern economies can find ways to work around limits on the supply of natural resources. One reason for this optimism is the fact that resource scarcity leads to high resource prices. These high prices in turn provide strong incentives to conserve the scarce resource and to find alternatives.

For example, after the sharp increases in oil prices during the 1970s, American consumers turned to smaller, more fuel-efficient cars, and industries in the United States also greatly intensified their efforts to reduce energy bills. The result is shown in **Figure 39.3**, which compares the growth rates of real GDP per capita and oil consumption before and after the 1970s energy crisis. Before 1973, there seemed to be a more or less one-to-one relationship between economic growth and oil consumption, but after 1973 the U.S. economy continued to deliver growth in real GDP per capita even as it substantially reduced its use of oil. This move toward conservation paused after 1990, as low real oil prices encouraged consumers to shift back to gas-greedy larger cars and SUVs. A sharp rise in oil prices from 2005 to 2008 encouraged renewed shifts toward oil conservation, although these shifts lost some steam as prices started falling again in late 2008.

The Tehachapi Pass Wind Farm, in Tehachapi, California, is one of the largest collections of wind generators in the world, with around 4,700 wind turbines.

Figure 39.3 U.S. Oil Consumption and Growth over Time

Until 1973, the real price of oil was relatively low and there was a more or less one-to-one relationship between economic growth and oil consumption. Conservation efforts increased sharply after the spike in the real price of oil in the mid-1970s. Yet the U.S. economy was still able to grow despite cutting back on oil consumption.

Data Sources: Energy Information Administration; Bureau of Economic Analysis.

Given such responses to prices, economists generally tend to see resource scarcity as a problem that modern economies handle fairly well, rather than a fundamental limit to long-run economic growth. Environmental issues, however, pose a more difficult problem because dealing with them requires effective political action.

Economic Growth and the Environment

Economic growth, other things equal, tends to increase the human impact on the environment. For example, China's spectacular economic growth has also brought a spectacular increase in air pollution in that nation's cities. It's important to realize, however, that other things aren't necessarily equal: countries can and do take action to protect their environments. In fact, air and water quality in today's advanced countries is generally much better than it was a few decades ago. London's famous "fog"—actually a form of air pollution called smog, which killed 4,000 people during a particularly intense two-week episode in 1952—is gone, thanks to regulations that virtually eliminated the use of coal heat. The equally famous smog of Los Angeles, although not extinguished, is far less severe than it was in the 1960s and early 1970s, again thanks to pollution regulations.

Despite these past environmental success stories, there is widespread concern today about the environmental impacts of continuing economic growth, reflecting a change in the scale of the problem. Environmental success stories have mainly involved dealing with *local* impacts of economic growth, such as the effect of widespread car ownership on air quality in the Los Angeles basin. Today, however, we are faced with *global* environmental issues—the adverse impacts on the environment of the Earth as a whole by worldwide economic growth. The biggest of these issues involves the impact of fossil-fuel consumption on the world's climate.

Burning coal and oil releases carbon dioxide into the atmosphere. There is broad scientific consensus that rising levels of carbon dioxide and other gases are causing a greenhouse effect on the Earth, trapping more of the sun's energy and raising the planet's overall temperature. And rising temperatures may impose high human and economic costs: rising sea levels may flood coastal areas; changing climate may disrupt agriculture, especially in poor countries; and so on.

The problem of climate change is clearly linked to economic growth. **Figure 39.4** shows carbon dioxide emissions from the United States, Europe, and China since 1980. Historically, the wealthy nations have been responsible for the bulk of these emissions because they have consumed far more energy per person than poorer countries. As China and other emerging economies have grown, however, they have begun to consume much more energy and emit much more carbon dioxide.

Is it possible to continue long-run economic growth while curbing the emissions of greenhouse gases? The answer, according to most economists who have studied the issue, is yes. It should be possible to reduce greenhouse gas emissions in a wide variety of ways, ranging from the use of non-fossil fuel energy sources such as wind, solar, and nuclear power; to preventive measures such as carbon sequestration (capturing carbon dioxide and storing it); to simpler things like designing buildings so that they require less energy to keep warm in winter and cool in summer. Such measures would impose costs on the economy, but the best available estimates suggest that even a large reduction in greenhouse gas emissions over the next few decades would only modestly dent the long-term rise in real GDP per capita.

The problem is how to make all of this happen. Unlike resource scarcity, environmental problems don't automatically provide incentives for changed behavior. Pollution is an example of a *negative externality*, a cost that individuals or firms impose on others without having to offer compensation. In the absence of government intervention, individuals and firms have no incentive to reduce negative externalities, which is

Figure 39.4 Climate Change and Growth

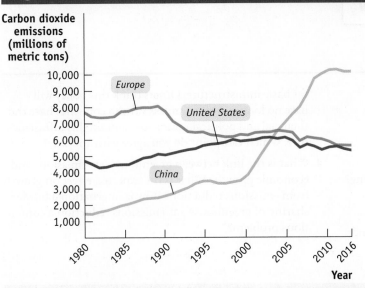

Greenhouse gas emissions are positively related to growth. As shown here by the United States and Europe, wealthy countries have historically been responsible for the great bulk of greenhouse gas emissions because of their richer and faster-growing economies. As China and other emerging economies have grown, they have begun to emit much more carbon dioxide.

Data Source: Boden et al. (2017), UNFCCC (2017), BP (2017).

why it took regulation to reduce air pollution in America's cities. And as Nicholas Stern, the author of an influential report on climate change, put it, greenhouse gas emissions are "the mother of all externalities."

So there is a broad consensus among economists—although there are some dissenters—that government action is needed to deal with climate change. There is also broad consensus that this action should take the form of market-based incentives, either in the form of a carbon tax—a tax per unit of carbon emitted—or a cap and trade system in which the total amount of emissions is capped, and producers must buy licenses to emit greenhouse gases. However, there is considerable dispute about how much action is appropriate, reflecting both uncertainty about the costs and benefits and scientific uncertainty about the pace and extent of climate change.

There are also several aspects of the climate change problem that make it much more difficult to deal with than, say, smog in Los Angeles. One is the problem of taking the long view. The impact of greenhouse gas emissions on the climate is very gradual: carbon dioxide put into the atmosphere today won't have its full effect on the climate for several generations. As a result, there is the political problem of persuading voters to accept pain today in return for gains that will benefit their children, grandchildren, or even great-grandchildren.

The added problem of international burden sharing presents a stumbling block for consensus, as it did at the United Nations Climate Change Conference in 2017. As Figure 39.4 shows, today's rich countries have historically been responsible for most greenhouse gas emissions, but newly emerging economies like China are responsible for most of the recent growth. Inevitably, rich countries are reluctant to pay the price of reducing emissions only to have their efforts frustrated by rapidly growing emissions from new players. On the other hand, countries like China, which are still relatively poor, consider it unfair that they should be expected to bear the burden of protecting an environment threatened by the past actions of rich nations.

Despite political issues and the need for compromise, the general moral of this story is that it is possible to reconcile long-run economic growth with environmental protection. The main question is how to get political consensus around the necessary policies.

Check Your Understanding

1. Explain the link between a country's growth rate, its investment spending as a percentage of GDP, and its domestic savings.

2. Which of the following is the better predictor of a future high long-run growth rate: a high standard of living today or high levels of savings and investment spending? Explain your answer.

3. Some economists think the best way to help African countries is for wealthier countries to provide more funds for basic infrastructure. Others think this policy will have no long-run effect unless African countries have the financial and political means to maintain this infrastructure. Which viewpoint do you agree with and why?

4. What is the link between greenhouse gas emissions and economic growth? What is the expected effect on growth from emissions reduction? Why is international burden sharing of greenhouse gas emissions reduction a contentious problem?

TACKLE THE AP® TEST: Multiple-Choice Questions

1. Economies experience more rapid economic growth when they do which of the following?
   a. invest in infrastructure
   b. limit human capital
   c. increase government spending
   d. eliminate public health programs
   e. raise taxes

2. Which of the following can lead to increases in physical capital in an economy?
   a. increased investment spending
   b. increased savings by domestic households
   c. increased savings from foreign households
   d. an inflow of foreign capital
   e. all of the above

3. Which of the following is true of sustainable long-run economic growth?
   a. It can continue in the face of the limited supply of natural resources.
   b. It was predicted by Thomas Malthus.
   c. Modern economies handle resource scarcity problems poorly.
   d. It is less likely when we find alternatives to natural resources.
   e. It results from decreases in total factor productivity.

4. Which of the following statements is true of environmental quality?
   a. It is typically not affected by government policy.
   b. Other things equal, it tends to improve with economic growth.
   c. There is broad scientific consensus that rising levels of carbon dioxide and other gases are raising the planet's overall temperature.

   d. Most economists believe it is not possible to reduce greenhouse gas emissions while economic growth continues.
   e. Most environmental success stories involve dealing with global, rather than local, impacts.

5. Which of the following is true of greenhouse gas emissions?
   a. They are unrelated to economic growth.
   b. They are positively related to economic growth.
   c. They are negatively related to economic growth.
   d. They come predominantly from poor countries.
   e. The amount a country emits increases as the country develops.

6. Which of the following is an example of a government infrastructure investment?
   a. roads
   b. powerlines
   c. ports
   d. information networks
   e. all of the above

7. To promote economic growth through investment in human capital, a government would need to invest in which of the following?
   a. roads and bridges
   b. public education
   c. research and development
   d. fossil fuels
   e. all of the above

TACKLE THE AP® TEST: Free-Response Questions

1. List and explain five different actions the government can take to promote long-run economic growth.

> **Rubric for FRQ 1 (10 points)**
>
> *A maximum of 10 points can be earned for any five of the six possible actions/descriptions.*
>
> **1 point:** Build infrastructure
>
> **1 point:** The government can provide roads, power lines, ports, rail lines, and related systems to support economic activity.
>
> **1 point:** Invest in human capital
>
> **1 point:** The government can improve access to quality education.
>
> **1 point:** Invest in research and development
>
> **1 point:** The government can promote technological progress by having government agencies support and participate in R&D.

> **1 point:** Provide political stability
>
> **1 point:** The government can create and maintain institutions that make and enforce laws that promote stability.
>
> **1 point:** Establish and protect property rights
>
> **1 point:** Growth is promoted by laws that define what property belongs to whom and by institutions that defend those property rights.
>
> **1 point:** Minimize government intervention
>
> **1 point:** The government can limit its intervention in the economy and promote competition.

2. What roles do physical capital, human capital, technology, and natural resources play in influencing the differences in long-run economic growth rates among countries? **(4 points)**

Economic Growth in Macroeconomic Models

> **In this Module, you will learn to:**
> - Explain how long-run economic growth is represented in macroeconomic models
> - Explain the use of supply-side fiscal policies to promote long-run economic growth
> - Model the effects of economic growth policies

Long-run economic growth is fundamental to solving many of today's most pressing economic problems. It is even more critical in poorer, less developed countries. But the policies we have studied in earlier sections to address short-run fluctuations and the business cycle may not encourage long-run economic growth. For example, an increase in household consumption can help an economy recover from a recession. However, when households increase consumption, they decrease their savings, which leads to decreased investment spending and slows long-run economic growth. In addition to understanding short-run stabilization policies, we need to understand the factors that influence economic growth and how choices by governments and individuals can promote or retard that growth in the long-run.

Long-run economic growth is the sustained rise in the quantity of goods and services the economy produces, as opposed to the short-run ups and downs of the business cycle. In Module 18, we looked at actual and potential output in the United States from 1989 to 2017. As shown in **Figure 40.1**, increases in potential output during that time represent long-run economic growth. The fluctuations of actual output compared to potential output are the result of the business cycle.

As we have seen throughout this section, long-run economic growth depends almost entirely on rising productivity. Good macroeconomic policy, including the policies discussed in Module 39 and the supply-side

Increased household consumption can help with short-term fluctuations but might slow long-term growth.

Joe Raedle/Getty Images

Figure 40.1 Actual and Potential Output from 1989 to 2017

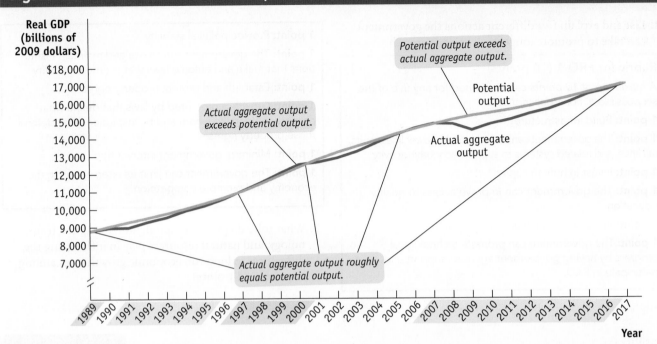

This figure shows the performance of actual and potential output in the United States from 1989 to 2017. The orange line shows estimates, produced by the Congressional Budget Office, of U.S. potential output. The blue line shows actual aggregate output. The purple-shaded years are periods in which actual aggregate output fell below potential output, and the green-shaded years are periods in which actual aggregate output exceeded potential output. As shown, significant shortfalls occurred in the recessions that hit in the early 1990s, just after 2000, and from 2007–2009 (the Great Recession). Actual aggregate output was above potential output in the boom of the late 1990s.

Data Source: Congressional Budget Office; Bureau of Economic Analysis.

fiscal policies presented later in this module, strives to foster increases in productivity, which in turn leads to long-run economic growth. In this Module, we will learn how to evaluate the effects of long-run growth policies using the production possibilities curve and the aggregate demand and supply model.

Long-Run Economic Growth and the Production Possibilities Curve

Recall from Section 1 that we defined the production possibilities curve as a graph that illustrates the trade-offs facing an economy that produces only two goods. In our example, we developed the production possibilities curve for Alex, a castaway facing a trade-off between producing fish and coconuts. Looking at **Figure 40.2**, we see that economic growth is shown as an outward shift of the production possibilities curve. Now let's return to the production possibilities curve model and use a different example to illustrate how economic growth policies can lead to long-run economic growth.

Figure 40.3 shows a hypothetical production possibilities curve for the fictional country of Kyland. In our previous production possibilities examples, the trade-off was between producing quantities of two different goods. In this example, our production possibilities curve illustrates Kyland's trade-off between two different *categories* of goods. The production possibilities curve shows the alternative combinations of investment goods and consumer goods that Kyland can produce. The consumer goods category includes everything purchased for consumption by households, such as food, clothing, and sporting goods. Investment goods include all forms of physical capital,

Figure 40.2 Economic Growth

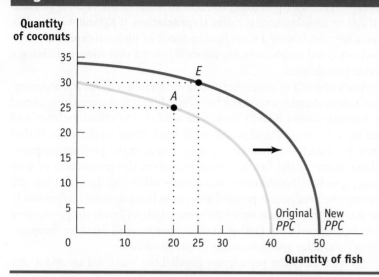

Economic growth results in an *outward shift* of the production possibilities curve because production possibilities are expanded. The economy can now produce more of everything. For example, if production is initially at point *A* (20 fish and 25 coconuts), it could move to point *E* (25 fish and 30 coconuts).

Figure 40.3 The Trade-off Between Investment and Consumer Goods

This production possibilities curve illustrates Kyland's trade-off between the production of investment goods and consumer goods. At point *A*, Kyland produces all investment goods and no consumer goods. At point *D*, Kyland produces all consumer goods and no investment goods. Points *B* and *C* represent two of the many possible combinations of investment goods and consumer goods.

that is, goods that are used to produce other goods. Kyland's production possibilities curve shows the trade-off between the production of consumer goods and the production of investment goods. Recall that the bowed-out shape of the production possibilities curve reflects increasing opportunity cost.

Kyland's production possibilities curve shows all possible combinations of consumer and investment goods that can be produced with full and efficient use of all of Kyland's resources. However, the production possibilities curve model does not tell us which of the possible points Kyland *should* select.

Figure 40.3 illustrates four points on Kyland's production possibilities curve. At point *A*, Kyland is producing all investment goods and no consumer goods. Investment in physical capital, one of the economy's factors of production, causes the production possibilities curve to shift outward. Choosing to produce at a point on the production possibilities curve that creates more capital for the economy will result in greater production possibilities in the future. Note that at point *A*, there are no consumer goods being produced, a situation which the economy cannot survive in the long run.

At point *D*, Kyland is producing all consumer goods and no investment goods. While this point provides goods and services for consumers in Kyland, it does not include the

Depreciation occurs when the value of an asset is reduced by wear, age, or obsolescence.

production of any physical capital. Over time, as an economy produces more goods and services, some of its capital is used up in that production. A loss in the value of physical capital due to wear, age, or obsolescence is called **depreciation**. If Kyland were to produce at point *D* year after year, it would soon find its stock of physical capital depreciating and its production possibilities curve would shift inward over time, indicating a decrease in production possibilities.

Points *B* and *C* represent a mix of consumer and investment goods for the economy. While we can see that points *A* and *D* would not be acceptable choices over a long period of time, the choice between points *B* and *C* would depend on the values, politics, and other details related to the economy and people of Kyland. What we do know is that the choice made by Kyland each year will affect the position of the production possibilities curve in the future. An emphasis on the production of consumer goods will make consumers better off in the short run but will prevent the production possibilities curve from moving farther out in the future. An emphasis on investment goods will shift the production possibilities curve out farther in the future but will decrease the quantity of consumer goods available in the short run.

So what does the production possibilities curve tell us about economic growth? Since long-run economic growth depends almost entirely on rising productivity, a country's decision regarding investment in physical capital, human capital, and technology affects its long-run economic growth. Governments can promote long-run economic growth, shifting the country's production possibilities curve outward over time, by investing in physical capital such as infrastructure. They can also encourage high rates of private investment in physical capital by promoting a well-functioning financial system, property rights, and political stability.

Government investment in infrastructure projects, such as transit rail systems, can promote long-run growth and encourage private investment spending.

Long-Run Economic Growth and the Aggregate Demand–Aggregate Supply Model

The aggregate demand and supply model we developed in Section 4 is another useful tool for understanding long-run economic growth. Recall that in the aggregate demand–aggregate supply model, the long-run aggregate supply (*LRAS*) curve shows the relationship between the aggregate price level and the quantity of aggregate output supplied when all prices, including nominal wages, are flexible. As shown in **Figure 40.4,** the long-run aggregate supply curve is vertical at the level of potential output, Y_P^1. While actual real GDP is almost always above or below potential output, reflecting the current phase of the business cycle, potential output is the level of output around which actual aggregate output fluctuates. Potential output in the United States has risen steadily over time. This corresponds to a rightward shift of the long-run aggregate supply curve, as shown in the shift to Y_P^2 and Y_P^3. Thus, the same government policies that promote an outward shift of the production possibilities curve promote a rightward shift of the long-run aggregate supply curve.

AP® EXAM TIP

The *LRAS* curve is vertical at the economy's potential output (also known as full employment output), which corresponds to the natural rate of unemployment and the NAIRU. Economic growth is illustrated in the *AD-AS* model by a rightward shift of the vertical *LRAS* curve. Long-run growth is distinct from short-run economic fluctuations, which are shown by changes in short-run equilibrium due to changes in *SRAS* or *AD*.

Distinguishing Between Long-Run Growth and Short-Run Fluctuations

When considering changes in real GDP, it is important to distinguish long-run growth from short-run fluctuations due to the business cycle. Both the production possibilities curve model and the aggregate demand–aggregate supply model can help us do this.

The points along a production possibilities curve are achievable if there is efficient use of the economy's resources. If the economy experiences a macroeconomic fluctuation due to the business cycle, such as unemployment due to a recession, production

Figure 40.4 The Long-Run Aggregate Supply Curve

The long-run aggregate supply (*LRAS*) curve shows the quantity of aggregate output supplied when all prices, including nominal wages, are flexible. It is vertical at potential output, Y_P^1, because in the long run a change in the aggregate price level has no effect on the quantity of aggregate output supplied. The growth in potential output over time can be shown as a rightward shift of the long-run aggregate supply curve.

falls to a point inside the production possibilities curve. On the other hand, long-run growth will appear as an outward shift of the production possibilities curve.

In the aggregate demand–aggregate supply model, fluctuations of actual aggregate output around potential output are illustrated by shifts of aggregate demand or short-run aggregate supply that result in a short-run macroeconomic equilibrium above or below potential output. In both panels of **Figure 40.5**, E_1 indicates a short-run equilibrium that differs from long-run equilibrium due to the business cycle. In the case of short-run fluctuations like these, adjustments in nominal wages will eventually bring the equilibrium level of real GDP back to the potential level. By contrast, we saw in Figure 40.4 that long-run economic growth is represented by a rightward shift of the long-run aggregate supply curve and corresponds to an increase in the economy's level of potential output.

Figure 40.5 From the Short Run to the Long Run

In panel (a), the initial equilibrium is E_1. At the aggregate price level, P_1, the quantity of aggregate output supplied, Y_1, exceeds potential output, Y_P. Eventually, low unemployment will cause nominal wages to rise, leading to a leftward shift of the short-run aggregate supply curve from $SRAS_1$ to $SRAS_2$ and a long-run equilibrium at E_2.

In panel (b), the reverse happens: at the short-run equilibrium, E_1, the quantity of aggregate output supplied is less than potential output. High unemployment eventually leads to a fall in nominal wages over time and a rightward shift of the short-run aggregate supply curve. The end result is long-run equilibrium at E_2.

Supply-Side Fiscal Policies and Economic Growth

As we have seen in previous Modules, the government can promote economic growth by influencing incentives for households and businesses to save and invest. Governments can implement policies to promote saving by, for example, reducing taxes on household savings. Governments can also implement policies to promote investment by, for example, offering investment tax credits and reducing government regulations that affect investments. Policies to promote economic growth by affecting the SRAS and LRAS curves are called **supply-side policies**. These policies can affect aggregate demand, aggregate supply, and potential output in the short run and long run, as shown in **Figure 40.6**.

Supply-side fiscal policies are government policies that seek to promote economic growth by affecting short-run and long-run aggregate supply.

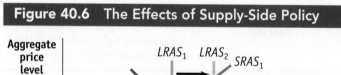

Figure 40.6   The Effects of Supply-Side Policy

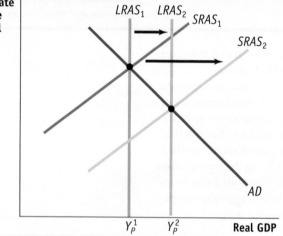

Government policies that incentivize households and firms to save and invest can increase potential output and create economic growth, shifting both the SRAS curve and the LRAS curve to a new short-run equilibrium to the right.

One potential issue faced by governments using supply-side fiscal policies to promote long-run economic growth is the effect large tax cuts could have on their budget. All other things equal, reductions in tax rates will move the government budget toward deficit. And larger budget deficits have the potential to create crowding out and decrease economic growth.

Proponents of supply-side economics note that lower tax rates could actually lead to higher government revenue if those lower tax rates are applied to sharply higher levels of income. That is, if all other things *are not* equal, the reduction in tax rates increases incentives for households to work and invest more. This idea can be shown using a Laffer curve, a hypothetical relationship between tax rates and total tax revenue that slopes upward at low tax rates (meaning higher taxes bring higher tax revenues) but turns downward when tax rates are very high (meaning higher taxes bring lower tax revenues). **Figure 40.7** illustrates the Laffer curve.

While almost all economists agree that tax cuts increase the incentives to work, save, and invest, they do not agree that tax cuts will lead to higher tax revenues or sharply higher potential output. What is clear is that supply-side fiscal policies have the potential to shift both the short-run and long-run aggregate supply curves which would lead to an increase in potential output in the AD–AS model.

Figure 40.7 The Laffer Curve

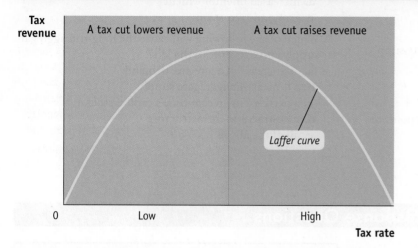

In the pink area on the left, the Laffer curve slopes upward, meaning higher taxes bring higher tax revenues when tax rates are low. In the green area to the right, the Laffer curve turns downward, meaning higher taxes bring lower tax revenues when tax rates are very high. The effect of a decrease in taxes on tax revenues depends on whether the tax rate is above or below the peak of the curve, where the pink and green areas meet.

MODULE 40 REVIEW

Adventures in AP® Economics

Watch the video: *Economic Growth*

Check Your Understanding

1. How are long-run economic growth and short-run fluctuations during a business cycle represented using the production possibilities curve model?

2. How are long-run economic growth and short-run fluctuations during a business cycle represented using the aggregate demand–aggregate supply model?

TACKLE THE AP® TEST: Multiple-Choice Questions

1. Which of the following will shift the production possibilities curve outward?
   a. technological progress
   b. an increase in the production of consumer goods
   c. a decrease in available labor resources
   d. depreciation of capital
   e. all of the above

2. In the production possibilities curve model, long-run economic growth is shown by a(n)
   a. outward shift of the *PPC*.
   b. inward shift of the *PPC*.
   c. movement from a point below the *PPC* to a point on the *PPC*.
   d. movement from a point on the *PPC* to a point below the *PPC*.
   e. movement from a point on the *PPC* to a point beyond the *PPC*.

3. The reduction in the value of an asset due to wear and tear is known as
   a. depreciation.
   b. negative investment.
   c. economic decline.
   d. disinvestment.
   e. net investment.

4. In the aggregate demand–aggregate supply model, long-run economic growth is shown by a
   a. leftward shift of the aggregate demand curve.
   b. rightward shift of the aggregate demand curve.
   c. rightward shift of the long-run aggregate supply curve.
   d. rightward shift of the short-run aggregate supply curve.
   e. leftward shift of the short-run aggregate supply curve.

5. Which of the following is listed among the key sources of growth in potential output?
   a. expansionary fiscal policy
   b. expansionary monetary policy
   c. a rightward shift of the short-run aggregate supply curve
   d. investment in human capital
   e. both a and b

6. A movement from a point below the *PPC* to a point on the *PPC* illustrates which of the following?
   a. increased inefficiency
   b. economic expansion

   c. long-run economic growth
   d. increased unemployment
   e. economic recession

7. Which of the following will cause the long-run aggregate supply curve to shift to the left?
   a. an increase in aggregate demand
   b. a decrease in aggregate supply
   c. a decrease in an economy's capital stock
   d. investment in infrastructure
   e. all of the above

TACKLE THE AP® TEST: Free-Response Questions

1. Refer to the graph provided.

a. Which point(s) could represent a downturn in the business cycle?
b. Which point(s) represent efficient production?
c. Which point(s) are attainable only after long-run economic growth?
d. How would long-run economic growth be represented on this graph?
e. Policy that results in an increase in the production of consumer goods without reducing the production of investment goods is represented by a movement between which two points?
f. Producing at which efficient point this year would lead to the most economic growth next year?

Rubric for FRQ 1 (9 points)

2 points: A downturn could be represented by points *E* or *F*.

3 points: Points *A*, *B*, and *C* represent efficient production.

1 point: Point *D* is attainable only after long-run economic growth.

1 point: Long-run economic growth would be represented by an outward shift of the curve.

1 point: Consumer goods increase and investment goods remain unchanged when moving from point *E* to point *C*.

1 point: Producing at point *A* would lead to the most economic growth.

2. Draw a separate, correctly labeled aggregate demand and supply graph to illustrate each of the following situations. On each of your graphs, include the relevant short-run aggregate supply curve(s), long-run aggregate supply curve(s), and aggregate demand curve(s).
   a. Expansionary fiscal policy moves the economy out of a recession.
   b. Investment in infrastructure by the government leads to long-run economic growth. **(6 points)**

Module 37

1. Economic growth is a sustained increase in the productive capacity of an economy and can be measured as changes in real GDP per capita. This measurement eliminates the effects of changes in both the price level and population size. Levels of real GDP per capita vary greatly around the world: more than half of the world's population lives in countries that are still poorer than the United States was in 1910.

2. Growth rates of real GDP per capita also vary widely. According to the **Rule of 70**, the number of years it takes for real GDP per capita to double is equal to 70 divided by the annual growth rate of real GDP per capita.

3. The key to long-run economic growth is rising **labor productivity**, also referred to as simply **productivity**, which is output per worker. Increases in productivity arise from increases in **physical capital** per worker and **human capital** per worker as well as advances in **technology**.

Module 38

4. The **aggregate production function** shows how real GDP per worker depends on physical capital per worker, human capital per worker, and technology. Other things equal, there are **diminishing returns to physical capital**: holding human capital per worker and technology fixed, each successive addition to physical capital per worker yields a smaller increase in productivity than the one before. Similarly, there are diminishing returns to human capital among other inputs. With *growth accounting*, which involves estimates of each factor's contribution to economic growth, economists have shown that rising *total factor productivity*, the amount of output produced from a given amount of factor inputs, is key to long-run growth. Rising total factor productivity is usually interpreted as the effect of technological progress. In most countries, natural resources are a less significant source of productivity growth today than in earlier times.

5. The world economy contains examples of success and failure in the effort to achieve long-run economic growth. East Asian economies have done many things right and achieved very high growth rates. In Latin America, where some important conditions are lacking, growth has generally been disappointing. In Africa, real GDP per capita declined for several decades, although there are recent signs of progress. The growth rates of economically advanced countries have converged, but the growth rates of countries across the world have not. This has led economists to believe that the convergence hypothesis fits the data only when factors that affect growth, such as education, infrastructure, and favorable policies and institutions, are held equal across countries.

Module 39

6. The large differences in countries' growth rates are largely due to differences in their rates of accumulation of physical and human capital, as well as differences in technological progress. A prime factor is differences in savings and investment rates, since most countries that have high investment in physical capital finance it by high domestic savings. Technological progress is largely a result of research and development, or R&D.

7. Government actions that contribute to growth include the building of **infrastructure**, particularly for transportation and public health; the creation and regulation of a well-functioning banking system that channels savings into investment spending; and the financing of both education and R&D. Government actions that slow growth are corruption, political instability, excessive government intervention, and the neglect or violation of property rights.

8. In regard to making economic growth sustainable, economists generally believe that environmental degradation poses a greater problem than natural resource scarcity does. Addressing environmental degradation requires effective governmental intervention, but the problem of natural resource scarcity is often well handled by the incentives created by market prices.

9. The emission of greenhouse gases is clearly linked to growth, and limiting emissions will require some reduction in growth. However, the best available estimates suggest that a large reduction in emissions would require only a modest reduction in the growth rate.

10. There is broad consensus that government action to address climate change and greenhouse gases should take the form of market-based incentives, like a carbon tax or a cap and trade system. It will also require rich and poor countries to come to some agreement on how the cost of emissions reductions will be shared.

Module 40

11. Long-run economic growth can be analyzed using the production possibilities curve and the aggregate demand–aggregate supply model. In these models, long-run economic growth is represented by an outward shift of the production possibilities curve and a rightward shift of the long-run aggregate supply curve.

12. Physical capital **depreciates** with use. Therefore, over time, the production possibilities curve will shift inward and the long-run aggregate supply curve will shift to the left if the stock of capital is not replaced.

13. Supply-side fiscal policy, which seeks to incentivize investment and saving and spur economic growth, has the potential to create long-run economic growth.

Key Terms

Rule of 70, p. 351
Labor productivity (productivity), p. 352
Physical capital, p. 352
Human capital, p. 353

Technology, p. 353
Aggregate production function, p. 355
Diminishing returns to physical capital, p. 355

Infrastructure, p. 366
Depreciation, p. 376
Supply-side fiscal policy, p. 378

AP® Exam Practice Questions

Multiple-Choice Questions

1. If real GDP grows by 5% per year, approximately how many years will it take for it to double?
   a. 150
   b. 75
   c. 35
   d. 15
   e. 5

2. What is the most important ingredient in long-run economic growth?
   a. increased labor productivity
   b. increased population
   c. low price level
   d. expansionary monetary and fiscal policies
   e. deficit spending

3. The technical means for the production of goods and services is known as
   a. physical capital.
   b. technology.
   c. human capital.
   d. productivity.
   e. machinery and equipment.

4. Which of the following is a major reason for productivity growth?
   a. financial investment
   b. an increase in aggregate demand
   c. a decrease in the amount of capital available per worker
   d. an increase in the price of capital
   e. technological progress

Refer to the following figure for Questions 5 and 6.

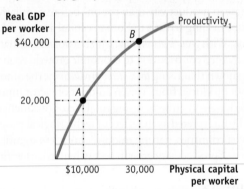

5. Assuming diminishing returns to physical capital, if physical capital per worker is $50,000, real GDP per worker will most likely equal which of the following?
   a. more than $60,000
   b. $60,000
   c. less than $60,000 but greater than $40,000
   d. $40,000
   e. $0

6. An upward shift of the curve could be caused by which of the following?
   a. an increase in real GDP per worker
   b. investment in physical capital
   c. diminishing returns to physical capital
   d. increases in population
   e. rising total factor productivity

7. Which of the following is true about the role of natural resources in productivity growth?
   a. They are a more important determinant of productivity than human or physical capital.
   b. They have played an increasingly prominent role in productivity growth in recent years.
   c. They play no role in determining productivity growth.
   d. They played a less important role in productivity growth in the 1800s.
   e. They result in higher productivity, other things equal.

8. According to the convergence hypothesis, over time, international differences in real GDP per capita will
   a. increase exponentially.
   b. increase slightly.
   c. decrease.
   d. remain the same.
   e. disappear.

9. When the government spends money to create and implement new technologies, it has invested in
   a. human capital.
   b. physical capital.
   c. infrastructure.
   d. research and development.
   e. political stability.

10. Which of the following is part of an economy's infrastructure?
    a. highways
    b. factories
    c. banks
    d. automobiles
    e. workers

11. If long-run economic growth can continue into the future despite limited natural resources, it is considered
    a. acceptable.
    b. equitable.
    c. economical.
    d. sustainable.
    e. expandable.

12. An outward shift of the production possibilities curve indicates which of the following?
    a. a decrease in cyclical unemployment
    b. long-run economic growth
    c. a reduction in productive resources
    d. a decrease in opportunity cost
    e. a decrease in potential output and the natural rate of unemployment

13. In the aggregate demand and supply model, a rightward shift of the *LRAS* curve indicates which of the following?
    a. long-run economic growth
    b. an increase in unemployment
    c. a decrease in real GDP
    d. an increase in the aggregate price level
    e. an economic recovery

14. Which of the following will lead to long-run economic growth?
    a. a decrease in nominal wages
    b. a decrease in the aggregate price level
    c. an increase in the production of consumer goods
    d. an increase in total factor productivity
    e. actual output that exceeds potential output

15. If an economy experiences long-run economic growth, which of the following is true of its potential output?
    a. It has increased.
    b. It has decreased.
    c. It is greater than actual output.
    d. It is less than actual output.
    e. It is no longer equal to *LRAS*.

16. Depreciation leads to
    a. a reduction in human capital.
    b. an increase in human capital.
    c. a reduction in physical capital.
    d. an advance in technology.
    e. an outward shift of the production possibilities curve.

17. The government can promote long-run economic growth by
    a. increasing education subsidies.
    b. increasing Social Security funding.
    c. decreasing unemployment compensation.
    d. increasing military spending.
    e. cutting taxes.

Use the following graph to answer Questions 18 and 19.

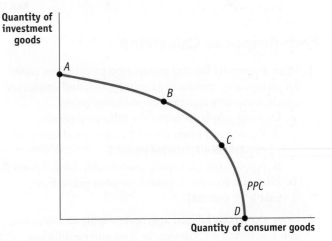

18. Which point on the graph will result in the least long-run growth?
    a. *A*
    b. *B*
    c. *C*
    d. *D*
    e. cannot be determined

19. How would economic growth be represented on the graph?
  a. a movement from D to C
  b. a movement from C to D
  c. a movement from A to B
  d. a movement from B to A
  e. an outward shift of the curve

20. All of the following will lead to growth EXCEPT
  a. increasing gross private domestic investment.
  b. increasing taxes.
  c. increasing productivity.
  d. decreasing the cost of technology.
  e. increasing human capital.

21. The key statistic used to track long-run economic growth is
  a. nominal GDP.   **d.** real GDP per capita.
  b. real GDP.   **e.** real net GDP per capita.
  c. nominal GDP per capita.

Use the following graph to answer Questions 22 and 23.

22. The *LRAS* is vertical because the aggregate price level
  a. is not flexible in the long run.
  b. has no effect on the aggregate quantity supplied.
  c. rises between P_1 and P_2.
  d. is constant in the long run.
  e. is positively related to aggregate output in the long run.

23. Long-run economic growth would be shown on the graph as a
  a. movement from P_1 to P_2.
  b. movement from P_2 to P_1.
  c. rightward shift of the curve.
  d. leftward shift of the curve.
  e. decrease in the slope of the curve.

24. Which of the following shifts of the *AD*, *SRAS*, and *LRAS* curves can be true if the economy experiences long-run economic growth?

	AD	SRAS	LRAS
a.	right	right	left
b.	left	left	right
c.	left	no change	right
d.	right	right	right
e.	no change	left	right

25. If an economy experiences long-run economic growth, which of the following is true of its full-employment level of output?
  a. It has increased.
  b. It has decreased.
  c. It is greater than actual output.
  d. It is less than actual output.
  e. It is no longer equal to *LRAS*.

Free-Response Questions

1. Draw a correctly labeled production possibilities curve for an economy producing capital goods and consumer goods, assuming constant opportunity costs.
  a. On your graph illustrate the following points:
    i. Production when the economy is producing only capital goods, labeled point A.
    ii. A point that is currently unattainable, labeled point B.
  b. Illustrate economic growth on your graph from part a. **(5 points)**

2. Draw a correctly labeled aggregate supply and demand graph showing an economy in long-run equilibrium.
  a. Label each of the following on your graph:
    i. equilibrium price level, *PL*.
    ii. equilibrium output level, *Y*.
    iii. *LRAS*.
  b. Assume the economy has experienced long-run economic growth. Illustrate a new long-run equilibrium on your graph from part a. **(6 points)**

3. Refer to the figure to answer the questions that follow.

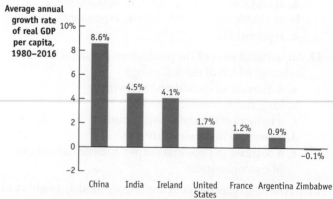

a. In how many years would it take the U.S. economy to double? Show your work.
b. Given the growth rate shown on the graph, how long will it take India to double its GDP per capita? Explain.
c. Use correctly labeled *LRAS* curves to show the change in Zimbabwe's economy between 1980 and 2016. **(5 points)**

Why are Some Countries Rich and Others Poor?

Growth Models, Miracles, and the Determinants of Economic Development

... the causes of the wealth and poverty of nations—the grand object of all enquiries of Political Economy.

—*Thomas Malthus in a letter to David Ricardo,*
January 26, 1817

Development and Growth

The determinants of wealth and poverty constitute pieces in one of the world's most important puzzles. As the pieces come together, the goal is to promote *economic development*, which is a sustained increase in the economic well-being and quality of life experienced in an economy. In order to compare development levels in different countries, Pakistani economist Mahbub ul Haq created the *Human Development Index* (HDI) on the basis of life expectancy, adult literacy rates, school enrollment rates, and GDP per capita. Since 1993, the United Nations Development Program has used the HDI as a gauge of well-being in its annual reports. In 2016, Norway received the highest HDI value of the 188 countries studied and the Central African Republic received the lowest. The United States came in 10th.[1]

Economic growth, commonly measured by increases in GDP, is necessary but not sufficient for economic development. Advancements in economic development require expenditures on, for example, health and education that boost GDP. Several other determinants of the quality of life, such as leisure time, environmental quality, and the distribution of income, don't make their way into the calculation of GDP. This makes GDP a flawed indicator of economic development. Even so, the relative objectivity and availability of GDP figures, and their positive correlation with many measures of the quality of life, make them a common focus in related studies.

Schools of Thought

Economists have studied the available data to identify common characteristics among rich and poor countries. Varying findings and interpretations have generated several broad schools of thought, with emphases that include technology, skills and knowledge, geography, outside influences, and governance.

The Solow Model

Economist Robert Solow set forth the neoclassical conception of growth in developing countries. Solow's model attributes growth to technological change, and each country is assumed to have the same technology. Productivity differences among countries are explained by differing amounts of capital per worker. Solow suggested that productivity in poor countries would catch up to that in rich countries because resources are allocated to the place where they are valued most highly, and (as implied by diminishing marginal returns) capital would be more valuable in countries that have little of it.

As an example, the first power plant in a country would be used to produce electricity for the most important uses—hospitals, schools, critical businesses—whereas the 10th power plant would satisfy less important needs, and the 100th would be even less valuable. Rational, profit-maximizing investors in

[1] See http://hdr.undp.org/sites/default/files/HDR2016_EN_Overview_Web.pdf.

power plants would place them in the countries where they would have the greatest value. Given the higher return from one more power plant in poor countries, where many businesses and homes are without power, and similarly high returns for other types of capital where it is most needed, this model predicts that capital will flow from rich countries into poor countries, thereby reducing the inequalities between them.

Human Capital

Economist Robert Lucas pointed out the inconsistencies between the Solow growth model and reality. In fact, capital moves mostly among rich countries. Lucas explained that the marginal product of capital between, for instance, India and the United States differs by a factor of 5, even when differences in *human capital* (education and knowledge) are taken into account. So why isn't all the new capital flowing into places such as India? Lucas points out that capital market imperfections, such as taxes on incoming capital and monopolies that control foreign trade, impede the free flow of capital to its most efficient uses.

There are also reasons why the marginal product of capital may not be relatively large in poor countries even though they have relatively little capital. Lucas suggests that positive externalities (that is, beneficial side effects) from human capital may equalize the marginal product of capital between India and the United States. The idea is that workers' skills, education, and experience rub off on other workers. One country may have twice the average education level of another, but by working with more knowledgeable people, the workers in the education-oriented country end up with *more than* twice the human capital. By Lucas's estimates, a 10% increase in the human capital of your co-workers will increase your own productivity by 3.6%.

Human capital and imperfect capital markets are two possible explanations for the difficulty some countries have in attracting capital investment and achieving economic growth. In related research, economists Greg Mankiw, David Romer, and David Weil found that by modifying the Solow model to accommodate differences in human capital, savings rates, and population growth, they could explain most of the international variation in incomes. However, the development of human capital is no silver bullet: several other studies have found no association between an increase in the average level of education and economic growth. The following sections provide an overview of alternative explanations for productivity differences among countries.

Location, Location, Location

They say that the three things most important to success in business are location, location, and location. The same could be said about growth and development on a larger scale. The fertile heartland of the United States and the oilfields of Saudi Arabia convey advantages not found in impoverished Laos or Haiti. But it is important to note that geographical problems are surmountable. A benefit of globalization is that transportation and communications reach around the world, helping countries with the narrowest comparative advantage in the production of a few goods or services to trade for virtually anything made anywhere. Japan and Singapore are examples of countries that have used export-oriented economies to overcome resource constraints and become wealthy. Size needn't be a problem, either. Many small countries have very high standards of living, including tiny Luxembourg and Qatar. Undesirable location and size are more than speed bumps on the road to success, but other factors have proven to be more important determinants of a country's potential for development.

Exploitation and Other Outside Influences

Without foreign involvement, poor countries sometimes languish in poverty, but when foreigners do become involved in the commerce of developing countries, the poor countries often get the short end of the stick. Corporations from rich countries sometimes find relatively lax rules or corruptible governments that allow them to exploit the natural resources and labor of poor countries. Consider the experience of countries referred to as *banana republics*—generally small, politically unstable countries whose economies are dominated by foreign corporations that produce and export a single good, such as bananas. In 1871, an American named Minor Keith arrived in Costa Rica to build a railroad and soon began planting bananas. Keith went on to help found the United Fruit Company (UFCO), whose plantations extended throughout Central America, South America, and the Caribbean. UFCO owned 112 miles of railroad and 11 ocean steamers; in its home-base country, Guatemala, it controlled telegraph lines, mail delivery to the United States, and all shipments in and out of the trade hub of Puerto Barrios. Most of the profits from UFCO operations escaped Guatemala, leaving that country poor. UFCO later changed its name to United Brands Company and, in the 1970s, sold its land holdings in Guatemala to Del Monte Corporation.

The United Fruit Company, like many other multinational corporations, provided benefits to its host countries as well. UFCO created jobs, built schools, and paid its workers well. Sometimes foreigners serve as movers and shakers, ushering in advances in health care, agriculture, and technology. For example, the 300-megawatt San Pedro de Macorís power plant in the Dominican Republic received $233 million in financing from companies in North Carolina and Great Britain, and engineering, procurement, and construction services from companies in Germany and Scotland. The affordable electricity delivered by this international team helps schools, hospitals, and factories on one of the poorest islands in the Western Hemisphere.

Many poorer countries face the disadvantage of producing raw materials such as metals, timber, and agricultural goods. Because many countries make these goods, competition leads to low and variable prices. Rich countries purchase raw materials such as iron ore, coffee beans, and timber from poor countries, process them into automobiles, instant coffee crystals, and fine furniture, and then sell them globally (including back to the poor countries) at a high markup thanks to brand names and quality distinctions with few substitutes.

Countries that produce raw materials also face competition from government-subsidized production in wealthier countries. Between 1995 and 2016, U.S. Department of Agriculture subsidies amounted to $353.5 billion.[2] Subsidies encourage the production of commodities even where substantial irrigation and soil enhancement are required, and surpluses are sold to relatively poor countries where farmers have difficulty competing with the subsidized prices. Likewise, Japanese farmers sell subsidized rice in Vietnam and other developing countries. The subsidies keep prices down, but in countries where most of the consumers are agricultural workers, lower prices on imported grains don't compensate for the loss of farm wages needed to purchase all goods and services.

Governance and Other Internal Influences

Hock Tan, the CEO of Broadcom Inc., received a compensation package worth $103 million in 2017. Some criticize the high salaries of leaders, and some leaders may well be overpaid, but it is difficult to overstate the importance of the person at the top. Leaders of corporations and countries orchestrate success stories, handle setbacks, and set the tone for ambition and morale. Most new businesses fail, and most countries are not wealthy. It took the guidance of CEO Greg Brenneman to turn Burger King around and the genius of President Sir Quett Ketumile Joni Masire to lead Botswana through democratization and three decades of rapid economic growth at the end of the twentieth century. In developing countries, leaders also determine whether international aid and trade revenues

[2] See https://farm.ewg.org/.

go toward investments in human and physical capital or into the pockets of corrupt officials. A change in leadership provides troubled countries and corporations with an immediate change in outlook and is often a first step for countries seeking reform.

No positive characteristic guarantees a country's development, and no negative characteristic inevitably spells doom, but a preponderance of either is the ticket to boom or gloom. Several countries on the continent of Africa struggle with multiple threats, including corrupt governance, disease, and warring factions. Even in these countries, progress is possible with solutions that might include inspirational new leaders, increased access to health care, assistance with loans from the World Bank or other international organizations, and new policies on education and trade. Other countries have strong positives but enough negatives to halt a developmental breakthrough. The trick, then, is to tip the scale. The next section describes such a transition in Southeast Asia.

The Asian Economic Miracle

Between 1970 and 1996, the historically poor countries of China, Hong Kong, Indonesia, Malaysia, Singapore, South Korea, Taiwan, and Thailand experienced GDP growth that averaged about 8% per year, compared to the 2.7% average growth rate of the rich industrial countries. These Southeast Asian countries had high levels of savings and investment, a growing quantity of high-quality labor, and rising productivity based on imported capital and technology. Their governments emphasized secondary education to improve human capital, and efficient transportation and communications networks. Export-oriented government policies lowered trade barriers for the purchase of raw materials. Budgetary restraint kept inflation in check, bolstering investor confidence. Stable prices and government encouragement prompted high household savings rates. Finally, exchange rates were managed so as to avoid sustained overvaluations of the Asian currencies and to promote investment from abroad. Several of the "Asian Tiger" economies were also boosted by cheap loans, and, as the Solow model would suggest, vast inflows of foreign capital.

Economists Paul Romer, Robert Lucas, Sérgio Rebelo, and others developed the *endogenous growth model* in the late 1980s and early 1990s to help explain the growth in Southeast Asia and elsewhere. While Solow's model holds that technological change is determined by forces outside the economy, this model treats the level of technology as *endogenous*, meaning that it is determined within the economic system. For example, private investment in research and development could hasten

Myruestory Photography/Getty Images

technical progress. Government policies could assist in that process by promoting education and training programs that build human capital, providing patents, and protecting property rights so that those who innovate to increase productivity reap greater rewards.

The Asian economic miracle lost its momentum in the mid- to late 1990s when inadequate bank regulation, cronyism, sliding exchange rates, and slow government responses to these problems dealt a blow to the rapid accumulation of capital. Existing productivity growth could not compensate for the waning flow of capital. Miracles do cease, but it is clear that developing countries can indeed become developed countries, regardless of whether they can sustain a rapid rate of growth in the long run.

Why Can't More Money Solve All the Problems?

Money alone is not the missing piece for a poor, isolated country aspiring to prosperity. Consider the tiny island of Barbareta off the coast of Honduras, on which there are coconut palms, fish, firewood, and very few people—for simplicity, let's imagine there are only three people. Suppose that by specializing, the first islander can catch enough fish to feed three people for a day, the second can harvest enough coconut milk to provide a day's beverages for three people, and the third can collect enough firewood for one day's cooking and heating fires for three people. With no money, the three islanders could make in-kind trades for what they want from each other, as long as each wants what the others have.

Money provides convenience as a medium of exchange, a store of value, and a unit of account. With two shells apiece that serve as money, each islander can purchase the items made by the other two for one shell per item, and in the end each would have two shells again. It is rumored that the notorious buccaneer Sir Henry Morgan buried treasure on the string of islands that includes Barbareta. If our three islanders discovered Morgan's buried treasure worth, say, $6 million, they would be "wealthy," with $2 million apiece, but they would not necessarily be better off. Having more money with which to purchase the same goods, they would each simply be able to pay more for their daily rations—up to $1 million per unit of fish, coconuts, or firewood—but this would create nothing but inflation.

This approach of adding more money into the equation has been tried. Most recently in Venezuela, the government printed large amounts of money in an effort to remedy a financial crisis. The result was hyperinflation that was projected to exceed 2000% in 2018. Development does not spring from more money chasing the same amount of goods and services. Solving the mystery of income inequality is a matter of explaining why poor countries can't make more stuff or improve their prospects for international trade.

Conclusion

Economists have much to say about recipes for economic development. Under the right conditions, investors would place capital in poor countries where it serves the greatest purpose. These conditions include adequacy in the areas of governance, education systems, entrepreneurialism, savings rates, population growth, and inflation control, not to mention compatible cultural, religious, and trade practices. The convergence of income levels predicted by neoclassical economic models is impeded in practice because many poor countries don't meet these conditions.

International aid and the forgiveness of debt can offer short-term relief, but they seldom provide long-term solutions. The eradication of agonizing poverty requires a confluence of changes, considerable time, and care to sidestep the pitfalls of corruption and exploitation. Economic growth stems chiefly from improvements in human and physical capital in an environment that is conducive to development.

Critical Thinking Questions

1. Consider again the story of Barbareta Island. For each of the following scenarios, explain how you would expect the outcome for the three inhabitants to differ from the original outcome:
   a. One of the islanders found the treasure alone, thus obtaining $6 million for himself.
   b. The treasure chest is filled with cans of tuna fish, which the islanders divide evenly.
   c. The treasure chest contains only a saw, a solar oven, and a spear gun.

2. The Central African Republic has the world's lowest level of GDP per capita: $700 in 2017. If you were the leader of that country, what specific steps would you take to effect change?

3. Research at Abdou Moumouni University (AMU) in Niger is reportedly hampered by the lack of a communications network. Suppose the McDonald's Corporation wants to invest in a new computer network for one university that is looking into lower-fat substances in which to fry food, and that scholars at both your school and AMU are working on the project. Under what assumptions would McDonald's be better off investing in a network at AMU rather than your school? How does this question relate to the issue of convergence according to the Solow growth model?

International Trade and Finance

lev dolgachov/AGE Fotostock

economics by example *Is Globalization a Bad Word?*

A Roller Coaster Ride for the Exchange Rate

"You should see, when they come in the door, the shopping bags they hand off to the coat check. I mean, they're just spending. It's Monopoly money to them." So declared a New York restaurant manager, describing the European tourists who, in the summer of 2008, accounted for a large share of her business. Meanwhile, American tourists in Europe were suffering sticker shock. One American, whose family of four was visiting Paris, explained his changing vacation plans: "We might not stay as long. We might eat cheese sandwiches."

Things were quite different just 10 years later when the U.S. dollar was much stronger and an article in the

New York Times bore the headline: "A Bounty of Europe Travel Deals." What happened? The answer is that there was a large shift in the relative values of the euro, the currency used by much of Europe, and the U.S. dollar. In 2008, the euro hit a high of 1.58 U.S. dollars per euro, making it cheap for Europeans to purchase U.S. dollars (in effect, each dollar costs Europeans US$0.63). But in 2018, the exchange rate fell to US$1.24 per euro, making it more expensive for Europeans to purchase dollars (each dollar costs Europeans US$0.81), and therefore it was cheaper for Americans to travel in Europe.

What causes the ups and downs of the relative value of the dollar and

the euro? What are the effects of such changes? These are among the questions addressed by *open-economy macroeconomics*, the branch of macroeconomics that deals with the relationships between national economies. In this section we'll learn about some of the key issues in open-economy macroeconomics: the determinants of a country's *balance of payments*, the factors affecting *exchange rates*, the different forms of *exchange rate policy* adopted by various countries, and the relationship between exchange rates and macroeconomic policy. In the final module we will apply what we have learned about macroeconomic modeling to conduct policy analysis.

MOD 41

Capital Flows and the Balance of Payments

In this Module, you will learn to:
- Explain the meaning of the balance of payments accounts
- Identify the determinants of international capital flows

Capital Flows and the Balance of Payments

In 2016, people living in the United States sold about $3.6 trillion worth of stuff to people living in other countries and bought about $3.2 trillion worth of stuff from other countries. What kind of stuff? All kinds. Residents of the United States (including employees of firms operating in the United States) sold airplanes, bonds, wheat, and many other items to residents of other countries. Residents of the United States bought cars, stocks, oil, and many other items from residents of other countries.

How can we keep track of these transactions? Earlier we learned that economists keep track of the domestic economy using the national income and product accounts. Economists keep track of international transactions using a different but related set of numbers, the *balance of payments accounts*.

Balance of Payments Accounts

A country's **balance of payments accounts** are a summary of the country's transactions with other countries.

To understand the basic idea behind the balance of payments accounts, let's consider a small-scale example: not a country, but a family farm. Let's say that we know the following about how last year went financially for the Costas, who own a small artichoke farm in California:

- They made $100,000 by selling artichokes.
- They spent $70,000 on running the farm, including purchases of new farm machinery, and another $40,000 buying food, paying utility bills for their home, and replacing their worn-out car.
- They received $500 in interest on their bank account but paid $10,000 in interest on their mortgage.
- They took out a new $25,000 loan to help pay for farm improvements but didn't use all the money immediately. So they put the extra in the bank.

How could we summarize the Costas' year? One way would be with a table like **Table 41.1**, which shows sources of cash coming in and money going out, characterized

A country's **balance of payments accounts** are a summary of the country's transactions with other countries.

Table 41.1	The Costas' Financial Year		
	Sources of cash	Uses of cash	Net
1. Sales and purchases of goods and services	Artichoke sales: $100,000	Farm operation and living expenses: $110,000	−$10,000
2. Interest payments	Interest received on bank account: $500	Interest paid on mortgage: $10,000	−$9,500
3. Loans and deposits	Funds received from new loan: $25,000	Funds deposited in bank: $5,500	+$19,500
Total	$125,500	$125,500	$0

under a few broad headings. Row 1 of Table 41.1 shows sales and purchases of goods and services: sales of artichokes; purchases of farm machinery, groceries, heating oil, a new car, and so on. Row 2 shows interest payments: the interest the Costas received from their bank account and the interest they paid on their mortgage. Row 3 shows cash coming in from new borrowing versus money deposited in the bank.

In each row we show the net inflow of cash from that type of transaction. So the net in Row 1 is − $10,000 because the Costas spent $10,000 more than they earned. The net in Row 2 is − $9,500, the difference between the interest the Costas received on their bank account and the interest they paid on the mortgage. The net in Row 3 is $19,500: the Costas brought in $25,000 with their new loan but put only $5,500 of that sum in the bank.

The last row shows the sum of cash coming in from all sources and the sum of all cash used. These sums are equal, by definition: every dollar has a source, and every dollar received gets used somewhere. (What if the Costas hid money under the mattress? Then that would be counted as another "use" of cash.)

A country's balance of payments accounts summarize its transactions with the world using a table similar to the one we just used to summarize the Costas' financial year.

Table 41.2 shows a simplified version of the U.S. balance of payments accounts for 2017. Where the Costa family's accounts show sources and uses of cash, the balance of payments accounts show payments from foreigners—in effect, sources of cash for the United States as a whole—and payments to foreigners.

Table 41.2	The U.S. Balance of Payments in 2017 (billions of dollars)		
	Payments from foreigners	Payments to foreigners	Net
1. Sales and purchases of goods and services	$2,332	$2,900	− $568
2. Factor income	927	710	217
3. Transfers	150	265	−115
Current account (1 + 2 + 3)			**−466**
4. Net increase in assets/Financial capital inflow	1,588	–	1,588
5. Net increase in liabilities/Financial capital outflow	–	1,212	1212
Financial account (4 − 5)			**376**
Total (statistical discrepancy)	–	–	**−90**

Source: Bureau of Economic Analysis.

Row 1 of Table 41.2 shows payments that arise from sales and purchases of goods and services. For example, the value of U.S. wheat exports and the fees foreigners pay to U.S. consulting companies appear in the Payments from Foreigners column of row 1; the value of U.S. oil imports and the fees American companies pay to Indian call centers—the people who often answer your toll-free calls—appear in the Payments to Foreigners column of row 1.

Row 2 shows *factor income*—payments for the use of factors of production owned by residents of other countries. Mostly this means investment income: interest paid on loans from overseas, the profits of foreign-owned corporations, and so on. For example, the profits earned by Disneyland Paris, which is owned by the U.S.-based Walt Disney Company, appear in the Payments from Foreigners column of row 2; the profits earned by the U.S. operations of Japanese auto companies appear in the Payments to Foreigners column. Factor income also includes labor income. For example, the wages of an American engineer who works temporarily on a construction site in Dubai are counted in the Payments from Foreigners column of row 2.

Profits from Disneyland Paris count as Payments from Foreigners in the U.S.'s factor income accounting.

A country's **balance of payments on the current account**, or **current account**, is its balance of payments on goods and services plus net international transfer payments and factor income.

A country's **balance of payments on goods and services** is the difference between the value of its exports and the value of its imports during a given period.

The **merchandise trade balance**, or **trade balance**, is the difference between a country's exports and imports of goods.

A country's **balance of payments on the financial account**, or **financial account**, is the difference between its sales of assets to foreigners and its purchases of assets from foreigners during a given period.

Row 3 shows *international transfers*—funds sent by residents of one country to residents of another. The main element here is the remittances that immigrants, such as the millions of Mexican-born workers employed in the United States, send to their families in their country of origin.

The next two rows of Table 41.2 show financial inflows from other countries into the United States and financial outflows from the United States into other countries. Because more capital flowed into the United States in 2017 than flowed out to other countries, the value for this category is positive.

In laying out Table 41.2, we have separated rows 1, 2, and 3 into one group and rows 4 and 5 into another. This reflects a fundamental difference in how these two groups of transactions affect the future.

When a U.S. resident sells a good, such as wheat, to a foreigner, that's the end of the transaction. But a financial asset, such as a bond, is different. Remember, a bond is a promise to pay interest and principal in the future. So when a U.S. resident sells a bond to a foreigner, that sale creates a liability: the U.S. resident will have to pay interest and repay principal in the future. The balance of payments accounts distinguish between those transactions that don't create liabilities and those that do.

Transactions that don't create liabilities are considered part of the **balance of payments on the current account**, often referred to simply as the **current account**: the balance of payments on goods and services plus factor income and net international transfer payments. The balance of row 1 of Table 41.2, −$568 billion, corresponds to the most important part of the current account: **the balance of payments on goods and services**, the difference between the value of exports and the value of imports during a given period.

By the way, if you read news reports on the economy, you may see references to another measure, the **merchandise trade balance**, sometimes referred to as the **trade balance** for short. This is the difference between a country's exports and imports of goods alone—not including services. Economists sometimes focus on the merchandise trade balance, even though it's an incomplete measure, because data on international trade in services aren't as accurate as data on trade in physical goods, and they are also slower to arrive.

The current account, as we've just learned, consists of international transactions that don't create liabilities. Transactions that involve the sale or purchase of assets, and therefore do create future liabilities, are considered part of the **balance of payments on the financial account**, or the **financial account** for short. (In the past, economists referred to the financial account as the *capital account*. We'll use the modern term, but you may run across the older term.)

So how does it all add up? The shaded rows of Table 41.2 show the bottom lines: the overall U.S. current account and financial account for 2017. As you can see, in 2017, the United States ran a current account deficit: the amount it paid to foreigners for goods, services, factors, and transfers was greater than the amount it received. Simultaneously, it ran a financial account surplus: the value of the assets it sold to foreigners was greater than the value of the assets it bought from foreigners.

In the official data, the U.S. current account deficit and financial account surplus almost, but not quite, offset each other. But that's just due to statistical error, reflecting the imperfection of official data. In fact, it's a basic rule of balance of payments accounting that the current account and the financial account must sum to zero:

(41-1) Current account (CA) + Financial account $(FA) = 0$

or

$$CA = -FA$$

Why must Equation 41-1 be true? We already saw the fundamental explanation in Table 41.1, which showed the accounts of the Costas family: in total, the sources of cash must equal the uses of cash. The same applies to balance of payments accounts. **Figure 41.1**, a variant on the circular-flow diagram we have found useful in discussing domestic macroeconomics, may help you visualize how this adding up works.

Instead of showing the flow of money *within* a national economy, Figure 41.1 shows the flow of money *between* national economies. Money flows into the United States from the rest of the world as payment for U.S. exports of goods and services, as payment for the use of U.S.-owned factors of production, and as transfer payments. These flows (indicated by the lower green arrow) are the positive components of the U.S. current account. Money also flows into the United States from foreigners who purchase U.S. assets (as shown by the lower red arrow)—the positive component of the U.S. financial account.

Figure 41.1 The Balance of Payments

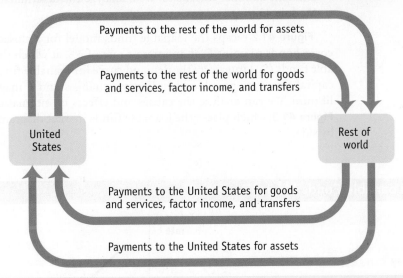

The green arrows represent payments that are counted in the current account. The red arrows represent payments that are counted in the financial account. Because the total flow into the United States must equal the total flow out of the United States, the sum of the current account plus the financial account is zero.

At the same time, money flows from the United States to the rest of the world as payment for U.S. imports of goods and services, as payment for the use of foreign-owned factors of production, and as transfer payments. These flows, indicated by the upper green arrow, are the negative components of the U.S. current account. Money also flows from the United States to purchase foreign assets, as shown by the upper red arrow—the negative component of the U.S. financial account. As in all circular-flow diagrams, the flow into a box and the flow out of a box are equal. This means that the sum of the red and green arrows going into the United States is equal to the sum of the red and green arrows going out of the United States. In other words, the current account and the financial account balance.

But what determines the current account and the financial account?

> **AP® EXAM TIP**
>
> The current and financial accounts must always balance. If there is a surplus in one account, there is a deficit in the other.

Modeling the Financial Account

A country's financial account measures its net sales of assets, such as currencies, securities, and factories, to foreigners. Those assets are exchanged for a type of capital called *financial capital*, which is funds from savings that are available for investment spending.

So we can think of the financial account as a measure of *capital inflows* in the form of foreign savings that become available to finance domestic investment spending.

What determines these capital inflows?

Part of our explanation will have to wait because some international capital flows are created by governments and central banks, which sometimes act very differently from private investors. But we can gain insight into the motivations for capital flows that are the result of private decisions by using the *loanable funds model* we developed in Module 28. In using this model, we make two important simplifications:

- We simplify the reality of international capital flows by assuming that all flows are in the form of loans. In reality, capital flows take many forms, including purchases of shares of stock in foreign companies and foreign real estate as well as *foreign direct investment*, in which companies build factories or acquire other productive assets abroad.

- We also ignore the effects of expected changes in *exchange rates*, the relative values of different national currencies. We'll analyze the determination of exchange rates in Module 43.

Figure 41.2 recaps the loanable funds model for a closed economy. Equilibrium corresponds to point *E*, at an interest rate of 4%, at which the supply curve for loanable funds (S_{LF}) intersects the demand curve for loanable funds (D_{LF}). If international capital flows are possible, this diagram changes and *E* may no longer be the equilibrium. We can analyze the causes and effects of international capital flows using **Figure 41.3**, which places the loanable funds market diagrams for two countries side by side.

Figure 41.2 The Loanable Funds Model Revisited

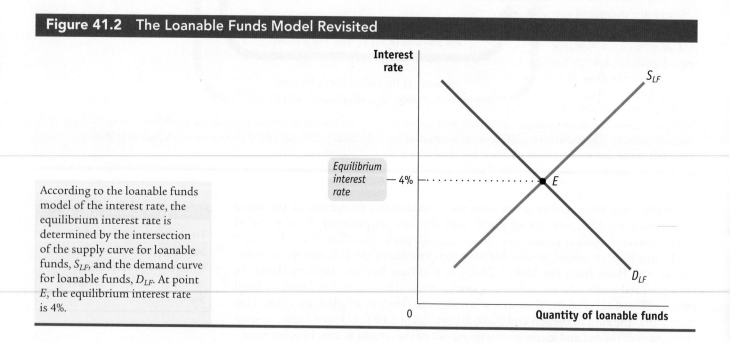

According to the loanable funds model of the interest rate, the equilibrium interest rate is determined by the intersection of the supply curve for loanable funds, S_{LF}, and the demand curve for loanable funds, D_{LF}. At point *E*, the equilibrium interest rate is 4%.

Figure 41.3 illustrates a world consisting of only two countries, the United States and Britain, assuming there are currently no capital flows between the two countries. Panel (a) shows the loanable funds market in the United States, where the equilibrium in the absence of international capital flows is at point E_{US} with an interest rate of 6%. Panel (b) shows the loanable funds market in Britain, where the equilibrium in the absence of international capital flows is at point E_B with an interest rate of 2%.

Will the actual interest rate in the United States remain at 6% and that in Britain at 2%? Not if it is easy for British residents to make loans to Americans. In that case,

Figure 41.3 Loanable Funds Markets in Two Countries

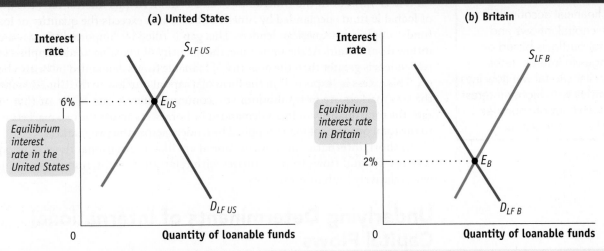

Here we show two countries, the United States and Britain, each with its own loanable funds market. The equilibrium interest rate is 6% in the U.S. market but only 2% in the British market. This creates an incentive for capital to flow from Britain to the United States.

British lenders, attracted by relatively high U.S. interest rates, will send some of their loanable funds to the United States. This capital inflow will increase the quantity of loanable funds supplied to American borrowers, pushing the U.S. interest rate down. At the same time, it will reduce the quantity of loanable funds supplied to British borrowers, pushing the British interest rate up. So international capital flows will narrow the gap between U.S. and British interest rates.

Let's further suppose that British lenders regard a loan to an American as being just as good as a loan to one of their own compatriots, and American borrowers regard a debt to a British lender as no more costly than a debt to an American lender. In that case, the flow of funds from Britain to the United States will continue until the gap between their interest rates is eliminated. In other words, international capital flows will equalize the interest rates in the two countries. **Figure 41.4** shows an

Figure 41.4 International Capital Flows

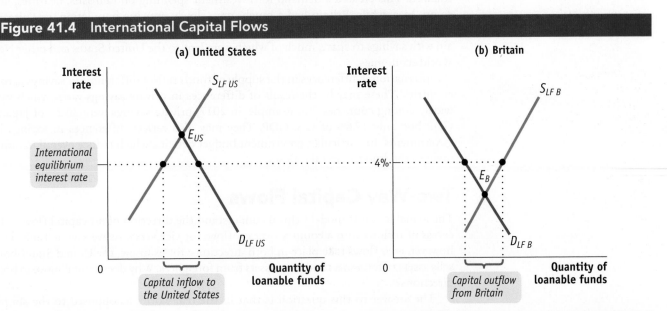

British lenders lend to borrowers in the United States, leading to equalization of interest rates at 4% in both countries. At that rate, American borrowing exceeds American lending; the difference is made up by capital inflows to the United States. Meanwhile, British lending exceeds British borrowing; the excess is a capital outflow from Britain.

international equilibrium in the loanable funds markets where the equilibrium interest rate is 4% in both the United States and Britain. At this interest rate, the quantity of loanable funds demanded by American borrowers exceeds the quantity of loanable funds supplied by American lenders. This gap is filled by "imported" funds—a capital inflow from Britain. At the same time, the quantity of loanable funds supplied by British lenders is greater than the quantity of loanable funds demanded by British borrowers. This excess is "exported" in the form of a capital outflow to the United States. And the two markets are in equilibrium at a common interest rate of 4%. At that interest rate, the total quantity of loans demanded by borrowers across the two markets is equal to the total quantity of loans supplied by lenders across the two markets.

In short, international flows of capital are like international flows of goods and services. Capital flows from countries with relatively low interest rates to countries with relatively high interest rates.

Underlying Determinants of International Capital Flows

The open-economy version of the loanable funds model helps us understand international capital flows in terms of the supply and demand for funds. But what underlies differences across countries in the supply and demand for funds? And why, in the absence of international capital flows, would interest rates differ internationally, creating an incentive for international capital flows?

International differences in the demand for funds reflect underlying differences in investment opportunities. In particular, a country with a rapidly growing economy, other things equal, tends to offer more investment opportunities than a country with a slowly growing economy. So a rapidly growing economy typically—though not always—has a higher demand for capital and offers higher returns to investors than a slowly growing economy in the absence of capital flows. As a result, capital tends to flow from slowly growing to rapidly growing economies.

The classic example is the flow of capital from Britain to the United States, among other countries, between 1870 and 1914. During that era, the U.S. economy was growing rapidly as the population increased and spread westward, and as the nation industrialized. This created a demand for investment spending on railroads, factories, and so on. Meanwhile, Britain had a much more slowly growing population, was already industrialized, and already had a railroad network covering the country. This left Britain with savings to spare, much of which were lent to the United States and other New World economies.

International differences in the supply of funds reflect differences in savings across countries. These may be the result of differences in private savings rates, which vary widely among countries. For example, in 2017, private savings were 26.2% of Japan's GDP but only 17.6% of U.S. GDP. They may also reflect differences in savings by governments. In particular, government budget deficits, which reduce overall national savings, can lead to capital inflows.

Two-Way Capital Flows

The loanable funds model helps us understand the direction of *net* capital flows—the excess of inflows into a country over outflows, or vice versa. As we saw in Table 41.2, however, *gross* flows take place in both directions: for example, the United States both sells assets to foreigners and buys assets from foreigners. Why does capital move in both directions?

The answer to this question is that in the real world, as opposed to the simple model we've just constructed, there are other motives for international capital flows besides seeking a higher rate of interest. Individual investors often seek to diversify against risk by buying both foreign and domestic stocks. Stocks in Europe may do well when stocks in the United States do badly, or vice versa, so investors in Europe try to reduce their risk by buying some U.S. stocks, even as investors in the United States try to reduce their risk by buying some European stocks. The result is capital flows in both directions. Meanwhile, corporations often engage in international investment as part of their business strategy—for example, auto companies may find that they can compete better in a national market if they assemble some of their cars locally. Such business investments can also lead to two-way capital flows, as, say, European carmakers build plants in the United States even as U.S. computer companies open facilities in Europe.

Finally, some countries, including the United States, are international banking centers: people from all over the world put money in U.S. financial institutions, which then invest many of those funds overseas.

The result of these two-way flows is that modern economies are typically both debtors (countries that owe money to the rest of the world) and creditors (countries to which the rest of the world owes money). Due to years of both capital inflows and outflows, at the end of 2016, the United States had accumulated foreign assets worth $24.5 trillion and foreigners had accumulated assets in the United States worth $32.5 trillion.

Nike, like many other companies, has opened plants in China to take advantage of low labor costs and to gain better access to the large Chinese market. Here, two Chinese employees assemble running shoes in a Nike factory in China.

MODULE 41 REVIEW

Check Your Understanding

1. Which of the balance of payments accounts do the following events affect?
   a. Boeing, a U.S.-based company, sells a newly built airplane to China.
   b. Chinese investors buy stock in Boeing from Americans.
   c. A Chinese company buys a used airplane from American Airlines and ships it to China.
   d. A Chinese investor who owns property in the United States buys a corporate jet, which he will keep in the United States so he can travel around America.

TACKLE THE AP® TEST: Multiple-Choice Questions

1. The current account includes which of the following?
   a. payments for goods and services, gross international transfer payments, and factor income
   b. payments for goods and services, net international transfer payments, and factor income
   c. sales of assets to foreigners minus purchases of assets from foreigners
   d. sales of assets to foreigners plus purchases of assets from foreigners
   e. payments for goods and services, net international transfers payments, and sales of assets to foreigners

2. The balance of payments on the current account plus the balance of payments on the financial account is equal to
   a. zero.
   b. one.
   c. the trade balance.
   d. net capital flows.
   e. the size of the trade deficit.

3. The financial account was previously known as the
   a. gross national product.
   b. capital account.
   c. trade deficit.
   d. investment account.
   e. trade balance.

4. The trade balance includes which of the following?
   a. capital inflows
   b. capital outflows
   c. net capital flows
   d. imports minus exports
   e. exports minus imports

5. Which of the following will increase the demand for loanable funds in a country?
   a. economic growth
   b. decreased investment opportunities
   c. a recession
   d. decreased private savings rates
   e. government budget surpluses

Questions 6 and 7 refer to panels (a) and (b) in the figure below.

6. The situation shown in these figures will lead to which of the following?
   a. capital inflows into the United States
   b. capital inflows into Britain
   c. increased exports to Britain
   d. increased imports to the United States
   e. capital outflows from the United States

7. In the long run, what will happen to interest rates in the United States and Britain?

	United States	Britain
a.	increase	increase
b.	increase	decrease
c.	decrease	increase
d.	decrease	decrease
e.	no change	increase

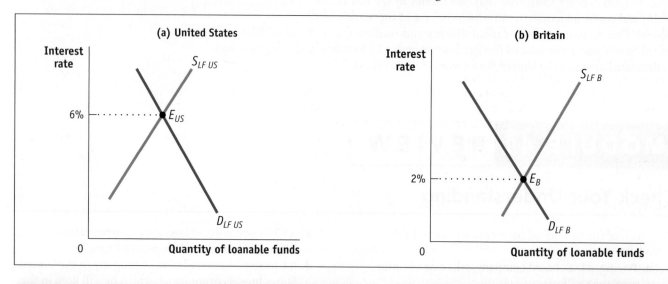

TACKLE THE AP® TEST: Free-Response Questions

1. a. How would a decrease in real income in the United States affect the U.S. current account balance? Explain.
   b. Suppose China financed a huge program of infrastructure spending by borrowing. How would this borrowing affect the U.S. balance of payments? Explain.

Rubric for FRQ 1 (4 points)

1 point: The current account balance would increase (or move toward a surplus).

1 point: The decrease in income would cause imports to decrease.

1 point: The increase in infrastructure spending in China would reduce the surplus in the U.S. financial account and reduce the deficit in the U.S. current account.

1 point: Because China is financing the program by borrowing, the demand for loanable funds in China would increase, causing an increase in the interest rate. It is likely that other countries would increase their lending to China, decreasing their lending to the United States. These capital outflows from the United States would reduce the U.S. surplus in the financial account and reduce the deficit in the current account.

2. Use two correctly labeled side-by-side graphs of the loanable funds market in the United States and China to show how a higher interest rate in the United States will lead to capital flows between the two countries. On your graphs, be sure to label the equilibrium interest rate in each country in the absence of international capital flows, the international equilibrium interest rate, and the size of the capital inflows and outflows. **(6 points)**

The Foreign Exchange Market

In this Module, you will learn to:
- Explain the role of the foreign exchange market and the exchange rate
- Discuss the importance of real exchange rates and their role in the current account

The Role of the Exchange Rate

We've just seen how differences in the supply of loanable funds from savings and the demand for loanable funds for investment spending lead to international capital flows. We've also learned that a country's balance of payments on the current account plus its balance of payments on the financial account add up to zero: a country that receives net capital inflows must run a matching current account deficit, and a country that generates net capital outflows must run a matching current account surplus.

The behavior of the financial account—reflecting inflows or outflows of capital—is best described as equilibrium in the international loanable funds market. At the same time, the balance of payments on goods and services, the main component of the current account, is determined by decisions in the international markets for goods and services. Given that the financial account reflects the movement of capital and the current account reflects the movement of goods and services, what ensures that the balance of payments really does balance? That is, what ensures that the two accounts actually offset each other?

The answer lies in the role of the *exchange rate*, which is determined in the *foreign exchange market*.

Understanding Exchange Rates

In general, goods, services, and assets produced in a country must be paid for in that country's currency. U.S. products must be paid for in dollars; most European products must be paid for in euros; Japanese products must be paid for in yen. Occasionally, sellers will accept payment in foreign currency, but they will then exchange that currency for domestic money.

International transactions, then, require a market—the **foreign exchange market**—in which currencies can be exchanged for each other. This market determines **exchange rates**, the prices at which currencies trade. (The foreign exchange market, in fact, is not located in any one geographic spot. Rather, it is a global electronic market that traders around the world use to buy and sell currencies.)

Table 42.1 shows exchange rates among the world's three most important currencies on August 15, 2018. Each entry shows the price of the "row" currency in terms of the "column" currency. For example, at that time, US$1 exchanged for €0.88, so it took €0.88

Currencies are traded in the **foreign exchange market**.

The prices at which currencies trade are known as **exchange rates**.

Susana Gonzalez/Bloomberg via Getty Images

Table 42.1	Exchange Rates, August 15, 2018		
	U.S. dollars	Yen	Euros
One U.S. dollar exchanged for	1	110.69	0.88
One yen exchanged for	0.009	1	0.008
One euro exchanged for	1.14	125.64	1

to buy US$1. Similarly, it took US$1.14 to buy €1. These two numbers reflect the same rate of exchange between the euro and the U.S. dollar: 1/1.14 = €0.88.

There are two ways to write any given exchange rate. In this case, there were €0.88 to US$1 and US$1.14 to €1. Which is the correct way to write it? The answer is that there is no fixed rule. In most countries, people tend to express the exchange rate as the price of a dollar in domestic currency. However, this rule isn't universal, and the U.S. dollar–euro rate is commonly quoted both ways. The important thing is to be sure you know which one you are using!

When a currency becomes more valuable in terms of other currencies, it **appreciates**.

When a currency becomes less valuable in terms of other currencies, it **depreciates**.

When discussing movements in exchange rates, economists use specialized terms to avoid confusion. When a currency becomes more valuable in terms of other currencies, economists say that the currency **appreciates**. When a currency becomes less valuable in terms of other currencies, it **depreciates**. Suppose, for example, that the value of €1 went from $1 to $1.25, which means that the value of US$1 went from €1 to €0.80 (because 1/1.25 = 0.80). In this case, we would say that the euro appreciated and the U.S. dollar depreciated.

Movements in exchange rates, other things equal, affect the relative prices of goods, services, and assets in different countries. Appreciation of a currency causes the country's net exports to decrease and depreciation causes the country's net exports to increase. Suppose, for example, that the price of an American hotel room is US$100 and the price of a French hotel room is €100. If the exchange rate is €1 = US$1, these hotel rooms have the same price. If the exchange rate is €1.25 = US$1, however, the French hotel room is 20% cheaper than the American hotel room (because at this rate €100 equals $80). If the exchange rate is €0.80 = US$1, the French hotel room is 25% more expensive than the American hotel room (because at this rate €100 equals $125).

But what determines exchange rates? Supply and demand in the foreign exchange market.

The Equilibrium Exchange Rate

For the sake of simplicity, imagine that there are only two currencies in the world: U.S. dollars and euros. Europeans who want to purchase American goods, services, and assets come to the foreign exchange market to exchange euros for U.S. dollars. That is, Europeans demand U.S. dollars from the foreign exchange market and, correspondingly, supply euros to that market. Americans who want to buy European goods, services, and assets come to the foreign exchange market to exchange U.S. dollars for euros. That is, Americans supply U.S. dollars to the foreign exchange market and, correspondingly, demand euros from that market. International transfers and payments of factor income also enter into the foreign exchange market, but to make things simple, we'll ignore these.

Figure 42.1 shows how the foreign exchange market works. The quantity of dollars demanded and supplied at any given euro–U.S. dollar exchange rate is shown on the horizontal axis, and the euro–U.S. dollar exchange rate is shown on the vertical axis. The exchange rate plays the same role as the price of a good or service in an ordinary supply and demand diagram.

The figure shows two curves, the demand curve for U.S. dollars and the supply curve for U.S. dollars. The key to understanding the slopes of these curves is that the level of the exchange rate affects exports and imports. When a country's currency appreciates (becomes more valuable), exports fall and imports rise. When a country's currency depreciates (becomes less valuable), exports rise and imports fall. To understand why the demand curve for U.S. dollars slopes downward, recall that the exchange rate, other things equal, determines the prices of American goods, services, and assets relative to those of European goods, services, and assets. If the U.S. dollar rises against the euro (the dollar appreciates), American products will become more expensive to Europeans relative to European products. So Europeans will buy less from the United States and will acquire fewer dollars in the foreign exchange market: the quantity of U.S. dollars demanded falls as the number of euros needed to buy a U.S. dollar rises. If the U.S. dollar falls against the euro (the dollar depreciates), American products will become relatively

Figure 42.1 The Foreign Exchange Market

The foreign exchange market matches up the demand for a currency from foreigners who want to buy domestic goods, services, and assets with the supply of a currency from domestic residents who want to buy foreign goods, services, and assets. Here the equilibrium in the market for dollars is at point E, corresponding to an equilibrium exchange rate of €0.95 per US$1.

cheaper for Europeans. Europeans will respond by buying more from the United States and acquiring more dollars in the foreign exchange market: the quantity of U.S. dollars demanded rises as the number of euros needed to buy a U.S. dollar falls.

A similar argument explains why the supply curve of U.S. dollars in Figure 42.1 slopes upward: the more euros required to buy a U.S. dollar, the more dollars Americans will supply. Again, the reason is the effect of the exchange rate on relative prices. If the U.S. dollar rises against the euro, European products look cheaper to Americans—who will demand more of them. This will require Americans to convert more dollars into euros.

The **equilibrium exchange rate** is the exchange rate at which the quantity of U.S. dollars demanded in the foreign exchange market is equal to the quantity of U.S. dollars supplied. In Figure 42.1, the equilibrium is at point E, and the equilibrium exchange rate is 0.95. That is, at an exchange rate of €0.95 per US$1, the quantity of U.S. dollars supplied to the foreign exchange market is equal to the quantity of U.S. dollars demanded.

To understand the significance of the equilibrium exchange rate, it's helpful to consider a numerical example of what equilibrium in the foreign exchange market looks like. Such an example is shown in **Table 42.2**. (This is a hypothetical table that isn't intended to match real numbers.) The first row shows European purchases of U.S. dollars, either to buy U.S. goods and services or to buy U.S. assets such as real estate or shares of stock in U.S. companies. The second row shows U.S. sales of U.S. dollars, either to buy European goods and services or to buy European assets. At the equilibrium

The **equilibrium exchange rate** is the exchange rate at which the quantity of a currency demanded in the foreign exchange market is equal to the quantity supplied.

Table 42.2 Equilibrium in the Foreign Exchange Market: A Hypothetical Example

European purchases of U.S. dollars (trillions of U.S. dollars) . . .	. . . to buy U.S. goods and services: 1.0	. . . to buy U.S. assets: 1.0	**Total purchases of U.S. dollars: 2.0**
U.S. sales of U.S. dollars (trillions of U.S. dollars) . . .	. . . to buy European goods and services: 1.5	. . . to buy European assets: 0.5	**Total sales of U.S. dollars: 2.0**
	U.S. balance of payments on the current account (CA): −0.5	**U.S. balance of payments on the financial account (FA): +0.5**	$CA + FA = 0$

exchange rate, the total quantity of U.S. dollars Europeans want to buy is equal to the total quantity of U.S. dollars Americans want to sell.

Remember that the balance of payments accounts divide international transactions into two types. Purchases and sales of goods and services are counted in the current account. (Again, we're leaving out transfers and factor income to keep things simple.) Purchases and sales of financial assets are counted in the financial account. At the equilibrium exchange rate, then, we have the situation shown in Table 42.2: the sum of the balance of payments on the current account plus the balance of payments on the financial account is zero.

Now let's consider how a shift in the demand for U.S. dollars affects equilibrium in the foreign exchange market. Suppose that for some reason capital flows from Europe to the United States increase—say, due to a change in the preferences of European investors. The effects are shown in **Figure 42.2**. The demand for U.S. dollars in the foreign exchange market increases as European investors convert euros into dollars to fund their new investments in the United States. This is shown by the shift of the demand curve from D_{USD1} to D_{USD2}. As a result, the U.S. dollar appreciates: the number of euros per U.S. dollar at the equilibrium exchange rate rises from XR_1 to XR_2.

Figure 42.2   An Increase in the Demand for U.S. Dollars

The demand curve for U.S. dollars shifts from D_{USD1} to D_{USD2}. So the equilibrium number of euros per U.S. dollar rises—the dollar *appreciates*. As a result, the balance of payments on the current account falls as the balance of payments on the financial account rises.

What are the consequences of this increased capital inflow for the balance of payments? The total quantity of U.S. dollars supplied to the foreign exchange market still must equal the total quantity of U.S. dollars demanded. So the increased capital inflow to the United States—an increase in the balance of payments on the financial account—must be matched by a decline in the balance of payments on the current account. What causes the balance of payments on the current account to decline? The appreciation of the U.S. dollar. A rise in the number of euros per U.S. dollar leads Americans to buy more European goods and services and Europeans to buy fewer American goods and services.

Table 42.3 shows how this might work. Europeans are buying more U.S. assets, increasing the balance of payments on the financial account from 0.5 to 1.0. This is offset by a reduction in European purchases of U.S. goods and services and a rise in U.S. purchases of European goods and services, both the result of the dollar's appreciation. *So any change in the U.S. balance of payments on the financial account generates an equal and opposite reaction in the balance of payments on the current account.* Movements in the exchange rate ensure that changes in the financial account and in the current account offset each other.

Table 42.3	Effects of Increased Capital Inflows			
European purchases of U.S. dollars (trillions of U.S. dollars) . . .	. . . to buy U.S. goods and services: 0.75 (down 0.25)	. . . to buy U.S. assets: 1.5 (up 0.5)	**Total purchases of U.S. dollars: 2.25**	
U.S. sales of U.S. dollars (trillions of U.S. dollars) . . .	. . . to buy European goods and services: 1.75 (up 0.25)	. . . to buy European assets: 0.5 (no change)	**Total sales of U.S. dollars: 2.25**	
	U.S. balance of payments on the current account (CA): −1.0 (down 0.5)	**U.S. balance of payments on the financial account (FA):** +1.0 (up 0.5)	$CA + FA = 0$	

Let's run this process in reverse. Suppose there is a reduction in capital flows from Europe to the United States—again due to a change in the preferences of European investors. The demand for U.S. dollars in the foreign exchange market falls, and the dollar depreciates: the number of euros per U.S. dollar at the equilibrium exchange rate falls. This leads Americans to buy fewer European products and Europeans to buy more American products. Ultimately, this generates an increase in the U.S. balance of payments on the current account. So a fall in capital flows into the United States leads to a weaker dollar, which in turn generates an increase in U.S. net exports. A shift in the supply curve for a currency will also affect the equilibrium exchange rate. For example, a tariff or quota on another country's goods will lead to fewer imports and therefore a lower demand for foreign currency. This results in a lower supply of domestic currency and a higher exchange rate.

Inflation and Real Exchange Rates

In 1994, on average, one U.S. dollar exchanged for 3.4 Mexican pesos. By 2014, the peso had fallen against the dollar by 77.4%, with an average exchange rate in early 2014 of 13.3 pesos per U.S. dollar. Did Mexican products also become much cheaper relative to U.S. products over that 20-year period? Did the price of Mexican products expressed in terms of U.S. dollars also fall by 77.4%? The answer to both questions is no, because Mexico had much higher inflation than the United States over that period. In fact, the relative price of U.S. and Mexican products changed little between 1994 and 2014, although the exchange rate changed a lot.

To account for the effects of differences in inflation rates, economists calculate **real exchange rates**, exchange rates adjusted for international differences in aggregate price levels. Suppose that the exchange rate we are looking at is the number of Mexican pesos per U.S. dollar. Let P_{US} and P_{Mex} be indexes of the aggregate price levels in the United States and Mexico, respectively. Then the real exchange rate between the Mexican peso and the U.S. dollar is defined as:

The exchange rates listed at currency exchange booths are nominal exchange rates. The current account responds only to changes in real exchange rates, which have been adjusted for differing levels of inflation.

(42-1) Real exchange rate = Mexican pesos per U.S. dollar $\times \dfrac{P_{US}}{P_{Mex}}$

To distinguish it from the real exchange rate, the exchange rate *unadjusted* for aggregate price levels is sometimes called the *nominal* exchange rate.

To understand the significance of the difference between the real and nominal exchange rates, let's consider the following example. Suppose that the Mexican peso depreciates against the U.S. dollar, with the exchange rate going from 10 pesos per U.S. dollar to 15 pesos per U.S. dollar, a 50% change. But suppose that at the same time the price of everything in Mexico, measured in pesos, increases by 50%, so that the Mexican price index rises from 100 to 150. We'll assume that there is no change in U.S. prices, so

Real exchange rates are exchange rates adjusted for international differences in aggregate price levels.

that the U.S. price index remains at 100. The initial real exchange rate is:

$$\text{Pesos per dollar} \times \frac{P_{US}}{P_{Mex}} = 10 \times \frac{100}{100} = 10$$

After the peso depreciates and the Mexican price level increases, the real exchange rate is:

$$\text{Pesos per dollar} = \frac{P_{US}}{P_{Mex}} = 15 \times \frac{100}{150} = 10$$

In this example, the peso has depreciated substantially in terms of the U.S. dollar, but the *real* exchange rate between the peso and the U.S. dollar hasn't changed at all. And because the real peso–U.S. dollar exchange rate hasn't changed, the nominal depreciation of the peso against the U.S. dollar will have no effect either on the quantity of goods and services exported by Mexico to the United States or on the quantity of goods and services imported by Mexico from the United States. To see why, consider again the example of a hotel room. Suppose that this room initially costs 1,000 pesos per night, which is $100 at an exchange rate of 10 pesos per dollar. After both Mexican prices and the number of pesos per dollar rise by 50%, the hotel room costs 1,500 pesos per night—but 1,500 pesos divided by 15 pesos per dollar is $100, so the Mexican hotel room still costs $100. As a result, a U.S. tourist considering a trip to Mexico will have no reason to change plans.

The same is true for all goods and services that enter into trade: *the current account responds only to changes in the real exchange rate, not the nominal exchange rate.* A country's products become cheaper to foreigners only when that country's currency depreciates in real terms, and those products become more expensive to foreigners only when the currency appreciates in real terms. As a consequence, economists who analyze movements in exports and imports of goods and services focus on the real exchange rate, not the nominal exchange rate.

Figure 42.3 illustrates just how important it can be to distinguish between nominal and real exchange rates. Between 1990 and 2013, Mexico's aggregate price level increased relative to the United States' level while the peso depreciated. The line labeled "Nominal exchange rate" shows the number of pesos exchanged for a U.S. dollar from 1990 to 2013. As you can see, the peso depreciated massively over that period. But the line labeled "Real exchange rate" indicates the cost of Mexican products to U.S. consumers: it was calculated using Equation 42.1, with price indexes for both Mexico and the United States set so that the value in 1990 was 100. In real terms, the peso depreciated between 1994 and

Figure 42.3 Real Versus Nominal Exchange Rates, 1990–2013

Between 1990 and 2013, the price of a dollar in Mexican pesos increased dramatically. But because Mexico had higher inflation than the United States, the real exchange rate, which accounts for the relative price of Mexican goods and services, ended up roughly where it started.

Data Source: OECD.

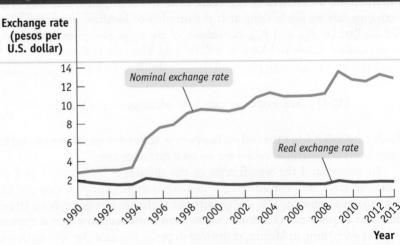

1995, and again in 2008, but not by nearly as much as the nominal depreciation. By 2013, the real peso–U.S. dollar exchange rate was just about back where it started.

Purchasing Power Parity

A useful tool for analyzing exchange rates, closely connected to the concept of the real exchange rate, is known as *purchasing power parity*. The **purchasing power parity** between two countries' currencies is the nominal exchange rate at which a given basket of goods and services would cost the same amount in each country. For example, suppose that a basket of goods and services that costs $100 in the United States costs 1,000 pesos in Mexico. Then the purchasing power parity is 10 pesos per U.S. dollar: at that exchange rate, 1,000 pesos = $100, so the market basket costs the same amount in both countries.

Calculations of purchasing power parities are usually made by estimating the cost of buying broad market baskets containing many goods and services—everything from automobiles and groceries to housing and telephone calls. But once a year the magazine *The Economist* publishes a list of purchasing power parities based on the cost of buying a market basket that contains only one item—a McDonald's Big Mac.

Nominal exchange rates almost always differ from purchasing power parities. Some of these differences are systematic: in general, aggregate price levels are lower in poor countries than in rich countries because services tend to be cheaper in poor countries. But even among countries at roughly the same level of economic development, nominal exchange rates vary quite a lot from purchasing power parity. **Figure 42.4** shows the nominal exchange rate between the Canadian dollar and the U.S. dollar, measured as the number of Canadian dollars per U.S. dollar, from 1990 to 2017, together with an estimate of the purchasing power parity exchange rate between the United States and Canada over the same period. The purchasing power parity didn't change much over the whole period because the United States and Canada had about the same rate of inflation. But at the beginning of the period the nominal exchange rate was below purchasing power parity, so a given market basket was more expensive in Canada than in the United States. By 2002, the nominal exchange rate was far above the purchasing power parity, so a market basket was much cheaper in Canada than in the United States.

Over the long run, however, purchasing power parities are pretty good at predicting actual changes in nominal exchange rates. In particular, nominal exchange rates between countries at similar levels of economic development tend to fluctuate around levels that lead to similar costs for a given market basket. In fact, by July 2005, the nominal exchange rate between the United States and Canada was C$1.22 per US$1— just about the purchasing power parity. And by 2006, the cost of living was once again higher in Canada than in the United States.

> The **purchasing power parity** between two countries' currencies is the nominal exchange rate at which a given basket of goods and services would cost the same amount in each country.

Figure 42.4 Purchasing Power Parity Versus the Nominal Exchange Rate, 1990–2017

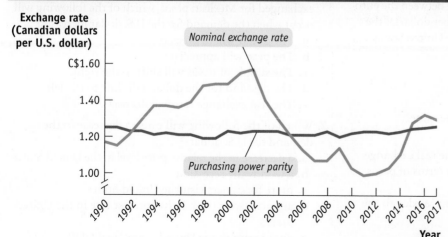

The purchasing power parity between the United States and Canada—the exchange rate at which a basket of goods and services would have cost the same amount in both countries— changed very little over the period shown, staying near C$1.20 per US$1. But the nominal exchange rate fluctuated widely.

Data Source: OECD.

Check Your Understanding

1. Suppose Mexico discovers huge reserves of oil and starts exporting oil to the United States. Describe how this would affect the following:
   a. the nominal peso–U.S. dollar exchange rate
   b. Mexican exports of other goods and services
   c. Mexican imports of goods and services

2. Suppose a basket of goods and services that costs $100 in the United States costs 800 pesos in Mexico and the current nominal exchange rate is 10 pesos per U.S. dollar. Over the next five years, the cost of that market basket rises to $120 in the United States and to 1,200 pesos in Mexico, although the nominal exchange rate remains at 10 pesos per U.S. dollar. Calculate the following:
   a. the real exchange rate now and five years from now, if today's price index in both countries is 100. [Reminder: Equation 15-1 provides the price index formula: (Cost of market basket in a given year/Cost of market basket in base year) × 100. For this problem, use the current year as the base year.]
   b. purchasing power parity today and five years from now

TACKLE THE AP® TEST: Multiple-Choice Questions

1. When the U.S. dollar buys more Japanese yen, what has happened to the value of the U.S. dollar and the Japanese yen?

	USD	Yen
a.	appreciated	appreciated
b.	appreciated	depreciated
c.	depreciated	appreciated
d.	depreciated	depreciated
e.	depreciated	not changed

2. The nominal exchange rate at which a given basket of goods and services would cost the same in each country describes
   a. the international consumer price index.
   b. appreciation.
   c. depreciation.
   d. purchasing power parity.
   e. the balance of payments on the current account.

3. What happens to the real exchange rate between the euro and the U.S. dollar (expressed as euros per dollar) if the aggregate price levels in Europe and the United States both fall?
   a. It is unaffected.
   b. It increases.
   c. It decreases.
   d. It may increase, decrease, or stay the same.
   e. It cannot be calculated.

4. Which of the following would cause the real exchange rate between pesos and U.S. dollars (in terms of pesos per dollar) to decrease?
   a. an increase in net capital flows from Mexico to the United States
   b. an increase in the real interest rate in Mexico relative to the United States
   c. a doubling of prices in both Mexico and the United States
   d. a decrease in oil exports from Mexico to the United States
   e. an increase in the balance of payments on the current account in the United States

5. Which of the following will decrease the supply of U.S. dollars in the foreign exchange market?
   a. U.S. residents increase their travel abroad.
   b. U.S. consumers demand fewer imports.
   c. Foreigners increase their demand for U.S. goods.
   d. Foreigners increase their travel to the United States.
   e. Foreign investors see increased investment opportunities in the United States.

6. In the foreign exchange market in which U.S. dollars are exchanged for Mexican pesos, which of the following will occur when the demand for the U.S. dollar increases?
   a. The dollar will depreciate.
   b. The peso will appreciate.
   c. The supply of pesos will shift to the right.
   d. The demand for the dollar will shift to the left.
   e. The real exchange rate will decrease.

7. Which of the following will cause a decrease in the demand for U.S. dollars?
   a. a decrease in the relative price level in the United States
   b. a worldwide recession
   c. more foreigners visit the United States
   d. an increase in the relative interest rate in the United States
   e. an increase in the United States' real GDP

TACKLE THE AP® TEST: Free-Response Questions

1. Draw a correctly labeled graph of the foreign exchange market showing the effect on the equilibrium exchange rate between the United States and Japan (the number of yen per U.S. dollar) if capital flows from Japan to the United States decrease due to a change in the preferences of Japanese investors. Has the U.S. dollar appreciated or depreciated?

Rubric for FRQ 1 (7 points)

1 point: The vertical axis is labeled "Exchange rate (yen per U.S. dollar)" and the horizontal axis is labeled "Quantity of U.S. dollars."

1 point: The supply of U.S. dollars is labeled and slopes upward.

1 point: The demand for U.S. dollars is labeled and slopes downward.

1 point: The initial equilibrium exchange rate is found at the intersection of the initial supply and demand curves and is labeled on the vertical axis.

1 point: The new demand for U.S. dollars is to the left of the initial demand.

1 point: The new equilibrium exchange rate is found where the initial supply curve and new demand curve intersect and is labeled on the vertical axis.

1 point: The U.S. dollar has depreciated.

2. Use a correctly labeled graph of the foreign exchange market between the United States dollar and the Euro to illustrate what would happen to the value of the U.S. dollar if there were an increase in the U.S. demand for imports from Europe. Explain your answer. **(6 points)**

Exchange Rate Policy and Macroeconomic Policy

In this Module, you will learn to:

- Explain the difference between fixed exchange rates and floating exchange rates
- Discuss the considerations that lead countries to choose different exchange rate regimes
- Describe the effects of currency devaluation and revaluation under a fixed exchange rate regime
- Explain how macroeconomic policy affects exchange rates under a floating exchange rate regime

Exchange Rate Policy

The nominal exchange rate is the price of a country's currency. Like other prices, it is determined by supply and demand. Unlike the price of wheat or oil, however, the exchange rate is the price of a country's currency *in terms of another country's currency*. Currency isn't a good or service produced by the private sector; it's an asset whose quantity is determined by government policy. For example, the Federal Reserve

Hossein Lohinejadian/Alamy

system determines the quantity of U.S. dollars. As a result, governments have much more power to influence nominal exchange rates than they have to influence ordinary prices.

The nominal exchange rate is a very important price. It determines the price of imports and the price of exports. In economies where exports and imports are large relative to GDP, movements in the exchange rate can have major effects on aggregate output and the aggregate price level. What influences this important price?

In market economies, the nominal exchange rate is determined by market forces—supply and demand in the foreign exchange market—but at different times and in different places, governments have adopted a variety of *exchange rate regimes*. (From now on, we'll adopt the convention that we mean the nominal exchange rate when we refer to the exchange rate.)

Exchange Rate Regimes

An *exchange rate regime* is a rule governing a country's policy toward the exchange rate. There are two main kinds of exchange rate regimes. A country has a **fixed exchange rate** when the government keeps the exchange rate against some other currency at or near a particular target. For example, Hong Kong has an official policy of setting an exchange rate of HK$7.80 per US$1. A country has a **floating exchange rate** when the government lets the exchange rate go wherever the market takes it. This is the policy followed by Britain, Canada, and the United States.

Fixed exchange rates and floating exchange rates aren't the only possibilities. At various times, countries have adopted compromise policies that lie somewhere between fixed and floating exchange rates. These include exchange rates that are fixed at any given time but are adjusted frequently, exchange rates that aren't fixed but are "managed" by the government to avoid wide swings, and exchange rates that float within a "target zone" but are prevented from leaving that zone. In this book, however, we'll focus on the two main exchange rate regimes: fixed and floating.

The immediate question about a fixed exchange rate is how it is possible for governments to fix the exchange rate when the exchange rate is determined by supply and demand.

How Can an Exchange Rate Be Held Fixed?

To understand how it is possible for a country to fix its exchange rate, let's consider the hypothetical country of Genovia, which has decided to fix the value of its currency, the geno, at US$1.50 to provide certainty for many Genovians who frequently travel to the United States.

The obvious problem is that $1.50 may not be the equilibrium exchange rate in the foreign exchange market: the equilibrium rate may be either higher or lower than the target exchange rate. **Figure 43.1** shows the foreign exchange market for genos, with the quantities of genos supplied and demanded on the horizontal axis and the exchange rate of the geno, measured in U.S. dollars per geno, on the vertical axis. Panel (a) shows the case in which the equilibrium value of the geno is *below* the target exchange rate. Panel (b) shows the case in which the equilibrium value of the geno is *above* the target exchange rate.

Consider first the case in which the equilibrium value of the geno is below the target exchange rate. As panel (a) shows, at the target exchange rate there is a surplus of genos in the foreign exchange market, which would normally push the value of the geno down. How can the Genovian government support the value of the geno to keep the rate where it wants? There are three possible answers, all of which have been used by governments at some point.

One way the Genovian government can support the geno is to "soak up" the surplus of genos by buying its own currency in the foreign exchange market. Government purchases or sales of currency in the foreign exchange market are called *exchange market intervention*. To buy genos in the foreign exchange market, of course, the Genovian government must have U.S. dollars to exchange for genos. In fact, most countries

A country has a **fixed exchange rate** when the government keeps the exchange rate against some other currency at or near a particular target.

A country has a **floating exchange rate** when the government lets the exchange rate go wherever the market takes it.

Figure 43.1 Exchange Market Intervention

(a) Fixing an Exchange Rate Above Its Equilibrium Value

(b) Fixing an Exchange Rate Below Its Equilibrium Value

In both panels, the imaginary country of Genovia is trying to keep the value of its currency, the geno, fixed at US$1.50. In panel (a), there is a surplus of genos on the foreign exchange market. To keep the geno from falling, the

Genovian government can buy genos and sell U.S. dollars. In panel (b), there is a shortage of genos. To keep the geno from rising, the Genovian government can sell genos and buy U.S. dollars.

maintain foreign exchange reserves, stocks of foreign currency (usually U.S. dollars or euros) that they can use to buy their own currency to support its price.

We mentioned earlier that an important part of international capital flows is the result of purchases and sales of foreign assets by governments and central banks. Now we can see why governments sell foreign assets: they are supporting their currency through exchange market intervention. As we'll see in a moment, governments that keep the value of their currency *down* through exchange market intervention must *buy* foreign assets. First, however, let's talk about the other ways governments fix exchange rates.

A second way for the Genovian government to support the geno is to try to shift the supply and demand curves for the geno in the foreign exchange market. Governments usually do this by changing monetary policy. For example, to support the geno, the Genovian central bank can raise the Genovian interest rate. This will increase capital flows into Genovia, increasing the demand for genos, at the same time that it reduces capital flows out of Genovia, reducing the supply of genos. So, other things equal, an increase in a country's interest rate will increase the value of its currency.

Third, the Genovian government can support the geno by reducing the supply of genos to the foreign exchange market. It can do this by requiring domestic residents who want to buy foreign currency to get a license and giving these licenses only to people engaging in approved transactions (such as the purchase of imported goods the Genovian government thinks are essential). Licensing systems that limit the right of individuals to buy foreign currency are called *foreign exchange controls*. Other things equal, foreign exchange controls increase the value of a country's currency.

So far we've been discussing a situation in which the government is trying to prevent a depreciation of the geno. Suppose, instead, that the situation is as shown in panel (b) of Figure 43.1, where the equilibrium value of the geno is *above* the target exchange rate and there is a shortage of genos. To maintain the target exchange rate, the Genovian government can apply the same three basic options in the reverse direction. It can intervene in the foreign exchange market, in this case *selling* genos and acquiring U.S. dollars, which it can add to its foreign exchange reserves. It can *reduce* interest rates to increase the supply of genos and reduce the demand. Or it can impose foreign exchange controls that limit the ability of foreigners to buy genos. All of these actions, other things equal, will reduce the value of the geno.

As we said, all three techniques have been used to manage fixed exchange rates. But we haven't said whether fixing the exchange rate is a good idea. In fact, the choice of exchange rate regime poses a dilemma for policy makers because fixed and floating exchange rates each have both advantages and disadvantages.

The Exchange Rate Regime Dilemma

Few questions in macroeconomics produce as many arguments as that of whether a country should adopt a fixed or a floating exchange rate. The reason there are so many arguments is that both sides have a case.

To understand the case for a fixed exchange rate, consider for a moment how easy it is to conduct business across state lines in the United States. There are a number of things that make interstate commerce trouble-free, but one of them is the absence of any uncertainty about the value of money: a dollar is a dollar, in both New York City and Los Angeles.

By contrast, a dollar isn't a dollar in transactions between New York City and Toronto. The exchange rate between the Canadian dollar and the U.S. dollar fluctuates, sometimes widely. If a U.S. firm promises to pay a Canadian firm a given number of U.S. dollars a year from now, the value of that promise in Canadian currency can vary by 10% or more. This uncertainty has the effect of deterring trade between the two countries. So one benefit of a fixed exchange rate is certainty about the future value of a currency.

In some cases, there is an additional benefit to adopting a fixed exchange rate: by committing itself to a fixed rate, a country is also committing itself not to engage in inflationary policies because such policies would destabilize the exchange rate. For example, in 1991, Argentina, which has a long history of irresponsible policies leading to severe inflation, adopted a fixed exchange rate of US$1 per Argentine peso in an attempt to commit itself to noninflationary policies in the future. (Argentina's fixed exchange rate regime collapsed disastrously in late 2001. But that's another story.)

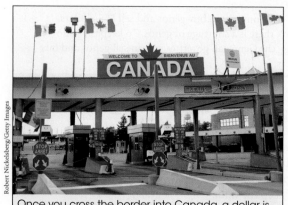

Once you cross the border into Canada, a dollar is no longer worth a dollar.

The point is that there is some economic value in having a stable exchange rate. Indeed, the presumed benefits of stable exchange rates motivated the international system of fixed exchange rates created after World War II. It was also a major reason for the creation of the euro.

However, there are also costs to fixing the exchange rate. To stabilize an exchange rate through intervention, a country must keep large quantities of foreign currency on hand, and that currency is usually a low-return investment. Furthermore, even large reserves can be quickly exhausted when there are large capital flows out of a country. If a country chooses to stabilize an exchange rate by adjusting monetary policy rather than through intervention, it must divert monetary policy from other goals, notably stabilizing the economy and managing the inflation rate. Finally, foreign exchange controls, such as import quotas and tariffs, distort incentives for importing and exporting goods and services. They can also create substantial costs in terms of red tape and corruption.

So there's a dilemma. Should a country let its currency float, which leaves monetary policy available for macroeconomic stabilization but creates uncertainty for everyone affected by trade? Or should it fix the exchange rate, which eliminates the uncertainty but means giving up monetary policy, adopting exchange controls, or both? Different countries reach different conclusions at different times. Most European countries, except for Britain, have long believed that exchange rates among major European economies, which do most of their international trade with each other, should be fixed. But Canada seems happy with a floating exchange rate with the United States, even though the United States accounts for most of Canada's trade.

Next we'll consider macroeconomic policy under each type of exchange rate regime.

Exchange Rates and Macroeconomic Policy

When the euro was created in 1999, there were celebrations across the nations of Europe—with a few notable exceptions. You see, some countries chose not to adopt the new currency. The most important of these was Britain, but other European countries, such as Switzerland and Sweden, also decided that the euro was not for them.

DANIEL SORABJI/AFP/Getty Images

Why did Britain say no? Part of the answer was national pride: for example, if Britain gave up the pound, it would also have to give up currency that bears the portrait of the queen. But there were also serious economic concerns about giving up the pound in favor of the euro. British economists who favored adoption of the euro argued that if Britain used the same currency as its neighbors, the country's international trade would expand and its economy would become more productive. But other economists pointed out that adopting the euro would take away Britain's ability to have an independent monetary policy and might lead to macroeconomic problems.

As this discussion suggests, the fact that modern economies are open to international trade and capital flows adds a new level of complication to our analysis of macroeconomic policy. Let's look at three policy issues raised by open-economy macroeconomics.

Devaluation and Revaluation of Fixed Exchange Rates

Historically, fixed exchange rates haven't been permanent commitments. Sometimes countries with a fixed exchange rate switch to a floating rate. A modern example is Argentina, which maintained a fixed exchange rate against the dollar from 1991 to 2001 but switched to a floating exchange rate at the end of 2001. In other cases, countries retain a fixed exchange rate regime but change the target exchange rate. Such adjustments in the target were common during the era following the 1944 adoption of the Bretton Woods system of monetary management, which established the rules for commercial and financial relations among the United States, Canada, Western Europe, Australia, and Japan. The agreement was designed to ensure exchange rate stability, prevent competitive devaluations, and promote economic growth between and within participating countries.

A reduction in the value of a currency that is set under a fixed exchange rate regime is called a **devaluation**. As we've already learned, a *depreciation* is a downward move in a currency. A devaluation is a depreciation that is due to a revision in a fixed exchange rate target. An increase in the value of a currency that is set under a fixed exchange rate regime is called a **revaluation**.

A devaluation, like any depreciation, makes domestic goods cheaper in terms of foreign currency, which leads to higher exports. At the same time, it makes foreign goods more expensive in terms of domestic currency, which reduces imports. The effect is to increase the balance of payments on the current account. Similarly, a revaluation makes domestic goods more expensive in terms of foreign currency, which reduces exports, and makes foreign goods cheaper in domestic currency, which increases imports. So a revaluation reduces the balance of payments on the current account.

Devaluations and revaluations serve two purposes under a fixed exchange rate regime. First, they can be used to eliminate shortages or surpluses in the foreign exchange market. For example, in 2010, some economists urged China to revalue the yuan so that it would not have to buy up so many U.S. dollars on the foreign exchange market.

A **devaluation** is a reduction in the value of a currency that is set under a fixed exchange rate regime.

A **revaluation** is an increase in the value of a currency that is set under a fixed exchange rate regime.

AP® EXAM TIP

A devaluation of a currency increases exports because they become cheaper to foreign buyers. A revaluation of a currency decreases exports because they become more expensive to foreign buyers.

Second, devaluation and revaluation can be used as tools of macroeconomic policy. By increasing exports and reducing imports, a devaluation increases aggregate demand. So a devaluation can be used to reduce or eliminate a recessionary gap. A revaluation has the opposite effect, reducing aggregate demand. So a revaluation can be used to reduce or eliminate an inflationary gap.

Monetary Policy Under a Floating Exchange Rate Regime

Under a floating exchange rate regime, a country's central bank retains its ability to pursue independent monetary policy: it can increase aggregate demand by cutting the interest rate or decrease aggregate demand by raising the interest rate. But the exchange rate adds another dimension to the effects of monetary policy. To see why, let's return to the hypothetical country of Genovia and ask what happens if the central bank cuts the interest rate.

Just as in a closed economy, a lower interest rate leads to higher investment spending and higher consumer spending. But the decline in the interest rate also affects the foreign exchange market. Foreigners have less incentive to move funds into Genovia because they will receive a lower rate of return on their loans. As a result, they have less need to exchange U.S. dollars for genos, so the demand for genos falls. At the same time, Genovians have *more* incentive to move funds abroad because the rate of return on loans at home has fallen, making investments outside the country more attractive. Thus, they need to exchange more genos for U.S. dollars and the supply of genos rises.

Figure 43.2 shows the effect of an interest rate reduction on the foreign exchange market. The demand curve for genos shifts leftward, from D_{G1} to D_{G2}, and the supply curve shifts rightward, from S_{G1} to S_{G2}. The equilibrium exchange rate, as measured in U.S. dollars per geno, falls from XR_1 to XR_2. That is, a reduction in the Genovian interest rate causes the geno to *depreciate*.

The depreciation of the geno, in turn, affects aggregate demand. We've already seen that a devaluation—a depreciation that is the result of a change in a fixed exchange

Figure 43.2 Monetary Policy and the Exchange Rate

Here we show what happens in the foreign exchange market if Genovia cuts its interest rate. Residents of Genovia have a reduced incentive to keep their funds at home, so they invest more abroad. As a result, the supply of genos shifts rightward, from S_{G1} to S_{G2}. Meanwhile, foreigners have less incentive to put funds into Genovia, so the demand for genos shifts leftward, from D_{G1} to D_{G2}. The geno depreciates: the equilibrium exchange rate falls from XR_1 to XR_2.

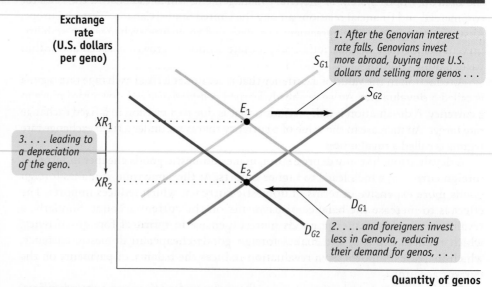

Exchange rate (U.S. dollars per geno)

1. After the Genovian interest rate falls, Genovians invest more abroad, buying more U.S. dollars and selling more genos . . .

3. . . . leading to a depreciation of the geno.

2. . . . and foreigners invest less in Genovia, reducing their demand for genos, . . .

Quantity of genos

rate—increases exports and reduces imports, thereby increasing aggregate demand. A depreciation that results from an interest rate cut has the same effect: it increases exports and reduces imports, increasing aggregate demand.

In other words, monetary policy under floating rates has effects beyond those we've described in looking at closed economies. In a closed economy, a reduction in the interest rate leads to a rise in aggregate demand because it leads to more investment spending and consumer spending. In an open economy with a floating exchange rate, the interest rate reduction leads to increased investment spending and consumer spending, but it also increases aggregate demand in another way: it leads to a currency depreciation, which increases exports and reduces imports, further increasing aggregate demand.

International Business Cycles

Up to this point, we have discussed macroeconomics, even in an open economy, as if all demand changes, or *shocks*, originated from the domestic economy. In reality, however, economies sometimes face shocks coming from abroad. For example, recessions in the United States have historically led to recessions in Mexico as a result of the close trade relationship between the two countries.

The key point is that changes in aggregate demand affect the demand for goods and services produced abroad as well as at home: other things equal, a recession leads to a fall in imports and an expansion leads to a rise in imports because changes in income affect the demand for *all* goods and services regardless of where they were produced. And one country's imports are another country's exports. This link between aggregate demand in different national economies is one reason business cycles in different countries sometimes—but not always—seem to be synchronized. The prime example is the Great Depression, which affected countries around the world.

For better or worse, trading partners tend to import each other's business cycles in addition to each other's goods, as was the case for Latin American countries after the U.S. financial crisis in 2008.

However, the extent of this link depends on the exchange rate regime. To see why, think about what happens if a recession abroad reduces the demand for Genovia's exports. A reduction in foreign demand for Genovian goods and services is also a reduction in demand for genos on the foreign exchange market. If Genovia has a fixed exchange rate, it responds to this decline with exchange market intervention. But if Genovia has a floating exchange rate, the geno depreciates. Because Genovian goods and services become cheaper to foreigners when the demand for exports falls, the quantity of goods and services exported doesn't fall by as much as it would under a fixed rate. At the same time, the fall in the geno makes imports more expensive to Genovians, leading to a fall in imports. Both effects limit the decline in Genovia's aggregate demand compared to what it would have been under a fixed exchange rate regime.

One of the virtues of floating exchange rates, according to their advocates, is that they help insulate countries from recessions originating abroad. This theory looked pretty good in the early 2000s: Britain, with a floating exchange rate, managed to stay out of a recession that affected the rest of Europe.

In 2008, however, a financial crisis that began in the United States produced a recession in virtually every country. In this case, it appears that the international linkages between financial markets were much stronger than any insulation from overseas disturbances provided by floating exchange rates.

MODULE 43 REVIEW

Check Your Understanding

1. Draw a diagram, similar to Figure 43.1, representing the foreign exchange situation of China when it kept the exchange rate fixed at a target rate of US$0.121 per yuan and the market equilibrium rate was higher than the target rate. Then show with a diagram how each of the following policy changes might eliminate the disequilibrium in the market.
   a. allowing the exchange rate to float more freely
   b. placing restrictions on foreigners who want to invest in China
   c. removing restrictions on Chinese who want to invest abroad
   d. imposing taxes on Chinese exports, such as clothing

2. In the late 1980s, Canadian economists argued that the high interest rate policies of the Bank of Canada weren't just causing high unemployment—they were also making it hard for Canadian manufacturers to compete with U.S. manufacturers. Explain this complaint using our analysis of how monetary policy works under floating exchange rates.

TACKLE THE AP® TEST: Multiple-Choice Questions

1. An increase in the supply of a currency with a floating exchange rate will cause which of the following?
   a. an increase in the demand for the currency
   b. appreciation of the currency
   c. depreciation of the currency
   d. the government to buy more of the currency
   e. the government to buy less of the currency

2. The United States has which of the following exchange rate regimes?
   a. fixed
   b. floating
   c. fixed, but adjusted frequently
   d. fixed, but managed
   e. floating within a target zone

3. An increase in the supply of a currency with a fixed exchange rate will cause which of the following?
   a. an increase in the demand for the currency
   b. appreciation of the currency
   c. depreciation of the currency
   d. the government to buy more of the currency
   e. the government to buy less of the currency

4. Devaluation of a currency is used to achieve which of the following?
   a. the elimination of a surplus in the foreign exchange market
   b. the elimination of a shortage in the foreign exchange market
   c. a reduction in aggregate demand

   d. a lower inflation rate
   e. a floating exchange rate

5. Monetary policy that reduces the interest rate will do which of the following?
   a. appreciate the domestic currency
   b. decrease exports
   c. increase imports
   d. depreciate the domestic currency
   e. prevent inflation

6. Revaluation of a currency will
   a. make domestic goods cheaper.
   b. lead to higher exports.
   c. make foreign goods more expensive.
   d. reduce imports.
   e. reduce aggregate demand.

7. Economic downturns are synchronized in different countries for all of the following reasons *except*
   a. governments often consult regarding economic policy.
   b. multinational corporations operate in more than one country.
   c. resources are traded, creating a link between countries' aggregate supply.
   d. countries' aggregate demand is linked through imports and exports.
   e. people move between countries through tourism and immigration.

TACKLE THE AP® TEST: Free-Response Questions

1. Suppose the United States and India were the only two countries in the world.
   a. Draw a correctly labeled graph of the foreign exchange market for U.S. dollars showing the equilibrium in the market.
   b. On your graph, indicate a fixed exchange rate set above the equilibrium exchange rate. Does the fixed exchange rate lead to a surplus or shortage of U.S. dollars? Explain and show the amount of the surplus/shortage on your graph.
   c. To bring the foreign exchange market back to an equilibrium at the fixed exchange rate, would the U.S. government need to buy or sell dollars? On your graph, illustrate how the government's buying or selling of dollars would bring the equilibrium exchange rate back to the desired fixed rate.

Rubric for FRQ 1 (9 points)

1 point: The vertical axis is labeled "Exchange rate (Indian rupees per U.S. dollar)" and the horizontal axis is labeled "Quantity of U.S. dollars."

1 point: Demand is downward-sloping and labeled; supply is upward-sloping and labeled.

1 point: The equilibrium exchange rate and the equilibrium quantity of dollars are labeled on the axes at the point where the supply and demand curves intersect.

1 point: The fixed exchange rate level is depicted above the equilibrium exchange rate.

1 point: The fixed exchange rate leads to a surplus.

1 point: The quantity supplied exceeds the quantity demanded at the higher fixed exchange rate.

1 point: The surplus is labeled as the horizontal distance between the supply and demand curves at the fixed exchange rate.

1 point: The U.S. government needs to buy dollars.

1 point: The new demand curve is shown to the right of the old demand curve, crossing the supply curve at the fixed exchange rate.

2. Suppose the United States and Australia were the only two countries in the world, and that both countries pursued a floating exchange rate regime. Note that the currency in Australia is the Australian dollar.
   a. Draw a correctly labeled graph showing equilibrium in the foreign exchange market for U.S. dollars.
   b. If the Federal Reserve pursues expansionary monetary policy, what will happen to the U.S. interest rate and international capital flows? Explain.
   c. On your graph of the foreign exchange market, illustrate the effect of the Fed's policy on the supply of U.S. dollars, the demand for U.S. dollars, and the equilibrium exchange rate.
   d. How does the Fed's monetary policy affect U.S. aggregate demand? Explain. **(10 points)**

Barriers to Trade

In this Module, you will learn to:
- Explain the pros and cons of protectionism
- Illustrate the effects of a tariff and an import quota

Trade Restrictions

It's natural for the citizens of a country to say, "We can make food, clothing, and almost everything we need. Why should we buy these goods from other countries and send our money overseas?" Module 4 explained the answer to this question: because specialization and trade make larger quantities of goods and services available to consumers. Yet the gains from trade are often overlooked, and many countries have experimented with a closed economy. Examples from the last century include Germany in 1933–1945, Spain in 1939–1959, Cambodia in 1975–1979, and Afghanistan in 1996–2001. The outcomes of these experiments were disappointing. By trying to make too many different products, these countries failed to specialize in what they were best at making; as a result, they ended up with less of most goods than trade would have provided.

A lack of transportation infrastructure can be a hindrance to trade for some countries.

Every country now has an open economy, although some economies are more open than others. **Figure 44.1** shows expenditures on imports as a percentage of GDP for select countries, which ranged from 12% in Brazil to 146% in Singapore. Several factors affect a country's approach to trade. Beyond the natural tendency for each country to want to be self-sufficient, special circumstances can limit the options for trade. For example, high transportation costs hinder trade for countries with primitive transportation systems as well as for countries that specialize in heavy, low-priced commodities such as bricks, drinking water, watermelons, or sand. Countries are wary of specialization that would make them overly reliant on other countries, because relationships with those countries could sour. And, as a matter of national pride, countries may prefer to make certain products on their own despite comparative disadvantages, such as food, art, weapons, and products that showcase technical know-how.

Figure 44.1 Imports of Goods and Services as a Percentage of GDP

International trade is an important part of every country's economy, but some economies are more open than others. In 2016, imports as a percentage of GDP ranged from 12% in Brazil to 146% in Singapore.

Data Source: The World Bank.

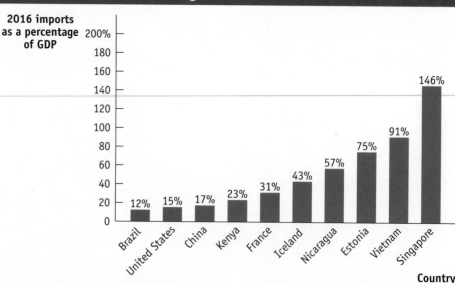

2016 imports as a percentage of GDP

Country	Percentage
Brazil	12%
United States	15%
China	17%
Kenya	23%
France	31%
Iceland	43%
Nicaragua	57%
Estonia	75%
Vietnam	91%
Singapore	146%

International trade can also have its casualties. As production shifts toward a country's comparative advantage, many workers in declining industries will lose their jobs and will remain structurally unemployed until or unless they can obtain the skills required in other industries. For example, as the United States imported more clothing from countries with a comparative advantage in textiles, workers in the Fruit of the Loom factory in Campbellsville, Kentucky, were among many who lost their jobs. Fortunately, the unemployment rates in Campbellsville and in the United States as a whole rose only temporarily. Many of these workers were able to adapt to the requirements of growing industries such as construction, automotive parts, health care, and software design, and were able to secure new jobs as a result.

Some industries may not initially be competitive at the international level, but they could attain a comparative advantage after a period of protection from lower-priced imports. This is the motivation for **protectionism**, the practice of limiting trade to protect domestic industries. *Tariffs* and *import quotas* are the primary tools of protectionism.

Protectionism is the practice of limiting trade to protect domestic industries.

Tariffs

The imposition of **tariffs**, which are taxes on imports, helps domestic industries and provides revenue for the government. The bad news is that tariffs make prices higher for domestic consumers and can spark trade wars. Early in American history, tariffs provided a majority of the revenue for the U.S. government, reaching a high of 97.9% in 1825. As the benefits of free trade came to light, and income and payroll taxes were adopted in the early 1900s, the use of tariffs diminished. By 1944, tariff revenue amounted to only about 1% of federal government revenue, which is still the case today.

Consider the U.S. market for ceramic plates, a hypothetical version of which is shown in **Figure 44.2**. The upward-sloping supply curve shows the supply from U.S. firms. The demand curve is for U.S. consumers only. If the United States had a closed economy, 5 million plates would sell for the no-trade equilibrium price of $15 each. However, suppose that an unlimited quantity of plates could be imported for the equilibrium price in the world market, $9. In the absence of trade restrictions,

Tariffs are taxes on imports.

> ### AP® EXAM TIP
>
> The effects of tariffs and quotas can be shown using supply and demand graphs. You should be able to illustrate and explain trade barriers using a graph for the AP® exam.

Figure 44.2 The U.S. Ceramic Plate Market with Imports

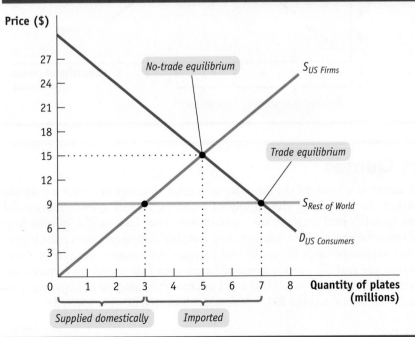

Without trade, 5 million plates would be sold at the no-trade equilibrium price of $15. An unlimited quantity of plates can be imported at the equilibrium world price of $9. With unrestricted trade, domestic firms will be unable to charge more than the world price, for which they are willing to supply 3 million plates. Domestic consumers will demand 7 million plates at a price of $9 each. The difference between the domestic demand and the domestic supply, 4 million plates, will be imported.

domestic firms would be unable to charge more than the world price. At the $9 world price, domestic firms would be willing to supply 3 million plates, but domestic consumers would demand 7 million. Four million imported plates would make up the difference between the 7 million plates demanded and the 3 million supplied in the domestic market.

Now suppose that the U.S. imposes a tariff of $3 per imported ceramic plate. As shown in **Figure 44.3**, that would effectively raise the curve that represents the supply from the rest of the world by $3. For every imported plate, the required payment would be $9 to the foreign suppliers plus $3 for the tariff, for a total of $12. Domestic firms would now be able to charge up to $12, for which they would be willing to supply 4 million plates, an increase of 1 million compared to the no-tariff situation. Domestic consumers would demand 6 million plates for $12, a decrease of 1 million from the no-tariff situation. Two million plates would be imported to make up the difference between the domestic supply of 4 million and the domestic demand of 6 million plates. Note that this is a drop of 2 million from the 4 million plates imported without the tariff. The tariff revenue would be 2 million × $3 = $6 million, as represented by the shaded rectangle in the figure.

Figure 44.3 A Tariff on Ceramic Plates

A tariff of $3 per imported ceramic plate effectively raises the curve that represents the supply from the rest of the world by $3. To receive an imported plate, one must pay $9 to the foreign suppliers plus $3 for the tariff, for a total of $12. Domestic firms can then charge up to $12, for which they are willing to supply 4 million plates. Domestic consumers demand 6 million plates for $12 each. Two million plates will be imported to make up the difference between the domestic supply and the domestic demand. This is 2 million less than the 4 million plates imported without the tariff.

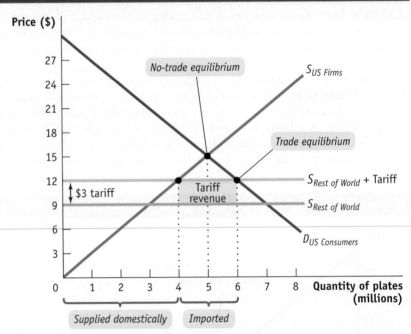

Import Quotas

An **import quota** is a limit on the quantity of a good that can be imported within a given period. By restricting the supply of imports, import quotas reduce the equilibrium quantity and increase the equilibrium price. Like tariffs, quotas help domestic firms compete with foreign suppliers, but they also cause prices to be higher for domestic consumers. Consider sugar, which Americans consume at a rate of about 11 million tons per year. To protect domestic sugar cane and sugar beet farmers, the U.S. Department of Agriculture (USDA) sets a quota for the amount of sugar that can be imported—1.5 million tons in 2017—before a substantial tariff is applied.

Figure 44.4   A Ceramic Plates Quota

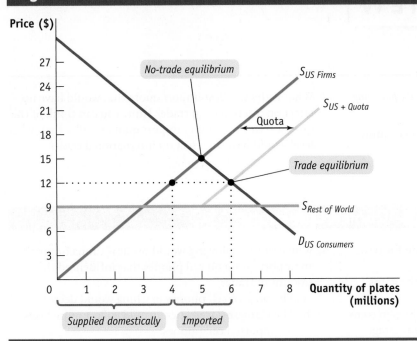

With an import quota of 2 million ceramic plates, consumers face the pink supply curve made up of the U.S. supply plus the 2 million plates that can be imported. Imports are not available for less than $9, so the pink U.S.-plus-quota supply curve does not extend below $9. At the $12 equilibrium price with the quota, a quantity of 6 million plates are purchased, 4 million of which are supplied domestically.

Suppose that the United States imposes an import quota of 2 million ceramic plates. That quota would prevent a trade equilibrium at the intersection of U.S. consumers' demand and the supply from the rest of the world because, as we saw in Figure 44.2, that equilibrium would require imports of 4 million plates. Instead, consumers would face the pink supply curve in **Figure 44.4**, which represents the U.S. supply plus the 2 million plates that could be imported with the quota. Imports would not be available for less than $9, so the U.S.-plus-quota supply curve does not extend below a price of $9. The equilibrium price with the quota is $12. Six million plates would be sold at that price, 4 million of which would be made domestically. Notice that the quota of 2 million plates would have the same effect on the price, imports, and domestic supply as the $3 tariff. One difference is that with the quota, no tariff revenue would be collected.

The use of tariffs and import quotas is seldom one-sided. When one country erects a trade barrier against another, retaliation is common. For instance, in 2018, after the Trump administration threatened to impose a tariff on imported steel, European Union leaders threatened to raise tariffs on items imported from the United States, such as bourbon and blue jeans. Escalating trade wars can obliterate the gains from trade, which motivates many countries to move in the opposite direction and negotiate the elimination of trade barriers. Trade agreements such as the North American Free Trade Agreement and the Dominican Republic–Central America Free Trade Agreement limit the use of tariffs, quotas, regulations, and other impediments to trade among the economies involved.

AP® EXAM TIP

Tariffs and quotas both affect the price and quantity in a market, but tariffs provide governments with revenues and quotas do not.

Check Your Understanding

Use the information provided in Figure 44.2 to answer the following questions:

1. What is the smallest tariff that would cause all ceramic plates to be supplied by U.S. firms?

2. What is the smallest import quota that would have no effect on international trade? Hint: You can think of the question this way: Every import quota smaller than what level would have an effect on international trade?

TACKLE THE AP® TEST: Multiple-Choice Questions

1. Which of the following is put forth as a reason for trade restrictions?
   a. National pride can take precedence over the gains from trade.
   b. Domestic industries need protection from foreign competition while they develop a comparative advantage.
   c. Citizens don't want to send their money overseas.
   d. Countries don't want to become overly reliant on other countries.
   e. All of the above are reasons.

2. The purpose of protectionism is to protect domestic
   a. resources.   d. exporters.
   b. consumption levels. e. all of the above
   c. industries.

3. Which of the following would result from a U.S. tariff on imported cars?
   a. The profit of U.S. car manufacturers would decrease.
   b. The price paid for cars in the United States would increase.
   c. More cars would be imported.
   d. Fewer domestically made cars would be sold in the United States.
   e. More cars from all sources would be sold in the United States.

4. An import quota is a
   a. minimum quantity of a good that may be imported.
   b. minimum quantity of a good that a factory must produce and sell overseas.
   c. maximum quantity of a good that may be imported.
   d. maximum quantity of a good that a factory may produce and sell overseas.
   e. maximum price that a company can charge for imports.

5. Which of the following would result if China imposed an import quota on cell phones that influenced the amount of trade?
   a. The price of cell phones in China would decrease.
   b. The Chinese government would collect more taxes on imported cell phones.
   c. More cell phones made outside of China would be sold in China.
   d. More cell phones made in China would be sold in China.
   e. More cell phones from all sources would be sold in China.

6. Which of the following is a difference between the effects of a tariff and the effects of a quota relative to the free-trade output?
   a. Domestic supply increases with a quota but not a tariff.
   b. Domestic price decreases with a tariff but not a quota.
   c. Government revenue decreases with a quota but not a tariff.
   d. Government revenue increases with a tariff but not a quota.
   e. Imports increase with a tariff but not a quota.

7. Which of the following is true regarding trade agreements?
   a. They increase tariffs.
   b. They increase regulations.
   c. They decrease impediments to trade.
   d. They enact quotas.
   e. They initiate trade wars.

TACKLE THE AP® TEST: Free-Response Questions

1. Suppose that rice is traded in the world market at a price of US$1 per pound, and that in the absence of trade, the equilibrium price of rice in Mexico is US$1.25 per pound.
   a. Draw a correctly labeled graph that shows the domestic supply and demand for rice in Mexico.
   b. Label the no-trade equilibrium and the trade equilibrium.
   c. Use labeled brackets to indicate the portions of the horizontal axis that represent
      i. the quantity of rice imported at the world price.
      ii. the quantity of rice supplied domestically at the world price.
   d. Suppose that Mexico imposes a tariff of US$0.15 per pound of imported rice.
      i. Label the new trade equilibrium.
      ii. Shade the area that represents the total tariff revenue.

2. Suppose that cheese is traded in the world market at a price of €3 per pound. Assume that France has no trade barriers and has supply and demand curves for cheese as shown in the graph.

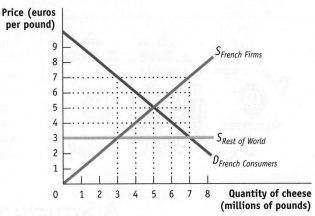

   a. How much cheese does France import?
   b. Suppose that France adopts an import quota of 2 million pounds of cheese.
      i. What will the price be at the new trade equilibrium?
      ii. How much cheese will French suppliers provide domestically with the quota in place?
      iii. If France imposed a tariff instead of a quota to restrict cheese imports, a tariff of what amount per pound would result in imports of 2 million pounds of cheese?
   c. Suppose that instead of any other trade restriction, France imposed a tariff of €4 per pound of cheese. How much cheese would France import? Explain. **(6 points)**

Rubric for FRQ 1 (6 points)

1 point: Graph shows "Price" on the vertical axis, "Quantity of Rice" on the horizontal axis, downward-sloping demand, upward-sloping supply, and the no-trade equilibrium.

1 point: Horizontal rest-of-world supply curve and trade equilibrium are presented as shown in the figure.

1 point: Graph shows correct indication of imported quantity.

1 point: Graph shows correct indication of domestically supplied quantity.

1 point: Horizontal rest-of-world supply + tariff curve and new trade equilibrium are presented as in the figure.

1 point: Shaded area that represents tariff revenue is presented as in the figure.

Putting It All Together

> **In this Module, you will learn to:**
> - Use macroeconomic models to conduct policy analysis
> - Improve your approach to free-response macroeconomics questions

Barcin/Getty Images

Having completed our study of basic macroeconomic models, we can use them to analyze scenarios and evaluate policy recommendations. In this Module we develop a step-by-step approach to macroeconomic analysis. You can adapt this approach to problems involving any macroeconomic model, including models of aggregate demand and supply, production possibilities, money markets, and the Phillips curve. By the end of this module you will be able to combine mastery of the principles of macroeconomics with problem solving skills to analyze a new scenario on your own.

A Structure for Macroeconomic Analysis

In our study of macroeconomics we have seen questions about the macroeconomy take many different forms. No matter what the specific question, most macroeconomic problems have the following components:

1. *A starting point.* To analyze any situation, you have to know where to start.
2. *A pivotal event.* This might be a change in the economy or a policy response to the initial situation.
3. *Initial effects of the event.* An event will generally have some initial, short-run effects.
4. *Secondary and long-run effects of the event.* After the short-run effects run their course, there are typically secondary effects and the economy will move toward its long-run equilibrium.

For example, you might be asked to consider the following scenario and answer the associated questions.

Assume the U.S. economy is currently operating at an aggregate output level above potential output. Draw a correctly labeled graph showing aggregate demand, short-run aggregate supply, long-run aggregate supply, equilibrium output, and the aggregate price level.

Now assume that the Federal Reserve conducts contractionary monetary policy. Identify the open market operation the Fed would conduct, and draw a correctly labeled graph of the money market to show the effect of the monetary policy on the nominal interest rate.

Show and explain how the Fed's actions will affect equilibrium in the aggregate demand and supply graph you drew previously. Indicate the new aggregate price level on your graph.

Assume Canada is the largest trading partner of the United States. Draw a correctly labeled graph of the foreign exchange market for the U.S. dollar showing how the change in the aggregate price level you indicate on your graph above will affect the foreign exchange market. What will happen to the value of the U.S. dollar relative to the Canadian dollar?

How will the Federal Reserve's contractionary monetary policy affect the real interest rate in the United States in the long run? Explain.

Taken as a whole, this scenario and the associated questions can seem overwhelming. Let's start by breaking down our analysis into four components.

1. **The starting point**
   Assume the U.S. economy is currently operating at an aggregate output level above potential output.

2. **The pivotal event**
   Now assume that the Federal Reserve conducts contractionary monetary policy.

3. **Initial effects of the event**
   Show and explain how the Fed's actions will affect equilibrium.

4. **Secondary and long-run effects of the event**
   Assume Canada is the largest trading partner of the United States. What will happen to the value of the U.S. dollar relative to the Canadian dollar?
   How will the Federal Reserve's contractionary monetary policy affect the real interest rate in the United States in the long run? Explain.

Now we are ready to look at each of the steps and untangle this scenario.

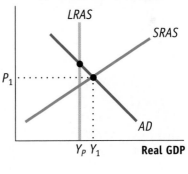

How will the Fed's monetary policy change nominal interest rates?

The Starting Point

Assume the U.S. economy is currently operating at an aggregate output level above potential output. Draw a correctly labeled graph showing aggregate demand, short-run aggregate supply, long-run aggregate supply, equilibrium output, and the aggregate price level.

To analyze a situation, you have to know where to start. You will most often use the aggregate demand–aggregate supply (*AD-AS*) model to evaluate macroeconomic scenarios. In this model, there are three possible starting points: long-run macroeconomic equilibrium, a recessionary gap, and an inflationary gap. This means that there are three possible "starting-point" graphs, as shown in **Figure 45.1**. The economy can be in long-run macroeconomic equilibrium with production at potential output as in panel (a); it can be in short-run macroeconomic equilibrium at an aggregate output level below potential output (creating a recessionary gap) as in panel (b); or it can be in short-run macroeconomic equilibrium at an aggregate output level above potential output (creating an inflationary gap) as in panel (c) and in our scenario.

> **AP® EXAM TIP**
>
> With the infinite number of possible changes in policy, politics, the economy, and markets around the world, don't expect to analyze a familiar scenario on the exam. But if you understand how to use the macroeconomic models (as we discuss in this module), you will be ready for whatever scenarios you face!

Figure 45.1 Analysis Starting Points

Panels (a), (b), and (c) represent the three basic starting points for analysis using the aggregate demand–aggregate supply model.

The Pivotal Event

Now assume that the Federal Reserve conducts contractionary monetary policy.

It is the events in a scenario that make it interesting. Perhaps a country goes into or recovers from a recession, inflation catches consumers off guard or becomes expected, consumers or businesses become more or less confident, holdings of money or wealth change, trading partners prosper or falter, or oil prices plummet or spike. The event can also be expansionary or contractionary monetary or fiscal policy.

While it's impossible to foresee all of the scenarios you might encounter, we can group the determinants of change into a reasonably small set of major factors that influence macroeconomic models. **Table 45.1** matches major factors with the curves they affect. With these influences in mind, it is relatively easy to proceed through a problem by identifying how the given events affect these factors. Most hypothetical scenarios involve changes in just one or two major factors. Although the real world is more complex, it is largely the same factors that change—there are just more of them changing at once.

Table 45.1	**Major Factors that Shift Curves in Each Model**	
Aggregate Demand and Aggregate Supply		
Aggregate Demand Curve	**Short-Run Aggregate Supply Curve**	**Long-Run Aggregate Supply Curve**
Expectations	Commodity prices	Productivity
Wealth	Nominal wages	Physical capital
Size of existing capital stock	Productivity	Human capital
Fiscal and monetary policy	Business taxes	Technology
Net exports		Quantity of resources
Interest rates		
Investment spending		
Supply and Demand		
Demand Curve	**Supply Curve**	
Income	Input prices	
Prices of substitutes and complements (related goods)	Prices of substitutes and complements (related goods) in production	
Tastes	Technology	
Consumer expectations	Producer expectations	
Number of consumers	Number of producers	
Loanable Funds Market		
Demand Curve	**Supply Curve**	
Investment opportunities	Private saving behavior	
Government borrowing	Capital inflows	
Money Market		
Demand Curve	**Supply Curve**	
Aggregate price level	Set by the Federal Reserve	
Real GDP		
Technology (related to money market)		
Institutions (related to money market)		
Foreign Exchange Market		
Demand	**Supply**	
Foreigners' purchases of domestic	Domestic residents' purchases of foreign	
Goods	Goods	
Services	Services	
Assets	Assets	

Note: It is the *real* exchange rate (adjusted for international differences in aggregate price levels) that affects imports and exports.

As shown in Table 45.1, many curves are shifted by changes in only two or three major factors. Even for the aggregate demand curve, which has the largest number of associated factors, you can simplify the task further by asking yourself, "Does the event influence consumer spending, investment spending, government spending, or net exports?" If so, aggregate demand shifts. A shift of the long-run aggregate supply curve is caused only by events that affect labor productivity or the number of workers.

In the supply and demand model there are five major factors that shift the demand curve and five major factors that shift the supply curve. Most examples using this model will represent a change in one of these 10 factors. The loanable funds market, money market, and foreign exchange market have their own clearly identified factors that affect supply or demand. With this information you can link specific events to relevant factors in the models to see what changes will occur. Remember that having correctly labeled axes on your graphs is crucial to a correct analysis.

Often, as in our scenario, the event is a policy response to an undesirable starting point such as a recessionary or inflationary gap. Expansionary policy is used to combat a recession, and contractionary policy is used to combat inflationary pressures. To begin analyzing a policy response, you need to fully understand how the Federal Reserve can implement each type of monetary policy (e.g., increase or decrease the money supply) and how that policy eventually affects the economy. You also need to understand how the government can implement expansionary or contractionary fiscal policy by raising or lowering taxes or government spending.

The Initial Effect of the Event

Show and explain how the Fed's actions will affect equilibrium.

We have seen that events will create short-run effects in our models. In the short run, fiscal and monetary policy both affect the economy by shifting the aggregate demand curve. As shown in panel (a) of **Figure 45.2**, expansionary policy shifts aggregate demand to the right, and as shown in panel (b), contractionary policy shifts aggregate demand to the left. To illustrate the effect of a policy response, shift the aggregate demand curve on your starting point graph and indicate the effects of the shift on the aggregate price level and aggregate output.

Figure 45.2 Monetary and Fiscal Policy Close Output Gaps

By shifting the aggregate demand curve, monetary and fiscal policy can close output gaps in the economy as shown in panel (a) for a recessionary gap and panel (b) for an inflationary gap.

Secondary and Long-Run Effects of the Event

Assume Canada is the largest trading partner of the United States. What will happen to the value of the U.S. dollar relative to the Canadian dollar?

How will the Federal Reserve's contractionary monetary policy affect the real interest rate in the United States in the long run? Explain.

Secondary Effects

In addition to the initial, short-run effects of any event, there will be secondary effects and the economy will move to its long-run equilibrium after the short-run effects run their course.

We have seen that negative or positive demand shocks (including those created by inappropriate monetary or fiscal policy) move the economy away from long-run macroeconomic equilibrium. As explained in Module 18, in the absence of policy responses, such events will eventually be offset through changes in short-run aggregate supply resulting from changes in nominal wage rates. This will move the economy back to long-run macroeconomic equilibrium.

If the short-run effects of an action result in changes in the aggregate price level or real interest rate, there will also be secondary effects throughout the open economy. International capital flows and international trade will be affected as a result of the initial effects experienced in the economy. A price level decrease, as in our scenario, will encourage exports and discourage imports, causing an appreciation in the domestic currency on the foreign exchange market. A change in the interest rate affects aggregate demand through changes in investment spending and consumer spending. Interest rate changes also affect aggregate demand through changes in imports or exports caused by currency appreciation and depreciation. These secondary effects act to reinforce the effects of monetary policy.

You've seen the speech, now, how would you analyze the proposed policy?

Long-Run Effects

While deviations from potential output are ironed out in the long run, other effects remain. For example, in the long run the use of fiscal policy affects the federal budget. Changes in taxes or government spending that lead to budget deficits (and increased federal debt) can "crowd out" private investment spending in the long run. The government's increased demand for loanable funds drives up the interest rate, decreases investment spending, and partially offsets the initial increase in aggregate demand. Of course, the deficit could be addressed by printing money, but that would lead to problems with inflation in the long run.

We know that in the long run, monetary policy affects only the aggregate price level, not real GDP. Because money is neutral, changes in the money supply have no effect on the real economy. The aggregate price level and nominal values will be affected by the same proportion, leaving real values (including the real interest rate as mentioned in our scenario) unchanged.

Analyzing Our Scenario

Now let's address the specific demands of our problem.

- Draw a correctly labeled graph showing aggregate demand, short-run aggregate supply, long-run aggregate supply, equilibrium output, and the aggregate price level.

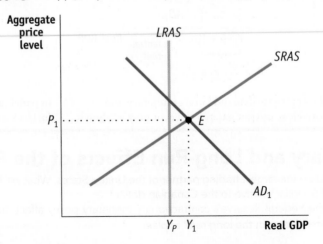

- Identify the open-market operation the Fed would conduct.

  The Fed would sell U.S. Treasury securities (bonds, bills, or notes).

- Draw a correctly labeled graph of the money market to show the effect of the monetary policy on the nominal interest rate.

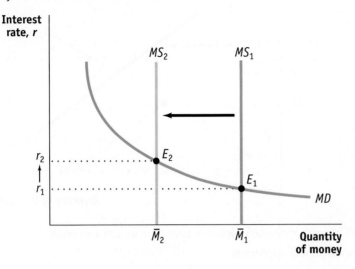

- Show and explain how the Fed's actions will affect equilibrium in the aggregate demand and supply graph you drew previously. Indicate the new aggregate price level on your graph.

  A higher interest rate will lead to decreased investment and consumer spending, decreasing aggregate demand. The equilibrium price level and real GDP will fall.

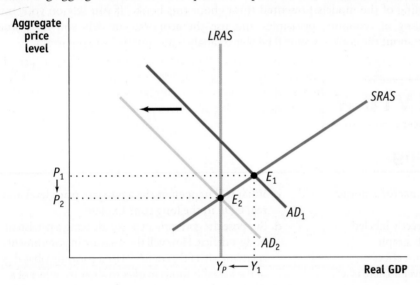

- Draw a correctly labeled graph of the foreign exchange market for the U.S. dollar showing how the change in the aggregate price level you indicate on your graph above will affect the foreign exchange market.

  The decrease in the U.S. price level will make U.S. exports relatively inexpensive for Canadians to purchase and will lead to an increase in demand for U.S. dollars with which to purchase those exports.

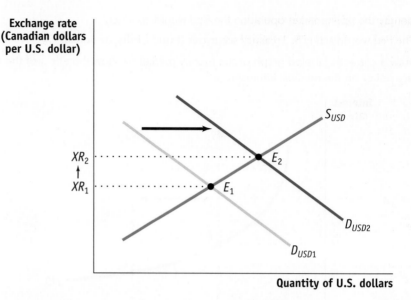

Exchange rate
(Canadian dollars
per U.S. dollar)

XR_2 .... E_2 — S_{USD}

XR_1 .... E_1

D_{USD2}

D_{USD1}

Quantity of U.S. dollars

- What will happen to the U.S. dollar relative to the Canadian dollar?

  The U.S. dollar will appreciate.

- How will the Federal Reserve's contractionary monetary policy affect the real interest rate in the United States in the long run? Explain.

  There will be no effect on the real interest rate in the long run because, due to the neutrality of money, changes in the money supply do not affect real values in the long run.

  Each AP exam presents students with new scenarios designed to test their understanding of the models presented throughout this book. If you rely on your understanding of economic principles and use the economic models you have studied throughout the course, you will be able to analyze any unfamiliar scenario!

MODULE 45 REVIEW

Check Your Understanding

1. The economy is operating in long-run macroeconomic equilibrium.
   a. Illustrate this situation using a correctly labeled aggregate demand–aggregate supply graph.
   b. Use your graph to show the short-run effect on real GDP and the aggregate price level if there is a decrease in government spending.
   c. What will happen to the aggregate price level and real GDP in the long run? Explain.
   d. Suppose the government is experiencing a persistent budget deficit. How will the decrease in government spending affect that deficit? Use a correctly labeled graph of the loanable funds market to show the effect of a decrease in government spending on the interest rate.

TACKLE THE AP® TEST: Multiple-Choice Questions

Questions 1–7 refer to the following scenario:

The United States and Mexico are trading partners. Suppose a flu outbreak significantly decreases U.S. tourism in Mexico and causes the Mexican economy to enter a recession. Assume that the money that would have been spent by U.S. tourists in Mexico is, instead, not spent at all.

1. Which of the following occurs as a result of the recession in Mexico?
   a. Output in Mexico decreases.
   b. Aggregate demand in the United States decreases.
   c. The price level in Mexico increases.
   d. Output in the United States decreases.
   e. The price level in the United States decreases.

2. What is the effect of Mexico's falling income on the demand for money and the nominal interest rate in Mexico?

	Demand for money	Nominal interest rate
a.	increases	decreases
b.	decreases	decreases
c.	increases	increases
d.	decreases	increases
e.	increases	no change

3. Given what happens to the nominal interest rate, if the aggregate price level in Mexico decreases, what will happen to the real interest rate?
  a. It will increase.
  b. It will decrease.
  c. It will not change.
  d. It will stabilize.
  e. The effect cannot be determined.

4. Suppose the aggregate price level in Mexico decreases relative to that in the United States. What is the effect of this price level change on the demand, and on the exchange rate, for Mexican pesos?

	Demand for pesos	Exchange rate
a.	increases	appreciates
b.	increases	depreciates
c.	decreases	appreciates
d.	decreases	depreciates
e.	decreases	no change

5. If the Mexican government pursues expansionary fiscal policy in response to the recession, what will happen to aggregate demand and aggregate supply in Mexico in the short run?

	Aggregate demand	Short-run aggregate supply
a.	increases	increases
b.	increases	decreases
c.	decreases	increases
d.	decreases	decreases
e.	increases	no change

6. Suppose the government of Mexico pursues an expansionary fiscal policy leading to an increased budget deficit and national debt. If the government borrows to finance the debt, what will happen in the market for loanable funds?

	Interest rate	Quantity of loanable funds
a.	increase	increase
b.	increase	decrease
c.	decrease	increase
d.	decrease	decrease
e.	increase	no change

7. How will a decrease in U.S. tourism to Mexico resulting from a flu outbreak affect Mexico's *LRAS* curve and long-run economic growth?

	LRAS	Long-run growth
a.	shift to the right	increase
b.	shift to the left	decrease
c.	shift to the right	decrease
d.	shift to the left	increase
e.	no change	no change

TACKLE THE AP® TEST: Free-Response Questions

1. Suppose the U.S. economy is experiencing a recession.
  a. Draw a correctly labeled aggregate demand–aggregate supply graph showing the aggregate demand, short-run aggregate supply, long-run aggregate supply, equilibrium output, and aggregate price level.
  b. Assume that energy prices increase in the United States. Show the effects of this increase on the equilibrium in your graph from part a.
  c. According to your graph, how does the increase in energy prices affect unemployment and inflation in the economy?
  d. Assume the United States and Canada are the only two countries in an open economy and that energy prices have remained unchanged in Canada. Draw a correctly labeled graph of the foreign exchange market for U.S. dollars, and use it to show the effect of increased U.S. energy prices on the demand for U.S. dollars. Explain.

Rubric for FRQ 1 (12 points)

1 point: The vertical axis is labeled "Aggregate price level" and the horizontal axis is labeled "Aggregate output" or "Real GDP."

1 point: The *AD* curve slopes downward, the *SRAS* curve slopes upward, and the *LRAS* curve is vertical.

1 point: The equilibrium is found where the *SRAS* curve crosses the *AD* curve, and the equilibrium aggregate price level and aggregate output are shown on the axes at this point.

1 point: The equilibrium is to the left of the *LRAS* curve.

1 point: The *SRAS* curve shifts to the left.

1 point: The equilibrium aggregate price level and output are shown on the axes at the new equilibrium (increased aggregate price level, decreased aggregate output).

1 point: It increases unemployment.

1 point: It increases the aggregate price level (inflation).

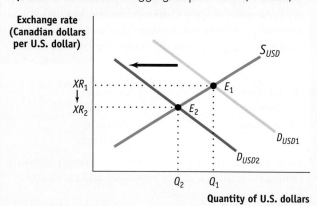

1 point: The vertical axis is labeled "Exchange rate (Canadian dollars per U.S. dollar)" and the horizontal axis is labeled "Quantity of U.S. dollars." Demand for U.S. dollars slopes downward and is labeled; supply of U.S. dollars slopes upward and is labeled.

1 point: The equilibrium exchange rate and quantity of U.S. dollars are shown on the axes at the intersection of the demand and supply curves.

1 point: The demand for U.S. dollars will decrease.

1 point: The inflation in the United States will lead to a decrease in the demand for U.S. exports (which must be purchased with U.S. dollars).

2. Assume the United States is operating below potential output.
   a. Draw a correctly labeled aggregate demand–aggregate supply graph showing equilibrium in the economy.
   b. Suppose the government decreases taxes. On your graph, show how the decrease in taxes will affect *AD*, *SRAS*, *LRAS*, equilibrium aggregate price level, and output.
   c. Assume the decrease in taxes led to an increased budget deficit and that the deficit spending was funded through government borrowing from the public. Use a correctly labeled graph of the market for loanable funds to show the effect of increased borrowing on the interest rate.
   d. Given the effect on the interest rate from part c, draw a correctly labeled graph of the foreign exchange market showing the effect of the change in the interest rate on the supply of U.S. dollars. Explain how the interest rate affects the supply of U.S. dollars.
   e. According to your graph from part d, what has happened to the value of the U.S. dollar? How will this affect U.S. exports and aggregate demand? **(12 points)**

SECTION 8 Review

 SECTION 8 Review Video

Adventures in AP® Economics Videos

Mod 42: Exchange Rates

Module 41

1. A country's **balance of payments accounts** summarize its transactions with the rest of the world. The **balance of payments on the current account**, or the **current account**, includes the **balance of payments on goods and services** together with balances on factor income and transfers. The **merchandise trade balance**, or **trade balance**, is a frequently cited component of the balance of payments on goods and services. The **balance of payments on the financial account**, or the **financial account**, measures capital flows. By definition, the balance of payments on the current account plus the balance of payments on the financial account is zero.

2. Capital flows respond to international differences in interest rates and other rates of return; they can be usefully analyzed using an international version of the loanable funds model, which shows how a country where the interest rate would be low in the absence of capital flows sends funds to a country where the interest rate would be high in the absence of capital flows. The underlying determinants of capital flows are international differences in savings and opportunities for investment spending.

Module 42

3. Currencies are traded in the **foreign exchange market**; the prices at which they are traded are **exchange rates**. When a currency rises against another currency, it **appreciates**; when it falls, it **depreciates**. The **equilibrium exchange rate** matches the quantity of that currency supplied to the foreign exchange market to the quantity demanded.

4. To correct for international differences in inflation rates, economists calculate **real exchange rates**, which multiply the exchange rate between two countries' respective currencies by the ratio of the countries' price levels. The current account responds only to changes in the real exchange rate, not the nominal exchange rate. **Purchasing power parity** is the exchange rate that makes the cost of a basket of goods and services equal in two countries. While purchasing power parity and the nominal exchange rate almost always differ, purchasing power parity is a good predictor of actual changes in the nominal exchange rate.

Module 43

5. Countries adopt different exchange rate regimes, rules governing exchange rate policy. The main types are **fixed exchange rates**, where the government takes action to keep the exchange rate at a target level, and **floating exchange rates**, where the exchange rate is free to fluctuate. Countries can fix exchange rates using exchange market intervention, which requires them to hold foreign exchange reserves that they use to buy any surplus of their currency. Alternatively, they can change domestic policies, especially monetary policy, to shift the demand and supply curves in the foreign exchange market. Finally, they can use foreign exchange controls.

6. Exchange rate policy poses a dilemma: there are economic payoffs to stable exchange rates, but the policies used to fix the exchange rate have costs. Exchange market intervention requires large reserves, and exchange controls distort incentives. If monetary policy is used to help fix the exchange rate, it isn't available to use for domestic policy.

7. Fixed exchange rates aren't always permanent commitments: countries with a fixed exchange rate sometimes engage in **devaluations** or **revaluations**. In addition to helping eliminate a surplus of domestic currency on the foreign exchange market, a devaluation increases aggregate demand. Similarly, a revaluation reduces shortages of domestic currency and reduces aggregate demand.

8. Under floating exchange rates, expansionary monetary policy works in part through the exchange rate: cutting domestic interest rates leads to a depreciation, and through that to higher exports and lower imports, which increases aggregate demand. Contractionary monetary policy has the reverse effect.

9. The fact that one country's imports are another country's exports creates a link between the business cycles in different countries. Floating exchange rates, however, may reduce the strength of that link.

Module 44

10. **Protectionism** is the practice of limiting trade to protect domestic industries. The idea is to allow domestic producers to gain enough strength to compete in global markets. Taxes on imports, known as **tariffs**, and limits on the quantities of goods that can be imported, known as **import quotas**, are the primary tools of protectionism.

Key Terms

Balance of payments accounts, p. 390
Balance of payments on the current account (current account), p. 392
Balance of payments on goods and services, p. 392
Merchandise trade balance (trade balance), p. 392
Balance of payments on the financial account (financial account), p. 392
Foreign exchange market, p. 399
Exchange rates, p. 399
Appreciates, p. 400
Depreciates, p. 400
Equilibrium exchange rate, p. 401
Real exchange rates, p. 403
Purchasing power parity, p. 405
Fixed exchange rate, p. 408
Floating exchange rate, p. 408
Devaluation, p. 411
Revaluation, p. 411
Protectionism, p. 417
Tariffs, p. 417
Import quota, p. 418

Multiple-Choice Questions

1. Which of the following transactions is counted in the U.S. current account?
   a. A French importer buys a case of California wine.
   b. An American working for a Brazilian company deposits her paycheck.
   c. An American buys a bond from a Japanese company.
   d. An American charity sends money to an African aid agency.
   e. A Chinese national buys stock in a U.S. company.

2. The difference between a country's exports and imports of goods is that country's
   a. balance of payments on its current account.
   b. balance of payments on its financial account.
   c. balance of payments on its capital account.
   d. merchandise trade balance.
   e. balance of payments on goods and services.

3. Which of the following relationships between the current account (*CA*) and the financial account (*FA*) must be true?
   a. $CA - FA = 0$
   b. $CA + FA = 0$
   c. $CA = FA$
   d. $CA = 1/FA$
   e. $(CA)(FA) = 1$

4. Which of the following is a reason for capital to flow into a country?
   a. a rapidly growing economy
   b. government budget surpluses
   c. higher savings rates
   d. lower interest rates
   e. a relatively high supply of loanable funds

Refer to the following graphs and information for Questions 5–7.

Suppose that Northlandia and Southlandia are the only two trading countries in the world, that each nation runs a balance of payments on both the current account and the financial account equal to zero, and that each nation sees the other's assets as identical to its own.

(a) Northlandia

(b) Southlandia

5. Given the situation depicted in the graphs, which of the following will happen?
   a. The interest rate in Northlandia will rise.
   b. The interest rate in Southlandia will fall.
   c. Capital will flow into Northlandia.
   d. Capital will flow into Southlandia.
   e. Southlandia will experience a balance of trade deficit.

6. Which of the following will happen in Southlandia?
   a. The quantity of loanable funds supplied will decrease.
   b. The supply of loanable funds will increase.
   c. The demand for loanable funds will decrease.
   d. The supply of loanable funds will decrease.
   e. The interest rate will decrease.

7. If the international equilibrium interest rate is 8%, which of the following will be true?
   a. Southlandia will experience a capital outflow of $250.
   b. Southlandia will experience a capital outflow of $700.
   c. Northlandia will experience a capital outflow of $250.
   d. Northlandia will experience a capital outflow of $300.
   e. The international equilibrium quantity of loanable funds will be $1,200.

8. Which of the following is traded in a foreign exchange market?
   a. imported goods only
   b. exported goods only
   c. both imported and exported goods
   d. international stocks and bonds
   e. currency

9. Which of the following will occur in the foreign exchange market as a result of capital inflow to the United States?
   a. a decrease in the demand for dollars
   b. a decrease in the dollar exchange rate
   c. an increase in the supply of dollars
   d. appreciation of the dollar
   e. a decrease in the quantity of dollars exchanged

10. The price in a foreign exchange market is a(n)
   a. real interest rate.
   b. nominal interest rate.
   c. tariff.
   d. exchange rate.
   e. discount rate.

Refer to the following graph and information for Questions 11–12.

The graph shows the foreign exchange market for the bern, the currency used in the country of Albernia.

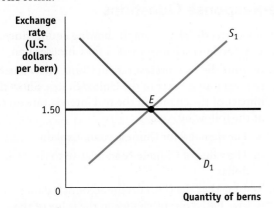

11. Given the equilibrium exchange rate on the graph, which of the following is true regarding the bern?
   a. It takes $1.50 to buy a bern.
   b. It takes $0.75 to buy a bern.
   c. It takes $0.67 to buy a bern.
   d. It takes 1.50 bern to buy a dollar.
   e. It takes 0.75 bern to buy a dollar.

12. How could depreciation of the bern be shown on the graph?
   a. a movement of the equilibrium exchange rate to 2
   b. a movement of the equilibrium exchange rate to 1
   c. a decrease in the equilibrium quantity of berns
   d. a rightward shift of the demand for berns
   e. a leftward shift of the supply of berns

13. Real exchange rates are adjusted for international differences in
   a. exchange rates.
   b. aggregate price levels.
   c. GDP per capita.
   d. capital flows.
   e. income.

14. Which of the following is true if two countries have purchasing power parity?
   a. The two countries' real GDP per capita is the same.
   b. The two countries' imports equal their exports.
   c. The nominal exchange rate ensures that goods cost the same amount in each country.
   d. There are no capital inflows or outflows between the two countries.
   e. The countries' exchange rates do not appreciate or depreciate.

15. When a government lets exchange rates be determined by foreign exchange markets, it is called
   a. an exchange rate regime.
   b. a fixed exchange rate.
   c. a floating exchange rate.
   d. a market exchange rate.
   e. a foreign exchange control.

16. Governments intervene to keep the value of their currency down in order to
   a. make domestic goods cheaper in the world market.
   b. decrease the price of imported goods.
   c. promote capital inflows.
   d. decrease exports.
   e. reduce aggregate demand.

17. A decrease in domestic interest rates will necessarily have which of the following effects in the foreign exchange market?
   a. The supply of the domestic currency will decrease.
   b. The demand for the domestic currency will decrease.
   c. The exchange rate will increase.
   d. The quantity of the domestic currency exchanged will rise.
   e. The quantity of the domestic currency exchanged will fall.

18. An import quota on a good will do which of the following?
   a. It will raise revenue for the government.
   b. It will reduce the domestic price of the good.
   c. It will raise the international price of the good.
   d. It will reduce the quantity of the good sold domestically.
   e. It will decrease domestic production of the good.

19. Which of the following is true of tariffs?
   a. They are limits on the quantity of a good that can be imported.
   b. They account for over 10% of federal government revenue in the United States.
   c. They can result in trade wars between countries.
   d. They do not protect domestic industries from competition.
   e. They decrease the price of goods.

20. A goal of protectionism is to
   a. generate revenue for the federal government.
   b. lower the price of goods for domestic consumers.
   c. increase world output through specialization and comparative advantage.
   d. decrease competition for domestic industries.
   e. raise the price of imported goods.

Questions 21 and 22 refer to the following graph.

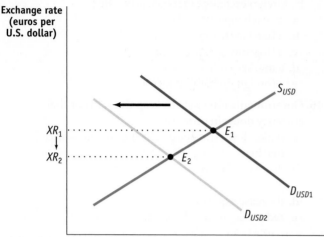

Exchange rate (euros per U.S. dollar)

Quantity of U.S. dollars

	Demand for USD	Demand for AUD	International Value of AUD
a.	no change	decreases	depreciates
b.	increases	no change	depreciates
c.	no change	decreases	appreciates
d.	decreases	no change	depreciates
e.	increase	increases	appreciates

21. Which of the following could cause the movement from D_{USD1} to D_{USD2}?
   a. More Americans travel to Europe.
   b. The aggregate price level in the United States falls.
   c. Exports from the United States increase.
   d. Interest rates in the United States rise.
   e. Europe goes into a recession.

22. When the exchange rate moves from XR_1 to XR_2, the U.S. dollar has
   a. appreciated.
   b. depreciated.
   c. revalued.
   d. become more valuable.
   e. caused the relative price level in the United States to rise.

23. Assume the aggregate price level in Mexico increases relative to the aggregate price level in Canada. What will happen to the exchange rate between Mexico and Canada (expressed as Mexican pesos per Canadian dollar)?
   a. It will increase.
   b. It will decrease.
   c. It remains unchanged.
   d. It will depreciate.
   e. The effect on the exchange rate cannot be determined.

24. Which of the following will result from the imposition of an import quota?
   a. an increase in government revenue
   b. an increase in imports
   c. a decrease in domestic supply
   d. an increase in domestic demand
   e. an increase in domestic price

25. Assume the U.S. dollar (USD) is exchanged for the Australian dollar (AUD). If GDP in Australia increases, what will happen to each of the following?

Free-Response Questions

1. Draw a correctly labeled graph showing equilibrium in the U.S. foreign exchange market for Chinese yuan.
   a. Assume the real interest rate in China falls relative to the real interest rate in the United States. Show the impact of the change in the real interest rate on each of the following.
      i. The demand for Chinese yuan. Explain.
      ii. The value of Chinese yuan relative to the U.S. dollar.
   b. Assume that the U.S. current account balance is zero. Based on the change in the value of the yuan, will the U.S. current account balance move to a surplus, move to a deficit, or stay the same? Explain. **(6 points)**

2. Assume the two countries, Xenia and Yania, have flexible exchange rates. The currency in Xenia is the xen dollar (XD), and the currency in Yania is the yan dollar (YD).
   a. Assume the current account in Yania is in deficit and the price level declines. Use a correctly labeled graph of the foreign exchange market to show the effect on the value of the YD.
   b. Will the current account deficit in Yania increase, decrease, or remain unchanged? Explain. **(5 points)**

3. Assume the economy of the country of Mininia is in a recession.
   a. Use a correctly labeled graph of *AD*, *SRAS*, and *LRAS* to illustrate each of the following:
      i. the equilibrium output and price level, labeled Q_1 and PL_1
      ii. the long-run equilibrium output, labeled Q_f
   b. Show the effect of an expansionary fiscal policy on your graph from part a. Label the new output level Q_2.
   c. Draw a correctly labeled graph of the foreign exchange market for the country's currency, the mina, relative to the U.S. dollar.
   d. How will the value of the mina be affected by the change in output shown on your graph from part b? Illustrate the effect on your graph from part c and explain. **(8 points)**

Is Globalization a Bad Word?
Comparative Advantage, Culture Clashes, and International Organizations

The Reverend Martin Luther King Jr. said of global interdependence: "We are all caught in an inescapable network of mutuality, tied into a single garment of destiny. . . . Did you ever stop to think that you can't leave for your job in the morning without being dependent on most of the world?" In all likelihood, he explained, the sponge you reach for in the bathroom is "handed to you by a Pacific Islander." Your soap comes from a French person. Your coffee, tea, or cocoa at breakfast comes from South American, Chinese, or West African citizens. Your toast comes "at the hands of an English-speaking farmer, not to mention the baker." And before breakfast is over, you have reaped benefits from work performed by people around the globe.

Interdependence is nothing new; spices, slaves, and silk were traded across the oceans centuries ago. But as clipper ships were replaced by ocean liners and airlines that crisscross the globe every day, the cross-pollination of cultures intensified, as did the scrutiny of the resulting mutual influences. Here we demystify the nebulous concept of globalization and explain its benefits, including economic incentives for cooperation and toleration, and its costs, such as exploitation and homogenization.

What Is Globalization?

We can now travel from one continent to another in the time it takes to walk from one end of New York's Manhattan Island to the other, and the modes of transportation are only getting faster. The Japan Aerospace Exploration Agency has completed successful tests of a supersonic jet plane that will someday carry 300 passengers from New York to Tokyo in less than 6 hours. New technologies allow instantaneous communication of information and overnight transfers of people and products around the globe, giving goods and influence a worldwide reach. In a nutshell, *globalization* is the creation of a worldwide scope for markets, communications, transportation, and ideas. The term has been used to convey a number of associated concepts, which include:

internationalization—the increase of international trade and interdependence

supraterritoriality—the de-emphasis on territorial boundaries

universalization—the spread of common ideas and goods across the globe

Westernization—the migration of Western culture

Political scientist Jan Aart Scholte argues that, of these, supraterritoriality is central to the meaning of globalization, citing economist Milton Friedman's observation that it has become possible "to produce products anywhere, using resources from anywhere, by a company located anywhere, to be sold anywhere." For example, Deere and Company produces tractors in Waterloo, Iowa, for export to 110 countries on 6 continents. Parts in its Augusta, Georgia, assembly plant come from 12 other countries. Deere also produces machinery in China for the Middle East, in Brazil for Europe, and in Germany and India for the United States. In all, the company does business in more than 160 countries.

What Can Be Gained from Globalization?

Our company buys denim in North Carolina, ships it to France where it is sewn into jeans, launders these jeans in Belgium, and markets them in Germany using TV commercials developed in England.

—Robert D. Haas, former CEO, Levi Strauss & Co.

Levi's jeans, like many other goods, are shuttled around the globe during the production process for several good reasons. As one of the first places in the world to use a cotton gin to separate seeds from fiber, North Carolina has more than 200 years of experience in the efficient production of high-quality cotton products. Barthélemy Thimonnier patented the first commercial sewing machine and ran the world's first garment factory in France in the 1830s. Having given the world denim as well, France knows a thing or two about sewing jeans. Belgium and England may not have enjoyed a first-mover advantage in commercial laundering or advertising—Texas claims the first laundromat and New York claims the first advertising firm—but they have developed expertise in these tasks.

When one country can make a good at a lower opportunity cost, meaning that it gives up less of other goods for each unit, it has a *comparative advantage* in producing that good. When a country can make more of a product than another country with the same resources, the more productive country has an *absolute advantage*. Economist David Ricardo reasoned that each country should specialize in the goods and services that it can produce most readily and cheaply and should trade those goods and services for what foreign countries can produce more efficiently. For example, India excels in information technology (IT) services, and, because of this, about half of the Fortune 500 companies are clients of Indian IT firms. Chile's warm winters and hard-working, low-paid workers give that country an advantage in the labor-intensive production of fresh fruits and vegetables, and Chile exports more than 800,000 tons of fruit to the United States each year. The American Midwest has a comparative advantage in wheat production: Thanks to its rich soil and moderate temperatures, the region exports 28.5 million metric tons of wheat annually. One of Ricardo's insights was that whenever a country has a comparative advantage over another country in the production of a good, it is a certainty that *both* countries can benefit from specialization and mutual trade.

The benefits of globalization extend beyond the efficiency of specialization and trade. Shared information serves as a public good for those who would otherwise have to reinvent solutions, cures, products, and processes on their own. International collaborations can contribute to the success of projects of grand importance, as with the International Space Station, efforts to track and propagate endangered species, and cures for deadly diseases. When several countries cooperate on a risky-but-important project, the potential costs of failure are shared, which makes more such projects possible.

International organizations can pool funds and disburse them for relief from disasters, including oil spills, droughts, cyclones, famines, and floods. When a devastating earthquake hit Nepal in 2015, assistance came from nonprofit organizations such as Oxfam, Save the Children, and AmeriCares, and from countries around the world. Cooperative international educational efforts include the work of the United Nations Educational, Scientific, and Cultural Organization (UNESCO). UNESCO's nearly 200 member nations have the goal of "education for all."

Finally, economic cooperation is a strong disincentive for bloodshed between countries. For example, France and the United Kingdom have an ongoing spat, but it's unlikely to come to military strikes because the two countries are economically interdependent—each sells tens of billions of dollars' worth of goods to the other each year. The loss of these enormous gains from trade, along with the other economic and political ramifications of war, would make the military option quite costly. Growing interdependence thus provides growing disincentives for avoidable belligerence.

What Are the Objections to Globalization?

It's not free trade, it's stupid trade.

—Craig Romero, Republican candidate for Louisiana's 3rd congressional district, on the Central American Free Trade Agreement

Despite the potential gains from cooperation, there is fervent opposition to globalization in many circles. Critics worry that the influence of multinational corporations rivals that of democratically elected representatives and concentrates power among those driven by profit. Intensified globalization might lead to a relatively homogeneous world market, causing cultures to lose their identities. And production might be shifted to countries that have low environmental or humanitarian standards, so that the exploitation of human and natural resources might be increased. This section explores the potential harm that could stem from the current trends in globalization.

The expansion of some cultures has led to the contraction of others. Some languages and dialects have been lost forever, and people in 119 countries now can eat food served by McDonald's. To critics of globalization, fast-food franchises are symbolic of a broader dissemination of unhealthy and unsustainable Western lifestyles. Seductive corporate advertising and contagious materialistic values could create a world in which everyone consumed at the rate of Western countries—and that would require the resources of at least five planets similar to earth.[1] Other things being equal, we might expect high-consumption countries also to be on the receiving end of influence, gaining ideas about how to live simply from countries with more sustainable economies. However, with an imbalance in marketing savvy, such a balance in influence is less likely.

Critics also argue that, in practice, globalization has perpetuated the imbalance of economic benefits rather than spreading the benefits far and wide. Income inequality is growing in most countries, and according to the *Global Wealth Report 2017* by the Credit Suisse Research Institute, half of the world's wealth is held by the richest 1 percent of people. Another problem is that profit-maximizing firms may shop for production sites in countries where labor or environmental protection standards are low. In related research, Dong-Sook S. Gills found that increased globalization has led to the exploitation of female workers

Homeland photos/Alamy

[1] To learn how many planets would be needed if everyone lived like you, see www.myfootprint.org/.

in Asia,[2] and Susmita Dasgupta, Nlandu Mamingi, and Craig Meisner found that globalization promoted pesticide use in Brazil, particularly on export crops.[3] Modern trade agreements, such as the North American Free Trade Agreement (NAFTA) and the Central American Free Trade Agreement (CAFTA), typically include provisions meant to protect humanitarian and environmental interests. However, the difficulty of monitoring and enforcement has meant limited success. Some workers also believe that, by de-emphasizing international boundaries, globalization invites levels of immigration and outsourcing that threaten domestic employment.

What Organizations Help to Keep Problems in Check?

The power and influence of governments tend to erode outside of national boundaries, causing a relative void of authority. Even the strongest armies have difficulty enforcing policies among rogue nations, and international law is only as binding as the multinational commitments to support it. At the same time, vital interests in the benefits of economic cooperation, in the ethical treatment of labor, and in the avoidance of global environmental catastrophes have spawned several organizations of considerable strength and controversy to offer international oversight.

The United Nations

The United Nations (UN) was founded in 1945 with 51 member countries and a charter "to maintain international peace and security; to develop friendly relations among nations; to cooperate in solving international economic, social, cultural and humanitarian problems and in promoting respect for human rights and fundamental freedoms; and to be a centre for harmonizing the actions of nations in attaining these ends." The organization now boasts 193 member countries, 15 agencies, and an extensive array of programs and bodies. Its initiatives include international conferences to establish agreements on the battle against global climate change. The latest activities of UN organizations are summarized online at www.unsystem.org.

The World Trade Organization

The General Agreement on Tariffs and Trade (GATT) signed in 1947 reduced barriers to the international trade of merchandise, which now represents 40% of global

production and 80% of global trade. In 1995, the World Trade Organization (WTO) replaced GATT as the global authority on rules of international trade. The WTO administers GATT principles and extends them with policies negotiated among its 164 member nations. Among these, the General Agreement on Trade in Services (GATS) is the service-industry equivalent to GATT. The objectives for GATS and GATT are to create "a credible and reliable system of international trade rules; ensuring fair and equitable treatment of all participants . . . ; stimulating economic activity through guaranteed policy bindings; and promoting trade and development through progressive liberalization."

The WTO has come under fire for allegedly placing commercial interests ahead of environmental protection. The Working Group on the WTO/Multilateral Agreement on Investment claims, for example, that WTO rulings have relaxed the environmental standards for Venezuelan oil refineries, undercut U.S. requirements that shrimp be caught using specific turtle-safe excluding devices, and neglected precautionary policies that call for the WTO to prepare for the worst in the context of environmental concerns. Whatever the intent and result of current WTO actions, the repercussions of globalization were certainly on the minds of its architects. The preamble to the 1994 Marrakesh agreement establishing the WTO states that

relations in the field of trade and economic endeavor should be conducted . . . while allowing for the optimal use of the world's resources in accordance with the objective of sustainable development, seeking both to protect and preserve the environment and to enhance the means for doing so in a manner consistent with their respective needs and concerns at different levels of economic development.

In support of this goal, umbrella clauses, such as Article 20 of the GATT, permit countries to act in the defense of human, animal, or plant life or health and to conserve nonrenewable natural resources.

The World Bank

Financial ministers from 44 governments gathered in Bretton Woods, New Hampshire, in 1944 as architects of the modern international economy. With fresh wounds from the Great Depression and World War II, they sought economic stability and revitalization for their countries. One result was the creation of the World Bank to assist with rebuilding war-torn Europe. With that task completed, the World Bank turned to less-developed countries, aiming to envelop them in the global economy and to reduce poverty by providing low- or no-interest loans for education, health, infrastructure, and communications. The World Bank and its 189 member countries also work together to combat negative repercussions of globalization, such as the spread of diseases across borders.

[2] "Globalization of Production and Women in Asia," *Annals of the American Academy of Political and Social Science 581* (2002), 106–120.
[3] "Pesticide Use in Brazil in the Era of Agroindustrialization and Globalization," *Environment and Development Economics 6*, no. 4 (2001), 459–482.

B Christopher/Alamy

As with all other international organizations and agreements, the World Bank has no shortage of detractors. There are charges that the World Bank actually exacerbates the problems of globalization by hastening development, promoting materialism, and neglecting environment health.[4]

The International Monetary Fund

Like the World Bank, the International Monetary Fund (IMF) was conceived as part of the Bretton Woods agreement. It serves as a stabilizing force for the currencies and economies of its 189 member countries by overseeing exchange-rate policies, lending to countries with balance-of-payment problems, and assisting with the development of monetary and fiscal policy.

The IMF defends globalization, saying that it transformed East Asia from one of the poorest areas to an area of greater prosperity: "And as living standards rose, it became possible to make progress on democracy and economic issues such as the environment and work standards. By contrast, in the 1970s and 1980s when many countries in Latin America and Africa pursued inward-oriented policies, their economies stagnated or declined, poverty increased and high inflation became the norm."[5]

Critics of the IMF, such as the Global Exchange organization, claim that the IMF and the World Bank trap countries by luring them into debt and then placing unwarranted demands on them. There are also concerns that the IMF causes poor countries to promote sweatshops and to accept exploitative

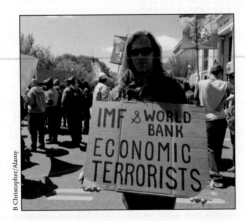
B Christopher/Alamy

inroads by large Western corporations. What is certain is that these organizations have come to symbolize desired order and assistance for some, and the pursuit of selfish ideals for others.

Conclusion

Innovations in travel and communications make the world's distances easily surmountable, and sharing has become commonplace in what communications theorist Marshall McLuhan dubbed "the global village"—a world made smaller by electronic media. Globalization brings with it the efficiency of specialization based on comparative advantage, along with better understanding of other cultures and incentives for the civilized resolution of disputes. It also creates homogenization, threats to the status quo, and a longer reach for powerful multinational corporations (Netmarketshare.com reports that Microsoft software runs 89% of the world's computers).

Perspectives on whether globalization provides a net gain depend on the observers' interests and priorities. With the aim of making the most of globalization, the world's nations seek policy guidance from international organizations with good intentions but checkered histories. The UN, the WTO, the World Bank, and the IMF face the ever-present possibility for corruption and the daunting challenge of reconciling differences in a world in which the ability to meet face-to-face has grown faster than the ability to see eye to eye.

Critical Thinking Questions

1. In what ways did you benefit from globalization by the time you finished breakfast this morning? Did you eat fruit from a tropical island, drink a beverage derived from foreign leaves or beans, put on clothes made in China, or use electronics made in South Korea? In what other ways do you gain from globalization?

2. What, in your opinion, are the worst aspects of globalization?

3. Intense controversy revolves around the WTO, the IMF, the UN, and other organizations that were formed to limit the negative aspects of globalization and promote its strengths. What standards—for example, along the lines of fairness, enforceability, sustainability, and cultural appropriateness—would you prescribe for new policies coming out of such organizations?

4. Suppose you're the new president of the WTO. What is the first new policy measure you would advocate to make the world a better place? Why do you suppose this measure has not yet been adopted?

[4] See www.econjustice.net/wbbb/.
[5] See www.imf.org/external/np/exr/ib/2000/041200to.htm.

SECTION

9

Behind the Demand Curve: Consumer Choice

> **economics by example** Why Is a Newspaper Heist So Easy?

Paying Whatever It Takes for Health

An allergic reaction can be fatal. Epinephrine is a drug used to treat allergic reactions to nuts, shellfish, latex, and bee stings, among other allergens. In an emergency, almost anyone can use an EpiPen® auto-injector to administer epinephrine to an allergy victim. The Mylan Corporation purchased the right to sell EpiPens in 2007. At that time a kit containing two pens cost less than $100. Over the next decade, Mylan raised the price of EpiPens aggressively, and in 2018, the price of a two-pen kit was around $600.

Millions of Americans are vulnerable to severe allergic reactions and purchase EpiPens for their homes, schools, and offices. With few alternatives available, as the price of EpiPens rose dramatically, customer outrage ensued. Protestors smashed a giant EpiPen replica in front of the Mylan offices in New York and the company was hit with a class-action lawsuit over the "skyrocketing" price of EpiPens. Mylan offered some discount coupons and a cheaper, generic version of the EpiPen but kept the price of its name-brand product high.

Mylan judged, correctly, that EpiPen customers were relatively *unresponsive* to price when it came to their purchasing decisions. That is, the large increase in the price of the kits had a relatively small effect on the quantity demanded by consumers.

Clearly, the demand for emergency allergy treatments is unusual in this respect. For many people, access to treatment could mean the difference between life and death. Now let's consider a very different and less urgent scenario. Suppose the price of a particular type of breakfast cereal increased by 500%. It is extremely unlikely that a consumer would be willing to pay six times the original price for a box of this particular cereal. Instead, they would likely switch to a different, cheaper option. In other words, consumers of breakfast cereal are much more responsive to price than consumers of emergency allergy treatments. How do we define *responsiveness*? Economists measure consumers' responsiveness to price with a particular number, called the *price elasticity of demand*.

In this section we take a closer look at the supply and demand model developed in Section 2 and present several economic concepts used to evaluate market results. We will see how the price elasticity of demand is calculated and why it is the best measure of how the quantity demanded responds to changes in price. We will then discover that the price elasticity of demand is only one of a family of related concepts, including the *income elasticity of demand* and the *price elasticity of supply*. We will look at how the price and the quantity bought and sold in a market affect consumer, producer, and overall welfare. And we will consider how consumers make choices to maximize their individual *utility*, the term economists use to describe "satisfaction."

Income Effects, Substitution Effects, and Elasticity

> **In this Module, you will learn to:**
> - Explain the law of demand on the basis of income and substitution effects
> - Calculate the price elasticity of demand, a measure of consumer responsiveness to price changes

Explaining the Law of Demand

In Section 2 we introduced the demand curve and the law of demand, which asserts that the demand curve has a negative slope. In this Module we present more detail about why the demand curve slopes downward and what we can learn from the shape of the curve. We begin with the *substitution* and *income effects*, which give the demand curve its shape.

The Substitution Effect

The **substitution effect** of a change in the price of a good is the change in the quantity of that good demanded as the consumer substitutes the good that has become relatively cheaper for the good that has become relatively more expensive.

When the price of a good increases, an individual will normally consume less of that good and more of other goods. Correspondingly, when the price of a good decreases, an individual will normally consume more of that good and less of other goods. This explains why the individual demand curve, which relates an individual's consumption of a good to the price of that good, normally obeys the law of demand and slopes downward.

An alternative way to think about why demand curves slope downward is to focus on opportunity costs. For simplicity, let's suppose there are only two goods between which to choose: good 1 and good 2. When the price of good 1 decreases, an individual doesn't have to give up as many units of good 2 in order to buy one more unit of good 1. That makes it attractive to buy more of good 1, whose price has gone down. Conversely, when the price of good 1 increases, one must give up more units of good 2 to buy one more unit of good 1, so consuming good 1 becomes less attractive and the consumer buys fewer.

The change in the quantity demanded as the good that has become relatively cheaper is substituted for the good that has become relatively more expensive is known as the **substitution effect**. When a good absorbs only a small share of the typical consumer's income, as with pillowcases and kites, the substitution effect is essentially the sole explanation of why the market demand curve slopes downward. However, there are some goods, like food and housing, that account for a substantial share of many consumers' incomes. In such cases, another effect, called the *income effect*, also comes into play.

A price hike on kites does not trigger a significant income effect because expenditures on kites are such a small portion of consumers' income. A price hike on homes, on the other hand, does cause a sizable income effect because consumers spend a large portion of their income on housing.

AP® EXAM TIP

The *substitution effect* comes from a change in the price of one good relative to the price of another good. The *income effect* comes from a change in purchasing power, which can result from a change in one or more prices or from a change in the actual income received.

The Income Effect

Consider the case of a family that spends half of its income on rental housing. Now suppose that the price of housing increases everywhere. This change will have a substitution effect on the family's demand: other things equal, the family will have an incentive to consume less housing—say, by moving to a smaller apartment—and more of other goods. But, in a real sense, the family will also be made poorer by that higher housing price—its income will buy less housing than before. When income is adjusted to reflect its true purchasing power, it is called *real income*, in contrast to *money income* or *nominal income*, which has not been adjusted. And this reduction in a consumer's real income will have an additional effect, beyond the substitution effect, on the amount of housing and other goods the family chooses to buy.

The **income effect** of a change in the price of a good is the change in the quantity of that good demanded that results from a change in the overall purchasing power of the consumer's income when the price of the good changes.

It's possible to give more precise definitions of the substitution effect and the income effect of a price change, but for most purposes, there are only two things you need to know about the distinction between these two effects.

First, for the majority of goods and services, the income effect is not important and has no significant effect on individual consumption. Thus, most market demand curves slope downward solely because of the substitution effect—end of story.

Second, when it matters at all, the income effect usually reinforces the substitution effect. That is, when the price rises on a good that absorbs a substantial share of income, consumers of that good become a bit poorer because their purchasing power falls. And for all *normal* goods—goods for which demand decreases when income falls—this effective reduction in income leads to a reduction in the quantity demanded and reinforces the substitution effect.

Module 5 introduced both normal goods and *inferior* goods—those goods, such as canned meat and ramen noodles, for which demand increases when income falls. In the case of an inferior good, the income and substitution effects work in opposite directions. For example, suppose the price of canned meat increases. The resulting substitution effect is a decrease in the quantity of canned meat demanded, because for both normal and inferior goods, the substitution effect of a price increase is a decrease in the quantity demanded. But the income effect of a price increase for canned meat is an *increase* in the quantity demanded. This makes sense because the price increase lowers the real income of the consumer, and as real income falls, the demand for an inferior good increases.

Could the *total effect* of a price increase—the combination of the income effect and the substitution effect—ever be an increase in the quantity demanded? In other words, might we see an increase in the price of ramen noodles lead to an increase in the quantity of ramen noodles demanded? It is conceivable. If a good were so inferior that the income effect exceeded the substitution effect, an increase in the price of that good would lead to an increase in the quantity of that good that is demanded. There is controversy over whether such goods, known as "Giffen goods," exist at all. If they do, they are very rare. You can generally assume that the income effect for an inferior good is smaller than the substitution effect, and so a price increase will lead to a decrease in the quantity demanded. Next, we will discuss an exact measure of the responsiveness of the quantity demanded to price changes.

> The **income effect** of a change in the price of a good is the change in the quantity of that good demanded that results from a change in the consumer's purchasing power when the price of the good changes.

Defining and Measuring Elasticity

As we saw in Section 1, *dependent variables* respond to changes in *independent variables*. For example, if two variables are negatively related and the independent variable increases, the dependent variable will respond by decreasing. Often the important question is not whether the variables are negatively or positively related, but how responsive the dependent variable is to changes in the independent variable. That is, *by how much* will the dependent variable change? If the price increases, we know from the law of demand that the quantity demanded will decrease. The question in this context is *by how much* will the quantity demanded decrease if the price goes up?

Economists use the concept of *elasticity* to measure the responsiveness of one variable to changes in another. For example, the *price elasticity of demand* measures the responsiveness of the quantity demanded to changes in the price—something a firm considering changing its price would certainly want to know! Elasticity can be used to measure responsiveness using any two related variables. We will start by looking at the price elasticity of demand and then move on to other types of elasticities commonly used by economists.

Think back to the opening example of price hikes for emergency allergy treatments. In order for a pharmaceutical company to know whether it could raise its revenue by

AP® EXAM TIP

Elasticity often appears on the AP® exam. Make sure you are able to calculate and interpret elasticity information.

raising the price of its drugs, it would have to know whether the price increase would decrease the quantity demanded by a lot or a little. That is, it would have to know the price elasticity of demand for its products.

Calculating the Price Elasticity of Demand

Figure 46.1 shows a hypothetical demand curve for another potentially life-saving medical product purchased by millions of Americans each year, flu vaccinations. At a price of $20 per vaccination, consumers would demand 10 million vaccinations per year (point *A*); at a price of $21, the quantity demanded would fall to 9.9 million vaccinations per year (point *B*).

Figure 46.1   The Demand for Vaccinations

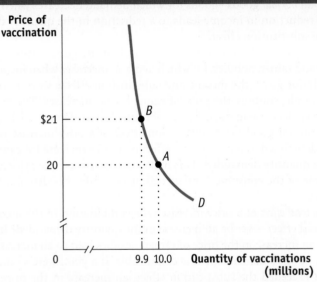

At a price of $20 per vaccination, the quantity of vaccinations demanded is 10 million per year (point *A*). When price rises to $21 per vaccination, the quantity demanded falls to 9.9 million vaccinations per year (point *B*). With the price elasticity of demand, one can measure the influence of price changes on the quantity demanded.

Figure 46.1, then, tells us the change in the quantity demanded for a particular change in the price. But how can we turn this information into a measure of price responsiveness? The answer is to calculate the price elasticity of demand. The **price elasticity of demand** compares the *percent change in quantity demanded* to the *percent change in price* as we move along the demand curve. As we'll see later, economists use percent changes to get a measure that doesn't depend on the units involved (say, a child-sized dose versus an adult-sized dose of vaccine). But before we get to that, let's look at how elasticity is calculated.

To calculate the price elasticity of demand, we first calculate the percent change in the quantity demanded and the corresponding percent change in the price as we move along the demand curve. These are defined as follows:

The **price elasticity of demand** is the ratio of the percent change in the quantity demanded to the percent change in the price as we move along the demand curve (dropping the minus sign).

$$\textbf{(46-1)} \quad \% \text{ change in quantity demanded} = \frac{\text{Change in quantity demanded}}{\text{Initial quantity demanded}} \times 100$$

and

$$\textbf{(46-2)} \quad \% \text{ change in price} = \frac{\text{Change in price}}{\text{Initial price}} \times 100$$

In Figure 46.1, we see that when the price rises from $20 to $21, the quantity demanded falls from 10 million to 9.9 million vaccinations, yielding a change in the quantity demanded of 0.1 million vaccinations. So the percent change in the quantity demanded is

$$\% \text{ change in quantity demanded} = \frac{-0.1 \text{ million vaccinations}}{10 \text{ million vaccinations}} \times 100 = -1\%$$

The initial price is $20 and the change in the price is $1, so the percent change in the price is

$$\text{\% change in price} = \frac{\$1}{\$20} \times 100 = 5\%$$

To calculate the price elasticity of demand, we find the ratio of the percent change in the quantity demanded to the percent change in the price:

(46-3) $\text{Price elasticity of demand} = \dfrac{\text{\% change in quantity demanded}}{\text{\% change in price}}$

In Figure 46.1, the price elasticity of demand is therefore

$$\text{Price elasticity of demand} = \frac{1\%}{5\%} = 0.2$$

The law of demand says that demand curves slope downward, so the price and the quantity demanded move in opposite directions. In other words, a positive percent change in the price (a rise in the price) leads to a negative percent change in the quantity demanded, and a negative percent change in the price (a fall in the price) leads to a positive percent change in the quantity demanded. This means that the price elasticity of demand, in strictly mathematical terms, is a negative number. However, it is inconvenient to repeatedly write a minus sign. So when economists talk about the price elasticity of demand, they usually drop the minus sign and report the absolute value of the price elasticity of demand. In this case, for example, economists would usually say "the price elasticity of demand is 0.2," taking it for granted that you understand they mean *minus* 0.2. We follow this convention here.

The larger the price elasticity of demand, the more responsive the quantity demanded is to the price. When the price elasticity of demand is large—when consumers change their quantity demanded by a large percentage compared with the percent change in the price—economists say that demand is highly elastic.

As we'll see shortly, a price elasticity of 0.2 indicates a small response of the quantity demanded to the price. That is, the quantity demanded will fall by a relatively small amount when the price rises. This is what economists call *inelastic* demand. In the next Module we'll see why inelastic demand is exactly what a pharmaceutical company needs for success with a strategy to increase revenue by raising the price of its flu vaccines.

> **AP® EXAM TIP**
>
> Be sure to use *absolute values* when computing the price elasticity of demand. In other words, always write the price elasticity of demand as a positive number.

An Alternative Way to Calculate Elasticities: The Midpoint Method

We've seen that price elasticity of demand compares the percent change in quantity demanded with the percent change in price. When we look at some other elasticities, which we will do shortly, we'll see why it is important to focus on percent changes. But at this point we need to discuss a technical issue that arises when you calculate percent changes in variables and how economists deal with it.

To better understand the issue let's consider a real example. Suppose you were trying to estimate the price elasticity of demand for gasoline by comparing gasoline prices and consumption in different countries. Because of high taxes, gasoline usually costs about twice as much per gallon in Europe as it does in the United States. So what is the percent difference between U.S. and European gas prices?

Well, it depends on which way you measure it. Because the price of gasoline in Europe is approximately twice as high as in the United States, it is 100% higher. Because the price of gasoline in the United States is one-half as high as in Europe, it is 50% lower.

In our previous example, we found an elasticity of demand for vaccinations of 0.200 when considering a movement from point *A* to point *B*. However, when going from point *B* to point *A*, the same elasticity formula would indicate an elasticity of

0.212. This is a nuisance: we'd like to have an elasticity measure that doesn't depend on the direction of change. A good way to avoid computing different elasticities for rising and falling prices is to use the *midpoint method* (sometimes called the *arc method*).

The **midpoint method** replaces the usual definition of the percent change in a variable, X, with a slightly different definition:

$$\textbf{(46-4)} \quad \% \text{ change in } X = \frac{\text{Change in } X}{\text{Average value of } X} \times 100$$

where the average value of X is defined as

$$\text{Average value of } X = \frac{\text{Starting value of } X + \text{Final value of } X}{2}$$

When calculating the price elasticity of demand using the midpoint method, both the percent change in the price and the percent change in the quantity demanded are found using average values in this way. To see how this method works, suppose you have the following data for chocolate bars:

	Price	Quantity demanded
Situation A	$0.90	1,100
Situation B	$1.10	900

To calculate the percent change in quantity going from situation A to situation B, we compare the change in the quantity demanded—a fall of 200 units—with the *average* of the quantity demanded in the two situations. So we calculate

$$\% \text{ change in quantity demanded} = \frac{-200}{(1{,}100 + 900)/2} \times 100 = \frac{-200}{1{,}000} \times 100 = -20\%$$

In the same way, we calculate the percent change in price as

$$\% \text{ change in price} = \frac{\$0.20}{(\$0.90 + \$1.10)/2} \times 100 = \frac{\$0.20}{\$1.00} \times 100 = 20\%$$

So in this case we would calculate the price elasticity of demand to be

$$\text{Price elasticity of demand} = \frac{\% \text{ change in quantity demanded}}{\% \text{ change in price}} = \frac{20\%}{20\%} = 1$$

Again, we drop the minus sign.

The important point is that we would get the same result, a price elasticity of demand of 1, whether we went up the demand curve from situation A to situation B or down from situation B to situation A.

To arrive at a more general formula for price elasticity of demand, suppose that we have data for two points on a demand curve. At point 1 the quantity demanded and the price are (Q_1, P_1); at point 2 they are (Q_2, P_2). Then the formula for calculating the price elasticity of demand is

$$\textbf{(46-5)} \quad \text{Price elasticity of demand} = \frac{\dfrac{Q_2 - Q_1}{(Q_1 + Q_2)/2}}{\dfrac{P_2 - P_1}{(P_1 + P_2)/2}}$$

As before, when reporting a price elasticity of demand calculated by the midpoint method, we drop the minus sign and report the absolute value.

> The **midpoint method** is a technique for calculating the percent change by dividing the change in a variable by the average, or midpoint, of the initial and final values of that variable.

AP® EXAM TIP

If an exam question requires you to calculate an elasticity and does not indicate which formula to use, that typically means the graders will accept the use of either formula, and you can use whichever formula you are most comfortable with.

Elasticity Estimates

In 1970, economists Hendrik S. Houthakker and Lester D. Taylor published a comprehensive study that estimated the price elasticities of demand for a wide variety of goods. Some of their results are summarized in **Table 46.1**. These estimates show a wide range of price elasticities. There are some goods, such as eggs, for which demand hardly responds at all to changes in the price; there are other goods, most notably foreign travel, for which the quantity demanded is very sensitive to the price.

Notice that Table 46.1 is divided into two parts: inelastic demand and elastic demand. Inelastic demand is *less responsive* to price changes than elastic demand. We'll explain the significance of that division in the next module.

Table 46.1	Some Estimated Price Elasticities of Demand	
Good		**Price elasticity of demand**
Inelastic demand		
Eggs		0.1
Beef		0.4
Stationery		0.5
Gasoline		0.5
Elastic demand		
Housing		1.2
Restaurant meals		2.3
Airline travel		2.4
Foreign travel		4.1

Source: Hendrick S. Houthakker and Lester D. Taylor, *Consumer Demand in the United States, 1929–1970* (Cambridge: Harvard University Press, 1970).

MODULE 46 REVIEW

Check Your Understanding

1. In each of the following cases, state whether the income effect, the substitution effect, or both are significant. In which cases do they move in the same direction? In opposite directions? Why?
   a. Orange juice represents a small share of Clare's spending. She buys more lemonade and less orange juice when the price of orange juice goes up. She does not change her spending on other goods.
   b. Apartment rents have risen dramatically this year. Since rent absorbs a major part of her income, Delia moves to a smaller apartment. Assume that rental housing is a normal good.
   c. The cost of a semester-long meal ticket at the student cafeteria rises, representing a significant increase in living costs. As a result, many students have less money to spend on weekend meals at restaurants and they choose to eat in the cafeteria instead. Assume that cafeteria meals are an inferior good.

2. The price of strawberries falls from $1.50 to $1.00 per carton, and the quantity demanded goes from 100,000 to 200,000 cartons. Use the midpoint method to find the price elasticity of demand.

3. The price elasticity of demand for movie tickets is 1 at the current price of $10 per ticket and the current consumption level of 4,000 tickets. Using the midpoint method, calculate the percentage by which the owners of movie theaters must reduce the price in order to sell 5,000 tickets.

4. The price elasticity of demand for ice cream sandwiches is 1.2 at the current price of $0.50 per sandwich and the current consumption level of 100,000 sandwiches. Calculate the change in the quantity demanded when price rises by $0.05. Use Equations 46-1 and 46-2 to calculate percent changes and Equation 46-3 to relate price elasticity of demand to the percent changes.

TACKLE THE AP® TEST: Multiple-Choice Questions

1. Which of the following statements is true?
   a. When a good absorbs only a small share of the typical consumer's income, the income effect explains the demand curve's negative slope.
   b. A change in consumption brought about by a change in purchasing power describes the substitution effect.
   c. In the case of an inferior good, the income effect is usually larger than the substitution effect.
   d. In the case of an inferior good, the income and substitution effects work in opposite directions.
   e. Normal goods and inferior goods differ in regard to the direction of the substitution effect caused by a price increase.

2. If there is an increase in the price of an inferior good on which consumers spend a large share of their income, which of the following will decrease the quantity of that good demanded?
   a. the Giffen effect
   b. the income effect only
   c. the substitution effect only
   d. the income effect and the substitution effect
   e. neither the income effect nor the substitution effect

3. If a decrease in price from $2 to $1 causes an increase in quantity demanded from 100 to 120, using the midpoint method, price elasticity of demand equals
   a. 0.17.   d. 2.5.
   b. 0.27.   e. 3.72.
   c. 0.40.

4. Which of the following is likely to have the highest price elasticity of demand?
   a. eggs
   b. beef
   c. housing
   d. gasoline
   e. foreign travel

5. If a 2% change in the price of a good leads to a 10% change in the quantity demanded of a good, what is the price elasticity of demand?
   a. 0.02   d. 10
   b. 0.2   e. 20
   c. 5

6. By convention, a price elasticity of demand of 5 indicates that a 1% increase in price leads to a _____ in the quantity demanded.
   a. 0.2% increase
   b. 0.2% decrease
   c. 0.5% increase
   d. 5% decrease
   e. 5% increase

7. The midpoint method of calculating elasticities determines the percent change in a variable as the change in the variable divided by
   a. the average value of the variable.
   b. the initial value of the variable.
   c. the final value of the variable.
   d. the highest value of the variable.
   e. the lowest value of the variable.

TACKLE THE AP® TEST: Free-Response Questions

1. a. Define the price elasticity of demand and provide the formula for calculating the price elasticity of demand using the midpoint method.
   b. Refer to the table provided. Using the midpoint method, calculate the price elasticity of demand for good X.

Good X	
Price	Quantity demanded
$2	800
$4	500

   c. Based on your calculation of the price elasticity of demand in part b, if the price increases by 10%, in what direction and by what percentage will the quantity demanded change?

2. Assume the price of an inferior good increases.
   a. In what direction will the substitution effect change the quantity demanded? Explain.
   b. In what direction will the income effect change the quantity demanded? Explain.
   c. Given that the demand curve for the good slopes downward, what is true of the relative sizes of the income and substitution effects for the inferior good? Explain. **(6 points)**

Rubric for FRQ 1 (5 points)

1 point: The price elasticity of demand measures the responsiveness of the quantity demanded to changes in the price.

1 point: $\dfrac{\left(\dfrac{\text{Change in quantity demanded}}{\text{average quantity demanded}}\right)}{\left(\dfrac{\text{change in price}}{\text{average price}}\right)}$

1 point: 0.69

1 point: The price will go down.

1 point: 6.9%

Interpreting Price Elasticity of Demand

In this Module, you will learn to:
- Explain the difference between elastic and inelastic demand
- Describe the relationship between elasticity and total revenue
- Illustrate how the price elasticity changes along a demand curve
- Identify the factors that determine price elasticity of demand

What the Price Elasticity of Demand Tells Us

Mylan Corporation believed it could sharply drive up prices for its emergency allergy treatments because the price elasticity of demand for those products was low. But what does that mean? How low does a price elasticity have to be for us to classify it as low? How high does it have to be for us to consider it high? And what determines whether the price elasticity of demand is high or low? To answer these questions, we need to look more deeply at the price elasticity of demand.

How Elastic Is Elastic?

As a first step toward classifying price elasticities of demand, let's look at two extreme cases. First, consider the demand for a good when people pay no attention to its price. Suppose, for example, that consumers would buy 1 million heart bypass surgeries per year regardless of the price. If that were true, the demand curve for these surgeries would look like the curve shown in panel (a) of **Figure 47.1**: it would be a vertical line at 1 million heart bypass surgeries. Since the percent change in the quantity demanded is

---

Figure 47.1   Two Extreme Cases of Price Elasticity of Demand

Panel (a) shows a perfectly inelastic demand curve, which is a vertical line. The quantity of heart bypass surgeries demanded is always 1 million, regardless of the price. As a result, the price elasticity of demand is zero—the quantity demanded is unaffected by the price. Panel (b) shows a perfectly elastic demand curve, which is a horizontal line. At a price of $5, consumers will buy any quantity of pink tennis balls, but they will buy none at a price above $5. As a result, the price elasticity of demand is infinite.

Photoevent/Getty Images

zero for *any* change in the price, the price elasticity of demand in this case is zero. The case of a zero price elasticity of demand is known as **perfectly inelastic** demand.

The opposite extreme occurs when even a tiny rise in the price will cause the quantity demanded to drop to zero or when even a tiny fall in the price will cause the quantity demanded to get extremely large. Panel (b) of Figure 47.1 shows the case of pink tennis balls; we suppose that tennis players don't have a color preference, and that other tennis ball colors, such as neon green and vivid yellow, are available at $5 per dozen balls. In this case, consumers will buy no pink tennis balls if they cost more than $5 per dozen. But if pink tennis balls cost less than $5 per dozen, consumers will buy no other color. The demand curve will therefore be a horizontal line at a price of $5 per dozen balls. If the price falls from above $5 to below $5, the quantity demanded will rise from zero to a number approaching infinity. So a horizontal demand curve implies an infinite price elasticity of demand. When the price elasticity of demand is infinite, economists say that demand is **perfectly elastic**.

The price elasticity of demand for the vast majority of goods is somewhere between these two extreme cases. Economists use one main criterion for classifying these intermediate cases: they ask whether the price elasticity of demand is greater or less than 1. When the price elasticity of demand is greater than 1, economists say that demand is **elastic**. When the price elasticity of demand is less than 1, they say that demand is **inelastic**. The borderline case is **unit-elastic** demand, where the price elasticity of demand is—surprise—exactly 1.

To see why a price elasticity of demand equal to 1 is a useful dividing line, let's consider a hypothetical example: a toll bridge operated by the state highway department. Other things equal, the number of drivers who use the bridge depends on the toll, the price the highway department charges for crossing the bridge: the higher the toll, the fewer the drivers who use the bridge.

Figure 47.2 shows three hypothetical demand curves that exhibit unit-elastic demand, inelastic demand, and elastic demand, respectively. In each case, point *A* shows the quantity demanded if the toll is $0.90 and point *B* shows the quantity demanded if the toll is $1.10. An increase in the toll from $0.90 to $1.10 is a 20% increase if we use the midpoint method to calculate the percent change.

Panel (a) shows what happens when the toll is raised from $0.90 to $1.10 and the demand curve is unit-elastic. Here the 20% increase in price leads to a fall in the quantity of cars using the bridge each day from 1,100 to 900, a 20% decline (again using the midpoint method). So the price elasticity of demand is 20%/20% = 1.

Panel (b) shows a case of inelastic demand when the toll is raised from $0.90 to $1.10. The same 20% increase in price reduces the quantity demanded from 1,050 to 950. That's only a 10% decline, so in this case the price elasticity of demand is 10%/20% = 0.5.

Panel (c) shows a case of elastic demand when the toll is raised from $0.90 to $1.10. The 20% price increase causes the quantity demanded to fall from 1,200 to 800, a 40% decline, so the price elasticity of demand is 40%/20% = 2.

Demand is **perfectly inelastic** when the quantity demanded does not respond at all to changes in the price. When demand is perfectly inelastic, the demand curve is a vertical line.

Demand is **perfectly elastic** when any price increase will cause the quantity demanded to drop to zero. When demand is perfectly elastic, the demand curve is a horizontal line.

Demand is **elastic** if the price elasticity of demand is greater than 1, **inelastic** if the price elasticity of demand is less than 1, and **unit-elastic** if the price elasticity of demand is exactly 1.

Total revenue is the total value of sales of a good or service. It is equal to the price multiplied by the quantity sold.

Larry Brownstein/Getty Images

When voters in San Francisco contemplated a toll increase from $6 to $9 for the Bay Bridge in 2018, at issue was the price elasticity of demand, which would determine the resulting drop in use.

Elasticity and Total Revenue

Why does it matter whether demand is unit-elastic, inelastic, or elastic? Because this classification indicates how changes in the price of a good will affect the *total revenue* earned by producers from the sale of that good. In many real-life situations, such as the one faced by Mylan, it is crucial to know how price changes affect total revenue. **Total revenue** is defined as the total value of sales of a good or service: the price multiplied by the quantity sold.

(47-1)   Total revenue = Price × Quantity sold

Figure 47.2 Unit-Elastic Demand, Inelastic Demand, and Elastic Demand

(a) Unit-Elastic Demand: Price Elasticity of Demand = 1

A 20% increase in the price . . .

$1.10

0.90

900 1,100

. . . generates a 20% decrease in the quantity of crossings demanded.

D_1

(b) Inelastic Demand: Price Elasticity of Demand = 0.5

A 20% increase in the price . . .

$1.10

0.90

950 1,050

. . . generates a 10% decrease in the quantity of crossings demanded.

D_2

(c) Elastic Demand: Price Elasticity of Demand = 2

A 20% increase in the price . . .

$1.10

0.90

800 1,200

. . . generates a 40% decrease in the quantity of crossings demanded.

D_3

Panel (a) shows a case of unit-elastic demand: a 20% increase in price generates a 20% decline in quantity demanded, implying a price elasticity of demand of 1. Panel (b) shows a case of inelastic demand: a 20% increase in price generates a 10% decline in quantity demanded, implying a price elasticity of demand of 0.5. Panel (c) shows a case of elastic demand: a 20% increase in price causes a 40% decline in quantity demanded, implying a price elasticity of demand of 2. All percentages are calculated using the midpoint method.

A useful graphical representation can help us understand why knowing the price elasticity of demand is crucial when we ask whether an increase in price will increase or decrease total revenue. Panel (a) of **Figure 47.3** shows the same demand curve as panel (a) of Figure 47.2. We see that 1,100 drivers will use the bridge if the toll is $0.90. So the total revenue at a price of $0.90 is $0.90 × 1,100 = $990. This value is equal to the area of the green rectangle, which is drawn with the bottom left corner at the point (0, 0) and the top right corner at (1,100, 0.90). In general, the total revenue at any given price is equal to the area of a rectangle whose height is the price and whose width is the quantity demanded at that price.

To get an idea of why total revenue is important, consider the following scenario. Suppose that the toll on the bridge is currently $0.90 but that the highway department must raise extra money for road repairs. One way to do this is to raise the toll on the bridge. But this plan might backfire, since a higher toll will reduce the number of drivers who use the bridge. And if traffic on the bridge dropped by a high enough percentage, a higher toll would actually reduce total revenue instead of increasing it. So it's important for the highway department to know how drivers will respond to a toll increase.

AP® EXAM TIP

When thinking of perfectly inelastic demand, think *I = Inelastic*, with the I representing the vertical perfectly inelastic demand curve. When thinking of perfectly elastic demand, think *E = Elastic*, with the horizontal middle line of the E representing the horizontal perfectly elastic demand curve.

Figure 47.3 Total Revenue

(a) Total Revenue by Area

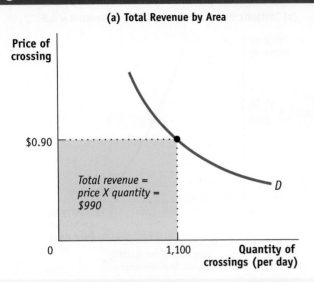

(b) Effect of a Price Increase on Total Revenue

The green rectangle in panel (a) represents the total revenue generated from 1,100 drivers who each pay a toll of $0.90. Panel (b) shows how total revenue is affected when the price increases from $0.90 to $1.10.

Due to the quantity effect, total revenue falls by area *A*. Due to the price effect, total revenue increases by area *C*. In general, the net effect can go either way, depending on the price elasticity of demand.

The graph shows how the toll increase affects total bridge revenue by examining panel (b) of Figure 47.3. At a toll of $0.90, total revenue is given by the sum of areas *A* and *B*. After the toll is raised to $1.10, total revenue is given by the sum of areas *B* and *C*. So when the toll is raised, revenue represented by area *A* is lost but revenue represented by area *C* is gained. These two areas have important interpretations. Area *C* represents the revenue gain that comes from the additional $0.20 paid by drivers who continue to use the bridge. That is, the 900 drivers who continue to use the bridge contribute an additional $0.20 × 900 = $180 per day to total revenue, represented by area *C*. But 200 drivers who would have used the bridge at a price of $0.90 no longer do so, generating a loss to total revenue of $0.90 × 200 = $180 per day, represented by area *A*. (In this particular example, because demand is unit-elastic—the same as in panel (a) of Figure 47.2—the rise in the toll has no effect on total revenue; areas *A* and *C* are the same size.)

Except in the rare case of a good with perfectly elastic or perfectly inelastic demand, when a seller raises the price of a good, two countervailing effects are present:

- *A price effect.* After a price increase, each unit sold sells at a higher price, which tends to raise revenue.

- *A quantity effect.* After a price increase, fewer units are sold, which tends to lower revenue.

But what is the net effect on total revenue: does it go up or down? The answer is that, in general, total revenue can go either way—an increase in price may either increase total revenue or decrease it. If the price effect, which tends to raise total revenue, is the stronger of the two effects, then total revenue goes up. If the quantity effect, which tends to reduce total revenue, is the stronger, then total revenue goes down. And if the strengths of the two effects are exactly equal—as in our toll bridge example where a $180 gain offsets a $180 loss—total revenue is unchanged by the price increase.

How do we know which effect, if either, is stronger? The size of the price elasticity of demand tells us. Specifically:

- If demand for a good is *unit-elastic* (the price elasticity of demand is 1), an increase in price does not change total revenue. In this case, the quantity effect and the price effect exactly offset each other.
- If demand for a good is *inelastic* (the price elasticity of demand is less than 1), a higher price increases total revenue. In this case, the price effect is stronger than the quantity effect.
- If demand for a good is *elastic* (the price elasticity of demand is greater than 1), an increase in price reduces total revenue. In this case, the quantity effect is stronger than the price effect.

Table 47.1 shows how the effect of a price increase on total revenue depends on the price elasticity of demand, using the same data as in Figure 47.2. When demand is unit-elastic, an increase in the price from $0.90 to $1.10 leaves total revenue unchanged at $990. When demand is inelastic, the price effect dominates the quantity effect; the same price increase leads to an increase in total revenue from $945 to $1,045. And when demand is elastic, the quantity effect dominates the price effect; the price increase leads to a decline in total revenue from $1,080 to $880.

Table 47.1	Price Elasticity of Demand and Total Revenue		
		Price of crossing = $0.90	Price of crossing = $1.10
Unit-elastic demand (price elasticity of demand = 1)			
Quantity demanded		1,100	900
Total revenue		$990	$990
Inelastic demand (price elasticity of demand = 0.5)			
Quantity demanded		1,050	950
Total revenue		$945	$1,045
Elastic demand (price elasticity of demand = 2)			
Quantity demanded		1,200	800
Total revenue		$1,080	$880

The price elasticity of demand also predicts the effect of a *fall* in price on total revenue. When the price falls, the same two countervailing effects are present, but they work in the opposite directions as compared to the case of an increase in price. There is the price effect of a lower price per unit sold, which tends to lower revenue. This is countered by the quantity effect of more units sold, which tends to raise revenue. Which effect dominates depends on the price elasticity. Here is a quick summary:

- When demand is *unit-elastic*, the two effects exactly balance each other out; so a fall in price has no effect on total revenue.
- When demand is *inelastic*, the price effect dominates the quantity effect; so a fall in price reduces total revenue.
- When demand is *elastic*, the quantity effect dominates the price effect; so a fall in price increases total revenue.

> **AP® EXAM TIP**
>
> If total revenue and price move in the same direction, the good is inelastic. If total revenue and price move in opposite directions, the good is elastic. If total revenue does not change when price changes, the good is unit-elastic.

Price Elasticity Along the Demand Curve

Suppose an economist says that "the price elasticity of demand for coffee is 0.25." What he or she means is that *at the current price* the elasticity is 0.25. In the previous discussion of the toll bridge, what we were really describing was the elasticity *at the price* of $0.90. Why this qualification? Because for the vast majority of demand curves, the price elasticity of demand at one point along the curve is different from the price elasticity of demand at other points along the same curve.

To see this, consider the table in **Figure 47.4**, which shows a hypothetical demand schedule. It also shows in the last column the total revenue generated at each price. The upper panel of the graph shows the corresponding demand curve. The lower panel illustrates the same data on total revenue: the height of a bar at each quantity demanded—which corresponds to a particular price—measures the total revenue generated at that price.

Figure 47.4 The Price Elasticity of Demand Changes Along the Demand Curve

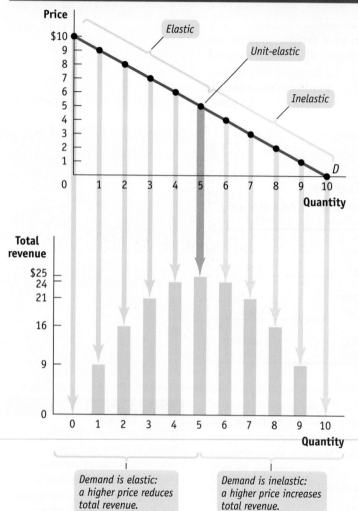

Demand Schedule and Total Revenue for a Linear Demand Curve		
Price	Quantity demanded	Total revenue
$0	10	$0
1	9	9
2	8	16
3	7	21
4	6	24
5	5	25
6	4	24
7	3	21
8	2	16
9	1	9
10	0	0

Demand is elastic: a higher price reduces total revenue.

Demand is inelastic: a higher price increases total revenue.

The upper panel shows a demand curve corresponding to the demand schedule in the table. The lower panel shows how total revenue changes along that demand curve: at each price and quantity combination, the height of the bar represents the total revenue generated. You can see that at a low price, raising the price increases total revenue. So demand is inelastic at low prices. At a high price, however, a rise in price reduces total revenue. So demand is elastic at high prices.

AP® EXAM TIP

For a straight, downward-sloping demand curve, the upper left segment of the demand curve is elastic and the bottom right segment is inelastic.

In Figure 47.4, you can see that when the price is low, raising the price increases total revenue: starting at a price of $1, raising the price to $2 increases total revenue from $9 to $16. This means that when the price is low, demand is inelastic. Moreover, you can see that demand is inelastic on the entire section of the demand curve where the price is below $5.

When the price is high, however, raising it further reduces total revenue: starting at a price of $8, for example, raising the price to $9 reduces total revenue from $16 to $9. This means that when the price is high, demand is elastic. Furthermore, you can see that demand is elastic over the section of the demand curve where the price exceeds $5.

For the vast majority of goods, the price elasticity of demand changes along the demand curve. So whenever you measure a good's elasticity, you are really measuring it at a particular point or section of the good's demand curve.

What Factors Determine the Price Elasticity of Demand?

Mylan was able to significantly raise its prices for emergency allergy treatments for two important reasons: there were few substitutes, and for many people the treatments were a medical necessity. People responded in various ways. Some paid the high prices, and some bought somewhat-less-expensive generic alternatives. Over time some people were able to travel to other countries where the prices for treatments are much lower. This experience illustrates the four main factors that determine elasticity: whether close substitutes are available, the share of income a consumer spends on the good, whether the good is a necessity or a luxury, and how much time has elapsed since the price change.

Whether Close Substitutes Are Available The price elasticity of demand tends to be high if there are other goods that consumers regard as similar and would be willing to consume instead. The price elasticity of demand tends to be low if there are no close substitutes.

Share of Income Spent on the Good The price elasticity of demand tends to be low when spending on a good accounts for a small share of a consumer's income. In that case, a significant change in the price of the good has little impact on how much the consumer spends. In contrast, when a good accounts for a significant share of a consumer's spending, the consumer is likely to be very responsive to a change in price. In this case, the price elasticity of demand is high.

Whether the Good Is a Necessity or a Luxury The price elasticity of demand tends to be low if a good is something you must have, like a life-saving medicine, or something you feel like you must have due to an addiction. The price elasticity of demand tends to be high if the good is a luxury—something you can easily live without.

You may want a Tesla, but you don't *need* one, so your price elasticity of demand for Teslas is probably high.

Time In general, the price elasticity of demand tends to increase as consumers have more time to adjust to a price change. This means that the long-run price elasticity of demand is often higher than the short-run elasticity.

A good illustration of the effect of time on the elasticity of demand is drawn from 2011 to 2013, when gasoline prices increased dramatically in the United States. Initially, consumption fell very little because there were no close substitutes for gasoline and because people needed to drive their cars to carry out the ordinary tasks of life. Over time, however, Americans changed their car buying and driving habits in ways that enabled them to gradually reduce their gasoline consumption. By 2013, the average household used 19% less gasoline and the average vehicle used 14% less gasoline than they had a decade earlier, confirming that the long-run price elasticity of demand for gasoline was indeed much higher than the short-run elasticity.

> **AP® EXAM TIP**
>
> Use this mnemonic to help remember that the determinants of price elasticity of demand are:
> **S** - Substitutes
> **P** - Proportion of income
> **L** - Luxury or necessity
> **A** - Addictive or habit forming
> **T** - Time

MODULE 47 REVIEW

Check Your Understanding

1. For each case, choose the condition that characterizes demand: elastic demand, inelastic demand, or unit-elastic demand.
   a. Total revenue decreases when price increases.
   b. When price falls, the additional revenue generated by the increase in the quantity sold is exactly offset by the revenue lost from the fall in the price received per unit.
   c. Total revenue falls when output increases.

   d. Producers in an industry find they can increase their total revenues by working together to reduce industry output.

2. For the following goods, is demand elastic, inelastic, or unit-elastic? Explain. What is the shape of the demand curve?
   a. demand by a snake-bite victim for an antidote
   b. demand by students for blue pencils

1. A perfectly elastic demand curve is
   a. upward-sloping.
   b. vertical.
   c. not a straight line.
   d. horizontal.
   e. downward-sloping.

2. Which of the following would cause the demand for a good to be relatively inelastic?
   a. The good has a large number of close substitutes.
   b. Expenditures on the good represent a large share of consumer income.
   c. There is ample time to adjust to price changes.
   d. The good is a necessity.
   e. The price of the good is in the upper left section of a linear demand curve.

3. Which of the following is true if the price elasticity of demand for a good is zero?
   a. The slope of the demand curve is zero.
   b. The slope of the demand curve is one.
   c. The demand curve is vertical.
   d. The demand curve is horizontal.
   e. The price of the good is high.

4. Which of the following is correct for a price increase? When demand is _____, total revenue will _____.

Demand	Total Revenue
a. inelastic	decrease
b. elastic	decrease
c. unit-elastic	increase
d. unit-elastic	decrease
e. elastic	increase

5. Total revenue is maximized when demand is
   a. elastic.
   b. inelastic.
   c. unit-elastic.
   d. zero.
   e. infinite.

6. The quantity demanded of a good with a high price elasticity of demand is necessarily
   a. very responsive to price changes.
   b. just slightly responsive to price changes.
   c. unresponsive to price changes.
   d. very small.
   e. very large.

7. If you are addicted to chocolate cake such that you buy one piece per day regardless of the price, your price elasticity of demand for chocolate cake is
   a. infinity.
   b. 1.
   c. more than 1 but less than infinity.
   d. 0.
   e. −1.

1. Draw a correctly labeled graph of a perfectly inelastic demand curve.
   a. What is the price elasticity of demand for this good?
   b. What is the slope of the demand curve for this good?
   c. Is this good more likely to be a luxury or a necessity? Explain.

1 point: A graph with "Price" (or "P") on the vertical axis, "Quantity" (or "Q") on the horizontal axis, and a vertical line labeled "Demand" (or "D")

1 point: Zero

1 point: Infinite or undefined

1 point: Necessity

1 point: Since you have to have a necessity (such as a life-saving medicine), you do not change the quantity you purchase when the price changes.

Rubric for FRQ 1 (5 points)

2. Draw a correctly labeled graph illustrating a demand curve that is a straight line and is neither perfectly elastic nor perfectly inelastic.
   a. On your graph, indicate the half of the demand curve along which demand is elastic.
   b. In the elastic range, how will an increase in price affect total revenue? Explain. **(4 points)**

Other Important Elasticities

In this Module, you will learn to:
- Measure the responsiveness of the demand for one good to changes in the price of another good using the cross-price elasticity of demand
- Measure the responsiveness of demand to changes in income using the income elasticity of demand
- Explain the significance of the price elasticity of supply, which measures the responsiveness of the quantity supplied to price changes
- Identify and describe the factors that influence the size of these various elasticities

Measuring Responses to Other Changes

We stated earlier that economists use the concept of *elasticity* to measure the responsiveness of one variable to changes in another. However, up to this point we have focused on the price elasticity of demand. Now that we have used elasticity to measure the responsiveness of quantity demanded to changes in price, we can look at how elasticity is used to understand the relationship between other important variables in economics.

The quantity of a good demanded depends not only on the price of that good but also on other variables. For example, demand curves shift because of changes in the prices of related goods and changes in consumers' incomes. It is often important to have a measure of these other effects, and the best measures are—you guessed it—elasticities. Specifically, we can best measure how the demand for a good is affected by prices of other goods using a measure called the *cross-price elasticity of demand*, and we can best measure how demand is affected by changes in income using the *income elasticity of demand*.

Finally, we can also use elasticity to measure supply responses. The *price elasticity of supply* measures the responsiveness of the quantity supplied to changes in price.

The Cross-Price Elasticity of Demand

The demand for a good is often affected by the prices of other, related goods—goods that are substitutes or complements. A change in the price of a related good shifts the demand curve of the original good, reflecting a change in the quantity demanded at any given price. The strength of such a "cross" effect on demand can be measured by the **cross-price elasticity of demand**, defined as the ratio of the percent change in the quantity demanded of one good to the percent change in the price of another.

> The **cross-price elasticity of demand** between two goods measures the effect of the change in one good's price on the quantity demanded of the other good. It is equal to the percent change in the quantity demanded of one good divided by the percent change in the other good's price.

$$\textbf{(48-1)} \quad \begin{array}{c} \text{Cross-price elasticity} \\ \text{of demand between} \\ \text{goods A and B} \end{array} = \frac{\text{\% change in quantity of A demanded}}{\text{\% change in price of B}}$$

When two goods are substitutes, like hot dogs and hamburgers, the cross-price elasticity of demand is positive: a rise in the price of hot dogs increases the demand for hamburgers—that is, it causes a rightward shift of the demand curve for hamburgers. If the goods are close substitutes, the cross-price elasticity will be positive and large; if they are not close substitutes, the cross-price elasticity will be positive and small. So when the cross-price elasticity of demand is positive, its size is a measure of how substitutable the two goods are.

When two goods are complements, like hot dogs and hot dog buns, the cross-price elasticity is negative: a rise in the price of hot dogs decreases the demand for hot dog buns—that is, it causes a leftward shift of the demand curve for hot dog buns. As with

AdShooter/Getty Images

substitutes, the size of the cross-price elasticity of demand between two complements tells us how strongly complementary they are: if the cross-price elasticity is only slightly below zero, they are weak complements; if it is a large negative number, they are strong complements.

Note that in the case of the cross-price elasticity of demand, the sign (plus or minus) is very important: it tells us whether the two goods are complements or substitutes. So we cannot drop the minus sign as we did for the price elasticity of demand.

Remember that elasticity is a *unit-free* measure—that is, it doesn't depend on the units in which goods are measured. To see the potential problem with units, suppose someone told you that "if the price of hot dog buns rises by $0.30, Americans will buy 10 million fewer hot dogs this year." If you've ever bought hot dog buns, you'll immediately wonder: is that a $0.30 increase in the price *per bun*, or is it a $0.30 increase in the price *per package* of buns? It makes a big difference what units we are talking about! However, if someone says that the cross-price elasticity of demand between buns and hot dogs is −0.3, you'll know that a 1% increase in the price of buns causes a 0.3% decrease in the quantity of hot dogs demanded, regardless of whether buns are sold individually or by the package. So elasticity is defined as a ratio of percent changes, which avoids confusion over units.

The Income Elasticity of Demand

The **income elasticity of demand** is the percent change in the quantity of a good demanded when a consumer's income changes divided by the percent change in the consumer's income; it measures how changes in income affect the demand for a good.

The **income elasticity of demand** measures how changes in income affect the demand for a good. It indicates whether a good is normal or inferior and specifies how responsive demand for the good is to changes in income. Having learned the price and cross-price elasticity formulas, the income elasticity formula will look familiar:

$$(48\text{-}2) \quad \text{Income elasticity of demand} = \frac{\%\text{ change in quantity demanded}}{\%\text{ change in income}}$$

Just as the cross-price elasticity of demand between two goods can be either positive or negative, depending on whether the goods are substitutes or complements, the income elasticity of demand for a good can also be either positive or negative. Recall that goods can be either *normal goods*, for which demand increases when income rises, or *inferior goods*, for which demand decreases when income rises. These definitions relate directly to the sign of the income elasticity of demand:

AP® EXAM TIP

A negative income elasticity identifies an inferior good (one you buy less of when your income goes up). A positive income elasticity identifies a normal good (one you buy more of when your income goes up).

- When the income elasticity of demand is positive, the good is a normal good.
- When the income elasticity of demand is negative, the good is an inferior good.

Economists often use estimates of the income elasticity of demand to predict which industries will grow most rapidly as the incomes of consumers grow over time. In doing this, they often find it useful to make a further distinction among normal goods, identifying which are *income-elastic* and which are *income-inelastic*.

The demand for a good is **income-elastic** if the income elasticity of demand for that good is greater than 1. The demand for a good is **income-inelastic** if the income elasticity of demand for that good is positive but less than 1.

The demand for a good is **income-elastic** if the income elasticity of demand for that good is greater than 1. When income rises, the demand for income-elastic goods rises *faster* than income. Luxury goods, such as second homes and international travel, tend to be income-elastic. The demand for a good is **income-inelastic** if the income elasticity of demand for that good is positive but less than 1. When income rises, the demand for income-inelastic goods rises as well, but more slowly than income. Necessities such as food and clothing tend to be income-inelastic.

The Price Elasticity of Supply

Mylan would not have been able to maintain its elevated price for emergency allergy treatments if a higher price had induced a large increase in the production of substitutes for the EpiPen. In fact, if the rise in price had attracted many new competitors into the market, the price would have been pushed back down. But that didn't happen because Mylan has a patent on its auto-injector and new products were slow to develop due to the life-and-death matter of avoiding design and manufacturing defects. This was another critical element in the ability of a few producers, including Mylan, to get significantly higher prices for their products: a low responsiveness in the quantity of output supplied to the higher price of emergency allergy treatments. To measure the response of producers to price changes, we need a measure parallel to the price elasticity of demand—the *price elasticity of supply*.

When the price of EpiPens shot up, product-development issues and Mylan's patent impeded a price-moderating response from competitors, but customers were quick to respond in their own way.

PACIFIC PRESS/Alamy

Measuring the Price Elasticity of Supply

The **price elasticity of supply** is defined the same way as the price elasticity of demand (although there is no minus sign to be eliminated here):

(48-3) Price elasticity of supply = $\dfrac{\text{\% change in quantity supplied}}{\text{\% change in price}}$

The only difference is that here we consider movements along the supply curve rather than movements along the demand curve.

Suppose the price of tomatoes rises by 10%. If the quantity of tomatoes supplied also increases by 10% in response, the price elasticity of supply of tomatoes is 1 (10%/10%) and supply is unit-elastic. If the quantity supplied increases by 5%, the price elasticity of supply is 0.5 and supply is inelastic; if the quantity increases by 20%, the price elasticity of supply is 2 and supply is elastic.

As in the case of demand, the extreme values of the price elasticity of supply have a simple graphical representation. Panel (a) of **Figure 48.1** shows the supply of cell phone frequencies, the portion of the radio spectrum that is suitable for sending and receiving cell phone signals. Governments own the right to sell the use of this part of the radio spectrum to cell phone operators inside their borders. But governments can't increase or decrease the number of cell phone frequencies they have to offer—for technical reasons, the quantity of frequencies suitable for cell phone operation is fixed. So the supply curve for cell phone frequencies is a vertical line, which we have assumed is set

The **price elasticity of supply** is a measure of the responsiveness of the quantity of a good supplied to changes in the price of that good. It is the ratio of the percent change in the quantity supplied to the percent change in the price as we move along the supply curve.

Figure 48.1 Two Extreme Cases of Price Elasticity of Supply

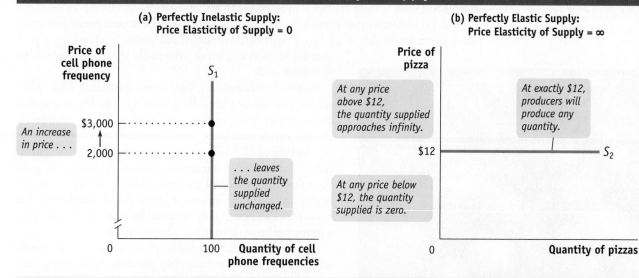

Panel (a) shows a perfectly inelastic supply curve, which is a vertical line. The price elasticity of supply is zero: the quantity supplied is always the same, regardless of price. Panel (b) shows a perfectly elastic supply curve, which is a horizontal line. At a price of $12, producers will supply any quantity, but they will supply none at a price below $12. If the price rises above $12, they will supply an extremely large quantity.

at the quantity of 100 frequencies. As you move up and down that curve, the change in the quantity supplied by the government is zero, whatever the change in price. So panel (a) illustrates a case of **perfectly inelastic supply**, meaning that the price elasticity of supply is zero.

Panel (b) shows the supply curve for pizza. We suppose that it costs $12 to produce a pizza, including all opportunity costs. At any price below $12, it would be unprofitable to produce pizza and all the pizza parlors would go out of business. At a price of $12 or more, there are many producers who could operate pizza parlors. The ingredients—flour, tomatoes, cheese—are plentiful. And if necessary, more tomatoes could be grown, more milk could be produced to make mozzarella cheese, and so on. So by allowing profits, any price above $12 would elicit the supply of an extremely large quantity of pizzas. The implied supply curve is therefore a horizontal line at $12. Since even a tiny increase in the price would lead to an enormous increase in the quantity supplied, the price elasticity of supply would approach infinity. A horizontal supply curve such as this represents a case of **perfectly elastic supply**.

As our cell phone frequencies and pizza examples suggest, real-world instances of both perfectly inelastic and perfectly elastic supply are easier to find than their counterparts in demand.

What Factors Determine the Price Elasticity of Supply?

Our examples tell us the main determinant of the price elasticity of supply: the availability of inputs. In addition, as with the price elasticity of demand, time may also play a role in the price elasticity of supply. Here we briefly summarize the two factors.

The Availability of Inputs The price elasticity of supply tends to be high when inputs are readily available and can be shifted into and out of production at a relatively low cost. It tends to be low when inputs are available only in a more-or-less fixed quantity or can be shifted into and out of production only at a relatively high cost.

Time The price elasticity of supply tends to increase as producers have more time to respond to a price change. This means that the long-run price elasticity of supply is typically higher than the short-run elasticity. In the case of epinephrine auto-injectors, Mylan's patent runs out in 2025, at which time we can expect new producers to enter the market with similar products in response to the high price.

The price elasticity of pizza supply is very high because the inputs needed to make more pizza are readily available. The price elasticity of cell phone frequencies is zero because an essential input—the radio spectrum—cannot be increased at all.

Many industries are like pizza and have high price elasticities of supply: they can be readily expanded because they don't require any hard-to-obtain resources. On the other hand, the price elasticity of supply is usually substantially less than perfectly elastic for goods that involve limited natural resources: minerals like gold or copper, agricultural products like coffee that mature slowly and only in particular types of soil, and renewable resources like ocean fish that can be exploited only up to a point without destroying the resource.

Given enough time, producers are often able to significantly change the amount they produce in response to a price change, even when production involves a limited natural resource. For example, given a few years, new gold deposits can be discovered and mined, new coffee trees can bear fruit, and new fisheries can be established.

There is **perfectly inelastic supply** when the price elasticity of supply is zero, so that changes in the price of the good have no effect on the quantity supplied. A perfectly inelastic supply curve is a vertical line.

There is **perfectly elastic supply** if the quantity supplied is zero below some price and approaches infinity above that price. A perfectly elastic supply curve is a horizontal line.

AP® EXAM TIP

If a straight-line supply curve intersects the horizontal axis, supply is inelastic; if it intersects the vertical axis, supply is elastic; if it intersects the origin, supply is unit elastic.

The supply of coffee responds slowly to price changes because coffee trees take 3 to 5 years to mature and require rich, porous soil.

For this reason, economists often make a distinction between the short-run elasticity of supply, usually referring to the elasticity over a few weeks or months, and the long-run elasticity of supply, usually referring to the elasticity over a period of years. In most industries, the long-run elasticity of supply is higher than the short-run elasticity of supply.

AP® EXAM TIP

Time gives firms a chance to adjust their size and find new sources of inputs. So the more time, the more ability to respond to price changes and the greater the elasticity of supply.

An Elasticity Menagerie

We've just run through quite a few different types of elasticity. Keeping them all straight can be a challenge, but all of these elasticities are important. So we provide a summary of all the types of elasticity we have discussed and their implications in **Table 48.1.**

Table 48.1	An Elasticity Menagerie	
Name	**Elasticity values**	**Significance**
Price elasticity of demand $= \dfrac{\% \text{ change in quantity demanded}}{\% \text{ change in price}}$ (dropping the minus sign)		
Perfectly inelastic demand	0	Price has no effect on quantity demanded (vertical demand curve).
Inelastic demand	Between 0 and 1	A rise in price increases total revenue.
Unit-elastic demand	Exactly 1	Changes in price have no effect on total revenue.
Elastic demand	Greater than 1, less than ∞	A rise in price reduces total revenue.
Perfectly elastic demand	∞	A rise in price causes quantity demanded to fall to 0. A fall in price leads to a quantity demanded that approaches infinity (horizontal demand curve).
Cross-price elasticity of demand $= \dfrac{\% \text{ change in quantity of } one\ good \text{ demanded}}{\% \text{ change in price of } another\ good}$		
Complements	Negative	Quantity demanded of one good falls when the price of another rises.
Substitutes	Positive	Quantity demanded of one good rises when the price of another rises.
Income elasticity of demand $= \dfrac{\% \text{ change in quantity demanded}}{\% \text{ change in income}}$		
Inferior good	Negative	Quantity demanded falls when income rises.
Normal good, income-inelastic	Positive, less than 1	Quantity demanded rises when income rises, but not as rapidly as income.
Normal good, income-elastic	Greater than 1	Quantity demanded rises when income rises, and more rapidly than income.
Price elasticity of supply $= \dfrac{\% \text{ change in quantity supplied}}{\% \text{ change in price}}$		
Perfectly inelastic supply	0	Price has no effect on quantity supplied (vertical supply curve).
Inelastic supply	Between 0 and 1	Quantity supplied rises by a smaller percentage than price.
Unit-elastic supply	Exactly 1	Quantity supplied rises by the same percentage as price.
Elastic supply	Greater than 1, less than ∞	Quantity supplied rises by a larger percentage than price.
Perfectly elastic supply	∞	Any fall in price causes quantity supplied to fall to 0. Any rise in price elicits a quantity supplied that approaches infinity (horizontal supply curve).

Check Your Understanding

1. After Chelsea's income increased from $12,000 to $18,000 a year, her purchases of music downloads increased from 10 to 40 music downloads a year. Calculate Chelsea's income elasticity of demand for music downloads using the midpoint method.

2. As the price of margarine rises by 20%, a manufacturer of baked goods increases its quantity of butter demanded by 5%. Calculate the cross-price elasticity of demand between butter and margarine. Are butter and margarine substitutes or complements for this manufacturer?

3. Using the midpoint method, calculate the price elasticity of supply for web-design services when the price per hour rises from $100 to $150 and the number of hours supplied increases from 300,000 hours to 500,000. Is supply elastic, inelastic, or unit-elastic?

TACKLE THE AP® TEST: Multiple-Choice Questions

1. If the cross-price elasticity between two goods is negative, this means that the two goods are
   a. substitutes.
   b. complements.
   c. normal.
   d. inferior.
   e. luxuries.

2. If Kylie buys 200 units of good X when her income is $20,000 and 300 units of good X when her income increases to $25,000, her income elasticity of demand, using the midpoint method, is
   a. 0.06.
   b. 0.5.
   c. 1.65.
   d. 1.8.
   e. 2.0.

3. The income elasticity of demand for a normal good is
   a. 0.
   b. 1.
   c. infinite.
   d. positive.
   e. negative.

4. A perfectly inelastic supply curve
   a. increases from left to right.
   b. decreases from left to right.
   c. is horizontal.
   d. is vertical.
   e. is U-shaped.

5. Which of the following leads to a more inelastic price elasticity of supply?
   a. the use of inputs that are easily obtained
   b. a high degree of substitutability between inputs
   c. a shorter time period in which to supply the good
   d. a more inelastic price elasticity of demand
   e. a small demand for the good

6. Zeke buys more cereal when his income falls. For Zeke, cereal
   a. is a normal good.
   b. has a positive income elasticity of demand.
   c. has a negative income elasticity of demand.
   d. has income-inelastic demand.
   e. has income-elastic demand.

7. A supply curve with a slope of zero has a price elasticity of supply that approaches
   a. 0.
   b. infinity.
   c. 1.
   d. −1.
   e. 100.

TACKLE THE AP® TEST: Free-Response Questions

1. Refer to the table below to answer the following questions.

Price of good A	Quantity of good A demanded	Quantity of good B demanded
$10	100	5
8	110	10

   a. Using the midpoint method, calculate the price elasticity of demand for good A.
   b. Give the formula for calculating the cross-price elasticity of demand between good B and good A.
   c. Using the midpoint method, calculate the cross-price elasticity of demand between good B and good A.
   d. What does your answer for part c tell you about the relationship between the two goods? Explain.

Rubric for FRQ 1 (5 points)

1 point: 0.43

1 point: % change in quantity of good B demanded/% change in price of good A or (change in Q_B/average Q_B)/(change in P_A/average P_A)

1 point: −3

1 point: They are complements.

1 point: Cross-price elasticity is negative—when the price of good A goes down, in addition to buying more of good A, people buy more of good B to go along with it.

2. Assume the price of corn rises by 20% and this causes suppliers to increase the quantity of corn supplied by 40%.
   a. Calculate the price elasticity of supply.
   b. In this case, is supply elastic or inelastic?
   c. Draw a correctly labeled graph of a supply curve illustrating the most extreme case of the category of elasticity you found in part b (either perfectly elastic or perfectly inelastic supply).
   d. What would likely be true of the availability of inputs for a firm with the supply curve you drew in part c? Explain. **(5 points)**

Consumer and Producer Surplus

In this Module, you will learn to:
- Explain the meaning of consumer surplus and its relationship to the demand curve
- Explain the meaning of producer surplus and its relationship to the supply curve

There is a lively market in second-hand college textbooks. At the end of each term, some students decide the money they can make by selling their used books is worth more to them than keeping the books. And some students prefer to buy a somewhat battered but less expensive used textbook rather than pay full price for a new one.

Textbook publishers and authors are not happy about these transactions because they cut into sales of new books. But both the students who sell used books and those who buy them clearly benefit from the existence of the used-book market. That is why many college bookstores facilitate their trade, buying used textbooks and selling them alongside the new books.

Can we put a number on what used textbook buyers and sellers gain from these transactions? Can we answer the question "*How much* do the buyers and sellers of textbooks gain from the existence of the used-book market?"

Yes, we can. In this Module we will see how to measure benefits from being able to purchase a good, such as those enjoyed by buyers of used textbooks. Those benefits are known as *consumer surplus*. And we will see that there is a corresponding measure, *producer surplus*, of the benefits sellers receive from being able to sell a good.

The concepts of consumer surplus and producer surplus are useful for analyzing a wide variety of economic issues. They let us quantify the benefits producers and consumers receive from the existence of a market. They also allow us to calculate how the welfare of consumers and producers is affected by changes in market prices. Such calculations play a crucial role in the evaluation of many economic policies.

What information do we need to calculate consumer and producer surplus? Surprisingly, all we need are the demand and supply curves for a good. That is, the supply and demand model isn't just a model of how a competitive market works—it's also a model of how much consumers and producers gain from participating in that market.

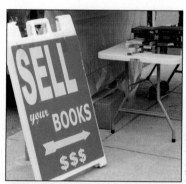

B Christopher/Alamy stockphoto

AP® EXAM TIP

On the AP® exam you may be asked to draw a graph and shade the areas that represent consumer and producer surplus.

So our first step will be to learn how consumer and producer surplus can be derived from the demand and supply curves. We will then see how these concepts can be applied to actual economic issues.

Consumer Surplus and the Demand Curve

First-year college students are often surprised by the prices of the textbooks required for their classes. The College Board estimates that in 2016–2017 students at public four-year schools, on average, spent $1,250 for books and supplies. But at the end of the semester, students might again be surprised to find out that they can sell back at least some of their textbooks for a sizable portion of the purchase price. The ability to purchase used textbooks at the start of the semester and to sell back used textbooks at the end of the semester is beneficial to students on a budget.

The market for used textbooks provides a convenient starting point for us to develop the concepts of consumer and producer surplus. We'll use these concepts to understand exactly how buyers and sellers benefit from a competitive market and how big those benefits are. In addition, these concepts assist in the analysis of what happens when competitive markets don't work well or there is interference in the market.

Let's begin by looking at the market for used textbooks, starting with the buyers. The key point, as we'll see in a minute, is that the demand curve is derived from their tastes or preferences—and those same preferences also determine how much they gain from the opportunity to buy used books.

Willingness to Pay and the Demand Curve

A used book is not as good as a new book—it will be battered and coffee-stained, may include someone else's highlighting, and may not be completely up to date. How much this bothers you depends on your preferences. Some potential buyers would prefer to buy the used book even if it is only slightly cheaper than a new one, while others would buy the used book only if it is considerably cheaper. Let's define a potential buyer's **willingness to pay** as the maximum price at which he or she would buy a good, in this case a used textbook. An individual won't buy the good if it costs more than this amount but is eager to do so if it costs less. If the price is equal to an individual's willingness to pay, he or she is indifferent between buying and not buying. For the sake of simplicity, we'll assume that the individual buys the good in this case.

The table in **Figure 49.1** shows five potential buyers of a used book that costs $200 new, listed in order of their willingness to pay. At one extreme is Ally, who will buy a used book even if the price is as high as $118. Bart is less willing to have a used book and will buy one only if the price is $90 or less. Cierra is willing to pay only $70, and Darrius, only $50. Emma, who really doesn't like the idea of a used book, will buy one only if it costs no more than $20.

How many of these five students will actually buy a used book? It depends on the price. If the price of a used book is $110, only Ally buys one; if the price is $80, Ally and Bart both buy used books, and so on, until you reach a price of $20, at which all five students are willing to purchase a book. So the information in the table can be used to construct the *demand schedule* for used textbooks.

We can use this demand schedule to derive the market demand curve shown in Figure 49.1. Because we are considering only a small number of consumers, this curve doesn't look like the smooth demand curves we have seen previously for markets that contained hundreds or thousands of consumers. This demand curve is step-shaped, with alternating horizontal and vertical segments. Each horizontal segment—each step—corresponds to one potential buyer's willingness to pay. However, we'll see shortly

A consumer's **willingness to pay** for a good is the maximum price at which he or she would buy that good.

Figure 49.1 The Demand Curve for Used Textbooks

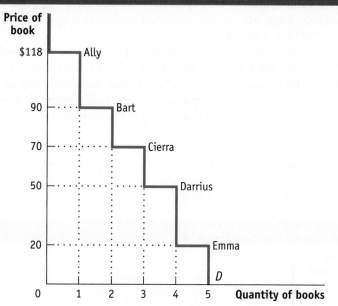

Potential buyers	Willingness to pay
Ally	$118
Bart	90
Cierra	70
Darrius	50
Emma	20

With only five potential consumers in this market, the demand curve is step-shaped. Each step represents one consumer, and its height indicates that consumer's willingness to pay—the maximum price at which each will buy a used textbook—as indicated in the table.

that for the analysis of consumer surplus it doesn't matter whether the demand curve is step-shaped, as in this figure, or whether there are so many consumers that the steps are tiny and the curve appears smooth.

Willingness to Pay and Consumer Surplus

Suppose that the campus bookstore makes used textbooks available at a price of $60. In that case Ally, Bart, and Cierra will buy books. Do they gain from their purchases, and if so, how much?

The answer, shown in **Table 49.1**, is that each student who purchases a book does achieve a net gain, but the amount of the gain differs among students. Ally would have been willing to pay $118, so her net gain is $118 − $60 = $58. Bart would have been willing to pay $90, so his net gain is $90 − $60 = $30. Cierra would have been willing to pay $70, so her net gain is $70 − $60 = $10. Darrius and Emma, however, won't be willing to buy a used book at a price of $60, so they neither gain nor lose.

The net gain that a buyer achieves from the purchase of a good is called that buyer's **individual consumer surplus**. What we learn from this example is that whenever a buyer pays a price less than his or her willingness to pay, the buyer achieves some individual consumer surplus.

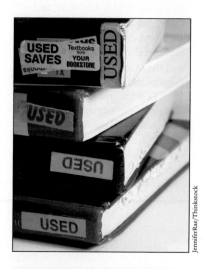

Individual consumer surplus is the net gain to an individual buyer from the purchase of a good. It is equal to the difference between the buyer's willingness to pay and the price paid.

Table 49.1 Consumer Surplus When the Price of a Used Textbook Is $60

Potential buyer	Willingness to pay	Price paid	Individual consumer surplus = Willingness to pay − Price paid
Ally	$118	$60	$58
Bart	90	60	30
Cierra	70	60	10
Darrius	50	—	—
Emma	20	—	—
All buyers			Total consumer surplus = $98

Total consumer surplus is the sum of the individual consumer surpluses of all the buyers of a good in a market.

The term **consumer surplus** is often used to refer to both individual and total consumer surplus.

The sum of the individual consumer surpluses achieved by all the buyers of a good is known as the **total consumer surplus** achieved in the market. In Table 49.1, the total consumer surplus is the sum of the individual consumer surpluses achieved by Ally, Bart, and Cierra: $58 + $30 + $10 = $98.

Economists often use the term **consumer surplus** to refer to both individual and total consumer surplus. We will follow this practice; it will always be clear in context whether we are referring to the consumer surplus achieved by an individual or by all buyers.

Total consumer surplus can be represented graphically. **Figure 49.2** reproduces the demand curve from Figure 49.1. Each step in that demand curve is one book wide and represents one consumer. For example, the height of Ally's step is $118, her willingness to pay. This step forms the top of a rectangle, the bottom of which lies on the price line showing the $60 price she actually pays for a book. The area of Ally's rectangle, ($118 − $60) × 1 = $58, is her consumer surplus from purchasing one book at $60. So the individual consumer surplus Ally gains is the *area of the dark blue rectangle* shown in Figure 49.2.

Figure 49.2 Consumer Surplus in the Used-Textbook Market

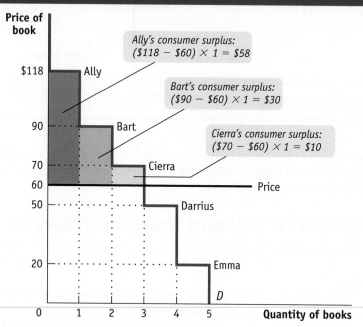

At a price of $60, Ally, Bart, and Cierra get individual consumer surpluses equal to the difference between their willingness to pay and the price, illustrated by the areas of the shaded rectangles. Both Darrius and Emma have a willingness to pay that is less than $60, so they are unwilling to buy a book in this market; they receive no consumer surplus. The total consumer surplus is given by the entire shaded area.

In addition to Ally, Bart and Cierra will also each buy a book when the price is $60. Like Ally, they benefit from their purchases, though not as much, because they each have a lower willingness to pay. Figure 49.2 shows the consumer surplus gained by Bart and Cierra as rectangles shaded with lighter blues. Darrius and Emma receive no consumer surplus because they do not buy books at a price of $60.

The total consumer surplus achieved in this market is just the sum of the individual consumer surpluses received by Ally, Bart, and Cierra. So the total consumer surplus is equal to the combined area of the three shaded rectangles in Figure 49.2, $98. Another way to say this is that total consumer surplus is equal to the area below the demand curve but above the price.

This is worth repeating as a general principle: *The total consumer surplus generated by purchases of a good at a given price is equal to the area below the demand curve but above that price.* The same principle applies regardless of the number of consumers.

When we consider large markets, this graphical representation becomes particularly helpful. Consider, for example, the sales of laptop computers to millions of potential buyers. Each potential buyer has a maximum price that he or she is willing to pay. With so many potential buyers, the step

Figure 49.3 Consumer Surplus

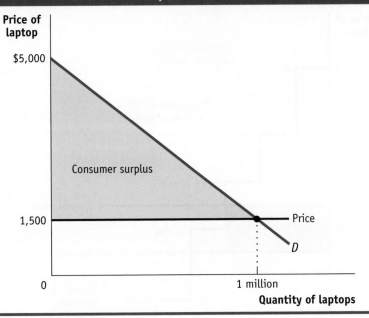

The demand curve for laptop computers is smooth because there are many potential buyers. At a price of $1,500, 1 million laptops are demanded. The consumer surplus at this price is equal to the shaded area: the area below the demand curve but above the price. The area of a triangle is $\frac{1}{2} \times$ the base of the triangle $\times$ the height of the triangle. So the total consumer surplus in this case is $\frac{1}{2} \times 1$ million $\times$ $3,500 = $1.75 billion. This is the total net gain to consumers generated from buying and consuming laptops when the price is $1,500.

representing each buyer's willingness to pay becomes very narrow and the demand curve appears smooth, like the one shown in **Figure 49.3**.

Suppose that at a price of $1,500, a total of 1 million laptops are purchased. How much do consumers gain from being able to buy those 1 million laptops? We could answer that question by calculating the individual consumer surplus of each buyer and then adding these numbers up to arrive at a total. But it is much easier just to look at Figure 49.3 and use the fact that total consumer surplus is equal to the shaded area below the demand curve but above the price. Recall that the area of a triangle is $\frac{1}{2} \times$ the base of the triangle $\times$ the height of the triangle. So the total consumer surplus in this case is $\frac{1}{2} \times 1$ million $\times$ $3,500 = $1.75 billion.

AP® EXAM TIP

You may be asked to calculate the size of the area that represents consumer surplus, which is bounded by the demand curve, the price line, and the vertical axis. Remember: the area of a triangle $= \frac{1}{2} \times$ base $\times$ height.

How Changing Prices Affect Consumer Surplus

It is often important to know how price *changes* affect consumer surplus. For example, we may want to know the harm to consumers from a frost in Florida that drives up the price of oranges, or consumers' gain from the introduction of fish farming that makes salmon steaks less expensive. The same approach we have used to derive consumer surplus can be used to answer questions about how changes in prices affect consumers.

Let's return to the example of the market for used textbooks. Suppose the bookstore decided to sell used textbooks for $40 instead of $60. By how much would this fall in price increase consumer surplus?

The answer is illustrated in **Figure 49.4**. As shown in the figure, there are two parts to the increase in consumer surplus. The first part, shaded dark blue, is the gain of those who would have bought books even at the higher price of $60. Each of the students who would have bought books at $60—Ally, Bart, and Cierra—now pays $20 less, and therefore each gains $20 in consumer surplus from the fall in price to $40. So the dark blue area represents the $20 $\times$ 3 = $60 increase in consumer surplus to those three buyers. The second part, shaded light blue, is the gain to those who would not have bought a book at $60 but are willing to pay more than $40. In this case that gain goes to Darrius, who would not have bought a book at $60 but does buy one at $40. He gains $10—the difference between his willingness to pay of $50 and the new price of $40. So the light blue area represents a further $10 gain in consumer surplus. The total increase in consumer surplus is the sum of the shaded areas, $70. Likewise, a rise in price from $40 to $60 would decrease consumer surplus by an amount equal to the sum of the shaded areas.

Figure 49.4 Consumer Surplus and a Fall in the Price of Used Textbooks

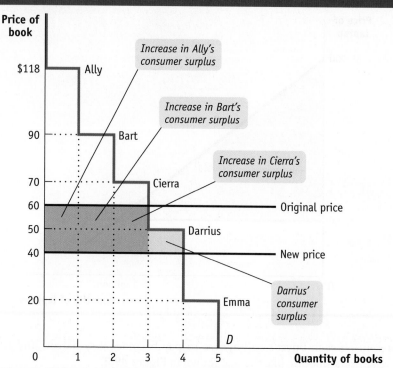

There are two parts to the increase in consumer surplus generated by a fall in price from $60 to $40. The first part is the dark blue rectangle that represents the $20 increase in consumer surplus for each person who would have bought a used textbook at the original price of $60. The second part is the light blue area that represents the increase in consumer surplus for those who would *not* have bought a used textbook at the original price of $60 but who buy at the new price of $40—namely, Darrius's increase in consumer surplus of $10. The total increase in consumer surplus is 3 × $20 + $10 = $70, represented by the sum of the shaded areas.

Producer Surplus and the Supply Curve

Just as some buyers of a good would have been willing to pay more for their purchase than the price they actually pay, some sellers of a good would have been willing to sell it for less than the price they actually receive. We can therefore carry out an analysis of producer surplus and the supply curve that is almost exactly parallel to that of consumer surplus and the demand curve.

Cost

Before we can find the producer surplus we must examine the underlying cost. Consider a group of students who are potential sellers of used textbooks. Because they have different preferences, the various potential sellers differ in regard to the lowest price they would accept for their books. The table in **Figure 49.5** shows the prices at which several different students would be willing to sell. Andrew is willing to sell the book as long as he can get at least $10; Betty won't sell unless she can get at least $30; Carlos requires $50; Donna requires $70; Emir requires $90.

A seller's **cost** is the lowest price at which he or she is willing to sell a good.

The lowest price at which a potential seller is willing to sell is called the seller's **cost**. So Andrew's cost is $10, Betty's is $30, and so on.

Using the term *cost*, which people normally associate with the monetary cost of producing a good, may sound a little strange when applied to sellers of used textbooks. The students don't have to manufacture the books, so it doesn't cost the student who sells a book anything to make that book available for sale, does it?

Yes, it does. A student who sells a book won't have it later, as part of his or her personal collection. So there is an *opportunity cost* to selling a textbook, even if the owner has completed the course for which it was required. And remember that one of the basic principles of economics is that the true measure of the cost of doing something is always its opportunity cost. That is, the real cost of something is what you must give up to get it.

Figure 49.5 The Supply Curve for Used Textbooks

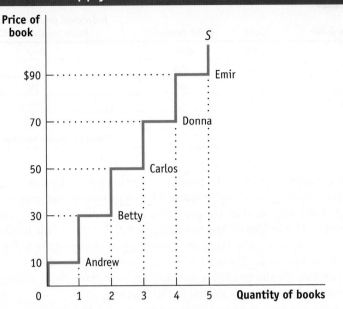

Potential sellers	Cost
Andrew	$10
Betty	30
Carlos	50
Donna	70
Emir	90

The supply curve illustrates sellers' cost, the lowest price at which a potential seller is willing to sell the good, and the quantity supplied at that price. Each of the five students has one book to sell and each has a different cost, as indicated in the accompanying table.

So it is appropriate to refer to the minimum price at which someone will sell a good as the "cost" of selling that good, even if he or she doesn't spend any money to make the good available for sale. Of course, in most real-world markets the sellers are also those who produce the good and therefore *do* spend money to make the good available for sale. In this case the cost of making the good available for sale *includes* monetary costs, but it may also include other opportunity costs.

Producer Surplus

Now we're ready to find the producer surplus. Suppose that Andrew sells his book for $60. Clearly he has gained from the transaction: he would have been willing to sell for only $10, so he has gained $50. This net gain, the difference between the price he actually gets and his cost—the minimum price at which he would have been willing to sell—is known as his **individual producer surplus**.

Just as we derived the demand curve from the willingness to pay of different consumers, we can derive the supply curve from the cost of different producers. The step-shaped curve in Figure 49.5 shows the supply curve implied by the costs shown in the accompanying table. At a price less than $10, none of the students are willing to sell; at a price between $10 and $30, only Andrew is willing to sell, and so on until you reach $90, the price at which all five students are willing to sell.

As in the case of consumer surplus, we can add the individual producer surpluses of each seller to calculate the **total producer surplus**, the total net gain to all sellers in the market. Economists use the term **producer surplus** to refer to either total or individual producer surplus. **Table 49.2** shows the net gain to each of the students who would sell a used book at a price of $60: $50 for Andrew, $30 for Betty, and $10 for Carlos. The total producer surplus is $50 + $30 + $10 = $90.

In upcoming modules we'll discuss profit. For now, we should note that in most cases producer surplus differs from profit because more types of costs—not just the lowest price at which the seller would provide the good—are subtracted from the amount sellers receive in the calculation of profit.

Individual producer surplus is the net gain to an individual seller from selling a good. It is equal to the difference between the price received and the seller's cost.

Total producer surplus in a market is the sum of the individual producer surpluses of all the sellers of a good in a market.

Economists use the term **producer surplus** to refer to both individual and total producer surplus.

Table 49.2	Producer Surplus When the Price of a Used Textbook Is $60		
Potential seller	Cost	Price received	Individual producer surplus = Price received − Cost
Andrew	$10	$60	$50
Betty	30	60	30
Carlos	50	60	10
Donna	70	—	—
Emir	90	—	—
All sellers			Total producer surplus = $90

As with consumer surplus, the producer surplus gained by those who sell books can be represented graphically. **Figure 49.6** reproduces the supply curve from Figure 49.5. Each step in that supply curve has a width that represents one book from one seller. The height of Andrew's step is $10, his cost. This forms the bottom of a rectangle, the top of which lies on the price line showing the $60 price he actually receives for his book. The area of this rectangle, ($60 − $10) × 1 = $50, is his producer surplus. So the producer surplus Andrew gains from selling his book is the *area of the dark red rectangle* shown in the figure.

Figure 49.6 Producer Surplus in the Used-Textbook Market

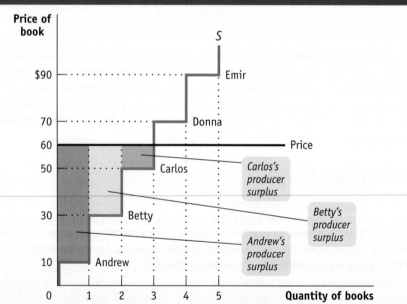

At a price of $60, Andrew, Betty, and Carlos each sell a book but Donna and Emir do not. Andrew, Betty, and Carlos get individual producer surpluses equal to the difference between the price and their cost, illustrated here by the shaded rectangles. Donna and Emir each have a cost that is greater than the price of $60, so they are unwilling to sell a book and so receive no producer surplus. The total producer surplus is given by the entire shaded area.

Let's assume that the campus bookstore is willing to buy all the used copies of this book that students are willing to sell at a price of $60. Then, in addition to Andrew, Betty and Carlos will also sell their books. They will benefit from their sales, though not as much as Andrew, because they have higher costs. Andrew, as we have seen, gains $50. Betty gains a smaller amount: since her cost is $30, she gains only $30. Carlos gains even less, only $10. Donna and Emir will not sell a book because their cost exceeds the price. The total surplus of $90 is represented in Figure 49.6 by the combined area of the three shaded rectangles.

Again, as with consumer surplus, we have a general rule for determining the total producer surplus from sales of a good: *The total producer surplus from sales of a good at a given price is the area above the supply curve but below that price.*

This rule applies both to examples like the one shown in Figure 49.6, where there are a small number of producers and a step-shaped supply curve, and to more realistic examples, where there are many producers and the supply curve is more or less smooth.

Consider, for example, the supply of wheat. **Figure 49.7** shows how producer surplus depends on the price per bushel. Suppose that, as shown in the figure, the price is $5 per bushel and farmers supply 1 million bushels. What is the benefit to the farmers from selling their wheat at a price of $5? Their producer surplus is equal to the shaded area above the supply curve but below the price of $5 per bushel: $1/2 \times 1$ million $\times \$4 = \$2$ million.

Figure 49.7 Producer Surplus

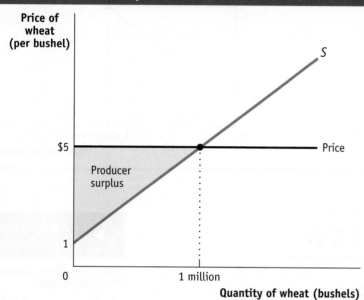

At a price of $5 per bushel, farmers supply 1 million bushels of wheat. The producer surplus at this price is equal to the shaded area above the supply curve but below the price: $1/2 \times 1$ million $\times \$4 = \$2$ million.

How Changing Prices Affect Producer Surplus

As in the case of consumer surplus, a change in price alters producer surplus. However, although a fall in price increases consumer surplus, it reduces producer surplus. Similarly, a rise in price reduces consumer surplus but increases producer surplus.

To see this, let's first consider a rise in the price of the good. Producers of the good will experience an increase in producer surplus, though not all producers gain the same amount. Some producers would have produced the good even at the original price; they will gain the entire price increase on every unit they produce. Other producers will enter the market because of the higher price; they will gain only the difference between the new price and their cost.

Figure 49.8 shows the effect on producer surplus of a rise in the price of wheat from $5 to $7 per bushel. The increase in producer surplus is the sum of the shaded areas, which consists of two parts. First, there is a dark red rectangle corresponding to the gains to those farmers who would have supplied wheat even at the original $5 price. The area of the dark red triangle is 1 million $\times \$2 = \$2$ million. Second, there is an additional light red triangle that corresponds to the gains to those farmers who would not have supplied wheat at the original price but are drawn into the market by the higher price. The area of the light red triangle is $1/2 \times 0.5$ million $\times \$2 = \$500,000$. So the total gain in producer surplus is $2 million + $500,000 = $2.5 million.

If the price were to fall from $7 to $5 per bushel, the story would run in reverse. The sum of the shaded areas would now be the decline in producer surplus, the decrease in the area above the supply curve but below the price. The loss would consist of two parts, the loss to farmers who would still grow wheat at a price of $5 (the dark red rectangle) and the loss to farmers who would no longer grow wheat because of the lower price (the light red triangle).

AP® EXAM TIP

The area on a graph that represents producer surplus is bounded by the supply curve, the price line, and the vertical axis.

Figure 49.8 A Rise in the Price Increases Producer Surplus

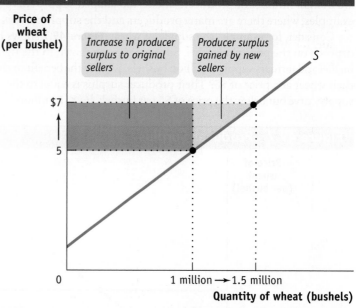

A rise in the price of wheat from $5 to $7 leads to an increase in the quantity supplied and an increase in producer surplus. The change in total producer surplus is given by the sum of the shaded areas: the total area above the supply curve but between the old and new prices. The dark red area represents the gain to the farmers who would have supplied 1 million bushels at the original price of $5; the triangular light red area represents the increase in producer surplus achieved by the farmers who supply the additional 500,000 bushels because of the higher price.

MODULE 49 REVIEW

Watch the video: **Consumer and Producer Surplus**

Check Your Understanding

1. Consider the market for cheese-stuffed jalapeño peppers. There are two consumers, Casey and Josey, and their willingness to pay for each pepper is given in the accompanying table. (Neither is willing to consume more than four peppers at any price.) Use the table (a) to construct the market demand schedule for peppers for prices of $0.00, $0.10, and so on, up to $0.90, and (b) to calculate the total consumer surplus when the price of a pepper is $0.40.

Quantity of peppers	Casey's willingness to pay	Josey's willingness to pay
1st pepper	$0.90	$0.80
2nd pepper	0.70	0.60
3rd pepper	0.50	0.40
4th pepper	0.30	0.30

2. Again consider the market for cheese-stuffed jalapeño peppers. There are two producers, Cara and Jamie, and their costs of producing each pepper are given in the accompanying table. (Neither is willing to produce more than four peppers at any price.) Use the table (a) to construct the market supply schedule for peppers for prices of $0.00, $0.10, and so on, up to $0.90, and (b) to calculate the total producer surplus when the price of a pepper is $0.70.

Quantity of peppers	Cara's cost	Jamie's cost
1st pepper	$0.10	$0.30
2nd pepper	0.10	0.50
3rd pepper	0.40	0.70
4th pepper	0.60	0.90

TACKLE THE AP® TEST: Multiple-Choice Questions

1. Refer to the graph below. What is the value of consumer surplus when the market price is $40?

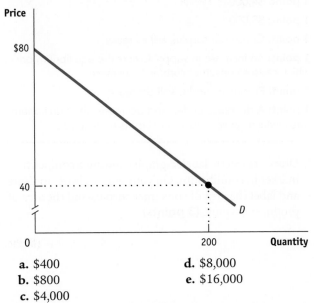

a. $400
b. $800
c. $4,000
d. $8,000
e. $16,000

2. Refer to the graph below. What is the value of producer surplus when the market price is $60?

a. $100
b. $150
c. $1,000
d. $1,500
e. $3,000

3. Other things equal, a rise in price will result in which of the following?
   a. Producer surplus will rise; consumer surplus will rise.
   b. Producer surplus will fall; consumer surplus will fall.
   c. Producer surplus will rise; consumer surplus will fall.
   d. Producer surplus will fall; consumer surplus will rise.
   e. Producer surplus will not change; consumer surplus will rise.

4. Consumer surplus is found as the area
   a. above the supply curve but below the price.
   b. below the demand curve but above the price.
   c. above the demand curve but below the price.
   d. below the supply curve but above the price.
   e. below the supply curve but above the demand curve.

5. Suppose a new policy allocates kidneys to patients needing a kidney transplant on the basis of who would receive the highest net benefit in terms of the expected increase in life span from a transplant. This policy would essentially be an attempt to maximize
   a. consumer surplus.   d. equity.
   b. producer surplus.   e. respect for elders.
   c. profit.

6. Producer surplus is shown on a graph by the area
   a. above the supply curve but below the price.
   b. below the demand curve but above the price.
   c. above the demand curve but below the price.
   d. below the supply curve but above the price.
   e. below the supply curve but above the demand curve.

7. Suppose there is a decrease in the price of swimsuits and no change in the market demand curve for swimsuits. Who receives the resulting increase in consumer surplus?
   a. Only buyers who purchased swimsuits at the original price.
   b. Only buyers who did not purchase swimsuits at the original price.
   c. Only sellers who sold swimsuits at the original price.
   d. Everyone who bought or sold swimsuits at the original price.
   e. Buyers who did, and who did not, purchase swimsuits at the original price.

1. Refer to the graph provided.

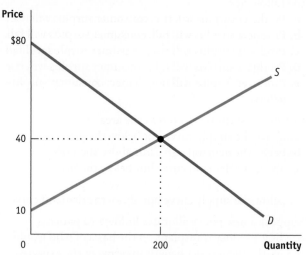

a. Calculate consumer surplus.
b. Calculate producer surplus.
c. If supply increases, what will happen to consumer surplus? Explain.
d. If demand decreases, what will happen to producer surplus? Explain.

Rubric for FRQ 1 (6 points)

1 point: $4,000

1 point: $3,000

1 point: Consumer surplus will increase.

1 point: An increase in supply lowers the equilibrium price, which causes consumer surplus to increase.

1 point: Producer surplus will decrease.

1 point: A decrease in demand decreases the equilibrium price, which causes producer surplus to decrease.

2. Draw a correctly labeled graph showing a competitive market in equilibrium. On your graph, clearly indicate and label the area of consumer surplus and the area of producer surplus. **(3 points)**

MOD 50

Efficiency and Deadweight Loss

In this Module, you will learn to:
- Define total surplus and discuss its relevance to market efficiency
- Explain how taxes affect total surplus and can create deadweight loss

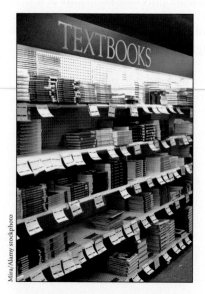

Consumer Surplus, Producer Surplus, and Efficiency

Markets are a remarkably effective way to organize economic activity: under the right conditions, they can make society as well off as possible given the available resources. The concepts of consumer and producer surplus can help us deepen our understanding of why this is so.

The Gains from Trade

Let's return to the market for used textbooks, but now consider a much bigger market—say, one at a large state university. There are many potential buyers and sellers, so the market is competitive. Let's line up incoming students who are potential buyers of a book in order of their willingness to pay, so that the entering student with the highest willingness to pay is potential buyer number 1, the student with the next highest willingness to pay is number 2, and so on. Then we can use their willingness to pay to derive a demand curve like the one in **Figure 50.1**. Similarly, we can line up outgoing students, the potential sellers of the book, in order of their cost, starting with the student with the lowest cost, followed by the student with the next lowest cost, and so on, to derive a supply curve like the one shown in the figure.

Figure 50.1 Total Surplus

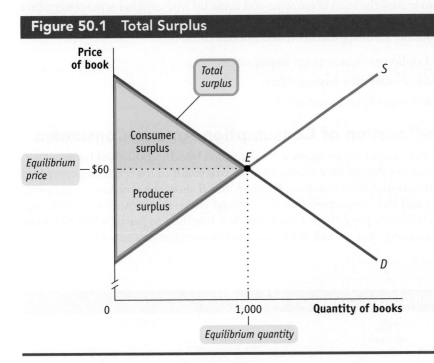

In the market for used textbooks, the equilibrium price is $60 and the equilibrium quantity is 1,000 books. Consumer surplus is given by the blue area, the area below the demand curve but above the price. Producer surplus is given by the pink area, the area above the supply curve but below the price. The sum of the blue and the pink areas is total surplus (indicated by the green triangle), the total benefit to society from the production and consumption of the good.

As we have drawn the curves, the market reaches equilibrium at a price of $60 per book, and 1,000 books are bought and sold at that price. The two shaded triangles show the consumer surplus (blue) and the producer surplus (pink) generated by this market. The sum of consumer and producer surplus, the total net gain to consumers and producers from trading in a market, is known as **total surplus**.

The striking thing about this picture is that both consumers and producers gain—that is, both consumers and producers are better off because there is a market for this good. But this should come as no surprise—it illustrates another core principle of economics: *There are gains from trade.* These gains from trade are the reason everyone is better off participating in a market economy than they would be if each individual tried to be self-sufficient.

But are we as well off as we could be? This brings us to the question of the efficiency of markets.

Total surplus is the total net gain to consumers and producers from trading in a market. It is the sum of consumer and producer surplus.

The Efficiency of Markets

A market is *efficient* if, once the market has produced its gains from trade, there is no way to make some people better off without making other people worse off. Note that market equilibrium is just *one* way of deciding who consumes a good and who sells a good. To better understand how markets promote efficiency, let's examine some alternatives. Consider the example of kidney transplants mentioned in the Module 49 problem set. More than 100,000 Americans are on the waiting list to obtain a new kidney, and around 4,000 people die each year while waiting for a transplant. There is no market for kidneys, and until December 2014, available kidneys went to whoever had been on the waiting list the longest. Of course, those who have been waiting the longest aren't necessarily those who would benefit the most from a new kidney. The policy adopted in late 2014 allocates kidneys on the basis of several criteria including the age and health of the recipient—indicators of how long the recipient is likely to benefit from the transplant. The result is an increase in the benefits received from the available kidneys. That is, total surplus in the exchange of kidneys has increased.

Could an alternative policy improve on the outcome in the market for used textbooks? Imagine a committee charged with improving on the market equilibrium by deciding who gets and who gives up a used textbook. The committee's ultimate goal would be to bypass the market outcome and come up with another arrangement that would increase total surplus.

Let's consider three approaches the committee could take:

1. It could reallocate consumption among consumers.

2. It could reallocate sales among sellers.

3. It could change the quantity traded.

The Reallocation of Consumption Among Consumers

The committee might try to increase total surplus by selling the used books to different consumers. **Figure 50.2** shows why this will result in lower surplus compared to the market equilibrium outcome. Points *A* and *B* show the positions of potential buyers Ana and Bob, respectively, on the demand curve. As we can see from the figure, Ana is willing to pay $70 for a book, but Bob is willing to pay only $50. Since the market equilibrium price is $60, under the market outcome Ana gets a book and Bob does not.

Figure 50.2 Reallocating Consumption Lowers Consumer Surplus

Ana (point *A*) has a willingness to pay of $70. Bob (point *B*) has a willingness to pay of only $50. At the market equilibrium price of $60, Ana purchases a book but Bob does not. If we rearrange consumption by taking a book from Ana and giving it to Bob, consumer surplus declines by $20 and, as a result, total surplus declines by $20. The market equilibrium generates the highest possible consumer surplus by ensuring that those who consume the good are those who most value it.

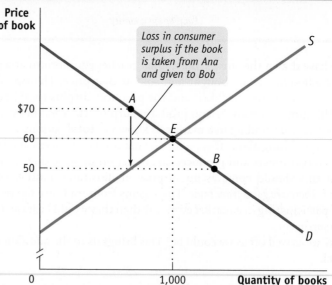

Now suppose the committee reallocates consumption. This would mean taking the book away from Ana and giving it to Bob. Since the book is worth $70 to Ana but only $50 to Bob, this change *reduces total consumer surplus* by $70 − $50 = $20. Moreover, this result of a decrease in total surplus doesn't depend on which two students we pick. Every student who buys a book at the market equilibrium price has a willingness to pay of $60 or more, and every student who doesn't buy a book has a willingness to pay of less than $60. So reallocating the good among consumers always means taking a book away from a student who values it more and giving it to one who values it less. This necessarily reduces total consumer surplus.

The Reallocation of Sales Among Sellers

The committee might try to increase total surplus by altering who sells their books, taking sales away from sellers who would have sold their books in the market equilibrium and instead compelling those who would not have sold their books in the market equilibrium to sell them. **Figure 50.3** shows why this will result in lower surplus. Here points X and Y show the positions on the supply curve of Xavier, who has a cost of $50, and Yvonne, who has a cost of $70. At the equilibrium market price of $60, Xavier would sell his book but Yvonne would not sell hers. If the committee reallocated sales, forcing Xavier to keep his book and Yvonne to sell hers, total producer surplus would be reduced by $70 − $50 = $20. Again, there is a decrease in total surplus no matter which seller and nonseller we choose to switch. Any student who sells a book at the market equilibrium price has a lower cost than any student who keeps a book. So reallocating sales among sellers necessarily increases total cost and reduces total producer surplus.

Figure 50.3 Reallocating Sales Lowers Producer Surplus

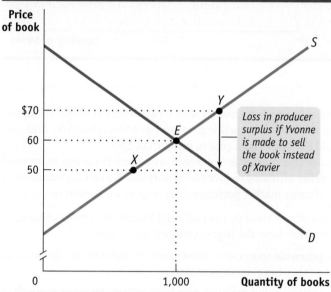

Yvonne (point Y) has a cost of $70, $20 more than Xavier (point X), who has a cost of $50. At the market equilibrium price of $60, Xavier sells a book but Yvonne does not. If we rearrange sales by preventing Xavier from selling his book and compelling Yvonne to sell hers, producer surplus declines by $20 and, as a result, total surplus declines by $20. The market equilibrium generates the highest possible producer surplus by ensuring that those who sell the good are those who most value the ability to sell it.

Changes in the Quantity Traded

The committee might try to increase total surplus by compelling students to trade either more books or fewer books than the market equilibrium quantity. **Figure 50.4** shows why this will result in lower surplus. It shows all four students: potential buyers Ana and Bob, and potential sellers Xavier and Yvonne. To reduce sales, the committee will have to prevent a transaction that would have occurred in the market equilibrium—that is, prevent Xavier from selling to Ana. Since Ana is willing to pay $70 and Xavier's cost is $50, preventing this transaction reduces total surplus by $70 − $50 = $20. Once again, this result doesn't depend on which two students we pick: any student who would have sold the book in the market equilibrium has a cost of $60 or less, and any student who would have purchased the book in the market equilibrium has a willingness to pay of $60 or more. So preventing any sale that would have occurred in the market equilibrium necessarily reduces total surplus.

Finally, the committee might try to increase sales by forcing Yvonne, who would not have sold her book at the market equilibrium price, to sell it to someone like Bob, who would not have bought a book at the market equilibrium price. Because Yvonne's cost is $70, but Bob is only willing to pay $50, this transaction reduces total surplus by $20.

Figure 50.4 Changing the Quantity Lowers Total Surplus

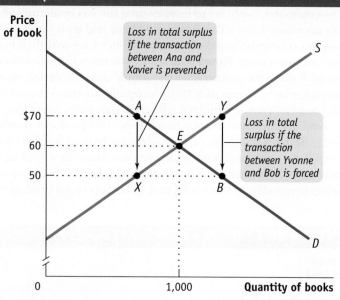

If Xavier (point *X*) were prevented from selling his book to someone like Ana (point *A*), total surplus would fall by $20, the difference between Ana's willingness to pay ($70) and Xavier's cost ($50). This means that total surplus falls whenever fewer than 1,000 books—the equilibrium quantity—are transacted. Likewise, if Yvonne (point *Y*) were compelled to sell her book to someone like Bob (point *B*), total surplus would also fall by $20, the difference between Yvonne's cost ($70) and Bob's willingness to pay ($50). This means that total surplus falls whenever more than 1,000 books are transacted.

And once again total surplus decreases no matter which two students we pick—anyone who wouldn't have bought the book has a willingness to pay of less than $60, and anyone who wouldn't have sold the book has a cost of more than $60.

The key point is that once this market is in equilibrium, there is no way to increase the gains from trade. Any other outcome reduces total surplus. We can summarize our results by stating that an efficient market performs four important functions:

1. It allocates consumption of the good to the potential buyers who most value it, as indicated by the fact that they have the highest willingness to pay.

2. It allocates sales to the potential sellers who most value the right to sell the good, as indicated by the fact that they have the lowest cost.

3. It ensures that every consumer who makes a purchase values the good more than every seller who makes a sale, so that all transactions are mutually beneficial.

4. It ensures that every potential buyer who doesn't make a purchase values the good less than every potential seller who doesn't make a sale, so that no mutually beneficial transactions are missed.

There are three caveats, however. First, although a market may be efficient, it isn't necessarily *fair*. In fact, fairness, or *equity*, is often in conflict with efficiency. We'll discuss this next.

The second caveat is that, under some well-defined conditions, markets can fail to deliver efficiency. When this occurs, markets no longer maximize total surplus. We'll take a closer look at market failures in later modules.

Third, even when the market equilibrium maximizes total surplus, this does not mean that it results in the best outcome for every *individual* consumer and producer. Other things equal, each buyer would like to pay a lower price and each seller would like to receive a higher price. So if the government were to intervene in the market—say, by lowering the price below the equilibrium price to make consumers happy or by raising the price above the equilibrium price to make sellers happy—the outcome would no longer be efficient. Although some people would be happier, society as a whole would be worse off because total surplus would be lower.

Equity and Efficiency

It's easy to get carried away with the idea that markets are always good and that economic policies that interfere with efficiency are bad. But that would be misguided because there is another factor to consider: society also cares about equity, or what's "fair." There is often a trade-off between equity and efficiency: policies that promote equity can come at the cost of decreased efficiency, and policies that promote efficiency can result in decreased equity. So it's important to realize that a society's choice to sacrifice some efficiency for the sake of equity, however it defines equity, may well be a valid one. It's also important to understand that fairness, unlike efficiency, can be very hard to define. Fairness is a concept about which well-intentioned people often disagree.

The trade-off between equity and efficiency is at the core of many debates over taxation. Consider the question of how the tax burden should vary with individuals' income. All taxes are ultimately paid out of income, so this question is relevant to more than just income taxes. Any tax that has high-income taxpayers pay a smaller percentage of their income than low-income taxpayers is a **regressive tax**. For instance, a sales tax is regressive, because high-income people generally spend a smaller proportion of their income than low-income people, so high-income taxpayers pay the sales tax on a relatively small portion of their income. Any tax that has all taxpayers pay the same percentage of their income is a **proportional tax**. A "flat" income tax of, say, 10% on all income would be an example of a proportional tax. Any tax that has high-income taxpayers pay a larger percentage of their income than low-income taxpayers is a **progressive tax**. The current U.S. income tax system is progressive.

Unfortunately, the most equitable taxes are generally not the most efficient taxes. For example, advocates of progressive income taxes emphasize the fairness of placing a heavier tax burden on high-income taxpayers. Critics argue that progressive income taxes create a growing disincentive for workers to increase their earnings. Such equity-efficiency trade-offs fuel debates and force tough decisions for policy makers. Next we'll see how to measure the efficiency loss caused by some particular taxes; later in this Module we'll discuss taxes that are efficient but not equitable.

> A **regressive tax** rises less than in proportion to income.
>
> A **proportional tax** rises in proportion to income.
>
> A **progressive tax** rises more than in proportion to income.

The Effects of Taxes on Total Surplus

To understand the economics of taxes, it's helpful to look at a simple type of tax known as an **excise tax**—a tax charged on each unit of a particular good or service that is sold. Most tax revenue in the United States comes from other kinds of taxes, but excise taxes are common. For example, there are federal excise taxes on gasoline, cigarettes, and foreign-made trucks, and many local governments impose excise taxes on services such as hotel room rentals. The lessons we'll learn from studying excise taxes apply to other, more complex taxes as well.

> An **excise tax** is a tax on sales of a particular good or service.

The Effect of an Excise Tax on Quantities and Prices

Suppose that the supply and demand for hotel rooms in the city of Potterville are as shown in **Figure 50.5**. We'll make the simplifying assumption that all hotel rooms are the same. In the absence of taxes, the equilibrium price of a room is $80 per night and the equilibrium quantity of hotel rooms rented is 10,000 per night.

Now suppose that Potterville's government imposes an excise tax of $40 per night on hotel rooms—that is, every time a room is rented for the night, the owner of the hotel must pay the city $40. For example, if a customer pays $80, $40 is collected as a tax, leaving the hotel owner with only $40. As a result, hotel owners are less willing to supply rooms at any given price.

What does this imply about the supply curve for hotel rooms in Potterville? To answer this question, we must compare the incentives of hotel owners *pre-tax* (before the tax is levied) to their incentives *post-tax* (after the tax is levied). From Figure 50.5 we know that

Figure 50.5 The Supply and Demand for Hotel Rooms in Potterville

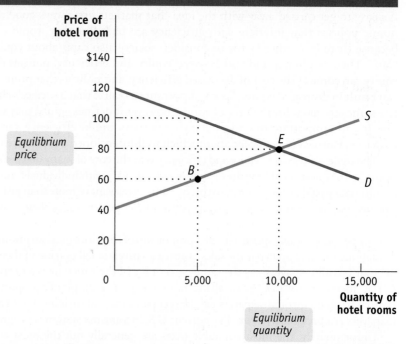

In the absence of taxes, the equilibrium price of hotel rooms is $80 per night, and the equilibrium number of rooms rented is 10,000 per night, as shown by point *E*. The supply curve, *S*, shows the quantity supplied at any given price, pre-tax. At a price of $60 per night, hotel owners are willing to supply 5,000 rooms, as shown by point *B*. But post-tax, hotel owners are willing to supply the same quantity only at a price of $100 per night: $60 for themselves plus $40 paid to the city as tax.

pre-tax, hotel owners are willing to supply 5,000 rooms per night at a price of $60 per room. But after the $40 tax per room is levied, they are willing to supply the same quantity, 5,000 rooms, only if they receive $100 per room—$60 for themselves plus $40 paid to the city as tax. Likewise, at every quantity supplied, the supply price—the price that producers must receive to produce a given quantity—has increased by $40. This implies that the post-tax supply curve shifts up by the amount of the tax compared to the pre-tax supply curve.

The upward shift of the supply curve caused by the tax is shown in **Figure 50.6**, where S_1 is the pre-tax supply curve and S_2 is the post-tax supply curve. As you can see,

Figure 50.6 An Excise Tax Imposed on Hotel Owners

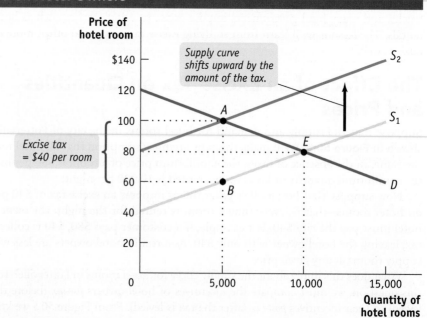

A $40 per room tax imposed on hotel owners shifts the supply curve from S_1 to S_2, an upward shift of $40. The equilibrium price of hotel rooms rises from $80 to $100 per night, and the equilibrium quantity of rooms rented falls from 10,000 to 5,000. Although hotel owners pay the tax, they actually bear only half the burden: the price they receive net of tax falls only $20, from $80 to $60. Guests who rent rooms bear the other half of the burden because the price they pay rises by $20, from $80 to $100.

the market equilibrium moves from E, at the equilibrium price of $80 per room and 10,000 rooms rented each night, to A, at a market price of $100 per room and only 5,000 rooms rented each night. In this case, $100 is the demand price of 5,000 rooms—but in effect hotel owners receive only $60, when you account for the fact that they have to pay the $40 tax. From the point of view of hotel owners, it is as if they were on their original supply curve at point B.

How do we know that 5,000 rooms will be supplied at a price of $100? Because the price *net of tax* is $60, and according to the original supply curve, 5,000 rooms will be supplied at a price of $60, as shown by point B in Figure 50.6.

An excise tax *drives a wedge* between the price paid by consumers and the price received by producers. As a result of this wedge, consumers pay more and producers receive less. In our example, consumers—people who rent hotel rooms—end up paying $100 per night, $20 more than the pre-tax price of $80. At the same time, producers—the hotel owners—receive a price net of tax of $60 per room, $20 less than the pre-tax price. In addition, the tax creates missed opportunities: 5,000 potential consumers who would have rented hotel rooms—those willing to pay $80 but not $100 per night—are discouraged from renting rooms. Correspondingly, 5,000 rooms that would have been made available by hotel owners for $80 are not offered when they receive only $60. Like a quota on sales as discussed in Module 9, this tax leads to inefficiency by distorting incentives and creating missed opportunities for mutually beneficial transactions.

It's important to recognize that as we've described it, Potterville's hotel tax is a tax on the hotel owners, not their guests—it's a tax on the producers, not the consumers. Yet the price received by producers, net of tax, is down by only $20, half the amount of the tax, and the price paid by consumers is up by $20. In effect, half the tax is being paid by consumers.

What would happen if the city levied a tax on consumers instead of producers? That is, suppose that instead of requiring hotel owners to pay $40 per night for each room they rent, the city required hotel *guests* to pay $40 for each night they stayed in a hotel. The answer is shown in **Figure 50.7**. If a hotel guest must pay a tax of $40 per night, then the price for a room paid by that guest must be reduced by $40 in order

This hotel receipt lists several taxes, each of which drives a wedge between the price paid by the consumer and the price received by the hotel owners.

Figure 50.7 An Excise Tax Imposed on Hotel Guests

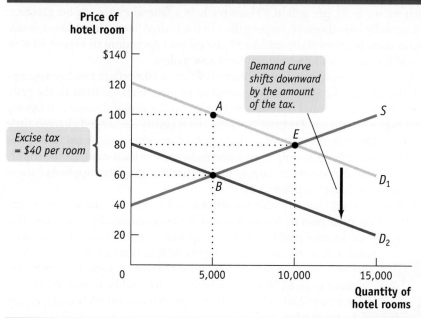

A $40 per room tax imposed on hotel guests shifts the demand curve from D_1 to D_2, a downward shift of $40. The equilibrium price of hotel rooms falls from $80 to $60 per night, and the quantity of rooms rented falls from 10,000 to 5,000. Although in this case the tax is officially paid by consumers, while in Figure 50.6 the tax was paid by producers, the outcome is the same: after taxes, hotel owners receive $60 per room but guests pay $100.

Tax incidence is the distribution of the tax burden.

for the quantity of hotel rooms demanded post-tax to be the same as that demanded pre-tax. So the demand curve shifts *downward*, from D_1 to D_2, by the amount of the tax. At every quantity demanded, the demand price—the price that consumers must be offered to demand a given quantity—has fallen by $40. This shifts the equilibrium from E to B, where the market price of hotel rooms is $60 and 5,000 hotel rooms are rented. In effect, hotel guests pay $100 when you include the tax. So from the point of view of guests, it is as if they were on their original demand curve at point A.

If you compare Figures 50.6 and 50.7, you will notice that the effects of the tax are the same even though different curves are shifted. In each case, consumers pay $100 per unit (including the tax, if it is their responsibility), producers receive $60 per unit (after paying the tax, if it is their responsibility), and 5,000 hotel rooms are bought and sold. *In fact, it doesn't matter who officially pays the tax—the equilibrium outcome is the same.*

This example illustrates a general principle of **tax incidence**, a measure of who really pays a tax: the burden of a tax cannot be determined by looking at who writes the check to the government. In this particular case, a $40 tax on hotel rooms brings about a $20 increase in the price paid by consumers and a $20 decrease in the price received by producers. Regardless of whether the tax is levied on consumers or producers, the incidence of the tax is the same. As we will see next, the burden of a tax depends on the price elasticities of supply and demand.

Price Elasticities and Tax Incidence

In the example shown in Figures 50.5 through 50.7, a tax on hotel rooms falls equally on consumers and producers, no matter on whom the tax is levied. This 50–50 split between consumers and producers is a result of our assumptions in this example. In the real world, the incidence of an excise tax usually falls unevenly between consumers and producers: one group bears more of the burden than the other.

What determines how the burden of an excise tax is allocated between consumers and producers? The answer depends on the shapes of the supply curve and the demand curve. *More specifically, the incidence of an excise tax depends on the price elasticity of supply and the price elasticity of demand.* We can see this by looking first at a case in which consumers pay most of an excise tax, and then at a case in which producers pay most of the tax.

When an Excise Tax Is Paid Mainly by Consumers

Figure 50.8 shows an excise tax that falls mainly on consumers: an excise tax on gasoline, which we set at $1 per gallon. (There really is a federal excise tax on gasoline, though it is actually only about $0.18 per gallon in the United States. In addition, states impose excise taxes between $0.08 and $0.58 per gallon.) According to Figure 50.8, in the absence of the tax, gasoline would sell for $2 per gallon.

The shapes of the supply and demand curves in Figure 50.8 reflect two key assumptions. First, the demand for gasoline is assumed to be price inelastic (that is, the price elasticity of demand is assumed to be less than one), so the demand curve is relatively steep. Recall that when demand is price inelastic, the quantity demanded changes little in response to a change in price. Second, the supply of gasoline is assumed to be price elastic (the price elasticity of supply is assumed to be greater than one), so the supply curve is relatively flat. A price-elastic supply means that the quantity supplied changes a lot in response to a change in price.

We have just learned that an excise tax drives a wedge, equal to the size of the tax, between the price paid by consumers and the price received by producers. This wedge drives the price paid by consumers up and the price received by producers down. But as we can see from Figure 50.8, in this case those two effects are very unequal in size. The price received by producers falls only slightly, from $2.00 to $1.95, but the price paid by consumers rises by a lot, from $2.00 to $2.95. This means that consumers bear the greater share of the tax burden.

Figure 50.8 An Excise Tax Paid Mainly by Consumers

The relatively steep demand curve here reflects a price-inelastic demand for gasoline. The relatively flat supply curve reflects a price-elastic supply. The pre-tax price of a gallon of gasoline is $2.00, and a tax of $1.00 per gallon is imposed. The price paid by consumers rises by $0.95 to $2.95, reflecting the fact that most of the burden of the tax falls on consumers. Only a small portion of the tax is borne by producers: the price they receive falls by only $0.05 to $1.95.

This example illustrates another general principle of taxation: *When the demand is price inelastic and the supply is price elastic, the burden of an excise tax falls mainly on consumers.* Why? A price-inelastic demand means that consumers have few substitutes and, therefore, little alternative to buying higher-priced gasoline. In contrast, a price-elastic supply results from the fact that producers have many production substitutes for their gasoline (that is, the crude oil from which gasoline is refined can be made into other things, such as plastic). This gives producers much greater flexibility in refusing to accept lower prices for their gasoline. And, not surprisingly, the party with the least flexibility—in this case, consumers—gets stuck paying most of the tax. This is a good description of how the burden is allocated between consumers and producers for most of the excise taxes actually collected in the United States, such as those on cigarettes and alcoholic beverages.

When an Excise Tax Is Paid Mainly by Producers

Figure 50.9 shows an example of an excise tax paid mainly by producers: a $5.00 per day tax on downtown parking in a small city. In the absence of the tax, the market equilibrium price of parking is $6.00 per day.

Figure 50.9 An Excise Tax Paid Mainly by Producers

The relatively flat demand curve here reflects a price-elastic demand for downtown parking, and the relatively steep supply curve results from a price-inelastic supply. When a tax of $5.00 per day is imposed on parking spaces, the price received by producers falls a lot, $4.50, reflecting the fact that they bear most of the tax burden. The price paid by consumers rises a small amount, $0.50, so they bear very little of the burden.

We've assumed in this case that the supply is price inelastic because the lots used for parking have very few alternative uses. This makes the supply curve for parking spaces relatively steep. The demand, however, is assumed to be price elastic: consumers can easily switch from the downtown spaces to other parking spaces a few minutes' walk from downtown, spaces that are not subject to the tax. This makes the demand curve relatively flat.

The tax drives a wedge between the price paid by consumers and the price received by producers. In this example, however, the tax causes the price paid by consumers to rise only slightly, from $6.00 to $6.50, but the price received by producers falls a lot, from $6.00 to $1.50. In the end, each consumer bears only $0.50 of the $5 tax burden, with producers bearing the remaining $4.50 for each parking space used.

Again, this example illustrates a general principle: *When the demand is price elastic and the supply is price inelastic, the burden of an excise tax falls mainly on producers.* Another real-world example is a tax on purchases of existing houses. In many American towns, house prices in desirable locations have risen as well-off outsiders have moved in and purchased homes from the less well-off original occupants, a phenomenon called gentrification. Some of these towns have imposed taxes on house sales intended to extract money from the new arrivals. But this ignores the fact that the demand for houses in a particular town is often price elastic because potential buyers can choose to move to other towns. Furthermore, the supply is often price inelastic because most sellers must sell their houses due to job transfers or to provide funds for their retirement. So taxes on home purchases are actually paid mainly by the less well-off sellers—not, as town officials imagine, by wealthy buyers.

The Benefits and Costs of Taxation

When a government is considering whether to impose a tax or how to design a tax system, it has to weigh the benefit of a tax against its cost. We may not think of a tax as something that is beneficial, but governments need money to provide things people want, such as streets, schools, national defense, and health care for those unable to afford it. The benefit of a tax is the revenue it raises for the government to pay for these services. Unfortunately, this benefit comes at a cost—a cost that is normally larger than the amount consumers and producers pay. Let's look first at what determines how much money a tax raises and then at the cost a tax imposes.

The Revenue from an Excise Tax

How much revenue does the government collect from an excise tax? In our hotel tax example, the revenue is equal to the area of the shaded rectangle in **Figure 50.10**.

Figure 50.10 **The Revenue from an Excise Tax**

The revenue from a $40 excise tax on hotel rooms is $200,000, equal to the tax rate, $40—the size of the wedge that the tax drives between the supply price and the demand price—multiplied by the number of rooms rented, 5,000. This is equal to the area of the shaded rectangle.

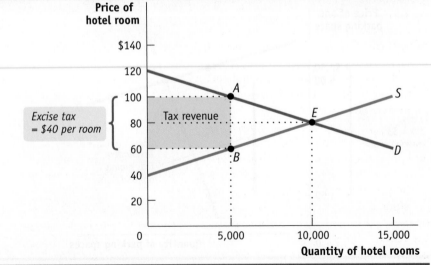

To see why this area represents the revenue collected by a $40 tax on hotel rooms, notice that the *height* of the rectangle is $40, equal to the tax per room. As we've seen, it is also the size of the wedge that the tax drives between the supply price (the price received by producers) and the demand price (the price paid by consumers). Meanwhile, the *width* of the rectangle is 5,000 rooms, equal to the equilibrium quantity of rooms given the $40 tax. With that information, we can make the following calculations.

The tax revenue collected is

$$\text{Tax revenue} = \$40 \text{ per room} \times 5{,}000 \text{ rooms} = \$200{,}000$$

The area of the shaded rectangle is

$$\text{Area} = \text{Height} \times \text{Width} = \$40 \text{ per room} \times 5{,}000 \text{ rooms} = \$200{,}000,$$

So,

$$\text{Tax revenue} = \text{Area of shaded rectangle}$$

This is a general principle: *The revenue collected by an excise tax is equal to the area of a rectangle with the height of the tax wedge between the supply price and the demand price and the width of the quantity sold under the tax.*

The Costs of Taxation

What is the cost of a tax? You might be inclined to answer that it is the amount of money taxpayers pay to the government—the tax revenue collected. But suppose the government uses the tax revenue to provide services that taxpayers want. Or suppose that the government simply hands the tax revenue back to taxpayers in the form of a rebate. Would we say in those cases that the tax didn't actually cost anything?

No—because a tax, like a quota, prevents mutually beneficial transactions from occurring. Consider Figure 50.10 once more. Here, with a $40 tax on hotel rooms, guests pay $100 per room but hotel owners receive only $60 per room. Because of the wedge created by the tax, we know that some transactions didn't occur that would have occurred without the tax. More specifically, we know from the supply and demand curves that there are some potential guests who would be willing to pay up to $90 per night and some hotel owners who would be willing to supply rooms if they received at least $70 per night. If these two sets of people were allowed to trade with each other without the tax, they would engage in mutually beneficial transactions—hotel rooms would be rented. But such deals would be illegal because the $40 tax would not be paid. In our example, 5,000 potential hotel room rentals that would have occurred in the absence of the tax, to the mutual benefit of guests and hotel owners, do not take place because of the tax.

So an excise tax imposes costs, over and above the tax revenue collected, in the form of inefficiency, which occurs because the tax discourages mutually beneficial transactions. You may recall from Module 9 that the cost to society of this kind of inefficiency—the value of the forgone mutually beneficial transactions—is called the **deadweight loss**. While most real-world taxes impose some deadweight loss, a badly designed tax imposes a larger deadweight loss than a well-designed one.

To measure the deadweight loss from a tax, we turn to the concepts of producer and consumer surplus. **Figure 50.11** shows the effects of an excise tax on consumer and producer surplus. In the absence of the tax, the equilibrium is at E and the equilibrium price and quantity are P_E and Q_E, respectively. An excise tax drives a wedge equal to the amount of the tax between the price received by producers and the price paid by consumers, reducing the quantity sold. In this case, with a tax of T dollars per unit, the quantity sold falls to Q_T. The price paid by consumers rises to P_C, the demand price of the reduced quantity. The price received by producers falls to P_P, the supply price of that quantity. The difference between these prices, $P_C - P_P$, is equal to the excise tax, T.

Be prepared to calculate the revenue earned from a tax. On a graph, this is the area of the rectangle that represents tax revenue. Remember: the area of a rectangle is the width times the height.

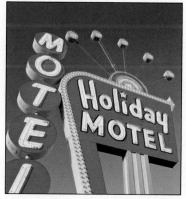

The **deadweight loss** (from a tax) is the decrease in total surplus resulting from the tax, minus the tax revenues generated.

Figure 50.11   A Tax Reduces Consumer and Producer Surplus

Before the tax, the equilibrium price and quantity are P_E and Q_E, respectively. After an excise tax of T per unit is imposed, the price to consumers rises to P_C and consumer surplus falls by the sum of the dark blue rectangle, labeled A, and the light blue triangle, labeled B. The tax also causes the price to producers to fall to P_P; producer surplus falls by the sum of the red rectangle, labeled C, and the pink triangle, labeled F. The government receives revenue from the tax, $Q_T \times T$, which is given by the sum of the areas A and C. Areas B and F represent the losses to consumer and producer surplus that are not collected by the government as revenue; they are the deadweight loss to society of the tax.

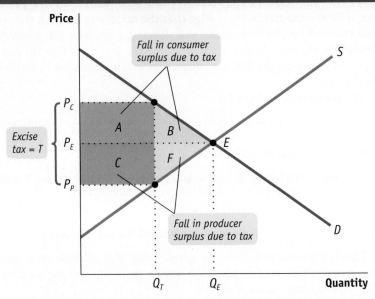

Using the concepts of producer and consumer surplus, we can show exactly how much surplus producers and consumers lose as a result of the tax. We learned previously that a fall in the price of a good generates a gain in consumer surplus that is equal to the sum of the areas of a rectangle and a triangle. Similarly, a price increase causes a loss to consumers that is represented by the sum of the areas of a rectangle and a triangle. So it's not surprising that in the case of an excise tax, the rise in the price paid by consumers causes a loss equal to the sum of the areas of a rectangle and a triangle: the dark blue rectangle labeled A and the area of the light blue triangle labeled B in Figure 50.11.

Meanwhile, the fall in the price received by producers leads to a fall in producer surplus. This loss in producer surplus is the sum of the areas of the red rectangle labeled C and the pink triangle labeled F in Figure 50.11.

Of course, although consumers and producers are hurt by the tax, the government gains revenue. The revenue the government collects is equal to the tax per unit sold, T, multiplied by the quantity sold, Q_T, or the area of a rectangle Q_T wide and T high. In the figure, this area is the sum of rectangles A and C. So the government gains part of what consumers and producers lose from an excise tax.

A portion of the loss to producers and consumers from the tax is not offset by a gain of tax revenue for the government. Specifically, triangles B and F represent the deadweight loss caused by the tax. That loss is the amount of total surplus that would have been generated by transactions that now do not take place because of the tax.

Figure 50.12 is a version of Figure 50.11 that leaves out rectangles A (the surplus shifted from consumers to the government) and C (the surplus shifted from producers to the government) and shows only the deadweight loss, drawn here as a triangle shaded yellow. The base of that triangle is equal to the tax wedge, T; the height of the triangle is equal to the reduction in the quantity transacted due to the tax, $Q_E - Q_T$. Clearly, the larger the tax wedge and the larger the reduction in the quantity transacted, the greater the inefficiency from the tax. But also note an important, contrasting point: if the excise tax somehow *didn't* reduce the quantity bought and sold in this market—if Q_T remained equal to Q_E after the tax was levied—the yellow triangle would disappear and the deadweight loss from the tax would be zero. So it is by discouraging transactions that an excise tax creates deadweight loss. Module 44 explains that at the international level, import quotas and tariffs (which are essentially taxes on imports) discourage transactions between countries, which likewise creates deadweight loss.

Figure 50.12 The Deadweight Loss of a Tax

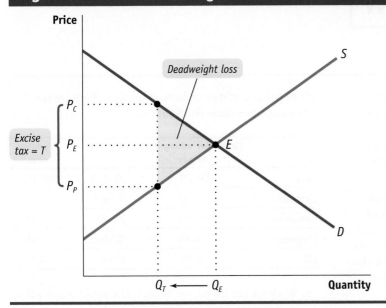

A tax leads to a deadweight loss because it creates inefficiency: some mutually beneficial transactions never take place because of the tax, namely the transactions from Q_T to Q_E. The yellow area in the graph represents the value of the deadweight loss, which is the total surplus that would have been gained from those discouraged transactions.

Some extreme forms of taxation, such as the regressive *poll tax* instituted by the government of British Prime Minister Margaret Thatcher in 1990, are notably unfair but very efficient. A poll tax is an example of a **lump-sum tax**, a tax that is the same for everyone regardless of any actions people take. The poll tax in Britain was widely perceived as much less fair than the tax structure it replaced, in which local taxes were proportional to property values.

Under the old British tax system, the highest local taxes were paid by the people with the most expensive houses. Because these people tended to be wealthy, they were also best able to bear the burden. But the old system definitely distorted incentives to engage in mutually beneficial transactions and created deadweight loss. People who were considering home improvements knew that by making their property more valuable such improvements would increase their tax bills. The result, surely, was that some home improvements that would have taken place without the tax did not take place because of it.

In contrast, a lump-sum tax does not distort incentives. Because under a lump-sum tax people have to pay the same amount of tax regardless of their actions, it does not cause them to substitute untaxed goods for a good whose price has been artificially inflated by a tax, as occurs with an excise tax. So lump-sum taxes, although unfair, are better than other taxes at promoting economic efficiency.

In considering the total amount of inefficiency caused by a tax, we must also take into account something not shown in Figure 50.12: the resources actually used by the government to collect the tax, and by taxpayers to pay it, over and above the amount of the tax. These lost resources are called the **administrative costs** of the tax. The most familiar administrative cost of the U.S. tax system is the time individuals spend filling out their income tax forms or the money they spend on accountants to prepare their tax forms for them. (The latter is considered an inefficiency from the point of view of society because accountants could instead be performing other, non-tax-related services.) Included in the administrative costs that taxpayers incur are resources used to evade the tax, both legally and illegally. The costs of operating the Internal Revenue Service, the arm of the federal government tasked with collecting the federal income tax, are actually quite small in comparison to the administrative costs paid by taxpayers. The total inefficiency caused by a tax can be measured by the sum of its deadweight loss and its administrative costs.

A **lump-sum tax** is a tax of a fixed amount paid by all taxpayers.

AP® EXAM TIP

Unless they cause a producer to go out of business, lump-sum taxes do not affect price or quantity, so they do not create deadweight loss.

The **administrative costs** of a tax are the resources used by the government to collect the tax, and by taxpayers to pay (or to evade) it, over and above the amount collected.

Check Your Understanding

1. Using the tables in Check Your Understanding Questions 1 and 2 in Module 49, find the equilibrium price and quantity in the market for cheese-stuffed jalapeño peppers. What is the total surplus in the equilibrium in this market, and how much of it does each consumer and producer receive?

2. Consider the market for butter, shown in the accompanying figure. The government imposes an excise tax of $0.30 per pound of butter. What is the price paid by consumers post-tax? What is the price received by producers post-tax? What is the quantity of butter sold? How is the incidence of the tax allocated between consumers and producers? Show this on the figure.

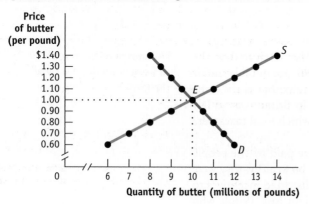

3. The accompanying table shows five consumers' willingness to pay for one can of diet soda each as well as five producers' costs of selling one can of diet soda each. Each consumer buys at most one can of soda; each producer sells at most one can of soda. The government asks your advice about the effects of an excise tax of

$0.40 per can of diet soda. Assume that there are no administrative costs from the tax.

	Consumer willingness to pay		Producer cost
Ana	$0.70	Zhang	$0.10
Bernice	0.60	Yves	0.20
Chizuko	0.50	Xavier	0.30
Dagmar	0.40	Walter	0.40
Ella	0.30	Vern	0.50

a. Without the excise tax, what is the equilibrium price and the equilibrium quantity of soda?

b. The excise tax raises the price paid by consumers post-tax to $0.60 and lowers the price received by producers post-tax to $0.20. With the excise tax, what is the quantity of soda sold?

c. Without the excise tax, how much individual consumer surplus does each consumer gain? How much individual consumer surplus does each consumer gain with the tax? How much total consumer surplus is lost as a result of the tax?

d. Without the excise tax, how much individual producer surplus does each producer gain? How much individual producer surplus does each producer gain with the tax? How much total producer surplus is lost as a result of the tax?

e. How much government revenue does the excise tax create?

f. What is the deadweight loss from the imposition of this excise tax?

TACKLE THE AP® TEST: Multiple-Choice Questions

1. At market equilibrium in a competitive market, which of the following is necessarily true?
   a. Consumer surplus is maximized.
   b. Producer surplus is maximized.
   c. Total surplus is maximized.
   d. Some buyers who do not make a purchase value the good more than some buyers who do make a purchase.
   e. The result is the best outcome for every individual seller.

2. Which of the following is true regarding equity and efficiency in competitive markets?
   a. Competitive markets ensure equity and efficiency.

   b. There is often a trade-off between equity and efficiency.
   c. Competitive markets lead to neither equity nor efficiency.
   d. There is general agreement about the level of equity and efficiency in a market.
   e. None of the above are true.

3. The following graph represents the toothpaste market, which begins with an equilibrium price of P_2 and an equilibrium quantity of Q_2. If an excise tax of $P_3 - P_1$ per unit is imposed on toothpaste sellers, the tax revenue will be represented by area(s) _____ and the deadweight loss will be represented by area(s) _____.

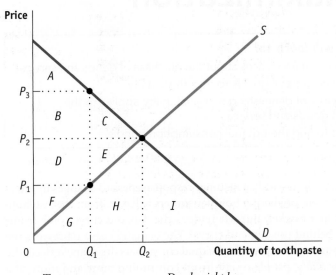

Price

A

P_3

B   C

P_2

D   E

P_1

F   H   I

G

0   Q_1 Q_2 **Quantity of toothpaste**

D

	Tax revenue	Deadweight loss
a.	B	E
b.	DE	GHI
c.	BD	GHI
d.	BD	CE
e.	DE	CE

4. An excise tax will be paid mainly by producers when
   a. it is imposed on producers.
   b. it is imposed on consumers.
   c. the price elasticity of supply is low and the price elasticity of demand is high.

   d. the price elasticity of supply is high and the price elasticity of demand is low.
   e. the price elasticity of supply is perfectly elastic.

5. Which of the following is the most likely to be a regressive tax?
   a. a tax of 12% of the value of each individual's property
   b. a personal income tax of 15% of the first $50,000 in income and 20% on all additional income
   c. a 10% tax on yachts
   d. a 25% tax on all income
   e. a 7% state sales tax on all goods

6. A lump-sum tax on the citizens of a country
   a. does not create deadweight loss.
   b. distorts incentives for production.
   c. is considered a progressive tax.
   d. collects taxes in proportion to the wealth of each citizen.
   e. is inferior to excise taxes at promoting economic efficiency.

7. An excise tax drives a wedge between the supply price and the demand price with a height equal to
   a. the deadweight loss caused by the tax.
   b. the amount of the tax per unit of the good.
   c. the total tax revenue collected with the tax.
   d. the pre-tax price of the good.
   e. the demand price of the good.

TACKLE THE AP® TEST: Free-Response Questions

1. Refer to the graph. Assume the government has imposed an excise tax of $60 on producers in this market.

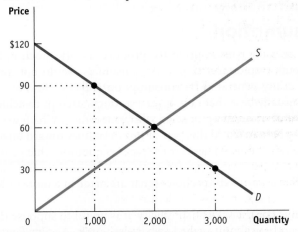

Price

$120

90

60

30

0   1,000   2,000   3,000   **Quantity**

S

D

   a. What quantity will be sold in the market?
   b. What price will consumers pay in the market?
   c. By how much will consumer surplus change as a result of the tax?
   d. By how much will producer surplus change as a result of the tax?
   e. How much revenue will the government collect from this excise tax?
   f. Calculate the deadweight loss created by the tax.

> **Rubric for FRQ 1 (6 points)**
> **1 point:** 1,000
> **1 point:** $90
> **1 point:** Consumer surplus will decrease by $45,000, from ½ ($2,000 × 60) = $60,000 before the tax to ½ ($1,000 × 30) = $15,000 after the tax.
> **1 point:** Producer surplus will decrease by $45,000, from ½ ($2,000 × 60) = $60,000 before the tax to ½ ($1,000 × 30) = $15,000 after the tax.
> **1 point:** $60 × 1,000 = $60,000
> **1 point:** ½ × $60 × 1,000 = $30,000

2. Draw a correctly labeled graph of a competitive market in equilibrium. Use your graph to illustrate the effect of an excise tax imposed on consumers. Indicate each of the following on your graph:
   a. the equilibrium price and quantity without the tax, labeled P_E and Q_E
   b. the quantity sold in the market post-tax, labeled Q_T
   c. the price paid by consumers post-tax, labeled P_C
   d. the price received by producers post-tax, labeled P_P
   e. the tax revenue generated by the tax, labeled "Tax revenue"
   f. the deadweight loss resulting from the tax, labeled "DWL" **(7 points)**

Utility Maximization

In this Module, you will learn to:
- Describe how consumers make choices about the purchase of goods and services
- Explain why consumers' general goal is to maximize utility
- Explain why the principle of diminishing marginal utility applies to the consumption of most goods and services
- Use marginal analysis to find the optimal consumption bundle

Utility is a measure of personal satisfaction.

A **util** is a unit of utility.

We have used the demand curve to study consumer responsiveness to changes in prices and discovered its usefulness in predicting how consumers will gain from the availability of goods and services in a market. But where does the demand curve come from? In other words, what lies behind the demand curve? The demand curve represents the tastes, preferences, and resulting choices of individual consumers. Its shape reflects the additional satisfaction, or *utility*, people receive from consuming more and more of a good or service.

Utility: It's All About Getting Satisfaction

When we analyze consumer behavior, we are looking into how people pursue their needs and wants and the subjective feelings that motivate purchases. Yet there is no simple way to measure subjective feelings. How much satisfaction do I get from eating my third cookie? Is it less or more than the satisfaction you receive from eating your third cookie? Does it even make sense to ask that question?

Luckily, we don't need to make comparisons between your feelings and mine. The analysis of consumer behavior that follows requires only the assumption that individuals try to maximize some personal measure of the satisfaction gained from consumption. That measure of satisfaction is known as **utility**, a concept we use to understand behavior but don't expect to measure explicitly in practice.

Utility and Consumption

We can think of consumers as using consumption to "produce" utility, much in the same way producers use inputs to produce output. As consumers, we do not make explicit calculations of the utility generated by consumption choices. However, we must make choices, and we usually base them on at least a rough attempt to achieve greater satisfaction. You can have either soup or salad with your dinner. Which would you enjoy more? You can go to Disney World this year or put the money toward buying a new car. Which would make you happier? These are the types of questions that go into utility maximization.

The concept of utility offers a way to study choices that are made in a more or less rational way.

How do we measure utility? For the sake of simplicity, it is useful to suppose that we can measure utility in hypothetical units called—what else?—**utils**. A *utility function* shows the relationship between a consumer's utility and the combination of goods and services—the *consumption bundle*—he or she consumes.

Figure 51.1 illustrates a utility function. It shows the total utility that Cassie, who likes fried clams, gets from an all-you-can-eat clam dinner. We suppose that her consumption bundle consists of a side of cole slaw, which comes with the meal, plus a number of clams to be determined. The table that accompanies the figure shows how Cassie's total utility depends on the number of clams; the curve in panel (a) of the figure shows that same information graphically.

Figure 51.1 Cassie's Total Utility and Marginal Utility

(a) Cassie's Utility Function

Quantity of clams	Total utility (utils)	Marginal utility per clam (utils)
0	0	
		15
1	15	
		13
2	28	
		11
3	39	
		9
4	48	
		7
5	55	
		5
6	60	
		3
7	63	
		1
8	64	
		−1
9	63	

(b) Cassie's Marginal Utility Curve

Panel (a) shows how Cassie's total utility depends on her consumption of fried clams. It increases until it reaches its maximum utility level of 64 utils at 8 clams consumed and decreases after that. Marginal utility is calculated in the table. Panel (b) shows the marginal utility curve, which slopes downward due to diminishing marginal utility. That is, each additional clam gives Cassie less utility than the previous clam.

Cassie's utility function slopes upward over most of the range shown, but it gets flatter as the number of clams consumed increases. And in this example it eventually turns downward. According to the information in the table in Figure 51.1, nine clams is a clam too far. Adding that additional clam actually makes Cassie worse off: it would hurt her stomach and lower her total utility. If she's rational, of course, Cassie will realize that and not consume the ninth clam.

So when Cassie chooses how many clams to consume, she will make this decision by considering the *change* in her total utility from consuming one more clam. This illustrates the general point: to maximize *total* utility, consumers must focus on *marginal* utility.

The Principle of Diminishing Marginal Utility

In addition to showing how Cassie's total utility depends on the number of clams she consumes, the table in Figure 51.1 also shows the **marginal utility** generated by consuming each additional clam—that is, the *change* in total utility from consuming one

The **marginal utility** of a good or service is the change in total utility generated by consuming one additional unit of that good or service.

Yarvin Market Journeys/Alamy

The **marginal utility curve** shows how marginal utility depends on the quantity of a good or service consumed.

According to the **principle of diminishing marginal utility**, each successive unit of a good or service consumed adds less to total utility than does the previous unit.

additional clam. The **marginal utility curve** shows how marginal utility depends on the quantity of clams consumed. The curve is constructed by plotting points at the midpoint between the numbered quantities since marginal utility is found as consumption levels change. For example, when consumption rises from 1 to 2 clams, marginal utility is 13. Therefore, we place the point corresponding to the marginal utility of 13 halfway between 1 and 2 clams.

The marginal utility curve slopes downward because each successive clam adds less to total utility than the previous clam. This is reflected in the table: marginal utility falls from a high of 15 utils for the first clam consumed to −1 for the ninth clam consumed. The fact that the ninth clam has negative marginal utility means that consuming it actually reduces total utility. (Restaurants that offer all-you-can-eat meals depend on the proposition that you can have too much of a good thing.) Not all marginal utility curves eventually become negative. But it is generally accepted that marginal utility curves do slope downward—that consumption of most goods and services is subject to *diminishing marginal utility*.

The basic idea behind the **principle of diminishing marginal utility** is that the additional satisfaction a consumer gets from one more unit of a good or service declines as the amount of that good or service consumed rises. Or, to put it slightly differently, the more of a good or service you consume, the closer you are to being satiated—reaching a point at which an additional unit of the good adds nothing to your satisfaction. For someone who almost never gets to eat a banana, the occasional banana is a marvelous treat (as it was in Eastern Europe before the fall of communism, when bananas were very hard to find). For someone who eats them all the time, a banana is just, well, a banana.

The Occasional Ups and Downs of Marginal Utility

Diminishing marginal utility is the norm, but it is not universal. In fact, there are a number of goods for which, at least over some range, marginal utility is surely *increasing*. For example, there are goods that require some experience to enjoy. The first time downhill skiing might involve a lot more fear than enjoyment. It only becomes a pleasurable activity if you do it enough to become reasonably competent. And even some less strenuous forms of consumption take practice; people who are not accustomed to drinking coffee say it has a bitter taste and can't understand its appeal. (The authors, on the other hand, regard coffee as one of the basic food groups.)

Another example would be goods that only deliver positive utility if you buy a sufficient quantity. The great Victorian economist Alfred Marshall, who more or less invented the supply and demand model, gave the example of wallpaper: buying only

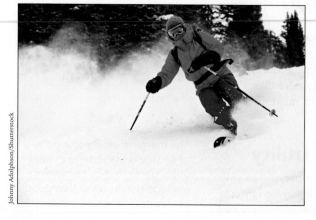

Johnny Adolphson/Shutterstock

enough to do half a room is worse than useless. If you need two rolls of wallpaper to finish a room, the marginal utility of the second roll is larger than the marginal utility of the first roll.

So why does it make sense to assume diminishing marginal utility? For one thing, most goods don't suffer from these qualifications: nobody needs to learn to like ice cream. Also, although most people don't ski and some people don't drink coffee, those who do ski or drink coffee do enough of it that the marginal utility of one more ski run or one more cup is less than that of the last. So *in the relevant range* of consumption, marginal utility is still diminishing.

The principle of diminishing marginal utility doesn't always apply, but it does apply in the great majority of cases, enough to serve as a foundation for our analysis of consumer behavior.

Budgets and Optimal Consumption

The principle of diminishing marginal utility explains why most people eventually reach a limit, even at an all-you-can-eat buffet where the cost of another clam is measured only in future indigestion. Under ordinary circumstances, however, it costs some additional resources to consume more of a good, and consumers must take that cost into account when making choices.

What do we mean by cost? As always, the fundamental measure of cost is *opportunity cost*. Because the amount of money a consumer can spend is limited, a decision to consume more of one good is also a decision to consume less of some other good.

Budget Constraints and Budget Lines

Consider Sammy, whose appetite is exclusively for clams and tomatoes. (There's no accounting for tastes.) He has a weekly income of $20 and since, given his appetite, more of either good is better than less, he spends all of it on clams and tomatoes. We will assume that clams cost $4 per pound and tomatoes cost $2 per pound. What are his possible choices?

Whatever Sammy chooses, we know that the cost of his consumption bundle cannot exceed the amount of money he has to spend. That is,

(51-1)   Expenditure on clams + Expenditure on tomatoes ≤ Total income

Consumers always have limited income, which constrains how much they can consume. So the requirement illustrated by Equation 51-1—that a consumer must choose a consumption bundle that costs no more than his or her income—is known as the consumer's **budget constraint**. It's a simple way of saying that a consumer can't spend more than the total amount of income available to him or her. In other words, consumption bundles are affordable when they obey the budget constraint. We call the set of all of Sammy's affordable consumption bundles his **consumption possibilities**. In general, whether or not a particular consumption bundle is included in a consumer's consumption possibilities depends on the consumer's income and the prices of goods and services.

Figure 51.2 shows Sammy's consumption possibilities. The quantity of clams in his consumption bundle is measured on the horizontal axis and the quantity of tomatoes on the vertical axis. The downward-sloping line connecting points *A* through *F* shows which consumption bundles are affordable and which are not. Every bundle on or inside this line (the shaded area) is affordable; every bundle outside this line is unaffordable. As an example of one of the points, let's look at point *C*, representing 2 pounds of clams and 6 pounds of tomatoes, and check whether it satisfies Sammy's budget constraint. The cost of bundle *C* is 6 pounds of tomatoes × $2 per pound + 2 pounds of clams × $4 per pound = $12 + $8 = $20. So bundle *C* does indeed satisfy Sammy's budget constraint: it costs no more than his weekly income of $20. In fact, bundle *C* costs exactly as much as Sammy's income. By doing the arithmetic, you can check that all the other points lying on the downward-sloping line are also bundles at which Sammy spends all of his income. If Sammy spends all of his income on clams (bundle *F*), he can purchase 5 pounds of clams; if he spends all of his income on tomatoes (bundle *A*), he can purchase 10 pounds of tomatoes.

The downward-sloping line has a special name, the **budget line (BL)**. It shows all the consumption bundles available to Sammy when he spends all of his income. It's downward-sloping because when Sammy is spending all of his income, say by consuming at point *A* on the budget line, then in order to consume more clams he must consume fewer tomatoes—that is, he must move from point *A* to a point further down, like *B*. In other words, when Sammy is on his budget line, the opportunity cost of consuming more clams is consuming fewer tomatoes, and vice versa. As Figure 51.2 indicates, any consumption bundle that lies above the budget line is unaffordable.

Do we need to consider the other bundles in Sammy's consumption possibilities—the ones that lie *within* the shaded region in Figure 51.2 bounded by the budget line? The answer, for all practical situations, is no: as long as Sammy doesn't get satiated—that

A **budget constraint** limits the cost of a consumer's consumption bundle to no more than the consumer's income.

A consumer's **consumption possibilities** are the set of all consumption bundles that are affordable, given the consumer's income and prevailing prices.

A consumer's **budget line (BL)** shows the consumption bundles available to a consumer who spends all of his or her income.

Figure 51.2 The Budget Line

Consumption bundle	Quantity of clams (pounds)	Quantity of tomatoes (pounds)
A	0	10
B	1	8
C	2	6
D	3	4
E	4	2
F	5	0

The *budget line (BL)* represents all the possible combinations of quantities of tomatoes and clams that Sammy can purchase if he spends all of his income. Also, it is the boundary between the set of affordable consumption bundles (the *consumption possibilities*) and the unaffordable ones.

is, as long as his marginal utility from consuming either good is always positive—and he doesn't get any utility from saving income rather than spending it, then he will always choose to consume a bundle that lies on his budget line.

Given Sammy's $20 per week budget, next we can consider the culinary dilemma of what point on his budget line Sammy will choose.

The Optimal Consumption Bundle

A consumer's **optimal consumption bundle** is the consumption bundle that maximizes the consumer's total utility given his or her budget constraint.

Because Sammy's budget constrains him to a consumption bundle somewhere along the budget line, a choice to consume a given quantity of clams also determines his tomato consumption, and vice versa. We want to find the consumption bundle—represented by a point on the budget line—that maximizes Sammy's total utility. This bundle is Sammy's **optimal consumption bundle**.

Table 51.1 shows hypothetical levels of utility Sammy gets from consuming various quantities of clams and tomatoes, respectively. According to the table, Sammy has a

Table 51.1	Sammy's Utility from Clam and Tomato Consumption		
Utility from clam consumption		Utility from tomato consumption	
Quantity of clams (pounds)	Utility from clams (utils)	Quantity of tomatoes (pounds)	Utility from tomatoes (utils)
0	0	0	0
1	15	1	11.5
2	25	2	21.4
3	31	3	29.8
4	34	4	36.8
5	36	5	42.5
		6	47.0
		7	50.5
		8	53.2
		9	55.2
		10	56.7

healthy appetite; the more of either good he consumes, the higher his utility. But because he has a limited budget, he must make a trade-off: the more pounds of clams he consumes, the fewer pounds of tomatoes, and vice versa. That is, he must choose a point on his budget line.

Table 51.2 shows how his total utility varies for the different consumption bundles along his budget line. Each of six possible consumption bundles, *A* through *F* from Figure 51.2, is given in the first column. The second column shows the level of clam consumption corresponding to each choice. The third column shows the utility Sammy gets from consuming those clams. The fourth column shows the quantity of tomatoes Sammy can afford *given* the level of clam consumption; this quantity goes down as his clam consumption goes up because he is sliding down the budget line. The fifth column shows the utility he gets from consuming those tomatoes. And the final column shows his *total utility*. In this example, Sammy's total utility is the sum of the utility he gets from clams and the utility he gets from tomatoes.

Table 51.2	Sammy's Budget and Total Utility				
Consumption bundle	Quantity of clams (pounds)	Utility from clams (utils)	Quantity of tomatoes (pounds)	Utility from tomatoes (utils)	Total utility (utils)
A	0	0	10	56.7	56.7
B	1	15	8	53.2	68.2
C	2	25	6	47.0	72.0
D	3	31	4	36.8	67.8
E	4	34	2	21.4	55.4
F	5	36	0	0	36.0

Figure 51.3 gives a visual representation of the data shown in Table 51.2. Panel (a) shows Sammy's budget line, to remind us that when he decides to consume more clams he is also deciding to consume fewer tomatoes. Panel (b) then shows how his total utility depends on that choice. The horizontal axis in panel (b) has two sets of labels: it shows both the quantity of clams, increasing from left to right, and the quantity of tomatoes, increasing from right to left. The reason we can use the same axis to represent consumption of both goods is, of course, that he is constrained by the budget line: the more pounds of clams Sammy consumes, the fewer pounds of tomatoes he can afford, and vice versa.

Clearly, the consumption bundle that makes the best of the trade-off between clam consumption and tomato consumption, the optimal consumption bundle, is the one that maximizes Sammy's total utility. That is, Sammy's optimal consumption bundle puts him at the top of the total utility curve.

As always, we can find the top of the curve by direct observation. We can see from Figure 51.3 that Sammy's total utility is maximized at point *C*—that his optimal consumption bundle contains 2 pounds of clams and 6 pounds of tomatoes. But we usually gain more insight into "how much" problems when we use marginal analysis. So next we turn to representing and solving the optimal consumption choice problem with marginal analysis.

Spending the Marginal Dollar

As we've just seen, we can find Sammy's optimal consumption choice by finding the total utility he receives from each consumption bundle on his budget line and then choosing the bundle at which total utility is maximized. But we can use marginal analysis instead, which leads to some useful guidelines for how much to buy. How do we do this? By thinking about choosing an optimal

Figure 51.3 Optimal Consumption Bundle

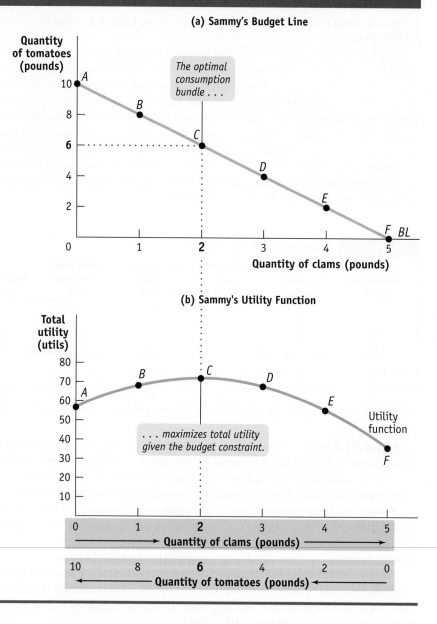

(a) Sammy's Budget Line

Quantity of tomatoes (pounds)

The optimal consumption bundle . . .

(b) Sammy's Utility Function

Total utility (utils)

. . . maximizes total utility given the budget constraint.

Utility function

Quantity of clams (pounds)

Quantity of tomatoes (pounds)

Panel (a) shows Sammy's budget line and his six possible consumption bundles. Panel (b) shows how his total utility is affected by his consumption bundle, which must lie on his budget line. The quantity of clams is measured from left to right on the horizontal axis, and the quantity of tomatoes is measured from right to left. As he consumes more clams, due to his fixed budget, he must consume fewer tomatoes. As a result, the quantity of tomatoes decreases as the quantity of clams increases. His total utility is maximized at bundle C, where he consumes 2 pounds of clams and 6 pounds of tomatoes. This is Sammy's *optimal consumption bundle.*

consumption bundle as a problem of *how much to spend on each good*. The marginal decision is a question of how to *spend the marginal dollar*—how to allocate an additional dollar between clams and tomatoes in a way that maximizes utility.

Our first step in applying marginal analysis is to ask if Sammy is made better off by spending an additional dollar on either good; and if so, by how much is he better off. To answer this question we must calculate the **marginal utility per dollar** spent on either clams or tomatoes—how much additional utility Sammy gets from spending an additional dollar on either good.

The **marginal utility per dollar** spent on a good or service is the additional utility from spending one more dollar on that good or service.

Marginal Utility per Dollar

We've already introduced the concept of marginal utility, the additional utility a consumer gets from consuming one more unit of a good or service; now let's see how this concept can be used to derive the related measure of marginal utility per dollar.

Table 51.3 shows how to calculate the marginal utility per dollar spent on clams and tomatoes, respectively.

Table 51.3 Sammy's Marginal Utility per Dollar

(a) Clams (price of clams = $4 per pound)				(b) Tomatoes (price of tomatoes = $2 per pound)			
Quantity of clams (pounds)	Utility from clams (utils)	Marginal utility per pound of clams (utils)	Marginal utility per dollar (utils)	Quantity of tomatoes (pounds)	Utility from tomatoes (utils)	Marginal utility per pound of tomatoes (utils)	Marginal utility per dollar (utils)
0	0			0	0		
		15	3.75			11.5	5.75
1	15			1	11.5		
		10	2.50			9.9	4.95
2	25			2	21.4		
		6	1.50			8.4	4.20
3	31			3	29.8		
		3	0.75			7.0	3.50
4	34			4	36.8		
		2	0.50			5.7	2.85
5	36			5	42.5		
						4.5	2.25
				6	47.0		
						3.5	1.75
				7	50.5		
						2.7	1.35
				8	53.2		
						2.0	1.00
				9	55.2		
						1.5	0.75
				10	56.7		

In panel (a) of the table, the first column shows different possible amounts of clam consumption. The second column shows the utility Sammy derives from each amount of clam consumption; the third column then shows the marginal utility, the increase in utility Sammy gets from consuming an additional pound of clams. Panel (b) provides the same information for tomatoes. The next step is to derive marginal utility *per dollar* for each good. To do this, we just divide the marginal utility of the good by its price in dollars.

To see why we divide by the price, compare the third and fourth columns of panel (a). Consider what happens if Sammy increases his clam consumption from 2 pounds to 3 pounds. This raises his total utility by 6 utils. But he must spend $4 for that additional pound, so the increase in his utility per additional dollar spent on clams is 6 utils/$4 = 1.5 utils per dollar. Similarly, if he increases his clam consumption from 3 pounds to 4 pounds, his marginal utility is 3 utils but his marginal utility per dollar is 3 utils/$4 = 0.75 utils per dollar. Notice that because of diminishing marginal utility, Sammy's marginal utility per pound of clams falls as the quantity of clams he consumes rises. As a result, his marginal utility per dollar spent on clams also falls as the quantity of clams he consumes rises.

So the last column of panel (a) shows how Sammy's marginal utility per dollar spent on clams depends on the quantity of clams he consumes. Similarly, the last column of panel (b) shows how his marginal utility per dollar spent on tomatoes depends on the quantity of tomatoes he consumes. Again, marginal utility per dollar spent on each good declines as the quantity of that good consumed rises because of diminishing marginal utility.

We will use MU_C and MU_T to represent the marginal utility per pound of clams and tomatoes, respectively. And we will use P_C and P_T to represent the price of clams (per pound) and the price of tomatoes (per pound), respectively. Then the marginal utility per dollar spent on clams is $\frac{MU_C}{P_C}$ and the marginal utility per dollar spent on tomatoes is $\frac{MU_T}{P_T}$. In general, the additional utility generated from an additional dollar spent on a good is equal to

$$(51\text{-}2) \quad \begin{array}{c}\text{Marginal utility}\\\text{per dollar spent}\\\text{on a good}\end{array} = \frac{\text{Marginal utility of one unit of the good}}{\text{Price of one unit of the good}}$$

$$= \frac{MU_{good}}{P_{good}}$$

Next we'll see how this concept helps us determine a consumer's optimal consumption bundle using marginal analysis.

AP® EXAM TIP

You may need to fill in or interpret a marginal utility table like Table 51.3 for the AP® exam. You may also be asked to determine how a change in price affects the quantity demanded for each good.

AP® EXAM TIP

To determine whether a consumer should buy more of one good or another, compare the marginal utility *per dollar* received from each good, not just the marginal utility received from each good.

Optimal Consumption

When you're deciding how much of one particular good to purchase, it's wise to buy more as long as the value of the marginal utility you receive from that good exceeds its price. When you're choosing the quantities of two goods to buy, there's another trick for finding the optimal consumption bundle. Let's consider **Figure 51.4**. As in Figure 51.3, we can measure both the quantity of clams and the quantity of tomatoes on the horizontal axis due to the budget constraint. Along the horizontal axis of Figure 51.4—also as in Figure 51.3—the quantity of clams increases as you move from left to right, and the quantity of tomatoes increases as you move from right to left. The curve labeled $\frac{MU_C}{P_C}$ in Figure 51.4 shows Sammy's marginal utility per dollar spent on clams as derived in Table 51.3. Likewise, the curve labeled $\frac{MU_T}{P_T}$ shows his marginal utility per dollar spent on tomatoes. Notice that the two curves, $\frac{MU_C}{P_C}$ and $\frac{MU_T}{P_T}$, cross at the optimal consumption bundle, point C, consisting of 2 pounds of clams and 6 pounds of tomatoes. Moreover, Figure 51.4 illustrates an important feature of Sammy's optimal consumption bundle: when Sammy consumes 2 pounds of clams and 6 pounds of tomatoes, his marginal utility per dollar spent is the same, 2, for both goods. That is, at the optimal consumption bundle, $\frac{MU_C}{P_C} = \frac{MU_T}{P_T} = 2$.

Figure 51.4 Marginal Utility per Dollar

Sammy's optimal consumption bundle is at point C, where his marginal utility per dollar spent on clams, $\frac{MU_C}{P_C}$, is equal to his marginal utility per dollar spent on tomatoes, $\frac{MU_T}{P_T}$. This illustrates the optimal consumption rule: *at the optimal consumption bundle, the marginal utility per dollar spent on each good and service is the same.* At any other consumption bundle on Sammy's budget line, such as bundle B in Figure 51.3, represented here by points B_C and B_T, consumption is not optimal: Sammy can increase his utility at no additional cost by reallocating his spending.

This isn't an accident. Consider another one of Sammy's possible consumption bundles—say, B in Figure 51.3, at which he consumes 1 pound of clams and 8 pounds of tomatoes. The marginal utility per dollar spent on each good is shown by points B_C and B_T in Figure 51.4. At that consumption bundle, Sammy's marginal utility per dollar spent on clams would be approximately 3, but his marginal utility per dollar spent on tomatoes would be only approximately 1. This shows that he has made a mistake: he is consuming too many tomatoes and not enough clams.

How do we know this? If Sammy's marginal utility per dollar spent on clams is higher than his marginal utility per dollar spent on tomatoes, he has a simple way to make himself better off while staying within his budget: spend $1 less on tomatoes and $1 more on clams. By spending an additional dollar on clams, he adds about 3 utils to his total utility; meanwhile, by spending $1 less on tomatoes, he subtracts only about

1 util from his total utility. Because his marginal utility per dollar spent is higher for clams than for tomatoes, reallocating his spending toward clams and away from tomatoes would increase his total utility. On the other hand, if his marginal utility per dollar spent on tomatoes is higher, he can increase his utility by spending less on clams and more on tomatoes. So if Sammy has in fact chosen his optimal consumption bundle, his marginal utility per dollar spent on clams and tomatoes must be equal.

This is a general principle known as the **optimal consumption rule**: *when a consumer maximizes utility in the face of a budget constraint, the marginal utility per dollar spent on each good or service in the consumption bundle is the same*. That is, for any two goods C and T, the optimal consumption rule says that at the optimal consumption bundle

$$(51\text{-}3) \quad \frac{MU_C}{P_C} = \frac{MU_T}{P_T}$$

It's easiest to understand this rule using examples in which the consumption bundle contains only two goods, but it applies no matter how many goods or services a consumer buys: the marginal utilities per dollar spent for each and every good or service in the optimal consumption bundle are equal.

The main reason for studying consumer behavior is to look behind the market demand curve. In Module 46 we explained how the *substitution effect* leads consumers to buy less of a good when its price increases. We used the substitution effect to explain, in general, why the individual demand curve obeys the law of demand. Marginal analysis adds clarity to the utility-maximizing behavior of individuals and explains more precisely how an increase in price leads to less marginal utility per dollar and therefore a decrease in the quantity demanded.

> The **optimal consumption rule** says that in order to maximize utility, a consumer must equate the marginal utility per dollar spent on each good and service in the consumption bundle.

> **AP® EXAM TIP**
>
> When the price of a good changes, the marginal utility per dollar spent on the good changes and so does the optimal consumption bundle.

MODULE 51 REVIEW

Check Your Understanding

1. Explain why a rational consumer who has diminishing marginal utility for a good would not consume an additional unit when it generates negative marginal utility, even when that unit is free.

2. In the following two examples, find all the consumption bundles that lie on the consumer's budget line. Illustrate these consumption possibilities in a diagram, and draw the budget line through them.
   a. The consumption bundle consists of movie tickets and buckets of popcorn. The price of each ticket is $10, the price of each bucket of popcorn is $5, and the consumer's income is $20. In your diagram, put movie tickets on the vertical axis and buckets of popcorn on the horizontal axis.

   b. The consumption bundle consists of underwear and socks. The price of each pair of underwear is $4, the price of each pair of socks is $2, and the consumer's income is $12. In your diagram, put pairs of socks on the vertical axis and pairs of underwear on the horizontal axis.

3. In Table 51.3 you can see that the marginal utility per dollar spent on clams and the marginal utility per dollar spent on tomatoes are equal when Sammy increases his consumption of clams from 3 pounds to 4 pounds and his consumption of tomatoes from 9 pounds to 10 pounds. Explain why 4 clams and 10 pounds of tomatoes is not Sammy's optimal consumption bundle. Illustrate your answer using a budget line like the one in Figure 51.3.

TACKLE THE AP® TEST: Multiple-Choice Questions

1. Generally, each successive unit of a good consumed will cause marginal utility to
   a. increase at an increasing rate.
   b. increase at a decreasing rate.
   c. increase at a constant rate.
   d. decrease.
   e. either increase or decrease.

2. Assume there are two goods, good X and good Y. Good X costs $5 and good Y costs $10. If your income is $200, which of the following combinations of good X and good Y is on your budget line?
   a. 0 units of good X and 18 units of good Y
   b. 0 units of good X and 20 units of good Y
   c. 20 units of good X and 0 units of good Y
   d. 10 units of good X and 12 units of good Y
   e. all of the above

3. The optimal consumption rule states that total utility is maximized when all income is spent and
   a. MU/P is equal for all goods.
   b. MU is equal for all goods.
   c. P/MU is equal for all goods.
   d. MU is as high as possible for all goods.
   e. the amount spent on each good is equal.

4. A consumer is spending all of her income and receiving 100 utils from the last unit of good A and 80 utils from the last unit of good B. If the price of good A is $2 and the price of good B is $1, to maximize total utility the consumer should buy
   a. more of good A.
   b. more of good B.

   c. less of good B.
   d. more of both goods.
   e. less of both goods.

5. The optimal consumption bundle is always represented by a point
   a. inside the consumer's budget line.
   b. outside the consumer's budget line.
   c. at the highest point on the consumer's budget line.
   d. on the consumer's budget line.
   e. at the horizontal intercept of the consumer's budget line.

6. Suppose the seventh carrot you consume provides a marginal utility of 3 utils and the eighth carrot provides a marginal utility of 2 utils. If you consume the eighth carrot your total utility will
   a. decrease by 1.   **d.** increase by 2.
   b. increase by 1.   **e.** decrease by 5.
   c. decrease by 2.

7. A second of which of the following is the most likely to provide more marginal utility than the first?
   a. refrigerator   **d.** t-shirt
   b. shoe   **e.** mailbox
   c. car

TACKLE THE AP® TEST: Free-Response Questions

1. Refer to the table provided. Assume you have $20 to spend.

Snacks (price = $4)		Drinks (price = $2)	
Quantity	Total utility (utils)	Quantity	Total utility (utils)
1	15	1	12
2	25	2	21
3	31	3	29
4	34	4	36
5	36	5	42
		6	47
		7	50
		8	52

   a. Draw a correctly labeled budget line.
   b. Determine the marginal utility and the marginal utility per dollar spent on the fourth drink.
   c. What is the optimal consumption rule?
   d. How many drinks and snacks should you purchase to maximize your total utility?

1 point: Graph with "Quantity of snacks" and "Quantity of drinks" as axis labels

1 point: Straight budget line with intercepts at 5 snacks and 0 drinks and at 0 snacks and 10 drinks

1 point: MU = 7 utils

1 point: MU/P = 3.5 utils per dollar

1 point: Total utility is maximized when the marginal utility per dollar is equal for all goods.

1 point: 6 drinks, 2 snacks

2. Assume you have an income of $100. The price of good X is $5, and the price of good Y is $20.
   a. Draw a correctly labeled budget line with "Quantity of good X" on the horizontal axis and "Quantity of good Y" on the vertical axis. Be sure to correctly label the horizontal and vertical intercepts.
   b. With your current consumption bundle, you spend all of your income and receive 100 utils from consuming your last unit of good X and 400 utils from consuming your last unit of good Y. Are you maximizing your total utility? Explain.
   c. What will happen to the total and marginal utility you receive from consuming good X if you decide to consume another unit of good X? Explain. **(4 points)**

Rubric for FRQ 1 (6 points)

SECTION 9 Review

SECTION 9 Review Video

Adventures in AP® Economics Videos

Mod 48: Elasticity
Mod 49: Consumer and Producer Surplus

Module 46

1. Changes in the price of a good affect the quantity consumed as a result of the **substitution effect**, and in some cases the **income effect**. Most goods absorb only a small share of a consumer's spending; for these goods, only the substitution effect—buying less of the good that has become relatively more expensive and more of the good that has become relatively cheaper—is significant. The income effect becomes substantial when there is a change in the price of a good that absorbs a large share of a consumer's spending, thereby changing the purchasing power of the consumer's income.

2. Many economic questions depend on the size of consumer or producer responses to changes in prices or other variables. *Elasticity* is a general measure of responsiveness that can be used to answer such questions.

3. The **price elasticity of demand**—the percent change in the quantity demanded divided by the percent change in the price (dropping the minus sign)—is a measure of the responsiveness of the quantity demanded to changes in the price. In practical calculations, it is usually best to use the **midpoint method**, which calculates percent changes in prices and quantities based on the average of the initial and final values.

Module 47

4. Demand can fall anywhere in the range from **perfectly inelastic**, meaning the quantity demanded is unaffected by the price, to **perfectly elastic**, meaning there is a unique price at which consumers will buy as much or as little as they are offered. When demand is perfectly inelastic, the demand curve is a vertical line; when it is perfectly elastic, the demand curve is a horizontal line.

5. The price elasticity of demand is classified according to whether it is more or less than 1. If it is greater than 1, demand is **elastic**; if it is less than 1, demand is **inelastic**; if it is exactly 1, demand is **unit-elastic**.

This classification determines how **total revenue**, the total value of sales, changes when the price changes. If demand is elastic, total revenue falls when the price increases and rises when the price decreases. If demand is inelastic, total revenue rises when the price increases and falls when the price decreases.

6. The price elasticity of demand depends on whether there are close substitutes for the good in question, whether the good is a necessity or a luxury, the share of income spent on the good, and the length of time that has elapsed since the price change.

Module 48

7. The **cross-price elasticity of demand** measures the effect of a change in one good's price on the quantity of another good demanded. The cross-price elasticity of demand can be positive, in which case the goods are substitutes, or negative, in which case they are complements.

8. The **income elasticity of demand** is the percent change in the quantity of a good demanded when a consumer's income changes divided by the percent change in income. The income elasticity of demand indicates how intensely the demand for a good responds to changes in income. It can be negative; in that case the good is an inferior good. Goods with positive income elasticities of demand are normal goods. If the income elasticity is

greater than 1, a good is **income-elastic**; if it is positive and less than 1, the good is **income-inelastic**.

9. The **price elasticity of supply** is the percent change in the quantity of a good supplied divided by the percent change in the price. If the quantity supplied does not change at all, we have an instance of **perfectly inelastic supply**; the supply curve is a vertical line. If the quantity supplied is zero below some price but infinite above that price, we have an instance of **perfectly elastic supply**; the supply curve is a horizontal line.

10. The price elasticity of supply depends on the availability of resources to expand production and on time. It is higher when inputs are available at relatively low cost and when more time has elapsed since the price change.

Module 49

11. The **willingness to pay** of each individual consumer determines the shape of the demand curve. When price is less than or equal to the willingness to pay, the potential consumer purchases the good. The difference between willingness to pay and price is the net gain to the consumer, the **individual consumer surplus**.

12. **Total consumer surplus** in a market, which is the sum of all individual consumer surpluses in a market, is

equal to the area below the market demand curve but above the price. A rise in the price of a good reduces consumer surplus; a fall in the price increases consumer surplus. The term **consumer surplus** is often used to refer to both individual and total consumer surplus.

13. The **cost** of each potential producer of a good, the lowest price at which he or she is willing to supply a unit of that good, determines the shape of the supply curve. If the price of a good is above a producer's cost, a sale generates a net gain to the producer, known as the **individual producer surplus**.

14. **Total producer surplus** in a market, the sum of the individual producer surpluses in a market, is equal to the area above the market supply curve but below the price. A rise in the price of a good increases producer surplus; a fall in the price reduces producer surplus. The term **producer surplus** is often used to refer to both individual and total producer surplus.

Module 50

15. **Total surplus**, the total gain to society from the production and consumption of a good, is the sum of consumer and producer surplus.

16. Usually, markets are efficient and achieve the maximum total surplus. Any possible reallocation of consumption or sales, or change in the quantity bought and sold, reduces total surplus. However, society also cares about equity. So government intervention in a market that reduces efficiency but increases equity can be a valid choice by society.

17. A tax that rises more than in proportion to income is a **progressive tax**. A tax that rises less than in proportion to income is a **regressive tax**. A tax that rises in proportion to income is a **proportional tax**.

18. An **excise tax**—a tax on the purchase or sale of a good—raises the price paid by consumers and reduces the price received by producers, driving a wedge between the two. **Tax incidence**—how the burden of the tax is divided between consumers and producers—does not depend on who officially pays the tax.

19. The incidence of an excise tax depends on the price elasticities of supply and demand. If the price elasticity of demand is higher than the price elasticity of supply, the tax falls mainly on producers; if the price elasticity of supply is higher than the price elasticity of demand, the tax falls mainly on consumers.

20. The tax revenue generated by a tax depends on the tax rate and on the number of units sold with the tax. Excise taxes cause inefficiency in the form of **deadweight loss** because they discourage some mutually beneficial transactions. Taxes also impose **administrative costs**: resources used to collect the tax, to pay it (over and above the amount of the tax), and to evade it.

21. An excise tax generates revenue for the government but lowers total surplus. The loss in total surplus exceeds the tax revenue, resulting in a deadweight loss to society. This deadweight loss is represented by a triangle, the area of which equals the value of the transactions discouraged by the tax. The greater the elasticity of demand or supply, or both, the larger the deadweight loss from a tax. If either demand or supply is perfectly inelastic, there is no deadweight loss from a tax.

22. A **lump-sum tax** is a tax of a fixed amount paid by all taxpayers. Because a lump-sum tax does not depend on the behavior of taxpayers, it does not discourage mutually beneficial transactions and therefore causes no deadweight loss.

Module 51

23. Consumers maximize a measure of satisfaction called **utility**. We measure utility in hypothetical units called **utils**.

24. A good's or service's **marginal utility** is the additional utility generated by consuming one more unit of the good or service. We usually assume that the **principle of diminishing marginal utility** holds: consumption of another unit of a good or service yields less additional utility than the previous unit. As a result, the **marginal utility curve** slopes downward.

25. A **budget constraint** limits a consumer's spending to no more than his or her income. It defines the consumer's **consumption possibilities**, the set of all affordable consumption bundles. A consumer who spends all of his or her income will choose a consumption bundle on the **budget line**. An individual chooses the consumption bundle that maximizes total utility, the **optimal consumption bundle**.

26. We use marginal analysis to find the optimal consumption bundle by analyzing how to allocate the marginal dollar. According to the **optimal consumption rule**, with the optimal consumption bundle, the **marginal utility per dollar** spent on each good and service—the marginal utility of a good divided by its price—is the same.

Key Terms

Substitution effect, p. 440
Income effect, p. 441
Price elasticity of demand, p. 442
Midpoint method, p. 444
Perfectly inelastic, p. 448
Perfectly elastic, p. 448
Elastic, p. 448
Inelastic, p. 448
Unit-elastic, p. 448
Total revenue, p. 448
Cross-price elasticity of demand, p. 455
Income elasticity of demand, p. 456
Income-elastic, p. 456
Income-inelastic, p. 456
Price elasticity of supply, p. 457

Perfectly inelastic supply, p. 458
Perfectly elastic supply, p. 458
Willingness to pay, p. 462
Individual consumer surplus, p. 463
Total consumer surplus, p. 464
Consumer surplus, p. 464
Cost, p. 466
Individual producer surplus, p. 467
Total producer surplus, p. 467
Producer surplus, p. 467
Total surplus, p. 473
Regressive tax, p. 477
Proportional tax, p. 477
Progressive tax, p. 477
Excise tax, p. 477

Tax incidence, p. 480
Deadweight loss, p. 483
Lump-sum tax, p. 485
Administrative costs, p. 485
Utility, p. 488
Util, p. 488
Marginal utility, p. 489
Marginal utility curve, p. 490
Principle of diminishing marginal utility, p. 490
Budget constraint, p. 491
Consumption possibilities, p. 491
Budget line (BL), p. 491
Optimal consumption bundle, p. 492
Marginal utility per dollar, p. 494
Optimal consumption rule, p. 497

AP® Exam Practice Questions

Multiple-Choice Questions

1. When the price of a normal good falls, consumers will _____ the quantity they want, in part because they now have more money to spend on these units, which economists call _____.
   a. increase   the substitution effect
   b. decrease   the unit effect
   c. increase   the price effect
   d. decrease   the quantity effect
   e. increase   the income effect

2. Suppose market prices for tomatoes were to increase by 10%, and tomato farmers wanted to know whether or not their overall total revenues would rise or fall as a consequence. The farmers could figure this out by calculating which of the following economic concepts?
   a. deadweight loss
   b. producer surplus
   c. diminishing marginal utility
   d. price elasticity of demand
   e. administrative costs

3. Suppose Jolene buys apples weekly. If the price of apples were to drop, Jolene would experience a(n) _____ in _____.
   a. decrease   total revenue
   b. increase   consumer surplus
   c. decrease   her budget constraint
   d. increase   marginal utility
   e. decrease   willingness to pay

4. Pizza and soda are often consumed together at Joe's Diner. Suppose that the price of pizza rises from $0.75 a slice to $1.25 a slice, and consequently April sales of pizza drop from 1,050 to 950 slices. Using the midpoint method and this information, an economist could conclude which of the following?
   a. The cross price elasticity of demand is 0.2.
   b. The price elasticity of supply is 0.1.
   c. The price elasticity of demand is 0.2.
   d. The income elasticity of demand is 0.5.
   e. The unit elasticity of demand is 0.1.

5. If the demand curve is a straight line with a slope of −1, then from the left end of the curve to the right,
   a. demand is unit-elastic.
   b. demand is elastic.
   c. demand inelastic.
   d. the price elasticity ranges from very high to very low.
   e. the price elasticity ranges from very low to very high.

6. If the price of an inferior good decreases, then consumers' purchasing power _____, and the income effect alone causes consumers to buy _____ of the good.
   a. decreases   more
   b. decreases   less
   c. increases   more
   d. increases   less
   e. remains the same   more

Use the following information to answer Questions 7–10.

Suppose the government levies a tax of $0.50 per pack on the buyers of cigarettes. Suppose also that the price elasticity of demand for cigarettes is 1.2 and the price elasticity of supply is 0.7.

7. Because this tax is levied on the sale of a specific good, it is a(n)
  a. excise tax.
  b. progressive tax.
  c. regressive tax.
  d. proportional tax.
  e. lump-sum tax.

8. After this tax is levied, total surplus will _____, and the price received by producers (not including the tax) will

_____.

a. increase	increase by exactly $0.50
b. decrease	fall by exactly $0.50
c. increase	fall by less than $0.50
d. decrease	fall by less than $0.50
e. increase	increase by more than $0.50

9. If economists were to study the tax incidence in this cigarette market, they would conclude which of the following?
  a. The burden of this tax falls entirely on consumers.
  b. The burden of this tax falls entirely on producers.
  c. The burden of this tax falls equally on consumers and producers.
  d. The burden of this tax falls more on consumers than on producers.
  e. The burden of this tax falls more on producers than on consumers.

10. In this example, cigarettes have
  a. perfectly inelastic demand.
  b. perfectly elastic demand.
  c. unit-inelastic demand.
  d. inelastic demand.
  e. elastic demand.

11. Jill is willing to sell her used calculator for $20. Her friend Jack is willing to pay $90 for a used calculator. They agree and trade at a price of $50. Which of the following is correct?
  a. Jill's cost is $50.
  b. Jack's individual consumer surplus is $30.
  c. Jill's individual producer surplus is $30.
  d. Jack's budget line is $90.
  e. Jill's deadweight loss is $70.

Refer to the figure for Questions 12–19.

12. Using the midpoint method, the price elasticity of demand between points C and E is _____ and economists would classify it as _____.
  a. 0.67   inelastic
  b. 1.5   elastic
  c. 1   unit-elastic
  d. 0.67   elastic
  e. 1.5   inelastic

13. Using the midpoint method, the price elasticity of supply between points J and E is _____ and economists would classify it as _____.
  a. 2.67   inelastic
  b. 0.375   elastic
  c. 0   perfectly inelastic
  d. 2.67   elastic
  e. 0.33   inelastic

14. Suppose the government levies a tax on the buyers of jeans that shifts the demand curve from D_1 to D_T. Using the diagram, determine the amount of the tax per pair of jeans sold.
  a. $50
  b. $40
  c. $30
  d. $20
  e. The exact amount of the tax cannot be determined.

15. Which of the following statements about the tax on jeans is true?
  a. Buyers bear the entire burden of the tax, since the tax was levied on them.
  b. Buyers bear most of the burden of the tax, since the tax was levied on them.
  c. Buyers bear most of the burden of the tax, since demand is more *inelastic* than supply.
  d. Buyers bear a smaller tax burden than sellers, since demand is more *elastic* than supply.
  e. Buyers and sellers share the tax burden equally.

16. How much revenue would the government collect from the tax on jeans?
  a. $1,250   **d.** $600
  b. $1,200   **e.** $300
  c. $750

17. Buyers in the jeans market gain _____ in consumer surplus before the imposition of the tax, and they gain _____ in consumer surplus after the imposition of the tax.
  a. $625 $400
  b. $400 $225
  c. $400 $625
  d. $625 $225
  e. $225 $400

18. Jeans and product X (not shown) have a cross-price elasticity of 3.7. After the imposition of the tax on jeans, buyers' consumption of product X would _____ because jeans and product X are _____.
  a. decrease   normal goods
  b. increase   substitutes
  c. decrease   complements
  d. increase   complements
  e. decrease   substitutes

19. The deadweight loss caused by the tax on jeans is
  a. $5.   **d.** $60.
  b. $30.   **e.** $75.
  c. $50.

Use the information from the following tables to complete Questions 20–22.

Quantity of ball toss games	Total utility (utils)
0	0
1	70
2	130
3	180
4	220
5	250
6	270
7	280

Quantity of video games	Total utility (utils)
0	0
1	30
2	55
3	75
4	90
5	100
6	105
7	109
8	112
9	114

20. If Jill purchased 5 video games and 1 ball toss game, she would receive _____ and _____.
  a. a marginal utility of 10 from her last video game | a marginal utility of 70 from her last ball toss game
  b. a marginal utility of 105 from her last video game | a marginal utility of 130 from her last ball toss game
  c. her highest possible marginal utility from video games | 170 total utils from both products
  d. less than her highest possible marginal utility from ball toss games | 90 utils of marginal utility from both products
  e. 100 utils in total utility from video games | a marginal utility of zero from ball toss games

21. At the arcade, Jill likes the video games, which cost $0.50 to play, and the ball toss, which costs $2 to play. She has $6 to spend at the arcade. If Jill maximizes her utility, she will
  a. spend all of her $6 on the ball toss because she likes it the best.
  b. achieve a total utility of 220.
  c. spend all of her $6 on video games because they are the cheapest.
  d. play 9 video games and 7 games of ball toss.
  e. find where the marginal utility of playing video games equals the marginal utility of playing ball toss.

22. Suppose that video games still cost $0.50 and the ball toss still costs $2, but Jill now has $10.50 to spend at the arcade. If Jill chooses her optimal consumption bundle,
  a. she will purchase 9 video games and 3 games of ball toss.
  b. her marginal utility per dollar spent on video games will be 10.
  c. her marginal utility from her last game of ball toss will be 40.
  d. her total utility will be 280.
  e. she will spend less than $10.50.

23. If razors and shaving cream are complements, their cross-price elasticity of demand will necessarily be
   a. greater than 1.
   b. less than − 1.
   c. 0.
   d. positive.
   e. negative.

24. The height of the demand curve at each quantity is determined by
   a. consumers' willingness to pay.
   b. the price of the good.
   c. the location of the supply curve.
   d. the marginal cost of production.
   e. the availability of inputs for making that good.

25. If marginal utility is positive and decreasing, then total utility is
   a. positive and decreasing.
   b. positive and increasing.
   c. positive and remaining the same.
   d. negative and decreasing.
   e. negative and increasing.

Free-Response Questions

1. On the island of Rockville, the equilibrium quantity of acres of land sold is currently 1,000, and the equilibrium price per acre is $500. Landowners have an elasticity of supply equal to 0. Consumers have an elasticity of demand greater than 1.
   a. Using a correctly labeled graph of supply and demand for acres of land, show the equilibrium price ($500) and equilibrium quantity (1,000).

   Now suppose that the government of Rockville imposes an excise tax of $20 per acre on the buyers of land.
   b. Show the effects of the tax on your graph from part a, and indicate the new equilibrium price and equilibrium quantity.
   c. Calculate the amount of tax revenue that is collected.
   d. Calculate the amount of deadweight loss.
   e. Who bears the burden of this tax? Explain. **(9 points)**

2. The table below shows the utility Milo receives each week from consuming various quantities of cheese and crackers. The price of cheese is $4 per pound and the price of crackers is $2 per box.

Cheese		Crackers	
Quantity (pounds)	Total utility (from cheese)	Quantity (boxes)	Total utility (from crackers)
1	200	1	100
2	360	2	200
3	440	3	250
4	480	4	270
5	500	5	280

   a. After what quantity of crackers does Milo begin to experience diminishing marginal utility?
   b. What is the marginal utility of the third pound of cheese?
   c. What is the marginal utility per dollar of the fourth pound of cheese? Show your work.
   d. Milo has a budget of $20, which he spends on 3 pounds of cheese and 4 boxes of crackers. To maximize his total utility from cheese and crackers, how should Milo adjust his consumption of cheese and crackers, if at all? Explain your answers using the concept of marginal analysis. **(5 points)**

3. Connor sells peanut butter and chocolate at his snack shop.
   a. Consumer demand is such that each day he can sell 50 jars of peanut butter for $4 each or 30 jars for $5 each. Is the price elasticity of demand for peanut butter elastic, inelastic, or unit-elastic? Explain.
   b. When the price of peanut butter is $4, Conner sells 20 chocolate bars per day, and when the price of peanut butter is $5, he sells 15 chocolate bars per day.
      i. Calculate the cross-price elasticity for peanut butter and chocolate. Show your work.
      ii. Based on your answer to part (i), are peanut butter and chocolate substitutes, complements, or unrelated?
   c. Jessica is one of Connor's customers. When Jessica's income increased by 10%, she bought 10% less peanut butter. For Jessica, is peanut butter necessarily a normal good, an inferior good, a luxury, or a necessity? Explain. **(5 points)**

Why Is a Newspaper Heist So Easy?

Diminishing Marginal Utility and the Price Elasticity of Demand

The Student Press Law Center tracks the epidemic of newspaper thefts in the United States. Dozens of times each year, a college campus is hit by a newspaper heist. The details are tawdry: typically, hundreds or even thousands of newspapers disappear on the day when an embarrassing story runs—say, on a fraternity party gone awry, a football star accused of violence, or two students photographed fighting. Why are newspaper thefts so easy? Sodas and candy bars cost as much as newspapers, but candy vending machines have elaborate mechanisms to prevent the removal of more than one item at a time. In contrast, newspaper vending machines allow the entire stack of papers to be taken after only one has been purchased, and school newspapers are often set out for free, with little fear that someone will take the whole pile. Here we explain how differing demands for various goods shape public policy, pricing decisions, and the distribution of newspapers.

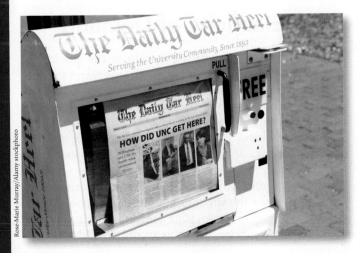

The Meaning of Life

Economics has been called the dismal science, but it is really about the meaning of life. The Dalai Lama, exiled Tibetan leader and winner of the Nobel Peace Prize, wrote in *The Meaning of Life* that "it is a fact that everybody wants happiness." The demand curve is simply a reflection of what makes us happy. The happier something makes us, the more we would be willing to exchange for it and the higher is our demand for

it. Other things being equal, relatively high demand boosts prices and spurs suppliers to provide more of what pleases us. Let's examine demand's foundation in happiness and the significance of the demand curve's shape.

There is no obvious measure of happiness. The benefits that consumers receive from goods and services could be measured, for example, in terms of giggles, goose bumps, satisfaction points, or smiles. Economists measure happiness in terms of *utility*, which they measure in units called *utils*. In agreement with the Dalai Lama, economists assume that human nature guides individuals to seek happiness. In economic terminology, the quest to be as happy as possible means that it is better to have more utils than fewer, and that we make decisions with the goal of maximizing our utility.

The sources of utility are subjective and result from personal tastes and preferences. Some people like sushi; others like their fish cooked. Some people like to shoot wild animals with cameras; others prefer to use rifles. These differences and the arbitrary nature of utility measurement make interpersonal utility comparisons impossible because there is no concrete gauge for such comparisons. You might report a gain of 100 utils from a day at the Five Flags amusement park, and I might report a gain of 1,000 utils, but who is to say that I really gained more happiness than you did? Fortunately, the simple fact that more utils are better is sufficient in many important areas of economic analysis, some of which we will explore here.

The additional utility gained from one more unit of a good is called the *marginal utility* of that good. According to the *"law" of diminishing marginal utility*, each additional unit of a good or service provides less happiness—that is, fewer utils—to the consumer than the one before it. This law explains the demand curve's negative slope. The height of the demand curve at each quantity indicates the most that consumers would be willing to pay for one more unit of the good. The demand curve's height at quantities of 1, 4, and 17, for example, is thus the number of dollars' worth of marginal utility that the 1st, 4th, and 17th units provide. The height of an individual's demand curve decreases because the utility from one more unit decreases as more units are consumed. The market demand is simply the sum of each individual's demand, so it, too, takes its negative slope from diminishing marginal utility.

Examples of Marginal Utility and Demand

Variations in the marginal utility of goods yield a varied crop of demand curves. A dollar will get you a soda or a can of soup, but each week, the average American purchases 19 cans of soda and only one can of soup. For a typical consumer of refrigerators, the marginal utility (and, therefore, the consumer's demand curve) starts relatively high and plummets after a quantity of one. Thus, owners of a good refrigerator are unlikely to respond to even the deepest discounts in refrigerator prices. For candy bars, marginal utility and demand typically begin low and fall gradually as more bars are consumed, depending on the consumer's sweet tooth. The differing demand curves for these goods explain why you'll see "buy one, get one free" sales on candy but not on refrigerators: the marginal utility of the second fridge doesn't warrant the promotion.

The marginal utility of newspapers is similar to that of refrigerators, but lower. Your first copy of the daily newspaper provides the latest information on current events, entertainment, sports, and any storms that are brewing. All this gives the first newspaper considerable marginal utility. Consequently, millions of people buy subscriptions to newspapers. For example, about 1.1 million people subscribe to the print version of the *New York Times*. (Another 2.5 million people subscribe to the digital version.) Here's the twist: The average U.S. citizen consumes 44 gallons of soft drinks, 99 pounds of poultry, and 10,837 kilowatt-hours of electricity in a year, but have you ever heard of anyone with more than one subscription to the same newspaper? Unless you're an art teacher in the midst of a large papier-mâché project or the owner of a new puppy, the marginal utility of a second copy of the print newspaper is minuscule. Although there might be some benefit from selling or giving extra papers to others, the marginal utility of a second print paper is usually so low that newspapers can give customers access to the entire box of papers without creating great losses.

Suppose the value of your marginal utility from today's newspaper drops from $3 for the first newspaper to $0 for the second copy. This precipitous drop in marginal utility means that the quantity of papers demanded is unlikely to change when the price changes. A change from one price above $3 to another price above $3 would not trigger a purchase because both prices exceed the value you place on a newspaper. A change from one price below $3 to another price below $3 would not cause you to buy another newspaper because you don't want a second paper at any price. Only if the price changed from above $3 to below $3 would any change take place: You would then make your first purchase. Once you've shelled out the cash to open the box and gain access to the newspapers, you have no interest in a second copy.

When the value of multiple copies increases as the result of, say, a desire to protest or cover up a story, newspapers are especially vulnerable to large-scale thievery. On the day the *Crimson White*—the student newspaper of the University of Alabama at Tuscaloosa—reported the firing of the head football coach for expenditures at a strip club, about 1,500 copies were stolen. After an article in the *Michigan Journal* reported that four fraternity members had been found in possession of alcohol and marijuana, 1,400 copies of the paper were stolen. Across the country, liberal and conservative groups have accused each other of stealing thousands of newspapers to suppress the "truth." Politics aside, the truth is that potential embarrassment breeds consumers who suddenly place a whole lot more value on a stack of identical newspapers.

Price Elasticity of Demand

The rate at which marginal utility falls as the quantity of a good rises determines consumers' sensitivity to price changes. The level of this sensitivity is of interest to firms, in part because it indicates whether a price hike will cause many customers to buy less, or profits to leap. Economists call the sensitivity of quantity demanded to price changes the *price elasticity of demand*. If you buy a lot more pairs of sunglasses when the price goes down a little, and a lot fewer when the price goes up, your demand for sunglasses is relatively elastic. If you persist in purchasing only one cell phone when the price goes up or down, your demand for cell phones is inelastic. To be precise, the value of the price elasticity of demand is

$$\frac{\text{percentage change in quantity demanded}}{\text{percentage change in price}}.$$

Consider a few real-world examples: a 10% increase in the price of coffee leads to about a 2.5% decrease in the quantity demanded, so coffee has a price elasticity of 2.5/10, or 0.25. (Because the price change is negative and the quantity change is positive, the price elasticity is actually a negative number. However, for simplicity, most economists discuss elasticities in absolute value terms, meaning that the negative signs are removed.)

A 10% increase in the price of restaurant meals leads to about a 23% decrease in the quantity demanded, so the price elasticity of restaurant meals is 23/10, or 2.3. When coffee and other goods have a price elasticity between 0 and 1, demand for them is described as *inelastic* because it is not particularly sensitive to price changes. When restaurant meals and other purchases have a price elasticity greater than 1, demand for them is described as *elastic* because it is highly sensitive to price changes.

Don't make the common mistake of confusing elasticity with the slope of the demand curve. At a given quantity and price, a steep demand curve is less elastic than a relatively flat demand curve, but there's more to elasticity than slope. The slope of the demand curve is found by dividing the change in price by the change in quantity; elasticity is found by dividing the percent change in quantity by the percent change in price. A straight demand curve with a constant slope has a different elasticity at every point because, even though price and quantity are changing at a constant rate, the *percent* changes in price and quantity are not constant. For example, an increase in quantity from 100 to 101 represents a 1% increase in quantity, whereas an equivalent increase in quantity by 1 from 10 to 11 represents a 10% increase in quantity. Thus, moving rightward along a straight demand curve, the slope stays the same, but elasticity decreases as the percent change in quantity falls and the percent change in price rises.

In general, the quantity demanded is more responsive to price changes, and, therefore, more elastic, for goods and services that

- have many substitutes
- are not essential to daily life
- require a large share of consumers' wealth
- are not needed in a hurry

The opposite is also true: goods and services have a relatively inelastic demand when they

- have few substitutes
- are necessities
- require a small share of consumers' wealth
- must be purchased without delay

Consider the price elasticity of demand for taxi rides in New York City and for the *New York Times*. Substitutes for taxis include buses, subways, bikes, Uber, Lyft, and feet. Many New Yorkers don't own cars, getting around just fine with alternative forms of transportation and considering it a luxury to hire a taxi. When New York City taxi fares increased by 25% a few years ago, riders said "hail no!" In contrast, the *New York Times* faces a relatively inelastic demand. The steep drop-off in marginal utility that occurs after the first newspaper is bought prevents more copies from being sold to existing customers as prices fall, and the price is low enough that modest price fluctuations involve only a small fraction of most people's income. Indeed, when the daily *New York Times* raised its newsstand price by 25%, circulation hardly budged.

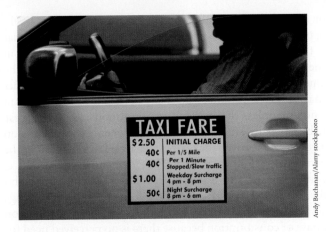

TAXI FARE
$2.50 INITIAL CHARGE
40¢ Per 1/5 Mile
40¢ Per 1 Minute Stopped/Slow traffic
$1.00 Weekday Surcharge 4 pm - 8 pm
50¢ Night Surcharge 8 pm - 6 am

Andy Buchanan/Alamy stockphoto

The Demand for Heart Surgery and Sin

In a way, the demand for open-heart surgery is similar to that for newspapers: most people don't need more than one, although those who require surgery would be willing to pay a lot more than $3 to get it. The marginal benefit of necessary surgery is life, and most people would pay whatever they could beg, borrow, or steal to get that benefit. Open-heart surgery and follow-up treatments can cost $325,000. Cancer treatment can cost $100,000 or more, and a bone marrow transplant can cost $675,000. For anyone who would pay everything possible to stay alive, the demand curve for these treatments is vertical at the quantity needed for survival, up to the maximum amount of funds that the person can obtain through all means.

The demand for life-saving surgery is inelastic because it is a necessity. Addiction can create a perceived necessity for drugs. Without discounting the deadly repercussions of illegal drug use, economists have used the concepts of supply and demand to argue for drug control via legalization. The legalization of drugs would increase the supply and cause the price to fall, but if the demand curve for drugs were vertical at the quantity users needed for their fixes, the quantity consumed would not change as prices changed. Lower prices would reduce profits for drug sellers and cut back on sellers' incentives to get people hooked on their products with free samples and other aggressive marketing techniques. This could result in fewer people becoming addicted while allowing taxation and more effective regulation. Such reasoning has led several states to legalize marijuana, and similar arguments have been made for the legalization of prostitution, as has occurred in Germany, India, and most of Nevada. Opponents argue that legalization can increase the demand by attracting consumers who don't currently use drugs or prostitutes out of respect for the law. Whichever side is right, the demand curve is at the crux of the issue.

Debates over so-called sin taxes to reduce the consumption of alcohol or tobacco revolve around the demand curve as well. Taxes lead to higher prices, but higher prices may or may not lead to substantially lower consumption levels, depending on the elasticity of demand. Studies suggest that a 10% increase in price leads to roughly a 4% decrease in the number of cigarettes smoked and a 3% decrease in the amount of beer consumed. From these numbers, it appears that sin taxes wouldn't take a large bite out of drinking and smoking unless the tax rates were enormous. However, these habits usually start at a young age when expenditures on alcohol and tobacco make up a relatively large portion of the consumers' incomes, and, therefore, demand for the products is more elastic. For example, the price elasticity of demand for young smokers is about three times that for the average smoker. Demand is also more elastic in the pre-addiction phase of consumption because there is no perceived need for a certain minimum quantity, or "fix."

The price elasticity of demand is critical to the pricing decisions of firms. If demand is inelastic, a price increase raises revenue because the quantity demanded decreases by a small proportion relative to the price increase. If demand is elastic, a price increase lowers revenue because the quantity demanded decreases by a large proportion relative to the price increase. In this case, profit might increase or decrease, depending on whether the reduction in costs (because fewer units are sold) is larger or smaller than the reduction in revenue. For example, suppose an increase in the price of pizza would decrease revenues by $1,000. But, because fewer pizzas would be made, the price increase would decrease costs by $1,200. In this case the price increase would increase profit by $1,200 − $1,000 = $200.

Conclusion

Your study of the underpinnings of demand will help you determine what shifts and shapes demand curves. Diminishing marginal utility is the reason for

the negative slope of the demand curve. As you get more of something, you generally receive less utility from the last unit received, so you are willing to pay less for additional units, as indicated by the decreasing height of your demand curve. Because the market demand curve is the sum of all the individual demand curves, its shape, too, is dictated by diminishing marginal utility.

The price elasticity of demand measures the responsiveness of the quantity demanded to the price. The price elasticity of demand is calculated as the percent change in the quantity demanded divided by the percent change in the price. This elasticity influences the effect of taxes on quantities purchased, the likely result of legalizing drugs, the revenue implications of raising product prices, and the differing optimal designs for vending machines that dispense candy and newspapers (unless the news stories have raised enough dander to warrant mass theft!).

Critical Thinking Questions

1. For the people you know who do, or do not, buy illegal drugs, is that demand (or lack thereof) determined by the fact that the drugs are illegal? What implications does this have for the government's drug enforcement policy?

2. For which goods do you have a relatively high price elasticity of demand?

3. Summarize in your own words the links among diminishing marginal utility, demand, and elasticity.

4. Explain whether you would expect the demand for the following goods to be elastic or inelastic, and why: software programs, cameras, notebook paper, peaches, textbooks, all carbonated beverages, A&W root beer.

Behind the Supply Curve: Profit, Production, and Costs

Scott Sinklier/Alamy

> **economics by example** *Could the Future Cost of Energy Change Life as We Know It?*

The Cost of Power

In Section 9 we examined the factors that affect consumer choice—the demand side of the supply and demand model. In this section we focus on the factors that affect producer choice and the supply side of the supply and demand model. Producers seek profit, which is the difference between total revenue and total cost. We turn to graphs to illustrate the story of what happens to various measures of revenue, cost, and profit as output changes. Different situations lead to different stories.

Consider the Upland Prairie Wind project in northwest Iowa, which cost around $500 million to build in 2018. The wind farm's 121 turbines have the capacity to produce 300 megawatts of electricity at a negligible additional cost

per kilowatt-hour, because the primary input—wind—is free.

Wisconsin's Nemadji Trail Energy Center natural gas–fired power plant, proposed for completion in 2025, will cost an estimated $700 million and have a capacity of up to 550 megawatts. The cost story at Nemadji Trail differs from that at Upland Prairie because each kilowatt-hour of electricity produced at Nemadji Trail will require the use of additional natural gas, which isn't free. But the larger capacity at Nemadji Trail will allow the cost of constructing the plant to be spread across more units of output.

The ability for power plants to cover their costs depends not only on the size of the costs but also on the prices sellers can charge per kilowatt-hour of

electricity, which range from 9 cents in Louisiana to 33 cents in Hawaii. Given the complexity of cost and revenue stories, the need to visualize them with graphs is clear. In this section you will learn several analytical tools used to inform production decisions.

After a discussion of profit maximization, we will investigate the production function, which shows the relationship between the inputs used for production and the output that is produced. Then we'll consider the costs that influence firms' decisions about supply. The final Module in this section introduces the models of market structure used to understand how the supply side of the economy works.

Defining Profit

Understanding Profit

The primary goal of most firms is to maximize profit. Other goals, such as maximizing market share or protecting the environment, may also figure into a firm's mission. But economic models generally start with the assumption that firms attempt to maximize profit. So we will begin with an explanation of how economists define and calculate profit. In the next Module we will look at how firms go about maximizing their profit.

In general, a firm's profit equals its *total revenue*—which is equal to the price of the output times the quantity sold, or $P \times Q$—minus the cost of all the inputs used to produce its output, its *total cost*. That is,

$$\text{Profit} = \text{Total Revenue} - \text{Total Cost}$$

However, there are different types of costs that may be used to calculate different types of profit. To start the discussion, we'll look at two different types of costs, *explicit costs* and *implicit costs*.

Explicit Versus Implicit Costs

Suppose that, after graduating from high school, you have two options: go to college or take a job immediately. You would like to continue your education but are concerned about the cost.

What exactly is the cost of attending college? Here it is important to remember the concept of opportunity cost, because the cost of getting a degree includes the income you forgo while in college. The opportunity cost of additional education, like any cost, can be broken into two parts: the *explicit cost* and the *implicit cost*.

An **explicit cost** is a cost that requires an outlay of money. For example, the explicit cost of a year of college includes tuition. In contrast, an **implicit cost** does not involve an outlay of money; instead, it is measured by the value, in dollar terms, of the benefits that are forgone. For example, the implicit cost of a year spent in college includes the additional income you would have earned if you had taken a full-time job instead.

A common mistake, both in economic analysis and in real business situations, is to ignore implicit costs and focus exclusively on explicit costs. But often the implicit cost of an activity is quite substantial—indeed, sometimes it is much larger than the explicit cost.

College students incur not only explicit costs, such as tuition, but also the implicit cost of forgone income.

An **explicit cost** is a cost that involves actually laying out money. An **implicit cost** does not require an outlay of money; it is measured by the value, in dollar terms, of benefits that are forgone.

Table 52.1 gives a breakdown of hypothetical explicit and implicit costs associated with spending a year in college instead of working. The explicit cost consists of tuition, books, supplies, and a computer for doing assignments—all of which require you to spend money. The implicit cost is the salary you would have earned if you had taken a full-time job instead. As you can see, the forgone salary is $32,000 and the explicit cost is $19,500, making the implicit cost more than the explicit cost in this example. As this shows, ignoring the implicit cost of an action can lead to a seriously misguided decision.

Table 52.1	Opportunity Cost of a Year of College		
Explicit cost		**Implicit cost**	
Tuition	$17,000	Forgone salary	$32,000
Books and supplies	1,000		
Computer	1,500		
Total explicit cost	19,500	Total implicit cost	32,000
Total opportunity cost = Total explicit cost + Total implicit cost = $51,500			

A slightly different way of looking at the implicit cost in this example can deepen our understanding of opportunity cost. The forgone salary is the cost of using your own resources—your time—in going to college rather than working. The use of your *time* for more education, despite the fact that you don't have to spend any money, is still costly to you. This illustrates an important aspect of opportunity cost: in considering the cost of an activity, you should include the cost of using any of your own resources for that activity. You can calculate the cost of using your own resources by determining what they would have earned in their next best alternative use.

The **accounting profit** of a business is the business's total revenue minus the explicit cost and depreciation.

The **economic profit** of a business is the business's total revenue minus the opportunity cost of its resources. It is usually less than the accounting profit.

Accounting Profit Versus Economic Profit

As the example of going to college suggests, taking account of implicit as well as explicit costs can be very important when making decisions. This is true whether the decisions affect individuals, groups, governments, or firms.

Consider the case of Babette's Cajun Café, a small restaurant in New Orleans. This year Babette brought in $110,000 in revenue. Out of that revenue, she paid $60,000 in expenses: the cost of food ingredients and other supplies, the cost of wages for her employees, and the rent for her restaurant space. We assume that Babette owns her restaurant equipment—items such as appliances and furnishings. The question is: Is Babette's restaurant profitable?

At first it might seem that the answer is obviously yes: she receives $110,000 from her customers and has expenses of only $60,000. Doesn't this mean that she has a profit of $50,000? Not according to her accountant, who reduces the number by $5,000 for the yearly *depreciation* (reduction in value) of the restaurant equipment. Depreciation occurs because equipment wears out over time. As a consequence, every few years Babette must replace her appliances and furnishings. The yearly depreciation amount reflects what an accountant estimates to be the reduction in the value of the machines due to wear and tear that year. This leaves $45,000, which is the business's **accounting profit**. That is, the accounting profit of a business is its total revenue minus its *explicit* cost and depreciation. The accounting profit is the number that Babette has to report on her income tax forms and that she would be obliged to report to anyone thinking of investing in her business.

Accounting profit is a useful number, but suppose that Babette wants to decide whether to keep her restaurant open or to take a different career path. To make this decision, she will need to calculate her **economic profit**—the total revenue she receives minus her *opportunity* cost, which includes implicit as well as explicit costs. In general, when economists use the simple term *profit*, they are referring to economic profit. (We adopt this simplification in this book.)

Why does Babette's economic profit differ from her accounting profit? Because she may have an implicit cost over and above the explicit cost her accountant has calculated. Businesses can face an implicit cost for two reasons. First, if the business owns its capital—its equipment, buildings, tools, inventory, and financial assets—it does not pay any money for its use, but it pays an implicit cost because it does not use the capital in some other way. Second, the owner devotes time and energy to the business that could have been used elsewhere—a particularly important factor in small businesses, whose owners tend to put in many long hours.

Jon Arnold Images Ltd/Alamy

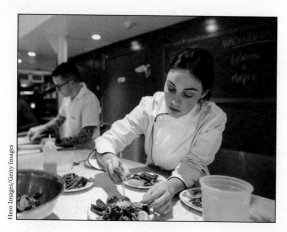

If Babette had rented her appliances and furnishings instead of owning them, her rent would have been an explicit cost. But because Babette owns her own equipment, she does not pay rent on it and her accountant deducts an estimate of its depreciation in the profit statement. However, this does not account for the opportunity cost of the equipment—what Babette forgoes by using it. Suppose that if she doesn't use the equipment in her own restaurant, Babette's most lucrative alternative is to sell the equipment for $55,000 and put the money into a bank account where it would earn yearly interest of $3,000. This $3,000 is an implicit cost of running the business. The **implicit cost of capital** is the opportunity cost of the capital used by a business; it reflects the income that could have been earned if the capital had been used in its next best alternative way. It is just as much a true cost as if Babette had rented her equipment instead of owning it.

Finally, Babette should take into account the opportunity cost of her own time. Suppose that instead of running her own restaurant, she could earn $44,000 as a chef in someone else's restaurant. That $44,000 is also an implicit cost of her business.

Table 52.2, in the column titled Case 1, summarizes the accounting for Babette's Cajun Café, taking both explicit and implicit costs into account. It turns out, unfortunately, that although the business makes an accounting profit of $45,000, its economic profit is actually negative. This means that Babette would be better off financially if she closed the restaurant and devoted her time and capital to something else. If, however, some of Babette's cost should fall sufficiently, she could earn a positive economic profit. In that case, she would be better off financially if she continued to operate the restaurant. For instance, consider the Case 2 column: here we assume that the salary Babette could earn as a chef employed by someone else has dropped to $39,000 (say, due to an increase in the availability of chefs). In this case, her economic profit is positive: she is earning more than her explicit and implicit costs and she should keep her restaurant open.

The **implicit cost of capital** is the opportunity cost of the capital used by a business—the income the owner could have realized from that capital if it had been used in its next best alternative way.

Table 52.2	Profit at Babette's Cajun Café	Case 1	Case 2
Revenue		$110,000	$110,000
Explicit cost		−60,000	−60,000
Depreciation		−5,000	−5,000
Accounting profit		**45,000**	**45,000**
Implicit cost of business			
Income Babette could have earned on capital used in the next best way		−3,000	−3,000
Income Babette could have earned as a chef in someone else's restaurant		−44,000	−39,000
Economic profit		**−2,000**	**3,000**

In real life, discrepancies between accounting profit and economic profit are extremely common. For example, farmers are well aware of the opportunity cost of farming their land rather than selling it to developers.

Normal Profit

In the example above, when Babette is earning an economic profit, her total revenue is higher than the sum of her implicit and explicit costs. This means that operating her restaurant makes Babette better off financially than she would be using her resources in any other activity. When Babette earns a negative economic profit (which can also be described as a *loss*), it means that Babette would be better off financially if she devoted her resources to her next best alternative. As this example illustrates, economic profits signal the best use of resources. A positive economic profit indicates that the current use is the best use of resources. A negative economic profit indicates that there is a better alternative use for resources.

But what about an economic profit *equal to zero*? It's tempting to think that earning zero profit is a bad thing. After all, the goal of most firms is to maximize profit. However, an economic profit equal to zero is not bad at all. An economic profit of zero means that the firm could not do any better using its resources in any alternative activity. Another name for an economic profit of zero is a **normal profit**. A firm earning a normal profit is earning just enough to keep it using its resources in its current activity. After all, it can't do any better in any other activity! In Module 59 we'll see that firms earning negative economic profit can sometimes minimize their losses by staying open for a while, but all such firms will close in the long run unless conditions change.

An economic profit equal to zero is also known as a **normal profit**. It is an economic profit just high enough to keep a firm engaged in its current activity.

> **AP® EXAM TIP**
>
> Remember that a firm with zero economic profit earns just enough to cover its implicit and explicit costs. The firm may have zero economic profit and a positive accounting profit.

MODULE 52 REVIEW

Check Your Understanding

1. Karma and Don run a furniture-refinishing business from their home. Which of the following represent an explicit cost of the business and which represent an implicit cost?
   a. supplies such as paint stripper, varnish, polish, and sandpaper
   b. basement space, which could otherwise be rented out as an apartment, that is instead being used as a workroom
   c. wages paid to a part-time helper
   d. a van that they inherited and use only for transporting furniture
   e. the job at a larger furniture restorer that Karma gave up in order to run the business

2. a. Suppose you are in business earning an accounting profit of $25,000. What is your economic profit if the implicit cost of your capital is $2,000 and the opportunity cost of your time is $23,000? Explain your answer.
   b. What does your answer to part a tell you about the advisability of devoting your time and capital to this business?

TACKLE THE AP® TEST: Multiple-Choice Questions

1. Which of the following is an example of an *implicit* cost of going out for lunch?
   a. the amount of the tip you leave the waiter
   b. the total bill you charge to your credit card
   c. the cost of gas to drive to the restaurant
   d. the value of the time you spent eating lunch
   e. all of the above

2. Which of the following is an *implicit* cost of attending college?
   a. tuition
   b. books
   c. laptop computer
   d. lab fees
   e. forgone salary

3. Accounting profit equals total revenue minus depreciation and total
   a. explicit cost only.
   b. implicit cost only.
   c. explicit cost plus total implicit cost.
   d. opportunity cost.
   e. explicit cost plus total opportunity cost.

4. Which of the following is considered when calculating economic profit but not accounting profit?
   a. implicit cost
   b. explicit cost
   c. total revenue
   d. marginal cost
   e. All of the above are considered when calculating accounting profit.

5. You sell T-shirts at your school's football games. Each shirt costs $5 to make and sells for $10. Each game lasts two hours, and you sell 100 shirts per game. During this time, you could be earning $8 per hour at your other job. What are your accounting profit and economic profit from selling shirts at a game?

	Accounting profit	Economic profit
a.	$1,000	$500
b.	$500	$1,000
c.	$500	$484
d.	$484	$500
e.	$500	$500

6. Opportunity costs include
  a. implicit costs only.
  b. explicit costs only.
  c. depreciation costs and explicit costs only.
  d. implicit costs and explicit costs.
  e. implicit costs and accounting profit only.

7. Earning an economic profit of zero is
  a. acceptable because the firm could make no better alternative use of its resources.
  b. a sign that the firm should shut down.
  c. acceptable during a recession but otherwise not.
  d. less desirable to a firm than earning an accounting profit of zero.
  e. equivalent to earning an accounting profit of zero if implicit costs exist.

TACKLE THE AP® TEST: Free-Response Questions

1. Your firm is selling 10,000 units of output at a price of $10 per unit. Your firm's total explicit cost is $70,000. Your firm's implicit cost of capital is $10,000, and your opportunity cost is $20,000.
  a. Calculate total revenue.
  b. Calculate total implicit cost.
  c. Calculate your accounting profit.
  d. Calculate your economic profit.
  e. Given the value of your economic profit calculated in part d, might there be a better use of your resources? Explain your answer.

Rubric for FRQ 1 (5 points)

1 point: Total revenue = $100,000

1 point: Total implicit cost = $30,000

1 point: Accounting profit = $30,000

1 point: Economic profit = $0

1 point: No. Because your firm earns normal profit, there is no better alternative use for your resources.

2. Mikey owns and operates Mikey's Meatloaf Stand, which sells meatloaf by the slice. Use the data in the table provided to answer the questions below.

Mikey's Meatloaf Stand: January	
Price per slice	$2
Slices sold	2,000
Explicit cost	$400
Depreciation	$100
Implicit cost of capital	$200

  a. Calculate Mikey's Meatloaf Stand's total revenue for January.
  b. Calculate Mikey's Meatloaf Stand's accounting profit for January.
  c. What additional information does Mikey need in order to determine whether or not to continue operating the Meatloaf Stand?
  d. Suppose these numbers remain unchanged in the long run. Explain how Mikey will determine whether or not to continue operating the business in the long run on the basis of these numbers. **(4 points)**

Profit Maximization

In this Module, you will learn to:
- Perform marginal analysis
- Determine the profit-maximizing level of output using the optimal output rule

Maximizing Profit

In the previous Module we learned about different types of profit, how to calculate profit, and how firms can use profit calculations to make decisions—for instance to determine whether to continue using resources for the same activity or not.

In this Module we ask the question: what quantity of output would maximize the producer's profit? First we will find the profit-maximizing quantity by calculating the total profit at each quantity for comparison. Then we will use marginal analysis to determine the *optimal output rule*, which turns out to be simple: as our discussion of marginal analysis in Module 1 suggested, a producer should increase production until marginal benefit equals marginal cost.

Consider Jennifer and Jason, who run an organic tomato farm. Suppose that the market price of organic tomatoes is $18 per bushel and that Jennifer and Jason can sell as many tomatoes as they would like at that price. We can use the data in **Table 53.1** to find their profit-maximizing level of output.

Michael Melford/Getty Images

Table 53.1	Profit for Jennifer and Jason's Farm When Market Price Is $18		
Quantity of tomatoes Q (bushels)	Total revenue TR	Total cost TC	Profit TR − TC
0	$0	$14	−$14
1	18	30	−12
2	36	36	0
3	54	44	10
4	72	56	16
5	90	72	18
6	108	92	16
7	126	116	10

The first column shows the quantity of output in bushels, and the second column shows Jennifer and Jason's total revenue from their output: the market value of their output. Total revenue (*TR*) is equal to the market price multiplied by the quantity of output:

(53-1) $TR = P \times Q$

In this example, total revenue is equal to $18 per bushel times the quantity of output in bushels.

The third column of Table 53.1 shows Jennifer and Jason's total cost, *TC*. Even if they don't grow any tomatoes, Jennifer and Jason must pay $14 to rent the land for their farm. As the quantity of tomatoes increases, so does the total cost of seeds, fertilizer, labor, and other inputs. You will learn more about firm costs in Module 55.

The fourth column shows their profit, equal to total revenue minus total cost:

(53-2) $\text{Profit} = TR - TC$

As indicated by the numbers in the table, profit is maximized at an output of five bushels, where profit is equal to $18. But we can gain more insight into the profit-maximizing choice of output by viewing it as a problem of marginal analysis, a task we'll dive into next.

Using Marginal Analysis to Choose the Profit-Maximizing Quantity of Output

The **principle of marginal analysis** provides a clear message about when to stop doing anything: proceed until the *marginal benefit* equals the *marginal cost*. To apply this principle, consider the effect on a producer's profit of increasing output by one unit. The marginal benefit of that unit is the additional revenue generated by selling it; this measure has a name—it is called the **marginal revenue** of that output. The general formula for marginal revenue is

(53-3) $\text{Marginal revenue} = \dfrac{\text{Change in total revenue generated by one additional unit of output}}{} = \dfrac{\text{Change in total revenue}}{\text{Change in quantity of output}}$

or, using the Greek uppercase delta (the triangular symbol Δ) to represent the change in a variable,

$$MR = \Delta TR/\Delta Q$$

The **optimal output rule** applies the principle of marginal analysis to the producer's decision of how much to produce. This rule states that profit is maximized by producing the quantity at which the marginal revenue of the last unit produced is equal to its marginal cost. Note that there may not be any particular quantity at which the marginal revenue exactly equals the marginal cost. We see an example of this in **Table 53.2**, which provides cost and revenue data for Jennifer and Jason's farm. In this case the producer should produce until one more unit would cause the marginal cost to rise above the marginal revenue, which producing the sixth unit would do for Jennifer and Jason.

Table 53.2	Short-Run Costs for Jennifer and Jason's Farm			
Quantity of tomatoes Q (bushels)	Total cost TC	Marginal cost of bushel $MC = \Delta TC/\Delta Q$	Marginal revenue of bushel MR	Net gain of bushel = MR − MC
0	$14			
		$16	$18	$2
1	30			
		6	18	12
2	36			
		8	18	10
3	44			
		12	18	6
4	56			
		16	18	2
5	72			
		20	18	−2
6	92			
		24	18	−6
7	116			

As a common simplification, we can think of marginal cost as rising steadily, rather than jumping from one level at one quantity to a different level at the next quantity. This ensures that the marginal cost will equal the marginal revenue at some quantity. We employ this simplified approach when we graph the data for Jennifer and Jason's farm in **Figure 53.1**.

Figure 53.1 The Firm's Profit-Maximizing Quantity of Output

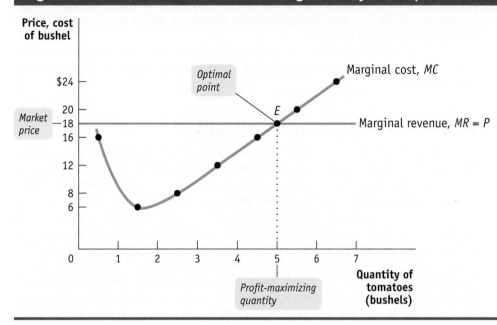

At the profit-maximizing quantity of output, the marginal revenue is equal to the marginal cost. It is located on the quantity axis below point *E*, where the marginal cost curve crosses the marginal revenue curve. Here, the profit-maximizing output is 5 bushels.

The second column contains the farm's total cost of output. The third column shows their marginal cost. Notice that, in this example, marginal cost initially falls as output rises but then begins to increase, so that the marginal cost curve has the "swoosh" shape seen in Figure 53.1. Later it will become clear that this shape has important implications for short-run production decisions.

The fourth column contains the farm's marginal revenue, which has an important feature: Jennifer and Jason's marginal revenue is assumed to be constant at $18 for every output level. The assumption holds true for a particular type of market—a perfectly competitive market—which we will study in Modules 58–60. For now we use this assumption just to make the calculations easier. The fifth and final column shows the calculation of the net gain per bushel of tomatoes, which is equal to the marginal revenue minus the marginal cost. As you can see, net gain is positive for the first through fifth bushels: producing each of these bushels raises Jennifer and Jason's profit. For the sixth and seventh bushels, however, the net gain is negative: producing them would decrease, not increase, profit. (You can verify this by reexamining Table 53.1.) So five bushels are Jennifer and Jason's optimal (profit-maximizing) output; if they produced one more unit, the marginal cost would rise above the market price, $18.

Figure 53.1 shows that Jennifer and Jason's profit-maximizing quantity of output is, indeed, the number of bushels at which the steadily rising marginal cost of production is equal to the marginal revenue (which is equivalent to the price in perfectly competitive markets). The figure illustrates the **marginal cost curve**, *MC*, which shows the relationship between marginal cost and output. We plot the marginal cost of increasing output from one to two bushels halfway between one and two, and so on. The horizontal line at $18 is Jennifer and Jason's **marginal revenue curve**, which shows the relationship between marginal revenue and output. Note that the marginal revenue stays the same regardless of how much Jennifer and Jason sell because we have assumed marginal revenue is constant.

Does this mean that the firm's production decision can be entirely summed up as "produce up to the point where the marginal cost of production is equal to the marginal revenue"? Not quite. Before applying the principle of marginal analysis to determine how much to produce, a potential producer must, as a first step, answer

The **marginal cost curve** shows how the cost of producing one more unit depends on the quantity that has already been produced.

The **marginal revenue curve** shows how marginal revenue varies as output varies.

an "either–or" question: Should I produce at all? If the answer to that question is yes, the producer then proceeds to the second step—a "how much" decision: maximizing profit by choosing the quantity of output at which the marginal cost is equal to the marginal revenue.

To understand why the first step in the production decision involves an "either–or" question, we need to ask how we determine whether it is profitable or unprofitable to produce at all.

When Is Production Profitable?

Recall from the previous Module that a firm's decision whether or not to stay in a given business in the long run depends on its *economic profit*—a measure based on the opportunity cost of resources used in the business. To put it a slightly different way: in the calculation of economic profit, a firm's total cost incorporates the implicit cost—the benefits forgone in the next-best use of the firm's resources—as well as the explicit cost in the form of actual cash outlays. In contrast, *accounting profit* is profit calculated using only the explicit costs incurred by the firm. This means that economic profit incorporates the opportunity cost of resources owned by the firm and used in the production of output, while accounting profit does not. As in the example of Babette's Cajun Café, a firm may make positive accounting profit while making zero or even negative economic profit. It's important to understand clearly that a firm's long-run decision to produce or not, to stay in business or to close down permanently, should be based on economic profit, not accounting profit.

We will assume, as we always do, that the cost numbers given in Tables 53.1 and 53.2 include all costs, implicit as well as explicit, and that the profit numbers in Table 53.1 are economic profit. What determines whether Jennifer and Jason's farm earns a profit or generates a loss? The answer is the market price of tomatoes—specifically, *whether selling the firm's optimal quantity of output at the market price results in at least a normal profit.*

In the next Modules, we look in detail at the two components used to calculate profit: firm revenue (which is determined by the level of production) and firm cost.

MODULE 53 REVIEW

Check Your Understanding

1. Suppose a firm can sell as many units of output as it wants for a price of $15 per unit and faces total costs as indicated in the table below. Use the optimal output rule to determine the profit-maximizing level of output for the firm.

Quantity	Total cost
0	$2
1	10
2	20
3	33
4	50
5	71

2. Use the data from Question 1 to graph the firm's marginal cost and marginal revenue curves and show the profit-maximizing level of output.

TACKLE THE AP® TEST: Multiple-Choice Questions

Use the data in the table provided to answer Questions 1–3.

Quantity	Total revenue	Total cost
0	$0	$14
1	18	30
2	36	36
3	54	44
4	72	56
5	90	72
6	108	92
7	126	116

1. What is the marginal revenue of the third unit of output?
   a. $8
   b. $14
   c. $18
   d. $44
   e. $54

2. What is the marginal cost of the first unit of output?
   a. $0
   b. $14
   c. $16
   d. $18
   e. $30

3. At what level of output is profit maximized?
   a. 0
   b. 1
   c. 3
   d. 5
   e. 7

4. A firm should continue to produce in the long run if its
   a. total revenue is less than its total costs.
   b. total revenue is greater than its total explicit costs.
   c. accounting profit is greater than its economic profit.
   d. accounting profit is not negative.
   e. economic profit is at least zero.

5. A firm earns a normal profit when its
   a. accounting profit equals 0.
   b. economic profit is positive.
   c. total revenue equals its total costs.
   d. accounting profit equals its economic profit.
   e. economic profit equals its total explicit and implicit costs.

6. Adherence to the principle of marginal analysis entails continuing activities until the
   a. total benefit exceeds the marginal benefit.
   b. total benefit equals the total cost.
   c. total benefit exceeds the total cost.
   d. marginal benefit equals the marginal cost.
   e. marginal benefit exceeds the marginal cost.

7. To maximize profit, a firm should produce the quantity at which marginal revenue equals marginal cost unless, in the long run, the firm would
   a. earn zero economic profit.
   b. earn less than normal profit.
   c. receive a price equal to its marginal revenue.
   d. earn positive accounting profit.
   e. earn positive economic profit.

TACKLE THE AP® TEST: Free-Response Questions

1. Use the data in the table provided to answer the following questions.

Quantity	Total revenue	Total cost
0	$0	$7
1	18	23
2	36	29
3	54	37
4	72	49
5	90	65
6	108	87
7	126	112

   a. What is the marginal revenue of the fourth unit?
   b. Calculate profit at a quantity of two. Explain how you calculated the profit.
   c. What is the profit-maximizing level of output? Explain how to use the optimal output rule to determine the profit-maximizing level of output.

> **Rubric for FRQ 1 (5 points)**
>
> **1 point:** $18
> **1 point:** $7
> **1 point:** $36 − $29 or $TR − TC$
> **1 point:** 5 units
> **1 point:** The optimal output rule states that profit is maximized when $MR = MC$. Here, MR never exactly equals MC, so in this case, the firm should produce the largest quantity at which MR exceeds MC. At a quantity of 5, $MC = 16 and $MR = 18. For the sixth unit, $MC = 22 and $MR = 18, and because $MC > MR$, the sixth unit would add more to total cost than it would to total revenue, so it should not be produced.

2. Use a graph to illustrate the typical shape of the two curves used to find a firm's profit-maximizing level of output on the basis of the optimal output rule. Assume all units of output can be sold for $5. Indicate the profit-maximizing level of output with a "$Q*$" on the appropriate axis. (You don't have enough information to provide a specific numerical answer.) **(3 points)**

The Production Function

In this Module, you will learn to:
- Discuss the importance of the firm's production function, the relationship between the quantity of inputs and the quantity of output
- Explain why production is often subject to diminishing returns to inputs

Inputs and Output

A **production function** is the relationship between the quantity of inputs a firm uses and the quantity of output it produces.

To produce goods or services for sale, a firm must transform inputs into output. The quantity of output a firm produces depends on the quantity of inputs; this relationship is known as the firm's **production function**. As we'll see, a firm's production function underlies its *cost curves*. As a first step, let's look at the characteristics of a hypothetical production function.

Production with Fixed and Variable Inputs

View Stock/Alamy

To understand the concept of a production function, let's consider a farm that we assume, for the sake of simplicity, produces only one output, wheat, and uses only two inputs, land and labor. This farm is owned by a couple named George and Martha. They hire workers to do the actual physical labor on the farm. Moreover, we will assume that all potential workers are of the same quality—they are all equally knowledgeable and capable of performing farmwork.

George and Martha's farm sits on 10 acres of land; no more acres are available to them, and they are currently unable to either increase or decrease the size of their farm by selling, buying, or leasing acreage. Land, in this case, is what economists call a **fixed input**—an input whose quantity is fixed for a period of time and cannot be varied. George and Martha, however, are free to decide how many workers to hire. The labor provided by these workers is called a **variable input**—an input whose quantity the firm can vary at any time.

A **fixed input** is an input whose quantity is fixed for a period of time and cannot be varied.

A **variable input** is an input whose quantity the firm can vary at any time.

The **long run** is the time period in which all inputs can be varied.

The **short run** is the time period in which at least one input is fixed.

The **total product curve** shows how the quantity of output depends on the quantity of the variable input for a given quantity of the fixed input.

In reality, whether or not the quantity of an input is really fixed depends on the time horizon. Given a long enough period of time, firms can adjust the quantity of any input. Economists define the **long run** as the time period in which all inputs can be varied. So there are no fixed inputs in the long run. In contrast, the **short run** is defined as the time period in which at least one input is fixed. Later, we'll look more carefully at the distinction between the short run and the long run. For now, we will restrict our attention to the short run and assume that at least one input (land) is fixed.

George and Martha know that the quantity of wheat they produce depends on the number of workers they hire. Using modern farming techniques, one worker can cultivate the 10-acre farm, albeit not very intensively. When an additional worker is added, the land is divided equally among all the workers: each worker has 5 acres to cultivate when 2 workers are employed, each cultivates 3 ⅓ acres when 3 are employed, and so on. So, as additional workers are employed, the 10 acres of land are cultivated more intensively and more bushels of wheat are produced.

The relationship between the quantity of labor and the quantity of output, for a given amount of the fixed input, constitutes the farm's production function. The production function for George and Martha's farm, where land is the fixed input and labor is the variable input, is shown in the first two columns of the table in **Figure 54.1**; the diagram shows the same information graphically. The curve in Figure 54.1 shows how the quantity of output depends on the quantity of the variable input for a given quantity of the fixed input; it is called the farm's **total product curve**. The physical quantity of output, bushels of wheat, is measured on the vertical axis; the quantity of the variable input, labor (that is, the number of workers employed), is measured on the horizontal axis. The total product curve here slopes upward, reflecting the fact that more bushels of wheat are produced as more workers are employed.

Figure 54.1 The Production Function and the Total Product Curve for George and Martha's Farm

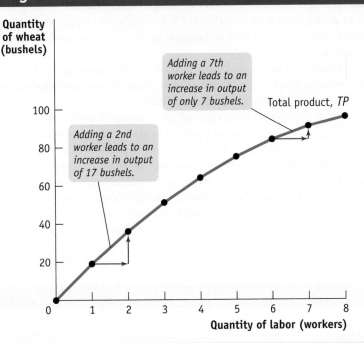

Quantity of labor L (workers)	Quantity of wheat Q (bushels)	Marginal product of labor MPL = ΔQ/ΔL (bushels per worker)
0	0	
		19
1	19	
		17
2	36	
		15
3	51	
		13
4	64	
		11
5	75	
		9
6	84	
		7
7	91	
		5
8	96	

The table shows the production function, the relationship between the quantity of the variable input (labor, measured in number of workers) and the quantity of output (wheat, measured in bushels) for a given quantity of the fixed input. It also shows the marginal product of labor on George and Martha's farm. The total product curve shows the production function graphically. It slopes upward because more wheat is produced as more workers are employed. It also becomes flatter because the marginal product of labor declines as more and more workers are employed.

Although the total product curve in Figure 54.1 slopes upward along its entire length, the slope isn't constant: as you move up the curve to the right, it flattens out. To understand this changing slope, look at the third column of the table in Figure 54.1, which shows the *change in the quantity of output* generated by adding one more worker. That is, it shows the **marginal product** of labor, or *MPL*: the additional quantity of output from using one more unit of labor (one more worker).

In this example, we have data at intervals of 1 worker—that is, we have information on the quantity of output when there are 3 workers, 4 workers, and so on. Sometimes data aren't available in increments of 1 unit—for example, you might have information on the quantity of output only when there are 40 workers and when there are 50 workers. In this case, you can use the following equation to calculate the marginal product of labor:

> The **marginal product** of an input is the additional quantity of output produced by using one more unit of that input.

(54-1) Marginal product of labor = Change in quantity of output produced by one additional unit of labor = $\dfrac{\text{Change in quantity of output}}{\text{Change in quantity of labor}}$

or

$$MPL = \frac{\Delta Q}{\Delta L}$$

Recall that Δ, the Greek uppercase delta, represents the change in a variable. Now we can explain the significance of the slope of the total product curve: it is equal to the marginal product of labor. The slope of a line is equal to "rise" over "run." This implies that the slope of the total product curve is the change in the quantity of output (the "rise") divided by the change in the quantity of labor (the "run"). And, as we can see from Equation 54-1, this is simply the marginal product of labor. So in Figure 54.1, the fact that the marginal product of the first worker is 19 also means that the slope of the total product curve in going from 0 to 1 worker is 19. Similarly, the slope of the total product curve in going from 1 to 2 workers is the same as the marginal product of the second worker, 17, and so on.

In this example, the marginal product of labor steadily declines as more workers are hired—that is, each successive worker adds less to output than the previous worker. So as employment increases, the total product curve gets flatter.

Figure 54.2 shows how the marginal product of labor depends on the number of workers employed on the farm. The marginal product of labor, MPL, is measured on the vertical axis in units of physical output—bushels of wheat—produced per additional worker, and the number of workers employed is measured on the horizontal axis. You can see from the table in Figure 54.1 that if 5 workers are employed instead of 4, output rises from 64 to 75 bushels; in this case the marginal product of labor is 11 bushels—the same number found in Figure 54.2. To indicate that 11 bushels is the marginal product when employment rises from 4 to 5, we place the point corresponding to that information halfway between 4 and 5 workers.

Figure 54.2   The Marginal Product of Labor Curve for George and Martha's Farm

The marginal product of labor curve plots each worker's marginal product, the increase in the quantity of output generated by each additional worker. The change in the quantity of output is measured on the vertical axis and the number of workers employed on the horizontal axis. The first worker employed generates an increase in output of 19 bushels, the second worker generates an increase of 17 bushels, and so on. The curve slopes downward due to diminishing returns to labor.

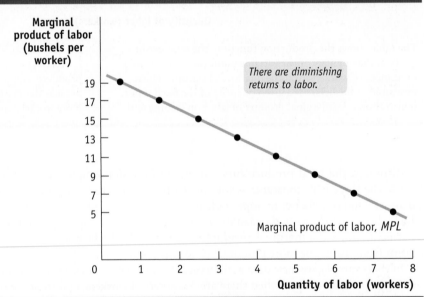

There are **diminishing returns to an input** when an increase in the quantity of that input, holding the levels of all other inputs fixed, leads to a decline in the marginal product of that input.

In this example the marginal product of labor falls as the number of workers increases. That is, there are *diminishing returns to labor* on George and Martha's farm. In general, there are **diminishing returns to an input** when an increase in the quantity of that input, holding the quantity of all other inputs fixed, reduces that input's marginal product. Due to diminishing returns to labor, the MPL curve is negatively sloped.

To grasp why diminishing returns can occur, think about what happens as George and Martha add more and more workers without increasing the number of acres farmed. As the number of workers increases, the land is farmed more intensively and the number of bushels increases. But each additional worker is working with a smaller share of the 10 acres—the fixed input—than the previous worker. As a result, output does not increase by as much when an additional worker is hired as it did when the previous worker was hired. So it's not surprising that the marginal product of the additional worker falls.

The next Module explains that opportunities for specialization among workers can allow the marginal product of labor to increase for the first few workers, but eventually diminishing returns set in as the result of redundancy and congestion. The crucial point to emphasize about diminishing returns is that, like many propositions in economics, it is an "other things equal" proposition: each successive unit of an input will raise production by less than the previous unit *if the quantity of all other inputs is held fixed*.

Production When All Inputs Are Variable

What would happen if the levels of other inputs were allowed to change? You can see the answer illustrated in **Figure 54.3**. Panel (a) shows two total product curves, TP_{10} and TP_{20}. TP_{10} is the farm's total product curve when its total area is 10 acres (the same curve as in Figure 54.1). TP_{20} is the total product curve when the farm's area has increased to 20 acres. Except when 0 workers are employed, TP_{20} lies everywhere above TP_{10} because with more acres available, any given number of workers produces more output.

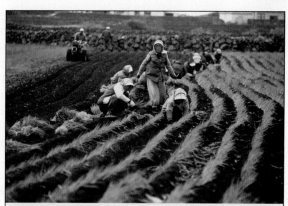

With diminishing returns to labor, each new worker added to a fixed amount of land contributes less to total output than the previous worker.

Panel (b) shows the corresponding marginal product of labor curves. MPL_{10} is the marginal product of labor curve given 10 acres to cultivate (the same curve as in Figure 54.2), and MPL_{20} is the marginal product of labor curve given 20 acres. Both curves slope downward because, in each case, the amount of land is fixed, albeit at different levels. But MPL_{20} lies everywhere above MPL_{10}, reflecting the fact that the marginal product of the same worker is higher when he or she has more of the fixed input to work with.

Figure 54.3 demonstrates a general result: the position of the total product curve depends on the quantities of other inputs. If you change the quantities of the other inputs, both the total product curve and the marginal product curve of the remaining input will shift. It is important to consider these shifts when making predictions on the basis of diminishing returns. Even Thomas Malthus, the Englishman who, in 1798, introduced the principle of diminishing returns to an input, was led astray by assumptions that other factors would remain largely unchanged.

Figure 54.3 Total Product, Marginal Product, and the Fixed Input

(a) Total Product Curves

(b) Marginal Product Curves

This figure shows how the quantity of output—illustrated by the total product curve—and marginal product depend on the level of the fixed input. Panel (a) shows two total product curves for George and Martha's farm, TP_{10} when their farm is 10 acres and TP_{20} when it is 20 acres. With more land, each worker can produce more wheat, so an increase in the fixed input shifts the total product curve up from

TP_{10} to TP_{20}. This also implies that the marginal product of each worker is higher when the farm is 20 acres than when it is 10 acres. As a result, an increase in acreage also shifts the marginal product of labor curve up from MPL_{10} to MPL_{20}. Panel (b) shows the marginal product of labor curves. Note that both marginal product of labor curves still slope downward due to diminishing returns to labor.

Malthus argued that as a country's population grew but its land area remained fixed, it would become increasingly difficult to grow enough food. Though more intensive cultivation of the land could increase crop yields, as the marginal product of labor diminished, each successive farmer would add less to the total than the last. In a country with a small population and abundant land (an accurate description of the United States at the time), Malthus argued, families would be large and the population would grow rapidly. Ultimately, the pressure of population on the land would reduce the condition of most people to a level at which starvation and disease held the population in check. (Arguments like this led the historian Thomas Carlyle to dub economics the "dismal science.")

Happily, Malthus's predictions have turned out to be wrong. The world population has increased from about 1 billion at the time when Malthus wrote to more than 7.5 billion in 2019, but in most parts of the world people eat better now than ever before. And where they do not, problems with food distribution or government corruption are typically to blame. Diminishing returns to labor can be mitigated by investments in capital and improvements in farming technology. Fortunately, since the eighteenth century, rapid capital accumulation and technological progress have relaxed the limits imposed by diminishing returns. Diminishing returns to labor imply that the marginal product declines when *all* other things—including capital and technology—remain the same. So the pleasing fact that Malthus's predictions were wrong does not invalidate the concept of diminishing returns.

MODULE 54 REVIEW

Check Your Understanding

1. Bernie's ice-making company produces ice cubes using a 10-ton machine and electricity (along with water, which we will ignore as an input for simplicity). The quantity of output, measured in pounds of ice, is given in the table below.

Quantity of electricity (kilowatts)	Quantity of ice (pounds)
0	0
1	1,000
2	1,800
3	2,400
4	2,800

a. What is the fixed input? What is the variable input?
b. Construct a table showing the marginal product of the variable input. Does it show diminishing returns?
c. Suppose a 50% increase in the size of the fixed input increases output by 100% for any given amount of the variable input. Construct a table showing the quantity of output and the marginal product in this case.

TACKLE THE AP® TEST: Multiple-Choice Questions

1. A production function shows the relationship between inputs and
   a. fixed costs.
   b. variable costs.
   c. total revenue.
   d. output.
   e. profit.

2. Which of the following defines the short run?
   a. less than a year
   b. when all inputs are fixed
   c. when no inputs are variable
   d. when only one input is variable
   e. when at least one input is fixed

3. The slope of the total product curve is also known as the
   a. marginal product.
   b. marginal cost.
   c. average product.
   d. average revenue.
   e. profit.

4. When the returns to an input are diminishing and a profit-maximizing firm chooses to hire more of that input, the total product curve has what kind of slope?
   a. negative and decreasing
   b. positive and decreasing
   c. negative and increasing
   d. positive and increasing
   e. positive and constant

5. Historically, the limits imposed by diminishing returns have been alleviated primarily by
   a. investments in capital and technology.
   b. population growth.
   c. new discoveries of land.
   d. the teachings of Thomas Malthus.
   e. the lessons of economic models.

6. Diminishing returns are a common result of
   a. more of one input being added to a fixed quantity of another input.
   b. the quantities of two inputs being decreased at the same time.
   c. the quantities of two inputs being increased at the same time.
   d. the profit of a firm being limited by increasing competition.
   e. the profit of a firm being limited by increasing input costs.

7. A horizontal marginal product curve would indicate that the total product curve is
   a. horizontal.
   b. vertical.
   c. downward-sloping.
   d. upward-sloping.
   e. downward-sloping and then upward-sloping.

TACKLE THE AP® TEST: Free-Response Questions

1. Draw a correctly labeled graph of a production function that exhibits diminishing returns to labor. Assume labor is the variable input and capital is the fixed input. Explain how your graph illustrates diminishing returns to labor.

Rubric for FRQ 1 (4 points)

1 point: Graph with vertical axis labeled "Quantity of output" or "Q" and horizontal axis labeled "Quantity of labor" or "L"

1 point: Upward-sloping curve labeled "Total product" or "TP"

1 point: The slope of the total product curve is positive and decreasing.

1 point: A positive and decreasing slope illustrates diminishing returns to labor because each additional unit of labor increases total product by less than the previous unit of labor.

2. Use the data in the table below to graph the production function and the marginal product of labor. Do the data illustrate diminishing returns to labor? Explain.

Quantity of labor	Quantity of output
0	0
1	25
2	47
3	66
4	82
5	95
6	105
7	112
8	116

(5 points)

Firm Costs

In this Module, you will learn to:
- Describe the various types of costs a firm faces, including fixed cost, variable cost, and total cost
- Explain how a firm's costs generate marginal cost curves and average cost curves

From the Production Function to Cost Curves

Now that we have learned about a firm's production function, we can use that knowledge to develop its cost curves. To see how a firm's production function is related to its cost curves, let's turn once again to George and Martha's farm. Once George and Martha know their production function, they know the relationship between inputs of labor and land and output of wheat. But if they want to maximize their profits, they need to translate this knowledge into information about the relationship between the quantity of output and cost. Let's see how they can do this.

To translate information about a firm's production function into information about its cost, we need to know how much the firm must pay for its inputs. We will assume that George and Martha face either an explicit or an implicit cost of $400 for the use of the land. As we learned previously, it is irrelevant whether George and Martha must rent the land for $400 from someone else (an explicit cost) or whether they own the land themselves and forgo earning $400 from renting it to someone else (an implicit cost). Either way, they pay an opportunity cost of $400 by using the land to grow wheat. Moreover, since the land is a fixed input for which George and Martha pay $400 whether they grow one bushel of wheat or one hundred, its cost is a **fixed cost (FC)**, which is a cost that does not depend on the quantity of output produced. In business, a fixed cost is often referred to as an "overhead cost."

We also assume that George and Martha must pay each worker $200. Using their production function, George and Martha know that the number of workers they must hire depends on the amount of wheat they intend to produce. So the cost of labor, which is equal to the number of workers multiplied by $200, is a **variable cost (VC)**, which is a cost that depends on the quantity of output produced. Adding the fixed cost and the variable cost of a given quantity of output gives the **total cost (TC)**, of that quantity of output. We can express the relationship among fixed cost, variable cost, and total cost as an equation:

(55-1)   Total cost = Fixed cost + Variable cost

or

$$TC = FC + VC$$

The table in **Figure 55.1** shows how total cost is calculated for George and Martha's farm. The second column shows the number of workers employed, L. The third column shows the corresponding level of output, Q, taken from the table in Figure 54.1. The fourth column shows the variable cost, VC, equal to the number of workers multiplied by $200. The fifth column shows the fixed cost, FC, which is $400 regardless of the quantity of wheat produced. The sixth column shows the total cost of output, TC, which is the variable cost plus the fixed cost.

A **fixed cost (FC)** is a cost that does not depend on the quantity of output produced. It is the cost of the fixed input.

A **variable cost (VC)** is a cost that depends on the quantity of output produced. It is the cost of the variable input.

The **total cost (TC)** of producing a given quantity of output is the sum of the fixed cost and the variable cost of producing that quantity of output.

AP® EXAM TIP

Understanding cost curves is crucial to understanding the market-structure models covered on the AP® Exam. Create note cards with definitions and formulas from this module to aid you in your studies.

Figure 55.1 The Total Cost Curve for George and Martha's Farm

Point on graph	Quantity of labor L (workers)	Quantity of wheat Q (bushels)	Variable cost VC	Fixed cost FC	Total cost TC = FC + VC
A	0	0	$0	$400	$400
B	1	19	200	400	600
C	2	36	400	400	800
D	3	51	600	400	1,000
E	4	64	800	400	1,200
F	5	75	1,000	400	1,400
G	6	84	1,200	400	1,600
H	7	91	1,400	400	1,800
I	8	96	1,600	400	2,000

The table shows the variable cost, fixed cost, and total cost for various output quantities on George and Martha's 10-acre farm. The total cost curve shows how the total cost (measured on the vertical axis) depends on the quantity of output (measured on the horizontal axis). The labeled points on the curve correspond to the rows of the table. The total cost curve slopes upward because the number of workers employed, and hence the total cost, increases as the quantity of output increases. The curve gets steeper as output increases due to diminishing returns to labor.

The first column labels each row of the table with a letter, from *A* to *I*. These labels will be helpful in understanding our next step: drawing the **total cost curve**, a curve that shows how total cost depends on the quantity of output.

George and Martha's total cost curve is shown in the diagram in Figure 55.1, where the horizontal axis measures the quantity of output in bushels of wheat and the vertical axis measures the total cost. Each point on the curve corresponds to one row of the table in Figure 55.1. For example, point *A* shows the situation when 0 workers are employed: output is 0, and the total cost is equal to the fixed cost, $400. Similarly, point *B* shows the situation when 1 worker is employed: output is 19 bushels, and the total cost is $600, equal to the sum of $400 in fixed cost and $200 in variable cost.

Like the total product curve, the total cost curve slopes upward: due to the increasing variable cost, the more output produced, the higher the farm's total cost. But unlike the total product curve, which gets flatter as employment rises, the total cost curve gets *steeper*. That is, the slope of the total cost curve is greater as the amount of

The **total cost curve** shows how total cost depends on the quantity of output.

output produced increases. As we will soon see, the steepening of the total cost curve is also due to diminishing returns to the variable input. Before we can see why, we must first look at the relationships among several useful measures of cost.

Two Key Concepts: Marginal Cost and Average Cost

We've just learned how to derive a firm's total cost curve from its production function. Our next step is to take a deeper look at total cost by deriving two extremely useful measures: *marginal cost* and *average cost*. As we'll see, these two measures of the cost of production have a somewhat surprising relationship to each other. Moreover, they will prove to be vitally important in later modules, where we will use them to analyze the firm's output decision and the market supply curve.

Marginal Cost

In Module 53, you learned that marginal cost is the added cost of doing something one more time. In the context of production, marginal cost is the change in total cost generated by producing one more unit of output. We've already seen that marginal product is easiest to calculate if data on output are available in increments of one unit of input. Similarly, marginal cost is easiest to calculate if data on total cost are available in increments of one unit of output because the increase in total cost for each unit is clear. When the data come in less convenient increments, it's still possible to calculate marginal cost over each interval. But for the sake of simplicity, let's work with an example in which the data come in convenient one-unit increments.

Selena's Gourmet Salsas produces bottled salsa; **Table 55.1** shows how its costs per day depend on the number of cases of salsa it produces per day. The firm has a fixed cost of $108 per day, shown in the second column, which is the daily rental cost of its food-preparation equipment. The third column shows the variable cost, and the fourth column shows the total cost. Panel (a) of **Figure 55.2** plots the total cost curve. Like the total cost curve for George and Martha's farm in Figure 55.1, this curve slopes upward, getting steeper as quantity increases.

Table 55.1	Costs at Selena's Gourmet Salsas			
Quantity of salsa Q (cases)	Fixed cost FC	Variable cost VC	Total cost TC = FC + VC	Marginal cost of case MC = $\Delta TC/\Delta Q$
0	$108	$0	$108	
				$12
1	108	12	120	
				36
2	108	48	156	
				60
3	108	108	216	
				84
4	108	192	300	
				108
5	108	300	408	
				132
6	108	432	540	
				156
7	108	588	696	
				180
8	108	768	876	
				204
9	108	972	1,080	
				228
10	108	1,200	1,308	

Figure 55.2 The Total Cost and Marginal Cost Curves for Selena's Gourmet Salsas

(a) Total Cost

8th case of salsa increases total cost by $180.

2nd case of salsa increases total cost by $36.

TC

(b) Marginal Cost

MC

Panel (a) shows the total cost curve from Table 55.1. Like the total cost curve in Figure 55.1, it slopes upward and gets steeper as we move up it to the right. Panel (b) shows the marginal cost curve. It also slopes upward, reflecting diminishing returns to the variable input.

The significance of the slope of the total cost curve is shown by the fifth column of Table 55.1, which indicates marginal cost—the additional cost of each additional unit. The general formula for marginal cost is

(55-2) $\quad$ Marginal cost = $\dfrac{\text{Change in total cost generated by one additional unit of output}}{}$ = $\dfrac{\text{Change in total cost}}{\text{Change in quantity of output}}$

or

$$MC = \frac{\Delta TC}{\Delta Q}$$

As in the case of marginal product, marginal cost is equal to "rise" (the increase in total cost) divided by "run" (the increase in the quantity of output). So just as marginal product is equal to the slope of the total product curve, marginal cost is equal to the slope of the total cost curve.

Now we can understand why the total cost curve gets steeper as it increases from left to right: as you can see in Table 55.1, marginal cost at Selena's Gourmet Salsas rises as output increases. And because marginal cost equals the slope of the total cost curve, a higher marginal cost means a steeper slope. Panel (b) of Figure 55.2 shows the marginal cost curve corresponding to the data in Table 55.1. Notice that, as in Figure 53.1, we plot the marginal cost for increasing output from 0 to 1 case of salsa halfway between 0 and 1, the marginal cost for increasing output from 1 to 2 cases of salsa halfway between 1 and 2, and so on.

Why does the marginal cost curve slope upward? Because there are diminishing returns to inputs in this example. As output increases, the marginal product of the variable input declines. This implies that more and more of the variable input must be used to produce each additional unit of output as the amount of output already produced rises. And since each unit of the variable input must be paid for, the additional cost per additional unit of output also rises.

Recall that the flattening of the total product curve is also due to diminishing returns: if the quantities of other inputs are fixed, the marginal product of an input falls as more of that input is used. The flattening of the total product curve as output

> **AP® EXAM TIP**
>
> Marginal cost is equal to the slope of the total cost curve.

increases and the steepening of the total cost curve as output increases are just flip-sides of the same phenomenon. That is, as output increases, the marginal cost of output also increases because the marginal product of the variable input decreases. Our next step is to introduce another measure of cost: *average cost*.

Average Cost

In addition to total cost and marginal cost, it's useful to calculate **average total cost (ATC)**, often simply called **average cost**. The average total cost of producing a given quantity of output is the total cost divided by the quantity; that is, it is equal to the total cost per unit of output. If we let *ATC* denote average total cost, the equation looks like this:

$$(55\text{-}3) \quad ATC = \frac{\text{Total cost}}{\text{Quantity of output}} = \frac{TC}{Q}$$

Average total cost is important because it tells the producer how much the *average* or *typical* unit of output costs to produce. Marginal cost, meanwhile, tells the producer how much *one more* unit of output costs to produce. Although they may look very similar, these two measures of cost typically differ. And confusion between them is a major source of error in economics, both in the classroom and in real life. **Table 55.2** uses data from Selena's Gourmet Salsas to calculate average total cost. For example, the total cost of producing 4 cases of salsa is $300, consisting of $108 in fixed cost and $192 in variable cost (from Table 55.1). So the average total cost of producing 4 cases of salsa is $300/4 = $75. You can see from Table 55.2 that as the quantity of output increases, the average total cost first falls, then rises.

Table 55.2	Average Costs for Selena's Gourmet Salsas			
Quantity of salsa Q (cases)	Total cost TC	Average total cost of case ATC = TC/Q	Average fixed cost of case AFC = FC/Q	Average variable cost of case AVC = VC/Q
1	$120	$120.00	$108.00	$12.00
2	156	78.00	54.00	24.00
3	216	72.00	36.00	36.00
4	300	75.00	27.00	48.00
5	408	81.60	21.60	60.00
6	540	90.00	18.00	72.00
7	696	99.43	15.43	84.00
8	876	109.50	13.50	96.00
9	1,080	120.00	12.00	108.00
10	1,308	130.80	10.80	120.00

Figure 55.3 plots the *ATC* data from Table 55.2 to yield the *average total cost curve*, which shows how average total cost depends on output. As before, the cost is measured on the vertical axis and the quantity of output is measured on the horizontal axis. The average total cost curve has a distinctive U shape that corresponds to how the average total cost first falls and then rises as output increases. Economists believe that such **U-shaped average total cost curves** are the norm for firms in many industries.

To help our understanding of why the average total cost curve is U-shaped, Table 55.2 breaks average total cost into its two underlying components, *average fixed cost* and *average variable cost*. The **average fixed cost**, or **AFC**, is the fixed cost divided by the quantity of output, also known as the fixed cost per unit of output. For example, if Selena's Gourmet Salsas produces 4 cases of salsa, the average fixed cost is $108/4 = $27 per case. The **average variable cost**, or **AVC**, is the variable cost divided

Figure 55.3 The Average Total Cost Curve for Selena's Gourmet Salsas

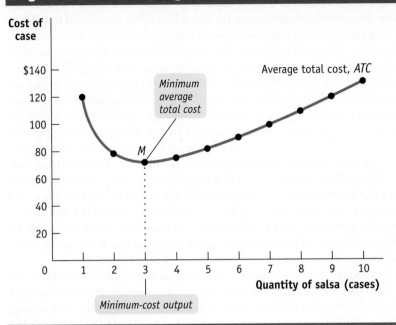

The average total cost curve at Selena's Gourmet Salsas is U-shaped. At low levels of output, the average total cost falls because the "spreading effect" of falling average fixed cost dominates the "diminishing returns effect" of rising average variable cost. At higher levels of output, the opposite is true and the average total cost rises. At point *M*, corresponding to an output of three cases of salsa per day, the average total cost is at its minimum level, the minimum average total cost.

by the quantity of output, also known as the variable cost per unit of output. At an output of 4 cases, the average variable cost is $192/4 = $48 per case. Writing these in the form of equations:

$$(55\text{-}4) \quad AFC = \frac{\text{Fixed cost}}{\text{Quantity of output}} = \frac{FC}{Q}$$

$$AVC = \frac{\text{Variable cost}}{\text{Quantity of output}} = \frac{VC}{Q}$$

The average total cost is the sum of the average fixed cost and the average variable cost. The average total cost curve has a U shape because these components move in opposite directions as output rises.

The average fixed cost falls as more output is produced because the numerator (the fixed cost) is a fixed number but the denominator (the quantity of output) increases as more is produced. Another way to think about this relationship is that, as more output is produced, the fixed cost is spread over more units of output; the end result is that the fixed cost *per unit of output*—the average fixed cost—falls. You can see this spreading effect in the fourth column of Table 55.2: the average fixed cost drops continuously as output increases. The average variable cost, however, rises as output increases. As we've seen, this reflects diminishing returns to the variable input: each additional unit of output adds more to the variable cost than the previous unit because increasing amounts of the variable input are required to make another unit.

So increasing output has two opposing effects on average total cost—the "spreading effect" and the "diminishing returns effect":

- *The spreading effect.* The larger the output, the greater the quantity of output over which the fixed cost is spread, leading to a lower average fixed cost.

- *The diminishing returns effect.* The larger the output, the greater the amount of the variable input required to produce additional units, leading to a higher average variable cost.

At low levels of output, the spreading effect is very powerful because even small increases in output cause large reductions in the average fixed cost. So at low levels of output, the spreading effect dominates the diminishing returns effect and causes the average total cost curve to slope downward. But when output is large, the average fixed cost is already quite small, so increasing output further has only a very small spreading effect. Diminishing returns, however, usually grow increasingly important as output rises. As a result, when output is large, the diminishing returns effect dominates the spreading effect, causing the average total cost curve to slope upward. At the bottom of the U-shaped average total cost curve, point M in Figure 55.3, the two effects exactly balance each other. At this point the average total cost is at its minimum level, the minimum average total cost.

Figure 55.4 brings together in a single picture the four cost curves that we have derived from the total cost curve for Selena's Gourmet Salsas: the marginal cost curve (MC), the average total cost curve (ATC), the average variable cost curve (AVC), and the average fixed cost curve (AFC). All are based on the information in Tables 55.1 and 55.2. As before, the cost is measured on the vertical axis and the quantity of output is measured on the horizontal axis.

Let's take a moment to note some features of the various cost curves. First of all, the marginal cost curve (MC) slopes upward—the result of diminishing returns that make an additional unit of output more costly to produce than the one before. The average variable cost curve (AVC) also slopes upward—again, due to diminishing returns—but is flatter than the marginal cost curve. This is because the higher cost of an additional unit of output is averaged across all units, not just the additional unit, in the average variable cost measure. Meanwhile, the average fixed cost curve (AFC) slopes downward because of the spreading effect.

Finally, notice that the marginal cost curve intersects the average total cost curve (ATC) from below, crossing it at its lowest point, point M in Figure 55.4. This last feature is our next subject of study.

When output increases, the average fixed cost falls because the fixed cost is spread over more units of output. But sooner or later the average variable cost increases due to diminishing returns.

AP® EXAM TIP

You may be required to draw these cost curves from memory on the AP® exam. Questions about the relationship between the curves are common.

Figure 55.4   The Marginal and Average Cost Curves for Selena's Gourmet Salsas

Here we have the family of cost curves for Selena's Gourmet Salsas: the marginal cost curve (MC), the average total cost curve (ATC), the average variable cost curve (AVC), and the average fixed cost curve (AFC). Note that the average total cost curve is U-shaped and the marginal cost curve crosses the average total cost curve at the bottom of the U, point M, corresponding to the minimum average total cost from Table 55.2 and Figure 55.3.

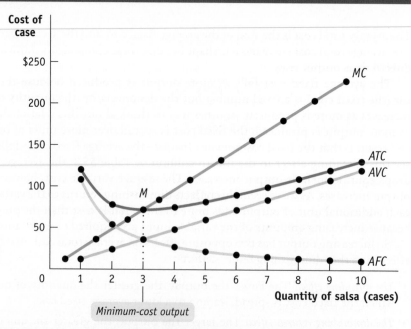

Minimum Average Total Cost

For a U-shaped average total cost curve, the average total cost is at its minimum level at the bottom of the U. Economists call the quantity of output that corresponds to the minimum average total cost the **minimum-cost output**. In the case of Selena's Gourmet Salsas, the minimum-cost output is three cases of salsa per day.

In Figure 55.4, the bottom of the U is at the level of output at which the marginal cost curve crosses the average total cost curve from below. Is this an accident? No—it reflects general principles that are always true about a firm's marginal cost and average total cost curves:

- At the minimum-cost output, the average total cost *is equal to* the marginal cost.
- At output less than the minimum-cost output, the marginal cost *is less than* the average total cost and the average total cost is falling.
- And at output greater than the minimum-cost output, the marginal cost *is greater than* the average total cost and the average total cost is rising.

To understand these principles, think about how your grade in one course—say, a 3.0 in physics—affects your overall grade point average. If your GPA before receiving that grade was more than 3.0, the new grade lowers your average. Similarly, if the marginal cost—the cost of producing one more unit—is less than the average total cost, producing that extra unit lowers the average total cost. This is shown in **Figure 55.5** by the movement from A_1 to A_2. In this case, the marginal cost of producing an additional unit of output is low, as indicated by the point MC_L on the marginal cost curve. When the cost of producing the next unit of output is less than the average total cost, increasing production reduces the average total cost. So any quantity of output at which the marginal cost is less than the average total cost must be on the downward-sloping segment of the U.

But if your grade in physics is more than the average of your previous grades, this new grade raises your GPA. Similarly, if the marginal cost is greater than the average total cost, producing that extra unit raises the average total cost. This is illustrated by the movement from B_1 to B_2 in Figure 55.5, where the marginal cost, MC_H, is higher than the average total cost. Any quantity of output at which the marginal cost is greater than the average total cost must be on the upward-sloping segment of the U.

The **minimum-cost output** is the quantity of output at which the average total cost is lowest—it corresponds to the bottom of the U-shaped average total cost curve.

Figure 55.5 The Relationship Between the Average Total Cost Curve and the Marginal Cost Curve

To see why the marginal cost curve (*MC*) must cut through the average total cost curve at the minimum average total cost (point *M*), corresponding to the minimum-cost output, we look at what happens if the marginal cost is different from the average total cost. If the marginal cost is *less* than the average total cost, an increase in output must reduce the average total cost, as in the movement from A_1 to A_2. If the marginal cost is *greater* than the average total cost, an increase in output must increase the average total cost, as in the movement from B_1 to B_2.

Finally, if a new grade is exactly equal to your previous GPA, the additional grade neither raises nor lowers that average—it stays the same. This corresponds to point M in Figure 55.5: when the marginal cost equals the average total cost, we must be at the bottom of the U because only at that point is the average total cost neither falling nor rising.

Does the Marginal Cost Curve Always Slope Upward?

Up to this point, we have emphasized the importance of diminishing returns, which lead to a marginal product curve that always slopes downward and a marginal cost curve that always slopes upward. In practice, however, economists believe that marginal cost curves often slope *downward* as a firm increases its production from zero up to some low level, sloping upward only at higher levels of production: marginal cost curves look like the curve labeled MC in **Figure 55.6**.

Figure 55.6 More Realistic Cost Curves

A realistic marginal cost curve has a "swoosh" shape. Starting from a very low output level, the marginal cost often falls as the firm increases output. That's because hiring additional workers allows greater specialization of their tasks and leads to increasing returns. Once specialization is achieved, however, diminishing returns to additional workers set in and the marginal cost rises. The corresponding average variable cost curve is now U-shaped, like the average total cost curve.

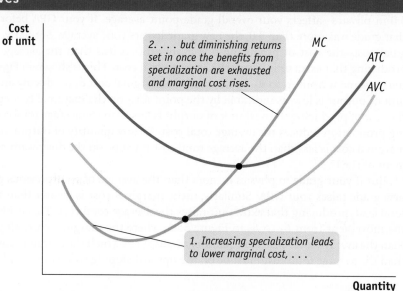

2. . . . but diminishing returns set in once the benefits from specialization are exhausted and marginal cost rises.

1. Increasing specialization leads to lower marginal cost, . . .

This initial downward slope occurs because a firm often finds that, when it starts with only a very small number of workers, employing more workers and expanding output allows its workers to specialize in various tasks. This, in turn, lowers the firm's marginal cost as it expands output. For example, one individual producing salsa would have to perform all the tasks involved: selecting and preparing the ingredients, mixing the salsa, bottling and labeling it, packing it into cases, and so on. As more workers are employed, they can divide the tasks, with each worker specializing in one aspect or a few aspects of salsa-making. This specialization leads to *increasing returns* to the hiring of additional workers and results in a marginal product of labor curve that initially slopes upward and a marginal cost curve that initially slopes downward. Once there are enough workers to have completely exhausted the benefits of further specialization, diminishing returns to labor set in and the marginal cost curve changes direction and slopes upward. So typical marginal cost curves actually have the "swoosh" shape shown by MC in Figure 55.6. For the same reason, average variable cost curves typically look like AVC in Figure 55.6: they are U-shaped rather than strictly upward-sloping.

However, as Figure 55.6 also shows, the key features we saw from the example of Selena's Gourmet Salsas remain true: the average total cost curve is U-shaped, and the marginal cost curve passes through the minimum point of the average total cost curve.

Figure 55.7 shows the relationship between the marginal product of labor curve and the marginal cost curve under the assumptions that labor is the only variable input and the wage rate remains unchanged. The horizontal axis on the top graph measures the quantity of labor; the horizontal axis on the bottom graph measures the quantity of output produced by the quantity of labor shown in the top graph. As the marginal product rises to its peak at the dotted line, the marginal cost falls, because less and less additional labor is needed to make each additional unit of output. To the right of the dotted line, the marginal cost rises as the marginal product falls, because more and more additional labor is needed to make each additional unit of output. The marginal product and the marginal cost go in opposite directions.

Figure 55.7 Links Between Productivity and Cost

If labor is the only variable input and the wage rate remains unchanged, the marginal cost falls as the marginal product rises and the marginal cost rises as the marginal product falls. Similarly, the average variable cost rises as the average product falls and the average variable cost falls as the average product rises.

The **average product** of an input is the total product divided by the quantity of the input. For example, if 5 workers produce 75 bushels of wheat, the average product of labor is $75/5 = 15$ bushels. The **average product curve** for labor, labeled *APL* in Figure 55.7, shows the relationship between the average product of labor and the quantity of labor. With labor as the only variable input and a fixed wage rate, the average product and the average variable cost go in opposite directions, just like the marginal product and the marginal cost. To the left of the dashed line in Figure 55.7, the average product is rising and the average variable cost is falling, while to the right of the dashed line, the average product is falling and the average variable cost is rising.

The **average product** of an input is the total product divided by the quantity of the input.

The **average product curve** for an input shows the relationship between the average product and the quantity of the input.

Check Your Understanding

1. Alicia sells apple pies out of a food truck. Alicia must pay $9.00 per day to rent a parking space for her truck. It costs her $1.00 to produce the first pie of the day; each subsequent pie costs 50% more to produce than the one before. For example, the second pie costs $1.00 × 1.5 = $1.50 to produce, the third pie costs $1.50 × 1.5 = $2.25 to produce, and so on.

   a. Calculate Alicia's marginal cost, variable cost, average fixed cost, average variable cost, and average total cost as her daily pie output rises from 0 to 6. (*Hint:* The variable cost of two pies is just the marginal cost of the first pie, plus the marginal cost of the second, and so on.)

   b. Indicate the range of pies for which the spreading effect dominates and the range for which the diminishing returns effect dominates.

   c. What is Alicia's minimum-cost output? Explain why making one more pie lowers Alicia's average total cost when output is lower than the minimum-cost output. Similarly, explain why making one more pie raises Alicia's average total cost when output is greater than the minimum-cost output.

TACKLE THE AP® TEST: Multiple-Choice Questions

1. When a firm is producing zero output, the total cost equals
   a. zero.
   b. the variable cost.
   c. the fixed cost.
   d. the average total cost.
   e. the marginal cost.

2. Marginal cost can be found at the change in either of which two types of cost when output increases by one?
   a. average variable cost or average total cost
   b. average fixed cost or average total cost
   c. total cost or fixed cost
   d. variable cost or fixed cost
   e. variable cost or total cost

3. Which of the following is correct about costs?
   a. *AVC* is the change in total cost generated by one additional unit of output.
   b. $MC = TC/Q$
   c. The average cost curve crosses at the minimum of the marginal cost curve.
   d. The *AFC* curve slopes upward.
   e. $AVC = ATC - AFC$

4. The slope of the total cost curve equals
   a. variable cost.
   b. average variable cost.
   c. average total cost.
   d. average fixed cost.
   e. marginal cost.

5. On the basis of the data in the table below, what is the marginal cost of the third unit of output?

Quantity	Variable cost	Total cost
0	$0	$40
1	20	60
2	50	90
3	90	130
4	140	180
5	200	240

   a. $40
   b. $50
   c. $60
   d. $90
   e. $130

6. Which of the following always decreases when the quantity of output increases?
   a. average variable cost
   b. marginal cost
   c. average fixed cost
   d. average total cost
   e. average product of labor

7. If labor is the only variable input and the wage rate is fixed, which of the following move in opposite directions each time the quantity of output increases?
   a. marginal cost and average variable cost
   b. average product of labor and marginal product of labor
   c. marginal cost and average product of labor
   d. marginal product of labor and average variable cost
   e. marginal cost and marginal product of labor

TACKLE THE AP® TEST: Free-Response Questions

1. Use the information in the table below to answer the following questions.

Quantity	Variable cost	Total cost
0	$0	$40
1	20	60
2	50	90
3	90	130
4	140	180
5	200	240

a. What is the firm's fixed cost? Explain how you know.

b. Draw one correctly labeled graph showing the firm's marginal and average total cost curves.

Rubric for FRQ 1 (6 points)

1 point: FC = $40

1 point: We can identify the fixed cost as $40 because when the firm is not producing, it still incurs a cost of $40. This could only be the result of a fixed cost because the variable cost is zero when output is zero.

1 point: Graph with correct labels ("Cost of unit" on vertical axis; "Quantity" on horizontal axis)

1 point: Upward-sloping MC curve plotted according to data, labeled "MC"

1 point: U-shaped ATC curve plotted according to the provided data, labeled "ATC"

1 point: MC curve crossing at minimum of ATC curve (Note: We have simplified this graph by drawing smooth lines between discrete points. If we had drawn the MC curve as a step function instead, the MC curve would have crossed the ATC curve exactly at its minimum point.)

2. Draw a correctly labeled graph showing a firm with a realistic "swoosh-shaped" MC curve and ATC, AVC, and AFC curves with their typical shapes. **(6 points)**

Long-Run Costs and Economies of Scale

In this Module, you will learn to:

- Explain why a firm's costs may differ between the short run and the long run
- Describe how a firm can enjoy economies of scale

Up to this point, we have treated fixed cost as completely outside the control of a firm because we have focused on the short run. But all inputs are variable in the long run: this means that in the long run, even "fixed cost" may change. *In the long run, in other words, a firm's fixed cost becomes a variable it can choose.* For example, given time, Selena's Gourmet Salsas can acquire additional food-preparation equipment or dispose of some of its existing equipment. In this Module, we will examine how a firm's costs behave in the short run and in the long run. We will also see that the firm will choose its fixed cost in the long run based on the level of output it expects to produce.

Short-Run Costs

Let's begin by supposing that Selena's Gourmet Salsas is considering whether to acquire additional capital in the form of food-preparation equipment. Acquiring additional machinery will affect its total cost in two ways. First, the firm will have to either rent or buy the additional equipment; either way, that will mean a higher fixed cost in the short run. Second, if the workers have more equipment, they will be more productive: fewer workers will be needed to produce any given output level, so the variable cost for each output level will be reduced.

The table in **Figure 56.1** shows how acquiring an additional machine affects costs. In our original example, we assumed that Selena's Gourmet Salsas had a fixed cost of $108. The left half of the table shows variable cost as well as total cost and average total

---

Figure 56.1 Choosing the Level of Fixed Cost for Selena's Gourmet Salsas

There is a trade-off between higher fixed cost and lower variable cost for any given output level, and vice versa. ATC_1 is the average total cost curve corresponding to a fixed cost of $108; it leads to lower fixed cost and higher variable cost. ATC_2 is the average total cost curve corresponding to a higher fixed cost of $216 but lower variable cost. At low output levels—4 or fewer cases of salsa per day—ATC_1 lies below ATC_2, meaning that the average total cost is lower with only $108 in fixed cost. But as output goes up, the average total cost is lower with the higher amount of fixed cost, $216: at more than 4 cases of salsa per day, ATC_2 lies below ATC_1.

	Low fixed cost (FC = $108)			High fixed cost (FC = $216)		
Quantity of salsa (cases)	High variable cost	Total cost	Average total cost of case ATC_1	Low variable cost	Total cost	Average total cost of case ATC_2
1	$12	$120	$120.00	$6	$222	$222.00
2	48	156	78.00	24	240	120.00
3	108	216	72.00	54	270	90.00
4	192	300	75.00	96	312	78.00
5	300	408	81.60	150	366	73.20
6	432	540	90.00	216	432	72.00
7	588	696	99.43	294	510	72.86
8	768	876	109.50	384	600	75.00
9	972	1,080	120.00	486	702	78.00
10	1,200	1,308	130.80	600	816	81.60

cost assuming a fixed cost of $108. The average total cost curve for this level of fixed cost is given by ATC_1 in Figure 56.1. Let's compare that to a situation in which the firm buys additional food-preparation equipment, doubling its fixed cost to $216 but reducing its variable cost at any given level of output. The right half of the table shows the firm's variable cost, total cost, and average total cost with this higher level of fixed cost. The average total cost curve corresponding to $216 in fixed cost is given by ATC_2 in Figure 56.1.

From the figure you can see that when output is small, 4 cases of salsa per day or fewer, average total cost is smaller when Selena forgoes the additional equipment and maintains the lower fixed cost of $108: ATC_1 lies below ATC_2. For example, at 3 cases per day, the average total cost is $72 without the additional machinery and $90 with the additional machinery. But as output increases beyond 4 cases per day, the firm's average total cost is lower if it acquires the additional equipment, raising its fixed cost to $216. For example, at 9 cases of salsa per day, the average total cost is $120 when fixed cost is $108 but only $78 when fixed cost is $216.

Why does average total cost change like this when fixed cost increases? When output is low, the increase in fixed cost from the additional equipment outweighs the reduction in variable cost from higher worker productivity—that is, there are too few units of output over which to spread the additional fixed cost. So if Selena plans to produce 4 or fewer cases per day, she would be better off choosing the lower level of fixed cost, $108, to achieve a lower average total cost of production. When planned output is high, however, she should acquire the additional machinery.

In general, for each output level there is some amount of fixed inputs such as capital and land—and a corresponding fixed cost—that minimizes the firm's average total cost for that output level. When the firm has a desired output level that it expects to maintain over time, it should choose the optimal fixed cost for that level—that is, the level of fixed cost that minimizes its average total cost.

Now that we are studying a situation in which fixed cost can change, we need to take *time* into account when discussing average total cost. All of the average total cost curves we have considered until now are defined for a given level of fixed cost—that is, they are defined for the short run, the period of time over which fixed cost doesn't vary. To reinforce that distinction, for the rest of this module we will refer to these average total cost curves as "short-run average total cost curves."

For most firms, it is realistic to assume that there are many possible choices of fixed cost, not just two. The implication: for such a firm, many possible short-run average total cost curves will exist, each corresponding to a different choice of fixed cost and so giving rise to what is called a firm's "family" of short-run average total cost curves.

At any given time, a firm will find itself on the short-run average total cost curve corresponding to the fixed cost of its current amount of fixed inputs. A change in output will cause the firm to move along its short-run curve. If the firm's current fixed cost does not minimize the average total cost of its desired level of output, given sufficient time, the firm will want to adjust its fixed cost. For example, suppose Selena produces 2 cases of salsa per day and minimizes her average total cost with a fixed cost of $108. If she then decides to increase her output to 8 cases per day for the foreseeable future, in the long run she should acquire more equipment and increase her fixed cost to a level that minimizes her average total cost at the 8-cases-per-day output level.

Long-Run Costs

Suppose we do a thought experiment and calculate the lowest possible average total cost that can be achieved for each output level. Economists have given this thought experiment a name: the *long-run average total cost curve*. Specifically, the **long-run average total cost curve**, or **LRATC**, is the relationship between output and average total cost when fixed cost has been chosen to minimize average total cost *for each level of output*. If there are many possible choices of fixed cost, the long-run average total cost curve will have the familiar, smooth U shape, as shown by *LRATC* in **Figure 56.2**.

The **long-run average total cost curve (LRATC)** shows the relationship between output and average total cost when fixed cost has been chosen to minimize average total cost for each level of output.

Figure 56.2 Short-Run and Long-Run Average Total Cost Curves

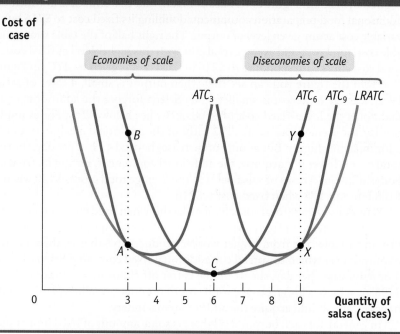

Short-run and long-run average total cost curves differ because a firm can choose its fixed cost in the long run. If Selena has the level of fixed cost that minimizes short-run average total cost at an output of 6 cases, and actually produces 6 cases, then she will be at point C on *LRATC* and ATC_6. But if she produces only 3 cases, she will move to point B. If she expects to produce only 3 cases for a long time, in the long run she will use less capital to reduce her fixed cost and move to point A on ATC_3. Likewise, if she produces 9 cases (putting her at point Y) and expects to continue this for a long time, she will increase her fixed cost in the long run and move to point X on ATC_9.

When output levels change significantly, so does the amount of capital that minimizes long-run average total cost.

ducu59us/Shutterstock

AP® EXAM TIP

Remember that the long run and the short run don't refer to predetermined periods of time. They are defined by whether or not all inputs are variable. In the short run at least one input is not variable, but in the long run all inputs are variable.

We can now draw the distinction between the short run and the long run more fully. In the long run, when a producer has had time to choose the fixed cost appropriate for its desired level of output, that producer will be at some point on the long-run average total cost curve. But if the output level is altered, the firm will no longer be on its long-run average total cost curve and will instead move along its current short-run average total cost curve. It will not be on its long-run average total cost curve again until it readjusts its fixed cost for its new output level.

Figure 56.2 illustrates this point. The curve ATC_3 shows the short-run average total cost if Selena has chosen the level of fixed cost that minimizes average total cost at an output of 3 cases of salsa per day. This is confirmed by the fact that at 3 cases per day, ATC_3 touches *LRATC*, the long-run average total cost curve. Similarly, ATC_6 shows the short-run average total cost if Selena's fixed cost minimizes the average total cost of producing 6 cases per day. We know this because ATC_6 touches *LRATC* at 6 cases per day. And ATC_9 shows the short-run average total cost if Selena's fixed cost minimizes the average total cost of producing 9 cases per day. It touches *LRATC* at 9 cases per day.

Suppose that Selena initially chose to be on ATC_6. If she actually produces 6 cases of salsa per day, her firm will be at point C on both its short-run and long-run average total cost curves. But what if Selena ends up producing only 3 cases of salsa per day? In the short run, her average total cost is indicated by point B on ATC_6; it is no longer on the *LRATC*. If Selena had known that she would be producing only 3 cases per day, she would have been better off acquiring less equipment and lowering her fixed cost to the one corresponding to ATC_3, thereby achieving a lower average total cost. Then her firm would have found itself at point A on the long-run average total cost curve, which lies below point B.

Suppose, conversely, that Selena ends up producing 9 cases per day even though she initially chose to be on ATC_6. In the short run her average total cost is indicated by point Y on ATC_6. But she would be better off purchasing more equipment and incurring a higher fixed cost in order to reduce her variable cost and move to ATC_9. This would allow her to reach point X on the long-run average total cost curve, which lies below Y. The distinction between short-run and long-run average total costs is extremely important in making sense of how real firms operate over time. A company that has to increase output suddenly to meet a surge in demand will typically find that in the short run its average total cost rises sharply because it is hard to get extra production out of existing facilities. But given time to build new factories or add machinery, short-run average total cost falls.

Returns to Scale

What determines the shape of the long-run average total cost curve? It is the influence of *scale*, the size of a firm's operations, on its long-run average total cost of production. Firms that experience *scale effects* in production find that their long-run average total cost changes substantially depending on the quantity of output they produce.

Economies of scale exist when long-run average total cost declines as output increases. As you can see in Figure 56.2, Selena's Gourmet Salsas experiences economies of scale over output levels ranging from 0 up to 6 cases of salsa per day—the output levels over which the long-run average total cost curve is declining. Economies of scale can result from **increasing returns to scale**, which exist when output increases more than in proportion to an increase in all inputs. For example, if Selena could double all of her inputs and make more than twice as much salsa, she would be experiencing increasing returns to scale. With twice the inputs (and costs) and more than twice the salsa, she would be enjoying decreasing long-run average total cost, and thus economies of scale. Increasing returns to scale therefore imply economies of scale, although economies of scale exist whenever long-run average total cost is falling, whether or not all inputs are increasing by the same proportion. When economies of scale end, the firm has reached its **minimum efficient scale**, which is the smallest quantity at which the firm's long-run average total cost is minimized. Selena's minimum efficient scale is 6, as shown by point *C* in Figure 56.2.

There are **diseconomies of scale** when long-run average total cost increases as output increases. Selena's Gourmet Salsas faces decreasing returns to scale at output levels greater than 6 cases, the output levels over which its long-run average total cost curve is rising. Diseconomies of scale can result from **decreasing returns to scale**, which exist when output increases less than in proportion to an increase in all inputs—doubling the inputs results in less than double the output. When output increases directly in proportion to an increase in all inputs—doubling the inputs results in double the output—the firm is experiencing **constant returns to scale**.

What explains these scale effects in production? The answer ultimately lies in the firm's technology of production. Economies of scale often arise from the increased *specialization* that larger output levels allow—a larger scale of operation means that individual workers can limit themselves to more specialized tasks, becoming more skilled and efficient at doing them. Another source of economies of scale is a very large initial setup cost; in some industries—such as auto manufacturing, electricity generating, and petroleum refining—it is necessary to pay a high fixed cost in the form of plant and equipment before producing any output. As we'll see when we study monopoly, economies of scale have important implications for how firms and industries behave and interact.

Diseconomies of scale—the opposite scenario—typically arise in large firms due to problems of coordination and communication: as a firm grows in size, it becomes ever more difficult and therefore costly to communicate and to organize activities. Although economies of scale induce firms to grow larger, diseconomies of scale tend to limit their size.

Sunk Costs

Although we have devoted much attention to costs that should be taken into account when making a decision, some costs should be ignored when doing so. This section presents these kinds of costs—what economists call *sunk costs*—and explains why they should be ignored.

To gain some intuition, consider the following scenario. You own a car that is a few years old, and you have just replaced the brake pads at a cost of $250. But then you find out that the entire brake system is defective and also must be replaced. This will cost you an

There are **economies of scale** when long-run average total cost declines as output increases.

There are **increasing returns to scale** when output increases more than in proportion to an increase in all inputs. For example, with increasing returns to scale, doubling all inputs would cause output to more than double.

The **minimum efficient scale** is the smallest quantity at which a firm's long-run average total cost is minimized.

There are **diseconomies of scale** when long-run average total cost increases as output increases.

There are **decreasing returns to scale** when output increases less than in proportion to an increase in all inputs.

There are **constant returns to scale** when output increases directly in proportion to an increase in all inputs.

AP® EXAM TIP

Don't mix up the concepts of diminishing returns and returns to scale. Diminishing returns is a short-run concept because at least one input is being held constant. Returns to scale is a long-run concept because all inputs are variable.

Greatstock/Alamy

additional $1,500. Alternatively, you could sell the car and buy another of comparable quality, but with no brake defects, by spending an additional $1,600. What should you do: fix your old car, or sell it and buy another?

Some might say that you should take the latter option. After all, this line of reasoning goes, if you repair your car, you will end up having spent $1,750: $1,500 for the brake system and $250 for the brake pads. If you were instead to sell your old car and buy another, you would spend only $1,600.

Although this reasoning sounds plausible, it is wrong. It ignores the fact that you have *already* spent $250 on brake pads, and that $250 is *nonrecoverable*. Because this $250 has already been spent and you cannot get it back, it should have no effect on your decision whether to repair your car and keep it or not. From a rational viewpoint, the real cost at this time of repairing and keeping your car is $1,500, not $1,750. So the correct decision is to repair your car and keep it rather than spend $1,600 on a new car.

In this example, the $250 that has already been spent and cannot be recovered is what economists call a **sunk cost**. Sunk costs should be ignored in making decisions because they have no influence on future costs and benefits. It's like the old saying, "There's no use crying over spilled milk": once something can't be recovered, it is irrelevant in making decisions about what to do in the future. This applies equally to individuals, firms, and governments—regardless of how much has been spent on a project in the past, if the future costs exceed the future benefits, the project should not continue.

It is often psychologically hard to ignore sunk costs. And if, in fact, you haven't yet incurred the costs, then you should take them into consideration. That is, if you had known at the beginning that it would cost $1,750 to repair your car, then the right choice *at that time* would have been to buy a new car for $1,600. But once you have already paid the $250 for brake pads, you should no longer include it in your decision making about your next actions. It may be hard to "let bygones be bygones," but it is the right way to make a decision.

A **sunk cost** is a cost that has already been incurred and is nonrecoverable. A sunk cost should be ignored in a decision about future actions.

Summing Up Costs: The Short and Long of It

If a firm is to make the best decisions about how much to produce, it has to understand how its costs relate to the quantity of output it chooses to produce. **Table 56.1** provides a quick summary of the concepts and measures of cost you have learned about.

Table 56.1	Concepts and Measures of Cost		
	Measurement	**Definition**	**Mathematical term**
Short run	Fixed cost	Cost that does not depend on the quantity of output produced	FC
	Average fixed cost	Fixed cost per unit of output	$AFC = FC/Q$
Short run and long run	Variable cost	Cost that depends on the quantity of output produced	VC
	Average variable cost	Variable cost per unit of output	$AVC = VC/Q$
	Total cost	The sum of fixed cost (short run) and variable cost	$TC = FC$ (short run) $+ VC$
	Average total cost (average cost)	Total cost per unit of output	$ATC = TC/Q$
	Marginal cost	The change in total cost generated by producing one more unit of output	$MC = \Delta TC/\Delta Q$
Long run	Long-run average total cost	Average total cost when fixed cost has been chosen to minimize average total cost for each level of output	$LRATC$

MODULE 56 REVIEW

Check Your Understanding

1. The accompanying table shows three possible combinations of fixed cost and average variable cost. For each choice, average variable cost is constant (it does not vary with the quantity of output produced).

Choice	Fixed cost	Average variable cost
1	$8,000	$1.00
2	12,000	0.75
3	24,000	0.25

   a. For each of the three choices, calculate the average total cost of producing 12,000, 22,000, and 30,000 units. For each of these quantities, which choice results in the lowest average total cost?

   b. Suppose that the firm, which has historically produced 12,000 units, experiences a sharp, permanent increase in demand that leads it to produce 22,000 units. Explain how its average total cost will change in the short run and in the long run.

   c. Explain what the firm should do instead if it believes the change in demand is temporary.

2. In each of the following cases, explain whether the firm is likely to experience economies of scale or diseconomies of scale and why.

   a. an interior design firm in which design projects are based on the expertise of the firm's owner

   b. a diamond-mining company

TACKLE THE AP® TEST: Multiple-Choice Questions

1. In the long run
   a. all inputs are variable.
   b. all inputs are fixed.
   c. some inputs are variable and others are fixed.
   d. a firm will go out of business.
   e. firms increase in size.

2. Which of the following is always considered the long run?
   a. 1 month
   b. 1 year
   c. 5 years
   d. 10 years
   e. none of the above

3. Which of the following statements is generally correct?
   a. Firms tend to experience economies of scale at high levels of output and diseconomies of scale at low levels of output.
   b. Fixed costs are the greatest in the long run.
   c. The average total cost of producing a particular quantity of output is the same in the short run and in the long run.
   d. The short-run average total cost curve intersects the long-run average total cost curve at its minimum point.
   e. The long-run average total cost curve is U-shaped.

4. When making decisions, which of the following costs should be ignored?
   a. average costs
   b. total costs
   c. marginal costs
   d. sunk costs
   e. None of the above—no costs should be ignored.

5. There is a different short-run average total cost curve for each level of
   a. variable cost.
   b. variable inputs.
   c. fixed cost.
   d. long-run average total cost.
   e. output prices.

6. If the long-run average total cost decreases as the quantity of output increases, the firm is necessarily experiencing
   a. constant returns to scale.
   b. increasing returns to scale.
   c. economies of scale.
   d. diminishing returns.
   e. decreasing returns to scale.

7. When the current amount of fixed cost minimizes the long-run average total cost for the quantity of output being produced, the short-run average total cost curve is necessarily
   a. horizontal.
   b. downward-sloping.
   c. above the long-run average total cost curve.
   d. below the long-run average total cost curve.
   e. touching the long-run average total cost curve.

1. Refer to the graph provided to answer the following questions.

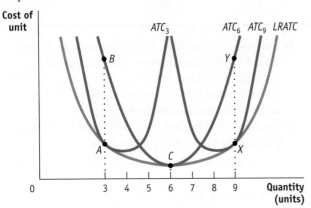

a. The same level of fixed cost that puts the firm at point *B* when the quantity is 3 minimizes short-run average total cost for what output level?

b. At an output level of 3, is the firm experiencing economies or diseconomies of scale? Explain.

c. In the long run, if the firm expects to produce an output of 9, the firm will produce on which short-run average total cost curve and at which point on the graph?

Rubric for FRQ 1 (5 points)

1 point: 6

1 point: economies of scale

1 point: At an output of 3, the *LRATC* is decreasing.

1 point: In the long run the firm will produce on *ATC₉*.

1 point: In the long run the firm will produce at point *X*.

2. Draw a correctly labeled graph showing a short-run average total cost curve and the corresponding long-run average total cost curve. On your graph, identify the areas of economies and diseconomies of scale. **(5 points)**

MOD 57

Introduction to Market Structure

In this Module, you will learn to:

- Explain the meaning and dimensions of market structure
- Describe the four principal types of market structure—perfect competition, monopoly, oligopoly, and monopolistic competition

You may have noticed that this section is titled "Behind the Supply Curve," but we have yet to mention any supply curve. The reason is that we need to identify the type of market we are looking at before we can discuss the supply curve in a market. In this Module we will learn about the basic characteristics of the four major types of markets in the economy.

Types of Market Structure

The real world holds a mind-boggling array of different markets. Patterns of firm behavior vary as widely as the markets themselves: in some markets, firms are extremely competitive; in others, they seem to coordinate their actions to limit competition; and some markets are monopolies in which there is no competition at all. In order to develop principles and make predictions about markets and firm behavior, economists have developed four primary models of market structure: *perfect competition, monopoly, oligopoly,* and *monopolistic competition.*

This system of market structure is based on two dimensions:

- the number of firms in the market (one, few, or many)
- whether the goods offered are identical or *differentiated*

Differentiated goods are goods that are different but considered at least somewhat substitutable by consumers (think Coca-Cola versus Pepsi).

Figure 57.1 provides a simple visual summary of the types of market structure classified according to these two dimensions. A more detailed summary appears at the end of the Module. In *perfect competition,* many firms each sell an identical product. In *monopoly,* a single firm sells a single, undifferentiated product. In *oligopoly,* a few firms—more than one but not a large number—sell products that may be either identical or differentiated. And in *monopolistic competition,* many firms each sell a differentiated product (think of producers of economics textbooks).

Pepsi and Coca-Cola are considered differentiated goods because they aren't the same, but one can serve as a substitute for the other.

Figure 57.1 Types of Market Structure

The behavior of any given firm and the market it occupies are analyzed using one of four models of market structure—monopoly, oligopoly, perfect competition, or monopolistic competition. This system for categorizing market structure is based on two dimensions: (1) whether products are differentiated or identical and (2) the number of firms in the industry—one, a few, or many.

Perfect Competition

Suppose that Yves and Zoe are neighboring farmers, both of whom grow organic tomatoes. Both sell their output to the same grocery store chains that carry organic foods; so, in a real sense, Yves and Zoe compete with each other.

Does this mean that Yves should try to stop Zoe from growing tomatoes or that Yves and Zoe should form an agreement to grow fewer tomatoes? Neither strategy would be effective because there are hundreds or thousands of organic tomato farmers (let's not forget Jennifer and Jason from Module 53!), and Yves and Zoe are competing with all those other growers as well as with each other. Because so many farmers sell organic tomatoes, if any one of them produced more or fewer, there would be no measurable effect on market prices.

When people talk about business competition, they often imagine a situation in which two or three rival firms are struggling for advantage. But economists know that when a business focuses on a few main competitors, it's actually a sign that competition is fairly limited.

As the example of organic tomatoes suggests, when the number of competitors is large, it doesn't even make sense to identify rivals and engage in aggressive competition because each firm is too small within the scope of the market to make a significant difference.

We can put it another way: Yves and Zoe are *price-takers*. A **price-taking firm** is one whose actions cannot affect the market price of the good or service it sells. As a result, a price-taking firm takes the market price as given. When there is enough competition—when competition is what economists call "perfect"—then every firm is a price-taker. There is a similar definition for consumers: a **price-taking consumer** is a consumer who cannot influence the market price of the good or service by his or her actions. That is, the market price is unaffected by how much or how little of the good the consumer buys.

Defining Perfect Competition

In a **perfectly competitive market**, all market participants, both consumers and producers, are price-takers. That is, neither consumption decisions by individual consumers nor production decisions by individual producers affect the market price of the good.

The supply and demand model is a model of a perfectly competitive market. It depends fundamentally on the assumption that no individual buyer or seller of a good, such as coffee beans or organic tomatoes, can individually affect the price at which he or she can buy or sell the good. For a firm, being a price-taker means that the demand curve is a horizontal line at the market price. If the firm charged more than the market price, buyers would go to any of the many alternative sellers of the same product. And it is unnecessary to charge a lower price because, as an insignificantly small part of the perfectly competitive market, the firm can sell all that it wants at the market price.

Instances in which consumers are able to affect the prices they pay are rare, so as a general rule, consumers are indeed price-takers. However, it is quite common for producers to have a significant ability to affect the prices they receive, a phenomenon we'll address later. An industry in which firms are price-takers is called a **perfectly competitive industry**. The model of perfect competition is appropriate for some but not all markets. Clearly, some industries aren't perfectly competitive; in later Modules we'll focus on industries that don't fit the perfectly competitive model.

Under what circumstances will all firms be price-takers? As we'll discover next, there are two necessary conditions for a perfectly competitive industry, and a third condition is often present as well.

Two Necessary Conditions for Perfect Competition

The markets for major grains, such as wheat and corn, are perfectly competitive: individual wheat and corn farmers, as well as individual buyers of wheat and corn, take market prices as given. In contrast, the markets for some of the food items made from these grains—in particular, breakfast cereals—are by no means perfectly competitive. There is intense competition among cereal brands, but not *perfect* competition. To understand the difference between the market for wheat and the market for shredded wheat cereal is to understand the two necessary conditions for perfect competition.

First, for an industry to be perfectly competitive, it must contain many firms, none of whom have a large *market share*. A firm's **market share** is the fraction of the total industry output accounted for by that firm's output. The distribution of market share constitutes a major difference between the grain industry and the breakfast cereal industry. There are thousands of wheat farmers, none of whom account for more than a tiny fraction of total wheat sales. The breakfast cereal industry, however, is dominated by four firms: Kellogg's, General Mills, Post, and Quaker. Kellogg's alone accounts for about one-third of all cereal sales. Kellogg's executives know that if they try to sell more corn flakes, they are likely to drive down the

The market for wheat is perfectly competitive—many firms, each with a small market share, sell the same standardized product and take the market price as given.

market price of corn flakes. That is, they know that their actions influence market prices—due to their tremendous size, changes in their production will significantly affect the overall quantity supplied. It makes sense to assume that firms are price-takers only when they are numerous and relatively small.

Second, an industry can be perfectly competitive only if consumers regard the products of all firms as equivalent. This clearly isn't true in the breakfast cereal market: consumers don't consider Cap'n Crunch to be a good substitute for Wheaties. As a result, the maker of Wheaties has some ability to increase its price without fear that it will lose all its customers to the maker of Cap'n Crunch. Contrast this with the case of a **standardized product**, sometimes known as a **commodity**, which is a product that consumers regard as the same good even when it comes from different firms. Because wheat is a standardized product, consumers regard the output of one wheat producer as a perfect substitute for that of another producer. This means that one farmer cannot increase the price for his or her wheat without losing all sales to other wheat farmers. So the second necessary condition for a perfectly competitive industry is that the industry output is a standardized product.

The market for breakfast cereal is competitive, but not perfectly competitive, because firms sell a differentiated product and may be able to charge a higher price than their competitors without losing all of their customers.

Free Entry and Exit

All perfectly competitive industries have many firms with small market shares, producing a standardized product. Most perfectly competitive industries are also characterized by one more feature: in the long run it is easy for new firms to enter the industry or for firms that are currently in the industry to leave. That is, no obstacles in the form of government regulations or limited access to key resources prevent new firms from entering the market. And no additional costs are associated with shutting down a company and leaving the industry. Economists refer to the arrival of new firms into an industry as *entry*; they refer to the departure of firms from an industry as *exit*. When there are no obstacles to entry into or exit from an industry, we say that the industry has **free entry and exit**.

Free entry and exit is not strictly necessary for perfect competition. However, it ensures that the number of firms in an industry can adjust to changing market conditions. And, in particular, it ensures that firms in an industry cannot act to keep other firms out.

To sum up, then, perfect competition depends on two necessary conditions. First, the industry must contain many firms, each having a small market share. Second, the industry must produce a standardized product. In addition, perfectly competitive industries are normally characterized by free entry and exit in the long run.

A good is a **standardized product**, also known as a **commodity**, when consumers regard the products of different firms as the same good.

An industry has **free entry and exit** when new firms can easily enter into the industry and existing firms can easily leave the industry.

Monopoly

The De Beers diamond monopoly based in South Africa was created in the 1880s by Cecil Rhodes, a British businessman. By 1880, mines in South Africa already dominated the world's supply of diamonds. However, there were many mining companies, all competing with each other. During the 1880s Rhodes bought the great majority of those mines and consolidated them into a single company, De Beers. By 1889, De Beers controlled almost all of the world's diamond production.

In other words, De Beers became a *monopolist*. But what does it mean to be a monopolist? And what do monopolists do?

Defining Monopoly

As we mentioned earlier, the supply and demand model of a market is not universally valid. Instead, it's a model of perfect competition, which is only one of several types of market structure. A market will be perfectly competitive only if there are many firms, all of which produce the same good. Monopoly is the most extreme departure from perfect competition.

A **monopolist** is a firm that is the only producer of a good that has no close substitutes. An industry controlled by a monopolist is known as a **monopoly**.

In practice, true monopolies are hard to find in the modern American economy, partly because of legal obstacles. A contemporary entrepreneur who tried to consolidate all the firms in an industry the way Rhodes did would soon find himself in court, accused of breaking *antitrust* laws, which are intended to prevent monopolies from emerging. However, monopolies do play an important role in some sectors of the economy.

Why Do Monopolies Exist?

A monopolist making profits will not go unnoticed by others. (Recall that this is "economic profit," revenue over and above the opportunity costs of the firm's resources.) But won't other firms crash the party, grab a piece of the action, and drive down prices and profits in the long run? If possible, yes, they will. For a profitable monopoly to persist, something must keep others from going into the same business; that "something" is known as a **barrier to entry**. There are four principal types of barriers to entry: control of a scarce resource or input, economies of scale, technological superiority, and government-created barriers.

Control of a Scarce Resource or Input

A monopolist that controls a resource or input crucial to an industry can prevent other firms from entering its market. Cecil Rhodes made De Beers into a monopolist by establishing control over the mines that produced the great bulk of the world's diamonds.

When De Beers controlled virtually all of the world's diamond production, it was a monopolist and the diamond industry was a monopoly.

Economies of Scale

Many Americans have natural gas piped into their homes for cooking and heating. Invariably, the local gas company is a monopolist. But why don't rival companies compete to provide gas?

In the early nineteenth century, when the gas industry was just starting up, companies did compete for local customers. But this competition didn't last long; soon local gas companies became monopolists in almost every town because of the large fixed cost of providing a town with gas lines. The cost of laying gas lines didn't depend on how much gas a company sold, so a firm with a larger volume of sales had a cost advantage: because it was able to spread the fixed cost over a larger volume, it had a lower average total cost than smaller firms.

The natural gas industry is one in which average total cost falls as output increases, resulting in economies of scale and encouraging firms to grow larger. In an industry characterized by economies of scale, larger firms are more profitable and drive out smaller ones. For the same reason, established firms have a cost advantage over any potential entrant—a potent barrier to entry. So economies of scale can both give rise to and sustain a monopoly.

A monopoly created and sustained by economies of scale is called a **natural monopoly**. The defining characteristic of a natural monopoly is that its minimum efficient scale is so large that the monopoly possesses economies of scale over the range of output that is relevant for the industry. The source of this condition is large fixed costs: when large fixed costs are required to operate, a given quantity of output is produced at lower average total cost by one large firm than by two or more smaller firms.

The most visible natural monopolies in the modern economy are local utilities— water, gas, and electricity, and, in some locations, internet service providers. As we'll see later, natural monopolies pose a special challenge to public policy.

Technological Superiority

A firm that maintains a consistent technological advantage over potential competitors can establish itself as a monopolist. For example, Apple has dominated the smartphone market since 2007, and captured as much as 92% of global smartphone profits in 2015.

But technological superiority is typically not a barrier to entry over the longer term: over time competitors will invest in upgrading their technology to match that of the technology leader. In fact, in the last few years firms such as Samsung and Huawei have used very similar products to erode Apple's market share.

We should note, however, that in certain high-tech industries, technological superiority is not a guarantee of success against competitors. Some high-tech industries are characterized by *network externalities*, a condition that arises when the value of a good to a consumer rises as the number of other people who also use the good rises. In these industries, the firm possessing the largest network—the largest number of consumers currently using its product—has an advantage over its competitors in attracting new customers, an advantage that may allow it to become a monopolist. Microsoft is often cited as an example of a company with a technologically inferior product—its computer operating system—that grew into a virtual monopolist through the phenomenon of network externalities.

Government-Created Barriers

In 2017 the pharmaceutical company Melinta Therapeutics introduced Baxdela, a drug for the treatment of serious skin infections. Although other drug companies had the know-how to produce Baxdela, no other firms challenged Melinta's monopoly. That's because the U.S. government had given Melinta the sole legal right to produce the drug in the United States. Baxdela is an example of a monopoly protected by government-created barriers.

The most important legally created monopolies today arise from *patents* and *copyrights*. A **patent** gives an inventor the sole right to make, use, or sell that invention for a period of time that in most countries lasts between 16 and 20 years. Patents are given to the creators of new products, such as drugs or mechanical devices. Similarly, a **copyright** gives the copyright holder—typically the creator of a literary or artistic work—the sole right to profit from that work, usually for a period equal to the creator's lifetime plus 70 years.

The justification for patents and copyrights is a matter of incentives. If inventors were not protected by patents, they would gain little reward from their efforts: as soon as a valuable invention was made public, others would copy it and sell products based on it. And if inventors could not expect to profit from their inventions, then there would be no incentive to incur the costs of invention in the first place. Likewise for the creators of literary or artistic works. So the law allows a monopoly to exist temporarily by granting property rights that encourage invention and creation. Patents and copyrights are temporary because the law strikes a compromise. The higher price for the good that holds while the legal protection is in effect compensates inventors for the cost of invention; conversely, the lower price that results once the legal protection lapses benefits consumers.

Because the lifetime of the temporary monopoly cannot be tailored to specific cases, this system is imperfect and leads to some missed opportunities. In some cases there can be significant welfare issues. For example, the violation of American drug patents by pharmaceutical companies in poor countries has been a major source of controversy, pitting the needs of poor patients who cannot afford to pay retail drug prices against the interests of drug manufacturers who have incurred high research costs to discover these drugs. To solve this problem, some American drug companies and poor countries have negotiated deals in which the patents are honored but the American companies sell their drugs at deeply discounted prices. (This is an example of *price discrimination*, which we'll learn more about in the next section.)

A **patent** gives an inventor a temporary monopoly in the use or sale of an invention.

A **copyright** gives the copyright holder for a literary or artistic work the sole right to profit from that work for a specified period of time.

Oligopoly

An industry with only a few firms is known as an **oligopoly**; a producer in such an industry is known as an **oligopolist**.

Oligopolists compete with each other for sales. But oligopolists aren't like producers in a perfectly competitive industry, who take the market as given. Oligopolists

An **oligopoly** is an industry with only a small number of firms. A producer in such an industry is known as an **oligopolist**.

know their decisions about how much to produce will affect the market price. That is, like monopolists, oligopolists have some *market power*. Economists refer to a situation in which firms compete but also possess market power—which enables them to affect market prices—as **imperfect competition**. There are two important forms of imperfect competition: oligopoly and *monopolistic competition*. Of these, oligopoly is probably the more important in practice.

Many familiar goods and services are supplied by only a few competing sellers, which means the industries in question are oligopolies. For example, most air routes are served by only two or three airlines: in recent years, regularly scheduled shuttle service between New York and Boston has been provided only by Delta, American, and JetBlue. Three firms—Chiquita, Dole, and Del Monte, which own huge banana plantations in Central America—control 65% of world banana exports. Most cola beverages are sold by Coca-Cola and Pepsi. This list could go on for many pages.

It's important to realize that an oligopoly isn't necessarily made up of large firms. What matters isn't size per se, but how many competitors there are. When a small town has only two grocery stores, grocery service there is just as much an oligopoly as air shuttle service between New York and Washington. Module 64 explains that, regardless of their size, the small number of competitors in an oligopoly makes it tempting—and often possible—for the firms to raise their profits by working together, or *colluding*, to limit direct competition and raise prices.

Why are oligopolies so prevalent? Essentially, an oligopoly is the result of the same factors that sometimes produce a monopoly, but in somewhat weaker form. An important source of oligopolies is the existence of economies of scale, which give bigger firms a cost advantage over smaller ones. When these effects are very strong, as we have seen, they lead to a monopoly; when they are not that strong, they lead to an industry with a small number of firms. For example, larger grocery stores typically have lower costs than smaller stores. But the advantages of large scale taper off once grocery stores are reasonably large, which is why two or three stores often survive in small towns.

Collage_Best/Getty Images

Sixty-five percent of the world's bananas are produced by three firms. An industry such as this with only a small number of firms is an oligopoly.

Is It an Oligopoly or Not?

In practice, it is not always easy to determine an industry's market structure just by looking at the number of firms. Many oligopolistic industries contain a number of small "niche" firms, which don't really compete with the major players. For example, the U.S. airline industry includes a number of regional airlines such as Mokulele Airlines, which flies propeller planes between the Hawaiian islands; if you count these carriers, the U.S. airline industry contains nearly one hundred firms, which doesn't sound like competition among a small group. But there are only a handful of national competitors like Delta and United, and on many routes, as we've seen, there are only two or three competitors.

To get a better picture of market structure, economists often use two measures of market power: *concentration ratios* and the *Herfindahl–Hirschman Index*. **Concentration ratios** measure the percentage of industry sales accounted for by the "X" largest firms, where "X" can equal any number of firms. For example, the four-firm concentration ratio is the percentage of sales accounted for by the four largest firms, and the eight-firm concentration ratio is the percentage of industry sales accounted for by the eight largest firms. If the largest four firms accounted for 25%, 20%, 15%, and 10% of industry sales, then the four-firm concentration ratio would equal 25 + 20 + 15 + 10 = 70. And if the next largest four firms in that industry accounted for 9%, 8%, 6%, and 2% of sales, the eight-firm concentration ratio would equal 70 + 9 + 8 + 6 + 2 = 95. The four- and eight-firm concentration ratios are the most commonly used. A higher concentration ratio signals that a market is more concentrated and therefore is more likely to be an oligopoly. For example, a market with a four-firm concentration ratio of 70 is more concentrated than a market with a four-firm concentration ratio of 40.

Another measure of market concentration is the **Herfindahl–Hirschman index**, or HHI. The HHI for an industry is the square of each firm's share of market sales summed over the firms in the industry. Unlike concentration ratios, the HHI takes into account the distribution of market sales among the top firms by squaring each firm's market share, thereby giving more weight to larger firms. For example, if an industry contains only three firms and their market shares are 60%, 25%, and 15%, then the HHI for the industry is:

$$HHI = 60^2 + 25^2 + 15^2 = 4,450$$

By squaring each market share, the HHI calculation produces numbers that are much larger when a larger share of an industry output is dominated by fewer firms. This is confirmed by the data in **Table 57.1**. Here, the indices for industries dominated by a small number of firms, like the internet search engine industry or the wide-body aircraft industry, are many times larger than the index for the ice cream and frozen desserts, which has numerous firms of approximately equal size.

Table 57.1	The HHI for Some Oligopolistic Industries	
Industry	**HHI**	**Largest firms**
Internet search engine	8,343	Google, Microsoft, Yahoo, Baidu
Wide-body aircraft	5,018	Boeing, Airbus
Computer operating systems	3,400	Microsoft, Apple, Google, Linux
Dog and cat food	2,019	Mars, Nestlé Purina, J.M. Smucker, Hill's, Blue Buffalo, Spectrum/United.
Automobiles	1,178	Volkswagen, GM, Ford, Toyota, Chrysler, Nissan, Honda, Hyundai-Kia
Movie distributors	1,307	Disney, Warner Bros., Sony Pictures, 20th Century Fox, Universal, Paramount, Lionsgate
Ice cream and frozen desserts	666	Unilever, Nestlé, Blue Bell

Data Sources: gs.statcounter.com; aviation-society.com; U.S. Census Bureau; the-numbers.com.

Monopolistic Competition

Leo manages the Wonderful Wok stand in the food court of a big shopping mall. He offers the only Chinese food in the mall, but there are more than a dozen alternatives, from Bodacious Burgers to Pizza Paradise. When deciding what to charge for a meal, Leo knows that he must take those alternatives into account: even people who normally prefer stir-fry won't order a $15 lunch from Leo when they can get a burger, fries, and drink for $4.

But Leo also knows that he won't lose all his business even if his lunches cost a bit more than the alternatives. Chinese food isn't the same thing as burgers or pizza. Some people will really be in the mood for Chinese that day, and they will buy from Leo even if they could have dined more cheaply on burgers. Of course, the reverse is also true: even if Chinese is a bit cheaper, some people will choose burgers instead. In other words, Leo does have some market power: he has *some* ability to set his own price.

How would you describe Leo's situation? He definitely isn't a price-taker, so he isn't in a situation of perfect competition. But you wouldn't exactly call him a monopolist, either. Although he's the only seller of Chinese food in that food court, he does face competition from other food vendors.

Yet it would also be wrong to call him an oligopolist. Oligopoly, remember, involves competition among a small number of interdependent firms in an industry protected by some—albeit limited—barriers to entry and whose profits are highly interdependent. Because of this

A restaurant in a food court is not a perfect competitor, a monopolist, or even an oligopolist. The many firms serving differentiated products in an industry with free entry satisfy the recipe for monopolistic competition.

interdependence, oligopolists have an incentive to collude. But in Leo's case there are *lots* of vendors in the shopping mall, too many to make collusion practical.

Defining Monopolistic Competition

Monopolistic competition is a market structure in which there are many competing firms in an industry, each firm sells a differentiated product, and there is free entry into and exit from the industry in the long run.

Economists describe Leo's situation as one of **monopolistic competition**. Monopolistic competition is particularly common in service industries such as the restaurant and gas station industries, but it also exists in some manufacturing industries. It involves three conditions:

- a large number of competing firms,
- differentiated products, and
- free entry into and exit from the industry in the long run.

In a monopolistically competitive industry, each producer has some ability to set the price of her differentiated product. But exactly how high she can set it is limited by the competition she faces from other existing and potential firms that produce similar, but not identical, products.

Large Numbers

In a monopolistically competitive industry there are many firms. Such an industry does not look either like a monopoly, where the firm faces no competition, or like an oligopoly, where each firm has only a few rivals. Instead, each seller has many competitors. For example, there are many vendors in a big food court, many gas stations along a major highway, and many hotels at a popular beach resort.

Differentiated Products

In a monopolistically competitive industry, each firm has a product that consumers view as somewhat distinct from the products of competing firms. Such product differentiation can come in the form of different styles or types, different locations, or different levels of quality. At the same time, though, consumers see these competing products as close substitutes. If Leo's food court contained 15 vendors selling exactly the same kind and quality of food, there would be perfect competition: any seller who tried to charge a higher price would have no customers. But suppose that Wonderful Wok is the only Chinese food vendor, Bodacious Burgers is the only hamburger stand, and so on. The result of this differentiation is that each vendor has some ability to set his or her own price: each firm has some—albeit limited—market power.

Free Entry and Exit in the Long Run

In monopolistically competitive industries, new firms, with their own distinct products, can enter the industry freely in the long run. For example, other food vendors would open outlets in the food court if they thought it would be profitable to do so. In addition, firms will exit the industry if they find they are not covering their costs in the long run.

Monopolistic competition, then, differs from the three market structures we have examined so far. It's not the same as perfect competition: firms have some power to set prices. It's not pure monopoly: firms face some competition. And it's not the same as oligopoly: there are many firms and free entry, which eliminates the potential for collusion that is so important in oligopoly. As we'll see in Modules 66 and 67, competition among the sellers of differentiated products is the key to understanding how monopolistic competition works.

Table 57.2 summarizes the characteristics of each market structure.

Now that we have introduced the idea of market structure and presented the four principal models of market structure, we can proceed in the next two sections to use the cost curves we have developed to build each of the four market structure models. These models will allow us to explain and predict firm behavior (for example, price and quantity determination) and analyze individual markets.

AP® EXAM TIP

Don't confuse monopolistic competition and monopoly or perfect competition. Monopolistic competition has low barriers to entry, unlike a monopoly, and a differentiated product, unlike a perfectly competitive firm.

AP® EXAM TIP

Create a chart showing the differences between the four types of market structures found in this module. These comparisons show up frequently on the AP® exam.

Table 57.2 Market Structure

Characteristic	Perfect Competition	Monopolistic Competition	Oligopoly	Monopoly
Number of firms	Many	Many	Few	One
Product differentiation	No	Yes	Yes or No	No
Control over price	None	Within narrow limits	Varies, depending on the degree of mutual interdependence and collusion	Considerable, limited by consumers' willingness to pay
Barriers to entry	None	Few if any	Considerable	Prohibitive
Example	Agriculture	Restaurants	Airlines	Utilities

MODULE 57 REVIEW

Adventures in AP® Economics

Watch the video: *Perfect Competition*

Check Your Understanding

1. In each of the following situations, what type of market structure do you think the industry represents?
   a. There are three producers of aluminum in the world, a good sold in many places.
   b. There are thousands of farms that produce indistinguishable soybeans, a commodity sold to thousands of buyers.
   c. Many designers sell high-fashion clothes. Each designer has a distinctive style and a somewhat loyal clientele.
   d. A small town in the middle of Alaska has one bicycle shop.

TACKLE THE AP® TEST: Multiple-Choice Questions

1. Which of the following is true for a perfectly competitive industry?
   a. There are many firms, each with a large market share.
   b. The firms in the industry produce a standardized product.
   c. There are barriers to entry.
   d. There are barriers to exit.
   e. There are a few firms, each with a small market share.

2. Which of the following is true for a monopoly?
   a. It consists of only one firm.
   b. A firm produces a product with many close substitutes.
   c. The industry allows free entry and exit.
   d. Firms are price-takers.
   e. The HHI is below 10,000.

3. Which of the following is true for an oligopoly?
   a. The firms typically experience diseconomies of scale.
   b. There are many firms.
   c. The firms have no market power.
   d. There is a small number of interdependent firms.
   e. It is impractical for the firms to collude.

4. Which of the following is true for a monopolistically competitive industry?
   a. There are many firms, each with a small market share.
   b. The firms in the industry produce a standardized product.
   c. Firms are price-takers.
   d. There are considerable barriers to entry.
   e. There is a small number of independent firms.

5. Which of the following is an example of differentiated products?
   a. Coca-Cola and Pepsi
   b. automobiles and bicycles
   c. trucks and gasoline
   d. stocks and bonds
   e. gold and silver

6. Which two market structures are normally characterized by free entry and exit in the long run?
   a. perfect competition and monopoly
   b. oligopoly and monopolistic competition
   c. perfect competition and monopolistic competition
   d. oligopoly and monopoly
   e. monopolistic competition and monopoly

7. Economies of scale are the defining characteristic of which market structure?
   a. perfect competition
   b. oligopoly
   c. monopolistic competition
   d. natural monopoly
   e. monopoly

TACKLE THE AP® TEST: Free-Response Questions

1. For each of the following characteristics, indicate which market structure(s) exhibit that characteristic.
   a. many sellers
   b. price-takers
   c. barriers to entry
   d. differentiated product

> **Rubric for FRQ 1 (7 points)**
>
> **a. 1 point:** perfect competition
>   **1 point:** monopolistic competition
> **b. 1 point:** perfect competition

> **c. 1 point:** monopoly
>   **1 point:** oligopoly
> **d. 1 point:** oligopoly
>   **1 point:** monopolistic competition

2. a. This module describes the demand curve for a perfectly competitive firm, which is a price taker. Draw a correctly labeled graph of a perfectly competitive firm's demand curve if the market price is $10.
   b. What does the firm's marginal revenue equal any time it sells one more unit of its output? **(3 points)**

SECTION 10 Review

SECTION 10 Review Video

Adventures in AP® Economics Videos

Mod 55: Production Costs
Mod 56: Returns to Scale
Mod 57: Perfect Competition

Module 52

1. The cost of using a resource for a particular activity is the opportunity cost of that resource. Some opportunity costs are **explicit costs**; they involve a direct payment of cash. Other opportunity costs, however, are **implicit costs**; they involve no outlay of money but represent the inflows of cash that are forgone. Both explicit and implicit costs should be taken into account when making decisions. Firms use capital and their owners' time, so firms should base decisions on **economic profit**, which takes into account implicit costs such as the opportunity cost of the owners' time and the **implicit cost of capital**. **Accounting profit**, which firms calculate for the purposes of taxes and public reporting, is often considerably larger than economic profit because it includes only explicit costs and depreciation, not implicit costs. Finally, **normal profit** is a term used to describe an economic profit equal to zero—a profit just high enough to justify the use of resources in an activity.

Module 53

2. A producer chooses output according to the **optimal output rule**: produce the quantity at which marginal revenue equals marginal cost. The **marginal revenue curve** shows the **marginal revenue** for each unit; the **marginal cost curve** shows the marginal cost for each unit. More generally, the **principle of marginal analysis** suggests that every activity should continue until marginal benefit equals marginal cost.

Module 54

3. The relationship between inputs and output is represented by a firm's **production function**. In the **short run**, the quantity of a **fixed input** cannot be varied but the quantity of a **variable input**, by definition, can. In the **long run**, the quantities of all inputs can be varied. For a given amount of the fixed input, the **total product curve** shows how the quantity of output changes as the quantity of the variable input changes. The **marginal product** of an input is the increase in output that results from using one more unit of that input.

4. There are **diminishing returns to an input** when its marginal product declines as more of the input is used, holding the quantity of all other inputs fixed.

Module 55

5. **Total cost**, represented by the **total cost curve**, is equal to the sum of **fixed cost**, which does not depend on output, and **variable cost**, which does depend on output. Due to diminishing returns, marginal cost—the increase in total cost generated by producing one more unit of output—normally increases as output increases.

6. **Average total cost** (also known as **average cost**) is the total cost divided by the quantity of output. Economists believe that **U-shaped average total cost curves** are typical because average total cost consists of two parts: **average fixed cost**, which falls when output increases (the spreading effect), and **average variable cost**, which rises with output (the diminishing returns effect).

7. When average total cost is U-shaped, the bottom of the U is the level of output at which average total cost is minimized, the point of **minimum-cost output**. This is also the point at which the marginal cost curve crosses the average total cost curve from below. Due to gains from specialization, the marginal cost curve may slope downward initially before sloping upward, giving it a "swoosh" shape.

8. The **average product** of an input is the total product divided by the quantity of the input, and the **average product curve** shows the relationship between the average product and the quantity of the input. When labor is the only variable input and the wage is constant, average variable cost falls when average product rises, and average variable cost rises when average product falls. Likewise, marginal cost rises when marginal product falls and vice versa.

Module 56

9. In the long run, a firm can change its fixed input and its level of fixed cost. By accepting higher fixed cost, a firm can lower its variable cost for any given output level, and vice versa. The **long-run average total cost curve** shows the relationship between output and average total cost when fixed cost has been chosen to minimize average total cost at each level of output. A firm moves along its short-run average total cost curve as it changes the quantity of output, and it returns to a point on both its short-run and long-run average total cost curves once it has adjusted fixed cost to its new output level. The **minimum efficient scale** is the

smallest quantity at which a firm's long-run average total cost is minimized.

10. As output increases, there are **economies of scale** if long-run average total cost decreases and **diseconomies of scale** if long-run average total cost increases. As all inputs are increased by the same proportion, there are **increasing returns to scale** if output increases by a larger proportion than the inputs, **decreasing returns to scale** if output increases by a smaller proportion, and **constant returns to scale** if output increases by the same proportion.

11. **Sunk costs** are expenditures that have already been made and cannot be recovered. Sunk costs should be ignored in making decisions about future actions because what is important is a comparison of future costs and future benefits.

Module 57

12. In a **perfectly competitive market** all firms are **price-taking firms** and all consumers are **price-taking consumers**—no one's actions can influence the market price. Consumers are normally price-takers, but firms often are not. In a **perfectly competitive industry**, every firm in the industry is a price-taker.

13. There are two necessary conditions for a perfectly competitive industry: there are many firms, none of which has a large **market share**, and the industry produces a **standardized product** or **commodity**—goods that consumers regard as equivalent. A third condition is often satisfied as well: **free entry and exit** into and from the industry.

14. There are four main types of market structure based on the number of firms in the industry and product differentiation: perfect competition, monopoly, oligopoly, and monopolistic competition.

15. A **monopolist** is a producer who is the sole supplier of a good without close substitutes. An industry controlled by a monopolist is a **monopoly**.

16. To persist, a monopoly must be protected by a **barrier to entry**. This can take the form of control of a natural resource or input, increasing returns to scale that give rise to a **natural monopoly**, technological superiority, or government rules that prevent entry by other firms, such as **patents** or **copyrights**.

17. Many industries are **oligopolies**, in which there are only a few sellers, known as **oligopolists**. Oligopolies exist for more or less the same reasons that monopolies exist, but in weaker form. They are characterized by **imperfect competition**: firms compete but possess some market power.

18. **Monopolistic competition** is a market structure in which there are many competing firms, each producing a differentiated product, and there is free entry and exit in the long run. Product differentiation takes three main forms: by style or type, by location, and by quality. The extent of imperfect competition can be measured by the **concentration ratio**, or the **Herfindahl–Hirschman Index**.

Key Terms

Explicit cost, p. 510
Implicit cost, p. 510
Accounting profit, p. 511
Economic profit, p. 511
Implicit cost of capital, p. 512
Normal profit, p. 513
Principle of marginal analysis, p. 516
Marginal revenue, p. 516
Optimal output rule, p. 516
Marginal cost curve, p. 517
Marginal revenue curve, p. 517
Production function, p. 520
Fixed input, p. 520
Variable input, p. 520
Long run, p. 520
Short run, p. 520
Total product curve, p. 520
Marginal product, p. 521
Diminishing returns to an input, p. 522
Fixed cost, p. 526

Variable cost, p. 526
Total cost, p. 526
Total cost curve, p. 527
Average total cost, p. 530
Average cost, p. 530
U-shaped average total cost curve, p. 530
Average fixed cost, p. 530
Average variable cost, p. 530
Minimum-cost output, p. 533
Average product, p. 535
Average product curve, p. 535
Long-run average total cost curve, p. 539
Economies of scale, p. 541
Increasing returns to scale, p. 541
Minimum efficient scale, p. 541
Diseconomies of scale, p. 541
Decreasing returns to scale, p. 541
Constant returns to scale, p. 541
Sunk cost, p. 542
Price-taking firm, p. 546

Price-taking consumer, p. 546
Perfectly competitive market, p. 546
Perfectly competitive industry, p. 546
Market share, p. 546
Standardized product, p. 547
Commodity, p. 547
Free entry and exit, p. 547
Monopolist, p. 548
Monopoly, p. 548
Barrier to entry, p. 548
Natural monopoly, p. 548
Patent, p. 549
Copyright, p. 549
Oligopoly, p. 549
Oligopolist, p. 549
Imperfect competition, p. 550
Concentration ratios, p. 550
Herfindahl–Hirschman Index, p. 550
Monopolistic competition, p. 552

AP® Exam Practice Questions

Multiple-Choice Questions

1. Consider the data about the cost of each year of college in the table below:

Opportunity Cost of a Year of College

Explicit cost		Implicit cost	
Tuition	$17,000	Forgone salary	$32,000
Books and supplies	1,000		
Computer	1,500		
Total explicit cost	19,500	Total implicit cost	32,000

Total opportunity cost = Total explicit cost + Total implicit cost
= $51,500

A rational person would attend another year of college if the additional income expected plus the value of improved quality of life were worth at least
- **a.** $17,000.
- **b.** $19,500.
- **c.** $32,000.
- **d.** $51,500.
- **e.** $83,500.

2. Comparing accounting profit to economic profit, accounting profit can
- **a.** only be greater than economic profit.
- **b.** only be less than economic profit.
- **c.** be equal to or more than economic profit.
- **d.** be equal to or less than economic profit.
- **e.** only be equal to economic profit.

3. Which kind of profit is just enough to keep a firm operating in the long run?
- **a.** normal
- **b.** economic
- **c.** accounting
- **d.** implicit
- **e.** explicit

Refer to the cost data in the table below to answer Question 4.

Quantity of tomatoes Q (bushels)	Total cost TC	Marginal cost of bushel MC = ΔTC/ΔQ
0	$14	
1	30	$16
2	36	6
3	44	8
4	56	12
5	72	16
6	92	20
7	116	24

4. If this business can sell all it can produce at a market price of $16, the firm should produce how many units in order to maximize profits?
- **a.** 1
- **b.** 3
- **c.** 5
- **d.** 6
- **e.** 7

5. Assume a perfectly competitive firm is producing at a level of output where marginal revenue is greater than marginal cost. What should the firm do to maximize profits?
- **a.** continue to produce at that level
- **b.** increase output
- **c.** decrease output
- **d.** raise prices
- **e.** lower prices

6. When a firm is producing where marginal cost is equal to marginal revenue, the firm
- **a.** may be making profits or losses.
- **b.** will definitely be maximizing profits.
- **c.** should produce more to maximize profits.
- **d.** should produce less to maximize profits.
- **e.** will definitely be minimizing losses.

7. A fixed input
- **a.** never changes.
- **b.** is a long-run phenomenon.
- **c.** does not change with the output level in the short run.
- **d.** causes marginal cost to fall as it is increased.
- **e.** causes marginal cost to rise as it is increased.

8. If marginal product is positive and declining as more workers are hired, then total product is
- **a.** decreasing at an increasing rate.
- **b.** decreasing at a decreasing rate.
- **c.** increasing at an increasing rate.
- **d.** increasing at a decreasing rate.
- **e.** increasing at a constant rate.

9. Diminishing marginal returns always involve
- **a.** too much plant capacity.
- **b.** a rapid expansion of plant size.
- **c.** a slow expansion of plant size.
- **d.** a fixed input.
- **e.** inputs that are all variable.

10. If marginal cost is positive and rising as more output is produced, then total cost is
- **a.** decreasing at an increasing rate.
- **b.** decreasing at a decreasing rate.
- **c.** increasing at an increasing rate.
- **d.** increasing at a decreasing rate.
- **e.** increasing at a constant rate.

11. Marginal cost rises due to
    a. diminishing marginal returns.
    b. increasing marginal returns.
    c. constant returns to scale.
    d. increasing returns to scale.
    e. increasing average returns.

12. The relationship between the marginal cost curve and the average cost curve is that when
    a. marginal cost is rising, average cost must be rising.
    b. average cost is falling, average cost must be falling.
    c. marginal cost is above average cost, average cost must be rising.
    d. marginal cost is below average cost, average cost must be rising.
    e. marginal cost is above average cost, average cost must be falling.

13. In the short run, what happens to average fixed cost as output increases?
    a. It remains constant.
    b. It falls and then rises after a certain output level.
    c. It rises initially, and then falls continuously.
    d. It falls continuously.
    e. It rises continuously.

14. If at the current level of output of 200 units, average variable cost is $10 per unit and average total cost is $15 per unit, then
    a. total fixed cost is equal to $1,000.
    b. total fixed cost is equal to $2,000.
    c. total fixed cost is equal to $3,000.
    d. marginal cost is equal to $5.
    e. marginal cost is equal to $25.

15. If labor is the only variable input and the wage rate is constant, marginal cost reaches its minimum when
    a. marginal product reaches its maximum.
    b. average product reaches its maximum.
    c. marginal product reaches its minimum.
    d. average product reaches its minimum.
    e. average cost reaches its minimum.

16. The spreading effect causes the average total cost curve to
    a. rise, while the diminishing returns effect causes it to fall.
    b. rise, as does the diminishing returns effect.
    c. fall, while the diminishing returns effect causes it to rise.
    d. fall, as does the diminishing returns effect.
    e. remain constant until the beginning of the diminishing marginal returns effect.

17. If marginal cost is rising and lies above average variable cost, then average total cost
    a. may be rising or falling.
    b. will definitely be rising.
    c. will definitely be falling.
    d. will definitely be constant.
    e. None of the above are correct.

18. If the average product of labor is rising as more workers are hired, then
    a. the marginal product of labor must be rising.
    b. the marginal product of labor must be falling.
    c. the marginal product of labor must be higher than the average product of labor.
    d. the average total cost must be rising.
    e. the marginal cost must be falling.

19. Which of the following causes the long-run average cost curve to eventually slope upward?
    a. economies of scale
    b. economies of scope
    c. diseconomies of scale
    d. overcrowding of the fixed factors of production
    e. diminishing marginal returns

20. When a firm makes production decisions, sunk costs should be
    a. set equal to the variable cost.
    b. set equal to the marginal cost.
    c. set equal to the total cost.
    d. subtracted from the fixed cost to determine profit.
    e. ignored.

21. Monopolistically competitive industries are characterized by
    a. standardized products, many firms, and easy entry and exit.
    b. standardized products, few firms, and easy entry and exit.
    c. differentiated products, many firms, and easy entry and exit.
    d. differentiated products, many firms, and high barriers to entry.
    e. differentiated products, few firms, and high barriers to entry.

22. Compared to a monopolistically competitive industry, an oligopoly has
    a. a higher Herfindahl–Hirschman Index, fewer firms, and more barriers to entry.
    b. a higher Herfindahl–Hirschman Index, more firms, and more barriers to entry.
    c. a higher Herfindahl–Hirschman Index, fewer firms, and fewer barriers to entry.
    d. a lower Herfindahl–Hirschman Index, fewer firms, and more barriers to entry.
    e. a lower Herfindahl–Hirschman Index, more firms, and more barriers to entry.

23. Compared to a monopoly, an oligopoly has
    a. a higher Herfindahl–Hirschman Index, fewer firms, and more barriers to entry.
    b. a higher Herfindahl–Hirschman Index, more firms, and more barriers to entry.

c. a lower Herfindahl–Hirschman Index, fewer firms, and fewer barriers to entry.

d. a lower Herfindahl–Hirschman Index, more firms, and more barriers to entry.

e. a lower Herfindahl–Hirschman Index, more firms, and fewer barriers to entry.

24. Diseconomies of scale can be caused by
    a. increasing returns to scale.
    b. overcrowding of the fixed factors of production.
    c. increasing average fixed cost.
    d. decreasing average fixed cost.
    e. communication problems.

25. In which of the following market structures are firms price-takers?
    a. perfect competition only
    b. perfect competition and monopolistic competition
    c. oligopoly only
    d. oligopoly and perfect competition
    e. monopoly and monopolistic competition

Free-Response Questions

1. One way to examine the marginal cost of a good is by looking at the opportunity cost using the production possibilities curve (PPC) model. Draw a correctly labeled PPC graph for computers and cell phones that exhibits constant opportunity cost. To the right of this PPC graph, draw another PPC graph for corn and grapes that exhibits increasing opportunity cost.
    a. Explain what the shape of each PPC implies about the resources used to make the goods.
    b. Indicate whether the marginal cost curve for the production of cell phones would be upward-sloping, downward-sloping, horizontal, vertical, or swoosh-shaped.
    c. Indicate whether the marginal cost curve for the production of corn would be upward-sloping, downward-sloping, horizontal, vertical, or swoosh-shaped. Explain.
    d. Given your answer to part c, indicate whether the total cost curve for corn production rises or falls as more corn is produced, and whether it does so at an increasing, decreasing, or constant rate.
    e. Assuming there is also a fixed cost of corn production, indicate whether the average fixed cost curve for corn production is upward-sloping, downward-sloping, horizontal, or vertical. **(9 points)**

2. Suppose RunCo Shoes produces running shoes using robots and a fixed amount of labor to oversee and repair the robots. The table below indicates how the number of pairs of running shoes produced and the total cost depend on the quantity of robots acquired.

Robots	Total output (pairs)	Total cost ($)
0	0	40
1	2	90
2	5	140
3	10	190
4	15	240
5	19	290
6	22	340
7	24	390
8	25	440

   a. What is the marginal product of the third robot?
   b. How many robots does RunCo need to acquire before it begins to experience diminishing marginal returns? Explain using numbers from the table.
   c. Calculate the marginal cost of the 15th pair of running shoes. Show your work.
   d. Suppose RunCo can sell any quantity of running shoes to retail stores for $30 per pair:
       i. How many robots should this firm hire in order to maximize profits?
       ii. Calculate the profit at this level of output. Show your work. **(6 points)**

3. Suppose Roland's Roller Blades operates with a nonzero fixed cost, an upward-sloping marginal cost, and a constant marginal revenue.
   a. Draw a correctly labeled graph for this firm and label the following:
       i. marginal cost (MC)
       ii. marginal revenue (MR)
       iii. average total cost (ATC)
       iv. average variable cost (AVC)
   b. Label the profit-maximizing quantity of output Q_m.
   c. Suppose that $MC = 5$, $MR = 3$, $ATC = 10$, $AVC = 7$, and $Q_m = 20$. What is the fixed cost? Show your work. **(5 points)**

Could the Future Cost of Energy Change Life as We Know It?

Production Costs and the Inescapable Demand for Energy

Researchers at the Post Carbon Institute, a nonprofit energy think tank, suggest that energy costs will increase dramatically as the supply of fossil fuels (oil, coal, and natural gas) decreases. Among other repercussions, skyrocketing energy costs would spell doom for transportation systems and the suburban neighborhoods, shopping malls, factories, and schools they serve. Because energy is consumed in the production, transportation, use, and disposal of most products, energy costs are built into the prices of almost everything we buy. A spike in oil prices in the 1970s was followed by double-digit inflation rates throughout the economy. Economic theory gives reason for cautious optimism: rising prices boost interest in new technology, which will temper energy costs to a greater or lesser extent, depending on the level of investment in that technology.

With our existing technology, energy from renewable sources such as the sun, wind, earth (geothermal), and water (hydroelectric) costs more than energy from fossil fuels. Even with energy from the cheapest sources, more than 6 million U.S. households require financial assistance from the federal Low Income Home Energy Assistance Program. Here we address the nature, cost structures, and market structures of this most critical of inputs.

An Introduction to Energy

Energy is the amount of physical work a system is capable of performing. *Power* is the rate of energy transfer per unit of time. The first law of thermodynamics implies that energy cannot be created, consumed, or destroyed because the amount of energy in the universe is fixed. So energy "production" refers not to the creation of energy but to its conversion into a usable form, and energy "use" does not mean that energy is destroyed but that it is dissipated into heat or other unusable forms.

From Where Does Energy Come?

The sun is the original and ultimate source of energy on Earth, fueling the plant life that feeds other living things, as well as the ancient plant life whose fossilized remains are burned as oil, natural gas, and coal. The water wheel is thought to have been invented around 350 C.E. as a way to capture energy from flowing water. Windmills were used to harness wind energy beginning about 950 C.E. James Watt used wood and coal fires to power the first modern steam engine in 1765, and to this day the standard unit of power (the watt), equal to 1/746 of a horsepower, or 1 amp times 1 volt, bears his last name. The first nuclear power plant went into operation in 1954, as did the first solar cell to produce significant amounts of electricity.

Today, most of our efforts to harness energy for commercial electricity production involve making turbines spin to create electrical currents. Nuclear fission and coal combustion create steam that turns turbines. Wind and flowing water apply direct force on turbines. You may have created electricity yourself by turning a crank or a bicycle wheel rigged for that purpose. An exception is solar energy collected by

Rolf Hicker Photography/Alamy stockphoto

a photovoltaic cell, which converts light energy into direct-current electricity without moving a thing.

Rocky Mountain Institute co-founder Amory Lovins describes two paths for energy dependence. The first is a "soft path" of many renewable energy sources, such as solar panels on millions of roofs or wind turbines on thousands of "wind farms." The second is a "hard path" of relatively few centralized fossil-fuel–based producers. Although Lovins made this observation in the context of environmental concerns, the distinctions between the two paths are also useful for discussions of market structures and production costs.

In 1850, the United States obtained most of its energy from decentralized sources—the muscles of humans and animals, followed by wood, water, wind, and coal. In 2018, the United States received about 90% of all its energy from large, centralized sources. Most of our energy comes from natural gas (33%); petroleum products (28%); coal (17%); renewable sources (12%); and nuclear power (10%). Electricity is a secondary source of energy because another source of energy must be harnessed to make it. The primary fuel sources for making electricity in the United States are natural gas (32%), coal (30%), uranium (20%), flowing water (7%), and wind (6%).

Where Does Energy Go?

Like the demand for labor, the demand for energy is derived from the demand for the services this input provides. Manufacturing industries create 32% of U.S. energy demand, transportation creates 29%, residential users create 21%, and nonmanufacturing commercial users, such as stores and restaurants, create 18%. Global growth in the number of homes, businesses, industrial plants, and vehicles leads to corresponding increases in the demand for energy.

Much of the energy that is tapped by consumers literally goes up in smoke or is lost to heat or respiration. *Energy conversion efficiency* refers to the percentage of energy from a source that is converted into useful energy rather than being spent in the process of making energy useful. Wind turbines convert about 30% of the wind's energy into electricity. Coal-fired power plants convert 30% to 35% of the energy in coal into electricity. The energy conversion efficiency of standard solar cells is about 20%, although experimental solar cells have reached efficiency levels in excess of 40%. If we captured one-half of 1% of the energy the earth receives from the sun with 20% energy conversion efficiency, no other energy source would be required.

What Does Energy Cost?

Expenditures on energy in the United States exceed $1 trillion annually. Energy costs also include important environmental and health costs. Here we examine the cost structure of energy production for large and small electricity producers. Several critical types of costs discussed in the preceding Modules are explained in this context. Their meanings are summarized here for convenience:

Fixed cost: a cost that does not change as more of the product is made

Variable cost: a cost that increases as more of the product is made

Total cost: fixed cost plus variable cost

Marginal cost: the cost of making one more unit of the product

Average fixed cost: the total fixed cost divided by the number of units made

Average variable cost: the total variable cost divided by the number of units made

Many Small Producers

The cost structure in an energy market depends on the scale of the production facilities, which tends to be either very large or very small. The 3,100 wind turbines at a wind farm near Palm Springs, California, produce as much energy as a midsize nuclear reactor. Environment Colorado plans to have solar panels installed on 1 million Colorado roofs by 2030. The roofs of the Zeeland Middle School in Michigan, a Harley-Davidson dealership in Hawaii, and the home of Minnesota resident Todd Volkmeier exemplify thousands of participants in this soft-path effort.

Mr. Volkmeier installed ten 165-watt solar panels on his roof. Why 10 and not 15 or 25? The answer is that diminishing marginal returns set in for panels, just as they do for workers. The marginal product of another rooftop panel will decrease as the roof becomes crowded and panels must be placed in less sunny spots, and it will fall to zero when the only place for a new panel is on top of another panel.

Let's consider the costs for energy producers such as Mr. Volkmeier. The $2,500 cost of the energy inverter that makes the solar energy usable by household appliances and the battery pack that stores energy for nighttime use is a *fixed cost*, because this expenditure does not change as energy production changes. In order to produce more energy per day with a given amount of sunlight, more panels must be added. Because solar panels are the input that is varied to produce more energy, their cost is a *variable cost*, which amounts to $600 per panel. The *total cost* is the sum of the total variable cost and the total fixed cost for a given amount of output. Mr. Volkmeier's total cost was $2,500 + (10 × $600) = $8,500.

The determination of the optimal number of panels for Mr. Volkmeier requires a closer look at the marginal cost and the marginal benefit. We know that, in general, the *marginal cost* is the cost to producers of one more unit of output. The marginal benefit for producers is the *marginal revenue*—the additional revenue gained from producing one more unit. If something is worth doing, it should be done as long as the marginal benefit exceeds the marginal cost; when the marginal benefit equals the marginal cost, it's time to stop. In the case of production, a good or service should be produced until the marginal revenue equals the marginal cost.

Let's track Mr. Volkmeier's marginal cost as he decides how many solar panels to install. This case illustrates the inverse relationship between marginal cost and marginal product—as the marginal product of solar panels decreases due to roof crowding, it takes more additional panels to increase productive capacity by a given amount, and the marginal cost of energy increases. Given the capacity of individual panels, we'll consider 165-watt increments. As long as there is unobstructed, sun-facing space on the roof, the marginal cost of adding 165 watts is $600—the cost of one panel—or $600/165 = $3.64 per watt. If the best available space requires that additional panels obstruct one-half of an existing panel, then it takes two additional panels to add 165 watts, bringing the marginal cost to $1,200 for 165 watts, or $7.27 per watt. If the best remaining roof space only gets one-third of the amount of sun necessary to bring a panel to its productive capacity, it will take three panels to increase Mr. Volkmeier's production by 165 watts, and the marginal cost is $1,800 for 165 watts, or $10.91 per watt. Finally, if the only place to put another panel is on top of an existing panel, the marginal cost of energy becomes infinite: There is no amount

that can be spent on additional panels to increase capacity.

A few more types of cost are important to consider. The *average fixed cost* is the total fixed cost divided by the quantity of output. To find the average fixed cost of producing 165 watts, we divide the total fixed cost of $2,500 by 165 to get $15.15. As output increases, the average fixed cost invariably decreases because the same total fixed cost is divided by a larger and larger quantity. For example, the average fixed costs of producing 330, 825, and 1,100 watts are $7.58, $3.03, and $2.27, respectively. When 250,000 watts are produced, the average fixed cost is 1 cent.

Average variable cost is the cost of the variable input (panels) divided by the quantity of output (watts). Suppose that the first four panels have prime locations in the sun, the next four create 50% obstruction for other panels, the four after that must go on the side with one-third as much sun, and additional panels provide no net gain. As a few examples of this calculation, the first two panels produce 330 watts at an average variable cost of (2 × $600)/330 = $3.64. The production of 825 watts requires four panels at full capacity plus two panels at half capacity, so the average variable cost is (6 × $600)/825 = $4.36. The production of 1,100 watts requires four panels at full capacity, four panels at half capacity, and two panels at one-third capacity, so the average variable cost is (10 × $600)/1,100 = $5.45.

Producers compare the average total cost with the price to determine whether profits or losses are in store. The average total cost is the sum of the average fixed cost and the average variable cost. It can also be found by dividing the total cost by the quantity of output. Because the total cost of producing 330 watts is $2,500 + (2 × $600) = $3,700, the average total cost is $3,700/330 = $11.21. Likewise, the average total cost of producing 825 and 1,100 watts is $7.39 and $7.73, respectively.

The accompanying table summarizes the marginal and average cost levels. Notice that as output increases, the average total cost decreases and then increases. The average total cost will generally fall as output increases at small levels of production because the increases in average variable cost are initially smaller than the decreases in average fixed cost, which can be dramatic. For example, going from 1 watt to 2 watts cuts down the average fixed cost from $2,500 to $1,250. At higher output levels, the average fixed cost decreases more gradually than the average variable cost increases, and the average total cost begins to rise at precisely the quantity at which the marginal cost rises above the average total cost.

Watts	Marginal cost	Average fixed cost	Average variable cost	Average total cost
330	$3.64	$7.58	$3.64	$11.21
825	7.27	3.03	4.36	7.39
1,100	10.91	2.27	5.45	7.73

Few Large Producers

If most rooftops held solar panels, the many small producers of identical units of energy would resemble the perfectly competitive model that economists describe as efficient. Instead, a majority of the electricity used in the United States comes from large coal-fired power plants and nuclear power plants. Relatively new coal-fired power plants include the Prairie State Energy Campus, completed in 2012 at a cost of $5 billion. This plant has a capacity of 1,600 megawatts (a megawatt is 1 million watts). The Watts Bar Nuclear Power Plant Unit 2 in Tennessee went online in 2016 with a capacity of 1,150 megawatts and a cost of about $4.5 billion after decades of construction delays.

Although there is diminishing marginal product from coal and uranium, the overarching cost of these types of operations is the cost of building the power plants themselves. The enormous fixed cost of these facilities makes the cost structure of coal-fired and nuclear energy producers different from that of soft-path producers. Consider the average fixed cost of nuclear power. The average fixed cost of the first million watts produced at the Watts Bar 2 plant is $4.5 billion/1 million = $4,500 per watt. In contrast, the average variable cost and the marginal cost are just pennies per kilowatt hour, because the primary input—uranium—is inexpensive. The same is true for coal.

The fixed costs of coal and nuclear power are prohibitive for any modest level of production. A competitive market divided among many coal or nuclear power producers could not survive because none of the plants would sell enough energy to cover the billions of dollars of fixed costs. The only way for such a plant to break even is to serve a large region and to sell mass quantities of electricity. When high fixed costs effectively eliminate access to the market by competing firms, the result is a *natural monopoly*—a single firm

that is more efficient than any number of competitive firms would be. Like energy utilities, water utilities are natural monopolies because the enormous cost of a water system infrastructure causes the average fixed cost to eclipse the marginal and average variable costs.

Is Energy Regulation a Good Idea?

Competition keeps prices in check, whereas a monopoly can sustain profits at the expense of consumers. Our reliance on natural monopolies raises the prospects for regulation to allow the monopolies to operate but moderate their prices. The importance of affordable energy to production, transportation, food supplies, heating, and cooling, among other essentials, makes energy prices a particular concern of government legislators.

By regulating prices, the government can prevent excessive prices, but it is also important for energy utilities to receive high enough prices to cover their expenses. Due to the high fixed costs, a regulated price set equal to the marginal cost would not provide a natural monopoly with adequate revenues to remain open in the long run. To ensure that consumers pay the smallest amount possible without sending the utility into debt, regulators can set the price equal to the average total cost of production. That way, all of the utility's costs are covered, but there is no economic profit.

Conclusion

Energy can be produced centrally by natural monopolies using fossil fuels or uranium, or locally by small producers of energy from alternative sources. There has been considerable interest and growth in alternative fuels during the past several decades, but, pollution costs aside, fossil fuels are typically less expensive and provide the large majority of energy in the United States. Decreasing stocks of oil and coal, dilemmas over the safe and secure storage of nuclear waste, ethical interests in conserving energy resources for future generations, and the demands of worldwide development force users to grapple with the spectrum of energy options. The high fixed costs of hard-path solutions invite monopolistic market structures and contentious regulations. Looking ahead, improvements in alternative energy technology could lower the costs of decentralized soft-path sources such as wind and solar and change the structure of energy markets.

Critical Thinking Questions

1. The Castle River Wind Farm in Alberta, Canada, operates 67 wind turbines and produces 125 million kilowatt-hours of electricity—enough to serve 20,000 homes. Why do you suppose the company erected 67 turbines, rather than, say, 50 or 100?

2. Some people believe that falling fossil-fuel supplies and rising energy prices will make transportation expensive and bring about "relocalization"—a return to communities with local economies, housing, schools, and amenities. Other people expect that investments in alternative fuels will prevent the need for Americans to change their way of life. What do the investments in alternative fuels that you see in your community suggest about which side is most likely to be right?

3. Which of the following power sources are most likely to come from natural monopolies? Which could be set up either as centralized power sources or as decentralized, soft-path sources?
   a. wind turbines
   b. hydroelectric power generation along a river
   c. coal
   d. oil
   e. solar
   f. nuclear

4. Of the six types of costs discussed above, which type is the most relevant when deciding how much of a good or service to produce? Why?

Market Structures: Perfect Competition and Monopoly

Citizen of the Planet/Alamy

> economics by example *Is Adam Smith Rolling Over in His Grave?*

Some Carrots Are More Expensive Than Others

Section 10 explained how factors including the number of firms in the industry, the type of product sold, and the existence of barriers to entry determine the market power of firms. We can think about the four basic market structures as falling along a spectrum from perfect competition at one end to monopoly at the other, with monopolistic competition and oligopoly lying in between. To shed more light on the market structure spectrum, consider two very different markets introduced in previous sections: the market for organic tomatoes and the market for diamonds.

In the United States, a growing interest in healthy living has steadily increased the demand for products such as organically grown fruits and vegetables. Over the past decade, the markets for these products have been healthy as well, with an average growth rate of 10% per year. It costs a bit more to grow crops without chemical fertilizers and pesticides, but consumers are willing to pay higher prices for the benefits of fruits and vegetables grown the "natural" way. The farmers in each area who pioneered organic farming techniques had little competition, and many prospered thanks to these higher prices.

But with profit as a lure for expanded production, the high prices are unlikely to persist. Over time, farmers already producing organically will increase their capacity, and conventional farmers will enter the organic food market, increasing supply and driving down price. With a large and growing number of buyers and sellers, undifferentiated products, and few barriers to entry, the organic food market increasingly resembles a *perfectly competitive* market.

In contrast, a *monopoly* has only one seller. For example, in the twentieth century, almost every diamond on the world market came from De Beers, a firm which still controls over one-third of the diamond market. Diamonds are valued not just for their beauty but also for their rarity. Yet geologists will tell you that diamonds aren't all that rare. In fact, they are among the more common gem-quality stones. Diamonds *seem* rare because De Beers and other firms limit the quantity supplied to the market. When a firm like De Beers controls the supply of a good, other firms find it difficult to enter the market and increase the available quantity of the good.

In this section we will study how markets like those for organic tomatoes and diamonds differ, and how these markets respond to market conditions. We will see how firms positioned at opposite ends of the spectrum of market power—from perfect competition to monopoly—make key decisions about output and prices. Then, in Section 12, we will complete our exploration of market structure with a closer look at oligopoly and monopolistic competition.

Introduction to Perfect Competition

> **In this Module, you will learn to:**
> - Determine the profit-maximizing quantity of output for a price-taking firm
> - Assess whether or not a competitive firm is profitable

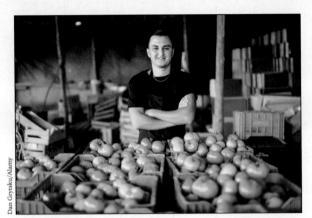
Dan Grytsku/Alamy

Recall the example of the market for organic tomatoes from our discussions in Section 10. Jennifer and Jason run an organic tomato farm, but many other organic tomato farmers, such as Yves and Zoe, sell their output to the same grocery store chains. Since organic tomatoes are a standardized product, consumers don't care which farmer produces the organic tomatoes they buy. And because so many farmers sell organic tomatoes, no individual farmer has a large market share, which means that no individual farmer can have a measurable effect on market prices. These farmers are price-taking producers and their customers are price-taking consumers. The market for organic tomatoes meets the two necessary conditions for perfect competition: there are many producers each with a small market share, and the firms produce a standardized product. In this Module, we build the model of perfect competition and use it to look at a representative firm in the market.

Production and Profit

AP® EXAM TIP

One of the most important concepts to learn in microeconomics is that firms maximize total profit by choosing the quantity of output that equates marginal revenue and marginal cost.

Jennifer and Jason's tomato farm will maximize its profit by producing bushels of tomatoes up until the marginal revenue equals the marginal cost. We know this from the producer's *optimal output rule* introduced in Module 53—profit is maximized by producing the quantity at which the marginal revenue of the last unit produced is equal to its marginal cost. Always remember, $MR = MC$ at the optimal quantity of output. This will be true for any profit-maximizing firm in any market structure.

We can review how to apply the optimal output rule with the help of **Table 58.1**, which provides various short-run cost measures for Jennifer and Jason's farm.

Table 58.1 Short-Run Costs for Jennifer and Jason's Farm

Quantity of tomatoes (bushels) Q	Variable cost VC	Total cost TC	Marginal cost of bushel $MC = \Delta TC/\Delta Q$	Marginal revenue of bushel MR	Net gain of bushel = $MR - MC$
0	$0	$14			
			$16	$18	$2
1	16	30			
			6	18	12
2	22	36			
			8	18	10
3	30	44			
			12	18	6
4	42	56			
			16	18	2
5	58	72			
			20	18	−2
6	78	92			
			24	18	−6
7	102	116			

The second column contains the farm's variable cost, and the third column shows its total cost based on the assumption that the farm incurs a fixed cost of $14. The fourth column shows the farm's marginal cost. Notice that, in this example, the marginal cost initially falls as output rises but then begins to increase, so the marginal cost curve has the familiar "swoosh" shape.

The fifth column contains the farm's marginal revenue, which has an important feature: Jennifer and Jason's marginal revenue is constant at $18 for every output level. The sixth and final column shows the calculation of the net gain per bushel of tomatoes, which is equal to the marginal revenue minus the marginal cost—or, equivalently in this case, the market price minus the marginal cost. As you can see, the net gain is positive for the 1st through 5th bushels; producing each of these bushels raises Jennifer and Jason's profit. For the 6th bushel, however, the net gain is negative: producing it would decrease, not increase, profit. So 5 bushels is Jennifer and Jason's profit-maximizing output; it is the level of output at which the marginal cost rises from a level below the market price to a level above the market price, passing through the market price of $18 along the way.

This example illustrates an application of the optimal output rule to the particular case of a price-taking firm—the **price-taking firm's optimal output rule**: *price equals marginal cost at the price-taking firm's optimal quantity of output.* In other words, a price-taking firm's profit is maximized by producing the quantity of output at which the market price is equal to the marginal cost of the last unit produced. Why? Because *in the case of a price-taking firm, the marginal revenue is equal to the market price.* A price-taking firm cannot influence the market price by its actions. It always takes the market price as given because it cannot lower the market price by selling more or raise the market price by selling less. So, for a price-taking firm, the additional revenue generated by producing one more unit is always the market price. In upcoming Modules, we will discuss market structures in which firms are *not* price-takers, and we will see that for those firms the marginal revenue is *not* equal to the market price.

Figure 58.1 shows Jennifer and Jason's profit-maximizing quantity of output. The figure shows the marginal cost curve, *MC*, drawn from the data in the fourth column of Table 58.1. We plot the marginal cost of increasing output from 1 to 2 bushels halfway between 1 and 2, and likewise for each incremental change. The horizontal line at $18 is Jennifer and Jason's marginal revenue curve. Remember from Module 53 that whenever

The **price-taking firm's optimal output rule** says that a price-taking firm's profit is maximized by producing the quantity of output at which the market price is equal to the marginal cost of the last unit produced.

Figure 58.1 The Price-Taking Firm's Profit-Maximizing Quantity of Output

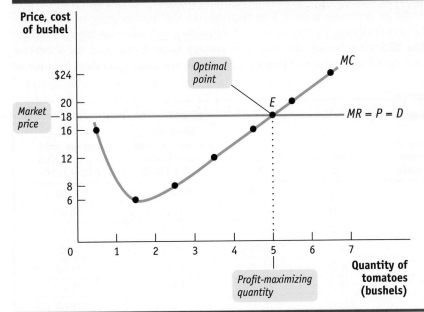

At the profit-maximizing quantity of output, the market price is equal to the marginal cost. It is located at the point where the marginal cost curve crosses the marginal revenue curve, which is a horizontal line at the market price and represents the firm's demand curve. Here, the profit-maximizing point is at an output of 5 bushels of tomatoes, the output quantity at point *E*.

a firm is a price-taker, its marginal revenue curve is a horizontal line at the market price: it can sell as much as it wants at the market price. Regardless of whether it sells more or less, the market price is unaffected. In effect, the individual firm faces a horizontal, perfectly elastic demand curve for its output—a demand curve that is equivalent to its marginal revenue curve. In fact, the horizontal line with the height of the market price represents the perfectly competitive firm's demand, marginal revenue, and *average revenue*—the average amount of revenue taken in per unit—because price equals average revenue whenever every unit is sold for the same price. The marginal cost curve crosses the marginal revenue curve at point E. Sure enough, the quantity of output at E is 5 bushels.

Does this mean that the price-taking firm's production decision can be entirely summed up as "produce up to the point where the marginal cost of production is equal to the price"? No, not quite. Before applying the principle of marginal analysis to determine how much to produce, a potential producer must answer a "yes–no" question: should it produce at all? If the answer is yes, the firm proceeds to the "how much" decision: maximizing profit by choosing the quantity of output at which the marginal cost is equal to the price.

To understand why the first step in the production decision involves this "yes–no" question, we need to ask how we determine whether it is profitable or unprofitable to produce at all. In the next Module we'll see that unprofitable firms shut down in the long run but tolerate losses in the short run up to a certain point.

When Is Production Profitable?

Remember from Module 52 that firms make their production decisions with the goal of maximizing *economic profit*—a measure based on the opportunity cost of resources used by the firm. In the calculation of economic profit, a firm's total cost incorporates the implicit cost—the benefits forgone in the next best use of the firm's resources—as well as the explicit cost in the form of actual cash outlays. In contrast, *accounting profit* is profit calculated using only the explicit costs incurred by the firm. This means that economic profit incorporates all of the opportunity cost of resources such as capital that is owned by the firm and used in the production of output, while accounting profit does not. A firm may make positive accounting profit while making zero or even negative economic profit. It's important to understand that a firm's decisions of how much to produce and whether or not to stay in business should be based on economic profit, not accounting profit.

So we will assume, as usual, that the cost numbers given in Table 58.1 include all costs, implicit as well as explicit. What determines whether Jennifer and Jason's farm earns a profit or generates a loss? This depends on the market price of tomatoes—specifically, *whether the market price is more or less than the farm's minimum average total cost*.

In **Table 58.2** we calculate the short-run average variable cost and the short-run average total cost for Jennifer and Jason's farm. These are short-run values because we

Table 58.2	Short-Run Average Costs for Jennifer and Jason's Farm			
Quantity of tomatoes Q (bushels)	Variable cost VC	Total cost TC	Short-run average variable cost of bushel AVC = VC/Q	Short-run average total cost of bushel ATC = TC/Q
1	$16.00	$30.00	$16.00	$30.00
2	22.00	36.00	11.00	18.00
3	30.00	44.00	10.00	14.67
4	42.00	56.00	10.50	14.00
5	58.00	72.00	11.60	14.40
6	78.00	92.00	13.00	15.33
7	102.00	116.00	14.57	16.57

take the fixed cost as given. (We'll turn to the effects of changing fixed cost shortly.) The short-run average total cost curve, ATC, is shown in **Figure 58.2**, along with the marginal cost curve, MC, from Figure 58.1. As you can see, average total cost is minimized at point C, corresponding to an output of 4 bushels—the *minimum-cost output*—and an average total cost of $14 per bushel.

Figure 58.2 Costs and Production in the Short Run

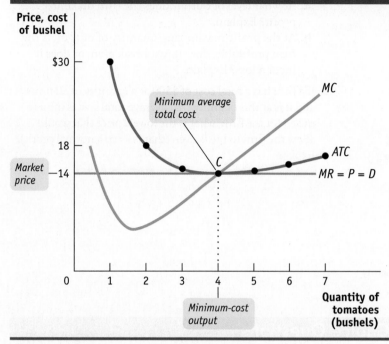

This figure shows the marginal cost curve, MC, and the short-run average total cost curve, ATC. When the market price is $14, output will be 4 bushels of tomatoes (the minimum-cost output), represented by point C. The price of $14 is equal to the firm's minimum average total cost, so at this price the firm breaks even.

To see how these curves can be used to decide whether production is profitable or unprofitable, recall that profit is equal to total revenue minus total cost, $TR - TC$. This means:

- If the firm produces a quantity at which $TR > TC$, the firm is profitable.
- If the firm produces a quantity at which $TR = TC$, the firm breaks even.
- If the firm produces a quantity at which $TR < TC$, the firm incurs a loss.

We can also express this idea in terms of revenue and cost per unit of output. If we divide profit by the number of units of output, Q, we obtain the following equation for profit per unit of output:

$$(58\text{-}1) \quad \text{Profit}/Q = TR/Q - TC/Q$$

TR/Q is average revenue, which is the market price (P). TC/Q is average total cost. So a firm is profitable if the market price for its product is more than the average total cost of the quantity the firm produces; a firm experiences a loss if the market price is less than the average total cost of the quantity the firm produces. This means:

- If the firm produces a quantity at which $P > ATC$, the firm is profitable.
- If the firm produces a quantity at which $P = ATC$, the firm breaks even.
- If the firm produces a quantity at which $P < ATC$, the firm incurs a loss.

In summary, in the short run a firm will maximize profit by producing the quantity of output at which $MC = MR$. A perfectly competitive firm is a price-taker, so it can sell as many units of output as it would like at the market price. This means that for a perfectly competitive firm it is always true that $MR = P$. The firm is profitable, or breaks even, as long as the market price is greater than, or equal to, the average total cost. In the next Module, we develop the perfect competition model using graphs to analyze the firm's level of profit.

Check Your Understanding

1. Refer to the graph provided.

a. At what level of output does the firm maximize profit? Explain.
b. At the profit-maximizing quantity of output, is the firm profitable, does it just break even, or does it incur a loss? Explain.

2. If a firm has a total cost of $500 at a quantity of 50 units, and it is at this quantity that average total cost is minimized for the firm, what is the lowest price that would allow the firm to break even (that is, earn a normal profit)? Explain.

TACKLE THE AP® TEST: Multiple-Choice Questions

1. A perfectly competitive firm will maximize profit at the quantity at which the firm's marginal revenue equals
   a. price.
   b. average revenue.
   c. total cost.
   d. marginal cost.
   e. demand.

2. Which of the following is true for a perfectly competitive firm?
   a. The market demand curve is horizontal.
   b. The firm can increase its profit by charging a higher price than other firms.
   c. The firm charges a price that exceeds the marginal revenue.
   d. The firm's marginal revenue curve is also its demand curve.
   e. To maximize profit, the firm sets its price above its marginal cost.

3. A firm is profitable if
   a. $TR < TC$.
   b. $AR < ATC$.
   c. $MC < ATC$.
   d. $ATC < P$.
   e. $ATC > MC$.

4. If a firm has a total cost of $200, its profit-maximizing level of output is 10 units, and it is breaking even (that is, earning a normal profit), what is the market price?
   a. $200
   b. $100
   c. $20
   d. $10
   e. $2

5. What is the firm's profit if the price of its product is $5 and it produces 500 units of output at a total cost of $1,000?
   a. $5,000
   b. $2,500
   c. $1,500
   d. −$1,500
   e. −$2,500

6. A price-taking firm should produce up to the point where the price equals the marginal cost if
   a. the firm produces at all.
   b. the price is below the average total cost, and up to where the price equals the average total cost otherwise.
   c. the firm has no fixed costs, but not otherwise.
   d. it seeks to maximize revenue rather than profit.
   e. it produces a service but not if it produces a good.

7. If a firm produces a quantity at which $P = ATC$, it will certainly
   a. incur a loss.
   b. break even.
   c. have a downward-sloping demand curve.
   d. maximize its profit.
   e. earn a profit, but it may or may not maximize its profit.

TACKLE THE AP® TEST: Free-Response Questions

1. Draw a correctly labeled graph showing a profit-maximizing perfectly competitive firm producing at its minimum average total cost.

Rubric for FRQ 1 (6 points)

1 point: Vertical axis and horizontal axis labels are correct ("Price, cost of unit" on vertical axis; "Quantity" on horizontal axis).

1 point: The line representing demand, marginal revenue, and price is horizontal and correctly labeled.

1 point: Marginal cost is "swoosh" shaped (upward-sloping) and correctly labeled.

1 point: Average total cost is U-shaped and correctly labeled.

1 point: Quantity is found where *MC* = *MR*.

1 point: Average total cost reaches its minimum point at the profit-maximizing level of output.

2. Refer to the table provided. Price is equal to $14.
   a. Calculate the firm's marginal cost at each quantity.
   b. Determine the firm's profit-maximizing level of output.
   c. Calculate the firm's profit at the profit-maximizing level of output. **(3 points)**

Short-Run Costs for Jennifer and Jason's Farm

Quantity of tomatoes (bushels)	Variable cost	Total cost
0	$0	$14
1	16	30
2	22	36
3	30	44
4	42	56
5	58	72
6	78	92
7	102	116

Graphing Perfect Competition

MOD 59

In this Module, you will learn to:
- Evaluate a perfectly competitive firm's situation using a graph
- Determine a perfectly competitive firm's profit or loss
- Explain how a firm decides whether to produce or shut down

We have just learned that for a perfectly competitive firm, a comparison of the market price to the firm's average total cost determines whether the firm is earning a profit, taking a loss, or breaking even with a normal profit of zero. Now we can evaluate the profitability of perfectly competitive firms in a variety of situations.

Interpreting Perfect Competition Graphs

Figure 59.1 illustrates how the market price determines whether a firm is profitable. It also shows how profit is depicted graphically. Each panel shows the marginal cost curve, *MC*, and the short-run average total cost curve, *ATC*. Average total cost is

Figure 59.1   Profitability and the Market Price

In panel (a) the market price is $18. The farm is profitable because the market price exceeds the minimum average total cost of $14. The farm's optimal output choice of 5 bushels is determined by the intersection of the price line and the marginal cost curve at point E. The average total cost of producing 5 bushels is $14.40, as shown by the height of the ATC curve at point Z. The vertical distance between point E and point Z indicates the farm's per-unit profit, $18.00 − $14.40 = $3.60. Total profit is given by the area of the shaded rectangle, $5 \times $3.60 = 18.00. In panel (b) the market price is $10; the farm is unprofitable because the price falls below the minimum average total cost of $14. If it continues to produce, the farm's optimal output choice is determined by point A, 3 bushels. The vertical distance between point A and point Y indicates the farm's per-unit loss, $14.67 − $10.00 = $4.67. The shaded rectangle represents the farm's total loss, $3 \times $4.67 = 14.00 (adjusted for rounding error).

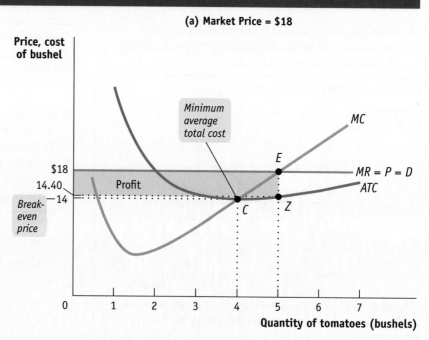

(a) Market Price = $18

(b) Market Price = $10

minimized at point C. Panel (a) shows the case in which the market price of tomatoes is $18 per bushel. Panel (b) shows the case in which the market price of tomatoes is lower, $10 per bushel.

In panel (a), we see that at a price of $18 per bushel the profit-maximizing quantity of output is 5 bushels, indicated by point E, where the marginal cost curve, MC, intersects the marginal revenue curve, MR—which for a price-taking firm is a horizontal line at the market price. At that quantity of output, average total cost is $14.40 per bushel, indicated by point Z. Since the price per bushel exceeds the average total cost per bushel, Jennifer and Jason's farm is profitable.

Jennifer and Jason's total profit when the market price is $18 is represented by the area of the shaded rectangle in panel (a). To see why, notice that total profit can be expressed in terms of profit per unit:

(59-1) $\text{Profit} = TR - TC = (TR/Q - TC/Q) \times Q$

or, equivalently, because market price, P, is equal to TR/Q and ATC is equal to TC/Q,

(59-2) $\text{Profit} = (P - ATC) \times Q$

The height of the shaded rectangle in panel (a) corresponds to the vertical distance between points E and Z. It is equal to $P - ATC = \$18.00 - \$14.40 = \$3.60$ per bushel. The shaded rectangle has a width equal to the output: $Q = 5$ bushels. So the area of the rectangle is equal to Jennifer and Jason's profit: 5 bushels $\times$ $3.60 profit per bushel = $18.

Panel (b) illustrates the very different outlook for the farm with a relatively low market price of $10 per bushel. In some cases the price is so low that a firm should simply shut down; we'll see how firms make that determination later in this Module. When the best a firm can do is produce at a loss, the price-taking firm's optimal output rule—produce until the price equals the marginal cost—will minimize that loss. So if Jennifer and Jason produce at all, they should produce until the price equals the marginal cost at point A, which corresponds to a quantity of 3 bushels. At that output level, Jennifer and Jason have an average total cost of $14.67 per bushel, indicated by point Y. The average total cost of producing 3 bushels exceeds the $10 market price, giving Jennifer and Jason's farm a loss, but the smallest loss possible.

How much do they lose by producing when the market price is $10? On average they lose $ATC - P = \$14.67 - \$10.00 = \$4.67$ per bushel, an amount corresponding to the vertical distance between points A and Y. Because they produce 3 bushels, the total value of the losses is $4.67 \times 3 = \$14.00$ (adjusted for rounding error), an amount represented by the area of the shaded rectangle in panel (b).

How does a producer know whether or not its business will be profitable? It turns out that the crucial test lies in a comparison of the market price to the firm's *minimum average total cost*. On Jennifer and Jason's farm, the average total cost reaches its minimum of $14 at an output of 4 bushels, indicated by point C. Whenever the market price exceeds the minimum average total cost, there are output levels for which the average total cost is less than the market price. In other words, the producer can find a level of output at which the firm makes a profit. So Jennifer and Jason's farm will be profitable whenever the market price exceeds $14. And they will achieve the highest possible profit by producing the quantity at which marginal cost equals price.

Conversely, if the market price is less than the minimum average total cost, there is no output level at which the price exceeds the average total cost. As a result, the firm will be unprofitable at any quantity of output. As we saw, at a price of $10—an amount less than the minimum average total cost—Jennifer and Jason did indeed lose money. By producing the quantity at which marginal cost equaled price, Jennifer and Jason did the best they could, but the best they could do was a loss of $14. Any other quantity would have increased the size of their loss.

The minimum average total cost of a price-taking firm is called its **break-even price**, the price at which it earns zero economic profit (also known as a *normal profit*). A firm will earn positive profit when the market price is above the break-even price, and it will suffer losses when the market price is below the break-even price. Jennifer and Jason's break-even price of $14 is the price at point C in Figure 59.1.

So whether a firm is profitable depends on a comparison of the market price of the good to the firm's break-even price—its minimum average total cost:

- When the market price exceeds the minimum average total cost, the firm is profitable.
- When the market price equals the minimum average total cost, the firm breaks even.
- When the market price is less than the minimum average total cost, the firm is unprofitable.

The **break-even price** of a price-taking firm is the market price at which it earns zero profit.

The Short-Run Production Decision

You might be tempted to say that if a firm is unprofitable because the market price is below its minimum average total cost, it shouldn't produce any output. In the short run, however, this conclusion isn't right. In the short run, sometimes the firm should produce even if price falls below minimum average total cost. The reason is that total cost includes *fixed cost*—cost that does not depend on the amount of output produced and can be altered only in the long run. In the short run, fixed cost must still be paid, regardless of whether or not a firm produces. For example, if Jennifer and Jason have rented a tractor for the year, they have to pay the rent on the tractor regardless of whether they produce any tomatoes. *Since it cannot be changed in the short run, their fixed cost is irrelevant to their decision about whether to produce or shut down in the short run.* Although fixed cost should play no role in the decision about whether to produce in the short run, another type of cost—variable cost—does matter. Part of the variable cost for Jennifer and Jason is the wage cost of workers who they must hire to help with planting and harvesting. Variable cost can be eliminated by *not* producing, which makes it a critical consideration when determining whether or not to produce in the short run.

Let's turn to **Figure 59.2**, which shows both the short-run average total cost curve, *ATC*, and the short-run average variable cost curve, *AVC*, drawn from the information in Table 58.2. Recall that the difference between the two curves—the vertical distance between them—represents average fixed cost, the fixed cost per unit of output, FC/Q. Because the marginal cost curve has a "swoosh" shape—falling at first before rising—the short-run average variable cost curve is U-shaped: the initial fall in marginal cost causes average variable cost to fall as well, and then the rise in marginal cost eventually pulls average variable cost up again. The short-run average variable cost curve reaches its minimum value of $10 at point *A*, at an output of 3 bushels.

Figure 59.2 The Short-Run Firm Supply Curve

When the market price equals or exceeds Jennifer and Jason's *shutdown price* of $10—the minimum average variable cost indicated by point *A*—they will produce the quantity at which the marginal cost equals the price. So at any price equal to or above the minimum average *variable* cost, the firm's short-run supply curve is its marginal cost curve. When the market price falls below the minimum average variable cost, the firm ceases operation in the short run. For the range of prices that causes the firm to shut down, the firm's supply curve lies along the vertical axis.

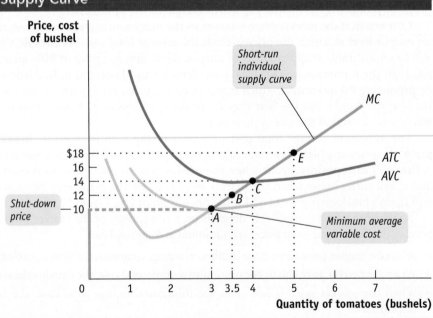

The Shut-Down Price

We are now prepared to analyze the optimal production decision in the short run. We have two cases to consider:

- When the market price is below the minimum average *variable* cost
- When the market price is greater than or equal to the minimum average *variable* cost

When the market price is below the minimum average variable cost, the price the firm receives per unit will not cover its variable cost per unit. A firm in this situation should cease production immediately. Why? Because there is no level of output at which the firm's total revenue covers its variable cost—the cost it can avoid by not operating. In this case the firm maximizes its profit by not producing at all—by, in effect, minimizing its loss. It will still incur a fixed cost in the short run, but it will no longer incur any variable cost. This means that the minimum average variable cost determines the **shut-down price**, the price at which the firm ceases production in the short run.

When the price is greater than the minimum average variable cost, however, the firm should produce in the short run. In this case, the firm maximizes profit—or minimizes loss—by choosing the output level at which its marginal cost is equal to the market price. For example, if the market price of tomatoes is $18 per bushel, Jennifer and Jason should produce at point *E* in Figure 59.2, corresponding to an output of 5 bushels. Note that point *C* in Figure 59.2 corresponds to the farm's break-even price of $14 per bushel. Since *E* lies above *C*, Jennifer and Jason's farm will be profitable; they will generate a per-bushel profit of $18.00 − $14.40 = $3.60 when the market price is $18.

What if the market price lies between the shut-down price and the break-even price—that is, between the minimum average *variable* cost and the minimum average *total* cost? This is the case for Jennifer and Jason's farm if the market price is between $10 and $14—say, $12. At $12, Jennifer and Jason's farm is not profitable; since the market price is below the minimum average total cost, the farm is losing (on average) the difference between the price and the average total cost on every unit produced. Yet even though the market price isn't covering Jennifer and Jason's average total cost, that price is covering their average variable cost and some—but not all—of their average fixed cost. If a firm in this situation shuts down, it will incur no variable cost but will incur the *full* fixed cost. As a result, shutting down will generate an even greater loss than continuing to operate.

Whenever the price falls between the minimum average total cost and the minimum average variable cost, the firm is better off producing some output in the short run. The reason is that by producing, it can cover its variable cost and at least some of its fixed cost, even though it is incurring a loss. In this case, the firm maximizes profit—that is, minimizes loss—by choosing the quantity of output at which its marginal cost is equal to the market price. So if Jennifer and Jason face a market price of $12 per bushel, their profit-maximizing output is given by point *B* in Figure 59.2, 3.5 bushels.

Note that the decision to produce when the firm is covering its variable cost but not all of its fixed cost is similar to the decision to ignore a *sunk cost*, a concept we studied in Module 56. You may recall that a sunk cost is a cost that has already been incurred and cannot be recouped; and because it cannot be changed, it should have no effect on any current decision. In the short-run production decision, fixed cost is effectively a sunk cost—the money has been spent (or in the case of rent, a contract requires it to be spent), and it can't be recovered. This comparison also illustrates why variable cost does indeed matter in the short run: it can be avoided by not producing.

What happens if the market price is exactly equal to the shut-down price, the minimum average variable cost? In this instance, the firm is indifferent between producing 3 units or 0 units. As we'll see shortly, this is an important point when looking at the behavior of an industry as a whole. For the sake of clarity, we'll assume that the firm, although indifferent, does indeed produce output when the market price is equal to the shut-down price.

A firm will cease production in the short run if the market price falls below the **shut-down price**, which is equal to the minimum average variable cost.

Putting everything together, we can now draw the **short-run firm supply curve** of Jennifer and Jason's farm, the red line in Figure 59.2; it shows how the profit-maximizing quantity of output in the short run depends on the price. As you can see, the curve is drawn in two segments. The upward-sloping red segment starting at point *A* shows the short-run profit-maximizing quantity when the market price is equal to or above the shut-down price of $10 per bushel. As long as the market price is equal to or above the shut-down price, Jennifer and Jason will produce the quantity of output at which the marginal cost is equal to the market price. So at market prices equal to or above the shut-down price, the firm's short-run supply curve corresponds to its marginal cost curve. But at any market price below the minimum average variable cost—in this case, $10 per bushel—the firm shuts down in the short run and output drops to zero. For that reason the firm's supply curve lies along the vertical axis for prices below the shut-down price.

Do firms sometimes shut down temporarily without going out of business? Yes. In fact, in some industries temporary shut-downs are routine. The most common examples are industries in which demand is highly seasonal, like outdoor amusement parks in climates with cold winters. Such parks would have to offer very low prices to entice customers during the colder months—prices so low that the owners would not cover their variable cost (principally wages and electricity). The wiser choice economically is to shut down until warm weather brings enough customers who are willing to pay a higher price.

Changing Fixed Cost

Although fixed cost cannot be altered in the short run, in the long run firms can acquire or get rid of machines, buildings, and so on. In the long run the level of fixed cost is a matter of choice, and a firm will choose the level of fixed cost that minimizes the average total cost for its desired output level. Now we will focus on an even bigger question facing a firm when choosing its fixed cost: whether to incur *any* fixed cost at all by continuing to operate.

In the long run, a firm can always eliminate its fixed cost by selling off its plant and equipment. If it does so, of course, it can't produce any output—it has exited the industry. In contrast, a new firm can take on some fixed cost by acquiring machines and other resources, which puts it in a position to produce—it can enter the industry. In most perfectly competitive industries the set of firms, although fixed in the short run, changes in the long run as some firms enter or exit the industry.

Consider Jennifer and Jason's farm once again. In order to simplify our analysis, we will sidestep the issue of choosing among several possible levels of fixed cost. Instead, we will assume that if they operate at all, Jennifer and Jason have only one possible choice of fixed cost: $14. Alternatively, they can choose a fixed cost of zero if they exit the industry. It is changes in fixed cost that cause short-run average total cost curves to differ from long-run total cost curves, so with this assumption, Jennifer and Jason's short-run and long-run average total cost curves are one and the same.

Suppose that the market price of organic tomatoes is consistently less than the break-even price of $14 over an extended period of time. In that case, Jennifer and Jason never fully cover their total cost: their business runs at a persistent loss. In the long run, then, they can do better by closing their business and leaving the industry. In other words, *in the long run* firms will exit an industry if the market price is consistently less than their break-even price—their minimum average total cost.

Conversely, suppose that the price of organic tomatoes is consistently above the break-even price of $14 for an extended period of time. Because their farm is profitable, Jennifer and Jason will remain in the industry and continue producing. But things won't stop there. The organic tomato industry meets the criterion of *free entry*: there are many potential organic tomato producers because the necessary inputs are easy to obtain. And the cost curves of those potential producers are likely to be similar to those of Jennifer and Jason, since the technology used by other producers is likely to be very similar to that used by Jennifer and Jason. If the price is high enough to generate profit for existing producers, it will also attract some of these potential producers into the industry. So *in the long run* a price in excess of $14 should lead to entry: new producers will come into the organic tomato industry.

As we will see shortly, exit and entry lead to an important distinction between the *short-run industry supply curve* and the *long-run industry supply curve*.

Summing Up: The Perfectly Competitive Firm's Profitability and Production Conditions

In this Module we've studied what's behind the supply curve for a perfectly competitive firm. A perfectly competitive firm is a price-taker and maximizes profit, or minimizes loss, by producing the quantity that equates price and marginal cost. The exception is if price is below minimum average variable cost in the short run, or below minimum average total cost in the long run, in which case the firm is better off shutting down. **Table 59.1** summarizes the perfectly competitive firm's profitability and production conditions. It also relates them to entry into and exit from the industry in the long run. Now that we understand how a perfectly competitive *firm* makes its decisions, we can go on to look at the supply curve for a perfectly competitive *market* and the long-run equilibrium in perfect competition.

Table 59.1 Summary of the Perfectly Competitive Firm's Profitability and Production Conditions	
Profitability condition (minimum *ATC* = break-even price)	**Result**
$P >$ minimum *ATC*	Firm profitable. Additional firms enter the industry in the long run.
$P =$ minimum *ATC*	Firm breaks even. No incentive for any firm to enter or exit the industry in the long run.
$P <$ minimum *ATC*	Firm unprofitable. The firm and other firms in the industry exit in the long run.
Production condition (minimum *AVC* = shut-down price)	**Result**
$P >$ minimum *AVC*	Firm produces in the short run. If $P <$ minimum *ATC*, firm covers variable cost and some but not all of fixed cost. If $P >$ minimum *ATC*, firm covers all variable cost and fixed cost.
$P =$ minimum *AVC*	Firm indifferent between producing in the short run or not. Just covers variable cost.
$P <$ minimum *AVC*	Firm shuts down in the short run. Does not cover variable cost.

Check Your Understanding

1. Draw a short-run diagram showing a U-shaped average total cost curve, a U-shaped average variable cost curve, and a "swoosh"-shaped marginal cost curve. On your diagram, indicate the range of prices for which the following actions are optimal.
   a. The firm shuts down immediately.
   b. The firm operates in the short run despite sustaining a loss.
   c. The firm operates while making a profit.

2. The state of Maine has a very active lobster industry, which harvests lobsters during the summer months. During the rest of the year, restaurants can obtain lobsters from producers in other parts of the world, but at a much higher price. Maine is also full of "lobster shacks," roadside restaurants serving lobster dishes that are open only during the summer. Supposing that the market demand for lobster dishes remains the same throughout the year, explain why it is optimal for lobster shacks to operate only during the summer.

TACKLE THE AP® TEST: Multiple-Choice Questions

For Questions 1–3, refer to the graph provided, and assume that the firm produces the profit-maximizing quantity.

Market Price = $20

1. The firm's total revenue is equal to
   a. $14.   d. $750.
   b. $20.   e. $1,000.
   c. $560.

2. The firm's total cost is equal to
   a. $14.   d. $750.
   b. $15.   e. $1,000.
   c. $560.

3. The firm is earning a
   a. profit equal to $5.   d. loss equal to $750.
   b. profit equal to $250.   e. loss equal to $250.
   c. loss equal to $15.

4. A firm should continue to produce in the short run as long as the price is at least equal to the
   a. *MR*.
   b. *MC*.
   c. minimum *ATC*.
   d. minimum *AVC*.
   e. *AFC*.

5. At prices that motivate the firm to produce at all, the short-run supply curve for a perfect competitor corresponds to which curve?
   a. the *ATC* curve
   b. the *AVC* curve
   c. the *MC* curve
   d. the *AFC* curve
   e. the *MR* curve

6. If a perfectly competitive firm decides to operate at a loss in the short run, it will minimize that loss by producing the quantity at which
   a. the *ATC* is minimized.
   b. the *AVC* is minimized.
   c. the *MC* equals the price.
   d. the *ATC* equals the price.
   e. the *AVC* equals the price.

7. If the price is between the *AVC* and the *ATC*, by producing, the firm will certainly cover
   a. neither its fixed cost nor its variable cost.
   b. all of its fixed cost but only some of its variable cost.
   c. all of its variable cost but only some of its fixed cost.
   d. both its fixed cost and its variable cost.
   e. its total cost and its economic profit.

TACKLE THE AP® TEST: Free-Response Questions

1. Draw a correctly labeled graph showing a perfectly competitive firm operating at a price that would lead it to stay open in the short run but shut down in the long run. Label the loss-minimizing quantity Q* and shade the area that represents the firm's loss.

Rubric for FRQ 1 (10 points)

1 point: Vertical axis is labeled "Price, cost of unit" or "Dollars per unit"; horizontal axis is labeled "Quantity" or "Q."

1 point: Demand curve is horizontal and labeled with some combination of "P," "MR," or "D."

1 point: MC is labeled and slopes upward in the shape of a swoosh.

1 point: Loss-minimizing quantity is labeled Q* on the horizontal axis where MC = MR.

1 point: ATC is labeled and U-shaped.

1 point: ATC is above price at the profit-maximizing output.

1 point: MC crosses ATC at the lowest point on ATC.

1 point: AVC is labeled and U-shaped.

1 point: AVC is below price at the profit-maximizing output.

1 point: Loss rectangle is correctly located and identified.

2. Refer to the graph provided.

a. Assuming it is appropriate for the firm to produce in the short run, what is the firm's profit-maximizing level of output?

b. Calculate the firm's total revenue.

c. Calculate the firm's total cost.

d. Calculate the firm's profit or loss.

e. If AVC were $22 at the profit-maximizing level of output, would the firm produce in the short run? Explain why or why not. **(5 points)**

Long-Run Outcomes in Perfect Competition

> **In this Module, you will learn to:**
> • Explain why industries behave differently in the short run than in the long run
> • Discuss what determines the industry supply curve in both the short run and the long run

Up to this point we have been discussing the perfectly competitive firm's short-run situation—whether to produce or not, and if so, whether the firm earns a positive profit, breaks even with a normal profit, or takes a loss. In this Module, we look at the long-run situation in a perfectly competitive market. We will see that perfect competition leads to some interesting and desirable market outcomes. Later, we will contrast these outcomes with the outcomes in imperfectly competitive markets.

The Industry Supply Curve

The **industry supply curve** (or market supply curve) shows the relationship between the price of a good and the total output of the industry as a whole.

Why will an increase in the demand for organic tomatoes lead to a large price increase at first, but a much smaller increase in the long run? The answer lies in the behavior of the **industry supply curve**, which represents the relationship between the price of a good and the total output of the industry as a whole. The industry supply curve is what we referred to in earlier modules as the supply curve or the market supply curve. But here we take some extra care to distinguish between the supply curve of an *individual firm* and the supply curve of the *industry as a whole*.

As you might guess from the previous Module, the industry supply curve must be analyzed in somewhat different ways for the short run and the long run. Let's start with the short run.

The Short-Run Industry Supply Curve

The **short-run industry supply curve** shows how the quantity supplied by an industry depends on the market price, given a fixed number of firms.

Recall that in the short run the number of firms in an industry is fixed. You may also remember that the industry supply curve is the horizontal sum of all of the individual firms' supply curves—you find it by summing the total output across all suppliers at every given price. We will do that exercise here under the assumption that all the firms are alike—an assumption that makes the derivation particularly simple. So let's assume that there are 100 organic tomato farms, each with the same fixed and variable costs as Jennifer and Jason's farm. Each of these 100 farms will have a short-run supply curve like the one in Figure 59.2 from the previous Module, which is reprinted here for your convenience.

At a price below $10, no farms will produce. At a price of more than $10, each farm will produce the quantity of output at which its marginal cost is equal to the market price. As you can see from Figure 59.2, this will lead each farm to produce 4 bushels if the price is $14 per bushel, 5 bushels if the price is $18, and so on. So if there are 100 organic tomato farms and the price of organic tomatoes is $18 per bushel, the industry as a whole will produce 500 bushels, corresponding to 100 farms × 5 bushels per farm. The result is the **short-run industry supply curve**, shown as S in **Figure 60.1**. This curve shows the quantity that producers in an industry will supply at each price, *taking the number of farms as given*.

The demand curve, labeled D in Figure 60.1, crosses the short-run industry supply curve at E_{MKT}, corresponding to a price of $18 and a quantity of 500 bushels. Point E_{MKT} is a *short-run market equilibrium*: the quantity supplied equals the quantity demanded, taking the number of farms as given. But the long run may look quite different because in the long run farms may enter or exit the industry.

Figure 59.2 The Short-Run Firm Supply Curve

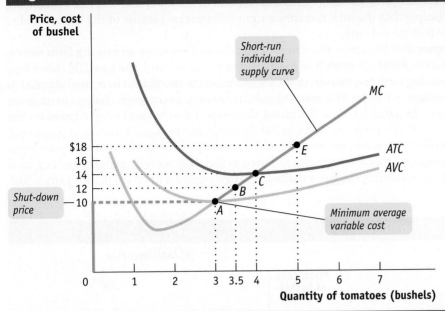

This figure from Module 59 is included here as a reminder of how each firm's short-run supply curve gets its shape. At any price equal to or above the minimum average *variable* cost, the firm's short-run supply curve is its marginal cost curve. When the market price falls below the minimum average variable cost, the firm ceases operation in the short run.

Figure 60.1 The Short-Run Market Equilibrium

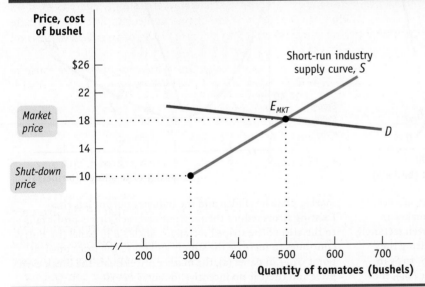

The short-run industry supply curve, S, is found by adding together the short-run firm supply curves of the 100 producers. Below the shut-down price of $10, no firm wants to produce in the short run. Above $10, the short-run industry supply curve slopes upward, as each firm increases output in response to higher prices. It intersects the demand curve, D, at point E_{MKT}, the point of short-run market equilibrium, corresponding to a market price of $18 and a quantity of 500 bushels.

The Long-Run Industry Supply Curve

Suppose that in addition to the 100 farms currently in the organic tomato business, there are many other potential organic tomato farms. Suppose also that each of these potential farms would have the same cost curves as each of the existing farms, like the farm owned by Jennifer and Jason, upon entering the industry.

What will lead additional farms to enter the industry? The existence of profit for the existing farms—that is, if the market price is above the break-even price of $14 per bushel, the existing farms will earn profit and more farms will enter the industry. For example, at a price of $18 per bushel, new farms will enter the industry.

What will happen as additional farms enter the industry? Clearly, the quantity supplied at any given price will increase, which means that the short-run industry supply

Module 60 Long-Run Outcomes in Perfect Competition **581**

curve will shift to the right. This shift will alter the market equilibrium and result in a lower market price. Existing farms will respond to the lower market price by reducing their output, but the total industry output will increase because of the larger number of farms in the industry.

Figure 60.2 illustrates the effects of this chain of events on an existing farm and on the market. Panel (a) shows how the market responds to entry, and panel (b) shows how one existing farm responds to entry. (Note that these two graphs have been rescaled in comparison to Figures 59.2 and 60.1 to better illustrate how profit changes in response to price.) In panel (a), S_1 is the initial short-run industry supply curve based on the existence of 100 producers. The initial short-run market equilibrium is at E_{MKT}, with an equilibrium market price of $18 and a quantity of 500 bushels. At this price existing farms are profitable, which is reflected in panel (b): an existing farm makes a total profit represented by the green shaded rectangle labeled A when the market price is $18.

Figure 60.2 The Long-Run Market Equilibrium

Point E_{MKT} of panel (a) shows the initial short-run market equilibrium. Each of the 100 existing producers makes an economic profit, illustrated in panel (b) by the green rectangle labeled A. Profit induces more firms to enter, shifting the short-run industry supply curve outward from S_1 to S_2 in panel (a). At the new short-run equilibrium point F_{MKT}, the market price has fallen and the industry output has risen. Existing firms reduce their output and each firm's profit falls to the area of the striped rectangle labeled B in panel (b). Entry continues to increase the supply and lower the price until, at point G_{MKT} in panel (a), the market price equals the break-even price and there is no incentive for entry or exit.

This profit will induce new producers to enter the industry, shifting the short-run industry supply curve to the right. For example, when the number of farms has increased to 167, the short-run industry supply curve is S_2. With this supply curve, the short-run market equilibrium is F_{MKT} at a market price of $16 and a quantity of 750 bushels. For $16, each farm produces 4.5 bushels, so the industry output is $167 \times 4.5 = 750$ bushels (rounded). From panel (b) you can see how the entry of 67 new farms affects an existing farm: the lower price causes the existing farm to reduce its output, and its profit falls to the area represented by the striped rectangle labeled B.

Although diminished, the remaining profit of existing farms at F_{MKT} means that entry will continue and the number of farms will continue to rise. When the number of farms rises to 250, the short-run industry supply curve shifts out to S_3, and the market equilibrium is at G_{MKT}, with 1,000 bushels supplied and demanded and a market price of $14 per bushel.

Like E_{MKT} and F_{MKT}, G_{MKT} is a short-run equilibrium, but it is also something more. Because the price of $14 is each farm's break-even price, an existing producer makes zero economic profit—neither a profit nor a loss, earning only the opportunity cost of the resources used in production—when producing its profit-maximizing output of 4 bushels. At this price there is no incentive either for potential producers to enter or for existing producers to exit the industry. So G_{MKT} corresponds to a **long-run market equilibrium**—a situation in which the quantity supplied equals the quantity demanded, given that sufficient time has elapsed for producers to either enter or exit the industry. In a long-run market equilibrium, all existing and potential producers have fully adjusted to their optimal long-run choices; as a result, no producer has an incentive to either enter or exit the industry.

For a better understanding of the difference between short-run and long-run equilibrium, consider the effect of an increase in demand on an industry with free entry that is initially in long-run equilibrium. Panel (b) in **Figure 60.3** shows how the market adjusts; panels (a) and (c) show how a representative existing firm behaves during the process.

A market is in **long-run market equilibrium** when the quantity supplied equals the quantity demanded, given that sufficient time has elapsed for entry into and exit from the industry to occur.

> ### AP® EXAM TIP
>
> When you are asked to draw side-by-side graphs for a representative firm and for the market in a perfectly competitive industry, draw dotted lines taking the equilibrium price from the market graph over to the firm graph to show your understanding that the firm is a price-taker.

Figure 60.3 The Effect of an Increase in Demand in the Short Run and the Long Run for a Constant-Cost Industry

An existing firm makes zero economic profit, operating at point X in panel (a) at the minimum of average total cost. Demand increases as D_1 shifts rightward to D_2, in panel (b), raising the market price from $14 to $18. Existing firms increase their output, and industry output moves along the short-run industry supply curve S_1 to a short-run equilibrium at point Y_{MKT}. Correspondingly, the existing firm in panel (a) moves from point X to point Y as its demand rises from D_{F1} to D_{F2}. But at a price of $18, existing firms are profitable. As shown in panel (b), in the long run new firms enter and the short-run industry supply curve shifts rightward. This continues until

the supply curve reaches S_2 and the new equilibrium point is Z_{MKT}. Like X_{MKT}, Z_{MKT} is a both a short-run and a long-run equilibrium point because the existing firms earn zero economic profit and there is no incentive for any firms to enter or exit the industry. Panel (c) shows how an existing firm responds to the decrease in its demand to D_{F3} by moving from point Y to point Z, returning to its initial output level and zero economic profit. The horizontal *long-run industry supply curve* passing through points X_{MKT} and Z_{MKT}, *LRS*, indicates that in the long run, firms will produce any amount that consumers demand at the break-even price of $14.

In panel (b) of Figure 60.3, D_1 is the initial demand curve and S_1 is the initial short-run industry supply curve. Their intersection at point X_{MKT} is both a short-run and a long-run market equilibrium because the equilibrium price of \$14 leads to zero economic profit—and therefore neither entry nor exit. Point X_{MKT} corresponds to point X in panel (a), where an existing firm is operating at the minimum of its average total cost curve.

Now suppose that the demand curve shifts out for some reason to D_2. As shown in panel (b), in the short run, industry output moves along the short-run industry supply curve, S_1, to the new short-run market equilibrium at point Y_{MKT}, the intersection of S_1 and D_2. The market price rises to \$18 per bushel, and industry output increases from Q_X to Q_Y. This corresponds to an existing firm's movement from point X to point Y in panel (a) as the firm increases its output in response to the rise in its demand curve (which also represents price and marginal revenue) from D_{F1} to D_{F2}.

But we know that point Y_{MKT} is not a long-run equilibrium because \$18 is higher than the minimum average total cost, so existing firms are making economic profit. This will lead additional firms to enter the industry. Over time entry will cause the short-run industry supply curve to shift to the right. In the long run, the short-run industry supply curve will have shifted out to S_2, and the equilibrium will be at point Z_{MKT}—with the price falling back to \$14 per bushel and industry output increasing yet again, from Q_Y to Q_Z. Like point X_{MKT} before the increase in demand, point Z_{MKT} is both a short-run and a long-run market equilibrium.

The effect of entry on an existing firm is illustrated in panel (c), in the movement from point Y to point Z along the firm's supply curve. The firm reduces its output in response to the fall in the market price, which lowers the firm's demand curve from D_{F2} to D_{F3}. The firm ultimately arrives back at its original output quantity, corresponding to the minimum of its average total cost curve. In fact, every firm that is now in the industry—the initial set of firms and the new entrants—will operate at the minimum of the firm's average total cost curve, at point Z. This means that the entire increase in industry output, from Q_X to Q_Z, comes from production by new entrants.

The line labeled LRS that passes through points X_{MKT} and Z_{MKT} in panel (b) is the **long-run industry supply curve**. It shows how the quantity supplied by an industry responds to the price, given that firms have had time to enter or exit the industry.

In this particular case, the long-run industry supply curve is horizontal at \$14. In other words, in this industry supply is *perfectly elastic* in the long run: given time to enter or exit, firms will supply any quantity that consumers demand at a price of \$14. Perfectly elastic long-run industry supply is characteristic of a **constant-cost industry**. In a constant-cost industry, the firms' cost curves are unaffected by changes in the size of the industry, either because there is a perfectly elastic supply of inputs, or because the industry's input demand is too small relative to the overall input market to influence the input price. For example, the wooden pencil industry can expand without causing a significant increase in the price of wood.

Increasing-Cost Industry

In an **increasing-cost industry**, even the long-run industry supply curve slopes upward. The usual reason for this is that producers must use a significant amount of an input that is in limited supply (that is, the input's supply is at least somewhat inelastic). As the industry expands, the price of that input is driven up. Consequently, the firms' production costs rise. An example is the cotton clothing industry, in which an expansion could drive up the price of cotton. **Figure 60.4** illustrates the short-run and long-run effects of an increase in demand in an increasing-cost industry. In panel (b), D_1 is the initial demand curve for cotton pants and S_1 is the initial short-run industry supply curve. The market equilibrium at point X_{MKT} corresponds to point X in panel (a), where an individual firm is operating at the minimum of its average total cost curve.

Now suppose that the demand curve shifts out to D_2. As shown in panel (b), in the short run, industry output expands along the short-run industry supply curve, S_1,

The **long-run industry supply curve** shows how the quantity supplied responds to the price once firms have had time to enter or exit the industry.

In a **constant-cost industry** the firms' cost curves are unaffected by changes in the size of the industry and the long-run industry supply curve is horizontal (perfectly elastic).

In an **increasing-cost industry** the firms' production costs increase with the size of the industry and the long-run industry supply curve is upward-sloping.

Figure 60.4 The Effect of an Increase in Demand in the Short Run and the Long Run in an Increasing-Cost Industry

In an increasing-cost industry, an increase in demand leads to a higher price both in the short run *and* in the long run. Suppose demand increases from D_1 to D_2 as shown in panel (b). This raises the market price to $42. Existing firms increase their output, and industry output expands along the short-run industry supply curve, S_1, to a short-run equilibrium at point Y_{MKT}. The increase in output from Q_X to Q_Y is the result of existing firms increasing their output as shown for a representative firm by the move from point X to point Y in panel (a). Because the new price is above the minimum average total cost, economic profit attracts new entrants in the long run, shifting the short-run industry supply curve rightward and lowering the market price. Meanwhile, industry expansion drives up the cost of inputs and shifts the firms' cost curves upward as shown in panel (c). This continues until the falling equilibrium price meets the rising minimum average total cost. As shown in panel (b), that occurs at equilibrium point Z_{MKT} with a price of $35. In the long run, an existing firm moves from point Y to point Z in panel (c) and earns zero economic profit. The upward-sloping line passing through points X_{MKT} and Z_{MKT}, labeled *LRS*, is the long-run industry supply curve.

to the new short-run market equilibrium at point Y_{MKT}, the intersection of S_1 and D_2. The market price rises from $30 to $42 per pair and the industry output increases from Q_X to Q_Y as a result of higher output levels at existing firms. This change is shown for a representative firm in panel (a) by a movement from point X to point Y in response to the increase in the firm's demand curve from D_{F1} to D_{F2}.

At the new market price, existing firms earn economic profit, so additional firms enter the industry in the long run. Entry shifts the short-run industry supply curve to the right and lowers the price of pants. At the same time, increasing demand for cotton drives up the cost of this input. The resulting rise in input costs shifts the marginal and average total cost curves upward for firms. This process continues until the falling market price and the rising minimum average total cost meet somewhere in between the initial price of $30 and the short-run price of $42. In Figure 60.4, they meet at a price of $35, after the short-run supply curve has shifted out to S_2 and the cost of making each pair of pants has risen by $5.

When the market reaches long-run equilibrium at point Z_{MKT}, each firm faces a demand curve of D_{F3} as shown in panel (c). Firms earn zero economic profit and there is no incentive for additional entry. Assuming that the cost increase is the same for each unit of output, each of the original firms ends up making the same quantity of output as it did before the increase in demand. If the cost increase is not the same for each unit of output, the cost curves will not shift straight up as they did here, so the new profit-maximizing quantity of output could be more or less than before. For this increasing-cost industry, the long-run industry supply curve *LRS* slopes upward as it passes through points X_{MKT} and Z_{MKT} in panel (b).

An expansion in the cotton clothing industry drives up the price of cotton.

A decrease in demand triggers the same process in reverse: the lower market price causes losses and, in the long run, the exit of firms. As firms exit, the market price rises. At the same time, the contraction of the industry lowers the cost of inputs and shifts the cost curves down until the falling minimum average total cost meets the rising market price.

Finally, it is possible for the long-run industry supply curve to slope downward, a condition that occurs when firms' production costs fall as the industry expands. This is the case in industries such as the electric car industry, in which increased output allows for economies of scale in the production of lithium batteries and other specialized inputs, and thus lower input prices.

Decreasing-Cost Industry

A downward-sloping industry supply curve indicates a **decreasing-cost industry**. **Figure 60.5** illustrates the short-run and long-run effects of an increase in demand in a decreasing-cost industry. In panel (b), D_1 is the initial demand curve for electric cars, S_1 is the initial short-run industry supply curve, and point X_{MKT} is the initial market equilibrium. If the demand curve shifts out to D_2, the new short-run market equilibrium is point Y_{MKT}. The market price rises from \$40,000 to \$49,000 per electric car, and industry output increases from Q_X to Q_Y. This corresponds to an existing firm's movement from point X to point Y in panel (a), caused by the increase in its demand curve from D_{F1} to D_{F2}.

Figure 60.5 The Effect of an Increase in Demand in the Short Run and the Long Run in a Decreasing-Cost Industry

In a decreasing-cost industry, an increase in demand leads to a higher price in the short run and a lower price in the long run. Suppose demand increases from D_1 to D_2 as shown in panel (b). Existing firms increase their output in response to the higher price, and industry output expands along the short-run industry supply curve, S_1, to a short-run equilibrium at point Y_{MKT}. Economic profit attracts new entrants in the long run, shifting the short-run industry supply curve rightward and lowering the market price. Meanwhile, industry expansion lowers the cost of inputs and shifts the firms' cost curves downward as shown in panel (c). This continues until the falling equilibrium price catches up to the falling minimum average total cost. As shown in panel (b), that occurs at equilibrium point Z_{MKT}. In the long run, an existing firm moves from Y to Z in panel (c) and earns zero economic profit. The downward-sloping line passing through points X_{MKT} and Z_{MKT}, labeled LRS, is the long-run industry supply curve.

At the new market price, economic profit attracts additional firms. Entry shifts the short-run industry supply curve to the right and lowers the price of electric cars. At the same time, increasing demand for lithium batteries allows for economies of scale in battery production and lowers the cost of this input. The resulting decrease in input costs shifts the marginal and average total cost curves downward for firms. This process continues until the falling market price catches up to the falling minimum average total cost somewhere below the initial price of $40,000. In Figure 60.5, that occurs at a price of $36,000, after the short-run supply curve has shifted out to S_2 in panel (b).

At the long-run equilibrium point Z_{MKT}, each firm faces a demand curve of D_{F3} as shown in panel (c). Firms earn zero economic profit and there is no incentive for additional entry. Assuming that the cost decrease is the same for each car produced, each firm ends up making the same quantity of cars as it did before the increase in demand. For a decreasing-cost industry, the long-run industry supply curve LRS slopes downward as it passes through points X_{MKT} and Z_{MKT} in panel (b).

Regardless of whether the long-run industry supply curve is horizontal, upward-sloping, or downward-sloping, the long-run price elasticity of supply is *higher* than the short-run price elasticity whenever there is free entry and exit. As shown in **Figure 60.6**, the long-run industry supply curve is always flatter than the short-run industry supply curve. The reason is entry and exit: a price increase caused by an increase in demand attracts new firms, resulting in a rise in industry output and an eventual fall in price; a price drop caused by a decrease in demand causes some firms to exit, leading to a fall in industry output and an eventual increase in price.

Figure 60.6 Comparing the Short-Run and Long-Run Industry Supply Curves

As a result of the entry and exit of firms in the long run, the long-run industry supply curve is always flatter—more elastic—than the short-run industry supply curve.

Efficiency in Long-Run Equilibrium

Our analysis leads us to three conclusions about efficiency in the long-run equilibrium of a perfectly competitive industry. These results will be important in our upcoming discussion of how monopoly gives rise to inefficiency.

First, when a perfectly competitive industry is in equilibrium, all firms produce the quantity of output that equates the marginal cost and the market price. This $P = MC$ outcome leads to allocative efficiency, meaning that it yields the mix of goods and services that society most values, as discussed in Module 3. This efficiency comes from the production of more of the good until the price consumers are willing to pay—an indication of the marginal benefit received from the good—equals the marginal cost of making it. After that point, the marginal cost exceeds the marginal benefit, so additional units should not be made.

Second, in a perfectly competitive industry with free entry and exit, each firm will earn zero economic profit in the long-run equilibrium. Each firm produces the quantity of output that minimizes its average total cost—corresponding to point Z in panel (c) of Figures 60.3, 60.4, and 60.5. As a result, a perfectly competitive industry achieves productive efficiency because the total cost of producing the industry's output is minimized.

Third, in the long-run market equilibrium of a perfectly competitive industry, the consumers who are willing to pay an amount greater than or equal to the sellers' marginal cost actually get the good. No mutually beneficial transactions go unexploited because the market price matches the consumers who are willing to pay the most for the good with the sellers who have a cost of production that is less than or equal to the market price.

So the long-run equilibrium of a perfectly competitive industry delivers efficiency. There is allocative efficiency because $P = MC$; there is productive efficiency because costs are minimized and no resources are wasted; and the goods are distributed to those who are willing to pay the most for them. Moreover, these conditions tend to persist over time as the situation changes: the force of competition makes producers responsive to changes in consumers' desires and to changes in technology.

MODULE 60 REVIEW

Check Your Understanding

1. Which of the following events will induce firms to enter an industry? Which will induce firms to exit? When will entry or exit cease? Explain your answers.
   a. A technological advance lowers the fixed cost of production of every firm in the industry.
   b. The wages paid to workers in the industry rise for an extended period of time.
   c. A permanent change in consumer tastes increases demand for the good.
   d. The price of a key input rises due to a long-term shortage of that input.

2. Assume that the egg industry is perfectly competitive and is in long-run equilibrium with a perfectly elastic long-run industry supply curve. Health concerns about cholesterol then lead to a decrease in demand. Construct a figure similar to Figure 60.3, showing the short-run behavior of the industry and how long-run equilibrium is reestablished.

TACKLE THE AP® TEST: Multiple-Choice Questions

1. In the long run, a perfectly competitive firm will earn
   a. a negative market return.
   b. a positive profit.
   c. a loss.
   d. a normal profit.
   e. excess profit.

2. With perfect competition, productive efficiency is generally attained in
   a. the short run but not the long run.
   b. the long run but not the short run.
   c. both the short run and the long run.
   d. neither the short run nor the long run.
   e. specific firms only.

3. Compared to the short-run industry supply curve, the long-run industry supply curve will be more
   a. elastic.   d. profitable.
   b. inelastic.   e. accurate.
   c. steeply sloped.

4. Which of the following is generally true in a perfectly competitive industry?
   a. A firm's supply curve lies above its marginal cost curve.
   b. Firms have fixed costs in the long run.
   c. The short-run market equilibrium is efficient if firms earn a positive profit.
   d. Firms face barriers to entry into the industry.
   e. Firms maximize profit at the output level at which $P = MC$.

5. What will happen in a perfectly competitive industry in response to firms earning a positive economic profit?
   a. Firms will exit the industry.
   b. The short-run industry supply curve will shift right.
   c. The short-run industry supply curve will shift left.
   d. Firm output will increase.
   e. Market price will increase.

6. In a perfectly competitive, decreasing-cost industry, the long-run industry supply curve is
   a. vertical.
   b. upward-sloping.
   c. horizontal.

   d. downward-sloping.
   e. upward-sloping at low quantities and downward-sloping at high quantities.

7. In a perfectly competitive, constant-cost industry, an increase in demand leads to which of the following in the long run?
   a. an increase in price
   b. an increase in the output of firms that were operating when the demand increased
   c. a decrease in industry output
   d. an increase in industry output
   e. positive profit for firms

TACKLE THE AP® TEST: Free-Response Questions

1. Draw a correctly labeled graph showing a perfectly competitive firm in long-run equilibrium.

Rubric for FRQ 1 (7 points)

1 point: Axes are correctly labeled.

1 point: Demand curve is horizontal and labeled with some combination of "P," "MR," or "D."

1 point: Marginal cost curve is labeled and slopes upward.

1 point: Profit-maximizing quantity is labeled on horizontal axis where $MC = MR$.

1 point: Average total cost curve is labeled and U-shaped.

1 point: Average total cost is equal to price at the profit-maximizing output.

1 point: Marginal cost curve crosses the average total cost curve at the lowest point on the average total cost curve.

2. Suppose that paper is produced in a perfectly competitive, increasing-cost industry.
   a. Draw correctly labeled side-by-side graphs for a representative firm and for the paper market in long-run equilibrium.
      i. Label the market equilibrium price "P_{M1}" and the equilibrium quantity "Q_{M1}."
      ii. Label the firm's marginal cost "MC_1," its average total cost "ATC_1," its demand curve "D_{F1}," and its profit-maximizing price and quantity "P_{F1}" and "Q_{F1}," respectively.
   b. Now suppose that increased reliance on digital communications causes a decrease in the demand for paper. Show the following on the graphs you drew for part (a):
      i. The new short-run market equilibrium price and quantity, labeled "P_{M2}" and "Q_{M2}."
      ii. The new short-run profit-maximizing price and quantity for the representative firm, labeled "P_{F2}" and "Q_{F2}."
   c. Now suppose the market and the representative firm have adjusted to a new long-run equilibrium.
      i. Label the new equilibrium market price and quantity "P_{M3}" and "Q_{M3}."
      ii. Explain how and why the representative firm's new average total cost curve differs from ATC_1.
      iii. Draw the long-run supply curve for the market and label it "LRS." **(8 points)**

Introduction to Monopoly

In this Module, you will learn to:
- Identify the profit-maximizing price and quantity for a monopolist
- Determine whether a monopoly is earning a profit or a loss

In this Module we turn to monopoly, the market structure at the opposite end of the spectrum from perfect competition. A monopolist's profit-maximizing decision is subtly different from that of a price-taking firm, but it has large implications for the output produced and the welfare created. We will see the crucial role that market demand plays in leading a monopolist to behave differently from a firm in a perfectly competitive industry.

The Monopolist's Demand Curve and Marginal Revenue

Recall the firm's optimal output rule: a profit-maximizing firm produces the quantity of output at which the marginal cost of producing the last unit of output equals marginal revenue—the change in total revenue generated by the last unit of output. That is, $MR = MC$ at the profit-maximizing quantity of output. Although the optimal output rule holds for *all* firms, decisions about price and the quantity of output differ between monopolies and perfectly competitive industries due to differences in the demand curves that monopolists and perfectly competitive firms face.

We have learned that even though the *market* demand curve always slopes downward, each of the firms that make up a perfectly competitive industry faces a horizontal, *perfectly elastic* demand curve like D_C in panel (a) of **Figure 61.1**. Any attempt by an individual firm in a perfectly competitive industry to charge more than the going market price will cause the firm to lose all its sales. However, a firm can sell as much as it likes

---

Figure 61.1 Comparing the Demand Curves of a Perfectly Competitive Firm and a Monopolist

(a) Demand Curve of a Perfectly Competitive Firm

Price

Market price — D_C

Quantity

(b) Demand Curve of a Monopolist

Price

D_M

Quantity

Because a firm in a perfectly competitive industry cannot affect the market price, it faces a horizontal demand curve like D_C in panel (a). A monopolist, on the other hand, can affect the price.

Because it is the sole supplier in the industry, its demand curve is the entire market demand curve, which slopes downward like D_M in panel (b). To sell more output, it must lower the price.

---

at the market price. We have seen that the marginal revenue of a perfectly competitive firm is simply the market price. As a result, the price-taking firm's optimal output rule is to produce the output level at which the marginal cost of the last unit produced is equal to the market price.

By contrast, a monopolist is the sole supplier of its good. So its demand curve is simply the market demand curve, which slopes downward, like D_M in panel (b) of Figure 61.1. This downward slope creates a "wedge" between the price of the good and the marginal revenue of the good. **Table 61.1** shows how this wedge develops. The first two columns show a hypothetical demand schedule for De Beers diamonds. For the sake of simplicity, we assume that De Beers is a monopoly, all diamonds are exactly alike, and the number of diamonds sold is far smaller than is actually the case. For instance, at a price of $500 per diamond, we assume that only 10 diamonds are sold. The demand curve implied by this schedule is shown in panel (a) of **Figure 61.2**.

Table 61.1	Demand, Total Revenue, and Marginal Revenue for the De Beers Diamond Monopoly		
Price of diamond P	Quantity of diamonds demanded Q	Total revenue $TR = P \times Q$	Marginal revenue $MR = \Delta TR/\Delta Q$
$1,000	0	$0	
			$950
950	1	950	
			850
900	2	1,800	
			750
850	3	2,550	
			650
800	4	3,200	
			550
750	5	3,750	
			450
700	6	4,200	
			350
650	7	4,550	
			250
600	8	4,800	
			150
550	9	4,950	
			50
500	10	5,000	
			−50
450	11	4,950	
			−150
400	12	4,800	
			−250
350	13	4,550	
			−350
300	14	4,200	
			−450
250	15	3,750	
			−550
200	16	3,200	
			−650
150	17	2,550	
			−750
100	18	1,800	
			−850
50	19	950	
			−950
0	20	0	

Radiant   Heart   Princess   Cushion   Asscher   Round

Oval   Emerald   Marquise   Pear

The third column of Table 61.1 shows De Beers's total revenue from selling each quantity of diamonds—the price per diamond multiplied by the number of diamonds sold. The last column shows marginal revenue, the change in total revenue from producing and selling another diamond.

After selling the first diamond, the marginal revenue a monopolist receives from selling one more unit is less than the price at which that unit is sold. For example, if De Beers sells 10 diamonds, the price at which the 10th diamond is sold is $500. But the marginal revenue—the change in total revenue in going from 9 to 10 diamonds—is only $50.

Figure 61.2   A Monopolist's Demand, Total Revenue, and Marginal Revenue Curves

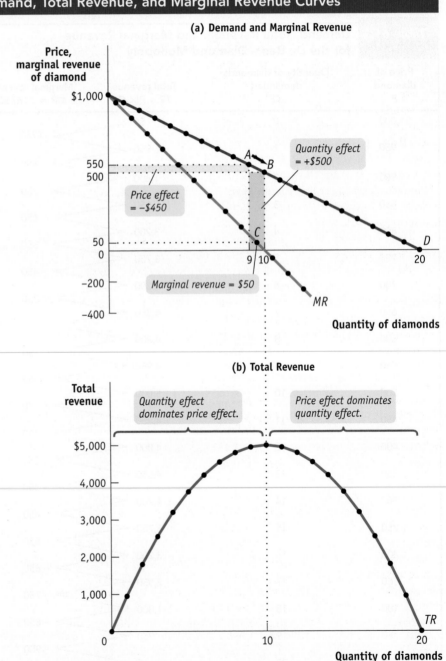

Panel (a) shows the monopolist's demand and marginal revenue curves for diamonds from Table 61.1. The marginal revenue curve lies below the demand curve. To see why, consider point A on the demand curve, where 9 diamonds are sold at $550 each, generating a total revenue of $4,950. To sell a 10th diamond, the price on all 10 diamonds must be cut to $500, as shown by point B. As a result, total revenue increases by the green area (the quantity effect: +$500) but decreases by the orange area (the price effect: −$450). So the marginal revenue from the 10th diamond is $500 − $450 = $50, which is much lower than its price of $500. Panel (b) shows the monopolist's total revenue curve for diamonds. Total revenue initially rises with an increase in output because the quantity effect dominates the price effect. Total revenue reaches its maximum at the level of output at which marginal revenue is zero. Total revenue then falls with an increase in output because the price effect dominates the quantity effect.

Why is the marginal revenue from that 10th diamond less than the price? Because an increase in production by a monopolist has two opposing effects on revenue:

- *A quantity effect*. One more unit is sold, increasing total revenue by the price at which the unit is sold (in this case, +$500).

- *A price effect*. In order to sell that last unit, the monopolist must cut the market price on *all* units sold. This decreases total revenue (in this case, by 9 × −$50 = −$450).

The quantity effect and the price effect are illustrated by the two shaded areas in panel (a) of Figure 61.2. Increasing diamond sales from 9 to 10 means moving down the demand curve from *A* to *B*, reducing the price per diamond from $550 to $500. The green-shaded area represents the quantity effect: De Beers sells the 10th diamond at a price of $500. This is offset, however, by the price effect. In order to sell that 10th diamond, De Beers must reduce the price on all its diamonds from $550 to $500. This price cut lowers the firm's revenue by 9 × $50 = $450, represented by the orange-shaded area. So, as point *C* indicates, the total effect on revenue of selling one more diamond—the marginal revenue—derived from an increase in diamond sales from 9 to 10 is only $500 − $450 = $50.

Point *C* lies on the monopolist's marginal revenue curve, labeled *MR* in panel (a) of Figure 61.2 and taken from the last column of Table 61.1. The crucial point about the monopolist's marginal revenue curve is that, except where the two curves meet on the left side of the graph, the marginal revenue curve is always *below* the demand curve. The marginal revenue from the first unit is equal to the price because there are no other units on which the price must be lowered to sell the first one. As more units are sold, the price effect creates an increasingly tall wedge between the monopolist's marginal revenue curve and the demand curve because, in order to sell an additional diamond, De Beers must cut the market price on all units sold.

In fact, this wedge exists for any firm that possesses market power, such as an oligopolist, except in the case of price discrimination, as we will discuss in Module 63. Having market power means that the firm faces a downward-sloping demand curve. As a result, a firm with market power that charges every customer the same price will experience a price effect. So for such a firm, the marginal revenue curve lies below the demand curve.

Take a moment to compare the monopolist's marginal revenue curve with the marginal revenue curve for a perfectly competitive firm, which has no market power. For the perfectly competitive firm there is no price effect from an increase in output: its marginal revenue curve is simply its horizontal demand curve. So for a perfectly competitive firm, the market price and the marginal revenue are always equal.

To understand how the quantity and price effects offset each other for a firm with market power, look at De Beers's total revenue curve in panel (b) of Figure 61.2. Notice that it is hill-shaped: as output rises from 0 to 10 diamonds, total revenue increases. This reflects the fact that *at low levels of output, the quantity effect is larger than the price effect*: as the monopolist sells more, it has to lower the price on only a few units, so the price effect is small. As output rises beyond 10 diamonds, total revenue actually falls. This reflects the fact that *at high levels of output, the price effect is larger than the quantity effect*: as the monopolist sells more, it now has to lower the price on many units of output, making the price effect very large. Correspondingly, the marginal revenue is negative at output levels above 10 diamonds. For example, to sell the 12th diamond, the price must be cut to $400 on the 11 diamonds that would otherwise sell for $450 each. So the quantity effect of gaining $400 is smaller than the price effect of losing $550, making the marginal revenue of the 12th diamond $400 − $550 = −$150.

Recall from Module 47 that the relationship between price changes and total revenue depends on the price elasticity of demand: a price cut increases total revenue along the section of the demand curve where the demand is elastic; a price cut has no effect on total revenue where the demand curve is unit elastic; and a price cut decreases total revenue where the demand is inelastic. So if you know how the price effect and the quantity effect change total revenue when the price changes, you know whether demand is elastic, unit elastic, or inelastic.

> **AP® EXAM TIP**
>
> The AP® exam sometimes asks questions about why a monopoly's marginal revenue is below its price. Be prepared to explain that the monopolist must lower its price on all units sold in order to sell more units.

The Monopolist's Profit-Maximizing Output and Price

To complete the story of how a monopolist maximizes profit, we now bring in the monopolist's marginal cost. Let's assume that there is no fixed cost of production and that the marginal cost of producing an additional diamond is constant at $200, no matter how many diamonds De Beers produces. Since the only cost of producing each diamond is the $200 marginal cost, that marginal cost will always equal the average total cost, and the marginal cost curve and the average total cost curve coincide as a horizontal line with a height of $200, as shown in **Figure 61.3**.

Figure 61.3   The Monopolist's Profit-Maximizing Output and Price

According to the optimal output rule, the profit-maximizing quantity of output for the monopolist is at $MR = MC$, shown by point A, where the marginal cost and marginal revenue curves cross at an output of 8 diamonds. The price De Beers can charge per diamond is found by going to the point on the demand curve directly above point A, shown by point B here—a price of $600 per diamond. A perfectly competitive industry produces the output level at which $P = MC$, given by point C, where the demand and marginal cost curves cross. So a competitive industry produces 16 diamonds, sells at a price of $200, and makes zero profit.

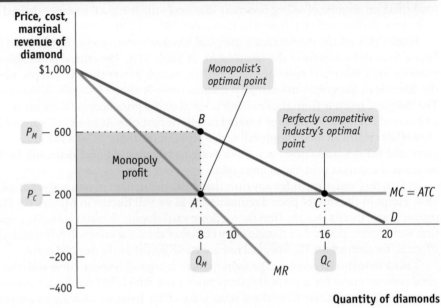

AP® EXAM TIP

Like a perfect competitor, a monopolist chooses the quantity at which $MR = MC$. The monopolist's price is found by going up from where $MR = MC$ to the demand curve, and then straight over to the price axis.

To maximize profit, the monopolist compares the marginal cost with the marginal revenue. If the marginal revenue exceeds the marginal cost, De Beers increases profit by producing more; if the marginal revenue is less than the marginal cost, De Beers increases profit by producing less. So the monopolist maximizes its profit by using the optimal output rule:

(61-1) $MR = MC$ at the monopolist's profit-maximizing quantity of output

The monopolist's optimal point is indicated by point A in Figure 61.3, where the marginal cost curve crosses the marginal revenue curve. The corresponding output level, 8 diamonds, is the monopolist's profit-maximizing quantity of output, Q_M. The price at which consumers demand 8 diamonds is $600, found by going straight up from point A to point B on the demand curve, so the monopolist's price, P_M, is $600. The average total cost of producing each diamond is $200, so the monopolist earns a profit of $600 − $200 = $400 per diamond, and total profit is $8 \times $400 = $3,200, as indicated by the shaded area.

Monopoly Versus Perfect Competition

When Cecil Rhodes consolidated many independent diamond producers into De Beers, he converted a perfectly competitive industry into a monopoly. We can now use our analysis to see the effects of such a consolidation.

Let's look again at Figure 61.3 and ask how this same market would work if, instead of being a monopoly, the industry were perfectly competitive. We will continue to assume that there is no fixed cost and that the marginal cost is constant, so the average total cost and the marginal cost are equal.

If the diamond industry consists of many perfectly competitive firms, each of those producers takes the market price as given. Because they don't need to lower their price in order to sell more units, each producer's marginal revenue is equal to the market price. So each firm within the industry uses the price-taking firm's optimal output rule:

(61-2) $P = MC$ at the perfectly competitive firm's profit-maximizing quantity of output

In Figure 61.3, this would correspond to producing at point C, where the price per diamond, P_C, is $200, equal to the marginal cost of production. So the profit-maximizing output of an industry under perfect competition, Q_C, is 16 diamonds.

Recall that the perfectly competitive outcome of $P = MC$ is allocatively efficient: by producing up to point C, the firm provides every unit for which consumers are willing to pay at least the marginal cost. But do firms in the perfectly competitive industry earn any profit at point C? No: the price of $200 is equal to the average total cost per diamond. So there is no economic profit in this industry when it produces at the perfectly competitive output level.

We've already seen that once the industry is consolidated into a monopoly, the result is very different. The monopolist's marginal revenue is influenced by the price effect, so that marginal revenue is less than the price. That is,

(61-3) $P > MR = MC$ at the monopolist's profit-maximizing quantity of output

So the monopolist does not meet the $P = MC$ condition for allocative efficiency. As we've already seen, the monopolist produces less than the competitive industry—8 diamonds rather than 16. The price with a monopoly is $600, compared to only $200 with perfect competition. The monopolist earns a positive profit, but the competitive industry does not.

We can see that compared to a competitive industry, a monopolist does the following:

- produces a smaller quantity: $Q_M < Q_C$
- charges a higher price: $P_M > P_C$
- earns a profit

Monopoly: The General Picture

In Figure 61.3 we worked with specific numbers and assumed that the marginal cost was constant and that there was no fixed cost, which meant that the average total cost curve was a horizontal line. **Figure 61.4** shows a more general picture of monopoly in action. Here we return to the usual assumption that the marginal cost curve has a "swoosh" shape and the average total cost curve is U-shaped.

Applying the optimal output rule, we see that the profit-maximizing level of output, identified as the quantity at which the marginal revenue curve and the marginal cost curve intersect (point A), is Q_M. The monopolist charges the highest price possible for this quantity, P_M, found at the height of the demand curve directly above Q_M (point B). At the profit-maximizing level of output, the monopolist's average total cost is ATC_M (point C).

Recalling how we calculated profit in Equation 59-1, profit is equal to the difference between total revenue and total cost. So we have

(61-4) Profit = $TR - TC$
$$= (P_M \times Q_M) - (ATC_M \times Q_M)$$
$$= (P_M - ATC_M) \times Q_M$$

Profit is equal to the area of the shaded rectangle in Figure 61.4, with a height of $P_M - ATC_M$ and a width of Q_M.

AP® EXAM TIP

Be prepared to draw and analyze the monopoly graph for the AP® exam. Remember, the monopolist's profit per unit is the difference between the price the firm charges and its ATC.

Figure 61.4 The Monopolist's Profit

In this case, the marginal cost curve has a "swoosh" shape and the average total cost curve is U-shaped. The monopolist maximizes profit by producing the level of output Q_M at which $MR = MC$, found directly below point A. It finds its monopoly price, P_M, from point B on the demand curve directly above point A. The average total cost of producing Q_M units is shown by the height of point C. Profit is given by the area of the shaded rectangle.

In the previous Module, we learned that a perfectly competitive industry can have profit *in the short run but not in the long run*. In the short run, price can exceed average total cost, allowing a perfectly competitive firm to make a profit. But we also know that this cannot persist. In the long run, any profit in a perfectly competitive industry will be competed away as new firms enter the market. In contrast, while a monopoly can earn a profit or a loss in the short run, barriers to entry make it possible for a monopolist to make positive profit in the long run.

MODULE 61 REVIEW

Adventures in AP® Economics

Watch the video: *Monopoly*

Check Your Understanding

1. Use the accompanying total revenue schedule of Emerald, Inc., a monopoly producer of 10-carat emeralds, to derive the items listed in parts a–d. Then answer part e.

Quantity of emeralds demanded	Total revenue
1	$100
2	186
3	252
4	280
5	250

   a. the demand schedule (Hint: the average revenue at each quantity indicates the price at which that quantity would be demanded.)
   b. the marginal revenue schedule
   c. the quantity effect component of marginal revenue at each output level
   d. the price effect component of marginal revenue at each output level
   e. What additional information is needed to determine Emerald, Inc.'s profit-maximizing output?

2. Replicate Figure 61.3 and use your graph to show what happens to the following items when the marginal cost of diamond production rises from $200 to $400. Use the information in Table 61.1 to identify specific numbers for prices and quantities on your graph.
   a. the marginal cost curve
   b. the profit-maximizing price and quantity
   c. the profit of the monopolist
   d. the quantity that would be produced if the diamond industry were perfectly competitive, and the associated profit

TACKLE THE AP® TEST: Multiple-Choice Questions

Refer to the graph provided for Questions 1–4.

Quantity of diamonds

1. The monopolist's profit-maximizing output is
   a. 0.   c. 5.   e. 10.
   b. 4.   d. 8.

2. The monopolist's total revenue equals
   a. $80.   c. $240.   e. $480.
   b. $160.   d. $300.

3. The monopolist's total cost equals
   a. $20.   c. $160.   e. $480.
   b. $80.   d. $240.

4. The monopolist is earning a profit equal to
   a. $0.   c. $80.   e. $240.
   b. $40.   d. $160.

5. How does a monopoly differ from a perfectly competitive industry with the same costs?
   a. The monopoly produces where $MR = MC$.
   b. The monopoly earns normal profit in the long run.
   c. The monopoly charges a lower price.
   d. The monopoly produces a smaller quantity.
   e. The monopoly can sell as many units as it wants at the equilibrium price.

6. A monopolist and a perfectly competitive firm both
   a. face a downward-sloping demand curve.
   b. have their marginal revenue curve below their demand curve.
   c. can earn profit in the long run.
   d. have a horizontal marginal revenue curve.
   e. maximize profit by producing the quantity at which marginal revenue equals marginal cost.

7. A price cut will lead to an increase in total revenue if the
   a. marginal revenue is zero.
   b. quantity effect is larger than the price effect.
   c. quantity effect is zero.
   d. demand curve is inelastic.
   e. demand curve is unit-elastic.

TACKLE THE AP® TEST: Free-Response Questions

1. **a.** Draw a correctly labeled graph showing a monopoly incurring a loss in the short run. Assume that the marginal cost curve is swoosh-shaped.
   b. At the quantity at which $MR = MC$, how does the size of the quantity effect compare with the size of the price effect? Explain.

Rubric for FRQ1 (9 points)

1 point: Axes are correctly labeled.

1 point: The demand curve is labeled and negatively sloped.

1 point: The marginal revenue curve is labeled, negatively sloped, and below the demand curve.

1 point: The profit-maximizing quantity is labeled on the horizontal axis where $MC = MR$.

1 point: Price is determined on the demand curve above the point where $MC = MR$.

1 point: The average total cost curve is labeled and U-shaped.

1 point: Average total cost is above price at the profit-maximizing output.

1 point: The marginal cost curve crosses the average total cost curve at the lowest point on the average total cost curve.

1 point: At that quantity, the quantity effect, which is positive, is larger than the price effect, which is negative. We know this because the MR—the sum of these effects—is positive.

2. **a.** Draw a graph showing a monopoly earning a normal profit in the short run. Assume that the marginal cost curve is swoosh-shaped.
   b. Can a monopolist earn a positive profit in the long run? Explain. **(9 points)**

Monopoly and Public Policy

> **In this Module, you will learn to:**
> - Compare the effects of monopoly and perfect competition on society's welfare
> - Explain how policy makers address the problems posed by monopoly

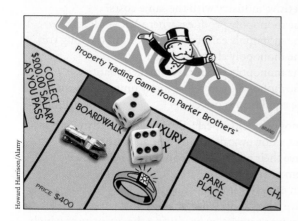

If you've ever played Hasbro's Monopoly game, you know that it's good to be a monopolist, but it's not so good to be a monopolist's customer. Players of the Monopoly game pay higher rents when they land on a monopoly. In real life, customers generally pay higher prices when the seller is a monopolist. But buyers and sellers always have conflicting interests when it comes to prices. Are the problems under monopoly any different from those under perfect competition?

The answer is yes, because monopoly is a source of inefficiency: the losses to consumers from monopoly behavior are larger than the gains to the monopolist. Because monopoly leads to net losses for the economy, governments often try either to prevent the emergence of monopolies or to limit their effects. In this Module, we will see why monopoly leads to inefficiency and examine the policies governments adopt in an attempt to prevent this inefficiency.

Welfare Effects of Monopoly

By holding output below the level at which the marginal cost equals the market price, a monopolist increases its profit but hurts consumers. To assess whether this is a net benefit or a net loss to society, we must compare the monopolist's gain in profit to the consumers' loss. What we learn is that the consumers' loss is larger than the monopolist's gain, so monopoly causes a net loss for society.

To see why, let's return to the case in which the marginal cost curve is horizontal, as shown in the two panels of **Figure 62.1**. Here the marginal cost curve is MC, the demand curve is D, and, in panel (b), the marginal revenue curve is MR.

Figure 62.1 Monopoly Causes Inefficiency

(a) Total Surplus with Perfect Competition

(b) Total Surplus with Monopoly

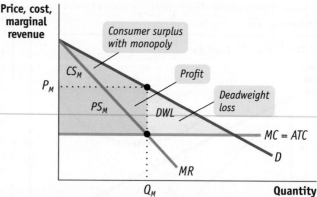

Panel (a) depicts a perfectly competitive industry: the output is Q_C and the market price is P_C. Since the price is exactly equal to the marginal cost of producing each unit, there is no producer surplus. So the consumer surplus is also the total surplus, represented by the blue-shaded area. Panel (b) depicts the industry under monopoly: the monopolist decreases output

to Q_M and charges P_M. Consumer surplus (the blue area) has shrunk: a portion of it has been captured as producer surplus and profit (the green area), and a portion is the lost value of mutually beneficial transactions that do not occur because of monopoly behavior, which we know as deadweight loss (the yellow area). As a result, total surplus falls.

Panel (a) shows what happens if this industry is perfectly competitive. The equilibrium output is Q_C; the price of the good, P_C, is equal to the marginal cost, which is also the average total cost because the marginal cost is the same for each unit and there is no fixed cost. Consumers pay firms exactly the marginal cost per unit of output, so there is no producer surplus in this equilibrium. The consumer surplus generated by the market is equal to the area of the blue-shaded triangle labeled CS_C in panel (a). Since there is no producer surplus when the industry is perfectly competitive, CS_C also represents the total surplus.

Panel (b) shows the results for the same market, but this time assuming that the industry is a monopoly. The monopolist produces the level of output Q_M, at which the marginal cost is equal to the marginal revenue, and it charges the price P_M. The industry now earns profit—which is also the producer surplus in this case—equal to the area of the green rectangle, PS_M. Note that this profit is part of what was consumer surplus in the perfectly competitive market, and the consumer surplus with the monopoly shrinks to the area of the blue triangle, CS_M.

By comparing panels (a) and (b), we see that in addition to the redistribution of surplus from consumers to the monopolist, another important change has occurred: the sum of producer surplus and consumer surplus—total surplus—is *smaller* under monopoly than under perfect competition. That is, the sum of CS_M and PS_M in panel (b) is less than the area CS_C in panel (a). Previously, we analyzed how taxes could cause *deadweight loss* for society. Here we show that a monopoly creates deadweight loss equal to the area of the yellow triangle, *DWL*. So monopoly produces a net loss for society.

This net loss arises because some mutually beneficial transactions do not occur. There are people for whom an additional unit of the good is worth more than the marginal cost of producing it but who don't consume it because they are not willing to pay the monopoly price, P_M. Indeed, by driving a wedge between the price and the marginal cost, a monopoly acts much like a tax on consumers, and produces the same kind of inefficiency.

When a sales tax or an excise tax is imposed on each unit of a good produced by a monopoly, even less of the good is sold, and the deadweight loss grows. However, a lump-sum tax—one that does not depend on the quantity sold—does not contribute to the deadweight loss unless it is so high that it causes the monopoly to close down. The reason is that a lump-sum tax does not affect the marginal cost or the marginal revenue, so the monopoly goes on producing the same profit-maximizing quantity.

We have seen that monopoly power detracts from the welfare of society as a whole and is a source of market failure. Is there anything government policy can do about it?

> **AP® EXAM TIP**
>
> Be prepared to identify and calculate the areas of consumer surplus, producer surplus, and deadweight loss for a monopoly on the AP® exam.

Preventing Monopoly Power

Policy toward monopolies depends crucially on what type of monopoly is involved. If the industry is *not* a natural monopoly, the best policy is generally to prevent a monopoly from arising or to break it up if it already exists. Government policy used to prevent or eliminate monopolies is known as *antitrust policy*, which we will discuss in Module 77. For now, let's focus on the more difficult problem of dealing with a natural monopoly.

Recall from Module 57 that a natural monopoly experiences economies of scale due to a large fixed cost. In that case, the average total cost would be high if the market were divided among many competing firms, but a single firm can bring the average total cost down by spreading the fixed cost across many units of output. For example, the fixed cost of building an oil pipeline is tremendous, but the average total cost becomes reasonable if the pipeline can carry billions of gallons of oil. If multiple pipelines each served a fraction of the same oil market, the average total cost of oil from each pipeline would be much higher.

Dealing with a Natural Monopoly

Breaking up a monopoly that isn't natural will provide gains to consumers that outweigh the loss to the firm. But it's not so clear whether a natural monopoly should be broken up, because large firms have lower average total costs than small firms. For example, a town government that tried to prevent a single gas company from acting as a natural monopoly would raise the cost of providing gas to its residents because two small gas companies would operate at a higher average total cost than one large gas company.

Yet even in the case of a natural monopoly, a profit-maximizing monopolist acts in a way that causes inefficiency—it charges consumers a price that is higher than the marginal cost and, by doing so, prevents some potentially beneficial transactions. Also, it can seem unfair that a firm that has managed to establish a monopoly position earns a large profit at the expense of consumers.

What can public policy do about this? There are two common answers.

With **public ownership** of a monopoly, the good is supplied by the government or by a firm owned by the government.

Public Ownership

In many countries, the preferred answer to the problem of natural monopoly has been **public ownership**. Instead of allowing a private monopolist to control an industry, the government establishes a public agency to provide the good and protect consumers' interests.

The advantage of public ownership, in principle, is that a publicly owned natural monopoly can set prices based on the criterion of efficiency rather than profit maximization. In a perfectly competitive industry, profit-maximizing behavior *is* efficient because firms charge a price equal to the marginal cost; that is why there is no economic argument for public ownership of, say, wheat farms.

Experience suggests, however, that public ownership as a solution to the problem of natural monopoly often works badly in practice. One reason is that publicly owned firms are often less eager than private companies to keep costs down or offer high-quality products. Another reason is that publicly owned companies all too often end up serving political interests—providing contracts or jobs to people with the right connections rather than to the most qualified individuals.

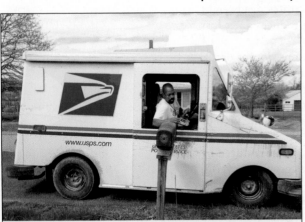

Public ownership of a natural monopoly, such as the United States Postal Service, can help to maintain efficient pricing for consumers.

Regulation

In the United States, the more common answer has been to leave the industry in private hands but subject it to regulation. In particular, most local utilities, such as electricity, water, natural gas, and so on, are covered by **price regulation** that limits the prices they can charge.

Price regulation limits the price that a monopolist is allowed to charge.

Figure 62.2 shows an example of price regulation of a natural monopoly—a highly simplified version of a local gas company. The company faces a demand curve, D, with an associated marginal revenue curve, MR. For simplicity, we assume that the firm's total cost consists of two parts: a fixed cost and a variable cost that is the same for every unit. So marginal cost is constant in this case, and the marginal cost curve (which here is also the average variable cost curve) is the horizontal line MC. The average total cost curve is the downward-sloping curve ATC; it slopes downward because the higher the output, the lower the average fixed cost (the fixed cost per unit of output). Because average total cost slopes downward over the range of output relevant for market demand, this is a natural monopoly.

Panel (a) illustrates a case of natural monopoly without regulation. The unregulated natural monopolist chooses the monopoly output Q_M and charges the price P_M.

Figure 62.2 Unregulated and Regulated Natural Monopoly

(a) Total Surplus with an Unregulated Natural Monopolist

(b) Total Surplus with a Regulated Natural Monopolist

This figure shows the case of a natural monopolist. In panel (a), if the monopolist is allowed to charge P_M, it makes a profit, shown by the green area; consumer surplus is shown by the blue area. If the monopolist is regulated and must charge the lower price, P_R, output increases from Q_M to Q_R and consumer surplus increases. Panel (b) shows what happens when the monopolist must charge a price equal to its average total cost where the average total cost curve crosses the demand curve, the price P_R^*. Output expands to Q_R^*, and consumer surplus is now the entire blue area. The monopolist makes zero profit. This is the greatest total surplus possible without the monopoly incurring losses.

Since the monopolist receives a price greater than its average total cost, she or he earns a profit, represented by the green-shaded rectangle in panel (a). Consumer surplus is given by the blue-shaded triangle.

Now suppose that regulators impose a price ceiling on local gas deliveries—one that falls below the monopoly price of P_M but above the firm's average total cost, say, at P_R in panel (a). At that price the quantity demanded is Q_R.

Does the company have an incentive to produce that quantity? Yes. If the price the monopolist can charge is fixed at P_R by regulators, the firm can sell any quantity between zero and Q_R for the same price, P_R. So the regulated price becomes the marginal revenue for the monopoly just like the market price is the marginal revenue for a perfectly competitive firm. With the marginal revenue being above the marginal cost and the price exceeding the average total cost, the firm expands output to meet the quantity demanded, Q_R. This policy has appeal because with the price ceiling, the monopolist produces a larger quantity at a lower price.

If regulators pursued allocative efficiency by setting a price ceiling equal to the marginal cost, the monopolist would not be willing to produce at all in the long run, because it would be producing at a loss. That is, the price ceiling has to be set high enough to allow the firm to cover its average total cost. Panel (b) shows a situation in which regulators have pushed the price down as far as possible, at the break-even level where the average total cost curve crosses the demand curve. At any lower price the firm loses money. The price here, P_R^*, is the best regulated price: the monopolist is just willing to operate and produces Q_R^*, the quantity demanded at that price. Consumers and society gain as a result.

The welfare effects of this regulation can be seen by comparing the shaded areas in the two panels of Figure 62.2. Consumer surplus is increased by the regulation, with the gains coming from two sources. First, profit is eliminated and added instead to consumer surplus. Second, the larger output and lower price lead to an overall welfare gain—an increase in total surplus. In fact, panel (b) illustrates the largest total surplus possible in this situation.

AP® EXAM TIP

You may be asked to explain what happens to consumer surplus, producer surplus, and deadweight loss when a monopoly is regulated. Remember that a regulated price equal to the average total cost is the lowest price that would not cause the firm to take losses and eventually close.

Check Your Understanding

1. What policy should the government adopt in the following cases? Explain.
   a. Internet service in Anytown, OH, is provided by cable. Customers feel they are being overcharged, but the cable company claims it must charge prices that let it recover the costs of laying cable.
   b. The only two airlines that currently fly to Alaska need government approval to merge. Other airlines wish to fly to Alaska but need government-allocated landing slots to do so.

2. True or false? Explain your answer.
   a. Society's welfare is lower under monopoly because some consumer surplus is transformed into profit for the monopolist.

   b. A monopolist causes inefficiency because there are consumers who are willing to pay a price greater than or equal to marginal cost but less than the monopoly price.

3. Suppose that instead of maximizing profit, a monopolist charges a price equal to marginal cost. Assuming constant marginal cost and no fixed cost, draw a diagram comparing the level of profit, consumer surplus, total surplus, and deadweight loss for this monopolist compared to a profit-maximizing monopolist.

TACKLE THE AP® TEST: Multiple-Choice Questions

1. Which of the following statements is true of a monopoly as compared to a perfectly competitive market with the same costs?
   a. Consumer surplus is smaller.
   b. Profit is smaller.
   c. Deadweight loss is smaller.
   d. Total surplus is larger.
   e. Quantity is larger.

2. Which of the following is true of a natural monopoly?
   a. It experiences diseconomies of scale.
   b. *ATC* is lower if there is a single firm in the market.
   c. It occurs in a market that relies on natural resources for its production.
   d. There are decreasing returns to scale in the industry.
   e. The government must provide the good or service to achieve efficiency.

3. Which of the following government actions is the most common for a natural monopoly in the United States?
   a. prevent its formation
   b. break it up using antitrust laws
   c. use price regulation
   d. take public ownership
   e. eliminate the market

4. Where the average total cost curve for a natural monopoly crosses the demand curve,
   a. the marginal cost curve is below the average total cost curve.
   b. the average total cost curve is rising.
   c. the marginal revenue curve is rising.

   d. the marginal revenue curve also crosses the demand curve.
   e. the marginal cost curve also crosses the demand curve.

5. Which of the following is most likely to be higher for a regulated natural monopoly than for an unregulated natural monopoly?
   a. product variety
   b. quantity
   c. price
   d. profit
   e. deadweight loss

6. A monopoly typically causes deadweight loss due to
   a. an absence of producer surplus.
   b. an absence of profit.
   c. low prices.
   d. high input costs.
   e. an inefficiently low quantity of output.

7. In order to allow a natural monopoly to continue operations in the long run, the regulated price must be at least as high as the
   a. average total cost where the average total cost curve meets the demand curve.
   b. marginal cost where the marginal cost curve meets the demand curve.
   c. minimum point of the average total cost curve.
   d. minimum point of the average variable cost curve.
   e. minimum point of the marginal cost curve.

TACKLE THE AP® TEST: Free-Response Questions

1. Draw a correctly labeled graph showing a profit-making natural monopoly. On your graph, indicate each of the following:
   a. the monopoly's profit-maximizing output (Q_M)
   b. the monopoly's price (P_M)
   c. the monopoly's profit
   d. the regulated price that would maximize consumer surplus without creating losses for the firm (P_R)

1 point: The marginal revenue curve is labeled, sloped downward, and below the demand curve.

1 point: The average total cost curve is labeled and downward-sloping (not U-shaped!).

1 point: The marginal cost curve is labeled and below the average total cost curve (it does not need to be flat).

1 point: The profit-maximizing output, Q_M, is shown on the horizontal axis where $MC = MR$.

1 point: The profit-maximizing price is found on the demand curve above the point where $MC = MR$.

1 point: The monopoly profit area is correctly shaded and labeled.

1 point: The regulated price is labeled on the vertical axis to the left of the point where the demand curve crosses the average total cost curve.

Rubric for FRQ 1 (9 points)

1 point: The axes are correctly labeled.

1 point: The demand curve is labeled and sloped downward.

2. Draw a correctly labeled graph of a natural monopoly. Use your graph to identify each of the following:
   a. consumer surplus if the market were somehow able to operate as a perfectly competitive market
   b. consumer surplus with the monopoly
   c. monopoly profit
   d. deadweight loss with the monopoly **(8 points)**

Price Discrimination

In this Module, you will learn to:
- Explain the meaning of price discrimination
- Discuss why price discrimination is common when producers have market power

Up to this point, we have considered only the case of a monopolist who charges all consumers the same price. However, monopolists want to maximize their profit, and often they do so by charging different prices for the same product. In this Module we look at how monopolists increase their profit by engaging in *price discrimination*.

Price Discrimination Defined

A monopolist who charges everyone the same price is known as a **single-price monopolist**. A small-town gas station with no competitors is an example of a single-price monopolist. Unlike gas stations, many monopolists find that they can increase their profit by selling the same good to different customers for different prices: they practice **price discrimination**.

A **single-price monopolist** charges all consumers the same price.

Sellers engage in **price discrimination** when they charge different prices to different consumers for the same good.

An example of price discrimination that travelers encounter regularly involves airline tickets. Although there are many airlines, most routes in the United States are served by only a few carriers, which gives those carriers market power and the ability to influence prices. Any regular airline passenger quickly learns that the simple question "How much will it cost me to fly there?" rarely has a simple answer. If you are willing to buy a nonrefundable ticket a month in advance and stay over a Saturday night, the round trip may cost only $250. But if you have to go on a business trip tomorrow, which happens to be Tuesday, and want to come back on Wednesday, the same round trip might cost $650. Yet the business traveler and the weekend vacationer receive the same product.

You might object that airlines are not usually monopolies—that in most flight markets the airline industry is an oligopoly. In fact, price discrimination takes place under oligopoly and monopolistic competition as well as monopoly. But it doesn't happen under perfect competition. Once we've seen why monopolists sometimes price-discriminate, we'll be in a good position to understand why it happens in other cases, too.

The Logic of Price Discrimination

To get a preliminary view of why price discrimination might be more profitable than charging all consumers the same price, imagine that Air Sunshine offers the only non-stop flights between Bismarck, North Dakota, and Ft. Lauderdale, Florida. Assume that there are no capacity problems—the airline can fly as many planes as the number of passengers warrants. Also assume that there is no fixed cost. The marginal cost to the airline of providing a seat is $200 no matter how many passengers it carries.

Further assume that the airline knows there are two kinds of potential passengers. First, there are business travelers, 2,000 of whom want to travel between the destinations each week. Second, there are students, 2,000 of whom also want to travel each week.

Whether the potential passengers take the flight depends on the price. The business travelers, it turns out, really need to fly on particular dates; they will take the plane as long as the price is no more than $650. Since they are flying purely for business, we assume that cutting the price below $650 will not lead to any increase in business travel. The students, however, have less money and more options; if the price goes above $250, they will take the bus or do something else for their vacation. The implied demand curve is shown in **Figure 63.1**.

Figure 63.1 Two Types of Airline Customers

Air Sunshine has two types of customers: business travelers willing to pay at most $650 per ticket and students willing to pay at most $250 per ticket. There are 2,000 of each kind of customer. Air Sunshine has a constant marginal cost of $200 per seat. If Air Sunshine could charge these two types of customers different prices, it would maximize its profit by charging business travelers $650 and students $250 per ticket. This price discrimination would allow Air Sunshine to capture all of the consumer surplus as profit.

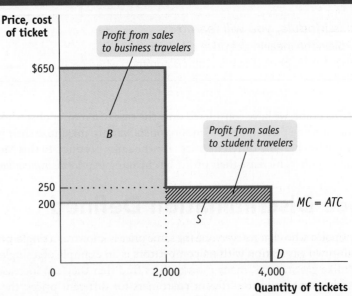

So what should the airline do? If it has to charge everyone the same price, its options are limited. It could charge $650; that way it would get as much as possible out of the business travelers but lose the student market. Or it could charge only $250; that way it would get both types of travelers but make significantly less money from sales to business travelers.

We can quickly calculate the profit from each of these alternatives. If the airline charged $650, it would sell 2,000 tickets to the business travelers, earning a total revenue of 2,000 × $650 = $1.3 million and incurring costs of 2,000 × $200 = $400,000; so its profit would be $900,000, illustrated by the shaded area B in Figure 63.1. If the airline charged only $250, it would sell 4,000 tickets, receiving revenue of 4,000 × $250 = $1,000,000 and incurring costs of 4,000 × $200 = $800,000; so its profit would be $200,000. If the airline must charge everyone the same price, charging the higher price and forgoing sales to students is clearly more profitable.

What the airline would really like to do, however, is charge the business travelers the full $650 but offer $250 tickets to the students. That's a lot less than the price paid by business travelers, but it's still above the marginal cost; so if the airline could sell those extra 2,000 tickets to students, it would make an additional ($250 − $200) × 2000 = $100,000 in profit. That is, it would make a profit equal to the areas B plus S in Figure 63.1.

It would be more realistic to suppose that there is some "give" in the demand of each group: at a price below $650, there would be some increase in business travel; and at a price above $250, some students would still purchase tickets. Even so, price discrimination adds to profit. The important point is that the two groups of consumers differ in their *sensitivity to price*—that a high price has a larger effect in discouraging purchases by students than by business travelers. As long as different groups of customers respond differently to the price, a monopolist will find that it can capture more consumer surplus and increase its profit by charging them different prices.

Price Discrimination and Elasticity

A more realistic description of the demand that airlines face would not specify particular prices at which different types of travelers would choose to fly. Instead, it would distinguish between the groups on the basis of their sensitivity to the price—their price elasticity of demand.

Suppose that a company sells its product to two easily identifiable groups of people—business travelers and students. It just so happens that business travelers are very insensitive to the price: they need a certain amount of the product whatever the price, but they cannot be persuaded to buy much more than that amount no matter how cheap it is. Students, though, are more flexible: offer a good enough price and they will buy quite a lot, but raise the price too high and they will switch to something else. Which approach is best for the company in this case?

The answer is the one already suggested by our simplified example: the company should charge business travelers, with their low price elasticity of demand, a higher price than it charges students, with their high price elasticity of demand.

The actual situation of the airlines is very much like this hypothetical example. Business travelers typically place a high priority on being in the right place at the right time and are not very sensitive to the price. But leisure travelers are fairly sensitive to the price—faced with a high price, they might take the bus, drive to another airport to get a lower fare, or skip the trip altogether.

So why doesn't an airline simply announce different prices for business and leisure customers? First, this would probably be illegal. (U.S. law places some limits on the

On many airline routes, the fare you pay depends on the type of traveler you are.

ability of companies to practice blatant price discrimination.) Second, even if it were legal, it would be a hard policy to enforce—business travelers might be willing to wear casual clothing and claim they were visiting family in Ft. Lauderdale in order to save $400.

What the airlines do—quite successfully—is impose rules that indirectly have the effect of charging business and leisure travelers different fares. Business travelers usually travel on weekdays and want to be home on the weekend, so the round-trip fare is much higher if you don't stay over a Saturday night. The requirement of a weekend stay for a cheap ticket effectively separates business travelers from leisure travelers. Similarly, business travelers often visit several cities in succession rather than make a simple round trip, so the fares for multi-city and one-way travel are relatively high. Many business trips are scheduled on short notice, so fares are much higher if you book close to the date of travel. Fares are also lower if you travel standby, taking your chances on whether you actually get a seat, because business travelers have to make it to that meeting but people visiting their relatives may have more flexibility in their travel plans. And because customers must show their ID at check-in, airlines make sure there are no resales of tickets between the two groups that would undermine their ability to price-discriminate—students can't buy cheap tickets and resell them to business travelers. Look at the rules that govern ticket pricing and you will see an ingenious implementation of profit-maximizing price discrimination.

Perfect Price Discrimination

Let's return to the example of business travelers and students traveling between Bismarck and Ft. Lauderdale illustrated in Figure 63.1 and ask what would happen if the airline could distinguish between the two groups of customers in order to charge each a different price.

Clearly, the airline would charge each group its *willingness to pay*—that is, the maximum that each group is willing to pay. For business travelers, the willingness to pay is $650; for students, it is $250. As we have assumed, the marginal cost is $200 and does not depend on output, making the marginal cost curve a horizontal line. And as we noted earlier, we can easily determine the airline's profit: it is the sum of the areas of rectangle *B* and rectangle *S*.

In this case, the consumers do not get any consumer surplus! The entire surplus is captured by the monopolist in the form of profit. When a monopolist is able to capture the entire surplus in this way, we say that the monopolist achieves **perfect price discrimination**.

In general, the greater the number of different prices charged, the closer the monopolist is to perfect price discrimination. **Figure 63.2** shows a monopolist facing a downward-sloping demand curve. We assume the monopolist is able to charge different prices to different groups of consumers, with the consumers who are willing to pay the most being charged the most. In panel (a) the monopolist charges two different prices; in panel (b) the monopolist charges three different prices. Two things are apparent:

- The greater the number of prices the monopolist charges, the lower the lowest price—that is, some consumers will pay prices that approach marginal cost.
- The greater the number of prices the monopolist charges, the more money is extracted from consumers.

With a very large number of different prices, the picture would look like panel (c), a case of perfect price discrimination. Here, every consumer pays the most he or she is willing to pay, and the entire consumer surplus is extracted as profit.

Both our airline example and the example in Figure 63.2 can be used to make another point: a monopolist who can engage in perfect price discrimination doesn't cause any allocative inefficiency! The reason is that the source of allocative inefficiency is eliminated: all potential consumers who are willing to purchase the good at a price

Perfect price discrimination takes place when a monopolist charges each consumer his or her willingness to pay—the maximum amount the consumer is willing to pay.

Figure 63.2 Price Discrimination

(a) Price Discrimination with Two Different Prices

(b) Price Discrimination with Three Different Prices

(c) Perfect Price Discrimination

Panel (a) shows a monopolist that charges two different prices; its profit is shown by the shaded area. Panel (b) shows a monopolist that charges three different prices; its profit, too, is shown by the shaded area. It is able to capture more of the consumer surplus and to increase its profit. That is, by increasing the number of different prices charged, the monopolist captures more of the consumer surplus and makes a larger profit. Panel (c) shows the case of perfect price discrimination, where a monopolist charges each consumer his or her willingness to pay. The monopolist's profit is given by the shaded triangle, and there is no consumer surplus.

equal to or above the marginal cost are able to do so. The perfectly price-discriminating monopolist manages to "scoop up" these consumers by offering some of them lower prices than others.

Perfect price discrimination is almost never possible in practice. At a fundamental level, firms' inability to achieve perfect price discrimination reveals a flaw in prices as economic signals. When prices work as economic signals, they convey the information needed to ensure that all mutually beneficial transactions will indeed occur: the market price signals the seller's cost, and a consumer signals willingness to pay by purchasing the good whenever that willingness to pay is at least as high as the market price. The problem in reality, however, is that prices are often not perfect signals: a consumer's true willingness to pay can be disguised, as by a business traveler who claims to be a student when buying a ticket in order to obtain a lower fare. When such disguises work, a monopolist cannot achieve perfect price discrimination. However, monopolists do

AP® EXAM TIP

A perfectly price-discriminating monopolist produces the efficient quantity, as there is no deadweight loss.

Costco and other discount clubs price discriminate by charging annual fees and providing volume discounts.

try to move in the direction of perfect price discrimination through a variety of pricing strategies. Common techniques for price discrimination include:

- *Advance purchase restrictions.* Prices are lower for those who purchase well in advance (or in some cases for those who purchase at the last minute). This separates those who are likely to shop for better prices from those who won't.

- *Volume discounts.* Often the price is lower if you buy a large quantity. For a consumer who plans to consume a lot of a good, the cost of the last unit—the marginal cost to the consumer—is considerably less than the average price. This separates those who plan to buy a lot, and so are likely to be more sensitive to price, from those who don't.

- *Two-part tariffs.* In a discount club like Costco or Sam's Club (which are not monopolists but monopolistic competitors), you pay an annual fee (the first part of the tariff) in addition to the price of the item(s) you purchase (the second part of the tariff). So the full price of the first item you buy is in effect much higher than that of subsequent items, making the two-part tariff behave like a volume discount.

Our discussion also helps explain why government policies on monopoly typically focus on preventing deadweight loss, not preventing price discrimination, unless that discrimination causes serious issues of equity. Compared to the pricing practices of a single-price monopolist, price discrimination—even when it is not perfect—can increase the efficiency of the market. When a single, medium-level price is replaced by a high price and a low price, some consumers who were formerly priced out of the market will be able to purchase the good. Price discrimination increases efficiency because more of the units for which the willingness to pay (as indicated by the height of the demand curve) exceeds the marginal cost are produced and sold.

Consider a drug that is disproportionately prescribed to senior citizens, who are often on fixed incomes and so are very sensitive to price. A policy that allows a drug company to charge senior citizens a low price and everyone else a high price will serve more consumers and create more total surplus than if everyone is charged the same price. But price discrimination that creates serious concerns about equity is likely to be prohibited—for example, an ambulance service that charges patients based on the severity of their emergency.

MODULE 63 REVIEW

Check Your Understanding

1. True or false? Explain your answer.
   a. A single-price monopolist sells to some customers that would not find the product affordable if purchasing from a price-discriminating monopolist.
   b. A price-discriminating monopolist creates more inefficiency than a single-price monopolist because it captures more of the consumer surplus.
   c. Under price discrimination, a customer with highly elastic demand will pay a lower price than a customer with inelastic demand.

2. Which of the following are cases of price discrimination and which are not? In the cases of price discrimination, identify the consumers with a high price elasticity of demand and those with a low price elasticity of demand.
   a. Damaged merchandise is marked down.
   b. Hotels have senior citizen discounts.
   c. Food manufacturers place discount coupons for their merchandise in newspapers.
   d. Airline tickets cost more during the summer peak flying season.

TACKLE THE AP® TEST: Multiple-Choice Questions

1. Which of the following characteristics is necessary in order for a firm to price-discriminate?
   a. free entry and exit
   b. differentiated product
   c. many sellers
   d. some control over price
   e. horizontal demand curve

2. Price discrimination
   a. is the opposite of volume discounts.
   b. is a practice limited to movie theaters and the airline industry.
   c. can lead to increased efficiency in the market.
   d. rarely occurs in the real world.
   e. helps to increase the profit of perfect competitors.

3. With perfect price discrimination, consumer surplus
   a. is maximized.
   b. equals zero.
   c. is increased.
   d. cannot be determined.
   e. is the area below the demand curve and above the marginal cost curve.

4. Which of the following is a common practice of single-price monopolists?
   a. two-part tariffs
   b. advance purchase restrictions
   c. volume discounts
   d. differentiating customers based on their price elasticity of demand
   e. operating where marginal revenue equals marginal cost

5. A price-discriminating monopolist will charge a higher price to consumers with
   a. a more inelastic demand.
   b. a less inelastic demand.
   c. higher income.
   d. lower willingness to pay.
   e. less experience in the market.

6. In order to carry out perfect price discrimination, a firm must know each
   a. customer's income.
   b. competitor's marginal cost.
   c. customer's willingness to pay.
   d. competitor's advertising budget.
   e. customer's price elasticity of demand.

7. A perfectly price-discriminating monopolist
   a. creates the highest possible consumer surplus.
   b. earns no more than a normal profit.
   c. creates deadweight loss.
   d. achieves allocative efficiency.
   e. produces less output than a single-price monopolist.

TACKLE THE AP® TEST: Free-Response Questions

1. a. Define price discrimination.
   b. Why do firms price-discriminate?
   c. In which market structures can firms price-discriminate? Explain why.
   d. Give an example of price discrimination.

> **Rubric for FRQ 1 (5 points)**
>
> **1 point:** Price discrimination is the practice of charging different prices to different customers for the same good.
>
> **1 point:** Firms price-discriminate to increase their profit.
>
> **1 point:** In order to price-discriminate, firms must be in the monopoly, oligopoly, or monopolistic competition market structure.

> **1 point:** Because rather than being price-takers, firms in these market structures have some degree of market power, which gives them the ability to charge more than one price.
>
> **1 point:** An example is different prices for movie tickets charged for people of different ages.

2. Draw a correctly labeled graph showing a monopoly with a horizontal average total cost curve practicing perfect price discrimination. On your graph, identify the monopoly's profit. What does consumer surplus equal in this case? Explain. **(6 points)**

SECTION
11
Review

▶ SECTION 11 Review Video

Adventures in AP® Economics Videos
Mod 59: Perfect Competition
Mod 61: Monopoly

Module 58

1. A producer chooses output according to the **price-taking firm's optimal output rule**: produce the quantity at which the price equals the marginal cost.

However, a firm that produces the optimal quantity may not be profitable.

Module 59

2. A firm is profitable if its total revenue exceeds its total cost or, equivalently, if the market price exceeds its **break-even price**—the minimum average total cost. If the market price exceeds the break-even price, the firm is profitable. If the market price is less than the minimum average total cost, the firm is unprofitable. If the market price is equal to the minimum average total cost, the firm breaks even. When profitable, the firm's per-unit profit is $P - ATC$; when unprofitable, its per-unit loss is $ATC - P$.

3. A firm's fixed cost is irrelevant to its optimal short-run production decision. That decision depends on the firm's **shut-down price**—its minimum average variable

cost—along with its marginal cost and the market price. When the market price is equal to or exceeds the shut-down price, the firm produces the quantity at which the marginal cost equals the market price. When the market price falls below the shut-down price, the firm ceases production in the short run. These decisions determine the shape of the **short-run firm supply curve**.

4. Fixed cost matters over time. If the market price is below the minimum average total cost for an extended period of time, firms will exit the industry in the long run. If the market price is above the minimum average total cost, existing firms are profitable and new firms will enter the industry in the long run.

Module 60

5. The **industry supply curve** depends on the time period (short run or long run). When the number of firms is fixed, the **short-run industry supply curve** applies. The short-run market equilibrium occurs where the short-run industry supply curve and the demand curve intersect.

6. With sufficient time for entry into and exit from an industry, the **long-run industry supply curve** applies. The **long-run market equilibrium** occurs at the intersection of the long-run industry supply curve and the demand curve. At this point, no producer has an incentive to enter or exit. The long-run industry supply curve is horizontal for a **constant-cost industry**. It may slope upward if the industry's demand represents a significant portion of the overall demand for an input, resulting in an **increasing-cost industry**. It may even slope

downward, as in the case of a **decreasing-cost industry**. But the long-run industry supply curve is always more elastic than the short-run industry supply curve.

7. In the long-run market equilibrium of a competitive industry, profit maximization leads each firm to produce at the same marginal cost, which is equal to the market price. Free entry and exit means that each firm earns zero economic profit—producing the output corresponding to its minimum average total cost. So the total cost of production of an industry's output is minimized and productive efficiency is achieved. The outcome is also allocatively efficient because the price equals the marginal cost, and every consumer with a willingness to pay greater than or equal to the marginal cost gets the good.

Module 61

8. The key difference between a monopoly and a perfectly competitive industry is that a single, perfectly competitive firm faces a horizontal demand curve but a monopolist faces a downward-sloping demand curve. This gives the monopolist market power, the ability to raise the market price by reducing output.

9. The marginal revenue of a monopolist is composed of a quantity effect (the price received from the additional unit) and a price effect (the reduction in the price at which all units are sold). Because of the price effect, a monopolist's marginal revenue is always less than the market price, and the marginal revenue curve lies below the demand curve.

10. At the monopolist's profit-maximizing output level, the marginal cost equals the marginal revenue, which is less than the market price. At the perfectly competitive firm's profit-maximizing output level, the marginal cost equals the market price. So in comparison to perfectly competitive industries, monopolies produce less, charge higher prices, and can earn profit in both the short run and the long run.

Module 62

11. A monopoly creates deadweight loss by charging a price above marginal cost: the loss in consumer surplus exceeds the monopolist's profit. This makes monopolies a source of market failure, and governments often make policies to prevent or end them.

12. A natural monopoly also causes deadweight loss. To limit such losses, governments sometimes impose **public ownership** and at other times impose **price regulation**. A price ceiling on a monopolist, as opposed to a perfectly competitive industry, need not cause shortages and can increase total surplus.

Module 63

13. Not all monopolists are **single-price monopolists**. Monopolists, as well as oligopolists and monopolistic competitors, often engage in **price discrimination** to make higher profit, using various techniques to differentiate consumers based on their sensitivity to price and then charging those with less elastic demand higher prices. A monopolist that achieves **perfect price discrimination** charges each consumer a price equal to his or her willingness to pay and captures the total surplus in the market. Although perfect price discrimination creates no allocative inefficiency, it is practically impossible to implement.

Key Terms

Price-taking firm's optimal output rule, p. 567
Break-even price, p. 573
Shut-down price, p. 575
Short-run firm supply curve, p. 576
Industry supply curve, p. 580
Short-run industry supply curve, p. 580
Long-run market equilibrium, p. 583
Long-run industry supply curve, p. 584
Constant-cost industry, p. 584
Increasing-cost industry, p. 584
Decreasing-cost industry, p. 586
Public ownership, p. 600
Price regulation, p. 600
Single-price monopolist, p. 603
Price discrimination, p. 603
Perfect price discrimination, p. 606

AP® Exam Practice Questions

Multiple-Choice Questions

1. According to the price-taking firm's optimal output rule, a perfectly competitive firm should produce the quantity at which marginal cost is equal to
  a. total cost.
  b. average variable cost.
  c. average fixed cost.
  d. marginal revenue but not price.
  e. marginal revenue and price.

2. A perfectly competitive firm is a price-taker because
  a. the government sets its price.
  b. it produces a differentiated product.
  c. a larger firm sets the price for the industry.
  d. intense competition prevents it from influencing the market price.
  e. a powerful consumer group establishes the market price.

3. Because a perfectly competitive firm is a price-taker, its short-run demand curve is
  a. perfectly elastic.
  b. perfectly inelastic.
  c. equal to its average total cost curve.
  d. downward-sloping.
  e. upward-sloping.

4. A perfectly competitive firm is guaranteed to be profitable when it produces a level of output where
  a. marginal revenue is equal to price.
  b. price is equal to average fixed cost.
  c. price is greater than average fixed cost.
  d. price is greater than average total cost.
  e. price is greater than average variable cost.

5. Average total cost is minimized by producing the level of output where the marginal cost
   a. is minimized.
   b. curve intersects the average total cost curve.
   c. curve intersects the average fixed cost curve.
   d. curve intersects the average variable cost curve.
   e. curve intersects the marginal revenue curve.

Use the data below for a perfectly competitive firm to answer Questions 6–8.

Quantity of tomatoes (bushels) Q	Variable cost VC	Total cost TC	Marginal cost of bushel MC = ΔTC/ΔQ	Marginal revenue of bushel MR	Net gain of bushel = MR − MC
0	$0	$14			
			$16	$18	$2
1	16	30			
			6	18	12
2	22	36			
			8	18	10
3	30	44			
			12	18	6
4	42	56			
			16	18	2
5	58	72			
			20	18	−2
6	78	92			
			24	18	−6
7	102	116			

6. Suppose an increase in the demand for tomatoes brings the market price up to $22. How many bushels should be produced in order to maximize profit?
   a. 7   d. 4
   b. 6   e. 3
   c. 5

7. Now suppose a decrease in the demand for tomatoes brings the market price down to $15. How many bushels should be produced in order to maximize profit?
   a. 7   d. 4
   b. 6   e. 3
   c. 5

8. What price represents the shut-down price in the short run?
   a. $8   d. $18
   b. $10   e. $20
   c. $16

9. Oscar sells bicycles in a perfectly competitive market. In the short run, at the quantity at which marginal revenue equals marginal cost, the market price is above Oscar's average variable cost and below his average total cost. Oscar should
   a. shut down his business.
   b. raise his price.

c. produce at a loss because he is covering his fixed costs.
d. produce at a loss because he is covering his variable costs.
e. produce at a profit because he is covering his variable costs.

10. The short-run supply curve for a perfectly competitive firm is its
   a. marginal cost curve above the average variable cost curve.
   b. marginal cost curve above the average fixed cost curve.
   c. average variable cost curve above the marginal cost curve.
   d. average variable cost curve above the average total cost curve.
   e. average variable cost curve above the average fixed cost curve.

11. For a perfectly competitive industry, the short-run industry supply curve is determined by
   a. horizontally summing all the firm's profit-maximizing output levels.
   b. horizontally summing all the firm's supply curves.
   c. vertically summing all the firm's profit-maximizing output levels.
   d. vertically summing all the firm's marginal cost curves.
   e. vertically summing all the firm's supply curves.

12. Tia sells hats in a perfectly competitive market. If, in the long run, the market price exceeds the minimum of Tia's average variable cost but is below the minimum of her average total cost, Tia should
   a. shut down her business if the situation continues for another year.
   b. shut down her business immediately.
   c. produce at a loss since she is covering her variable cost.
   d. produce at a loss since she is covering her fixed cost.
   e. produce at a loss since she is covering her marginal cost.

13. In the long run for a perfectly competitive constant-cost industry, if existing firms are producing where the price is greater than the average total cost, firms will enter the industry, the price will
   a. fall, and existing firms will increase production.
   b. fall, and existing firms will decrease production.
   c. rise, and existing firms will increase production.
   d. rise, and existing firms will decrease production.
   e. remain constant, and existing firms will increase production.

14. For a perfectly competitive increasing-cost industry, an increase in demand will cause the price to
    a. rise and the cost of inputs to fall.
    b. rise and the cost of inputs to rise.
    c. fall and the cost of inputs to fall.
    d. fall and the cost of inputs to rise.
    e. remain constant and the cost of inputs to rise.

15. The long-run industry supply curve for a perfectly competitive firm is
    a. flatter and more elastic than the short-run supply curve.
    b. flatter and more inelastic than the short-run supply curve.
    c. steeper and more elastic than the short-run supply curve.
    d. steeper and more inelastic than the short-run supply curve.
    e. more horizontal and more inelastic than the short-run supply curve.

16. The demand curve for a monopolist producing a normal good is downward-sloping because of
    a. the substitution effect being larger than the income effect.
    b. the income effect being larger than the substitution effect.
    c. diminishing marginal returns.
    d. price discrimination.
    e. diminishing marginal utility.

17. The marginal revenue curve for a monopolist lies below the demand curve because of
    a. the income effect.
    b. the quantity effect.
    c. price discrimination.
    d. the price effect.
    e. the substitution effect.

18. If a monopolist charges a price such that marginal revenue is greater than marginal cost, then the monopolist
    a. will earn profit.
    b. will earn losses.
    c. will break even.
    d. can improve its profit by reducing its price.
    e. can improve its profit by raising its price.

19. For a monopolist, when marginal revenue is positive,
    a. the quantity effect outweighs the price effect.
    b. the price effect outweighs the quantity effect.
    c. total revenue is rising at an increasing rate.
    d. total revenue is declining at an increasing rate.
    e. total revenue is declining at a declining rate.

20. Relative to a competitive industry with the same costs, a monopolist charges
    a. a higher price and produces more output.
    b. a lower price and produces more output.
    c. a higher price and produces less output.
    d. a lower price and produces less output.
    e. a higher price and produces the same level of output.

21. If a monopolist finds that demand is elastic at the level of output where marginal revenue is equal to marginal cost, the monopolist will
    a. maintain that level of output.
    b. increase output.
    c. decrease output.
    d. raise the price.
    e. lower the price.

22. A perfectly competitive industry will likely have
    a. more consumer surplus, more producer surplus, and more deadweight loss than a monopoly.
    b. more consumer surplus, less producer surplus, and less deadweight loss than a monopoly.
    c. less consumer surplus, more producer surplus, and more deadweight loss than a monopoly.
    d. more consumer surplus, less producer surplus, and more deadweight loss than a monopoly.
    e. less consumer surplus, more producer surplus, and less deadweight loss than a monopoly.

23. If a regulatory commission wants to ensure that a monopolist produces the largest quantity of output that is consistent with earning a normal profit, it will require the monopolist to charge a price equal to its
    a. marginal cost.
    b. average fixed cost.
    c. average variable cost.
    d. average total cost.
    e. total cost.

24. In order to practice price discrimination, a firm must have
    a. market power.
    b. customers of different ages.
    c. customers with the same price elasticity of demand.
    d. customers with different income levels.
    e. customers in different locations.

25. Perfect price discrimination will result in
    a. more output and more consumer surplus.
    b. more output and less consumer surplus.
    c. less output and more producer surplus.
    d. less output and less consumer surplus.
    e. less output and more consumer surplus.

Free-Response Questions

1. Holly's Cutlery is one of many producers of knives in a perfectly competitive market. Holly's Cutlery is earning a greater-than-normal profit. Draw correctly labeled side-by-side graphs showing the market for knives and the marginal cost, average total cost, demand, and marginal revenue curves for Holly's Cutlery.
   a. Show what will happen to each of the following in the long run:
      i. the industry supply curve for knives
      ii. the price of knives
      iii. Holly's Cutlery's output compared to the initial level
   b. On your graph for part a, shade the area that represents Holly's Cutlery's initial economic profit and explain what will happen to it in the long run.
   c. Now assume that in order to ensure overall public safety, the local government grants Holly's Cutlery the exclusive right to produce knives. Draw a correctly labeled graph showing Holly's Cutlery's output level and price, assuming Holly's Cutlery makes a greater-than-normal economic profit. Does Holly's Cutlery produce the allocatively efficient level of output? Explain.
   d. Shade in the area of deadweight loss, if any, in the graph for part c. **(14 points)**

2. The Desert Oasis Water Company is a natural monopoly in the town of Dryville. The firm experiences a constant marginal cost and is currently operating at a loss.
   a. Using a correctly labeled graph, illustrate the market for water in Dryville.
      i. Label the profit-maximizing quantity Q_1.
      ii. Label the profit-maximizing price P_1.
      iii. Shade the area that represents the firm's loss.
      iv. Label the allocatively efficient quantity Q_S.
   b. In an effort to achieve the allocatively efficient quantity, the government of Dryville is considering a lump-sum subsidy (a fixed contribution of money) for the Desert Oasis Water Company. Assuming that the firm would continue to operate with or without the subsidy, what effect will this subsidy have on the firm's output level? Explain. **(7 points)**

3. Gary's Greenhouse is a single-price monopolist that sells tulips and earns a normal profit.
   a. Draw a correctly labeled graph for Gary's Greenhouse showing the following:
      i. the profit-maximizing price and quantity, labeled as P_m and Q_m
      ii. the area of total cost, shaded completely
   b. Label a point A to indicate the left end of the inelastic portion of the demand curve. **(7 points)**

Is Adam Smith Rolling Over in His Grave?

Perfect Competition, Efficiency, and the Father of Modern Economics

The celebrated eighteenth-century economist Adam Smith worshipped the workings of free markets, and his words are still quoted in support of unbridled capitalism. However, Smith's role as the patron saint of unconstrained markets may be unwarranted: Smith abhorred market power, and the market efficiency he glorified was achieved only by relatively rare perfectly competitive markets. Do a few detours from Smith's market model matter? In a word, yes. And if you've seen prices that differ among gas stations or among burger joints, you've seen evidence that competition is seldom perfect. Here we discuss the splendor of markets at their best and some neglected truths about Adam Smith.

Statue of Adam Smith outside of the St Giles Cathedral in Edinburgh, Scotland, the city where he did most of his work.

The Beauty of Perfectly Competitive Markets

Adam Smith is often proclaimed the patriarch of modern economics. His most famous saying first appeared in his 1776 book, *The Wealth of Nations*, in which he wrote that the individual decision maker

> *intends only his own gain; and he is in this, as in many other cases, led by an invisible hand to promote an end which was no part of his intention. . . . By pursuing his own interest, he frequently promotes that of the society more effectually than when he really intends to promote it.*

The notion of the market embodying an "invisible hand" by which self-interested behavior yields efficient outcomes for society has captured the fancy of generations of economists and policy makers.

Efficiency is a matter of attaining the largest possible gains with the least possible waste. The efficiency of markets stems largely from conditions that occur at market equilibrium, where the supply-and-demand curves intersect to establish quantity and price. Smith explained how a competitive market tends toward a price that is fair to both buyers and sellers, and that this price allocates resources as well as possible from the broad standpoint of society. Suppose you were a benevolent, all-knowing dictator. After eliminating war, hunger, and acne, you could

advance the well-being of society by allocating resources to achieve three types of efficiency:

- *productive efficiency*, achieved when firms minimize the average cost of producing their goods
- *allocative efficiency*, achieved when each type of good is produced until the benefit from another unit of the good no longer exceeds the cost of producing another unit
- *distributive efficiency*, achieved when goods go to those who value them the most

Remarkably, perfectly competitive markets can achieve all three of these outcomes without your help as dictator. Let's examine how that happens, beginning with a quick review of the conditions for perfect competition.

In a perfectly competitive market, a large number of firms sell the same good to a large number of buyers. Competitors can enter and leave the market easily, and everyone involved in the market has full information about what is available from whom at what price. Under these conditions, a firm that charged more than its competitors would get no business. Firms need not charge *less* than the equilibrium price because they can sell all they want at the equilibrium price (after all, demand equals supply at equilibrium). So, each firm in a perfectly competitive market ends up as a *price-taker*, taking on the equilibrium price determined by supply and demand in the market.

Consider the online market for rubber clown noses—those bright-red semispheres that fit over a real nose and make onlookers smile. In this market there are many buyers and sellers, the noses are all pretty much the same, ample information on both prices and suppliers is available through a quick internet search, and it's possible for almost anyone with access to a computer to enter or exit the market. If one online seller of clown noses tried to charge significantly more than other sellers, the high-priced seller would lose its customers to the competition. Perfect competition isn't all funny business; markets for agricultural products, such as corn and sugar, also approximate the perfectly competitive model.

Productive Efficiency

Perfectly competitive markets achieve productive efficiency thanks to the ease of entry and exit by firms seeking economic profit. If ClownAntics.com isn't using the lowest-cost methods of clown nose production, competitors, such as TheClownShop.com, will. Rival firms can undercut the price charged by an inefficient firm and steal its business. If the market price for clown noses exceeds the average cost of producing them, other informed entrepreneurs, such as Betty at ClownCostumes.com, will be attracted to the market by the smell of profit, and the entrance of new firms will increase the supply and lower the equilibrium price. This process will continue until the lowest-cost method of nose making no longer provides economic profit. This situation leaves no room for the use of inefficient production methods in a perfectly competitive industry.

Allocative Efficiency

Remember that the supply curve represents the increasing marginal cost of producing each unit and that the demand curve represents the decreasing marginal value of each unit to consumers. At quantities of output less than the equilibrium quantity, the demand curve lies above the supply curve, indicating that, up to the equilibrium quantity, the value to consumers of each unit exceeds the cost of making it. For instance, if the marginal value of another clown nose is $7 and the marginal cost is $3, that nose provides a net gain to society and should be made. However, it would be inefficient to produce beyond the equilibrium quantity because marginal value falls below marginal cost at the point of equilibrium. If another clown nose would cost $4 to make and it would be worth only $2, it would be unwise for society to allocate resources for another nose. It follows that to produce the equilibrium quantity is to produce all those units that are worth more than they cost to provide.

Like the equilibrium quantity, the equilibrium price is established at the intersection of supply and demand, meaning that the price equals both the marginal cost and the marginal value of the last nose sold. The condition for allocative efficiency is often stated as the equality of marginal cost and price because if the price that buyers are willing to pay is above the marginal cost, consumers must value another nose at more than the cost of making one, and too few clown noses are being made. Conversely, if buyers are not willing to pay a price as high as the marginal cost, the marginal value is below the marginal cost and too many noses have been made.

Distributive Efficiency

The well-being of society is maximized if clown noses go to those who value them the most—presumably clowns. A perfectly competitive market is up to the task of maximizing well-being. Consider a simplified market with 5 potential buyers: Alfie, Buttons, Chuckles, Dot, and Ernie, each of whom is interested in, at most, 1 clown nose. The values these clowns receive from a rubber nose are, respectively, $12, $8, $6, $3, and $1. Suppose the marginal cost of producing

the first 5 clown noses is $2, $4, $6, $8, and $10, as shown in the accompanying table. Three noses should be produced, because any additional noses would be valued at less than the cost of producing them.

Buyer	Buyer's Marginal Value	Seller's Marginal Cost
Alfie	$12	$2
Buttons	$8	$4
Chuckles	$6	$6
Dot	$3	$8
Ernie	$1	$10

In our example, the equilibrium price is $6 because that is the only price that equates supply and demand. Three of the clowns—Alfie, Buttons, and Chuckles—are willing to pay the $6 equilibrium price. Because those who place the highest value on noses are willing to pay the highest price, clown noses will be rightly allocated to the true nose lovers.

In contrast, imagine that a lottery rather than a market is used to allocate 3 noses. If names are drawn out of a hat, the recipients are equally likely to be any of the 5 clowns. Suppose Buttons, Dot, and Ernie win the lottery. The total value created by the noses is the sum of the recipients' marginal values: $8 + $3 + $1 = $12; this amount falls below the $12 + $8 + $6 = $26 worth of value obtained through the market allocation. In both cases the cost of producing 3 noses is $2 + $4 + $6 = $12, but the net gain is the highest with the help of the market. Nonetheless, lotteries are common for allocating dorm rooms and student tickets for popular football games, among other valuable goods and services.

Trouble in Paradise: Market Failure and Immorality

The previous example demonstrates how buyers and sellers can enhance the well-being of society merely by acting out of self-interest. Adam Smith marveled at the potential for markets to allocate resources efficiently without government assistance, as if they were guided by the invisible hand of a benevolent dictator. To Smith, competition was the great enforcer that held greed at bay. Should one merchant decide to charge an excessive price, another merchant would swiftly provide the same product for less money. This is the case under perfect competition. Those who cite Smith's work to support a more general disdain for government policies should consider two issues about which Smith's message is often misinterpreted: market failure and morality. This section introduces the sources of market failure and discusses the overlap between markets and morality.

Market Power Matters

The cruelest of our revenue laws, I will venture to affirm, are mild and gentle, in comparison to some of those which the clamor of our merchants and manufacturers has extorted from the legislature, for the support of their own absurd and oppressive monopolies.

—Adam Smith, *The Wealth of Nations*

Although Smith venerated competitive markets, he abhorred monopoly power and trade secrets. In *The Wealth of Nations*, Smith wrote of "the mean rapacity, the monopolizing spirit, of merchants and manufacturers, who neither are, nor ought to be, the rulers of mankind." The celebrated efficiency of competitive markets is jeopardized when individual sellers or buyers have *market power*, meaning that they can restrict supply and increase prices, or when any of the other conditions for perfect competition are violated.

Legal, technical, and economic barriers are among the deterrents to potential competitors in some markets. For example, when Grace VanderWaal writes a song, she owns the *copyright* to it, which makes it illegal for competitors to sell the song without her permission. Facebook was built on a *proprietary technology platform*, meaning that competitors can't use the technology because Facebook owns it. And cable companies such as Spectrum have a competitive advantage in small markets because it would be prohibitively expensive to create multiple cable networks to serve one small area, so the first company to serve the area is often the only one.

Neglected Costs and Benefits

In order for the equilibrium quantity of a good or service to be efficient, buyers and sellers must also bear, or *internalize*, the full cost and benefit of that product. Otherwise, the market equilibrium differs from the true equilibrium of marginal costs and marginal benefits felt by society. Consider the following examples:

• As the Anheuser-Busch brewery makes beverages in St. Louis, Missouri, it releases hundreds of thousands of pounds of suspected pollutants, such as hydrochloric acid, into the air in a typical year. Because consumers don't bear the full health cost of these emissions, without intervention, the equilibrium quantity would be too large.

• Heart disease is the leading cause of death in the United States. If buyers don't have full information on the health costs associated with their food choices, or if insurance spreads some of those costs to other people, then private decisions about the production and consumption of unhealthy food won't reflect all of the costs, and the equilibrium quantity will be too large.

• If studying economics increases people's contributions to society by making them wiser voters and more productive workers, the demand curve for economics classes will understate the value of economics to society, and the equilibrium number of students will be too small.

Such benefits and costs that aren't borne by those buying or selling the products are called *externalities*, and they thwart the efficiency of competitive markets. What is to be done when the invisible hand of perfect competition loses its touch? Economists Richard Lipsey and Kelvin Lancaster advanced the general theory of second-best, which demonstrates that, when one of the conditions for perfect competition is not met, intervention to remedy the situation can lead to a better outcome than a hands-off approach, even if every other condition is met. Thus, if free markets cultivate market power, pollution, and study benefits that aren't internalized, then antitrust legislation, environmental regulations, and funding for education may be warranted to achieve the best possible situation.

Imperfect information is another source of market failure. Do you have full information on the prices of competing doctors, restaurants, and hotels where you live and travel? If not, policies requiring the posting of prices could improve efficiency and social well-being, and such policies do exist for restaurants and hotels in some countries. You'll learn about more sources of market failure as well as government failure in Section 14.

Morality and the Market

Smith believed that markets would overcome immoral behavior. He believed that benevolence would spring from market forces because, through trade, people gain in proportion to what they give and thus are prompted to develop ways to give more. But as with market failure, problems with morals have persisted in a way that Smith hoped they would not. Recent examples include the corporate ethics scandals at Apple, Facebook, Samsung, Uber, Volkswagen, and Wells Fargo.

Tension exists between the desire for complete freedom and the desire to avoid the moral bankruptcy that threatens the efficiency of markets. The contemporary Adam Smith Institute is a self-proclaimed "free-market think tank," but Smith himself was a moral philosopher, and his theories assumed a foundation of righteousness and human decency. He wrote of every person being "left perfectly free to pursue his own interest in his own way" on the premise that markets compel ethical behavior.

Smith wrote at length about the morality that underpinned his laissez-faire disposition. In the context of children whose parents are poor role models, Smith wrote that "the example of that bad conduct commonly corrupts their morals; so that, instead of being useful to society by their industry, they become public nuisances by their vices and disorders." In his book *The Theory of Moral Sentiments* (1759), Smith argued that an individual should examine his or her behaviors as would an impartial spectator. By Smith's standard, an action is wrong if an individual feels a sentiment of disapproval when she or he considers that action. Several other schools of thought provide questions that assist decision making when markets and morals intersect:

Utilitarianism: Does this action bring the greatest good to the greatest number of people?

Ethical egoism: Is this action good for me?

The common good: Is this action good for society as a whole?

Virtue: Does this action reflect balance between vices?

Rights: Does this action respect the moral rights of everyone?

Kantianism: Would I want everyone to perform this action?

Justice: Is this action fair and just? Does it treat equals equally?

Role models: What would my hero do?

The newspaper test: Would I be embarrassed if this action appeared in a newspaper headline?

Smith would have us ruled neither by big government nor by big business. And he would have us behave in such ways as to win the approval of impartial observers. Would these observers approve of the exploitation of labor, the neglect of health and environmental concerns, exorbitant prices, or pressure on buyers to purchase items they don't really need? Probably not—meaning that the progenitor of modern economics would disapprove of the license for unchecked business behavior that some see as his legacy.

Conclusion

Adam Smith wrote about how markets can achieve miraculous efficiency and how constraints on otherwise efficient markets can distort the incentives for socially optimal behavior. Smith would not have liked artificial controls on prices, quantities, or wages; nor would he have favored government subsidies or tax breaks. However, the markets that are efficient are those that involve many informed sellers of an identical product and no barriers to entry or exit by competitors. Smith probably would have appreciated such measures as nutrition information labels on food packages, restrictions on monopoly power, and harsh punishments for deceptive advertising. Likewise, the enforcement of health and environmental standards that prevent firms from imposing pollution costs on society is in the spirit of Smith's sensibilities.

Like the lessons of Adam Smith, much of what is learned in economics classes—such as the common model of supply and demand—is based on the assumption of perfectly competitive markets. Given the reality of market imperfections, Smith would probably want individuals to relish free markets within reason, while maintaining high moral standards and accepting measures that deal with market failure.

Critical Thinking Questions

1. What markets in your local economy most closely resemble Adam Smith's ideal of perfect competition?

2. What conditions for perfect competition does the hamburger market in your area violate?

3. Summarize the potential pros and cons of free markets.

4. Which of the questions to guide decision making do you feel is the most appropriate?

Market Structures: Imperfect Competition

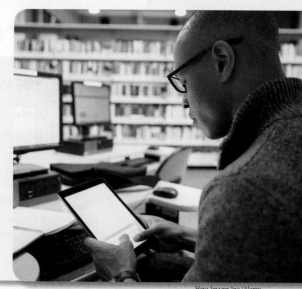

Hero Images Inc./Alamy

economics by example *What's Behind the Music Industry's Woes?*

Corporate Misdeeds and the Differentiation Dance

Apple is one of several companies hoping to furnish your electronic devices with virtual libraries. In 2015, a U.S. circuit court ruled that Apple had conspired with five publishers to raise the price of eBooks, behavior known as *price-fixing*. Each company agreed to limit its supply of eBooks to achieve price targets above the $9.99 price charged by Amazon.com. What the companies did was illegal. Apple ended up paying a $450 million settlement for their actions, and the other companies paid settlements as well. Other industries recently investigated for price-fixing range from insurance to college education to computer chips. Despite its illegality, some firms attempt to fix

the prices of their products in order to raise their profits.

In the fast-food market, the legal practice of *product differentiation* occupies the minds of marketing executives. Fast-food producers go to great lengths to convince you they have something special to offer beyond the ordinary burger: it's flame broiled or 100% beef or super-thick or lathered with special sauce. Or maybe they offer chicken or fish or roast beef. The differentiation dance goes on in the pizza industry as well. Pizza Hut offers cheese in the crust. Papa John's claims "better ingredients." Dominoes has a "new recipe," and if you don't want thin crust, the alternative isn't "regular," it's "hand

tossed"! The slogans and logos for fast-food restaurants often seem to differ more than the food itself.

To understand why some companies engage in illegal price-fixing and why fast-food joints go to great lengths to differentiate their patties and pizzas, we need to understand the two market structures in between perfect competition and monopoly in the spectrum of market power—oligopoly and monopolistic competition. The models of these two market structures are at the same time more complicated and more realistic than those we studied in the previous section. Indeed, they describe the behavior of most of the firms in the real world.

Introduction to Oligopoly

> **In this Module, you will learn to:**
> - Explain why oligopolists have an incentive to act in ways that reduce their combined profit
> - Explain how oligopolies can benefit from collusion

In Module 57 we learned that an oligopoly is an industry with only a few firms. But what number constitutes a "few"? There is no standard answer, and it is not always easy to determine an industry's market structure just by looking at the number of firms. Economists use various measures to gain a better picture of market structure, including concentration ratios and the Herfindahl–Hirschman Index, as explained in Module 57.

In addition to having a small number of firms in the industry, an oligopoly is characterized by **interdependence**, a relationship in which the outcome (profit) of each firm depends on the actions of the other firms in the market. This is not true for monopolies because, by definition, a monopoly has no other firms to consider. On the other hand, perfectly competitive markets contain so many firms that no one firm has a significant effect on the outcome of the others. However, in an oligopoly—an industry with few firms—the outcome for each firm depends on the behavior of the others. Interdependence makes studying a market much more interesting because firms must observe and predict the behavior of other firms. But such a market is also more complicated. To understand the strategies of oligopolists, we must do more than find the point where the *MC* and *MR* curves intersect!

> Firms are **interdependent** when the outcome (profit) of each firm depends on the actions of the other firms in the market.

Understanding Oligopoly

How much will a firm produce? Up to this point, the answer has always been: a firm will produce the quantity that maximizes its profit. When a firm is a perfect competitor or a monopolist, we can assume that the firm will use its cost curves to determine its profit-maximizing output. When it comes to oligopoly, however, we run into some difficulties.

A Duopoly Example

Let's begin by looking at the simplest version of the oligopoly puzzle: an industry in which there are only two firms—a **duopoly**—and each is known as a **duopolist**.

Imagine that only two firms sell dictionary apps for smartphones and that the apps sold by the two firms are indistinguishable from each other. Once a company has incurred the fixed cost of creating an app, the marginal cost of selling the app to another customer is very low (to keep things simple we will assume that the marginal cost is zero). In this case the companies are concerned only with the revenue they receive from sales.

> An oligopoly consisting of only two firms is a **duopoly**. Each firm is known as a **duopolist**.

Table 64.1 shows a hypothetical demand schedule for dictionary apps and the total revenue of the industry at each price-quantity combination.

If this were a perfectly competitive industry, each firm would have an incentive to sell more as long as the market price was above the marginal cost. Since the marginal cost is zero, this would mean that at equilibrium, dictionary apps would be provided for free. Firms would sell more until the price equaled zero, yielding a total output of 12 million apps and zero revenue for both firms.

However, with only two firms in the industry, it would seem foolish to allow the price and revenue to plummet to zero. Like a monopolist, each firm sees that profits will be higher if the two firms charge a higher price, and sell a smaller quantity, than they would in a perfectly competitive industry.

What will the two firms do?

Table 64.1	Demand Schedule for Dictionary Apps	
Price of app	Quantity of apps demanded (millions)	Total revenue (millions)
$12	0	$0
11	1	11
10	2	20
9	3	27
8	4	32
7	5	35
6	6	36
5	7	35
4	8	32
3	9	27
2	10	20
1	11	11
0	12	0

One possibility is that the two companies will engage in **collusion**—they will cooperate to raise their joint profits. The strongest form of collusion is a **cartel**, a group of firms with an agreement to work together to limit output and increase price, and therefore profit. The world's most famous cartel is the Organization of the Petroleum Exporting Countries (OPEC).

As its name indicates, OPEC is actually a cartel made up of governments rather than firms. There's a reason for this: cartels among firms are illegal in the United States and many other jurisdictions, whereas organizations of governments can often evade restrictions on firm behavior. But let's ignore the law for a moment. Suppose the firms selling dictionary apps were to form a cartel and that this cartel decided to act as if it were a monopolist, maximizing total industry profits. It's obvious from Table 64.1 that in order to maximize the combined profits of the firms, this cartel should set a price of $6 per app and provide a combined total of 6 million apps, leading to revenue of $36 million, the maximum possible. Then the only question would be how many of those 6 million apps does each firm get to sell. A "fair" solution might be for each firm to sell 3 million apps and receive revenues of $18 million.

But even if the two firms agreed on such a deal, they might have a problem: each of the firms would have an incentive to break its word and sell more than the agreed-upon quantity at less than the agreed-upon price.

OPEC representatives meet regularly to discuss the cartel's policies of cooperation.

Firms engage in **collusion** when they cooperate to raise their joint profits. A **cartel** is a group of firms that agree to restrict output in order to increase prices and their joint profits.

Collusion and Competition

Suppose that the presidents of the two app sellers were to agree that each would charge $6 per app and sell 3 million apps over the next year. Both would understand that this plan maximizes their combined profits. And both would have an incentive to cheat.

To see why, consider what would happen if one firm honored its agreement to charge $6, but the other ignored its promise and lowered its price to $5 per app, the price at which 7 million apps are demanded. The industry's total revenue would fall from $36 million ($6 × 6 million apps) to $35 million ($5 × 7 million apps). However, the cheating firm would have the best price, attract all of the customers, and receive the entire $35 million in total revenue rather than half of $36 million. Since we are assuming a marginal cost of zero, this would mean a $17 million increase in profit over the $18 million the firm would have earned by charging $6.

AP® EXAM TIP

To make sense of the discussions of cartels and related matters that might appear on the exam, remember that collusion is illegal in the United States but legal in some parts of the world.

But then the other firm would see that by lowering its price to $4, it could sell 8 million apps and receive $32 million in revenue. As long as the price remained above the marginal cost, these firms would have an incentive to undercut each other's prices. More generally, the incentive to cheat motivates firms in an oligopoly to lower their price and sell more than the quantity that maximizes their joint profits, rather than maintaining a higher price and limiting output as a true monopolist would.

In the oil industry, among others, some firms cheat on collusive agreements by producing more than the agreed upon quantity, which has the effect of increasing the market quantity and decreasing the market price. Let's examine how this affects firm profits. We know that a profit-maximizing monopolist sets marginal cost (which in the dictionary app example is zero) equal to marginal revenue. But what is marginal revenue? Recall that producing an additional unit of a good has two effects:

1. A positive *quantity effect*: one more unit is sold, increasing total revenue by the price at which that unit is sold.

2. A negative *price effect*: in order to sell one more unit, the monopolist must cut the market price on *all* units sold.

The negative price effect is the reason marginal revenue for a monopolist is less than the market price. But when considering the effect of increasing production, an oligopolist is concerned only with the price effect on its *own* units of output, not on those of its fellow oligopolists. In the apps example, both duopolists suffer a negative price effect if one firm decides to lower the price and sell additional apps. But each firm cares only about the portion of the negative price effect that falls on the apps it sells.

This tells us that an individual firm in an oligopolistic industry faces a smaller price effect from an additional unit of output than a monopolist; therefore, the marginal revenue that such a firm calculates is higher. So it will seem to be profitable for any one firm in an oligopoly to increase output, even if that increase reduces the profits of the industry as a whole. But if everyone thinks that way, the result is that everyone earns a lower profit!

Until now, we have been able to analyze firm behavior by asking what a firm should do to maximize profits. But even if both duopolists are trying to maximize profits, what does this predict about their behavior? Will they engage in collusion, reaching and holding to an agreement that maximizes their combined profits? Or will they engage in **noncooperative behavior**, with each firm acting in its own self-interest, even though this has the effect of driving down everyone's profits? Both strategies can be carried out with a goal of profit maximization. Which strategy will actually describe their behavior?

When firms act in their own self-interest, ignoring the effects of their actions on each other's profits, they engage in **noncooperative behavior**.

If there were dozens or hundreds of firms, it would be safe to assume they would behave noncooperatively. Yet, when there are only a handful of firms in an industry, it's hard to determine whether collusion will actually occur. Now you see why oligopoly presents a puzzle: there are only a small number of players, making collusion a real possibility.

Since collusion is ultimately more profitable than noncooperative behavior, firms have an incentive to collude if they can. One way to do so is to formalize it—sign an agreement (maybe even make a legal contract) or establish some financial incentives for the companies to set their prices high. But in the United States and many other nations, firms can't do that—at least not legally. A contract among firms to keep prices high would be unenforceable, and it could be a one-way ticket to jail. The same goes for an informal agreement. In fact, executives from rival firms rarely meet without lawyers present, who make sure that the conversation does not stray into inappropriate territory. Even hinting at how nice it would be if prices were higher can bring an unwelcome interview with the Justice Department or the Federal Trade Commission.

Bryan Smith/Zuma Press

A contract among firms to keep prices high would be unenforceable, and could be a one-way ticket to jail.

In 2017, the Justice Department announced that Bumble Bee Foods paid a $25 million fine for fixing the price of canned tuna, and Höegh Autoliners paid a $21 million fine for price-fixing and other actions to suppress competition in the ocean shipping industry. In the same year, the attorneys general in 45 states filed suit against 18 pharmaceutical companies, alleging conspiracy to fix prices on generic drugs.

Sometimes, oligopolistic firms just ignore the rules. More often they develop strategies for making the best of the situation depending on what they know, or assume, about the other firms' behavior. As in the dictionary app example, some firms repeatedly undercut each other's prices—charging a bit less than the others to steal their customers—until the price reaches the level of the marginal cost, as under perfect competition.

Understandably, oligopolists would prefer to avoid direct price competition that leaves them earning zero economic profit. One alternate strategy for limiting competition is to produce products that are not perfect substitutes but are instead differentiated. We'll examine this strategy in more detail in Module 68. For now, we note that producing differentiated products allows oligopolists to cultivate a loyal set of customers and to charge prices higher than the marginal cost.

We have seen that collusion is another approach to dodging the profit-suppressing effects of competition. In the next Module, we examine efforts to collude that do not involve formal agreements.

In the absence of collusion, price competition among oligopolists can be intense, as with the price wars that led to $99 airfares from New York to Paris in 2018.

James Leynse/Getty Images

MODULE 64 REVIEW

Check Your Understanding

1. Explain whether each of the following characteristics will increase or decrease the likelihood that a firm will collude with other firms in an oligopoly to restrict output.
   a. The firm's initial market share is small. (Hint: Think about the price effect.)
   b. The firm has a cost advantage over its rivals.
   c. The firm's customers face additional costs when they switch from one firm's product to another firm's product.
   d. The firm and its rivals are currently operating at maximum production capacity, which cannot be altered in the short run.

TACKLE THE AP® TEST: Multiple-Choice Questions

1. When firms cooperate to raise their joint profits, they are necessarily
   a. colluding.
   b. in a cartel.
   c. a monopoly.
   d. in a duopoly.
   e. in a competitive industry.

2. Within a group of firms, if the actions of the firms affect each other's profits, the firms are necessarily
   a. colluding.
   b. duopolists.
   c. in a cartel.
   d. monopolists.
   e. interdependent.

3. An agreement among several producers to restrict output and increase profit is necessary for
  a. cooperation.
  b. collusion.
  c. monopolization.
  d. a cartel.
  e. competition.

4. Oligopolists are tempted to produce more than the quantity that would maximize industry profits because when they increase output,
  a. the price effect is zero.
  b. the quantity effect is zero.
  c. the price effect equals the quantity effect.
  d. the price effect is larger than the quantity effect.
  e. the price effect is spread across multiple firms.

5. Which of the following will make it easier for firms in an industry to maintain positive economic profit?
  a. a ban on cartels
  b. a small number of firms in the industry

  c. a lack of product differentiation
  d. low start-up costs for new firms
  e. the assumption by firms that other firms have variable output levels

6. Oligopolistic firms that engage in direct price competition will stop undercutting each other's prices when the price reaches the
  a. price a monopoly would charge.
  b. profit-maximizing price for the industry as a whole.
  c. price a perfectly competitive firm would charge.
  d. lowest price that ensures positive economic profits for each firm.
  e. marginal revenue.

7. In the United States, price-fixing is
  a. unheard of.
  b. only seen among monopolies.
  c. encouraged by the Federal Trade Commission.
  d. common among perfectly competitive firms.
  e. illegal.

TACKLE THE AP® TEST: Free-Response Questions

1. Refer to the table provided to answer the following questions. Assume that marginal cost is zero.

Demand Schedule	
Price	Quantity
$24	0
22	1
20	2
18	3
16	4
14	5
12	6
10	7
8	8
6	9
4	10
2	11
0	12

a. If the market is perfectly competitive, what will the market equilibrium price and quantity be in the long run? Explain.
b. If the market is a duopoly and the firms collude to maximize joint profits, what will market price and quantity be? Explain.
c. If the market is a duopoly and the firms collude to maximize joint profits, what is each firm's total revenue if the firms split the market equally?

> **Rubric for FRQ 1 (7 points)**
>
> **1 point:** If the market is perfectly competitive, price will be zero.
>
> **1 point:** If the market is perfectly competitive, quantity will be 12.
>
> **1 point:** Price equals marginal cost in the long-run equilibrium of a perfectly competitive market, so price will be zero, at which price the quantity is 12.
>
> **1 point:** If the market is a duopoly, price will be $12.
>
> **1 point:** If the market is a duopoly, quantity will be 6.
>
> **1 point:** In order to maximize joint profits, the two firms would act as a monopoly, setting marginal revenue equal to marginal cost and finding price on the demand curve above the profit-maximizing quantity. Marginal revenue passes through zero (going from 2 to −2) after the 6th unit, making 6 the profit-maximizing quantity. The most consumers would pay for 6 units is $12, so that is the profit-maximizing price.
>
> **1 point:** Total revenue is $12 × 6 = $72. By dividing this equally, each firm receives $36.

2. **a.** What are two major deterrents to cartels among oligopolistic industries in the United States?
  b. Although we do not see cartels in the United States, we do see interdependence among oligopolists. Explain why firms in an oligopoly are interdependent, but firms in a perfectly competitive market or a monopoly are not. **(4 points)**

Game Theory

In this Module, you will learn to:
- Use game theory to enhance your understanding of oligopoly
- Analyze a prisoners' dilemma using a payoff matrix
- Determine dominant strategies and Nash equilibria in a variety of games

Games Oligopolists Play

If you eat tuna salad, you most likely consume the product of StarKist or Bumble Bee, the two largest firms in the U.S. tuna market. The tuna oligopoly includes a few smaller firms, but to keep things simple we'll treat this market as a duopoly. Each firm in a duopoly realizes that its profit depends on what its competitor does, and that its competitor's profit depends on what it does. That is, the two firms are interdependent—each firm's decision significantly affects the profit of the other firm (or firms, in the case of more than two).

In effect, the two firms are playing a "game" in which the profit of each player depends not only on its own actions but on those of the other player (or players). In order to better understand how oligopolists behave, economists and mathematicians developed **game theory**—the study of behavior in such interdependent games. Game theory has many applications, not just to economics but also to military strategy, politics, and other social sciences.

Let's see how game theory helps us understand oligopoly.

Game theory is the study of behavior in situations of interdependence.

A player's reward in a game, such as an oligopolist's profit, is that player's **payoff**.

A **payoff matrix** shows how the payoff to each of the participants in a two-player game depends on the actions of both. Such a matrix helps us analyze situations of interdependence.

The Prisoners' Dilemma

Game theory deals with any situation in which the reward to any one player—the **payoff**—depends not only on his or her own actions but also on those of other players in the game. In the case of oligopolistic firms, the payoff is simply the firm's profit.

When there are only two players, as in a tuna duopoly, the interdependence between the players can be represented with a **payoff matrix** like that shown in **Figure 65.1**. Each

Figure 65.1 A Payoff Matrix

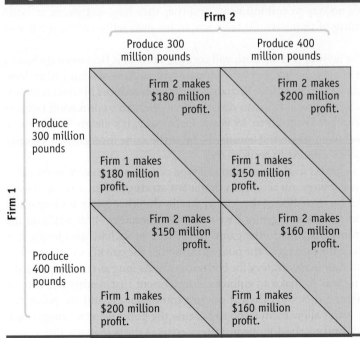

Two firms must decide how much tuna to produce. The profits of the two firms are *interdependent*: each firm's profit depends not only on its own decision but also on the other's decision. Each row represents an action by Firm 1; each column represents an action by Firm 2. Both firms will be better off if they both choose the lower output, but it is in each firm's individual interest to choose the higher output.

The **prisoners' dilemma** is a game based on two premises: (1) each player has an incentive to choose an action that benefits him- or herself at the other player's expense; and (2) when both players follow that incentive, both are worse off than if they had acted cooperatively.

An action is a **dominant strategy** when it is a player's best action regardless of the action taken by the other player.

In the movie *Murder by Numbers*, loosely based on a real 1924 murder case, the police know that high schoolers Richard and Justin were involved in a crime. Yet there is insufficient evidence to convict the suspects, so the police offer a lighter sentence in exchange for a confession from either one of them.

row corresponds to an action by one player; each column corresponds to an action by the other. For simplicity, let's assume that each firm can pick only one of two alternatives: produce 300 million pounds of tuna or produce 400 million pounds.

The matrix contains four boxes, each divided by a diagonal line. Each box shows the payoff to the two firms that results from a pair of choices; the number below the diagonal shows Firm 1's profits, the number above the diagonal shows Firm 2's profits.

These payoffs show that the combined profit of the two firms is maximized if they each produce 300 million pounds. However, either firm can increase its own profits by producing 400 million pounds if the other produces only 300 million pounds. But if both produce the larger quantity, both will have lower profits than if they had both held their output down.

The particular situation shown here is a version of the famous—and seemingly paradoxical—case of interdependence known as the **prisoners' dilemma**, a type of game in which the payoff matrix implies the following:

- Each player has an incentive, regardless of what the other player does, to cheat—to take an action that benefits him or her at the other's expense.

- When both players cheat, both are worse off than they would have been if neither had cheated.

The original illustration of the prisoners' dilemma occurred in a fictional story about two accomplices in crime—let's call them Richard and Justin—who have been caught by the police. The police have enough evidence to put the suspects behind bars for 5 years. They also know that the pair have committed a more serious crime, one that carries a 20-year sentence; unfortunately, they don't have enough evidence to convict the young men on that charge. To do so, they would need each of the suspects to implicate the other in the second crime.

So the police put the suspects in separate cells and say the following to each: "Here's the deal: if neither of you confesses, you know that we'll send both of you to jail for 5 years. If you confess and implicate your partner, and he doesn't do the same, we reduce your sentence from 5 years to 2. But if your partner confesses and you don't, you'll get the maximum of 20 years. And if both of you confess, we'll give you both 15 years."

Figure 65.2 shows the payoffs that face each suspect, depending on the decision to remain silent or to confess. (Usually higher payoffs are better than lower payoffs. This case is an exception: a higher number of years in prison is bad, not good!) Let's assume that the suspects have no way to communicate and that they have not sworn an oath to cooperate or anything of that sort. So each acts in his own self-interest. What will they do?

The answer is clear: both will confess. Look at it first from Richard's point of view: he is better off confessing, regardless of what Justin does. If Justin doesn't confess, Richard's confession reduces his own sentence from 5 years to 2. If Justin does confess, Richard's confession reduces his sentence from 20 to 15 years. Either way, it's clearly in Richard's interest to confess. And because he faces the same incentives, it's clearly in Justin's interest to confess, too.

To confess in this situation is a type of action that economists call a *dominant strategy*. An action is a **dominant strategy** when it is the player's best action regardless of the action taken by the other player. It's important to note that not all games have a dominant strategy—it depends on the structure of payoffs in the game. In the case of Richard and Justin, it is clearly in the interest of the police to structure the payoffs so that confessing is a dominant strategy for both suspects. As long as the two prisoners have no way to make an enforceable agreement that neither will confess (something they can't do if they can't communicate, and the police certainly won't allow them to do so because the police want to compel each one to confess), the dominant strategy exists as the best alternative.

Figure 65.2 The Prisoners' Dilemma

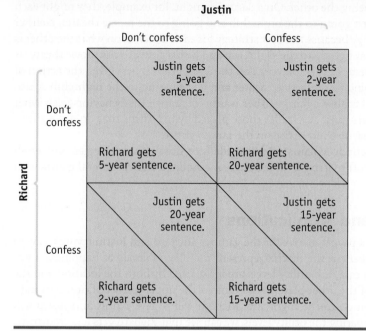

Justin

	Don't confess	Confess
Don't confess	Justin gets 5-year sentence. / Richard gets 5-year sentence.	Justin gets 2-year sentence. / Richard gets 20-year sentence.
Confess	Justin gets 20-year sentence. / Richard gets 2-year sentence.	Justin gets 15-year sentence. / Richard gets 15-year sentence.

Richard

Each of two suspects, held in separate cells, is offered a deal by the police—a light sentence if he confesses and implicates his accomplice but his accomplice does not do the same. The sentence is heavy for a suspect if he does not confess but his accomplice does. It is in the joint interest of both suspects not to confess; it is in each one's individual interest to confess.

If each prisoner acts rationally in his own interest, both will confess. Yet if neither of them confesses, both will receive a much lighter sentence! In a prisoners' dilemma, each player has a clear incentive to act in a way that hurts the other player—but when both make that choice, it leaves both of them worse off.

When Richard and Justin both confess, they reach an *equilibrium* of the game. We have used the concept of equilibrium many times in this book; it is an outcome in which no individual or firm has any incentive to change his or her action. In game theory, this kind of equilibrium, in which each player takes the action that is best for him or her, given the actions taken by other players, is known as a **Nash equilibrium**, after the mathematician and Nobel Laureate John Nash. (Nash's life was chronicled in the best-selling biography *A Beautiful Mind*, which was made into a movie.) Because the players in a Nash equilibrium do not take into account the effect of their actions on others, this is also known as a **noncooperative equilibrium**.

Now look back at Figure 65.1: the two firms face a prisoners' dilemma just like Richard and Justin did after their crimes. Each firm is better off producing the higher output, regardless of what the other firm does. Yet if both produce 400 million pounds, both are worse off than if they had followed an agreement to produce only 300 million pounds. In both cases, then, the pursuit of individual self-interest—the effort to maximize profit or to minimize jail time—has the perverse effect of hurting both players.

Prisoners' dilemmas appear in many situations. Examples include business competitors deciding whether to advertise high or low prices, athletes deciding whether to use illegal performance-enhancing drugs, and countries deciding whether to spend more or less on military hardware.

A **Nash equilibrium**, also known as a **noncooperative equilibrium**, is the result when each player in a game chooses the action that maximizes his or her payoff, given the actions of other players.

More Games

We can use payoff matrices to analyze any number of games played by individuals and firms. The equilibria of many of these games differ from what we've seen in the prisoners' dilemma. For example, in the prisoners' dilemma, the Nash equilibrium happens to be an equilibrium of two dominant strategies—a *dominant strategy equilibrium*—but Nash equilibria can exist when there is no dominant strategy at all. Also, a game can have multiple Nash equilibria.

Mathematician and Nobel Laureate John Forbes Nash, Jr., proposed one of the key ideas in game theory.

Let's return to Richard and Justin, who are disheartened by the mutual distrust that led them to confess to their crime. After serving their jail time, each wants nothing more than to avoid seeing the other. On a Saturday night, for example, they might each have to choose between going to the nightclub and going to the movie theater. Neither has a dominant strategy because the best strategy for each depends on what the other is doing. However, Richard going to the nightclub and Justin going to the movie theater is a Nash equilibrium because each player takes the action that is best given the action of the other. Richard going to the movie theater and Justin going to the nightclub is also a Nash equilibrium, because again, neither wants to change his behavior given what the other is doing. This game resembles those played by two firms that do not want to locate in the same area, or to advertise on the same website.

The following section explains tricks to identify dominant strategies and Nash equilibria using a payoff matrix. We'll use these methods to analyze several games with varying outcomes.

Approaches and Applications

Figure 65.3 provides a payoff matrix for the game of Richard and Justin trying to avoid each other. The numbers in the matrix represent the players' levels of happiness, measured in utils. In each case, the utility levels are influenced by both the location and the presence or absence of the other player. For example, the upper-left set of numbers indicates that if both men go to the nightclub, Richard will receive 2 utils and Justin will receive 4 utils. By comparing the utility levels, we can see that Richard gets less enjoyment out of the nightclub than Justin, and that both players would be happier if they were not in the same place. If, instead, Richard goes to the nightclub and Justin goes to the movie theater, Richard will receive 4 utils while Justin receives 6, as indicated by the upper-right set of numbers.

Here's a trick for finding dominant strategies and Nash equilibria. Begin by supposing that Justin goes to the nightclub. In the "Nightclub" column for Justin, we see that Richard receives 2 utils by going to the nightclub and 5 utils by going to the movie

Figure 65.3   A Game of Avoidance

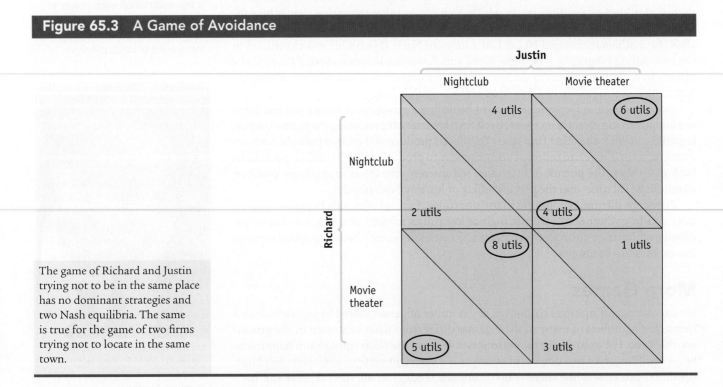

The game of Richard and Justin trying not to be in the same place has no dominant strategies and two Nash equilibria. The same is true for the game of two firms trying not to locate in the same town.

theater. Circle the best outcome for Richard, which is the 5 utils received by going to the movie theater. Then suppose that Justin goes to the movie theater. Circle the best outcome for Richard, which is to receive 4 utils by going to the nightclub.

Now look at things from Justin's point of view. If Richard goes to the nightclub, the options for Justin are to receive 4 utils by going to the nightclub or 6 utils by going to the movie theater. Circle the best outcome for Justin: 6 utils. Finally, suppose that Richard goes to the movie theater. Circle the best outcome for Justin in that case, which is to receive 8 utils by going to the nightclub.

Justin has a dominant strategy if there are two circles around his outcomes in the same column. In this game Justin does not have a dominant strategy, because he has one circle in the "Movie theater" column and one circle in the "Nightclub" column. Richard has a dominant strategy if there are two circles around his outcomes in the same row. Here Richard does not have a dominant strategy, because he has only one circle in each row.

A combination of strategies is a Nash equilibrium if the box representing that combination contains two circles. In this game, there are two circles in the box representing Richard going to the movie theater and Justin going to the nightclub, so that is a Nash equilibrium. The two circles in the box representing Richard going to the nightclub and Justin going to the movie theater indicate a second Nash equilibrium.

The same outcome of two Nash equilibria and no dominant strategy occurs when two grocery store chains, Chain 1 and Chain 2, consider opening a store in a town that can only support one grocery store. Just like Richard and Justin, if one of them is there, the other doesn't want to be there. So the two Nash equilibria are: Chain 1 there and Chain 2 not there, and Chain 2 there and Chain 1 not there. Whichever chain can commit to being in that town first has the *first-mover advantage* of being able to ward off the other chain.

Sometimes firms face differing choices. For example, suppose that Juice Tree is deciding whether to raise its price on orange juice, while competitor Juice Max is deciding whether to spend more on advertising. **Figure 65.4** shows hypothetical profits for each firm, depending on the chosen strategies. For example, if Juice Tree raises its

> **AP® EXAM TIP**
>
> Whenever there are two circles in the same box, a Nash equilibrium exists. Whenever there are two circles in a column (or row) for a player, a dominant strategy exists.

Figure 65.4 Differing Choices

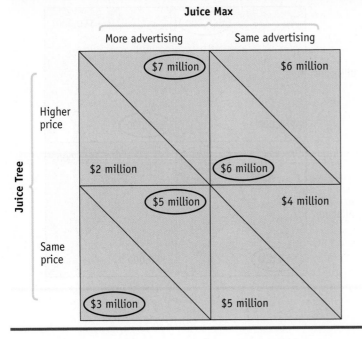

> Players don't always face the same choices. In this game, Juice Tree is deciding whether to raise its price on orange juice, while competitor Juice Max is deciding whether to spend more on advertising. Juice Max has a dominant strategy of spending more on advertising, while Juice Tree has no dominant strategy. There is one Nash equilibrium of Juice Tree keeping the same price and Juice Max spending more on advertising.

price and Juice Max doesn't advertise more, some of Juice Tree's customers will switch to Juice Max, increasing Juice Max's profit from $4 million to $6 million. In this case, Juice Tree's profit increases from $5 million to $6 million, indicating that the price effect of receiving more per unit is larger than the quantity effect of losing customers. The story changes if Juice Max advertises more: Juice Tree's profit decreases from $3 million to $2 million if it raises its price, because Juice Max is better able to draw attention to Juice Tree's higher prices and attract its customers.

Using the circle trick, we find one Nash equilibrium where Juice Tree keeps its price the same and Juice Max advertises more. The two circles around Juice Max's payoffs in the left column indicate that Juice Max has a dominant strategy of advertising more. Juice Tree does not have a dominant strategy because its best strategy depends on the strategy of Juice Max—Juice Tree is better off raising its price if Juice Max doesn't advertise more, and better off not raising its price if Juice Max does advertise more.

Spending more on advertising is a wise strategy for Juice Max, but the cost of more advertising can exceed the benefit. Suppose Ally and Barto offer competing painting services, and each must decide whether to rent a billboard to attract customers. **Figure 65.5** shows each painter's annual profits depending on the chosen strategies. Remember that oligopolists are not identical, so differing characteristics can result in differing payoffs for two firms in analogous situations. In this case, Barto is relatively unknown

Figure 65.5 Differing Payoffs

Even when facing the same choices, differences among oligopolists can cause them to receive different payoffs in analogous situations. In this example of painters Ally and Barto, Ally is well known in the area but Barto is a newcomer. This makes it a dominant strategy for Barto to rent a billboard to make customers aware of his services, whereas Ally is better off not renting a billboard if Barto rents one. The one Nash equilibrium in this case is for Barto to rent a billboard and for Ally not to.

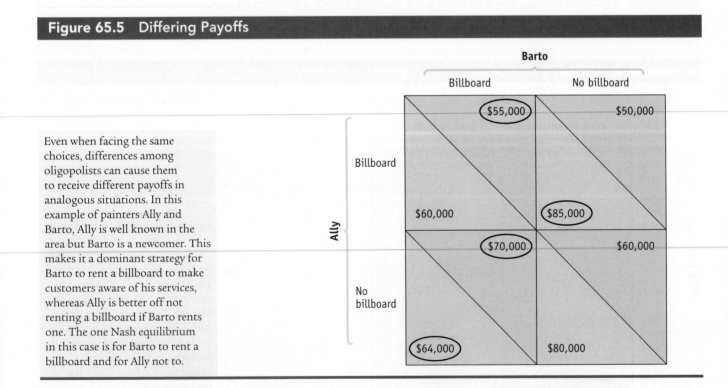

among the potential customers, and receives a net gain from billboard advertising regardless of Ally's decision. If Barto does not rent a billboard, Ally receives a net gain of $5,000 from a billboard. But if Barto does rent a billboard, he attracts so many new customers that Ally cannot gain enough to cover the cost of a billboard, and Ally loses $4,000 by renting one.

Applying the circle trick, the two circles around Barto's payoffs in the left column indicate that Barto has a dominant strategy of advertising. There are not two circles around Ally's payoffs in any one row, so she does not have a dominant strategy. The two circles in the box for Ally not getting a billboard and Barto getting a billboard indicate that neither side would want to take a different action given what the other is doing, so that combination is a Nash equilibrium.

We can explore more possible outcomes by supposing that the annual cost of renting a billboard decreases by $4,000. As shown with green numbers in **Figure 65.6**, this increases each profit level associated with renting a billboard by $4,000. Notice that if Barto rents a billboard, Ally receives a profit of $64,000 with or without a billboard. Which number do we circle when applying the circle trick to two identical choices? Both! This indicates that Ally is indifferent between the two strategies if Barto has a billboard. If Barto doesn't have a billboard, Ally earns more profit with a billboard. Because Ally is sometimes indifferent about having a billboard and sometimes she is better off with one, we describe having a billboard as a *weakly dominant strategy* for Ally. Having a billboard is again a dominant strategy for Barto. And now there are two Nash equilibria: both having a billboard, and Ally having no billboard while Barto does have a billboard. If Ally and Barto had to decide whether to rent billboards year after year, this would be considered a *repeated game*. The next Module explains how repeated games create new options for strategy and cooperation.

Figure 65.6   Adjusting for Changes

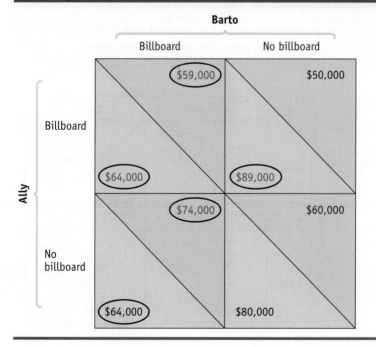

Barto

Billboard | No billboard

Ally

Billboard: $59,000, $50,000, $64,000, $89,000

No billboard: $74,000, $60,000, $64,000, $80,000

Changes in prices, taxes, or related policies can change the payoffs of a game. If the change only affects one strategy, as with a $4,000 decrease in the cost of renting a billboard, be careful to adjust only the payoffs for that strategy. The changes in this figure relative to Figure 65.5 are shown in green. The lower cost makes renting a billboard a weakly dominant strategy for Ally, meaning that the payoffs from that strategy are at least as good, and in some cases better, than the payoffs from the alternative strategy. The lower rental cost also creates an additional Nash equilibrium of both players renting a billboard.

Check Your Understanding

1. Suppose world leaders Nikita and Margaret are engaged in an arms race and face the decision of whether to build a missile. Answer the following questions using the information in the payoff matrix below, which shows how each set of actions will affect the utility of the players (the numbers represent utils gained or lost).

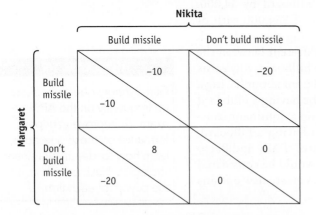

Nikita

a. Identify any Nash equilibria that exist in this game, and explain why they do or do not exist.

b. Which set of actions maximizes the total payoff for Nikita and Margaret?

c. Why is it unlikely that they will choose the payoff-maximizing set of actions without some communication?

2. Consider a new version of the game in which Richard and Justin must decide whether to go to the nightclub or the movie theater (see page 628). In this version, rather than being disheartened, the two men bond in jail and want nothing more than to be in the same place after their release. Describe any dominant strategies and Nash equilibria in this game.

TACKLE THE AP® TEST: Multiple-Choice Questions

1. Each player has an incentive to choose an action that, when both players choose it, makes them both worse off than if neither had chosen it. This situation describes
   a. a dominant strategy.
   b. the prisoners' dilemma.
   c. interdependence.
   d. Nash equilibrium.
   e. game theory.

2. Which of the following is true of every Nash equilibrium?
   a. It is the only Nash equilibrium in the game.
   b. Neither player wants to independently change his or her strategy.
   c. It is also a dominant strategy equilibrium.
   d. Each player receives the same payoff.
   e. There is no better outcome in the payoff matrix for either player.

3. A situation in which each player in a game chooses the action that maximizes his or her payoff, given the actions of the other players and ignoring the effects of his or her action on the payoffs received by others, is known as a
   a. dominant strategy.
   b. cooperative equilibrium.
   c. Nash equilibrium.
   d. strategic situation.
   e. prisoners' dilemma.

4. In the context of the Richard and Justin story in the Module, suppose that Justin discovers Richard's action (confess or don't confess) before choosing his own action.

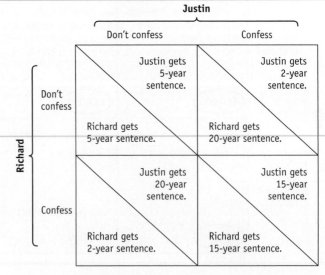

Based on the payoff matrix provided, Justin will
   a. confess whether or not Richard confessed.
   b. not confess only if Richard confessed.

c. not confess only if Richard didn't confess.
d. not confess regardless of whether or not Richard confessed.
e. confess only if Richard did not confess.

5. Which of the following is true on the basis of the payoff matrix provided in Question 4?
  a. Justin has no dominant strategy, but Richard does.
  b. Richard has no dominant strategy, but Justin does.
  c. Both Richard and Justin have a dominant strategy.
  d. Neither Richard nor Justin has a dominant strategy.
  e. Justin has a dominant strategy only if Richard confesses.

6. Relative to the Nash equilibrium outcome in the classic prisoners' dilemma game, the opportunity to successfully cooperate would

a. lead both players to change their strategies.
b. lead one player to change his or her strategy, but not the other.
c. have no effect on the payoffs received by the two players.
d. make the two players indifferent between the two strategies.
e. lead to a better payoff for one player but not the other.

7. Which of the following is necessarily true if both players have a dominant strategy in a game?
  a. There are multiple Nash equilibria in the game.
  b. There are multiple dominant strategy equilibria in the game.
  c. At least one player has a weakly dominant strategy.
  d. The players will follow a cooperative strategy.
  e. There is a dominant strategy equilibrium that is also a Nash equilibrium.

TACKLE THE AP® TEST: Free-Response Questions

1. Refer to the payoff matrix provided, which indicates the profits earned by two producers in various scenarios. You and your competitor must decide whether or not to market a new product.

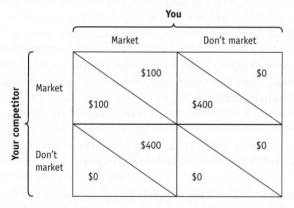

a. If you market the new product and your competitor does not, how much profit will you earn?
b. If you market the new product, what should your competitor do?
c. Do you have a dominant strategy? Explain.
d. Does this situation have a Nash equilibrium? Explain.

Rubric for FRQ 1 (6 points)
1 point: $400
1 point: Market the new product
1 point: Yes, I have a dominant strategy.
1 point: Profits are greater (either $100 or $400 versus $0) if I market the new product, regardless of what my competitor does.

1 point: Yes, there is a Nash equilibrium.
1 point: Both players marketing the product is a Nash equilibrium because neither side wants to change to not marketing, given what the other side is doing. (In fact, in this case both sides want to market the product regardless of what the other side is doing, so it is a dominant strategy equilibrium as well as a Nash equilibrium.)

2. Suppose there are two firms in an oligopoly, Firm A and Firm B. If both firms charge a low price, each earns $2 million in profit. If both firms charge a high price, each earns $3 million in profit. If one firm charges a high price and one charges a low price, customers flock to the firm with the low price, and that firm earns $4 million in profit while the firm with the high price earns $1 million in profit.
  a. Draw a clearly labeled payoff matrix for this game and fill in each of the payoffs. Arrange the matrix so that Firm A is on the left, and make the upper-left set of strategies the low-price option for both firms.
  b. Identify the dominant strategy for each player, if one exists.
  c. Identify the Nash equilibria in this game, if any exist.
  d. Now suppose a tax on high-priced goods causes a $500,000 decrease in the payoffs received from charging a high price. Redraw the payoff matrix with adjustments for this change. **(5 points)**

MOD 66

Oligopoly in Practice

In this Module, you will learn to:
- Discuss the legal constraints of antitrust policy
- Explain how repeated interactions among oligopolists can result in collusion in the absence of any formal agreement
- Explain the cause and effect of price wars, product differentiation, price leadership, and nonprice competition
- Describe the importance of oligopoly in the real world

We have described how oligopolists can form cartels that collude to raise prices and lower output. Fortunately, conspiratorial dealings are not the norm. But how do oligopolies usually work in practice? The answer depends both on the legal framework that limits what firms can do and on the underlying ability of firms in a given industry to cooperate without formal agreements. In this Module we will explore a variety of oligopoly behaviors and how antitrust laws limit oligopolists' attempts to raise their profits.

The Legal Framework

To understand oligopoly pricing in practice, we must be familiar with the legal constraints under which oligopolistic firms operate. In the United States, oligopoly first became an issue during the second half of the nineteenth century, when the growth of railroads—themselves an oligopolistic industry—created a national market for many goods. Large firms producing oil, steel, and many other products soon emerged. The industrialists quickly realized that profits would be higher if they could limit price competition. So, many industries formed cartels—that is, they signed formal agreements to limit production and raise prices. Until 1890, when the first federal legislation against such cartels was passed, this was perfectly legal.

However, although these cartels were legal, their agreements weren't legally *enforceable*—members of a cartel couldn't ask the courts to force a firm that was violating its agreement to reduce its production. And firms often did violate their agreements, for the reason already suggested by our duopoly example in Module 64: there is always a temptation for each firm in a cartel to produce more than it is supposed to.

In 1881, clever lawyers at John D. Rockefeller's Standard Oil Company came up with a better way to thwart price competition—the so-called *trust*. In a trust, shareholders of all the major companies in an industry placed their shares in the hands of a board of trustees who controlled the companies. This, in effect, merged the companies into a single firm that could then engage in monopoly pricing. In this way, the Standard Oil Trust established what was essentially a monopoly of the oil industry, and it was soon followed by trusts in sugar, whiskey, lead, cottonseed oil, and linseed oil.

Eventually, there was a public backlash, driven partly by concern about the economic effects of the trust movement and partly by fear that the owners of the trusts were simply becoming too powerful. The result was the Sherman Antitrust Act of 1890, which was intended both to prevent the creation of more monopolies and to break up existing ones. At first this law went largely unenforced. But over the decades that followed, the federal government became increasingly committed to making it difficult for oligopolistic industries either to become monopolies or to behave like them. Such efforts are known to this day as **antitrust policy**.

Carnegie, Morgan, and Rockefeller established trusts in the steel, electricity, and oil markets, among others, in the late 19th and early 20th centuries.

Antitrust policy involves efforts by the government to prevent oligopolistic industries from becoming or behaving like monopolies.

One of the most striking early actions of antitrust policy was the breakup of Standard Oil in 1911. Its components formed the nuclei of many of today's large oil companies—Standard Oil of New Jersey became Exxon, Standard Oil of New York became Mobil, and so on. In the 1980s a long-running antitrust case led to the breakup of Bell Telephone, which once had a monopoly on both local and long-distance phone service in the United States. In 2000, a U.S. district judge ruled that Microsoft was a monopoly and should be split into two companies, but a federal appeals court overturned the decision. The Justice Department also reviews proposed mergers between companies in the same industry, such as AT&T and T-Mobile, and prohibits mergers that it believes will reduce competition.

Among advanced countries, the United States is unique in its long tradition of antitrust policy. Until recently, other advanced countries did not have policies against price-fixing, and some even supported the creation of cartels, believing that it would help their own firms compete against foreign rivals. But the situation has changed radically over the past 30 years, as the European Union (EU)—an international body with the duty of enforcing antitrust policy for its member countries—has converged toward U.S. practices. Today, EU and U.S. regulators often target the same firms because price-fixing has "gone global" as international trade has expanded. During the early 1990s, the United States instituted an amnesty program in which a price-fixer receives a much-reduced penalty if it provides information on its co-conspirators. In addition, Congress substantially increased maximum fines levied upon conviction. With the help of such policies, the Justice Department has recently collected billions of dollars in fines from sellers of auto parts, air transportation, and LCD panels, among other goods and services. As one lawyer commented, "You get a race to the courthouse" as each conspirator seeks to be the first to come clean.

In 2011, executives from AT&T, T-Mobile USA, and Sprint Nextel testified before the Senate Judiciary Committee regarding their proposed merger. The companies eventually abandoned the merger amid concerns about antitrust violations.

Life has gotten much tougher over the past few years if you want to operate a cartel. So what's an oligopolist to do?

Tacit Collusion

Clearly, the players in any prisoners' dilemma would be better off if they had some way of enforcing cooperative behavior. In terms of the examples from the previous Module, criminals Richard and Justin would benefit from successfully swearing to a code of silence, and the tuna producers would benefit from signing an enforceable agreement not to produce more than 300 million pounds of tuna. But we know that in the United States and many other countries, an agreement setting the output levels of two oligopolists isn't just unenforceable, it's illegal. So it seems that a noncooperative equilibrium is the only possible outcome. Or is it?

Overcoming the Prisoners' Dilemma: Repeated Interaction and Tacit Collusion

Richard and Justin are playing what is known as a *one-shot* game—they play the game with each other only once. They get to choose once and for all whether to confess or remain silent, and that's it. However, most of the games that oligopolists play aren't one-shot games; instead, the players expect to play the game repeatedly with the same rivals.

An oligopolist usually expects to be in business for many years, and knows that a decision today about whether to cheat is likely to affect the decisions of other firms in the future. A smart oligopolist doesn't just decide what to do based on the effect on

A firm engages in **strategic behavior** when it attempts to influence the future actions of other firms.

A strategy of **tit for tat** involves playing cooperatively at first, then doing whatever the other player did in the previous period.

profit in the short run. Instead, it engages in **strategic behavior**, taking into account the effects of its action on the future actions of other players. And under some conditions oligopolists that behave strategically can manage to behave as if they had a formal agreement to collude.

Suppose that our two firms expect to be in the tuna business for many years and therefore expect to play the game of cheat versus collude many times. Would they really betray each other time and again? Probably not. Suppose that each firm considers two strategies. In one strategy, it always cheats, producing 400 million pounds of tuna each year, regardless of what the other firm does. In the other strategy, it starts with good behavior, producing only 300 million pounds in the first year, and watches to see what its rival does. If the other firm also keeps its production down, each firm will stay cooperative, producing 300 million pounds again for the next year. But if one firm produces 400 million pounds, the other firm will also produce 400 million pounds the following year. This latter strategy—start by behaving cooperatively, but thereafter do whatever the other player did in the previous period—is generally known as **tit for tat**.

Playing "tit for tat" is a form of strategic behavior because it is intended to influence the future actions of other players. The tit-for-tat strategy offers a reward to the other player for cooperative behavior—if you behave cooperatively, so will I. It also provides a punishment for cheating—if you cheat, don't expect me to be nice in the future.

For each of these strategies, the payoff to each firm would depend on which strategy the other chooses. Consider the following four possibilities, illustrated in **Figure 66.1**:

1. If one firm plays "tit for tat" and so does the other, both firms will make a profit of $180 million each year.

2. If one firm plays "always cheat" but the other plays "tit for tat," the one that always cheats makes a profit of $200 million the first year but only $160 million per year thereafter.

3. If one firm plays "tit for tat" but the other plays "always cheat," the one that plays tit for tat makes a profit of only $150 million in the first year but $160 million per year thereafter.

4. If one firm plays "always cheat" and the other does the same, both firms will make a profit of $160 million each year.

Figure 66.1 How Repeated Interaction Can Support Collusion

A strategy of tit for tat involves playing cooperatively at first, then following the other player's move. This rewards good behavior and punishes bad behavior. If the other player cheats, playing "tit for tat" will lead to only a short-term loss in comparison to playing "always cheat." But if the other player plays "tit for tat," also playing "tit for tat" leads to a long-term gain. So a firm that expects other firms to play "tit for tat" may well choose to do the same, leading to successful tacit collusion.

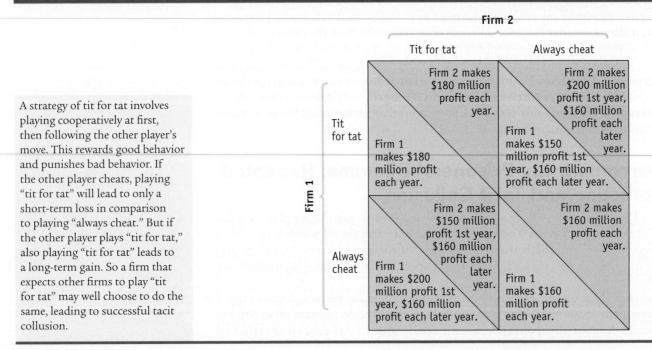

Which strategy is better? In the first year, one firm does better playing "always cheat," whatever its rival's strategy: it assures itself that it will get either $200 million or $160 million. (Which of the two payoffs it actually receives depends on whether the other plays "tit for tat" or "always cheat.") This is better than what it would get in the first year if it played "tit for tat": either $180 million or $150 million. But by the second year, a strategy of "always cheat" gains the firm only $160 million per year for the second and all subsequent years, regardless of the other firm's actions. Over time, the total amount gained by playing "always cheat" is less than the amount gained by playing "tit for tat": for the second and all subsequent years, it would never get any less than $160 million and would get as much as $180 million if the other firm played "tit for tat" as well. Which strategy, "always cheat" or "tit for tat," is more profitable depends on two things: how many years each firm expects to play the game and what strategy its rival follows.

If the firm expects the tuna business to end in the near future, it is in effect playing a one-shot game. So it might as well cheat and grab what it can. Even if the firm expects to remain in the tuna business for many years (therefore to find itself repeatedly playing this game) and, for some reason, expects the other firm will always cheat, it should also always cheat. That is, the firm should follow a variation on the Golden Rule: "Do unto others before they do unto you."

But if the firm expects to be in the business for a long time and thinks the other firm is likely to play "tit for tat," it will make more profits over the long run by playing "tit for tat," too. It could have made some extra short-term profit by cheating at the beginning, but this would provoke the other firm into cheating, too, and, in the end, would mean less profit.

The lesson of this story is that when oligopolists expect to compete with each other over an extended period of time, each individual firm will often conclude that it is in its own best interest to be helpful to the other firms in the industry. So it will restrict its output in a way that raises the profit of the other firms, expecting them to return the favor. Despite the fact that firms have no way of making an enforceable agreement to limit output and raise prices (and are in legal jeopardy if they even discuss prices), they manage to act "as if" they had such an agreement. When this type of unspoken agreement comes about, we say that the firms are engaging in **tacit collusion**.

Business decisions in real life are nowhere near as simple as those in our tuna story; nonetheless, in most oligopolistic industries, most of the time, the sellers do appear to succeed in keeping prices above their noncooperative level. Tacit collusion, in other words, is the normal state of oligopoly.

When firms limit production and raise prices in a way that raises each other's profits, even though they have not made any formal agreement, they are engaged in **tacit collusion**.

Constraints on Collusion

Although tacit collusion is common, it is usually far from perfect. It rarely allows an industry to push prices all the way up to their monopoly level. A variety of factors make it hard for an industry to coordinate on high prices.

Large Numbers

Suppose that there were three firms instead of two in the tuna industry and that each was currently producing only 200 million pounds. In that case any one firm that decided to produce an extra 100 million pounds would gain more in short-term profits—and lose less once another firm responded in kind—than in our original example because it has fewer units on which to feel the price effect. The general point is that the more firms there are in an oligopoly, the less incentive any one firm has to behave cooperatively, taking into account the impact of its actions on the profits of the other firms. Larger numbers of firms in an industry also make the monitoring of price and output levels more difficult, and typically indicate low barriers to entry.

Complex Products and Pricing Schemes

In our simplified tuna example the two firms produce only one product. In reality, however, oligopolists often sell thousands or even tens of thousands of different products. A Walmart Supercenter sells over 100,000 items! Under these circumstances, as when there are a large number of firms, keeping track of what other firms are producing and what prices they are charging is difficult. This makes it hard to determine whether a firm is cheating on the tacit agreement.

Differences in Interests

In the tuna example, a tacit agreement for the firms to split the market equally is a natural outcome, probably acceptable to both firms. In other situations, however, firms often differ both in their perceptions about what is fair and in their real interests.

For example, suppose that one firm in a duopoly is a long-established producer and the other a more recent entrant into the industry. The long-established firm might feel that it deserves to continue producing more than the newer firm, but the newer firm might feel that it is entitled to 50% of the business.

Alternatively, suppose that the newer firm's marginal costs are lower than the long-established firm's. Even if they could agree on market shares, they would then disagree about the profit-maximizing level of output.

Bargaining Power of Buyers

Often oligopolists sell not to individual consumers but to large buyers—other industrial enterprises, nationwide chains of stores, and so on. These large buyers are in a position to bargain for lower prices from the oligopolists: they can ask for a discount from an oligopolist, and warn that they will go to a competitor if they don't get it. An important reason large retailers like Target are able to offer lower prices to customers than small retailers is precisely their ability to use their size to extract lower prices from their suppliers.

These difficulties in enforcing tacit collusion have sometimes led companies to defy the law and engage in price-fixing. We've already discussed the case of the eBook industry. An older, classic example was the U.S. electrical equipment conspiracy of the 1950s, which led to the indictment of and jail sentences for some executives. The industry was one in which tacit collusion was especially difficult because of all the reasons just mentioned. There were many firms—40 companies were indicted. They produced a very complex array of products, often more or less custom-built for particular clients. They differed greatly in size, from giants like General Electric to family firms with only a few dozen employees. And the customers in many cases were large buyers like electrical utilities, which would normally try to force suppliers to compete for their business. Tacit collusion just didn't seem practical—so executives met secretly and illegally to decide who would bid what price for which contract.

Because tacit collusion is often hard to achieve, most oligopolies charge prices that are well below what the same industry would charge if it were controlled by a monopolist—or what they would charge if they were able to collude explicitly. In addition, sometimes tacit collusion breaks down and aggressive price competition amounts to a **price war**. Recent price wars in the hamburger, airline, and grocery industries caused prices to collapse to their noncooperative level, or even lower.

A **price war** occurs when tacit collusion breaks down and aggressive price competition causes prices to collapse.

Product Differentiation and Price Leadership

In many oligopolies firms produce products that consumers regard as similar but not identical. A $10 difference in the price of a car won't make many customers switch from a Ford to a Chrysler, or vice versa. Sometimes the differences between products are real, like differences between Froot Loops and Wheaties; sometimes, they exist mainly in the minds of consumers, like differences between brands of canned peas. Either way, the effect is to reduce the intensity of competition among the firms: consumers will not all rush to buy whichever product is cheapest.

As you might imagine, oligopolists welcome the extra market power that comes when consumers think that their product is different from that of competitors. In many oligopolistic industries, firms make considerable efforts to create the perception that their product is unique—that is, they engage in **product differentiation**.

A firm that tries to differentiate its product may do so by altering what it actually produces, adding "extras," or choosing a different design. It may also use advertising and marketing campaigns to create a differentiation in the minds of consumers, even though its product is more or less identical to the products of rivals.

Generic pharmaceutical drugs provide a classic case of products that may be perceived as being significantly different even when they're not. For instance, the pain relievers ibuprofen and acetaminophen are marketed under a number of brand names in advertising campaigns that imply some special superiority, yet the same drugs are sold in generic forms at much lower prices.

Whatever the nature of product differentiation, oligopolists producing differentiated products often reach a tacit understanding not to compete on price. For example, back when the great majority of cars sold in the United States were produced by the Big Three auto companies (General Motors, Ford, and Chrysler), there was an unwritten rule that none of the three companies would try to gain market share by making its cars noticeably cheaper than those of the other two.

But then who would decide on the overall price of cars? The answer was normally General Motors: as the biggest of the three, it would announce its prices for the year first; and the other companies would adopt similar prices. This pattern of behavior, in which one company tacitly sets prices for the industry as a whole, is known as **price leadership.**

Interestingly, firms that have a tacit agreement not to compete on price often engage in vigorous **nonprice competition**—adding new features to their products, spending large sums on ads that proclaim the inferiority of their rivals' offerings, and so on.

Perhaps the best way to understand the mix of cooperation and competition in such industries is with a political analogy. During the long Cold War between the United States and the Soviet Union, the two countries engaged in intense rivalry for global influence. They not only provided financial and military aid to their allies; they sometimes supported forces trying to overthrow governments allied with their rival (as the Soviet Union did in Vietnam in the 1960s and early 1970s, and as the United States did in Afghanistan from 1979 until the collapse of the Soviet Union in 1991). They even sent their own soldiers to support allied governments against rebels (as the United States did in Vietnam and the Soviet Union did in Afghanistan). But they did not get into direct military confrontations with each other; open warfare between the two superpowers was regarded by both as too dangerous—and tacitly avoided.

Price wars aren't as serious as military wars, but the principle is the same.

How Important Is Oligopoly?

We have seen that, across industries, oligopoly is far more common than either perfect competition or monopoly. When we try to analyze oligopoly, the economist's usual way of thinking—asking how self-interested individuals would behave, then analyzing their interaction—does not work as well as we might hope because we do not know whether rival firms will engage in noncooperative behavior or manage to engage in some kind of collusion. Given the prevalence of oligopoly, then, is the analysis we developed in earlier Modules, which was based on perfect competition, still useful?

The conclusion of the great majority of economists is yes. For one thing, important parts of the economy are fairly well described by perfect competition. And even

Product differentiation is an attempt by a firm to convince buyers that its product is different from the products of other firms in the industry.

In **price leadership**, one firm sets its price first, and other firms then follow.

Firms that have a tacit understanding not to compete on price often engage in intense **nonprice competition**, using advertising and other means to try to increase their sales.

Cars line up for gasoline in 1973 after the U.S. government imposed price controls on the oil industry.

though many industries are oligopolistic, in many cases the limits to collusion keep prices relatively close to marginal costs—in other words, the industry behaves "almost" as if it were perfectly competitive.

It is also true that predictions from supply and demand analysis are often valid for oligopolies. For example, Module 8 explained how price controls can produce shortages. Strictly speaking, this conclusion is certain only for perfectly competitive industries. But in the 1970s, when the U.S. government imposed price controls on the definitely oligopolistic oil industry, the result was indeed shortages and lines at the gas pumps.

How important is it to analyze the behavior of oligopolists? Most economists adopt a pragmatic approach. As we have seen here, the analysis of oligopoly is far more difficult and messy than that of perfect competition; so in situations where they do not expect the complications associated with oligopoly to be crucial, economists prefer to adopt the working assumption of perfectly competitive markets. They always keep in mind the possibility that oligopoly might be important; they recognize that there are important issues, from antitrust policies to price wars, that make trying to understand oligopolistic behavior crucial.

MODULE 66 REVIEW

Check Your Understanding

1. For each of the following industry practices, explain whether the practice supports the conclusion that there is tacit collusion in this industry.
   a. For many years the price in the industry has changed infrequently, and all the firms in the industry charge the same price. The largest firm publishes a catalog containing a "suggested" retail price. Changes in price coincide with changes in the catalog.
   b. There has been considerable variation in the market shares of the firms in the industry over time.
   c. Firms in the industry build into their products unnecessary features that make it hard for consumers to switch from one company's products to another's.
   d. Firms meet yearly to discuss their annual sales forecasts.
   e. Firms tend to adjust their prices upward at the same time.

TACKLE THE AP® TEST: Multiple-Choice Questions

1. Having which of the following makes it easier for oligopolies to coordinate on raising prices?
   a. a large number of firms
   b. differentiated products
   c. buyers with bargaining power
   d. identical perceptions of fairness
   e. complex pricing schemes

2. If the bike shops in Cycle City do not have a formal agreement on pricing, but they increase their profits by adopting the prices of a price leader, these firms are necessarily participating in

   a. antitrust policy making.
   b. nonprice competition.
   c. a tit-for-tat strategy.
   d. tacit collusion.
   e. the formation of a trust.

3. When was the first federal legislation against cartels passed?
   a. 1776   d. 1900
   b. 1800   e. 1980
   c. 1890

4. Antitrust policy is designed to
   a. limit competition.
   b. prevent citizens from trusting disreputable politicians.
   c. regulate untrustworthy advertising claims.
   d. combat moral decay.
   e. prevent oligopolists from behaving like monopolists.

5. Oligopolists engage in tacit collusion in order to
   a. raise prices.
   b. increase output.
   c. share profits.
   d. increase market share.
   e. do all of the above.

6. When a firm considers how its behavior will affect the future actions of its competitors, it necessarily engages in
   a. price-fixing.
   b. strategic behavior.
   c. monopoly behavior.
   d. tit-for-tat behavior.
   e. a price war.

7. Firms successfully engaged in tacit collusion are unlikely to
   a. engage in nonprice competition.
   b. engage in product differentiation.
   c. engage in price leadership.
   d. engage in a price war.
   e. have higher prices than firms with no tacit collusion.

TACKLE THE AP® TEST: Free-Response Questions

1. Like other firms, universities face temptations to collude in order to limit the effects of competition and avoid price wars. (In fact, the U.S. Department of Justice formally accused a group of universities of price-fixing in 1991.) Answer the following questions about behavior in the market for higher education.
   a. Describe one factor of the market for higher education that invites tacit collusion.
   b. Describe one factor of the market for higher education that works against tacit collusion.
   c. Explain one way in which universities could engage in illegal collusion.
   d. What are three ways in which universities engage in product differentiation?
   e. Explain how price leadership might work in the university setting.
   f. What forms of nonprice competition do you see universities engaged in?

> **Rubric for FRQ 1 (6 points)**
>
> **1 point:** The fact that universities offer a small number of products—a small number of programs with a small number of tuition levels—invites tacit collusion. They may also have similar perceptions of the tuition level that families can afford.
>
> **1 point:** Factors that work against tacit collusion in the market for higher education include the large number of universities and the bargaining power of the better applicants.

> **1 point:** Universities could engage in illegal collusion by holding meetings to establish uniform tuition rates, divvying up applicants so that each is accepted by a limited number of schools (to avoid competition), or sharing information on scholarship offerings so that applicants will receive similar offers from the competing schools.
>
> **1 point:** Universities seek product differentiation in regard to athletic programs, facilities, academic standards, location, overseas programs, faculty, graduation requirements, and class size, among other areas.
>
> **1 point:** Price leadership could be achieved in the university setting if one school, perhaps a large or prestigious university, announced its tuition early and then other schools based their tuition on that announcement.
>
> **1 point:** Universities can engage in nonprice competition by offering better food, bigger dorm rooms, more accomplished faculty members, plush student centers, and similar amenities.

2. Indicate whether each of the following circumstances makes it more likely that oligopolists will behave noncooperatively or engage in tacit collusion. Explain your answers.
   a. It is difficult for a firm to detect whether another firm has raised output.
   b. The firms have coexisted while maintaining high prices for a long time.
   c. Each oligopolist expects several new firms to enter the market in the future. **(6 points)**

Introduction to Monopolistic Competition

In this Module, you will learn to:
- Determine prices and profit in monopolistic competition, both in the short run and in the long run
- Explain how monopolistic competition can lead to inefficiency and excess capacity

Understanding Monopolistic Competition

In Module 57, we learned that a monopolistically competitive industry consists of many producers, all competing for the same consumers but offering differentiated products. How does such an industry behave?

As the term *monopolistic competition* suggests, this market structure combines some features typical of monopoly with others typical of perfect competition. Because each firm offers something distinct, such as a special recipe for fried chicken or a convenient location for gasoline, it is in a way like a monopolist: it faces a downward-sloping demand curve and has some market power—the ability within limits to determine the price of its product. However, unlike a pure monopolist, a monopolistically competitive firm does

face competition: the amount of its product it can sell depends on the prices and products offered by other firms in the industry.

The same, of course, is true of an oligopoly. In a monopolistically competitive industry, however, there are *many* producers, as opposed to the small number that defines an oligopoly. This means that the "puzzle" of oligopoly—whether firms will collude or behave noncooperatively—does not arise in the case of monopolistically competitive industries. If all the gas stations or all the restaurants in a town could agree—explicitly or tacitly—to raise prices, it would be in their mutual interest to do so. But such collusion is virtually impossible when the number of firms is large and, by implication, there are no barriers to entry. So in situations of monopolistic competition, we can safely assume that firms behave noncooperatively and ignore the potential for collusion.

Monopolistic Competition in the Short Run

We introduced the distinction between short-run and long-run equilibrium when we studied perfect competition in Module 60. The short-run equilibrium of an industry takes the number of firms as given. The long-run equilibrium, by contrast, is reached only after enough time has elapsed for firms to enter or exit the industry. To analyze monopolistic competition, we focus first on the short run and then on how an industry moves from the short run to the long run.

Panels (a) and (b) of **Figure 67.1** show two possible situations that a typical firm in a monopolistically competitive industry might face in the short run. In each case, the firm looks like any monopolist: it faces a downward-sloping demand curve, which implies a downward-sloping marginal revenue curve.

We assume that every firm has an upward-sloping marginal cost curve but that it also faces some fixed costs, so that its average total cost curve is U-shaped. This assumption doesn't matter in the short run; but, as we'll see shortly, it is crucial to understanding the long-run equilibrium.

AP® EXAM TIP

In a monopolistically competitive industry there are many firms and low barriers to entry, as in a perfectly competitive industry. However, the sale of differentiated products gives the monopolistically competitive firms some monopoly power.

Figure 67.1 The Monopolistically Competitive Firm in the Short Run

(a) A Profitable Firm

(b) An Unprofitable Firm

The firm in panel (a) can be profitable for some output quantities: the quantities for which its average total cost curve, *ATC*, lies below its demand curve, D_P. The profit-maximizing output quantity is Q_P, the output at which the marginal revenue, MR_P, is equal to the marginal cost, *MC*. The firm charges price P_P and earns a profit, represented by the area of the green shaded rectangle. The firm in panel (b), however, is unprofitable because its average total cost curve lies above its demand curve, D_U, for every output quantity. The best that it can do if it produces at all is to produce quantity Q_U and charge price P_U. This generates a loss, indicated by the area of the orange shaded rectangle.

In each case the firm, in order to maximize its profit or minimize its loss, sets marginal revenue equal to marginal cost. So how do these two figures differ? In panel (a) the firm is profitable; in panel (b) it is unprofitable.

In panel (a) the firm faces the demand curve D_P and the marginal revenue curve MR_P. It produces the profit-maximizing output Q_P, the quantity at which the marginal revenue is equal to the marginal cost, and sells it at the price P_P. This price is above the average total cost at this output, ATC_P. The firm's profit is indicated by the area of the green-shaded rectangle.

In panel (b) the firm faces the demand curve D_U and the marginal revenue curve MR_U. It chooses the quantity Q_U at which the marginal revenue is equal to the marginal cost. However, in this case the price P_U is *below* the average total cost ATC_U; so at this quantity the firm loses money. Its loss is equal to the area of the orange shaded rectangle. Since Q_U is the profit-maximizing quantity—which means, in this case, the loss-minimizing quantity—there is no way for a firm in this situation to make a profit. We can confirm this by noting that at every quantity of output, the average total cost curve in panel (b) lies above the demand curve D_U. Because $ATC > P$ at every quantity of output, this firm always suffers a loss.

As this comparison suggests, the key to whether a firm with market power is profitable or unprofitable in the short run lies in the relationship between its demand curve and its average total cost curve. In panel (a) the demand curve D_P crosses the average total cost curve, meaning that some of the demand curve lies above the average total cost curve. So there are some price–quantity combinations available at which price is higher than average total cost, indicating that the firm can choose a quantity at which it makes positive profit.

In panel (b), by contrast, the demand curve D_U does not cross the average total cost curve—it always lies below it. So the price corresponding to each quantity demanded is always less than the average total cost of producing that quantity. There is no quantity at which the firm can avoid losing money.

These figures, showing firms facing downward-sloping demand curves and their associated marginal revenue curves, look just like ordinary monopoly graphs. The "competition" aspect of monopolistic competition comes into play, however, when we move from the short run to the long run.

Monopolistic Competition in the Long Run

Obviously, an industry in which existing firms are losing money, like the one in panel (b) of Figure 67.1, is not in long-run equilibrium. When existing firms are losing money, some firms will *exit* the industry. The industry will not be in long-run equilibrium until the persistent losses have been eliminated by the exit of some firms.

In the long run, profit lures new firms to enter an industry.

It is less obvious that an industry in which existing firms are earning profits, like the one in panel (a) of Figure 67.1, is also not in long-run equilibrium. Given there is *free entry* into the industry, persistent profits earned by the existing firms will lead to the entry of additional producers. The industry will not be in long-run equilibrium until the persistent profits have been eliminated by the entry of new producers.

How will entry or exit by other firms affect the profit of a typical existing firm? Because the differentiated products offered by firms in a monopolistically competitive industry are available to the same set of customers, entry or exit by other firms will affect the demand curve facing every existing producer. If new gas stations open along a highway, each of the existing gas stations will no longer be able to sell as much gas as before at any given price. So, as illustrated in panel (a) of **Figure 67.2**, entry of additional producers into a monopolistically competitive industry will lead to a *leftward* shift of the demand curve and the marginal revenue curve facing a typical existing producer.

Figure 67.2 Entry and Exit Shift Existing Firms' Demand Curves and Marginal Revenue Curves

Entry will occur in the long run when existing firms are profitable. In panel (a), entry causes each existing firm's demand curve and marginal revenue curve to shift to the left. The firm receives a lower price for every unit it sells, and its profit falls. Entry will cease when firms make zero profit. Exit will occur in the long run when existing firms are unprofitable. In panel (b), exit from the industry shifts each remaining firm's demand curve and marginal revenue curve to the right. The firm receives a higher price for every unit it sells, and profit rises. Exit will cease when the remaining firms make zero profit.

Conversely, suppose that some of the gas stations along the highway close. Then each of the remaining stations will be able to sell more gasoline at any given price. As illustrated in panel (b), the exit of firms from an industry leads to a *rightward* shift of the demand curve and marginal revenue curve facing a typical remaining producer.

The industry will be in long-run equilibrium when there is neither entry nor exit. This will occur only when every firm earns zero profit. So in the long run, firms just manage to cover their costs at their profit-maximizing output quantities.

We have seen that a firm facing a downward-sloping demand curve will earn positive profit if any part of that demand curve lies above its average total cost curve; it will incur a loss if its entire demand curve lies below its average total cost curve. To earn zero profit, the firm must be in a borderline position between these two cases; its demand curve must just touch its average total cost curve. That is, the demand curve must be just *tangent* to the average total cost curve at the firm's profit-maximizing output quantity—the output quantity at which marginal revenue equals marginal cost.

If this is not the case, the firm operating at its profit-maximizing quantity will find itself making either a profit or a loss, as illustrated in the panels of Figure 67.1. But we also know that free entry and exit means that this cannot be a long-run equilibrium. Why? In the case of a profit, new firms will enter the industry, shifting the demand curve of every existing firm leftward until all profit is eliminated. In the case of a loss, some existing firms exit and so shift the demand curve of every remaining firm to the right until all losses are eliminated. All entry and exit ceases only when every existing firm makes zero profit at its profit-maximizing quantity of output.

Figure 67.3 shows a typical monopolistically competitive firm earning zero profit. The firm produces Q_{MC}, the output at which $MR_{MC} = MC$, and charges price P_{MC}. At this price and quantity, represented by point Z, the demand curve is just tangent to its average total cost curve. The firm earns zero profit because the price, P_{MC}, is equal to the average total cost, ATC_{MC}.

AP® EXAM TIP

Like a monopolist, a monopolistically competitive firm faces a downward-sloping demand curve and a marginal revenue curve that is below the demand curve. Unlike a monopolist, a monopolistically competitive firm will necessarily earn zero economic profit in the long run.

Figure 67.3 The Long-Run Equilibrium

If existing firms are profitable, new firms will enter and shift each existing firm's demand curve leftward. If existing firms are unprofitable, each remaining firm's demand curve shifts rightward as some firms exit the industry. Entry and exit will cease when every existing firm earns zero profit at its profit-maximizing quantity. So, in long-run equilibrium, the demand curve of each firm is tangent to its average total cost curve at its profit-maximizing quantity: at the profit-maximizing quantity, Q_{MC}, the price, P_{MC}, equals the average total cost, ATC_{MC}.

The normal long-run condition of a monopolistically competitive industry, then, is that each firm is in the situation shown in Figure 67.3. Each firm acts like a monopolist, facing a downward-sloping demand curve and setting marginal cost equal to marginal revenue so as to maximize profit. But this is just enough to achieve zero economic profit. The firms in the industry are like monopolists without monopoly profit.

Monopolistic Competition Versus Perfect Competition

In a way, long-run equilibrium in a monopolistically competitive industry looks a lot like long-run equilibrium in a perfectly competitive industry. In both cases, there are many firms; in both cases, profits have been competed away; in both cases, the price received by every firm is equal to the average total cost of production.

However, we will see that the two versions of long-run equilibrium are different in ways that are economically significant.

Price, Marginal Cost, and Average Total Cost

Figure 67.4 compares the long-run equilibrium of a typical firm in a perfectly competitive industry with that of a typical firm in a monopolistically competitive industry. Panel (a) shows a perfectly competitive firm facing a market price equal to its minimum average total cost; panel (b) reproduces Figure 67.3, which shows a monopolistically competitive firm in long-run equilibrium. Comparing the panels, we see two important differences.

Figure 67.4 Comparing Long-Run Equilibrium in Perfect Competition and Monopolistic Competition

Panel (a) shows the situation of the typical firm in long-run equilibrium in a perfectly competitive industry. The firm operates at the minimum-cost output Q_{PC}, sells at the competitive market price P_{PC}, and makes zero profit. It is indifferent to selling another unit of output because P_{PC} is equal to its marginal cost, MC_{PC}. Panel (b) shows the situation of the typical firm in long-run equilibrium in a monopolistically competitive industry. At Q_{MC} it makes zero profit because its price P_{MC} just equals average total cost, ATC_{MC}. At Q_{MC} the firm would like to sell another unit at price P_{MC} because P_{MC} exceeds marginal cost, MC_{MC}. But it is unwilling to lower the price to make more sales. It therefore produces less than the minimum-cost output level and has excess capacity.

First, in the case of the perfectly competitive firm shown in panel (a), the price, P_{PC}, received by the firm at the profit-maximizing quantity, Q_{PC}, is equal to the firm's marginal cost of production, MC_{PC}, at that quantity of output. By contrast, at the profit-maximizing quantity chosen by the monopolistically competitive firm in panel (b), Q_{MC}, the price, P_{MC}, is *higher* than the marginal cost of production, MC_{MC}.

This difference translates into a difference in the attitude of firms toward consumers. A wheat farmer who can sell as much wheat as he likes at the going market price would not get particularly excited if you offered to buy some more wheat at the market price. Since he has no desire to produce more at that price and can sell the wheat to someone else, you are not doing him a favor.

But if you decide to fill up your tank at Jamil's gas station rather than at Katy's, you are doing Jamil a favor. He is not willing to cut his price to get more customers—he's already made the best of that trade-off. If he gets a few more customers than he expected at the posted price, that's good news: an additional sale at the *posted* price increases his revenue more than it increases his cost because the posted price exceeds the marginal cost.

The fact that monopolistic competitors, unlike perfect competitors, want to sell more at the going price is crucial to understanding why they engage in activities like advertising that help increase sales.

The other difference between monopolistic competition and perfect competition that is visible in Figure 67.4 involves the position of each firm on its average total cost curve. In panel (a), the perfectly competitive firm produces at point Q_{PC}, at the bottom of the U-shaped *ATC* curve. That is, each firm produces the productively efficient quantity at which average total cost is minimized—the *minimum-cost output*. As a consequence, the total cost of industry output is also minimized.

Under monopolistic competition, in panel (b), the firm produces at Q_{MC}, on the *downward-sloping* part of the U-shaped *ATC* curve: it produces less than the quantity that would minimize average total cost. This failure to produce enough to minimize average total cost is sometimes described as the **excess capacity** issue. The typical vendor in a food court or a gas station along a road is not big enough to take maximum advantage of available cost savings. So the total cost of industry output is not minimized in the case of a monopolistically competitive industry.

Some people have argued that, because every monopolistic competitor has excess capacity, monopolistically competitive industries are inefficient. But the issue of efficiency under monopolistic competition turns out to be a subtle one that does not have a clear answer.

Is Monopolistic Competition Inefficient?

A monopolistic competitor, like a monopolist, charges a price that is above marginal cost. As a result, some people who are willing to pay at least as much for an egg roll at Wonderful Wok as it costs to produce it are deterred from doing so. In monopolistic competition, some mutually beneficial transactions go unexploited.

Furthermore, it is often argued that monopolistic competition is subject to a further kind of inefficiency: that the excess capacity of every monopolistic competitor implies *wasteful duplication* because monopolistically competitive industries offer too many varieties. According to this argument, it would be better if there were only two or three vendors in the food court, not six or seven. If there were fewer vendors, they would each have lower average total costs and so could offer food more cheaply.

Is this argument against monopolistic competition right—that it lowers total surplus by causing inefficiency? Not necessarily. It's true that if there were fewer gas stations along a highway, each gas station would sell more gasoline and so would have a lower cost per gallon. But there is a drawback: motorists would be inconvenienced because gas stations would be farther apart. The numerous firms and the diversity of products offered in a monopolistically competitive industry are beneficial to consumers. So the higher price consumers pay because excess capacity is offset to some extent by the value they receive from greater diversity.

In other words, there is a trade-off: more producers mean higher average total costs but also more locations and greater product diversity. Does a monopolistically competitive industry arrive at the socially optimal point in this trade-off? Probably not, but it is hard to say whether there are too many firms or too few! Most economists now believe that duplication of effort and excess capacity in monopolistically competitive industries are not large problems in practice.

AP® EXAM TIP

Like monopolists and oligopolists, monopolistically competitive firms are allocatively inefficient both in the short run and in the long run because they charge a price that exceeds the marginal cost.

Firms in a monopolistically competitive industry have **excess capacity**: they produce less than the output at which average total cost is minimized.

MODULE 67 | REVIEW

Check Your Understanding

1. Suppose a monopolistically competitive industry composed of firms with U-shaped average total cost curves is in long-run equilibrium. For each of the following changes, explain how the industry is affected in the short run and how it adjusts to a new long-run equilibrium.
   a. a technological change that increases fixed cost for every firm in the industry
   b. a technological change that decreases marginal cost for every firm in the industry

2. Why is it impossible for firms in a monopolistically competitive industry to join together to form a monopoly that is capable of maintaining positive economic profit in the long run?

3. Indicate whether the following statements are true or false, and explain your answers.
   a. Like a firm in a perfectly competitive industry, a firm in a monopolistically competitive industry is willing to sell a good at any price that equals or exceeds marginal cost.
   b. Suppose there is a monopolistically competitive industry in long-run equilibrium that possesses excess capacity. All the firms in the industry would be better off if they merged into a single firm and produced a single product, but whether consumers would be made better off by this is uncertain.
   c. Fads and fashions are more likely to arise in industries characterized by monopolistic competition or oligopoly than in those characterized by perfect competition or monopoly.

TACKLE THE AP® TEST: Multiple-Choice Questions

1. Which of the following is a characteristic of monopolistic competition?
   a. a standardized product
   b. many sellers
   c. substantial barriers to entry
   d. positive long-run profits
   e. a perfectly elastic demand curve

2. Which of the following necessarily exists for a monopolistic competitor in the short run?
   a. positive economic profit
   b. normal profit
   c. loss
   d. allocative efficiency
   e. competition

3. Which of the following necessarily exists for a monopolistic competitor in the long run?
   a. loss
   b. excess capacity
   c. positive economic profit
   d. productive efficiency
   e. allocative efficiency

4. Which of the following best describes a monopolistic competitor's demand curve?
   a. upward-sloping
   b. downward-sloping
   c. U-shaped
   d. horizontal
   e. vertical

5. The long-run outcome in a monopolistically competitive industry results in
   a. inefficiency because firms earn positive economic profits.
   b. efficiency due to excess capacity.
   c. inefficiency due to product diversity.
   d. efficiency because price exceeds marginal cost.
   e. a trade-off between higher average total cost and more product diversity.

6. Which of the following is generally true for a firm in a monopolistically competitive industry but not for a monopolist?
   a. The firm can earn positive economic profit in the long run.
   b. The firm faces a downward-sloping demand curve.
   c. The firm's ATC curve will be tangent to its demand curve in the long run.
   d. The firm is a price-taker.
   e. The firm has no reason to advertise.

7. Which of the following will necessarily eliminate profits in a monopolistically competitive industry in the long run?
   a. rising barriers to entry
   b. increasing production costs
   c. increasing advertising costs
   d. the entry of new firms
   e. the exit of firms

TACKLE THE AP® TEST: Free-Response Questions

1. Draw a correctly labeled graph for a monopolistically competitive firm that is taking a loss in the short run. Shade the area that represents the firm's loss.

Rubric for FRQ 1 (7 points)

---

1 point: Correctly labeled axes

1 point: Downward-sloping demand curve

1 point: Marginal revenue curve below the demand curve

1 point: Loss-minimizing quantity below where $MC = MR$

1 point: Loss-minimizing price on demand curve above where $MC = MR$

1 point: U-shaped average total cost curve above the demand curve at every quantity

1 point: Correct loss area shaded

2. Draw a correctly labeled graph for a monopolistically competitive firm in long-run equilibrium. Label the distance along the quantity axis that represents excess capacity. **(6 points)**

Product Differentiation and Advertising

MOD 68

In this Module, you will learn to:
- Explain why oligopolists and monopolistic competitors differentiate their products
- Discuss the economic significance of advertising and brand names

In Module 66 we saw that product differentiation often plays an important role in oligopolistic industries. In such industries, product differentiation reduces the intensity of competition between firms when tacit collusion cannot be achieved. Module 67 explained that product differentiation is even more crucial in monopolistically competitive industries. Because tacit collusion is virtually impossible when there are many producers, product differentiation is the only way monopolistically competitive firms can acquire some market power. In this Module, we look at how oligopolists and monopolistic competitors differentiate their products in order to maximize profits.

AP® EXAM TIP

Product differentiation allows oligopolists and monopolistic competitors to decrease competition, increase market power, and ultimately increase sales.

How Firms Differentiate Their Products

How do firms in the same industry—such as fast-food vendors, gas stations, or chocolate makers—differentiate their products? Sometimes the difference is mainly in the minds of consumers rather than in the products themselves. We'll discuss the role of advertising and the importance of brand names in achieving this kind of product differentiation later in this Module. But, in general, firms differentiate their products by—surprise!—actually making them different.

The key to product differentiation is that consumers have different preferences and are willing to pay somewhat more to satisfy those preferences. Each producer can carve out a market niche by producing something that caters to the particular preferences of some group of consumers better than the products of other firms. There are three important forms of product differentiation: differentiation by style or type, differentiation by location, and differentiation by quality.

Differentiation by Style or Type

The sellers in the Central Mall's food court offer different types of fast food: hamburgers, pizza, Chinese food, Mexican food, and so on. Each consumer arrives at the food court with some preference for one or another of these offerings. This preference may depend on the consumer's mood, diet, or meals eaten earlier that day. These preferences will not make consumers indifferent to price: if Wonderful Wok were to charge $15 for an egg roll, everybody would go to Bodacious Burgers or Pizza Paradise instead. But some people will choose a more expensive meal if that type of food is closer to their preference. So the products of the different vendors are substitutes, but they aren't *perfect* substitutes—they are *imperfect substitutes.*

Vendors in a food court aren't the only sellers who differentiate their offerings by type. Clothing stores concentrate on women's or men's clothes, on business attire or sportswear, on trendy or classic styles, and so on. Auto manufacturers offer sedans, minivans, sport-utility vehicles, and sports cars, each type aimed at drivers with different needs and tastes.

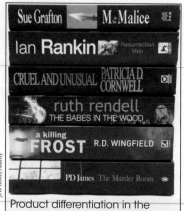

Product differentiation in the mystery book market allows publishers to acquire some market power.

Books offer yet another example of differentiation by type and style. Mysteries are differentiated from romances; among mysteries, we can differentiate among hard-boiled detective stories, whodunits, and police procedurals. And no two writers of hard-boiled detective stories are exactly alike: Ian Rankin and Sue Grafton each have their devoted fans, for example.

In fact, product differentiation is characteristic of most consumer goods. As long as people differ in their tastes, producers find it possible and profitable to offer variety.

Differentiation by Location

Gas stations along a road offer differentiated products. True, the gas may be exactly the same. But the location of the stations is different, and location matters to consumers: it's more convenient to stop for gas near your home, near your workplace, or near wherever you are when the gas gauge gets low.

In fact, many monopolistically competitive industries supply goods differentiated by location. This is especially true in service industries, from dry cleaners to hairdressers, where customers often choose the seller who is closest rather than cheapest.

Differentiation by Quality

Do you have a craving for chocolate? How much are you willing to spend on it? You see, there's chocolate and then there's *chocolate:* although ordinary chocolate may not be very expensive, gourmet chocolate can cost several dollars per bite.

With chocolate, as with many goods, there is a range of possible qualities. You can get a usable bicycle for less than $100; you can get a much fancier bicycle for 10 times as much.

It all depends on how much the additional quality matters to you and how much you will miss the other things you could have purchased with that money.

Because consumers vary in what they are willing to pay for higher quality, producers can differentiate their products by quality—some offering lower-quality, inexpensive products and others offering higher-quality products at a higher price.

Product differentiation, then, can take several forms. Whatever form it takes, however, there are two important features of industries with differentiated products: *competition among sellers* and *value in diversity*.

Competition among sellers means that even though sellers of differentiated products are not offering identical goods, they are to some extent competing for a limited market. If more businesses enter the market, each will find that it sells a lower quantity at any given price. For example, if a new gas station opens along a road, each of the existing gas stations will sell a bit less.

Value in diversity refers to the gain to consumers from the proliferation of differentiated products. A food court with eight vendors makes consumers happier than one with only six vendors, even if the prices are the same, because some customers will get a meal that is closer to what they had in mind. A road on which there is a gas station every two miles is more convenient for motorists than a road where gas stations are five miles apart. When a product is available in many different qualities, fewer people are forced to pay for more quality than they need or to settle for lower quality than they want. In other words, there are benefits to consumers from a greater diversity of available products.

As we'll see next, competition among the sellers of differentiated products is the key to understanding how monopolistic competition works.

Some customers are willing to pay more for higher quality chocolate, while others prefer to pay less for lower quality. A diverse market satisfies many needs and desires.

Controversies About Product Differentiation

Up to this point, we have assumed that products are differentiated in a way that corresponds to some real desire of consumers. There is real convenience in having a gas station in your neighborhood; Indian food and Mexican food are really different from each other.

In the real world, however, some instances of product differentiation can seem puzzling if you think about them. What is the real difference between Crest and Colgate toothpaste? Between Energizer and Duracell batteries? Or a Marriott and a Hilton hotel room? Most people would be hard-pressed to answer these questions. Yet the producers of these goods make considerable efforts to convince consumers that their products are different from and better than those of their competitors.

No discussion of product differentiation is complete without spending at least a bit of time on the two related issues—and puzzles—of *advertising* and *brand names*.

The Role of Advertising

Wheat farmers don't advertise their product, but car dealers do. That's not because farmers are shy and car dealers are outgoing; it's because advertising is worthwhile only in industries in which firms have at least some market power. The purpose of advertisements is to persuade people to buy more of a seller's product at the going price. A perfectly competitive firm, which can sell as much as it likes at the going market price, has no incentive to spend money persuading consumers to buy more. Only a firm that has some market power, and which therefore charges a price that is above marginal cost, can gain from advertising. (Some industries that are very competitive, like the milk industry, do advertise—but these ads are sponsored by an association on behalf of the industry as a whole, not on behalf of a particular farm.)

Given the influence of advertising, it's easy to see why firms with market power would spend money on it. But the big question about advertising is, *why* is it influential? A related question is whether advertising, from society's point of view, is a waste of resources.

AP® EXAM TIP

Exam questions might ask which types of firms engage in advertising. Firms in perfectly competitive markets don't need to advertise because they can sell as much as they want at the market price. Oligopolists advertise to differentiate their products and boost demand. The same is true for the monopolistically competitive firms (see Module 67). Monopolies sometimes advertise in order to increase demand for their products.

Not all advertising poses a puzzle. Much of it is straightforward: it's a way for sellers to inform potential buyers about what they have to offer (or, occasionally, for buyers to use *want ads* to inform potential sellers about what they want). Nor is there much controversy about the economic usefulness of ads that provide information: the car ad that says "four-wheel drive, 22 mpg, automatic transmission" tells you things you need to know.

But what information is being conveyed when a famous actor proclaims the virtues of one or another toothpaste or a sports heroine declares that some company's batteries are better than those inside that pink mechanical rabbit? Surely nobody believes that the sports star is an expert on batteries—or that she chose the company that she personally believes makes the best batteries, as opposed to the company that offered to pay her the most. Yet companies believe, with good reason, that money spent on such promotions increases their sales—and that they would be in big trouble if they stopped advertising but their competitors continued to do so.

Why are consumers influenced by ads that do not really provide any information about the product? One answer is that consumers are not as rational as economists typically assume. Perhaps consumers' judgments, or even their tastes, can be influenced by things that economists think ought to be irrelevant, such as which company has hired the most charismatic celebrity to endorse its product. And there is surely some truth to this. Consumer rationality is a useful working assumption; it is not an absolute truth.

However, another answer is that consumer response to advertising is not entirely irrational because ads can serve as indirect *signals* in a world in which consumers don't have good information about products. To take a common example, suppose that you need to avail yourself of some local service that you don't use regularly—body work on your car, say, or furniture moving. You find a number of companies listed online, some with a simple Facebook page and others with their own professionally made website. You know that those websites are expensive to design; still, it may be quite rational to call one of the companies with a nice website. After all, the nice website probably means that the company is relatively large and successful—otherwise, the investment in professional website design wouldn't have been worthwhile.

The same principle may partly explain why ads feature celebrities. You don't really believe that the pop star prefers that watch; but the fact that the watch manufacturer is willing and able to pay her fee tells you that it is a major company that is likely to stand behind its product. According to this reasoning, an expensive advertisement serves to establish the quality of a firm's products in the eyes of consumers.

The possibility that it is rational for consumers to respond to advertising also has some bearing on the question of whether advertising is a waste of resources. If ads work by manipulating only the weak-minded, the $207 billion U.S. businesses spent on advertising in 2017 was unproductive—except to the extent that ads sometimes provide entertainment. To the extent that advertising conveys important information, however, it is an economically productive activity after all.

Brand Names

You're on the bus returning from a sports competition and the team is looking for a place to eat. On your right you see a sign for Dave's Doggone-Good Hotdogs; on your left you see a sign for Sonic, KFC, or some other national chain. Which one do you choose?

Unless they are familiar with the area, most people will head for the chain. In fact, most fast-food restaurants in the United States are members of major chains; the same is true of most motels and many, if not most, stores in shopping malls.

Chain fast-food restaurants and motels are only part of a broader phenomenon: the role of **brand names**, names owned by particular companies that differentiate their products in the minds of consumers. In many cases, a company's brand name is the most important asset it possesses. Clearly, McDonald's is worth far more than the sum of the deep-fat fryers and hamburger grills the company owns.

What can a giant pink bunny tell us about batteries? Nothing, but it might send a signal that these batteries are worth buying.

A **brand name** is a name owned by a particular firm that distinguishes its products from those of other firms.

AP® EXAM TIP

If the exam asks for examples of nonprice competition, you can mention advertising and brand name development, which competitors use to modify consumers' perceptions about their products and gain more sales without lowering prices.

In fact, companies often go to considerable lengths to defend their brand names, suing anyone else who uses them without permission. You may ask for a box of kleenex when you have a runny nose or a band-aid when you have a cut, but unless the product in question comes from Kleenex or Johnson & Johnson, legally the seller must describe it as a facial tissue or an adhesive bandage.

As with advertising, with which they are closely linked, the social usefulness of brand names is a source of dispute. Does the preference of consumers for known brands reflect consumer irrationality? Or do brand names convey real information? That is, do brand names create unnecessary market power, or do they serve a real purpose?

As in the case of advertising, the answer is probably some of both. On the one hand, brand names often do create unjustified market power. Consumers often pay more for brand-name goods in the supermarket even though consumer experts assure us that the cheaper store brands are equally good. Similarly, many common medicines, like aspirin, are cheaper—with no loss of quality—in their generic form.

On the other hand, for many products the brand name does convey information. A traveler arriving in a strange town can be sure of what awaits in a Holiday Inn or a McDonald's; a tired and hungry traveler may find this preferable to trying an independent hotel or restaurant that might be better—but might be worse.

In addition, brand names offer some assurance that the seller is engaged in repeated interaction with its customers and so has a reputation to protect. If a traveler eats a bad meal at a restaurant in a tourist trap and vows never to eat there again, the restaurant owner may not care, since the chance is small that the traveler will be in the same area again in the future. But if that traveler eats a bad meal at McDonald's and vows never to eat a McDonald's again, that matters to the company. This gives McDonald's an incentive to provide consistent quality, thereby assuring travelers that quality controls are in place.

saknakorn/Shutterstock

MODULE 68 REVIEW

Check Your Understanding

1. For each of the following types of advertising, explain whether it is likely to be useful or wasteful from the standpoint of consumers.
   a. advertisements explaining the benefits of aspirin
   b. advertisements for Bayer aspirin
   c. advertisements that state how long a plumber or an electrician has been in business

2. Some industry analysts have stated that a successful brand name is like a barrier to entry. Explain why this might be true.

TACKLE THE AP® TEST: Multiple-Choice Questions

1. Which of the following is true about product differentiation?
   a. Its purpose is to differentiate expensive and inexpensive raw materials.
   b. Its purpose is to differentiate raw materials from normal goods.
   c. It leads to lower prices.
   d. It can be based on style but not on quality.
   e. It can be based on location.

2. In which of the following market structures will individual firms advertise?
   a. perfect competition only
   b. oligopoly only
   c. monopolistic competition only
   d. oligopoly and monopolistic competition only
   e. perfect competition, oligopoly, and monopolistic competition

3. Advertising is an attempt to affect which of the following?
   a. consumer tastes and preferences
   b. consumer income
   c. the price of complements
   d. the price of substitutes
   e. input prices

4. Brand names generally serve to
   a. waste resources.
   b. decrease firm profits.
   c. confuse consumers.
   d. decrease information.
   e. signal quality.

5. Which of the following is true of advertising expenditures in monopolistic competition? Monopolistic competitors
   a. will not advertise.
   b. use only informational advertising.
   c. always waste resources on advertising.
   d. attempt to create popular brand names.
   e. earn long-run profits through advertising.

6. Companies often hire celebrities to promote their product because
   a. it signals that the product is made by a legitimate company.
   b. the celebrities are considered experts on the product.
   c. celebrities purchase a large share of the product.
   d. celebrities typically promote products for free.
   e. all consumers believe whatever celebrities say.

7. Which of the following is certainly true?
   a. Travelers typically avoid restaurants with familiar brand names when they travel.
   b. Two gas stations selling the same product in different locations are an example of product differentiation.
   c. Firms in a perfectly competitive market have an incentive to advertise.
   d. Product differentiation is good for firms but bad for consumers.
   e. It is irrational for consumers to respond to advertising.

TACKLE THE AP® TEST: Free-Response Questions

1. Refer to the table below showing the effects of running television commercials on a firm's total revenue. Assume that each commercial costs $1,000 to run.

Number of commercials	Total revenue
0	$20,000
1	30,000
2	38,000
3	44,000
4	48,000
5	50,000
6	50,500

   a. What is the marginal revenue from running the second commercial?
   b. Should the firm run a third commercial? Explain.
   c. If the firm has no variable costs aside from the cost of commercials, how many commercials should the firm run to maximize profits? Explain.

Rubric for FRQ 1 (5 points)

1 point: $8,000

1 point: Yes, it should run a third commercial.

1 point: Because the marginal revenue of $6,000 exceeds the marginal cost of $1,000

1 point: The firm should run five commercials.

1 point: Marginal revenue exceeds marginal cost for the first five commercials. Marginal revenue is less than marginal cost for the sixth commercial.

2. Explain two ways in which product differentiation can be useful to consumers and two ways in which it can be detrimental to consumers. **(4 points)**

Module 64

1. Many industries are oligopolies, characterized by a small number of **interdependent** sellers. The smallest type of oligopoly, a **duopoly**, has only two sellers, known as **duopolists**. Oligopolies exist for more or less the same reasons that monopolies exist, but in weaker form. They are characterized by imperfect competition: firms compete but possess market power.

2. Predicting the behavior of oligopolists poses something of a puzzle. The firms in an oligopoly could maximize their combined profits by acting as a **cartel**, setting output levels for each firm as if they were a single monopolist; to the extent that firms manage to do this, they engage in **collusion**. But each individual firm has an incentive to produce more than the agreed upon quantity of output—to engage in **noncooperative behavior**. Informal collusion is likely to be easier to achieve in industries in which firms face capacity constraints.

Module 65

3. The situation of interdependence, in which each firm's profit depends noticeably on what other firms do, is the subject of **game theory**. In the case of a game with two players, the **payoff** of each player depends on both its own actions and on the actions of the other; this interdependence can be shown in a **payoff matrix**. Depending on the structure of payoffs in the payoff matrix, a player may have a **dominant strategy**—an action that is always the best regardless of the other player's actions.

4. Some duopolists face a particular type of game known as a **prisoners' dilemma**; if each acts independently on its own interest, the resulting **Nash equilibrium** or **noncooperative equilibrium** will be bad for both.

Module 66

5. Firms that expect to play a game repeatedly tend to engage in **strategic behavior**, trying to influence each other's future actions. A particular strategy that seems to work well in such situations is **tit for tat**, which often leads to **tacit collusion**. In order to limit the ability of oligopolists to collude and act like monopolists, most governments pursue **antitrust policy** designed to make collusion more difficult. In practice, however, tacit collusion is widespread.

6. A variety of factors make tacit collusion difficult: a large number of firms, complex products and pricing, differences in interests, and buyers with bargaining power. When tacit collusion breaks down, there can be a **price war**. Oligopolists try to avoid price wars in various ways, such as through **product differentiation** and through **price leadership**, in which one firm sets prices for the industry. Another approach is **nonprice competition**, such as advertising.

Module 67

7. Monopolistic competition is a market structure in which there are many competing producers, each producing a differentiated product, and there is free entry and exit in the long run.

8. Short-run profits will attract the entry of new firms in the long run. This reduces the quantity each existing producer sells at any given price and shifts its demand curve to the left. Short-run losses will induce exit by some firms in the long run. This shifts the demand curve of each remaining firm to the right.

9. In the long run, the demand curve for each existing firm in a monopolistically competitive industry is tangent to its average total cost curve. There are zero profits in the industry and no entry or exit.

10. In long-run equilibrium, firms in a monopolistically competitive industry sell at a price greater than marginal cost. They also have **excess capacity** because they produce less than the minimum-cost output; as a result, they have higher costs than firms in a perfectly competitive industry. Whether or not monopolistic competition is inefficient is ambiguous because consumers value the product diversity that it creates.

Module 68

11. Product differentiation takes three main forms: style or type, location, and quality. Firms will engage in advertising to increase demand for their products and enhance their market power. Advertising and **brand names** that provide useful information to consumers are valuable to society. Advertisements can be wasteful from a societal standpoint when their only purpose is to create market power.

Key Terms

Interdependent, p. 620
Duopoly, p. 620
Duopolist, p. 620
Collusion, p. 621
Cartel, p. 621
Noncooperative behavior, p. 622
Game theory, p. 625
Payoff, p. 625

Payoff matrix, p. 625
Prisoners' dilemma, p. 626
Dominant strategy, p. 626
Nash equilibrium, p. 627
Noncooperative equilibrium, p. 627
Antitrust policy, p. 634
Strategic behavior, p. 636

Tit for tat, p. 636
Tacit collusion, p. 637
Price war, p. 638
Product differentiation, p. 639
Price leadership, p. 639
Nonprice competition, p. 639
Excess capacity, p. 647
Brand name, p. 652

AP® Exam Practice Questions

Multiple-Choice Questions

1. A difference between oligopolists and monopolistic competitors is that only
   a. monopolistic competitors collude.
   b. oligopolists engage in product differentiation.
   c. monopolistic competitors can form a cartel.
   d. oligopolists can earn economic profit in the long run.
   e. monopolistic competitors can incur losses.

2. In studying market structures, economists have observed that when an industry has a relatively large number of firms, the firms are more likely to engage in _____ and prices are likely be relatively _____.

a.	collusion	high
b.	noncooperative behavior	low
c.	a dominant strategy	high
d.	strategic behavior	low
e.	tit for tat	high

3. The government would attempt to enforce antitrust policy under which of the following circumstances?
   a. to prevent cartels from agreeing to limit quantities and set prices
   b. to prevent firms' strategic behavior that leads to tacit collusion
   c. to prevent firms' interdependence that leads to tit-for-tat behavior
   d. to prevent duopolists from engaging in product differentiation that leads to higher prices
   e. to prevent excess capacity because of the unnecessary waste that it creates

4. Government regulators should be concerned with _____ if firms in an industry have _____.

a.	a prisoners' dilemma	found a Nash equilibrium
b.	encouraging competition	started a price war
c.	regulating profits	low barriers to entry
d.	enforcing antitrust policy	acted as a cartel and not just in tacit collusion
e.	increasing nonprice competition	differentiated their products

5. Brand names can lead to higher prices because
   a. they are a sign that firms have formed a cartel and engaged in collusion.
   b. maximizing profits requires firms to follow a dominant strategy.
   c. they turn firms into monopolies.
   d. price leadership occurs when one firm sets a high price and others follow.
   e. they create additional market power for firms even if they provide information to consumers.

6. Which of the following is the most likely to lead to lower prices in an oligopoly?
   a. the formation of a cartel
   b. tacit collusion
   c. low barriers to entry
   d. price leadership
   e. product differentiation

Use the information and table below to answer Questions 7 and 8.

Suppose that Firm A and Firm B are the only companies that make a common food preservative. The marginal cost of production is zero and the industry demand schedule for the preservative in a typical month is as follows:

Price (per pound)	Quantity demanded (millions of pounds)
$6	0
5	10
4	20
3	30
2	40
1	50
0	60

7. If the two companies agree to each produce half of the quantity that maximizes their combined profits and to share the revenue equally, what is the dollar amount (in millions) of revenue that each firm collects?

a. $100
b. $90
c. $50
d. $45
e. $40

8. Suppose Firm A continues to honor the production agreement from Question 7 while Firm B breaks it and produces more. Now what is the maximum dollar amount (in millions) that Firm B would collect?

a. $100
b. $90
c. $50
d. $45
e. $40

Suppose a breakfast cereal market consists of only two firms, Firm X and Firm Y. Each firm sets either high prices or low prices for one month at a time. Use the information on each firm's monthly profit in the payoff matrix below to answer Questions 9–12.

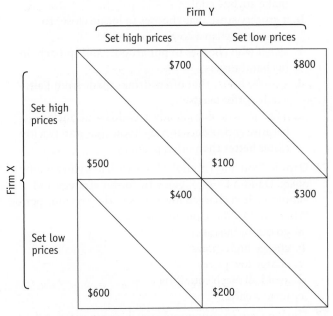

9. Which of the following statements is true?

a. Firm X and Firm Y are engaged in a prisoners' dilemma.
b. At the noncooperative equilibrium, the total profits for both firms combined are equal to $1,200.
c. At the Nash equilibrium, the total profits for both firms combined are equal to $1,000.
d. At the noncooperative equilibrium, the total profits for both firms combined are equal to $900.
e. At the Nash equilibrium, the total profits for both firms combined are equal to $500.

10. Which of the following accurately describes the dominant strategies of Firm X and Firm Y?

	Dominant strategy for Firm X	Dominant strategy for Firm Y
a.	no dominant strategy	high prices
b.	high prices	no dominant strategy
c.	low prices	high prices
d.	low prices	low prices
e.	low prices	no dominant strategy

11. Suppose the same payoff matrix applies every month. For the current month, Firm X has set low prices and Firm Y has set high prices. If each firm follows a tit-for-tat strategy, then

a. Firm X would set high prices next time, earn $500 for one month, and then $200 thereafter.
b. Firm X would set low prices next time, earn $600 for one month, and then $200 thereafter.
c. Firm X would set high prices next time, earn $100 for one month, and then $500 the following month.
d. Firm X would set low prices next time, earn $200 for one month, and then $200 the following month.
e. Firm X would set high prices next time, earn $100 for one month, and then $600 the following month.

12. Suppose all the profit payoffs for Firm X double, but they remain the same for Firm Y. Which of the following is a true statement?

a. The noncooperative equilibrium would remain the same.
b. The dominant strategy would change for Firm X but remain the same for Firm Y.
c. There would be a second Nash equilibrium.
d. Firm Y would be more likely to engage in a tit-for-tat strategy.
e. Both firms would be more likely to engage in tacit collusion.

13. Which of the following works in favor of tacit collusion in an oligopolistic industry?

a. The bargaining power of large buyers can keep prices low.
b. Over time, firms realize it is in their best interest to collectively restrict output.
c. Selling thousands of products makes it hard to keep track of competitors' output and prices.
d. With a larger number of sellers, there is less incentive for any one firm to cooperate.
e. The threat of enforcement of antitrust policy is always present.

14. Which of the following business tactics are ways that firms in an oligopolistic industry attempt to legally collude?

a. engaging in nonprice competition
b. using price leadership for signaling
c. lowing prices in a trade war
d. differentiating their products
e. advertising

15. In a monopolistically competitive soda industry, assume the following facts: a typical firm produces 10,000 beverage cans in a month; the price per can is $1.00; average total cost is $0.50 at the current production level; and marginal cost is $0.25 at the current production level. What will happen to the equilibrium quantity and profits for a typical firm in the soda industry in the long run?

	Equilibrium quantity for a typical firm	Profit for a typical firm
a.	increase	decrease
b.	decrease	remain the same
c.	remain the same	increase
d.	decrease	decrease
e.	decrease	increase

16. Economists have argued that there may be inefficiencies in monopolistically competitive industries. Which of the following is a reason cited for this inefficiency?
   a. There is excess capacity at the chosen production level.
   b. The price is too low.
   c. There is zero profit in the long run.
   d. Price is set equal to marginal cost.
   e. Production occurs along the upward-sloping section of the average total cost curve.

Use the following graph of a typical firm in a monopolistically competitive industry to answer Questions 17–19.

17. What price and quantity combination would we expect from a profit-maximizing firm in this monopolistically competitive industry?
   a. P_6, Q_1 **d.** P_3, Q_5
   b. P_5, Q_2 **e.** P_2, Q_4
   c. P_4, Q_3

18. Firms in this industry are earning _____ and over time we would expect these profits or losses to _____.

a.	economic losses	remain the same
b.	economic profits	increase
c.	economic losses	decrease
d.	economic profits	decrease
e.	economic losses	increase

19. Over time, what will happen to the number of firms in this industry and the output per firm?

	Number of firms	Output per firm
a.	decrease	increase
b.	increase	decrease
c.	decrease	decrease
d.	increase	increase
e.	decrease	remain the same

20. Which of the following is NOT an example of product differentiation?
   a. a clothing store that advertises jean jackets that will make anyone cool
   b. a grocery store that chooses to locate closer to customers than a competing grocer
   c. a chef who chooses to put arugula and spinach on his hamburgers
   d. a coffee house that offers drinks made from Fair Trade coffee beans
   e. a farmer who doesn't advertise his watermelons because consumers already know that watermelon tastes better than other produce

21. Daddio Don and Fabulous Fred are hairstyling oligopolists. Daddio Don follows a tit-for-tat strategy and Fabulous Fred charged low prices in the previous period. What will Daddio Don do now?
   a. go out of business
   b. charge high prices
   c. charge low prices
   d. avoid all Nash equilibria
   e. form a cartel

22. The long run in a monopolistically competitive industry is characterized by
   a. productive efficiency.
   b. allocative efficiency.
   c. firms earning positive economic profits.
   d. firms operating at the minimum of their average total cost curves.
   e. firms with excess capacity.

23. In the short run, Martha's Zen Bakery earns profit in a monopolistically competitive industry. What will happen in this industry in the long run?

  a. Martha's demand curve will shift to the left.
  b. Martha's profit will increase.
  c. Other firms will exit the industry.
  d. Nonprice competition will become impossible.
  e. Product differentiation will become impossible.

Use the payoff matrix provided to answer Questions 24 and 25. The values in the matrix represent the profits that WeSellLights and the Lighting Barn will earn depending on each firm's strategy to build or not build a new store. The first entry in each box represents the profit for WeSellLights; the second entry is the profit for the Lighting Barn.

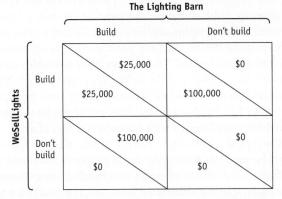

The Lighting Barn

24. If WeSellLights believes that the Lighting Barn will not build a new store, WeSellLights will

  a. not build a new store and it will earn no profit.
  b. not build a new store because not building is the dominant strategy.
  c. build a new store and earn a $25,000 profit.
  d. build a new store and earn a $100,000 profit.
  e. be indifferent as to whether or not to build a new store.

25. Assume that WeSellLights offers the Lighting Barn $30,000 not to build a new store. Given that new information, in which case will a Nash equilibrium occur?

  a. If both companies build a new store.
  b. If WeSellLights builds a new store and the Lighting Barn does not.
  c. If WeSellLights does not build a new store and the Lighting Barn does.
  d. If neither company builds a new store.
  e. A Nash equilibrium does not exists.

Free-Response Questions

1. The hot dog stand industry in Frankland is monopolistically competitive. A typical stand produces and sells 10,000 hot dogs during the summer season. For that stand, the price per hot dog is $3.00, the average total cost is $1.00 at the current production level, and the marginal cost is $0.50 at the current production level.

  a. Draw a correctly labeled graph of this typical hot dog stand under current market conditions, labeling the equilibrium quantity and the equilibrium price with the numbers provided.
  b. Calculate the economic profit or loss for the typical hot dog stand.
  c. On your graph from part a, shade in the area of the profit or loss.

Now assume that the government imposes a $20,000 lump-sum license fee for the summer season.

  d. What happens to the price and quantity for the typical hot dog stand as a result of the license fee? Explain.
  e. Show the impact of the license fee on the graph from part a and provide a clear label for anything that changed.
  f. What will happen to the number of hot dog stands over the course of the season? Explain. **(10 points)**

2. The following diagram shows the pricing strategies and payoffs for the two bubble gum firms in town.

  a. Does Big Bubble Co. have a dominant strategy? Explain.
  b. Does Long Lasting Flavor Co. have a dominant strategy? Explain.
  c. Does this situation have any Nash equilibria? Explain. **(6 points)**

3. The drone industry is made up of a small number of interdependent firms.

  a. What market structure best describes this industry?
  b. Suppose drone makers try to collude by agreeing to restrict output and raise prices. Aside from issues of legality, what else would make it difficult for this form of collusion to succeed?
  c. Explain how price leadership could lead to relatively high prices in the drone industry.
  d. If one firm lowers its price this period, how would a competitor following the tit-for-tat strategy respond next period? **(4 points)**

What's Behind the Music Industry's Woes?
The Sound of Market Power

Secrets can make or break market power. Sometimes the critical secrets are held by sellers. In 1925, the Coca-Cola Company deposited the formula for its market-dominating soft drink in an Atlanta bank and set a policy that only two company officials would be privy to the formula at any given time. Stashed in a vault in Louisville, Kentucky, is Colonel Sanders's secret recipe for the eleven herbs and spices that make Kentucky Fried Chicken (KFC) finger-lickin' good. For greater security, incomplete sets of KFC's ingredients are mixed in two separate locations and then combined in a third location so that no one at any single location can identify all the seasonings. Such trade secrets create informational barriers that prevent competitors from entering a market and pilfering profits.

Michael Tercha/Chicago Tribune/Getty Images

In the case of the music industry, the consumers hold the most influential secrets, and they work to break down the barriers to competition. Music fans, perhaps even you, secretly copy music files and try to hide their true identities while swapping music files online. The songs are copyrighted, but relative secrecy and advancing technology allow the practice to compete with retail music venues. Is this development the death knell for the $17 billion global music industry? And how did the industry become so lucrative in the first place? The answers play to the tune of market power.

Power in the Marketplace

When copyrights or other barriers to competition result in a *monopoly*, the one producer in that market can restrict the quantity sold and raise the price in pursuit of profit. For instance, copyrights and unique skills make glass artist Stephen Rolfe Powell the only producer of his unique style of colorful glass "vessels." Powell can make a sizable number of vessels in a month, but by selling fewer than he is able to make, he keeps his artwork relatively scarce and can charge more than $20,000 for a vessel. This would not be the case if the market were flooded with his unique works of art.

The typical monopoly is inefficient from the standpoint of society because the monopolist holds output below the level at which the marginal cost of production equals the price consumers are willing to pay. Additional units could be made for a marginal cost below the value to consumers, creating a deadweight loss equal to the difference between the missed benefits and the avoided costs. For example, if Powell could produce another glass vessel using $5,000 worth of materials, equipment, fuel, and time, and a consumer would be willing to pay $20,000 for it, that vessel would create $15,000 worth of net benefits.

It might not be in Powell's best interest to create that net gain, however, if he charges the same price for each vessel. Suppose Powell can either sell 8 vessels per month for $22,000 each or drop the price to $20,000 and sell 9. At the lower price he gains $20,000 − $5,000 = $15,000 in profit from the ninth unit but loses $2,000 on each of the 8 units he could otherwise sell for $22,000, for a net loss of ($2,000 × 8) − ($15,000) = $1,000. Powell is better off selling fewer units at the higher price. More generally, firms with market power often produce less than the quantity that is efficient for society and charge more than the price that would exist in a competitive market.

Stephen Rolfe Powell, Salacious Tickling Snooper, 36.25 × 17.5 × 17.5 inches, 2009

An *oligopoly* exists when a small number of firms dominate the market. As in a monopoly, firms in an oligopoly can influence prices and quantities to their advantage, although the ability to earn profit typically falls as the number of firms in the market increases. To remedy that problem, producers of similar products sometimes organize into *cartels*, which are groups of firms that work together to restrict output and raise prices as a monopoly would. Cartels are prohibited in most countries including the United States.

Market power can be measured by the market share held by the biggest competing firms. A *four-firm concentration ratio*, for example, is the sum of the market shares of the four largest firms in a market. The market structure is considered an oligopoly if the four-firm concentration ratio is 40 percent or more. The United States has oligopolies in industries that include tobacco, soft drinks, computer software, and cellular service, all of which have a four-firm concentration ratio higher than 90 percent. There are three major groups in the music industry—Universal, Sony, and Warner—and together they hold about 80 percent of the market.

Barriers to Entry in the Music Industry

In a competitive market, the existence of profit attracts competitors, which increases the supply until the price falls to equal the minimum average cost. Profits continue in markets with barriers to competitors. These barriers may include legal barriers, such as patents, licenses, and copyrights; information barriers, such as secret recipes; the control of resources, such as diamond mines; and economies of scale, as with a small town that cannot support a second movie theater.

Thanks to barriers to competition, the music industry enjoyed $40 billion in annual sales at its peak. Particular songs are copyrighted so that a single firm controls their sale. Music companies have the incentive to develop relationships with radio stations and concert venues that enable the corporations to promote their own artists over those of smaller, independent record companies and to influence the amount of airtime granted to particular songs. Competing firms that crop up and pose threats are often acquired through mergers. The history of the music industry resembles a feeding frenzy, with big fish, such as Sony and Universal, devouring former threats, such as CBS Records and PolyGram, and merging with others, such as BMG, EMI, and Geffen Records.

From the perspective of Eagles singer and drummer Don Henley, "The industry, which was once composed of hundreds of big and small record labels, is now controlled by just a handful of unregulated, multinational corporations determined to continue their mad rush toward further consolidation and merger." According to economic theory, the market

power held by music companies is not simply a reason for high prices, but also a source of diminished quality. Henley writes that since the days of greater competition ended, the variety of music has eroded, as have the meaningful relationships between artists and music company executives and the "unique and personal way" in which music once touched listeners.

With their "Say YES to Creativity and NO to Concentration" campaign, members of the Independent Music Companies Association (IMPALA) fought the consolidation of major music companies in the early 2000s. They said that "to flourish, creativity requires diversity, plurality, fair competition and an open society."[1] IMPALA successfully fought the proposed merger of Time Warner and EMI in 2000. IMPALA also fought the Sony-BMG merger in 2004 and the Universal-EMI merger in 2012, and the association is vigilant against new merger proposals, threatening legal actions to prevent them.

Music Piracy and Patchwork in the Barriers to Entry

Music piracy can involve *stream-ripping* music by converting it from a streaming platform such as Spotify to a downloadable file, *counterfeiting* CDs to mislead consumers into thinking they're buying a legal product, and *bootlegging* by recording and selling music from live or broadcast performances. The International Federation of the Phonographic Industry estimates that 35 percent of all internet users access unlicensed music. The Recording Industry Association of America (RIAA) blames illegal file sharing for slumping music sales since 1999. In a 2018 news release, RIAA president Mitch Glazier wrote that music piracy poses "a systemic threat not only to the American creative industries, but to the growth of the legitimate U.S. streaming economy and our digital future."[2]

Pernicious symptoms of market power may have contributed to the decline in music sales. *Rolling Stone* magazine's ranking of the top 500 albums reveals that the perceived quality of music has gone downhill since the early 1970s. As suggested by Don Henley, the lack of competition may have led to reluctance among the consolidated music groups to take risks with new artists and unconventional approaches. Conservative tactics and complacency may have opened the door for competitors such as mp3unsigned.com, which offers free music by groups that have

---

[1] See https://corpwatch.org/article/impala-say-yes-creativity-and-no-concentration.

[2] See www.riaa.com/new-notorious-markets-report-u-s-trade-rep-calls-stream-ripping-websites-phenomena-continue-threaten-american-creative-community/.

not yet signed a contract with a music label. Regardless of whether you're a fan of independent bands, the ability to find alternative music online has an appeal similar to that of used bookstores, where one can finally find an array of titles beyond those on the best-seller list.

The music industry has responded to piracy with efforts to maintain and rebuild barriers. The RIAA has initiated thousands of lawsuits for alleged copyright violations. Legal competitors in the music-downloading business have also been accused of thwarting competition. For example, Apple allegedly told music companies that music included in Amazon's "MP3 Daily Deal" would not be promoted on the iTunes website, and Apple has been slow to give music companies control over the prices of songs and albums. To the extent that anticompetitive behavior leads to higher prices or limited offerings, it may, in fact, encourage the use of illegal files.

Music Lessons

Historically, the music industry has weathered many a technology-based storm. Along the way, eight-track tapes lost a war over media formats, cassette tapes allowed illegal copying that records did not, and CD burners dramatically improved the quality of copied music. After some casualties, the industry has always adapted with new strategies and business models, more recent examples being low-priced music downloads and subscription streaming services.

Firms in *contestable markets*, into which competitors could enter, can be enticed to offer the prices, quantities, and qualities of a competitive industry to forestall the entry of new competitors. Rampant music piracy in the oligopolistic music industry provides a persistent, if illegal, threat of competition. No sooner did a court dismember the original Napster peer-to-peer (P2P) music-sharing service than myriad alternatives came on the scene. As lawsuits against second-generation P2P systems such as Grokster proceeded, "censorship-resistant"

file-sharing programs such as Freenet were waiting in the wings, followed by the availability of stream-ripping software such as Streamosaur. Given the unlikely prospects of reining in the expanding universe of music-pirating technology, the music industry is starting to act more like a competitive firm, taking risks with innovative acts, lowering prices, and providing more variety. Along these lines, Universal and Warner are investing in independent labels such as Canada's Maple Music to help them identify promising new artists.

When something is cheap or free, it is sometimes said that it can be bought "for a song," but saying that pirated music can be had for a song is misleading (and a bad pun). As consumers consider piracy and the music industry addresses its clandestine competition, it is important for both to assess the true costs inherent in music piracy. Some of the cost is imposed on workers in the retail music industry—musicians, advertisers, software developers, secretaries, maintenance workers, and so on—whose wages and employment are jeopardized by illegal activities. The pirates also face costs. The *expected legal cost* is the probability of detection multiplied by the fine if detected. *Risk-averse* people are uncomfortable with the uncertain prospect of being caught and being punished. The *risk burden* is the amount above the expected legal cost that a risk-averse individual would pay to avoid uncertainty about being caught. The *guilt burden* is the amount an individual would pay to avoid feeling guilty about breaking the law and depriving workers in the music industry of compensation. Music piracy also takes time and thus imposes an opportunity cost equal to the value of the next-best alternative use of the time spent obtaining the music.

When similar music is available from both legal and illegal sources, consumers must compare the price of legal music with the sum of the expected legal cost, the risk burden, the guilt burden, and the opportunity cost of time required for piracy. The common $1.29 price of legal downloads may be the industry's closest approximation of that sum (in this case, minus the opportunity cost of time spent downloading the music, which is paid by the consumer for either type of download). The music industry sells more than 1 billion digital songs each year, so apparently the price is right for many consumers. The continuing popularity of music piracy indicates that, for many other people, either the legal price is too high or the limited legal offerings are inadequate.

The lessons from the music industry are relevant to a broad set of related industries. Movies and audiobooks can be stream-ripped, counterfeited, or bootlegged. Piracy and counterfeiting are growing problems for textbook publishers in an industry dominated by a similarly small number of large companies. And the power of the large media companies, such as 21st Century Fox, WarnerMedia, and Comcast (parent company to NBC), may become diluted by a growing number of free, online news and entertainment services, and alternatives such as satellite radio, that are made available by advancing technology.

ents run out. Movie theaters, convention centers, and school food-service providers typically forbid consumers to bring food in from elsewhere in order to maintain a monopoly. And the recording industry fights to uphold the copyrights to songs for the same reason. New technology makes stream-ripping and file sharing available-yet-illegal competition for the big music-recording firms. As consumers grapple with their consciences and firms weigh the wisdom of litigating against young perpetrators, artists and fans alike argue that the temptation to steal music would be eased if the music industry would offer prices and variety that more closely resemble the competitive ideal.

Conclusion

Around 200 years ago, seashells inscribed with ancient Chinese characters turned up in Xiaotun, China, and commanded handsome profits from scholars and collectors. Dealers kept the source a secret to maintain their monopoly. Villagers caught up in the trade of these "dragon bones" subsequently engaged in fights and lawsuits. In the music industry, the dragon bones are songs and the secrets are held by clandestine copiers of music, but the fierce fight for market power is the same. Market power confers profits that cannot be maintained in a competitive industry, and that power comes from barriers to entry. When the walls come tumbling down, competitors enter the market and bring profits down as well. Competition is good for consumers in terms of price, quantity, and quality, but it's bad for business.

Firms have long fought to establish and maintain what barriers they could. In the 15th and 16th centuries, spices such as nutmeg, cinnamon, and myrrh garnered high profits in Europe. In hopes of preventing competitors from entering the market, spice merchants claimed that their source was Africa, although the goods really came from the Far East. Today, pharmaceutical companies create barriers with patents and update products when old patents run out.

Critical Thinking Questions

1. What would you guess is the four-firm concentration ratio for seafood restaurants in your town? What is the four-firm concentration ratio for steak restaurants? How is the market power in these markets reflected in the relative price and quality of seafood and steak available in your town?

2. What barriers to entry exist in the following industries?
   a. electric power utilities
   b. word-processing software
   c. cold remedies
   d. textbooks
   e. family medicine

3. Who are the three highest-paid people you can think of? Is there market power in their industries? What barriers to entry exist for labor market participants who might want to compete for the positions of those three people? Are the lowest-paying jobs those with the fewest barriers to entry?

4. What strategies would you adopt in regard to music piracy if you were a music-industry CEO?

5. Suppose that by providing more exposure to new bands, music piracy increased the demand for legal music. Would that justify the illegal act of piracy?

Factor Markets

Jim West/Alamy; David Schaffer/Getty Images

economics by example *Immigration: How Welcoming Should Lady Liberty Be?*

From Whence Wages Arise

Does higher education pay? Yes, it does: In the modern economy, employers are willing to pay a premium for workers with more education. In fact, the size of that premium has increased a lot over the last few decades. Back in 1973 workers with advanced degrees, such as law degrees or MBAs, earned only 76% more than those who had only graduated from high school. By 2017, the premium for an advanced degree had risen to over 100%.

Who decided that the wages of workers with advanced degrees would rise so much compared with those of high school grads? The answer, of course, is that nobody decided it. Wage rates are prices, the prices of different kinds of

labor; and they are decided, like other prices, by supply and demand.

Still, there is a qualitative difference between the wage rate of high school grads and the price of, say, textbooks: the wage rate isn't the price of a *good*; it's the price of a *factor of production*. And although markets for factors of production are in many ways similar to those for goods, there are also some important differences.

In this section, we examine *factor markets*, the markets in which the factors of production such as labor, land, and capital are traded. Factor markets, like product markets, play a crucial role in the economy: they allocate resources

to firms and help ensure that those resources are used efficiently.

In *King Lear*, Shakespeare wrote that "all friends shall taste the wages of their virtue." This section concludes with a Module focused on the *marginal productivity theory of income distribution*, which qualifies Shakespeare's prediction with insights about the wages that workers "taste." How do they compare with the lowest wages that workers would accept? How do they compare with the workers' contributions to revenue? And what controversies surround the markets for labor among other factors of production? Read on, or as Shakespeare wrote, "O, see, see!"

Introduction and Factor Demand

In this Module, you will learn to:
- Describe features that make markets for factors of production—resources such as labor, land, capital, and entrepreneurship—different from goods markets
- Explain how factor markets determine the factor distribution of income
- Discuss how the demand for a factor of production is determined

The Economy's Factors of Production

You may recall that we have already defined a factor of production in the context of the circular-flow diagram: it is any resource that is used by firms to produce goods and services. To help distinguish factors of production from goods and services, remember that goods and services are consumed by households, but factors of production are not. The markets in which factors of production are bought and sold are called *factor markets*, and the prices in factor markets are known as *factor prices*.

What are these factors of production, and why do factor prices matter?

The Factors of Production

Economists divide factors of production into four principal classes. The first is *labor*, the work done by human beings. The second is *land*, which encompasses resources provided by nature. The third is capital, which can be divided into two categories: **physical capital**—often referred to simply as "capital"—consists of manufactured productive resources such as equipment, buildings, tools, and machines. In the modern economy, **human capital**, the improvement in labor created by education and knowledge, and embodied in the workforce, is at least equally significant. Technological progress has boosted the importance of human capital and made technical sophistication essential to many jobs, thus helping to create a premium for workers with advanced degrees. The final factor of production, *entrepreneurship*, is a unique resource that is not purchased in an easily identifiable factor market like the other three. It refers to innovation and risk-taking activities that bring together resources for production.

Why Factor Prices Matter: The Allocation of Resources

The factor prices determined in factor markets play a vital role in the important process of allocating resources among firms.

Consider the example of Houston, Texas, which was ravaged by Hurricane Harvey in 2017. The city had an urgent need for workers to haul hurricane debris to landfills. What ensured that those needed workers actually came? The factor market: the high demand for workers drove up wages. The city of Houston paid workers 50% more than the normal wage for debris removal. Workers doing repairs on homes and businesses also received above-normal wages. Over time, these higher wages drew workers from far and near to manage the mounds of wreckage.

In other words, the market for a factor of production—cleanup workers—allocated that factor of production to where it was needed.

In this sense factor markets are similar to goods markets, which allocate goods among consumers. But there are two features that make factor markets special. Unlike in a goods market, demand in a factor market is what we call **derived demand**.

AP® EXAM TIP

The factors of production are sometimes referred to as *inputs* on the AP® exam.

Physical capital—often referred to simply as "capital"—consists of manufactured productive resources such as equipment, buildings, tools, and machines.

Human capital is the improvement in labor created by education and knowledge that is embodied in the workforce.

Like most firms, this solar farm uses inputs from each of the four classes of factors of production: land, labor, physical and human capital, and entrepreneurship.

The demand for a factor is a **derived demand**. It results from (that is, it is *derived* from) the demand for the output being produced.

Higher wages helped Houston attract workers to clear the debris from Hurricane Harvey.

That is, demand for the factor is derived from demand for the product made by that factor—the firm's output. The second feature is that factor markets are where most people earn the largest shares of their income (government transfers being the next largest source of income in the economy).

Factor Incomes and the Distribution of Income

Most American families get the majority of their income in the form of wages and salaries—that is, they get their income by selling their labor. Some people, however, get most of their income from owning physical capital. For example, when you own stock in a company, what you really own is a share of that company's physical capital. Some people get much of their income from rents earned on land they own. And successful entrepreneurs earn income in the form of profit from businesses they own individually (or as a partnership), which is classified as *proprietors' income*.

Factor prices have a major influence on how the economic "pie" is sliced among different groups. For example, a higher wage rate, other things equal, means that a larger proportion of the total income in the economy goes to people who derive their income from their labor and less goes to those who derive their income from capital, land, or entrepreneurship. Economists refer to how the economic pie is sliced as the "distribution of income." Specifically, factor prices determine the **factor distribution of income**—how the total income of the economy is divided among labor, land, capital, and entrepreneurship.

The factor distribution of income in the United States has been reasonably stable over the past few decades. In other times and places, however, large changes have taken place in the factor distribution. One notable example: during the Industrial Revolution, the share of total income earned by landowners fell sharply, while the share earned by capital owners rose.

The **factor distribution of income** is the division of total income among land, labor, capital, and entrepreneurship.

The Factor Distribution of Income in the United States

When we talk about the factor distribution of income, what are we talking about in practice?

In the United States, as in all advanced economies, payments to labor account for most of the economy's total income. **Figure 69.1** shows the factor distribution of income in the United States in 2017: in that year, 67.8% of total income in the economy took the form of "compensation of employees"—a number that

---

Figure 69.1   Factor Distribution of Income in the United States in 2017

In 2017, compensation of employees accounted for most income earned in the United States—67.8% of the total. Most of the remainder—consisting of earnings paid in the form of interest, corporate profits, and rent—went to owners of physical capital. Finally, proprietors' income—9.1% of the total—went to individual owners of businesses as compensation for their labor, entrepreneurship, and capital expended in their businesses.

Data Source: Bureau of Economic Analysis.

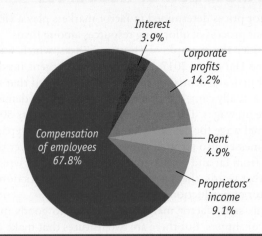

Interest 3.9%

Corporate profits 14.2%

Compensation of employees 67.8%

Rent 4.9%

Proprietors' income 9.1%

---

includes both wages and benefits such as health insurance. This number has been quite stable over the long run; 45 years earlier, in 1972, compensation of employees was similar, at 72.2% of total income.

Much of what we call compensation of employees is really a return on human capital. A surgeon isn't just supplying the services of a pair of ordinary hands (at least the patient hopes not!); that individual is also supplying the result of many years and hundreds of thousands of dollars invested in training and experience. We can't directly measure what fraction of wages is really a payment for education and training, but many economists believe that labor resources created through additional human capital have become *the* most important factor of production in modern economies.

The income of surgeons is largely a return on human capital.

Marginal Productivity and Factor Demand

All economic decisions are about comparing costs and benefits—and usually about comparing marginal costs and marginal benefits. This goes both for a consumer, deciding whether to buy more goods or services, and for a firm, deciding whether to hire an additional worker.

Although there are some important exceptions, most factor markets in the modern American economy are perfectly competitive. This means that most buyers and sellers of factors are price-takers because they are too small relative to the market to do anything but accept the market price. And in a competitive labor market, it's clear how to define the marginal cost an employer pays for a worker: it is simply the worker's wage rate. But what is the marginal benefit of that worker? To answer that question, we return to the production function, which relates inputs to output. We begin by examining a firm that is a price-taker in the output market—that is, it operates in a perfectly competitive industry.

Marginal Product of Labor

Figure 69.2 shows the production function for wheat on George and Martha's farm, as introduced in Module 54. Panel (a) uses the total product curve to show how total wheat production depends on the number of workers employed on the farm; panel (b) shows how the *marginal product of labor*, the increase in output from employing one more worker, depends on the number of workers employed. The table in Figure 69.2 shows the numbers behind the figure. Note that sometimes the marginal product (*MP*) is called the *marginal physical product* or *MPP*. These two terms are the same; the extra "P" just emphasizes that the term refers to the quantity of physical output being produced, not the monetary value of that output.

If workers are paid a daily wage of $200 each and George and Martha can sell an unlimited amount of wheat for $20 per bushel, how many workers should George and Martha employ to maximize profit?

In Module 54 we showed how to answer this question in several steps. First, we used information from the production function to derive the firm's total cost and its marginal cost. Then we used the *price-taking firm's optimal output rule*: a price-taking firm's profit is maximized by producing the quantity of output at which the marginal cost is equal to the market price. Having determined the optimal quantity of output, we went back to the production function to find the optimal number of workers—which was simply the number of workers needed to produce the optimal quantity of output.

Figure 69.2 The Production Function for George and Martha's Farm

(a) Total Product

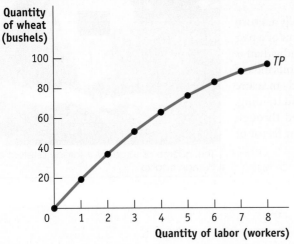

Quantity of labor L (workers)	Quantity of wheat Q (bushels)	Marginal product of labor $MPL = \Delta Q/\Delta L$ (bushels per worker)
0	0	
		19
1	19	
		17
2	36	
		15
3	51	
		13
4	64	
		11
5	75	
		9
6	84	
		7
7	91	
		5
8	96	

(b) Marginal Product of Labor

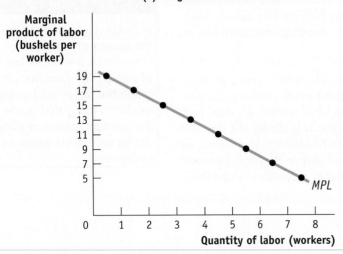

Panel (a) shows how the quantity of output of wheat on George and Martha's farm depends on the number of workers employed.

Panel (b) shows how the marginal product of labor depends on the number of workers employed.

Marginal Revenue Product and Factor Demand

As you might have guessed, marginal analysis provides a more direct way to find the number of workers that maximizes a firm's profit. This alternative approach is just a different way of looking at the same thing. But it gives us more insight into the demand for factors as opposed to the supply of goods. To see how this alternative approach works, suppose that George and Martha are deciding whether to employ another worker. The increase in *cost* from employing another worker is the wage rate, *W*, at which the firm can hire any number of workers in a perfectly competitive labor market. The *benefit* to George and Martha from employing another worker is the additional revenue gained from the hire. To determine the change in revenue, we can multiply the marginal product of labor, *MPL*, by the marginal revenue received from selling the additional output, *MR*. This amount—the additional revenue generated by employing one more unit of labor—is known as the **marginal revenue product** of labor (*MRPL*):

The **marginal revenue product** of a factor is the additional revenue generated by employing one more unit of that factor.

(69-1)   Marginal revenue product of labor $(MRPL) = MPL \times MR$

So should George and Martha hire another worker? Yes, if the resulting increase in revenue exceeds the cost of the additional worker—that is, if $MRPL > W$. Otherwise, they should not.

The hiring decision is made using marginal analysis, by comparing the marginal benefit from hiring another worker ($MRPL$) with the marginal cost (W). And as with any decision that is made on the margin, the optimal choice is made by equating marginal benefit with marginal cost (or if they're never equal, by continuing to hire until the marginal cost of one more unit would exceed the marginal benefit). So to maximize profit, George and Martha will employ workers up to the point at which, for the last worker employed,

$$\textbf{(69-2)} \quad MRPL = W$$

This rule isn't limited to labor; it applies to any factor of production. The marginal revenue product of any factor is its marginal product times the marginal revenue received from the good it produces. And as a general rule, profit-maximizing, price-taking firms will keep adding more units of each factor of production until the marginal revenue product of the last unit employed is equal to the factor's price.

This rule is consistent with our previous analysis. We saw that a profit-maximizing firm chooses the level of output at which the marginal revenue of the good it produces equals the marginal cost of producing that good. It turns out that if the level of output is chosen so that marginal revenue equals marginal cost, then it is also true that with the amount of labor required to produce that output level, the marginal revenue product of labor will equal the wage rate.

Now let's look more closely at why firms should choose the level of employment that equates $MRPL$ and W, and at how that decision helps us understand factor demand.

The table in **Figure 69.3** shows the marginal revenue product of labor on George and Martha's farm when the price of wheat (and thus the marginal revenue for this price-taking firm) is $20 per bushel. In Figure 69.3, the horizontal axis shows the number of workers employed; the vertical axis measures the marginal revenue product

Figure 69.3 The Marginal Revenue Product Curve

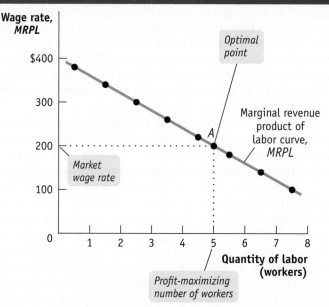

Quantity of labor L (workers)	Marginal product of labor MPL (bushels per worker)	Marginal revenue product of labor $MRPL = MPL \times MR$
0		
	19	$380
1		
	17	340
2		
	15	300
3		
	13	260
4		
	11	220
5		
	9	180
6		
	7	140
7		
	5	100
8		

This curve shows how the marginal revenue product of labor depends on the number of workers employed. It slopes downward because of diminishing returns to labor in production.

To maximize profit, George and Martha choose the level of employment at which the marginal revenue product of labor is equal to the market wage rate, at point A.

The marginal revenue product curve of a factor shows how the marginal revenue product of that factor depends on the quantity of the factor employed.

of labor and the wage rate. The curve shown is the **marginal revenue product curve** of labor. This curve, like the marginal product of labor curve, slopes downward because of diminishing returns to labor in production. That is, the marginal revenue product of each worker is less than that of the preceding worker because the marginal product of each worker is less than that of the preceding worker. For a firm that is not a price-taker, the curve also slopes downward because marginal revenue decreases as more units are sold.

We have just seen that to maximize profit, George and Martha hire workers until the wage rate is equal to the marginal revenue product of the last worker employed. Let's use the example to see how this principle really works.

Assume that George and Martha currently employ 3 workers and that these workers must be paid the market wage rate of $200 per day. Should they employ an additional worker? Looking at the table in Figure 69.3, we see that since George and Martha have 3 workers, the marginal revenue product of an additional worker is $260. So if they employ an additional worker, they will increase their revenue by $260 but increase their cost by only $200, yielding a $60 increase in profit. In fact, a firm can always increase profit by employing one more unit of a factor of production as long as the marginal revenue product of that factor exceeds the factor price.

Alternatively, suppose that George and Martha employ 8 workers. By reducing the number of workers to 7, they can save $200 in wages. In addition, the marginal revenue product of the 8th worker is only $100. So, by reducing employment by one worker, they can increase profit by $200 − $100 = $100. In other words, a firm can always increase profit by employing one less unit of a factor of production as long as the marginal revenue product of that factor is less than the factor price.

Using this method, we can see from the table in Figure 69.3 that the profit-maximizing employment level is 5 workers, given a wage rate of $200. The marginal revenue product of the 5th worker is $220, so adding the 5th worker results in $220 of additional revenue ($20 of additional profit). But George and Martha should not hire more than 5 workers: the marginal revenue product of the 6th worker is only $180, $20 less than the cost of that worker. So, to maximize profit, George and Martha should employ workers up to but not beyond the point at which the marginal revenue product of the last worker employed is equal to the wage rate.

Look again at the marginal revenue product curve in Figure 69.3. To determine the profit-maximizing level of employment, we set the marginal revenue product of labor equal to the price of labor—a wage rate of $200 per worker. This means that the profit-maximizing level of employment is at point *A*, corresponding to an employment level of 5 workers. If the wage rate were higher than $200, we would simply move up the curve and decrease the number of workers employed; if the wage rate were lower than $200, we would move down the curve and increase the number of workers employed.

A small farm like George and Martha's, with no worker whose marginal revenue product happens to equal the wage rate, hires workers until the marginal revenue product of another worker would fall below the wage rate. For a larger farm with many employees, the marginal revenue product of labor falls only slightly when an additional worker is employed, so there will be some worker whose marginal revenue product almost exactly equals the wage rate. (In keeping with the George and Martha example, this means that some worker generates a marginal revenue product of approximately $200.) In this case, as Equation 69-2 implies, the firm maximizes profit by choosing a level of employment at which the marginal revenue product of the last worker hired *equals* (to a very good approximation) the wage rate.

In the interest of simplicity, we will assume from now on that firms use this rule to determine the profit-maximizing level of employment. This means that *the marginal revenue product of labor*

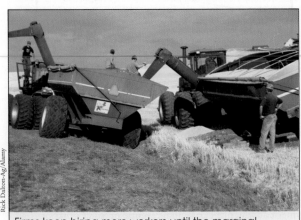

Firms keep hiring more workers until the marginal revenue product of labor equals the wage rate.

Rick Dalton-Ag/Alamy

curve is the individual firm's labor demand curve. And in general, a firm's marginal revenue product curve for any factor of production is that firm's individual demand curve for that factor.

Because many firms are not price-takers, let's now consider the marginal revenue product for a firm in an imperfectly competitive market. Suppose John and Abigail own the only pizzeria in their town, and like all monopolists, they must lower their price in order to sell more pizzas. In this case, due to the *price effect* of charging a lower price on all units so that one more can be sold, the marginal revenue gained from each pizza is less than its price. **Table 69.1** shows the calculation of the marginal revenue product for each of John and Abigail's workers. For example, by hiring the 3rd worker, they are able to produce 18 additional pizzas. The marginal revenue received from these pizzas is $9.69, so the marginal revenue product of the 3rd worker is 18 × $9.69 = $169.74.

AP® EXAM TIP

Given the total product and product price, you may be expected to calculate the marginal product, marginal revenue product, and total revenue for the AP® exam.

Table 69.1	Marginal Revenue Product of Labor with Imperfect Competition in the Product Market					
Quantity of Labor L	Quantity of Output Q	Marginal Product of labor MPL	Product Price P	Total Revenue $TR = P \times Q$	Marginal Revenue $MR = \Delta TR / \Delta Q$	Marginal Revenue Product of labor $MRPL = MPL \times MR$
0	0			$0.00		
		20			$10.00	$200.00
1	20		$10.00	200.00		
		19			9.61	182.59
2	39		9.81	382.59		
		18			9.43	169.74
3	57		9.69	552.33		
		16			8.96	143.36
4	73		9.53	695.69		
		13			8.67	112.71
5	86		9.40	808.40		

Shifts of the Factor Demand Curve

As in the case of ordinary demand curves, it is important to distinguish between movements along the factor demand curve and shifts of the factor demand curve. What causes factor demand curves to shift? There are three main causes:

- Changes in the prices of goods
- Changes in the supply of other factors
- Changes in technology

AP® EXAM TIP

Although the factor demand curve looks and acts like other demand curves you have studied, the causes of a shift in demand are different.

Changes in the Prices of Goods

Remember that factor demand is derived demand: if the price of the good that is produced with a factor changes, so will the marginal revenue received from the good and thus the marginal revenue product of the factor. That is, in the case of labor demand, if P changes, MR changes, and $MRPL = MPL \times MR$ will change at any given level of employment.

Figure 69.4 illustrates the effects of changes in the price of wheat on George and Martha's demand for labor, assuming that $200 is the current wage rate. Panel (a) shows the effect of an *increase* in the price of wheat. Note that in this example, the price increase is the same as the marginal revenue increase because $P = MR$ in a perfectly competitive market. This increase shifts the marginal revenue product of labor curve upward because $MRPL$ rises at any given level of employment. If the wage rate remains unchanged at $200, then the optimal point moves from point A to point B: the profit-maximizing level of employment rises from 5 to 8 workers.

Figure 69.4 Shifts of the Marginal Revenue Product Curve

Panel (a) shows the effect of an increase in the price of wheat on George and Martha's demand for labor. The increase in price (and thus marginal revenue) shifts the marginal revenue product of labor curve upward from $MRPL_1$ to $MRPL_2$. If the market wage rate remains at $200, the profit-maximizing quantity of labor rises from 5 workers to 8 workers, shown by the movement from point A to point B. Panel (b) shows the effect of a decrease in the price of wheat. The marginal revenue product of labor curve shifts downward, from $MRPL_1$ to $MRPL_3$. At the market wage rate of $200, the profit-maximizing quantity of labor falls from 5 workers to 2 workers, shown by the movement from point A to point C.

Panel (b) shows the effect of a *decrease* in the price of wheat. This shifts the marginal revenue product of labor curve downward. If the wage rate remains unchanged at $200, then the optimal point moves from point A to point C: the profit-maximizing level of employment falls from 5 to 2 workers.

Changes in the Supply of Other Factors

Goods and services are made using a combination of different factors, and the productivity of each factor generally depends on the supplies of other factors. Suppose that George and Martha clear a woodland on their property to make more land available to cultivate. Each worker now produces more wheat because each one has more land to work with. The increase in productivity raises the marginal product of labor on the farm at any given level of employment. This has the same effect as an increase in the price of wheat, which is illustrated in panel (a) of Figure 69.4: the marginal revenue product of labor curve shifts upward, and at any given wage rate the profit-maximizing level of employment rises. Similarly, suppose George and Martha cultivate less land. This leads to a fall in the marginal product of labor at any given employment level. Each worker produces less wheat because each has less land to work with. As a result, the marginal revenue product of labor curve shifts downward—as in panel (b) of Figure 69.4—and the profit-maximizing level of employment falls.

Changes in Technology

In general, the effect of technological progress on the demand for any given factor can go either way: improved technology can either increase or decrease the demand for a given factor of production.

How can technological progress decrease factor demand? Consider horses, which were once an important factor of production. The development of substitutes for horse power, such as automobiles and tractors, greatly reduced the demand for horses.

The usual effect of technological progress, however, is to increase the demand for a given factor, often because it raises the marginal product of the factor. In particular, although there have been persistent fears that machinery would reduce the demand for labor, over the long run the U.S. economy has seen both wage increases and increases in employment, suggesting that technological progress has increased labor demand.

MODULE 69 REVIEW

Check Your Understanding

1. Suppose that the government places price controls on the market for college professors, imposing a wage that is lower than the market wage. Describe the effect of this policy on the production of college degrees. What sectors of the economy do you think would be adversely affected by this policy? What sectors of the economy might benefit?

2. **a.** Suppose service industries, such as retailing and banking, experience an increase in demand. These industries use relatively more labor than nonservice industries. Does the demand curve for labor shift to the right, shift to the left, or remain unchanged?

   b. Suppose diminishing fish populations off the coast of Maine lead to policies restricting the use of the most productive types of nets in that area. The result is a decrease in the number of fish caught per day by commercial fishers in Maine. The price of fish is unaffected due to growing supplies from elsewhere. Does the demand curve for fishers in Maine shift to the right, shift to the left, or remain unchanged?

TACKLE THE AP® TEST: Multiple-Choice Questions

1. Which of the following is an example of *physical* capital?
   a. manual labor
   b. welding equipment
   c. farm land
   d. lumber
   e. education

2. Which of the following will shift a factor's demand curve to the right?
   a. a technological advance that replaces that factor
   b. a decrease in demand for the good being produced
   c. a decrease in that factor's marginal product
   d. an increase in the price of that factor
   e. an increase in the price of the good being produced

3. Factor market demand is called a *derived* demand because it
   a. derives its name from the Latin word *factorus*.
   b. is derived from the market wage received by workers.
   c. is derived from the productivity of workers.
   d. is derived from the product market.
   e. derives its shape from the price of the factor.

4. Which factor of production receives the largest portion of income in the United States?
   a. land
   b. labor
   c. physical capital
   d. entrepreneurship
   e. interest

5. An individual firm's demand curve for labor is
   a. downward-sloping.
   b. upward-sloping.
   c. horizontal at the level of the product price.
   d. vertical.
   e. U-shaped.

6. Which of the following curves represents an individual firm's demand curve for labor?
   a. marginal revenue
   b. marginal product of labor
   c. marginal revenue product of labor
   d. average product of labor
   e. average revenue

7. If Roland Bike Works expands the number of assembly lines in its mountain bike factory, its *MRPL* curve will
   a. shift upward.
   b. shift downward.
   c. remain unchanged.
   d. shift to the left.
   e. become vertical.

1. The table below shows the quantity of umbrellas that Umbrellarama can produce with various quantities of workers. Umbrellarama can sell all of the output it produces at a price of $15.

Quantity of labor (workers)	Quantity of umbrellas
0	0
1	300
2	550
3	700
4	800
5	850
6	890

   a. What is the marginal revenue product of labor of the 3rd worker?
   b. Draw a correctly labeled graph showing the firm's demand curve for labor.
   c. What happens to the demand curve for labor if the price of umbrellas increases to $20? Show the result on your graph from part b.
   d. Assume that a technological advance doubles the productivity of workers. Calculate the total quantity that will now be produced with each quantity of labor.

1 point: $MRPL = 150 \times \$15 = \$2{,}250$

1 point: The vertical axis is labeled "$MRPL$" and/or "Wage rate"; the horizontal axis is labeled "Quantity of labor."

1 point: $MRPL$ is downward-sloping and labeled.

1 point: $MRPL$ is plotted using correct numbers (see graph).

1 point: The demand curve for labor shifts to the right.

1 point: $MRPL$ curve is shown shifted to the right.

1 point: The new quantities produced are 600; 1,100; 1,400; 1,600; 1,700; and 1,780.

2. Draw separate, correctly labeled graphs illustrating the effect of each of the following changes on the demand for labor. Adopt the usual *ceteris paribus* assumption that all else remains unchanged in each case.
   a. The price of the product being produced decreases.
   b. Worker productivity increases.
   c. Firms invest in more capital to be used by workers.
   (5 points)

Rubric for FRQ 1 (7 points)

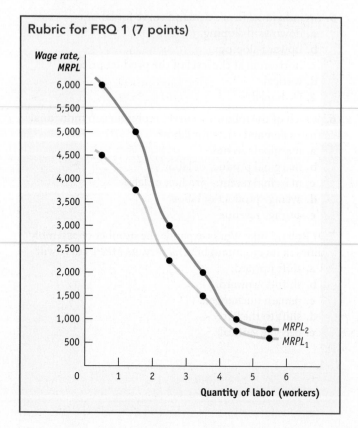

The Markets for Land and Capital

In this Module, you will learn to:
- Determine supply and demand in the markets for land and capital
- Find equilibrium in the land and capital markets
- Explain how the demand for factors leads to the marginal productivity theory of income distribution

In Figure 69.1 we saw the factor distribution of income and found that approximately 68% of total income in the economy took the form of compensation for employees. Because labor is such an important resource, it is often used as the example in discussions of factor markets. But land and capital are critical resources as well, and their markets have unique characteristics worthy of examination. In this Module we look more closely at the markets for land and capital before moving on to discuss the labor market further in Module 71.

Land and Capital

In the previous Module we used a labor market example to explain why a firm's individual demand curve for a factor is its marginal revenue product curve. Now we look at the distinguishing characteristics of demand and supply in land and capital markets, and how the equilibrium price and quantity of these factors are determined.

Demand in the Markets for Land and Capital

The result that we derived for demand in the labor market also applies to other factors of production. For example, suppose that a farmer is considering whether to rent an additional acre of land for the next year. He or she will compare the cost of renting that acre with the additional revenue generated by farming an additional acre—the marginal revenue product of an acre of land. To maximize profit, the farmer will rent more land up until the marginal revenue product of an acre of land is equal to the rental cost per acre. The same is true for capital: the decision of whether to rent an additional piece of equipment comes down to a comparison of the additional cost of the equipment with the additional revenue it generates.

What if the farmer already owns the land or the firm already owns the equipment? As discussed in Module 52 in the context of Babette's Cajun Café, even if you own land or capital, there is an implicit cost—the opportunity cost—of using it for a given activity because it could otherwise be used for something else, such as renting it out to other firms. So a profit-maximizing firm employs additional units of land and capital until the cost of the last unit employed, explicit or implicit, is equal to the marginal revenue product of that unit. We call the cost of renting a unit of land or capital for a set period of time its **rental rate**. The rental rate is also the owner's opportunity cost of using the land or capital rather than renting it out.

As with labor, due to diminishing returns, the marginal revenue product curve and therefore the individual firm's demand curves for land and capital slope downward.

The **rental rate** of either land or capital is the cost, explicit or implicit, of using a unit of that asset for a given period of time.

Even if a farmer owns her tractor, her opportunity cost of using it is the rental rate, because if she didn't use the tractor herself, she could rent it out to another farmer at that rate.

Supply in the Markets for Land and Capital

Figure 70.1 illustrates the markets for land and capital. The red curve in panel (a) is the supply curve for land. As we have drawn it, the supply curve for land is relatively steep and therefore relatively inelastic. This reflects the fact that finding new supplies of land for production is typically difficult and expensive—for example, creating new farmland through expensive irrigation.

Figure 70.1 Equilibria in the Land and Capital Markets

(a) The Market for Land

(b) The Market for Capital

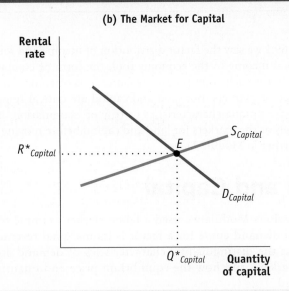

Panel (a) illustrates equilibrium in the market for land; panel (b) illustrates equilibrium in the market for capital. The supply curve for land is relatively steep, reflecting the high cost of increasing the quantity of productive land. The supply curve for capital, by contrast, is relatively flat because the supply of capital is relatively responsive to price changes.

The red curve in panel (b) is the supply curve for capital. In contrast to the supply curve for land, the supply curve for capital is relatively flat and therefore relatively elastic. That's because the supply of capital is relatively responsive to price changes: capital is typically paid for with the savings of investors, and the amount of savings that investors make available is relatively responsive to the rental rate for capital.

As in the case of supply curves for goods and services, the supply curve for a factor of production will shift as the factor becomes more or less available. For example, the supply of farmland could decrease as a result of a drought, or the supply of capital could increase as a result of a government policy to promote investment. Because of diminishing returns, when the supply of land or capital changes, its marginal product will change. When the supply of land or capital decreases, the marginal product and rental rate increase. For example, if the number of available delivery trucks decreased, the additional benefit from the last truck used would be higher than before—it would serve more critical delivery needs—and firms would pay more for it. Likewise, when the supply of land or capital increases, the marginal product and rental rate decrease.

Equilibrium in Land and Capital Markets

The equilibrium rental rate and quantity in the land and capital markets are found at the intersection of the supply and demand curves in Figure 70.1. Panel (a) shows the equilibrium in the market for land. Summing all of the firm demand curves for land gives us the market demand curve for land. The equilibrium rental rate for land is R^*_{Land}, and the equilibrium quantity of land employed in production is Q^*_{Land}. In a competitive land market, each unit of land will be paid the *equilibrium marginal revenue product* of land. The **equilibrium marginal revenue product** of a factor is the additional revenue generated by the last unit of that factor employed in the entire market for that factor.

Panel (b) shows the equilibrium in the market for capital. The equilibrium rental rate for capital is $R^*_{Capital}$, and the equilibrium quantity of capital employed is $Q^*_{Capital}$. In a competitive capital market, each unit of capital will be paid the equilibrium marginal revenue product of capital.

> The **equilibrium marginal revenue product** of a factor is the additional revenue generated by the last unit of that factor employed in the factor market as a whole.

Economic Rent

When the payment for a factor of production is higher than it would need to be to employ that factor, the factor is earning **economic rent**. Consider the 512 acres of flat land in Ouray, Colorado, which is ringed by mountains too steep to build or farm on. Because the land is in fixed supply, the supply curve is vertical as shown in **Figure 70.2**, and the monthly rental rate is determined by the level of demand. The land would be there even if the rental rate were zero, as it would be if the demand curve were D_1. Since no payment is needed to make the land available, the entire payment for the land is economic rent. If the demand curve were D_2, the rental rate would be $1,000 an acre, and the economic rent would be $1,000 \times 512 = \$512,000$. If the demand curve were D_3, the rental rate would be $4,000 per acre, and the economic rent would be $4,000 \times 512 = \$2,048,000$.

When studying competitive factor markets remember that all inputs are paid the equilibrium marginal revenue product *in that market*.

> **Economic rent** is the payment to a factor of production in excess of the minimum payment necessary to employ that factor.

Figure 70.2 Demand, the Rental Rate, and Economic Rent

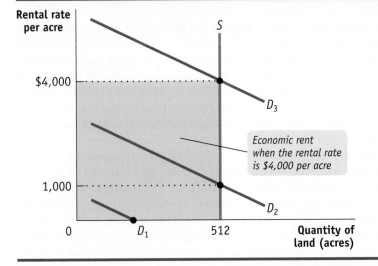

When the supply of a factor of production is fixed, the rental rate is determined by the level of demand. For example, if the demand curve for land were D_1, the annual rental rate would be zero. If the demand curve were D_2, the rental rate would be $1,000 per acre. And if the demand curve were D_3, the rental rate would be $4,000 per acre. The shaded area of the graph represents the economic rent of $4,000 \times 512 = \$2,048,000$ that exists when the rental rate is $4,000 per acre.

The appropriate distribution of the economic rent from land is a source of debate. Socialists argue that land should be publicly owned so that its benefits can be shared broadly. Critics argue that markets provide incentives for resources to be allocated to their most productive uses, whereas publicly owned land might not be allocated with the same attention to opportunity costs.

With private land ownership, portions of the economic rent can be redistributed using a land tax, which creates no deadweight loss when land is in fixed supply. Recall from Section 9 that many types of taxes cause deadweight loss by reducing the equilibrium quantity and eliminating some mutually beneficial exchanges. When the quantity of land is fixed, a tax on land does not decrease the quantity of land

Economic rent is similar to producer surplus, except that economic rent applies to factor markets and producer surplus applies to product markets.

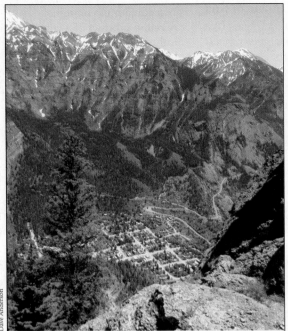

When a factor of production, such as the land in this Colorado town, would be available regardless of its price, the entire payment for that factor is economic rent.

According to the **marginal productivity theory of income distribution**, every factor of production is paid the equilibrium marginal revenue product.

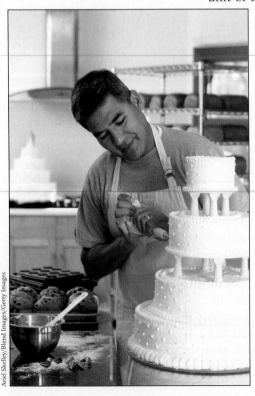

that is bought and sold, so there is no deadweight loss. The entire burden of the tax is placed on landowners in the form of a loss of economic rent. Although a land tax is appealing from an efficiency standpoint, there is no consensus on the level of taxation that is fair to landowners.

Workers receive economic rent as well. If you earn $12 per hour, but you would be willing to work for as little as $8 per hour, you receive $4 of economic rent per hour. If you love your job so much that you would work for free, your income is pure economic rent.

Now that we know how equilibrium rental rates and quantities are determined in factor markets, we can learn how these markets influence the factor distribution of income. To do this, we look more closely at marginal productivity in factor markets.

Marginal Productivity Theory

The **marginal productivity theory of income distribution** sums up what we have learned about payments to factors when goods markets and factor markets are perfectly competitive. According to this theory, each factor is paid the value of the additional revenue generated by the last unit of that factor employed in the factor market as a whole—its equilibrium marginal revenue product. To understand why the marginal productivity theory of income distribution is important, look back at Figure 69.1, which shows the factor distribution of income in the United States, and ask yourself this question: who or what determined that labor would get 67.8% of total U.S. income? Why not 90% or 50%?

The answer, according to this theory, is that the division of income among the economy's factors of production isn't arbitrary: in the economy-wide factor market, the price paid for each factor is equal to the contribution to revenue made by the last unit of that factor hired. If a unit of labor is paid more than a unit of capital, it is because at the equilibrium quantity of each factor, the marginal revenue product of labor exceeds the marginal revenue product of capital.

So far we have treated factor markets as if every unit of each factor were identical—that is, as if all land were identical, all labor were identical, and all capital were identical. But in reality factors differ considerably with respect to productivity. For instance, land resources differ in their ability to produce crops, and workers have different skills and abilities. Rather than thinking of one land market for all land resources in an economy, and similarly one capital market and one labor market, we can instead think of different markets for different types of land, capital, and labor. For example, the market for computer programmers is different from the market for pastry chefs.

When we consider that there are separate factor markets for different types of factors, the marginal productivity theory of income distribution still holds. That is, when the labor market for pastry chefs is in equilibrium, the wage rate earned by all pastry chefs is equal to the market's equilibrium marginal revenue product—the marginal revenue product of the last pastry chef hired in that market. The marginal productivity theory can explain the distribution of income among different types of land, labor, and capital as well as the distribution of income among the factors of production. In Module 73 we look more closely at the distribution of income between different types of labor and the extent to which the marginal productivity theory of income distribution explains differences in workers' wages.

MODULE 70 REVIEW

Check Your Understanding

1. Explain how each of the following events would affect the equilibrium rental rate and the equilibrium quantity in the land market.
   a. Developers improve the process of filling in coastal waters with rocks and soil to form large new areas of land.
   b. New fertilizers improve the productivity of each existing acre of farmland.

2. Explain the following statement: "When firms in different industries all compete for the same land, the marginal revenue product of the last unit of land rented will be equal across all firms, regardless of whether they are in different industries."

TACKLE THE AP® TEST: Multiple-Choice Questions

1. The implicit cost of capital that you own is
   a. the rental rate.
   b. greater than the rental rate.
   c. the original purchase price of the capital.
   d. greater than the original purchase price of the capital.
   e. zero because you already own it.

2. A very steep supply curve for land indicates that
   a. the supply of land is elastic.
   b. the quantity of land supplied is very responsive to price changes.
   c. it is very costly to increase the quantity of land supplied.
   d. an increase in the demand for land would have a relatively small effect on the price of land.
   e. a decrease in the demand for land would have a relatively large effect on the quantity of land supplied.

3. The explicit cost of land you don't own is equal to the
   a. rental rate.
   b. interest rate.
   c. profit received from using that land.
   d. market wage rate.
   e. marginal product of land.

4. A firm will continue to employ more land until its marginal revenue product of land is
   a. zero.
   b. maximized.
   c. equal to the rental rate.
   d. equal to the wage rate.
   e. equal to the marginal revenue product of labor and capital.

5. According to the marginal productivity theory of income distribution,
   a. each unit of a factor will be paid its marginal revenue product.
   b. as more of a factor is used, its marginal productivity increases.
   c. factors that receive higher payments are less productive.
   d. capital should receive the highest portion of factor income.
   e. each factor is paid the equilibrium marginal revenue product.

6. The entire payment for land that is in fixed supply constitutes
   a. a tax.
   b. a subsidy.
   c. deadweight loss.
   d. economic rent.
   e. price discrimination.

7. When a land tax is used to distribute the economic rent from land that is in fixed supply, the resulting deadweight loss is
   a. equal to the size of the tax.
   b. equal to the price paid for the land.
   c. larger than the size of the tax but smaller than the price paid for the land.
   d. negative.
   e. zero.

1. Refer to the table below. Assume that the rental rate for capital is $100 per unit and the price of the product is $10.

Quantity of capital (units)	Quantity of output
0	0
1	30
2	55
3	70
4	78
5	85
6	89

a. What is the MRP of the 2nd unit of capital?

b. Will the firm employ the 2nd unit of capital? Explain.

c. How many units of capital will the firm hire? Explain.

Rubric for FRQ 1 (5 points)

1 point: $MRP = 25 \times \$10 = \$250$

1 point: Yes, they will employ the second unit.

1 point: Because the MRP of $250 is greater than the rental rate of $100

1 point: 3

1 point: Because the MRP exceeds the rental rate for the first 3 units

2. Draw a correctly labeled graph for a land market in which land is in fixed supply. Label each of the following on your graph: the axes, the supply and demand curves for land, the equilibrium rental rate, and the equilibrium quantity of land employed. Shade and label the area that represents economic rent. **(5 points)**

MOD 71

The Market for Labor

In this Module, you will learn to:
- Describe how a worker's decision about time preference gives rise to labor supply
- Determine the equilibrium wage and level of employment in the labor market

In Module 69 we looked at the determinants of labor demand and how the wage rate influences the quantity of labor demanded by firms. Now we complete our development of the labor market model by adding the supply of labor and exploring the determination of equilibrium wage and quantity in the labor market.

The Supply of Labor

There are only 24 hours in a day, so to supply labor is to give up leisure, which presents a dilemma of sorts. For this and other reasons, as we'll see, the labor market looks different from markets for goods and services.

Work Versus Leisure

In the labor market, the roles of firms and households are the reverse of what they are in markets for goods and services. A good such as coffee is supplied by firms and demanded by households; labor, though, is demanded by firms and supplied by households. How do households decide how much labor to supply?

As a practical matter, most people have limited control over their work hours: sometimes a worker has little choice but to take a job for a set number of hours per week. However, there is often flexibility to choose among different careers and employment situations that involve varying numbers of work hours. There is a range of part-time and full-time jobs; some are strictly 9:00 A.M. to 5:00 P.M., others have much longer or shorter work hours. Some people work two jobs; others don't work at all. And self-employed people have many work-hour options.

To simplify our study of labor supply, we will imagine an individual who can choose to work as many or as few hours as he or she likes. Why wouldn't such an individual work as many hours as possible? Because workers are human beings, and have other uses for their time. An hour spent on the job is an hour not spent on other, presumably more pleasant, activities. So the decision about how much labor to supply involves making a decision about *time allocation*—how many hours to spend on different activities.

By working, people earn income that they can use to buy goods. The more hours an individual works, the more goods he or she can afford to buy. But this increased purchasing power comes at the expense of a reduction in **leisure**, the time spent not working. Leisure doesn't necessarily mean time goofing off. It could mean time spent with one's family, pursuing hobbies, exercising, and so on. And though purchased goods yield utility, so does leisure. Indeed, we can think of leisure itself as a normal good, which most people would like to consume more of as their incomes increase.

How does a rational individual decide how much leisure to consume? By making a marginal comparison, of course. In analyzing consumer choice, we asked how a utility-maximizing consumer uses a marginal *dollar*. In analyzing labor supply, we ask how an individual uses a marginal *hour*.

Consider Clive, an individual who likes both leisure and the goods money can buy. Suppose that his wage rate is $20 per hour. In deciding how many hours he wants to work, he must compare the marginal utility of an additional hour of leisure with the additional utility he gets from $20 worth of goods. If $20 worth of goods adds more to his total utility than an additional hour of leisure, he can increase his total utility by giving up an hour of leisure in order to work an additional hour. If an extra hour of leisure adds more to his total utility than $20 worth of goods, he can increase his total utility by working one fewer hour in order to gain an hour of leisure.

At Clive's optimal level of labor supply, then, the marginal utility he receives from one hour of leisure is equal to the marginal utility he receives from the goods that his hourly wage can purchase. This is very similar to the *optimal consumption rule* we encountered previously, except that it is a rule about time rather than money.

Our next step is to ask how Clive's decision about time allocation is affected when his wage rate changes.

Time spent working is time not spent on leisure activities.

Leisure is time available for purposes other than earning money to buy marketed goods.

Wages and Labor Supply

Suppose that Clive's wage rate increases from $20 to $30 per hour. How will he change his time allocation?

You could argue that Clive will work longer hours because his incentive to work has increased: by giving up an hour of leisure, he can now gain $30 instead of $20. But you could equally well argue that he will work less because he doesn't need to work as many hours to generate the income required to pay for the goods he wants.

As these opposing arguments suggest, the quantity of labor Clive supplies can either rise or fall when his wage rate rises. To understand why, let's recall the distinction between the *substitution effect* and the *income effect*. We have seen that a price change affects consumer choice in two ways: by changing the opportunity cost of a good in terms of other goods (the substitution effect) and by making the consumer richer or poorer (the income effect).

Now think about how a rise in Clive's wage rate affects his demand for leisure. The opportunity cost of leisure—the amount of money he gives up by taking an hour off instead of working—rises. Other things equal, that substitution effect gives him an incentive to consume less leisure and work longer hours. Conversely, a higher wage rate makes Clive richer—and, other things equal, this income effect leads him to want to consume *more* leisure and supply less labor because leisure is a normal good.

So in the case of labor supply, the substitution effect and the income effect work in opposite directions. If the substitution effect is so powerful that it dominates the income effect, an increase in Clive's wage rate leads him to supply *more* hours of labor. If the income effect is so powerful that it dominates the substitution effect, an increase in the wage rate leads him to supply *fewer* hours of labor.

We see, then, that the **individual labor supply curve**—the relationship between the wage rate and the number of hours of labor supplied by an individual worker—does not necessarily slope upward at every wage rate.

Figure 71.1 illustrates the two possibilities for the slope of the labor supply curve. If the substitution effect dominates the income effect, the individual labor supply curve slopes upward, as it does here up to a wage of $40. So an increase in the wage rate from $20 to $30 per hour leads to a *rise* in the number of hours worked from 40 to 50. However, if the income effect dominates the substitution effect, the quantity of labor supplied goes down when the wage rate increases and the labor supply curve slopes downward. For instance, a rise in the wage rate from $50 to $60 leads to a *fall* in the number of hours worked from 50 to 40.

The **individual labor supply curve** shows how the quantity of labor supplied by an individual depends on that individual's wage rate.

Figure 71.1 The Individual Labor Supply Curve

When the substitution effect of a wage increase dominates the income effect, the individual labor supply curve slopes upward, as it does in this graph up to a wage of $40 per hour. Here a rise in the wage rate from, for example, $20 to $30 per hour increases the number of hours worked from 40 to 50. But when the income effect of a wage increase dominates the substitution effect, the individual labor supply curve slopes downward. Here a rise in the wage rate from, say, $50 to $60 per hour reduces the number of hours worked from 50 to 40.

Economists refer to an individual labor supply curve that contains both upward-sloping and downward-sloping segments as a "backward-bending labor supply curve." At lower wage rates, the substitution effect dominates the income effect. At higher wage rates, the income effect eventually dominates the substitution effect.

Is a backward-bending labor supply curve a real possibility? Yes: many labor economists believe that income effects on the supply of labor may be somewhat stronger than substitution effects at high wage rates. You may know a doctor or dentist who only works four days a week, which supports this belief. The most compelling piece of evidence comes from Americans' increasing consumption of leisure over the past century. At the end of the nineteenth century, wages adjusted for inflation were only about one-eighth what they are today; the typical work week was 70 hours, and very few workers retired at age 65. Today the typical work week is less than 40 hours, and most people retire at age 65 or earlier. So it seems that Americans have chosen to take advantage of higher wages in part by consuming more leisure.

Shifts of the Labor Supply Curve

Now that we have examined how income and substitution effects shape the individual labor supply curve, we can turn to the market labor supply curve. In any labor market, the market supply curve is the horizontal sum of the individual labor supply curves of all workers in that market. Although the individual labor supply curve can bend backward at very high wage rates, we will assume that the market labor supply curve has the more common upward-sloping shape. A change in any factor *other than the wage* that alters workers' willingness to supply labor causes a shift of the market labor supply curve. A variety of factors can lead to such shifts, including changes in preferences and social norms, changes in population, changes in opportunities, and changes in wealth.

AP® EXAM TIP

You may be asked to identify, graph, and analyze shifts of the labor supply curve for the AP® exam.

Changes in Preferences and Social Norms

Changes in preferences and social norms can lead workers to increase or decrease their willingness to work at any given wage. A striking example of this phenomenon is the large increase in the number of employed women—particularly married, employed women—that has occurred in the United States since the 1960s. Before that time, women who could afford to largely avoided working outside the home. Changes in preferences and norms in post–World War II America (helped along by the invention of labor-saving home appliances such as washing machines, the trend for more people to live in cities, and higher female education levels) have induced large numbers of American women to join the workforce—a phenomenon often observed in other countries that experience similar social and technological changes.

Changes in Population

Changes in the population size generally lead to shifts of the labor supply curve. A larger population tends to shift the labor supply curve rightward as more workers are available at any given wage; a smaller population tends to shift the labor supply curve leftward due to fewer available workers. Currently the size of the U.S. labor force grows by approximately 0.5% per year, a result of immigration from other countries and, in comparison to many developed countries, a relatively high birth rate. As a result, the labor supply curve in the United States is shifting to the right.

Changes in Opportunities

At one time, teaching was the only occupation considered suitable for well-educated women. However, as opportunities in other professions opened up to women starting in the 1960s, many women left teaching and chose other careers.

This generated a leftward shift of the supply curve for teachers, reflecting a fall in the willingness to work at any given wage and forcing school districts to pay more to maintain an adequate teaching staff. These events illustrate a general result: when superior alternatives arise for workers in another labor market, the supply curve in the original labor market shifts leftward as workers move to the new opportunities. Similarly, when opportunities diminish in one labor market—say, layoffs in the manufacturing industry due to increased foreign competition—the supply in alternative labor markets increases as workers move to these other markets.

Women can now choose among myriad careers.

Changes in Wealth

A person whose wealth increases will buy more normal goods, including leisure. So when a class of workers experiences a general increase in wealth—say, due to a stock market boom—the income effect from the wealth increase will shift the labor supply curve associated with those workers leftward as workers consume more leisure and work less. Note that *the income effect caused by a change in wealth shifts the labor supply curve,* but *the income effect from a wage rate increase*—as we discussed in the case of the individual labor supply curve—*is a movement along the labor supply curve.*

Such an increase in the wealth levels of many families over recent decades has led to a shift of the summertime labor supply curve for teenagers. The Bureau of Labor Statistics reports that in 1980, 71% of Americans between the ages of 16 and 19 were in the summer workforce. Twenty years later that number had fallen to 62%, and by 2017, it was 41%. One explanation for the decline in the summer labor supply is that more students are using their summers to study. But an important factor in the decline is that, due to increasing household affluence, many teenagers no longer feel pressured to contribute to household finances by taking a summer job. That is, the income effect leads to a reduced labor supply.

Equilibrium in the Labor Market

Now that we have discussed the labor supply curve, we can use the supply and demand curves for labor to determine the equilibrium wage and level of employment in the labor market.

Figure 71.2 illustrates the labor market as a whole. The *market labor demand curve,* like the market demand curve for a good, is the horizontal sum of all the individual labor demand curves of all the firms that hire labor. Recall that a firm's labor demand curve is the same as its marginal revenue product of labor curve.

The equilibrium wage rate is the wage rate at which the quantity of labor supplied is equal to the quantity of labor demanded. In Figure 71.2, this leads to an equilibrium wage rate of W^* and the corresponding equilibrium employment level of L^*. The equilibrium wage rate is also known as the market wage rate.

Figure 71.2 Equilibrium in the Labor Market

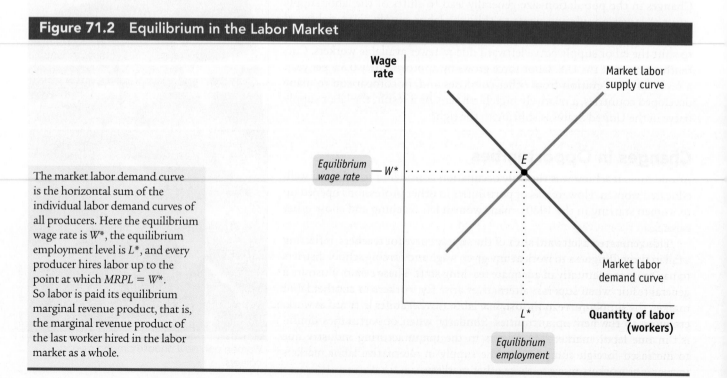

The market labor demand curve is the horizontal sum of the individual labor demand curves of all producers. Here the equilibrium wage rate is W^*, the equilibrium employment level is L^*, and every producer hires labor up to the point at which $MRPL = W^*$. So labor is paid its equilibrium marginal revenue product, that is, the marginal revenue product of the last worker hired in the labor market as a whole.

So far we have assumed that the labor market is perfectly competitive, but that isn't always the case. Next we'll examine the workings of an imperfectly competitive labor market.

When the Labor Market Is Not Perfectly Competitive

There are important differences when considering an imperfectly competitive factor market rather than a perfectly competitive market. One major difference involves the **marginal factor cost**, which is the additional cost of employing one more unit of a factor of production. For example, the marginal factor cost of labor (*MFCL*) is the additional cost of hiring one more unit of labor. With perfect competition in the labor market, each firm is so small that it can hire as much labor as it wants at the market wage. The firm's hiring decision does not affect the market. This means that with perfect competition in the labor market, the additional cost of hiring another worker (the *MFCL*) is always equal to the market wage, and each firm faces a horizontal labor supply curve, as shown in **Figure 71.3**.

The **marginal factor cost** is the additional cost of employing an additional unit of a factor of production.

Figure 71.3 Firm Labor Supply in a Perfectly Competitive Labor Market

In a perfectly competitive labor market, an individual firm faces a labor supply curve that is horizontal at the market equilibrium wage because the firm is so small relative to the market that it can hire all the labor that it wants at the market wage. For this reason, the labor supply curve for a firm in a perfectly competitive labor market is equivalent to the marginal factor cost of labor curve.

A firm faces a very different labor supply curve in a labor market characterized by imperfect competition: it is upward-sloping, and the marginal factor cost is above the market wage. Unlike a perfect competitor that is small and cannot affect the market, a firm in an imperfectly competitive labor market is large enough to affect the market wage. For example, a labor market in which there is only one firm hiring labor is called a **monopsony**. A **monopsonist** is the single buyer of a factor. Perhaps you've seen a small town where one firm, such as a meatpacking company or a lumber mill, is the only significant employer—that's an example of a monopsony. Since the firm faces the upward-sloping labor market supply curve, if it wants to hire more workers it has to offer higher wages to attract them. The higher wages go to all workers, not

A **monopsonist** is a single buyer in a factor market. A market in which there is a monopsonist is a **monopsony**.

just the workers hired last. Therefore, the additional cost of hiring an additional worker (the *MFCL*) is *higher* than the wage: it is the wage plus the raises paid to workers who would have been willing to work for less. **Table 71.1** shows a calculation of the *MFCL*.

Table 71.1	Marginal Factor Cost of Labor with Imperfect Competition in the Labor Market		
Quantity of Labor *L*	Wage *W*	Total Labor Cost = *L* × *W*	Marginal Factor Cost of Labor *MFCL*
0	$0	$0	
			$6
1	6	6	
			8
2	7	14	
			10
3	8	24	
			12
4	9	36	
			14
5	10	50	

The fact that a firm in an imperfectly competitive labor market must raise the wage to hire more workers means that the *MFCL* curve is *above* the labor supply curve, as shown in **Figure 71.4**. The explanation for this is similar to the explanation for why the monopolist's marginal revenue curve is below the demand curve. To sell one more, the monopolist has to lower the price, so the additional revenue is the price minus the losses on the units that would otherwise sell at the higher price. Here, to hire an additional worker, the monopsonist has to raise the wage, so the marginal factor cost is the wage plus the wage increase for those workers who could otherwise be hired at the lower wage.

Figure 71.4 Supply of Labor and Marginal Factor Cost in an Imperfectly Competitive Market

The marginal factor cost of labor curve is above the market labor supply curve because, to hire more workers in an imperfectly competitive labor market (such as a monopsony), the firm must raise the wage and pay everyone more. This makes the additional cost of hiring another worker higher than the wage rate.

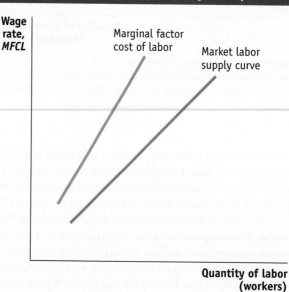

Equilibrium in the Imperfectly Competitive Labor Market

In a perfectly competitive labor market, firms hire labor until the marginal revenue product of labor equals the market wage. With imperfect competition in a factor market, a firm will hire additional workers until the marginal revenue product of labor equals the marginal factor cost of labor. Note that the wage in a perfectly competitive labor market is equivalent to the marginal factor cost, so the term *marginal factor cost* is generally applicable to the analysis of hiring decisions in both perfectly competitive and imperfectly competitive labor markets. Thus, we can generalize and say that every type of firm hires workers up to the point at which the marginal revenue product of labor equals the marginal factor cost of labor:

$$(71\text{-}1) \quad \text{Hire workers until } MRPL = MFCL$$

Equilibrium in the labor market with imperfect competition is shown in **Figure 71.5**. Once an imperfectly competitive firm has determined the optimal number of workers to hire, L^*, it finds the wage necessary to hire that number of workers by starting at the point on the labor supply curve above the optimal number of workers, and looking straight to the left to see the wage level at that point, W^*.

Figure 71.5 Equilibrium in an Imperfectly Competitive Labor Market

The equilibrium quantity of labor is found where the marginal revenue product of labor equals the marginal factor cost, at L^*. The equilibrium wage, W^*, is found on the vertical axis at the height of the market supply curve directly above L^*.

Let's put the information we just learned together, again referring to Figure 71.5: In an imperfectly competitive labor market, the firm must offer a higher wage to hire more workers, so the marginal factor cost curve is above the labor supply curve. The equilibrium quantity of labor is found where the marginal revenue product equals the marginal factor cost, as represented by L^* on the graph. The firm will pay the wage required to hire L^* workers, which is found on the supply curve above L^*. The labor supply curve shows that the quantity of labor supplied is equal to L^* at a wage of W^*. The equilibrium wage in the market is thus W^*. Note that, unlike the wage in a perfectly competitive labor market, the wage in the imperfectly competitive labor market is less than the marginal factor cost of labor.

Module 13 explained how a minimum wage could cause unemployment in a perfectly competitive labor market. We can use the monopsony model in **Figure 71.6** to examine the effect of a minimum wage in an imperfectly competitive labor market. Without a minimum wage, the marginal revenue product equals the marginal factor cost at point A, which corresponds to a quantity of 100 workers. Point B shows that the firm must pay $8 per hour to attract 100 workers. With a minimum wage of $12 per hour, point C on the supply curve indicates that the firm can hire up to 110 workers without increasing the wage rate. This means that the marginal factor cost for each of the first 110 workers is $12. In order to hire more than 110 workers, the firm must raise the wage rate above $12—just as it did without a minimum wage—so the marginal factor cost returns to its original level.

Figure 71.6   A Minimum Wage in an Imperfectly Competitive Labor Market

In the absence of a minimum wage, this monopsonist would find the point where $MRPL = MFCL$ (point A), hire the corresponding 100 workers, and pay them the $8 wage found on the market labor supply curve for that quantity of workers (point B). With a $12 minimum wage, point C on the supply curve shows that up to 110 workers could be hired without raising the wage above $12, so the marginal factor cost for the first 110 workers is $12. For larger quantities of labor, the firm must raise its wage for all workers in order to hire any additional workers, just as it did without a minimum wage. That raises the marginal factor cost back up to the original level. The firm will again hire workers until $MRPL = MFCL$ (point D), which now occurs at a quantity of 110 workers.

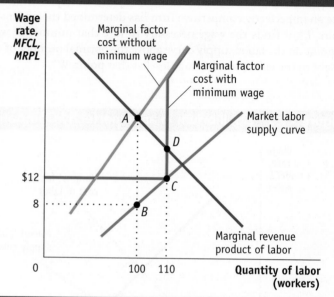

With the minimum wage, the marginal factor cost equals the marginal revenue product at point D, which corresponds to a quantity of 110 workers. So, 10 more workers are hired with the minimum wage than without the minimum wage. This makes sense in the context of an imperfectly competitive labor market because, up to the quantity of labor supplied at the minimum wage, the firm can hire another worker without raising the wage for all workers. For example, suppose that without the minimum wage the firm had to raise the wage to $8.50 in order to hire the 101st worker. The cost of hiring that worker would be the $8.50 wage plus the additional $0.50 paid to each of the first 100 workers; a total of $8.50 + ($0.50 \times 100) = $58.50. With the $12 minimum wage, however, up to 110 workers can be hired without raising the wage any higher, so that 101st worker would cost only $12. Studies of real-world labor markets—most famously by economists David Card and Alan Krueger—support the prospect that minimum wages do not cause unemployment in imperfectly competitive labor markets.

In Modules 69–71 we have learned how firms determine the optimal amount of land, labor, or capital to hire in factor markets. But often there are different combinations of factors that a firm can use to produce the same level of output. In the next Module, we look at how a firm chooses between alternative input combinations for producing a given level of output.

MODULE 71 REVIEW

Adventures in
AP® Economics

Watch the video: *Factor Markets*

Check Your Understanding

1. Formerly, Clive was free to work as many or as few hours per week as he wanted. A new law limits the maximum number of hours he can work per week to 35. Explain under what circumstances, if any, he is made
   a. worse off.
   b. equally well off.
   c. better off.

2. Explain in terms of the income and substitution effects how a decrease in the wage rate can induce a worker to increase the number of hours worked.

TACKLE THE AP® TEST: Multiple-Choice Questions

1. Which of the following is necessarily true if you work more when your wage rate increases?
   a. The income effect is large.
   b. The substitution effect is small.
   c. The income effect dominates the substitution effect.
   d. The substitution effect dominates the income effect.
   e. The income effect equals the substitution effect.

2. Which of the following will cause you to work more as your wage rate decreases?
   a. the income effect but not the substitution effect
   b. the substitution effect but not the income effect
   c. both the income effect and the substitution effect
   d. an increased desire for leisure
   e. a large inheritance

3. Which of the following will shift the supply curve for labor to the right?
   a. a decrease in the labor force participation rate of women
   b. a decrease in population
   c. an increase in wealth
   d. a decrease in the opportunity cost of leisure
   e. an increase in labor market opportunities for women

4. An increase in the wage rate will
   a. shift the labor supply curve to the right.
   b. shift the labor supply curve to the left.
   c. cause an upward movement along the labor supply curve.
   d. cause a downward movement along the labor supply curve.
   e. have no effect on the quantity of labor supplied.

5. The quantity of labor demanded in an imperfectly competitive factor market is determined by the intersection of which two curves?
   a. marginal revenue and marginal factor cost
   b. marginal product and supply
   c. supply and marginal revenue product
   d. marginal revenue product and marginal factor cost
   e. marginal product and marginal factor cost

6. Which of the following is necessarily true for a firm in a perfectly competitive labor market?
   a. The labor supply curve is horizontal.
   b. The labor demand curve is horizontal.
   c. The marginal revenue product curve for labor is above the demand curve for labor.
   d. The firm has difficulty finding enough workers due to competition from other firms.
   e. The firm must increase its wage in order to hire more workers.

7. When a minimum wage is imposed on a monopsony, the marginal factor cost of labor becomes
   a. vertical at the current quantity of labor.
   b. horizontal until it meets the supply curve.
   c. downward-sloping to the left of the supply curve.
   d. downward-sloping to the right of the supply curve.
   e. steeper than it was without the minimum wage at all quantities of labor.

1. Assume the demand curve for a firm's product is as shown below and that the firm can hire as many workers as it wants for a wage of $80 per day.

a. What is the market structure of the factor market in which the firm hires labor? Explain.

b. What is the market structure of the product market in which the firm sells its output? Explain.

c. Define marginal factor cost. What is the marginal factor cost of labor for this firm?

d. If the last worker hired produces an additional 20 units of output, what is the last worker's $MRPL$? Explain.

Rubric for FRQ 1 (8 points)

1 point: The firm hires labor in a perfectly competitive labor market.

1 point: The firm is a price-taker in the labor market. (It can hire all that it wants for $80 per day.)

1 point: The firm sells its output in a perfectly competitive product market.

1 point: The horizontal demand curve indicates that the firm is a price-taker in the product market (it can sell all the output it wants at the market price of $5).

1 point: the additional cost of hiring one more unit of a factor

1 point: $80

1 point: $100

1 point: $MRPL = MPL \times MR$, $MPL = 20$, $MR = \$5$, so $MRPL = 20 \times \$5 = \$100$.

---

2. Maggie's Pizzeria hires delivery drivers from a perfectly competitive labor market.

a. Draw correctly labeled side-by-side graphs of delivery driver supply and demand for Maggie's Pizzeria and for the entire delivery driver market.

b. On your graphs, show how an increase in the supply of delivery drivers would affect the equilibrium wage and the number of drivers hired, both by Maggie's Pizzeria and in the delivery driver market as a whole. **(8 points)**

MOD 72

The Cost-Minimizing Input Combination

In this Module, you will learn to:
- Explain how firms determine the optimal input mix
- Apply the cost-minimization rule for employing inputs

In the past three Modules we discussed the markets for factors of production—land, capital, and labor—and how firms determine the optimal quantity of each factor to employ. But firms don't determine how much of each input to employ separately. Production requires multiple inputs, and firms must decide what *combination* of inputs to use to produce their output. In this Module, we will look at how firms decide the optimal combination of factors for producing the desired level of output.

Alternative Input Combinations

In many instances a firm can choose among a number of alternative combinations of inputs that will produce a given level of output. For example, on George and Martha's wheat farm, the decision might involve labor and capital. To produce their optimal quantity of wheat, they could choose to have a relatively *capital-intensive* operation by investing in several tractors and other mechanized farm equipment and hiring relatively little labor. Alternatively, they could have a more *labor-intensive* operation by hiring a lot of workers to do much of the planting and harvesting by hand. The same amount of wheat can be produced using many different combinations of capital and labor. George and Martha must determine which combination of inputs will maximize their profits.

To begin our study of the optimal combination of inputs, we'll look at the relationship between two inputs used for production. Depending on the situation, inputs can be either substitutes or complements.

Additional capital can take the place of some labor, and vice versa.

Substitutes and Complements in Factor Markets

In Section 2 we discussed substitutes and complements in the context of the supply and demand model. Two goods are *substitutes* if a rise in the price of one good makes consumers more willing to buy the other good. For example, an increase in the price of oranges will cause some buyers to purchase tangerines instead. When buyers tend to consume two goods together, the goods are known as *complements*. For example, cereal and milk are considered complements because many people consume them together. If the price of cereal increases, people will buy less cereal and therefore need less milk. The decision about how much of a good to buy is influenced by the prices of related goods.

The concepts of substitutes and complements also apply to a firm's purchase of inputs. And just as the price of related goods affects consumers' purchasing decisions, the price of other inputs can affect a firm's decision about how much of an input it will use. In some situations, capital and labor are substitutes. For example, George and Martha can produce the same amount of wheat by substituting more tractors for fewer farm workers. Likewise, vending machines can substitute for sales clerks.

Capital and labor can also be complements when more of one increases the marginal product of the other. For example, a farm worker is more productive when George and Martha buy a tractor, and each tractor requires a worker to drive it. Office workers are more productive when they can use faster computers, and doctors are more productive with modern medical imaging equipment and data entry software. In these cases the quantity and quality of capital available affect the marginal product of labor, and thus the demand for labor. Given the relationship between inputs, how does a firm determine which of the possible combinations to use?

Capital can often substitute for labor, as when vending machines substitute for human vendors.

Determining the Optimal Input Mix

If several alternative input combinations can be used to produce the optimal level of output, a profit-maximizing firm will select the input combination with the lowest cost. This process is known as cost minimization.

Cost Minimization

How does a firm determine the combination of inputs that maximizes profit? Let's consider this question using an example.

Imagine you manage a grocery store chain and you need to decide the right combination of self-checkout stations and cashiers at a new store. **Table 72.1** shows the alternative combinations of capital (self-checkout stations) and labor (cashiers) you can hire to check out customers shopping at the store. If the store puts in 20 self-checkout stations, you will need to hire 1 cashier to monitor every 5 stations for a total of 4 cashiers. However, trained cashiers are faster than customers at scanning goods, so the store could check out the same number of customers using 10 cashiers and only 10 self-checkout stations.

Table 72.1	Cashiers and Self-Checkout Stations	
	Capital (self-checkout stations)	Labor (cashiers)
	Rental rate = $1,000/month	Wage rate = $1,600/month
a.	20	4
b.	10	10

If you can check out the same number of customers using either of these combinations of capital and labor, how do you decide which combination of inputs to use? By finding the input combination that costs the least—the cost-minimizing input combination.

Many stores have replaced some of their cashiers with self-checkout stations in efforts to reach the cost-maximizing combination of labor and capital.

Assume that the cost to rent, operate, and maintain a self-checkout station for a month is $1,000 and hiring a cashier costs $1,600 per month. The cost of each input combination from Table 72.1 is shown below.

a.	Cost of capital	$20 \times \$1,000 = \$20,000$
	Cost of labor	$4 \times \$1,600 = \underline{\$\ 6,400}$
	TOTAL	$\$26,400$
b.	Cost of capital	$10 \times \$1,000 = \$10,000$
	Cost of labor	$10 \times \$1,600 = \underline{\$16,000}$
	TOTAL	$\$26,000$

Clearly, your grocery store chain would choose the lower cost combination, combination b, and hire 10 cashiers and put 10 self-checkout stations in the new store.

When firms must choose among alternative combinations of inputs, they evaluate the cost of each combination and select the one that minimizes the cost of production. This can be done by calculating the total cost of each alternative combination of inputs, as shown in this example. However, because the number of possible combinations can be very large, it is more practical to use marginal analysis to find the cost-minimizing level of output—which brings us to the cost-minimization rule.

The Cost-Minimization Rule

A firm determines the cost-minimizing combination of inputs using the **cost-minimization rule**: employ factors so that the marginal product per dollar spent on each factor is the same.

We already know that the additional output that results from employing an additional unit of an input is the marginal product (*MP*) of that input. Firms want to receive the highest possible marginal product from each dollar spent on inputs. To do this, firms apply the **cost-minimization rule** by adjusting their combination of inputs until the marginal product per dollar is equal for all inputs, while maintaining their desired level of output. When the inputs are labor and capital, this amounts to equating the marginal product of labor (*MPL*) per dollar spent on wages to the marginal product of capital (*MPK*) per dollar spent to rent capital:

$$(72\text{-}1) \quad \frac{MPL}{\text{Wage}} = \frac{MPK}{\text{Rental rate}}$$

To understand why cost minimization occurs when the marginal product per dollar is equal for all inputs, let's start by looking at two counterexamples. Consider a situation in which the marginal product of labor per dollar is greater than the marginal product of capital per dollar. This situation is described by Equation 72-2:

$$(72\text{-}2) \quad \frac{MPL}{\text{Wage}} > \frac{MPK}{\text{Rental rate}}$$

Suppose the marginal product of labor is 20 units and the marginal product of capital is 100 units. If the wage is $10 and the rental rate for capital is $100, then the marginal product per dollar will be 20/$10 = 2 units of output per dollar for labor and 100/$100 = 1 unit of output per dollar for capital. The firm is receiving 2 additional units of output for each dollar spent on labor and only 1 additional unit of output for each dollar spent on capital. In this case, the firm gets more additional output for its money by hiring labor, so it should hire more labor and rent less capital. Because of diminishing returns, as the firm hires more labor, the marginal product of labor falls, and as it rents less capital, the marginal product of capital rises. The firm will continue to substitute labor for capital until the falling marginal product of labor per dollar meets the rising marginal product of capital per dollar and the two are equivalent. That is, the firm will adjust its quantities of labor and capital until the marginal product per dollar spent on each input is equal, as in Equation 72-1.

Next, consider a situation in which the marginal product of capital per dollar is greater than the marginal product of labor per dollar. This situation is described by Equation 72-3:

$$(72\text{-}3) \quad \frac{MPL}{\text{Wage}} < \frac{MPK}{\text{Rental rate}}$$

Let's continue with the assumption that the marginal product of labor for the last unit of labor hired is 20 units and the marginal product of capital for the last unit of capital rented is 100 units. If the wage is $10 and the rental rate for capital is $25, then the marginal product per dollar will be 20/$10 = 2 units of output per dollar for labor and 100/$25 = 4 units of output per dollar for capital. The firm is receiving four additional units of output for each dollar spent on capital and only two additional units of output for each dollar spent on labor. In this case, the firm gets more additional output for its money by renting capital, so it should rent more capital and hire less labor. Because of diminishing returns, as the firm rents more capital, the marginal product of capital falls, and as it hires less labor, the marginal product of labor rises. The firm will continue to rent more capital and hire less labor until the falling marginal product of capital per dollar meets the rising marginal product of labor per dollar to satisfy the cost-minimization rule. That is, the

A firm will adjust the quantities of its inputs until the marginal product per dollar spent on each input is the same.

firm will adjust its quantities of capital and labor until the marginal product per dollar spent on each input is equal.

The cost-minimization rule is analogous to the optimal consumption rule (introduced in Module 51), which has consumers maximize their utility by choosing the combination of goods so that the marginal utility per dollar is equal for all goods.

So far in this section we have learned how factor markets determine the equilibrium price and quantity in the markets for land, labor, and capital and how firms determine the combination of inputs they will employ. But how well do these models of factor markets explain the distribution of factor incomes in our economy? In Module 70 we considered how the marginal productivity theory of income distribution explains the factor distribution of income. In the final Module in this section we look at the distribution of income in *labor* markets and consider to what extent the marginal productivity theory of income distribution explains wage differences.

MODULE 72 REVIEW

Check Your Understanding

1. A firm produces its output using only capital and labor. Labor costs $100 per worker per day and capital costs $200 per unit per day. If the marginal product of the last worker employed is 500 and the marginal product of the last unit of capital employed is 1,000, is the firm employing the cost-minimizing combination of inputs? Explain.

TACKLE THE AP® TEST: Multiple-Choice Questions

1. An automobile factory can employ either assembly line workers or robotic arms to produce automobile engines. In this case, labor and capital are considered
   a. independent.
   b. complements.
   c. substitutes.
   d. supplements.
   e. human capital.

2. If an increase in the amount of capital employed by a firm leads to an increase in the marginal product of labor, labor and capital are considered
   a. independent.
   b. complements.
   c. substitutes.
   d. supplements.
   e. human capital.

3. If a firm is producing its desired level of output and the marginal product of labor per dollar is greater than the marginal product of capital per dollar, which of the following is necessarily true?
   a. The marginal product of labor is greater than the marginal product of capital.
   b. The wage rate for labor is less than the rental rate for capital.
   c. The firm should employ more labor and less capital.
   d. The firm should employ less labor and more capital.
   e. The firm should increase its desired level of output.

4. The cost-minimization rule states that costs are minimized when
   a. *MP* per dollar is equal for all factors.
   b. (*MP* × *P*) is equal for all factors.
   c. each factor's *MP* is the same.
   d. *MRP* is maximized.
   e. *MFC* is minimized.

5. The Orange Computer Company currently produces its desired level of output. Its marginal product of labor is 400, its marginal product of capital is 1,000, the wage rate is $20, and the rental rate of capital is $100. In this case, the firm should
   a. employ more capital and more labor.
   b. employ less labor and less capital.
   c. employ less labor and more capital.
   d. employ less capital and more labor.
   e. not change its employment of capital or labor.

6. The Grapefruit Computer Company currently produces its desired level of output. Its marginal product of labor is 10, its marginal product of capital is 50, the wage rate is $20, and the rental rate of capital is $100. In this case, the firm should
   a. employ more capital and more labor.
   b. employ less labor and less capital.
   c. employ less labor and more capital.
   d. employ less capital and more labor.
   e. not change its employment of capital or labor.

7. Which of the following is necessarily true if a firm is producing its desired level of output and its marginal product of labor exceeds its marginal product of capital?
   a. The firm should employ more labor and less capital.
   b. The firm should employ more capital and less labor.
   c. The firm should not change its employment of capital or labor.
   d. The firms should employ more of both capital and labor.
   e. More information is needed to determine the optimal combination of capital and labor.

TACKLE THE AP® TEST: Free-Response Questions

1. Answer the following questions under the assumption that firms use only two inputs and seek to maximize profit.
   a. Would it be wise for a firm that does not have the cost-minimizing combination of inputs to employ more of the input with the highest marginal product and less of the input with the lowest marginal product? Explain.
   b. What is the cost-minimization rule?
   c. When a firm hires more labor and rents less capital, what happens to the marginal product of labor per dollar and the marginal product of capital per dollar? Explain.

Rubric for FRQ 1 (5 points)

1 point: No, it would not be wise.

1 point: The input with the highest marginal product might be much more expensive than the input with the lowest marginal product, making the marginal product per dollar higher for the input with the lowest marginal product. When that is the case, costs would be lower if the firm employed more of the input with the lowest marginal product (but the highest marginal product per dollar) and less of the input with the highest marginal product (but the lowest marginal product per dollar.)

1 point: The cost-minimization rule says that firms should adjust their combination of inputs to equalize the marginal product per dollar spent on each input.

1 point: The marginal product of labor per dollar decreases and the marginal product of capital per dollar increases.

1 point: Each factor has diminishing marginal returns. So when more labor is hired, the marginal product of labor (and thus the marginal product of labor per dollar) decreases.

Likewise, when less capital is rented, the marginal product of capital (and thus the marginal product of capital per dollar) increases because the units of capital that are given up had a lower marginal product than those that remain.

2. Refer to the table below. Assume that the wage is $10 per day and the price of pencils is $1.

Quantity of labor (workers)	Quantity of pencils produced
0	0
1	40
2	90
3	120
4	140
5	150
6	160
7	166

   a. What is the *MPL* of the 4th worker?
   b. What is the *MPL* per dollar of the 5th worker?
   c. How many workers would the firm hire if it hired every worker for whom the marginal product per dollar is greater than or equal to 1 pencil per dollar?
   d. If the marginal product per dollar spent on labor is 1 pencil per dollar, the marginal product of the last unit of capital rented is 100 pencils per dollar, and the rental rate is $50 per day, is the firm minimizing its cost? Explain. **(5 points)**

Theories of Income Distribution

In this Module, you will learn to:
- Explain the labor market applications of the marginal productivity theory of income distribution
- Identify and describe sources of wage disparities and the role of discrimination

In Module 70, we introduced the factor distribution of income and explained how the *marginal productivity theory of income distribution* helps to explain how income is divided among factors of production in an economy. We also considered how the markets for factors of production are broken down. There are different markets for different types of factors. For example, there are different labor markets for different types of labor, such as for computer programmers, pastry chefs, and economists. In this Module, we look more closely at the marginal productivity theory of income distribution and the extent to which it explains wage disparities between workers.

Hola Images/Getty Images

The Marginal Productivity Theory of Income Distribution

According to the marginal productivity theory of income distribution, the division of income among the economy's factors of production is determined by each factor's marginal revenue product at the market equilibrium. If we consider an economy-wide factor market, the price paid for *all* factors in the economy is equal to the increase in revenue generated by the last unit of the factor employed in the market. But what about the distribution of income among different labor markets and workers? Does the marginal productivity theory of income distribution help to explain why some workers earn more than others?

Marginal Productivity and Wage Inequality

A large part of the observed inequality in wages can be explained by considerations that are consistent with the marginal productivity theory of income distribution. In particular, there are three well-understood sources of wage differences across occupations and individuals.

Compensating differentials are wage differences across jobs that reflect the fact that some jobs are less pleasant or more dangerous than others.

The first is the existence of **compensating differentials**: across different types of jobs, wages are often higher or lower depending on how attractive or unattractive the job is. Workers in unpleasant or dangerous jobs receive a higher wage than workers in jobs that require the same skill, training, and effort but lack the unpleasant or dangerous qualities. For example, truckers who haul hazardous chemicals are paid more than truckers who haul bread. For any *particular* job, the marginal productivity theory of income distribution generally holds true. For example, hazardous-load truckers are paid a wage equal to the equilibrium marginal revenue product of those truckers, which is the contribution to revenue of the last person employed in the market for hazardous-load truckers.

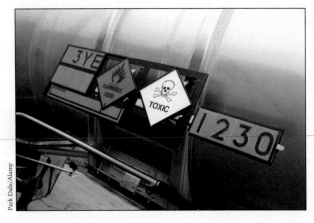

Park Dale/Alamy

A second reason for wage inequality that is clearly consistent with marginal productivity theory is differences in natural skill or aptitude that can be described as *talent*. People differ in their abilities: a more talented person, by producing a better product that commands a higher price compared to a less talented person, generates a higher marginal revenue product. And these differences in the marginal revenue product translate into differences in earning potential. We all know that this is true in sports: practice is important, but 99.99% (at least) of the population just doesn't have what it takes to control a soccer ball like Neymar or swim like Katie Ledecky. The same is true, though less obvious, in other labor markets.

A third, very important reason for wage differences is differences in the quantity of *human capital*. Recall that human capital—education and training—is at least as important in the modern economy as physical capital in the form of buildings and machines. Different people "embody" quite different quantities of human capital, and a person with more human capital typically generates a higher marginal revenue product by producing more or better products. So differences in human capital account for substantial differences in wages. People with high levels of human capital, such as surgeons or engineers, generally receive high wages.

The most direct way to see the effect of human capital on wages is to look at the relationship between education levels and earnings. **Figure 73.1** shows earnings by education level for full-time workers 25 years or older in 2017. As you can see, higher education levels are generally associated with higher median earnings. For example,

Figure 73.1 Earnings by Education Level, 2017

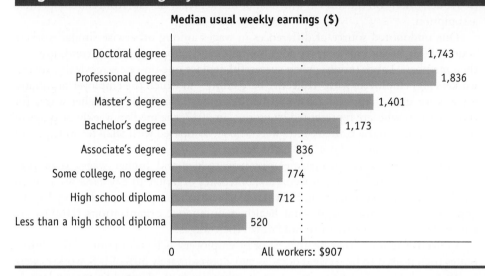

Median usual weekly earnings ($)

Education Level	Earnings
Doctoral degree	1,743
Professional degree	1,836
Master's degree	1,401
Bachelor's degree	1,173
Associate's degree	836
Some college, no degree	774
High school diploma	712
Less than a high school diploma	520

All workers: $907

It is clear that education pays: those with a high school diploma earn more than those without one, and those with a college degree earn substantially more than those with only a high school diploma.

Data Source: Bureau of Labor Statistics.

workers without a high school diploma had median earnings 27% less than those with a high school diploma and 56% less than those with a bachelor's degree. One exception is that workers with a doctoral degree (such as professors, who have a PhD) had median earnings 5% less than those with a professional degree (such as lawyers, who have a JD, and physicians, who have an MD).

It's also important to realize that formal education is not the only source of human capital; on-the-job training and experience are also very important. This point was highlighted by a 2014 National Science Foundation report on earnings differences between male and female scientists and engineers who hold the highest possible degree in their field. The study was motivated by concerns over the male–female earnings gap: the median salary for women in this category is about 19% less than the median salary for men. The study found that, on average, women in these occupations are younger than men and have less experience than their male counterparts. According to the study, differences in age and experience, along with workers' particular field, job, and degree-granting institution, explained most, but not all, of the earnings differential.

Earnings differences arising from differences in human capital are not necessarily "fair." A society in which non-White children often receive an inferior education because they live in underfunded school districts, and then go on to earn low wages because of their differing educational opportunities, may have labor markets that are well described by marginal productivity theory. Even so, many people consider the resulting distribution of income unfair.

Still, many observers think that actual wage differentials cannot be entirely explained by compensating differentials, differences in talent, and differences in human capital. They believe that market power, *efficiency wages*, and discrimination also play an important role. We will examine these forces next.

Market Power

The marginal productivity theory of income distribution is based on the assumption that factor markets are perfectly competitive. In such markets we can expect workers to be paid the equilibrium value of their marginal product, regardless of who they are. But how valid is this assumption?

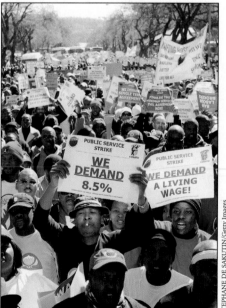

Union members rally to demand higher wages.

In the previous Modules, we studied markets that are *not* perfectly competitive; now let's touch briefly on the ways in which labor markets may deviate from the competitive assumption.

One undoubted source of differences in wages among otherwise similar workers is **unions**—organizations that try to raise wages and improve working conditions for their members. Labor unions, when successful, replace one-on-one wage deals between workers and employers with "collective bargaining," in which the employer negotiates wages with union representatives. Without question, this leads to higher wages for those workers who are represented by unions. In 2017, the median weekly earnings of union members in the United States were $1,041, compared with $829 for workers not represented by unions—about a 20% difference.

Just as workers can sometimes organize to demand higher wages than they would otherwise receive, employers can sometimes organize to pay *lower* wages than would result from competition. For example, health care workers—including doctors and nurses—sometimes argue that health maintenance organizations (HMOs) are engaged in a collective effort to hold down their wages.

Collective action, either by workers or by employers, is less common in the United States than it used to be. Several decades ago, approximately 30% of U.S. workers were union members. Today, however, union membership in the United States is relatively limited: 6.4% of the employees of private businesses are represented by unions. And although there are fields such as health care in which a few large firms account for a sizable share of employment in certain geographical areas, the sheer size of the U.S. labor market and the ease with which most workers can move in search of higher-paying jobs probably mean that concerted efforts to hold wages below the unrestrained market equilibrium level rarely occur and even more rarely succeed.

> **Unions** are organizations of workers that try to raise wages and improve working conditions for their members by bargaining collectively.

Efficiency Wages

A second source of wage inequality is the payment of **efficiency wages**—wages above the equilibrium level that employers use to incentivize hard work and reduce worker turnover. Suppose a worker performs a job that is extremely important but difficult for the employer to monitor. This would be true, for example, for childcare providers. Then it often makes sense for the employer to pay more than the worker could earn in an alternative job—that is, more than the equilibrium wage. Why? Because earning a premium makes losing this job and having to take the alternative job quite costly for the worker. A worker who happens to be observed performing poorly and is therefore fired is now worse off for having to accept a lower-paying job. The threat of losing a job that pays a premium motivates the worker to perform well and avoid being fired. Paying a premium also reduces worker turnover—the frequency with which an employee leaves a job voluntarily—and the associated costs of recruiting and training new workers. Although it may take no more effort and skill to be a childcare provider than to be an office worker, efficiency wages show why it often makes economic sense to pay a caregiver more than the equilibrium wage of an office worker.

> **Efficiency wages** are wages that exceed the market equilibrium wage rate. Employers use efficiency wages to motivate hard work and reduce worker turnover.

Henry Ford was an early adopter of efficiency wages. He paid workers $5 a day to build automobiles back in 1914, when the average daily wage for auto workers was less than $2.50. Efficiency wages allowed Ford to attract and retain the best workers and to keep them on task, even when worker performance was hard to track. For similar reasons, in 2017, Adobe, Amazon, Capital One, ExxonMobil, Facebook, Google, and Microsoft were among dozens of companies that paid their student interns more than the median income for U.S. workers.

On the downside, much like the minimum wages discussed in Module 8, efficiency wages lead to unemployment. Some workers

Some employers pay *efficiency wages*—wages above the equilibrium wage rate—to promote loyalty and motivate hard work, especially in jobs, such as childcare, that are difficult to monitor.

Caiaimage/Robert Daly/Getty Images

actively searching for a high-paying efficiency-wage job are unable to get one, while more fortunate but equally deserving workers are able to find work. As a result, two workers with the same skills and experience may earn different wages: the worker who is lucky enough to get an efficiency-wage job earns more than the worker who gets a standard job (or who remains unemployed while searching for a higher-paying job).

Discrimination

It is an ugly fact that throughout history there has been discrimination against workers who are considered to be of the wrong race, ethnicity, gender, or other characteristic. How does this fit into our economic models?

The main insight economic analysis offers is that discrimination is *not* a natural consequence of market competition. On the contrary, market forces tend to work against discrimination. To see why, consider the incentives that would exist if social convention dictated that women be paid, say, 30% less than men with equivalent qualifications and experience. A company whose management was itself unbiased would then be able to reduce its costs by hiring women rather than men—and such companies would have an advantage over other companies that hired men despite their higher cost. The result would be to create an excess demand for female workers, which would tend to drive up their wages.

But if market competition works against discrimination, how is it that so much discrimination has taken place? The answer is twofold. First, when labor markets don't work well, employers may have the ability to discriminate without hurting their profits. For example, market interferences (such as unions or minimum-wage laws) or market failures (such as efficiency wages) can lead to wages that are above their equilibrium levels. In these cases, there are more job applicants than there are jobs, leaving employers free to discriminate among applicants. In research published in the *American Economic Review*, economists Marianne Bertrand and Sendhil Mullainathan documented discrimination in hiring by sending fictitious résumés to prospective employers on a random basis. Applicants with "White-sounding" names, such as Emily Walsh, were 50% more likely to be contacted than applicants with "African-American-sounding" names, such as Lakisha Washington. Also, applicants with White-sounding names and good credentials were much more likely to be contacted than those without such credentials. By contrast, potential employers seemed to ignore the credentials of applicants with African-American-sounding names.

Second, discrimination has sometimes been institutionalized in government policy. This institutionalization has made it easier to maintain discrimination against market pressure. For example, until the mid-1950s, African-Americans were barred from attending "Whites-only" public schools and universities in many states and were forced to attend schools that tended to be inferior. Although market competition tends to work against *current* discrimination, it is not a remedy for the lingering repercussions of past discrimination on victims' income, education, and experience.

Wage Disparities in Practice

Wage rates in the United States cover a very wide range. In 2018, hundreds of thousands of workers received the legal federal minimum of $7.25 per hour. At the other extreme, the chief executives of several companies were paid more than $100 million for the year, which works out to $20,000 per hour even if they worked 100-hour weeks. Leaving out these extremes, there is still a huge range of wage rates. Are people really that different in their marginal productivities? Do workers really differ that much in their value to firms?

A particular source of concern is the existence of systematic wage differences across gender and ethnicity. **Figure 73.2** compares median weekly earnings in 2018 of workers 25 years or older classified by gender and ethnicity. As a group, White males had the highest earnings. Women (averaging across all ethnicities) earned only about 78% as much; African-American workers (male and female combined) only 69% as much; and Hispanic workers only 67% as much.

Figure 73.2 Median Weekly Earnings by Gender and Ethnicity, 2018

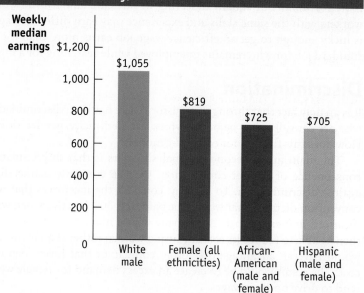

The U.S. labor market continues to show large differences across workers according to gender and ethnicity. Women are paid substantially less than men; African-American and Hispanic workers are paid substantially less than White male workers.

Data Source: Bureau of Labor Statistics.

We are a nation founded on the belief that all men are created equal—and if the Constitution were rewritten today, we would say that *all people* are created equal. So why do the people receive such unequal pay? The pay differences may involve some differences in marginal productivity, but we also must allow for the possibility of other influences.

Is the Marginal Productivity Theory of Income Distribution Really True?

Although the marginal productivity theory of income distribution is a well-established part of economic theory, it is a source of some controversy. There are two main objections to it.

First, in the real world we see large disparities in income among workers who, in the eyes of some observers, should receive the same payment. Perhaps the most conspicuous examples in the United States are the large differences in the average wages between women and men and among various racial and ethnic groups. Do these wage differences really reflect differences in marginal productivity, or is something else going on?

Second, many people wrongly believe that the marginal productivity theory of income distribution gives a *moral* justification for the distribution of income, implying that the existing distribution is fair and appropriate. This misconception sometimes leads other people, who believe that the current distribution of income is unfair, to reject marginal productivity theory.

So Does Marginal Productivity Theory Hold?

The main conclusion you should draw from this discussion is that the marginal productivity theory of income distribution is not a perfect description of how factor incomes are determined but that it works pretty well. The deviations are important to consider. But, by and large, in a modern economy with well-functioning labor markets, factors of production are paid the equilibrium marginal revenue product—the marginal revenue product of the last unit employed in the market as a whole.

We should emphasize, once again, that this does not mean that the factor distribution of income is morally justified.

MODULE 73 REVIEW

Check Your Understanding

1. Assess each of the following statements. Do you think they are true, false, or ambiguous? Explain.
   a. The marginal productivity theory of income distribution is inconsistent with the presence of income disparities associated with gender, race, or ethnicity.
   b. Companies that engage in workplace discrimination but whose competitors do not are likely to earn less profit as a result of their actions.
   c. Workers who are paid less because they have less experience are not the victims of discrimination.

TACKLE THE AP® TEST: Multiple-Choice Questions

1. Which group of U.S. workers had the lowest median earnings in 2018?
   a. White males
   b. females (all ethnicities)
   c. African-Americans (male and female)
   d. Hispanics (male and female)
   e. African-American males

2. Which of the following sources of wage differences is inconsistent with the marginal productivity theory of income distribution?
   a. human capital
   b. compensating differentials
   c. education
   d. efficiency wages
   e. talent

3. Compensating differentials mean that which of the following leads to higher wages for some jobs?
   a. danger
   b. discrimination
   c. marginal productivity
   d. market power
   e. a surplus of labor

4. Which of the following is a result of efficiency wages?
   a. compensating differentials
   b. surpluses of labor
   c. shortages of labor
   d. discrimination
   e. a lack of motivation among workers

5. Which of the following statements regarding the marginal productivity theory of income distribution is correct?
   a. Each worker should earn a wage based on his or her marginal productivity.
   b. The wage rate should equal the rental rate.
   c. Workers with higher marginal products always receive a higher wage than workers with lower marginal products.
   d. The factor distribution of income is morally justified.
   e. With well-functioning labor markets, each factor is paid the equilibrium marginal revenue product of that factor.

6. Which of the following statements about human capital is true?
   a. Experience is a source of human capital.
   b. After accounting for differences in human capital, on average, men and women earn the same amount of income.
   c. Human capital comes from natural aptitude.
   d. There is general consensus that earnings differences arising from differences in human capital are fair.
   e. Human capital is the money humans hold in savings accounts.

7. Discrimination is
   a. a natural consequence of market competition.
   b. more likely when there is a surplus of labor in a market.
   c. absent from today's labor markets.
   d. never institutionalized into government policy.
   e. less likely when a minimum wage is in place.

TACKLE THE AP® TEST: Free-Response Questions

1. Explain the most likely reason for the wage differences among similar workers in each of the following situations.
   a. Test pilots for new jet aircraft earn higher wages than airline pilots.
   b. College graduates usually have higher earnings in their first year on the job than workers without college degrees have in their first year on the job.
   c. Experienced AP® teachers command higher salaries than new AP® teachers for teaching the same class.

   > **Rubric for FRQ 1 (6 points)**
   > **1 point:** Compensating differentials
   > **1 point:** Being a test pilot is more dangerous.

   > **1 point:** Differences in human capital
   > **1 point:** Education leads to higher productivity.
   > **1 point:** Differences in human capital
   > **1 point:** On-the-job experience increases the marginal product of experienced teachers.

2. List three different economic concepts that explain wage differences when the marginal productivity theory of income distribution does not. Explain each. **(6 points)**

SECTION 13 Review

SECTION 13 Review Video

Adventures in AP® Economics Videos

Mod 71: Factor Markets

Module 69

1. Just as there are markets for goods and services, there are markets for factors of production, including labor, land, and both **physical capital** and **human capital**. These markets determine the **factor distribution of income**.

2. A profit-maximizing firm hiring from a perfectly competitive factor market will keep employing more units of a factor until the factor's price is equal to the **marginal revenue product**—the marginal product of the factor multiplied by the marginal revenue of the output

   it produces. The **marginal revenue product curve** is therefore the firm's demand curve for a factor. Factor demand is often referred to as a **derived demand** because it is derived from the demand for the producer's output.

3. The market demand curve for labor is the horizontal sum of the individual demand curves of firms in that market. It shifts for three main reasons: changes in output price, changes in the supply of other factors, and technological changes.

Module 70

4. When a perfectly competitive labor market is in equilibrium, the market wage is equal to the **equilibrium marginal revenue product** of labor, the additional revenue generated by the last worker hired in the labor market as a whole. The same principle applies to other factors of production: the **rental rate** of land or capital is equal to the equilibrium marginal revenue product.

   This insight leads to the **marginal productivity theory of income distribution**, which states that each factor is paid the marginal revenue product of the last unit of that factor employed in the factor market as a whole. The payment to a factor in excess of the minimum amount necessary to employ that factor is called **economic rent**.

Module 71

5. Labor supply is the result of decisions about time allocation, with each worker facing a trade-off between **leisure** and work. An increase in the hourly wage rate tends to increase work hours via the substitution effect but decrease work hours via the income effect. If the net result is that a worker increases the quantity of labor supplied in response to a higher wage, the **individual labor supply curve** slopes upward. If the net result is that a worker decreases work hours, the individual labor supply curve—unlike supply curves for goods and services—slopes downward.

6. The market labor supply curve is the horizontal sum of the individual labor supply curves of all workers in that market. It shifts for four main reasons: changes in preferences and social norms, changes in population, changes in opportunities, and changes in wealth.

7. When a firm is not a price-taker in a factor market due to imperfect competition, the firm will consider the marginal revenue product and the **marginal factor cost** when determining how much of a factor to employ. The marginal factor cost is equivalent to the wage (or the price of the factor) in a perfectly competitive market.

8. A **monopsonist** is the single buyer of a factor. A market in which there is a monopsonist is a **monopsony**.

Module 72

9. Firms will determine the optimal input combination using the **cost-minimization rule**: when a firm uses the cost-minimizing combination of inputs, the marginal product of labor divided by the wage rate is equal to the marginal product of capital divided by the rental rate.

Module 73

10. Large disparities in wages raise questions about the validity of the marginal productivity theory of income distribution. Many disparities can be explained by **compensating differentials** and by differences in talent, job experience, and human capital across workers. Market interference in the forms of **unions** and collective action by employers also creates wage disparities. Above-equilibrium wages known as **efficiency wages** result from employers' attempts to increase worker performance despite monitoring difficulties. Free markets tend to diminish discrimination, but discrimination remains a real source of wage disparity. Discrimination is typically maintained either through problems in labor markets or (historically) through institutionalization in government policies.

Key Terms

Physical capital, p. 665
Human capital, p. 665
Derived demand, p. 665
Factor distribution of income, p. 666
Marginal revenue product, p. 668
Marginal revenue product curve, p. 670
Rental rate, p. 675

Equilibrium marginal revenue product, p. 677
Economic rent, p. 677
Marginal productivity theory of income distribution, p. 678
Leisure, p. 681
Individual labor supply curve, p. 682

Marginal factor cost, p. 685
Monopsonist, p. 685
Monopsony, p. 685
Cost-minimization rule, p. 692
Compensating differentials, p. 696
Unions, p. 698
Efficiency-wages, p. 698

AP® Exam Practice Questions

Multiple-Choice Questions

1. The four principal classes of factors of production are
   a. money, capital, land, and labor.
   b. money, capital, labor, and entrepreneurship.
   c. money, labor, land, and entrepreneurship.
   d. land, labor, capital, and entrepreneurship.
   e. land, labor, entrepreneurship, and money.

2. Because it results from the demand for automobiles, the demand for automobile workers is a/an
   a. derived demand.
   b. irrational demand.
   c. elastic demand.
   d. inelastic demand.
   e. unit elastic demand.

3. In the United States, the percentage of factor income earned by labor is close to
- **a.** 10%.
- **b.** 30%.
- **c.** 50%.
- **d.** 70%.
- **e.** 90%.

4. For a perfectly competitive firm in both the product market and the factor market, the demand curve for labor slopes downward due to
- **a.** market power.
- **b.** economies of scale.
- **c.** diseconomies of scale.
- **d.** diminishing marginal returns.
- **e.** increasing marginal returns.

5. If marginal product is positive and falling as the firm hires more workers, then
- **a.** total product is rising at a decreasing rate.
- **b.** total product is falling at a decreasing rate.
- **c.** average product must be falling.
- **d.** the marginal revenue product of labor is increasing.
- **e.** the diminishing returns to labor are decreasing.

Use the following production data for a firm operating in both a perfectly competitive product market and a perfectly competitive factor market to answer Questions 6–8.

Number of workers	Total output/hour
1	10
2	22
3	30
4	36
5	40
6	43
7	45
8	46

6. Based on the production data above, at what level of employment does the firm begin to experience diminishing marginal returns?
- **a.** There are no diminishing marginal returns.
- **b.** 3 workers
- **c.** 4 workers
- **d.** 5 workers
- **e.** 6 workers

7. Assume the firm sells its product for $2 each and must pay each worker $8 per hour. What is the marginal revenue product of labor for the second worker?
- **a.** $10
- **b.** $22
- **c.** $24
- **d.** $60
- **e.** $176

8. Assume the firm sells its product for $2 each and must pay each worker $8 per hour. How many workers should the firm hire in order to maximize profit?
- **a.** 2 workers
- **b.** 3 workers
- **c.** 5 workers
- **d.** 6 workers
- **e.** 8 workers

9. Which of the following would shift the demand curve for labor to the right?
- **a.** a decrease in the wage rate
- **b.** an increase in the wage rate
- **c.** an increase in labor productivity
- **d.** a decrease in the final price of the product produced
- **e.** a decrease in the availability of physical capital per worker

10. Suppose a firm produces coffee mugs in a perfectly competitive output market. Which of the following would shift the firm's demand curve for labor to the left?
- **a.** an increase in the demand for mugs
- **b.** a decrease in the price of mugs
- **c.** an increase in the price of mugs
- **d.** improvements in technology that increase the marginal product of labor
- **e.** an increase in the availability of physical capital per worker

11. Suppose a firm hires labor in a perfectly competitive labor market. If the marginal revenue product is less than the wage, the firm should definitely
- **a.** shut down in the short run.
- **b.** shut down in the long run.
- **c.** hire more workers.
- **d.** hire fewer workers.
- **e.** not change the number of workers it hires.

12. Compared to the supply curve for capital, the supply curve for land is
- **a.** flatter, more elastic, and more responsive to factor prices.
- **b.** flatter, less elastic, and less responsive to factor prices.
- **c.** steeper, more elastic, and more responsive to factor prices.
- **d.** steeper, less elastic, and less responsive to factor prices.
- **e.** steeper, more elastic, and less responsive to factor prices.

13. The supply curve for labor slopes downward when
- **a.** the substitution effect outweighs the income effect.
- **b.** the income effect outweighs the substitution effect.
- **c.** the substitution effect equals the income effect.
- **d.** workers experience an overall decrease in wealth.
- **e.** wage rates are at very low levels.

14. The supply curve for labor may shift to the left due to
    a. an increase in wealth.
    b. an increase in the wage rate due to the income effect.
    c. a decrease in the wage rate due to the income effect.
    d. an increase in the wage rate due to the substitution effect.
    e. a decrease in the wage rate due to the substitution effect.

15. For a monopsony, the marginal factor cost of labor curve lies above the supply curve at every quantity of labor due to
    a. diminishing marginal returns.
    b. increasing marginal returns.
    c. different workers receiving different wage rates.
    d. all workers receiving the same wage rate.
    e. decreasing opportunity cost of leisure.

16. Compared to a competitive labor market, a firm with monopsony power in the labor market would pay a
    a. higher wage rate and hire more workers.
    b. higher wage rate and hire fewer workers.
    c. lower wage rate and hire more workers.
    d. lower wage rate and hire fewer workers.
    e. lower wage rate but hire the same amount of workers.

17. Assume an effective minimum wage is imposed on a monopsony labor market, and the minimum wage is set below the wage that would exist in a perfectly competitive market. Employment would
    a. decrease, and there would be unemployment.
    b. decrease, and there would be a shortage of workers.
    c. increase, but there would be a shortage of workers.
    d. increase, but there would be unemployment.
    e. increase, and there would be no shortages or surpluses of labor.

18. Assume a firm is operating as a monopolist in the product market and as a perfect competitor in the factor market. The firm's demand curve for labor will be
    a. horizontal due to the competitive labor market.
    b. horizontal due to the effects of market power.
    c. downward-sloping due to diminishing marginal returns and decreasing marginal revenue.
    d. downward-sloping due solely to diminishing marginal returns.
    e. downward-sloping due solely to decreasing marginal revenue.

19. If a former monopolist in the product market begins to face competition as firms enter the market, the firm's demand curve for labor would
    a. not change.
    b. become more elastic.
    c. become less elastic.
    d. show the effects of more rapidly diminishing marginal returns.
    e. show the effects of less rapidly diminishing marginal returns.

20. Suppose that a firm is currently producing its desired quantity of output and that the firm's marginal product of labor is 20, its marginal product of capital is 100, the wage rate for labor is $5, and the rent for capital is $25. All data are per hour. The firm should
    a. employ more labor and rent more capital.
    b. employ less labor and rent less capital.
    c. employ less labor and rent more capital.
    d. employ more labor and rent less capital.
    e. employ the current amount of labor and rent the current amount of capital.

21. According to marginal productivity theory, a factor of production will be paid based on the
    a. increase in revenue generated by the last unit of the factor employed in the market.
    b. increase in output generated by the last unit of the factor employed in the market.
    c. average revenue generated by the factor of production employed in the market.
    d. average output generated by the factor of production employed in the market.
    e. average revenue generated by all factors of production employed in the market.

22. According to marginal productivity theory, wage inequality in perfectly competitive markets can be attributed to
    a. compensating differentials.
    b. union activity.
    c. discrimination.
    d. efficiency wages.
    e. the similarity in quality and quantity of human capital among all workers.

23. An increase in which of the following practices would help to minimize wage inequality in labor markets?
    a. discrimination
    b. compensating differentials
    c. efficiency wages
    d. educational opportunities for the poor
    e. the wages paid to workers that produce a higher value of marginal product

24. Efficiency wages are wages that
    a. are below the market equilibrium wage.
    b. are above the market equilibrium wage.
    c. never deviate from the market equilibrium wage.
    d. result in lower levels of worker productivity.
    e. necessitate greater amounts of worker supervision.

25. Firms that pay efficiency wages do so primarily to
    a. save money on wages.
    b. increase customer loyalty.
    c. increase worker productivity and loyalty.
    d. replace workers with machines.
    e. reduce wage inequality.

Free-Response Questions

1. Quinn and Courtney manage a factory in the toy airplane industry, which is perfectly competitive in both the product market and the factor market. They have compiled the following per-day data on worker productivity:

Number of workers	0	1	2	3	4	5	6
Marginal product	−	6	5	4	3	2	1

a. The price of toy airplanes is $100, the wage per worker is $200, and the rent per machine is $400. Assume the firm always produces the profit-maximizing quantity of airplanes using the cost-minimizing combination of inputs. If the marginal product of capital is 4, how many workers do Quinn and Courtney hire?

b. Draw a graph of Quinn and Courtney's supply and demand curves for labor using the data from part a above. Be sure to indicate the equilibrium wage rate and the number of workers hired. Label all curves and axes.

c. Explain why the demand curve for labor slopes the way it does.

d. On your factor market graph from part b, show the effect of a decrease in the supply of workers in the toy airplane industry. Add the subscript "new" to the label of anything that changes.
(7 points)

2. The Pelican Perch Hotel hires workers in a perfectly competitive labor market.

a. Draw side-by-side graphs for the hotel and the labor market and show the following:
   i. the equilibrium wage and quantity of workers in the market, labeled W_E and Q_{E1}, respectively
   ii. the labor supply curve for the hotel, labeled S_H
   iii. the quantity of workers hired by the hotel, labeled Q_1

b. Suppose a minimum wage higher than W_E is imposed on the labor market. On your graph from part a, show the following:
   i. the new wage in the market, labeled W_{Min}
   ii. the quantity of workers hired in the market, labeled Q_{E2}
   iii. the quantity of workers hired by the hotel, labeled Q_2
   (7 points)

3. Colby Coal Inc. is the only employer of labor in town.

a. Identify the market structure in which Colby Coal hires labor.

b. Draw a correctly labeled graph of the labor market for Colby Coal and identify the following:
   i. the quantity of labor employed, labeled Q_M
   ii. the wage rate Colby Coal will pay, labeled W_M

c. Suppose the government breaks up Colby Coal into many smaller firms, creating a perfectly competitive labor market. On your graph from part a, label the new equilibrium quantity of employment Q_C and the new wage rate W_C.
   (7 points)

Immigration: How Welcoming Should Lady Liberty Be?

The Costs and Benefits of Relatively Open Borders

Give me your tired, your poor,
Your huddled masses yearning to breathe free,
The wretched refuse of your teeming shore.
Send these, the homeless, tempest-tossed, to me:
I lift my lamp beside the golden door.

From "The New Colossus" by Emma Lazarus (1883)

The words above, engraved at the base of the Statue of Liberty, remind us that the United States is a proud nation of immigrants. Since 1820, more than 85 million immigrants have entered the United States. Foreign-born individuals make up 14% of the U.S. population, 17% of its workforce, 25% of its doctors, 6% of its prison inmates, and 15% of its unemployed. Immigration issues are complex, and entire books are devoted to the details. This overview merely starts the conversation about the costs and benefits of

immigration, its influence on the labor market, and policies to limit the number of immigrants greeted by what Lazarus described as Lady Liberty's "beacon-hand" of "world-wide welcome."

Arguments Against Immigration

Criticism of immigration centers on the drawbacks of population growth, competition for jobs, and overburdened public assistance programs. Some Americans fear that immigrants with different languages and customs will alter the way of life in the United States. Others associate immigration with terrorism. Anti-immigration sentiment has influenced recent elections in the United States, Australia, and several European countries.

Rapid mass migration, like the flood of emigrants from Europe to North America that took place between 1870 and 1913, can provoke nationalism and increase competition for resources. A national non-profit group called the Carrying Capacity Network (CCN) considers the current level of immigration into the United States to be excessive, and lists among the repercussions: traffic congestion, air pollution, water and energy shortages, overcrowded schools, declines in purchasing power, a lower quality of life, tax increases, and soil erosion. These claims are debatable, but they come from some respected sources. The board of the CCN has included such celebrated environmentalists and ecological economists as L. Hunter Lovins, Herman E. Daly, and Robert Costanza.

Despite annual expenditures of $4 billion on border protection in the United States, the Federation for American Immigration Reform (FAIR) estimates that 12.5 million illegal immigrants lived in this country in 2017. In 2018, President Donald Trump asked Congress for $25 billion to enhance the system of border walls and fences between Mexico and the United States. Congress allocated $1.6 billion to the project, and the president vowed to fight for more.

Illegal immigration stresses the tight budgets for schools, medical care, public transportation, criminal

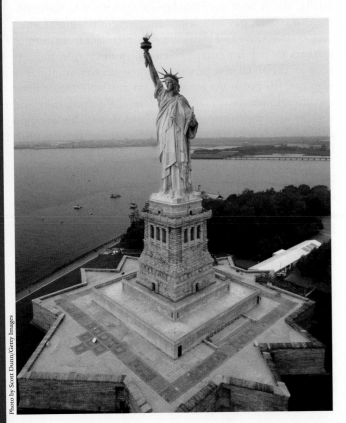

Photo by Scott Dunn/Getty Images

Michael Dwyer/Alamy

justice systems, and public infrastructure. The burden of illegal immigrants falls disproportionately on border states, most notably California, Texas, and Florida. FAIR estimates that the state of Florida spends $6.3 billion per year on illegal immigrants and their children.[1] The same immigrants pay about $1 billion in taxes, for a net cost of roughly $5.3 billion per year.

About 80% of immigrants have less education than the average American and earn correspondingly lower wages. Lower household incomes mean greater reliance on social services, including welfare and food stamps. Current legislation prevents immigrants from collecting food stamps for at least five years after entry into the United States, and immigrants can't collect Supplemental Security Income (SSI) from the federal government until they achieve citizenship, which takes at least five years. However, there are exceptions for immigrant children within the food stamp program (SNAP), and most immigrants have been in the country for more than five years. U.S. immigration policy favors immigrants with family connections, refugees, and workers who have been invited by U.S. employers. One alternative would be to follow the lead of Canada, Australia, and New Zealand by placing more weight on the economic potential of workers, and less on family connections, when selecting visa recipients. Proponents argue that this would place a lighter burden on social services and bring in more workers ready to contribute to gross domestic product.

Arguments for Immigration

The first human inhabitants of North America are thought to have crossed a land bridge from present-day Russia to Alaska roughly 50,000 years ago. The first Europeans crossed the Atlantic around the year 1001. So every American is either an immigrant or a descendant of immigrants, without whom

the benefits of this great melting pot of ideas, customs, and productivity would be unrealized.

Foreign-born workers create jobs in the United States. Consider Charlie Woo, who emigrated from Hong Kong to the United States in 1968 to pursue an education and a new life. In 1979, he opened a toy wholesaling business in a run-down warehouse district in Los Angeles. Woo's Megatoys company became the centerpiece of Toytown, the business district that eventually employed 4,000 workers and generated $500 million in annual revenues. Entrepreneurial immigrants such as Woo bring new ideas, energy, and jobs to the marketplace. Almost half of the *Fortune 500* companies (the 500 largest U.S. companies based on total revenues) were founded by immigrants or their children.[2] Immigrants also fill jobs in rural locations where labor is scarce, and in low-paying blue-collar industries, such as textile manufacturing, meatpacking, poultry processing, and crop harvesting, that go largely unfilled by U.S. citizens. In so doing, they contribute to U.S. growth and prosperity.

In many ways immigration represents an ideal source of labor. Beyond providing hard work for low pay, immigrant workers tend to respond to market forces by supplying their services when and where they are most needed. There is evidence that the supply of both legal and illegal immigration fluctuates with business cycles. The Homeland Security Department's Office of Immigration Statistics reports that the number of people caught attempting to cross the southwestern border between the United States and Mexico increased by about 50% during the prosperous late 1990s and fell sharply during the recessions of the 2000s. The flow of working-age immigrants into the country also assists "pay-as-you-go" entitlement programs, such as Social Security and Medicare, which collect from current workers to pay for current retirees. Immigration policies such as the H-1B visa program, which admits immigrants who can fill positions for which no available U.S. citizen qualifies, lower the average age of the U.S. population, and thereby increase the proportion of people who are working and paying taxes rather than receiving benefits from entitlement programs.

As immigrant families become established over several generations, their purchases and tax payments grow, and their net effect on state and local benefits becomes positive.[3] Alan Greenspan, former chair of the Federal Reserve, sees immigration as beneficial, saying that "unless immigration is uncapped . . . the continuous reduction in the number of available workers willing to take jobs . . . would intensify inflationary pressures or squeeze profit margins, with either outcome capable of bringing our growing prosperity to an end."[4]

[1] See www.fairus.org/issue/publications-resources/fiscal-burden-illegal-immigration-united-states-taxpayers.

[2] See www.brookings.edu/blog/the-avenue/2017/12/04/almost-half-of-fortune-500-companies-were-founded-by-american-immigrants-or-their-children/.

[3] See National Academies of Sciences, Engineering, and Medicine, *The Economic and Fiscal Consequences of Immigration* (Washington, DC: The National Academies Press, 2017).

[4] See www.bc.edu/bc_org/mvp/fincon/greenspanspeech.html.

Economists estimate that immigration's effect on the wages of U.S.-born workers falls in the range from slightly negative to slightly positive. For example, Gianmarco Ottaviano and Giovanni Peri estimated that immigration between 1990 and 2006 increased the wages of U.S.-born workers by about 1%.[5] George Borjas estimated that immigration into the United States depresses wages by $152 billion annually but increases profits by $160 billion.[6] In theory at least, we could use taxes and transfer programs, such as SNAP (food stamps) and related welfare programs, to redistribute some of the gains in corporate profits to the workers whose wages may be lowered—primarily those without high school diplomas.

A wave of immigration-related legislation followed the 9/11 terrorist attacks: the USA Patriot Act, the Enhanced Border Security and Visa Entry Reform Act, and the Homeland Security Act. Starting in 2017, President Donald Trump placed further limits on entry into the United States by immigrants, refugees, and visitors from designated countries. By increasing the difficulty of entering the United States, these laws provided a glimpse of the effects of more restricted immigration. Groups claiming damage from the new procedures include U.S. companies trying to attract customers from overseas, refugees seeking asylum from oppressive regimes, and educational institutions trying to capitalize on America's reputation for academic excellence. Tightened restrictions after 9/11 helped reduce the number of student visas issued in the United States from 299,000 in 2001 to 220,000 in 2003. The more recent entry restrictions brought the number of new refugees admitted into the United States down from 85,000 in 2016 to 54,000 in 2017.

As for the burden that immigration places on the border states, a line must be drawn between legal and illegal immigration. Florida may spend $5.3 billion annually on illegal immigrants (net of their tax payments), but legal immigrants are another story—their numbers are limited and the requirements are strict. For instance, before certifying a permanent worker's visa, the U.S. Department of Labor verifies that there are not enough qualified U.S. workers available to fill the position and that the employment of a foreign worker would not lower the wages or worsen the working conditions of U.S. workers.

Border states absorb much of the expense of educating immigrant children, but investments in education are a primary determinant of the productivity and wealth of a region. Thus, Florida's expenditure on the education of immigrants helps to create a versatile, skilled workforce. Immigrants don't simply fill a need for blue-collar workers. They also help remedy the severe shortage of medical personnel, particularly in rural areas. The U.S. Department of Health and Human Services estimates that by 2025, the demand for primary care doctors in Florida will exceed the supply by 3,060.[7] Immigrants

are currently easing shortages of doctors, nurses, dentists, and mental health workers across the country. The American Immigration Law Foundation (AILF) points out that the "enhanced use of immigration policy" would further ease these shortages.[8] At present, about 2.1 million immigrants account for 17% of health care providers in the United States, including 24% of nursing, psychiatric, and home health aides; 15% of health care practitioners and technicians; and 10% of all therapists.[9]

Sorting Out the Claims

Perhaps the best way to sort fact from fiction in the immigration debate is to weigh the claims against theory and evidence. Despite immigration in record numbers, U.S. crime rates have declined markedly during the past 25 years and the standard of living has remained among the highest in the world by almost every measure. Except during occasional recessions, the U.S. unemployent rate has remained relatively low, indicating that immigrant workers are creating jobs or filling labor needs.

[5] See "Rethinking the Effect of Immigration on Wages," *Journal of the European Economic Association* 10, no 1 (February 2012): 152–197.

[6] See *Heaven's Door: Immigration Policy and the American Economy* (Princeton, NJ: Princeton University Press, 2001).

[7] See https://bhw.hrsa.gov/sites/default/files/bhw/health-workforce-analysis/research/projections/primary-care-state-projections2013-2025.pdf.

[8] See www.mcknights.com/report-immigration-policies-need-to-be-altered-to-fill-vital-roles/article/100741/.

[9] See www.migrationpolicy.org/article/foreign-born-health-care-workers-united-states.

Economic theory and data support the contention that ample supplies of manual labor suppress wages for low-skilled jobs. The relative lack of interest among U.S.-born workers in migrant agricultural work and other forms of unpleasant manual labor diminishes the competition between U.S.-born workers and immigrants. Meanwhile, the benefits of a plentiful labor supply are enjoyed by producers and consumers of food, clothing, and other critical goods and services that immigrant workers provide, and by immigrants, who would generally earn less in their home countries. The same is true for the labor supply in high-skilled jobs—immigrants fill needs in health care and high-tech fields, allowing producers to earn higher profits and giving consumers lower prices and a more abundant supply of goods and services.

Pollution and stresses on natural resources do indeed grow with the population, but remember that immigration is a transfer of people from one place to another, not a source of population growth for the planet. Immigrants who adopt the American lifestyle and have families that resemble American families will have fewer children than do people in many of the countries from which large numbers of immigrants come, including Mexico, India, and the Philippines. The most serious pollution problems, such as climate change, are global problems, and it makes little difference where the pollutants are released. If we so desire, the productivity gains and the sharing of ideas achieved with immigration will allow us to devote more funds and better policy-making efforts to the ubiquitous issues of resource scarcity and pollution.

Conclusion

A central message of economics is that the wisdom of actions depends on the relative size of costs and benefits, many of which are overlooked by casual observers. Immigration is no exception. Appropriate policy making requires an understanding of the contributions and burdens of people who follow the immigrant path of the founders of the United States. The benefits of immigration include job creation, inflation control, and diversity in skills and ideas. Increased expenditures on education, infrastructure, and public assistance are among the burdens.

Income disparities among nations, and skills gaps within nations, intensify the interest in immigration. Natural tendencies to avoid competition for jobs, and to steer tax dollars away from expenditures on

immigrants, collide with desires to pay low prices and fill large needs for manual laborers; health care professionals; and workers with skills in science, math, and technology. Relevant policies touch the lives of would-be immigrants and virtually every U.S. citizen. The best decisions on pending policies will come not from emotional or political decisions but from cost-benefit analyses that go beyond direct tax and profit measures to cover every facet of Lady Liberty's promised welcome.

Critical Thinking Questions

1. In your opinion, what are the two largest costs and benefits of immigration?

2. With the United States unlikely to ever close its borders entirely, immigration policy is primarily a matter of degree. Some people argue that the costs associated with additional immigrants exceed the benefits after 100,000 immigrants per year. Others favor limits far higher than the current rate of more than 1 million immigrants per year. On the basis of your understanding of the issue, how many immigrants would you welcome into the country each year? Defend your answer.

3. Immigrants to the United States are helping to fill persistent needs for workers in health care and high-tech careers. A national campaign in the United Kingdom is urging residents to close their own skills gaps by seeking additional training in fields that are experiencing labor shortages. Are Americans well enough aware of the skills gap and the role immigrants play? Should a similar informational campaign be run in the United States? Are there alternative ways in which the United States' skills gap could be handled?

4. Many immigrants enter the country with relatively few marketable skills beyond a willingness to perform manual labor for a low wage. Are you aware of unemployed Americans who would be willing to pick crops or perform similarly unpleasant tasks for the minimum wage? Discuss the costs and benefits of paying manual laborers a more desirable wage, which might attract more U.S.-born workers to those jobs.

5. Does a nation of past immigrants have a moral obligation to welcome new immigrants? Explain your answer.

SECTION 14

Market Failure and the Role of Government

economics by example *Why Not Split the Check?*

Incentives Matter, for Better or Worse

Rivers are critical sources of drinking water and can be beautiful places to swim, fish, and boat. They are also recipients of industrial waste, sewage, and farm runoff containing chemical fertilizers, herbicides, and pesticides. Each year, millions of pounds of toxic chemicals enter the Mississippi River, causing problems for those who want to use the water for other purposes. At the mouth of the Mississippi River lies a "dead zone" spread across thousands of square miles of the Gulf of Mexico. Nitrogen and phosphorus pollution in the dead zone unleashes algae blooms that deplete oxygen in the water and make it unviable for sea creatures.

The dead zone was larger than ever in 2018, but some of the Mississippi River's worst pollutants—polychlorinated biphenyls known as PCBs—are on the decline. For most of the last century, manufacturers used PCBs in everything from cables and caulking to paints and plastics. Levels of PCBs in waterways have slowly declined since 1979, when many industries phased out their use. But the industries didn't do this out of the goodness of their hearts; they did it in response to a ban on PCBs by the Environmental Protection Agency. Without such government intervention, manufacturers would have had few incentives to take the environmental effects of their actions into account.

Neglected pollution is one of several reasons why markets sometimes fail to deliver efficient quantities of goods and services. We've already seen that inefficiency can arise from market power, which allows monopolists and colluding oligopolists to charge prices that exceed the marginal cost and prevent mutually beneficial transactions from occurring. In this section we will consider other reasons for inefficient market outcomes. In Modules 74 and 75, we will see that inefficiency can arise from *externalities*, which create a conflict between the best interests of an individual or a firm and the best interests of society as a whole. In Module 76, we will focus on how the characteristics of goods often determine whether markets can deliver them efficiently. In Modules 77 and 78, we will look at the role of government in addressing market power and income inequality. The investigation of sources of inefficiency will deepen our understanding of the types of policy that can make society better off.

Introduction to Externalities

In this Module, you will learn to:
- Explain what externalities are and why they can lead to inefficiency in a market economy
- Discuss why the optimal amount of pollution is not zero
- Describe how, according to the Coase theorem, private individuals can sometimes remedy externalities
- Explain why some approaches to externality problems are more likely to yield efficient outcomes than others

Externalities

Much of our behavior affects other people in ways we fail to consider. For example, the National Safety Council estimates that drivers who are texting or talking on cell phones account for more than one in four traffic accidents. Billboards urge people not to use phones while driving. But a growing number of people say that voluntary standards aren't enough; they want the use of hand-held cell phones while driving made illegal, as it already is in over a dozen states and the District of Columbia, as well as in Japan, Israel, and many other countries.

Why not leave the decision up to the driver? Because driving while talking isn't just a risk to the driver; it puts many other people at risk. You might take a call while driving if the benefit is worth the risk to you, neglecting the costs you could impose on other drivers.

The use of cell phones while driving endangers people not involved in the decision to use them.

An **external cost** is an uncompensated cost that an individual or a firm imposes on others.

An **external benefit** is a benefit that an individual or a firm confers on others without receiving compensation.

External costs and benefits are known as **externalities**.

External costs are **negative externalities**, and external benefits are **positive externalities**.

Market failure occurs when the outcome in a market is inefficient.

The environmental cost of pollution is perhaps the best-known and most important example of an **external cost**—an uncompensated cost that an individual or a firm imposes on others. Another important, and certainly familiar, external cost is traffic congestion—an individual who chooses to drive during rush hour increases congestion and so increases the travel time of other drivers.

We'll see in the next Module that there are also important examples of **external benefits**, benefits that individuals or firms confer on others without receiving compensation. For example, when you plant a tree in your yard, you provide the external benefit of beauty to passersby. External costs and external benefits are jointly known as **externalities**. External costs are called **negative externalities**, and external benefits are called **positive externalities**.

Externalities lead to inefficient market outcomes. Economists describe the problem of inefficiency in a market as **market failure**. In this Module, we'll examine how externalities cause market failure by looking at a case study of pollution. Other sources of market failure include *public goods*, market power, and imperfect information, which are discussed in Module 75, Module 76, and Enrichment Module C, respectively.

The Economics of Pollution

Pollution is a bad thing. Yet most pollution is a side effect of activities that provide us with good things: our air is polluted by power plants generating the electricity that lights our cities, and our rivers are sullied by fertilizer runoff from farms that grow our food. Why shouldn't we accept a certain amount of pollution as the cost of a good life?

Actually, we do. Even highly committed environmentalists don't think that we can or should completely eliminate pollution—*some* pollution comes as the unavoidable cost of producing the most basic goods and services, such as food, clothing, and health care.

What environmentalists typically argue is that unless there is a strong and effective environmental policy, our society will generate *too much* pollution—too much of a bad thing. And the great majority of economists agree.

To see why, we need a framework that lets us think about how much pollution a society *should* have. We'll then be able to see why a market economy, left to itself, will produce more pollution than it should. We'll start by adopting a framework to study the problem under the simplifying assumption that the amount of pollution emitted by a polluter is directly observable and controllable.

Costs and Benefits of Pollution

How much pollution should society allow? We learned previously that "how much" decisions made by individuals or firms involve comparing the marginal benefit from an additional unit of something with the marginal cost of that additional unit. The same is true for society as a whole.

The **marginal social cost** of something, be it a good, service, activity, or pollutant, is the additional cost imposed on society as a whole by one additional unit. For example, each additional ton of sulfur dioxide released into the atmosphere by a coal-fired power plant increases the harm of this acidic pollution to waterways, plants, and human health.

The **marginal social benefit** of something is the additional benefit to society from one additional unit. So the marginal social benefit of pollution is the additional benefit to society from one more unit of pollution. This concept may seem counterintuitive—what's good about pollution? However, pollution avoidance requires the use of money and inputs that could be used for other purposes. For example, to reduce the quantity of sulfur dioxide they emit, power companies must either buy expensive low-sulfur coal or install special scrubbers to remove sulfur from their emissions. The more sulfur dioxide they are allowed to emit, the lower are these avoidance costs. If we calculated how much money the power industry would save if it were allowed to emit an additional ton of sulfur dioxide, that savings would be the marginal benefit to society of emitting that ton of sulfur dioxide.

Using hypothetical numbers, **Figure 74.1** shows how we can determine the **socially optimal quantity** of pollution—the quantity that makes society as well off as possible, taking all costs and benefits into account. The upward-sloping marginal social cost curve, labeled *MSC*, shows how the marginal cost to society of an additional ton of pollution emissions varies with the quantity of emissions. (An upward slope is likely because nature can often safely handle low levels of pollution but is increasingly harmed by additional units as pollution reaches high levels.)

The marginal social benefit curve, labeled *MSB*, is downward-sloping because the first units of pollution can be used for the most beneficial purposes, such as heating hospitals and homes. Subsequent units of pollution enable less critical uses of energy and therefore provide smaller benefits. If pollution is reduced at the power plants, the first few units of pollution avoidance come from the lowest-cost avoidance methods; increasingly more expensive technology must be used to achieve further reductions. As a result, the marginal social benefit of being able to emit another ton of pollution is relatively high at low levels of pollution.

The socially optimal quantity of pollution in this example isn't zero. It's Q_{OPT}, the quantity corresponding to point *O*, where the marginal social benefit curve crosses the marginal social cost curve. At Q_{OPT}, the marginal social benefit from an additional ton of emissions and its marginal social cost are equalized at $200. But will a market economy, left to itself, arrive at the socially optimal quantity of pollution? No, it won't.

The effects of pollution.

Ted Spiegel/Getty Images

The **marginal social cost** of something is the additional cost imposed on society as a whole by one additional unit.

The **marginal social benefit** of something is the additional benefit to society as a whole from one additional unit.

The **socially optimal quantity** of something is the quantity that society would choose if all the costs and benefits were fully accounted for.

Figure 74.1 Why a Market Economy Produces Too Much Pollution

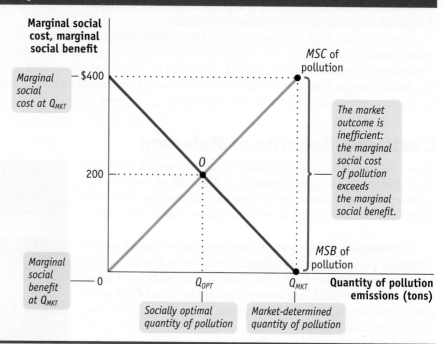

Pollution yields both costs and benefits. The socially optimal quantity of pollution is Q_{OPT}; at that quantity, the marginal social benefit of pollution is equal to the marginal social cost, in this case $200. The market-determined quantity of pollution will be Q_{MKT}, the quantity at which the marginal social benefit of pollution equals the price polluters pay for each unit of pollution they emit: $0. This is an inefficiently high quantity of pollution because the marginal social cost, $400, greatly exceeds the marginal social benefit, $0.

For polluters, the benefits of emissions take the form of monetary savings: by emitting more sulfur dioxide, a power company saves the cost of buying expensive, low-sulfur coal or installing pollution-control equipment. So the benefits of pollution accrue directly to the polluters.

The costs of pollution, however, fall on people who typically have no say in the decision about how much pollution takes place. For example, people who would like to fish or swim in rivers have no say in decisions about the efforts to reduce coal ash contamination from power plants upstream.

In a market economy without government intervention, only the benefits of pollution are taken into account in choosing the quantity of pollution. So the quantity of emissions won't be the socially optimal quantity Q_{OPT}, it will be Q_{MKT}, the quantity at which the marginal social benefit of an additional ton of pollution is zero, but the marginal social cost of that additional ton is much larger—$400. The quantity of pollution in a market economy without government intervention will be higher than its socially optimal quantity.

The reason is that, in the absence of government intervention, those who derive the benefit from pollution—the owners of polluting firms—don't have to compensate those who bear the cost of pollution. Assuming the polluter is not also the pollution victim, the entire cost of pollution is external, which gives polluters no incentive to limit the amount of emissions. For example, before the Clean Air Act of 1970, power plants in the Midwest used the cheapest type of coal available, despite the fact that cheap coal generated more pollution.

Private Solutions to Externality Problems

When externalities are present, can the private sector achieve efficient outcomes without government intervention? In an influential 1960 article, economist and Nobel laureate Ronald Coase pointed out that in an ideal world, private negotiations could indeed resolve externality problems. According to the **Coase theorem**, payments between the parties involved can achieve an efficient solution to externality problems, provided that the legal rights of the parties are clearly defined and the costs of making a deal are sufficiently low. In some cases it takes a lot of time, or even money, to bring the relevant parties together, negotiate a payment, and carry out the terms of the deal. The costs of making a deal are known as **transaction costs**.

To get a sense of Coase's argument, imagine two neighbors, Justin and Adele, who both like to barbecue in their backyards. Justin likes to blast music while barbecuing, but this annoys Adele, who can't stand loud music. Who prevails? You might think it depends on the legal rights involved in the case: if the law says that Justin has the right to play music at whatever volume he wants, Adele just has to suffer; if the law says that Justin needs Adele's consent to play loud music in his backyard, Justin can't blast his favorite bands while barbecuing.

But as Coase pointed out, the outcome need not be determined by legal rights, because Adele and Justin can make a private deal as long as the legal rights are clearly defined. Even if Justin has the right to play loud music, Adele could pay him not to. Even if Justin can't play loud music without an OK from Adele, he can offer to pay her to give that OK. These payments allow them to reach an efficient solution regardless of who has the legal upper hand.

Suppose playing loud music is worth $30 to Justin, and quiet is worth $50 to Adele. If Justin has the right to play loud music, Adele could pay Justin any amount between $30 and $50, say $40, not to. With this payment, both parties would be better off than if loud music were played—Justin would have $40 in cash rather than $30 worth of music, and Adele would pay $40 for $50 worth of quiet. If, instead, playing loud music is worth $80 to Justin and quiet is worth $50 to Adele, there is no amount that Adele would pay, and Justin would accept, to stop playing loud music. In both cases we have the efficient outcome: if the benefit of loud music to Justin exceeds its cost to Adele, the blasting will occur; if the benefit to Justin is less than the cost to Adele, the volume will be low.

The implication of Coase's analysis is that externalities need not lead to inefficiency because individuals have an incentive to make mutually beneficial deals—deals that lead them to take externalities into account when making decisions. When individuals *do* take externalities into account when making decisions, economists say that they **internalize the externalities**. If externalities are fully internalized, as when Justin must forgo a payment from Adele equal to the external cost he imposes on her in order to play music, the outcome is efficient even without government intervention.

Why can't individuals always internalize externalities? Our barbecue example implicitly assumes the transaction costs are low enough for Justin and Adele to be able to make a deal. In many situations involving externalities, however, transaction costs prevent individuals from making efficient deals. Examples of transaction costs include the following:

- *The costs of communication among the interested parties.* Such costs may be particularly high if many people are involved or the people involved don't know each other.

- *The costs of making legally binding agreements.* Such costs may be high if expensive legal services are required.

- *Costly delays involved in bargaining.* Even if there is a potentially beneficial deal, both sides may hold out in an effort to extract more favorable terms, leading to increased effort and forgone utility.

In some cases, transaction costs are low enough to allow individuals to resolve externality problems. For example, while filming *A League of Their Own* on location in a neighborhood ballpark, director Penny Marshall paid a man $100 to stop using his noisy chainsaw nearby. But in many other cases, transaction costs are too high to make it possible to deal with externalities through private action. For example, millions of people are adversely affected by pollution from power plants. It would be prohibitively expensive to strike a deal among all those people and all those power companies.

When transaction costs prevent the private sector from dealing with externalities, it is time to look for government solutions.

According to the **Coase theorem**, payments between private parties can achieve an efficient solution to externality problems as long as **transaction costs**—the costs to individuals of making a deal—are sufficiently low.

AP® EXAM TIP

For the AP® exam, remember that private negotiations are the key to Coase's solution to externality problems. Be prepared to identify and explain the reasons Coasian bargaining can fail.

When individuals take external costs or benefits into account, they **internalize the externalities**.

Policies Toward Pollution

Before 1970 there were no rules governing the amount of sulfur dioxide that power plants in the United States could emit. In 1970, the Clean Air Act set rules restricting sulfur dioxide emissions; thereafter, pollution levels declined significantly. Economists argued, however, that a more flexible system of rules that exploited the effectiveness of markets could achieve lower pollution levels at a lower cost. This theory was put into effect in 1990 with a modified version of the Clean Air Act. And guess what? The economists were right!

Next, we'll look at the policies governments use to deal with pollution and at how economic analysis has been used to improve those policies.

Environmental Standards

Environmental standards are rules that protect the environment by specifying limits for or actions by producers and consumers.

Because the economy, and life itself, depend on a viable environment, external costs that threaten the environment—air pollution, water pollution, habitat destruction, and so on—are worthy of attention. Protection of the environment has become a major focus of government in every advanced nation. In the United States, the Environmental Protection Agency is the principal enforcer of environmental policies at the national level and is supported by the actions of state and local governments.

How does a country protect its environment? At present the main policy tools are **environmental standards**, rules that protect the environment by specifying limits for or actions by producers and consumers. A familiar example is the law that requires almost all vehicles to have catalytic converters, which reduce the emission of chemicals that can cause smog and lead to health problems. Other standards require communities to treat their sewage, factories to limit their pollution emissions, and homes to be painted with lead-free paint, among many other examples.

Environmental standards are helping to erase the Los Angeles smog.

Environmental standards came into widespread use in the 1960s and 1970s with considerable success. Since the United States passed the Clean Air Act in 1970, for example, the emission of air pollutants has fallen by more than a third, even though the population has grown by nearly two-thirds and the size of the economy has more than doubled.

Despite these successes, environmental standards are inflexible and often don't allow reductions in pollution to be achieved at the lowest possible cost. For example, two power plants might be ordered to reduce pollution by the same percentage, even if their costs of achieving that objective are very different. A more efficient policy would allow more pollution at the plant where it is more expensive to reduce pollution levels, and less pollution where it is more easily avoided.

How does economic theory suggest that pollution should be controlled? We'll examine two approaches: taxes and tradable permits. As we'll see, either approach can achieve the efficient outcome at the minimum feasible cost.

Emissions Taxes

One way to deal with pollution directly is to charge polluters an *emissions tax*, a tax that depends on the amount of pollution a firm produces. For example, rather than being required to use specific pollution reduction technology, power plants might be charged $200 for every ton of sulfur dioxide they emit.

Consider the socially optimal quantity of pollution, Q_{OPT}, shown in Figure 74.1. At that quantity of pollution, the marginal social benefit and the marginal social cost of an additional ton of emissions are equal at $200. But in the absence of government intervention, power companies have no incentive to limit pollution to the socially optimal quantity Q_{OPT}; instead, they will push pollution up to the quantity Q_{MKT}, at which the marginal social benefit is zero.

It's now easy to see how an emissions tax can solve the problem. If power companies are required to pay a tax of $200 per ton of emissions, they face a marginal cost of $200 per ton and have an incentive to reduce emissions to Q_{OPT}, the socially optimal quantity. This illustrates a general result: an emissions tax equal to the marginal social cost at the socially optimal quantity of pollution induces polluters to internalize the externality—to take into account the true cost to society of their actions. Module 75 explains more ways that taxes can bring decision makers to internalize negative externalities.

The term *emissions tax* may convey the misleading impression that taxes are a solution to only one kind of external cost, pollution. In fact, taxes can be used to discourage any activity that generates negative externalities, such as driving during rush hour or operating a noisy bar in a residential area. Emissions taxes do present a challenge: In practice, government officials usually aren't sure at what level the tax should be set. If they set the tax too low, there will be too little improvement in the environment; if they set it too high, emissions will be reduced by more than is efficient. This uncertainty cannot be eliminated, but the nature of the risks can be changed with the alternative strategy of issuing tradable emissions permits.

Tradable Emissions Permits

Tradable emissions permits are licenses to emit limited quantities of pollutants that can be bought and sold by polluters. They are usually issued to polluting firms according to some formula reflecting their history. For example, each power plant might be issued permits equal to 50% of its emissions before the system went into effect. The more important point, however, is that these permits are *tradable*. A system of tradable emissions permits, commonly known as a *cap and trade program*, creates a market in rights to pollute. Firms with differing costs of reducing pollution can use this market to engage in mutually beneficial transactions: those that find it easier to reduce pollution will sell some of their permits to those that find it more difficult. In the end, those with the lowest cost will reduce their pollution the most and those with the highest cost will reduce their pollution the least.

Suppose that the market price of a permit to emit one ton of sulfur dioxide is $200. Then every plant has an incentive to limit its emissions of sulfur dioxide to the point where its marginal benefit of emitting another ton of pollution is $200. If a plant must pay $200 for the right to emit an additional ton of sulfur dioxide, it faces the same incentives as a plant facing an emissions tax of $200 per ton. Even for plants that have more permits than they plan to use, by *not* emitting a ton of sulfur dioxide, a plant frees up a permit that it can sell for $200, so the opportunity cost of a ton of emissions to the plant's owner is $200.

In short, tradable emissions permits have the same cost-minimizing advantage over environmental standards as emissions taxes: either system ensures that those who can reduce pollution most cheaply are the ones who do so. The socially optimal quantity of pollution shown in Figure 74.1 could be efficiently achieved either way: by imposing an emissions tax of $200 per ton of pollution or by issuing tradable permits to emit Q_{OPT} tons of pollution.

It is important to realize that emissions taxes and tradable permits do more than induce polluting industries to reduce their output. Unlike rigid environmental standards, emissions taxes and tradable permits provide incentives to create and use technology that emits less pollution. The main effect of the permit system for sulfur dioxide has been to change *how* electricity is produced rather than to reduce the nation's electricity output. For example, power companies have shifted to the use of alternative fuels such as low-sulfur coal and natural gas; they have also installed scrubbers that take much of the sulfur dioxide out of a power plant's emissions.

The main problem with tradable emissions permits is the flip-side of the problem with emissions taxes: because it is difficult to determine the optimal quantity of pollution, governments find themselves either issuing too many permits, or too few. And there must be vigilant monitoring of compliance if the system is to work.

Tradable emissions permits are licenses to emit limited quantities of pollutants that can be bought and sold by polluters.

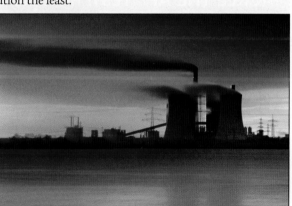

Emissions taxes and tradable emissions permits can guide power companies toward the efficient level of pollution.

AVTG/Getty Images

AP® EXAM TIP

Cap and trade programs reward producers who reduce emissions with the ability to gain revenue from the sale of emissions permits they no longer need.

After relying on environmental standards for decades, in 1995 the U.S. government began a cap and trade system for sulfur dioxide emissions by issuing permits to power plants based on their historical consumption of coal. The cap of 8.95 million tons set for 2010 and beyond is about half the level of emissions in 1980. Economists who have analyzed the sulfur dioxide cap and trade system point to another reason for its success: It would have been much more expensive—80% more to be exact—to reduce emissions by this much using a non-market-based regulatory policy.

MODULE 74 REVIEW

Check Your Understanding

1. Wastewater runoff from large poultry farms adversely affects residents in neighboring homes. Explain the following:
   a. Why is this considered an externality problem?
   b. Will the outcome be efficient if there is neither government intervention nor a private deal?
   c. How is the socially optimal outcome determined and how does it compare with the no-intervention, no-deal outcome?

2. According to Yasmin, any student who borrows a book from the university library and fails to return it on time imposes a negative externality on other students. She claims that rather than charging a modest fine for late returns, the library should charge a huge fine, so that borrowers will never return a book late. Is Yasmin's economic reasoning correct?

TACKLE THE AP® TEST: Multiple-Choice Questions

1. The socially optimal level of pollution is
   a. less than that created by the market, but not zero.
   b. more than that created by the market.
   c. whatever the market creates.
   d. determined by firms.
   e. zero.

2. Which of the following is a source of negative externalities?
   a. loud conversations in a library
   b. smokestack scrubbers
   c. a beautiful view
   d. national defense
   e. a decision to purchase dressy but uncomfortable shoes

3. Inefficiencies created by externalities can be dealt with through
   a. government actions only.
   b. private actions only.
   c. market outcomes only.
   d. either private or government actions.
   e. neither private nor government actions.

4. The Coase theorem asserts that, under the right circumstances, inefficiencies created by externalities can be dealt with through
   a. lawsuits.
   b. private bargaining.
   c. vigilante actions.
   d. government policies.
   e. mediation.

5. Which of the following makes it more likely that private solutions to externality problems will succeed?
   a. high transaction costs
   b. high prices for legal services
   c. delays in the bargaining process
   d. a small number of affected parties
   e. loosely defined legal rights

6. The inflexibility of which of the following tools makes it inefficient even when correctly applied?
   a. environmental standards
   b. emissions taxes
   c. tradable emissions permits
   d. Coasian bargaining
   e. cap and trade programs

7. A drawback of tradable emissions permits is that
   a. there is no incentive to further reduce emissions if the firm has enough permits to cover its current pollution level.
   b. the firm with the highest cost of reducing emissions typically ends up having to reduce emissions the most.
   c. every firm must reduce emissions by the same amount.
   d. permits do not encourage the use of emissions-reducing technology.
   e. governments may provide too many or too few permits.

TACKLE THE AP® TEST: Free-Response Questions

1. Draw a correctly labeled graph showing the market-determined quantity of pollution, and explain why that quantity will be chosen in the absence of intervention and private deals. On the same graph, show the socially optimal level of pollution.

Rubric for FRQ 1 (6 points)

1 point: The vertical axis is labeled "Marginal social cost, marginal social benefit" or "Dollars per unit" and the horizontal axis is labeled "Quantity of pollution" or "Q."

1 point: The marginal social cost curve is labeled and upward-sloping.

1 point: The marginal social benefit curve is labeled and downward-sloping.

1 point: The market-determined level of pollution is shown on the horizontal axis where the marginal social benefit curve reaches the horizontal axis.

1 point: In the absence of intervention and private deals, the marginal cost to a polluter of polluting is zero. Thus, pollution will continue until the marginal social benefit (all of which goes to the polluter) equals the polluter's marginal cost of zero, which occurs at the horizontal intercept of the marginal social cost curve.

1 point: The socially optimal level of pollution is shown on the horizontal axis below the intersection of MSC and MSB.

2. **a.** Define the marginal social cost of pollution.
   b. Define the marginal social benefit of pollution, and explain why polluting more can provide benefits to a firm even when it could produce the same quantity of output without polluting as much.
   c. Define the socially optimal level of pollution.
   (4 points)

Externalities in Markets for Goods and Services

In this Module, you will learn to:
- Differentiate private benefits and costs from social benefits and costs
- Explain the effects of externalities in markets for goods and services
- Apply Pigouvian taxes and subsidies

Production, Consumption, and Externalities

Nobody imposes external costs out of malice. Pollution, traffic congestion, and other negative externalities are side effects of activities that are otherwise desirable, like electricity generation, manufacturing, or driving. We've just learned how government regulators can move the market to the socially optimal quantity when the externalities can be directly controlled. But in some cases it's not possible to directly control

A flock of positive externalities.

Peter Barritt/Alamy

the externalities—only the activities that cause them can be influenced. In these situations, government policies must be geared to changing the levels of production and consumption that create externalities, which in turn changes the levels of the externalities themselves.

This approach, although slightly more complicated, has several advantages. First, for activities that generate external *costs*, it gives us a clear understanding of how the desirable activity is affected by policies designed to manage its side effects. Second, it helps us think about a question that is different but related to the problem of external costs: what should be done when an activity generates external *benefits*. It's important to remember that not all externalities are negative. In fact, we encounter many positive externalities every day; for example, a neighbor's bird-feeder has the external benefit of maintaining the local wild bird population for everyone's enjoyment. And a beautiful flower garden in front of a neighbor's house can be enjoyed by many passersby.

Using the approach of targeting the activity behind the externalities, we'll now turn our attention to the topic of positive externalities.

Private Versus Social Benefits

Flu shots are another source of positive externalities because getting a flu shot provides benefits to people beyond the person getting the shot. Under some conditions, getting a flu vaccination reduces the expected number of *other* people who get the flu by as much as 1.5 people. This prompted one economist to suggest a new T-shirt slogan, one particularly suited for the winter months: "Kiss Me, I'm Vaccinated!" When you get vaccinated against the flu, it's likely that you're conferring a substantial benefit on those around you—a benefit for others that you are not compensated for. In other words, getting a flu shot generates a positive externality.

The government can directly control the external costs of pollution because it can measure emissions. In contrast, it can't observe the reduction in flu cases caused by you getting a flu shot, so it can't directly control the external benefits—say, by rewarding you based on how many fewer people caught the flu because of your actions. So if the government wants to influence the level of external benefits from flu vaccinations, it must target the original activity—getting a flu shot.

From the point of view of society as a whole, a flu shot carries both costs (the price you pay for the shot, which compensates the vaccine maker and your health care provider for the inputs and factors of production necessary to grow the vaccine and deliver it to your bloodstream) and benefits. Those benefits include the private benefit that accrues to you from not getting the flu yourself, but they also include the external benefits that accrue to others from a lower likelihood of catching the flu.

So far we have studied goods in the absence of external benefits, so the marginal benefit to the consumer has been no different from the marginal benefit to society. When a good like a flu shot creates positive externalities, we call the marginal benefit to the consumer the **marginal private benefit**. Module 74 explained that the marginal benefit to society is called the *marginal social benefit*. The difference between the marginal private benefit (*MPB*) and the marginal social benefit (*MSB*) is the **marginal external benefit** (*MEB*) that indicates the increase in external benefits to society from one additional unit of the good:

$$(75\text{-}1) \quad MSB = MPB + MEB$$

The demand curve represents the marginal benefit that accrues to *consumers of the good*: the marginal private benefit. It does not incorporate the benefits to society as a whole from consuming the good—in this case, the reduction in the number of flu cases.

The **marginal private benefit** of a good is the marginal benefit that accrues to consumers of a good, not including any external benefits.

The **marginal external benefit** of a good is the addition to external benefits created by one more unit of the good.

Figure 75.1 shows that the marginal social benefit curve, *MSB*, corresponds to the demand and marginal private benefit curve, $D = MPB$, *shifted upward* by the amount of the marginal external benefit.

Figure 75.1 Positive Externalities and Consumption

Consumption of flu shots generates external benefits, so the marginal social benefit curve, *MSB*, of flu shots, is above the demand and marginal private benefit curve, $D = MPB$, by the amount of the marginal external benefit. Without government action, the market produces Q_{MKT}. The market quantity is lower than the socially optimal quantity of consumption, Q_{OPT}, at which the marginal social benefit equals the marginal social cost (*MSC*). At Q_{MKT}, the marginal social benefit of another flu shot, P_{MSB}, is greater than the marginal private benefit to consumers of another flu shot, P_{MKT}. The yellow deadweight loss area represents the lost opportunities for net gains that could be achieved by producing Q_{OPT} rather than Q_{MKT}. A Pigouvian subsidy to consumers, equal to the marginal external benefit, moves consumption to Q_{OPT} by lowering the price paid by consumers to P_{CNS} and raising the price received by producers to P_{OPT}.

Recall that in a competitive market, the market supply curve is the horizontal sum of the individual firms' supply curves, which are the same as their marginal cost curves. So the market supply curve, *S*, indicates the marginal cost to firms (identified in the next section as the *marginal private cost, MPC*). Because there are no external costs, the marginal cost to firms is also the marginal social cost, *MSC*. That is, with no external costs, $S = MPC = MSC$.

An individual has no incentive to consider the external benefits generated by his or her actions. As a result, in the absence of government intervention, too few people will choose to be vaccinated. Figure 75.1 illustrates this point. In the absence of government intervention, the market equilibrium will be at point E_{MKT}, with Q_{MKT} flu shots being bought and sold at the market price of P_{MKT}. At that point, the marginal cost to society of another flu shot is equal to the marginal benefit gained by the individual consumer who purchases that flu shot, measured by the market price.

With the marginal social benefit curve and the marginal social cost curve, we can find the socially optimal quantity of a good or activity that generates external benefits: it is the quantity Q_{OPT} that corresponds to point *O* at which the marginal social benefit equals the marginal social cost. Because the external benefit is not accounted for in market decisions, Q_{MKT} is less than Q_{OPT}. The yellow deadweight loss

Your flu shot provides positive externalities to those whom you would otherwise make sick.

area represents the lost opportunities for net gains that could be achieved by producing Q_{OPT} rather than Q_{MKT}.

Left to its own, a market will bring about too little production and consumption of a good or activity that generates external benefits. Correspondingly, without government action, the price to consumers of such a good or activity is too high: at the market output level Q_{MKT}, the unregulated market price is P_{MKT} and the marginal benefit to consumers of an additional flu shot is lower than P_{MSB}, the true marginal benefit to society of an additional flu shot.

Pigouvian Subsidies

> A **Pigouvian subsidy** is a payment designed to correct for the effects of external benefits.

How can the economy be induced to produce Q_{OPT}, the socially optimal level of flu shots shown in Figure 75.1? Economist Arthur Pigou emphasized the usefulness of subsidies and taxes to guide decision makers to socially optimal outcomes. A **Pigouvian subsidy** is a payment designed to correct for the effects of external benefits. The optimal Pigouvian subsidy, shown in Figure 75.1, is equal to the marginal external benefit of consuming another unit of flu shots. In this example, a Pigouvian subsidy works by lowering the price consumers pay to P_{CNS} and raising the price producers receive to P_{OPT}: consumers pay a price for a flu shot that is equal to the price the producers receive *minus* the subsidy. Many high schools, colleges, and communities offer subsidized flu shots in hopes of reaching the socially optimal level in a way that would make Pigou proud.

Technology Spillover

> A **technology spillover** is an external benefit that results when new technological knowledge spreads among firms.

The most important single source of external benefits in the modern economy is the creation of knowledge. In high-tech industries such as the semiconductor, software design, and bioengineering industries, innovations by one firm are quickly emulated by rival firms and put to use in the development of further advancements in related industries. This spreading of cutting-edge technological information among firms is known as **technology spillover**. Such spillovers often take place through face-to-face contact. For example, bars and restaurants in California's Silicon Valley are famed for their technical chitchat. Workers know that the best way to keep up with the latest technological innovations is to hang around in the right places, have a drink, and gossip. Such informal contact helps to spread useful knowledge to other firms, which may also explain why so many high-tech firms are clustered close to one another.

> The **marginal private cost** of a good is the marginal cost of producing that good, not including any external costs.

Private Versus Social Costs

Now let's consider a case in which the production of a good creates external costs—namely, the livestock industry. Whatever it is—cows, pigs, chicken, sheep, or salmon—livestock farming produces prodigious amounts of what is euphemistically known as "muck." But that's not all: scientists estimate that the amount of methane gas produced by livestock currently rivals the amount caused by the burning of fossil fuels in the creation of greenhouse gases. From the point of view of society as a whole, then, the cost of livestock farming includes both direct production costs (payments for factors of production and inputs) and the external environmental costs imposed as a by-product of farming.

When a good like pork involves negative externalities, there is a difference between the marginal cost to the *firm*, which we distinguish as the **marginal private cost**, and the marginal cost to *society*, the marginal social cost of the good (or likewise of a service or activity). The difference between the marginal private cost (*MPC*) and the marginal social cost (*MSC*) is the

The social cost of livestock production is felt beyond the farm.

Photodisc/Getty images

marginal external cost (MEC)—the increase in external costs to society from an additional unit of the good:

The **marginal external cost** of a good is the increase in external costs to society created by one more unit of the good.

$$(75\text{-}2) \quad MSC = MPC + MEC$$

Figure 75.2 shows the marginal social cost curve, *MSC*, of livestock; it corresponds to the industry supply and marginal private cost curve, *S = MPC*, *shifted upward* by the amount of the marginal external cost. In the absence of government intervention, the market equilibrium will be at point E_{MKT}, yielding an equilibrium quantity of Q_{MKT} and an equilibrium price of P_{MKT}.

Figure 75.2 Negative Externalities and Production

Livestock production generates external costs, so the marginal social cost curve, *MSC*, of livestock, corresponds to the supply and marginal private cost curve, *S = MPC*, shifted upward by the marginal external cost. Without government action, the market produces the quantity Q_{MKT}. That market quantity is greater than the socially optimal quantity of livestock production, Q_{OPT}, at which the marginal social cost equals the marginal social benefit. At Q_{MKT}, the market price, P_{MKT}, is less than P_{MSC}, the true marginal cost to society of livestock production. The yellow deadweight loss area represents society's net losses from producing Q_{OPT} rather than Q_{MKT}. A Pigouvian tax on livestock production equal to its marginal external cost moves the production to Q_{OPT} by raising the price paid by consumers to P_{OPT} and lowering the price received by producers to P_{PRD}.

The ever-important socially optimal quantity of a good is the quantity at which *the marginal social benefit equals the marginal social cost*. In the livestock example, this criterion is met at point *O*, where the *MSC* curve crosses the *D = MPB = MSB* curve. Why does the demand curve also represent the marginal private benefit and marginal social benefit curves in this case? Because although the demand curve represents the marginal benefit to consumers—the marginal private benefit—there are no external benefits to separate the marginal private benefit from the marginal social benefit. That means that when *MSC = D* and there are no external benefits, it is also true that *MSC = MPB = MSB*.

Unfortunately, the market equilibrium quantity Q_{MKT} is greater than Q_{OPT}, the socially optimal quantity of livestock. The yellow deadweight loss area represents society's net losses from producing Q_{OPT} rather than Q_{MKT}.

Left to its own, the market produces too much of a good that generates an external cost in production, and the price to consumers of such a good is too low: P_{MKT} is less than P_{MSC}, the true marginal cost to society of another unit of livestock. A tax can bring decision makers to internalize negative externalities. Taxes designed to correct

AP® EXAM TIP

When a positive externality exists, the socially optimal quantity is higher than the market equilibrium quantity and the deadweight loss triangle points to the right. When a negative externality exists, the socially optimal quantity is lower than the market equilibrium quantity and the deadweight loss triangle points to the left.

Taxes designed to correct for the effects of external costs are known as **Pigouvian taxes**.

A good is subject to a **network externality** when the value of the good to an individual depends on how many other people also use the good.

for the effects of external costs are known as **Pigouvian taxes**. As Figure 75.2 shows, an optimal Pigouvian tax on livestock production, equal to the marginal external cost, moves the market to the socially optimal level of production, Q_{OPT}. The Pigouvian tax works by raising the price paid by consumers to P_{OPT} and lowering the price received by producers to P_{PRD}: the consumers pay a price equal to what the producers receive *plus* the tax.

Network Externalities

There is one type of externality that has no inherently favorable or adverse effect on society at large, but does affect other users of the associated good or service. Suppose you were the only user of Twitter in the world. What would it be worth to you? The answer, of course, is nothing. Twitter derives its value only from the fact that other people also use Twitter and you can send or receive tweets. In general, the more people who use Twitter, the more valuable it is to you.

A **network externality** exists when the value to an individual of a good or service depends on how many other people use the same good or service. Sometimes referred to as the "fax machine effect," the phenomenon of network externalities is so named because the classic examples involve networks of telephones, computers, and transportation systems. When it comes to sharing digital information, it helps to have more users of the same software, hardware, and online networking services. In other contexts, it's better to have more users of the same stock exchanges, gauges of railroad line, and sizes of electrical plugs, among many examples. Congestion creates a form of negative network externality: it can make things worse for you when more people use the same highway, elevator, swimming pool, or computer network.

The private benefit of network externalities, like Twitter and other social media platforms, depends on others using it.

MODULE 75 REVIEW

Adventures in AP® Economics

Watch the video: *Externalities and Deadweight Loss*

Check Your Understanding

1. When is the supply curve also the marginal social cost curve? When they are not the same, what specific measure indicates the distance between these two curves?

2. For each of the following cases, explain whether an external cost or an external benefit is created and identify an appropriate policy response.

a. Trees planted in urban areas improve air quality and lower summer temperatures.

b. Water-saving toilets reduce the need to pump water from rivers and aquifers. The cost of a gallon of water to homeowners is virtually zero.

c. Old computer monitors contain toxic materials that pollute the environment when improperly disposed of.

TACKLE THE AP® TEST: Multiple-Choice Questions

1. When there are no external benefits, the demand curve is also which of the following curves?
   a. *MSB*
   b. *MEB*
   c. *MPC*
   d. *MSC*
   e. *S*

2. An efficient Pigouvian subsidy for a good is set equal to the good's
   a. external cost.
   b. marginal social benefit.
   c. marginal external cost.
   d. marginal external benefit.
   e. price at which *MSC* = *MSB*.

3. Which of the following is true in the case of a positive externality?
   a. $MSC > MSB$
   b. $MPB > MSC$
   c. $MSB > MPB$
   d. $MPB > MSB$
   e. $MSC > MPC$

4. One example of a source of external benefits is
   a. technology spillover.
   b. traffic congestion.
   c. pollution.
   d. subsidies for polluters.
   e. taxes on environmental conservation.

5. Marginal social benefit equals marginal private benefit plus
   a. marginal external benefit.
   b. marginal private cost.
   c. total external benefit.
   d. total external cost.
   e. marginal social cost.

6. If external costs cause the socially optimal quantity to fall below the market quantity, the resulting deadweight loss is represented by the area between these two quantities that is
   a. above the MPC curve and below the MSC curve.
   b. above the MSB curve and below the MPC curve.
   c. above the MSB curve and below the MSC curve.
   d. above the S curve and below the D curve.
   e. above the MPC curve and below the MSB curve.

7. When you join Snapchat, the value of this social media platform increases for your friends who are already using Snapchat. This is an example of a
   a. negative externality.
   b. marginal external cost.
   c. Pigouvian subsidy.
   d. network externality.
   e. technology spillover.

TACKLE THE AP® TEST: Free-Response Questions

1. The purchase of antivirus software by one person provides benefits to other people because they are less likely to receive a virus from the software purchaser. Draw a correctly labeled graph showing how the market will determine the quantity of antivirus software purchased. On the same graph, show the socially optimal quantity of antivirus software. Shade and label the area that represents deadweight loss. List two different government policies that could bring about the optimal quantity of antivirus software.

1 point: Upward-sloping supply (or equivalently, marginal cost) curve (Note that with no external costs, marginal private cost equals marginal social cost.)

1 point: Downward-sloping demand (or equivalently, marginal private benefit) curve

1 point: The market quantity of antivirus software is found at the intersection of supply and demand and shown on the horizontal axis.

1 point: Downward-sloping marginal social benefit curve drawn above demand curve

1 point: The optimal quantity of antivirus software is found at the intersection of supply and marginal social benefit and shown on the horizontal axis.

1 point: The correct deadweight-loss area is shaded and labeled.

1 point: A Pigouvian subsidy equal to the marginal external benefit at the socially optimal quantity

1 point: A government regulation requiring the optimal quantity of antivirus software

Rubric for FRQ 1 (9 points)

1 point: Vertical axis labeled "Price, marginal social benefit" or "Dollars per unit," horizontal axis labeled "Quantity of antivirus software" or "Q"

2. The use of plastic water bottles creates external costs as the result of plastic production, bottle transportation, litter, and waste disposal. Draw a correctly labeled graph showing how the market will determine the quantity of water bottles purchased. On the same graph, show the marginal external cost, the socially optimal quantity of water bottles, and the size of a Pigouvian tax that could be used to achieve the socially optimal quantity of water bottles. **(6 points)**

Public Goods

In this Module, you will learn to:
- Characterize public goods and explain why markets fail to supply efficient quantities of public goods
- Define common resources and explain why they are overused
- Define artificially scarce goods and explain why they are underconsumed
- Describe how government intervention in the production and consumption of these types of goods can make society better off
- Discuss why finding the right level of government intervention is often difficult

In this Module we examine another important reason markets sometimes fail. Here we focus on how the characteristics of goods often determine whether markets can deliver them efficiently. When goods have the "wrong" characteristics, the resulting market failures resemble those associated with externalities or market power. After a close look at these additional sources of inefficiency we will consider solutions that can improve the well-being of society.

Private Goods—and Others

What is the difference between installing a new bathroom in a house and building a municipal sewage system? What is the difference between growing apples and fishing in the open ocean?

These are not trick questions. In each case there is a basic difference in the characteristics of the goods involved. Bathroom appliances and apples have the characteristics necessary to allow markets to work efficiently. Public sewage systems and fish in the sea do not.

Let's look at these crucial characteristics and why they matter.

Characteristics of Goods

Goods like bathroom fixtures and apples have two characteristics that are essential if a good is to be provided in efficient quantities by a market economy.

- They are **excludable**: suppliers of the good can prevent people who do not pay from consuming it.

- They are **rival in consumption**: the same unit of the good cannot be consumed by more than one person at the same time.

When a good is both excludable and rival in consumption, it is called a **private good**. Apples are an example of a private good. They are *excludable*: the farmer can sell a bushel to one consumer without having to provide apples to everyone in the community. And they are *rival in consumption*: if I eat an apple, that apple cannot be consumed by someone else.

Not all goods possess these two characteristics. Some goods are **nonexcludable**—the supplier cannot prevent consumption of the good by people who do not pay for it. Fire protection is one example: a fire department that puts out fires before they spread protects the whole city, not just people who have made contributions to the Firemen's Benevolent Association. An improved environment is another: pollution can't be ended for some users of a river while leaving the river foul for others.

Nor are all goods rival in consumption. Goods are **nonrival in consumption** if more than one person can consume the same unit of the good at the same time. TV programs

Zoonar GmbH/Alamy

A good is **excludable** if the supplier of that good can prevent people who do not pay from consuming it.

A good is **rival in consumption** if the same unit of the good cannot be consumed by more than one person at the same time.

A good that is both excludable and rival in consumption is a **private good**.

When a good is **nonexcludable**, the supplier cannot prevent consumption by people who do not pay for it.

A good is **nonrival in consumption** if more than one person can consume the same unit of the good at the same time.

are nonrival in consumption: your decision to watch a show does not prevent other people from watching the same show.

Because goods can be either excludable or nonexcludable, and either rival or nonrival in consumption, there are four types of goods, illustrated by the matrix in **Figure 76.1**:

- *Private goods*, which are excludable and rival in consumption, like apples
- *Public goods*, which are nonexcludable and nonrival in consumption, like a public sewer system
- *Common resources*, which are nonexcludable but rival in consumption, like fish in the ocean
- *Artificially scarce goods*, which are excludable but nonrival in consumption, like songs from music-streaming services such as Spotify.

AP® EXAM TIP

Be prepared to classify goods according to the four different types for the AP® exam.

Figure 76.1 Four Types of Goods

	Rival in consumption	**Nonrival in consumption**
Excludable	**Private goods** • Apples • Bathroom fixtures	**Artificially scarce goods** • Streaming music • Computer software
Non-excludable	**Common resources** • Fish in the ocean • Clean river water	**Public goods** • Public sanitation • National defense

There are four types of goods. The type of a good depends on (1) whether or not it is excludable—whether a producer can prevent someone from consuming it; and (2) whether or not it is rival in consumption—whether it is impossible for the same unit of a good to be consumed by more than one person at the same time.

Of course there are many other characteristics that distinguish between types of goods—necessities versus luxuries, normal versus inferior, and so on. Why focus on whether goods are excludable and rival in consumption? We explore this question next.

Why Markets Can Supply Only Private Goods Efficiently

As we learned in earlier Modules, markets are typically the best means for a society to deliver goods and services to its members; that is, markets are efficient except in the case of market power, externalities, or other instances of market failure. One source of market failure is rooted in the nature of the good itself: markets cannot supply goods and services efficiently unless they are private goods—excludable and rival in consumption.

To see why excludability is crucial, suppose that a farmer had only two choices: either produce no apples or provide a bushel of apples to every resident of the community who wants it, whether or not that resident pays for it. It seems unlikely that anyone would grow apples under those conditions.

Yet the operator of a public sewage system consisting of pipes that anyone can dump sewage into faces pretty much the same problem as our hypothetical farmer. A sewage system makes the whole city cleaner and healthier—but that benefit accrues to all the city's residents, whether or not they pay the system operator. The general point is that if a good is nonexcludable, rational consumers won't be willing to pay for it—they will "free ride" on anyone who *does* pay. So there is a **free-rider problem**. Examples of the free-rider problem are familiar from daily life. One example you may have encountered happens when students are required to do a group project. There is often a tendency of some group members to shirk their responsibilities, relying on others in the group to get the work done. The shirkers *free-ride* on someone else's effort.

Goods that are nonexcludable suffer from the **free-rider problem**: individuals have no incentive to pay for their own consumption and instead will "free ride" on anyone who does pay.

When the benefits from a group project are nonexcludable, there is a temptation to free-ride on the efforts of others.

Because of the free-rider problem, the forces of self-interest alone do not lead to an efficient level of production for a nonexcludable good. Even though consumers would benefit from increased production of the good, no one individual is willing to pay for more, and so no producer is willing to supply it. The result is that nonexcludable goods suffer from *inefficiently low production* in a market economy. In fact, in the face of the free-rider problem, self-interest may not ensure that any amount of the good—let alone the efficient quantity—is produced.

Artificially scarce goods, which are excludable and nonrival in consumption, suffer from a different kind of inefficiency. As long as a good is excludable, it is possible to earn a profit by making it available only to those who pay. Therefore, producers are willing to supply an excludable good. Consider pay-per-view movies. The marginal cost of letting an additional viewer watch a pay-per-view movie is zero because it is nonrival in consumption. So the efficient price to the consumer is also zero—or, to put it another way, individuals should watch pay-per-view movies up to the point where their marginal benefit is zero. But if the movie provider actually charges viewers $4, viewers will consume the good only up to the point where their marginal benefit is $4. When consumers must pay a price greater than zero for a good that is nonrival in consumption, the price they pay is higher than the marginal cost of allowing them to consume that good, which is zero. So in a market economy goods that are nonrival in consumption suffer from *inefficiently low consumption*.

Now we can see why private goods are the only goods that will be produced and consumed in efficient quantities in a competitive market. (That is, a private good will be produced and consumed in efficient quantities in a market free of market power, externalities, and other sources of market failure.) Because private goods are excludable, producers can charge for them and so have an incentive to produce them. And because they are also rival in consumption, it is efficient for consumers to pay a positive price—a price equal to the marginal cost of production. If one or both of these characteristics are lacking, a market economy will lack the incentives to bring about efficient quantities of the good.

Yet there are crucial goods that don't meet these criteria—and in these cases, the government can offer assistance.

Public Goods

A **public good** is both nonexcludable and nonrival in consumption.

A **public good** is the exact opposite of a private good: it is both nonexcludable and nonrival in consumption. A public sewage system is an example of a public good: if a river is kept clean by piping sewage elsewhere, no one who lives near the river can be excluded from the benefits of clean water, and your protection from sewage contamination does not prevent your neighbor from being protected as well.

Here are some other examples of public goods:

- *Disease prevention.* When a disease is stamped out, no one can be excluded from the benefit, and one person's health doesn't prevent others from being healthy.

- *National defense.* A strong military protects all citizens.

- *Scientific research.* New findings that particular substances are dangerous or healthy provide widespread benefits that are not excludable or rival.

Because these goods are nonexcludable, they suffer from the free-rider problem, so private firms would produce inefficiently low quantities of them. And because they are nonrival in consumption, it would be inefficient to charge people for consuming them. As a result, society must find nonmarket methods for providing these goods.

Providing Public Goods

Public goods are provided in a variety of ways. The government doesn't always get involved—in many cases a non-governmental solution has been found for the free-rider problem. But these solutions are usually imperfect in some way.

Some public goods are supplied through voluntary contributions. For example, private donations help support public radio and a considerable amount of scientific research. But private donations are insufficient to finance large programs of great importance, such as the Centers for Disease Control and Prevention and national defense.

Some public goods are supplied by self-interested individuals or firms because those who produce them are able to make money in indirect ways. A classic example is radio broadcasts, which in most cases are supported entirely by advertising. The downside of such indirect funding is that it skews the nature

On the prowl: a British TV detection van checks for unlicensed TV viewers to prevent broadcast television from becoming a public good.

and quantity of the public goods that are supplied, while imposing additional costs on consumers. Radio stations broadcast the programs that yield the most advertising revenue, which are not necessarily the programs people most enjoy. And listeners must endure many commercials.

Some potentially public goods are deliberately made excludable and therefore subject to charge, like pay-per-view movies. In the United Kingdom, where most television programming is paid for by a yearly license fee assessed on every television owner (£150.50, or about $200 in 2018), television viewing is made excludable by the use of "television detection vans": vans that roam neighborhoods in an attempt to detect televisions in non-licensed households and fine them. However, as noted earlier, when suppliers charge a price greater than zero for a nonrival good, consumers will consume an inefficiently low quantity of that good.

In small communities, a high level of social encouragement or pressure can be brought to bear on people to contribute money or time to provide the efficient level of a public good. Volunteer fire departments, which depend both on the volunteered services of the firefighters themselves and on contributions from local residents, are a good example. But as communities grow larger and more anonymous, social pressure is increasingly difficult to apply, compelling larger towns and cities to tax residents and depend on salaried firefighters for fire protection services.

As this last example suggests, when other solutions fail, it is up to the government to provide public goods. Indeed, the most important public goods—national defense, the legal system, disease control, fire protection in large cities, and so on—are provided by the government and paid for by taxes. Economic theory tells us that the provision of public goods is one of the crucial roles of government.

How Much of a Public Good Should Be Provided?

In some cases, the provision of a public good is an "either–or" decision: a city can either have a sewage system—or not. But in most cases, governments must decide not only whether to provide a public good but also *how much* of that public good to provide. For example, street cleaning is a public good—but how often should the streets be cleaned? Once a month? Twice a month? Every other day?

Imagine a city with only two residents, Ted and Alice. Assume that the public good in question is street cleaning and that Ted and Alice truthfully tell the government how much they value a unit of the public good, one unit being one street cleaning per month. Specifically, each of them tells the government his or her *willingness to pay* for another unit of the public good supplied—an amount that corresponds to that individual's *marginal private benefit* from another unit of the public good.

Using this information along with information on the cost of providing the good, the government can use marginal analysis to find the efficient level of providing the public good: the level at which the *marginal social benefit* of the public good is equal to the marginal social cost of producing it. Recall that the marginal social benefit of a good is the benefit that accrues to society as a whole from the consumption of one additional unit of the good.

But what is the marginal social benefit of another unit of a public good—a unit that generates utility for *all* consumers, not just one consumer, because it is non-excludable and nonrival in consumption? This question leads us to an important principle: *In the special case of a public good, the marginal social benefit of a unit of the good is equal to the sum of the marginal private benefits enjoyed by all consumers of that unit.* Or to consider it from a slightly different angle, if a consumer could be compelled to pay for a unit before consuming it (the good is made excludable), then the marginal social benefit of a unit is equal to the *sum* of each consumer's willingness to pay for that unit. Using this principle, the marginal social benefit of an additional street cleaning per month is equal to Ted's marginal private benefit from that additional cleaning *plus* Alice's marginal private benefit.

Why? Because a public good is nonrival in consumption—Ted's benefit from a cleaner street does not diminish Alice's benefit from that same clean street, and vice versa. Because Ted and Alice can simultaneously "consume" the same unit of street cleaning, the marginal social benefit is the *sum* of their marginal private benefits. And the efficient quantity of a public good is the quantity at which the marginal social benefit is equal to the marginal social cost of providing it.

Figure 76.2 illustrates the efficient provision of a public good, showing three marginal benefit curves. Panel (a) shows Ted's marginal private benefit curve from street cleaning, MPB_T: he would be willing to pay $25 for the city to clean its streets once a month, an additional $18 to have it done a second time, and so on. Panel (b) shows Alice's marginal private benefit curve from street cleaning, MPB_A. Panel (c) shows the marginal social benefit curve from street cleaning, MSB: it is the vertical sum of Ted's and Alice's marginal private benefit curves, MPB_T and MPB_A.

To maximize society's welfare, the government should increase the quantity of street cleanings until the marginal social benefit of an additional cleaning would fall below the marginal social cost. Suppose that the marginal social cost is $6 per cleaning. Then the city should clean its streets 5 times per month, because the marginal social benefit of each of the first 5 cleanings is more than $6, but going from 5 to 6 cleanings would yield a marginal social benefit of only $2, which is less than the marginal social cost.

One fundamental rationale for the existence of government is that it provides a way for citizens to tax themselves in order to provide public goods—particularly a vital public good like national defense.

Of course, if society really consisted of only two individuals, they would probably manage to strike a deal to provide the good. But imagine a city with a million residents, each of whose marginal private benefit from a good is only a tiny fraction of the marginal social benefit. It would be impossible for people to reach a voluntary agreement to pay for the efficient level of a good like street cleaning—the potential for free-riding would make it too difficult to make and enforce an agreement among so many people. But they could and would vote to tax themselves to pay for a citywide sanitation department.

Voting as a Public Good

As the economist Mancur Olson pointed out in his famous book *The Logic of Collective Action: Pubilc Goods and the Theory of Groups*, voting is a public good, one that suffers from severe free-rider problems. It's a sad fact that many Americans who are eligible to vote don't bother to. As a result, their interests tend to be ignored by politicians. But what's even sadder is that this self-defeating behavior may be completely rational.

Imagine that you are one of a million people who would stand to gain the equivalent of $100 each if a plan to improve public schools is passed in a statewide referendum.

Figure 76.2 A Public Good

(a) Ted's Marginal Private Benefit Curve

Marginal benefit

$25, 18, 12, 7, 3, 1

MPB_T

Quantity of street cleanings (per month)

(b) Alice's Marginal Private Benefit Curve

Marginal benefit

$21, 17, 13, 9, 5, 1

MPB_A

Quantity of street cleanings (per month)

(c) The Marginal Social Benefit Curve

Marginal benefit, marginal cost

$46, 35, 25, 16, 8, 2, 1

21, 17, 13, 9, 5, 1

25, 18, 12, 7, 3

The marginal social benefit curve of a public good equals the vertical sum of private marginal benefit curves.

MSB

$MSC = \$6$

Efficient quantity of the public good

Quantity of street cleanings (per month)

Panel (a) shows Ted's marginal private benefit curve, MPB_T, and panel (b) shows Alice's marginal private benefit curve, MPB_A. Panel (c) shows the marginal social benefit of the public good, equal to the *sum* of the marginal private benefits to all consumers (in this case, Ted and Alice). The marginal social benefit curve, MSB, is the vertical sum of the marginal private benefit curves MPB_T and MPB_A. At a constant marginal social cost of $6, there should be 5 street cleanings per month, because the marginal social benefit of going from 4 to 5 cleanings is $8 ($3 for Ted plus $5 for Alice), but the marginal social benefit of going from 5 to 6 cleanings is only $2.

And suppose that the opportunity cost of the time it would take you to vote is $10. Will you be sure to go to the polls and vote for the referendum? If you are rational, the answer is no! The reason is that it is very unlikely that your vote will decide the issue, and the benefits of the measure are nonexcludable: You benefit if the measure passes, even if you didn't bother to vote. If the measure doesn't pass, your vote would not have changed the outcome. Either way, by not voting—by free-riding on those who do vote—you save $10.

Of course, many people do vote out of a sense of civic duty. But because political action is a public good, in general people devote too little effort to defending their own interests. Is this a reason to distrust democracy? Winston Churchill said it best: "Democracy is the worst form of government, except for all the other forms that have been tried."

Common Resources

A **common resource** is a good that is nonexcludable but is rival in consumption. An example is the stock of fish in a fishing area, like the fisheries off the coast of New England. Traditionally, anyone with a boat could go out to sea and catch fish—fish in the sea were a nonexcludable good. Yet the total number of fish is limited: the fish that one person catches are no longer available to be caught by someone else. So fish in the sea are rival in consumption.

Other examples of common resources include clean air, water, and the diversity of animal and plant species on the planet (biodiversity). In each of these cases the fact that the good is rival in consumption, and yet nonexcludable, poses a serious problem.

The Problem of Overuse

Because common resources are nonexcludable, individuals cannot be charged for their use. But the resources are rival in consumption, so an individual who uses a unit depletes the resource by making that unit unavailable to others. As a result, a common resource is subject to **overuse**: an individual will continue to use it until his or her marginal private benefit is equal to his or her marginal private cost, ignoring the cost that this action inflicts on society as a whole.

Fish are a classic example of an overused common resource. Particularly in heavily fished waters, each fisher's catch imposes a cost on others by reducing the fish population and making it harder for others to catch fish. But fishers have no personal incentive to take this cost into account. As a result, from society's point of view, too many fish are caught. Traffic congestion is another example of overuse of a common resource. A major highway during rush hour can accommodate only a certain number of vehicles per hour. Each person who decides to drive to work alone, rather than carpool or work at home, causes many other people to have a longer commute, but there is no incentive for individual drivers to take these consequences into account.

In the case of a common resource, as in the earlier examples involving marginal external costs, the *marginal social cost* of your use of that resource is higher than your *marginal private cost*, the cost to you of using an additional unit of the good. **Figure 76.3** illustrates this point. It shows the demand curve for fish, which measures

AP® EXAM TIP

For the AP® exam, you should be able to explain and identify solutions to the overuse of common resources.

Figure 76.3   A Common Resource

The supply curve S, which shows the marginal private cost of production of the fishing industry, is composed of the individual supply curves of the individual fishers. But each fisher's marginal private cost does not include the cost that his or her actions impose on others: the depletion of the common resource. As a result, the marginal social cost curve, *MSC*, lies above the supply curve; in an unregulated market, the quantity of the common resource used, Q_{MKT}, exceeds the efficient quantity of use, Q_{OPT}.

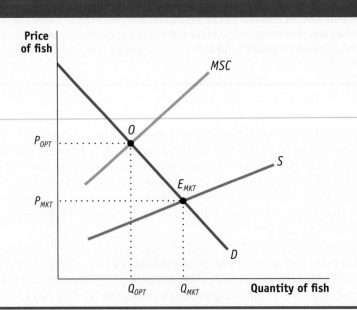

the marginal private benefit of fish (as well as the marginal social benefit because there are no external benefits from catching and consuming fish). The figure also shows the supply curve for fish, which measures the marginal private cost of production in the fishing industry. We know that the industry supply curve is the horizontal sum of each individual fisher's supply curve—equivalent to his or her marginal private cost curve. The fishing industry supplies the quantity Q_{MKT} at which its marginal private cost equals the price. But the efficient quantity is Q_{OPT}, the quantity of fish that equates the marginal social benefit (as indicated by the demand curve) to the marginal social cost, not to the fishing industry's marginal private cost of production. Thus, the market outcome results in overuse of the common resource.

As we noted, there is a close parallel between the problem of managing a common resource and the problem posed by negative externalities. In the case of an activity that generates a negative externality, the marginal social cost of production is greater than the marginal private cost of production, the difference being the marginal external cost imposed on society. Here, the loss to society arising from a fisher's depletion of the common resource plays the same role as the external cost when there is a negative externality. In fact, many negative externalities (such as pollution) can be thought of as involving common resources (such as clean air).

The Efficient Use and Maintenance of a Common Resource

Because common resources pose problems similar to those created by negative externalities, the solutions are also similar. To ensure efficient use of a common resource, society must find a way to get individual users of the resource to take into account the costs they impose on others. This is the same principle as that of getting individuals to internalize a negative externality that arises from their actions.

There are three principal ways to induce people who use common resources to internalize the costs they impose on others:

- Tax or otherwise regulate the use of the common resource
- Create a system of tradable licenses for the right to use the common resource
- Make the common resource excludable and assign property rights to some individuals

The first two solutions overlap with the approaches to private goods with negative externalities. Just as governments use Pigouvian excise taxes to temper the consumption of alcohol, they use alternative forms of Pigouvian taxes to reduce the use of common resources. For example, in London and elsewhere there are "congestion charges" on those who drive during rush hour, in effect charging them for the use of highway space, a common resource. Likewise, visitors to national parks in the United States must pay an entry fee that is essentially a Pigouvian tax.

A second way to correct the problem of overuse is to create a system of tradable licenses for the use of the common resource, much like the tradable emissions permit systems designed to address negative externalities. The policy maker issues the number of licenses that corresponds to the efficient level of use of the good. For example, hundreds of fisheries around the world have adopted *individual transferable quotas* that are effectively licenses to catch a certain quantity of fish. Making the

If it weren't for fees and restrictions, some common resources would be overrun.

licenses tradable ensures that the right to use the good is allocated efficiently—that is, those who end up using the good (those willing to pay the most for a license) are those who gain the most from its use.

But when it comes to common resources, often the most natural solution is simply to assign property rights. At a fundamental level, common resources are subject to overuse because *nobody owns them*. The essence of ownership of a good—the *property right* over the good—is that you can limit who can and cannot use the good as well as how much of it can be used. When a good is nonexcludable, in a very real sense no one owns it because a property right cannot be enforced—and consequently no one has an incentive to use it efficiently. So one way to correct the problem of overuse is to make the good excludable and assign property rights over it to someone. The good now has an owner who has an incentive to protect the value of the good—to use it efficiently rather than overuse it. This solution is applicable when currently nonexcludable goods can be made excludable, as with the privatization of parks and even roads, but it cannot be applied to resources that are inherently nonexcludable, including the air and flowing water.

Artificially Scarce Goods

An **artificially scarce good** is a good that is excludable but nonrival in consumption.

An **artificially scarce good** is a good that is excludable but nonrival in consumption. As we've already seen, pay-per-view movies are a familiar example. The marginal cost to society of allowing an individual to watch a movie is zero because one person's viewing doesn't interfere with another person's viewing. Yet cable companies and movie-streaming services prevent an individual from seeing a movie if he or she hasn't paid. Goods like computer software and audio files, which are valued for the information they embody (and are sometimes called "information goods"), are also artificially scarce.

Markets will supply artificially scarce goods because their excludability allows firms to charge people for them. However, since the efficient price is equal to the marginal cost of zero and the actual price is something higher than that, the good is "artificially scarce" and consumption is inefficiently low. The problem is that, unless the producer can somehow earn revenue from producing and selling the good, none will be produced, which is likely to be worse than a positive but inefficiently low quantity.

We have seen that, in the cases of public goods, common resources, and artificially scarce goods, a market economy will not provide adequate incentives for efficient levels of production and consumption. Fortunately for the sake of market efficiency, most goods are private goods. Food, clothing, shelter, and most other desirable things in life are excludable and rival in consumption, so the types of market failure discussed in this module are important exceptions rather than the norm.

MODULE 76 REVIEW

Check Your Understanding

1. For each of the following goods, indicate whether it is excludable, whether it is rival in consumption, and what kind of good it is.
   a. a public space such as a park
   b. a cheese burrito
   c. information from a website that is password-protected
   d. publicly announced information about the path of an incoming hurricane

2. Which of the goods in Question 1 will be provided by a private producer without government intervention? Which will not be? Explain your answer.

TACKLE THE AP® TEST: Multiple-Choice Questions

1. Which of the following types of goods are always nonrival in consumption?
   a. public goods
   b. private goods
   c. common resources
   d. inferior goods
   e. goods provided by the government

2. The free-rider problem occurs in the case of
   a. private goods.
   b. common resources.
   c. artificially scarce goods.
   d. motorcycles.
   e. all of the above.

3. Public goods are provided through which of the following means?
   a. the government only
   b. voluntary contributions only
   c. self-interested individuals and firms only
   d. the government and voluntary contributions only
   e. the government, voluntary contributions, and self-interested individuals and firms

4. Market provision of a public good will lead to
   a. the efficient quantity of the good and an inefficiently high price.
   b. the efficient quantity of the good and the efficient price.
   c. an inefficiently high quantity of the good and the efficient price.
   d. an inefficiently low quantity of the good and an inefficiently high price.
   e. an inefficiently high quantity of the good and an inefficiently low price.

5. The Pineland community has a public forest where citizens can harvest (cut down) as many trees as they desire. Which of the following would most likely worsen the overuse of this common resource?
   a. a Pigouvian tax on each tree harvested
   b. a government regulation that bans chainsaws in the forest
   c. tradable licenses for tree harvesting
   d. the assignment of property rights to the forest
   e. a subsidy for tree harvesting

6. A common resource is
   a. excludable and nonrival in consumption.
   b. excludable and rival in consumption.
   c. nonexcludable and nonrival in consumption.
   d. nonexcludable and rival in consumption.
   e. a public good that is excludable.

7. The marginal social benefit curve for a public good is the
   a. horizontal sum of the marginal private benefit curves of all consumers.
   b. vertical sum of the marginal private benefit curves of all consumers.
   c. horizontal sum of the marginal external benefit curves of all consumers.
   d. vertical sum of the marginal external benefit curves of all consumers.
   e. demand curve of the consumer who values the public good the most.

TACKLE THE AP® TEST: Free-Response Questions

1. Suppose Austin and Ally are the only soccer enthusiasts in a small town where any number of public soccer clinics could be put on by visiting experts for $80 each. There are no external costs involved. Austin's marginal private benefit curve for soccer clinics is horizontal at $60. Ally's marginal private benefit curve is a straight line starting at $100 on the vertical axis and ending at 10 clinics on the horizontal axis. Draw a correctly labeled graph for soccer clinics showing the marginal social cost, the marginal social benefit, and each resident's marginal private benefit. Label the quantity of clinics that Austin would purchase if he were the only resident as Q_{Austin}. Label the quantity of clinics that Ally would purchase if she were the only resident as Q_{Ally}. Label the optimal quantity of clinics for society as $Q_{Optimal}$.

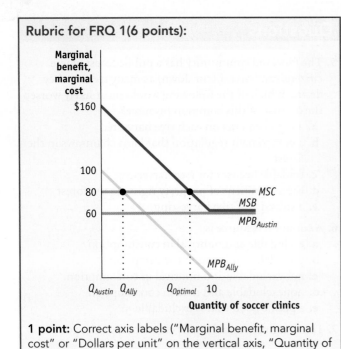
2. Imagine that the city of Townville has 1,000 residents and, as a public good for the benefit of every member of the community, pays $100,000 per year to rent equipment to fight a serious problem with mosquitoes.
   a. Identify and explain the two characteristics shared by every public good.
   b. Suppose a new resident moves to Townville. What is the additional cost of providing the public good to the new community member? Explain. **(6 points)**

MOD 77

Public Policy to Promote Competition

In this Module, you will learn to:

- Identify the three major antitrust laws and describe how they are used to promote competition
- Explain how government regulation is used to prevent inefficiency in the case of natural monopoly
- Discuss the pros and cons of using marginal cost pricing and average cost pricing to regulate prices in natural monopolies

Promoting Competition

We have seen that, in general, equilibrium in a competitive market with no externalities is efficient. On the other hand, imperfectly competitive markets—for example, those with a monopoly or an oligopoly—generally create inefficient outcomes. Concern about the higher prices, lower quantities, and lower quality of goods that can result from imperfect competition has led to public policies to promote competition. These policies include antitrust laws and direct government regulation.

Public policy toward monopoly depends crucially on whether or not the industry in question is a natural monopoly. The most common approach to a natural monopoly is for the government to allow one firm to exist but to regulate that firm to increase the quantity and lower the price relative to the monopoly outcome.

In this Module, we first focus on ways to promote competition in cases that don't involve natural monopolies. If the industry is *not* a natural monopoly, the best policy is to prevent a monopoly from arising or to break it up if it already exists. These policies are carried out through antitrust laws. Later in this Module we will turn to the more difficult problem of dealing with a natural monopoly.

Antitrust Policy

As we discussed in Module 66, imperfect competition first became an issue in the United States during the second half of the nineteenth century when industrialists formed trusts to facilitate monopoly pricing. By having shareholders place their shares in the hands of a board of trustees, major companies in effect merged into a single firm. That is, they created monopolies.

Eventually, there was a public backlash, driven partly by concern about the economic effects of the trust movement and partly by fear that the owners of the trusts were simply becoming too powerful. The result was the Sherman Antitrust Act of 1890, which was intended both to prevent the creation of more monopolies and to break up existing ones. Following the Sherman Act, the government passed several other acts intended to clarify antitrust policy.

The Sherman Antitrust Act of 1890

Credit card companies charge merchants "swipe fees" of roughly 1.5% to 3.5% of the purchase price for accepting payments with their card. When the American Express Company barred merchants from offering discounts to customers who use credit cards with lower swipe fees, and from educating consumers about how different companies charge different fees, merchants cried foul. In support of the merchants, the U.S. Department of Justice and many state attorneys general argued that these rules hindered competition among credit card companies that could bring the fees down.

These plaintiffs sought protection under the cornerstone of U.S. antitrust policy, the Sherman Antitrust Act. This act was the first of three major federal antitrust laws in the United States, followed by the Clayton Antitrust Act and the Federal Trade Commission Act, both passed in 1914. The Department of Justice, which has an Antitrust Division charged with enforcing antitrust laws, describes the goals of antitrust laws as protecting competition, ensuring lower prices, and promoting the development of new and better products. It emphasizes that firms in competitive markets attract consumers by cutting prices and increasing the quality of products or services. Competition and profit opportunities also stimulate businesses to find new and more efficient production methods.

Credit card companies that take steps to prevent competition may find themselves in violation of antitrust laws.

The Sherman Antitrust Act of 1890 has two important provisions, each of which outlaws a particular type of activity. The first provision makes it illegal to create a contract, combination, or conspiracy that unreasonably restrains interstate trade. The second provision outlaws the monopolization of any part of interstate commerce. In addition, under the law, the Department of Justice is empowered to bring civil claims and criminal prosecutions when the law is violated. Indeed, it was the Department of Justice that filed suit against Microsoft in the web browser case. The initial court ruling, by the way, was that Microsoft should be broken up into one company that sold Windows and another that sold other software components. After that ruling was overturned on appeal, a final settlement kept Microsoft intact but prohibited various forms of predatory behavior and practices that could create barriers to entry.

As the ambiguities of the Microsoft case suggest, the law provides little detail regarding what constitutes "restraining trade." And the law does not make it illegal to *be* a monopoly but to "monopolize," that is, to take illegal actions to become a monopoly. If you are the only firm in an industry because no other firm chooses to enter the market, you are not in violation of the Sherman Act.

The two provisions of the Sherman Act give very broad, general descriptions of the activities it makes illegal. The act does not provide details regarding specific actions or activities that it prohibits. The vague nature of the Sherman Act led to the subsequent passage of two additional major antitrust laws.

The Clayton Antitrust Act of 1914

The Clayton Antitrust Act of 1914 was intended to clarify the Sherman Act, which did not identify specific firm behaviors that were illegal. The Clayton Act outlaws four specific firm behaviors: price discrimination, anticompetitive practices, anticompetitive mergers and acquisitions, and interlocking directorates (two corporate boards of directors that share at least one director in common).

You are already familiar with the topic of price discrimination from our discussion of market structures. The Clayton Act makes it illegal for a firm to charge different prices to different customers for the same product. Obviously, there are exceptions to this rule that allow the price discrimination we see in practice, for example, at movie theaters where children pay a different price than adults.

By prohibiting the anticompetitive practice of *exclusive dealing*, the Clayton Act makes it illegal for a firm to refuse to do business with you just because you also do business with its competitors. If a firm had the dominant product in a given market, exclusive dealing could allow it to gain monopoly power in other markets. For example, a company that sells an extremely popular office desk—the only one of its kind—could set a condition that customers who want to purchase the desk must also purchase all of their office supplies from the company. This would allow the company to expand its existing market power into the market for office supplies.

The Clayton Act also outlaws *tying arrangements* because, if it did not, a firm could expand its monopoly power for a dominant product by "tying" the purchase of one product to the purchase of a dominant product in another market. Tying arrangements occur when a firm stipulates that it will sell you a specific product, say a printer, only if you buy something else, such as printer paper, at the same time. In this case, tying the printer and paper together expands the firm's printer market power into the market for paper. In this way, as with exclusive dealing, tying arrangements can lessen competition by allowing a firm to expand its market power from one market into another.

Mergers and acquisitions happen fairly often in the U.S. economy; most are not illegal despite stipulations in the Clayton Act. The Justice Department regularly reviews proposed mergers between companies in the same industry and, under the Clayton Act, bars any that they determine would significantly reduce competition. To evaluate proposed mergers, they often use measures discussed in Module 57: *concentration ratios* and the *Herfindahl–Hirschman Index*. But the Justice Department is not the only agency responsible for enforcing antitrust laws. Another of our major antitrust laws created and empowers the Federal Trade Commission to enforce antitrust laws.

The Federal Trade Commission Act of 1914

Passed in 1914, the Federal Trade Commission Act prohibits unfair methods of competition in interstate commerce and created the Federal Trade Commission (FTC) to enforce the Act. The FTC Act outlaws unfair competition, including "unfair or deceptive acts." The FTC Act also outlaws some of the same practices included in the Sherman and Clayton Acts. In addition, it specifically outlaws price fixing (including the setting of minimum resale prices), output restrictions, and actions that prevent the entry of new firms. The FTC's goal is to promote lower prices, higher output, and free entry—all characteristics of competitive markets (as opposed to monopolies and oligopolies).

Dealing with Natural Monopoly

Antitrust laws are designed to promote competition by preventing business behaviors that concentrate market power. Breaking up a monopoly that isn't natural is clearly a good idea: the gains to consumers outweigh the loss to the firm. But what if a market is a natural monopoly? As you will recall, a natural monopoly exists when economies of scale make it efficient to have only one firm in a market. For instance, the Board of Water and Light in Lansing, Michigan, plans to build a $500 million natural gas power plant by 2021. If many power plants competed for customers in the Lansing area, none would sell enough energy to warrant the cost of each plant. Here we see the spreading effect from Module 55 in action—having just one plant allows the production level to be relatively high and the average fixed cost to be tolerably low.

Now we turn from promoting competition to establishing a natural monopoly while also seeking public policy to prevent the relatively high prices and low quantities that result when there is only one firm. The goal in these circumstances is to retain the advantage of lower average total cost that results from a single producer and still curb the inefficiency associated with a monopoly. In Module 62, we presented two ways to do this—public ownership and price regulation.

While there are a few examples of public ownership in the United States, such as Amtrak, a provider of passenger rail service, the more common answer has been to leave the industry in private hands but subject it to regulation.

The Federal Trade Commission promotes fair practices, free entry by firms, and the virtues of competitive markets.

Price Regulation

Most water, sewer, and power utilities are natural monopolies with regulated prices. By having only one firm produce in the market, society benefits from increased efficiency. That is, the average cost of production is lower due to economies of scale. But without price regulation, the natural monopoly would be tempted to restrict its output and raise its price. How, then, do regulators determine an appropriate price?

Since the purpose of regulation is to achieve efficiency in the market, a logical place to set the price is at the level at which the marginal cost curve intersects the demand curve. This is called **marginal cost pricing**. (Because we are no longer discussing situations with externalities, we will refer to a single marginal cost that is both the marginal social cost and the marginal private cost.) We have seen that it is allocatively efficient for a firm to set its price equal to its marginal cost. So should regulators require marginal cost pricing?

Figure 77.1 illustrates this situation. In the case of a natural monopoly, the firm is operating on the downward-sloping portion of its average total cost curve (it is experiencing economies of scale). When the average total cost is falling, the marginal cost must be below the average total cost, pulling it down. If the firm had to set its price equal to its marginal cost and sell Q_1 units (the quantity demanded when $P = MC$), the price would be below the average total cost and the firm would incur a loss: for each unit sold, the firm would lose the difference between the average total cost and the price. The firm would not continue to operate at a loss in the long run unless it received a subsidy equal to the amount of the loss. The government could require the efficient price and subsidize the firm, resulting in an overall increase in

Marginal cost pricing occurs when regulators set a monopoly's price equal to its marginal cost to achieve efficiency.

Allowing public utilities to operate as natural monopolies saves these firms money due to economies of scale. Regulating the prices that natural monopolies charge passes some of the savings on to consumers.

Figure 77.1 Price Setting for a Regulated Monopoly

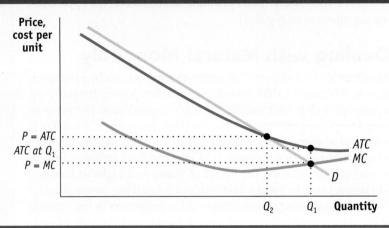

This figure shows the marginal cost curve, *MC*, and the average total cost curve, *ATC*. When the price is set equal to the marginal cost (where the *MC* curve crosses the demand curve), the firm incurs a loss. When the price is set equal to the average total cost (where the *ATC* curve crosses the demand curve) the firm breaks even, but the quantity is below the allocatively efficient level.

Average cost pricing occurs when regulators set a monopoly's price equal to its average cost to prevent the firm from incurring a loss.

efficiency for society. But firm subsidies funded from tax revenues are often politically unpopular. What other options do regulators have?

If regulators want to set the price so that the firm does not require a subsidy, they can set the price at which the demand curve intersects the average total cost curve and the firm breaks even. This is called **average cost pricing**. As Figure 77.1 illustrates, average cost pricing results in output level Q_2 (the quantity demanded when $P = ATC$). The result, a lower quantity at a higher price than with marginal cost pricing, seems to fly in the face of what antitrust regulation is all about. But remember that there are always trade-offs, and it may be best to avoid subsidizing a loss even if it results in less than the allocatively efficient quantity.

Allowing a natural monopoly to exist permits the firm to produce at a lower average total cost than if multiple firms produced in the same market. And price regulation seeks to prevent the inefficiency that results when an unregulated monopoly limits its output and raises its price. This all looks terrific: consumers are better off, monopoly profits are avoided, and overall welfare increases. Unfortunately, things are rarely that easy in practice. The main problem is that regulators don't always have the information required to set the price exactly at the level at which the demand curve crosses the average total cost curve. Sometimes they set it too low, creating shortages; at other times they set it too high, increasing inefficiency. Also, regulated monopolies, like publicly-owned firms, tend to exaggerate their costs to regulators and to provide inferior quality to consumers.

MODULE 77 REVIEW

Check Your Understanding

1. Would each of the following business practices be legal under antitrust law? Explain.
   a. You have a patent for a superior electric car and therefore are the only person able to sell that type of electric car. You require buyers of your car to also purchase a service contract from you (even though other firms provide excellent service for your car).
   b. You have invented a new type of coffee maker that is easy to use and makes incredible cappuccinos and espressos. In order to buy your coffee maker,

   you require purchasers to also buy all of their coffee-making supplies and accessories from you.
   c. You own a car dealership and plan to buy the dealership across the street and merge the two companies. There are several other car dealerships in town.

2. Wind farms generate clean energy but have a high fixed cost. Explain why policy makers who don't want to pay subsidies would choose average cost pricing over marginal cost pricing in the market for wind energy.

TACKLE THE AP® TEST: Multiple-Choice Questions

1. The Sherman Antitrust Act of 1890 sought to do which of the following?
   a. break up existing monopolies
   b. prevent the creation of new monopolies
   c. stop monopoly behavior engaged in by trusts
   d. respond to the increasing power of trusts in the economy
   e. all of the above

2. A natural monopoly exists when, over the relevant range, increasing the output level results in a lower
   a. total cost.
   b. average total cost.
   c. average variable cost.
   d. average fixed cost.
   e. marginal cost.

3. Which of the following is the most common policy approach to a natural monopoly?
   a. public ownership
   b. price regulation
   c. quantity regulation
   d. quality regulation
   e. a breakup of the monopoly into smaller firms

For questions 4 and 5, refer to the graph below.

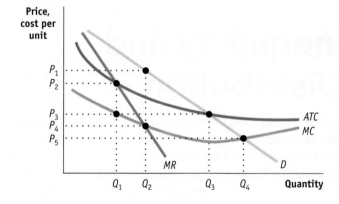

4. Without government intervention, a monopolist will produce _____ and charge _____.
   a. Q_3 P_3
   b. Q_2 P_4
   c. Q_2 P_1
   d. Q_1 P_3
   e. Q_1 P_2

5. The lowest regulated price the government could expect this monopolist to maintain in the long run is
   a. P_1.
   b. P_2.
   c. P_3.
   d. P_4.
   e. P_5.

6. Unlike other monopolies, a natural monopoly is characterized by a high
   a. marginal cost.
   b. variable cost.
   c. fixed cost.
   d. marginal revenue.
   e. price.

7. If the regulated price of a natural monopoly is set where the marginal cost curve intersects the demand curve, the firm will certainly
   a. shut down in the long run.
   b. shut down in the short run.
   c. produce the quantity at which marginal revenue equals average total cost.
   d. increase its output.
   e. make a profit.

TACKLE THE AP® TEST: Free-Response Questions

1. a. Draw a correctly labeled graph showing a natural monopoly. On your graph, label the price and quantity the monopoly will choose if unregulated as P_U and Q_U, respectively.
   b. On the same graph, shade in and label consumer surplus and the firm's profit in the absence of regulation.
   c. On the same graph, label the lowest price that regulators could expect the monopoly to maintain in the long run as P_R and the resulting quantity as Q_R.
   d. What happens to the size of consumer surplus when the firm is required to charge P_R rather than P_U? What happens to the firm's profit?

Rubric for FRQ 1 (10 points)

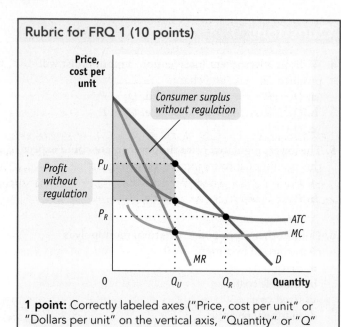

1 point: Correctly labeled axes ("Price, cost per unit" or "Dollars per unit" on the vertical axis, "Quantity" or "Q" on the horizontal axis)

1 point: Downward-sloping *ATC* curve

1 point: Downward-sloping *MC* curve below the *ATC* curve

1 point: Unregulated quantity Q_U shown on the horizontal axis where $MC = MR$

1 point: Unregulated price P_U found on a downward-sloping demand curve above Q_U and shown on the vertical axis

1 point: Correct profit rectangle

1 point: Consumer surplus triangle shown below the demand curve and above the price

1 point: Regulated price and quantity P_R and Q_R shown on the appropriate axes, corresponding to where the demand curve crosses the average total cost curve

1 point: Consumer surplus will increase

1 point: Profit will decrease to zero

2. List and explain three different public policy approaches to monopoly. **(6 points)**

Income Inequality and Income Distribution

In this Module, you will learn to:
- Describe the causes and consequences of poverty
- Explain how income inequality in America has changed over time
- Discuss how Social Security and similar programs affect poverty and income inequality

The descriptive *positive* branch of economics offers information about the extent of poverty and income inequality. *Normative* economics presents more challenging questions about how to weigh equity in the distribution of income against associated losses in efficiency. For example, the redistribution of income from the rich to the poor reduces income inequality, but the taxes used to collect money for the poor generally cause deadweight loss. How much income redistribution is appropriate? That is a subject of debate, and although there may not be a single "right" answer, the tools of economics do much to inform the debate. In this Module, we look at the problem of poverty and the issue of income distribution, and learn how public policy can affect them.

The Problem of Poverty

For at least the past 75 years, every U.S. president has promised to do his best to reduce poverty. In 1964 President Lyndon Johnson went so far as to declare a "war on poverty," creating a number of new programs to aid the poor. Antipoverty programs account for a significant part of the U.S. *welfare state*— the system whereby the government takes responsibility for the welfare of its citizens— although social insurance programs, including Social Security and Medicare, are an even larger part.

What, exactly, do we mean by poverty? Any definition is somewhat arbitrary. Since 1965, however, the U.S. government has maintained an official definition of the **poverty threshold**, a minimum annual income that is considered adequate to purchase the necessities of life. Families whose incomes fall below the poverty threshold are considered poor.

The official poverty threshold depends on the size and composition of a family. In 2018 the poverty threshold for an adult living alone was $12,140; for a household consisting of two adults and two children, it was $25,100.

Trends in Poverty

Contrary to popular misconceptions, although the official poverty threshold is adjusted each year to reflect changes in the cost of living, it has *not* been adjusted upward over time to reflect the long-term rise in the standard of living of the average American family. As a result, as the economy grows and becomes more prosperous, and average incomes rise, you might expect the percentage of the population living below the poverty threshold to steadily decline.

Somewhat surprisingly, however, this hasn't happened. **Figure 78.1** shows the U.S. **poverty rate**—the percentage of the population living below the poverty threshold—from 1959 to 2016. As you can see, the poverty rate fell steeply during the 1960s and early 1970s. Since then, however, it has fluctuated up and down, with no clear trend. In fact, in 2016 the poverty rate was higher than it had been in the 1970s.

President Johnson signing the War on Poverty bill in 1964.

The **poverty threshold** is the annual income below which a family is officially considered poor.

The **poverty rate** is the percentage of the population with incomes below the poverty threshold.

Figure 78.1   Trends in the U.S Poverty Rate, 1959–2016

The poverty rate fell sharply from the 1960s to the early 1970s but has not shown a clear trend since then.
Data Source: U.S. Census Bureau.

Who Are the Poor?

In 2016, about 40.6 million Americans were in poverty—12.7% of the population, or about one in eight persons. No particular stereotype is valid for a majority of America's poor, although poverty rates are disproportionately high among some groups. Almost one-quarter of the poor in 2016 were African-American and slightly more than one-quarter were Hispanic. Within these two groups, poverty rates were well above the national average: 22.0% of African-Americans and 19.4% of Hispanics. But there was also widespread poverty among non-Hispanic Whites, who had a poverty rate of 8.8%.

There is also a correlation between family makeup and poverty. Female-headed families with no husband present had a very high poverty rate: 26.6%. Married couples were much less likely to be poor, with a poverty rate of only 5.1%; still, about 38% of poor families were married couples.

What really stands out from the data, however, is the association between poverty and lack of adequate employment. Adults who work full time are very unlikely to be poor: only 2.2% of full-time workers were poor in 2016. Adults who worked part time or not at all during the year made up 64.6% of the poor in 2016. Many industries, particularly in the retail and service sectors, now rely primarily on part-time workers. Part-time work typically lacks benefits such as health plans, paid vacation days, and retirement benefits, and it also usually pays a lower hourly wage than comparable full-time work. As a result, many of the poor are members of what analysts call the *working poor*: workers whose income falls at or below the poverty threshold.

What Causes Poverty?

Poverty is often blamed on lack of education, and educational attainment clearly has a strong positive effect on income level—on average, those with more education earn higher incomes than those with less education. For example, in 2017 the average hourly wage of workers with a college degree was 82% higher than that of workers with only a high school diploma. Lack of proficiency in English is also a barrier to higher income. For example, Mexican-born male workers in the United States—two-thirds of whom have not graduated from high school and many of whom have poor English skills—earn less than half of what native-born men earn. And it's important not to overlook the role of racial and gender discrimination; although less pervasive today than 50 years ago, discrimination still erects formidable barriers to advancement for many Americans. Non-Whites earn less and are less likely to be employed than Whites with comparable levels of education. Studies find that African-American males suffer persistent discrimination by employers in favor of Whites, African-American women, and Hispanic immigrants. Women earn lower incomes than men with similar qualifications.

In addition, one important source of poverty that should not be overlooked is bad luck. Many families find themselves impoverished when a wage-earner loses a job or a family member falls seriously ill. In fact, medical expenses are the primary cause of personal bankruptcies. Other forms of bad luck among the major causes of bankruptcies include pay cuts, unexpected car expenses, divorce, and storm damage to personal property.

Consequences of Poverty

The consequences of poverty are often severe, particularly for children. Currently, 21% of children in the United States live in poverty. Poverty is often associated with a lack of access to health care, which can lead to further health problems that erode the ability to attend school and work later in life. Recent medical studies have shown that children raised in severe poverty tend to suffer from lifelong learning disabilities. Affordable housing is also frequently a problem, leading poor families to move often, disrupting school and work schedules.

One of the most vexing problems facing any society is how to break what researchers call the *cycle of poverty*: children who grow up with

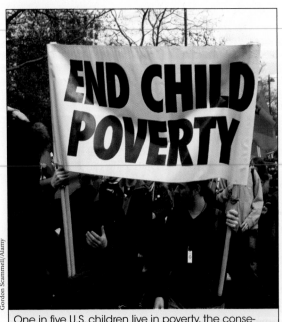

Gordon Scammell/Alamy

One in five U.S. children live in poverty, the consequences of which can include poor health and lifelong learning disabilities.

disadvantaged socioeconomic backgrounds are far more likely to remain trapped in poverty as adults, even after we account for differences in ability. They are more likely to be unemployed or underemployed, to engage in crime, and to suffer chronic health problems.

Even bright children who come from poor families are unlikely to finish college. A long-term study conducted by the U.S. Department of Education compared the college outcomes of students with high and low socioeconomic status (a measure based on the parents' education, income, and occupations) who scored among the top 25% on a rigorous math test. Among those talented students from families with low socioeconomic status, only 29% finished college. By contrast, 74% of the equally talented students from high-status families finished college. This tells us that poverty, to an important degree, is self-perpetuating: the children of the poor start at such a disadvantage relative to other Americans that it is very hard for them to achieve a better life.

Early childhood intervention has offered some hope of breaking the cycle. A study by the RAND Corporation found that high-quality early-childhood programs that focus on education and health care lead to significant social, intellectual, and financial advantages for kids who would otherwise be at risk of dropping out of high school and of engaging in criminal behavior. Children in programs like Head Start were less likely to engage in such destructive behaviors and more likely to end up with a job and to earn a high salary later in life.

A study by researchers at the University of Pittsburgh looked at early-childhood intervention programs from a dollars-and-cents perspective, finding that every $1 spent on early-childhood intervention programs provides between $4 and $7 worth of benefits to society. The observed external benefits to society of high-quality preschool education are so large that the Brookings Institution predicts that providing these programs to every American child would result in an increase in GDP by almost 2%, and would contribute over 3 million more jobs to the economy.

Economic Inequality

The United States is a rich country. In 2017, the average U.S. household had an income of more than $86,000, far exceeding the poverty threshold. How is it possible, then, that so many Americans still live in poverty? The answer is that income is unequally distributed, with many households earning much less than the average and others earning much more.

Table 78.1 shows the distribution of pre-tax income among U.S. families in 2017—income before federal income taxes are paid—as estimated by the Census Bureau. Households are grouped into *quintiles*, each containing 20% or one-fifth of the population. The first, or bottom, quintile contains households whose income puts them below the 20th percentile in income, the second quintile contains households whose income

Table 78.1	U.S. Income Distribution in 2017		
Income group	Income range	Average income	Percent of total U.S. income
Bottom quintile	Less than $24,638	$13,258	3.1%
Second quintile	$24,638 to $47,110	35,401	8.2
Third quintile	$47,111 to $77,552	61,564	14.3
Fourth quintile	$77,553 to $126,855	99,030	23.0
Top quintile	More than $126,855	221,846	51.5
Top 5%	More than $237,034	385,289	22.3
Mean Income = $86,220		**Median Income = $61,372**	

Data Source: U.S. Census Bureau.

Mean household income is the average income across all households.

Median household income is the income of the household lying in the middle of the income distribution.

When billionaire Elon Musk walks into a room filled with ordinary wage-earners, it has a large effect on the average income and a small effect on the median income of people in the room.

The **Lorenz curve** shows the percentage of all income received by the poorest members of the population, from the poorest 0% to the poorest 100%.

The **Gini coefficient** is a number that summarizes a country's level of income inequality based on how unequally income is distributed.

puts them between the 20th and 40th percentiles, and so on. The Census Bureau also provides data on the 5% of families with the highest incomes.

For each group, Table 78.1 shows three numbers. The second column shows the range of incomes that define the group. For example, in 2017, the bottom quintile consisted of households with annual incomes of less than $24,638; the next quintile of households with incomes between $24,638 and $47,110; and so on. The third column shows the average income in each group, ranging from $13,258 for the bottom fifth to $385,289 for the top 5%. The fourth column shows the percentage of total U.S. income received by each group.

At the bottom of Table 78.1 are two useful numbers for thinking about the incomes of American households. **Mean household income**, also called average household income, is the total income of all U.S. households divided by the number of households. **Median household income** is the income of a household in the exact middle of the income distribution—the level of income at which half of all households have lower income and half have higher income. It's very important to realize that these two numbers do not measure the same thing. Economists often illustrate the difference by asking people first to imagine a room containing several dozen more or less ordinary wage-earners, and then to think about what happens to the mean and median incomes of the people in the room if the CEO of a major corporation walks in. The mean income soars, because the CEO's multimillion-dollar income pulls up the average, but median income hardly rises at all because the person in the middle of the income distribution is still one of the ordinary wage-earners. This example helps explain why economists generally regard median income as a better guide to the economic status of typical American families than mean income: mean income is strongly affected by the incomes of a relatively small number of very-high-income Americans, who are not representative of the population as a whole; median income is not.

What we learn from Table 78.1 is that income in the United States is quite unequally distributed. The average income of the poorest fifth of families is less than a quarter of the average income of families in the middle, and the richest fifth have an average income more than three times that of families in the middle. On average, the incomes of the richest fifth of the population are about 15 times as high as those of the poorest fifth. In fact, the distribution of income in America has become more unequal since 1980, rising to a level that has made it a significant political issue. Earlier in the last century, U.S. income inequality declined in the 1930s and 1940s, was stable for more than 30 years after World War II, but began rising again in the late 1970s.

We can visualize income inequality with the *Lorenz curve* as shown in **Figure 78.2**. The **Lorenz curve** indicates the percentage of all income received by the poorest members of the population, starting from the poorest 0% who receive 0% of the income and ending with the poorest 100% who receive 100% of the income. If income were equally distributed—that is, if the poorest 20% of the population received 20% of the income, the poorest 40% of the population received 40% of the income, and so on—the Lorenz curve would coincide with the *line of equality*. However, from the data in Table 78.1, we know, for example, that the poorest 20% receive 3.1% of the income and the poorest 40% receive 3.1% + 8.3% = 11.4% percent of the income, so the Lorenz curve falls below the line of equality.

It's often convenient to have a single number that summarizes a country's level of income inequality. The **Gini coefficient**, the most widely used measure of inequality, is the ratio of area A in Figure 78.2, between the line of equality and the Lorenz curve, to area B, below the line of equality. So we have

$$\text{Gini coefficient} = A/(A + B)$$

A country with a perfectly equal distribution of income would have a Gini coefficient of 0, because the Lorenz curve would follow the line of equality, and area A would be zero. At the other extreme, the highest possible value for the Gini coefficient

Figure 78.2 The Lorenz Curve

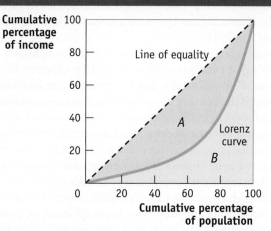

The Lorenz curve indicates the percentage of all income received by the poorest members of the population, starting from the poorest 0% who receive 0% of the income and ending with the poorest 100% who receive 100% of the income. If everyone received the same income, the Lorenz curve would follow the line of equality. Income inequality causes the Lorenz curve to fall below the line of equality.

is 1—the level it would attain if all of a country's income went to just one person. In that case, area *A* would equal area *A* + *B*, because the Lorenz curve would lie along the horizontal axis until the richest person was included, at which point it would jump up to a height of 100%.

One way to get a sense of what Gini coefficients mean in practice is to look at international comparisons. **Figure 78.3** shows the most recent estimates of the Gini coefficient for many of the world's countries. A few countries in Africa have Gini coefficients around 0.6. Elsewhere, the highest levels of income inequality are found in Latin America, where countries such as Brazil have Gini coefficients around 0.5. The most equal

AP® EXAM TIP

The College Board's *Course Description* for AP® microeconomics recommends coverage of the Lorenz curve and the Gini coefficient, which suggests that these concepts are worth studying in preparation for the AP® exam.

Figure 78.3 Income Inequality Around the World

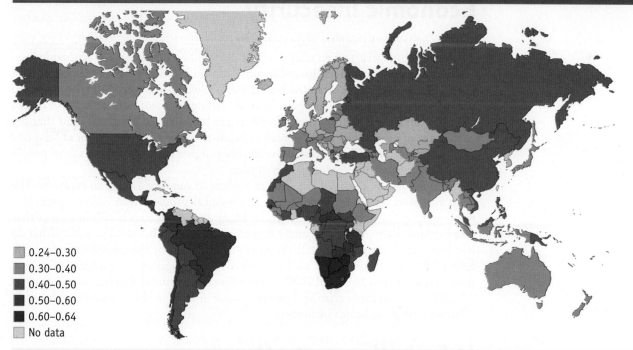

0.24–0.30
0.30–0.40
0.40–0.50
0.50–0.60
0.60–0.64
No data

The highest levels of income inequality are found in Africa and Latin America. The most equal distributions of income are in Europe, especially in Scandinavia. Compared to other wealthy countries, the United States, with a Gini coefficient of 0.415 in 2016, has unusually high inequality.

Data Sources: World Bank, CIA World Factbook, various years depending on data availability.

distributions of income are in Europe, especially in Scandinavia; countries with very equal income distributions, such as Sweden, have Gini coefficients around 0.25. Compared to other wealthy countries, the United States has high income inequality, with a Gini coefficient of 0.415 in 2016.

How serious an issue is income inequality? In a direct sense, high income inequality means that some people don't share in a nation's overall prosperity. As we've seen, rising inequality explains how it's possible that the U.S. poverty rate has failed to fall for the past 35 years even though the country as a whole has become considerably richer. Also, extreme inequality, as found in Latin America, is often associated with political instability, because of tension between a wealthy minority and the rest of the population.

It's important to realize, however, that the data shown in Table 78.1 overstate the true degree of inequality in the United States among other countries, for several reasons. One is that the data represent a snapshot for a single year, whereas the incomes of many individual families fluctuate over time. That is, many of those near the bottom in any given year are having an unusually bad year and many of those at the top are having an unusually good one. Over time, their incomes will revert to a more normal level. So a table showing average incomes within quintiles over a longer period, such as a decade, would not show as much inequality. Furthermore, a family's income tends to vary over its life cycle: most people earn considerably less in their early working years than they will later in life, and then experience a considerable drop in income when they retire. Consequently, the numbers in Table 78.1, which combine young workers, mature workers, and retirees, show more inequality than would a table that compares families of similar ages.

Despite these qualifications, there is a considerable amount of genuine inequality in the United States. Moreover, the fact that families' incomes fluctuate from year to year isn't entirely good news. Measures of inequality in a given year *do* overstate true inequality. But those year-to-year fluctuations are part of a problem that worries even affluent families—economic insecurity.

Economic Insecurity

The rationale for the welfare state rests in part on the benefits of reducing economic insecurity, which afflicts even relatively well-off families. One source of economic insecurity is the risk of a sudden loss of income, as occurs when a family member loses a job and either spends an extended period without work or is forced to take a new job that pays considerably less. In a given year, according to recent estimates, about one in six American families will see their income cut in half. Related estimates show that the percentage of people who find themselves below the poverty threshold for at least one year over the course of a decade is several times higher than the percentage of people below the poverty threshold in any given year.

Even if a family doesn't face a loss in income, it can face a surge in expenses. The most common reason for such surges is a medical problem that requires expensive treatment, such as heart disease or cancer. Many Americans have health insurance that covers a large share of their expenses in such cases, but a substantial number either do not have health insurance or rely on insurance provided by the government. In 2018, around 30 million Americans were uninsured. The Congressional Budget Office estimates that between 2019 and 2027, the number of uninsured Americans will grow by 13 million as a result of changes Congress made in 2017 in the requirements for individuals to purchase health insurance.

U.S. Antipoverty Programs

U.S. antipoverty programs include three huge programs—Social Security, Medicare, and Medicaid—several other fairly big programs, including Temporary Assistance for Needy Families, the Supplemental Nutrition Assistance Program, and the Earned Income

Tax Credit, and a number of smaller programs. **Table 78.2** shows one useful way to categorize these programs, along with the amount spent on each listed program in 2017.

Table 78.2	Major U.S. Welfare State Programs, 2017	
	Monetary transfers	**In-kind**
Means-tested	Temporary Assistance for Needy Families: $16 billion	Supplemental Nutrition Assistance Program: $70 billion
	Supplemental Security Income: $56 billion	Medicaid: $376 billion
	Earned Income Tax Credit: $79 billion	
Not means-tested	Social Security: $793 billion Unemployment insurance: $30 billion	Medicare: $709 billion

Data Source: Department of Labor, Bureau of Economic Analysis, Department of Health & Human Services.

First, the table distinguishes between programs that are **means-tested** and those that are not. In means-tested programs, benefits are available only to families or individuals whose income and/or wealth falls below some minimum. Basically, means-tested programs are poverty programs designed to help only those with low incomes. By contrast, non-means-tested programs provide their benefits to everyone, although, as we'll see, in practice they tend to reduce income inequality by increasing the incomes of the poor by a larger proportion than the incomes of the rich.

Second, the table distinguishes between programs that provide monetary transfers that beneficiaries can spend as they choose and those that provide **in-kind benefits**, which are given in the form of goods or services rather than money. As the numbers suggest, in-kind benefits are dominated by Medicare and Medicaid, which pay for health care.

A **means-tested** program is available only to individuals or families whose incomes fall below a certain level.

An **in-kind benefit** is a benefit given in the form of goods or services.

A **negative income tax** is a program that supplements the income of low-income workers.

Means-Tested Programs

When people use the term *welfare*, they're often referring to monetary aid to poor families. The main source of such monetary aid in the United States is Temporary Assistance for Needy Families, or TANF. This program does not aid everyone who is poor; it is available only to poor families with children and only for a limited period of time.

TANF was introduced in the 1990s to replace a highly controversial program known as Aid to Families with Dependent Children, or AFDC. The older program was widely accused of creating perverse incentives for the poor, including encouraging family breakup. Partly as a result of the change in programs, the benefits of modern "welfare" are considerably less generous than those available a generation ago, once the data are adjusted for inflation. Also, TANF contains time limits, so welfare recipients—even single parents—must eventually seek work. As you can see from Table 78.2, TANF is a relatively small part of the modern U.S. welfare state.

Other means-tested programs, though more expensive, are less controversial. The Supplemental Security Income program aids disabled Americans who are unable to work and have no other source of income. The Supplemental Nutrition Assistance Program (formerly known as the Food Stamp Program) helps low-income families and individuals to buy food staples.

Finally, economists use the term **negative income tax** for a program that supplements the earnings of low-income workers. For example, in the United States, the Earned Income Tax Credit (EITC) provides additional income to millions of workers. It has become more generous as traditional welfare has become less generous. As an incentive to work, only workers who earn income are eligible for the EITC. And as an incentive to work more, over a certain range of incomes, the more

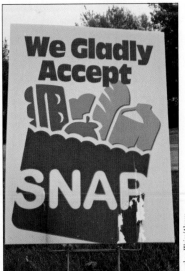

The Supplemental Nutrition Assistance Program helps those with low incomes put food on the table. Purchases are made using an electronic benefits transfer card that works like a debit card but can be used only to purchase food.

Jonathan Weiss/Alamy

a worker earns, the higher the amount of EITC received. That is, the EITC acts as a negative income tax for low-wage workers. In 2018, married couples with two children earning less than $14,290 per year received EITC payments equal to 40% of their earnings. Payments were slightly lower for single-parent families or workers without children. At higher incomes, the EITC is phased out, disappearing at an income of $51,492 in 2018.

Social Security and Unemployment Insurance

Social Security, the largest program in the U.S. welfare state, is a non-means-tested program that guarantees retirement income to qualifying older Americans. It also provides benefits to workers who become disabled and "survivor benefits" to family members of workers who die. Social Security is supported by a dedicated tax on wages: the Social Security portion of the payroll tax pays for Social Security bene-

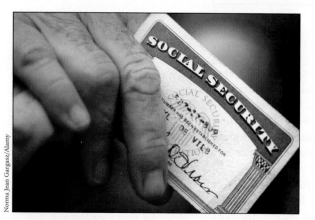

fits. The benefits workers receive on retirement depend on their taxable earnings during their working years: the more you earn up to the maximum amount subject to Social Security taxes ($128,400 in 2018), the more you receive in retirement. However, benefits are not strictly proportional to earnings. Instead, they're determined by a formula that gives high earners more than low earners, but with a sliding scale that makes the program relatively more generous for low earners.

Because most senior citizens don't receive pensions from their former employers, and most can't live off the income from their assets, Social Security benefits are an enormously important source of income. Fully 64% of Americans 65 and older rely on Social Security for more than half their income, and 35% of those 65 or older rely on Social Security for 90% or more of their income.

Unemployment insurance, although a much smaller amount of government transfers than Social Security, is another key social insurance program. It provides workers who lose their jobs with about 35% of their previous salary until they find a new job or until 26 weeks have passed. (This period is sometimes extended when the economy is in a slump.) Unemployment insurance is financed by a tax on employers.

The Debate over Income Redistribution

The goals of income redistribution seem laudable: to help the poor, protect everyone from financial risk, and ensure that people can afford essential health care. But good intentions don't always make for good policy. There is an intense debate about how large the antipoverty programs should be, a debate that partly reflects differences in philosophy but also reflects concern about the possibly counterproductive effects of antipoverty programs. Disputes about the role of government in income redistribution are also one of the defining issues of modern politics.

Problems with Income Redistribution

There are two different lines of argument against antipoverty programs. One is based on philosophical concerns about the proper role of government. Some political theorists believe that governments should not redistribute income—that government's role should be limited to maintaining the rule of law, providing public goods, and managing externalities.

The more conventional argument against income redistribution involves the trade-off between efficiency and equity. A government with extensive antipoverty programs requires more revenue, and thus higher tax rates, than one that limits itself mainly to the provision of public goods such as national defense. **Table 78.3** shows "social expenditure," a measure that roughly corresponds to welfare state spending, as a percentage

Table 78.3	Social Expenditure and Average Tax Rates	
	Social expenditure as percent of GDP (2016)	Average tax rate (2017)
U.S.	19.3%	31.7%
Portugal	24.1	41.4
France	31.5	47.6

Data Sources: OECD Social Expenditure Database; OECD Taxing Wages Database.

of GDP in the United States, Portugal, and France; it also compares this with an estimate of the average income tax rate for single workers with no children, including payroll taxes paid by employers and state and local income taxes. As you can see, France's large welfare state goes along with a high average rate of taxation. Some, but not all, economists believe that this high rate of taxation is a major reason the French work substantially fewer hours per year than Americans—the idea being that the high tax rate makes additional hours of work less financially rewarding.

The trade-off between antipoverty programs and high marginal tax rates seems to suggest that we should try to hold down the cost of these programs. One way to do this is to means-test benefits: make them available only to those who need them. But means-testing, it turns out, creates a different kind of trade-off between equity and efficiency. Consider the following example: suppose there is some means-tested benefit worth $2,000 per year that is available only to families with incomes of less than $20,000 per year. Now suppose that a family currently has an income of $19,500 but that one family member is deciding whether to take a new job that will raise the family's income to $20,500. Well, taking that job will actually make the family worse off because it will gain $1,000 in earnings but lose the $2,000 government benefit.

This situation, in which earning more actually leaves a family worse off through lost benefits, is known as a *notch*. It is a well-known problem with programs that aid the poor and behaves much like a high marginal tax rate on income. Most welfare state programs are designed to avoid creating a notch. This is typically done by setting a sliding scale for benefits such that they fall off gradually as the recipient's income rises. As long as benefits are reduced by less than a dollar for every additional dollar earned, there is an incentive to work more if possible. In the past, the combined effects of the major means-tested programs shown in Table 78.2, plus additional means-tested programs such as housing aid that are offered by some state and local governments, sometimes created very high effective marginal tax rates. For example, one 2005 study found that a family consisting of two adults and two children that raised its annual income from $20,000—just above the poverty threshold in 2005—to $35,000, would find almost all of its increase in after-tax income offset by the loss of benefits from means-tested programs. The Congressional Budget Office reported improved incentives to work in 2016, when the average effective marginal tax rate for low- and moderate-income workers was 31%.

The Politics of Income Redistribution

In 1791, in the early phase of the French Revolution, France had a sort of congress, the National Legislative Assembly, in which representatives were seated according to social class: nobles, who pretty much liked the way things were, sat on the right; commoners, who wanted big changes, sat on the left. Ever since, it has been common in political discourse to talk about politicians as being on the "right" (more conservative) or on the "left" (more liberal).

But what do modern politicians on the left and right disagree about? In the United States, they largely disagree about the appropriate size of antipoverty programs.

It would be an oversimplification to say that political debate is all about government's involvement in income redistribution. Yet political scientists have found that once you carefully rank members of Congress from right to left, a congressperson's position in that ranking does a very good job of predicting his or her votes on proposed legislation. Modern politics isn't completely one-dimensional—but it comes pretty close.

The same studies that show a strong left–right spectrum in U.S. politics also show strong polarization between the major parties on this spectrum. Thirty years ago there was a substantial overlap between the parties: some Democrats were to the right of some Republicans, or, if you prefer, some Republicans were to the left of some Democrats. Today, however, the rightmost Democrats appear to be to the left of the leftmost Republicans. There's nothing necessarily wrong with this. Although it's common to decry "partisanship," it's hard to see why members of different political parties shouldn't have different views about policy.

Can economic analysis help resolve this political conflict? Only up to a point.

Some of the political controversy over the welfare state involves differences in opinion about the trade-offs we have just discussed: if you believe that the disincentive effects of generous benefits and high taxes are very large, you're likely to look less favorably on welfare state programs than if you believe they're fairly small. Economic analysis, by improving our knowledge of the facts, can help resolve some of these differences.

To an important extent, however, differences of opinion on income redistribution reflect differences in values and philosophy. And those are differences economics can't resolve.

MODULE 78 REVIEW

Adventures in AP® Economics

Watch the video: *The Gini Coefficient and the Lorenz Curve*

Check Your Understanding

1. Recall that the poverty threshold is not adjusted to reflect changes in the standard of living. As a result, is the poverty threshold a relative or an absolute measure of poverty? That is, does it define poverty according to how poor someone is relative to others or according to some fixed measure that doesn't change over time? Explain.

2. Suppose that the incomes of members of an economy become more similar.
   a. Will the Lorenz curve move upward and to the right, upward and to the left, or downward and to the left?
   b. Will the area labeled A in Figure 78.2 become larger, become smaller, or remain the same?
   c. Will the area labeled B in Figure 78.2 become larger, become smaller, or remain the same?
   d. Will the Gini coefficient become larger, become smaller, or remain the same?

TACKLE THE AP® TEST: Multiple-Choice Questions

1. Which of the following is true of the U.S. poverty rate?
   a. It fell in the 1960s.
   b. There has been a clear upward trend since 1973.
   c. It was lower in 2016 than in 1973.
   d. It has remained unchanged since the mid 1970s.
   e. It has been steadily decreasing since 1959.

2. In 2016, the poorest 20% of households received approximately what percent of total income?
   a. 1%   d. 10%
   b. 3%   e. 17%
   c. 7%

3. If one person received all of the income in an economy, the Lorenz curve would
   a. rise steadily until the middle of the graph, and then fall.
   b. be upward-sloping.
   c. be downward-sloping.
   d. be vertical on the left side of the graph.
   e. lie along the horizontal axis except at the far right side of the graph.

4. Programs designed to help only those with low incomes are called
   a. welfare programs.
   b. in-kind programs.
   c. means-tested programs.
   d. income maintenance programs.
   e. social programs.

5. If a country has a perfectly equal distribution of income, its Gini coefficient equals
   a. 0.
   b. 1.
   c. 10.
   d. 50.
   e. 100.

6. If everyone in the economy earned exactly the same income, the Lorenz curve would be
   a. vertical.
   b. horizontal.
   c. downward-sloping.
   d. straight.
   e. upward-sloping and then downward-sloping.

7. Which of the following statements about poverty is true?
   a. The poverty rate has steadily declined over the past two decades.
   b. Most governments seek an increase in the Gini coefficient.
   c. Married couples are more likely to be poor than single individuals.
   d. Bright students from poor families are almost as likely to finish college as bright students from rich families.
   e. High-quality preschool education helps to end the poverty cycle.

TACKLE THE AP® TEST: Free-Response Questions

1. There are 100 households in the economy of Equalor. Initially, 99 of them have an income of $10,000 each, and one household has an income of $1,010,000.
   a. What is the median income in this economy? What is the mean income?

   Through its antipoverty programs, the government of Equalor now redistributes income: it collects $990,000 from the richest household and distributes it equally among the remaining 99 households.
   b. What is the median income in this economy now? What is the mean income? Which indicator (mean or median household income) is a better indicator of the typical Equalorian household's income?

2. Again consider the economy of Equalor described in Question 1, in which the total income is $2 million.
   a. Draw a correctly labeled graph showing the points on the Lorenz curve for the poorest 0%, 20%, 40%, 60%, 80%, and 100% of the population before the redistribution of income.
   b. On the graph you have already drawn, repeat your answer to part a for the situation after the redistribution of income. Indicate the points that have changed with an "X."
   c. What is the Gini coefficient after the redistribution of income? **(5 points)**

Rubric for FRQ 1 (5 points)

1 point: median income = $10,000

1 point: mean income = $20,000

1 point: median income = $20,000

1 point: mean income = $20,000

1 point: median household income

Module 74

1. When pollution can be directly observed and controlled, government policies should be geared directly to producing the **socially optimal quantity** of pollution, the quantity at which the **marginal social cost** of pollution is equal to the **marginal social benefit** of pollution. In the absence of government intervention, a market produces too much pollution because polluters take only their benefit from polluting into account, not the costs imposed on others.

2. The cost to society of pollution from a power plant is an example of an **external cost**; the benefit to neighbors of beautiful flowers planted in your yard is an example of an **external benefit**. External costs and benefits are jointly known as **externalities**, with external costs called **negative externalities** and external benefits called **positive externalities**. Externalities are among the sources of inefficiency in markets, which economists describe as **market failures**.

Module 75

5. When a good yields external benefits, such as **technology spillovers**, the marginal social benefit of the good is equal to the **marginal private benefit** accruing to consumers plus its **marginal external benefit**. Without government intervention, the market produces too little of the good. An optimal **Pigouvian subsidy** for the good, equal to the marginal external benefit, moves the market to the socially optimal quantity of production. This yields higher output and a higher price to producers.

6. When there are external costs from production, the marginal social cost of a good exceeds its **marginal private**

3. According to the **Coase theorem**, when externalities exist, bargaining will cause individuals to **internalize the externalities**, making government intervention unnecessary, as long as property rights are clearly defined and **transaction costs**—the costs of making a deal—are sufficiently low. However, in many cases transaction costs are too high to permit such deals.

4. Governments often deal with pollution by imposing **environmental standards**, an approach, economists argue, that is usually inefficient. Two efficient (cost-minimizing) methods for reducing pollution are emissions taxes and **tradable emissions permits**. These two methods also provide incentives for the creation and adoption of production technologies that cause less pollution.

cost to producers, the difference being the **marginal external cost**. Without government action, the market produces too much of the good. The optimal **Pigouvian tax** on the good is equal to its marginal external cost, yielding lower output and a higher price to consumers. A system of tradable production permits for the right to produce the good can also achieve efficiency at minimum cost.

7. Communications, transportation, and high-technology goods are frequently subject to **network externalities**, which arise when the value of the good to an individual is greater when more people use the good.

Module 76

8. Goods may be classified according to whether or not they are **excludable**, meaning that people can be prevented from consuming them, and whether or not they are **rival in consumption**, meaning that one person's consumption of them affects another person's consumption of them.

9. Free markets can deliver efficient levels of production and consumption for **private goods**, which are both excludable and rival in consumption. When goods are **nonexcludable**, **nonrival in consumption**, or both, free markets cannot achieve efficient outcomes.

10. When goods are nonexcludable, there is a **free-rider problem**: consumers will not pay for the good, leading to inefficiently low production. When goods are nonrival in consumption, any positive price leads to inefficiently low consumption.

11. A **public good** is nonexcludable and nonrival in consumption. In most cases a public good must be supplied by the government. The marginal social benefit of a public good is equal to the sum of the marginal private benefits to each consumer. The efficient quantity of a public good is the quantity at which the marginal social benefit equals the marginal social cost of providing the good. As with a positive externality, the marginal social benefit is greater than any one individual's marginal private benefit, so no individual is willing to provide the efficient quantity.

12. One rationale for the presence of government is that it allows citizens to tax themselves in order to provide public goods. Governments use cost-benefit analysis to determine the efficient provision of a public good. Such analysis is difficult, however, because individuals have an incentive to overstate the good's value to them.

13. A **common resource** is rival in consumption but nonexcludable. It is subject to **overuse**, because an individual does not take into account the fact that his or her use depletes the amount available for others. This is similar to the problem with a negative externality: the marginal social cost of an individual's use of a common resource is always higher than his or her marginal private cost. Pigouvian taxes, the creation of a system of tradable licenses, and the assignment of property rights are possible solutions.

14. **Artificially scarce goods** are excludable but nonrival in consumption. Because no marginal cost arises from allowing another individual to consume the good, the efficient price is zero. A positive price compensates the producer for the cost of production but leads to inefficiently low consumption.

Module 77

15. Antitrust laws and regulation are used to promote competition. When the industry in question is a natural monopoly, price regulation is used.

16. The Sherman Act, the Clayton Act, and the Federal Trade Commission Act were the first major antitrust laws.

17. **Marginal cost pricing** and **average cost pricing** are examples of price regulation used in the case of natural monopoly to allow efficiencies from large-scale production without allowing the deadweight loss that results from unregulated monopoly.

Module 78

18. Despite the fact that the **poverty threshold** is adjusted according to the cost of living but not according to the standard of living, and that the average income in the United States has risen substantially over the last 30 years, the **poverty rate**, the percentage of the population with an income below the poverty threshold, is no lower than it was 30 years ago. There are various causes of poverty: lack of education, the legacy of discrimination, and bad luck. The consequences of poverty are particularly harmful for children.

19. **Median household income**, the income of a family at the center of the income distribution, is a better indicator of the income of the typical household than **mean household income** because it is not distorted by the inclusion of a small number of very wealthy households. The **Lorenz curve** indicates the percentage of all income received by the poorest members of the population, starting with the poorest 0% and ending with the poorest 100%. The **Gini coefficient**, a number that summarizes a country's level of income inequality, is used to compare income inequality across countries.

20. **Means-tested** programs target aid to people whose income falls below a certain level. The major **in-kind benefits** programs are Medicare and Medicaid, which pay for medical care. Due to concerns about the effects on incentives to work and on family cohesion, aid to poor families has become significantly less generous even as the **negative income tax** has become more generous. Social Security, the largest U.S. welfare program, has significantly reduced poverty among the elderly. Unemployment insurance is another key social insurance program.

Key Terms

External cost, p. 712
External benefit, p. 712
Externalities, p. 712
Negative externalities, p. 712
Positive externalities, p. 712
Market failure, p. 712
Marginal social cost, p. 713
Marginal social benefit, p. 713
Socially optimal quantity, p. 713
Coase theorem, p. 715
Transaction costs, p. 715
Internalize the externalities, p. 715
Environmental standards, p. 716
Tradable emissions permits, p. 717
Marginal private benefit, p. 720

Marginal external benefit, p. 720
Pigouvian subsidy, p. 722
Technology spillover, p. 722
Marginal private cost, p. 722
Marginal external cost, p. 723
Pigouvian taxes, p. 724
Network externality, p. 724
Excludable, p. 726
Rival in consumption, p. 726
Private good, p. 726
Nonexcludable, p. 726
Nonrival in consumption, p. 726
Free-rider problem, p. 727
Public good, p. 728
Common resource, p. 732

Overuse, p. 732
Artificially scarce good, p. 734
Marginal cost pricing, p. 739
Average cost pricing, p. 740
Poverty threshold, p. 743
Poverty rate, p. 743
Mean household income, p. 746
Median household income, p. 746
Lorenz curve, p. 746
Gini coefficient, p. 746
Means-tested, p. 749
In-kind benefit, p. 749
Negative income tax, p. 749

Multiple-Choice Questions

1. The poverty rate is
   a. the total number of people who earn less than $23,850 annually.
   b. the percentage of households that file for bankruptcy in a year.
   c. the percentage of the population that earns less than the poverty threshold.
   d. the percentage of the labor force that is unemployed at some point during a year.
   e. the percentage of the population that is in the lowest income quintile.

2. Which of the following conditions contributes to the resolution of externality problems as suggested by the Coase theorem?
   a. It is awkward for the parties involved to approach each other about the problem.
   b. There is ambiguity about the legal rights of the parties involved.
   c. There are many parties involved.
   d. Transaction costs are high.
   e. The legal rights of the parties involved are clearly defined.

3. When the production of a good creates negative externalities, which of the following leads to the socially optimal quantity of output?
   a. a price ceiling set equal to the marginal external cost
   b. a price floor set equal to the marginal private cost
   c. a Pigouvian tax set equal to the marginal external cost
   d. a Pigouvian subsidy set equal to the marginal external cost
   e. average cost pricing

4. Which of the following policy changes would be the most likely to provide a gain in efficiency while achieving the same goal of reducing pollution?
   a. environmental standards instead of emissions taxes
   b. Pigouvian taxes instead of tradable emissions permits
   c. emissions taxes instead of Pigouvian taxes
   d. environmental standards instead of in-kind benefits
   e. tradable emissions permits instead of environmental standards

5. When the economy is producing the socially optimal amount of pollution, it is necessarily true that
   a. the marginal social benefit of pollution exceeds the marginal social cost.

   b. the marginal external cost of pollution equals the marginal external benefit.
   c. no pollution is being emitted.
   d. the marginal social benefit of pollution equals the marginal social cost.
   e. the marginal external cost of pollution is zero.

6. Market failure caused by a positive externality will involve
   a. deadweight loss.
   b. overconsumption.
   c. pollution.
   d. marginal external costs.
   e. taxation.

The graph below shows the marginal social cost, supply, and marginal social benefit in an industry that generates pollution. Use this graph to answer Questions 7 and 8.

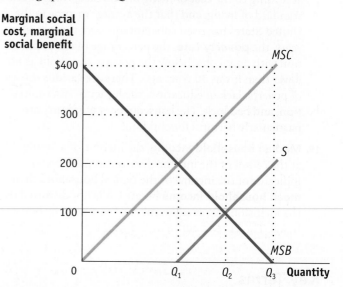

7. Suppose the industry is currently producing the quantity Q_2 and the price is $100. If a Pigouvian tax equal to the marginal external cost is imposed, what will happen to society's total surplus and the deadweight loss in the industry?

	Total surplus	Deadweight loss
a.	decrease	stay the same
b.	increase	decrease
c.	increase	increase
d.	decrease	decrease
e.	increase	stay the same

8. The marginal social cost (*MSC*) and the marginal external cost (*MEC*) at the socially optimal equilibrium would be

	MSC	*MEC*
a.	$200	$200
b.	$100	$0
c.	$200	$100
d.	$100	$200
e.	$200	$0

9. When external benefits exist, the marginal external benefit is the difference between the
   a. marginal external cost and the marginal private benefit.
   b. marginal private benefit and the price.
   c. supply and the demand.
   d. marginal social benefit and the marginal private benefit.
   e. marginal social cost and the marginal private cost.

10. Which of the following curves is the same as the marginal social cost curve at every level of output in a perfectly competitive market with no external costs?
    a. marginal social benefit
    b. marginal external cost
    c. marginal external benefit
    d. marginal private benefit
    e. supply

11. Which of the following is accurate for goods provided by markets?
    a. Artificially scarce goods are likely to be produced in inefficiently large quantities.
    b. Common resources are likely to suffer from inefficiently low consumption levels.
    c. Private goods that are popular are likely to suffer from overuse problems.
    d. Public goods are likely to suffer from inefficiently low production.
    e. Artificially scarce goods are likely to suffer from the free-rider problem.

12. Which of the following is an example of market failure?
    a. Most people can't buy as many pairs of shoes as they would like.
    b. Most stores can't sell as much merchandise as they would like.
    c. Fishing in many waterways brings the quantity of fish below its socially optimal level.
    d. People typically pay more for a good than they would like to pay.
    e. Stores typically must charge a price that is less than they would like to charge.

13. Which of the following characteristics apply to private goods and common resources?

	Private goods	*Common resources*
a.	nonrival in consumption	nonexcludable
b.	rival in consumption	excludable
c.	nonexcludable	rival in consumption
d.	excludable	nonrival in consumption
e.	rival in consumption	nonexcludable

14. Based on economic analysis, why do so many people decide not to vote?
    a. The benefits of voting are nonexcludable.
    b. The costs of voting are nonrival.
    c. The benefits of voting are rival.
    d. The costs of voting are excludable.
    e. The benefits of voting outweigh the costs.

15. Which of the following statements regarding the passage of laws intended to promote competition in the marketplace is true?
    a. The Sherman Antitrust Act was intended to clarify the Clayton Act.
    b. The Clayton Antitrust Act made price discrimination illegal.
    c. The Federal Trade Commission Act made anticompetitive mergers illegal.
    d. The Sherman Antitrust Act outlawed price fixing.
    e. The Clayton Antitrust Act made it legal for two boards of directors to share a director in common.

16. Which of the following statements regarding a natural monopoly is accurate?
    a. The FTC will try to break up the natural monopoly because it is inefficient.
    b. Marginal cost pricing would lead to an efficient outcome and monopoly profits.
    c. The cost of producing any given quantity of the good produced by the natural monopoly would increase if multiple firms produced it.
    d. Regulators require the natural monopoly to produce the quantity that equates marginal cost and marginal benefit.
    e. The information required for average cost pricing is readily available to regulators.

17. Which of the following welfare state programs provides in-kind benefits?
    a. Temporary Assistance for Needy Families
    b. Medicaid
    c. the Earned Income Tax Credit
    d. Social Security
    e. Supplemental Security Income

18. Which of the following welfare state programs is not means-tested?
    a. Temporary Assistance for Needy Families (TANF)
    b. Medicaid
    c. the Earned Income Tax Credit
    d. Social Security
    e. Supplemental Security Income

19. A Gini coefficient of 0.5 would indicate
    a. that the richest 50% of the population receives all of the income.
    b. more income inequality than a Gini coefficient of 0.4.
    c. that a country has perfect income equality.
    d. that a country has perfect income inequality.
    e. that the poorest 10% of the population receives half as much income as the richest 10% of the population.

20. Which of the following combinations correctly describes the changes since the 1970s in the poverty threshold and in the mean income as compared to the median income in the United States?

Poverty threshold	Mean income compared to median income
a. not adjusted for the standard of living	rose faster
b. adjusted for the cost of living	declined
c. adjusted for the standard of living	declined
d. not adjusted for the cost of living	rose faster
e. not adjusted for the standard of living	remained the same

21. Suppose the production of a smartphone imposes $10 worth of pollution costs on people unrelated to the sale or purchase of smartphones. This $10 is part of the smartphones'
    a. marginal private cost and marginal external cost.
    b. marginal private cost and marginal social cost.
    c. marginal external cost and marginal social cost.
    d. marginal social cost, but not marginal external cost.
    e. marginal external cost, but not marginal social cost.

22. If everyone in Equalville earns the same income, the Lorenz curve for Equalville is
    a. flat.
    b. circular.
    c. upward-sloping and then downward-sloping.
    d. straight and upward-sloping.
    e. curved and upward-sloping.

23. Markets for public goods generally experience problems with
    a. overconsumption.
    b. free riders.

c. consumers fighting over the use of products.
d. market power.
e. particularly high marginal external costs.

24. A Pigouvian subsidy is appropriate in a market with a significant
    a. marginal external cost.
    b. marginal external benefit.
    c. difference between the marginal private cost and the marginal social cost.
    d. difference between the equilibrium price and the marginal social cost.
    e. Pigouvian tax.

25. Implementing which of the following for low-income workers would be an effective way to prevent means-tested antipoverty programs from creating a disincentive to work?
    a. a high marginal tax rate
    b. a high average tax rate
    c. a program that eliminates benefits for those who work
    d. a notch-based program
    e. a low marginal tax rate

Free-Response Questions

1. Suppose there are 100 residents on the island of Mahalo. Whenever someone purchases a palm tree to plant on the island, everyone on the island receives the same benefits from the tree, which include beauty, shade, and erosion control. The table below shows the total social cost (which is also the total private cost) and the total private benefit received *per resident* depending on the quantity of palm trees purchased. Use this information to answer the questions that follow.

Quantity of palm trees	Total social cost (total private cost)	Total private benefit per resident
0	$0	$0
1	200	8
2	400	12
3	600	14
4	800	15

   a. Does the purchase of palm trees create a negative externality, a positive externality, or no externality? Explain.
   b. Draw a graph that depicts the marginal social cost and the marginal social benefit of palm trees.
   c. What quantity of palm trees would be purchased if they were sold in a private market? Explain.
   d. What is the socially optimal quantity of palm trees? Explain.
   e. In this situation are palm trees a private good, a public good, or a common resource?
   f. What could be an appropriate governmental policy response to this situation? Explain. **(10 points)**

2. The Burginville Bowl puts on concerts in an outdoor venue. They contract with the city of Burginville to put on 50 concerts per year, so the supply of concerts is perfectly inelastic.
   a. Draw a correctly labeled graph of the market for these concerts and label the market price P_1.
   b. Assume the music from the outdoor concerts is enjoyed by everyone who is close enough to hear it from their homes.
      i. On your graph, draw the marginal social benefit and label it *MSB*.
      ii. Label the socially optimal quantity Q_s.
      iii. Is there a positive externality, a negative externality, or no externality?
      iv. Is there a deadweight loss? Explain. **(7 points)**

3. The country of Nina has a Gini coefficient of 0. The country of Pinta has a Gini coefficient of 1.
   a. On a correctly labeled graph, draw the Lorenz curve for Nina.
   b. On your graph, draw any one point that lies on the Lorenz curve for Pinta and label it *X*.
   c. The country of Santa Maria has a Gini coefficient of 0.5, and wants to enact tax legislation to move its Lorenz curve closer to that of Nina. Should Santa Maria adopt a tax that is regressive, progressive, or proportional? Explain. **(5 points)**

section 14 economics by example

Why Not Split the Check?
A Briefing on Market Failure

Last Friday, somewhere near you, a group of students slurped root beers at a popular hamburger restaurant. Frosted mugs cluttered the table like miniature Manhattan skyscrapers. Gossip and wisecracks filled the air. When it came time to pay, a student with a root beer-foam mustache murmured, "Let's just split the check." Those who had emptied several mugs greeted the motion with nods. Those still sipping their first root beer had blank faces. One light drinker whispered something about fairness. An equal splitting of the check seemed inevitable. Then a baseball player leaned up to the table, his face illuminated by the restaurant's red neon sign. "My friends," he inserted into the awkward silence, "check splitting is an injustice to those who had fewer drinks, and that practice creates an incentive for overindulgence." The others looked puzzled. But as he leaned back, the light struck his Economics Club T-shirt, and they knew that logic was on his side. Let's explore the errors in check-splitters' ways, and uncover other common sources of market failure.

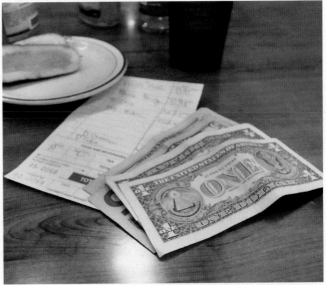

Image Source/Alamy

Market Failure

Ideal market conditions yield efficient allocations of inputs and outputs. *Market failure* occurs when markets do *not* bring about the best outcomes for society. Here we review the sources of market failure—externalities, imperfect competition, imperfect information, and public goods—and discuss ways to avoid it. As you'll see, some of the solutions to market failure are as simple as paying for your own root beers.

Externalities

Externalities are costs or benefits felt beyond, or external to, the people causing them. When you take good care of your health and avoid catching a cold, you create positive externalities because other people won't catch a cold from you. When you leave sweaty clothing in your locker, the resulting bad odor is a negative externality imposed on passersby. Likewise, to emit toxins into the air or water during a manufacturing process, smoke in public, keep a lot of loud dogs in your yard, catch fish that other fishers are angling for, or paint your house a dreadful shade of green is to impose negative externalities on other people.

You may not think of root beer as a source of negative externalities, but when you buy a root beer with a group that is splitting the check, you impose a cost on everyone in that group. Suppose a root beer costs $2 and you have 10 people in your group. Suppose also that diminishing marginal utility leads you to value your first 5 root beers at $3, $2.50, $1.25, $0.50, and $0.10, respectively. If you were not splitting the check, you would buy 2 root beers for $2 each because the first 2 root beers are worth more than $2 (that is, $3 and $2.50) to you. You wouldn't pay $2 for a third root beer that's worth $1.25 to you.

The situation changes when you're splitting the check equally among 10 people. In that case each root beer raises the bill by $2, but it raises your share of the bill by only $2/10 = 20 cents. Thus, it's rational for you to purchase 4 root beers—all of those that are worth at least 20 cents to you—even though the last 2 are worth less than the $2 price that the group pays.

The problem grows because everyone in the group faces the same incentive to overconsume. If your friends share your preference for root beer, each of the 10 friends will consume 4 beverages, bringing the total bill up to $80. Each friend's share of the bill will be $8—twice what they would have paid on their own and 75 cents more than the $3 + $2.50 + $1.25 + $0.50 = $7.25 value of the root beers to them. Notice that you cannot improve on your situation by reducing the number of drinks you order. If you ordered 3 root beers, you would reduce your share of the bill by $0.20 and you would receive $0.60 cents less worth of beverage. By splitting the check, your group creates negative externalities that harm everyone in the group.

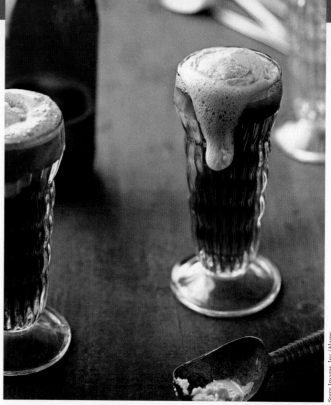

To eliminate an externality problem, find a way to have everyone internalize, or feel for themselves, the full costs or benefits of their decisions. In the root beer example, that means having everyone pay his or her own bill. The negative externalities from goods such as gasoline, cigarettes, and alcohol are internalized if *excise taxes* (taxes levied on particular goods such as these) approximate the associated external costs. Positive externalities lead to the underconsumption of such things as flu shots, education, tree planting, and clean energy. This problem arises because consumers neglect the external benefits when deciding how much to buy. By paying a subsidy equal to the external benefit each unit provides, the government can bring consumers to internalize the benefits conferred on others.

Because goods that create positive externalities are underconsumed and goods that create negative externalities are overconsumed from a societal standpoint, another solution is to require people to purchase the efficient quantity of these goods. It is common for governments to require a particular number of childhood immunizations and education through high school, while limiting the volume of toxic emissions and the number of pets that can be kept in a household. For example, in the interest of neighborhood serenity, no resident in the city of Sauk Rapids, Minnesota, may keep more than two dogs and four cats.

Imperfect Competition

Hawaiian shirts sell for $30 and up in the gift shop of the Honolulu International Airport. In downtown Honolulu, the Daiei supermarket sells similar Hawaiian shirts for $14.

Both places sell shirts that are made in Hawaii at comparable costs; most of the price differential stems from differing levels of competition. Daiei faces competition from hundreds of other shirt sellers, and if the managers were to raise their prices significantly above marginal cost, competitors would undercut their prices and steal away some of their customers and profits. When price equals marginal cost, consumers keep buying until their marginal benefit equals the price, and because price equals marginal cost, the efficiency condition of marginal cost equaling marginal benefit is satisfied.

Prices are higher at the airport because the number of sellers is limited and their clientele is captive. That gives the airport gift shop *market power*—the ability to influence prices. It is market power that allows a single operator of ballpark concession stands to charge relatively more for hot dogs and allows a campus bookstore to charge more for batteries than do competing stores in a distant shopping area.

robertharding/Alamy

In the absence of competitors who would undercut excessive prices, the gift shop can charge prices above the marginal cost of production. Suppose that it costs $14 to put each Hawaiian shirt on the market (that is, the $14 downtown price equals the marginal cost, as is the case in perfectly competitive markets). Different consumers place a variety of values on Hawaiian shirts, from 0 to more than $100. When the price is $30, consumers who value the shirts in the range between $14 and $30 are dissuaded from purchasing shirts, even though they value shirts at more than the $14 cost of production. When someone who values a shirt at, say, $20 does not buy one because the price is $30, society experiences a deadweight loss equal to the $20 − $14 = $6 net benefit the consumer would have received if the price had been $14. Imperfect competition leads to market failure as a result of lost opportunities for net gains such as this.

Imperfect Information

McDonald's Restaurant and Doug's Restaurant are both located on North Canal Boulevard in Thibodaux, Louisiana. Why would visitors eat at McDonald's when they could

encounter local cuisine at Doug's? One reason involves *imperfect information*, which exists when at least one buyer doesn't know the true benefit of a good or service, or at least one seller doesn't know the true cost of providing a good or service. As far as visitors know, Doug's may or may not be a good place to eat. In contrast, most visitors know exactly what is on the menu at McDonald's and how it will taste. The additional investment of time and money needed to determine food quality at unknown restaurants like Doug's stands in the way of competition and thereby thwarts market efficiency. More broadly, although plenty of businesses charge prices above marginal cost, consumers' fear of the unknown hinders competition from new entries.

When buyers and sellers don't share the same information, the problem of *asymmetric information* arises. For example, those in the marriage market use ease of attraction as a signal of the unseen qualities of a potential mate. Employers and shoppers likewise use college degrees, grades, name brands, and prices as imperfect signals of quality among workers and products when perfect information is not available. Nobel laureate George Akerlof pointed out that there is asymmetric information between buyers and sellers of used cars: sellers know things about the quality of their cars that potential buyers do not. Suppose that used cars are either good or bad, and that good used cars are worth $20,000, whereas bad used cars are worth $10,000. Given the uncertainty about whether a car will be a "lemon" (bad), buyers are unlikely to pay $20,000 for a used car. If, in the buyer's estimation, there is a 20% chance that the car is a lemon and an 80% chance that it's worth $20,000, the expected value of the car (the sum of each probability times the outcome that occurs with that probability) is $(0.2)(\$10,000) + (0.8)(\$20,000) = \$18,000$. Thus, sellers of good used cars won't get fair prices for their cars, but sellers of lemons will. The result is that owners of good used cars are more likely to hold on to their cars, and the used car market may be made up primarily of lemons.

For this reason, many buyers of used cars (and homes and boats) invest in a professional evaluation of their contemplated purchase to try to gain more of the information held by the seller. Car buyers are also wise to request a vehicle identification number (VIN) check on their car at a website such as www.carfax.com, which will reveal information on odometer readings, the number of previous owners, any major accidents in the vehicle's past, and other potential problems that sellers know about and buyers otherwise don't.

Adverse selection occurs when it costs varying amounts of money to serve different customers, but sellers cannot distinguish between high-need and low-need buyers. It would make sense for people who take more physical risks to buy more health insurance; for big eaters to patronize all-you-can-eat restaurants; and for people with terminal diseases to buy more life insurance. In efforts to limit adverse selection, insurance companies typically require physical exams and may not cover preexisting illnesses. All-you-can-eat restaurants and employers have a harder time dodging the adverse-selection bullet because they cannot discriminate on the basis of appetite or family size.

Moral hazard is the tendency for those with insurance against a problem to take fewer precautions to avoid that problem. Knowing that a hospital stay can cost $2,000 or more per day, people with insurance may be more likely to take up skydiving than are people who must pay their entire medical bill themselves. Laid-off workers covered by unemployment insurance take more time to find new jobs than do those who are ineligible or whose coverage has lapsed. And people with fire insurance may take more risks with candles in their homes because they will not have to pay the entire price of a new house if there is a fire. Since insurance companies can't monitor the risk-taking behavior of their customers, they use cost-sharing approaches such as copayments and experienced-based premiums to force insured people to internalize some of the costs of taking risks. People respond to incentives in rational ways, so the more they have to pay for their mistakes, the less likely they will be to make them.

The solutions to imperfect information are themselves imperfect and costly. Car and human checkups intended to level the informational playing field sometimes miss problems. High copayments place a financial burden on the poor. Only a 100% copayment would bring decision makers to internalize the full costs of their behaviors, and that would eliminate the risk-sharing benefits of insurance. When solutions are unavailable or incomplete, the information problems explained here obscure true marginal benefits or marginal costs and deter the efficient convergence of the two.

Public Goods

A handful of spy satellites spin 100 miles above the earth, recording a constant video stream of activities below. These billion-dollar detectives are intended to make the world safer by tracking military, drug, and terrorist activities. The U.S. National Reconnaissance Office operates satellites to intercept messages, draw maps, and gather visual information for U.S. intelligence agencies. As useful as spy satellites are to society, it would be difficult for a spy satellite market to bring about the efficient number of them because there are incentives for beneficiaries to receive the benefits of satellites without helping out with the costs.

Konstantin Shaklein/Alamy

A few relevant terms are useful in explaining why this is the case. A good or service is *nonrival in consumption* if one person's consumption of it does not affect anyone else's consumption of it. A street band is nonrival in consumption because one person's enjoyment of the music doesn't prevent others from enjoying it. In contrast, shoes are rival in consumption because if one person is wearing them, another person cannot. A good or service is *nonexcludable* if it is impossible to prevent other people from benefiting as long as one person is benefiting from it. A streetlight is nonexcludable because, if it is lighting the way for one driver, other drivers can benefit from the same light. Lockers are excludable because you can lock your locker and prevent others from entering. Goods and services that are both nonrival in consumption and nonexcludable are called *public goods*.

The challenge of creating the efficient number of spy satellites, as with street bands and streetlights, is that they are public goods. Everyone can benefit from them no matter who pays for them. Thus, the temptation is to be a *free rider* and enjoy the benefits of someone else's expenditures. If the Central Intelligence Agency (CIA) went from door to door asking everyone to pitch in to pay for the next satellite, it would be rational from an individual standpoint for many people to contribute less than their fair share of the price, and perhaps nothing, in hopes that others would purchase the satellite. The result is that private markets for public goods generally don't bring about the efficient quantity of output.

A common solution to the free-rider problem is for the government to collect taxes from the beneficiaries of public goods and use the revenues to purchase them in appropriate quantities. The spy satellites are indeed paid for with tax dollars, as are streetlights, police and fire departments, the Environmental Protection Agency, and the military.

It's Not Only Root Beer

Getting back to our root beer story, it's interesting to note that restaurants are not the only place where checks are split. The great benefit from health insurance is that it allows people to spread the risks and rising costs of health care. The downside is that, as with root beer, people make decisions about additional health care purchases knowing that they will personally bear only a small fraction of the price of these services. Between 1960 and 2016, the share of health care costs paid out of pocket dropped from 56 percent to 11 percent. According to health economist Devon Herrick, "A primary reason why health care costs are soaring is that most of the time when people enter the medical marketplace, they are spending someone else's money."[1] If the doctor asked whether you'd like to use an X-ray to rule out the possibility that the frozen pizza you dropped on your foot broke a toe, you might consider your copayment

[1] See www.ncpathinktank.org/commentaries/why-are-health-costs-rising.

for the procedure rather than the full cost of an X-ray and request X-rays that are not justified by their true cost. Similarly, if your car is dented by an errant baseball, you might weigh the benefit of getting it fixed against your share of the repair cost, not including the portion that the insurance company would pay. Like moral hazard problems, the problems caused by splitting checks with insurance companies could be diminished by charging consumers higher copayments. When costs and benefits are internalized, people generally make more efficient decisions.

Conclusion

Sometimes market incentives drive decisions away from what is best for society. When individuals don't bear the cost of their personal consumption choices, the incentive is to buy too much of goods and services that place burdens on others and too little of goods and services that benefit others. When barriers to competition exist, people can expect prices above marginal cost and lost opportunities to produce goods that are valued beyond their production cost. When information is imperfect, people cannot respond appropriately to true marginal costs and marginal benefits. And when goods are nonrival in consumption and nonexcludable, people have incentives to minimize expenditures on these public goods

in hopes of free-riding on the purchases of others. In these cases, markets fail to create all the net benefits they otherwise could, and the government may be able to nudge the outcomes in a direction more favorable to society.

Critical Thinking Questions

1. Do you consider the burden you impose on others when you and your friends order root beers and split the check? Do you consider the burden you impose on others when you order new shoes, thus creating production, transportation, and disposal externalities? Do you think about the congestion and pollution you create when you decide how many car trips to take?

2. Do you ever participate in adverse selection? How might adverse selection cause you to pay higher interest rates on your credit card balances?

3. Are you ever affected by moral hazard? How might moral hazard influence your decision to go waterskiing?

4. Why do you suppose there are 50 McDonald's restaurants within 10 miles of the tourism mecca of Orlando, Florida, but only 17 within the same distance of Oxnard, California (a town with a similar population size)? *Hint:* This difference is not caused by differing numbers of restaurant meals being eaten in the two cities.

AP® Macroeconomics Exam
Practice Test

Multiple-Choice Questions

Refer to the figure below to answer Question 1.

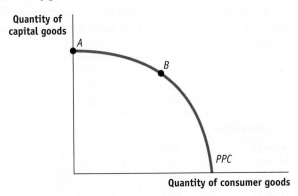

Quantity of capital goods

A

B

PPC

Quantity of consumer goods

1. A movement from point *B* to point *A* illustrates which of the following?
   a. a choice to produce only capital goods
   b. an advance in technology
   c. a decrease in available resources used to produce consumer goods
   d. an increase in the price of capital goods
   e. an increase in efficiency

Refer to the figure below to answer Question 2.

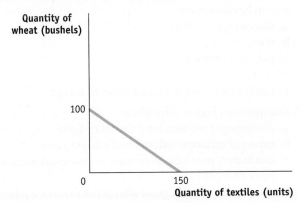

Quantity of wheat (bushels)

100

0   150
Quantity of textiles (units)

2. A country can produce either 100 bushels of wheat or 150 units of textiles, as shown on the graph above. If an advance in technology affects only the production of wheat, what happens to the slope of the production possibilities curve and the opportunity cost of wheat?

	Slope	*Opportunity cost of wheat*
a.	no change	no change
b.	decrease	decrease
c.	increase	decrease
d.	no change	increase
e.	decrease	increase

3. According to the concept of comparative advantage, which of the following is true when countries specialize and trade?
   a. Each country obtains an absolute advantage.
   b. Total world output increases.
   c. The production possibilities curve for both countries shifts outward.
   d. Prices fall in both countries.
   e. Deadweight loss is created.

Refer to the figure below to answer Question 4.

Quantity of corn (bushels)

800

Country A's PPC

400

Country B's PPC

0   200   500   **Quantity of computers**

4. Using equal amounts of labor hours, two countries, Country A and Country B, can produce corn and computers as shown. Based on the information provided, which of the following is true?
   a. Country A has an absolute advantage in the production of corn and computers.
   b. Country B has an absolute advantage in the production of corn and computers.
   c. Country A has a comparative advantage in the production of computers.
   d. Country B has a comparative advantage in the production of corn.
   e. Country A has an absolute advantage in the production of corn.

5. If the price of a complimentary good increases, which of the following will happen to the price and the quantity sold in a market?

	Price	*Quantity sold*
a.	increase	increase
b.	increase	decrease
c.	decrease	increase
d.	decrease	decrease
e.	increase	no change

6. If the wages of workers producing a good decrease, the price and quantity of the good sold will change in which of the following ways?

	Price	Quantity
a.	increase	increase
b.	increase	decrease
c.	decrease	increase
d.	decrease	decrease
e.	increase	no change

7. If real gross domestic product is declining, the economy is most likely experiencing which of the following?
   a. increasing unemployment
   b. negative long-run economic growth
   c. inflationary pressures
   d. an increase in aggregate demand
   e. a recovery

8. In the circular-flow model of an economy, which of the following is an injection into the flow of money?
   a. savings
   b. imports
   c. exports
   d. consumption
   e. taxes

9. Which of the following is not counted in a country's GDP?
   a. goods exported to other countries
   b. changes in inventories
   c. domestically produced capital goods
   d. financial assets, such as stocks and bonds
   e. newly produced services

10. Which of the following is true of the relationship between real GDP and nominal GDP?
    a. Real GDP is higher than nominal GDP when there is inflation in the economy.
    b. Real GDP is equal to nominal GDP when the economy is at full employment.
    c. Real GDP minus nominal GDP equals the rate of inflation.
    d. Real GDP is nominal GDP adjusted for changes in the price level.
    e. Real GDP increases when nominal GDP increases.

11. Which of the following transactions would be included in the calculation of GDP?
    a. Lee buys a used car.
    b. Kylie buys a new softball bat.
    c. Eric mows his own lawn rather than paying someone else $25 to mow it.
    d. Ray resells his ticket to a football game.
    e. Kumar volunteers for 3 hours per week as a tutor at the local high school.

12. If the real interest rate is 1% and the nominal interest rate is 4%, the expected rate of inflation is
    a. 0%.   d. 3%.
    b. 1%.   e. 5%.
    c. 2%.

13. Suppose that last year the price level increased and the production of goods and services increased. Nominal GDP has necessarily
    a. increased but real GDP decreased.
    b. increased but the value of real GDP cannot be determined.
    c. stayed the same but real GDP increased.
    d. increased and real GDP increased.
    e. decreased but real GDP increased.

14. Given the information provided below, what are the number of unemployed and the labor participation rate (*LFPR*)?

Population	1,000
Labor force	800
Employment	600

	Unemployed	*LFPR*
a.	200	80%
b.	400	80%
c.	200	25%
d.	400	60%
e.	400	25%

15. A worker who is laid off due to a recession is experiencing which type of unemployment?
    a. temporary
    b. frictional
    c. cyclical
    d. structural
    e. seasonal

16. Which of the following could lead the unemployment rate to be overstated?
    a. discouraged workers
    b. teenage workers
    c. part-time workers
    d. retired workers
    e. workers deciding which job offer to accept

17. Substitution bias results when
    a. discouraged workers leave the labor force.
    b. expected inflation reduces real interest rates.
    c. consumers purchase alternative goods in response to price changes.
    d. the demand for one good affects the price of a related good.
    e. buyers choose imports over domestically produced goods and services.

18. If the general price level doubles and at the same time a worker's real wage rate increases, what must be true of the worker's nominal wage rate?
    a. It doubled.
    b. It increased by less than double.
    c. It increased by more than double.
    d. It decreased.
    e. It did not change.

19. Which of the following is true of the natural rate of unemployment?
 a. It equals the actual rate of unemployment in short-run equilibrium.
 b. It includes both frictional and structural unemployment.
 c. It measures cyclical unemployment.
 d. It changes with the business cycle.
 e. It increases over time.

20. A Canadian recession will affect the United States' aggregate supply and demand in which of the following ways?

	Aggregate supply	Aggregate demand
a.	increase	increase
b.	increase	decrease
c.	decrease	increase
d.	decrease	decrease
e.	no change	decrease

21. Which of the following will shift the aggregate demand curve to the right?
 a. contractionary monetary policy
 b. a decrease in the aggregate price level
 c. a decrease in the value of household assets
 d. a decrease in the consumer confidence index
 e. an increase in planned business investment

22. If the marginal propensity to consume in an economy is 0.8 and the government increases spending by $5 million, GDP will increase by how much?
 a. $1 million
 b. $5 million
 c. $25 million
 d. $50 million
 e. $100 million

23. In the short run, a decrease in aggregate demand will change the price level and aggregate output in which of the following ways?

	Price level	Aggregate output
a.	increase	increase
b.	increase	decrease
c.	decrease	increase
d.	decrease	decrease
e.	increase	no change

24. Which of the following is the most likely to cause a leftward shift in the long-run aggregate supply curve?
 a. a decrease in the wage rate
 b. a decrease in short-run aggregate supply
 c. contractionary fiscal policy
 d. a deadly disease that decreases the size of the labor force
 e. a long-term decrease in demand

25. If an economy is in long-run equilibrium, how will an increase in aggregate demand affect real GDP and nominal wages in the long run?

	Real GDP	Nominal wages
a.	increase	increase
b.	increase	decrease
c.	decrease	increase
d.	decrease	decrease
e.	no change	increase

26. The long-run aggregate supply curve is always
 a. vertical and below potential output.
 b. horizontal and at potential output.
 c. upward-sloping at all output levels.
 d. vertical and at potential output.
 e. horizontal at all output levels.

27. An economy experiences inflationary pressures when the equilibrium level of output is
 a. too low.
 b. above the full employment level of output.
 c. equal to the full employment level of output.
 d. decreasing.
 e. in long-run equilibrium.

28. Which of the following policies might provide a remedy when the equilibrium output in an economy is above the potential level of output?
 a. Increase government spending.
 b. Decrease the federal funds rate.
 c. Increase transfer payments.
 d. Raise taxes.
 e. Buy more government securities.

29. Which of the following would cause the aggregate demand curve to shift to the right?
 a. an increase in taxes
 b. a decrease in consumer wealth
 c. an increase in consumer confidence
 d. a decrease in exports
 e. an increase in savings

30. Which of the following is a liability for a commercial bank?
 a. deposits
 b. loans
 c. reserves
 d. Treasury securities
 e. its building and equipment

31. If the interest rate is 2%, what is the present value of $1 paid to you in one year?
 a. less than $1
 b. $1
 c. $1.02
 d. $1.04
 e. $1.20

32. Which of the following is a component of the M1 money supply?
    a. gold
    b. cash
    c. savings deposits
    d. Treasury bills
    e. certificates of deposit

33. Which of the following will decrease the ability of the banking system to create money?
    a. a decrease in the amount of cash people hold
    b. a decrease in the reserve requirement
    c. an increase in the amount of excess reserves held by banks
    d. an increase in banks' willingness to make loans
    e. a decrease in the discount rate

34. If the reserve ratio is 10%, what is the maximum amount of money that could be created by a new deposit of $1,000?
    a. $1,000
    b. $1,010
    c. $1,100
    d. $10,000
    e. $20,000

35. Advances in information technology such as ATMs have had what effect on the demand for money and the interest rate?

	Money demand	Interest rate
a.	increase	increase
b.	increase	decrease
c.	decrease	increase
d.	decrease	decrease
e.	no change	decrease

36. Which of the following will decrease the demand for money?
    a. an increase in the aggregate price level
    b. a decrease in the use of mobile devices for payments
    c. an increase in the interest rate
    d. a decrease in the supply of money
    e. a decrease in real GDP

37. Which of the following will increase the interest rate in the market for loanable funds?
    a. a decrease in the expected rate of return from investment spending
    b. an increase in government budget deficits
    c. an increase in the aggregate savings rate
    d. a decrease in expected inflation
    e. an increase in capital inflows

38. Which of the following is true of the money supply curve?
    a. It shifts to the right when the interest rate increases.
    b. It shifts to the left when the savings rate decreases.
    c. It is vertical.
    d. It shows a positive relationship between the interest rate and the quantity of loanable funds.
    e. It shifts to the left when the Federal Reserve buys Treasury bills.

39. Crowding out occurs when government borrowing leads to an increase in
    a. real GDP.
    b. inflation.
    c. consumer confidence.
    d. unemployment.
    e. interest rates.

40. According to the quantity theory of money, the money supply multiplied by the velocity of money is equal to
    a. nominal GDP.
    b. real GDP.
    c. full employment real GDP.
    d. the price level.
    e. a constant value.

41. An open market purchase of securities by a central bank will lead to which of the following?
    a. a decrease in the demand for money
    b. a decrease in interest rates
    c. an increase in investment demand
    d. a decrease in aggregate demand
    e. a decrease in the price level

42. The Federal Reserve will take action to decrease the federal funds rate in an attempt to
    a. increase unemployment.
    b. increase the money supply.
    c. reduce inflation.
    d. increase real GDP.
    e. discourage investment.

43. An increase in expected inflation is likely to have which of the following effects?
    a. shift the long-run Phillips curve to the right
    b. shift the short-run Phillips curve downward
    c. increase the actual inflation rate
    d. decrease the natural unemployment rate
    e. shift the short-run aggregate supply curve to the right

44. Which of the following policies could the Federal Reserve implement to combat inflation?
    a. lower the reserve requirement
    b. raise the discount rate
    c. buy Treasury securities
    d. raise taxes
    e. reduce government spending

45. Which of the following is a contractionary fiscal policy?
    a. raising the reserve requirement
    b. decreasing transfer payments
    c. decreasing taxes
    d. raising government spending
    e. increasing the federal funds rate

46. If a country currently has a positive national debt and a balanced budget, how would a decrease in taxes affect the country's deficit and debt?

	Deficit	*Debt*
a.	increase	increase
b.	increase	decrease
c.	decrease	increase
d.	decrease	decrease
e.	decrease	no change

47. A country's national debt is
    a. the amount the country owes to foreigners.
    b. the difference between the country's tax revenue and government spending in a given year.
    c. the sum of the country's past deficits and surpluses.
    d. always positive.
    e. higher when gross domestic product is increasing.

48. Which of the following is an example of contractionary monetary policy?
    a. decreasing taxes
    b. increasing government spending
    c. lowering the discount rate
    d. lowering the reserve requirement
    e. selling Treasury securities

49. During a recession, the U.S. Federal Reserve might _____ its purchase of Treasury bills in order to _____ the Federal funds rate and _____ aggregate demand.

	Treasury bill purchases	*Federal funds rate*	*Aggregate demand*
a.	increase	decrease	increase
b.	increase	decrease	decrease
c.	decrease	decrease	increase
d.	decrease	increase	increase
e.	decrease	increase	decrease

50. The short-run Phillips curve shows a _____ relationship between the rate of inflation and the _____ rate.

a.	negative	unemployment
b.	positive	interest
c.	negative	employment
d.	positive	GDP growth
e.	negative	inflation

51. Which of the following is true of the long-run Phillips curve?
    a. It shows a negative relationship between the unemployment rate and the inflation rate.
    b. It shows a negative relationship between the unemployment rate and the interest rate.
    c. It shifts upward when expected inflation increases.
    d. It is vertical at the natural rate of unemployment.
    e. It shifts to the right when a central bank pursues expansionary monetary policy.

52. An increase in which of the following over time best describes economic growth?
    a. nominal GDP
    b. real GDP per capita
    c. nominal GDP per capita
    d. the labor force
    e. aggregate demand

53. Which of the following is true of an increase in labor productivity in an economy?
    a. It will shift the long-run aggregate supply curve to the left.
    b. It will decrease the wages of workers.
    c. It will reduce the size of the labor force.
    d. It will shift the production possibilities curve outward.
    e. It results from a decrease in the availability of capital.

54. Which of the following is most likely to lead to long-run economic growth?
    a. a more restrictive immigration policy
    b. higher trade barriers
    c. increased government funding of education
    d. contractionary fiscal policy
    e. negative net investment

55. Which of the following transactions will be recorded in the financial account of the United States?
    a. A U.S. firm sells $100 million worth of its product to Mexico.
    b. Chinese imports to the United States increase by $200 million.
    c. The wages paid by U.S. firms to workers in India increase by $20 million.
    d. Canada purchases $50 million of new U.S. Treasury bills.
    e. The United States' trade balance moves from deficit to surplus.

56. The exchange rate is the price of
    a. goods expressed in terms of another nation's currency.
    b. one nation's currency expressed in terms of another country's currency.
    c. the same basket of goods purchased in two countries.
    d. exported goods, adjusted for inflation.
    e. imported goods expressed in the other country's currency.

57. Which of the following would cause the U.S. dollar to depreciate relative to the Canadian dollar?
    a. an increase in net capital flows from Canada to the United States
    b. an increase in the real interest rate in Canada relative to the United States
    c. an increase in the balance of payments on the current account in the United States
    d. a doubling of prices in both Canada and the United States
    e. a decrease in exports from Canada to the United States

58. If a country's inflation rate rises, which of the following will happen to the demand for and value of the country's currency on the foreign exchange market?

Demand	Value
a. shift right	depreciate
b. shift right	appreciate
c. shift left	appreciate
d. shift left	depreciate
e. no change	depreciate

59. If foreign investors decrease investment in the United States, what will happen to the value of the dollar in the foreign exchange market and U.S. net exports?

Value of the U.S. dollar	U.S. net exports
a. appreciate	increase
b. appreciate	decrease
c. depreciate	increase
d. depreciate	decrease
e. no change	no change

60. Which of the following is an example of U.S. direct foreign investment?
 a. a U.S. citizen spending while traveling abroad
 b. a U.S. manufacturer building a factory in another country
 c. a U.S. investor purchasing corporate bonds from a Mexican company
 d. a U.S. worker sending money to a family member living abroad
 e. a U.S. bank loaning money to an international company

Free-Response Questions

1. Assume the country of Boland is currently in long-run equilibrium.
 a. Draw a correctly labeled production possibilities curve if Boland produces only corn and textiles. On your graph, label point X, a point that illustrates a productively efficient output combination for Boland.
 b. Draw a correctly labeled aggregate supply and aggregate demand graph for Boland. Show each of the following:
  i. equilibrium output, labeled Y_1
  ii. equilibrium price level, labeled PL_1

 c. Assume the government of Boland has a balanced budget and decides to raise government spending.
  i. What effect will the reduction in taxes have on Boland's budget?
  ii. Show the short-run effect of the reduction in taxes on your graph from part b, labeling the new equilibrium output and price level Y_2 and PL_2, respectively.
 d. Draw a correctly labeled graph of the loanable funds market. Suppose the government borrows money to pay for the increased spending. Show the effect of this borrowing on your graph from part c.
  i. Label the equilibrium interest rate before the government borrowing i_1.
  ii. Label the equilibrium interest rate after the government borrowing i_2.
 e. How will the change in the interest rate depicted in your graph from part d affect real GDP in the long run? Explain. **(10 points)**

2. Suppose a firm in the United States sells $5 million worth of its output to consumers in Canada.
 a. How will this transaction affect each of the following?
  i. Canada's current account balance
  ii. the United States' current account balance
  iii. aggregate demand in Canada
 b. Suppose there is an increase in U.S. financial investment in Canada.
  i. Draw a correctly labeled graph of the foreign exchange market for Canadian dollars and show how an increase in U.S. financial investment in Canada affects equilibrium in the market.
  ii. What happens to the value of the Canadian dollar relative to the U.S. dollar? **(6 points)**

3. Assume the expected rate of inflation is zero.
 a. Draw a correctly labeled graph showing the short-run and long-run Phillips curves. On your graph, identify each of the following:
  i. the nonaccelerating inflation rate of unemployment, labeled N
  ii. a point on the short-run Phillips curve indicating an unemployment rate below the natural rate of unemployment, labeled A
 b. Now assume the inflation rate associated with point A in part a is incorporated into inflationary expectations. Show the effect of this change in expectations on your graph from part a. **(5 points)**

AP® Microeconomics Exam
Practice Test

Multiple-Choice Questions

1. The study of microeconomics includes measuring the
   a. profit of a corporation.
   b. national output level.
   c. money supply.
   d. overall level of prices.
   e. number of people employed in the economy.

2. Economic models are
   a. exact replicas of the real world using the concept of *ceteris paribus*.
   b. exact replicas of the real world using the concept of *laissez-faire*.
   c. simplifications of the real world using the concept of *laissez-faire*.
   d. simplifications of the real world using the concept of *ceteris paribus*.
   e. simplifications of the real world using the concept of *caveat emptor*.

3. What does a straight production possibilities curve indicate?
   a. no specialization of resources and increasing opportunity costs
   b. no specialization of resources and decreasing opportunity costs
   c. no specialization of resources and constant opportunity costs
   d. specialization of resources and decreasing opportunity costs
   e. specialization of resources and constant opportunity costs

4. Which of the following is an example of a positive economic statement?
   a. A college education should be provided tuition-free to all students.
   b. Economics is the study of scarcity and choice.
   c. Governments should never run budget deficits.
   d. Large universities ought to do more to prepare students to make ethical decisions.
   e. Corporate income taxes in the United States should not be increased.

5. If a curve on a two-dimensional graph represents a direct or positive relationship between two variables, what change in the variable on the vertical axis is associated with an increase in the variable on the horizontal axis?
   a. a decrease, as shown by a movement down along the curve
   b. a decrease, as shown by a movement up along the curve
   c. an increase, as shown by a movement down along the curve
   d. an increase, as shown by a shift of the curve to the right
   e. an increase, as shown by a movement up along the curve

6. Which of the following would cause an increase in the quantity demanded of tea?
   a. an increase in the supply of coffee, a substitute
   b. a decrease in the price of coffee, a substitute
   c. a decrease in the price of tea
   d. a decrease in the supply of sugar, a complement
   e. an increase in the price of sugar, a complement

7. Which of the following would occur in the market for grapefruits if an increase in popularity caused the price of grapefruits to rise?
   a. a shift of the demand curve to the left
   b. a shift of the supply curve to the right
   c. a movement down along the supply curve
   d. a movement up along the supply curve
   e. a movement down along the demand curve

8. Assuming relatively elastic supply and demand curves, which of the following would occur if the market quantity were to fall below the equilibrium quantity due to a quota in a competitive market?
   a. a deadweight loss
   b. a market surplus
   c. a violation of the law of demand
   d. a less elastic demand
   e. the development of a horizontal demand curve

9. A new price ceiling set below the equilibrium price in a competitive market with relatively elastic supply and demand would result in which of the following?
   a. an increase in the quantity demanded and an increase in the quantity supplied
   b. an increase in the quantity demanded and no change in the quantity supplied
   c. an increase in the quantity demanded and a decrease in the quantity supplied
   d. a decrease in the quantity demanded and an increase in the quantity supplied
   e. a decrease in the quantity demanded and no change in the quantity supplied

Refer to the table provided to respond to Questions 10 and 11. The numbers in the table represent the numbers of solar panels or bicycles that can be produced by the countries of Alpha and Omega each day if they completely specialize in one good or the other using the same resources. Assume that each country faces constant opportunity costs.

	Quantity of Panels	Quantity of Bicycles
Alpha	12	24
Omega	5	15

10. What do the numbers in the table indicate about Omega?
    a. It has a comparative advantage in the production of bicycles.
    b. It has a comparative advantage in the production of panels.
    c. The opportunity cost of producing 1 panel is $\frac{1}{3}$ of a bicycle.
    d. It should focus its effort on the production of panels only.
    e. Since Omega does not have an absolute advantage in producing either good, Omega cannot carry out mutually beneficial trade with Alpha.

11. If something changed in Omega that allowed it to make up to 15 panels or up to 45 bicycles,
    a. Omega's opportunity cost of producing 1 bicycle would be 3 panels.
    b. Omega would have the comparative advantage in the production of panels.
    c. Omega would not trade with Alpha, since Omega now has an absolute advantage in producing both goods.
    d. there would be no change in the good in which Omega should specialize in order to maximize the gains from trade.
    e. Omega would be willing to trade 4 bicycles for 1 panel.

12. Due to the spreading effect, as output increases,
    a. marginal product initially rises and then falls.
    b. marginal product initially falls and then rises.
    c. marginal product remains constant at large levels of output.
    d. average fixed cost rises.
    e. average fixed cost falls.

13. Which of the following is true when marginal product is decreasing?
    a. Average product is necessarily decreasing.
    b. Average product is necessarily increasing.
    c. Average product could be increasing or decreasing.
    d. Total cost is increasing at a decreasing rate.
    e. Marginal cost is decreasing.

14. For what type of good does a decrease in income lead to an increase in demand?
    a. a normal good
    b. an inferior good
    c. a good with price-elastic demand
    d. a good with price-inelastic demand
    e. a good with price-unit-elastic demand

15. Which of the following curves always falls as output increases?
    a. the marginal cost curve
    b. the average variable cost curve
    c. the average total cost curve
    d. the average fixed cost curve
    e. the total fixed cost curve

16. If a firm's long-run average total cost falls as output rises, the firm is experiencing
    a. economies of scale.
    b. economies of scope.
    c. diseconomies of scale.
    d. increasing marginal returns.
    e. diminishing marginal returns.

17. If a firm experiencing decreasing returns to scale doubles all of its inputs, which of the following will occur?
    a. Output will decrease.
    b. Output will less than double.
    c. Output will more than double.
    d. Total cost will decrease.
    e. Fixed cost will decrease.

18. What is necessarily true about a perfectly competitive market?
    a. In the long run economic profits are positive.
    b. In the short run there are no fixed costs.
    c. Productive efficiency will be achieved in the short run.
    d. Allocative efficiency is not achieved in the short run.
    e. Productive efficiency will be achieved in the long run.

19. What is one way to distinguish implicit costs from explicit costs?
    a. Checks are only written for explicit costs.
    b. Checks are only written for implicit costs.
    c. All costs are implicit, but some are also explicit.
    d. All costs are explicit, but some are also implicit.
    e. All opportunity costs are implicit.

20. What does the Herfindahl–Hirschman Index measure?
    a. the degree of comparative advantage one nation has relative to another
    b. the amount of specialization and trade between nations
    c. opportunity cost differences between firms
    d. the amount of market concentration in a given industry
    e. the amount of government intervention in a market

21. Which two market structures are characterized by free entry into and exit from the industry in the long run?
    a. monopolistic competition and monopoly
    b. monopolistic competition and perfect competition
    c. monopolistic competition and oligopoly
    d. oligopoly and perfect competition
    e. monopoly and perfect competition

22. If supply increases and the demand curve is downward-sloping, which of the following is necessarily true?
  a. consumer surplus increases
  b. consumer surplus decreases
  c. consumer surplus is unaffected
  d. producer surplus is unaffected
  e. producer surplus increases

23. Firms generally produce the quantity that equates marginal revenue with
  a. price, because that minimizes average total cost.
  b. average total cost, because that minimizes total cost.
  c. average variable cost, because that stabilizes costs.
  d. marginal cost, because that minimizes average total cost.
  e. marginal cost, because that maximizes profit or minimizes loss.

24. For a competitive firm, if marginal revenue exceeds marginal cost at the current level of output and the firm is currently earning economic losses, what could the firm certainly do?
  a. increase output to ensure economic profits
  b. decrease output to ensure economic profits
  c. increase output to reduce economic losses
  d. decrease output to reduce economic losses
  e. shut down to reduce economic losses

Use the following figure to answer Question 25.

25. At the equilibrium price, producer surplus is
  a. $6.   **d.** $16.
  b. $8.   **e.** $24.
  c. $12.

26. The price below which a firm in a perfectly competitive industry will shut down in the long run is determined by the minimum of
  a. marginal cost.
  b. average total cost.
  c. total cost.
  d. total variable cost.
  e. average fixed cost.

27. To maximize utility, a consumer will always select a consumption bundle represented by a point
  a. on the consumer's budget line.
  b. below the consumer's budget line.
  c. above the consumer's budget line.
  d. as far to the right along the budget line as possible.
  e. as high on the budget line as possible.

28. In a perfectly competitive industry, the long-run supply curve is flatter and more elastic than the short-run supply curve due to
  a. the availability of more substitutes.
  b. the availability of more complements.
  c. economies of scale.
  d. diseconomies of scale.
  e. easy exit and entry of firms.

29. Jennifer owns a hot dog vending business. Each month she spends $1,000 on fixed capital and $2,000 on buns, hot dogs, and supplies. Jennifer's monthly total revenue is $3,000. In order to start this business, Jennifer had to quit her teaching job, in which she earned $2,500 per month and had no work-related expenses. Jennifer earns
  a. an accounting profit of $5,500.
  b. an accounting profit of $3,000.
  c. a normal profit.
  d. an economic profit of $0.
  e. an economic profit of −$2,500.

30. When marginal revenue is positive and decreasing for a monopolist, what is happening to total revenue?
  a. It is increasing at an increasing rate.
  b. It is decreasing at the same rate as marginal revenue.
  c. It is decreasing faster than marginal revenue.
  d. It is increasing at a decreasing rate.
  e. It is decreasing slower than marginal revenue.

31. What type of tax would collect $1,000 from a person with a $10,000 income, $2,000 from a person with a $20,000 income, and $4,000 from a person with a $40,000 income?
  a. a progressive tax
  b. a proportional tax
  c. a regressive tax
  d. an excise tax
  e. a tax incidence

32. What would happen to the consumer surplus that was lost if a perfectly competitive market became a monopoly facing the same demand and costs?
  a. All of it would be gained by the monopolist.
  b. Some of it would be gained by the monopolist, and the rest would be part of the deadweight loss.
  c. It would all be part of the deadweight loss.
  d. It would be paid to the government in taxes.
  e. It would be transferred to the Federal Trade Commission.

33. Which of the following is a distinguishing characteristic of a natural monopoly, assuming that it is capable of earning positive economic profit?
   a. Profit is maximized at the output level that equates marginal revenue and marginal cost.
   b. Profit is maximized at the output level that equates price and marginal cost.
   c. The average total cost curve crosses the demand curve twice in the economies of scale region.
   d. The average total cost curve crosses the demand curve in the diseconomies of scale region.
   e. The marginal cost curve crosses the average total cost curve at the minimum point of the average total cost curve.

34. Which of the following is true of a natural monopoly? If regulators
   a. set a price ceiling equal to marginal cost, firms will not be willing to produce in the long run unless they are subsidized.
   b. set a price ceiling equal to average total cost, there will be no deadweight loss.
   c. set a price ceiling above the average total cost, the firm will not be able to make a profit.
   d. choose not to set a price ceiling, the firm will be a price-taker and the market will determine the price.
   e. split the monopolist into several smaller firms, the average total cost will decrease.

35. The efficient use of a common resource is most likely to be achieved by
   a. subsidizing use of the resource.
   b. taxing use of the resource.
   c. eliminating requirements for tradable licenses for the right to use the resource.
   d. eliminating private property rights.
   e. making the resource nonexcludable.

36. Which of the following is a result of perfect price discrimination?
   a. a gain in producer surplus
   b. a gain in consumer surplus
   c. less output overall
   d. marginal revenue less than price
   e. marginal revenue greater than price

37. An oligopoly is a market with
   a. only one firm.
   b. fewer firms than in a monopolistically competitive market, and the existence of interdependent firms.
   c. more firms than in a perfectly competitive market, and the existence of interdependent firms.
   d. more firms than in a monopoly, and the existence of independent firms.
   e. more firms than in a monopolistically competitive market, and the existence of independent firms.

38. The numbers in the following payoff matrix indicate profits for firms Alpha and Beta.

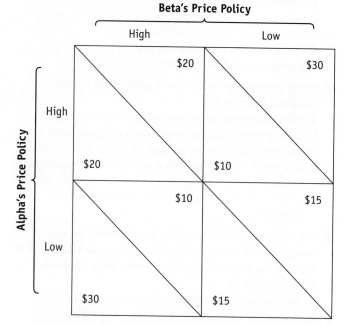

Which of the following is true?
   a. Charging a high price is a dominant strategy for Alpha.
   b. Charging a high price is a dominant strategy for Beta.
   c. Beta will charge a high price if Alpha charges a high price.
   d. Alpha will charge a high price if Beta charges a high price.
   e. Charging a low price is a dominant strategy for Alpha.

39. In the long run, a monopolistically competitive firm will earn
   a. positive or negative economic profit, depending on the situation.
   b. positive economic profit due to barriers to entry.
   c. normal profit.
   d. positive economic profit due to a differentiated product.
   e. positive economic profit due to price discrimination.

40. If a country had perfect income equality, its Lorenz curve would be
   a. U-shaped.
   b. L-shaped.
   c. V-shaped.
   d. straight.
   e. downward-sloping.

41. The labor demand curve for a firm hiring in a perfectly competitive labor market is
   a. the firm's marginal revenue product curve.
   b. the firm's marginal product curve.
   c. horizontal.
   d. the firm's average product curve.
   e. the firm's marginal revenue curve.

42. Suppose Brenda's Boat Taxis rents capital in a perfectly competitive capital market. Brenda's Boat Taxis should rent more capital if which condition is true?
- **a.** The marginal revenue product of capital is equal to the rental rate.
- **b.** The average revenue product of capital is equal to the rental rate.
- **c.** The marginal revenue product of capital is less than the rental rate.
- **d.** The marginal revenue product of capital is greater than the rental rate.
- **e.** The average revenue product of capital is less than the rental rate.

Use the following per day employment and output data for Lenny's Lattes to answer Questions 43 and 44.

Number of workers	Total number of lattes
0	0
1	10
2	30
3	60
4	100
5	125
6	140

43. If lattes sell in a perfectly competitive market for $4 each, what is the marginal revenue product of the third worker?
- **a.** $4
- **b.** $12
- **c.** $60
- **d.** $120
- **e.** $240

44. If lattes sell in a perfectly competitive market for $4 each and workers are paid $80 per day, how many workers should Lenny hire to maximize profit?
- **a.** 2
- **b.** 3
- **c.** 4
- **d.** 5
- **e.** 6

45. Which of the following is always horizontal?
- **a.** the demand curve facing a firm that sells its product in a perfectly competitive market
- **b.** the labor demand curve for a firm hiring in a perfectly competitive labor market
- **c.** the labor supply curve for a monopsony
- **d.** the demand curve for a monopoly
- **e.** the long-run industry supply curve in a goods market

46. If Keno's Cars is the only employer in a small town, that firm is a
- **a.** monopolist.
- **b.** monopolistic competitor.
- **c.** monopsonist.
- **d.** perfectly competitive firm.
- **e.** Keynesian.

47. The marginal factor cost curve of labor for a monopsonist is
- **a.** upward-sloping and above the supply curve at every quantity of labor beyond one.
- **b.** downward-sloping and above the supply curve at every quantity of labor beyond one.
- **c.** upward-sloping and below the supply curve at every quantity of labor beyond one.
- **d.** downward-sloping and below the supply curve at every quantity of labor beyond one.
- **e.** upward-sloping and coincident with the supply curve of labor.

48. A perfectly competitive firm's short-run supply curve
- **a.** does not exist.
- **b.** is perfectly elastic.
- **c.** is the same as the firm's marginal cost curve at every price.
- **d.** is that portion of the firm's marginal cost curve that lies above the *ATC* curve.
- **e.** is that portion of the firm's marginal cost curve that lies above the *AVC* curve.

49. Higher wages paid in order to motivate hard work and reduce worker turnover are called
- **a.** compensating differentials.
- **b.** union wages.
- **c.** efficiency wages.
- **d.** equilibrium wages.
- **e.** marginal productivity wages.

50. To minimize the cost of producing a given quantity of output, a firm should
- **a.** equate the marginal product of capital per dollar spent on capital and the marginal product of labor per dollar spent on labor.
- **b.** equate the total amount spent on labor and the total amount spent on capital.
- **c.** make the marginal revenue product of capital per dollar spent on capital greater than the marginal revenue product of labor per dollar spent on labor.
- **d.** equate the marginal revenue product of capital and the marginal revenue product of labor.
- **e.** hire mostly the factor of production that has the lowest cost per unit of the factor.

51. The Coase theorem suggests that when transaction costs are low, mutually beneficial deals between private parties cause externalities to be
- **a.** internalized.
- **b.** inefficiently large.
- **c.** inefficiently small.
- **d.** taxed by the government.
- **e.** produced in illegal markets.

52. A market with external costs and no external benefits will do which of the following?
 a. produce too much output
 b. produce too little output
 c. have a price that is too high
 d. experience deadweight gains
 e. produce the socially optimal quantity

53. The deadweight loss caused by an excise tax
 a. consists of lost producer and consumer surplus.
 b. results in gains to consumers but losses to producers.
 c. results in gains to producers but losses to consumers.
 d. results from overproduction.
 e. results from externalities.

54. What is true if marginal social benefit exceeds marginal social costs at the market level of output?
 a. A negative externality exists, and the government could correct for it with a Pigouvian tax.
 b. A negative externality exists, and the government could correct for it with a Pigouvian subsidy.
 c. A positive externality exists, and the government could correct for it with a Pigouvian tax.
 d. A positive externality exists, and the government could correct for it with a Pigouvian subsidy.
 e. The market outcome is ideal, since there are positive marginal benefits.

55. What taxes are designed to reduce external costs?
 a. Pigouvian taxes
 b. income taxes
 c. Okun's taxes
 d. Keynesian taxes
 e. sales taxes

56. Company A and Company B are monopolistically competitive firms that make winter coats. If Company A adds fuzzy trim to its coats and Company B doesn't, then Company A is necessarily practicing
 a. price leadership.
 b. tit-for-tat strategy.
 c. product differentiation.
 d. tacit collusion.
 e. cartel behavior.

57. Which of the following suggests that solutions to externalities can be achieved in the private sector when transaction costs are low and property rights are clearly defined?
 a. the law of supply
 b. the law of demand
 c. the optimal consumption rule
 d. the optimal output rule
 e. the Coase theorem

Use the graph provided to answer Questions 58 and 59.

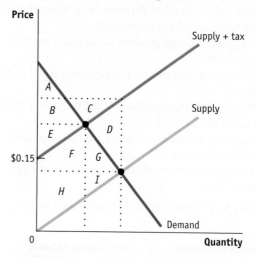

58. Suppose the peanut market is at equilibrium as shown in this graph. If an excise tax of $0.15 per unit is imposed on producers, the consumer surplus that would result after the imposition of the tax is represented by which area?
 a. *A, B, C, D, E, F, G*
 b. *A, B, C, D*
 c. *E, F, H*
 d. *A, B, E*
 e. *A, B*

59. What area represents the deadweight loss that would result from the imposition of the $0.15 tax on producers?
 a. *A, B, E*
 b. *G, I*
 c. *C*
 d. *D*
 e. *F*

60. What is the term for a situation in which distorted incentives arise because an individual has private information about his or her own actions but someone else bears the costs of a lack of care or effort?
 a. moral hazard
 b. adverse selection
 c. upper hand
 d. game theory
 e. prisoner's dilemma

Free-Response Questions

1. Patent Ted's Pharmaceutical Company is the only maker of a drug that cures laziness. The table below provides a portion of Patent Ted's demand schedule. Patent Ted's demand curve is linear.

Price	Quantity demanded
$101	0
100	1
51	50
50	51
1	100
0	101

a. Draw Patent Ted's demand curve on a graph.
b. Draw Patent Ted's marginal revenue curve on the graph for part a.
   i. What is the marginal revenue for the first unit?
   ii. What is the marginal revenue for the 51st unit?
c. Label as *A* the point along the quantity axis at which the price elasticity of demand is 1.
d. Each pill costs Patent Ted $10 to produce. Draw the company's marginal cost curve on the graph.
e. On the graph, label the profit-maximizing price *P** and the profit-maximizing quantity *Q**.
f. Suppose Patent Ted has no fixed cost. Completely shade-in the area on the graph that represents profit.
g. In a few years, the patent on these pills will expire and this market will become perfectly competitive. If there are no other changes related to the production or demand for these pills, what price will firms charge in the perfectly competitive market? Explain your answer. **(10 points)**

2. Suppose that Ann's Oregon Omelets uses both labor and capital such that the marginal product per hour of labor is 5 omelets and the marginal product per hour of capital is 15 omelets. The wage is $25 per hour, and the capital rents for $75 per hour.
   a. What should Ann do if she wants to minimize her cost at the current level of output? Explain.
   b. Now assume that the wage rate rises to $30 per hour while the marginal product of labor rises to 6 omelets and everything else remains the same. What should Ann do if she wants to minimize her cost? Explain.
   c. Using the data from part b and assuming Ann buys her labor in a perfectly competitive labor market, draw a correctly labeled graph of Ann's labor supply and labor demand. **(6 points)**

3. The country of MeTee has a perfectly competitive hot dog market with supply and demand curves as shown in the accompanying graph.

a. If the government imposed a price ceiling of $3.50 per pack of hot dogs, would the quantity of hot dogs sold in the market increase, decrease, or stay the same? Explain your answer.
b. Now suppose there is no price ceiling, but the government bans all hot dogs. Calculate the deadweight loss that results from this ban. Show your work.
c. Now suppose that there is no price ceiling or ban, but that the government collects a $2.00 excise tax from consumers on each pack of hot dogs purchased. Indicate the values of each of the following:
   i. the consumer surplus
   ii. the total revenue received by sellers of hot dogs
   iii. the total tax revenue collected by the government of MeTee **(6 points)**

EM

Enrichment Modules

Module A Financial Markets and Crises

Module B Behavioral Economics

Module C The Economics of Information

Module D Indifference Curves and Consumer Choice

Hopefully this sampling of economics has kindled your interest in more than just exam content. If you've wondered what the financial crisis of 2008 was all about, you'll enjoy Enrichment Module A, which tells the story of the Great Recession. Have you questioned the rationality of buyers or sellers? Enrichment Module B explains how economists deal with behavior that isn't so rational. If you've ever bought a used car, you know that even rational people sometimes don't have all the information they would like. Enrichment Module C explains how imperfect information affects markets and discusses related problems and remedies. In Enrichment Module D you will learn how economists use indifference curves to illustrate preferences and to model various aspects of consumer choice. Finally, the Financial Literacy Handbook that follows Enrichment Module D will help you navigate your own financial situation. While these Modules cover material in greater depth than is expected for the current AP® exams, they provide interesting background and insights for subsequent coursework, and they offer advice for making good economic decisions and developing sound financial habits.

Financial Markets and Crises

> **In this Module, you will learn to:**
> - Describe the importance of a well-functioning financial system
> - List the causes of financial crises in the economy
> - Identify the macroeconomic consequences of financial crises
> - Explain the factors leading to the financial crisis of 2008

The Role of Financial Markets

These days, almost everyone is connected in some way to *financial markets*. When you receive a paycheck, pay a bill, borrow money, or use a credit card, the financial markets assist with the transaction. And a Federal Deposit Insurance Corporation (FDIC) study found that about 91% of U.S. households have some form of checking or savings account.

In Module 22, we learned about the three tasks of a financial system: to reduce transaction costs, to reduce risk, and to provide liquidity. The financial system performs these tasks largely through financial intermediaries, such as banks and mutual funds. In Module 25, we looked at what banks do and how problems in the banking system can adversely affect the economy. Past problems have led to financial regulations that help to ensure a safe and efficient financial system. But what happens in an economy when its financial markets do not function well—or even worse, collapse? In this Module we will take another look at the role of financial markets in the economy and the causes and consequences of financial crises, including the 2008 financial crisis.

The Importance of an Efficient Financial System

A well-functioning financial system promotes the saving and investing required for long-run economic growth. Depository institutions such as banks are a major part of an economy's financial system and are necessary to facilitate the flow of funds from lenders to borrowers. Let's take a look at the role the banking system and other **financial markets**—the markets that channel private saving into investment spending—play in an economy and how problems in the financial system can result in macroeconomic downturns.

Financial markets are the markets (banking, stock, and bond) that channel private saving into investment spending.

The Purpose of the Banking System

Banks and other depository institutions are financial intermediaries that use liquid assets in the form of deposits to finance the illiquid investments of borrowers. When individuals deposit their savings in a depository institution, they are providing that institution with a short-term loan. In turn, the depository institution uses those funds to make long-term loans to other borrowers. Depositors are paid interest on their deposits, and lenders pay interest on their loans. Because depository institutions receive the difference between the lower interest rate paid to depositors and the higher interest rate received from borrowers, they earn profits by converting their short-term deposit liabilities into long-term loans. This conversion is known as maturity transformation. Because deposits are short-term loans, depositors can demand to be repaid at any time. However, the loans made by depository institutions are long-term, and borrowers cannot be forced to repay their loans until the end of the loan period.

Other financial institutions also engage in maturity transformation and are part of the banking system. But instead of taking deposits, these institutions—known as **shadow banks**—borrow funds in short-term credit markets in order to invest in longer-term assets. Like depository institutions, shadow banks can earn profits as a result of the difference between the amount paid to borrow in the short-term credit market and the return received from the long-term asset. Increasing profits in the shadow banking market since 1980 have led to a steady increase in shadow banking in the United States.

> A **shadow bank** is a financial institution that engages in maturity transformation but does not accept deposits.

You may recall seeing the maturity transformation function of financial markets in the circular-flow diagram (see Figures 10.1 and 10.2). Financial markets take private savings that would otherwise leak out of the circular flow and inject it back into the economy through loans. In this way, financial markets facilitate the investment that drives economic growth.

Risks of the Banking System: Banking Crises

Because a well-functioning financial system is crucial to economic growth, we need to understand the risk to an economy of a banking system failure. Individual bank failures are not uncommon; banks fail every year, as shown in **Figure A.1**. In 2017, the FDIC reported 8 bank failures, down from 157 failures in 2010 in the wake of the financial crisis. Like other businesses in the economy, banks can fail for a variety of reasons. However, there is a big difference between the failure of a single bank and the failure of the banking system.

Fears of a bank failure can lead many depositors to panic and attempt to withdraw their funds at the same time, a phenomenon described in Module 25 as a *bank run*. The U.S. economy has experienced two periods of widespread bank failures: the National Banking Era (1883–1912) and the Great Depression (1929–1941). **Table A.1** shows the number of failures that occurred during each of those periods of panic. Current banking regulations protect U.S. depositors and the economy as a whole against bank runs. So modern bank failures generally take place through an orderly process overseen by regulators and often go largely unnoticed by depositors or the general public.

A **banking crisis**—which is much less common, and far more dangerous to the economy, than individual bank failures—occurs when a large part of the banking sector, either depository institutions or shadow banks, fails or threatens to fail. Banking crises that involve large segments of the banking system are comparatively rare. The failure of a large number of banks at the same time can occur either because many institutions

> A **banking crisis** occurs when a large part of the banking system fails.

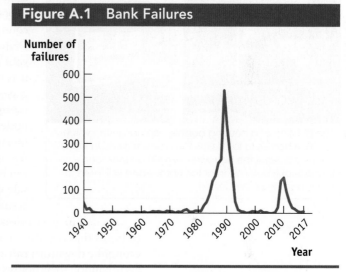

Figure A.1 Bank Failures

Table A.1	Bank Failures during the National Banking Era and the Great Depression		
National Banking Era (1883–1912)		**Great Depression (1929–1941)**	
Panic dates	**Number of failures**	**Panic dates**	**Number of failures**
September 1873	101	November–December 1930	806
May 1884	42	April–August 1931	573
November 1890	18	September–October 1931	827
May–August 1893	503	June–July 1932	283
October–December 1907	73*	February–March 1933	Bank Holiday

*This underestimates the scale of the 1907 crisis because it doesn't take into account the role of trusts.

make the same mistake or because mistakes from one institution spread to others through links in the financial system.

Banking crises often occur as a result of asset bubbles. In an **asset bubble**, the price of an asset, such as housing, is pushed above a reasonable level by investor expectations of future price increases. Eventually the market runs out of new buyers, the future price increases do not materialize, and the bubble bursts, leading to a decrease in the asset price. People who borrowed money to purchase the asset based on the expectation that prices would rise end up with a large debt when prices decrease instead. For example, individuals who borrow to purchase a house may find themselves "underwater," meaning that the value of their house is below the amount borrowed to purchase it.

Imagine that, during the recent housing boom, you purchase a house valued at $100,000 and pay for it with a $95,000 mortgage and a $5,000 down payment. At first, the value of your house increases, because investors demand more houses to resell at a profit after housing prices increase. In a few years, you have paid off some of your mortgage and you find yourself with a $93,000 mortgage on the same house; however, it is now worth $120,000! You have a more expensive house, but you didn't have to pay any more for it. You now have $27,000 of equity in your house. A few years later, the price increases that investors counted on for their profits end, so they stop buying houses. Demand in the housing market falls, and, with it, the value of your house. Now you find yourself living in the same house, but it is worth only $80,000. You have paid off more of your mortgage, but you still owe $90,000. You find yourself with a $90,000 mortgage on a house that is now worth $80,000. Your mortgage is underwater. If you stay in your house and continue to make your mortgage payments, being underwater may not make much difference to you. However, if you want or need to sell your house, it can become a real problem. The amount you would receive in the sale would not be enough to pay off your mortgage. You would actually have to *pay* to sell your house.

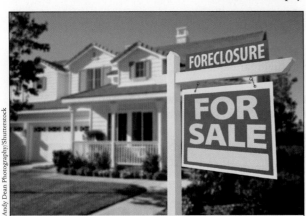

The bursting of a housing bubble can cause the value of some homes to fall below the amount owed in loans for the homes. If the borrowers default on their loans, lenders take possession of the homes and sell them to recoup some of their losses.

The fall in asset prices from a bursting asset bubble exposes financial institutions to losses that can affect confidence in the financial system as a whole. For example, an economic downturn can cause people with underwater mortgages to default on them and abandon their houses rather than paying to sell them. When default rates on mortgages increase, financial institutions experience losses that undermine confidence in the financial system. If the loss in confidence is sufficiently severe, it can lead to an economy-wide banking crisis.

Institutions in financial markets are linked to each other through their mutual dependence on confidence in the banking system and the value of long-term assets. In an especially severe banking crisis, links in the financial system can increase the odds of even more bank failures. Bank failures can lead to a downward spiral, as each failure increases rumors and fears and further weakens confidence, thereby creating more bank failures. For example, when financial institutions have engaged in leverage by financing investments with borrowed funds, the institutions that loaned the funds may recall their loans if they are worried about default from failure of the borrowing institution. In addition, when financial institutions are in trouble, they try to reduce debt and raise cash by selling assets. When many banks try to sell similar assets at the same time, prices fall. The decrease in asset prices further hurts the financial position of banks, reinforcing the downward spiral in the banking system.

As we have discussed, a well-developed financial system is a central part of a well-functioning economy. However, banking systems come with an inherent risk of banking crises. And banking crises, when left unchecked, can lead to a more widespread *financial crisis*.

Financial Crises: Consequences and Prevention

Some economists believe that to have a developed financial system is to face the risk of financial crises. Understanding the causes and consequences of financial crises is a key to understanding how they can be prevented.

What Is a Financial Crisis?

A **financial crisis** is a sudden and widespread disruption of financial markets. Such a crisis can occur when people suddenly lose faith in the ability of financial institutions to provide liquidity by bringing together those with cash to offer and those who need it. Since the banking system provides liquidity for buyers and sellers of everything from homes and cars to stocks and bonds, banking crises can easily turn into more widespread financial crises, as happened in 2008. In addition, an increase in the number and size of shadow banks in the economy can increase the scope and severity of financial crises, because shadow banks are not subject to the same regulations as depository institutions.

A **financial crisis** is a sudden and widespread disruption of financial markets.

The Consequences of Financial Crises

Financial crises have a significant negative effect on the economy and are closely associated with recessions. Historically, the origins of the worst economic downturns, such as the Great Depression, were tied to severe financial crises that led to decreased output and high unemployment (especially long-term unemployment). Recessions caused by financial crises tend to inflict sustained economic damage, and recovery from them can be very slow. **Figure A.2** shows the unemployment rate and duration associated with selected banking crises around the world.

When a financial system fails, there can be an economy-wide credit crunch, meaning that borrowers lose access to credit—either they cannot get credit at all, or they must pay high interest rates on loans. The lack of available or affordable credit in turn causes consumers and businesses to cut back on spending and investing, which leads to a recession. In addition, a financial crisis can lead to a recession because of a decrease in the price of assets. Decreases in housing prices are especially significant because real estate is often an individual's largest asset. Consumers who become poorer as a result of the decrease in the price of housing respond by reducing their spending to pay off debt and rebuild their assets, deepening the recession.

Finally, financial crises can also lead to a decrease in the effectiveness of expansionary monetary policy intended to combat a recession. Typically, the Fed decreases the target interest rate to provide an incentive to increase spending during a recession. However, with a financial crisis, depositors, depository institutions, and borrowers all lose confidence in the system. As a result, even very low interest rates may not stimulate lending or borrowing in the economy.

Government Regulation of Financial Markets

Before the Great Depression, the U.S. government pursued a laissez-faire approach to banking. That is, the government let market forces determine the success or failure of banks, just as they did in other markets. However, since the Great Depression, considerable government regulation of financial markets has been implemented to prevent the severe economic downturns that can result from financial crises. In general, governments can take three major actions to diminish the effects of banking crises: they act as a lender of last resort, guarantee deposits, and provide private credit market financing.

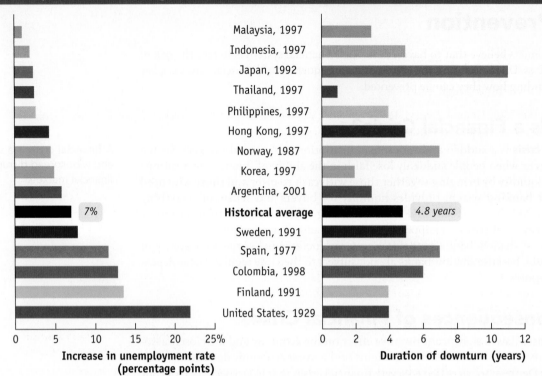

Economists Carmen Reinhart and Kenneth Rogoff have compared employment performance across several countries in the aftermath of a number of severe banking crises. For each country, the bar on the left shows the rise in the unemployment rate during and following the crisis, and the bar on the right shows how long it took for unemployment to begin to fall.

On average, severe banking crises have been followed by a 7 percentage point rise in the unemployment rate, and in many cases it has taken four years or more before unemployment even begins to fall, let alone return to precrisis levels.

Data Source: Carmen M. Reinhart and Kenneth S. Rogoff, "The Aftermath of Financial Crises," *American Economic Review 99*, no. 2 (2009): 466–472.

When governments act as a lender of last resort (usually through a central bank, such as the Federal Reserve), they provide funds to banks that are unable to borrow through private credit markets. Access to credit can help solvent banks—banks that have assets in excess of their liabilities—withstand bank runs without requiring them to sell off assets. In the case of financially unsound banks that are truly insolvent and will eventually go bankrupt, the government creates confidence in the banking system by guaranteeing the banks' liabilities. Deposit guarantees assure depositors that they will receive their deposits, preventing possible bank runs that would result from fear that deposits could be lost. Finally, governments have the ability to provide credit to shadow banks and to purchase private debt to keep the economy afloat when a banking crisis causes private credit markets to dry up.

The 2008 Financial Crisis

In 2008, the combination of a burst housing market bubble, a loss of faith in the liquidity of financial institutions, and an unregulated shadow banking system led to a widespread disruption of financial markets.

Causes of the 2008 Financial Crisis

The collapse of Lehman Brothers—a large shadow bank—set off the 2008 financial crisis, first in the United States and eventually across the globe. Although a number of factors led to the bank's collapse and the subsequent worldwide economic downturn, economists have identified four major causes of the 2008 financial crisis:

1. Macroeconomic conditions
2. A housing bubble
3. Financial system linkages
4. Failure of government regulation

Prior to the 2008 financial crisis, the economy experienced a long period of low inflation, stable growth, and low global interest rates. These macroeconomic conditions encouraged risk taking by shadow banks because they made it easy and cheap to borrow money. The banks searched for new ways to invest the funds they borrowed from short-term credit markets to earn higher returns in financial markets. One way to invest was through **securitization**, assembling a group of loans into a pool and selling shares of that pool to investors. Before the 2008 crisis, Lehman Brothers had been borrowing heavily in short-term credit markets and investing in subprime mortgages. **Subprime lending**—lending to home-buyers at risk of not being able to afford their payments—had been a part of the banking industry for a long time, but subprime borrowing increased in the period leading up to the crisis. Subprime mortgages started to be packaged into so-called low-risk securities by pooling them together as **collateralized debt obligations**. These debt obligations are a type of financial **derivative**, a financial contract that has value based on the performance of another asset, index, or interest rate. Unfortunately, the shadow banks invested in these derivatives without accurately assessing their risk. When the real estate bubble burst, people began to default on their subprime mortgages and the value of the collateralized debt obligations fell. Because real estate markets represent a large part of the economy and shadow banks had invested heavily in subprime mortgages, the defaults quickly exposed the fragility of the financial system.

In 2008, when rumors of Lehman's exposure in the housing market spread, the shadow bank was no longer able to borrow in short-term credit markets to finance its long-term obligations. Without access to credit, Lehman Brothers went bankrupt.

Chains of debt linked Lehman to other financial institutions. **Credit default swaps** had been created to spread the risk of default on loans, but in fact they concentrated that risk. AIG was a large insurance company that provided those swaps. When the housing bubble burst, the large number of defaults caused AIG to collapse soon after Lehman Brothers.

The 2008 crisis was like a traditional bank run—except that it was in the shadow banking system. The fall of Lehman Brothers led to a credit freeze, withdrawals of mutual funds, and a fall in derivative prices.

Finally, relaxed regulation of investment banks in the shadow banking sector failed to prevent the start and spread of the financial crisis. Prior to 2008, risk taking by shadow banks increased for several reasons. To begin with, given the vital importance of the financial system to the economy as a whole, many people thought the government would step in to prevent severe problems. That is, large financial institutions were considered "too big to fail." This led to the problem of **moral hazard**, which exists when a party takes excessive risks because it believes it will not bear all of the costs that could result. At the same time, the large profits earned by shadow banks further encouraged increased risk taking. Initially, the high-risk shadow banking activities were not a problem, because economic conditions were good. When the housing bubble burst, however, everything changed. It became clear that derivatives, which were thought to mitigate or eliminate default risk, only hid it. Because much of the existing government regulation did not apply to shadow banks, it could not prevent their activities from continuing to crisis.

Securitization involves assembling a pool of loans and selling shares of that pool to investors.

Subprime lending involves lending to home-buyers who don't meet the usual criteria for being able to afford their payments.

A **collateralized debt obligation** is an asset-backed security tied to corporate debt or mortgages.

A **derivative** is a financial contract that has value based on the performance of another asset, index, or interest rate.

A **credit default swap** is an agreement that the seller will compensate the buyer in the event of a loan default.

Moral hazard involves a distortion of incentives when someone else bears the costs of a lack of care or effort.

Consequences of the 2008 Financial Crisis

The 2008 financial crisis caused significant, prolonged damage to economies across the globe, with consequences that continued years later. For example, by the end of 2009, the United States' economy had lost over 7 million jobs, causing the

Figure A.3 Unemployment in the Aftermath of the 2008 Crisis

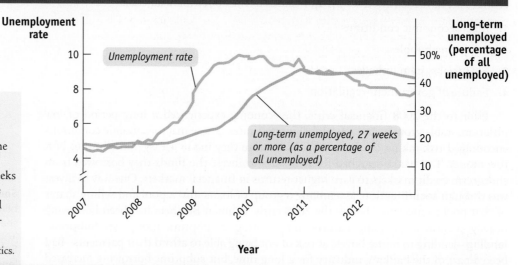

After 2008, the unemployment rate increased dramatically and remained high. Long-term unemployment, measured by the percentage of the unemployed who were out of work for 27 weeks or longer, increased at the same time. By 2011, almost half of all unemployed workers were long-term unemployed.

Data Source: Bureau of Labor Statistics.

unemployment rate to increase dramatically and remain high for years after, as shown in **Figure A.3**. In particular, the crisis led to an increase in long-term unemployment, which rose to almost half of the total unemployment in the economy.

The recession in the U.S. economy sent ripples throughout the world, and many countries have seen only a weak recovery. For example, **Figure A.4** shows that it took more than five years for the United States to get back to the precrisis level of real GDP. In addition, in 2011–2012, fear of a second crisis related to public debt in southern Europe and Ireland further hampered economic recovery from the crisis.

Figure A.4 Crisis and Recovery in the United States and the European Union

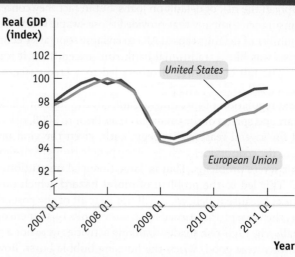

In the aftermath of the 2008 financial crisis, aggregate output in the European Union and the United States fell dramatically. Real GDP, shown here as an index with each economy's peak precrisis quarter set to 100, declined by more than 5%. By late 2011, real GDP in the United States had only barely recovered to precrisis levels, and aggregate output in the European Union had still not reached its precrisis peak.

Data Sources: Bureau of Economic Analysis; Eurostat.

Government Response to the 2008 Financial Crisis

The intervention of the U.S. government and the Federal Reserve at the start of the financial crisis helped to calm financial markets. The federal government bailed out some failing financial institutions and instituted the Troubled Asset Relief Program (TARP), which involved the purchase of assets and equity from financial institutions to help strengthen the markets.

The Federal Reserve pursued an expansionary monetary policy, decreasing the federal funds rate to zero. The Fed also implemented programs to foster improved conditions in financial markets, significantly changing its own balance sheet. For example, the Fed acted as a lender of last resort by providing liquidity to financial institutions, it provided credit to borrowers and investors in key credit markets, and it put downward pressure on long-term interest rates by purchasing longer-term securities.

Financial Crises and the Future

The 2008 financial crisis highlighted the importance of financial markets and the need to ensure a well-functioning financial system. In 2010, the Wall Street Reform and Consumer Protection Act, known as the Dodd-Frank Act, was enacted to overhaul financial regulation in the aftermath of the crisis. The Dodd-Frank Act contains four main elements:

1. Consumer protection

2. Derivatives regulation

3. Shadow bank regulation

4. Resolution authority over nonbank financial institutions

Increases in the complexity of financial instruments played a large role in the financial crisis of 2008, as consumers purchased assets they either didn't understand or were not able to afford. The Consumer Financial Protection Bureau (CFPB) was created by the Dodd-Frank Act to protect borrowers from abusive practices that became prevalent due to the complexity of these instruments. The proliferation of derivatives was another important factor in the crisis, because derivatives, which had been designed to spread risk, worked to conceal risk prior to 2008. As a result, the new law also contains stipulations designed to make financial markets transparent so that asset risk is no longer concealed.

In the event of future financial crises, the shadow bank regulation and resolution authority can extend government control to cover non-bank financial institutions. The Dodd-Frank Act gives a special panel the ability to designate financial institutions that have the potential to create a banking crisis. These designated shadow banks are then subject to banklike regulation. In addition, the government now has the authority to seize control of financial institutions that require a bailout during a crisis, the way it already did with commercial banks. This power, called resolution authority, allows the government to guarantee a wide range of financial institution debts in a crisis. In May 2018, Congress passed a bill to roll back rules enacted as part of the Dodd-Frank law to prevent another financial crisis. The new bill leaves fewer than ten large banks subject to the strict requirements of the original law while exempting small and medium-sized banks from the regulations.

Going forward, financial regulation faces several challenges. First of all, the idea that a financial institution can be "too big to fail" is still prevalent and the problem of moral hazard still exists. And, while new regulation has been put in place in the United States, it is not clear how these regulations can or will be applied in other countries. The 2008 financial crisis highlighted the global nature of financial markets and the worldwide linkages that must be acknowledged in order for regulation to be effective.

Finally, regulation that addresses what happened in 2008 may not be effective in addressing financial crises in the future. World economies and world financial markets are ever changing; regulation must be dynamic and able to respond to the current situation, not merely the most recent crisis.

The Dodd-Frank Act created the Consumer Financial Protection Bureau to protect borrowers from abusive practices that became more prevalent as financial instruments became more complex.

Check Your Understanding

1. Draw a circular-flow diagram that includes households, firms, factor markets, markets for goods and services, and financial markets. Circle the section of the diagram that illustrates maturity transformation and briefly explain the maturity transformation process.

2. What are the four major causes of the 2008 financial crisis? Briefly describe each one.

3. What are the four main elements of the Dodd-Frank Act? Briefly describe each one.

Multiple Choice Review Questions

1. A shadow bank is a financial institution that does not
   a. allow customers into its physical location.
   b. have any form of government regulation.
   c. invest in long-term assets.
   d. accept deposits.
   e. participate in a financial market.

2. Converting short-term liabilities into long-term assets is called
   a. maturity transformation.
   b. subprime lending.
   c. credit swapping.
   d. leveraging.
   e. pooling.

3. In an asset bubble, the price of an asset
   a. drops dramatically because of buyer panic.
   b. begins to decline as demand falls.
   c. rises steadily as the economy grows.
   d. increases due to expectations of price gains.
   e. fluctuates wildly as markets change.

4. A sudden and widespread disruption of financial markets is called a(n)
   a. credit crunch.
   b. financial crisis.
   c. bank panic.
   d. credit default swap.
   e. economic depression.

5. Which of the following was not a cause of the 2008 financial crisis?
   a. a housing bubble
   b. a stock market crash
   c. macroeconomic conditions
   d. failed government regulation
   e. financial system linkages

Discussion Starters

1. Why is an efficient financial system important?

2. What is a shadow bank? Using specific examples, explain how these shadow banks differ from traditional banks.

3. How can an asset bubble lead to an economy-wide banking crisis?

4. What are some of the possible consequences of a financial crisis?

5. What was the role of moral hazard in the 2008 financial crisis?

6. What regulatory changes have we seen in the recovery since the 2008 financial crisis? What impact have they had?

Behavioral Economics

In this Module, you will learn to:
- Identify barriers to rational decision making
- Discuss the role of psychology in consumer behavior
- Explain why assumptions of rationality are useful despite limits on the rationality of humans

Consumers and Rationality

Nytro Multisport recently advertised the Scott Plasma RC triathlon bike for $7,299.95. Aside from the question of whether it is rational for anyone to pay that much money for a bicycle, why would the retailer not simply charge $7,300? The nickel difference is 1/145,999th of the price. Could that matter? Ads routinely offer products for $19.95 rather than $20. Gasoline prices typically end in 9/10ths of a cent. And Apple arguably revived the music industry by charging 99 cents for iTunes music downloads. Traditional economic theory does nothing to explain the importance of shaving a price down from an even number to an essentially equivalent odd number, yet some 90% of advertised prices end in "9" or "5." Psychological influences clearly matter, whether or not those influences can be categorized as rational. A melding of psychology and economics, **behavioral economics** is the study of economic decision making as influenced by the limits of the human mind.

Courtesy Scott Sports SA

> **Behavioral economics** is the study of economic decision making as influenced by the limits of the human mind.
>
> **Homo economicus** ("economic man") is a fictional economic actor who makes self-interested, informed, rational judgments in pursuit of wealth and leisure.

Homo economicus

Economists have made great strides with models starring "economic man" or **Homo economicus**, a fictional economic actor and amalgamation of all people, who makes self-interested, informed, rational judgments in pursuit of wealth and leisure. In neoclassical models, *Homo economicus* represents the typical member of society. *Homo economicus* is a reasonable depiction of the average economic decision maker in the many contexts in which variations in behaviors either average out across people or are unimportant. In those contexts, the neoclassical models form the basis for useful conclusions. For example, these models predict that people will buy more of a product when the price falls, work more when the wage rises, and prefer some money to none at all. In this Module, however, we'll explore challenges to the assumptions about *Homo economicus* and the implications of irrationality among economic actors.

Behavioral economics unveils *Homo economicus* and finds an individual who is sensitive, flawed, and biased in ways that can disrupt the efficient allocation of resources. Human decisions can go awry due to the scarcity of time, intelligence, and information. The importance of the psychological side of economic behavior is still controversial, but acceptance of the field of behavioral economics has grown considerably over the past four decades. Herbert Simon, Daniel Kahneman, and Richard Thaler won Nobel Prizes in economics in 1978, 2002, and 2017, respectively, for their research on behavioral economics. In addition, the *Journal of Behavioral Economics* was established in 1970. And a surge in popularity in the 1980s and 1990s led scholars at virtually every top economics department in North America to dive into the field of behavioral economics. Now it is your turn.

Homo misinformicus

There are differing schools of thought about the extent of information problems and behavioral anomalies. The work of neoclassical economists such as Milton Friedman, Arthur Pigou, and Gary Becker placed considerable reliance on *rational choice theory*, which holds that decision makers are able to compare all of their alternatives with full information about their choices. For example, based on this theory, one would predict that if Nytro Multisport lowers the price of the Scott Plasma RC triathalon bike from $7,299.95 down to $7,000.00, it will sell more bikes. The assumption is that consumers are aware of the product, its virtues, and the price change. However, unless you are a bicycle enthusiast, chances are that you did not know much about the Scott Plasma RC before reading this Module. In reality, information is imperfect, and consumers do not know every product's availability, quality, or price. The large amounts of money people pay for internet access, smartphones, and college education exemplify the value placed on information. Yet the cost of perfect information is prohibitive—no one has the time or money to become all-knowing. The result is ill-informed behavior, such as people paying more than necessary for a Scott Plasma RC because they are unaware of the deals that are available at particular bike shops.

Researchers in the field of behavioral economics study the rationality of market participants under realistic constraints on time, information, and intelligence. Because information takes time and sometimes money to obtain, it is appropriate to continue seeking information until the marginal benefit of doing so no longer exceeds the marginal cost. This is why rational people often act on incomplete information. For example, if you live in a large city, you wouldn't want to call every shoe store in town to check prices before buying a new pair of shoes. After you call a few stores, the likely savings from additional calls falls below the value of your time.

Many uses of information are not so rational. In defiance of rationality, individuals often respond to the way in which information is presented. For example, would a half-empty glass of soda pop sound as appealing to you as a half-full glass of soda pop? Psychologists Daniel Kahneman and Amos Tversky found that respondents who were presented with four identical outcomes with differing descriptions overwhelmingly preferred a disease-control program that would save 200 out of 600 people to a program that would allow 400 out of 600 people to die. In other words, it is perceived as better to have one-third of a population live than to have two-thirds of a population die.

Helen Sessions/Alamy

It takes time to acquire information about the prices and products available to consumers; at some point, the marginal cost of information gathering exceeds the marginal benefit. So shoppers typically buy shoes and other goods on the basis of incomplete information.

Descriptions also drive perceptions of products and policies. For example, New York Super Fudge Chunk ice cream is one of Ben and Jerry's top sellers, whereas Bovinity Divinity and Dastardly Mash, though similarly chewy and chocolaty, were discontinued for lack of interest. Similarly, policies that environmentalists say would weaken current standards have gained steam due to appealing names such as the Clear Skies Initiative and the Healthy Forests Initiative. And, while the prospect of higher wages motivates employees to work harder, so does the prospect of loftier job titles, such as vice president or office manager.

Uninformed consumers may buy too much of products that have health risks, such as junk food; pay more for products or services than they are worth, such as counterfeit watches; or purchase products that are inferior in price or quality to those available elsewhere, such as full-priced triathlon bicycles. Uninformed managers face the same problems when purchasing from vendors. Incomplete information and irrational behavior stab at the heart of *Homo economicus*. With perfect information and rationality at the foundation of efficient decision making in many economic models, there is reason to be concerned about error, bias, and incomplete information.

Psychology and Economics

In *Blink: The Power of Thinking Without Thinking*, Malcolm Gladwell explains that by necessity or instinct, many decisions are made on the basis of first impressions. Snap judgments can lead to less-than-optimal choices when products—such as new cars—or people—such as potential employees, marital prospects, or presidential candidates—look better than they really are. Gladwell calls this the *Warren Harding Error* in reference to the twenty-ninth president of the United States, who looked winningly presidential to over 60% of the voters, but turned out to be a poor leader with a scandal-ridden administration. Harding reportedly said of himself, "I am not fit for this office and never should have been here." Clearly, Harding, and those who voted for him, made some mistakes due to limits on information and intelligence.

Bounded Rationality

Dubious about models based on rationality and full information, Nobel laureate Herbert Simon explained that rationality is bounded by limitations in the ability of decision makers to formulate and solve complex problems. In *Models of My Life*, Simon argued that even Albert Einstein could not match the mental gymnastics ascribed to the fictional "economic man." Simon coined the phrase **bounded rationality** to describe the limits on optimal decision making that result from imperfect intelligence and the scarcity of time and information. Bounded rationality causes missteps, as when a price that ends in "99" makes a consumer perceive the amount as being lower than it really is.

Simon also studied the *judgmental heuristics*—rules of thumb—that people use to simplify decisions when constrained by time, information, or cognitive ability. Consumers and managers are like chess players: they cannot fully analyze every possible sequence of actions that will follow their move. Instead, they must rely on instincts, experience, advice, short-cuts, and guesswork. For example, rather than making pricing decisions by evaluating the consumer response and subsequent profit from every possible price point, many managers use the simple "keystone" technique of doubling the wholesale price of each good to establish the retail price.

Status quo bias causes people to stick with what they have despite equally attractive alternatives. In *Smart Choices: A Practical Guide to Making Better Decisions*, John Hammond, Ralph Keeney, and Howard Raiffa describe a natural experiment in which the state governments of New Jersey and Pennsylvania both adopted the same two options for automobile insurance, but each selected a different default plan. Under plan A, insurance premiums were lower but drivers had a limited right to litigate after an accident. Under plan B, the premiums were higher but litigation options were broader. In New Jersey, drivers received plan A unless they specified a preference for plan B; Pennsylvania drivers were assigned to plan B unless they opted for plan A. The result was that the majority of drivers in each state stuck with the status quo, meaning that they felt the best plan was the plan they were given in the first place.

Have you experienced status quo bias? Think about your family's choice of where to live and your favorite sports teams, politicians, and brand names. In some cases, the choice might be clear. In other cases, perhaps you've stuck with the status quo despite the existence of equally attractive alternatives. Herbert Simon felt that status quo bias and judgmental heuristics led to decisions that were satisfactory but not optimal, and described this type of decision making as *satisficing*.

Neoclassical theories rest on assumptions of rationality that are sometimes at odds with observed human behavior. For example, some theories of consumer choice are valid under the assumption that the largest amount an individual would be willing to pay for a good and the smallest amount he or she would accept in exchange for an identical good are the same. However, researchers have found *endowment effects*, meaning that people place a higher value on what they have than on what they don't have. In a famous example, Daniel Kahneman, Jack Knetsch, and Richard Thaler found that, after randomly selecting half the students in a class to receive coffee mugs, the largest amount that the average student without a mug was willing to pay to buy one was less than half as much as the smallest amount that the average student with a mug was willing to accept to give one up.

When decisions are made quickly, options can look better than they really are. Malcolm Gladwell calls this the *Warren Harding Error*, after the president who looked the part while campaigning, but once in office, even called himself unfit for the job.

Bounded rationality describes the limits on optimal decision making that result from imperfect intelligence and the scarcity of time and information.

Bounded rationality causes missteps, as when a price that ends in "99" makes a consumer perceive the amount as being lower than it really is.

Lower premiums or broader options for litigation? Most drivers stuck with the status quo.

Behavioral economists use the concept of *loss aversion* to explain evidence that consumers consider sunk costs—those costs that have already been incurred and cannot be recovered—in their decision making. No matter how much money one has sunk into a project, it would be rational to abandon that project if the future benefits do not exceed the future costs. Yet some people choose to overeat in order to finish expensive meals, go to bad plays because they paid a lot for season tickets, or stick with a failing stock because they have invested so much money in it. Rather than ignoring the sunk cost as they always should, these people mistakenly let irrecoverable losses sway their decisions.

Excessive Optimism

Crime provides an important example of bounded rationality in the form of *excessive optimism*—some criminals are unrealistically confident that things will go their way. Neoclassical models treat crime as a rational activity, the price of which is the expected punishment. This implies that more severe punishments or higher rates of apprehension or conviction will deter crime. Yet a study by one of your authors, Dave Anderson, of the knowledge and mindset of criminals found that most criminals do not have the information required to perform cost-benefit analysis before committing their crimes. Specifically, 76% of the convicted criminals in the study either had no thought that they might be caught or had no idea of the punishment for their crime, or both. Among the violent offenders, 89% lacked the information needed for cost-benefit analysis. So in order to solve the crime problem, policy makers must go beyond the tenets of neoclassical economics and be open to solutions that address psychological problems and informational shortcomings.

Unfortunately, crime is just the tip of the iceberg of poor decisions caused by excessive optimism. Here are some additional examples:

- People underestimate the risks of common but unpublicized events such as work-related falls and motor vehicle accidents, and overestimate the risk of uncommon but dramatic, highly publicized events such as earthquakes, homicides, airplane crashes, and rare types of cancer. The result is inadequate safety precautions against the large risks and overinvestment in precautions against the small risks.

- More than half of all new businesses fail within five years, which may indicate excessive optimism among entrepreneurs. It is also possible that the potential benefits of a successful business outweigh the high risks of failure, but decision makers who underestimate the risks are prone to overinvest.

- The majority of Americans believe they are smarter than average and have better-than-average chances of winning the lottery, being professionally successful, and avoiding disease and automobile accidents. In the business world, most managers think they are more capable than the average manager.

- A common reason that many lawsuits go to trial is unrealistic optimism on the part of one side or both sides about the strength of their case. In a representative study, the average plaintiff's attorney expected a jury award 27% higher than the amount anticipated by the average defense attorney.

Even when good information is available, people may not use it wisely. Because people are capable of stubbornness, bias, and misjudgment to their own downfall, the improper use of information can lead to unfortunate and inefficient resource allocations.

Framing

It is standard procedure at several international hotel chains to place a card in the bathrooms of guest rooms with a message like this one:

> Save Our Planet. Every day millions of gallons of water are used to wash towels . . . A towel on the rack means "I will use again." Thank you for helping us conserve the Earth's vital resources.

If the hotels were really bent on saving Earth's resources, they would provide recycling bins, organic cotton sheets, and carpets made from recycled fibers. The pitch to avoid washing towels may have more to do with saving the financial resources of the hotels, but customer participation depends on how the appeal is framed.

Context matters, and **framing** is the creation of context for a product or idea. Richard Thaler found that a typical consumer would pay no more than $1.50 for a good brand of beer from a grocery store, but would pay up to $2.65 for an identical beer from a fancy hotel, even if a friend was bringing the beer from either source to the consumer to drink at a beach. Brand managers spend millions of dollars to frame their brand names because, for example, consumers perceive apparel differently after seeing Olympic skier Lindsey Vonn wear it, and they perceive a hotel differently knowing that singer Pharrell Williams stays there. Consumers pay more for a cup of coffee at Starbucks than at McDonald's, not because the Starbucks coffee itself is necessarily better (a *Consumer Reports* taste test suggests that McDonald's coffee is actually better), but because of the image and ambiance in which Starbucks coffee is framed.

> **Framing** is the creation of context for a product or idea.

The strategy of *odd* or *just-below* pricing—setting prices that end in an odd number or just below an even dollar amount—is about framing as well. In terms of damage to the pocketbook, there's little difference between paying $4.99 and paying $5.00. But the human mind finds it easier to accept a price of $4.99. Consumers subconsciously downplay the importance of the cents at the end of a price, and place more emphasis on the dollar amount at the beginning. Thus, $4.99 might seem close to $4.00, even though it is only a penny shy of $5.00. Also, prices ending in "99" or "95" convey the idea of a discount to bargain-hungry shoppers. Marketing professor Robert Schindler and management consultant Thomas Kibarian tested the influence of prices with odd-numbered endings by sending out three versions of a direct mail catalog for women's clothing. The catalogs were identical except for the prices, which ended with either 00, 99, or 88. The catalogs with prices ending in 99 generated 8% more sales volume and attracted more consumers than those with prices ending in the even numbers. Managers at upscale department stores such as Nordstrom are aware of the psychology of pricing as well, but they use the contrasting strategy of ending prices with even numbers, symbolic of their high-end brand image.

At Nordstrom, prices ending in even numbers convey an upscale image.

Bounded Willpower

It's rational to spend money, retire, or take vacations that decrease earnings, as long as the value of the resulting benefits exceeds the value of the money forgone. Yet sometimes people forgo money in irrational ways. **Bounded willpower**—willpower constrained by limits on the determination needed to do difficult things—can be the cause. The effects include spending too much money and earning too little money, but it isn't all about money. Bounded willpower can also explain decisions to do too little homework, procrastinate too much, overeat, or throw a career-ending temper tantrum in front of the boss.

> **Bounded willpower** is willpower constrained by limits on the determination needed to do difficult things.

In the analysis of behavior, it is important not to categorize everything that causes problems as irrational. Economists Gary Becker and Kevin Murphy pointed out that even the use of potentially addictive substances can be rational if the benefits outweigh the costs. They showed that people who care more about the present than the future are more prone to addiction because they discount future problems related to health, relationships, and finances when weighing them against ongoing desires for addictive substances. Becker and Murphy argue that when heavy drinkers and smokers say they want to quit but cannot, it may be a matter of the long-term benefits of quitting falling below the short-term costs of making that adjustment.

While some addictions may be rational, humans are subject to temptations and emotions that can lead them astray. Anger, jealousy, frustration, and embarrassment can overcome willpower and trigger irrational responses. Take, for example, the Wendy's customer who shot manager Renal Frage due to anger over not receiving enough packets of chili sauce. Similar examples appear frequently in the news.

Bounded Self-Interest

Neoclassical economic models rest on assumptions of self-interested behavior, which is seldom in short supply. But some behaviors exhibit elements of altruism uncharacteristic of *Homo economicus*. Billionaire businessman and investor Warren Buffett is apparently not *Homo economicus*, having pledged to give at least half of his fortune to charity. Americans recycle tens of millions of tons of materials each year to the benefit of the environment and future generations. And the Bureau of Labor Statistics estimates that each year more than a quarter of all Americans volunteer some of their time to help less fortunate individuals. Charitable efforts can be self-serving if they bring attention, gratitude, tax advantages, or other benefits to the donors. But to the extent that some decisions are made selflessly, **bounded self-interest**—self-interest that leaves room for concerns about the welfare of others—represents a third category of deviance from neoclassical economic models.

Bounded self-interest is self-interest that leaves room for concerns about the welfare of others.

Economists have examined the human struggle between self-interest and fairness with experiments involving *ultimatum games* and *dictator games*. In an ultimatum game, one person, whom we shall call *the divider*, has an amount of money, say $10, to divide between herself and another person, whom we shall call *the recipient*. After the divider makes the allocation, the recipient can either accept that division or reject it. If the allocation is rejected by the recipient, neither side gets anything. A rational, wealth-maximizing recipient will accept any positive share of the money, because some money is better than the alternative of no money. When working with such recipients, a rational, wealth-maximizing divider would allocate the smallest possible positive amount to the recipient: one cent. However, much experimentation has revealed strong interest in fair allocations, and punishment for those who make unfair allocations. Daniel Kahneman, Jack Knetsch, and Richard Thaler found that the typical recipient rejects anything less than a 23% share of the money to be divided, and that the average divider offers 45% of the money to the recipient. Related research has found fairness to be important even with changes in the culture of the participants, the amount of money at stake, and opportunities to learn from experience with the game.

In the dictator game, the recipient has no choice but to accept the divider's allocation. Thus, a rational, wealth-maximizing divider would give nothing to the recipient. Kahneman, Knetsch, and Thaler gave 161 students the option of dividing $20 evenly with an anonymous other student or giving the other student $2 while keeping $18. Even though the recipients had no say in the matter, 76% of the dividers gave half of the money to the recipient, again exhibiting substantial interest in fairness.

Would you divide $20 evenly between you and an anonymous recipient if you didn't have to?

Clearly there is more to decision making than wealth maximization. Customers may pay more for a product that causes less harm to other people or the environment, as managers at Toyota discovered when their relatively expensive but environmentally friendly Prius Hybrid flew out of showrooms faster than the company could make more. Attracting a new employee by offering a salary that eclipses the salary of existing employees can cause considerable strife due to those employees' interests in fairness, so employers should take the fairness of their salaries into consideration. And money can't separate most parents from their children: the 2016 Modern Family Index reveals that a majority of parents sacrifice financial gains in their careers to spend more time with their kids.

Evolving Models

Just as many anthropologists theorize that *Homo ergaster* evolved into modern men and women, in contemporary economic theory, the traditional model of *Homo economicus* is evolving into a modern conception of economic men and women. Behavioral economists have adapted earlier notions of economic man to capture decision making under the constraints on human rationality, willpower, and self-interest. Some strange behaviors can be traced to rational foundations, but others are sufficiently suspect to warrant policy that addresses the possibility of misinformation, mistakes, and psychosis.

We've seen that the information that neoclassical theory treats as fully and freely available is often incomplete and costly. We've also seen that market participants do not always put the information they have to its best use. The key question is whether problems with information justify an abandonment of neoclassical precepts, some revisions and expansions in rational choice theory, or none of the above. Most contemporary economists stake out a middle ground, leaning toward the neoclassical side. Despite their flaws, neoclassical models provide useful guidance and predictive power. Experiments demonstrate that people—not to mention rats, dolphins, and other decision makers broadly defined—generally respond to incentives in rational ways: they all tend to follow the money, cheese, or sardines. That being said, worthwhile improvements in theories and policy making can be achieved by acknowledging psychological influences beyond the desire for money and leisure. Consumers, managers, employees, and all other participants in an economy are more or less flawed, biased, emotional, benevolent, undisciplined, and uninformed, which helps to explain myriad behaviors that neoclassical models do not predict.

ENRICHMENT MODULE B REVIEW

Check Your Understanding

1. Identify the cause of each of the following types of behavior:
   a. Nelson employs a worker whose family desperately needs the income, even though the worker's wage exceeds the revenue that worker brings into Nelson's firm.
   b. Roberto will pay more for the same steak in a restaurant with fancy tablecloths than in a restaurant without them.
   c. Alesia opens a new hardware store despite market research indicating insufficient consumer demand for the store's products.
   d. Karen knows she should stop eating chocolate, but she eats more anyway.

2. What do experiments with the ultimatum game reveal about the typical participant?

Multiple-Choice Review Questions

1. Behavioral economics is a combination of economics and which field?
   a. animal science
   b. government
   c. business
   d. psychology
   e. sociology

2. Who unquestionably represents a self-interested, informed, rational decision maker?
   a. *Homo misinformicus*
   b. *Homo economicus*
   c. *Homo ergaster*
   d. Malcolm Gladwell
   e. Warren Harding

3. A price that ends in "99" can be perceived as being significantly lower than a price that ends in "00" due to
   a. judgmental heuristics.
   b. bounded rationality.
   c. satisficing.
   d. loss aversion.
   e. bounded willpower.

4. Status quo bias causes people to
   a. try new things.
   b. favor what they have.
   c. prefer alternatives to the default option.
   d. always spend as little money as possible.
   e. overspend on items that will increase their social status.

5. Research suggests that criminals commit more than the rational number of crimes due to excessive
   a. optimism.
   b. pessimism.
   c. wealth.
   d. information.
   e. investments in stocks.

6. Suppose the Eat-It Truck Stop and the Royal Palace Restaurant serve food of the same quality. Which of the following is the most likely to allow the Royal Palace Restaurant to charge higher prices?
   a. bounded self-interest
   b. the dictator game
   c. framing
   d. sunk costs
   e. loss aversion

7. Bounded self-interest can most easily explain why
   a. people consider sunk costs.
   b. workers seek higher wages.
   c. consumers are more willing to buy goods if their prices end in "99."
   d. businesses carry out framing techniques.
   e. donors give anonymously to charity.

Discussion Starters

1. Which of your behaviors might be considered irrational? Do you consider sunk costs? Do emotions ever put you on an irrational path?

2. How gullible are you? Do you tend to believe what you hear from your friends and what you read on the internet? Have you ever learned that you were fooled by these or other information sources?

3. Do you sometimes exhibit altruism? In what instances have you forgone money for the benefit of others?

4. Would a product's effects on the environment influence your decision to buy it? Can you name the greenhouse gases that cause global warming? What sorts of costs weigh against the benefits of obtaining this information?

5. As a manager, would you set prices so that they ended in "99"? Why or why not? Does this approach ever work on you as a consumer?

6. What evidence have you seen of the failure or success of neoclassical models? Have you noticed changes in the price or quality of goods as the number of competitors changed? Does the quantity of a good demanded decrease as its price increases?

The Economics of Information

In this Module, you will learn to:
- Identify the special problems posed by information that some people have and other people do not.
- Explain how information asymmetries can lead to the problem of adverse selection
- Discuss ways that firms can deal with imperfect information using screening and signaling
- Explain how information asymmetries can lead to the problem of moral hazard

Private Information: What You Don't Know Can Hurt You

Markets can handle situations in which nobody knows what is going to happen. However, markets have much more trouble with situations in which *some people know things that other people don't know*—situations involving **private information** (also known as **asymmetric information**). As we will see, private information can distort economic decisions and sometimes prevent mutually beneficial economic transactions from taking place.

Why is some information private? The most important reason is that people generally know more about themselves than other people do. For example, you know whether or not you are a careful driver; but unless you have already been in several accidents, your auto insurance company does not have that information. You are more likely to have a better estimate than your health insurance company of whether or not you will need an expensive medical procedure. And if you are selling your used car, you are more likely to be aware of any problems with it than the buyer is.

But why should such differences in who knows what be a problem? It turns out that there are two distinct sources of trouble: *adverse selection*, which arises from having private information about the way things are, and *moral hazard*, which arises from having private information about what people do.

Private information is information that some people have and others do not; it is also known as **asymmetric information**.

Adverse Selection: The Economics of Lemons

Suppose that someone offers to sell you an almost brand-new car—purchased just three months ago, with only 2,000 miles on the odometer and no dents or scratches. Will you be willing to pay almost as much for that car as you would pay for the same model purchased new from a car dealership?

Probably not, for one main reason: you cannot help but wonder why this car is being sold. Has the owner discovered that something is wrong with it—that it is a "lemon"? Having driven the car for a while, the owner knows more about it than you do—and people are more likely to sell cars that give them trouble.

You might think that the extra information held by sellers of used cars provides a distinct advantage to the sellers. But potential buyers know that potential sellers are likely to offer them lemons—they just don't know exactly which car is a lemon. Because potential buyers of a

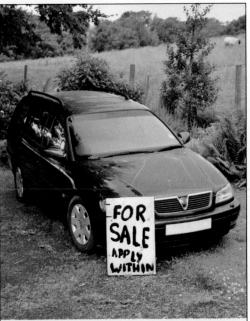

Is the most you would pay for a used car influenced by the fact that the seller knows more about the car than you do?

used car know that potential sellers are more likely to sell lemons than good cars, buyers will offer a lower price than they would if they had a guarantee of the car's quality. Worse yet, this poor opinion of used cars tends to be self-reinforcing, precisely because it depresses the prices that buyers offer. Used cars sell at a discount because buyers expect a disproportionate share of those cars to be lemons. Even a used car that is not a lemon would sell only at a large discount because buyers don't know whether it's a lemon or not. But potential sellers who have good cars are unwilling to sell them at a deep discount, except under exceptional circumstances. So it is relatively uncommon for good used cars to be offered for sale, and used cars that are offered for sale have a tendency to be lemons. (This is why people who have a compelling reason to sell a car, such as moving overseas, make a point of revealing that information to potential buyers—as if to say "This car is not a lemon!")

The end result, then, is not only that used cars sell for low prices but also that there are a large number of used cars with hidden problems. Equally important, many potentially beneficial transactions—sales of good used cars by people who would like to get rid of them to people who would like to buy them—end up being frustrated by the inability of potential sellers to convince potential buyers that their cars are worth the higher price demanded. So some mutually beneficial trades between those who want to sell used cars and those who want to buy them go unexploited.

Although economists sometimes refer to situations like this as the "lemons problem" (the issue was introduced in a famous 1970 paper by economist and Nobel laureate George Akerlof entitled "The Market for Lemons"), **adverse selection** is the more formal name for the problem of one person knowing more than other people about the way things are. Because potential sellers know more about the quality of what they are selling than potential buyers, they have an incentive to select the worst things to sell.

Adverse selection applies to more than just used cars. It is a problem for many parts of the economy—notably for insurance companies, and most notably for health insurance companies. Suppose that a health insurance company were to offer a standard policy to everyone with the same premium (the basic monthly fee for the policy). The premium would reflect the *average* risk of incurring a medical expense. But that would make the policy look very expensive to healthy people, who know that they are less likely than the average person to incur medical expenses. So healthy people would be less likely than less healthy people to buy the policy, leaving the health insurance company with exactly the customers it doesn't want: people with a higher-than-average risk of needing medical care, who would find the premium to be a good deal. In order to cover its expected losses from this less healthy customer pool, the health insurance company is compelled to raise premiums, driving away more of the remaining healthier customers, and so on. Because the insurance company can't determine who is healthy and who is not, it must charge everyone the same premium, thereby discouraging healthy people from purchasing policies and encouraging unhealthy people to buy policies.

Adverse selection can lead to an *adverse selection death spiral*: the relatively unhealthy customers drive up the insurance company's average cost per customer, which leads to higher premiums, which drive away the healthier remaining customers, which raises the company's average cost even higher, and so on. Eventually, only the least healthy customers are willing to pay the elevated premiums, which prevents the spreading of costs necessary for a viable insurance market, so the market for health insurance collapses. Because of the severe adverse selection problems, governments in many advanced countries assume the role of providing health insurance to their citizens. The U.S. government, through its various health insurance programs including Medicare, Medicaid, and the Children's Health Insurance Program, now disburses more than half the total payments for medical care in the United States.

Adverse selection occurs when one person knows more about the way things are than other people do. Adverse selection exists, for example, when sellers offer items of particularly low (hidden) quality for sale, and when the people with the greatest need for insurance are those most likely to purchase it.

The death spiral: Adverse selection can push healthy people out of the health insurance market, which raises the average cost of insuring a customer, resulting in higher premiums, causing more people to drop out, and so on.

In general, people or firms faced with the problem of adverse selection follow one of several well-established strategies for dealing with it. One strategy is **screening**: using observable information to make inferences about private information. If you apply to purchase health insurance, you'll find that the insurance company will demand documentation of your health status in an attempt to "screen out" less healthy applicants, whom they will refuse to insure or will insure only at very high premiums. Auto insurance also provides a very good example. An insurance company may not know whether you are a careful driver, but it has statistical data on the accident rates of people who resemble your profile—and it uses those data in setting premiums. A 19-year-old male who drives a sports car and has already had a fender-bender is likely to pay a very high premium. A 40-year-old female who drives a minivan and has never had an accident is likely to pay much less. In some cases, this may be quite unfair: some adolescent males are very careful drivers, and some mature women drive their minivans as if they were fighter jets. But nobody can deny that the insurance companies are right on average.

Another strategy is for people who are good prospects to somehow *signal* their private information. **Signaling** involves taking some action that wouldn't be worth taking unless they were indeed good prospects. Reputable used-car dealers often offer warranties—promises to repair any problems with the cars they sell that arise within a given amount of time. This isn't just a way of insuring their customers against possible expenses; it's a way of credibly showing that they are not selling lemons. As a result, more sales occur and dealers can command higher prices for their used cars.

Finally, in the face of adverse selection, it can be very valuable to establish a good **reputation**: a used-car dealership will often advertise how long it has been in business to show that it has continued to satisfy its customers. As a result, new customers will be willing to purchase cars and to pay more for that dealer's cars.

Adverse selection can be reduced through **screening**: using observable information about people to make inferences about their private information.

Adverse selection can be diminished by people **signaling** their private information through actions that credibly reveal what they know.

A long-term **reputation** allows an individual to assure others that he or she isn't concealing adverse private information.

Moral Hazard

In the late 1970s, New York and other major cities experienced an epidemic of suspicious fires—fires that appeared to be deliberately set. Some of the fires were probably started by teenagers for amusement, others by gang members struggling over turf. But investigators eventually became aware of patterns in a number of the fires. Particular landlords who owned several buildings seemed to have an unusually large number of their buildings burn down. Although it was difficult to prove, police had few doubts that most of these fire-prone landlords were hiring professional arsonists to torch their own properties.

Why burn your own buildings? These buildings were typically in declining neighborhoods, where rising crime rates and middle-class flight had led to a decline in property values. But the insurance policies on the buildings were written to compensate owners based on historical property values, and so would pay the owner of a destroyed building more than the building was worth in the current market. For a corrupt landlord who knew the right people, this presented a profitable opportunity.

The arson epidemic became less severe during the 1980s, partly because insurance companies began making it difficult to overinsure properties and partly because a boom in real estate values made many previously arson-threatened buildings worth more unburned.

The arson episodes make it clear that it is a bad idea for insurance companies to let customers insure buildings for more than their value—it gives the customers some destructive incentives. However, you might think that the incentive problem would go away as long as the insurance is no more than 100% of the value of what is being insured.

But, unfortunately, anything close to 100% insurance still distorts incentives—it induces policyholders to behave differently from how they would in the absence of insurance. The reason is that preventing fires requires effort and cost on the part of a building's owner. Fire alarms and sprinkler systems have to be kept in good

Would you be more careful to avoid a fire if you didn't have fire insurance?

repair, fire safety rules have to be strictly enforced, and so on. All of this takes time and money—time and money that the owner may not find worth spending if the insurance policy will provide close to full compensation for any losses.

Of course, the insurance company could specify in the policy that it won't pay if basic safety precautions have not been taken. But it isn't always easy to tell how careful a building's owner has been—the owner knows, but the insurance company does not.

The point is that the building's owner has private information about his or her own actions; the owner knows whether he or she has really taken all appropriate precautions. As a result, the insurance company is likely to face greater claims than if it were able to determine exactly how much effort a building owner exerts to prevent a loss. The problem of distorted incentives known as **moral hazard** arises when an individual has private information about his or her own actions but someone else bears the costs of a lack of care or effort.

To deal with moral hazard, it is necessary to give individuals with private information some personal stake in what happens, a stake that gives them a reason to exert effort even if others cannot verify that they have done so. Moral hazard is the reason salespeople in many stores receive a commission on sales: it's hard for managers to be sure how hard the salespeople are really working, and if they were paid only straight salary, they would not have an incentive to exert effort to make those sales. Similar logic explains why many stores and restaurants, even if they are part of national chains, are actually franchises, licensed outlets owned by the people who run them.

Insurance companies deal with moral hazard by requiring a **deductible**: they compensate for losses only above a certain amount, so that coverage is always less than 100%. The insurance on your car, for example, may pay for repairs only after the first $500 in loss. This means that a careless driver who gets into a fender-bender will end up paying $500 for repairs even if he is insured, which provides at least some incentive to be careful and reduces moral hazard.

In addition to reducing moral hazard, deductibles provide a partial solution to the problem of adverse selection. Your insurance premium often drops substantially if you are willing to accept a large deductible. This is an attractive option to people who know they are low-risk customers; it is less attractive to people who know they are high-risk—and so are likely to have an accident and end up paying the deductible. By offering a menu of policies with different premiums and deductibles, insurance companies can screen their customers, inducing them to sort themselves out on the basis of their private information.

As the example of deductibles suggests, moral hazard limits the ability of the economy to allocate risks efficiently. You generally can't get full (100%) insurance on your home or car, even though you would like to buy full insurance, and you bear the risk of large deductibles, even though you would prefer not to.

Moral hazard arises when an individual knows more about his or her own actions than other people do. This leads to a distortion of incentives to take care or to exert effort when someone else bears the costs of the lack of care or effort.

A **deductible** is a sum specified in an insurance policy that the insured individuals must pay before being compensated for a claim; deductibles reduce moral hazard.

ENRICHMENT MODULE C REVIEW

Check Your Understanding

1. Your car insurance premiums are lower if you have had no moving violations for several years. Explain how this feature tends to decrease the potential inefficiency caused by adverse selection.

2. A common feature of home construction contracts is that when it costs more to construct a building than was originally estimated, the contractor must absorb the additional cost. Explain how this feature reduces

the problem of moral hazard but also forces the contractor to bear more risk than she would like.

3. True or false? Explain your answer, stating what concept discussed in this Module accounts for the feature.
   a. People with higher deductibles on their auto insurance generally drive more carefully.
   b. People with higher deductibles on their auto insurance pay lower premiums.

Multiple-Choice Review Questions

1. Which of the following is true about private information?
   a. Everyone has access to it.
   b. It has no value.
   c. Adverse selection arises when people take fewer precautions because they are insured.
   d. It can distort economic decisions.
   e. Moral hazard arises when sellers have private information about the quality of goods.

2. Due to adverse selection,
   a. mutually beneficial trades go unexploited.
   b. people buy lemons rather than other fruit.
   c. sick people buy less insurance.
   d. private information is available to all.
   e. public information is available to no one.

3. When colleges use grade point averages to make admissions decisions, they are employing which strategy?
   a. signaling
   b. screening
   c. profit maximization
   d. marginal analysis
   e. adverse selection

4. Moral hazard is the result of
   a. asymmetric information.
   b. signaling.
   c. toxic waste.
   d. adverse selection.
   e. public information.

5. A deductible is used by insurance companies to
   a. allow customers to pay for insurance premiums using payroll deduction.
   b. deal with moral hazard.
   c. make public information private.
   d. compensate policyholders fully for their losses.
   e. avoid all payments to policyholders.

6. The used car market has been described as the "market for lemons" because in that market,
   a. information problems make the owners of flawed cars more likely to sell them than the owners of good cars.
   b. moral hazard causes buyers of used cars to drive recklessly and damage the cars.
   c. buyers often get a sour look on their faces when they hear the asking price for a car.
   d. the documents used to transfer the title to a car are traditionally yellow, like a lemon.
   e. used cars are often dented, like the skin of a lemon.

7. Which of the following would increase the problem of adverse selection in the health insurance industry?
   a. higher insurance premiums
   b. a legal requirement that everyone must buy health insurance
   c. mandatory health screening for health insurance applicants
   d. a taxpayer-funded system that provides health care to everyone at no cost except for the tax payment
   e. lower insurance premiums for individuals whose good health is verified by a thorough physical examination

Free-Response Review Questions

1. Identify whether each of the following situations reflects moral hazard or adverse selection. Propose a potential solution to reduce the inefficiency that each situation creates.
   a. When you buy a second-hand car, you do not know whether it is a lemon (low quality) or a plum (high quality), but the seller knows.
   b. People with dental insurance might not brush their teeth as often, knowing that if they get cavities, the insurance will pay for the fillings.
   c. A company does not know whether individual workers on an assembly line are working hard or slacking off.
   d. When making a decision about hiring you, prospective employers do not know whether or not you are a productive worker.

> **Rubric for FRQ 1 (8 points)**
> **1 point:** Adverse selection
> **1 point:** Sellers could offer a warranty with the car that pays for repair costs.

> **1 point:** Moral hazard
> **1 point:** Each insured person can be made to pay a co-payment of a certain dollar amount each time he or she gets a filling.
> **1 point:** Moral hazard
> **1 point:** Pay the workers "piece rates," that is, pay them according to how much they have produced each day.
> **1 point:** Adverse selection
> **1 point:** Provide potential employers with references from previous employers.

2. Suppose individuals or corporations (for example home-buyers or banks) believe that the government will "bail them out" in the event that their decisions lead to a financial collapse. This is an example of what problem created by asymmetric information? How does this situation lead to inefficiency? What is a possible remedy for the problem? **(3 points)**

Discussion Starters

1. In what situations have you experienced asymmetric information? What screening or signaling was involved?

2. Describe a situation in which you experienced moral hazard by taking fewer precautions when the cost of damage would be at least partially someone else's

problem. For example, you might have done this when a product was under warranty, a car or home was being rented, or insurance would cover the cost of damage.

3. Describe a case in which you used a seller's reputation to deal with asymmetric information.

EM D

Indifference Curves and Consumer Choice

> **In this Module, you will learn to:**
> - Explain how economists use indifference curves to illustrate a person's preferences
> - Discuss the importance of the marginal rate of substitution, the rate at which a consumer is just willing to substitute one good for another
> - Use indifference curves and the budget line to find a consumer's optimal consumption bundle

Mapping the Utility Function

In Module 51, we introduced the concept of a utility function, which determines a consumer's total utility given his or her consumption bundle. Here we will extend the analysis by learning how to express total utility as a function of the consumption of two goods. This will deepen our understanding of the trade-offs involved when choosing the optimal consumption bundle. We will also see how the optimal consumption bundle itself changes in response to changes in the prices of goods. We begin by examining a different way of representing a consumer's utility function, based on the concept of *indifference curves*.

Indifference Curves

Ingrid is a consumer who buys only two goods: housing, measured by the number of rooms in her house or apartment, and restaurant meals. How can we represent her utility function in a way that takes account of her consumption of both goods?

One way is to draw a three-dimensional picture, or "utility hill," as shown in **Figure D.1**. The distance along the horizontal axis measures the quantity of housing Ingrid consumes in terms of the number of rooms; the distance along the vertical axis measures the number of restaurant meals she consumes. The altitude or height of the hill at each point is indicated by a contour line, along which the height of the hill is constant. For example, point *A*, which corresponds to a consumption

A. Astes/Alamy

Figure D.1   Ingrid's Utility Function

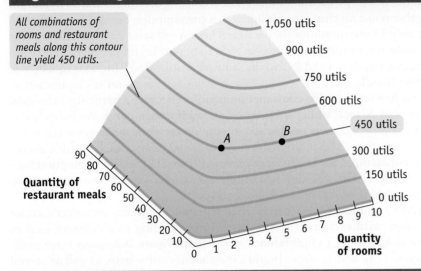

All combinations of rooms and restaurant meals along this contour line yield 450 utils.

The three-dimensional hill shows how Ingrid's total utility depends on her consumption of housing and restaurant meals. Point A corresponds to consumption of 3 rooms and 30 restaurant meals. That consumption bundle yields Ingrid 450 utils, corresponding to the height of the hill at point A. The lines running around the hill are contour lines, along which the height is constant. So point B and every other point along the same contour line as point A generates the same level of utility.

bundle of 3 rooms and 30 restaurant meals, and point *B*, which corresponds to a bundle of 6 rooms and 15 restaurant meals, lie on the contour line labeled 450. So the total utility Ingrid receives from consuming either of these bundles is 450 utils.

A three-dimensional picture like Figure D.1 helps us think about the relationship between consumption bundles and total utility. But anyone who has ever used a topographical map to plan a hiking trip knows that it is possible to represent a three-dimensional surface in only two dimensions. A topographical map doesn't offer a three-dimensional view of the terrain; instead, it conveys information about altitude solely through the use of contour lines.

The same principle can be applied to the representation of a utility function. In **Figure D.2**, Ingrid's consumption of rooms is measured on the horizontal axis and her consumption of restaurant meals on the vertical axis. The curve here corresponds to the contour line in Figure D.1, drawn at a total utility of 450 utils. This curve shows all

Figure D.2   An Indifference Curve

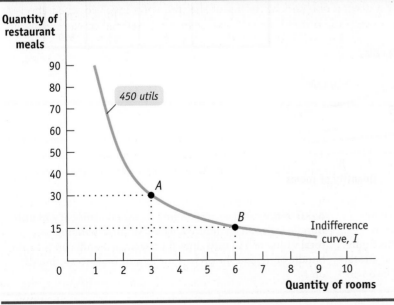

An indifference curve is a contour line along which total utility is constant. In this case, we show all the consumption bundles that yield Ingrid 450 utils. Consumption bundle A, consisting of 3 rooms and 30 restaurant meals, yields the same total utility as bundle B, consisting of 6 rooms and 15 restaurant meals. That is, Ingrid is indifferent between bundle A and bundle B.

the consumption bundles that yield a total utility of 450 utils. As we've seen, one point on that contour line is A, a consumption bundle consisting of 3 rooms and 30 restaurant meals. Another point on that contour line is B, a consumption bundle consisting of 6 rooms but only 15 restaurant meals. Because B lies on the same contour line, it yields Ingrid the same total utility—450 utils—as A. We say that Ingrid is *indifferent* between A and B: because bundles A and B yield the same total utility level, Ingrid is equally well off with either bundle.

A contour line representing consumption bundles that give a particular individual the same amount of total utility is known as an **indifference curve**. An individual is always indifferent between any two bundles that lie on the same indifference curve. For a given consumer, there is an indifference curve corresponding to each possible level of total utility. For example, the indifference curve in Figure D.2 shows consumption bundles that yield Ingrid 450 utils; different indifference curves would show consumption bundles that yield Ingrid 400 utils, 500 utils, and so on.

A collection of indifference curves that represents a given consumer's entire utility function, with each indifference curve corresponding to a different level of total utility, is known as an **indifference curve map**. **Figure D.3** shows three indifference curves—I_1, I_2, and I_3—from Ingrid's indifference curve map, as well as several consumption bundles, A, B, C, and D. The accompanying table lists each bundle, its composition of rooms and restaurant meals, and the total utility it provides. Because bundles A and B generate the same number of utils, 450, they lie on the same indifference curve, I_2.

Although Ingrid is indifferent between A and B, she is certainly not indifferent between A and C: as you can see from the table, C generates only 391 utils, fewer than A or B. So Ingrid prefers consumption bundles A and B to bundle C. This is evident from the graph because C is on indifference curve I_1, and I_1 lies below I_2. Bundle D, though,

An **indifference curve** shows all the consumption bundles that yield the same amount of total utility for an individual.

The entire utility function of an individual can be represented by an **indifference curve map**—a collection of indifference curves, each of which corresponds to a different total utility level.

Figure D.3   An Indifference Curve Map

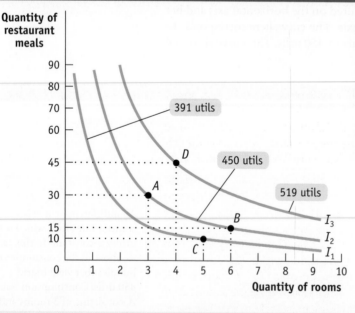

Consumption bundle	Quantity of rooms	Quantity of meals	Total utility (utils)
A	3	30	450
B	6	15	450
C	5	10	391
D	4	45	519

The utility function can be represented in greater detail by increasing the number of indifference curves drawn, each corresponding to a different level of total utility. In this figure, bundle C lies on an indifference curve corresponding to a total utility of 391 utils. As in Figure D.2, bundles A and B lie on an indifference curve corresponding to a total utility of 450 utils. Bundle D lies on an indifference curve corresponding to a total utility of 519 utils. Ingrid prefers any bundle on I_2 to any bundle on I_1, and she prefers any bundle on I_3 to any bundle on I_2.

generates 519 utils, more than A and B. So bundle D is on indifference curve I_3, which lies above I_2. Clearly, Ingrid prefers D to either A or B. And, even more strongly, she prefers D to C.

As you will see shortly, the indifference curve map tells us all we need to know in order to find a consumer's optimal consumption bundle. That is, it's important that Ingrid has higher total utility along indifference curve I_2 than she does along I_1, but it doesn't matter how much higher her total utility is. In other words, we don't have to measure utils in order to understand how consumers make choices.

Consumer theory requires an ordinal measure of utility—one that ranks consumption bundles in terms of desirability—so that we can say bundle X is better than bundle Y. The theory does not, however, require cardinal utility, which actually assigns a specific number to the total utility yielded by each bundle.

Properties of Indifference Curves

No two individuals have the same indifference curve map because no two individuals have the same preferences. But economists believe that, regardless of the person, every indifference curve map has two general properties. These properties are explained below and illustrated in panels A1 and A2 of **Figure D.4**.

a. *Indifference curves never cross.* Suppose that we tried to draw an indifference curve map like the one depicted in panel A1, in which two indifference curves cross at A. What is the total utility at A? Is it 100 utils or 200 utils? Indifference curves cannot cross because each consumption bundle must correspond to one unique total utility level—not, as shown at A, two different total utility levels.

b. *The farther out an indifference curve lies—the farther it is from the origin—the higher the level of total utility it indicates.* The reason, illustrated in panel A2, is that we assume that more is better—we consider only the consumption bundles for which the consumer is not satiated. Bundle B, on the outer indifference curve, contains more of both goods than bundle A on the inner indifference curve. So B, because it generates a higher total utility level (200 utils), lies on a higher indifference curve than A.

Furthermore, economists believe that, for most goods, consumers' indifference curve maps also have two additional properties. They are explained here and illustrated in panels B1 and B2 of Figure D.4:

c. *Indifference curves slope downward.* Here, too, the reason is that more is better. Panel B1 shows four consumption bundles on the same indifference curve: W, X, Y, and Z. By definition, these consumption bundles yield the same level of total utility. But as you move along the curve to the right, from W to Z, the quantity of rooms consumed increases. The only way a person can consume more rooms without gaining utility is by giving up some restaurant meals. So the indifference curve must slope downward.

d. *Indifference curves have a convex shape.* Panel B2 shows that the slope of each indifference curve changes as you move down the curve to the right: the curve gets flatter. If you move up an indifference curve to the left, the curve gets steeper. So the indifference curve is steeper at A than it is at B. When this occurs, we say that an indifference curve has a *convex* shape—it is bowed-in toward the origin. This feature arises from diminishing marginal utility, a principle we discussed in Module 51. Recall that when a consumer has diminishing marginal utility, consumption of another unit of a good generates a smaller increase in total utility than the previous unit consumed. Next we will examine in detail how diminishing marginal utility gives rise to convex-shaped indifference curves.

Goods that satisfy all four properties of indifference curve maps are called *ordinary goods*. The vast majority of goods in any consumer's utility function fall into this category. Next we will define ordinary goods more precisely and see the key role that diminishing marginal utility plays for them.

Properties of All Indifference Curves

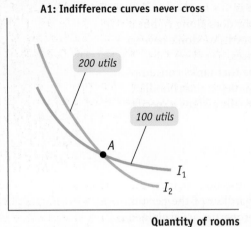

A1: Indifference curves never cross

Quantity of restaurant meals

200 utils

100 utils

A

I_1

I_2

Quantity of rooms

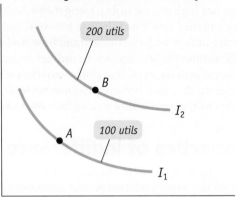

A2: The farther out an indifference curve lies, the higher the level of total utility

Quantity of restaurant meals

200 utils

B

I_2

A

100 utils

I_1

Quantity of rooms

Additional Properties of Indifference Curves for Ordinary Goods

B1: Indifference curves slope downward

Quantity of restaurant meals

W

X

Y

Z

I

Quantity of rooms

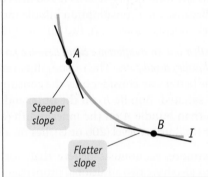

B2: Indifference curves have a convex shape

Quantity of restaurant meals

A

Steeper slope

B

I

Flatter slope

Quantity of rooms

Indifference Curves and Consumer Choice

Above, we used indifference curves to represent the preferences of Ingrid, whose consumption bundles consist of rooms and restaurant meals. Our next step is to show how to use Ingrid's indifference curve map to find her utility-maximizing consumption bundle, given her budget constraint, which exists because she must choose a consumption bundle that costs no more than her total income.

It's important to understand how our analysis here relates to what we did in Module 51. We are not offering a new theory of consumer behavior in this Module—consumers are assumed to maximize total utility as before. In particular, we know that consumers will follow the *optimal consumption rule*: the optimal consumption bundle lies on the budget line, and the marginal utility per dollar is the same for every good in the bundle.

But as we will see shortly, we can derive this optimal consumer behavior in a somewhat different way—a way that yields deeper insights into consumer choice.

The Marginal Rate of Substitution

The first element of our approach is a new concept, the *marginal rate of substitution*. We'll see that this concept is tied closely to the shape of the indifference curve, which gets flatter moving from left to right, as illustrated in **Figure D.5**.

Figure D.5 The Changing Slope of an Indifference Curve

Consumption bundle	Quantity of rooms	Quantity of restaurant meals
V	2	30
W	3	20
X	4	15
Y	5	12
Z	6	10

This indifference curve is downward-sloping and convex, implying that restaurant meals and rooms are ordinary goods for Ingrid. As Ingrid moves down her indifference curve from V to Z, she gives up restaurant meals in exchange for a larger number of rooms. However, the terms of that trade-off change. As she moves from V to W, she is willing to give up 10 restaurant meals in return for 1 more room. As her consumption of rooms rises and her consumption of restaurant meals falls, she is willing to give up fewer restaurant meals in return for each additional room. The flattening of the slope as she moves from left to right arises from diminishing marginal utility.

We have just seen that for most goods, consumers' indifference curves are downward-sloping and convex. Figure D.5 shows such an indifference curve. The points labeled V, W, X, Y, and Z all lie on this indifference curve—that is, they represent consumption bundles that yield Ingrid the same level of total utility. The table accompanying the figure shows the components of each of the bundles. As we move along the indifference curve from V to Z, Ingrid's consumption of housing steadily increases from 2 rooms to 6 rooms, her consumption of restaurant meals steadily decreases from 30 meals to 10 meals, and her total utility is kept constant. As we move down the indifference curve, then, Ingrid is trading more of one good for less of the other, with the *terms* of that trade-off—the ratio of additional rooms consumed to restaurant meals sacrificed—chosen to keep her total utility constant.

Notice that the quantity of restaurant meals that Ingrid is willing to give up in return for an additional room changes along the indifference curve. As we move from V to W, housing consumption rises from 2 to 3 rooms and restaurant meal consumption falls from 30 to 20—a trade-off of 10 restaurant meals for 1 additional room. But as we move from Y to Z, housing consumption rises from 5 to 6 rooms and restaurant meal consumption falls from 12 to 10, a trade-off of only 2 restaurant meals for an additional room.

To put it in terms of slope, the slope of the indifference curve between V and W is −10: the change in restaurant meal consumption, −10, divided by the change in housing consumption, 1. Similarly, the slope of the indifference curve between Y and Z is −2. So the indifference curve gets flatter as we move down it to the right—that is, it has a convex shape, one of the four properties of an indifference curve for ordinary goods.

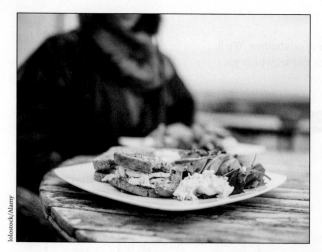

Why does the trade-off change in this way? Let's think about it intuitively and then work through it more carefully. When Ingrid moves down her indifference curve, whether from V to W or from Y to Z, she gains utility from her additional consumption of housing but loses an equal amount of utility from her reduced consumption of restaurant meals. But at each step, the initial position from which Ingrid begins is different. At V, Ingrid consumes only a small quantity of rooms; because of diminishing marginal utility, her marginal utility per room at that point is high. At V, then, an additional room adds a lot to Ingrid's total utility. But at V she already consumes a large quantity of restaurant meals, so her marginal utility of restaurant meals is low at that point. This means that it takes a large reduction in her quantity of restaurant meals consumed to offset the increased utility she gets from the extra room of housing.

At Y, in contrast, Ingrid consumes a much larger quantity of rooms and a much smaller quantity of restaurant meals than at V. This means that an additional room adds fewer utils, and a restaurant meal forgone costs more utils, than at V. So Ingrid is willing to give up fewer restaurant meals in return for another room of housing at Y (where she gives up 2 meals for 1 room) than she is at V (where she gives up 10 meals for 1 room).

Now let's express the same idea—that the trade-off Ingrid is willing to make depends on where she is starting from—by using a little math. We do this by examining how the slope of the indifference curve changes as we move down it. Moving down the indifference curve—reducing restaurant meal consumption and increasing housing consumption—will produce two opposing effects on Ingrid's total utility: lower restaurant meal consumption will reduce her total utility, but higher housing consumption will raise her total utility. And since we are moving down the indifference curve, these two effects must exactly cancel out:

Along the indifference curve:

(D-1)   (Change in total utility due to lower restaurant meal consumption) +
(Change in total utility due to higher housing consumption) = 0

or, rearranging terms,

Along the indifference curve:

(D-2)   − (Change in total utility due to lower restaurant meal consumption) =
(Change in total utility due to higher housing consumption)

Let's now focus on what happens as we move only a short distance down the indifference curve, trading off a small increase in housing consumption in place of a small decrease in restaurant meal consumption. Following our notation from before, let's use MU_R and MU_M to represent the marginal utility of rooms and restaurant meals, respectively, and ΔQ_R and ΔQ_M to represent the changes in room and meal consumption, respectively. In general, the change in total utility caused by a small change in consumption of a good is equal to the change in consumption multiplied by the *marginal utility* of that good. This means that we can calculate the change in Ingrid's total utility generated by a change in her consumption bundle using the following equations:

(D-3)   Change in total utility due to a change in restaurant meal consumption $= MU_M \times \Delta Q_M$

and

(D-4)   Change in total utility due to a change in housing consumption $= MU_R \times \Delta Q_R$

So we can write Equation D-2 in symbols as:

Along the indifference curve:

$$\textbf{(D-5)} \quad -MU_M \times \Delta Q_M = MU_R \times \Delta Q_R$$

Note that the left-hand side of Equation D-5 has a negative sign; it represents the loss in total utility from decreased restaurant meal consumption. This must equal the gain in total utility from increased room consumption, represented by the right-hand side of the equation.

What we want to know is how this translates into the slope of the indifference curve. To find the slope, we divide both sides of Equation D-5 by ΔQ_R, and again by $-MU_M$, in order to get the ΔQ_M, ΔQ_R terms on one side and the MU_R, MU_M terms on the other. This results in:

Along the indifference curve:

$$\textbf{(D-6)} \quad \frac{\Delta Q_M}{\Delta Q_R} = \frac{MU_R}{MU_M}$$

The left-hand side of Equation D-6 is the slope of the indifference curve; it is the rate at which Ingrid is willing to trade rooms (the good on the horizontal axis) for restaurant meals (the good on the vertical axis) without changing her total utility level. The right-hand side of Equation D-6 is the negative of the ratio of the marginal utility of rooms to the marginal utility of restaurant meals—that is, the ratio of what she gains from one more room to what she gains from one more meal, with a negative sign in front.

Putting all this together, Equation D-6 shows that, along the indifference curve, the quantity of restaurant meals Ingrid is willing to give up in return for a room, $\frac{\Delta Q_M}{\Delta Q_R}$, is exactly equal to the negative of the ratio of the marginal utility of a room to that of a meal, $-\frac{MU_R}{MU_M}$. Only when this condition is met will her total utility level remain constant as she consumes more rooms and fewer restaurant meals.

Economists have a special name for the ratio of the marginal utilities found in the right-hand side of Equation D-6: the **marginal rate of substitution**, or ***MRS***, of rooms (the good on the horizontal axis) in place of restaurant meals (the good on the vertical axis). That's because as we slide down Ingrid's indifference curve, we are substituting more rooms for fewer restaurant meals in her consumption bundle. As we'll see shortly, the marginal rate of substitution plays an important role in finding the optimal consumption bundle.

Recall that indifference curves get flatter as you move down them to the right. The reason, as we've just discussed, is diminishing marginal utility: as Ingrid consumes more housing and fewer restaurant meals, her marginal utility from housing falls and her marginal utility from restaurant meals rises. So her marginal rate of substitution, which is equal to the negative of the slope of her indifference curve, falls as she moves down the indifference curve.

The flattening of indifference curves as you slide down them to the right—which reflects the same logic as the principle of diminishing marginal utility—is known as the principle of **diminishing marginal rate of substitution**. It says that the more of one good an individual consumes in proportion to a second good, the less of the second good he or she is willing to give up in exchange for another unit of the first good.

We can illustrate this point by referring to Figure D.5. At point *V*, a bundle with a low proportion of rooms to restaurant meals, Ingrid is willing to forgo 10 restaurant meals in return for 1 room. But at point *Y*, a bundle with a high proportion of rooms to restaurant meals, she is willing to forgo only 2 restaurant meals in return for 1 room.

From this example we see that, in Ingrid's utility function, rooms and restaurant meals possess the two additional properties that characterize ordinary goods. Ingrid requires additional rooms to compensate her for the loss of a meal, and vice versa; so her indifference curves for these two goods slope downward. And her indifference

The **marginal rate of substitution**, or ***MRS***, of good *R* in place of good *M* is equal to $\frac{MU_R}{MU_M}$, the ratio of the marginal utility of *R* to the marginal utility of *M*.

The principle of **diminishing marginal rate of substitution** states that the more of one good a person consumes in proportion to a second good, the less of the second good he or she is willing to substitute for another unit of the first good.

curves are convex: the slope of her indifference curve—*the negative of* the marginal rate of substitution—becomes flatter as we move down it. In fact, an indifference curve is convex only when it has a diminishing marginal rate of substitution. These two conditions are equivalent.

With this information, we can define *ordinary goods*, which account for the great majority of all goods. A pair of goods are **ordinary goods** in a consumer's utility function if they possess two properties: the consumer requires more of one good to compensate for less of the other, and the consumer experiences a diminishing marginal rate of substitution when substituting one good for the other.

Next we will see how to determine Ingrid's optimal consumption bundle using indifference curves.

The Tangency Condition

Now let's put some of Ingrid's indifference curves on the same diagram as her budget line to illustrate her optimal consumption choice. **Figure D.6** shows Ingrid's budget line, *BL*, when her income is $2,400 per month, housing costs $150 per room each month, and restaurant meals cost $30 each. What is her optimal consumption bundle?

> Two goods are **ordinary goods** in a consumer's utility function when (1) the consumer requires additional units of one good to compensate for fewer units of the other, and (2) the consumer experiences a diminishing marginal rate of substitution when substituting one good for the other.

Figure D.6   The Optimal Consumption Bundle

> The budget line, *BL*, shows Ingrid's possible consumption bundles, given an income of $2,400 per month, when rooms cost $150 per month and restaurant meals cost $30 each. I_1, I_2, and I_3 are indifference curves. Consumption bundles such as *B* and *C* are not optimal because Ingrid can move to a higher indifference curve. The optimal consumption bundle is *A*, where the budget line is just tangent to the highest possible indifference curve.

To answer this question, we consider three of Ingrid's indifference curves: I_1, I_2, and I_3. Of these curves, I_3 represents the highest total utility level, but Ingrid cannot afford to reach that level because she is constrained by her income: no consumption bundle on her budget line yields that much total utility. But she shouldn't settle for the total utility level generated by *B* or *C*, which both lie on I_1: there are other bundles on her budget line, such as *A*, that clearly yield more total utility than *B* or *C*.

In fact, *A*—a consumption bundle consisting of 8 rooms and 40 restaurant meals per month—is Ingrid's optimal consumption choice. The reason is that *A* lies on the highest indifference curve Ingrid can reach given her income.

At the optimal consumption bundle *A*, Ingrid's budget line *just touches* the relevant indifference curve—the budget line is *tangent* to the indifference curve. This **tangency condition** between the indifference curve and the budget line applies to the optimal consumption bundle when the indifference curves have the typical convex shape.

> The **tangency condition** between the indifference curve and the budget line holds when the indifference curve and the budget line just touch. This condition determines the optimal consumption bundle when the indifference curves have the typical convex shape.

To see why, let's look more closely at how we know that a consumption bundle that *doesn't* satisfy the tangency condition can't be optimal. Reexamining Figure D.6, we can see that consumption bundles B and C are both affordable because they lie on the budget line. However, neither is optimal. Both of them lie on the indifference curve I_1, which cuts through the budget line at both points. But because I_1 cuts through the budget line, Ingrid can do better: she can move down the budget line from B or up the budget line from C, as indicated by the arrows. In each case, this allows her to get onto a higher indifference curve, I_2, which increases her total utility.

However, Ingrid cannot do any better than I_2: any other indifference curve either cuts through her budget line or doesn't touch it at all. And the bundle that allows her to achieve I_2, of course, is her optimal consumption bundle.

The Slope of the Budget Line

Figure D.6 shows us how to use a graph of the budget line and the indifference curves to find the optimal consumption bundle, the bundle at which the budget line and the indifference curve are tangent. But rather than rely on drawing graphs, we can determine the optimal consumption bundle by using a bit more math. As you can see from Figure D.6, the budget line and the indifference curve have the same slope at the optimal consumption bundle, A. Why? Because two curves can only be tangent to each other if they have the same slope at the point where they meet. Otherwise, they would cross each other at that point. And we know that if a point is on an indifference curve that crosses the budget line (like I_1, in Figure D.6), it can't be on the indifference curve that contains the optimal consumption bundle (like I_2).

So we can use information about the slopes of the budget line and the indifference curve to find the optimal consumption bundle. To do that, we must first analyze the slope of the budget line, a fairly straightforward task. We know that Ingrid will get the highest possible utility by spending all of her income and consuming a bundle on her budget line. So we can represent Ingrid's budget line, made up of the consumption bundles available to her when she spends all of her income, with the equation:

(D-7) $(Q_R \times P_R) + (Q_M \times P_M) = N$

where N stands for Ingrid's income. To find the slope of the budget line, we divide its vertical intercept (where the budget line hits the vertical axis) by its horizontal intercept (where it hits the horizontal axis) and then add a negative sign. The vertical intercept is the point at which Ingrid spends all her income on restaurant meals and none on housing (that is, $Q_R = 0$). In that case the number of restaurant meals she consumes is:

(D-8) $Q_M = \dfrac{N}{P_M} = \dfrac{\$2,400}{(\$30 \text{ per meal})} = 80 \text{ meals}$

$= \text{Vertical intercept of budget line}$

At the other extreme, Ingrid spends all her income on housing and none on restaurant meals (so that $Q_M = 0$). This means that at the horizontal intercept of the budget line, the number of rooms she consumes is:

(D-9) $Q_R = \dfrac{N}{P_R} = \dfrac{\$2,400}{(\$150 \text{ per room})} = 16 \text{ rooms}$

$= \text{Horizontal intercept of budget line}$

Now we have the information needed to find the slope of the budget line. It is:

(D-10) $\text{Slope of budget line} = -\dfrac{\text{Vertical intercept}}{\text{Horizontal intercept}} = -\dfrac{\dfrac{N}{P_M}}{\dfrac{N}{P_R}} = -\dfrac{P_R}{P_M}$

The **relative price** of good R in terms of good M is equal to $\frac{P_R}{P_M}$, the rate at which R trades for M in the market.

Notice the negative sign in Equation D-10; it's there because the budget line slopes downward. The $\frac{P_R}{P_M}$ quantity is known as the **relative price** of rooms in terms of restaurant meals, to distinguish it from an ordinary price in terms of dollars. Because buying one more room requires Ingrid to give up the quantity $\frac{P_R}{P_M}$ of restaurant meals, or 5 meals, we can interpret the relative price $\frac{P_R}{P_M}$ as the rate at which a room trades for restaurant meals in the market; it is the price—in terms of restaurant meals—Ingrid has to "pay" to get one more room.

Looking at this another way, the slope of the budget line—the negative of the relative price—tells us the opportunity cost of each good in terms of the other. The relative price illustrates the opportunity cost to an individual of consuming one more unit of one good in terms of how much of the other good in his or her consumption bundle must be forgone. This opportunity cost arises from the consumer's limited resources—his or her limited budget. It's useful to note that Equations D-8, D-9, and D-10 give us all the information we need about what happens to the budget line when relative price or income changes. From Equations D-8 and D-9 we can see that a change in income, N, leads to a parallel shift of the budget line: both the vertical and horizontal intercepts will shift. That is, how far out the budget line is from the origin depends on the consumer's income. If a consumer's income rises, the budget line moves outward. If the consumer's income shrinks, the budget line shifts inward. In each case, the slope of the budget line stays the same because the relative price of one good in terms of the other does not change.

In contrast, a change in the relative price $\frac{P_R}{P_M}$ will lead to a change in the slope of the budget line. Next, we'll analyze in greater detail these changes in the budget line and examine how the optimal consumption bundle changes when either the relative price or income changes.

Prices and the Marginal Rate of Substitution

Now we're ready to bring together the slope of the budget line and the slope of the indifference curve to find the optimal consumption bundle. From Equation D-6, we know that the slope of the indifference curve at any point is equal to the negative of the marginal rate of substitution:

$$\textbf{(D-11)} \quad \text{Slope of indifference curve} = -\frac{MU_R}{MU_M}$$

The **relative price rule** says that at the optimal consumption bundle, the marginal rate of substitution between two goods is equal to their relative price.

As we've already noted, at the optimal consumption bundle the slope of the budget line and the slope of the indifference curve are equal. We can write this formally by putting Equations D-10 and D-11 together, which gives us the **relative price rule** for finding the optimal consumption bundle:

$$\textbf{(D-12)} \quad \textit{At the optimal consumption bundle:} \ -\frac{MU_R}{MU_M} = -\frac{P_R}{P_M}$$

$$\textit{or, cancelling the negative signs,} \ \frac{MU_R}{MU_M} = \frac{P_R}{P_M}$$

That is, at the optimal consumption bundle, the marginal rate of substitution between any two goods is equal to the ratio of their prices. To put it in a more intuitive way, starting with Ingrid's optimal consumption bundle, the rate at which she would trade a room for more restaurant meals along her indifference curve, $\frac{MU_R}{MU_M}$, is equal to the rate at which rooms are traded for restaurant meals in the market, $\frac{P_R}{P_M}$.

What would happen if this equality did not hold? We can see by examining **Figure D.7**. There, at point B, the slope of the indifference curve, $-\dfrac{MU_R}{MU_M}$, is greater in absolute value than the slope of the budget line, $-\dfrac{P_R}{P_M}$. This means that, at B, Ingrid values an additional room in place of meals *more* than it costs her to buy an additional room and forgo some meals. As a result, Ingrid would be better off moving down her budget line toward A, consuming more rooms and fewer restaurant meals—and because of that, B could not have been her optimal bundle! Likewise, at C, the slope of Ingrid's indifference curve is less in absolute value than the slope of the budget line. The implication is that, at C, Ingrid values additional meals in place of a room *more* than it costs her to buy additional meals and forgo a room. Again, Ingrid would be better off moving along her budget line—consuming more restaurant meals and fewer rooms—until she reaches A, her optimal consumption bundle.

But suppose we transform the last term of Equation D-12 in the following way: divide both sides by P_R and multiply both sides by MU_M. Then the relative price rule becomes the optimal consumption rule:

$$\textbf{(D-13)} \quad \textit{Optimal consumption rule:} \quad \frac{MU_R}{P_R} = \frac{MU_M}{P_M}$$

So using either the optimal consumption rule or the relative price rule, we find the same optimal consumption bundle.

Figure D.7 Understanding the Relative Price Rule

The *relative price* of rooms in terms of restaurant meals is equal to the negative of the slope of the budget line. The *marginal rate of substitution* of rooms for restaurant meals is equal to the negative of the slope of the indifference curve. The *relative price rule* says that at the optimal consumption bundle, the marginal rate of substitution must equal the relative price. This point can be demonstrated by considering what happens when the marginal rate of substitution is not equal to the relative price. At consumption bundle B, the marginal rate of substitution is larger than the relative price; Ingrid can increase her total utility by moving down her budget line, BL. At C, the marginal rate of substitution is smaller than the relative price, and Ingrid can increase her total utility by moving up the budget line. Only at A, where the relative price rule holds, is her total utility maximized, given her budget constraint.

Preferences and Choices

Now that we have seen how to represent the optimal consumption choice in an indifference curve diagram, we can turn briefly to the relationship between consumer preferences and consumer choices.

When we say that two consumers have different preferences, we mean that they have different utility functions. This in turn means that they will have indifference curve maps with different shapes. And those different maps will translate into different consumption choices, even among consumers with the same income and who face the same prices.

To see this, suppose that Ingrid's friend Lars also consumes only housing and restaurant meals. However, Lars has a stronger preference for restaurant meals and a weaker preference for housing. This difference in preferences is shown in **Figure D.8**, which shows *two* sets of indifference curves: panel (a) shows Ingrid's preferences and panel (b) shows Lars's preferences. Note the difference in their shapes.

Suppose, as before, that rooms cost $150 per month and restaurant meals cost $30. Let's also assume that both Ingrid and Lars have incomes of $2,400 per month, giving them identical budget lines. Nonetheless, because they have different preferences, they will make different consumption choices, as shown in Figure D.8. Ingrid will choose 8 rooms and 40 restaurant meals, whereas Lars will choose 4 rooms and 60 restaurant meals.

Figure D.8 Differences in Preferences

(a) Ingrid's Preferences and Her Optimal Consumption Bundle

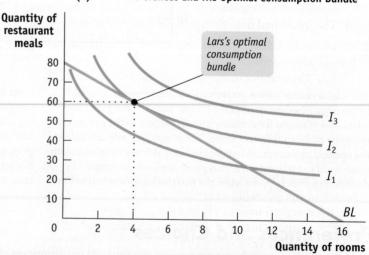

(b) Lars's Preferences and His Optimal Consumption Bundle

Ingrid and Lars have different preferences, reflected in the different shapes of their indifference curve maps. So they will choose different consumption bundles even when they have the same options. Each has an income of $2,400 per month and faces prices of $30 per meal and $150 per room. Panel (a) shows Ingrid's consumption choice: 8 rooms and 40 restaurant meals. Panel (b) shows Lars's choice: even though he has the same budget line, he consumes fewer rooms (4) and more restaurant meals (60).

ENRICHMENT MODULE D REVIEW

Check Your Understanding

1. The accompanying table shows Samantha's preferences for consumption bundles composed of chocolate kisses and licorice drops.

Consumption bundle	Quantity of chocolate kisses	Quantity of licorice drops	Total utility (utils)
A	1	3	6
B	2	3	10
C	3	1	6
D	2	1	4

a. With chocolate kisses on the horizontal axis and licorice drops on the vertical axis, draw hypothetical indifference curves for Samantha and locate the bundles on the curves. Assume that both items are ordinary goods.

b. Suppose you don't know the number of utils provided by each bundle. Assuming that more is better, predict Samantha's ranking of each of the four bundles to the extent possible. Explain your answer.

2. On panel A1 of Figure D.4, draw a point B anywhere on the 200-util indifference curve and a point C anywhere on the 100-util indifference curve (but *not* at the same location as point A). By comparing the utils generated by bundles A and B and those generated by bundles A and C, explain why indifference curves cannot cross.

3. Lucinda and Kyle each consume 3 comic books and 6 video games. Lucinda's marginal rate of substitution of books for games is 2 and Kyle's is 5.

a. For each person, find another consumption bundle that yields the same total utility as the current bundle. Who is less willing to trade games for books? In a diagram with books on the horizontal axis and games on the vertical axis, how would this be reflected in differences in the slopes of their indifference curves at their current consumption bundles?

b. Find the relative price of books in terms of games at which Lucinda's current bundle is optimal. Is Kyle's bundle optimal given this relative price? If not, how should Kyle rearrange his consumption?

Multiple-Choice Review Questions

1. Which of the following is true along an individual's indifference curve for ordinary goods?
   a. The slope is constant.
   b. Total utility changes.
   c. The individual is indifferent between any two points.
   d. The slope is equal to the ratio of the prices of the consumption bundles.
   e. The individual doesn't care if utility is maximized.

2. Which of the following is/are true of indifference curves for ordinary goods?
   I. They cannot intersect.
   II. They have a negative slope.
   III. They are convex.
   a. I only
   b. II only
   c. III only
   d. I and II only
   e. I, II, and III

3. Moving from left to right along an indifference curve, which of the following increases?
   a. the marginal utility of the vertical axis good
   b. the marginal utility of the horizontal axis good
   c. the absolute value of the slope
   d. the marginal rate of substitution
   e. the demand for the vertical axis good

4. If the quantity of good X is measured on the horizontal axis and the quantity of good Y is measured on the vertical axis, the marginal rate of substitution is equal to
   a. $\dfrac{\Delta Q_X}{Q_Y}$.
   b. $\dfrac{MU_X}{MU_Y}$.
   c. $\dfrac{P_X}{P_Y}$.
   d. the ratio of the slope of the budget line and the slope of the indifference curve.
   e. 1, at the optimal level of consumption.

5. If the quantity of good X is again measured on the horizontal axis and the quantity of good Y is measured on the vertical axis, which of the following is true? The optimal consumption bundle is found where
   a. $\dfrac{MU_X}{MU_Y} = \dfrac{P_X}{P_Y}$.
   b. the slope of the indifference curve equals the slope of the budget line.
   c. the indifference curve is tangent to the budget line.
   d. $\dfrac{MU_X}{P_X} = \dfrac{MU_Y}{P_Y}$.
   e. all of the above are true.

Free-Response Review Questions

1. Each of the combinations of song and movie downloads shown in the table below give Kathleen an equal level of utility.

Quantity of songs	Quantity of movies
0	8
1	6
2	4
3	2
4	0

   a. Graph Kathleen's indifference curve.
   b. Economists believe that each individual indifference curve for ordinary goods exhibits what two properties?
   c. Does Kathleen's indifference curve exhibit the two properties from part b? Explain.

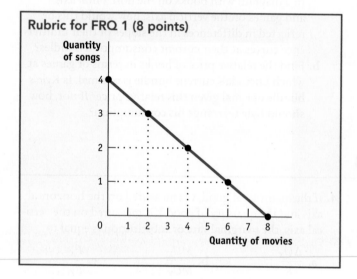
2. Kathleen has $20 to spend on song and movie downloads each week. The price of a song download is $2 and the price of a movie download is $5.
   a. Graph Kathleen's budget line.
   b. Suppose all of Kathleen's indifference curves have the same shape and slope as the one in Question 1. How many song and movie downloads will Kathleen purchase to maximize her utility? Explain. **(4 points)**

Discussion Starters

1. What would it indicate about your preferences for two goods if your indifference curves were vertical? Can you think of examples of pairs of goods for which this is the case?

2. Suppose that on a Saturday afternoon you must divide your time between studying and playing sports, and both activities are free. Could you use a budget constraint and indifference curves to model this decision?

3. Consider the dilemma of how much money to spend now and how much to set aside for the future. Is this another trade-off that could be modeled with a budget constraint and indifference curves? What makes it possible to spend more now than you actually have? If you spend less than you have now, what can you do with your money so that the amount you have to spend in the future grows? What rate associated with these opportunities affects the slope of the budget constraint?

Financial Literacy Handbook

By Laura Adams ("The Money Girl")

Part 1 Take It to the Bank

Part 2 Get Interested in Money Math

Part 3 Learn to Earn

Part 4 Save and Invest Money

Part 5 Give Yourself Some Credit

Part 6 Borrow Without Sorrow

Part 7 Manage Your Money

Part 8 Protect Yourself from Risk

Take It to the Bank

Part 1

A bank account is a safe and convenient place to accumulate savings and to keep the money you need to pay bills and to make everyday cash purchases. Keeping a large amount of cash at home or in your wallet isn't as safe because your money could be lost or stolen.

Overview of Banks

Banks can be small community institutions that have just one or a few locations, or they can be huge companies with thousands of branch locations all over the country. There are internet-only banks with no physical location to visit and only a website address. In addition to holding your money, banks also offer a variety of services to help you manage your money.

Banks stay in business by using the money you deposit to make a profit by offering loans to other customers or businesses. They lend to customers who want to borrow money for big purchases like cars or homes. They also lend to small and large businesses for making purchases like inventory and equipment.

When you take a loan from a bank, you're charged interest, which is an additional charge on top of the amount you borrow. To stay profitable, a bank must receive more money in interest from borrowers than it pays out in the form of loans to customers.

Despite the benefits banking institutions offer, about one-quarter of Americans are "unbanked" or "underbanked" and use no or few basic financial services. According to the Federal Deposit Insurance Corporation (FDIC), these individuals typically have low income. FDIC data shows that for households with annual income of less than $15,000 per year, 25.6% have no bank account at all.

Individuals may not use banks for a variety of reasons, including the lack of a conveniently located branch office or the desire to avoid bank fees. However, some potential customers do not take advantage of the services banks offer because they don't understand how banks work or how much nonbank alternatives cost. In this section you'll learn why going without banking services is both expensive and inconvenient.

FINANCE TIP

You can use the Electronic Deposit Insurance Estimator (EDIE) at fdic.gov/deposit to make sure your deposits in various bank accounts are fully covered by the FDIC.

Types of Financial Institutions

When you're ready to open a bank account, there are three main types of institutions to choose from: savings and loan associations, commercial banks, and credit unions.

Savings and Loan Associations and Commercial Banks

Savings and loan associations (S&Ls) and commercial banks operate under federal and state regulations. They specialize in taking deposits for checking and savings accounts, making home loans (known as mortgages) and other personal and business loans, facilitating the flow of money into and out of accounts, and providing various financial services for individuals and businesses.

Have you ever wondered what would happen to your money if your bank went out of business or failed? Most banks insure your deposits through the FDIC up to the maximum amount allowed by law, which is currently $250,000 per depositor per account type for each insured bank.

FDIC insurance means that if your bank permanently closes for any reason, you won't lose your money. You'll know a bank is properly insured if it displays the FDIC logo at a local branch, on advertising materials, or online. To learn more, visit fdic.gov.

Credit Unions

Credit unions are nonprofit organizations owned by their customers, who are called members. Credit union members typically have something in common, like working for the same employer, working in the same profession, or living in the same geographic area. You must qualify to become a member of a credit union to be able to use its financial services.

Credit unions offer many of the same services as commercial banks and S&Ls. Most also offer insurance for your deposits through the National Credit Union Administration (NCUA), which gives the same coverage (up to $250,000 per depositor) as the FDIC. Just look for the official NCUA sign at credit union branches and websites. To learn more, visit ncua.gov.

Why Keep Money in a Bank?

While it's possible to keep your money at home and manage your personal finances using a cash-only system, here are five reasons why it's better to use an insured bank or credit union:

1. **Safety**: Money you deposit in a bank account is safe from loss, theft, or destruction. Even the best hiding places for money can be found by a thief or be susceptible to a flood or fire.

2. **Insurance**: Deposits covered by FDIC or NCUA insurance are protected by a fund backed by the full faith and credit of the U.S. government. So if your bank closes and can't return your money, the FDIC or NCUA will pay the insured portion of your deposits.

3. **Convenience**: Money in a bank account can be accessed in a variety of ways. You can make deposits by visiting a local branch or setting up electronic direct deposit. Some institutions have remote deposit services where you deposit a paper check by taking a picture of it with a mobile device or scanner and uploading it online. You can use online bill pay to send funds in the form of a paper check or electronic transfer.

4. **Low cost**: Different banks offer accounts with a variety of benefits, such as interest paid, debit cards, online banking, account alerts, bill pay, and overdraft protection. Many bank services are free to their customers, which makes using a bank to get cash or pay bills less expensive than alternatives, such as a check-cashing service. Some check cashers charge a fee that's a percentage of the check value, plus an additional flat fee. For instance, cashing a $1,000 check at a check-cashing service could cost 1.5%, or $15.

5. **Business relationship**: Building a relationship with a bank may give you the opportunity to qualify for premium banking services, loans, and credit cards that can improve your financial future.

> **FINANCE TIP**
> Did you know that funds deposited electronically into your bank account are available sooner than those deposited by a paper check?

Types of Bank Accounts

The two main types of bank accounts are deposit accounts and non-deposit accounts.

Deposit Accounts

Deposit accounts allow you to add money to or withdraw money from your account at any time. Examples of deposit accounts are checking, savings, and money market accounts.

Checking Account A checking account, also known as a payment account, is the most common type of bank account. It's a real workhorse that allows you to make purchases or pay bills using paper checks, a debit or check card, online bill pay, automatic transfer, or cash withdrawal from an automatic teller machine (ATM). The institution keeps a record of your deposits and withdrawals and sends you a monthly account statement. The best checking accounts offer no fees, no minimum balance requirement, free checks and debit cards, and online account access.

Savings Account A savings account is a safe place to keep money, and it earns you interest. It doesn't give you as much flexibility or access to your money as a checking account. While there's typically no limit on the number of deposits you can make into a savings account, Federal rules prohibit you from making more than six withdrawals or transfers per month. Savings accounts typically don't come with paper checks, but they may offer a debit or ATM card that you can use a maximum of three times per month.

If your balance dips below a certain amount, you may be charged a monthly fee. The institution keeps a record of your transactions and sends you a monthly account statement.

Savings accounts are perfect for your short-term savings goals, like a down payment on a car or holiday gift-giving. Interest rates on savings accounts vary, so it's important to shop around locally or online for the highest offers. Interest rates on savings accounts are variable, which means they're subject to change and can decrease after you open an account. (You'll learn more about compounded interest in Part 2 of this handbook.)

> **FINANCE TIP**
> *Rewards checking accounts* pay a relatively high rate of interest when you follow certain requirements, such as receiving e-statements, having at least one direct deposit per month, and using a debit card for a certain number of purchases each month.

> **FINANCE TIP**
> Use the power of the internet to shop for the best bank accounts. Sites like findabetterbank.com and bankrate.com gather up-to-date information about the best offers nationwide.

Money Market Account (MMA) A money market account has features of both a savings and a checking account. You can make up to six withdrawals or transfers per month, including payments by check, debit card, and online bill pay. You're paid relatively high interest rates, especially if you maintain a high minimum balance, such as $5,000 or more.

Money market accounts are a great choice when you start to accumulate more savings. Interest rates vary and are subject to change, so always do your research to find the best money market account offer.

There are also special types of deposit accounts known as *time deposits*, where you're restricted from withdrawing your money for a certain period of time.

Certificate of Deposit (CD) A certificate of deposit is a time deposit that requires you to give up the use of your money for a fixed term or period of time, such as 3 months, 12 months, or 5 years. In exchange for this restricted access, banks typically pay higher interest rates than for savings or money market accounts (where you can withdraw money on demand). In general, the longer the term of the CD, the higher the interest rate you receive.

For instance, a six-month CD might pay 1% interest and a five-year CD might pay 3%. If you take money out of a CD before the end of the term, or maturity date, you generally have to pay a penalty. So before putting money in a CD, be sure that you won't need it until after the maturity date and that you understand all the charges and fees associated with early withdrawals.

Non-deposit Accounts

Many banks offer non-deposit accounts that can be investments, such as stocks, bonds, or mutual funds. It's important to remember that non-deposit products are never insured by the FDIC or NCUA and may lose some or all of their value.

How Old Do You Have to Be to Open a Bank Account?

Many banks offer checking and savings accounts for young people. Some require you to open a joint account with a parent or guardian; however, some offer independent student accounts when you reach age 16.

The earlier you open up a bank account and start saving on a regular basis, the better. Having a checking and savings account established before you go to college will help you manage money and make necessary purchases. Money you earn from a job, get from a relative, or receive as a gift can be set aside for your future needs.

How to Maintain a Checking Account

It's important to maintain your checking account on a regular basis so you know exactly how much money you have at all times. You should reconcile each monthly statement's ending balance against your records so you never miss a transaction, such as an unexpected fee. Never write checks or make debit card purchases that exceed your balance.

Using ATM and Debit Cards

An ATM card allows you to use ATMs to make deposits, check your account balance, transfer funds between accounts, and make cash withdrawals 24 hours a day. You typically have to pay a fee for each ATM cash withdrawal at banks other than your own—unless your bank gives you free access to a network of ATMs or reimburses your ATM fees.

A debit card, also known as a check card, looks like a credit card because it typically has a MasterCard or VISA logo. A debit card can be used just like an ATM or credit card or to make purchases where accepted by merchants. When you use a debit card, money is deducted immediately from your bank account and credited to the merchant's account. This reduces your available balance.

If you make a debit card purchase for more than your available balance, your transaction will be declined. However, if you enroll in overdraft protection, you authorize your bank to cover your transaction—but typically at the cost of a large service fee.

Prepaid Cards A prepaid card may look like a debit or credit card, but it isn't linked to a bank or credit account. Prepaid cards may come loaded with a set value or may require you to add money to the card. The card value goes down each time you make a purchase. Prepaid cards have many fees—such as a purchase fee, monthly fees, ATM withdrawal fees, transaction fees, balance inquiry fees, and more—which generally makes them more expensive to use than a bank debit card.

Writing Checks

With the popularity of debit cards and online banking, people don't use paper checks as much anymore. However, if you need to write one, it's easy to fill in the blanks. Always write clearly using dark ink and never cross out a mistake—it's better to start over with a fresh check.

Reconciling Your Checking Account

Each month you'll receive a statement that shows activity in your account. The statement should include a reconciliation worksheet that you can follow. Reconciling or balancing your account is the process of making sure the information on the bank statement matches your records. Always keep track of your deposits, checks, debit card purchases, ATM withdrawals, and fees. You can use a paper or digital check register. Most financial software programs allow you to automatically download bank and credit card account transactions. Not having to enter each of your transactions manually saves time and makes account reconciliation simple.

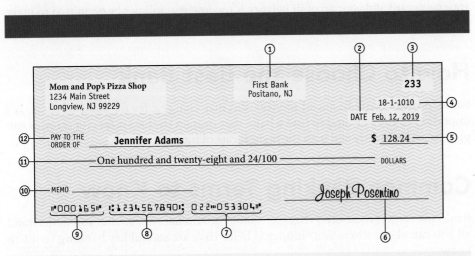

1. **Bank name**: This may be preprinted on each check.

2. **Date**: Enter the month, day, and year.

3. **Check number**: If your checks don't have preprinted numbers, label them with consecutive numbers.

4. **Bank ID numbers**: This may be preprinted on each check.

5. **Amount**: Enter the amount to pay in figures.

6. **Signature**: Sign your name exactly as you signed it on documents you completed when you opened the account.

7. **Check number**: This may be preprinted on each check.

8. **Account number**: This should be preprinted on each check.

9. **Bank routing number**: This should be preprinted on each check to identify your bank's unique routing number.

10. **Memo**: Write a quick note to remind yourself of the reason for the check.

11. **Amount**: Enter the amount to pay in words and draw a line over unused space so nothing can be added later.

12. **Payee**: Enter the person or company to pay.

Online and mobile banking isn't particularly risky, but it is important to be careful when making online transactions. Use these tips to avoid risk when you're making purchases or banking using a mobile device:

1. **Use a secured network** instead of public Wi-Fi so your personal information can't be exposed to criminals. The web address of a secured network begins with "https" instead of "http."

2. **Guard your mobile device** like you would your wallet, because it may contain information others can use to access your accounts if it were lost or stolen.

3. **Create strong passwords** for your devices (to turn them on or wake them from sleep mode) and for your online accounts. Most passwords are at least eight characters long and use a combination of letters, numbers, and symbols. Security experts also recommend that you change your important passwords frequently and never use the same password for more than one account.

4. **Don't lend your mobile devices** or share your passwords with anyone you don't know or trust.

5. **Log off** from financial accounts and close the browser window or app when you finish using them.

6. **Only download trusted apps** from sources like your bank or other legitimate financial institutions.

7. **Delete text messages** from your bank once you've read them.

8. **Don't divulge personal information** such as your social security number or account number. A financial institution or authorized agency will *never* ask you for personal information over the internet or even on the phone.

Overdraft Protection

Having overdraft protection means your debit card purchases and ATM withdrawals will be processed, even if your bank account balance isn't high enough to cover them. You must give written permission for overdraft protection because using it typically comes with expensive nonsufficient funds (NSF) fees. However, you can opt out of overdraft protection and avoid the potential charges. This means that if you try to use your debit card and your account balance is too low, you will not be permitted to make the purchase.

How to Choose the Best Bank

Banks provide many financial services and may charge a fee for some of them. It's important to shop around to find a bank that charges the lowest fees for services you plan to use frequently and pays the highest rate of interest.

Common Banking Terms to Know

Banks use certain vocabulary that you should be familiar with so that you understand all you can about where your money is held. Here are several key banking terms to know:

account statement—a paper or electronic record of account activity, service charges, and fees, issued by the bank on a regular basis

bounced or **bad check**—slang for a check that is rejected due to insufficient funds in the account

check—a paper form that authorizes a bank to release funds from the payer's account to the payee

cleared or **canceled checks**—paper checks that have been processed and paid by a bank

deposit slip or **ticket**—a printed form you complete that lists cash and checks to be deposited into an account

direct deposit—an electronic payment method typically used by an employer or government agency

electronic payment or **transaction**—a deposit or charge to an account that happens without the use of a paper form

endorsement—the payee's signature on the back of a paper check that is required to deposit or to take cash out of an account

payee—the person or company to whom a check is made payable

payer—the person or company who writes a check or pays another party

reconciliation—the process of comparing a bank account statement to your records and resolving any differences until you determine an identical account balance

service charge (or **maintenance charge**)—a fee charged by a bank to maintain your account

Part 1 Review Questions

1. How do banks make money?

2. Describe the similarities and differences between commercial banks and credit unions. Why do you think someone would choose one over the other?

3. In your own words, describe why it's better to keep your money in a financial institution instead of holding large amounts of cash.

4. Give several reasons why someone would open more than one type of bank account.

5. Come up with at least five questions you should ask before deciding to put your money in a financial institution.

Project

Research the savings and loan associations, commercial banks, and credit unions in your town. Choose one of each type of financial institution and speak to a manager or associate. What services do they provide their customers? How do they attract new customers? What measures to they take to secure their customers' financial information?

Get Interested in Money Math

Part 2

Whether you're shopping at the grocery store, choosing a car loan, or figuring out how much to invest for retirement, managing money comes down to the numbers. Making the best decisions for your personal finances always begins by doing some simple money math.

Pay Attention to Interest

When you borrow money by taking out a loan for college, a car, or any other expense, you'll be charged interest. Additionally, if you don't pay off a credit card balance in full by the statement due date, you'll also be charged interest on the balance owed. Lenders make money by charging interest to a borrower as a percentage of the amount of the loan or credit card balance due.

When you deposit money in a bank account that pays interest—for example, a savings account or CD—you become the lender and the bank is the borrower. The bank pays you interest for keeping money on deposit.

Interest is typically expressed as an annual percentage rate, or APR. To keep more of your money, it's wise to shop around and borrow at the lowest interest rates. Likewise, lend your money and deposit it in the bank that offers the highest possible interest rates, so you earn more.

How Simple and Compound Interest Work

But how does your money actually earn interest? There are two basic types of interest: simple interest and compound interest.

Simple Interest Simple interest is, well, pretty simple! That's because it's calculated on the original principal amount.

Say you borrow $100 from your friend John at a 5% annual rate of simple interest for a term of 3 years. Here's how the interest would be calculated for the loan:

Loan year	Principal amount (dollars)	APR (percent)	Annual interest earned (dollars) (Principle × APR)	Balance due (dollars)
1	$100	5%	$5	$105
2	100	5	5	110
3	100	5	5	115

Notice that the 5% APR is always calculated on the original principal amount of $100. At the end of the third year you have to pay $100 plus $15 in interest. In other words, your $100 loan cost a total of $115.

Compound Interest Compound interest is more complex because it's calculated on the original principal amount and also on the accumulated interest of a deposit or loan. Compound interest allows you to earn interest on a growing principal balance, which allows you to accumulate interest at a much faster rate.

Say you get the same loan of $100 for 3 years from your friend John, but this time he charges you 5% interest that compounds annually. Here's how the interest would be calculated:

Loan year	Principal amount (dollars)	APR (percent)	Annual interest earned (dollars) (Principle × APR)	Balance due (dollars)
1	$100	5%	$5	$105
2	105	5	5.25	110.25
3	110.25	5	5.51	115.76

Notice that the 5% APR is calculated on an increasing principal balance. At the end of the third year you'd owe the original amount of $100 plus interest of $15.76. Your $100 loan cost $115.76 with annual compounding interest. This table also shows you how much you'd earn if you deposited $100 in the bank and earned a 5% annual return that compounds annually.

Interest can be compounded according to variety of schedules, such as annually, semiannually, monthly, or daily. **Table 2.1** shows how much you'd pay if John charged you 5% compounded semiannually, or every 6 months.

Table 2.1	Semiannual Compound Interest Calculation			
Loan year	Principal amount (dollars)	Semiannual percentage rate (percent)	Annual interest earned (dollars)	Balance due (dollars)
1 (January)	$100	2.5%	$2.50	$102.50
1 (July)	102.50	2.5	2.56	105.06
2 (January)	105.06	2.5	2.63	107.69
2 (July)	107.69	2.5	2.69	110.38
3 (January)	110.38	2.5	2.76	113.14
3 (July)	113.14	2.5	2.83	115.97

At the end of the third year you'd owe the original loan amount of $100 plus $15.97 of interest—in other words, with semiannual compounding your $100 loan would cost $115.97. Likewise, this table shows how much you could earn from $100 in savings if compounded semiannually at a 5% annual rate of return.

Remember that the more frequent the compounding, the faster the interest grows. Annual percentage yield (APY) is the amount of interest you'll earn on an annual basis, including the effect of compounding. APY is expressed as a percentage and will be higher the more often your money compounds.

What Is the Rule of 72?

How long would it take you to double your money through savings and investments? It's easy to figure it out using a handy formula called the Rule of 72. If you divide 72 by the interest rate you earn, the answer is the number of years it will take for your initial savings amount to double in value.

For example, if you earn an average annual return of 1% on a bank savings account, dividing 1 into 72 tells you that your money will double in 72 years. But if you earn 6% on an investment, your money will take only 12 years to double (72 ÷ 6 = 12).

You can also estimate the interest rate you'd need to earn to double your money within a set number of years by dividing 72 by the number of years. For instance, if you put $500 in an account that you want to grow to $1,000 in 12 years, you'll need an interest rate of 6% (72 ÷ 12 = 6).

Understand Credit Cards

Using credit cards without fully understanding the relevant money math is a recipe for financial disaster. Credit cards start charging interest the day you make a purchase, take a cash advance, or transfer a balance from another account.

You're typically charged a daily rate that's equal to the APR divided by 365 (the 365 days in a year). Rates may be different for each transaction category and depending on your credit rating. For instance, your APR could be 11.99% for new purchases, 23.99% for cash advances, and 5% for balance transfers. Balances accumulate day after day until you pay them off in full.

You can make a monthly minimum payment and carry over the remaining balance from month to month. But that's not a wise way to manage credit cards because the interest starts racking up. Additionally, if you make a late payment, you're charged a late fee that gets added to your outstanding balance—and interest is calculated on that amount, too.

The bright spot in using a credit card wisely is that you're given a grace period for new purchases that allows you to avoid all interest charges—if you pay your balance in full by the billing statement due date. Note that there is generally no grace period for cash advances or balance transfers.

Credit cards are powerful financial tools that can enhance your life if you use them responsibly. But abusing them by making purchases that you can't afford to pay off in full each month can be devastating to your financial future. Your credit report history will also be harmed if you make late payments. You'll learn more about how to establish and maintain a good credit history in Part 5.

Calculate Credit Card Payoff

Question: If you buy a 4K TV for $2,000 using a credit card that charges 23.99% APR, how long would it take to pay off, if you only make minimum payments of 3% of your outstanding balance down to a minimum of $15 per month?

Answer: It would take over 16 years! So, if you're 17 years old right now, you'd celebrate your thirty-third birthday before you finally pay off the TV. Due to the high rate of credit card interest, the total cost of the TV would actually be $5,328. That's an increase of more than 266% on the TV's original purchase price. Only making minimum payments can easily double or triple the price of any item charged to a credit card, which is why it's so important to pay off credit card balances in full every month.

Amortization

Gradually paying off a debt's principal and interest in regular installments over time is called amortization. Loans that amortize, such as a car loan or home mortgages, have fixed interest rates and charge equal monthly payments, though each payment is made up of a slightly different amount of principal and interest.

Take a look at **Table 2.2** to see how each payment is split up for the first six months on a three-year $20,000 car loan with an interest rate of 7%.

Table 2.2	Amortization Schedule			
Payment month	Loan balance (dollars)	Monthly payment (dollars)	Interest portion of payment (dollars)	Principal portion of payment (dollars)
1	$20,000	$617.54	$116.67	$500.88
2	19,499.12	617.54	113.74	503.80
3	18,995.32	617.54	110.81	506.74
4	18,488.58	617.54	107.85	509.69
5	17,978.89	617.54	104.88	512.67
6	17,466.22	617.54	101.89	515.66

Notice that each month's beginning loan balance is reduced by the prior month's principal portion paid. The interest portion is slightly lower each month because it's calculated on an ever-decreasing principal balance.

How to Become a Millionaire

If you think that the only way to become a millionaire is to win the lottery, think again! Thanks to the power of compounding interest it's easy—if you get an early start. **Table 2.3** shows you how.

If you start saving and investing just $250 a month as soon as you get your first job, you could amass a million dollars by the time you're in your 60s. But if you wait until you're over 40 years old to get started and invest the same amount, you'd be close to 90 before becoming a millionaire!

Table 2.3	At What Age Could You Become a Millionaire?			
Age to begin saving	Amount to save each month (dollars)	Average APR (percent)	Years to become a millionaire	Age you're a millionaire!
18	$250	7%	46	64
20	250	7	46	66
25	250	7	45	70
30	250	7	45	75
40	250	7	45	86

Millionaire Case Study

Steve and Jessica are both 25 years old and work for the same company. They have the same financial goal: to retire at age 65 with one million dollars in savings. Steve starts contributing to his company's retirement plan right away, but Jessica waits 10 years, until she's 35 years old, to begin investing. Here's what happens: Steve can reach his million-dollar goal by contributing $400 a month and earning an average 7% annual return. But since Jessica gets a late start, she has to contribute much more than Steve. Jessica must contribute $850 a month with the same 7% rate of return to reach her million-dollar goal, as shown in **Figure 1**.

Figure 1 Saving To Be a Millionaire

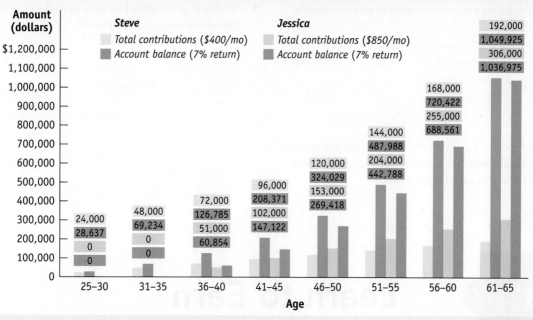

Steve
- Total contributions ($400/mo)
- Account balance (7% return)

Jessica
- Total contributions ($850/mo)
- Account balance (7% return)

You'll notice that Steve only had to invest $192,000 over a 40-year period to amass over one million dollars. However,

Jessica had to invest $306,000, or 60% more than Steve, over a 30-year period to accumulate approximately the same amount.

The Power of Saving Early Case Study

Ava and Jay are both 25 years old, but they begin saving for retirement at different times. Ava begins saving $200 per month right away, but Jay decides to buy a new car instead. Jay ends up delaying his retirement savings for 10 years. After his 35th birthday, he finally gets started and saves $300 per month. They both earn an average annual return of 8%.

Here's what happens: When Jay reaches age 65, he has almost $450,000. But Ava has amassed close to $700,000. The benefit of choosing to invest earlier, rather than later, really pays off for Ava because she has $250,000 more than Jay to spend during retirement, as demonstrated in **Figure 2**.

Figure 2 Saving for Retirement

If you start saving now, you can potentially save $250,000 more than if you wait!

Amount saved for retirement by age 65: $698,201

Amount saved for retirement by age 65: $447,107

Start contributing $200/month at age 25: $96,000 invested

Start contributing $300/month at age 35: $108,000 invested

The sooner you start saving and investing, the more you will benefit from the power of compounding interest!

Part 2 Review Questions

1. What is the difference between simple and compound interest?

2. Using the Rule of 72, how long will it take you to double your savings if you have $3,200 in an account making 4% interest?

3. Why is it generally a bad idea to make only minimum payments on your credit card?

Project

Imagine you deposit $125 in a savings account each month. It pays 3% annually, which is compounded monthly. How much interest will you earn for the year?

Part 3

Learn to Earn

How can you earn enough money to cover your expenses and save for the future? It starts by having the education and skills to get a good job or to start your own business. Every work experience builds your level of knowledge, boosts your resume, helps you know what work you like best, and makes you more attractive to potential employers.

What Is a Resume?

A resume is a summary of your education, skills, and work experience—that you submit to a potential employer in person or online—that highlights many of your outstanding traits and experiences. It should be a one-page document that is succinct and well written.

Employers typically conduct a background check to verify data in your resume, so never include false information. Lying on a resume or job application can disqualify you for a job or cause an employer to fire you later on.

At the top of a resume, list your name, address, phone number, and e-mail address. The body should include sections titled "Objective," "Experience," "Skills," "Education," and "Honors or Awards." Tailor each resume to the particular job you apply for so the employer knows you have the skills to be successful.

If you have trouble creating a resume, ask for help from family, friends, or a professional resume writer, who can help you articulate the skills and experiences you have to offer a potential employer. You can also use free online resources such as careeronestop. org and myfuture.com.

What Is a Job Application?

In addition to your resume, many potential employers require you to complete a job or employment application. The application can be customized by the employer, but it typically asks for personal information, references, and specifics about the job you're applying for. Submitting an impressive resume and application will make you stand out from other applicants.

There are certain questions that an employer is not allowed to ask applicants under federal and some state and local laws. These may include topics such as your age, race, religion, citizenship status, and whether you are disabled, pregnant, or married. You can learn more about employment laws at the U.S. Department of Labor website at www.dol.gov.

Types of Income

The money you make falls into one of two basic categories: earned income and passive income.

Earned Income

Earned income is the income you receive by working for a company or someone who pays you, or from a business that you own and run. Earned income includes your hourly wages, salaries, tips, commissions, and bonuses. This is the most common way to make money. Of course, if you stop working, you stop earning. However, if you save and invest your earned income wisely, you can turn it into passive income.

Passive Income

Passive income is generated from assets you buy or create, such as financial investments, rental real estate, or something you have created, such as a book or a song. If you buy a house and rent it for more than your mortgage and other expenses, the profit is passive income. If you write and publish a book or a song that pays royalties, that is intellectual property that pays passive income. The benefit of passive income is that you get paid with little or no additional work on your part. That makes it possible to retire and still receive money to pay your everyday living expenses.

Although you must have income to meet your financial needs, an income doesn't give you lasting wealth unless you save or invest some amount of it on a regular basis. Even those with high incomes can live paycheck to paycheck and end up with no true wealth. Likewise, those with modest incomes can save small amounts of money over a long period of time and accumulate a nest egg for a healthy financial future.

Getting a Paycheck

It might surprise you to know that if you get a job earning $600 a week, you don't actually receive $600 a week. Although your gross income or pay will be $600, you'll have payroll taxes deducted from each paycheck before you receive it, which include federal, state, Medicare, and Social Security taxes. You may also have voluntary deductions for workplace benefits such as health insurance, life insurance, and contributions to a retirement account. The remaining amount that you'll have to spend after taxes and deductions is called your net income or net pay.

When you take a new job, one of the forms you must complete is the W-4. It tells your employer how much tax should be taken out, or withheld, from each of your paychecks. If too little tax is withheld during the year, you'll owe money to the government's Internal Revenue Service (IRS) on tax day (which is usually April 15 unless that date falls on a weekend or holiday). If too much tax is withheld, the IRS will pay a refund, but you will lose the use of your money until the refund payment arrives. So it is good to have your payroll withholding match the actual amount of tax you'll owe.

Significant events—such as marriage, divorce, the birth or adoption of a child, buying a home, or taking an additional job—will affect how much tax you owe. Additionally, earning income from savings accounts or investments affects the tax you owe. Any time your personal situation changes, you can file a new W-4 with your employer

FINANCE TIP

Employers are required to pay 50% of FICA on behalf of their employees. If you become your own boss, you must pay self-employment tax, which includes 100% of the Social Security and Medicare tax owed.

to make sure the right amount of tax is withheld so you don't have any surprises on tax day. You can learn more by visiting the IRS website at irs.gov and searching for Publication 505, Tax Withholding and Estimated Tax.

How Payroll Withholding Works

Employers are required to withhold four different types of tax from your paycheck:

1. **Federal income tax** is paid to the IRS for expenses such as salaries of elected officials, the military, welfare assistance programs, public education, and interest on the national debt.

2. **State income tax** is generally paid to your state's revenue department for expenses such as salaries of state employees and maintenance of state highways and parks. Depending on where you live, there may also be payroll deductions for county and city tax.

3. **Social Security tax** provides income for eligible taxpayers who are retired or disabled, or who survive a relative who was receiving benefits. The program's official name is OASDI, which stands for Old-Age, Survivors, and Disability Insurance.

4. **Medicare tax** provides hospital insurance benefits to eligible individuals who are over the age of 65 or have certain medical conditions. Social Security and Medicare taxes are collectively called the Federal Insurance Contributions Act (FICA) tax.

Filing an Income Tax Return

By April 15th of each year you must complete and file, by mail or electronically, a federal tax return to the IRS for income from the prior year. Most states also require a state tax return at the same time. Whether you must file a tax return depends on your income, tax filing status, age, and whether or not you are a dependent. The filing requirements apply even if you don't owe any tax.

If you don't file taxes on time, you'll be charged a late payment penalty, plus interest on any amount owed. Willfully failing to file a return is a serious matter because it's against the law and may result in criminal prosecution.

If you are an unmarried dependent student, you must file a tax return if your earned or unearned income exceeds certain limits. You may also owe tax on certain scholarships and fellowships for education. Tax rules are subject to change each year, so be sure to visit irs.gov and review IRS Publication 501, Exemptions, Standard Deduction, and Filing Information, for income limits and up-to-date information.

In January and February of each year, you'll receive official forms from institutions that paid you, such as your employer, bank, or investment brokerage or firm. These forms provide the data you need to complete your taxes. Even if you don't receive these official tax documents, you must still declare all your income on a tax return. So be sure to request any missing information.

The IRS does not require a tax filing for individuals who earn under a certain minimum income threshold. However, you should file a tax return each year in case you are owed a refund—for instance, if you had income tax withheld from your pay or you qualify for refundable tax benefits.

In addition to individuals and families, the IRS (and certain states) also taxes corporations, trusts, and estates.

How Much Income Tax Do You Pay?

The United States has a marginal or progressive tax system, which means that people with more earned income pay tax at a higher rate or percentage. A tax bracket is a range of income that's taxed at a certain rate. Currently, there are seven federal tax brackets that range from 10% up to 37%. So, someone with very little income may pay 10% while someone with high income could pay as much as 37% on their highest range of income for just federal income tax.

Every year the IRS adjusts many tax provisions as the cost of living goes up or down. It uses the Consumer Price Index (CPI) to calculate the prior year's inflation rate and adjusts income limits for tax brackets, tax deduction amounts, and tax credit values accordingly. All of these variables affect the net amount of tax you must pay.

Here's a table showing the federal income tax brackets and rates for 2018 for some different types of taxpayers:

2018 Federal Income Tax Brackets and Rates

Tax rate	Single filers	Married joint filers	Head of household filers
10%	$0–$9,525	$0–$19,050	$0–$13,600
12%	$9,526–$38,700	$19,051–$77,400	$13,601–$51,800
22%	$38,701–$82,500	$77,401–$165,000	$51,801–$82,500
24%	$82,501–$157,500	$165,001–$315,000	$82,501–$157,500
32%	$157,501–$200,000	$315,001–$400,000	$157,501–$200,000
35%	$200,001–$500,000	$400,001–$600,000	$200,001–$500,000
37%	$500,001 +	$600,001 +	$500,001 +

You'll notice that if you're single and earn $40,000, you're in the 22% tax *bracket* for 2018. However, the following table shows that your effective or net federal tax rate would be only 11.9%:

Net Federal Tax Rate for Single Filer Earning $40,000

Income tax bracket	Income taxed	Federal tax rate	Federal tax due
$0–$9,525	$9,525	10%	$953
$9,526–$38,700	$29,175	12%	$3,501
$38,701–$40,000	$1,300	22%	$286
Totals	$40,000		$4,740

As you can see, the effective tax rate = $4,740 ÷ $40,000 = 11.9%.

Although earning $40,000 means you're in the 22% tax bracket, your entire income is not taxed at this rate. A portion is taxed at 10%, another at 12%, and another at 22%, which generally makes your effective or net tax rate lower than your tax bracket rate.

There are four ways to file your federal and state tax returns:

1. *Free File* is tax preparation software provided free of charge at irs.gov for individuals with income below a certain amount. You're guided through a series of questions to calculate your tax liability, and your federal and state returns are filed electronically.

2. *Fillable forms* are free online tax forms at irs.gov that you can complete and file electronically without the help of software, regardless of your income. State tax forms are not included.

3. *Tax software* can be purchased to help you prepare your federal and state returns and file them electronically.

4. *Tax preparers* are tax professionals who prepare your federal and state returns and file them electronically. Visit irs.gov for a list of authorized e-file providers or ask people you know to recommend a reputable tax accountant.

Not Every State Collects Income Tax In addition to federal taxes, you may have to pay state tax on your income. Each state has its own tax system. The following nine states don't collect any tax from income that residents earn: Alaska, Florida, Nevada, New Hampshire, South Dakota, Tennessee, Texas, Washington, and Wyoming.

FINANCE TIP

Use an online calculator at taxfoundation.org or taxact.com to find out how much federal tax you really pay (your effective tax rate) based on your income and tax filing status.

Part 3 Review Questions

1. List several reasons that people work. What are some reasons people change jobs throughout their lifetime?

2. What are some "marketable skills" you possess? Think about skills you've developed and used in past jobs, volunteer opportunities, and even in school.

3. What are four different kinds of taxes withheld from your paycheck? What is the money ultimately used for?

4. Briefly describe how tax brackets work in the U.S. tax system.

Project

Research how the United States government spent last year's tax dollars. What percentages went to discretionary spending, mandatory spending, and interest on federal debt? What do discretionary and mandatory spending pay for?

Part 4

Save and Invest Money

Going to college. Buying a car. Starting a business. Retiring from work. Any financial goal or dream that you have can become a reality if you get in the habit of consistently setting aside small amounts of money over time. Starting this routine at a young age will really pay off and allow you to control your financial future.

Though we tend to use the terms *saving* and *investing* interchangeably, they're not the same. The difference has to do with financial risk. Investors walk a line between wanting to make money and not wanting to lose money. Saving money in a bank keeps it completely safe but pays a lower rate of return than some other investments. Investments that pay higher rates of return come with higher risk—the chance you could lose some or all of your money.

It's important to understand that, most often, high-return investments come with higher risk. And low-return investments or savings usually come with low risk.

Types of Savings Accounts

You will probably earn only a small amount of interest on savings. But the purpose of having savings is to keep your funds completely safe and accessible. Money you need to spend in the short term for planned purchases and emergencies should be kept in a federally insured savings account, so you can't lose it.

There are three basic types of savings accounts you can open at most banks and credit unions: a savings account, a money market account, and a certificate of deposit. Review Part 1 of this handbook for an explanation of these accounts and the protection offered by the Federal Deposit Insurance Corporation, or FDIC.

Investing Basics

Looking at the period from 1928 to 2017, we see that investing money in the stock market has historically rewarded investors with average returns nearing 10%. Even from 2004 to 2013—the decade that includes the most recent economic recession—investors earned approximately 9% on average.

So why would you put money in a bank savings account that might earn 0.1% to 1% instead? Because investing money always involves some amount of risk—the potential to lose money as well as the potential to make money.

Financial analysts make forecasts based on what happened in the past. But they include the disclaimer "Past performance does not guarantee future results." In other words, even the smartest analyst can't predict how much an investment will be worth in the future. Therefore, it's very important to invest with wisdom and caution.

The purpose of investing money is to increase your wealth over a long time period so you can achieve goals like paying for retirement or purchasing a home. Whether you should save or invest depends on your time horizon, which is the amount of time between now and when you'll actually need to spend the money. If you have a long time horizon—such as 10 years or more—investing makes sense. When you have a short time horizon—such as a year or less—many financial advisors recommend that you stick with an insured savings account.

What Is the Securities Investor Protection Corporation (SIPC)?

Investments, or securities, are not guaranteed by any federal agency such as the FDIC. There is no insurance against losing money in an investment. However, the Securities Investor Protection Corporation (SIPC) is a nongovernment entity that gives you limited protection in certain situations. They step in when an investment brokerage firm fails or when fraud is the cause of investor loss. The SIPC replaces missing securities up to $500,000 per customer. You can learn more at sipc.org.

Types of Investments

The earlier you start investing, the more money you'll have to pay for your financial dreams and goals. There are four basic types of financial securities and products that you can purchase for your investment portfolio. They are stocks, bonds, mutual funds, and exchange-traded funds.

Stocks

Stocks are issued by companies—such as Apple, Starbucks, and Disney—that want to raise money. When you buy shares of a stock, you purchase an ownership interest in a company and your shares can go up or down in value over time. Stocks are bought and sold on exchanges, such as the New York Stock Exchange or the NASDAQ, and you can monitor their prices in real time online.

Stocks are one of the riskiest investments because the price per share can be volatile, swinging up or down in a short period of time. People can't be sure about which stocks will increase in value over the short or long term. However, historically, stocks have rewarded investors with higher returns than other major investment classes, such as cash or bonds.

Bonds

Bonds are loans you give to a corporation or government entity, known as the issuer, who wants to raise money for a specific project. Projects paid for by a bond include things such as building a factory or a school. Bonds pay a fixed interest rate over a set period of time. The time can range from weeks to 30 years. In general, interest is higher for longer-term bond terms and for bonds issued by companies with better credit.

Bonds are also called fixed-income investments because the return is guaranteed. In return for a higher degree of safety than stocks, you receive a relatively low rate of return. (Remember that lower risk investments give you a lower return and higher risk investments typically offer higher returns.) But these conservative investments still have some risk. For example, a bond issuer can default on repayment. Agencies such as Standard and Poor's (standardandpoors.com) do research and offer a rating system of bond safety.

Mutual Funds

Mutual funds are products that bundle combinations of investments, such as stocks, bonds, and other securities. They're operated by professional money managers who invest the fund's money according to stated objectives, such as achieving maximum growth or earning fixed income. Mutual fund shares are purchased directly from the fund company or from investment brokers and can go up or down in value over time.

In general, mutual funds composed of stock have the greatest potential risk and reward; however, there's a wide range of risk within this category. Mutual funds composed of bonds also have a range of risk but are considered more conservative than stock funds.

Exchange-Traded Funds (ETFs)

Exchange-traded funds are products that bundle combinations of investments—just like mutual funds—but trade like a stock on an exchange throughout the day. These securities are growing in popularity due to their flexibility and low cost. The cost to operate an ETF is very low compared to many mutual funds.

Other Types of Investments

Other types of investments include real estate, precious metals (such as gold and silver), and businesses, just to name a few. They generally require more expertise and skill to buy and sell than the four types of securities covered here. The drawback to these alternative investments is that they aren't as liquid, or sold as easily, as the mainstream investments described above.

FINANCE TIP

You can reduce risk by diversification, which means owning a variety of investments in your portfolio.

What Is Financial Risk?

To be a successful investor, you need to understand the financial risks of different types of investments and gauge your own tolerance for risk. Many brokerage firms offer a questionnaire that can help you determine this.

What seems safe to one person may be deemed very risky by another. Your tolerance for risk is reflected in how you react when your investments decline in value. Someone who doesn't like risk is considered risk averse. A risk-averse person is willing to miss out on higher rates of return in exchange for financial safety. A more risk-tolerant person is willing to accept investment losses in exchange for potential higher returns.

There is no right or wrong risk style that you should adopt. It just comes down to your personal feelings and preferences for how you want to manage your investments.

Ways to Invest

You have many choices when it comes to investing your money. The two most common are brokerage accounts and retirement accounts.

Brokerage Accounts

Brokerage accounts are available at local and online brokerage firms that are licensed to place investment orders, such as buying or selling shares of a stock, a mutual fund, or an ETF. You own the assets in a brokerage account and must pay tax each year on the earnings, which are called capital gains.

Retirement Accounts

Retirement accounts are special accounts you can open at a variety of institutions, such as local or online banks and brokerage firms, that allow you to save for retirement. One of the advantages is that they allow you to pay less tax.

There are different kinds of retirement accounts available for individuals, as part of an employee benefit package at work, and for the self-employed. Investment options include many of the instruments already mentioned, such as stocks, bonds, mutual funds, ETFs, or even bank CDs.

When you invest through a retirement account—as opposed to a regular brokerage account—you defer, or avoid paying, tax on your earnings. That means you save money on taxes and have more money for retirement! However, if you withdraw funds from a retirement account that weren't previously taxed, you are typically subject to an early withdrawal penalty, in addition to ordinary income tax.

The most commonly used retirement accounts include individual retirement arrangements, the 401(k) plan, and the 403(b) plan. In order to have enough money to live comfortably for decades during retirement, it's important to get in the habit of saving money in a retirement account.

Individual Retirement Arrangement (IRA) The IRA is a personal account available to anyone, regardless of age, who has taxable income. You can begin making contributions to an IRA as soon as you get your first job. However, you're in charge of it, not your employer. With a traditional IRA you generally don't pay tax on contributions or earnings until after you retire and start taking withdrawals. In other words, taxes on the account are deferred until sometime in the future. With a Roth IRA, you pay tax on your contributions up front. However, you never pay tax on them again or on any amount of earnings. You get a huge tax benefit with a Roth because your entire account grows completely tax free.

401(k) Plan The 401(k) plan is a retirement account offered by many companies. You authorize a portion of your wages to be contributed to the plan before income tax is withheld from your paycheck. A 401(k) plan offers participants a set menu of investment choices. You can contribute amounts up to certain allowable limits each year. Many employers also offer a Roth 401(k) option that allows you to make after-tax contributions.

403(b) Plan The 403(b) plan is a retirement account offered by certain organizations such as schools, churches, and hospitals. It's similar to a 401(k) in most aspects and also limits contributions each year. This plan may also include a Roth option.

Retirement Accounts for Employees

There are two main types of retirement programs found in the workplace: defined benefit plans and defined contribution plans.

- A **defined benefit plan** is funded and managed by an employer and is commonly known as a pension. Employees don't pay into the plan, pick investments, or manage the money in any way. Defined benefit plans give retired workers a specific, defined benefit, such as $800 per month for the rest of their life. The benefit paid depends on various factors, such as age, length of employment, and salary history. These plans have become rare in the workplace because they're expensive to operate. However, some large companies, government agencies, and labor unions offer them.

- A **defined contribution plan** is established by an employer but requires that the employee manage it. This type of plan includes the 401(k) and 403(b) plans. The retirement benefit that an employee will receive depends on the amount that's invested and the performance of the chosen investments over the years. Defined contribution plans are more common because they're less risky for an employer to administer.

What Is Employer Matching?

If you could earn a guaranteed 100% return on your money, would you be interested? Many employers match a certain amount of the money you put in a workplace retirement plan. Say your employer matches 100% of your contributions to a 401(k) up to 3% of your salary. If you earn $30,000 a year and contribute $75 a month or $900 a year, that's a contribution of 3% of your salary. With matching, your employer would also contribute $900. So you'd invest $900 and automatically get $900 from your company—an immediate 100% return on your money!

How Much Will Social Security Pay in Retirement?

As a young person, it's not possible to know exactly how much you'll receive in Social Security retirement benefits. These benefits are calculated based on various factors, such as the current law, your future earnings, how long you pay payroll or self-employment taxes, the age you elect to start receiving benefits, and your military service.

However, according to the Social Security Administration, the benefit replaces only about 40% of your preretirement earnings, if you have average income. As of 2017, the average monthly benefit for a retired worker was $1,360. The maximum monthly benefit was $2,788; however, higher benefits may be possible if you choose to delay benefits until after you reach full retirement age.

Therefore, it's important not to count on Social Security retirement benefits as your sole source of income during retirement. The program was created as a supplement for personal savings, not as a substitute for having a retirement plan.

Investing for Education

Just as there are special accounts that allow you to invest for retirement and pay less tax, there are two education savings accounts, or ESAs, to be familiar with: 529 plans and Coverdells.

- A **529 plan** is a savings or investment vehicle that allows you to contribute money to pay for qualified expenses at a college, university, or vocational school. Starting in 2018, individuals can also spend up to $10,000 per year for eligible K–12 tuition. There are prepaid plans, where you prepay all or a portion of the future cost, and investment plans, where you choose specific investments. Contributions and earnings in a 529 plan grow tax free.

- A **Coverdell account** allows you to contribute money to pay for any level of education, from kindergarten through graduate school. It differs from a 529 plan in that it has more restrictions, such as how much can be contributed each year and the age of the student who will use the funds.

You can learn more about 529s and Coverdells at savingforcollege.com and finaid.org.

Part 4 Review Questions

1. What is the difference between *saving* and *investing*?
2. Briefly describe each of the four kinds of mainstream investments described in this Part.
3. Briefly describe the different kinds of retirement accounts. Why is it a good idea to invest in retirement accounts as soon as you start working?

Project

What does it mean to "diversify" your savings plan? Research different kinds of savings and investments and come up with a plan that provides a good balance of both.

Give Yourself Some Credit

How is it possible to make a major purchase, like a home, if you don't have the cash? The answer is credit. If you're "creditworthy," you can be trusted to borrow money and pay it back over time.

What Is Credit?

Credit is the ability to borrow money that you promise to repay with interest. Credit is an important part of your financial life because it allows you to do the following:

- **Make a large purchase and pay for it over time**. If you don't have enough money saved up to buy a car, having credit allows you to get a loan and repay it over a set period of time.
- **Stay safe in an emergency situation**. If your car breaks down and you don't have enough to pay for the repair, having a credit card or line of credit allows you to get back on the road and repay the balance over time.
- **Avoid having to carry cash or paper checks**. When you're making a large purchase, like a computer or furniture, using a credit card is safer than carrying around a large amount of cash or paper checks that could be stolen.
- **Make online purchases and reservations**. When you need to buy something over the internet—such as books, clothes, or travel reservations—it's convenient to use a credit card.

If you don't have credit, the only way to get a loan or credit card is to have someone with good credit cosign an account. A cosigner might be a family member or friend who guarantees to take full responsibility for the debt if you don't repay it.

How do you become creditworthy, so that a potential creditor—such as a bank or credit card company—will allow you to borrow money? While each institution has different guidelines for evaluating a potential borrower, the following five criteria are generally used:

1. **Credit score**: How likely are you to make on-time payments based on your credit history? In this section you'll learn more about what a credit score is.
2. **Income**: Do you have a steady job and have enough income to repay a debt?
3. **Debt**: Do you have existing debts? If so, will you have enough money to pay your current debt and make payments on a new debt?
4. **Financial ratios**: How much debt do you have relative to your income?
5. **Collateral**: Will you secure a debt by pledging property (like a car or home) that a lender could sell if you don't make payments?

Understanding Credit Reports

Your credit history is maintained by three major nationwide credit reporting agencies: Equifax (equifax.com), Experian (experian.com), and TransUnion (transunion.com). These agencies receive information about you from your creditors and list it on your credit report. They are interested in things such as whether you make payments on time, your outstanding debt balances, and your available credit limits. Credit reporting agencies don't make credit decisions; they simply report information provided to them on your credit reports.

Each of your credit reports from the three agencies is slightly different, but they generally contain the following four types of information:

1. **Personal information** includes your name, current and previous addresses, Social Security number, birth date, and employer.

2. **Account information** lists your open accounts and your closed accounts for up to a certain period of time.

3. **Credit inquiries** include a list of companies and employers that have made inquiries about you because you applied for a credit account or job.

4. **Public information** is data that is available in the public records about you, including bankruptcies, foreclosures, liens for unpaid income taxes, and legal judgments.

The information in your credit report sticks with you for a long time. Credit accounts with negative information (for example, late payments) remain on your credit report for seven years from the date your payment became past due, even after you close the account or pay it off in full. Credit accounts with positive information remain on your credit report for 10 years after you close the account or pay it off in full.

Understanding Credit Scores

Just as your schoolwork determines your final grade in various classes, the information in your credit reports is used to calculate your credit scores. One of the most confusing things about credit scores is that there isn't just one. Your credit score depends on the particular scoring model that's used to calculate it. Companies can create their own scoring systems or use brand-name scores calculated by other firms, like the FICO (Fair Isaac Corporation) Score or the VantageScore.

Your credit score is different from the final grade you receive for a class because it isn't figured once and filed away. Your credit score is calculated fresh every time it is requested. Therefore, it's a snapshot of your credit behavior up to that moment in time.

Poor credit may indicate that you've mismanaged your finances by making late payments or maxing out credit accounts. However, having too little credit history can also be a reason for having a low credit score.

Having poor credit means you'll be viewed as a risky customer who may not repay a debt. You'll either be turned down for credit or charged an interest rate that's higher than the rate offered to a customer with good credit. Why? In exchange for taking a financial risk on a customer with poor credit, lenders protect themselves financially by charging higher interest rates, which means you have to make higher monthly payments.

How Much Can Poor Credit Cost You? Dora has excellent credit and goes to her bank to apply for a $15,000 car loan. After a few days the bank's lending representative calls her with good news—she's been approved! She can borrow $15,000 at 4% APR for a term of four years, which makes her monthly payment $338.69. The total amount of interest she'll pay on the loan principal is $1,256.92.

On the other hand, let's imagine Dora didn't have excellent credit and the bank charged her 12% APR instead of 4%. At this higher interest rate, her monthly payment would be $395.01. She'd pay a total of $3,960.36 in interest—or $2,703.44 more than if her credit was in good shape.

The larger a loan, the more poor credit costs you. **Table 5.1** below shows different scenarios for a home mortgage of $150,000 paid over 30 years. Not having excellent credit means you could pay an additional $127,493.41 in interest—on top of the original loan amount of $150,000.

Table 5.1	The Cost of Poor Credit			
Credit status	APR (percent)	Monthly payment (dollars)	Total interest paid (dollars)	Cost of having poor credit (dollars)
Excellent	3.75%	$694.67	$100,082.42	$0
Good	5.00	805.23	139,883.68	39,801.26
Average	7.50	1,048.82	227,575.83	127,493.41

Other Ways Having Poor Credit Hurts Your Finances Did you know that having poor credit scores can cost you even if you don't want a loan or credit card? Here are five ways that having poor credit affects your personal finances:

1. **Paying high insurance premiums**: In most U.S. states, insurance companies are allowed to factor in your credit when setting car and home insurance rates. Having poor credit means you'll be quoted rates that could be double or triple the amount that someone with excellent credit would pay. That's because consumers with poor credit have been found to file more insurance claims.

2. **Paying high security deposits**: You may be asked to pay higher deposits for an apartment and for utilities such as power, gas, water, and phone accounts.

3. **Getting declined as a tenant**: You could be turned down for an apartment or house to rent because property managers prefer tenants who demonstrate good payment history.

4. **Getting turned down for government benefits**: You might not qualify for certain types of federal or state benefits that require a good credit history.

5. **Getting denied a job**: You might be turned down for a job by an employer who requires a credit check. Employers can't get your credit scores or see your entire credit report, but they can find out if you've had credit problems.

> **FINANCE TIP**
>
> To find out your credit score, you can visit the credit bureau websites mentioned earlier and purchase the information from them. You may also buy your FICO Score at myfico.com, or get several scores for free at creditkarma.com.

How to Establish Credit

The information in your credit report has a ripple effect throughout your entire financial life. How can you get started building good credit? Knowing how credit scores are calculated can help you improve them.

Each credit scoring model values the information in your credit report differently and uses a unique score range. The popular FICO Score uses a scale from 300 to 850 and values the following five factors:

1. **Payment history** (35%): making payments for bills and credit accounts on time

2. **Credit utilization** (30%): having lower amounts of debt relative to your available credit limits on credit cards and lines of credit

3. **Length of credit history** (15%): having credit accounts for a longer period of time

4. **Type of credit used** (10%): having a mix of credit types, including loans and credit cards

5. **Applications for credit** (10%): having fewer requests for new credit accounts

How to Build Your Credit

It may be difficult to get approved for a credit card before you've established a good credit history. However, everyone over age 18 can get a secured credit card, which can help you build credit for the first time—as long as it reports payment transactions to the credit agencies. With a secured credit card, you must make a refundable upfront deposit (as little as $200) that serves as your credit limit.

To build good credit, focus on actions within your control that have the biggest influence on typical scoring models. These include paying bills on time and not maxing out credit cards. But remember that it takes time to build good credit—it's a marathon, not a sprint.

How to Protect Your Credit

To protect the integrity of your credit, you should check your credit report on a regular basis. It's up to you to make sure that the information in your credit report is correct. Errors or fraudulent activity can hurt your credit scores without you knowing it.

Checking your credit reports is easy, and it never hurts your credit scores. You can purchase your credit report from any of the three credit agencies, but you're entitled to a free report from each once a year at annualcreditreport.com. You can report inaccuracies or put a stop to fraud by placing a credit alert or credit freeze on your credit reports. The Fair Credit Reporting Act (FCRA) is a federal law that regulates how your credit information can be used and your consumer credit rights. You can learn more on the Federal Trade Commission website at ftc.gov.

> **FINANCE TIP**
>
> To stay on top of your credit more than once a year, space out your requests and get a free report from a different credit agency every four months at annualcreditreport.com.

Part 5 Review Questions

1. Briefly describe the criteria a creditor uses to evaluate a potential borrower.

2. Why is it important to maintain an excellent credit score? Name ways that bad credit can hurt someone. How can good credit help you achieve some of your own financial goals?

3. Why do you think lenders have an interest in your credit history?

4. Do you think it's fair that consumers with good credit scores typically pay less for credit accounts, such as credit cards, loans, and certain insurance products? Why or why not?

Project

Imagine that your best friend just got approved for a credit card with a $500 available credit limit. He or she is excited to use a credit card for the first time and wants to go on a shopping spree. If you know that he or she doesn't have much money to pay off the credit card bill, what advice would you offer?

Part 6

Borrow Without Sorrow

It can be easy to get into financial trouble if you borrow money that you can't repay. Getting behind on bills—such as payments for a car loan, student loan, or credit card—results in large late fees and long-term damage to your credit history. Therefore, it's important to know how to use debt responsibly and to make wise choices that are best for your financial future.

What to Know About Debt

Before you apply for credit or take on any amount of debt, ask yourself some important questions:

- Do I really need this item?
- Can I wait until I save enough cash to pay for it?
- What's the total cost of the credit, including interest and fees?
- Can I afford the monthly payments?

There are many different kinds of debt, but they fall into two main categories: installment loans and revolving credit.

Installment Loan Basics

An installment loan is an agreement you make with a creditor to borrow a certain
amount of money and repay it in equal monthly payments, or installments, for a set
period of time. The length or term of the loan could be very short or in excess of 30
years, and the loan may be secured or unsecured.

Secured loans are backed by collateral, which is something of value that you pledge
to the lender. For instance, a car you finance is collateral for the car loan. And a house is
collateral for a home loan, which is also known as a mortgage. Collateral protects lenders because they can sell it to repay your debt if you don't make payments as agreed.

Unsecured loans are not backed by any collateral. They're often called personal or
signature loans because you sign an agreement where you promise to repay the debt.
For instance, credit card debt and student loans are both forms of unsecured loans.

When you take an installment loan, your monthly payment will depend on three
factors:

1. **Principal amount**: The less you borrow, the lower your monthly payment will be.

2. **Interest rate**: The lower the rate, the lower your monthly payment will be.

3. **Loan term**: The longer the term, the lower your monthly payment will be; however,
   this generally results in paying more total interest.

Common Types of Installment Loans

Installment loans give consumers money to buy many different products and services,
such as cars, homes, or a college education.

Consumer Loans

Consumer installment loans, also called personal or signature loans, are commonly
used for small purchases, such as buying a computer or paying for unexpected
expenses. You can apply for an unsecured consumer loan from local banks, credit
unions, or online lenders.

Auto Loans

Installment loans to buy a new or used vehicle are available from local banks, credit
unions, online lenders, and some car dealers. You may be required to make a down payment on the purchase price—especially if you don't have good credit.

For example, if you want to buy a used car that costs $10,000, the lender may
require that you pay 20% or $2,000 up front in order to borrow the remaining balance
of $8,000.

As previously mentioned, the car you buy becomes collateral for the loan. If you don't make payments as agreed, the lender can repossess, or take back, the vehicle to pay off the outstanding loan balance. The lender typically holds the title of the car until the loan is paid off in full.

The term or repayment period for a car loan is typically 2 to 7 years. Choosing a longer loan term reduces the monthly payment but can significantly increase the amount of total interest you have to pay.

What's Being "Upside Down"? A new car depreciates, or loses its value, very quickly—especially in the first three years—depending on the make and model. For example, a $20,000 car might be worth only $15,000 after a year. But your outstanding loan balance could be over $16,000 if you made a low or no down payment (depending on the loan terms).

When you owe more for a car than it's worth, you're "upside down" on the loan. If you want to trade or sell the car, you have to pay extra out of pocket to pay off the loan. Making a down payment helps you avoid this common financial problem of being upside down—and helps reduce your monthly loan payment. So, even if you have good credit, it's wise to make a down payment on a car loan.

What's a Car Title? A car title is a document that shows who purchased a vehicle and lists information including the vehicle identification number (VIN), make, year of manufacture, purchase price, registered owner name and address, and legal owner if any money is owed. When a car is sold, the title must be transferred to the new owner.

What's Vehicle Leasing? Instead of owning a car, you can lease one for a set period of time. After the lease term (usually two, three, or four years) expires, you have to return the vehicle to the leasing company. Monthly lease payments may be less than a loan payment for the same vehicle and term. However, after you pay off a car loan the vehicle belongs to you. You can sell it for cash or continue to drive it for many years without having to make a car payment. Therefore, purchasing a car is more cost effective when you keep it for the long term.

Student Loans

Student loans are funds you can use for education expenses, such as tuition, books, room and board, and other living expenses while you attend college. There are two main types of unsecured installment loans that may be available to you or your parents: federal student loans and private student loans.

Federal student loans are issued by the federal government, and most don't require a credit check for approval. Most students qualify for some type of federal loan, up to certain limits, depending on their income or their parents' financial qualifications. To apply, you must complete the Free Application for Federal Student Aid (FAFSA). You can submit it online at the U.S. Department of Education website at studentaid.ed.gov.

Here are three types of federal student loans:

- **Stafford Loan** is the main federal loan for students. It can be subsidized by the federal government or unsubsidized. To receive a subsidized Stafford Loan, you must demonstrate financial need. The government pays, or subsidizes, the interest on the loan while you're in school.

  Unsubsidized Stafford Loans require you to pay all the interest; however, you can defer making payments until after graduation. All students, regardless of financial need, can get an unsubsidized Stafford Loan.

- **Perkins Loan** is a subsidized federal loan given to students who have the greatest financial need. The government pays the loan interest during school and for a nine-month grace period after graduating or withdrawing from school.

- **Parent Loan for Undergraduate Students (PLUS)** is an unsubsidized federal loan for parents of students. A credit check is made to verify that the parents have no adverse credit history.

Private student loans originate from a private lender, such as an online institution, a local bank, or a credit union. Private education loans are generally used to bridge the gap between the cost of college and the amount you can borrow from the government.

Eligibility for a private loan depends on your or your parents' financial qualifications and credit scores. You submit an application directly to a private lender and don't have to complete any federal forms.

Private student loans typically have higher interest rates and less repayment flexibility than federal loans. Therefore, always apply for a federal student loan first.

> **FINANCE TIP**
>
> If you want to learn more about completing the FAFSA and paying for college, finaid.org is a leading resource for financial aid—including loans, scholarships, grants, and fellowships.

Home Loans

You can get a home loan or mortgage from local banks, credit unions, or online lenders. Home loans can be used to

- buy real estate, such as a house or condominium,
- buy a parcel of vacant land,
- build a home, or
- borrow against the equity or value of a home you already own.

There are three main types of home loans:

1. A **purchase loan** is used to buy a home and is secured by the property. You must make a down payment that's typically 5% to 20% of the purchase price. The loan term is typically 30 years, but 15- and 20-year mortgages are also common.

2. An **equity loan** is secured by your home and can be used for any purpose. *Equity* is the current market value of your property less the amount of outstanding debt you owe. For instance, if your home is worth $200,000 and your mortgage balance is $140,000, you have $60,000 in equity.

3. A **refinance loan** replaces an existing home loan by paying it off and creating a brand new loan that has better terms, such as a lower interest rate. Refinancing at a lower interest rate may allow you to lower your monthly payments and save money.

What Is Foreclosure? Foreclosure is a legal process a home lender uses to collect the balance of an unpaid debt when a borrower defaults or stops making loan payments as agreed. The lender can take legal title to the property, evict the borrower(s), and sell the property to pay off the debt, according to state laws.

Revolving Credit Basics

Revolving credit is different from an installment loan (such as a car or student loan) because it doesn't have a fixed number of payments or a final due date. The account revolves, or stays open indefinitely, as long as the borrower makes minimum monthly payments. The lender approves a maximum loan amount, or credit limit, to use at any time. Credit cards, retail store credit cards, and home equity lines of credit (HELOCs) are common types of revolving credit.

Applying for a Credit Card

If you're under age 21, you must show that you have income or an eligible cosigner to qualify for a credit card. The law requires that you receive a Federal Truth in Lending Disclosure Statement from any company that offers you credit. Be sure to read it carefully so you understand the terms and can compare cards based on these features:

- annual percentage rate (APR) for purchases, promotions, cash advances, and balance transfers
- your credit limit
- potential fees and penalties

- how balances are calculated
- rewards or rebates for purchases
- additional protections (such as travel insurance or extended warranties)

Managing a Credit Card

A credit card gives you the ability to make purchases now and pay for them later. For example, if you have a credit card with a $1,000 credit limit, you can use it to buy products or services, or take cash advances that total up to $1,000. However, you should never max out a credit card because that hurts your credit.

This flexibility makes credit cards powerful financial tools that can help you in an emergency situation. But credit cards can also devastate your finances if you get over your head in debt that you can't repay.

Because credit cards are so convenient for consumers and come with unsecured risk for lenders, card companies charge relatively high interest rates that can exceed 30%. Every time you make a credit card purchase, you're borrowing money that must be paid back. You'll also have to pay interest charges if you don't pay off your balance in full by the monthly statement due date. See Part 5 for more information on understanding and establishing credit.

Paying Off Your Credit Card

Credit cards issue an account statement each month that lists transactions from the previous month. The lowest amount you can pay—your "minimum payment"—varies depending on the card, but may range from 2% to 4% of your outstanding balance. For instance, if you owe $500, your minimum payment could be 3%, or $15. The remaining balance of $485 will continue to accrue interest, in addition to any new transactions you make or late fees that may apply.

However, if you pay off your entire credit card balance by the due date on your statement each month, you can use a credit card without paying any interest charges or late fees. That's because no interest charges accrue during this "grace period."

✓ Tips to Reduce the Cost of Borrowing

The cost of borrowing money depends on several factors, such as current interest rates, your credit rating, the APR you're offered, loan fees, and how long it takes you to repay the debt. Here are 10 tips to reduce the cost of borrowing:

1. **Shop around for the lowest APR** for a loan or credit card before you accept an offer.
2. **Finance an item based on the total price** (including interest) that you can afford—not just on a monthly payment amount.
3. **Repay loans over a shorter term** so you pay less total interest over the life of a loan.
4. **Pay off credit card purchases in full each month** so you're never charged interest or late fees.
5. **Make payments on time** so you're never penalized with expensive late fees or an increased APR on a credit card.

6. **Build a good credit history** so you have high credit scores and will be offered low interest rates by lenders and credit card companies. Establishing credit was covered in Part 5 of this handbook.
7. **Make a bigger down payment** so you'll owe less and receive lower APR offers from auto and home lenders.
8. **Take out federal student loans** before accepting private education loans so you qualify for the most favorable interest rates and repayment terms.
9. **Claim tax benefits** that come with education loans, such as the student loan interest tax deduction, which may allow you to reduce the amount of tax you owe.
10. **Never take a payday loan**, which is a short-term unsecured advance against your next paycheck. The interest rate for one of these loans can be over 15% for just two weeks—which translates into a sky-high APR that can exceed 400%!

Part 6 Review Questions

1. What are the advantages and disadvantages of borrowing money?

2. What goals do you have that might require you to borrow money?

3. Briefly describe the different kinds of student loans. How can you be sure you don't borrow more than you can comfortably pay back, taking other lifetime financial burdens (such as buying a home or car, or having children) into consideration?

4. What are some important rules to remember when it comes to managing a credit card the right way?

5. Why should credit cards and loans never be viewed as "free money"?

Project

Come up with five questions to ask when you are comparing different kinds of loans or credit. For example, one question can be "What is my minimum monthly payment?"

Manage Your Money

Part 7

Building wealth and creating financial security can be easy if you have a reliable income and manage your money wisely. Good money management starts with never spending more than you make each month. Your financial life will always be a balancing act between the short-term gratification of spending to fulfill your current wants versus the long-term benefit of saving. Striking the right balance will allow you to have enough money to fulfill your future wants and needs.

It's your job to have the willpower to resist unnecessary spending and get into the habit of saving for the future on a regular basis. If you use your financial resources responsibly, you'll be able to have a secure future and make your dreams a reality.

Setting Financial Goals

A financial goal is something you want to do with your money in a certain period of time. Goals can be short-term, like buying a car this year or taking a vacation next summer. Or goals can be long-term, like accumulating a large nest egg for retirement. Retirement is one of the most important goals for everyone. Why? Because as you grow older, you may neither want nor be able to work. The hope is that we save enough money so it's possible to enjoy life and pursue other interests besides work when desired.

In Part 3 you learned that Social Security benefits are likely to provide you with a small amount of income after you retire. You'll need additional savings for everyday expenses, such as housing, food, and medical costs—otherwise you won't have a comfortable lifestyle as you grow older.

Though you have many years to go, saving enough for retirement generally takes decades to achieve. That's why it's critical that you begin saving for the future as early as possible. Financial success doesn't happen overnight—so the earlier you start saving for retirement, the better.

What Is Social Security?

Social Security is a group of benefits paid to eligible taxpayers who are retired, disabled, or who survive a relative who was receiving benefits. The funds for Social Security come from taxes withheld from your paycheck. The amount you'll receive in retirement depends on how many years you work, how much payroll or self-employment tax you pay during your career, the age you elect to start receiving benefits, and the future financial health of the Social Security system. Visit ssa.gov for more information.

Creating a Budget

It's easy for everyday purchases like snacks, magazines, and music to get out of control if you're not watching them carefully. Keeping your expenses as low as possible can add up to huge savings over time. For instance, let's say bringing your lunch to work four days a week saves you $8 a day, or $32 a week. If you invested $32 a week for 40 years at a moderate rate of return, that savings would grow to over $330,000.

The best way to take control of your money is to create a budget, also known as a spending plan. A spending plan helps you understand how much money you have and where it goes, so you can prioritize expenses and set objectives to achieve your short- and long-term financial goals.

Managing money the right way is all about making choices and sacrifices—like whether to spend money on a night out with friends or save it to buy a car. You'll always have many needs and wants competing for your limited financial resources. You can apply an economic mindset to your financial planning too! It's up to you to choose your priorities and decide the best way to spend your money.

Four Steps to Preparing a Successful Budget

Knowing exactly how much you have to spend and where you spend it gives you power over your finances. You can keep track of your financial information on paper, using a computer spreadsheet or a mobile app, or by importing transactions from your bank or credit card accounts into a financial program, like Quicken.

Here are four easy steps to creating a successful spending plan:

• **Step #1**—Enter your net monthly income.

To stay in control of your money and reach your financial goals, you must know how much money you have coming in each month. Recall that net income, or take-home pay, is the amount you have left after taxes and other voluntary workplace deductions. Enter this amount at the top of your spending plan because it's what you actually have to spend each month.

• **Step #2**—Enter your fixed and variable expenses.

Many people don't achieve financial success because they spend money carelessly. It's critical that you keep a close watch on your spending so it never exceeds your net income. Enter all your expenses below your income.

Fixed expenses don't change from month to month and may include your rent, insurance, phone and internet bill, or loan payment. Variable expenses can change each month and can include discretionary spending, like dining out, using transportation services, or buying clothes.

Organize your expenses into major categories—such as rent, insurance, groceries, dining out, clothes, and entertainment—and enter the total amounts.

• **Step #3**—Compare your income and expenses.

When you compare your total take-home pay to your total expenses, you may be pleased that you have money left over or disappointed that there's none to spare. Discretionary income is the amount of money you have left over each month after all your essential living expenses are paid.

You must spend less than you make in order to have enough discretionary income to save and invest for your future. Living paycheck to paycheck may satisfy immediate wants and needs, but it won't empower you to achieve long-term financial success.

- **Step #4**—Set priorities and make changes.

The final step is to create new spending guidelines. Decide how much you want to allocate toward each of your short- and long-term financial goals and enter them as separate categories in your spending plan. You may need to reduce spending in other categories or find ways to earn extra income to cover all your expenses.

It's up to you to figure out the best way to balance your spending and saving so you enjoy life today and put away enough money for a safe and secure tomorrow.

What Does "Pay Yourself First" Mean?

"Pay yourself first" is a common saying in personal finance that means saving money should be your top priority. Putting your savings on autopilot is the best way to remove the temptation to spend it! A portion of each paycheck can be deposited automatically in a savings or retirement account before you receive the balance. That way you pay yourself before paying your living expenses or making discretionary purchases.

Tracking Your Wealth

A spending plan is the perfect way to track your income and expenses. But to monitor the big picture of your finances, you need to know your net worth. Your net worth can be summed up in this simple equation:

$$\text{net worth} = \text{assets} - \text{liabilities}$$

Assets are items you own that have real value, such as cash in the bank, vehicles, investments, real estate, personal belongings, and money owed to you. Liabilities are your debts and financial obligations to others, such as an auto loan, credit card debt, or money you borrowed from a friend.

If you have more assets than you owe in liabilities, your net worth will be a positive number. But if you owe more than you own, your net worth will be a negative number. The goal is to raise your net worth over time by increasing your assets or decreasing your liabilities, so you build wealth.

Paying Bills

Paying bills on time is one of the most important money management responsibilities. Late payments can result in expensive fees and damage to your credit. Thanks to online banking, it's never been easier to manage bills and pay them on time.

Most local and internet-only banks offer free bill pay, which allows you to pay any company or individual with the click of a button. If a company you want to pay accepts electronic payments, your funds will transfer electronically. If not, the bill pay service prints and mails a paper check on your behalf to any payee in the United States that has a mailing address.

E-bills and e-statements can be sent to your e-mail, bill pay center, or both. You can set up a bill to be paid automatically on a certain date and e-mail you when the transaction is complete. Or you can log on to your bill pay center and manually initiate a payment for up to one year into the future. You can set up reminder alerts for all your recurring bills so no payment due date ever falls through the cracks.

One of the most surprising facts about wealthy people is that most of them weren't born that way. About 80% of the wealthiest people in the United States are first-generation millionaires. They accumulated wealth by working hard and saving and investing money. That means anyone who is disciplined with his or her money can achieve financial security. Here are 10 tips to manage your money like a millionaire:

1. **Live below your means.** Spending less than you make is a choice. Saving money, and not overspending, is how you build wealth.

2. **Know where your money goes.** If you don't have a spending plan to track your money, you won't know if you're making wise decisions. Getting ahead financially starts with taking control of your cash flow.

3. **Create an emergency fund.** Having money set aside for unexpected expenses is a safety net that you should never be without. That's how you'll make it through a financial rough patch, such as suddenly losing your job or having large unexpected expenses. Make a goal to accumulate at least six months' worth of your living expenses to keep on hand at all times.

4. **Focus on net worth instead of income.** No matter how much you earn, you can grow rich by slowly increasing your net worth over time. But even if you have a large income, you'll never grow rich if you don't get in the habit of setting aside money for the future.

5. **Have long-term financial goals.** Wealthy people know what they want to achieve and then work backward so they have a plan for what to do each year, month, week, or day to stay on track and meet their goals. Set objectives to achieve your goals.

6. **Begin saving for retirement early.** If you think you're too young to start saving for retirement, think again. Creating wealth for your future rarely happens overnight—unless you beat huge odds by having a winning lottery ticket or a big inheritance.

7. **Save and invest at least 15% of your income.** Make it a habit to save 15% to 20% of your income, starting with your first job, and adjust your lifestyle so you can easily live on the rest.

8. **Automate your savings and investments.** It's easier to save money that you never see. Participate in a workplace retirement account or have your paycheck split between a checking and savings account so your savings are on autopilot.

9. **View money as a tool.** Money is only as useful as what you do with it. So decide what's important to you and use money to achieve your needs and your dreams. Push away short-term gratification in favor of important, long-term goals like saving for retirement.

10. **Realize when you've made a money mistake.** Everyone makes mistakes with their money from time to time. If you overspend or make unwise decisions, stop and make the choice to get back on track right away.

Part 7 Review Questions

1. Do you think that writing down your goals and reviewing them on a regular basis could help increase your chances of accomplishing them? Why or why not?

2. What is the relationship between spending and the ability to build wealth?

3. Why does tracking how you spend money help you make better financial decisions?

4. What is the purpose of an emergency fund, and how much should be in it?

Project

Choose a savings goal that you'd like to achieve in one year. Create a savings plan and keep track of your progress over the next few months.

Protect Yourself from Risk

Life is full of events that no one can predict. It's impossible to know if you'll get into a car accident, have your laptop stolen, or need to visit the emergency room for a broken bone. While you can't prevent these kinds of catastrophes, you can protect your personal finances by having enough of the right kinds of insurance.

Insurance is a special type of contract between you and an insurance company. The company agrees that when certain events—defined in an insurance policy—occur, they'll meet certain expenses or provide a payout. For example, with a car insurance policy, the insurer agrees to pay some amount of the cost to repair your car if you're in an accident. Health insurance pays a certain amount of your medical expenses if you need to go to the doctor.

Insurance eliminates or reduces the potential financial loss you could experience from an unforeseen event and protects the income and assets that you work hard for.

Types of Insurance

There are many different types of insurance products that can be purchased from an insurance company or a licensed insurance agent, either in person or online. The types you should have depend on your age and life circumstances. There are eight major types of insurance: health, disability, life, auto, homeowner's, renter's, long-term care, and umbrella.

Health Insurance

Without health insurance you could get stuck with a huge bill if you have any kind of medical need, from a broken bone to a chronic illness. Even a quick trip to the emergency room can cost thousands of dollars.

The federal government, through the Affordable Care Act (ACA), may provide a financial subsidy, which reduces the monthly cost of health insurance, depending on your income and family size.

Many employers offer group health insurance to their employees, or you can purchase an individual policy on your own. You can stay on your parents' health policy until you are 26 years old—unless you're offered insurance through your work.

Visit healthcare.gov to explore your health insurance options.

Disability Insurance

A disability is a physical or mental condition that limits your ability to perform various types of activities. If you're unable to work due to a disability, accident, or illness, disability insurance replaces a portion of your income, typically 60%. Unless you have plenty of savings in an emergency fund, a disability could leave you unable to pay for everyday living expenses, such as housing or groceries. Remember that health insurance only covers a portion of your medical bills—not your everyday living expenses.

Many employers offer some type of disability coverage for employees, or if you're self-employed you can purchase an individual policy on your own. Professionals—such as surgeons, athletes, or dancers—who want to protect their financial health if their ability to do their jobs is compromised should always have disability coverage. Every disability policy is different, but there are two main types: short-term disability (STD) and long-term disability (LTD). A short-term policy usually pays you for a maximum of two years, while a long-term policy could provide benefits that last your entire life.

Life Insurance

Life insurance provides a lump-sum payment, known as a death benefit, to one or more named beneficiaries when the insured person dies. It's important to have life insurance when your death would cause a financial burden for those you leave behind—such as a spouse or child.

Many employers offer life insurance for employees, or you can purchase your own policy. There are two basic kinds of life insurance: term and permanent.

- **Term life insurance** provides less expensive coverage for a set period of time, such as 10 or 20 years, and pays the policy's death benefit amount to the beneficiary.
- **Permanent life insurance** provides lifetime coverage that pays a death benefit and accumulates a cash value that the beneficiary can withdraw later in life. This type of policy is much more expensive that a term life policy.

A good rule of thumb is to purchase life insurance with a benefit that's 10 times your income. So if you make $50,000 a year, you might need coverage that would pay your beneficiary $500,000. However, factors such as your family size, debt, and assets, and the lifetime income needs of a surviving partner, spouse, or child are critical considerations.

Auto Insurance

Most U.S. states require you to have some amount of insurance for vehicles such as cars, trucks, motorcycles, and recreational vehicles. The required insurance types and minimum amounts vary depending on the state in which you live.

Auto insurance is a package of coverages that may include the following:

- **Collision** pays for damage to your vehicle caused by getting into an accident with another vehicle, even if you are at fault.
- **Comprehensive** pays for damage to your vehicle due to something other than a collision, such as fire, hail, or theft.
- **Property damage liability** pays for damage you cause to someone else's property, such as their vehicle or fence, or a city's stop sign.
- **Bodily injury liability** pays for injuries you cause to another person. It's important to have enough liability because if you're involved in a serious accident, you could be sued for a large sum of money.
- **Personal injury protection** pays for medical expenses of the driver and passengers of the policyholder's car regardless of who's at fault, in certain states.
- **Uninsured and underinsured motorist coverage** pays when you're in an accident with an at-fault driver who has insufficient or no insurance to pay for your loss.

The cost of auto insurance varies depending on many factors, such as your age, driving record, and credit history (in most states), the type and age of your vehicle, and the amount and type of coverage you choose. So remember to factor in the cost of insurance when choosing a new ride.

Homeowner's Insurance

When you have a home mortgage, the lender requires you to purchase and maintain insurance for the property. Basic homeowner's insurance pays for damage to your property or personal belongings caused by a covered event, such as a natural disaster or theft. Homeowner's insurance also includes liability coverage that protects you if someone gets hurt while on your property.

Renter's Insurance

When you rent an apartment or home, your landlord's insurance doesn't cover your personal belongings or liability. Renter's insurance pays for damage to your possessions (such as clothes, jewelry, electronics, furniture, artwork, household goods, and sporting equipment) if they're damaged by a covered event, such as a natural disaster, wind storm, theft, or faulty plumbing. It can also reimburse your living expenses if you're forced to move out temporarily while repairs are being made. And as with homeowner's insurance, the liability protection keeps you safe if someone is injured on the property and involves you in a lawsuit.

If you rent a home or apartment, you should never go without renter's insurance. According to the National Association of Insurance Commissioners (NAIC), the national average cost of a renter's policy in 2015 was only $188. So it's a very inexpensive way to protect your finances from an unforeseen crisis!

Long-Term Care Insurance

If you have a long-term illness or disability that keeps you from taking care of yourself, long-term care (LTC) insurance pays a certain amount of day-to-day care that isn't covered by other types of insurance. Remember that disability insurance only replaces a portion of your lost income if you're unable to work due to a disability. And health insurance only pays for a portion of your medical bills.

Individuals who require long-term care may need help with activities of daily living, such as dressing, bathing, eating, and walking. Long-term care insurance generally covers care provided in your home by a visiting professional or in an assisted living facility.

Umbrella Insurance

As you build wealth, you may find that you need additional liability insurance protection to cover the total value of your assets. An umbrella policy gives you broad coverage from losses above the limits of your existing policies.

For instance, say you have $100,000 of auto insurance liability and a million dollar umbrella policy. If you were in a car accident that caused serious injuries to another driver that exceeded $100,000, your umbrella policy would give you protection up to one million dollars.

What Is an Insurance Deductible?

Many types of insurance—such as health, auto, renter's, and homeowner's—require you to pay a certain amount of expenses before the policy covers your remaining costs. This out-of-pocket expense is called your deductible. For example, if you have a medical bill for $2,000 and your deductible is $500, then you must pay $500 before the policy will pay all or a portion of the remaining $1,500 in covered benefits.

Extended Product Warranties

If you've ever purchased a product like a computer or a TV, the salesperson probably gave you a sales pitch for an extended product warranty. These warranties give you additional protection if something breaks after the manufacturer's warranty expires. They can also cover issues that the manufacturer doesn't.

While the added protection of an extended product warranty can come in handy, the cost can be very high. Product warranties are typically very profitable for retailers, who train salespeople to sell them aggressively. If the benefit isn't worth the cost, never let a salesperson talk you into buying something you don't need.

When to Purchase an Extended Product Warranty

Consider the following to know when you should purchase an extended product warranty:

- **Look at the price of the warranty versus the price of the product**. If you spend $100 for a printer and the extended warranty is $40, that increases the price 40% for a relatively inexpensive product. However, spending $150 for a warranty on a $2,000 computer may be worthwhile, since it has many expensive parts that could break.

- **Consider the likelihood that you'll need extra coverage**. Will you use the product on a daily basis or in an environment where it could be damaged easily? Does the manufacturer have a reputation for making quality products?

- **Understand the coverage provided**. Does the warranty simply duplicate what's already available from the manufacturer, and how long does it last? What about parts and labor—are they also covered by the policy? Are the rules of the warranty clear and do they make sense for your situation? If the coverage is thin or it's too difficult to file a claim, then the warranty would be useless.

- **Remember coverage offered by your credit card**. Many credit cards offer built-in extended warranty coverage as a card benefit. So it might make sense to purchase a product with your credit card to take advantage of the extra protection.

Identity Theft

Identity theft is a serious and growing crime. It happens when a criminal steals your personal information and uses it to commit fraud. A thief can use data—such as your name, date of birth, Social Security number, driver's license number, bank account number, or credit card number—to wreak havoc on your finances. An identity criminal can open new phone accounts, credit cards, or loans in your name, then go on a spending spree and leave you with a huge bill. Thieves have even filed fictitious tax returns and applied for driver's licenses in their victims' names.

Many insurance companies offer identity theft insurance to cover expenses that you may incur as a victim, such as lost wages, attorney fees, and certified mailing costs. You may have the option to add this protection to your homeowner's or renter's policy.

There are also companies that specialize in identity theft protection, credit monitoring, and identity restoration. These services may be sold through insurance agents, credit card companies, credit reporting agencies, or banks and credit unions. Be sure to read the fine print of these policies before signing up so you understand if do-it-yourself safeguards may be just as effective.

It's impossible to completely prevent identity theft; however, if you catch it early, you can stop it quickly and with less potential hassle and expense.

What to Do If You're the Victim of Identity Theft

Once your identity is jeopardized, getting it corrected can cost time and money. So be sure to keep an eye on your accounts and immediately take the following actions if you see any suspicious activity:

Step #1—Place an initial fraud alert on your credit report with one of the major credit reporting agencies (Equifax, Experian, TransUnion). They must inform the other two agencies on your behalf.

This alert makes it more difficult for a thief to open additional accounts in your name because a business must take additional steps to contact you directly to verify your identity. An initial fraud alert lasts for 90 days; however, you can renew it for free as needed.

Step #2—Request your credit reports from each of the three major credit reporting agencies. Placing a fraud alert also gives you access to free copies of your credit reports. It's a good idea to request copies that reveal only the last four digits of your Social Security number.

If you know which of your accounts have been compromised, contact those companies directly to discuss the fraudulent activity. Take notes about what actions are being taken and follow up in writing. Be sure to send all communication regarding an identity theft case by certified mail and ask for a return receipt. It's important to create a record that proves you have been diligent to resolve unauthorized charges on your account.

Step #3—Submit an identity theft report to the Federal Trade Commission (FTC) and then the local police. Having these formal reports will help you prove that you've been an identity theft victim to credit reporting agencies, businesses, and debt collectors. If a thief opened new accounts in your name and made large purchases, this could damage your credit history unless the creditor is willing to remove the account or the fraudulent charges from your report.

Visit the FTC website at consumer.ftc.gov to submit an identity theft report or to learn more.

✓ Tips to Stay Safe from Identity Theft

Here are 10 tips to help you protect yourself and stay safe from identity theft:

1. **Never carry confidential information that you don't need.** Unless you plan to use them, remove your Social Security card, paper checks, and financial cards from your wallet and leave them at home so they can't be lost or stolen.

2. **Don't share your Social Security number.** There are only a few situations where you might need to provide it, such as for a new job, in tax-related matters, or when applying for credit or insurance. Never reveal your confidential information over the phone or internet to any person or company that you don't trust entirely.

3. **Keep a close watch over your debit and credit cards.** When you hand a financial card to a store clerk or restaurant server, watch to make sure that it isn't copied and get it back as soon as possible. Also, never loan your financial cards to anyone.

4. **Shred all documents with personal information.** Make confetti out of receipts, financial account statements, and unwanted credit card offers before putting them in the garbage. Identity thieves dumpster dive for paperwork and can even use the last few digits of a confidential number against you.

5. **Check your credit reports once a year.** If an identity thief opens an account in your name, it will show up on your credit reports. That's why it's important to review them on a periodic basis at annualcreditreport.com.

6. **Resist clicking on links in e-mails.** Thieves can pose as a legitimate organization—such as the IRS, a bank, or PayPal—and send "phishing" e-mails with links to phony sites that ask for confidential information. Genuine companies never ask you for personal information over the phone or internet. Instead of clicking on a hyperlink, enter a website address directly into an internet browser.

7. **Use a secure internet connection.** Don't access a website where you enter confidential information using a public computer or an open Wi-Fi connection. Hackers can track what you're doing over an unsecured internet connection. Also, never send any personal information to a website unless the address begins with "https," which means that it's secure. You should also be careful to keep the antivirus and spyware software current on your computer.

8. **Create strong online usernames and passwords.** Each password for your financial accounts should be unique, with no fewer than eight characters made up of uppercase and lowercase letters, numbers, and symbols. They should never include your Social Security number, name, address, or birth date.

9. **Opt for e-bills and e-statements when possible.** Criminals can change your mailing address so they receive your mail and have access to your personal information. Therefore, reducing the amount of paper documents you send and receive with confidential information is beneficial.

10. **Monitor your bank and credit card account activity.** Review your accounts online or view monthly statements to watch out for unauthorized transactions.

Part 8 Review Questions

1. Why do you think most U.S. states require drivers to have some amount of auto insurance for liability? Do you agree with this requirement? Why or why not?

2. Why does your driving record affect your auto insurance rates?

3. Imagine your best friend has enrolled in a photography program at a fine arts school. He is required to purchase nearly $3,000 worth of photography equipment for his courses and will be keeping it all in his new apartment. What kind of insurance would you suggest he get, if any, and why?

4. Who should have renter's insurance, and why is it a good idea?

5. Why do you think mortgage lenders require homeowners to have a certain amount of homeowner's insurance?

6. Describe several precautions you or your family take to stay safe from identity theft.

Project

Research health insurance plans online, taking into account your specific situation and needs. Start by making a list of how you use health insurance (frequency of doctor visits, need for special dental or vision services, etc.) and decide what kind of insurance policy would fit your needs best. Is it one with a high deductible but low monthly premium? Or is it different? Once you have selected the right fit, list the details of the plan and explain why this plan was the best fit for you.

Glossary/Glosario

Italicized terms within definitions are key terms that are defined elsewhere in this glossary.

Los *términos en cursiva* dentro de las definiciones son términos clave que se definen en otras partes de este glosario.

English

Español

A

absolute advantage the advantage conferred by the ability to produce more of a good or service with a given amount of time and resources; different from *comparative advantage*. (p. 25)

ventaja absoluta ventaja conferida por la capacidad de producir más de un bien o servicio cuando se dispone de una cantidad dada de tiempo y recursos; no es lo mismo que *ventaja comparativa*. (pág. 25)

absolute value the value of a number without a minus sign, whether or not the number was negative to begin with. (p. 39)

valor absoluto valor de una cifra sin el signo de menos, haya sido o no una cifra negativa inicialmente. (pág. 39)

accounting profit a business's *total revenue* minus the *explicit cost* and *depreciation* (p. 511)

utilidad contable *ingresos totales* de un negocio menos los *costes explícitos* y la *depreciación* (pág. 511)

AD–AS model model in which the *aggregate supply curve* and the *aggregate demand curve* are used together to analyze economic fluctuations. (p. 184)

modelo AD-AS modelo en el que la *curva de oferta agregada* y la *curva de demanda agregada* se emplean juntas para analizar fluctuaciones económicas. (pág. 184)

administrative costs (of a tax) the resources used by the government to collect the tax, and by taxpayers to pay (or to evade) it, over and above the amount collected. (p. 485)

costes administrativos (de un impuesto) recursos que emplea el gobierno para recaudar el impuesto y que emplean los contribuyentes para pagarlo (o para evadirlo), por encima del importe recaudado. (pág. 485)

adverse selection when one person knows more about the way things are than other people do; for example, when sellers offer items of particularly low (hidden) quality for sale, and when the people with the greatest need for insurance are those most likely to purchase it. (p. EM-20)

selección adversa cuando una persona sabe más que otras personas acerca de cómo son las cosas; por ejemplo, cuando los vendedores ofrecen para la venta artículos de una calidad particularmente mala (oculta), y cuando las personas con la mayor necesidad de un seguro son aquéllas con la mayor probabilidad de comprarlo. (pág. EM-20)

aggregate demand curve shows the relationship between the *aggregate price level* and the quantity of *aggregate output* demanded by *households*, businesses, the government, and the rest of the world. (p. 166)

curva de demanda agregada permite apreciar la relación entre el *nivel de precios agregados* y la cantidad de *producción agregada* exigida por los *hogares*, los negocios, el gobierno y el resto del mundo. (pág. 166)

aggregate output the economy's total production of goods and services for a given time period. (pp. 11, 114)

producción agregada producción total de bienes y servicios en la economía durante un período de tiempo dado. (págs. 11, 114)

aggregate price level a measure of the overall level of prices in the *economy*. (p. 140)

nivel de precios agregados medida del nivel total de precios en la *economía*. (pág. 140)

aggregate production function a hypothetical function that shows how *productivity* (output per worker) depends on the quantities of *physical capital* per worker and *human capital* per worker as well as the state of *technology*. (p. 355)

función de producción agregada función hipotética que nos permite apreciar cómo la *productividad* (producción por trabajador) depende de las cantidades de *capital físico* por trabajador y de *capital humano* por trabajador, así como del estado de la *tecnología*. (pág. 355)

aggregate spending the total spending on domestically produced *final goods and services* in the *economy*; the sum of *consumer spending*, *investment spending*, *government purchases of goods and services*, and *exports* minus *imports*. (p. 107)

gastos agregados total de gastos en los *bienes y servicios finales* producidos internamente en la *economía*; suma de los *gastos de consumo*, los *gastos de inversión*, la compra por el gobierno de bienes y servicios, y las *exportaciones* menos las *importaciones*. (pág. 107)

aggregate supply curve shows the relationship between the *aggregate price level* and the quantity of *aggregate output* supplied in the *economy*. (p. 174)

curva de oferta agregada permite apreciar la relación entre el *nivel de precios agregados* y la cantidad de *producción agregada* ofertada en la *economía*. (pág. 174)

allocative efficiency achieved by an *economy* if it produces at the point along its *production possibilities* curve that makes consumers as well off as possible. (p. 17)

eficiencia en la distribución una *economía* la alcanza si produce en el punto a lo largo de su *curva de posibilidades de producción* que permite a los consumidores vivir en la posición más acomodada posible. (pág. 17)

English

Español

English	Español
antitrust policy involves efforts by the government to prevent *oligopolistic* industries from becoming or behaving like *monopolies*. (p. 634)	**política antimonopolio** implica esfuerzos de parte del gobierno para impedir que algunas industrias *oligopolísticas* se conviertan en *monopolios* o se comporten como tales. (pág. 634)
appreciation when a currency becomes more valuable in terms of other currencies. (p. 400)	**apreciación** ocurre cuando una moneda aumenta en su valor en relación con otras divisas. (pág. 400)
artificially scarce good a good that is *excludable* but *nonrival in consumption*. (p. 734)	**bien en escasez artificial** bien que es *excluible* pero que *no tiene rival en su consumo*. (pág. 734)
asset bubble situation in which the price of an asset increases to a high level due to expectations of future price gains; can cause a *banking crisis*. (p. EM-4)	**burbuja de activos** coyuntura en la que el precio de un activo aumenta hasta un nivel alto debido a expectativas de ganancias futuras; puede desencadenar una *crisis bancaria*. (pág. EM-4)
asymmetric information see *private information* (p. EM-19)	**información asimétrica** véase *información privada o reservada* (pág. EM-19)
automatic stabilizers government spending and taxation rules that cause *fiscal policy* to be automatically *expansionary* when the *economy* contracts and automatically *contractionary* when the economy expands. (p. 204)	**estabilizadores automáticos** reglas gubernamentales sobre gastos e impuestos que hacen que la *política fiscal* automáticamente se torne *expansiva* cuando la *economía* se contrae y automáticamente se torne *contractiva* cuando la economía se expande. (pág. 204)
autonomous change in aggregate spending an initial rise or fall in *aggregate spending* that is the cause, not the result, of a series of income and spending changes. (p. 164)	**cambio autónomo en los gastos agregados** subida o caída iniciales en *gastos agregados* que son la causa y no el resultado de una serie de cambios en los ingresos y los egresos. (pág. 164)
average cost see *average total cost* (p. 530)	**coste promedio** véase *coste total promedio* (pág. 530)
average cost pricing occurs when regulators set a monopoly's price equal to its average cost to prevent the firm from incurring a loss. (p. 740)	**fijación del precio con base en el coste promedio** ocurre cuando los reguladores fijan el precio de un monopolio de manera que sea equivalente a su coste promedio a fin de impedir que la empresa genere una pérdida. (pág. 740)
average fixed cost (AFC) the *fixed cost* per unit of output. (p. 530)	**coste fijo promedio** *coste fijo* por unidad de producción. (pág. 530)
average product the total product divided by the quantity of an input. (p. 535)	**producto promedio** producto total dividido entre la cantidad de un insumo. (pág. 535)
average product curve shows the relationship between the *average product* and the quantity of an input. (p. 535)	**curva de producto promedio** permite apreciar la relación entre el *producto promedio* y la cantidad de un insumo. (pág. 535)
average total cost (ATC) *total cost* divided by quantity of output produced; also known as *average cost*. (p. 530)	**coste total promedio** *coste total* dividido entre la cantidad de producción producida; también denominado *coste promedio* (pág. 530)
average variable cost (AVC) the *variable cost* per unit of output. (p. 530)	**coste variable promedio** *coste variable* por unidad de producción. (pág. 530)

B

English	Español
balance of payments accounts a summary of a country's transactions with other countries. (p. 390)	**cuentas de la balanza de pagos** resumen de las transacciones que un país efectúa con otros países. (pág. 390)
balance of payments on goods and services the difference between the value of a country's *exports* and the value of its *imports* during a given period. (p. 392)	**balanza de pagos de bienes y servicios** diferencia entre el valor de las *exportaciones* de un país y el valor de sus *importaciones* en un período de tiempo dado. (pág. 392)
balance of payments on the current account a country's balance of payments on goods and services plus net international transfer payments and factor income; also known as the *current account*. (p. 392)	**balanza de pagos de la cuenta corriente** balanza de pagos de un país respecto de los bienes y servicios más los pagos netos de las transferencias internacionales y los ingresos de factores; también denominado *cuenta corriente*. (pág. 392)
balance of payments on the financial account the difference between a country's sales of assets to foreigners and its purchases of assets from foreigners during a given period; also known as the *financial account*. (p. 392)	**balanza de pagos de la cuenta financiera** diferencia entre las ventas a extranjeros de los activos de un país y las compras efectuadas a extranjeros durante un período de tiempo dado; también denominado *cuenta financiera*. (pág. 392)
balanced budget multiplier the factor by which a change in both spending and taxes changes *real GDP*. (p. 203)	**multiplicador del presupuesto equilibrado** factor mediante el cual un cambio tanto en los gastos como en los impuestos modifica el *PIB real*. (pág. 203)

English

Español

English	Español
bank a *financial intermediary* that provides *liquid* assets in the form of *bank deposits* to lenders and uses those funds to finance borrowers' *investment spending* on *illiquid* assets. (p. 222)	**banco** *intermediario financiero* que ofrece a los prestamistas activos *líquidos* en forma de *depósitos bancarios* y hace uso de dichos fondos para financiar los *gastos de inversión* que hacen los prestatarios para adquirir activos *ilíquidos*. (pág. 222)
bank deposit a claim on a *bank* that obliges the bank to give the depositor his or her cash when demanded. (p. 222)	**depósito bancario** compromiso de un *banco* que lo obliga a entregar a los depositarios su dinero cuando el depositario lo exija. (pág. 222)
bank reserves the currency that *banks* hold in their vaults plus their deposits at the Federal Reserve. (p. 235)	**reservas bancarias** moneda corriente que los *bancos* mantienen en sus arcas más los depósitos que mantienen en el Banco de la Reserva Federal. (pág. 235)
bank run a phenomenon in which many of a *bank's* depositors try to withdraw their funds due to fears of a bank failure. (p. 237)	**pánico bancario** fenómeno en el que muchos de los depositarios de un *banco* tratan de retirar sus fondos debido a temores de que el banco pudiera desplomarse. (pág. 237)
banking crisis occurs when a large part of the banking system fails. (p. EM-3)	**crisis bancaria** ocurre cuando fracasa una parte importante del sistema bancario. (pág. EM-3)
bar graph a graph that uses bars of various heights or lengths to indicate values of a variable. (p. 43)	**gráfico de barras** gráfico que hace uso de barras de diferentes alturas o longitudes para indicar valores de una variable. (pág. 43)
barrier to entry protects a *monopolist* (and allows it to persist and earn *economic profits*) by preventing other firms from entering the industry. (p. 548)	**barrera al ingreso** protege a un *monopolista* (y le permite persistir y obtener *utilidades económicas*) al impedir que otras empresas incursionen en la industria. (pág. 548)
base year year arbitrarily chosen for comparison when calculating a *price index;* the price level compares the price of the *market basket* of goods in a given year to its price in the base year. (p. 141)	**año base** año de referencia elegido arbitrariamente cuando se computa un *índice de precios;* el nivel de precios compara el precio de la *canasta familiar* de bienes en un año dado con su precio en el año base. (pág. 141)
behavioral economics the study of economic decision making as influenced by the limits of the human mind. (p. EM-11)	**economía conductual** estudio de la toma de decisiones económicas y la influencia que en el proceso ejerce la mente humana. (pág. EM-11)
black market a market in which goods or services are bought and sold illegally—either because it is illegal to sell them at all or because the prices charged are legally prohibited by a *price ceiling.* (p. 81)	**mercado negro** mercado en el que los bienes y servicios se compran y se venden ilegalmente, ya sea porque es totalmente ilícito venderlos o porque los precios que se cobran son prohibidos legalmente por un *techo de precios* establecido. (pág. 81)
bounded rationality describes the limits on optimal decision making that result from imperfect intelligence and the scarcity of time and information. (p. EM-13)	**racionalidad limitada** describe los límites en la toma de decisiones óptimas que se dan por inteligencia imperfecta y por falta de tiempo e información. (pág. EM-13)
bounded self-interest self-interest that leaves room for concerns about the welfare of others. (p. EM-16)	**interés propio limitado** interés propio que deja espacio para inquietudes relacionadas con el bienestar de los demás. (pág. EM-16)
bounded willpower willpower constrained by limits on the determination needed to do difficult things. (p. EM-15)	**voluntad limitada** voluntad restringida por límites en la determinación que se precisa para lograr cosas difíciles. (pág. EM-15)
brand name a name owned by a particular firm that distinguishes its products from those of other firms. (p. 652)	**nombre de marca** marca de propiedad de una empresa particular que distingue sus productos de los de otras empresas. (pág. 652)
break-even price the market price at which a price-taking firm earns zero profit; the minimum *average total cost* of such a firm. (p. 573)	**precio de equilibrio** precio de mercado en el que la empresa aceptadora de precios obtiene cero ganancias; *coste total promedio* mínimo de dicha empresa. (pág. 573)
budget balance the difference between tax revenue and government spending. (p. 217)	**equilibrio presupuestario** diferencia entre los ingresos fiscales y los gastos del gobierno. (pág. 217)
budget constraint limits the cost of a consumer's consumption bundle to no more than the consumer's income. (p. 491)	**restricción presupuestaria** limita el coste de lo que el consumidor compra a no más que los ingresos del consumidor. (pág. 491)
budget deficit the difference between tax revenue and government spending when government spending exceeds tax revenue. (p. 217)	**déficit presupuestario** diferencia entre los ingresos fiscales y los gastos del gobierno cuando los gastos son mayores que los ingresos fiscales. (pág. 217)
budget line (BL) shows the consumption bundles available to a consumer who spends all of his or her income. (p. 491)	**rubro del presupuesto** permite apreciar los grupos de consumo al alcance del consumidor que gasta la totalidad de sus ingresos. (pág. 491)

English

Español

budget surplus the difference between tax revenue and government spending when tax revenue exceeds government spending. (p. 217)	**superávit presupuestario** diferencia entre los ingresos fiscales y los gastos del gobierno cuando los ingresos son mayores que los gastos del gobierno. (pág. 217)
business cycle the alternation between economic downturns, known as *recessions*, and economic upturns, known as *expansions*. (p. 10)	**ciclo de negocios** alternación entre desaceleraciones económicas, llamadas *recesiones*, y auges económicos, conocidos como *expansiones*. (pág. 10)

C

capital manufactured goods used to make other goods and services; also called *physical capital*. (p. 3)	**capital** bienes fabricados que se emplean para hacer otros bienes y servicios; también denominado *capital físico*. (pág. 3)
capital inflow the total inflow of foreign funds minus the total outflow of domestic funds to other countries. (p. 217)	**afluencia de capital** afluencia total de divisas menos el egreso total de fondos nacionales pagados a otros países. (pág. 217)
cartel a group of producers that agree to restrict output in order to increase prices and their joint profits. (p. 621)	**cartel** grupo de productores que conviene en restringir la producción con el fin de aumentar los precios y sus utilidades conjuntas. (pág. 621)
causal relationship a relationship between two *variables* in which the value taken by one variable directly influences or determines the value taken by the other variable. (p. 35)	**relación causal** relación entre dos *variables* en la que el valor tomado por una variable influye directamente o determina el valor tomado por la otra variable. (pág. 35)
central bank an institution that oversees and regulates the banking system and controls the *monetary base*. (p. 243)	**banco central** institución que vigila y regula el sistema bancario y controla la *base monetaria*. (pág. 243)
ceteris paribus assumption see *other things equal assumption* (p. 13)	**supuesto ceteris paribus** véase *supuesto de que todos los demás factores seguirán iguales* (pág. 13)
change in demand a shift of the *demand curve*, which changes the *quantity demanded* at any given price. (p. 52)	**cambio en la demanda** desplazamiento de la *curva de demanda*, el cual modifica la *cantidad demandada* a un precio dado cualquiera. (pág. 52)
change in supply a shift of the *supply curve*, which changes the *quantity supplied* at any given price. (p. 60)	**cambio en la oferta** desplazamiento de la *curva de oferta*, el cual modifica la *cantidad ofertada* a un precio dado cualquiera. (pág. 60)
Coase theorem states that payment between private parties can achieve an efficient solution to externality problems as long as *transaction costs* are sufficiently low. (p. 714)	**teorema de Coase** explica que el pago entre particulares puede llegar a una solución de eficiencia siempre y cuando los *costes de transacción* sean lo suficientemente bajos. (pág. 714)
collateralized debt obligation an asset-backed security tied to corporate debt or mortgages. (p. EM-7)	**obligación de deuda colaterizada** título valor respaldado por un activo y ligado a deudas corporativas o a hipotecas. (pág. EM-7)
collusion when sellers cooperate to raise their joint profits. (p. 621)	**colusión** cuando los vendedores colaboran entre sí con el fin de aumentar sus utilidades conjuntas. (pág. 621)
command economy an *economy* in which industry is publicly owned and a central authority makes production and consumption decisions. (p. 2)	**economía planificada** *economía* en la que la industria es de propiedad pública y una autoridad central toma las decisiones de producción y consumo. (pág. 2)
commercial bank a depository *bank* that accepts deposits and is covered by *deposit insurance*. (p. 247)	**banco comercial** *banco* depositario que acepta depósitos y está amparado por un *seguro de depósitos bancarios*. (pág. 247)
commodity see *standardized product* (p. 547)	**insumo** véase *producto normalizado* (pág. 547)
commodity money a good used as a *medium of exchange* that has intrinsic value in other uses. (p. 226)	**dinero mercancía** bien que se usa como *medio de intercambio* y que tiene un valor intrínseco en otros usos. (pág. 226)
commodity-backed money a *medium of exchange* with no intrinsic value whose ultimate value is guaranteed by a promise that it can be converted into valuable goods. (p. 226)	**dinero respaldado por materia prima** *medio de intercambio* que no tiene ningún valor intrínseco y cuyo valor definitivo está garantizado por la promesa de que se puede convertir en bienes de valor. (pág. 226)
common resource *nonexcludable* and *rival in consumption*; you can't stop others from consuming the good, and when they consume it, less of the good is available for you. (p. 732)	**recurso común** *no excluible y rival en su consumo*; uno no puede impedir que otros consuman el bien y cuando lo consumen, uno tiene alcance a una menor cantidad del bien. (pág. 732)
comparative advantage the advantage conferred by an individual if the *opportunity cost* of producing the good or service is lower for that individual than for other people. (p. 25)	**ventaja comparativa** ventaja conferida por una persona si el *coste de oportunidad* para producir el bien o servicio es menor para esa persona que para otras. (pág. 25)

English

Español

English	Español
compensating differentials wage differences across jobs that reflect the fact that some jobs are less pleasant or more dangerous than others. (p. 696)	**diferenciales compensatorios** diferenciales salariales entre empleos que reflejan el hecho de que algunos empleos son menos agradables o más peligrosos que otros. (pág. 696)
competitive market a market in which there are many buyers and sellers of the same good or service, none of whom can influence the price at which the good or service is sold. (p. 50)	**mercado competitivo** mercado en el que muchos compran y venden el mismo bien o servicio, y ninguno de ellos puede influir en el precio al que se vende dicho bien o servicio. (pág. 50)
complements two goods (often consumed together) for which a rise in the price of one of the goods leads to a decrease in the demand for the other good. (p. 56)	**complementos** dos bienes (que a menudo se consumen juntos) para los cuales un aumento del precio de uno de los bienes lleva a una disminución en la demanda del otro bien. (pág. 56)
concentration ratios measure of the percentage of industry sales accounted for by the "X" largest firms; for example, the four-firm concentration ratio or the eight-firm concentration ratio. (p. 550)	**tasas de concentración** miden el porcentaje de las ventas de una industria que se le atribuyen a la cantidad equis de las empresas más grandes; por ejemplo, la tasa de concentración de cuatro empresas o la tasa de concentración de ocho empresas. (pág. 550)
constant returns to scale when output increases directly in proportion to an increase in all inputs. (p. 541)	**rendimientos constantes de escala** cuando la producción aumenta en proporcionalidad directa con un aumento en todos los insumos. (pág. 541)
constant-cost industry an industry with a horizontal *(perfectly elastic) long-run supply curve*; the firms' cost curves are unaffected by changes in the size of the industry. (p. 584)	**industria de costes constantes** industria que cuenta con una *curva de oferta a largo plazo* horizontal *(perfectamente elástica)*; las curvas de costes de las empresas no se ven afectadas por los cambios de tamaño de la industria. (pág. 584)
consumer price index (CPI) measures the cost of the *market basket* of a typical urban American family. (p. 141)	**índice de precios de consumo (IPC)** mide el coste de la *canasta familiar* de una familia estadounidense urbana típica. (pág. 141)
consumer spending *household* spending on goods and services. (p. 104)	**gastos de consumo** gastos del *hogar* en bienes y servicios. (pág. 104)
consumer surplus the net gain received from purchasing a good or service; often used to refer to both *individual consumer surplus* and *total consumer surplus*. (p. 464)	**superávit del consumidor** ganancia neta obtenida al comprar un bien o servicio; se refiere tanto al *superávit del consumidor individual* como al *superávit total del consumidor*. (pág. 464)
consumption function shows how a *household's consumer spending* varies with the household's current *disposable income*. (p. 157)	**función de consumo** permite apreciar cómo los *gastos de consumo* de un *hogar* varían en relación con el *ingreso disponible* de dicho hogar en la actualidad. (pág. 157)
consumption possibilities the set of all consumption bundles that are affordable, given a consumer's income and prevailing prices. (p. 491)	**posibilidades de consumo** total de todos los conjuntos de consumo que están al alcance del consumidor según sus ingresos y los precios vigentes. (pág. 491)
contractionary fiscal policy *fiscal policy* that reduces *aggregate demand*. (p. 198)	**política fiscal contractiva** *política fiscal* que reduce la *demanda agregada*. (pág. 198)
contractionary monetary policy *monetary policy* that reduces *aggregate demand*. (p. 296)	**política monetaria contractiva** *política monetaria* que reduce la *demanda agregada*. (pág. 296)
copyright gives the copyright holder for a literary or artistic work the sole right to profit from that work for a specified period of time. (p. 549)	**derechos de autor** dan al creador de una obra literaria o artística el derecho exclusivo a obtener utilidades de su obra durante un período de tiempo específico. (pág. 549)
cost the lowest price at which a seller is willing to sell a good. (p. 466)	**coste** el precio más bajo al cual un vendedor está dispuesto a vender un bien. (pág. 466)
cost-minimization rule employ factors so that the *marginal product* per dollar spent on each factor is the same; this rule is used by a firm to determine the cost-minimizing combination of inputs. (p. 692)	**regla de minimizar costes** emplear factores de manera que el *producto marginal* por dólar dedicado a cada factor sea equivalente; la empresa determina la combinación de insumos destinados a minimizar costes según esta regla. (pág. 692)
cost-push inflation *inflation* caused by a significant increase in the price of an *input* with economy-wide importance. (p. 309)	**inflación impulsada por costes** *inflación* causada por un aumento significativo en el precio de un *insumo* con importancia en toda la economía. (pág. 309)
credit default swap an agreement that the seller will compensate the buyer in the event of a loan default. (p. EM-7)	**seguro de impago de deuda** acuerdo de que el vendedor compensará al comprador en caso de que haya un incumplimiento en el pago de la deuda. (pág. EM-7)
cross-price elasticity of demand (between two goods) measures the effect of the change in one good's price on the quantity demanded of another good; is equal to the percent change in the quantity demanded of one good divided by the percent change in the other good's price. (p. 455)	**elasticidad de la demanda por cruce de precios** (entre dos productos) mide el efecto que el cambio en el precio de un bien tiene en la cantidad demandada de otro bien; es igual al cambio porcentual en la cantidad demandada de un bien dividida entre el cambio porcentual en el precio del otro bien. (pág. 455)

English

Español

English	Español
crowding out occurs when a government deficit drives up the *interest rate* and leads to reduced *investment spending*. (p. 268)	**efecto expulsión** ocurre cuando el déficit gubernamental empuja la *tasa de interés* en sentido ascendente y lleva a la disminución en los *gastos de inversión*. (pág. 268)
current account see *balance of payments on the current account* (p. 392)	**cuenta corriente** véase *balanza de pagos de la cuenta corriente*. (pág. 392)
curve any line on a graph, regardless of whether it is a straight line or a curved line. (p. 35)	**curva** cualquier línea en un gráfico, sea una línea recta o una línea curva. (pág. 35)
cyclical unemployment the deviation of the actual rate of *unemployment* from the *natural rate*. (p. 128)	**desempleo cíclico** desviación de la tasa de *desempleo* real a partir de su *tasa natural*. (pág. 128)
cyclically adjusted budget balance an estimate of what the *budget balance* would be if *real GDP* were exactly equal to *potential output*. (p. 287)	**equilibrio presupuestario con ajustes cíclicos** estimado de lo que sería el *equilibrio presupuestario* si el *PIB real* fuese exactamente equivalente al *potencial de producción*. (pág. 287)

D

English	Español
deadweight loss the value of foregone mutually beneficial transactions; (from a tax) the decrease in *total surplus* resulting from the tax, minus the tax revenues generated. (pp. 91, 483)	**pérdida irrecuperable de eficiencia** valor de transacciones evitadas que son mutuamente beneficiosas; (a partir de un impuesto) disminución del *superávit total* que resulta de un gravamen, menos los ingresos fiscales generados. (págs. 91, 483)
debt-GDP ratio the government's debt as a percentage of *GDP*. (p. 290)	**proporción de deuda a PIB** deuda gubernamental como porcentaje del *PIB*. (pág. 290)
decreasing returns to scale when output increases less than in proportion to an increase in all inputs. (p. 541)	**rendimientos decrecientes de escala** cuando la producción aumenta menos que en proporcionalidad con un aumento en todos los insumos. (pág. 541)
decreasing-cost industry an industry with a downward-sloping *long-run supply curve*; the firms' production costs decrease as the industry grows. (p. 586)	**industria de costes decrecientes** industria con una *curva de oferta a largo plazo* que presenta una inclinación descendente; los costes de producción de las empresas disminuyen a medida que crece la industria . (pág. 586)
deductible a sum specified in an insurance policy that the insured individuals must pay before being compensated for a claim; reduces *moral hazard*. (p. EM-22)	**deducible** suma que se detalla en una póliza de seguros que los asegurados han de pagar antes de que se les pague una reclamación; reduce el *riesgo moral*. (pág. EM-22)
deflation a falling overall price level. (p. 11)	**deflación** caída generalizada del nivel de precios. (pág. 11)
demand curve a graphical representation of the *demand schedule*; shows the relationship between *quantity demanded* and price. (p. 52)	**curva de demanda** representación gráfica de la *tabla de demanda*; permite apreciar la relación entre la *cantidad demandada* y el precio. (pág. 52)
demand price the price of a given quantity at which consumers will demand that quantity. (p. 89)	**precio de demanda** precio de una cantidad, llegado al cual los consumidores exigen dicha cantidad. (pág. 89)
demand schedule shows how much of a good or service consumers will be willing and able to buy at different prices. (p. 51)	**tabla de demanda** permite apreciar qué cantidad de un bien o servicio los consumidores están dispuestos a comprar y tienen la capacidad de comprar a diferentes precios. (pág. 51)
demand shock an event that shifts the *aggregate demand curve*. (p. 185)	**crisis de demanda** evento que desplaza la *curva de demanda agregada*. (pág. 185)
demand-pull inflation *inflation* caused by an increase in *aggregate demand*. (p. 309)	**inflación arrastrada por la demanda** *inflación* causada por un aumento en la *demanda agregada*. (pág. 309)
dependent variable in a *causal relationship*, the variable that is determined by the *independent variable*. (p. 35)	**variable dependiente** en una *relación causal*, la variable que es determinada por la *variable independiente*. (pág. 35)
depreciation when the value of an asset is reduced by wear, age, or obsolescence; also, when a currency becomes less valuable in terms of other currencies. (pp. 376, 400)	**depreciación** ocurre cuando el valor de un activo se ve reducido por desgaste, edad u obsolescencia, o cuando una moneda pierde valor en relación con otras divisas. (págs. 376, 400)
depression a very deep and prolonged economic downturn. (p. 10)	**depresión** desaceleración económica muy profunda y prolongada. (pág. 10)
derivative a financial contract that has value based on the performance of another asset, index, or *interest rate*. (p. EM-7)	**derivado** contrato financiero cuyo valor se basa en el rendimiento de otro activo, índice o *tasa de interés*. (pág. EM-7)

English

Español

English	Español
derived demand demand for a factor is a derived demand because it results from (that is, it is *derived* from) the demand for the output being produced. (p. 665)	**demanda derivada** la demanda por un factor es una demanda derivada porque es el resultado de la demanda por la producción que se está produciendo. (pág. 665)
devaluation reduction in the value of a currency that is set under a *fixed exchange rate regime*. (p. 411)	**devaluación** reducción en el valor de una moneda que está fijada bajo un régimen de cambio de divisas fijo. (pág. 411)
diminishing marginal rate of substitution principle that states the more of one good a person consumes in proportion to a second good, the less of the second good he or she is willing to substitute for another unit of the first good. (p. EM-31)	**tasa marginal de sustitución decreciente** principio que explica que cuanto más consuma una persona de un bien en proporción a otro bien, menos dispuesta estará dicha persona a reemplazar el segundo bien por otra unidad del primer bien. (pág. EM-31)
diminishing returns to an input when an increase in the quantity of an input, holding the levels of all other inputs fixed, leads to a decline in the *marginal product* of that input. (p. 522)	**rendimientos decrecientes de un insumo** cuando un aumento en la cantidad de ese insumo, manteniendo fijos todos los demás insumos, conduce a una disminución en su *producto marginal*. (pág. 522)
diminishing returns to physical capital exhibited by an *aggregate production function* when, holding the amount of *human capital* per worker and the state of *technology* fixed, each successive increase in the amount of *physical capital* per worker leads to a smaller increase in *productivity*. (p. 355)	**rendimientos decrecientes del capital físico** en una *función de producción agregada* cuando, manteniendo la cantidad de *capital humano* por trabajador y el estado de la *tecnología* fijos, cada aumento sucesivo en la cantidad de *capital físico* por trabajador conduce a un aumento más pequeño en la *productividad*. (pág. 355)
discount rate the *interest rate* the Federal Reserve charges on *loans* to *banks*. (p. 251)	**tasa de descuento** *tasa de interés* que fija el Banco de la Reserva Federal en *préstamos* que hace a *bancos*. (pág. 251)
discouraged workers nonworking people who are capable of working but have given up looking for a job due to the state of the job market. (p. 120)	**trabajadores desalentados** personas que no están empleadas y que tienen la capacidad de trabajar pero que han dejado de buscar empleo debido al estado del mercado laboral. (pág. 120)
discretionary fiscal policy *fiscal policy* that is the result of deliberate actions by policy makers rather than rules. (p. 204)	**política fiscal discrecional** *política fiscal* que es el resultado de acciones deliberadas de las autoridades en lugar de ser producto de las reglas. (pág. 204)
diseconomies of scale when *long-run average total cost* increases as output increases. (p. 541)	**deseconomías de escala** cuando el *coste total promedio a largo plazo* aumenta a medida que aumenta la producción. (pág. 541)
disinflation the process of bringing the *inflation rate* down. (p. 137)	**desinflación** proceso de bajar la *tasa de inflación*. (pág. 137)
disposable income income plus *government transfers* minus taxes; the total amount of *household* income available to spend on consumption and to save. (p. 105)	**ingreso disponible** ingresos más *transferencias gubernamentales* menos los impuestos; cantidad total de ingresos que se puede utilizar en el *hogar* para el consumo y los ahorros. (pág. 105)
dominant strategy a player's best action regardless of the action taken by the other player. (p. 626)	**estrategia dominante** la mejor acción de un jugador independientemente de cualquier acción que tome el otro jugador. (pág. 626)
duopolist each of the two firms in a *duopoly*. (p. 620)	**duopolista** cada una de las dos empresas en un *duopolio*. (pág. 620)
duopoly an *oligopoly* consisting of only two firms. (p. 620)	**duopolio** *oligopolio* que consta de solamente dos empresas. (pág. 620)

E

English	Español
economic aggregates economic measures that summarize data across many different markets. (p. 5)	**agregados económicos** medidas económicas que resumen datos a través de varios mercados. (pág. 5)
economic growth an increase in the maximum amount of goods and services an *economy* can produce. (p. 12)	**crecimiento económico** aumento en la cantidad máxima de bienes y servicios que puede producir una *economía*. (pág. 12)
economic profit a business's *total revenue* minus the *opportunity cost* of its resources; usually less than the *accounting profit*. (p. 511)	**utilidad económica** *ingresos totales* de un negocio menos el *coste de oportunidad* de sus recursos; generalmente es menos que las *utilidades contables*. (pág. 511)
economic rent the payment to a factor of production in excess of the minimum payment necessary to employ that factor. (p. 677)	**renta económica** pago de un factor de producción en exceso del pago mínimo necesario para emplear dicho factor. (pág. 677)
economics the study of scarcity and choice. (p. 2)	**economía (ciencia)** estudio de la escasez y de las opciones disponibles. (pág. 2)
economies of scale when *long-run average total cost* declines as output increases. (p. 541)	**economías de escala** cuando el *coste total promedio a largo plazo* disminuye a medida que aumenta la producción. (pág. 541)

English

Español

English	Español
economy a system for coordinating a society's productive and consumptive activities. (p. 2)	**economía (sistema)** sistema para la coordinación de las actividades de producción y de consumo de una sociedad. (pág. 2)
efficiency wages wages that exceed the market equilibrium wage rate; employers use efficiency wages to motivate hard work and reduce worker turnover. (pp. 128, 698)	**salarios de eficiencia** salarios fijados por encima de la tasa de equilibrio salarial; los empleadores los utilizan como incentivo para lograr un mejor desempeño de los empleados. (págs. 128, 698)
efficient describes a market or *economy* in which there is no way to make anyone better off without making at least one person worse off. (p. 16)	**eficiente** describe un mercado o una *economía* en los que no es posible mejorar la condición de una persona sin empeorar la condición de otra. (pág. 16)
elastic demand when the *price elasticity of demand* is greater than 1. (p. 448)	**demanda elástica** cuando la *elasticidad del precio de la demanda* es mayor que 1. (pág. 448)
employed people who are currently holding a job in the *economy*, either full time or part time. (p. 119)	**empleado** persona que a la fecha tiene empleo en la *economía*, ya sea con dedicación total o dedicación parcial. (pág. 119)
employment the number of people who are currently working for pay in the *economy*. (p. 11)	**empleo** cantidad de personas que actualmente están trabajando por remuneración en la *economía*. (pág. 11)
entrepreneurship the efforts of entrepreneurs in organizing *resources* for production, taking risks to create new enterprises, and innovating to develop new products and production processes. (p. 3)	**espíritu emprendedor** los esfuerzos de los empresarios emprendedores para organizar *recursos* de producción y tomar riesgos a fin de crear empresas nuevas e innovar con miras a desarrollar nuevos productos o procesos de producción. (pág. 3)
environmental standards rules that protect the environment by specifying limits for or actions by producers and consumers. (p. 716)	**normas ambientales** reglas que protegen el medio ambiente al fijar límites en lo que hacen tanto productores como consumidores. (pág. 716)
equilibrium an economic situation when no individual would be better off doing something different; a *competitive market* is in equilibrium when the price has moved to a level at which the *quantity demanded* of goods equals the *quantity supplied* of that good. (p. 68)	**equilibrio** coyuntura económica en la que ninguna persona estaría en mejor condición si hiciera algo diferente;un *mercado competitivo* está en equilibrio cuando el precio se ha desplazado a un nivel en el que la *cantidad demandada* de un bien es igual a la *cantidad ofertada* de dicho bien. (pág. 68)
equilibrium exchange rate the *exchange rate* at which the quantity of a currency demanded in the *foreign exchange market* is equal to the quantity supplied. (p. 401)	**tasa de cambio en equilibrio** *tasa de cambio* en la que la cantidad demandada de una divisa en el *mercado de divisas* es equivalente a la cantidad ofertada. (pág. 401)
equilibrium marginal revenue product the additional revenue generated by the last unit of a factor employed in the factor market as a whole. (p. 677)	**producto de ingreso marginal en equilibrio** ingresos adicionales generados por la última unidad de un factor empleado en el mercado de factores en su conjunto. (pág. 677)
equilibrium price the price of a good at which the *quantity demanded* of that good equals the *quantity supplied* of that good; also known as the *market-clearing price*. (p. 68)	**precio de equilibrio** precio de un bien al que la *cantidad demandada* de dicho bien es equivalente a la *cantidad ofertada* del mismo bien; también denominado *precio de compensación*. (pág. 68)
equilibrium quantity the quantity of a good bought and sold at its *equilibrium price*. (p. 68)	**cantidad de equilibrio** cantidad de un bien comprado y vendido a su *precio de equilibrio*. (pág. 68)
excess capacity when firms in a *monopolistically competitive* industry produce less than the output at which *average total cost* is minimized. (p. 647)	**capacidad en exceso** cuando las empresas de una industria *competitiva monopolista* producen menos que la producción en la que el *coste promedio total* se minimiza. (pág. 647)
excess demand see *shortage* (p. 71)	**demanda excesiva** véase *escasez* (pág. 71)
excess reserves a *bank's* reserves over and above its *required reserves*. (p. 240)	**reservas en exceso** las reservas de un *banco* en exceso de las reservas obligatorias. (pág. 240)
excess supply see *surplus* (p. 70)	**oferta excesiva** véase *superávit* (pág. 70)
exchange rate effect (of a change in the *aggregate price level*) the change in *net exports* caused by a change in the value of the domestic currency, which leads to a change in the relative price of domestic and foreign goods and services (p. 169)	**efecto del tipo de cambio** (de un cambio en el *nivel de precios agregados*) cambio en las exportaciones netas causado por un cambio en el valor de la moneda nacional, el qual conduce a un cambio en el precio relativo de los bienes y servicios nacionales y extranjeros. (pág. 169)
exchange rates the prices at which currencies trade. (p. 399)	**tasas de cambio** precios a los cuales se intercambian divisas. (pág. 399)
excise tax a tax on sales of a particular good or service. (p. 477)	**impuesto de consumo** gravamen por la venta de un bien o servicio en particular. (pág. 477)

English

Español

English	Español
excludable a good is excludable if the supplier of that good can prevent people who do not pay from consuming it. (p. 726)	**excluible** un bien es excluible si el proveedor de dicho bien puede impedir que las personas que no pagan por el mismo lo puedan aprovechar. (pág. 726)
expansion a period of economic upturn in which output and employment are rising; also referred to as *recovery*. (p. 10)	**expansión** período de auge económico en el que la producción y el empleo están creciendo; también denominado *recuperación*. (pág. 10)
expansionary fiscal policy *fiscal policy* that increases *aggregate demand*. (p. 197)	**política fiscal expansiva** *política fiscal* mediante la cual se aumenta la *demanda agregada*. (pág. 197)
expansionary monetary policy *monetary policy* that increases *aggregate demand*. (p. 296)	**política monetaria expansiva** *política monetaria* mediante la cual se aumenta la *demanda agregada*. (pág. 296)
expenditure approach an approach to calculating *GDP* by adding up *aggregate spending* on domestically produced *final goods and services* in the *economy*—the sum of *consumer spending, investment spending, government purchases of goods and services,* and *exports* minus *imports*. (p. 107)	**enfoque de gastos** enfoque para computar el *PIB* sumando los *gastos agregados* en *bienes y servicios finales* producidos internamente en la *economía*. Se trata de la suma de los *gastos de consumo*, los *gastos de inversión*, las compras de bienes y servicios por el gobierno, y las *exportaciones* menos las *importaciones*. (pág. 107)
explicit cost a cost that involves actually laying out money. (p. 510)	**coste explícito** coste que implica un desembolso de dinero. (pág. 510)
exports goods and services sold to other countries. (p. 107)	**exportaciones** bienes y servicios que se venden a otros países. (pág. 107)
external benefit a benefit that an individual or a firm confers on others without receiving compensation. (p. 712)	**beneficio externo** beneficio que una persona o empresa confiere a otros sin recibir ningún pago. (pág. 712)
external cost an uncompensated cost that an individual or a firm imposes on others (p. 712)	**coste externo** coste no remunerado que una persona o empresa impone a otros. (pág. 712)
externalities *external costs* and *external benefits* (p. 712)	**externalidades** *costes externo y beneficios externos* (pág. 712)

F

English	Español
factor distribution of income the division of total income among land, *labor, capital,* and *entrepreneurship*. (p. 666)	**distribución del ingreso entre factores** división del total de ingresos entre terreno, *mano de obra, capital y espíritu emprendedor*. (pág. 666)
factor markets where *resources*, especially *capital* and *labor*, are bought and sold. (p. 105)	**mercados de factores** mercados en los que los *recursos*, sobre todo el *capital* y la *mano de obra*, se compran y se venden. (pág. 105)
federal funds rate the *interest rate* that *banks* charge other banks for *loans*, as determined in the *federal funds market*. (p. 251)	**tasa federal de fondos** *tasa de interés* que los *bancos* cobran a otros bancos por concepto de *préstamos*, tal como se determina en el mercado federal de fondos. (pág. 251)
fiat money a *medium of exchange* whose value derives entirely from its official status as a means of payment. (p. 227)	**dinero fiduciario** *medio de intercambio* cuyo valor se deriva totalmente de su estatus oficial como medio de pago. (pág. 227)
final goods and services goods and services sold to the final, or end, user. (p. 108)	**bienes y servicios finales** bienes y servicios vendidos al usuario final o definitivo. (pág. 108)
financial account see *balance of payments on the financial accounts* (p. 392)	**cuenta financiera** véase *balanza de pagos de la cuenta financiera* (pág. 392)
financial asset a paper claim that entitles the buyer to future income from the seller. (p. 218)	**activo financiero** papel que le da derecho al comprador a ingresos futuros provenientes de un vendedor. (pág. 218)
financial crisis a sudden and widespread disruption of *financial markets*. (p. EM-5)	**crisis financiera** interrupción repentina y generalizada de los *mercados financieros*. (pág. EM-5)
financial intermediary an institution that transforms the funds it gathers from many individuals into *financial assets*. (p. 221)	**intermediario financiero** institución que transforma los fondos que recoge de muchas personas en *activos financieros*. (pág. 221)
financial markets the markets (banking, *stock*, and *bond*) that channel *private savings* and foreign lending into *investment spending*, *government borrowing*, and foreign borrowing. (pp. 106, EM-2)	**mercados financieros** mercados (bancario, *bursátil y de bonos*) que canalizan *ahorros privados y particulares* y préstamos del extranjero en *gastos de inversión, empréstitos gubernamentales* y préstamos al extranjero. (págs. 106, EM-2)

English

Español

financial risk uncertainty about future outcomes that involve financial losses and gains. (p. 219)	**riesgo financiero** incertidumbre acerca de los resultados futuros que implican pérdidas y ganancias financieras. (pág. 219)
firm an organization that produces goods and services for sale. (p. 104)	**empresa** entidad que produce bienes y servicios para la venta. (pág. 104)
fiscal policy the use of government purchases of goods and services, government transfers, or tax policy to stabilize the *economy*. (p. 171)	**política fiscal** uso de la compra de bienes y servicios por parte del gobierno, transferencias gubernamentales o políticas impositivas para estabilizar la *economía*. (pág. 171)
fixed cost (*FC*) a cost that does not depend on the quantity of output produced; the cost of the *fixed input*. (p. 526)	**coste fijo** coste que no depende de la cantidad de producción producida; coste del *insumo fijo*. (pág. 526)
fixed exchange rate exchange rate regime in which the government keeps the *exchange rate* against some other currency at or near a particular target. (p. 408)	**tasa de cambio fija** régimen de cambio de divisas en el que el gobierno mantiene la *tasa de cambio* con respecto a otras divisas en una meta dada o cerca de dicha cifra. (pág. 408)
fixed input an input whose quantity is fixed for a period of time and cannot be varied. (p. 520)	**insumo fijo** insumo cuya cantidad se fija por un período de tiempo y no se puede variar. (pág. 520)
floating exchange rate exchange rate regime in which the government lets the *exchange rate* go wherever the market takes it. (p. 408)	**tasa de cambio flotante** régimen de cambio de divisas en el que el gobierno permite que la *tasa de cambio* vaya hacia dondequiera que el mercado la lleve. (pág. 408)
foreign exchange market the market in which currencies are traded. (p. 399)	**mercado de divisas** mercado en el cual se compran y venden divisas extranjeras. (pág. 399)
framing the creation of context for a product or idea. (p. EM-15)	**marco conceptual** creación de un contexto para un producto o una idea. (pág. EM-15)
free entry and exit when new firms can easily enter into an industry and existing firms can easily leave that industry. (p. 547)	**entrada y salida libres** cuando las empresas nuevas pueden ingresar fácilmente en la industria y las empresas existentes pueden salirse fácilmente de ella. (pág. 547)
free-rider problem goods that are *nonexcludable* suffer from the free-rider problem. Individuals have no incentive to pay for their own consumption and instead will take a "free ride" on anyone who does pay. (p. 727)	**problema del polizón** los bienes que *no son excluibles* sufren del problema del polizón. Las personas no tienen ningún incentivo para pagar por lo que consumen y en lugar aprovechan para ser "polizones" de cualquiera que sí pague. (pág. 727)
frictional unemployment *unemployment* due to the time workers spend in job search. (p. 125)	**desempleo de fricción** *desempleo* atribuible al tiempo que los trabajadores dedican a la búsqueda de empleo. (pág. 125)
full-employment level of output the level of *real GDP* the economy can produce if all resources are fully employed. (p. 180)	**nivel de producción de pleno empleo** el nivel del *PIB real* que la economía puede producir si se emplean todos los recursos disponibles. (pág. 180)
future value the amount to which some current amount of money will grow as interest accumulates over a specified period of time. (p. 230)	**valor futuro** cantidad a la que crecerá alguna suma actual de dinero a medida que acumula intereses durante un período de tiempo especificado. (pág. 230)

G

gains from trade an economic principle that states that people can get more of what they want through *trade* than they could if they tried to be self-sufficient; this increase in *output* is due to *specialization*. (p. 22)	**ganancias logradas de un intercambio** principio económico que manifiesta que las personas pueden obtener más de lo que desean mediante un *intercambio* que lo que podrían lograr si fuesen autosuficientes; este aumento en la *producción* se debe a la *especialización*. (pág. 22)
game theory the study of behavior in situations of *interdependence*. (p. 625)	**teoría de juego** estudio de la conducta en situaciones de *interdependencia*. (pág. 625)
GDP see *gross domestic product*. (p. 107)	**PIB** véase *producto interno bruto*. (pág. 107)
GDP deflator (for a given year) 100 times the ratio of *nominal GDP* to *real GDP* in that year. (p. 144)	**deflactor del PIB** (para un año dado) 100 veces el cociente entre el *PIB nominal* y el *PIB real* en dicho año. (pág. 144)
GDP per capita *GDP* divided by the size of the population; equivalent to the average *GDP* per person. (p. 115)	**PIB per cápita** *PIB* dividido entre el número de habitantes; es equivalente al *PIB* promedio por persona. (pág. 115)
Gini coefficient a number that summarizes a country's level of income inequality based on how unequally income is distributed. (p. 746)	**coeficiente Gini** cifra que resume el nivel de desigualdad en los ingresos de un país con base en la inequidad con la que se distribuyen los ingresos. (pág. 746)
government borrowing the amount of funds borrowed by the government in the *financial markets*. (p. 106)	**empréstito gubernamental** cantidad de fondos que el gobierno toma en préstamo en los *mercados financieros*. (pág. 106)

English

Español

English	Español
government debt the accumulation of past *budget deficits*, minus past *budget surpluses*. (p. 288)	**deuda gubernamental** acumulación de *déficits presupuestarios* del pasado menos los *superávits presupuestarios* del pasado. (pág. 288)
government spending total expenditures on goods and services by federal, state, and local governments (p. 105)	**gasto público** total de gastos por concepto de bienes y servicios de los gobiernos federal, estatales y locales. (pág. 105)
government transfers payments that the government makes to individuals without expecting a good or service in return. (p. 106)	**transferencias gubernamentales** pagos efectuados por el gobierno a personas sin esperar a cambio un bien o un servicio. (pág. 106)
gross domestic product (GDP) the total value of all *final goods and services* produced in the *economy* during a given year. (p. 107)	**producto interno bruto (PIB)** valor total de todos los *bienes y servicios finales* producidos en la *economía* durante un año dado. (pág. 107)

H

English	Español
Herfindahl–Hirschman Index (HHI) the square of each firm's share of market sales summed over the industry; gives a picture of the industry market structure. (p. 550)	**índice Herfindahl-Hirschman (IHH)** cuadrado de la proporción de las ventas en el mercado de la industria que posee cada empresa; da una imagen de la estructura del mercado de dicha industria. (pág. 550)
Homo economicus ("economic man") a fictional economic actor who makes self-interested, informed, rational judgments in pursuit of wealth and leisure. (p. EM-11)	***Homo economicus*** ("hombre económico") actor económico ficticio que toma decisiones informadas, racionales y de interés propio en su búsqueda de riqueza y ocio. (pág. EM-11)
horizontal axis see *x-axis* (p. 35)	**eje horizontal** véase *eje x* (pág. 35)
horizontal intercept indicates the value of the *x*-variable when the value of the *y*-variable is zero. (p. 36)	**intersección horizontal** indica el valor de la variable *x* cuando el valor de la variable *y* es cero. (pág. 36)
household a person or group of people who share income. (p. 104)	**hogar** persona o grupo de personas que comparten sus ingresos. (pág. 104)
human capital the improvement in labor created by the education and knowledge that is embodied in the workforce. (pp. 353, 665)	**capital humano** mejora en la mano de obra creada por la educación y los conocimientos de los integrantes de la fuerza laboral. (págs. 353, 665)

I

English	Español
illiquid describes an asset if it cannot be quickly converted into cash without much loss of value. (p. 219)	**ilíquido** describe un activo si éste no se puede convertir rápidamente en dinero en efectivo sin perder mucho de su valor. (pág. 219)
imperfect competition industry in which no one firm has a *monopoly*, but producers nonetheless realize that they can affect market prices. (p. 550)	**competencia imperfecta** industria en la que ninguna empresa tiene un *monopolio*, pero los productores reconocen que aun así pueden afectar los precios del mercado. (pág. 550)
implicit cost a cost that does not require an outlay of money; it is measured by the value, in dollar terms, of benefits that are foregone. (p. 510)	**coste implícito** coste que no precisa un desembolso de dinero; se mide según el valor, en términos de dólares, de los beneficios que son inevitables. (pág. 510)
implicit cost of capital the *opportunity* cost of the capital used by a business—the income the owner could have realized from that capital if it had been used in its next best alternative way. (p. 512)	**coste implícito del capital** *coste de oportunidad* del capital empleado por un negocio; ingresos que el propietario hubiera realizado de dicho capital si éste se hubiese utilizado en la siguiente mejor manera alternativa. (pág. 512)
import quota a limit on the quantity of a good that can be imported within a given period. (p. 418)	**cuota de importaciones** límite de la cantidad de un bien que se puede importar dentro de un período de tiempo dado. (pág. 418)
imports goods and services purchased from other countries. (p. 107)	**importaciones** bienes y servicios que se compran a otros países. (pág. 107)
incentives rewards or punishments that motivate particular choices. (p. 2)	**incentivos** premios o castigos que motivan a seleccionar una opción u otra. (pág. 2)
income approach an approach to calculating *GDP* by adding up the total factor income earned by households from firms in the economy, including rent, wages, interest, and profit. (p. 107)	**enfoque en ingresos** manera de computar el *PIB* mediante la suma total de los ingresos de factores ganados por los hogares de empresas en la economía, incluidos el arriendo, los salarios, los intereses y las utilidades. (pág. 107)

English

Español

income effect the change in the quantity of a good demanded that results from a change in the consumer's purchasing power when the price of the good changes. (p. 441)	**efecto de los ingresos** cambio en la cantidad de un bien que se demanda a raíz de un cambio en el poder adquisitivo del consumidor cuando cambia el precio del bien. (pág. 441)
income elasticity of demand the percent change in the quantity of a good demanded when a consumer's income changes divided by the percent change in the consumer's income; it measures how changes in income affect the demand for a good. (p. 456)	**elasticidad de la demanda según los ingresos** cambio porcentual en la cantidad de un bien demandado cuando los ingresos de un consumidor cambian dividido entre el cambio porcentual en los ingresos del consumidor; mide cómo los cambios en el ingreso afectan la demanda de un bien. (pág. 456)
income-elastic demand when the *income elasticity of demand* for a good is greater than 1. (p. 456)	**demanda elástica según los ingresos** cuando la *elasticidad de la demanda según los ingresos* por un bien es mayor que 1. (pág. 456)
income-inelastic demand when the *income elasticity of demand* for a good is positive but less than 1. (p. 456)	**demanda inelástica según los ingresos** cuando la *elasticidad de la demanda según los ingresos* por un bien es positiva pero menor que 1. (pág. 456)
increasing returns to scale when output increases more than in proportion to an increase in all inputs; for example, doubling all inputs would cause output to more than double. (p. 541)	**rendimientos crecientes de escala** cuando la producción aumenta más en proporción a un aumento en todos los insumos; por ejemplo, si se duplicaran todos los insumos, la producción aumentaría a más del doble. (pág. 541)
increasing-cost industry an industry with an upward-sloping *long-run supply curve;* the firms' production costs increase with the size of the industry. (p. 584)	**industria de costes crecientes** industria en la que la *curva de oferta a largo plazo* presenta una inclinación ascendente; los costes de producción de las empresas aumentan a la par que el tamaño de la industria. (pág. 584)
independent variable in a *causal relationship,* the variable that determines the *dependent variable.* (p. 35)	**variable independiente** en una *relación causal,* la variable que determina la *variable dependiente.* (pág. 35)
indifference curve shows all the consumption bundles that yield the same amount of total *utility* for an individual. (p. EM-26)	**curva de indiferencia** permite apreciar todos los conjuntos de consumo que producen el mismo nivel total de *utilidad* para una persona. (pág. EM-26)
indifference curve map a collection of *indifference curves,* each of which corresponds to a different total *utility* level; represents an individual's entire *utility function.* (p. EM-26)	**mapa de la curva de indiferencia** colección de *curvas de indiferencia,* cada una de las cuales corresponde a un nivel total de utilidad diferente; representa la totalidad de la función de *utilidad* de una persona. (pág. EM-26)
individual choice decisions by individuals about what to do, which necessarily involve decisions about what not to do. (p. 2)	**opción individual** decisiones que toman las personas sobre qué hacer, las cuales necesariamente implican decisiones sobre qué no hacer. (pág. 2)
individual consumer surplus the net gain to an individual buyer from the purchase of a good; equal to the difference between the buyer's willingness to pay and the price paid. (p. 463)	**superávit del consumidor individual** ganancia neta de un comprador individual gracias a la compra de un bien; es equivalente a la diferencia entre la voluntad del comprador de pagar y el precio pagado. (pág. 463)
individual demand curve illustrates the relationship between *quantity demanded* and price for an individual consumer. (p. 57)	**curva de demanda individual** ilustra la relación entre la *cantidad demandada* y el precio para un consumidor individual. (pág. 57)
individual labor supply curve shows how the quantity of labor supplied by an individual depends on that individual's wage rate. (p. 682)	**curva de oferta de mano de obra individual** permite apreciar cómo la cantidad de mano de obra que proporciona una persona depende de la tasa salarial de dicha persona. (pág. 682)
individual producer surplus the net gain to an individual seller from selling a good; equal to the difference between the price received and the seller's *cost.* (p. 467)	**superávit del productor individual** ganancia neta para un vendedor individual por la venta de un bien; es equivalente a la diferencia entre el precio recibido y los *costes* del vendedor. (pág. 467)
individual supply curve illustrates the relationship between *quantity supplied* and price for an individual producer. (p. 65)	**curva de oferta individual** ilustra la relación entre la *cantidad ofertada* y el precio para un productor individual. (pág. 65)
industry supply curve shows the relationship between the price of a good and the total output of the industry as a whole; also known as *market supply curve.* (p. 580)	**curva de oferta de la industria** permite apreciar la relación entre el precio de un bien y la producción total de toda la industria; también denominado *curva de oferta del mercado.* (pág. 580)
inefficient allocation of sales among sellers a form of inefficiency resulting from *price floors* in which those who would be willing to sell the good at the lowest price are not always those who manage to sell it. (p. 83)	**distribución ineficiente de las ventas entre los vendedores** forma de ineficiencia que resulta de los *pisos de precios* en los que aquellos dispuestos a vender el bien al precio más bajo no siempre son quienes logran venderlo. (pág. 83)

English

Español

English	Español
inefficient allocation to consumers a form of inefficiency often resulting from *price ceilings* in which people who want a good badly and are willing to pay a high price don't get it, and those who care relatively little about the good and are only willing to pay a relatively low price do get it. (p. 80)	**distribución ineficiente a los consumidores** forma de ineficiencia que a menudo resulta de tener *techos de precios* en los que las personas que desean mucho un bien y están dispuestas a pagar un precio alto no lo obtienen, y aquellas a quienes les importa relativamente poco dicho bien y están dispuestas a pagar un precio relativamente bajo sí lo obtienen. (pág. 80)
inefficiently high quality a form of inefficiency resulting from *price floors* in which sellers offer high-quality goods at a high price, even though buyers would prefer a lower quality at a lower price. (p. 84)	**calidad ineficientemente buena** forma de ineficiencia que es el resultado de *pisos de precios* en los que los vendedores ofrecen bienes de buena calidad a un precio alto, aunque los compradores preferirían una calidad inferior a un precio menor. (pág. 84)
inefficiently low quality a form of inefficiency resulting from *price ceilings* in which sellers offer low-quality goods at a low price even though buyers would prefer a higher quality at a higher price. (p. 80)	**calidad ineficientemente mala** forma de ineficiencia que es el resultado de *techos de precios* en los que los vendedores ofrecen bienes de mala calidad a un precio bajo, aunque los compradores preferirían una mejor calidad a un precio más alto. (pág. 80)
inelastic demand when the *price elasticity of demand* is less than 1. (p. 448)	**demanda inelástica** cuando la *elasticidad del precio de demanda* es menor que 1. (pág. 448)
inferior good when a rise in income decreases the demand for a good; an inferior good is usually considered less desirable than more expensive alternatives. (p. 56)	**bien inferior** cuando un aumento en los ingresos disminuye la demanda de un bien; por lo general un bien inferior se considera menos deseable que otras alternativas más costosas. (pág. 56)
inflation a rising overall price level. (p. 11)	**inflación** aumento generalizado del nivel de precios. (pág. 11)
inflation rate the percentage increase in the overall level of prices per year. (p. 134)	**tasa de inflación** aumento porcentual en el nivel generalizado de precios por año. (pág. 134)
inflation targeting when the *central bank* sets an explicit target for the *inflation rate* and sets *monetary policy* in order to hit that target. (p. 298)	**inflación objetivo** ocurre cuando el *banco central* fija un objetivo explícito para la *tasa de inflación* y define la *política monetaria* de manera que se llegue a dicho objetivo. (pág. 298)
inflation tax a reduction in the value of money held by the public caused by *inflation*. (p. 308)	**impuesto inflacionario** reducción en el valor del dinero que está en manos del público; atribuible a la *inflación*. (pág. 308)
inflationary gap when *aggregate output* is above *potential output*. (p. 189)	**brecha inflacionaria** ocurre cuando la *producción agregada* está por encima del *potencial de producción*. (pág. 189)
infrastructure roads, power lines, ports, information networks, and other underpinnings for economic activity. (p. 366)	**infraestructura** vías públicas, tendidos eléctricos, puertos, redes de información y otros apuntalamientos de la actividad económica. (pág. 366)
in-kind benefit a benefit given in the form of goods or services. (p. 749)	**beneficio en especie** beneficio que se da en forma de bienes o servicios. (pág. 749)
input a good or service that is used to produce another good or service. (p. 63)	**insumo** bien o servicio que se utiliza para producir otro bien o servicio. (pág. 63)
interdependence when the outcome (profit) of each firm depends on the actions of the other firms in the market. (p. 620)	**interdependencia** cuando el resultado (las utilidades) de cada empresa depende de lo que hagan las otras empresas en el mercado. (pág. 620)
interest rate the price, calculated as a percentage of the amount borrowed, charged by lenders to borrowers for the use of their savings for one year. (p. 216)	**tasa de interés** precio, computado como un porcentaje de la cantidad tomada en préstamo, que los prestamistas cobran a los prestatarios por el uso de sus ahorros durante un año. (pág. 216)
interest rate effect (of a change in the *aggregate price level*) the change in investment and *consumer spending* caused by altered *interest rates* that result from changes in the demand for money. (p. 168)	**efecto de interés** (de un cambio en el *nivel de precios agregados*) cambio que ocurre en los gastos de inversión y de *consumo* a raíz de alteraciones en *las tasas de interés* como resultado de cambios en la demanda por dinero. (pág. 168)
intermediate goods and services goods and services bought from one firm by another firm to be used as inputs into the production of *final goods and services*. (p. 108)	**bienes y servicios intermedios** bienes y servicios comprados a una empresa por otra a fin de usarlos como insumos en la producción de *bienes y servicios finales*. (pág. 108)
internalize the externalities when individuals take *external costs* or *external benefits* into account, they internalize the externalities. (p. 715)	**internalizar las externalidades** cuando las personas tienen en cuenta los *costes o beneficios externos* internalizan las externalidades. (pág. 715)
inventories stocks of goods and raw materials held to facilitate business operations. (p. 107)	**inventarios** existencias de bienes y materia prima que se mantiene para facilitar las operaciones comerciales de un negocio. (pág. 107)

English

Español

inventory investment the value of the change in total *inventories* held in the *economy* during a given period. Inventory investment is unplanned when a difference between actual sales and expected sales leads to the change in inventories; actual inventory investment is the sum of planned and unplanned inventory investment. (p. 161)	**inversión en inventario** valor del cambio en la totalidad de *inventarios* que se mantienen en la *economía* durante un período de tiempo dado. Una inversión en inventario no es planeada cuando la diferencia entre las ventas reales y las ventas esperadas conduce a un cambio en los inventarios; una inversión en inventario real es la suma de las inversiones en inventario planeadas y no planeadas. (pág. 161)
investment bank a *bank* that trades in *financial assets* and is not covered by deposit insurance. (p. 247)	**banco de inversiones** *banco* que comercia con en *activos financieros* y que no está amparado por ningún seguro de depósitos bancarios. (pág. 247)
investment spending spending on new productive *physical capital*, such as machinery and structures, and on changes in *inventories*. (p. 106)	**gastos de inversión** gastos en *capital físico* nuevo y productivo, tal como maquinaria y estructuras, y en cambios en los *inventarios*. (pág. 106)
investment tax credit an amount that firms are allowed by law to deduct from their taxes based on their *investment spending*. (p. 267)	**crédito fiscal a la inversión** cantidad que las empresas están autorizadas por ley a deducir de sus impuestos con base a sus *gastos de inversión*. (pág. 267)

L

labor the effort of workers. (p. 3)	**trabajo** esfuerzo de los trabajadores. (pág. 3)
labor force the number of people who are either currently holding a job (full time or part time) in the economy or are actively looking for work but aren't currently employed; the sum of *employment* and *unemployment*. (pp. 11, 119)	**fuerza laboral** número de personas que están empleadas activamente en la economía (con dedicación total o parcial) o están buscando empleo activamente pero están desempleadas; suma de los *empleados* y los *desempleados*. (págs. 11, 119)
labor force participation rate the percentage of the population aged 16 or older that is in the *labor force*. (p. 119)	**tasa de participación de la fuerza laboral** porcentaje de la población de los 16 años de edad en adelante que forma parte de la *fuerza laboral*. (pág. 119)
labor productivity output per worker; also known simply as *productivity*. (p. 352)	**productividad de la mano de obra** producción por trabajador; también denominado *productividad*. (pág. 352)
land all *resources* that come from nature, such as minerals, timber, and petroleum. (p. 3)	**terrenos** todos los *recursos* que provienen de la naturaleza, tales como los minerales, la madera y el petróleo. (pág. 3)
law of demand states that a higher price for a good or service, other things being equal, leads people to demand a smaller quantity of that good or service. (p. 52)	**ley de la demanda** manifiesta que un precio más alto por un bien o servicio, si los demás factores son iguales, conduce a que las personas exijan una cantidad menor de dicho bien o servicio. (pág. 52)
law of supply states that, other things being equal, the price and quantity supplied of a good are positively related. (p. 60)	**ley de la oferta** manifiesta que, si los demás factores son iguales, el precio y la cantidad ofertados de un bien están relacionados de manera positiva. (pág. 60)
leisure the time available for purposes other than earning money to buy marketed goods. (p. 681)	**ocio** tiempo disponible para efectos que no sean ganar dinero que se usa par comprar bienes comercializados. (pág. 681)
liability a requirement to pay money in the future. (p. 218)	**obligación** requisito de pagar dinero en el futuro. (pág. 218)
license gives its owner the right to supply a good or service; a form of *quantity control*, as only those who are licensed can supply the good or service. (p. 88)	**licencia** da al licenciatario el derecho a suministrar un bien o servicio; forma de *control de cantidad*, ya que solamente aquellos que cuenten con la debida licencia pueden ofertar el bien o servicio. (pág. 88)
linear relationship the relationship between two *variables* when the *curve* that shows their relationship is a straight line, or linear. (p. 35)	**relación lineal** relación entre dos *variables* cuando la *curva* que nos permite apreciar la relación es una línea recta o lineal. (pág. 35)
liquid describes an asset if it can be quickly converted into cash without much loss of value. (p. 219)	**líquido** describe un activo si éste se puede convertir rápidamente en dinero en efectivo sin mucha pérdida de valor. (pág. 219)
loan a lending agreement between an individual lender and an individual borrower. (p. 220)	**préstamo** convenio para otorgar un crédito entre un prestamista individual y un prestatario individual. (pág. 220)
loanable funds market a hypothetical market that brings together those who want to lend money and those who want to borrow money. (p. 264)	**mercado de fondos prestables** mercado hipotético que une a aquellos deseosos de prestar dinero y a aquellos deseosos de recibir dinero en préstamo. (pág. 264)

English

Español

English	Español
long run the time period in which all inputs can be varied. (p. 520)	**largo plazo** período de tiempo en el que se pueden variar todos los insumos. (pág. 520)
long-run aggregate supply curve shows the relationship between the *aggregate price level* and the quantity of *aggregate output* supplied that would exist if all prices, including *nominal wages*, were fully flexible. (p. 179)	**curva de oferta agregada a largo plazo** permite apreciar la relación entre el *nivel de precios agregados* y la cantidad de *producción agregada* ofertada que existiría si todos los precios, inclusive los *salarios nominales*, fueran totalmente flexibles. (pág. 179)
long-run average total cost curve (*LRATC*) shows the relationship between output and *average total cost* when *fixed cost* has been chosen to minimize average total cost for each level of output. (p. 539)	**curva de costes totales promedio a largo plazo** permite apreciar la relación entre producción y *coste total promedio* cuando se han seleccionado los *costes fijos* para minimizar el coste total promedio para cada nivel de producción. (pág. 539)
long-run industry supply curve shows how the quantity supplied responds to the price once producers have had time to enter or exit the industry. (p. 584)	**curva de oferta de la industria a largo plazo** permite apreciar cómo la cantidad ofertada responde al precio una vez que los productores han tenido tiempo para ingresar o salir de la industria. (pág. 584)
long-run market equilibrium when the quantity supplied equals the quantity demanded, given that sufficient time has elapsed for entry into and exit from the industry to occur. (p. 583)	**equilibrio del mercado a largo plazo** cuando la cantidad ofertada equivale a la cantidad demandada, dado que ha transcurrido suficiente tiempo para que se dé el ingreso y la salida de la industria. (pág. 583)
long-run Phillips curve (*LRPC*) shows the relationship between *unemployment* and *inflation* after expectations of inflation have had time to adjust to experience. (p. 318)	**curva de Phillips a largo plazo (*CPLP*)** permite apreciar la relación entre *desempleo* e *inflación* después de que se le haya dado a las expectativas de inflación tiempo suficiente para ajustarse a la experiencia. (pág. 318)
long-term interest rates *interest rates* on *financial assets* that mature a number of years in the future. (p. 256)	**tasas de interés a largo plazo** *tasas de interés* sobre *activos financieros* que se vencen en unos cuantos años en el futuro. (pág. 256)
Lorenz curve shows the percentage of all income received by the poorest members of the population, from the poorest 0% to the poorest 100%. (p. 746)	**curva de Lorenz** permite apreciar el porcentaje de todos los ingresos percibidos por los integrantes más pobres de la población, desde el más pobre al 0% al más pobre al 100%. (pág. 746)
lump-sum tax a tax of a fixed amount paid by all taxpayers, independent of the taxpayer's income. (pp. 203, 485)	**impuesto de suma fija** impuesto de importe fijo que pagan todos los contribuyentes, independientemente de cuáles sean los ingresos percibidos por el contribuyente. (págs. 203, 485)

M

English	Español
macroeconomics the branch of *economics* that is concerned with the overall ups and downs of the *economy*. (p. 5)	**macroeconomía** rama de la *economía (ciencia)* que trata de las subidas y bajadas generales de la *economía (sistema)*. (pág. 5)
marginal analysis the study of the costs and benefits of doing a little bit more of an activity versus a little bit less. (p. 3)	**análisis marginal** estudio de los costes y beneficios de hacer un poco más de una actividad en contraste con un poco menos. (pág. 3)
marginal cost curve shows how the cost of producing one more unit depends on the quantity that has already been produced. (p. 517)	**curva de costes marginales** permite apreciar cómo el coste de producir una unidad más depende de la cantidad que ya se haya producido. (pág. 517)
marginal cost pricing occurs when regulators set a *monopoly's* price equal to its marginal cost to achieve efficiency. (p. 739)	**fijación de precio según los costes marginales** ocurre cuando los reguladores fijan el precio para un *monopolio* y dicho precio es equivalente a sus costes marginales; se hace con el fin de lograr la eficiencia. (pág. 739)
marginal external benefit the addition to *external benefits* created by one more unit of the good. (p. 720)	**beneficio externo marginal** incorporación de *beneficios externos* creados por una unidad más de un bien. (pág. 720)
marginal external cost the increase in *external costs* to society created by one more unit of the good. (p. 723)	**coste externo marginal** aumento en los *costes externos* para la sociedad creados por una unidad más del bien. (pág. 723)
marginal factor cost the additional cost of employing an additional unit of a factor of production. (p. 685)	**coste de los factores marginal** coste adicional de emplear una unidad adicional de un factor de producción. (pág. 685)
marginal private benefit the marginal benefit that accrues to consumers of the good, not including any *external benefits*. (p. 720)	**beneficio privado marginal** beneficio marginal de un bien que corresponde a los consumidores, sin incluir ningún *beneficio externo*. (pág. 720)
marginal private cost the marginal cost of producing the good, not including any *external costs*. (p. 722)	**coste privado marginal** coste marginal de producir ese bien, sin incluir ningún *coste externo*. (pág. 722)

English

Español

English	Español
marginal product the additional quantity of output produced by using one more unit of an input. (p. 521)	**producto marginal** cantidad adicional de producción producida por el uso de una unidad más de un insumo. (pág. 521)
marginal productivity theory of income distribution states that every *factor of production* is paid the *equilibrium marginal revenue product*. (p. 678)	**teoría de productividad marginal de la distribución de ingresos** a cada *factor de producción* se le paga el *producto de ingreso marginal en equilibrio*. (pág. 678)
marginal propensity to consume (MPC) the increase in *consumer spending* when *disposable income* rises by $1. (p. 157)	**propensión marginal al consumo (PMC)** aumento en los *gastos del consumidor* cuando el *ingreso disponible* aumenta 1$. (pág. 157)
marginal propensity to save (MPS) the increase in household savings when *disposable income* rises by $1. (p. 158)	**propensión marginal al ahorro (PMA)** aumento de los ahorros del hogar cuando el *ingreso disponible* aumenta 1$. (pág. 158)
marginal rate of substitution (MRS) the ratio of the *marginal utility* of one good to the marginal utility of another; equal to MU_R/MU_M, for good R in place of good M. (p. EM-31)	**tasa marginal de sustitución (TMS)** relación entre la *utilidad marginal* de un bien y la utilidad marginal de otro; es equivalente a UM_R/UM_M, donde el bien R sustituye el bien M. (pág. EM-31)
marginal revenue the change in *total revenue* generated by an additional unit of output. (p. 516)	**ingreso marginal** cambio en el *ingreso total* generado por una unidad adicional de producción. (pág. 516)
marginal revenue curve shows how *marginal revenue* varies as output varies. (p. 517)	**curva de ingreso marginal** permite apreciar cómo los *ingresos marginales* varían en la medida en que varía la producción. (pág. 517)
marginal revenue product the additional revenue generated by employing one more unit of a factor. (p. 668)	**producto de ingreso marginal** ingresos adicionales generados al emplear una unidad más de un factor. (pág. 668)
marginal revenue product curve shows how the *marginal revenue product* of a factor depends on the quantity of that factor employed. (p. 670)	**curva del producto de ingreso marginal** permite apreciar cómo el *producto del ingreso marginal* de dicho factor depende de la cantidad del factor que se emplee. (pág. 670)
marginal social benefit the additional gain to society as a whole from an additional unit. (p. 713)	**beneficio social marginal** ganancia adicional para toda la sociedad de una unidad adicional. (pág. 713)
marginal social cost the additional cost imposed on society as a whole by one additional unit. (p. 713)	**coste social marginal** coste adicional impuesto sobre toda la sociedad por una unidad adicional. (pág. 713)
marginal utility the change in total *utility* generated by consuming one additional unit of a good or service. (p. 489)	**utilidad marginal** cambio en la *utilidad* total generado por el consumo de una unidad adicional de un bien o servicio. (pág. 489)
marginal utility curve shows how *marginal utility* depends on the quantity of a good or service consumed. (p. 490)	**curva de utilidad marginal** permite apreciar cómo la *utilidad marginal* depende de la cantidad de un bien o servicio que se ha consumido. (pág. 490)
marginal utility per dollar the additional *utility* from spending one more dollar on a good or service. (p. 494)	**utilidad marginal por dólar** *utilidad* adicional obtenida al gastar un dólar más en un bien o servicio. (pág. 494)
marginally attached workers people who would like to be employed and have looked for a job in the recent past but are not currently looking for work. (p. 120)	**trabajadores vinculados marginalmente** personas que quisieran estar empleadas y han buscado empleo recientemente, pero actualmente no están buscando empleo. (pág. 120)
market basket a hypothetical set of consumer purchases of goods and services. (p. 140)	**canasta familiar** conjunto hipotético de compras de bienes y servicios que hace el consumidor. (pág. 140)
market economy an *economy* in which the decisions of individual producers and consumers largely determine what, how, and for whom to produce, with little government involvement in the decisions. (p. 2)	**economía de mercado** *economía* en la que las decisiones que toman los productores y consumidores individuales determinan en gran parte qué, cómo y para quién se produce, con poca intervención del gobierno en las decisiones. (pág. 2)
market failure when the outcome in a market is ineffective (p. 712)	**fallo de mercado** cuando el resultado en un mercado es ineficiente. (pág. 712)
market share the fraction of the total industry output accounted for by a given firm's output. (p. 546)	**proporción del mercado** fracción de la producción total de la industria que está representada por la producción de una empresa. (pág. 546)
market supply curve see *industry supply curve* (p. 65)	**curva de oferta del mercado** véase *curva de oferta de la industria* (pág. 65)
market-clearing price see *equilibrium price* (p. 68)	**precio de compensación** véase *precio de equilibrio* (pág. 68)
maximum point the point along a *curve* with the largest value of *y*. (p. 40)	**punto máximo** punto a lo largo de una *curva* con el valor más alto de *y*. (pág. 40)
mean household income the average income across all *households*. (p. 746)	**media de ingresos del hogar** ingresos promedio teniendo en cuenta todos los *hogares*. (pág. 746)

English

Español

means-tested program program available only to individuals or families whose incomes fall below a certain level. (p. 749)	**programa de selección según los medios** programa disponible solamente para personas o familias cuyos ingresos caen por debajo de cierto nivel. (pág. 749)
median household income the income of the *household* lying in the middle of the income distribution. (p. 746)	**ingresos medios de los hogares** ingresos del *hogar* que yacen en la mitad de la distribución de ingresos. (pág. 746)
medium of exchange an asset that individuals acquire for the purpose of trading for goods and services rather than for their own consumption. (p. 225)	**medio de intercambio** activo que las personas adquieren con el fin de intercambiarlo por bienes y servicios en lugar de consumirlo. (pág. 225)
menu costs the real costs of changing listed prices. (p. 135)	**costes de menú** costes reales de cambiar los precios de una lista de precios. (pág. 135)
merchandise trade balance the difference between a country's *exports* and *imports* of goods; also known as *trade balance* (p. 392)	**balanza comercial de mercancía** diferencia entre las *exportaciones* e *importaciones* de bienes de un país; también denominado *balanza comercial*. (pág. 392)
microeconomics the branch of *economics* that studies how individuals, *households,* and firms make decisions and how those decisions interact. (p. 5)	**microeconomía** rama de la *economía* en la que se estudia cómo las personas, los *hogares* y las empresas toman decisiones y cómo dichas decisiones interactúan. (pág. 5)
midpoint method a technique for calculating the percent change by dividing the change in a *variable* by the average, or midpoint, of the initial and final values of that variable. (p. 444)	**método del punto intermedio** técnica para computar el cambio porcentual dividiendo el cambio en una *variable* entre el promedio o punto intermedio de los valores inicial y final de dicha variable. (pág. 444)
minimum efficient scale the smallest quantity at which a firm's long-run average total costs is minimized. (p. 541)	**la escala mínima eficiente** la cantidad reducida en la que se minimizan los costos totales promedio a largo plazo de una empresa. (pág. 541)
minimum point the point along a *curve* with the smallest value of *y*. (p. 40)	**punto mínimo** punto a lo largo de una *curva* con el valor más pequeño de *y*. (pág. 40)
minimum wage a legal floor on the hourly wage rate paid for a worker's labor. (p. 82)	**salario mínimo** piso legal en la tasa salarial por hora que se paga por el trabajo de un trabajador. (pág. 82)
minimum-cost output the quantity of output at which *average total cost* is lowest; corresponds to the bottom of the *U-shaped average total cost curve.* (p. 533)	**producción al coste mínimo** cantidad de producción en la que el *coste total promedio* es más bajo; corresponde a la parte más baja de la *curva de costes totales promedio en forma de U.* (pág. 533)
model a simplified representation used to better understand a real-life situation. (p. 13)	**modelo** representación simplificada que se usa para entender con más claridad una coyuntura de la vida real. (pág. 13)
monetarism asserts that *GDP* will grow steadily if the *money supply* grows steadily. (p. 326)	**monetarismo** afirma que el *PIB* crecerá de manera uniforme si el *dinero en circulación* crece con constancia. (pág. 326)
monetary aggregate an overall measure of the *money supply.* (p. 227)	**agregado monetario** medición general del *dinero en circulación.* (pág. 227)
monetary base the sum of currency in circulation and *bank reserves.* (p. 241)	**base monetaria** suma de dinero en circulación más las *reservas bancarias.* (pág. 241)
monetary neutrality the concept that changes in the *money supply* have no real effects on the *economy.* (p. 302)	**neutralidad monetaria** concepto de que los cambios en el *dinero en circulación* no tienen efectos reales en la *economía.* (pág. 302)
monetary policy the central bank's use of changes in the quantity of money or the *interest rate* to stabilize the *economy.* (p. 172)	**política monetaria** uso por el banco central de cambios en la cantidad de dinero o *la tasa de interés* con el fin de estabilizar la *economía.* (pág. 172)
money any asset that can easily be used to purchase goods and services. (p. 224)	**dinero** todo activo que se pueda utilizar fácilmente para comprar bienes y servicios. (pág. 224)
money demand curve (MD) shows the relationship between the quantity of money demanded and the *interest rate.* (p. 258)	**curva de demanda de dinero** permite apreciar la relación entre la cantidad de dinero demandada y la *tasa de interés.* (pág. 258)
money multiplier the ratio of the *money supply* to the *monetary base*; indicates the total number of dollars created in the banking system by each $1 addition to the *monetary base.* (p. 241)	**multiplicador monetario** relación entre el *dinero en circulación* y la *base monetaria*; indica el número total de dólares creados en el sistema bancario por cada adición de 1$ a la *base monetaria.* (pág. 241)
money supply the total value of *financial assets* in the *economy* that are considered *money.* (p. 225)	**dinero en circulación** valor total de los *activos financieros* en la *economía* que se consideran *dinero.* (pág. 225)
money supply curve shows the relationship between the quantity of money supplied and the *interest rate.* (p. 260)	**curva del dinero en circulación** permite apreciar la relación entre la cantidad de dinero en circulación y la *tasa de interés.* (pág. 260)
monopolist the only producer of a good that has no close *substitutes.* (p. 548)	**monopolista** el único productor de un bien que no tiene *sustitutos* cercanos. (pág. 548)

English

Español

English	Español
monopolistic competition market structure in which there are many competing firms in an industry, each firm sells a differentiated product, and there is *free entry* into and exit from the industry in the *long run*. (p. 552)	**competencia monopolística** estructura de mercado en la que muchas empresas compiten en una industria, cada empresa vende un producto diferenciado y existe una *entrada y una salida libres* de la industria a *largo plazo*. (pág. 552)
monopoly an industry controlled by a *monopolist*. (p. 548)	**monopolio** industria controlada por un *monopolista*. (pág. 548)
monopsonist a single buyer in a factor market. (p. 685)	**monopsonista** un comprador único en un mercado de factores. (pág. 685)
monopsony a market in which there is a *monopsonist*. (p. 685)	**monopsonio** mercado en el que hay un *monopsonista*. (pág. 685)
moral hazard a distortion of incentives when someone else bears the costs of a lack of care or effort; arises when an individual knows more about his or her own actions than other people do. (pp. EM-7, EM-22)	**riesgo moral** distorsión de incentivos cuando otra persona responde por los costes de la falta de atención o esfuerzo; surge cuando una persona tiene más información sobre sus propias acciones que otras. (págs. EM-7, EM-22)
movement along the demand curve a change in the *quantity demanded* of a good that is the result of a change in that good's price. (p. 53)	**movimiento a lo largo de la curva de demanda** cambio en la *cantidad demandada* de un bien. Es el resultado de un cambio en el precio de dicho bien. (pág. 53)
movement along the supply curve a change in the *quantity supplied* of a good arising from a change in the good's price. (p. 62)	**movimiento a lo largo de la curva de oferta** cambio en la *cantidad ofertada* de un bien. Es el resultado de un cambio en el precio de dicho bien. (pág. 62)

N

English	Español
Nash equilibrium the result when each player in a game chooses the action that maximizes his or her payoff, given the actions of other players; also called *noncooperative equilibrium*. (p. 627)	**equilibrio de Nash** resultado que se obtiene cuando cada jugador de un juego opta por la acción que maximiza sus ganancias, dadas las acciones de los demás jugadores; también denominado *equilibrio no cooperativo*. (pág. 627)
national accounts see *national income and product accounts* (p. 104)	**cuentas nacionales** véase *cuentas nacionales de rentas y productos* (pág. 104)
national income and product accounts keep track of the flows of money among different sectors of the *economy*; in the United States, calculated by the Bureau of Economic Analysis; also known as *national accounts* (p. 104)	**cuentas nacionales de rentas y productos** lleva el control de los movimientos de dinero entre los diversos sectores de la *economía*; en Estados Unidos las computa la Oficina de Análisis Económico; también denominado *cuentas nacionales*. (pág. 104)
national savings the sum of private savings and the *budget balance*; the total amount of savings generated within the *economy*. (p. 217)	**ahorros nacionales** suma de los ahorros privados y el *equilibrio presupuestario*; total de ahorros generados dentro de la *economía*. (pág. 217)
natural monopoly when *economies of scale* provide a large cost advantage to a single firm that produces all of an industry's output. (p. 548)	**monopolio natural** cuando las *economías de escala* ofrecen una ventaja grande en costes a una sola empresa que produce toda la producción de una industria. (pág. 548)
natural rate of unemployment the *unemployment rate* that arises from the effects of *frictional* plus *structural unemployment*. (p. 128)	**tasa natural de desempleo** *tasa de desempleo* que surge de los efectos del *desempleo de fricción* y del *desempleo estructural*. (pág. 128)
negative externalities *external costs*. (p. 712)	**externalidades negativas** *costes externos*. (pág. 712)
negative income tax a program that supplements the income of low-income workers. (p. 749)	**impuesto sobre la renta negativo** programa que complementa los ingresos de los trabajadores de bajos ingresos. (pág. 749)
negative relationship the relationship between two *variables* when an increase in one variable is associated with a decrease in the other variable. (p. 36)	**relación negativa** relación entre dos *variables* en la que un aumento en una variable se asocia con una disminución en la otra variable. (pág. 36)
net exports the difference between the value of *exports* and the value of *imports*; $(X - M)$. (p. 109)	**exportaciones netas** diferencia entre el valor de las *exportaciones* y el valor de las *importaciones*; $(X - M)$. (pág. 109)
net present value the *present value* of current and future benefits minus the *present value* of current and future costs. (p. 232)	**valor presente neto** *valor presente* de los beneficios actuales y futuros menos el *valor presente* de los costes actuales y futuros. (pág. 232)
network externality when the value of a good to an individual depends on how many people also use the good. (p. 724)	**externalidad de red** cuando el valor de un bien para una persona depende de qué cantidad de personas también usan el bien. (pág. 724)

English

Español

English	Español
nominal GDP the total value of all *final goods and services* produced in the *economy* during a given year, calculated with the prices current in the year in which the *output* is produced. (p. 115)	**PIB nominal** valor total de todos los *bienes y servicios finales* producidos en la *economía* durante un año dado y computados con los precios vigentes en el año en que se produce la *producción*. (pág. 115)
nominal interest rate the interest rate actually paid for a *loan*. (p. 136)	**tasa de interés nominal** tasa de interés que en efecto se paga por un *préstamo*. (pág. 136)
nominal wage the dollar amount of the wage paid. (p. 175)	**salario nominal** cantidad en dólares que se paga por concepto salarial. (pág. 175)
nonaccelerating inflation rate of unemployment (NAIRU) the *unemployment rate* at which *inflation* does not change over time. (p. 318)	**tasa de desempleo no aceleradora de la inflación** *tasa de desempleo* en la cual la *inflación* no varía a través del tiempo. (pág. 318)
noncooperative behavior when firms act in their own self-interest, ignoring the effects of their actions on each other's profits. (p. 622)	**conducta no cooperativa** cuando las empresas funcionan exclusivamente en su interés propio, haciendo caso omiso de los efectos que sus acciones podrían tener en las utilidades de los demás. (pág. 622)
noncooperative equilibrium see *Nash equilibrium*. (p. 627)	**equilibrio no cooperativo** véase *equilibrio de Nash*. (pág. 627)
nonexcludable when a good is nonexcludable, the supplier cannot prevent consumption by people who do not pay for it. (p. 726)	**no excluible** cuando un bien no es excluible el proveedor no puede impedir que lo consuman personas que no han pagado por él. (pág. 726)
nonlinear curve a *curve* along which the *slope* changes. (p. 38)	**curva no lineal** *curva* a lo largo de la cual la *pendiente* cambia. (pág. 38)
nonlinear relationship the relationship between two *variables* when the *curve* that shows their relationship is not a straight line, or is nonlinear. (p. 35)	**relación no lineal** relación entre dos *variables* cuando la *curva* en la que se aprecia su relación no es rectilínea o no es lineal. (pág. 35)
nonprice competition when firms that have a tacit understanding not to compete on price use advertising and other means to try to increase their sales. (p. 639)	**competencia no basada en el precio** cuando las empresas que tienen un acuerdo tácito de no competir por precio utilizan la publicidad u otros medios para tratar de aumentar sus ventas. (pág. 639)
nonrival in consumption a good is nonrival in consumption if more than one person can consume the same unit of the good at the same time. (p. 726)	**no rival en el consumo** un bien no es rival en el consumo si más de una persona puede consumir la misma unidad del bien al mismo tiempo. (pág. 726)
normal good when a rise in income increases the demand for a good; most goods are normal goods. (p. 56)	**bien normal** cuando un aumento en los ingresos aumenta la demanda por un bien; la mayoría de los bienes son bienes normales. (pág. 56)
normal profit an *economic profit* equal to zero; an economic profit just high enough to keep a firm engaged in its current activity. (p. 513)	**utilidades normales** *utilidades económicas* equivalentes a cero; utilidades económicas justo lo suficientemente altas para mantener a una empresa en marcha realizando su actividad actual. (pág. 513)
normative economics the branch of economic analysis that makes prescriptions about the way the *economy* should work. (p. 5)	**economía normativa** rama del análisis económico que formula prescripciones sobre la manera como ha de funcionar la *economía*. (pág. 5)

O

English	Español
oligopolist a producer in an *oligopoly*. (p. 549)	**oligopolista** productor en un *oligopolio*. (pág. 549)
oligopoly an industry with only a small number of firms. (p. 549)	**oligopolio** industria con tan solo una cantidad pequeña de empresas. (pág. 549)
open market operation a purchase or sale of *government debt* by the Federal Reserve. (p. 252)	**operación de mercado abierto** compra o venta de la *deuda gubernamental* por el Banco de la Reserva Federal. (pág. 252)
opportunity cost the real cost of an item: the value of the next best alternative that you must give up in order to get that item. (p. 4)	**coste de oportunidad** coste real de un artículo: valor de la siguiente mejor alternativa que se tiene que entregar para obtenerlo. (pág. 4)
optimal consumption bundle the consumption bundle that maximizes the consumer's total *utility* given his or her *budget constraint*. (p. 492)	**conjunto de consumo óptimo** conjunto de consumo que maximiza la *utilidad* total para el consumidor dadas sus *restricciones presupuestarias*. (pág. 492)

English

Español

English	Español
optimal consumption rule says that in order to maximize *utility*, a consumer must equate the *marginal utility per dollar* spent on each good and service in the consumption bundle. (p. 497)	**regla de consumo óptimo** explica que a fin de maximizar la utilidad, el consumidor tiene que equilibrar la *utilidad marginal por dólar* dedicado a cada bien o servicio en el conjunto de consumo. (pág. 497)
optimal output rule says that profit is maximized by producing the quantity of output at which the *marginal revenue* of the last unit produced is equal to its marginal cost. (p. 516)	**regla de producción óptima** explica que las utilidades se maximizan al producir la cantidad de producción en la que el *ingreso marginal* de la última unidad producida es equivalente a su coste marginal. (pág. 516)
ordinary goods in a consumer's *utility function*, goods for which (1) the consumer requires additional units of one good to compensate for fewer units of another, and vice versa; and (2) the consumer experiences a *diminishing marginal rate of substitution* when substituting one good for the other. (p. EM-32)	**bienes ordinarios** en la función de utilidad de un consumidor, bienes por los cuales (1) el consumidor requiere unidades adicionales de un bien para compensar las pocas unidades de otro, y viceversa; y (2) el consumidor experimenta una *tasa marginal de sustitución decreciente* cuando se sustituye un bien por otro. (pág. EM-32)
origin the point where the *(horizontal)* x-axis and *(vertical)* y-axis meet. (p. 35)	**origen** punto en el cual se encuentran el *eje x (horizontal)* y el *eje y (vertical)*. (pág. 35)
other things equal assumption in the development of a *model*, the assumption that all other relevant factors remain unchanged; also known as the *ceteris paribus assumption*. (p. 13)	**supuesto de que todos los demás factores seguirán iguales** en la creación de un *modelo*, supuesto de que todos los demás factores pertinentes seguirán sin cambio; también denominado *supuesto ceteris paribus*. (pág. 13)
output the quantity of goods and services produced. (p. 11)	**producción** cantidad de bienes y servicios producidos. (pág. 11)
output gap the percentage difference between actual *aggregate output* and *potential output*. (p. 189)	**brecha de producción** diferencia porcentual entre la *producción agregada* real y el *potencial de producción*. (pág. 189)
overuse the depletion of a common resource that occurs when individuals ignore the fact that their use depletes the amount of the resource remaining for others. (p. 732)	**consumo excesivo** agotamiento de un recurso común que sucede cuando las personas hacen caso omiso del hecho de que ese consumo agota la cantidad de ese recurso que queda para uso de los demás. (pág. 732)

P

English	Español
patent gives an inventor a temporary *monopoly* in the use or sale of an invention. (p. 549)	**patente** da al inventor un *monopolio* temporal en el uso o la venta de una invención. (pág. 549)
payoff the reward received by a player in a game, such as the profit earned by an *oligopolist*. (p. 625)	**pago** premio recibido por un jugador, tales como las utilidades obtenidas por un *oligopolista*. (pág. 625)
payoff matrix shows how the *payoff* to each of the participants in a two-player game depends on the actions of both. Such a matrix helps us analyze situations of *interdependence*. (p. 625)	**matriz de pago** permite apreciar cómo el *pago* a cada uno de los participantes en un juego de dos jugadores depende de las acciones de ambos. Tal matriz nos sirve para analizar coyunturas de *interdependencia*. (pág. 625)
perfect price discrimination when a *monopolist* charges each consumer his or her *willingness to pay*—the maximum that the consumer is willing to pay. (p. 606)	**discriminación de precios perfecta** cuando un *monopolista* cobra a cada consumidor en función de su *voluntad de pago*; el máximo que el consumidor paga por voluntad propia. (pág. 606)
perfectly competitive industry an industry in which firms are *price takers*. (p. 546)	**industria perfectamente competitiva** industria en la que las empresas son *aceptadoras de precios*. (pág. 546)
perfectly competitive market a market in which all market participants are *price takers*. (p. 546)	**mercado perfectamente competitivo** mercado en el que todos los participantes en el mercado son *aceptadores de precios*. (pág. 546)
perfectly elastic demand when any price increase will cause the *quantity demanded* to drop to zero; when demand is perfectly elastic, the *demand curve* is a horizontal line. (p. 448)	**demanda perfectamente elástica** cuando como resultado de cualquier aumento de precio la *cantidad demandada* cae a cero; cuando la demanda es perfectamente elástica la *curva de demanda* es una línea horizontal. (pág. 448)
perfectly elastic supply when the quantity supplied is zero below some price and approaches infinity above that price; a perfectly elastic *supply curve* is a horizontal line. (p. 458)	**oferta perfectamente elástica** cuando la cantidad ofertada es cero por debajo de cierto precio y se aproxima al infinito por encima de dicho precio; una *curva de oferta* perfectamente elástica es una línea horizontal. (pág. 458)

English

Español

English	Español
perfectly inelastic demand when the *quantity demanded* does not respond at all to changes in the price; when demand is perfectly inelastic, the *demand curve* is a vertical line. (p. 448)	**demanda perfectamente inelástica** cuando la *cantidad demandada* no parece responder a todos los cambios en el precio; cuando la demanda es perfectamente inelástica la *curva de demanda* es una línea vertical. (pág. 448)
perfectly inelastic supply when the price elasticity of supply is zero, so that changes in the price of the good have no effect on the quantity supplied; a perfectly inelastic *supply curve* is a vertical line. (p. 458)	**oferta perfectamente inelástica** cuando la elasticidad del precio de la oferta es cero, de manera que los cambios en el precio del bien no tienen ningún efecto en la cantidad ofertada; una *curva de oferta* perfectamente inelástica es una línea vertical. (pág. 458)
physical asset a claim on a tangible object that gives the owner the right to dispose of the object as he or she wishes. (p. 218)	**activo físico** derecho sobre un objeto tangible que da al propietario el derecho de disponer de dicho objeto según desee. (pág. 218)
physical capital often referred to simply as *capital*—consists of manufactured (human-made) productive resources, such as equipment, buildings, tools, and machines, used to produce other goods and services. (pp. 352, 665)	**capital físico** a menudo se le dice simplemente *capital*. Consta de recursos productivos manufacturados (hechos por el hombre) tales como equipos, edificaciones, herramientas y maquinaria, que se usan para producir otros bienes y servicios. (págs. 352, 665)
pie chart a chart that shows the share of a total amount that is accounted for by various components, usually expressed in percentages. (p. 43)	**gráfico circular** cuadro en el que se aprecia la proporción un total que está representado por diversos componentes, generalmente expresados como porcentajes. (pág. 43)
Pigouvian subsidy a payment designed to correct for the effects of *external benefits*. (p. 722)	**subsidio pigouviano** pago diseñado para corregir los efectos de *beneficios externos*. (pág. 722)
Pigouvian taxes taxes designed to correct for the effects of *external costs*. (p. 724)	**impuestos pigouvianos** impuestos diseñados para corregir los efectos de *costes externos*. (pág. 724)
planned investment spending the *investment spending* that businesses intend to undertake during a given period. (p. 160)	**gastos de inversión planificados** *gastos de inversión* que las empresas tienen la intención de emprender durante un período de tiempo dado. (pág. 160)
positive economics the branch of economic analysis that describes the way the *economy* actually works. (p. 5)	**economía positiva** rama del análisis económico que describe la manera en la que realmente funciona la *economía*. (pág. 5)
positive externalities *external benefits*. (p. 712)	**externalidades positivas** *beneficios externos*. (pág. 712)
positive relationship the relationship between two *variables* when an increase in one variable is associated with an increase in the other variable. (p. 35)	**relación positiva** relación entre dos *variables* cuando un aumento en una variable se asocia con un aumento en la otra variable. (pág. 35)
potential output the level of *real GDP* the *economy* would produce if all prices, including *nominal wages*, were fully flexible. (p. 179)	**potencial de producción** nivel del *PIB real* que la *economía* produciría si todos los precios, incluidos los *salarios nominales*, fueran totalmente flexibles. (pág. 179)
poverty rate the percentage of the population with incomes below the *poverty threshold*. (p. 743)	**tasa de pobreza** porcentaje de la población con ingresos por debajo del *umbral de pobreza*. (pág. 743)
poverty threshold the annual income below which a family is officially considered poor. (p. 743)	**umbral de pobreza** ingresos anuales por debajo de los cuales a una familia se le considera pobre. (pág. 743)
present value (of $1 realized one year from now) the amount of money you must lend out today in order to have $1 in one year; the value to you today of $1 realized one year from now; $1/(1 + r)$. (p. 231)	**valor presente** (de 1$ realizado dentro de un año contado a partir de ahora) cantidad de dinero que una persona tiene que prestar hoy para tener 1$ en un año. Se trata del valor que tiene para una persona hoy 1$ realizado dentro de un año; $1\$ /(1 + r)$. (pág. 231)
price ceiling a maximum price that sellers are allowed to charge for a good or service. (p. 77)	**techo de precios** precio máximo que a los vendedores se les permite cobrar por un bien o servicio. (pág. 77)
price controls legal restrictions on how high or low a market price may go; typically take the form of either a *price ceiling* or a *price floor*. (p. 77)	**controles de precios** restricciones legales de cuán alto o cuán bajo puede subir o bajar el precio de mercado; casi siempre se presenta en la forma de ya sea un *techo de precios* o bien de un *piso de precios*. (pág. 77)
price discrimination when firms charge different prices to different consumers for the same good. (p. 603)	**discriminación por precio** cuando los vendedores cobran precios diferentes a diferentes clientes por el mismo bien. (pág. 603)
price elasticity of demand the ratio of the percent change in the *quantity demanded* to the percent change in the price as we move along the *demand curve* (dropping the minus sign). (p. 442)	**elasticidad del precio de demanda** relación entre el cambio porcentual en la *cantidad demandada* y el cambio porcentual en el precio a medida que avanzamos en la *curva de demanda* (sin el signo de menos). (pág. 442)

English	Español
price elasticity of supply a measure of the responsiveness of the quantity of a good supplied to changes in the price of that good; the ratio of the percent change in the quantity supplied to the percent change in the price as we move along the *supply curve*. (p. 457)	**elasticidad de precio de oferta** medida de la reacción de la cantidad de un bien ofertado a lo cambios en el precio de ese bien; relación entre el cambio porcentual en la cantidad ofertada y el cambio porcentual en el precio a medida que avanzamos en la *curva de oferta*. (pág. 457)
price floor a minimum price that buyers are required to pay for a good or service. (p. 77)	**piso de precios** precio mínimo que se les exige pagar a los compradores por un bien o servicio. (pág. 77)
price index measures the cost of purchasing a given *market basket* in a given year; the index value is normalized so that it is equal to 100 in the selected *base year*. (p. 141)	**índice de precios** mide el coste de comprar una *canasta familiar* dada en un año dado; el valor del índice se normaliza de manera que sea igual a 100 en el *año base* escogido. (pág. 141)
price leadership one firm sets its price first, and other firms then follow. (p. 639)	**liderazgo en precios** una empresa fija el precio primero y luego las otras empresas la siguen. (pág. 639)
price regulation limits the price that a *monopolist* is allowed to charge. (p. 600)	**reglamentación de precios** limita el precio que se le permite cobrar a un *monopolista*. (pág. 600)
price stability when the overall price level is changing only slowly if at all. (p. 12)	**estabilidad de precios** cuando el nivel de precios en general apenas cambia lentamente o no cambia. (pág. 12)
price war when *tacit collusion* breaks down and aggressive price competition causes prices to collapse. (p. 638)	**guerra de precios** cuando se desploma una *colusión tácita* y la competencia de precios tenaz hace colapsar los precios. (pág. 638)
price-taking consumer a consumer whose actions have no effect on the market price of the good or service he or she buys. (p. 546)	**consumidor aceptador de precios** consumidor cuyas acciones no tienen ningún efecto en el precio de mercado del bien o servicio que ha comprado. (pág. 546)
price-taking firm a firm whose actions have no effect on the market price of the good or service it sells. (p. 546)	**empresa aceptadora de precios** empresa cuyas acciones no tienen ningún efecto en el precio de mercado del bien o servicio que vende. (pág. 546)
price-taking firm's optimal output rule says that a *price-taking firm's* profit is maximized by producing the quantity of output at which the market price is equal to the marginal cost of the last unit produced. (p. 567)	**regla sobre la producción óptima de empresas aceptadores de precios** explica que las utilidades de una *empresa aceptadora de precios* se maximizan produciendo la cantidad de producción en la cual el precio de mercado es igual al coste marginal de la última unidad producida. (pág. 567)
principle of diminishing marginal utility states that each successive unit of a good or service consumed adds less to total *utility* than does the previous unit. (p. 490)	**principio de la utilidad marginal decreciente** explica que cada unidad sucesiva de un bien o servicio que se consume agrega menos a la *utilidad* total que la unidad anterior. (pág. 490)
principle of marginal analysis says that every activity should continue until marginal benefit equals marginal cost. (p. 516)	**principio del análisis marginal** explica que toda actividad debería proseguir hasta que el beneficio marginal sea equivalente al coste marginal. (pág. 516)
prisoners' dilemma a game based on two premises: (1) each player has an incentive to choose an action that benefits itself at the other player's expense; and (2) when both players follow this incentive, both are worse off than if they had acted cooperatively. (p. 626)	**dilema del prisionero** juego basado en dos premisas: (1) cada jugador tiene un incentivo para escoger una acción que lo beneficie a costas del otro jugador; y (2) cuando ambos jugadores actúan de tal manera a ambos les va peor que si hubieran actuado de manera cooperativa. (pág. 626)
private good a good that is both *excludable* and *rival in consumption*. (p. 726)	**bien privado** bien que es tanto *excluible* como *rival en el consumo*. (pág. 726)
private information information that some people have and others do not; also known as *asymmetric information*. (p. EM-19)	**información privada o reservada** información que algunas personas tienen y otras no; también denominado *información asimétrica*. (pág. EM-19)
private savings *disposable income* minus *consumer spending*; disposable income that is not spent on consumption but rather often goes into *financial markets*. (p. 106)	**ahorros privados** *ingresos disponibles* menos los *gastos de consumo*; ingresos disponibles que no se utilizan para consumir sino pasan a los *mercados financieros*. (pág. 106)
producer price index (PPI) measures the prices of goods and services purchased by producers. (p. 144)	**índice de precios del productor (IPP)** mide los precios de bienes y servicios que compran los productores. (pág. 144)
producer surplus refers to both *individual* and *total producer surplus*. (p. 467)	**superávit del productor** se refiere tanto al *superávit del productor individual* como al *superávit total del productor*. (pág. 467)

English

Español

English	Español
product differentiation an attempt by a firm to convince buyers that its product is different from the products of other firms in the industry. (p. 639)	**diferenciación de productos** intento que hace la empresa de convencer a los compradores de que su producto es diferente a los productos de otras empresas en la industria. (pág. 639)
product markets where goods and services are bought and sold. (p. 104)	**mercados de productos** mercados en los cuales se compran y se venden bienes y servicios. (pág. 104)
production function the relationship between the quantity of inputs a firm uses and the quantity of output it produces. (p. 520)	**función de producción** relación entre la cantidad de insumos que emplea una empresa y la cantidad de producción que produce. (pág. 520)
production possibilities curve (PPC) illustrates the *trade-offs* facing an *economy* that produces only two goods; shows the maximum quantity of one good that can be produced for each possible quantity of the other good produced. (p. 15)	**curva de posibilidades de producción (CPP)** ilustra las *compensaciones* que enfrenta una *economía* que produce solo dos bienes; permite apreciar la cantidad máxima de un bien que se puede producir por cada cantidad posible producida del otro bien. (pág. 15)
productive efficiency achieved by an *economy* if it produces at a point on its *production possibilities curve*. (p. 17)	**eficiencia productiva** la logra una *economía* si produce en un punto de su *curva de posibilidades de producción*. (pág. 17)
productivity see *labor productivity* (p. 352)	**productividad** véase *productividad de la mano de obra* (pág. 352)
progressive tax a tax that rises more than in proportion to income. (p. 477)	**impuesto progresivo** impuesto que aumenta más que en proporcionalidad directa con los ingresos. (pág. 477)
property rights establish ownership and grant individuals the right to trade goods and services with each other. (p. 2)	**derechos de propiedad** establece la propiedad y otorga a las personas el derecho a intercambiar bienes y servicios unas con otras. (pág. 2)
proportional tax a tax that rises in proportion to income. (p. 477)	**impuesto proporcional** impuesto que aumenta en proporcionalidad directa con los ingresos. (pág. 477)
protectionism the practice of limiting trade to protect domestic industries. (p. 417)	**proteccionismo** práctica de limitar el comercio con el fin de proteger las industrias nacionales. (pág. 417)
public good both *nonexcludable* and *nonrival in consumption*. (p. 728)	**bien público** ni *excluible* ni *no rival en el consumo*. (pág. 728)
public ownership (of a *monopoly*) when a good is supplied by the government, or by a firm owned by the government, instead of by a *monopolist*. (p. 600)	**propiedad pública** (de un *monopolio*) cuando un bien es ofertado por el gobierno o por una empresa de propiedad del gobierno en lugar de por un *monopolista*. (pág. 600)
purchasing power parity (between two countries' currencies) the nominal *exchange rate* at which a given basket of goods and services would cost the same amount in each country. (p. 405)	**paridad en el poder adquisitivo** (entre las divisas de dos países) *tasa de cambio* nominal a la cual una canasta de bienes y servicios costaría la misma cantidad en cada uno de los países. (pág. 405)

Q

English	Español
quantity control an upper limit on the quantity of some good that can be bought or sold; also known as a *quota*. (p. 88)	**control de cantidad** límite superior de la cantidad que se puede comprar o vender de algún bien, también denominado *cuota*. (pág. 88)
quantity demanded the actual amount of a good or service consumers are willing and able to buy at some specific price; shown as a single point in the *demand schedule* or along a *demand curve*. (p. 52)	**cantidad demandada** cantidad precisa de un bien o servicio que los consumidores están dispuestos (y tienen la capacidad) de comprar a un precio específico; se aprecia en un único punto en la *tabla de demanda* o a lo largo de una *curva de demanda*. (pág. 52)
quantity supplied the actual amount of a good or service people are willing to sell at some specific price. (p. 60)	**cantidad ofertada** cantidad precisa de un bien o servicio que las personas están dispuestas a vender a algún precio específico. (pág. 60)
Quantity Theory of Money emphasizes the positive relationship between the price level and the *money supply*; relies on the velocity equation ($M \times V = P \times Y$). (p. 328)	**teoría cuantitativa del dinero** enfatiza la relación positiva entre el nivel de precios y el *dinero en circulación*; se basa en la ecuación de velocidad ($M \times V = P \times Y$). (pág. 328)
quota see *quantity control* (p. 88)	**cuota** véase *control de cantidad* (pág. 88)
quota rent the earnings that accrue to the license-holder from ownership of the right to sell the good; this is the difference between the demand and supply price at the quota amount and is equal to the market price of the *license* when the licenses are traded. (p. 91)	**alquiler de cuota** ganancias que acumula el licenciatario por ser propietario del derecho de vender el bien; es la diferencia entre el precio de demanda y el precio de oferta establecidos según la cuota y es igual al precio de mercado de la *licencia* cuando las licencias se comercializan. (pág. 91)

English

Español

English	Español
rate of return (on a project) is the profit earned on the project expressed as a percentage of its cost. (p. 265)	**tasa de rentabilidad** (de un proyecto) utilidades obtenidas en un proyecto expresadas como un porcentaje de su coste. (pág. 265)
real exchange rates *exchange rates* adjusted for international differences in *aggregate price levels*. (p. 403)	**tasas de cambio reales** *tasas de cambio* ajustadas a las diferencias internacionales en los *niveles de precios agregados*. (pág. 403)
real GDP the total value of all *final goods and services* produced in the *economy* during a given year, calculated using the prices of a selected *base year* in order to remove the effects of price changes. (p. 115)	**PIB real** valor total de todos los *bienes y servicios finales* producidos en la *economía* durante un año dado, computado haciendo uso de los precios de un *año base* escogido a fin de eliminar los efectos de los cambios de precios. (pág. 115)
real income income divided by the price level to adjust for the effects of *inflation* or *deflation*. (p. 133)	**ingresos reales** ingresos divididos entre el nivel de precios a fin de ajustarse a los efectos de la *inflación* o *deflación*. (pág. 133)
real interest rate the *nominal interest rate* minus the rate of *inflation*. (p. 136)	**tasa de interés real** *tasa de interés nominal* menos la tasa de *inflación*. (pág. 136)
real wage the wage rate divided by the price level to adjust for the effects of *inflation* or *deflation*. (p. 133)	**salario real** tasa salarial dividida entre el nivel de precios a fin de ajustarse a los efectos dela *inflación* o *deflación*. (pág. 133)
real wealth effect (of a change in the *aggregate price level*) the change in *consumer spending* caused by the altered purchasing power of consumers' assets. (p. 168)	**Efecto de riqueza real** (de un cambio en el *nivel de precio agregado*) el cambio en los gastos de consumo causado por el cambio en el poder *adquisitivo de los consumidores*. (pág. 168)
recession a period of economic downturn when output and employment are falling. (p. 10)	**recesión** período de desaceleración económica cuando la producción y el empleo están en caída. (pág. 10)
recessionary gap when *aggregate output* is below *potential output*. (p. 188)	**brecha recesiva** cuando la *producción agregada* se encuentra por debajo del *potencial de producción*. (pág. 188)
recovery see *expansions* (p. 10)	**recuperación** véase *expansiones* (pág. 10)
regressive tax a tax that rises less than in proportion to income. (p. 477)	**impuesto regresivo** impuesto que aumenta menos en proporcionalidad con los ingresos. (pág. 477)
relative price the rate at which good R trades for good M in the market; equal to P_R/P_M (p. EM-34)	**precio relativo** precio al que el bien R se intercambia por el bien M en el mercado; es equivalente a P_R/P_M (pág. EM-34)
relative price rule states that, at the *optimal consumption bundle*, the *marginal rate of substitution* between two goods is equal to their *relative price*. (p. EM-34)	**regla del precio relativo** en el *conjunto de consumo óptimo* la *tasa marginal de sustitución* entre dos bienes es equivalente a sus precios relativos. (pág. EM-34)
rental rate the cost, explicit or implicit, of using a unit of an asset, either land or *capital*, for a given period of time. (p. 675)	**canon de alquiler** sea de terrenos o de *capital*, es el coste, explícito o implícito, de hacer uso de una unidad de dicho activo por un período de tiempo dado. (pág. 675)
reputation long-term credibility that allows an individual to assure others that he or she isn't concealing adverse *private information*. (p. EM-21)	**reputación** credibilidad a largo plazo que permite que una persona asegure a otras que no está ocultando ninguna *información reservada o privada* adversa. (pág. EM-21)
required reserve ratio the smallest fraction of deposits that the Federal Reserve allows *banks* to hold. (p. 236)	**tasa de reservas obligatorias** fracción más pequeña de los depósitos que el Banco de la Reserva Federal autoriza que retengan los *bancos*. (pág. 236)
reserve ratio the fraction of *bank deposits* that a *bank* holds as reserves. (p. 236)	**tasa de reserva** fracción de los *depósitos bancarios* que un *banco* retiene como reservas. (pág. 236)
reserve requirements rules set by the Federal Reserve that determine the *required reserve ratio* for banks. (p. 238)	**requisitos de reserva** reglas que fija el Banco de Reserva Federal en las que se determina la *tasa de reservas obligatorias* para los *bancos*. (pág. 238)
resource anything that can be used to produce something else. (p. 3)	**recurso** cualquier cosa que se pueda utilizar para producir otra cosa. (pág. 3)
revaluation an increase in the value of a currency that is set under a *fixed exchange rate regime*. (p. 411)	**revaloración** aumento en el valor de una divisa que se encuentra bajo un régimen de cambio de divisas fijo. (pág. 411)
rival in consumption a good is rival in consumption if the same unit of the good cannot be consumed by more than one person at the same time. (p. 726)	**rival en el consumo** bien rival en el consumo si la misma unidad del bien no puede ser consumida por más de una persona a la vez. (pág. 726)
Rule of 70 a mathematical formula that tells us that the time it takes a variable that grows gradually over time to double is approximately 70 divided by that variable's annual growth rate. (p. 351)	**regla del 70** fórmula matemática que nos explica que el tiempo que una variable que crece paulatinamente precisa para duplicarse es de aproximadamente 70 dividido entre la tasa de crecimiento anual de la variable. (pág. 351)

English

Español

S

English	Español
savings–investment spending identity an accounting fact that states that savings and *investment spending* are always equal for the *economy* as a whole. (p. 216)	**identidad de gastos de ahorros para invertir** hecho contable que explica que los ahorros y los *gastos de inversión* siempre son iguales para la *economía* en conjunto. (pág. 216)
scarce in short supply; when a *resource* is not available in sufficient quantities to satisfy all the various ways a society wants to use it. (p. 3)	**escaso** de oferta insuficiente; cuando no se dispone de un *recurso* en cantidades suficientes para satisfacer las diversas necesidades en que la sociedad desea aprovecharlo. (pág. 3)
scatter diagram a diagram in which each point corresponds to an actual observation of the *x*-variable and the *y*-variable. (p. 42)	**diagrama de dispersión** diagrama en el que cada punto corresponde a una observación directa de la variable *x* y de la variable *y*. (pág. 42)
screening using observable information about people to make inferences about their *private information*; a way to reduce *adverse selection*. (p. EM-21)	**selección** uso de información observable sobre las personas con el fin de inferir sobre su *información reservada o privada*; manera de reducir las *selecciones adversas*. (pág. EM-21)
securitization involves assembling a pool of *loans* and selling shares of that pool to investors. (p. EM-7)	**titulización** implica reunir un conjunto de *préstamos* y vender a inversionistas acciones de dicho conjunto. (pág. EM-7)
shadow bank a financial institution that engages in *maturity transformation* but does not accept deposits. (p. EM-3)	**banco en la sombra** institución financiera que maneja transformaciones de vencimiento pero que no acepta depósitos. (pág. EM-3)
shoe-leather costs the increased costs of transactions caused by *inflation*. (p. 135)	**costes directos** costes mayores de las transacciones ocasionados por la *inflación*. (pág. 135)
short run the time period in which at least one input is fixed. (p. 520)	**a corto plazo** período de tiempo en el que por lo menos un insumo es fijo. (pág. 520)
shortage when the quantity of a good or service demanded exceeds the *quantity supplied*; occurs when the price is below its *equilibrium* level; also known as *excess demand*. (p. 71)	**escasez** cuando la cantidad de un bien o servicio en demanda es mayor que la *cantidad ofertada*; sucede cuando el precio está por debajo de su nivel de *equilibrio*; también denominado *demanda excesiva*. (pág. 71)
short-run aggregate supply curve shows the positive relationship between the *aggregate price level* and the quantity of *aggregate output* supplied that exists in the *short run*, the time period when many production costs can be taken as fixed. (p. 175)	**curva de oferta agregada a corto plazo** permite apreciar la relación entre el *nivel de precios agregados* y la cantidad de *producción agregada* ofertada que existe *a corto plazo*, el período de tiempo en el que muchos de los costes de producción se pueden adoptar como costes fijos. (pág. 175)
short-run equilibrium aggregate output the quantity of *aggregate output* produced in the short-run macroeconomic equilibrium. (p. 184)	**producción agregada de equilibrio a corto plazo** cantidad de *producción agregada* producida en el equilibrio macroeconómico a corto plazo. (pág. 184)
short-run equilibrium aggregate price level the *aggregate price level* in the short-run macroeconomic equilibrium. (p. 184)	**nivel de precios agregados de equilibrio a corto plazo** *nivel de precios agregados* en el equilibrio macroeconómico a corto plazo. (pág. 184)
short-run firm supply curve shows how an individual firm's profit-maximizing level of output depends on the market price, taking the *fixed cost* as given. (p. 576)	**curva de oferta individual a corto plazo** permite apreciar cómo el nivel de producción para maximizar las utilidades de una empresa individual depende del precio de mercado, tomando el *coste fijo* como un hecho dado. (pág. 576)
short-run industry supply curve shows how the quantity supplied by an industry depends on the market price, given a fixed number of firms. (p. 580)	**curva de oferta de la industria a corto plazo** permite apreciar cómo la cantidad ofertada por una industria depende del precio de mercado, dado un número fijo de empresas. (pág. 580)
short-run Phillips curve (*SRPC*) represents the negative short-run relationship between the *unemployment rate* and the *inflation rate*. (p. 312)	**curva de Phillips a corto plazo** representa la relación negativa a corto plazo entre la *tasa de desempleo* y la *tasa de inflación*. (pág. 312)
short-term interest rates the *interest rates* on *financial assets* that mature within a year. (p. 256)	**tasa de interés a corto plazo** *tasa de interés* sobre *activos financieros* que se vencen antes de concluir un año. (pág. 256)
shut-down price the price at which a firm ceases production in the *short run*; equal to minimum *average variable cost*. (p. 575)	**precio de cierre definitivo** precio al cual una empresa deja de producir *a corto plazo*; es equivalente al *coste variable promedio* mínimo. (pág. 575)
signaling revealing *private information* through actions that establish credibility; a way to reduce *adverse selection*. (p. EM-21)	**señalización** revelar *información reservada o privada* mediante acciones que establecen credibilidad; manera de reducir la *selección adversa*. (pág. EM-21)

English

Español

English	Español
single-price monopolist firm that charges all consumers the same price. (p. 603)	**monopolista de precio único** empresa que cobra a todos los consumidores el mismo precio. (pág. 603)
slope a measure of how steep a *curve* is; indicates how sensitive the *y*-variable is to a change in the *x*-variable. (p. 37)	**pendiente** medida de la profundidad de una *curva*; indica la sensibilidad de la variable *y* y cómo reacciona a cambios en la variable *x*. (pág. 37)
social insurance government programs intended to protect families against economic hardship. (p. 195)	**seguro social** programas del gobierno que tienen por fin proteger a las familias contra toda índole de dificultades económicas. (pág. 195)
socially optimal quantity the quantity that society would choose if all the costs and benefits of pollution were fully accounted for. (p. 713)	**cantidad socialmente óptima** cantidad que la sociedad escogería si se tuvieran en cuenta todos los costes y beneficios de la contaminación. (pág. 713)
specialization situation in which each person specializes in the task that he or she is good at performing. (p. 22)	**especialización** coyuntura en la que cada persona se especializa en la tarea que realiza bien. (pág. 22)
spending multiplier the ratio of the total change in *real GDP* caused by an *autonomous change in aggregate spending* to the size of that autonomous change; indicates the total rise in *real GDP* that results from each $1 of an initial rise in spending. (p. 164)	**multiplicador de gastos** relación entre el cambio total en el *PIB real* ocasionado por *cambios autónomos en los gastos agregados* y las dimensiones de ese cambio autónomo; indica el aumento total en el *PIB real* que resulta de cada 1$ de un aumento inicial en los gastos. (pág. 164)
stabilization policy the use of government policy to reduce the severity of *recessions* and rein in excessively strong *expansions*. (p. 192)	**política de estabilización** uso de las políticas gubernamentales para reducir la gravedad de las *recesiones* y controlar las *expansiones* excesivas. (pág. 192)
stagflation the combination of *inflation* and stagnating (or falling) *aggregate output*. (p. 186)	**estanflación** combinación de *inflación* y estancamiento (o caída) de la *producción agregada*. (pág. 186)
standardized product describes a good produced by different firms, but that consumers regard as the same good; also known as a *commodity*. (p. 547)	**producto normalizado** describe un bien cuando los consumidores consideran que los productos de diferentes empresas son el mismo bien; también denominado *insumo*. (pág. 547)
sticky wages *nominal wages* that are slow to fall even in the face of high *unemployment* and slow to rise even in the face of *labor shortages*. (p. 175)	**salarios rígidos** *salarios nominales* que descienden lentamente incluso a la luz de *desempleo* alto y que suben lentamente incluso a la luz de escasez de *mano de obra*. (pág. 175)
store of value a means of holding purchasing power over time. (p. 226)	**valor refugio** manera de retener el poder adquisitivo a través del tiempo. (pág. 226)
strategic behavior when a firm attempts to influence the future behavior of other firms. (p. 636)	**conducta estratégica** cuando una empresa trata de influir en la conducta futura de otras empresas. (pág. 636)
structural unemployment *unemployment* that results when workers lack the skills required for the available jobs, or there are more people seeking jobs in a *labor market* than there are jobs available at the current wage rate. (p. 126)	**desempleo estructural** *desempleo* que se genera cuando los trabajadores carecen de las destrezas necesarias para los empleos disponibles o cuando hay más personas buscando empleo en un *mercado laboral* que empleos disponibles a la tasa salarial vigente. (pág. 126)
subprime lending involves lending to home-buyers who don't meet the usual criteria for being able to afford their payments. (p. EM-7)	**crédito subprime** implica prestar a compradores de casa que no satisfacen los criterios habituales para poder efectuar el pago de las cuotas. (pág. EM-7)
substitutes two goods for which a rise in the price of one of the goods leads to an increase in the demand for the other good. (p. 56)	**sustitutos** dos bienes para los cuales el aumento del precio de un bien conduce al aumento en la demanda del otro bien. (pág. 56)
substitution bias bias that occurs in the *consumer price index* because, over time, items with prices that have risen more receive too much weight (because households substitute away from them), while items with prices that have risen least are given too little weight (because households shift their spending toward them). (p. 143)	**sesgo de sustitución** sesgo que sucede en el *índice de precios de consumo* porque, a través del tiempo, artículos con mayores subidas de precio reciben demasiado peso (porque los hogares los sustituyen por otros), mientras que artículos con subidas de precio menores reciben demasiado poco peso (porque los hogares empiezan a utilizar sus ingresos para comprarlos). (pág. 143)
substitution effect the change in the quantity of a good demanded as the consumer substitutes the good that has become relatively cheaper for the good that has become relatively more expensive. (p. 440)	**efecto de sustitución** cambio en la cantidad de un bien que se demanda cuando el consumidor reemplaza el bien que se ha vuelto relativamente más costoso con el bien que se ha tornado relativamente menos costoso. (pág. 440)
sunk cost a cost that has already been incurred and is nonrecoverable; should be ignored in a decision about future actions. (p. 542)	**coste hundido** coste que ya se ha pagado y que no se puede recuperar; debe pasarse por alto cuando se toma una decisión acerca de acciones futuras. (pág. 542)

English

Español

English	Español
supply and demand model a *model* of how a *competitive market* works. (p. 50)	**modelo de oferta y demanda** *modelo* de cómo funciona un *mercado competitivo*. (pág. 50)
supply curve shows the relationship between the *quantity supplied* and the price. (p. 60)	**curva de oferta** permite apreciar la relación entre la *cantidad ofertada* y el precio. (pág. 60)
supply price the price of a given quantity at which producers will supply that quantity. (p. 89)	**precio de la oferta** precio de una cantidad dada en la cual los productores ofertarán esa cantidad. (pág. 89)
supply schedule shows how much of a good or service producers would supply at different prices. (p. 60)	**tabla de oferta** permite apreciar cuánto de un bien o servicio ofertarían los productores a precios diferentes. (pág. 60)
supply shock an event that shifts the *short-run aggregate supply curve*. (p. 185)	**choque de oferta** evento que hace desplazar la *curva de la oferta agregada a corto plazo*. (pág. 185)
supply-side fiscal policies government policies that seek to promote economic growth by affecting *short-run* and *long-run aggregate supply curves*. (p. 378)	**políticas fiscales del lado de la oferta** políticas gubernamentales que buscan promover el crecimiento económico al afectar las *curvas de oferta agregada de corto y largo plazo*. (pág. 378)
surplus when the *quantity supplied* of a good or service exceeds the *quantity demanded;* occurs when the price is above its *equilibrium* level; also known as *excess supply*. (p. 70)	**superávit** cuando la *cantidad ofertada* de un bien o servicio es mayor que la *cantidad demandada*; sucede cuando el precio está por encima de su nivel de *equilibrio*; también denominado *oferta excesiva*. (pág. 70)

T

English	Español
tacit collusion when firms limit production and raise prices in a way that raises each other's profits, even though they have not made any formal agreement. (p. 637)	**colusión tácita** cuando las empresas limitan su producción y aumentan sus precios de manera que aumenten las utilidades de unos y otros, pese a que no cuentan con un convenio formal. (pág. 637)
tangency condition on a graph of a consumer's *budget line* and available *indifference curves* of available *consumption bundles*, the point at which an indifference curve and the budget line just touch; this condition determines the *optimal consumption bundle* when the *indifference curves* have the typical convex shape. (p. EM-32)	**condición tangencial** en un gráfico del *rubro del presupuesto* del consumidor y las *curvas de indiferencia* disponibles de los *conjuntos de consumo* disponibles, el punto en el cual hay contacto entre la curva de indiferencia y el rubro del presupuesto; esta coyuntura determina el *conjunto de consumo óptimo* cuando las *curvas de indiferencia* tienen la forma convexa característica. (pág. EM-32)
target federal funds rate the Federal Reserve's desired level for the *federal funds rate*; the Federal Reserve can achieve this target through *open market operations*. (p. 295)	**tasa de los fondos federales objetivo** nivel deseado del Banco de la Reserva Federal para la tasa de fondos federales; el Banco de la Reserva Federal puede lograr este objetivo a través de *operaciones de mercado abierto*. (pág. 295)
tariffs taxes on *imports*. (p. 417)	**aranceles** impuestos que se cobran por las importaciones. (pág. 417)
tax incidence the distribution of the tax burden. (p. 480)	**incidencia tributaria** distribución de la carga impositiva. (pág. 480)
tax multiplier the factor by which a change in tax collections changes *real GDP*. (p. 202)	**multiplicador impositivo** factor mediante el cual un cambio en las recaudaciones tributarias cambia el *PIB real*. (pág. 202)
tax revenue the total amount the government receives from *taxes*. (p. 105)	**ingresos fiscales** total de ingresos que el gobierno recibe mediante *impuestos*. (pág. 105)
taxes required payments to the government. (p. 105)	**impuestos** pagos que se exige pagar al gobierno. (pág. 105)
Taylor rule for monetary policy rule for setting the *federal funds rate* that takes into account both the *inflation rate* and the *output gap*. (p. 297)	**regla Taylor sobre política monetaria** regla para fijar la *tasa de fondos federales* que tiene en cuenta tanto la *la tasa de inflación* como la *brecha de producción*. (pág. 297)
technology the technical means for producing goods and services. (pp. 20, 353)	**tecnología** los medios técnicos para producir bienes y servicios. (págs. 20, 353)
technology spillover an *external benefit* that results when new technological knowledge spreads among firms. (p. 722)	**desbordamiento de tecnología** *beneficio externo* que resulta cuando los conocimientos acerca de una tecnología se distribuyen entre varias empresas. (pág. 722)
terms of trade indicate the rate at which one good can be exchanged for another. (p. 25)	**términos del comercio** indican el ritmo al cual un bien se puede intercambiar con otro. (pág. 25)
time-series graph a graph with successive dates on the *horizontal (x-) axis* and the values of a variable that occurred on those dates on the *vertical (y-) axis*. (p. 41)	**gráfico de una serie temporal** gráfico con fechas sucesivas en el *eje horizontal (x)* y los valores de una variable que ocurrió en esas fechas en el *eje vertical (y)*. (pág. 41)

English

Español

English	Español
tit for tat a strategy that involves playing cooperatively at first, then doing whatever the other player did in the previous period. (p. 636)	**toma y daca** estrategia que implica jugar de manera cooperativa al principio y luego hacer lo que el otro jugador hizo en el período anterior. (pág. 636)
total consumer surplus the sum of the *individual consumer surpluses* of all the buyers of a good in a market. (p. 464)	**superávit total del consumidor** suma de los *superávits de los consumidores individuales* de todos los compradores de un bien en un mercado. (pág. 464)
total cost (TC) the sum of the *fixed cost* and the *variable cost* of producing a given quantity of output. (p. 526)	**coste total** suma de los *costes fijos* y el *coste variable* de producir una cantidad dada de producción. (pág. 526)
total cost curve shows how *total cost* depends on the quantity of output. (p. 527)	**curva de costes totales** permite apreciar cómo el *coste total* depende de la cantidad de producción. (pág. 527)
total producer surplus the sum of the *individual producer surpluses* of all the sellers of a good in a market. (p. 467)	**superávit total de los productores** suma de los *superávits de los productores individuales* de todos los vendedores de un bien en el mercado. (pág. 467)
total product curve shows how the quantity of output depends on the quantity of the variable input, for a given quantity of the *fixed input*. (p. 520)	**curva del producto total** permite apreciar cómo la cantidad de producción depende de la cantidad del insumo variable para una cantidad dada del *insumo fijo*. (pág. 520)
total revenue the total value of sales of a good or service; equal to the price multiplied by the quantity sold. (p. 448)	**ingresos totales** valor total de las ventas de un bien o servicio; es igual al precio multiplicado por la cantidad vendida. (pág. 448)
total surplus the total net gain to consumers and producers from trading in a market; the sum of *consumer surplus* and *producer surplus*. (p. 473)	**superávit total** ganancia neta total de los consumidores y productores producto de intercambios en el mercado; suma de los *superávits de consumidores* y los *superávits de productores*. (pág. 473)
tradable emissions permits licenses to emit limited quantities of pollutants that can be bought and sold by polluters. (p. 717)	**permisos comerciables de emisiones** licencias para emitir cantidades limitadas de contaminantes que los contaminadores pueden comprar y vender. (pág. 717)
trade when, in a *market economy*, individuals provide goods and services to others and receive goods and services in return. (p. 22)	**intercambio** cuando, en una *economía de mercado*, las personas ofertan bienes y servicios a otros y reciben bienes y servicios a cambio. (pág. 22)
trade balance see *merchandise trade balance* (p. 392)	**balanza comercial** véase *balanza comercial de mercancía* (pág. 392)
trade-off when you give up something in order to have something else. (p. 15)	**compensación** cuando se sacrifica algo con el objetivo de obtener otra cosa. (pág. 15)
transaction costs the costs to individuals of making a deal. (pp. 218, 715)	**costes de transacción** gastos que implica negociar y ejecutar una transacción. (págs. 218, 715)

U

English	Español
underemployed workers who would like to work more hours or who are overqualified for their jobs. (p. 120)	**subempleados** trabajadores que quisieran trabajar más horas o que están sobrecualificados para los empleos que tienen. (pág. 120)
unemployed people who are actively looking for work but aren't currently *employed*. (p. 119)	**desempleados** personas que están buscando trabajo activamente pero que actualmente no tienen *empleo*. (pág. 119)
unemployment the number of people who are actively looking for work but aren't currently *employed*. (p. 11)	**desempleo** número de personas que están buscando trabajo activamente pero que actualmente no tienen *empleo*. (pág. 11)
unemployment rate the percentage of the *labor force* that is *unemployed*. (pp. 11, 119)	**tasa de desempleo** porcentaje de la *fuerza laboral* que está *desempleada*. (págs. 11, 119)
unions organizations of workers that try to raise wages and improve working conditions for their members by bargaining collectively. (p. 698)	**sindicatos** organizaciones de trabajadores que aspiran a subir los salarios y mejorar las condiciones de trabajo para sus afiliados mediante negociaciones colectivas. (pág. 698)
unit of account a measure used to set prices and make economic calculations. (p. 226)	**unidad de cuenta** medición que se usa para fijar precios y realizar cómputos económicos. (pág. 226)
unit-of-account costs arise from the way *inflation* makes money a less reliable unit of measurement. (p. 136)	**costes de la unidad de cuenta** surgen a raíz de la manera en la que la *inflación* le resta fiabilidad al dinero como unidad de medición. (pág. 136)
unit-elastic demand when the *price elasticity of demand* is exactly 1. (p. 448)	**demanda elástica unitaria** cuando la *elasticidad precio de la demanda* es exactamente. (pág. 448)

English

Español

U-shaped average total cost curve falls at low levels of output and then rises at higher levels. (p. 530)	**curva de costes totales promedio en forma de U** desciende a niveles bajos de producción y luego asciende a niveles más altos. (pág. 530)
util a unit of *utility*. (p. 488)	**útil** unidad de *utilidad*. (pág. 488)
utility a measure of personal satisfaction. (p. 488)	**utilidad** medición de satisfacción personal. (pág. 488)

V

value added (of a producer) the value of a producer's sales minus the value of its purchases of inputs. (p. 110)	**valor agregado** (de un productor) valor de las ventas de un productor menos el valor de sus compras de insumos. (pág. 110)
value-added approach an approach to calculating *GDP* by surveying firms and adding up their contributions to the value of *final goods and services*. (p. 108)	**enfoque de valor agregado** enfoque para computar el *PIB* mediante una encuesta a empresas y la suma de sus aportes al valor de los *bienes y servicios finales*. (pág. 108)
variable a measure that can take on more than one value. (p. 34)	**variable** medición que puede adoptar más de un valor. (pág. 34)
variable cost (VC) a cost that depends on the quantity of output produced; the cost of the *variable input*. (p. 526)	**coste variable** coste que depende de la cantidad de producción; coste del *insumo variable*. (pág. 526)
variable input an input whose quantity the firm can vary at any time. (p. 520)	**insumo variable** insumo cuya cantidad la empresa puede variar en cualquier momento. (pág. 520)
velocity of money the ratio of *nominal GDP* to the *money supply*; a measure of the number of times the average dollar bill is spent per year. (p. 328)	**velocidad del dinero** relación entre el *PIB nominal* y el *dinero en circulación*; medición del número de veces que el billete promedio de un dólar se utiliza para pagar durante un año. (pág. 328)
vertical axis see *y-axis* (p. 35)	**eje vertical** véase *eje y* (pág. 35)
vertical intercept indicates the value of the *y*-variable when the value of the *x*-variable is zero. (p. 36)	**intersección vertical** indica el valor de la variable *y* cuando el valor de la variable *x* es cero. (pág. 36)

W

wasted resources a form of inefficiency in which people expend money, effort, and time to cope with the *shortages* caused by the *price ceiling* or *surpluses* caused by the *price floor*. (p. 80)	**recursos desperdiciados** forma de ineficiencia en la que las personas usan dinero, esfuerzo y tiempo para lidiar con las *escaseces* ocasionadas por el *techo de precios* o con los *superávits* ocasionados por el *piso de precios*. (pág. 80)
wealth the value of a *household*'s accumulated savings. (p. 218)	**riqueza** valor de los ahorros acumulados en un *hogar*. (pág. 218)
wedge the difference between the *demand price* and the *supply price* of a good, such that the price paid by buyers ends up being higher than that received by the sellers; often created by a *quantity control*, or *quota*. (p. 91)	**cuña** diferencia entre el *precio de demanda* y el *precio de oferta* de un bien de manera que el precio pagado por los compradores termina siendo más alto que el que reciben los vendedores; a menudo se crea con un *control de cantidad* o una *cuota*. (pág. 91)
willingness to pay the maximum price at which a consumer would buy a good. (p. 462)	**voluntad de pago** el precio máximo que un consumidor pagaría para comprar un bien. (pág. 462)

X

x-axis the solid horizontal line on a graph that intersects with the *y-axis* at the *origin*; also called the *horizontal axis*. (p. 35)	**eje x** la línea horizontal en un gráfico que se cruza con el *eje y* en el *origen*; también denominado *eje horizontal*. (pág. 35)

Y

y-axis the solid vertical line on a graph that intersects with the *x-axis* at the *origin*; also called the *vertical axis*. (p. 35)	**eje y** la línea vertical en un gráfico que se cruza con el *eje x* en el *origen*; también denominado *eje vertical*. (pág. 35)

Z

zero bound the lower bound of zero on the *nominal interest rate*: it cannot go below zero. (p. 319)	**límite de cero** límite inferior de cero en la *tasa de interés nominal*: no puede bajar por debajo de cero. (pág. 319)

Index

Note: **Boldface** type indicates key terms.